Hood's Texas Brigade:

A Compendium

Some Other Books By
COLONEL HAROLD B. SIMPSON

BRAWLING BRASS, NORTH & SOUTH
GAINES' MILL TO APPOMATTOX
TEXAS IN THE WAR, 1861-1865
TOUCHED WITH VALOR
RED GRANITE FOR GRAY HEROES
THE MARSHALL GUARDS
HISTORY OF HOOD'S TEXAS BRIGADE (4 VOLS.)
AUDIE MURPHY: AMERICAN SOLDIER

Hood's Texas Brigade:

A Compendium

By

COLONEL
HAROLD B. SIMPSON

Hill Jr. College Press • Hillsboro, Texas • 1977

E
580. 3
.S55

Composed By
The LeWay Composing Service, Ft. Worth, Tex.
Printed By
Sprint Press Incorp., Ft. Worth, Tex.
Bound By
The Library Binding Co., Waco, Tex.

73055

Not for fame or reward, not for place or rank,
Not lured by ambition or goaded by necessity,
But in simple obedience to duty as they understood it,
These men suffered all, sacrificed all, endured all
   . . . and died.

       — Confederate Monument, Arlington National Cemetery

Preface

This book completes the four volume history of Hood's Texas Brigade, Longstreet's Corps, Army of Northern Virginia, CSA. Research for the history commenced during the summer of 1960 with a lengthy visit to the National Archives, Washington, D.C. Seventeen years later the research and writing has been completed. Volume One, *Hood's Texas Brigade in Poetry and Song* was published in 1968; Volume Two, *Hood's Texas Brigade: Lee's Grenadier Guard,* appeared in 1970; Volume Three, *Hood's Texas Brigade in Reunion and Memory,* was finished in 1972; and this one, Volume Four, is finished five years later. Together the four volumes comprise a definitive history of the Brigade. However, each volume is separately indexed and can stand alone as a specialized study.

By far the two most important sources used in compiling the service records of the men in the seventy-two companies included in this book were the Bi-Monthly Muster Rolls and the microfilm copies of the Service Records of Confederate Soldiers. The task of researching these records was enormous. Some 10,000 records of individual soldiers consisting of an estimated 128,000 entries were read and pertinent data extracted therefrom.

The 147 photographs of members of the Brigade that appear in the book were collected over a seventeen year period from various books, magazines and from relatives of the soldiers. Most of the photographs have never before been published. Many of them are wartime photographs and thus are a good source for depicting Confederate uniforms, accouterments and arms.

A confession is good for the soul; the section of the book entitled "Brigade Trivia" was added for the purpose of providing enjoyment for the general reader and for those persons interested in the Civil War who did not have a relative in Hood's Texas Brigade. Pages of rosters, even informational rosters, like those in this book, are of little interest but to the scholar, relative and writer. On the other hand, human relations experiences, unusual events and facts are of interest to most readers.

Complete rosters for the 1st, 4th and 5th Texas Infantry Regiments, the 3rd Arkansas and the 18th Georgia Infantry Regiments, the Infantry Battalion of Hampton's South Carolina Legion and Company D (Rowan Artillery), 1st North Carolina

Artillery Regiment comprise Part One of the book. Of these regiments only the three Texas Regiments served with the Brigade during the entire war. The 3rd Arkansas joined the Brigade during the reorganization of Lee's Army in November, 1862, and served with it until Appomattox. The 18th Georgia joined the Texans in the Fall of 1861 and the infantry companies of Hampton's South Carolina Legion were assigned to the Brigade after the battle of Seven Pines (June 1, 1862). Both the Georgians and South Carolinans left the Hood's Texas Brigade upon the reorganization of the Army of Northern Virginia in November, 1862. Reilly's Battery, Company D (Rowan Artillery), 1st North Carolina, Artillery Regiment was never assigned or even attached to the Texas Brigade but did give the Brigade close support during some of the bitterest battles of the war from 2nd Manassas to Gettysburg. The infantrymen of the Texas Brigade and the Reilly's artillerists considered themselves to be an integral unit.

By actual count, using the original Bi-Monthly Muster Rolls, 7,268 men were assigned to Hood's Texas Brigade during the war. Of this number, 4,346 served with the 1st, 4th and 5th Texas Infantry Regiments. The remaining 2,926 men who fought with the Texans were with the 3rd Arkansas and 18th Georgia Infantry Regiments and the Infantry Battalion (eight companies) of Hampton's South Carolina Legion when these units were assigned to the Brigade. Another 2,459 men served with the two regiments and the battalion but not during the period their unit was assigned to the Brigade. There was a total of 249 men assigned to Reilly's Battery during the war, of this number 205 were with the Battery when it supported the Brigade.

The Texas regiments experienced severe losses due to disease and sickness during the first fall and winter that they were in Virginia. Like the other Confederate soldiers from the deep South, the Texans were not acclimatized to the cold damp winters of northern Virginia. To compound their problem they were insufficiently clothed and housed and too far from home to receive the extra clothing required to maintain good health. Too, many of the men were physically unfit for the rigors of military campaigning. It is doubtful if the members of the original companies were even physically examined prior to leaving Texas for Virginia. Embued with patriotism, many of the men concealed serious defects for a chance "to get at the enemy before the war was over." Almost 20% of the men in the Texas Regiments died of disease or were discharged for disabilities related to sickness between September, 1861, and March, 1862, a seven month period.

Although men recruited for the Brigade after 1861 were supposed to have been passed by a local "examining surgeon" who certified them "to be free from all bodily defects and mental infirmity," no doubt, recruiting personnel often bypassed the surgeon to help fill the ranks of their much depleted companies. There is at least one case on record where a man was recruited on the grounds of the State Insane Asylum at Austin, Texas. After several peculiar antics in camp and battle the soldier was examined by a brigade physician and his background revealed. The man and his brother were both discharged and ordered back to the Lone Star State.

During the first winter of the war (February and March, 1862) each Texas Company sent a recruiting party back to the county in which it was raised to fill the ranks depleted by sickness and death. Usually the recruiting party consisted of an officer, a non-commissioned officer and a private, and the County Court House was recruiting headquarters. The first recruiting drive proved to be a most profitable one as 1,159 new soldiers entered the ranks of the three Texas Regiments. Company F of the 1st Texas Regiment from Tyler County garnered the most recruits, 63. Subsequent recruiting drives netted few soldiers. Only 51 men were recruited during February and March, 1863, and but 47 the following year. Without replacements the companies withered away to a handful of men by the winter of 1864-65.

The Texas Brigade fought in all of the major engagements of the Army of Northern Virginia, except Chancellorsville. However, its casualties at Chickamauga more than compensated for the losses suffered by any one of Lee's Brigade during the May 1-4, 1863, engagement. To my knowledge, this is the first book to contain a full informational roster and a statistical analysis of a brigade in Lee's Army. Hood's Brigade was fairly typical, except perhaps for its great number of casualties, of the other fighting brigades in the Army of Northern Virginia. Statistics concerning this Brigade could well serve as a fair sample for computations for the rest of Lee's Army.

Many acknowledgements are due for assistance given me in the compilation of this detailed study.

Annielee Wright, my secretary, must be singled out for special attention for the hundreds of hours of work expended typing and proofing the seventy-two company rosters. So must Tom

Lemmons, history teacher at the Carter-Riverside High School in Fort Worth, who spent the summer of 1977 at the Confederate Research Center, Hill Junior College, compiling statistics and digging out "Brigade Trivia".

Several students at Hill Junior College spent hours checking rosters and indexing the book. Credit for this goes to Betty Gilmore in particular, and her co-workers, Sue Sumner, Tina Campbell, Judy Miller, Arlene Bruton, Brian Childers, and James Wilson.

Josephine Cobb and Elmer O. Parker of the National Archives in Washington and Carol Carefoot of the Texas State Archives at Austin were most helpful in providing data and referring me to sources of information.

In the physical preparation of the book many thanks are due Ms. LeNelle Campbell, Mrs. Mary Terry, Mrs. Joyce Parkhurst, Mrs. Bea Connor, Mrs. Dianne Long, Miss Susan Skelly and Mrs. Connie Brynterson of LeWay Composing Company of Fort Worth; Bob Williams of Sprint Press in Fort Worth; and Frank Jasek and Clarence Kedrowski of the Library Binding Company in Waco, Texas.

I appreciate the efforts of the large number of descendants of soldiers of Hood's Texas Brigade who searched through drawers, trunks and attics to provide me with a photograph of their forebear.

To all of these, many thanks.

Harold B. Simpson
November, 1977

Contents

PART THREE
STATISTICAL CHARTS & SUMMARIES

PART FOUR
BRIGADE TRIVIA

Part One

Rosters

Headquarters, Hood's Texas Brigade
1st Texas Infantry Regiment
4th Texas Infantry Regiment
5th Texas Infantry Regiment
3rd Arkansas Infantry Regiment
18th Georgia Infantry Regiment
Hampton's So. Carolina Legion (Infantry Battalion)
Rowan Artillery (Co. D), 1st No. Carolina Arty. Regiment

HDQTRS., HOOD'S TEXAS BRIGADE
FIELD, STAFF & BAND

A SHORT ORGANIZATIONAL HISTORY

The Texas Brigade of Infantry that fought in the Army of Northern Virginia (1861-1865) was organized on October 22, 1861, per General Orders No. 15 issued by the Confederate War Department at Richmond. The Brigade was originally comprised of the 1st, 4th and 5th Texas Infantry Regiments, the only Texas troops to fight in the Eastern Theater. During the course of the war several non-Texas regiments were assigned for varying periods of time to the Brigade. On November 20, 1861, the 18th Georgia Infantry Regiment, commanded by Colonel William T. Wofford, was assigned to the Texas Brigade, thus bringing it up to its full brigade complement of four regiments. On June 1, 1862, the eight infantry companies of Hampton's South Carolina Legion, commanded by Lieutenant Colonel Martin W. Gary, were assigned to the Brigade. When the Army of Northern Virginia was re-organized in early November, 1862, the Texas Brigade lost both the Georgia and South Carolina infantry. The 18th Georgia and Hampton's South Carolina Infantry were transferred to brigades consisting of men from their respective states. To fill the void left by the departing units, in early November, 1862, the 3rd Arkansas Infantry Regiment, commanded by Colonel Van H. Manning, and the only Arkansas Infantry in the Army of Northern Virginia, was assigned to the Texas unit. This brought the Brigade, once again, up to full strength. The three original Texas Regiments and the Arkansas Regiment comprised the organization of the Brigade until the end at Appomattox.

The first commander of the Texas Brigade in Virginia was Brigadier-General Louis T. Wigfall, who had commanded the 1st Texas Infantry, the cornerstone regiment of the Brigade. The 1st Texas Infantry was the first of the three Texas Regiments to reach Virginia. Wigfall was selected by the Texas Legislature on November 16, 1861, to represent the Lone Star State in the Confederate Senate. He left the Brigade on February 20, 1862, to take up his new position in Richmond. Upon the departure of

Wigfall, Colonel James J. Archer assumed temporary command of the Brigade. Archer was the commander of the 5th Texas Infantry and senior colonel in the Brigade. Colonel John Bell Hood, commander of the 4th Texas Infantry, was promoted to Brigadier-General on March 8, 1862, and succeeded Colonel Archer as the Brigade Commander on March 12. Although Hood was to command the Brigade for only about six months, the unit bore his name throughout the war, regardless of subsequent commanders. Hood and "his Texans" combined their talents to give the Confederacy one of its best combat units. When Hood was advanced to two stars and given command of a division in October, 1862, he was succeeded in command by Colonel William T. Wofford, commander of the 18th Georgia Infantry. When Wofford and his Georgians were transferred out of the Brigade upon the re-organization of Lee's Army in early November, 1862, Jerome Bonaparte Robertson, commander of the 5th Texas, was promoted to Brigadier-General and command of the Brigade. Robertson was to command the Texans in Lee's Army longer than any other officer, until February, 1864, some fifteen months. Brigadier-General John Gregg, a Texan who was transferred into the Brigade from the Army of Tennessee, succeeded to command in February, 1864, when Robertson was re-assigned to the Trans-Mississippi Department. When Gregg was killed at Darbytown Road (October 7, 1864), the command of the Brigade passed to Colonel Frederick S. Bass, the senior colonel and commander of the 1st Texas Infantry. Bass commanded the much depleted unit until February, 1865, when Colonel Robert M. Powell rejoined the organization after his release from prison camp. Powell, the senior colonel of the Brigade and former commander of the 5th Texas, had been wounded and captured at Gettysburg (July 2, 1863). Powell was the commander of "Hood's Texas Brigade" when the survivors, some 600 men, laid down their well used Enfield rifles and their tattered battle flags at Appomattox on April 12, 1865.

During much of the early part of the war, the Texas Brigade was supported by a North Carolina Artillery battery of six guns — Company D, 1st North Carolina Artillery Regiment. This Company or Battery was raised in Rowan County, North Carolina, and was known originally as the "Rowan Artillery" before it received its alphabetical designation. After James Reilly was appointed captain of the unit on June 28, 1861, it was generally referred to as "Reilly's Battery." This Battery supported the Texas Brigade during four of the major battles of the war, 2nd Manassas (August

29-30, 1862), Antietam (September 17, 1862), Fredericksburg (December 13-15, 1862), and Gettysburg (July 2-3, 1863). Reilly's Battery was assigned to Major B. W. Frobel's Artillery Battalion in the summer of 1862, and to Major M. W. Henry's Artillery Battalion just prior to Gettysburg. The infantrymen of the Texas Brigade regarded the North Carolina Artillerymen as unofficial members of their unit.

Key

(1) Original member of Brig. Hdqtrs. (2) Paroled at Appomattox.
K (Killed), W (Wounded), POW (Prisoner of War)
AWOL (Absent Without Leave)

OFFICERS, FIELD OR LINE

ARCHER, JAMES J. Colonel
>Prom. to Bvt. Maj. for gallantry in Mexican War: Orig. cmdr., 5th Tex. Inf. Regt.: Asgnd. cmd., Tex. Brig., Feb. 20, 1862: Returned to cmd. of 5th Tex. Inf., Mar. 12, 1862: Prom., B-Gen., June 3, 1862 & asgnd. cmd., Hatton's Tenn. Brig.: POW, Gettysburg (July 1, 1863): Confined at Johnson's Is. Prison Camp: Exchanged, Summer, 1864: Died, Richmond, Oct. 24, 1864. Note: Archer, prior to joining the CSA, had been a Capt. in the 9th Inf. Regt., US Army.

BASS, FREDERICK S. Colonel
>Orig. Capt., Co. E, 1st Tex. Inf. Regt.: Prom., Maj., Oct. 18, 1861, & asgnd. to Regmtl. Hdqtrs., 1st Tex. Inf.: Prom., Lt.-Col., Spring, 1864: Prom., Col., Summer, 1864, & asgnd. cmd., 1st Tex. Inf.: W., Darbytown Rd. (Oct. 7, 1864): Asgnd. cmd., Hood's Tex. Brig., Oct. 7, 1864: Returned to 1st Tex. Inf. Regt., as cmdr., Feb., 1865: Paroled at Appomattox (Apr. 12, 1865). Note: Bass was prom., Brig-Gen., near end of war, but was never informed of the promotion. He died at the Tex. Conf. Home at Austin, July 9, 1897, and was buried in the State Cemetery in that city.

GREGG, JOHN Brig.-General
>Org. & cmded. 7th Tex. Inf. Regt., Summer, 1861: Prom., Brig.-Gen., Aug. 29, 1862: W., Chickamauga (Sept. 20, 1863): Asgnd. cmd., Hood's Tex. Brig., Feb., 1864: K., Darbytown Rd. (Oct. 7, 1864). Note: Gregg had been a member of the Texas Secession Convention, Jan., 1861, and was a Texas delegate to the Provisional Confederate Congress at Montgomery, Apr., 1861.

HOOD, JOHN BELL Brig.-General
>Commissioned 1Lt. (Cav.) CSA, Apr., 1861: Prom., Capt., Maj., & Lt. Col., Spring & Summer, 1861: Prom., Col. & asgnd. cmd., 4th Tex. Inf. Regt., Sept. 30, 1861: Prom., Brig.-Gen. & asgnd. cmd. Tex. Brig., Mar. 12, 1862: Prom., Maj.-Gen., Oct. 10, 1862

& asgnd. cmd. of a div. in Longstreet's Cmd., Army of No. Va.: W., Gettysburg (July 2, 1862): W., Chickamauga (Sept. 20, 1863): Leg amputated: Prom., Lt.-Gen., Feb. 1, 1864 & asgnd. a corps in Army of Tenn.: Prom., full Gen., CSA, July 18, 1864 & asgnd. cmd., Army of Tenn.: Paroled, Natchez, Miss., May 31, 1865. Note: Hood was the youngest and the eighth and last Confederate officer to be promoted to full general: Prior to the war Hood had been a Lieut. in the 2nd US Cav. Regt.

(2) POWELL, ROBT. M. Colonel

Orig. Capt., Co. D, 5th Tex. Inf. Regt.: Detach serv. in Richmond, Winter, 1861-62: Prom., Maj., Aug. 22, 1862 & asgnd. to Regmtl. Hdqtrs., 5th Tex. Inf.: Prom., Lt.-Col., Aug. 30, 1862: Prom. to Col. & cmd., 5th Tex. Inf. Regt., Nov. 1, 1862: W. & POW, Gettysburg (July 2, 1863): Confined to Johnson's Island (Ohio) prison camp: Transfd. to Fortress Monroe, Jan. 27, 1865: Paroled, Feb. 6, 1865 & assumed cmd., Hood's Tex. Brig.: Paroled, Appomattox (Apr. 12, 1865).

ROBERTSON, JEROME B. Brig.-General

Orig. Capt., Co. I, 5th Tex. Inf. Regt.: Prom., Lt.-Col., Oct. 10, 1861 & asgnd. to Regmtl. Hdqtrs., 5th Tex. Inf.: Prom., Col., June 2, 1862 & took cmd., 5th Tex. Inf.: W., Gaines' Mill (June 27, 1862): W., 2nd Manassas (Aug. 30, 1862): Asgnd. cmd., Hood's Tex. Brig., Oct. 22, 1862: Prom., Brig-Gen., Nov. 1, 1862: W., Gettysburg (July 2, 1863): Court-Martialed, Feb. 25, 1864: Asgnd. to Trans-Miss. Dept.: Asgnd. cmd., Reserve Forces of Tex., June 24, 1864: Paroled, Houston, Tex., July 12, 1865.

(1) WIGFALL, LOUIS T. Brig.-General

Orig. cmdr., 1st Tex. Inf. Regt.: Prom., Brig.-Gen. & cmd. the Tex. Brigade, Nov. 12, 1861: Resgnd. from Army, Feb. 21, 1862, to accept appt. as a Senator from Tex. to the Confederate Congress. Note: Wigfall fled to England after the war. He returned to the US and died in Texas, Feb. 18, 1874. Wigfall is buried in the Episcopal Cemetery at Galveston, Tex.

WOFFORD, WM. T. Colonel

Orig. Col., 18th Ga. Inf. Regt.: Asgnd., cmd. Hood's Tex. Brigade, mid-Sept., 1862: Transfd. to T.R.R. Cobb's Ga. Brig., Nov., 1862: Prom., Brig.-Gen., Jan. 17, 1863: Asgnd., cmd., Dept. of Ga., Jan. 23, 1865: Paroled, Resaca, Ga., May 2, 1865. Note: Wofford served as the Capt. of a Ga., Mtd. Btln. during the Mexican War.

OFFICERS, STAFF

ADJUTANTS (AAG)

EWELL, BENJ. S. Colonel

Transfd. with Gen. Hood to Army of Tenn., Spring, 1864.

KERR, JOHN W. Captain

See "Inspector-Generals" following.

PRICE, FRANCIS L. Captain

Orig. 4Sgt., Co. B, 4th Tex. Inf. Regt.: Prom., 1Sgt., Co. B, Oct. 9, 1861: Prom., Regmtl. Adj., 4th Tex. Inf., July 24, 1862:

Prom., Asst. Adj. Gen., Nov., 1862: Prom., Capt., Spring, 1863: POW, Gettysburg (July 2, 1863): Confined at Johnson's Is., Ohio: Exchanged, Feb. 24, 1865.

QUATTLEBAUM, PAUL J. Major
2Lt. in Reg. US Army (9th Inf. Regt.) prior to war: Orig. Maj., 5th Tex. Inf. Regt.: Appt. Maj., Oct. 2, 1861: Resgnd., Nov. 1, 1861 & transfd. to Hdqtrs., Hood's Tex. Brig. as Asst. Adj. Gen., Nov. 2, 1861: Resgnd., Feb. 22, 1862.

SELLERS, WM. H. Colonel
Orig. 1Lt., Co. A, 5th Tex. Inf. Regt.: Appt. Regmtl. Adj.-Gen., 5th Tex. Inf., Oct. 6, 1861: Asgnd. as Actg. Asst. Adj. Gen. of Brig., Feb., 1862, to replace Quattlebaum: Appt. Asst. Adj. Gen., Apr., 1862: Transfd. to Hood's Div.

INSPECTOR-GENERALS

(2) KERR, JOHN W. Captain
Orig. 2Lt., Co. I, 5th Tex. Inf. Regt.: Prom., 1Lt., Oct. 23, 1861: Appt. Adj., 5th Tex. Inf. Regt., Aug. 1, 1862: Appt. Actg. Asst. Brigade Adj., Oct. 22, 1862: Prom., Capt., Nov. 2, 1863: Prom., Brigade Insp.-Gen., Dec. 3, 1863: Paroled, Appomattox (Apr. 12, 1865).

SHOTWELL, JOHN I. Captain
Orig. 3Lt., Co. B, 1st Tex. Inf. Regt.: On detached service with Div. Provost Guard, July, 1863: Prom., Capt., Jan. 5, 1864: Actg. Insp.-Gen., Tex. Brig., Spring, 1864: Actg. Aide de Camp to Gen. Gregg, Sept., 1864: Actg. Insp.-Gen., Tex. Brig., Oct., 1864: Transfd. to "Foreign Btln." raised by Maj. Garnett Andrews, Dec., 1864.

SURGEONS

(1) CROSS, GEO. WARREN
Orig. Surgeon of the Texas Brigade: Brother-in-law to Gen. L. T. Wigfall: Appt. Surg., 3rd Tex. Cav. Regt., May 21, 1861: Asgnd. as Surg. to Gen. Ben McCulloch's Brig., July, 1861: Transfd. to 5th Tex. Inf. Regt., Nov. 18, 1861: Appt. Surg., Tex. Brig., Dec., 1861: Died at Dumfries, Va., Jan. 19, 1862.

ERSKINE, J. H.
Appt. Brig. Surg., July, 1862: No other record.

ASST. SURGEONS

HERNDON, Z. B.
Commissioned an Asst. Surg., CSA, July 19, 1861: Appt. Asst. Regmtl. Surg., 5th Tex. Inf., Dec. 24, 1861: On detached service, Tex. Brig. Hosp., Jan. 4, 1862: No other record.

JONES, S. A.
Appt. Asst. Brig. Surg., July, 1862: No other record.

RICHARDSON, W. F.
A physician by profession but enl. as a Pvt. at 29 on Aug. 1, 1861 in Co. L, 1st Tex. Inf. Regt.: Appt. 3Sgt., Sept., 1861: Reduced to Pvt., Mar., 1862: Detailed as Surg. at Brig. sick camp, May,

1862: Dischgd. as Pvt. and prom. to rank of Brig. Asst. Surg., Sept. 13, 1862: Transfd. to Conf. Medical Dept., Richmond, Nov., 1862.

SCHERCK, A.
>   Appt. Asst. Brig. Surg., July, 1862: No other record.

WORK, JOHN
>   Appt. Asst. Regmtl. Surg., 1st Tex. Inf., Oct. 17, 1862: Placed in charge of Brig. Field Hosp., Summer, 1863: Transfd. to hosp. duty in Richmond, July 15, 1864.

YOUNG, J. F.
>   Appt. Asst. Brig. Surg., July, 1862: Medical Purveyor & Asst. Surg., Hood's Corps, Army of Tenn., Spring, 1864: Paroled, Greensboro, No. Car., Apr. 26, 1865.

DENTIST

DE GRAFFENRIED, THOS. T.
>   Orig. Pvt., Co. B, 5th Tex. Inf. Regt.: Detailed to Tex. Hosp. as a nurse, Sept. 18, 1862 to Dec., 1863: Sick most of 1864 in various hospitals around Richmond: Detailed as Brig. Dentist by Col. Bass, Nov., 1864: Paroled, Appomattox (Apr. 12, 1865).

COMMISSARY SUBSISTENCE OFFICERS (ACS)

(2) BURNS, ROBT. Major
>   Orig. Pvt., Co. A, 5th Tex. Inf. Regt.: Asgnd. as clerk in Regmtl. Adj. Office, Nov. 4, 1861 to May 7, 1862: Prom., Capt. & appt. Regmtl. Comsy. Off., May 7, 1862: Appt. Brig. Comsy. Off., Aug., 1863: Prom., Maj.: Returned to Tex., Feb. 15, 1865.

HAMILTON, TILFORD A. Major
>   Enl. as a Pvt. in Co. F, 1st Tex. Inf. Regt. at Camp McLeod, Va., Sept. 20, 1861: Detailed as Brig. QM Sgt., Mar., 1862: Detailed to Brig. Comsy. Dept., May, 1862: Detailed as Brig. Comsy. Sgt., Sept., 1862: Appt. Brig. Comsy. Off., Feb. 1, 1863: Prom. to Maj., Spring, 1863: K., Wilderness (May 6, 1864).

NOBLE, MILTON C. Second Lieutenant
>   Enl. at age 20 as a Pvt. in Co. F, 1st Tex. Inf. Regt., at Camp McLeod, Va., Sept. 20, 1861: Elect., 3Lt., Oct. 22, 1862: Prom., 2Lt., Apr. 6, 1863: Detailed as Asst. Brig. Comsy. Off., July, 1863: On "leave of indulgence", Feb. 24, 1865.

POPE, JAS. W. Captain
>   Orig. Pvt., Co. E, 1st Tex. Inf. Regt.: Appt. Regmtl. Comsy. Off., Feb. 3, 1862 & prom. to Capt.: Released from duty as Regmtl. Comsy. Off., July, 1863 when Conf. Govt. abolished Regmtl. Comsy. Office: Asgnd. to Brig. Comsy. Dept. as Comsy. Officer.

(1) STEWART, W. H.
>   Orig. Pvt., Co. A, 4th Tex. Inf. Regt.: Appt. Regmtl. QM Sgt., 4th Tex. Inf., Oct. 1, 1861: Appt. Brig. Comsy. Off., Nov. 18, 1861: Resigned, Nov. 20, 1862.

QUARTERMASTER OFFICERS

EWING, E. H. Major
>   Appt. Brig. QM Off., July, 1862: Later in war served as QM on Hood's Staff, Army of Tenn.

(1)　GEORGE, MOSES B.　Major

Enl. at 28: Orig. Pvt., Co. D, 4th Tex. Inf. Regt.: Appt. QM Off., Tex. Brig., Dec. 9, 1861: Appt. QM Off., Hood's Div., Fall, 1862.

(2)　LITTLEFIELD, J. H.　Major

Orig. 1Sgt., Co. E, 5th Tex. Inf. Regt.: Prom., Capt. & appt. Regmtl. QM Off., 5th Tex. Inf., Oct. 31, 1861: Prom., Maj. & appt. QM Off., Tex. Brig., Summer, 1862: Paroled, Appomattox (Apr. 12, 1865).

NORWOOD, WALTER N.　Captain

Orig. 3Sgt., Co. E, 5th Tex. Inf. Regt.: Prom., 1Sgt., Co. E, Nov. 1, 1861: W., Gaines' Mill (June 27, 1862): Prom., 3Lt., July 22, 1862: Prom., 2Lt., Sept., 1862: Appt. Asst. QM Off., 5th Tex. Inf. Regt., Nov. 1, 1862: Detailed as Asst. Brig. QM, Jan., 1863: Prom., Capt.: Asgnd. as Asst. Brig. QM, Sept. 26, 1864.

ORDNANCE OFFICERS

RANDALL, W. P.　Lieutenant

Orig. 2Cpl., Co. L, 1st Tex. Inf. Regt.: Prom., 5Sgt., June 5, 1862: W., 2nd Manassas (Aug. 30, 1862): Prom., 3Sgt.: Elect., 2Lt., May 20, 1863: POW, Chickamauga (Sept. 19, 1863): Exchanged: Appt. Ordn. Off., Tex. Brig., Mar., 1864: K., Wilderness (May 6, 1864).

SUBLETT, DAVE L.　Lieutenant

Orig. 2Lt., Co. E, 4th Tex. Inf. Regt.: Appt. Aide de Camp to Gen. Hood, Mar. 17, 1862: Prom., 1Lt. & appt. Ordn. Off., Tex. Brig., May 1, 1862: Asgnd. Actg. Ordn. Off., Hood's Div., Sept., 1862: Prom., Capt.

PROVOST MARSHAL

BRADFORD, J. W.　Captain

Appt., July, 1862: No other record.

AIDE DE CAMPS

BUCKLEY, EDW. C.

See list of "QM Sgts." following.

CHAMBERS, THOS. JEFFERSON

Appt. Aide de Camp to Gen. Hood, July, 1862. Note: Chambers, an important Tex. political figure, at age 60, came to Va., and volunteered his services early in the war. He was assassinated in Tex., Mar. 15, 1865.

DWYER, JOS. E.

Appt. Aide de Camp to Gen. Hood, Mar. 28, 1862: No other record.

SCOTT, JOHN G.

Orig. Pvt., Co. G, 1st Tex. Inf. Regt.: Detached duty, Brig. Comsy., Mar. 10, 1862: Appt. Aide de Camp to Gen. J. B. Robertson, Nov. 12, 1862.

SMITH, JOHN S.

Orig. Pvt. Co. E, 4th Tex. Inf. Regt.: Detached serv. at Brig. Hdqtrs., from Nov. 13, 1861: Asgnd. as Aide de Camp to Gen. Hood, Spring, 1862: Prom., 1Lt. & asgnd. to Hdqtrs., Hood's Div., Jan. 21, 1863.

SUBLETT, DAVE L.
See list of "Ordnance Officers" above.

NON-COMMISSIONED OFFICERS

SERGEANT-MAJOR
BARCLAY, THOS.
Orig. Pvt., Co. F, 1st Tex. Inf. Regt.: Appt. 1Cpl., Sept. 7, 1862:
Appt. Actg. Brig. Sgt. Maj., Feb. 3, 1863: Detailed as a clerk in
Brig. Adj. Office, Mar. & Apr., 1863: Paroled, Farmville, Va.,
Apr. 13, 1865.

QUARTERMASTER-SERGEANTS
BUCKLEY, EDW. C.
Enl. at 22: Orig. Pvt., Co. L, 1st Tex. Inf. Regt.: Served as Aide
de Camp to Gen. Hood at Gaines' Mill (June 27, 1862): Appt.
Brig. QM Sgt., July, 1862: Appt. Div. QM Clerk, Feb., 1863:
Asgnd. as Clerk for Maj. George, QM, Hood's Corps, Army of
Tenn., July, 1864.
(2) SHELTON, WM. A
Orig. Pvt., Co. L, 1st Tex. Inf. Regt.: W., Seven Pines (June 1,
1862): Prom., 4Sgt.: Detailed as QM Sgt., Tex. Brig., Feb., 1863:
Paroled, Appomattox (Apr. 12, 1865).
HAMILTON, TILFORD A.
See list of "Commissary Subsistence Officers" above.

COMMISSARY SUBSISTENCE-SERGEANT
HAMILTON, TILFORD A.
See list of "Commissary Subsistence Officers" above.

ORDNANCE-SERGEANT
(2) ROBINSON, JAS.
Orig. Pvt., Co. E, 4th Tex. Inf.: Appt. Brig. Ordn. Sgt., May 20,
1862: Returned to Co. E, 4th Tex. Inf., Feb., 1864: Paroled,
Appomattox (Apr. 12, 1865).

SPECIALISTS

FARRIERS OR BLACKSMITHS
BRIEGER, JOHN G.
Enl. in Co. F, 4th Tex. Inf., Mar. 24, 1862 at Lyons, Tex.:
Detailed as Brig. Blacksmith, Jan.-Sept., 1864: W. & POW,
Darbytown Rd. (Oct. 7, 1864): Confined at Pt. Lookout, Md.:
Paroled, June 9, 1865.
(2) HARDOIN, SERAND H.
Enl. in Co. F, 4th Tex. Inf., Mar. 18, 1862 at Hopkinsville, Tex.:
Asgnd. duty as Brig. Blacksmith, June 25, 1862: Asgnd. duty as
Blacksmith of Div. (Hood's) Wagon Train, July, 1864: Paroled at
Appomattox (Apr. 12, 1865).

FORAGEMASTER

(1) HUNT, JAS. F.
> Orig. Pvt., Co. E, 4th Tex. Inf.: Actg. Brig. Foragemaster, Dec. 1, 1861: Appt. Brig. Foragemaster, May, 1862: Deserted, Jan. 1, 1863.

WHEELWRIGHT

(1) SIMPSON, HIRAM
> Orig. Pvt., Co. H, 5th Tex. Inf. Regt.: Detailed as Brig. Wheelwright, Nov. 20, 1861: Sick in various hospitals around Richmond, Feb.-Aug., 1862: AWOL in Tex., Fall, 1862: Dropped from rolls for prolonged absence, Oct., 1864.

WAGONMASTER

BARTON, OLIVER P.
> Orig. 4Sgt., Co. I, 5th Tex. Inf.: Detailed as Brig. Wagonmaster, Mar. 24, 1862 to May 25, 1864: W. (thigh), Wilderness (May 6, 1864): Accidentally wounded, Darbytown Rd. (Oct. 7, 1864): Finger amputated: Paroled, Montgomery, Ala., May 9, 1865.

1ST TEX. VOL. INF. REGT.
HDQTRS. - FIELD, STAFF & BAND

Originally organized as an overstrength Battalion (Cos. A thru H) June, 1861. Organized as a Regiment (Cos. I, K, L added), Aug., 1861: Co. M was added July, 1862, making the 1st Texas Infantry the only twelve company regiment in the Army of Northern Virginia.

Key

(1) Original member of Hdqtrs. (2) Paroled at Appomattox.
K (Killed), W (Wounded), POW (Prisoner of War)
AWOL (Absent Without Leave)

OFFICERS, FIELD & LINE

BASS, FREDERICK S.   Colonel
    See roster, "Hdqtrs., Hood's Tex. Brig."

(1)   RAINEY, ALEXIS T.   Colonel
    Orig. Capt., Co. H: Prom. to Maj., Sept., 1861 & transfd. to Regmt. Hdqtrs. (Orig. Maj. of Regt.): Prom., Lt-Col., Nov. 12, 1861: Prom., Col., Jan. 2, 1862: W., Gaines' Mill (June 27, 1862): Returned to Tex. on disability furlough, June 27, 1862, and never returned to Regt.

(1)   WIGFALL, LOUIS T.   Colonel
    Orig. Col., 1st Tex. Inf. Regt.: See roster, "Hdqtrs., Hood's Tex. Brig."

BLACK, HARVEY H.   Lieut.-Colonel
    Orig. Capt., Co. A: Prom., Maj., Dec. 12, 1861 & asgnd. to Regmtl. Hdqtrs.: Prom., Lt-Col., Jan. 2, 1862: K., Eltham's Landing (May 7, 1862).

HARDING, RICHARD J.   Lieut.-Colonel
    Orig. 1Sgt., Co. B: Elect., 1Lt.: Elect., Capt.: W., Gettysburg (July 2, 1863): Prom., Lt-Col., Spring, 1864, & asgnd. to Regmtl. Hdqtrs., 1st Tex. Inf.: W., Cold Harbor (June 3, 1864): Relieved from active duty by medical examining board, Summer, 1864.

(1)   McLEOD, HUGH   Lieut-Colonel
    Orig. Lt-Col., 1st Tex. Inf. Regt.: Died of pneumonia in Va., Jan. 2, 1862: Body, on being shipped back to Tex., passed through New Orleans Jan. 15, and lay in state there prior to being returned to Austin for burial in the State Cemetery.

WORK, PHILLIP A.   Lieut.-Colonel
    Orig. Capt., Co. F: Asgnd. to Regmtl. Hdqtrs., & prom. to Lt-Col., May 19, 1862: Sick at Selma, Ala., Sept. 19, 1863: Resgnd. on account of health, Jan. 5, 1864.

CLOPTON, DR. ALBERT GALLATIN Major
>Orig. Capt., Co. D: Asgnd. to Regmtl. Hdqtrs., & prom. to Maj., Jan. 2, 1862: Transfd. to Medical Dept., Richmond.

DALE, MATT Major
>Orig. 2Lt., Co. G: Asgnd. to Regmtl. Hdqtrs., & prom. to Maj., May 19, 1862: K., Antietam (Sept. 17, 1862).

WOODWARD, JOHN R. Major
>Orig. Capt., Co. G: Detailed to recruiting service in Tex., Feb.-Apr., 1862: Appt. Actg. Maj. of Regt., May, 1863: W., Gettysburg (July 2, 1863): Died of wound at Front Royal, Va., July 22, 1863.

KENNEDY, JAS. H. Ensign/Lieut.
>Orig. Pvt. in Co. G.: Detailed as orderly to Col. Bass, Feb. 24, 1863: Appt. 1Sgt., Co. G., Apr. 7, 1863: Appt. Ensign, 1st Tex. Inf. Regt., July 18, 1864.

OFFICERS, STAFF

ADJUTANTS

FONTAINE, HENRY B.
>Orig. Pvt. in Co. F: Transfd. to Co. B, April 26, 1862: Appt. Regmtl. Adj., May 18, 1862: Returned to Co. B, July, 1862: Performed duty with "Hood's Minstrel Show," Dec., 1862: Transfd. to Trans-Miss. Army: Elect. Capt. of Artillery.

FORSYTH, A. P.
>Orig. 1Cpl., Co. L: Prom., 3Sgt., June 5, 1862: Appt. Regmtl. Sgt.-Maj., Aug. 30, 1862: Prom., 2Lt., Oct. 23, 1862: Appt. Regmtl. Adj., Dec., 1862: Asgnd. to recruiting duty in Tex., Spring, 1863: Dischgd. for disability, July 18, 1864.

(1) HENDERSON, JAS. F.
>Orig. 3Lt., Co. A: Appt. Regmtl. Adj., Oct. 1, 1861.

(2) LEETE, JOHN H.
>Orig. 1Sgt., Co. A: Appt. Regmtl. Sgt.-Maj., Sept. 17, 1862: W., Wilderness (May 6, 1864): Appt. Regmtl. Adj., 1865: Paroled, Appomattox (April 12, 1865).

LORD, H. H.
>Actg. Adj., Winter, 1864-65: W., Charles City Rd., near Richmond, Mar. 4, 1865.

SHROPSHIRE, J. WINKFIELD
>Orig. 1Sgt., Co. D: Appt. Regmtl. Adj., July 12, 1862: W., Antietam (Sept. 17, 1862): Resgnd. from army, Feb. 3, 1863.

SURGEONS

(1) EWING, A.
>Orig. Pvt., Co. A: Appt. Regmtl. Surg., July 19, 1861: Transfd. to Gen. Pemberton's cmd. at Jackson, Miss., March 23, 1863.

TAYLOR, ARCH
>Appt. Regmtl. Surg., Aug. 13, 1863.

WATERS, H. W.
>Appt. Regmtl. Surg., April 7, 1863: Left with wounded at Gettysburg — POW.

ASST. SURGEONS

CROMBIE, ANDREW C.
>Orig. Pvt., Co. G: Detailed to Medical Staff, 1st Tex. Inf. Regt.: Appt. Asst. Regmtl. Surg., March 24, 1863: K., in RR wreck on way to Ga. for battle of Chickamauga, Sept., 1863.

(2) MERRITT, G. A.
>Appt. Asst. Regmtl. Surg., Feb. 24, 1864: Paroled, Appomattox (April 12, 1865).

SNOW, HENRY
>Orig. Pvt., Co. F: Elect. 1Lt.: W., Gaines' Mill (June 27, 1862): Detailed as Asst. Surg., Regmtl. Hdqtrs., Spring, 1862: Returned to Co. F: Resgnd. from army, June 18, 1863.

(1) WARE, G. S.
>Orig. Pvt., Co. F: Appt. Asst. Regmtl. Surg., July 19, 1861: Resgnd. from army, Oct. 23, 1862.

WORK, JOHN
>See roster, "Hdqtrs., Hood's Tex. Brig."

COMMISSARY SUBSISTENCE OFFICER (ACS)

(1) POPE, JAS. W.
>See roster, "Hdqtrs., Hood's Tex. Brig."

QUARTERMASTER OFFICER

MILLS, C. STYLES
>Orig. Pvt., Co. E: Appt. Regmtl. QM, April 14, 1862: In charge of Train (wagons) in Hood's Div., Sept. 1 to Oct. 1, 1862.

CHAPLAIN

VICK, IREDELL R.
>Jnd. Co. K as a Pvt. from Co. C, 3rd Ark. Inf. Regt., June 13, 1863: W., Chickamauga (Sept. 19, 1863): Appt. Regmtl. Chaplain, July 15, 1864.

NON-COMMISSIONED OFFICERS

SERGEANT-MAJORS

FORSYTH, A. P.
>See preceding list of "Adjutants."

HORTON, ALFRED M.
>Orig. 2Sgt., Co. H: Appt. Regmtl. Sgt.-Maj., June 18, 1862: K., 2nd Manassas (Aug. 30, 1862).

LEETE, JOHN H.
>See preceding list of "Adjutants."

(1) TODD, GEO. T.
>Orig. Pvt., Co. A: Appt. Regmtl. Sgt.-Maj., Aug., 1861: Elect. Capt. of Co. A, May 16, 1862: Returned to Co. A: W., Antietam (Sept. 17, 1862): Resgnd. from serv., Oct. 30, 1863: Left Co. A, Dec. 1, 1863: Re-entered Conf. serv. as Adj., W. P. Lane's Tex. Cav. Regt.

COLOR-SERGEANTS

BRANARD, GEO. A.

    Orig. 4Cpl., Co. L: Appt. Regmtl. Color-Sgt., May 11, 1862: W., Knoxville, Nov. 27, 1863 — disabled: Served as Sgt. in Brig. Ambulance Corps: Retired for disability, Feb., 1865.

BRONAUGH, D. B.

    Orig. Pvt., Co. A: Resgnd. from Co. A, May 16, 1862: Detailed as Regmtl. Color-Sgt. for battle of Antietam (Sept. 17, 1862).

WALKER, D. F.

    Orig. Pvt., Co. A: Prom., 5Sgt.: Served as Regmtl. Color-Sgt., April, 1862: Detailed as Regmtl. Butcher, Sept., 1862: Detailed as Brig. Butcher, Jan., 1863: POW, near Sweetwater, Tenn., Nov. 11, 1863.

QUARTERMASTER-SERGEANT

(1)   MAHONEY, J. P.

    Orig. Pvt., Co. L: Appt. Regmtl. QM-Sgt., Oct. 15, 1861: On detchd. serv. with QM Depot in Richmond, April, 1862.

COMMISSARY (SUBSISTENCE)-SERGEANTS

(2)   ALDRICH, COLLIN Q.

    Orig. Pvt., Co. I: Detailed as Co. Comsy.-Sgt., Sept. 25, 1861: Appt. Regmtl. Comsy. Clerk, Dec., 1862: Appt. Regmtl. Comsy.-Sgt., July 31, 1863: Paroled, Appomattox (April 12, 1865).

SCOTT, JOHN G.

    Orig. Pvt., Co. G: Appt. Regmtl. Comsy.-Sgt., April, 1862: Appt. aide-de-camp on staff of Gen. J. B. Robertson, Nov. 12, 1862.

ORDNANCE-SERGEANTS

DUNHAM, M. A.

    Orig. Pvt., Co. B: Detailed to recruiting serv. in Tex., Feb.-April, 1862: W., Gaines' Mill (June 27, 1862): W., 2nd Manassas (Aug. 30, 1862): Transfd. to Co. M, 1st Tex. Inf. Regt., Sept., 1862: W., Antietam (Sept. 17, 1862): Appt. Regmtl. Ordn.-Sgt., Aug. 15, 1863.

LAZARUS, S. S.

    Orig. Pvt., Co. L: Appt. Regmtl. Ordn.-Sgt., May 21, 1862: Returned to Co. L, April 1, 1863: W., Chickamauga (Sept. 19, 1863): Disabled & detailed to QM Depot, Montgomery, Ala.

MAHLE, HENRY B.

    Orig. Pvt., Co. G: Prom., 3Sgt., Nov. 1, 1862: Actg. Asst. Ordn.-Sgt., May, 1863: W., Wilderness (May 6, 1864).

MYNATT, W. PARK

    Orig. Pvt., Co. G: Prom., 1Cpl.: POW, Antietam (Sept. 17, 1862): Paroled & rejnd. Co., Dec. 2, 1862: Appt. Regmtl. Ordn.-Sgt., March 25, 1863: Elect., 2Lt., Aug. 12, 1863, & returned to Co. G: W., Chickamauga (Sept. 19, 1863): Died of wound, Sept. 25.

WOOD, CHAS. W.

    Pvt. in Co. E: Detailed as Regmtl. Ordn.-Sgt., April, 1862: W., Gaines' Mill (June 27, 1862): Died of wound.

HOSPITAL STEWARD

(2) FORT, WM. A.

Orig. 2Sgt., Co. D: Reduced to Pvt.: Detailed as Surgeon's Asst., June, 1862: Appt. Regmtl. Hosp. Steward, Sept., 1862: Additional duty as Regmtl. Druggist: Paroled, Appomattox (April 12, 1865).

BAND

DRUM-MAJOR

SHARP, CHARLEY F.

Orig. Drummer, Co. F: Appt. Regmtl. Drum-Maj., April 30, 1862.

FIFER

ALLEN, E. A.

Orig. Musician (Fifer), Co. E: Appt. Regmtl. Fifer, May 28, 1862: Elect., 2Lt., Co. E, Oct. 21, 1862: W., Wilderness (May 6, 1864): Foot amputated.

BUGLER

RIDLEY, JAS. M.

Orig. Musician (Drummer), Co. K: Reduced to ranks, June 1, 1862: AWOL, Gaines' Mill (June 27, 1862): Asgnd. to Regmtl. Hdqtrs. as Bugler, Fall, 1862: Self-inflicted wound while in Richmond Hosp., Spring, 1863: Reduced to ranks, Aug. 1, 1863: Deserted to Tex., Spring, 1864.

BAND MEMBER

SHEPARD, W. G.

Orig. Pvt., Co. L: W., Chickamauga (Sept. 19, 1863): Detailed as a Regmtl. Musician, Fall, 1864.

SPECIALISTS

FARRIER

STEDMAN, B. B. ("Bug")

Orig. Pvt., Co. F: Prom., 3Cpl.: Co. Flag Bearer, Gaines' Mill (June 27, 1862): Resgnd. from Co. & appt. Regmtl. Farrier & Blacksmith, Oct. 1, 1862: Missing since Dec. 20, 1863 — presumed deserted.

WAGONMASTERS

BRADSTON, SAMUEL J.

See Co. I: Served as Regmtl. Wagonmaster early part of 1864.

COOK, ABRAM P.

Orig. Pvt., Co. G: Asgnd. as Regmtl. Wagon Master, Fall, 1862: Paroled, Appomattox (April 12, 1865).

COMPANY A — *MARION RIFLES*

Company was organized in Marion County, Texas, and mustered into Confederate service "for one year" at New Orleans, May 16, 1861, by Lt. C. W. Phifer, CSA.

Key

(1) Original member of Company. (2) Paroled at Appomattox.
K (Killed), W (Wounded), POW (Prisoner of War)
AWOL (Absent Without Leave)

ORIGINAL OFFICERS

(1) BLACK, HARVEY H. Capt. — See roster, "Regmtl. Hdqtrs., 1st Tex. Inf."
(1) WIMBERLY, W. G. 1Lt. — Elect., Capt., Jan., 1862: Relieved from duty when Co., re-org., May 16, 1862: Resgnd. and returned to Tex.
(1) WATERHOUSE, JACK 2Lt. — Cmded. Co. at Eltham's Landing (May 7, 1862): Relieved from duty when Co., re-org. May 16, 1862: Resgnd. and returned to Tex.
(1) HENDERSON, JAS. F. 3Lt. — See roster, "Regmtl. Hdqtrs., 1st Tex. Inf."

ORIGINAL NON-COMMISSIONED OFFICERS

(1) LEETE, JOHN H. 1Sgt. — See roster, "Regmtl. Hdqtrs., 1st Tex. Inf."
(2)
(1) BUSH, G. H. 2Sgt. — Enrolled at Jefferson, Tex., Apr. 29, 1861, age 25: Dischgd. for disability (chronic diarrhea), Feb. 23, 1862.
(1) WIMBERLY, JOHN 3Sgt. — K. near Potomac River, 1861.
(1) POSTLEWAITE, CHAS. S. 4Sgt. — See list of "Other Officers" following.
(1) CRAWFORD, J. K. ("Bull") 1Cpl. — W., Gaines' Mill (June 27, 1862).
(1) GILLIAN, J. W. 2Cpl. — Deserted, July 13, 1862 (enlmt. expired).
(1) CAMPBELL, ARGYLE ("Gulie") 3Cpl. — Prom., 3Sgt.: W., Chickamauga (Sept. 19, 1863): Missing, Darbytown Rd. (Oct. 7, 1864).
(1) LANEY, WES. W. 4Cpl. — See list of "Other Officers" following.

OTHER OFFICERS

LANEY, WES. W. Capt. — Orig. 4Cpl. of Co.: Elect. Lt.: W., Eltham's Landing (May 7, 1862): W., Chickamauga (Sept. 19, 1863): Elect. Capt., Jan., 1864: W., Wilderness (May 6, 1864).

TODD, GEO. T.   Capt. — See roster, "Regmtl Hdqtrs., 1st Tex. Inf."

POWELL, T. D.   1Lt. — Resgnd., May 14, 1863.

ROBINSON, HARRY H.   1Lt. — Orig. Pvt. in Co.: Elect., 3Lt., May 16, 1862: W., 2nd Manassas (Aug. 30, 1862): W., Chickamauga (Sept. 19, 1863): Elect., 2Lt.: Elect. 1Lt.: Paroled, Appomattox (April 12, 1865).

THOMPSON, G. B.   2Lt. — Orig. Pvt. in Co.: Elect., 2 Lt., May 16, 1862: Confined in Richmond jail by civilian authorities, Jan. to June, 1863: AWOL, July 13, 1863.

POSTLEWAITE, CHAS. S.   3Lt. — Orig. 4Sgt. of Co.: Elect., 3 Lt.: Relieved from duty when Co., re-org., May 16, 1862: Resgnd.

MUSICIANS

(1)   WALKER, DICK — Enl. at Jefferson, Tex., Apr. 27, 1861, age 50: Dischgd., May 13, 1862, "incapable of performing duty of soldier because of hernia.

PRIVATES

(1)
(2)   ALFORD, JULIUS, C. — Prom., 1 Cpl., Dec. 1862: Prom., 2Sgt., Fall, 1864: Paroled, Appomattox (Apr. 12, 1865).

(1)   ALFORD, J. W. ("Will") — Died of disease, Ashland, Va., Apr. 12, 1862.

(1)
(2)   ALLEN, JAS. L. — Appt. 2Cpl., May 16, 1862: Reduced to Pvt., Dec., 1862: W. (face), Wilderness (May 6, 1864): Paroled, Appomattox (Apr. 12, 1865).

(1)   ALLEN, T. B. ("Ben") — W., Chickamauga (Sept. 19, 1863): Prom., 1Cpl., Oct. 31, 1863: W., Wilderness (May 6, 1864).

(1)   ALLEN, THOS. — Deserted, May 27, 1862 (enlmt. expired).

(1)   ARMSTRONG, GEO. W. — W., Antietam (Sept. 17, 1862): Detailed to "Texas Iron Works," April, 1864.

(1)   BAKER, GREEN — W., Antietam (Sept. 17, 1862).

(1)   BARRON, CHAS. S. S. — Appt., 5Sgt., May 16, 1862: Prom., 1Sgt., Oct. 1, 1862: Reported AWOL, Oct. 31, 1863: POW, Rodney, Miss., Nov. 7, 1863.

(1)   BELL, THOS. H. — Confined to Hosp., Medical College of Va., July 19-23, 1861: Dischgd. for disability, Oct. 26, 1861.

BIRD, ROSS — Hospitalized, Richmond, Apr., 1862: Deserted, June 11, 1862 (enlmt. expired).

(1)   BLACKBURN, FRANK E. — W., Antietam (Sept. 17, 1862): K., Chickamauga (Sept. 19, 1863).

(1)   BLALOCK, JAS. M. — Sick in hosp., Richmond, Summer, 1862: Prom., 2Cpl., Sept., 1862: AWOL, Winter, 1863-64: Reduced to. Pvt.: W., Cold Harbor (June 3, 1864): W., Darbytown Rd. (Oct. 7, 1864): Furloughed to Tex.

(1)   BOBO, C. W. — Died of disease at Richmond, Va., April 19, 1862.

(1)   BOWERS, GUS — Deserted, May 27, 1862 (enlmt. expired).

(1)   BRACKNELL, W. N. — This soldier was sick with lung disease and rheumatism in hospitals all over the South during 1863 — Chimborazo in Richmond, General Hospitals in Lynchburg, and

Farmville, Va., Episcopal Hosp. at Williamsburg, and a CSA hospital in Atlanta, Ga.: Reported AWOL, Nov. 1, 1863: POW, Rodney, Miss., Nov. 7, 1863: Confined to Camp Morton, Ind. for rest of war.

(1) BREWER, T. E. ("Dick") — W., Antietam (Sept. 17, 1862): Prom., 3Cpl.: W., Chickamauga (Sept. 19, 1863).

(1) BRONAUGH, D. B. — See roster, "Regmtl. Hdqtrs., 1st Tex., Inf."

(1) BROOKSHIRE, J. H. — Dischgd., Aug. 12, 1862, term of enlistment expired.

(1) BROWNING, R. HENRY — Died of disease at Richmond, Va., April 9, 1862.

BUFFALO, DAVID — Deserted, June 11, 1862 (enlmt. expired).

(1) CAROLAN, P. J. — Dischgd., Aug. 12, 1862, enlistment terminated.

(1) CHASE, RILEY — Dischgd., Aug. 12, 1862, enlistment terminated.

(1) COX, J. M. — Dischgd., Aug. 12, 1862, enlistment terminated.

(1) DERRICK, E. P. — W., 2nd Manassas (Aug. 30, 1862): W., Antietam (Sept. 17, 1862): K., Gettysburg (July 2, 1863).

(1) DOUGHERTY, HUGH — W., 2nd Manassas (Aug. 30, 1862): K., Chickamauga (Sept. 19, 1863).

(1) EIDSON, JOHN, W. M. — Prom., 4Cpl., July, 1862: Dischgd., Sept. 16, 1862, as a non-conscript, underage (17).

(1) ELLIOTT, W. A. ("Bill") — Sick furlough to Ala., Summer & Fall, 1862: Sick in Richmond Hosp., Winter & Spring, 1863 (hemorrhoids & rheumatism): Confined by civil authorities in Richmond jail, May, 1863: Paroled, Columbia, S.C., May 4, 1865.

EPPERSON, H. J. — W., Antietam (Sept. 17, 1862): POW, Gerardstown, Va., July 19, 1863: Paroled, Camp Delaware, June 19, 1865.

(1) ETLEY, JOHN — K., Eltham's Landing (May 7, 1862).

(1) EWING, DR. A. — See roster, "Regmtl. Hdqtrs., 1st Tex. Inf."

(1) FLOYD, J. W. — Dischgd. for disability, May 1, 1862.

(1) FRAZOR (or FRAZIER), O. C. — Sick in Hosp., Summer, 1862: Dischgd., Nov. 8, 1862, enlistment terminated.

(1) GAINES, JOHN — W., Gettysburg (July 2, 1863): W., Wilderness (May 6, 1864).

(1) GOFORTH, JOHN C. — Appt. a teamster in Tex. Brig., Sept., 1862: W., Wilderness (May 6, 1864). K., Chaffin's Farm (Sept. 29, 1864).

(1) GRAHAM, CHAS. J. — Recruiting duty in Tex., Feb.-Apr., 1862: Dischgd., enlistment terminated: May have later jnd., 18th Tex. Inf. Regt.

(1) GRAY, JOHN T. (or F.) — Prom., 2Sgt.: W., Chickamauga (Sept. 19, 1863): Prom., 1Sgt.: Missing, Darbytown Rd. (Oct. 7, 1864).

(1) HARROWER, W. J. — Deserted, May 19, 1862 (enlmt. expired).

HAWKINS, JOHN C. — Enl., June 2, 1862: Prom., 3Cpl.: POW, Chickamauga (Sept. 19, 1863): Confined in Camp Douglas, Federal prison at Chicago: Released May 23, 1865.

(1) HEMPSTEAD, STEPHAN — Enl., May 27, 1861: POW, Antietam (Sept. 17, 1862): Confined to Fed. prison in St. Louis.

(1) HENNESY (or HENNESSY), HUGH — W., Eltham's Landing (May 7, 1862): Dischgd., Aug. 12, 1862, enlmt. expired.

(1) HIGGINS, PATRICK — W., Eltham's Landing (May 7, 1862).

(1) HILL, JAS. C. — Appt., 1Sgt., May 16, 1862: K., Antietam (Sept. 17, 1862).

(1) HINES, S. M. — Asgnd. as a scout along the Occoquan R., Winter, 1861-62: No other record.

HINNANT, BOYNTON C. — Prom., 2Cpl.: Resgnd., May 16, 1862.

(1) HINNANT, HENRY H. — W., Eltham's Landing (May 7, 1862): Died, May 31, from wound.

HOLLAND, B. F. — Enl., Dec. 1, 1863: W., Wilderness (May 6, 1864).

(1) HUDSON, GEORGE W. — Sick in Richmond hosp., Nov., 1862-Aug., 1863: Detailed as a hosp. attendant at Charlottesville, Va., Sept., 1863-Aug., 1864: Dischgd. from service, Feb. 1, 1865.

(1) JACOBY, M. — W., Gaines' Mill (June 27, 1862): Leg amputated: Returned to Tex.

(1) JOHNSON, H. R. — Enl., Apr. 25, 1861, at Jefferson, Tex.: Dischgd., July 15, 1861, for "inability to perform duty."

JONES, C. (or E.) D. — Hospitalized, Summer, 1862: K., Antietam (Sept. 17, 1862).

(1) JONES, W. R. — Died of pneumonia at Fredericksburg, Va., Mar. 30, 1862.

JOYNER, JAS. A. — Hospitalized, Richmond, Spring, 1862: Deserted, June 11, 1862 (enlmt. expired).

(1) KENNEDY, JOHN H. — Paroled, Talladega, Ala., June 30, 1865.

(1) LANE, BEN R. — W., Gaines' Mill (June 27, 1862): W., Antietam (Sept. 17, 1862): Detailed to QM Office in Richmond, Oct., 1863.

(1) LEFTWICH, M. L. — No record available: Probably discharged when 1 year enlistment terminated, Summer, 1862.

(1) LUSK, H. H. — Sick, May, 1861: Dischgd. for disability, Aug. 11, 1861.

(1) MAHON, TOM — W., Eltham's Landing (May 7, 1862): Died of wound, May 19, 1862.

(1) MALONE, JAS. K. — Prom., 3Cpl., May 16, 1862: W., Antietam (Sept. 17, 1862): Jailed by civil authorities in Richmond, Va., April, 1863.

(1) MASON, WILEY C. — Enl. at Jefferson, Tex., Apr. 27, 1861, age 33: Dischgd. for disability, Oct. 31, 1861.

(1) MATHEWS, G. M. — Detailed to Litter Corps, Sept., 1862: Paroled,
(2) Appomattox (April 12, 1865).

(1) McLENDON, W. F. — Sick, Summer, 1861: Detailed as Scout, Fall, 1862: K., Gettysburg (July 2, 1863).

(1) McRUNNELS, W. A. — Transfd. to Capt. W. E. Jones Co., Va. Mtd. Vols., June 22, 1861.

(1) MURPHY, PATRICK — Born in Ireland, enlisted at age 37: Dischgd., Aug. 12, 1862, enlistment expired.

(1) ORR, H. V. — Dischgd., Aug. 12, 1862, enlistment expired.

(1) OWEN, W. E. — Deserted, June 11, 1862 (enlmt. expired).

(1) PAGE, P. R. — Sick in hosp., Spring, 1862 (acute dysentery): Dischgd., Aug. 12, 1862, expiration of term of service.

PARKER, WM. — Enlisted, May 27, 1861: POW, Apr. 2, 1865, at Hatcher's Run, Va.

(1) RINTS, JOS. — Born in Germany, enlisted at age 50: Sick in hosp., Spring & Summer, 1862: Dischgd., Aug. 12, 1862, enlistment expired.

(1) ROBINSON, HARRY H. — See list of "Other Officers" above.
(2)
(1) ROGERS, GEO. L. — W., Eltham's Landing (May 7, 1862): K., Wilderness (May 6, 1864).
(1) ROGERS, W. T. — Prom., 3Cpl., Nov., 1862: W., Cold Harbor (June 3, 1864): Hospitalized, Richmond, Summer, 1864.
(1) ROGERS, WALTER R. — Dischgd., Aug. 13, 1861 on Surg. Cert. of disability.
(1) SEDBERRY, J. D. — Dischgd., Dec. 9, 1861, physical disability.
(1) SETSER, P. — W., Eltham's Landing (May 7, 1862): Died from wound.
(1) SLAUGHTER, DANIEL S. — W., accidentally in camp, Dec. 28, 1862: Sick in hosp., Spring, 1863: Dischgd. for disability, July 31, 1863.
(1) SLAUGHTER, E. — Died of disease at Fredericksburg, Va., April 4, 1862.
(1) SMITH, D. W. — Deserted, June 11, 1862 (enlmt. expired).
     SMITH, ED. D. — Prom., 3Cpl., July, 1862: Prom., 5Sgt., Sept., 1862: Prom., 4Sgt., July, 1863: W., Chickamauga (Sept. 19, 1863): Sick, Howard's Grove Hosp., Richmond, Summer, 1864: Retired by Medical Bd. Aug. 16, 1864.
     SMITH, J. H. — Dischgd., Aug. 12, 1862, expiration of term of service.
(1) STEPT, GOLDSON — No record available: Probably dischgd., Aug., 1862, when term of service expired.
(1) SWEENEY, J. A. — No record available: Probably dischgd., Aug., 1862, when term of service expired.
(1) TADLOCK, CARTER — Confined by civil authorities in Richmond jail, May, 1863: Paroled near Richmond, May 4, 1865.
(1) TANNER, THOS. — Dischgd., Aug. 11, 1861, physically disabled.
(1) THOMPSON, G. B. — See list of "Other Officers" above.
(1) TODD, GEO. T. — See list of "Other Officers" above.
(1) TODD, JAS. — "Exchanged at Muster (May 16, 1861) for his brother, Geo. T. Todd."
     TODD, LOUIS B. — Prom., 2Sgt.: POW, Gerardstown, Va., July 19, 1863.
(1) VEAL, JOHN C. — Dischgd., Aug. 12, 1862, enlmt. expired: Re-enl. in Co., Mar. 25, 1863: W., Chickamauga (Sept. 19, 1863): Hospitalized, Atlanta, Ga.: Paroled, Durham Station, N.C., Apr. 26, 1865.
(1) WALKER, DAVID F. — See roster, "Regmtl. Hdqtrs., 1st Tex. Inf."
     WALTON, DOUG D. — Asgnd. to recruiting duty in Tex., Feb.-April, 1862: Never returned to Va., term of enlistment expired.
     WHITTAKER, WILLIS — Asgnd. to recruiting duty in Tex., Feb.-April, 1862: W., Antietam (Sept. 17, 1862): Arm amputated.
(1) WILLIAMS, CHAS. B. — Detailed as a carpenter at Brig. Hdqtrs.: Dischgd., Aug. 12, 1862, term of enlmt. expired.
(1) WILLINGHAM, W. J. — Dischgd., Fall, 1862, enlistment expired.
(1) WRIGHT, HENRY CLAY — W. & POW, Gettysburg (July 2, 1863): Died of wound, Aug. 19, 1863.
(1) WRIGHT, JOHN K. — W., Gaines' Mill (June 27, 1862): Dischgd., Aug. 12, 1862, term of service expired.

COMPANY B — *LIVINGSTON GUARDS*

Company was organized at Livingston, Polk County, Texas, and mustered into Confederate service "for one year" at New Orleans, May 16, 1861, by Lt. C. W. Phifer, CSA.

Key

(1) Original member of Hdqtrs. (2) Paroled at Appomattox.
K (Killed), W (Wounded), POW (Prisoner of War)
AWOL (Absent Without Leave).

ORIGINAL OFFICERS

(1)   MOORE, D. D.   Capt. — Resgnd. Sept. 1861.
(1)   DeWALT, K. B. 1Lt. — Elect. Capt.: Not re-elect. when Co. re-org., May 16, 1862: Resgnd.
(1)   LOWE, HENRY B. 2Lt. — Detailed to recruiting duty in Tex., Feb.-Apr., 1862: Not re-elected when Co. re-org., May 16, 1862: Re-enl. as 3Sgt., Oct. 13, 1862: Prom., 1Sgt., July 2, 1863: AWOL, Dec. 26, 1863: Dischgd., Feb. 4, 1864.
(1)   SHOTWELL, JOHN I. 3Lt. — Elect., 3Lt., Apr. 29, 1861: Elect., 2Lt., May 16, 1861: Elect., 1Lt., May 16, 1862: W., Antietam (Sept. 17, 1862): See roster, "Hdqtrs., Hood's Tex. Brigade."

ORIGINAL NON-COMMISSIONED OFFICERS

(1)   HARDING, R. J.   1Sgt. — See List of "Other Officers" following.
(1)   SHOTWELL, THOS. B.   2Sgt. — K., Gaines' Mill (June 27, 1862).
(1)   McGEE, SAM H. 3Sgt. — Discharged for sickness, Dec. 22, 1861: Re-enl. in Co. C, Apr. 7, 1862.
(1)   BRADFORD, C. L. 4Sgt. — See list of "Other Officers" following.
(1)   NETTLES, W. THOS. 1Cpl. — W., Yorktown, Va., April, 1862: Dischgd. for disability.
(1)   SHOTWELL, WM. B. 2Cpl. — Dischgd., Aug. 25, 1861, Surg. Cert. of Disability.
(1)   SANDERSON, ADOLPH D. 3Cpl. — Prom., 5Sgt.: Detailed to recruiting duty in Tex., Feb.-Apr., 1863: Prom., 4Sgt.: K., Chickamauga (Sept. 20, 1863).
(1)   BARTEE, FERDINAND 4Cpl. — In hosp. (chronic bronchitis), spring, 1862: Dischgd., Aug. 14, 1862 on "official order from Gen. Lee", enlmt. expired.

OTHER OFFICERS

HARDING, R. J. Capt. — See roster, "Regmtl. Hdqtrs., 1st Tex. Inf."
BRADFORD, C. L. ("Champ") Lt. — Orig. 4Sgt. of Co.: Elect., 2Lt., May 16, 1862: AWOL, Feb. 9, 1865.
WALKER, WM. F. Lt. — Orig. Pvt. in Co.: Elect., 3Lt., May 20, 1862: K., Cold Harbor (June 3, 1864).

MUSICIANS

(1) COLLINS, BENJAMIN FRANKLIN — Hotel clerk, enlisted at age 15, 5 feet tall, unhealthy: Dischgd., Aug. 1, 1861, bronchitis.
(1) MEEKINS, I. RODERICK — Prom., 2Cpl.: Served as Co. Color Guard: K., Gettysburg (July 2, 1863).

PRIVATES

(1) ANDERSON, M. B. — W., Antietam (Sept. 17, 1862): Dischgd. for disability.
(1) BARFIELD, G. W. — W., Antietam (Sept. 17, 1862): Prom., 5Sgt.: W., Chickamauga (Sept. 19, 1863).
(1) BASS, RICHARD — Hospitalized most of 1862 (chronic dysentery): Absent on "sick furlough" most of 1863.
(1) BASS, RICHARD W. — Died, Richmond, Va., June 2, 1861.
(1) BATTISE, IKE ("Indian") — Carried on CSA Rolls as "Isaac (Indian)": An Alabama-Coushatta Indian: Dischgd., May 20, 1862: Returned to Tex. & jnd. Capt. Charley Bullock's Co. from Tyler County.
BEAN, C. — Deserted, May 5, 1862.
(1) BOWLING, B. L. — Sick, Spring, 1862 (pneumonia): W., Antietam (Sept. 17, 1862): POW, Gettysburg (July 4, 1863), left with wounded: Died as POW, Aug. 5, 1864, Point Lookout, Md.
(1) BRADFORD, JAS. J. — Dischgd. on Surg. Cert. for "Rheumatism & dropsy," Feb. 19, 1862.
(1) BURKE, THOS. — Born in Ireland, age 53 when enl.: Dischgd., Aug. 14, 1862. Term of serv. (1 yr.) expired: Later jnd. Co. G, 3Btln., Tex. Cav. (Coastal Service).
(1) BUTLER, CHAS. W. — Prom., 3Sgt.: Prom., 2Sgt.: W., Antietam (Sept. 17, 1862): Prom., 1Sgt.: K., Gettysburg (July 2, 1863).
(1) BUTLER, JOHN B. — Detchd. serv. with Div. Provost Guard, July, 1863: Detailed, Spring, 1864, to procure cattle for Brig. Comsy.
(1) BYRNES, J. LARRY — Born in Ireland, age 37 when enl.: Dischgd., Aug. 14, 1862, one yr. enlistment completed.
(1) CANTERBERRY, JORDAN M. — Prom., 4Cpl.: W., Gaines' Mill (June 27, 1862): Reduced to Pvt.: W., Chickamauga (Sept. 20, 1863): Transfd. out of Co.
CARR, FRANK M. — Enl., at Livingston, Tex., Apr. 29, 1862: W., Gaines' Mill (June 27, 1862): Dischgd. Oct., 1862, as non-conscript, underage (17).

(1)   CHOATE, RUFUS R. — W., Antietam (Sept. 17, 1862): K., Chickamauga (Sept. 20, 1863).

COFFIN, ISAAC — Deserted, May 6, 1862 (enlmt. expired).

(1)   COX, W. H. — Asgnd. to Litter Corps., Spring, 1862: Dischgd., Aug. 14, 1862, one yr. enlistment up.

CROBERT, JOHN — Detailed to Litter Corps: Dischgd. from Co. A, 1st Tex., and transfd. to 8th La. Inf. Regt.

DERRICK, GEO. A. — No information available.

(1)   DERRICK, JOHN — Dischgd., Aug. 14, 1862, enlmt. expired.

(1)   DONNELLY, M. E. — K., Chickamauga (Sept. 19, 1863).

(1)   DORTCH, JOS. S. — K., Malvern Hill (July 1, 1862).

(1)   DUNHAM, C. R. — Prom., 3Cpl.: Detailed as Co. Color Bearer, Sept., 1862: POW, Antietam (Sept. 17, 1862): Paroled and rejnd. Co.: K., Chickamauga (Sept. 20. 1863).

(1)   DUNHAM, M. A. — See roster, "Regmtl. Hdqtrs., 1st Tex. Inf."

(1)   DUNHAM, SID H. — Prom., 1Sgt., Sept. 20, 1863: Reduced to Pvt.: Reported AWOL: Transfd. to Trans-Mississippi Army: K., Mansfield (April 8, 1864).

(1)   ELLIS, RICHARD H. — K., Chickamauga (Sept. 20, 1863).

EVANS, JAMES M. — Jnd. Co., June 5, 1861, at Richmond: Transfd. to Va. regt. and killed in battle.

FONTAINE, HENRY B. — See roster, "Regmtl. Hdqtrs., 1st Tex. Inf."

(1)   GARNER, JAMES W. — Hospitalized, May 12, 1862, pneumonia: Sick, Fall, 1862: K., Gettysburg (July 2, 1863).

(1)   GARNER, WM. — W., Malvern Hill (July 1, 1862): Hospitalized until Dec., 1862: Nurse, White Sulphur Springs Hosp., Va., Summer & Fall, 1863: Retired for disability, July, 1864: Asgnd. as "RR Agent" in Trans-Miss. Dept. by Gen. E. Kirby Smith.

(1)   GIBSON, WM. W. — Hospitalized, May 14 (diarrhea) & Sept. 30, 1862: Deserted, Nov. 26, 1862 (enlmt. expired).

(1)   HADEN, J. E. — Nurse at Camp Lee Hosp., Richmond, Aug. 1, 1861: Asgnd. as Hosp. Steward, Camp Lee Hosp., Feb., 1862: Appt. Hosp. Steward in Trans-Miss. Dept., Aug. 25, 1862.

HAM, GEO. W. — Transfd. to Co. B, from Co. K, 5th Tex. Inf., Mar. 1, 1863.

(1)   HAZLETT, J. S. — Duty as teamster, June, 1862: Dischgd. as a non-conscript, Aug., 1862, overage (52).

HINES, SY — Deserted, May 5, 1862.

(1)   JOHNSON, GEO. H. — W., Antietam (Sept. 17, 1862): K., Chickamauga (Sept. 19, 1863).

(1)   JONES, ENOCH C. — Dischgd., Aug., 1862, enlmt. expired.

(1)   KENDRICH, WM. — Dischgd., Aug. 14, 1862, enlmt. expired.

(1)   KENNEDY, T. JEFF — Dischgd., Aug., 1862, enlmt. expired.

(1)   KIRKSEY, J. NEWTON — Prom., Sgt.: W., Chickamauga (Sept. 19, 1863): Reduced to 1Cpl.

(1)   LAW, NAPOLEAN — Dischgd., Aug., 1862, enlmt. expired.

(1)   LEWIS, W. GREEN — W., Malvern Hill (July 1, 1862): Hospitalized for wound most of 1862 & 1863.

(1)   LOVE, ROBT. B. — Asgnd. to recruiting duty in Tex., Feb.-Apr., 1862: W., Malvern Hill (July 1, 1862): Right foot amputated.

LOWE, DANIEL B. — W., Gettysburg (July 2, 1863): Prom., 1Sgt., Aug., 1863: AWOL, Winter, 1863-64: W., Wilderness (May 6, 1864): Dischgd. for disability, Mar. 15, 1865.

(1) McANALLY, THOS. — K., Malvern Hill (July 1, 1862).

(1) McCLANNAHAN, JAS. E. — K., Malvern Hill (July 1, 1862).

(1) McDONALD, WM. — W., Gaines' Mill (June 27, 1862).

(1) McNULTY, HAINES — Born in England, enl., at age 39: Dischgd., Aug. 14, 1862, enlmt. expired.

(1) MEECE, CALVIN W. — Transfd. to Co. K, 5th Tex. Vol. Inf. Regt., Mar. 1, 1863.

(1) MEEKINS, P. P. — Prom., 2Cpl.: Deserted, Jan. 22, 1864 "with Enfield Rifle and accouterments."

(1) MORRIS, BENJ. F. — Asgnd. as a teamster: Deserted Oct. 15, 1862 at Culpeper, Va. (enlmt. expired).

(1) MORRIS, W. L. — Dischgd., Aug., 1862, when enlmt. expired.

(1) O'GORMAN, JOHN — Dischgd., Aug. 14, 1862, enlmt. expired.

(1) PANKEY, W. O. — Detailed as a teamster, Spring, 1862: W., Gaines' Mill (June 27, 1862): Finger shot off: W., Antietam (Sept. 17, 1862): "Wounded Furlough," Sept., 1862: AWOL, May, 1863.

(1) PROBERT, JOHN — Prom., Sgt.: K., Gaines' Mill (June 27, 1862).

(1) QUIGLEY, JOHN — Born in Ireland, enl., at age 36: Dischgd., Aug. 14, 1862, enlmt. expired.

(1) SANDEL, WILBORN — Dischgd., Aug. 1, 1861 on Surg. Cert. of disability (bronchitis & measles): Age 17.

(1) SCOTT, THOS J. — Sick in hosp., Spring, 1863: AWOL, Summer, 1863: Arrested in Penn. by Feds., July 22, 1863: Confined at Ft. Millis, Pa.: Took oath to Federals, Jan. 1, 1864, and agreed "to work for Fed. Govt."

(1) SCOTT, WM. G. — W., Gaines' Mill (June 27, 1862): Dischgd., Aug. 26, 1862, on Surg. Cert. of disability.

(1) SMITH, URIAH — Prom., 2Sgt., Fall, 1861: Reduced to Pvt., July, 1862: AWOL, Nov., 1863: Supposed to have jnd. a unit in the Trans-Miss. Army.

(1) STEVENS, JAS. P. — Prom., 1Cpl.: W., 2nd Manassas (Aug. 30, 1862): Prom., Sgt.: K., Chickamauga (Sept. 20, 1863).

(1) THOMASON, H. J. — Deserted in New Orleans, May 17, 1861.

TRENCKMAN (or TRINKMAN), A. — W., Malvern Hill (July 1, 1862): K., Antietam (Sept. 17, 1862).

(1) VICTORY, JOHN — Prom., 4Sgt.: W., Antietam (Sept. 17, 1862): Prom., 3Sgt.: W., Gettysburg (July 2, 1863): Died of wound.

(1) WALKER, GEO. A. — Hosp. orderly, 1862-1864: K., Chaffin's Farm (Sept. 29, 1864).

(1) WALKER, W. W. — Dischgd., Aug. 13, 1861 on Surg. Cert. of disability.

(1) WALKER, WM. F. — See list of "Other Officers" above.

(1) WARD, J. V. — Deserted, May 23, 1861, in Tenn.

(1) WARD, SAM L. — W., Antietam (Sept. 17, 1862): Dischgd., Aug. 12, 1862, enlmt. expired.

(1) WEST, DR. JACOB — A medical doctor by profession: Dischgd., Nov. 15, 1861, Surg. Cert. for disability (lung disease).

(1) WESTBROOK, NATHANIEL G. — Hospitalized for pneumonia, May, 1864: K., Chaffin's Farm (Sept. 29, 1864).
(1) WILLIAMS, ZACK — Prom., 2Cpl.: K., Malvern Hill (July 1, 1862).
(1) WOODWARD, M. W. — Dischgd. in Aug., 1862, termination of enlistment.
(1) WOODWARD, SAM J. — Asgnd. to duty with Litter Corps., Summer, 1862: W., Antietam (Sept. 17, 1862): W., Wilderness (May 6, 1864): POW, Darbytown Rd. (Oct. 7, 1864): Released, May 13, 1865.
(1) ZELUFF, WM. M. — Dischgd., Aug., 1862, termination of enlistment.

1ST TEX. VOL. INF. REGT.

COMPANY C — *PALMER GUARDS*

Company was organized in Harris County, Texas, and mustered into Confederate service "for one year" at New Orleans, May 19, 1861, by Lt. C. W. Phifer, CSA.

Key

(1) Original member of Company. (2) Paroled at Appomattox.
K (Killed), W (Wounded), POW (Prisoner of War)
AWOL (Absent Without Leave)

ORIGINAL OFFICERS

(1) DICKINSON, A. G. Capt. — Resgnd., Jan. 1, 1862: Returned to Tex.: Appt. Cmdr. of Post of San Antonio, Tex., Oct., 1863.
(1) PERRY, B. F. 1Lt. — Elect. Capt., Jan., 1862: Resgnd., May, 1862.
(1) DECATUR, HARRY E. 2Lt. — Prom., 1Lt., Jan., 1862: Asgnd. recruiting duty in Tex., Feb.-Apr., 1862: K., Eltham's Landing (May 7, 1862).
(1) DEANE, J. G. 3Lt. — Prom., 2Lt., May 31, 1861: Deserted, Winter, 1861-62.

ORIGINAL NON-COMMISSIONED OFFICERS

(1) SAMUEL, D. B. 1Sgt. — Resgnd., Apr. 3, 1862.
(1) O'BURNE, JOHN 2Sgt. — Reduced to a Pvt.: Reported AWOL, Oct. 31, 1862: Deserted, Dec., 1862.
(1) CASWELL, JAS. 3Sgt. — Deserted, May 19, 1862.
(1) GHOLSTON, WEST 4Sgt. — Sick in Richmond Hosp., Spring, 1862: Took amnesty oath, Apr. 24, 1865, Charleston, W. V.
(1) MILLER, HORATIO 1Cpl. — Enl. in Tex., jnd. Co. in New Orleans, May 19, 1861: No other record.

(1) LOYD, FRANK 2Cpl. — Deserted, April 1, 1862.

(1) SEARLE, EDWIN B. 3Cpl. — Reduced to Pvt., Mar., 1862: Prom., 2Sgt., Jan., 1863: Elect., 1Sgt., Apr., 1863: W., Chickamauga (Sept. 19, 1863): Hospitalized at Griffin, Ga.: Deserted, Jan. 22, 1864, near Morristown, Tenn., "taking all of his equip.": Captured and "in arrest," April, 1864: Deserted, July 26, 1864, to the enemy (3rd Del. Inf. Regt.).

(1) FERGUSON, J. A. 4Cpl. — Dischgd., Aug. 29, 1861 on Surg. Cert. of disability.

OTHER OFFICERS

RICE, D. K. Capt. — Orig. Pvt. in Co.: Elect., 3Lt., Jan., 1862: Elect., 1Lt., May 7, 1862: Elect., Capt., May 16, 1862: Asgnd. to recruiting duty in Tex., Feb.-Apr., 1863: Actg. Maj., Sept. 1, 1863: Actg. Lt.-Col., Nov. 5, 1863: In arrest, Dec., 1863: Absent, sick (pneumonia) in Richmond, Fall & Winter, 1864: Paroled, Appomattox (Apr. 12, 1865).

BUCKNER, A. W. 1Lt. — Recruited in Tex. as a Pvt., Mar. 30, 1862: Elect., 3Lt., Nov., 1862: Elect., 2Lt., Dec., 1862: Elect., 1Lt., May, 1863: Paroled, Appomattox (April 12, 1865).

GERALD, W. A. Lt. — Recruited in Tex., as a Pvt., Apr. 7, 1862: Elect., Lt., May, 1863: K., Gettysburg (July 2, 1863).

HOFFMAN, F. L. 1Lt. — Enl. at Camp Wigfall, Va., Aug. 18, 1861, as a Pvt.: Elect., 1Sgt., April 3, 1862: Elect., 1Lt.: K., Antietam (Sept. 17, 1862).

NADLE, W. B. 1Lt. — Enl. in Tex. as a Pvt., and jnd. Co. at New Orleans, May 27, 1861: Elect., 2Lt.: Elect., 1Lt.: Reported AWOL "right before Battle of Sharpsburg" (Sept. 17, 1862): Reduced to Pvt.

MILLER, HENRY BENJAMIN 2Lt. — Orig. Pvt. in Co., Enl. at New Orleans, May 19, 1861: Prom., 1Cpl., May 31, 1861: Elect., 2Lt., Jan., 1862: AWOL & under arrest, Apr., 1862: Deserted, July 15, 1864.

TINNIN, ROBT. N. 2Lt. — Enl. in Tex., jnd. Co. in New Orleans, May 19, 1861: Elect., 3Lt., Dec. 6, 1862: Elect., 2Lt., Jan., 1863: W., Gettysburg (July 2, 1863): W., Wilderness (May 6, 1864): W., Darbytown Rd. (Oct. 7, 1864); Paroled, Greensboro, N. Car., May 16, 1865.

PRIVATES

ADAMS, SAMUEL — Enl. at Pensacola, Fla., jnd. Co. in New Orleans, May 27, 1861: No other record.

(1) AMILE, AUGUST — Enl. in Tex., jnd. Co. in New Orleans, May 19, 1861: No other record.

ANDERSON, JAS. — Enl. at Pensacola, Fla., jnd. Co. in New Orleans, May 27, 1861: Sick, Sept., 1862: Deserted, Dec., 1862.

(2)   ARMSTRONG, J. W. — Recruited in Tex., Mar. 30, 1862: W., Chickamauga (Sept. 19, 1863): W., Knoxville (Nov. 28, 1863): Paroled, Appomattox (April 12, 1865).

(2)   ARMSTRONG, O. G. — Enl. at Pensacola, Fla., and jnd. Co. in New Orleans, May 27, 1861: Prom., 3Cpl., Apr. 12, 1862: Prom., 4Sgt.: W., Gaines' Mill (June 27, 1862): Reduced to ranks at own request, Oct. 1, 1863: Paroled, Appomattox (Apr. 12, 1865).

       ARNOLD, J. H. — Recruited in Tex., Mar. 30, 1862: Detailed to recruiting service in Tex., Feb.-Apr., 1863: Detchd. duty as a shoemaker, Dec., 1863: Prom., 4Sgt., March 1, 1864: K., Wilderness (May 6, 1864).

       ASHLEY, ED — K., 2nd Manassas (Aug. 30, 1862).

       BICKNELL, JAS. — Enl. at Pensacola, Fla., and jnd. Co. at New Orleans, May 27, 1861: Deserted, May 19, 1862 (enlistment expired).

(1)   BOURNE, F. — Enl. at New Orleans, May 19, 1861: No other record.

(1)   BOURNE, S. — Enl. at New Orleans, May 19, 1861: No other record.

(1)   BRANEGHAN, JOHN — Enl. at New Orleans, May 19, 1861: Deserted, May 19, 1862 (enlistment expired).

(2)   BUCKNER, A. W. — See list of "Other Officers" above.

       BUCKNER, J. B. — Recruited in Tex., Mar. 30, 1862: Died in Richmond Hosp., Apr., 1863.

(1)   CALHOUN, T. J. — W., Malvern Hill (July 1, 1862): Leg amputated.

       CANADA, J. P. — Recruited in Tex., Mar. 30, 1862: Prom., 4Cpl., May, 1863: W., Gettysburg (July 2, 1863).

       CARDINAL, ALFRED — Recruited in Tex., and jnd. Co. at New Orleans, May 26, 1861: Deserted, Dec. 1862 (enlmt. expired).

       CARNES, D. A. — Sick in hosp., White Sulphur Springs, Va., Oct., 1862: Dischgd. from service, Oct. 10, 1862.

       CARNES, THOS. — Enl. in Tex. for 12 mos., jnd. Co. at New Orleans, May 26, 1861: Dischgd., Aug. 19, 1862, enlmt. expired.

       CARTER, JACOB — Enl. for 12 mos. at Pensacola, Fla., and jnd. Co. at New Orleans, May 27, 1861: No other record.

       CHAPMAN, J. H. — Recruited in Tex., Mar. 30, 1862: Prom., 4Cpl., May, 1862: Prom., 2Sgt.: POW, July 20, 1863, near Bunker Hill, Va.

(1)   CLAY, T. H. — Resgnd., Aug., 1862, enlmt. expired.

(1)   CONNELLY, THOS. — In Regmtl. guardhouse, Apr., 1862: Sick, June, 1862. No other record.

(1)   COOPER, HENRY — Resgnd., Aug., 1862, enlmt. expired.

(1)   COYLE, THOS. — Dischgd., Aug. 19, 1862 as a non-conscript, overage (36).

(1)   CREIGER, J. — Resgnd., Aug., 1862, enlmt. expired.

       CREAMER, THOS. — Died, Oct. 25, 1862, Winder Hosp., Richmond.

(1)   DAFFT, J. W. — Deserted, May, 1862 (enlmt. expired).

(1)   DAY, PATRICK — Deserted in New Orleans, May 21, 1861.

(1)   DELANO, R. H. — Resgnd., Aug., 1862, enlmt. expired.

(1)   DONNELLY, ROBT. — Prom., 4Cpl., Apr. 12, 1862: W., Eltham's Landing (May 7, 1862): "Not heard from in 12 months — supposed dead."

(1)   DUFFY, W. B. — Deserted, May 19, 1862 (enlmt. expired).

(1)   DUNLISS, JOHN — Resgnd., Aug., 1862, enlmt. expired.

ENLAW, J. D. — Enl., Sharon, Tex., Mar. 26, 1862: W., Gaines' Mill (June 27, 1862): Dischgd. for disability (heart trouble), Oct. 28, 1862.

ENRIGHT, THOS. — Enl. in Tex. for 12 mos., jnd. Co. at New Orleans, May 19, 1861: No other record.

(1)   ESCAN, JOHN — Enl. in Tex. for 12 mos., jnd. Co. at New Orleans, May 19, 1861: No other record.

(1)   FITZGERALD, E. T. — Enl. in Tex. for 12 mos., jnd. Co. in New Orleans, May 19, 1861: No other record.

(2)   FREEMAN, H. F. M. — Recruited in Tex., Mar. 30, 1862: W., Malvern Hill (July 1, 1862): W., Wilderness (May 6, 1864): Paroled, Appomattox (April 12, 1865).

(2)   FREEMAN, J. N. — Recruited in Tex., Mar. 30, 1862: Prom., 3Cpl., Oct. 1, 1863: W., Wilderness (May 6, 1864): Prom., 4Sgt.: Paroled, Appomattox (April 12, 1865).

GAGE, G. L. — K., Antietam (Sept. 17, 1862).

GERALD, W. A. — See list of "Other Officers" above.

(1)   GERARD, J. — Deserted in New Orleans, May 21, 1861.

(1)   GILES, MOSES A. J. — Prom., 3Sgt.: On recruiting detail in Tex., Feb.-Apr., 1862: W., Gaines' Mill (June 27, 1862): Leg amputated.

GOODWIN, THOS. — Enl. in Tex. for 12 mos., jnd. Co. at New Orleans, May 26, 1861: Deserted, May 19, 1862 (enlmt. expired).

GRAHAM, HARRISON — Enl. in Tex., jnd. Co. at New Orleans, May 26, 1861: Prom., 4Sgt., 2Sgt., and 1Sgt.: Reduced to ranks by court-martial, Apr., 1863: W., Darbytown Rd., (Oct. 7, 1864): Paroled, Lynchburg, Va., Apr., 1865.

GRIFFIN, J. L. — Enl., Mar. 26, 1863: Prom., 4Cpl., Oct. 1, 1863: W., Wilderness (May 6, 1864).

(1)   GUY, WM. — Enl. in Tex. for 12 mos., jnd. Co. in New Orleans, May 19, 1861: Sick, Richmond Hosp., Spring, 1862: No other record.

HARRIS, A. B. — Enlisted in Tex., Mar. 30, 1862: On recruiting service in Tex., Feb.-Apr., 1863: K., Chickamauga (Sept. 20, 1863).

(1)   HARTMAN, WM. — Sick in Richmond Hosp., June, 1862: Dischgd., Aug. 19, 1862.

(1)   HENDRICKS, HANDSOM H. — Sick (rheumatism), Spring, 1862: Detchd. serv. Pioneer Corps, 1863: K., Wilderness (May 6, 1864).

(1)   HIGGINS, W. — Deserted in New Orleans, May 21, 1861.

(1)   HINDLE, H. — Deserted in New Orleans, May 21, 1861.

(1)   HODGE, R. — Deserted in New Orleans, May 21, 1861.

HOFFMAN, F. L. — See list of "Other Officers" above.

(1)   HOLLY, BERNARD ("Barny") — Prom., 1Cpl., March 10, 1862. Deserted, May 19, 1862 (enlmt. expired).

(1)   HOLLY, N. T. — Enl., New Orleans, May 19, 1861: No other record available, may have resgnd. after 1 yr. enlmt. expired.

(1)   HOLT, D. — Enl., New Orleans, May 19, 1861: No other record available, may have resgnd. after 1 yr. enlmt. expired.

(1)   HOWARD, CHAS. — Deserted in New Orleans, May 21, 1861.

JACKSON, J. D. — Recruited in Tex., Mar. 30, 1862: Died of typhoid fever in Chimborazo Hosp., Richmond, June 27, 1862. Buried in Hollywood Cemetery, Richmond.

(1)   JAGGERS, ALFRED — Deserted in New Orleans, May 22, 1861.

(1)   JARRAL, THOS. — Enl., New Orleans, May 19, 1861: Deserted, May 19, 1862 (enlmt. expired).

JOHNSON, ALFRED — Enl. in Tex., and jnd. Co. at New Orleans, May 26, 1861: POW, near Dumfries, Va., May 8, 1862.

JOHNSON, CHAS. — Enl. at Pensacola, Fla. and jnd. Co. at New Orleans, May 27, 1861: Deserted, May 19, 1862 (enlmt. expired).

(1)   KAUFMAN, ISAAC — Jnd. Co. in New Orleans, May 19, 1861: No other record, may have resgnd. after 1 yr. enlmt. expired.

KELLY, CHAS. L. — Recruited in Tex., April 7, 1862: Dischgd. on Surg. Cert., June 5, 1862 (hemiplegia).

(1)   KENNEY, THOS. — Enl., New Orleans, May 19, 1861: No other record, may have resgnd. after 1 yr. enlmt. expired.

KHALEN, HENRY — Enl. in Tex., and jnd. Co. at New Orleans, May 26, 1861. No other record, may have resgnd. after 1 yr. enlmt. expired.

(1)   KING, JOHN — Deserted in New Orleans, May 22, 1861.

(1)   KING, WM. — Enl., New Orleans, May 19, 1861: Prom., Sgt.: Deserted, May 19, 1862 (enlmt. expired).

KING, WM. M. — Recruited in Tex., Apr. 7, 1862: Sick in hosp. in Lynchburg, Va., June, 1862 (diarrhea). Transfd. to Co. E., 4th Tex. Inf. Regt., Dec. 31, 1863.

LALLUS, B. F. — Enl. at Pensacola, Fla., and jnd. Co. at New Orleans, May 27, 1861: Deserted, May 19, 1862 (enlmt. expired).

(1)   LAMB, THOS. — Enl., New Orleans, May 19, 1861: Deserted, May 19, 1862 (enlmt. expired).

LASSITER, S. — Recruited in Tex., Mar. 30, 1862: Sick in Richmond, Spring, 1862: W., Chickamauga (Sept. 20, 1863): AWOL, Spring, 1864.

(1)   LOGAN, JOHN A. — Dischgd., May 22, 1861 at New Orleans as "incompetent to do duty."

(1)   LONG, JAS. — Enl., New Orleans, May 19, 1861: No other record available, may have resgnd. after 1 yr. enlmt. expired.

(1)   LORIO, R. — Deserted at New Orleans, May 22, 1861.

(1)   LORMY, CHAS. — Enl., New Orleans, May 19, 1861: No other record, may have resgnd. after 1 yr. enlmt. expired.

LONGHEAD, JOHN N. — Enl. in Tex., and jnd. Co. at New Orleans, May 26, 1861: W., Gaines' Mill (June 27, 1862): Dischgd., Aug. 19, 1862.

(1)   LOWERY, PHILLIP — Enl., New Orleans, May 19, 1861: Deserted, May 19, 1862 (enlmt. expired).

(1)   LYONS, JOS. D. — Enl., New Orleans, May 19, 1861: Deserted, May 19, 1862 (enlmt. expired).

(1)   MACKAY, W. A. — Enl., New Orleans, May 19, 1861: No other record, may have resgnd. after 1 yr. enlmt. expired.

McCARTER, J. D. P. — Recruited in Tex., Mar. 30, 1862: Prom., 3Cpl.: Prom., 2Cpl., May, 1863: Prom., 5Sgt., Oct. 1, 1863: Prom., 1Sgt., Mar. 1, 1864.

(1)   McCARTHY, ED — Deserted at New Orleans, May 22, 1861.

McGEE, S. H. — Enl., Apr. 7, 1862: W. & POW, Antietam (Sept. 17, 1862): Paroled, Sept. 27, 1862: W., furlough, Nov., 1862: Dischgd., July, 1864.

McGINNIS, J. H. — Recruited in Tex., Apr. 7, 1862: Sick in hosp. since enlistment: Missing at Gettysburg (July 2, 1863).

McGINNIS, JOHN H. — Recruited in Tex., Apr. 7, 1862: Prom., 2Cpl., June 1, 1862: Sick (bronchitis), Summer, 1862: Prom., 1Cpl., Oct., 1862: Prom., 5Sgt., Feb., 1863: W., Chickamauga (Sept. 20, 1863): Died from wound, Sept. 21, 1863.

McMANNUS, G. W. — Recruited in Tex., Mar. 30, 1862: Sick (dysentery), May, 1862: W. & POW, Antietam (Sept. 17, 1862): Paroled: Sick in hosp., Dec., 1862.

McNEW, G. W. — Recruited in Tex., Mar. 30, 1862: W., Gaines' Mill (June 27, 1862): W., Malvern Hill (July 1, 1862): In hosp. at Petersburg, Va., Spring, 1863: Disabled & dischgd., June 30, 1863.

(1)   McRAE, C. G. — Enl., New Orleans, May 19, 1861: No other record. See "C. G. McRae," Co. F., 1st Tex. Inf. Regt., probably same man.

(1)   MILLER, HENRY BENJ. — See list of "Other Officers" above.

MORRISSEY, JAS. — Enl. in Tex. and jnd. Co. at New Orleans, May 20, 1861: No other record, may have resgnd. after 1 yr. enlmt. expired.

(1)   MULVEY, JOS. P. — Enl. in Tex. for one yr., jnd. Co. in New Orleans, May 19, 1861: Dischgd., Aug. 19, 1862 for disability.

MUNROE, AUGUST — Enl. in Tex., for one yr. and jnd. Co. May 20, 1861: No other record, may have resgnd. after 1 yr. enlmt. expired.

MURCHISON, R. J. — Recruited in Tex., Mar. 30, 1862: Dischgd. for disability (neuralgia), Sept. 15, 1862.

MURPHY, PAT — Enl. in Tex., and jnd. Co. at New Orleans, May 20, 1861: Arrested by civilian authorities and confined in Richmond jail, Mar., 1862.

NADLE, W. B. — See list of "Other Officers" above.

(2)   NEIL, J. P. — Recruited in Tex., Mar. 30, 1862: W., Chickamauga (Sept. 19, 1863): W., Wilderness (May 6, 1864): Paroled, Appomattox (April 12, 1865).

NELSON, J. W. — Recruited in Tex., Apr. 7, 1862: Died, Spring, 1862.

NEWMAN, WM. — Enl. at Pensacola, Fla., and jnd. Co. at New Orleans, May 27, 1861: Dischgd., June 22, 1861.

NICHOLSON, JACKSON — Enl. at Pensacola, Fla. and jnd. Co. at New Orleans, May 27, 1861: Prom., 5Sgt., Apr. 3, 1862: Deserted, May 27, 1862 (enlmt. expired).

(1)   ODELL, THOS. — Enl. in Tex. for one yr., jnd. in New Orleans, May 19, 1861: Present for duty, Mar. & Apr., 1862: No other record, may have resgnd. after 1 yr. enlmt. expired.

O'ROURKE, MICHAEL — Enl. at Pensacola, Fla., and jnd. Co. at New Orleans, May 27, 1861: Prom., Sgt.: Dischgd., Dec. 27, 1862 as "never having acquired domicile."

PARKER, W. — Recruited in Tex., Apr. 7, 1862: Died of lung disease, May 21, 1862.

PEY, W. P. — Enlisted by Col. Wigfall in Va., July 1, 1861: Deserted, Apr. 1, 1862 "with rifle and accouterments."

PHILLIPS, THOS. C. — Recruited in Tex., Mar. 30, 1862: Sick, Summer, 1862: Dischgd., Oct. 5, 1862, on physical disability.

(1) PICKETT, WM. — Enl. in Tex., jnd. Co. in New Orleans, May 19, 1861: AWOL, May 31, 1861.

PIERCE, G. W. — Recruited in Tex., Mar. 30, 1862: W. and POW, Gettysburg (July 2, 1863): Exchanged, Aug. 31, 1863.

PIERCE, W. M. — Enl. in Tex., Mar. 30, 1862: Sick (rubeola and diarrhea), Summer, 1862: Dischgd. for disability (acute bronchitis), Oct. 23, 1862.

RAINEY, JAS. — Enl. in Tex., and jnd. Co. at New Orleans, May 26, 1861: AWOL: Returned to duty, Aug. 29, 1863: W., Chickamauga (Sept. 20, 1863).

(1) REESE, HENRY B. — Deserted at New Orleans, May 22, 1861.

(1) REILLY, RICHARD — Enl. in Texas, jnd. Co. in New Orleans, May 19, 1861: Deserted at New Orleans, May 22, 1861.

(1) RHODES, J. W. — Enl. in Tex. for one year, jnd. Co. in New Orleans, May 19, 1861: Sick in hosp., Manchester, Va., Mar., 1862: Deserted, May, 1862 (enlmt. expired).

(1) RICE, D. K. — See list of "Other Officers" above.

(2)

(1) ROBINSON, GEO. W. — Enl. in Tex. for one year, jnd. Co. in New Orleans, May 19, 1861: Deserted, May 27, 1862 (enlmt. expired).

ROGERS, JAS. H. — Recruited in Tex., Mar. 30, 1862: Sick in Richmond Hosp., Fall, 1862: Extra duty as orderly, Feb., 1864: Paroled at Ashland, Va., May 2, 1865.

(1) ROUSSEAU, G. W. — Enl. in Tex. for one yr., jnd. Co. in New Orleans, May 19, 1861: Present for duty, Mar. & Apr., 1862: No record after that date, may have resgnd. after 1 yr. enlmt. expired.

SALTER, JAS. M. — Recruited in Tex., Mar. 30, 1862: AWOL, Spring, 1863: POW, Gettysburg (July 3, 1863): Sent to Fed. Prison at Ft. Delaware: Exchanged, Mar. 12, 1864: Hospitalized, Richmond, Mar. 20, 1864 (pneumonia).

(1) SAWYER, JOHN — Jnd. Co. at New Orleans, May 26, 1861: Deserted, June, 1862 (enlmt. expired).

(1) SCOTT, JAS. — Deserted, May 21, 1861, at New Orleans.

(1) SICORBY, JAS. — Deserted at New Orleans, May 22, 1861.

(1) SKIDMORE, JOS. — Deserted, June, 1862 (enlmt. expired).

(1) SMITH, CHAS. W. — No record of arriving in Va. from Tex.

(1) SMITH, HENRY W. — Detailed as a Regmtl. teamster, Spring, 1862: W., Eltham's Landing (May 7, 1862).

SMITH, W. HENEGAR — Enl. at Pensacola, Fla., and jnd. Co. at New Orleans, May 27, 1861. Detailed as a Regmtl. teamster, Apr., 1862: Deserted, May 19, 1862 (enlmt. expired).

(1) STAMPER, WM. T. — Enl. in Tex., jnd. Co. in New Orleans, May 19, 1861: W., Antietam (Sept. 17, 1862): Prom., 3Cpl., May, 1863: W., Chickamauga (Sept. 20, 1863): Received "wound furlough" from Medical Board, Feb. 21, 1864 for 60 days: served as a tailor in the C.S. Clothing Depot, Richmond, June-Nov., 1864.

STEWART, JOS. — Enl. at Pensacola, Fla., and jnd. Co. at New Orleans, May 27, 1861: Prom., 5Sgt., March 1, 1864: K., near Chester Station, Va., June 17, 1864.

(1) STOVAL, WM. — Enl. in Tex. for one yr., jnd. Co. in New Orleans, May 18, 1861: No other record, may have resgnd. after 1 yr. enlmt. expired.

SULLERS, J. G. — Enl. at Pensacola, Fla., and jnd. Co. at New Orleans, May 27, 1861: No other record, may have resgnd. after 1 yr. enlmt. expired.

(1) TABOR, CHAS. C. — Enl. in Tex. for one yr., jnd. Co. in New Orleans, May 19, 1861: Deserted, June, 1862 (enlmt. expired): POW, Falmouth, Va., Aug. 15, 1863.

TAYLOR, JOS. — Enl. in Tex., jnd. Co. in New Orleans, May 19, 1861: Detailed as a Regmtl. butcher, Spring, 1862: W., Eltham's Landing (May 7, 1862): Deserted, June, 1862 (enlmt. expired).

(1) THOMASON, C. G. — Deserted, April 1, 1862 (enlmt. expired).

(1) TINNIN, ROBT. N. — See list of "Other Officers" above.

TROTTER, J. W. — Recruited in Tex., Apr. 7, 1862: W., Eltham's Landing (May 7, 1862): Prom., 1Sgt.: W., Malvern Hill (July 1, 1862): Dischgd. for disability.

TRULOCK, EMANUEL M. — Enl. in Tex., Mar. 30, 1862: Sick, Summer, 1862: Dischgd., Sept. 24, 1862, "for permanent disease of the heart."

VINSON, ABRAHAM — Recruited in Tex., Apr. 7, 1862: Sick in hosp. most of 1862, 1863 & 1864 with rheumatism: Dischgd. for disability, Oct. 31, 1864.

VINSON, W. — Recruited in Tex., Apr. 7, 1862: K., 2nd Manassas (Aug. 30, 1862).

VINSON, W. H. — Recruited in Tex., Apr. 7, 1862: K., 2nd Manassas (Aug. 30, 1862).

WALL, D. R. — Recruited in Tex., Mar. 30, 1862: W., Wilderness (May 6, 1862).

(1) WARD, WM. E. — Deserted, April 1, 1862, "with rifle and accouterments."

WATSON, CHAS. — Enl. in Tex., Apr. 7, 1862: W., Antietam (Sept. 17, 1862): Leg amputated: Died, Sept. 20, 1862.

WESTON, THOS. — In Regmtl. Guardhouse, Apr., 1862: Deserted, June, 1862 (enlmt. expired).

WHITTLE, J. W. — Recruited in Tex., Mar. 30, 1862: Prom., 1Cpl.: Died in Richmond Hosp., Mar. 14, 1863.

(1) WILLIAMS, JAS. — Prom., 2Cpl., Apr. 12, 1862: W. & POW, Knoxville (Nov., 1864): Leg amputated.

WINN, JAS. — Recruited in Tex., Mar. 30, 1862: Prom., 3Cpl.: Prom., 2Cpl.: W., Gaines' Mill (June 27, 1862): Prom., 1Cpl., May, 1863: W. & POW, Gettysburg (July 2, 1863).

(1) WRIGHT, EUGENE — Deserted at New Orleans, May 22, 1861.

WRIGHT, FRANK — Enl. in Tex., and jnd. Co. at New Orleans, May 20, 1861: Deserted, June, 1862 (enlmt. expired).

YAGER, W. B. — Recruited in Tex., Apr. 7, 1862: Sick in Farmerville, Va., Aug., 1864: Permanently disabled, returned to Tex.

(1) YOUNG, FRED — Enl. in Tex., for one yr., jnd. Co. in New Orleans, May 19, 1861: Deserted, June, 1862 (enlmt. expired).

COMPANY D — *STAR RIFLES*

Company was organized in Marion County, Texas, and mustered into Confederate service "for one year" at New Orleans, June 6, 1861 by Lt. A. W. Pope, CSA.

Key

(1) Original member of Company. (2) Paroled at Appomattox.
K (Killed), W (Wounded), POW (Prisoner of War)
AWOL (Absent Without Leave)

ORIGINAL OFFICERS

(1)   CLOPTON, DR. ALBERT GALLATIN Capt. — See roster, "Regmtl. Hdqtrs., 1st Tex. Inf."

(1)   HEWITT, W. M. 1Lt. — Prom., Capt., Feb., 1862: Cmd. Co. at Eltham's Landing (May 7, 1862): Not re-elected when Co. re-org., May 16, 1862: Resgnd.

(1)   HENDERSON, WM. W. 2Lt. — Asgnd. to recruiting service in Tex., Feb.-Apr., 1862: Prom., 1Lt.: Not re-elect. when Co. re-org., May 16, 1862: Resgnd.

(1)   CARTRIGHT, C. R. 3Lt. — Not re-elect. when Co. re-org., May 16, 1862: Resgnd.

ORIGINAL NON-COMMISSIONED OFFICERS

(1)   SHROPSHIRE, WINKFIELD 1Sgt. — See roster, "Regmtl. Hdqtrs., 1st Tex. Inf."

(1)   FORT, WM. A. 2Sgt. — See roster, "Regmtl. Hdqtrs., 1st Tex. Inf."
(2)

(1)   CARLOW, JAS. S. 3Sgt. — No record available.

(1)   FLOYD, ROBT. Y. H. 4Sgt. — Prom., 1Sgt., May, 1862: Hosp., Richmond, Nov., 1862-June, 1863 (rheumatism): W., Gettysburg (July 2, 1863): Present & accounted for until Dec., 1864.

(1)   MORRISS, SIMON 1Cpl. — Prom., 2Sgt.: K., Gettysburg (July 2, 1863).

(1)   THOMAS, JACK M. 2Cpl. — See list of "Other Officers" following.

(1)   HENDERSON, JOHN B. 3Cpl. — Enl., May 27, 1861, at Linden, Tex.: Fought at Gaines' Mill (June 27, 1862), no record after that.

(1)   McDOWELL, JAS. F. 4Cpl. — W., Eltham's Landing (May 7, 1862): Prom., 3Sgt., Dec., 1862: Died of pneumonia, Richmond Hosp., Jan. 22, 1863: Personal effects consisted of, "1, pocket-book containing in notes $70.25; 1, silver watch; 1, gold ring, & 1, bundle of clothing."

OTHER OFFICERS

CONNALLY, U. S. ("Scott") Capt. — Orig. Pvt. in Co.: Elect., Lt., Jan., 1862: Detailed to recruiting service in Tex., Spring, 1862: Elect., Capt., May 15, 1862: Died from consumption (TB.), Atlanta, Ga., Nov. 20, 1862.

MOSS, HENRY E. Capt. — Orig. Pvt. in Co.: Elect., Lt., May 15, 1862: Elect., Capt., Nov. 8, 1862: Cmd. Co. at Chickamauga (Sept. 19-20, 1863): Dischgd. on Surg. Cert. for disability, July 25, 1864.

OLIVER, A. C. 1Lt. — Orig. Pvt. in Co.: Elect., 2Lt.: Elect., 1Lt.: W., White Oak Swamp (Aug. 16, 1864): Paroled, Appomattox (Apr. 12, 1865).

THOMAS, JACK M. 1Lt. — Orig., 2Cpl. in Co.: Prom., 1Cpl.: Elect., 2Lt., March 15, 1862: Cmd. Co. at 2nd Manassas (Aug. 30, 1862): Elect., 1Lt.: W., Chickamauga (Sept. 19, 1863): Died from wound.

McALPINE, JAS. M. 2Lt. — Orig. Pvt. in Co.: Elect., 2Lt., March 15, 1862: POW, Wilderness (May 6, 1864): Deserted, took oath to the Fed. Govt.: Dropped from rolls, Jan., 1865.

TOBIN, J. J. 2Lt. — Orig. Pvt. in Co.: Prom., 2Lt., Feb., 1862: Not re-elect. when Co. re-org., May 16, 1862: Resgnd.

PRIVATES

(1)   ADAMS, A. J. — Enl. in Tex., jnd. Co. in New Orleans, June 6, 1861:
(2)   Paroled, Appomattox (Apr. 12, 1865): No other record.
(1)   ADAMS, Dr. T. J. — A physician by profession: Enl. at Linden, Tex., May 27, 1861: Dischgd. for disability (rheumatism), Dec. 5, 1862.

(1)   ALLEN, YOUNG D. — Enl. at New Orleans, May 26, 1861: Sick, Summer, 1862: Dischgd. as a non-conscript, overage (42), Sept. 2, 1862.

(1)   BARKER, S. D. ("Dug") — Enl. in Tex. for 12 mos., jnd. Co. in New Orleans, June 6, 1861: Deserted, June 14, 1862 (enlmt. expired).

(1)   BARTLETT, DAN W. — Enl., May 26, 1861 at New Orleans: W., Antietam (Sept. 17, 1862): Arm amputated: Disabled, returned to Tex., May 23, 1863.

      BEAN, JOHN A. — Transfd. into Co. D from Co. E, 1st Tex. Inf. Regt., Apr., 1862: Deserted at Lynchburg, Va., June 14, 1862 (enlmt. expired).

(1)   BERNARD (or BARNARD), JOE C. — Dischgd. for disability (chronic diarrhea), Dec. 4, 1861.

(1)   BLACKWELL, JAS. — One of Hood's trusted scouts: Prom., Sgt.: W., 2nd Manassas (Aug. 30, 1862): Dischgd. for disability, Oct. 10, 1862.

(1)   BLALOCK, RUBE W. — Prom., 3Cpl.: POW, 7 Pines (June 1, 1862): Exchanged, Aug. 5, 1862: Died from bayonet wound in abdomen, Spotsylvania (May 10, 1864).

(1)   BROWN, E. B. — K., Antietam (Sept. 17, 1862).

(1)   BRYAN, FELIX B. — W., Wilderness (May 6, 1864): Wound furlough granted, May 18, 1864: Did not return to Co.

(1)   BRYAN, THOS. J. — Died of colic at Camp Quantico, Va., Oct. 18, 1861.

(1)   CHILDS (or CHILES), JOS. C. — Prom., 4Cpl., Nov., 1862: Prom., 3Cpl., Nov., 1863: AWOL, Jan., 1864: POW, Chaffin's Farm (Sept. 29, 1864): Exchanged, Mar. 17, 1865.

(1)   COLLEY, ALBERT W. — Enl. in Tex. for 12 mos., jnd. Co. at New Orleans, June 6, 1861: No other information: Probably served out enlistment.

(1)   COLLEY, WM. R. — Drowned at Camp Pulaski, La., June 12, 1861.

(1)   CONNALLY, J. R. ("Ruddy") — K., Antietam (Sept. 17, 1862).

(1)   CONNALLY, U. S. ("Scott") — See list of "Other Officers" above.

(1)   COOK, JOHN P. — W., Chickamauga (Sept. 20, 1863).

(1)   COVEY, THOS. J. — Dischgd., Sept. 12, 1862, as a non-conscript, underage (17).

(1)   COVEY, CHAS. F. — K., Eltham's Landing (May 7, 1862).

(1)   DAVENPORT, SEABORNE D. — Asgnd. as the Enrolling Off., Clarke

(2)   County, Tex., July, 1863: Paroled, Appomattox (Apr. 12, 1865).

(1)   DAY, WM. — Born in Ireland: POW at Wainsboro, Pa., July 7, 1863, following the battle of Gettysburg.

(1)   DENNIS, ANDREW ("Pone") — K., Gaines' Mill (June 27, 1862).

(1)   DICKSON (or DIXON), J. T. — W., Seven Pines (June 1, 1862): Prom.,

(2)   1Cpl.: W., Antietam (Sept. 17, 1862): Paroled, Appomattox (Apr. 12, 1865).

(1)   DOBBS, WM. C. — K., Gettysburg (July 2, 1863).

(1)   DRUMGOOLE, JOHN — POW, Gettysburg (July 2, 1863): Deserted, took oath to Federal Government.

(1)   DUBOISE, WM. — Deserted at Richmond, May 22, 1862.

(1)   DUDLEY, JAS. J. — Dischgd. for disability (bronchial trouble), Jan. 12, 1862.

(1)   DUNKLIN, JAS. P. — W., Antietam (Sept. 17, 1862): POW, Chickamauga (Sept. 19, 1863): Confined in Fed. Prison in New Orleans.

(1)   DURHAM, JAKE J. — Sick in Richmond Hosp., Sept., 1862: W., Chickamauga (Sept. 19, 1863): Died from wound, Sept. 22, 1863.

(1)   DURHAM, WM. L. — W., Freeman's Ford (Aug. 22, 1862): W., and

(2)   POW, Chickamauga (Sept. 19, 1863): W., Darbytown Rd. (Oct. 7, 1864): Received Texas Gold Medal for bravery, Feb., 1865: Paroled, Appomattox (Apr. 12, 1865).

(1)   EASLEY, JAS. S. — W., Chickamauga (Sept. 19, 1863): W., Wilderness (May 6, 1864): AWOL, Aug., 1864.

(1)   ELLINGTON, W. M. — Dischgd. as a non-conscript, Sept. 2, 1862, underage (17).

(1)   FRAZIER, EBENEZER — Dischgd. for disability, June 13, 1862 (chronic rheumatism).

(1)   GIBSON, ROBT. H. — K., Gettysburg (July 2, 1863).

       GLAZE, JOHN R. — Dischgd. as a non-conscript, Aug. 26, 1862, underage (17).

(1) GLAZE, P. H. — Present for duty for entire war except for 40 day
(2)   furlough to Tex., Jan.-Feb., 1864: Paroled, Appomattox (April
        12, 1865).
(1) GRAHAM, CHAS. M. — Dischgd. on Surg. Cert. of disability, Nov. 3,
        1861 (hernia).
(1) GROGARD, THOS. F. — Dischgd. on a Surg. Cert. for disability, Sept.
        5, 1861.
(1) HARTZO, C. F. — Dischgd. on Surg. Cert. for disability, Nov. 18, 1861
        (lung disease).
(1) HASS, HENRY J. — W., Gettysburg (July 2, 1863): W., Wilderness
        (May 6, 1864): Dischgd., June 26, 1864.
(1) HENDERSON, B. F. — Dischgd. for disability, July 30, 1861 (severe
        measles).
(1) HEWETT, JOS. — Asgnd. to recruiting serv. in Tex., Feb.-Apr., 1862:
        dischgd. for disability, Apr. 30, 1862.
(1) HINES, BEN C. — Sick in Richmond hospitals, June-Oct., 1862:
        Deserted, Nov. 1, 1862 (enlmt. expired).
(1) HOPKINS, F. COLUMBUS — W., Siege of Knoxville (Nov., 1863):
        Detailed as forager, Winter, 1863-64, bushwacked: K., Wilderness
        (May 6, 1864).
(1) HOUSTON, A. A. — Enl. in Tex., jnd. Co. at New Orleans, May 26,
        1861: No other record available.
(1) HUGHES, A. FRANK — Died at Medical College Hosp. in Richmond,
        Aug. 26, 1861, "Personal effects, 1 pocket book with $2.00":
        Buried in Hollywood Cemetery, Richmond, Aug. 27, 1861.
(1) INGRAM, J. S. — Deserted, Pocahontas, Ala., June 23, 1861.
(1) JACKSON, WALTER C. — Hospitalized with fever, Apr., 1862: K.,
        Antietam (Sept. 17, 1862).
(1) LINDSEY, DAVE P. — On detached duty as Hosp. Steward, Oct.,
        1861, and blacksmith, Nov., 1861 and Mar., 1862: Dischgd.,
        Sept. 5, 1862, as a non-conscript, overage (38).
(1) LOCKETT, WM. H. — W., Seven Pines (June 1, 1862): Dischgd., Sept.
        2, 1862 as a non-conscript, overage (36).
(1) MATTHEWS, SOL E. — Died of pneumonia in Fredericksburg, Va.
        Hosp., Feb. 27, 1862.
(1) McALPINE, JAS. M. — See list of "Other Officers" above.
(1) McALPINE, THOS. J. — Dischgd., Sept. 12, 1862, as a non-conscript,
        underage.
    McCELON (or McCLELLAND), WM. K. — K., Gettysburg (July 2,
        1863).
(1) McCOY, H. C. — W., Antietam (Sept. 17, 1862); Prom., 1Cpl.: AWOL,
        Apr. 18, 1864, presumed deserted.
    MILES, AQUILLA — W., 2nd Manassas (Aug. 30, 1862): W.,
        Chickamauga (Sept. 20, 1863): Retired for disability, Nov. 3,
        1864.
(1) MILES, J. FOSTER — W., Antietam (Sept. 17, 1862): K., Gettysburg
        (July 2, 1863).
(1) MILLICAN, LARKIN — Dischgd., Surg. Cert., Feb. 27, 1862 (chronic
        diarrhea).
(1) MITCHELL, B. FRANK — Dischgd., Surg. Cert., Dec. 5, 1861 (chronic
        diarrhea & typhoid fever).

(1) MIXON, C. M. ("Chap") — K., Darbytown Rd. (Oct. 7, 1864).
(1) MOODY, SAM. O. — Enl. at 17 years: Dischgd., Feb. 22, 1862 for disability (chronic diarrhea).
(1) MOORE, JOHN B. — W., Wilderness (May 6, 1864): W., Darbytown Rd. (Oct. 7, 1864): Died of wound.
(2) MOORE, W. O. — Paroled, Appomattox (April 12, 1865): No other record.
     MOSS, A. M. — Transfd. into Co. D from 8th Ga. Inf. Regt., 1861: AWOL, Apr. 1, 1864.
(2) MOSS, G. F. — Transfd. into Co. D from 8th Ga. Inf. Regt., 1861: Paroled, Appomattox (Apr. 12, 1865).
(1) MOSS, HENRY E. — See list of "Other Officers" above.
(1) MOSS, WM. O. — Asgnd. to recruiting service in Tex., Spring, 1862: W., Chickamauga (Sept. 19, 1863): Died of wound.
(1) MURRAY, W. W. — W., Gaines' Mill (June 27, 1862): Dischgd., Sept. 28, 1862, as a non-conscript, overage (37).
(1) NEWMAN, J. F. — Dischgd. for disability, Mar. 5, 1862.
(1) OLIVER, A. C. — See list of "Other Officers" above.
(2)
(2) OLIVER, F. T. — W., Chaffin's Farm (Sept. 29, 1864): Paroled, Appomattox (Apr. 12, 1865).
(1) OLIVER, H. B. — Died of pneumonia, Fredericksburg, Va. Hosp., Feb. 28, 1862.
(1) OLIVER, JOHN A. — Died of pneumonia, Fredericksburg, Va. Hosp., April 1, 1862.
(1) OLIVER, S. W. — Detailed as Co. Wagonmaster, May 24, 1862: W.,
(2) Gettysburg (July 2, 1863): Paroled, Appomattox (Apr. 12, 1865).
(1) OLIVER, W. A. T. — Prom., 5Sgt., Mar., 1862: W., Antietam (Sept. 17, 1862): POW, Gettysburg (July 5, 1863), detailed to stay with wounded at Cashtown, PA: Exchanged, Dec. 25, 1863.
(1) OLIVER, WM. H. — W., Chickamauga (Sept. 20, 1863): Died of wound, Sept. 26, 1863.
(1) O'REAR, J. PINK — W., and POW, Darbytown Rd. (Oct. 7, 1864): Leg amputated: Returned to Tex.
(1) PERRYMAN, T. G. — Dischgd. as a non-conscript, Sept. 8, 1862, overage (35).
(1) PETTY, THOS. B. — Present & accounted for up to June 30, 1862: No record after that date.
(1) PICKETT, JAMES L. — Died of pneumonia in Fredericksburg, Va. Hosp. Mar. 25, 1862.
(1) PORTER, J. W. — Sick in Richmond Hosp., Summer, 1862: Dischgd., Sept. 15, 1862, as a non-conscript.
(1) POWELL, E. C. — Prom., 3Sgt.: W., Malvern Hill (July 1, 1862): W.,
(2) Antietam (Sept. 17, 1862): W., (3 times), Chickamauga (Sept. 18-20, 1863): Disabled: Detailed as hosp. nurse: Paroled, Appomattox (Apr. 12, 1865).
(1) REYNOLDS, S. F. — Enl. for 12 mos. on May 26, 1861 in Cass County, Tex.: Deserted, June 14, 1862, Lynchburg, Va. (enlmt. expired).

(1)   RICHARDSON, A. F. − Enl. in Tex. for 12 mos. and jnd. Co., June 6, 1861 at New Orleans: Died, Aug. 10, 1861 & buried in Hollywood Cemetery in Richmond.

(1)   ROBINSON, JOHN C. − W., Chickamauga (Sept. 20, 1863): Retired for disability, Oct., 1864.

(1)   ROBINSON, WM. H. − Enl., May 26, 1861 in Cass County, Tex.: No other information available.

(1)   SARTIN, JOHN W. − Dischgd., Aug. 26, 1862, as a non-conscript, underage (17).

(1)   SARTIN, WM. C. − Died of pneumonia in Richmond, Va., Apr. 18, 1862.

(1)   SASSER, WM. R. − Enl. for 12 mos. in Cass Co., Tex., May 26, 1861: No other info. available.

(1)   SHAW, JOHN A. − Prom., 3Sgt.: Dischgd., Sept. 2, 1862, as a non-conscript, overage (36).

(1)   SIMMS, DAVE F. − W., Gaines' Mill (June 27, 1862): Wound furlough, Summer & Fall, 1862: Detailed as a teamster, Summer, 1864: Disabled for field duty.

(1)   SLADE, THOS. C. − Sick in hospitals most of 1861 & 1862 (rheumatism): Sick furlough to Tex., Fall, 1862: AWOL: Turned self in to Conf. Hdqtrs., Bonham, Tex. for re asgnmt., Dec. 19, 1863.

(1)   SMITH, J. W. − W., Eltham's Landing (May 7, 1862): W., Spotsylvania
(2)   C. H. (May 10, 1864): Paroled, Appomattox (Apr. 12, 1865).

(1)   SMITH, JUDSON − Dischgd. for disability (chronic diarrhea), Feb. 17, 1862.

(1)   SNELGROVE (or SNELLGROVE), J. P. − Furlough to Tex., Jan. & Feb., 1863: W., Chickamauga (Sept. 20, 1863): W., Darbytown Rd. (Oct. 7, 1864).

(1)   SNOW, GEORGE L. − Prom., 2Cpl., June 15, 1862: Sick in hosp., Spring, 1863; Fall, 1863; and Spring, 1864 (debilitas): W., Darbytown Rd. (Oct. 7, 1864): Paroled, New Orleans, May 26, 1865.

(1)   SNOW, ROBT. M. − Died in Richmond of pneumonia, Jan. 1, 1862.

(1)   SNOW, WM. M. − W., Chickamauga (Sept. 19, 1863): Detailed by Medical Board for hosp. duties, Mar. 2, 1864.

(1)   STORY, D. F. − Prom., 2Sgt., July, 1863: W., Siege of Knoxville
(2)   (Nov., 1863): W., Wilderness (May 6, 1864), lost part of hand: Paroled, Appomattox (Apr. 12, 1865).

(1)   TAYLOR, WM. H. − Dischgd., Feb. 14, 1862, for disability (chronic diarrhea).

(1)   THERRELL, ABE S. − K., Antietam (Sept. 17, 1862).

(1)   THOMAS, LUCIAN W. − W., Antietam (Sept. 17, 1862): POW, Gettysburg (July 2, 1863): Died at Ft. Delaware Prison, May 26, 1865.

(1)   TOBIN, J. J. − See list of "Other Officers" above.

       WARE, HENRY − Dischgd., Sept. 2, 1862, as a non-conscript, overage (37).

(1)   WATSON, JOHN W. − Enl., May 26, 1861 in Cass Co., Tex.: Dischgd. for disability (pneumonia), Dec. 17, 1861.

       WHITE, JOE G. − Dischgd., Sept. 2, 1862, as a non-conscript, underage (17).

(1) WILLIAMS, W. E. — Enl. at 16 for 1 yr. in Cass Co., Tex., May 26, 1861: Dischgd. for disability (typhoid fever), Dec. 4, 1861.

(1) WISE, CHAS. A. — Enl. for 12 mos. in Cass Co., Tex., Apr. 26, 1861: Left service Feb. 10, 1862, cause unknown.

(1) WOOD, A. J. — Prom., 4Sgt., May, 1862: W., Antietam (Sept. 17, 1862): W., Chickamauga (Sept. 19, 1863).

(1) WOOD, BAILEY P. — Dischgd. for disability, July 13, 1861.

(1) WOOD, JACK P. — W., Antietam (Sept. 17, 1862): Discharged, disabled by wound.

1ST TEX. VOL. INF. REGT.

COMPANY E — *MARSHALL GUARDS*

Company organized in Harrison County, Texas, and mustered into Confederate service "for one year" at New Orleans, June 6, 1861 by Lt. A. W. Pope, CSA.

Key

(1) Original member of Company. (2) Paroled at Appomattox.
K (Killed), W (Wounded), POW (Prisoner of War)
AWOL (Absent Without Leave)

ORIGINAL OFFICERS

(1) BASS, FREDERICK S. Capt. — See roster, "Hdqtrs., Hood's Tex.
(2)   Brig."
(1) BAXTER, ELI N. 1Lt. — Resgnd., Mar. 18, 1862, to engage in the "recruiting service in Texas."
(1) TAYLOR, J. K. 2Lt. — Detailed to recruiting duty in Tex., Spring, 1862: Not re-elect. in the May 18, 1862, reorganization: Returned to Tex.
(1) BURNS, A. D., Sr. 3Lt. — Appt. a Maj. in a Conf. Cav. Regt., Mar., 1862.

ORIGINAL NON-COMMISSIONED OFFICERS

(1) OCHILTREE, THOS. PECK 1Sgt. — Returned to Tex., Summer, 1862: Served on staff of B/Gen. Samuel B. Maxey as Asst. Adj. Gen.: Prom. to Maj.
(1) LANGLEY, THOS H. 2Sgt. — Dischgd. for disability, Mar. 4, 1862:
(2)   Re-enl. as a Pvt., May 3, 1863 at Suffolk, Va.: Detailed as a "forager for leather," East Tenn., Feb., 1864: Hospitalized in Richmond, June, 1864: Paroled, Appomattox (Apr. 12, 1865).

(1) PRESTON, W. B. 3Sgt. — Reduced to Pvt.: Detailed to Tex. on recruiting duty, Feb.-Apr., 1862: AWOL, never returned to Co. from Tex.: 12 mos. enlmt. expired.

(1) STAUTS, G. W. 4Sgt. — See list of "Other Officers" following.

(1) HUGHES, PRATT 1Cpl. — Hospitalized at Chimborazo (Richmond) for pleurisy, May, 1862: Dischgd., Aug. 31, 1862, 12 mos. enlmt. expired.

(1) ERNEST, E. A. 2Cpl. — AWOL, Nov. 15, 1862: Returned to Co., Mar. 10, 1863: Deserted, Aug., 1863.

(1) PRESCOTT, W. D. 3Cpl. — Prom., 1Sgt., June, 1862: W., Chickamauga (Sept. 19, 1863).

(1) WILLINGHAM, T. W. 4Cpl. — Reduced to Pvt.: W., Antietam (Sept. 17, 1862): W., Chickamauga (Sept. 19, 1863): Prom., Cpl.: K., Wilderness (May 6, 1864).

OTHER OFFICERS

WEBB, BERRY W. Capt. — Orig. Pvt. in Co.: Elect., Lt., May 18, 1862: W., Antietam (Sept. 17, 1862): Elect., Capt., Oct. 18, 1862: W., Wilderness (May 6, 1864): Retired for disability on Surg. Cert., Nov. 24, 1864.

ALLEN, E. A. 2Lt. — See roster, "Regmtl. Hdqtrs., 1st Tex. Inf."

HAYES, JAS. H. 2Lt. — Orig. Pvt. in Co.: Elect., 2Lt.: Not re-elect. in the May 18, 1862, re-organization: Returned to Tex.

HOPE, ADAM 3Lt. — Orig. Pvt. in Co.: Elect., 3Lt., Mar. 4, 1862: Not re-elect. in the May 18, 1862, re-organization: Returned to Tex.

MADISON, _____, Lt. — Prom., Lt.: Sent to Tex. to arrest deserters, Aug., 1864: No other record.

PERRY, CLINTON E. 2Lt. — Enl. as a Pvt. at Camp McLeod, Va., Sept. 22, 1861: Elect., 2Lt., May 18, 1862: K., Antietam (Sept. 17, 1862).

STAUTS, G. W. 3Lt. — Orig. 4Sgt. of Co.: Elect., 3Lt., Oct. 21, 1863: W., Wilderness (May 6, 1864).

WOODSON, CHAS. 1Lt. — Orig. Pvt. in Co.: Elect., 1Sgt.: Elect., 3Lt., May 18, 1862: Elect., 2Lt.: Elect., 1Lt.: W., Wilderness (May 6, 1864): Sent to Tex., Aug., 1864, to arrest deserters.

MUSICIAN

(1) ALLEN, E. A. — See list of "Other Officers" above.

PRIVATES

AUSTIN, HOWELL C. — Dischgd. from Serv. for disability, May 29, 1862.

(1) BEAN, JOHN A. — Transfd. from Co. E to Co. D, 1st Tex. Inf. Regt., Apr., 1862.

(1)   BLUDWORTH, WM. — Prom., 2Sgt., Apr., 1862: Deserted, June 30, 1862 (enlmt. expired).

(1)   BOONE, JOHN R. — Dischgd., Aug. 28, 1862, as a non-conscript, underage (17).

       BRADFIELD, JAS. O. — Originally enl. in Cobb's Ga. Legion, Dec. 8, 1861: Transfd. into Co. E, 1st Tex. Inf. Regt., July 25, 1862: Sick much of 1862 & 1863: AWOL, Jan., 1864: Paroled, Shreveport, La., June 13, 1865.

(1)   BRAZEAL, W. SAMUEL — W., and POW, Antietam (Sept. 17, 1862): Paroled, Sept. 30, 1862: No other record.

(1)   BULLOCK, JAS. H. — Prom., Sgt.: Died at Ashland, Va., hosp., Apr. 28, 1862.

       BURKE, JOHN — An outstanding scout: W., near Fredericksburg, Va., Aug. 10, 1862: Detailed to scouting service for Gen. Jeb Stuart, Feb., 1863: "Confidential Scout" for Gen. Lee: Dischgd. to serve on Gov. Murrah's (Tex.) staff, Apr., 1864.

(1)   BURNHAM, S. H. — Dischgd., Aug. 26, 1862 as a non-conscript, overage (38).

       BURNS, JOHN — Enl., Sept. 22, 1862: Sick in Ga., June, 1862: No other record.

(1)   BURNS, R. S. — Enl. in Tex., jnd. in New Orleans, May 28, 1861: No other record.

       CAMPBELL, J. D. — W., Antietam (Sept. 17, 1862): Accidentally W., in camp, Feb. 21, 1863: W. and POW, Gettysburg (July 2, 1863).

(1)   CAMPBELL, WM. M. — W., Gaines' Mill (June 27, 1862): K., Antietam (Sept. 17, 1862).

(1)   CHILDERS, RICHARD — Sick in Hosp., Richmond, Summer, 1862: POW, Gettysburg, July, 1863: Sent to Ft. Delaware Prison: Took oath to Federals, jnd., 3rd Md. Cav. Regt., USA.

(1)   CHIVERS, M. A. — Died of disease (cerebritas), July, 1862.

(2)   CLARK, J. A. — Transfd. into Co. E from Hampton's So. Car. Legion, July, 1862: Sick in hosp. most of 1863: Paroled, Appomattox (Apr. 12, 1865).

(1)   CLARK, ROBT. L. — W., Antietam (Sept. 17, 1862): Dischgd., Nov. 19, 1862: Died in Tex. soon after reaching home.

(1)   CLARK, W. T. — Dischgd. for chronic diarrhea, Feb. 23, 1862.

(1)   COLEMAN, J. H. — Enl. in Tex., jnd. Co. in New Orleans, May 28, 1861: No other record.

(1)   COLEMAN, W. H. — Prom., 5Sgt., Jan. 15, 1863: Prom., 4Sgt.,
(2)   Summer, 1864: Present for duty, June, 1861 through Aug., 1864: Paroled, Appomattox (Apr. 12, 1865).

       COLLINS, Rev. W. C. — Dischgd., Aug. 28, 1862 as a non-conscript, clergyman.

       CUNNINGHAM, V. A. — Dischgd., Aug. 28, 1862, as a non-conscript, overage (38).

(1)   DAVIS, D. D. — K., near Richmond, June 3, 1862.

       DUNN, DAVID C. — Enl. at Camp Pulaski, La., June 13, 1861: Dischgd., Aug. 28, 1862, as a non-conscript, overage (37).

(1)   EWING, E. M. — POW, Frederick, Md., Sept. 15, 1862: No other record.

(1)   FIELDS, C. H. — W., Antietam (Sept. 17, 1862): Deserted, Aug., 1863.

(1) FINNEY, W. — Enl. in Tex. for 1 yr., jnd. Co. in New Orleans, June 6, 1861: No other record.

GILLETTE, MARCUS — Enl., Sept. 22, 1861, at Camp McLeod, Va.: W., Antietam (Sept. 17, 1862): Detailed to Medical Purveyor's Office, Richmond, Aug., 1863.

(1) GILLIAN, J. W. — This same soldier was listed as the Orig. 2Cpl. of Co. A: He is also carried as a Pvt. in Co. E.

(1) HAYES, JAS. H. — See list of "Other Officers" above.

HAYNES, W. D. — Enl., June 13, 1861: Sick in hosp., Fall, 1862: AWOL, Feb., 1863, fined $30: W., Darbytown Rd. (Oct. 7, 1864): Furloughed, 35 days, Oct. 28, 1864.

(2) HEARD, GEO. F. — W., Antietam (Sept. 17, 1862): W., Gettysburg (July 2, 1863): Paroled, Appomattox (April 12, 1865).

(1) HENDRICK, JAS. H. — W., Antietam (Sept. 17, 1862): W., Wilderness (May 6, 1864): Died of wound.

(1) HOPE, ADAM — See list of "Other Officers" above.

JOYCE, ROBT. F. — Appt., 1Cpl., Oct. 30, 1863: POW while on foraging detail near Mossy Creek, Tenn., Jan. 22, 1864.

KIMBALL, J. D. — Died of disease, buried in Hollywood Cemetery, Richmond, Sept. 2, 1862.

(1) KING, S. A. — K., Wilderness (May 6, 1864).

(1) LANGLEY, WM. S. — Sick in hosp., Winchester, Va., Sept., 1862: K., Gettysburg (July 2, 1863).

LAWSON, J. A. — Prom., 2Sgt., June, 1862: K., Gaines' Mill (June 27, 1862).

(1) LEVY, LEWIS M. — Hospitalized (diarrhea), May, 1862: Dischgd., Aug. 28, 1862, as a non-conscript, underage (17).

(1) LINDSEY, J. A. — Prom., 3Sgt.: Detailed to Tex. on recruiting duty, Feb.-Apr., 1863: W., Chickamauga (Sept. 19, 1863).

(2) LONGINO, J. T. — Enl., Camp Pulaski, La., June 13, 1861: Prom., 3Cpl., June, 1862: Prom., 2Sgt., Aug., 1862: W. and POW, Gettysburg (July 2, 1863): Paroled: Detailed to Ordn. Dept., 1st Corps, Army of Northern Virginia, Apr., 1864: Returned to Co.: Paroled, Appomattox (Apr. 12, 1865).

(1) MARKS, JOS. — Left sick near Shepardstown, Md., Sept. 19, 1862: Deserted.

MARSHALL, ROBT. J. — Enl., June 13, 1861 at Camp Pulaski, La.: W., Antietam (Sept. 17, 1862): W., Chickamauga (Sept. 20, 1863): Died of wound, Sept. 22, 1863.

MARTIN, J. W. — Enl. for 1 yr., May 28, 1861, at New Orleans: Hospitalized, 2 wks. with rubeola, June, 1862: Deserted, Nov. 15, 1862 (enlmt. expired).

(1) MAYS, FRANKLIN M. — W., Wilderness (May 6, 1864): Paroled,
(2) Appomattox (Apr. 12, 1865).

(1) McKAY, THOS. — Dischgd., Aug. 28, 1862, as a non-conscript, overage (45).

(1) McKINNEY (or McKENNY), A. M. — No record available.

(1) McQUEEN, GEO. — Deserted, July 13, 1862 (enlmt. expired).

(1) MILLER, JOHN — With Co., until July 1, 1862: No other record.

(1) MILLS, C. STILES — See roster "Regmtl. Hdqtrs., 1st Tex. Inf."

(1) MORRISON, C. H. — Deserted, June 1, 1862 (enlmt. expired).

MULLAY, J. C. K. — POW, Williamsport, Md., July 13, 1863: Paroled: On detchd. duty to Navy Dept., Feb., 1864: AWOL, Mar., 1864: Appt. Lt. in Co. A, 6th Tex. Cav. Regt.: Paroled, Marshall, Tex., June 7, 1865.

(1) NORWOOD, JAS. K. — Enl., June 6, 1861 at New Orleans: Detailed as a Brig. Teamster, Jan., 1863: Detailed as Div. Wagonmaster, Mar., 1864: Deserted, picked up by Federals at Charleston, W. Va., Mar. 20, 1865.

(1) PAGE, ELLIS G. — Enl. for 12 mos. at New Orleans, May 28, 1861: No other record.

(1) PEAL, N. B. — Dischgd., Jan. 20, 1862, for disability (lung disease).

(1) PEERS, J. M. — Dischgd., Aug. 28, 1862, as a non-conscript, overage (41).

(1) PEET, GEO. A. — Enl. at New Orleans, May 28, 1862: No other record.

PERRY, CLINTON E. — See list of "Other Officers" above.

PERRY, EUGENE OSCEOLA — Jnd. Co., Sept. 22, 1861: Sick in Richmond, Summer, 1862: W., Antietam (Sept. 17, 1862): 60-day recuperation furlough: W., Chickamauga (Sept. 20, 1863): Detailed as Division Wagon Master, Feb., 1864: K., Wilderness (May 6, 1864).

PERRY, HOWARD EARLE — Prom., Cpl.: K., Antietam (Sept. 17, 1862).

(2) PERRY, SIDNEY FRANKLIN ("Bose") — Enl. at Camp McLeod, Va., Sept. 22, 1861: W., Antietam (Sept. 17, 1862): Paroled, Appomattox (Apr. 12, 1865).

PHILLIPS, Rev. H. B. — Enl. at Camp McLeod, Va., Sept. 21, 1861: Minister by profession: Dischgd. for disability (lung disease & typhoid fever), Dec. 1, 1861.

(1) POAGUE, JAS. R. — Died of disease near Manassas, Va., Oct. 1, 1861.

(1) POPE, BEN S. — Dischgd. for disability ("general bad health"), July 11, 1861.

(1) POPE, JAS. W. — See roster, "Regmtl. Hdqtrs., 1st Tex. Inf."

PURNELL, W. T. — Enl., June 13, 1861, Camp Pulaski, La.: Sick, Summer, 1862, "unfit for field service:" Detailed as a nurse in hosp. at Staunton, Va., most of 1863 & 1864: Paroled, Staunton, Va., May 17, 1865.

(1) RAWLS, W. P. — Enl. for 12 mos. at New Orleans, May 28, 1861: No other record.

ROBINSON, JOS. T. — Enl. at Huntsville, Ala., June 17, 1861: Dischgd. as a non-conscript, Aug. 28, 1862, overage (36).

(1) RUDDER, JOSEPH F. — W., & POW, Antietam (Sept. 17, 1862).

(2) SANDS, RILEY G. — Jnd. Co. E, Aug. 15, 1862, from C. R. Wheat's La. Battalion: W., Wilderness (May 6, 1864): Paroled, Appomattox (April 12, 1865).

(1) SCOTT, W. C. — Prom., Cpl.: W., Gaines' Mill (June 27, 1862).

(1) SLOAN, T. M. — Dischgd. on surg. cert., July, 1862: Re-enlisted later in war.

(1) SMITH, JOHN — Dischgd. for "poor health," Jan., 1862.

(1) SMITH, JOHN W. — Prom., 5Sgt.: W., Gaines' Mill (June 27, 1862): Prom., 1Sgt., July, 1862: W., Antietam (Sept. 17, 1862): W., Wilderness (May 6, 1864).

SPRATTING, J. B. — K., Occoquan, Va., Feb. 5, 1862.

(1) STEEL, THOS. J. — Prom., 5Sgt., July 21, 1862: W., 2nd Manassas (Aug. 30, 1862): Arm amputated.

(1) STEPHENS, RHODES B. — Prom., 4Cpl.: K., 2nd Manassas (Aug. 30, 1862). (Was to be dischgd. for overage, Aug. 28, 1862, but elected to go into battle.)

(1) STONE, HENRY W. — Prom., 5Sgt.: Dischgd., July 21, 1862, as a non-conscript, underage (17).

(1) TAYLOR, J. M. — Dischgd. for disability (lung disease), Dec. 19, 1861.

(1) TRICE, J. J. — Dischgd., Aug. 28, 1862, as a non-conscript, overage (36).

TRIMBLE, LEE W. — Prom., Cpl., Dec., 1862: Reduced to ranks, March 28, 1863: Patient in Tex. Hosp., Richmond, Summer, 1863: AWOL, Sept. 19, 1863 at Battle of Chickamauga: In CSA hosp., Shreveport, La., Mar. 17, 1864.

(2) TROWBRIDGE, J. W. — Captured by enemy cav. while scouting on the Occoquan near Dumfries, Va., March, 1862: Exchanged, Aug. 5, 1862: Detailed to Signal Serv., Feb., 1863: Courier at Brig. Hdqtrs.: Paroled, Appomattox (Apr. 12, 1865).

(1) TURNER, E. J. B. — Enl. for 12 mos. at New Orleans, May 28, 1861: Detailed as a Regmtl. Butcher, Apr., 1862: Deserted, July 13, 1862 (enlmt. expired).

(1) TURNER, W. E. — Enl., New Orleans, May 28, 1861: Dischgd. for disability, Oct. 29, 1861.

TURRENTINE, M. B. — Dischgd., Aug. 28, 1862 as a non-conscript, overage (35).

VANDERGRAFF, J. S. — Enl., Spring, 1862, at Quantico, Va.: Transfd. to Navy, Apr., 1863: Prom., Lt.

WALKER, D. M. — K., 2nd Manassas (Aug. 30, 1862): Was to be dischgd. for underage, Aug. 28, 1862, but elect. to go into battle.

(1) WATSON, SAMUEL T. — Captured by enemy cav. while scouting on the Occoquan near Dumfries, Va., Mar., 1962: Exchanged Aug. 5, 1862: W., Antietam (Sept. 17, 1862): Detailed to Signal Serv., Feb., 1863: Courier at Brig. Hdqtrs.: Paroled, Appomattox (Apr. 12, 1865).

(1) WEBB, BERRY W. — See list of "Other Officers" above.

WEBB, J. W. — W., 2nd Manassas (Aug. 30, 1862): Prom., 2Cpl., Nov., 1862: Prom., 4Sgt., Jan. 15, 1863: "On furlough of indulgence," Feb., 1864: Deserted, March 12, 1864.

WEBB, STEVE W. — Enl., June 6, 1861 for 1 yr.: On recruiting serv. to Tex., Spring, 1862: Did not return to Co., probably finished out enlmt. in Tex.

WHITTAKER, M. — Enl., Camp Pulaski, La., June 15, 1861: Dischgd., Aug. 28, 1862, as a non-conscript, overage (35).

(1) WIGGS, A. F. — Enl. at New Orleans, May 28, 1861: Sick (dysentery) in hosp., Winter & Spring, 1863: Dischgd. for disability (eye disease), June 19, 1863.

(1) WILSON, DAVID L. — Enl., New Orleans, May 28, 1861: Dischgd. for "poor health," Jan., 1862.

WOOD, C. W. — See roster, "Regmtl. Hdqtrs., 1st Tex. Inf."

(1)   WOODSON, CHAS. — See list of "Other Officers" above.
       WOODWARD, W. F. — Detailed to recruiting serv. in Tex., Spring,
       1862: Dischgd., Aug. 28, 1862, as a non-conscript, overage (36).

1ST TEX. VOL. INF. REGT.

COMPANY F — WOODVILLE RIFLES

Company was organized in Tyler County, Texas, and mustered
into Confederate service "for one year" at New Orleans on May
28, 1861 by Lt. A. W. Pope, CSA.

Key

(1) Original member of Company. (2) Paroled at Appomattox.
K (Killed), W (Wounded), POW (Prisoner of War)
AWOL (Absent Without Leave)

ORIGINAL OFFICERS

(1)   WORK, PHILIP A. Capt. — See roster, "Regmtl. Hdqtrs., 1st Tex.
       Inf."
(1)   WILSON, (or WILLSON), SAM A. 1Lt. — Detailed to recruiting duty
       in Tex., Feb.-Apr., 1862: Elect., Capt.: W., Antietam (Sept. 17,
       1862): W. and POW, Gettysburg (July 2, 1863).
(1)   SAUNDERS, ROBT. M. 2Lt. — Dropped from Rolls during re-org. of
       Co., May 16, 1862: Left for Tex. to raise his own Co.
(1)   ROCK, T. D. 3Lt. — Reduced to Pvt., May 16, 1862 when Co. was
       re-org.: POW, Gettysburg (July 2, 1863).

ORIGINAL NON-COMMISSIONED OFFICERS

(1)   NIX, W. P. 1Sgt. — Dischgd., Jan. 5, 1862, poor health (TB).
(1)   RATCLIFF, E. B. 2Sgt. — Detailed to recruiting serv. in Tex.,
       Feb.-Apr., 1862: Deserted, June 26, 1862 (enlmt. expired).
(1)   MAY, R. B. 3Sgt. — W., Eltham's Landing (May 7, 1862): Dischgd.,
       July 24, 1862 on Surg. Cert. of disability.
(1)   SMITH, W. V. 4Sgt. — Prom., 3Sgt., Feb., 1863: Prom., 2Sgt., June,
       1863: W., Chickamauga (Sept. 19, 1863): K., Spotsylvania C. H.
       (May 10, 1864).
(1)   GILDER, O. P. 1Cpl. — Enl., New Orleans, May 28, 1861: Dischgd.,
       Jan. 21, 1862 for disability (chronic bronchitis & dysentery).
(1)   KITCHEN, C. 2Cpl. — Enl., New Orleans, May 28, 1861: Dischgd. for
       disability (lung condition), Aug. 1, 1861.

(1) SUMNER, D. W. 3Cpl. — Reduced to Pvt., Fall, 1861: Detailed as courier to Maj. Randolph in Ordn. Dept., Dec., 1862: Detailed as orderly to Div. Chief of Ordnance, July, 1863: POW, Gettysburg (July 2, 1863).

(1) PERRYMAN, JAS. E. 4Cpl. — Prom., 1Sgt.: W., Antietam (Sept. 17, 1862): W., Chickamauga (Sept. 20, 1863).

OTHER OFFICERS

RIGSBY, A. J. Capt. — Orig. Pvt. in Co.: Elect., 2Lt., Oct. 21, 1862: Elect., 1Lt., June 26, 1863: W., Wilderness (May 6, 1864): Elect., Capt.: POW, Chaffin's Farm (Sept. 29, 1864).

BURROUGHS, J. J. Lt. — Elect., Lt.: No other record.

NOBLE, MILTON C. 1Lt. — See roster, "Hdqtrs., Hood's Tex. Brig."

RUNNELS, PERRY Lt. — Orig. Pvt. in Co.: Prom. to 2Sgt., Mar. 13, 1862: Elect., Lt.: K., Antietam (Sept. 17, 1862).

SNOW, HENRY 1Lt. — See roster, "Regmtl. Hdqtrs., 1st Tex. Inf."

TOMPKINS, E. JASPER 2Lt. — Orig. Pvt. in Co.: W., Malvern Hill (July 1, 1862): Elect., 2Lt.

MUSICIAN

(1) SHARP, CHAS. F. — See roster, "Regmtl. Hdqtrs., 1st Tex. Inf."

PRIVATES

(1) ALLEN, W. A. — K., Gaines' Mill (June 27, 1862).

(1) AMBROSE, JOHN — K., Gaines' Mill (June 27, 1862).

(1) BARCLAY, THOS. — See roster, "Hdqtrs., Hood's Tex. Brig."

BARLOW, JOHN — Enl., Woodville, Tex., Apr. 22, 1862: Died at University Hosp. (Richmond), July 7, 1862 (typhoid fever).

(1) BENEDICT, JACOB — W., Malvern Hill (July 1, 1862): No other record.

(1) BOSTWICK, C. — Dischgd., Aug. 28, 1862, as a non-conscript, overage.

BRADHAM, BENJ. — Enl., Woodville, Tex., Apr. 21, 1862: Prom., 5Sgt., June 10, 1863: W., Chickamauga (Sept. 20, 1863): Prom., 4Sgt., Feb., 1864: POW, Wilderness (May 6, 1864): imprisoned at Elmira, N. Y.: Paroled, June 19, 1865.

BRADY, THOS. F. — Enl., Woodville, Tex., Apr. 8, 1862: sick or on furlough most of 1862: POW, Nov. 8, 1863, Lookout Mtn., Tenn.

BULEY, NATHAN — Enl., Woodville, Tex., Mar. 22, 1862: Died at sick camp near Richmond, June 2, 1862.

(1) BULLOCK, JAS. M. — Prom., 2Cpl.: Detchd. as courier for B/Gen. J. B. Robertson.

(1) BUSH, JAS. — K., Eltham's Landing (May 7, 1862).

CHANCE, DAN — Enl., Woodville, Tex., Apr. 21, 1862: Absent sick (typhoid), Fall, 1862: Sick furlough, Winter, 1862-63: AWOL, Spring, 1863.

CHANCE, E. M. ("Dock") — Enl., Woodville, Tex., Apr. 9, 1862: Sick (hepatitis), Summer & Fall, 1862: No other record.

CHANCE, J. B. ("Zeke") — Enl., Woodville, Tex., Apr. 4, 1862: No other record.

COLLIER, JOS. W. — Enl., Mar. 26, 1862: Prom., 5Sgt., May 1, 1863: Prom., 4Sgt.: Captured on patrol in Va., Aug. 8, 1863.

(2)   CRAVEY, JOHN ("Jack") — Enl., Apr. 10, 1862: W., Wilderness (May 6, 1864): Paroled, Appomattox (Apr. 12, 1865).

CRIER, EMANUEL — Enl., Mar. 22, 1862: Sick most of 1862: K., Chickamauga (Sept. 19, 1863).

CRIER, M. T. — Enl., Mar. 22, 1862: W., Gaines' Mill (June 27, 1862): W., 2nd Manassas (Aug. 30, 1862): W., Gettysburg (July 2, 1863): Died, July 4, 1863.

CRIER, WM. — Enl., Mar. 22, 1862: Prom., 2Cpl., Apr., 1863: Prom., Color-Cpl., Oct., 1863: W., & POW, Siege of Knoxville (Nov. 25, 1863): Exchanged, Nov. 29, 1863: Died of wound.

(1)   DEAN, A. D. — "Detached as guard for Hood's Minstrels," Dec. 15, 1862: AWOL, Feb., 1863.

DURHAM, RICHARD — Enl., Mar. 28, 1862: Died in Richmond (typhoid fever), June 23, 1862.

DURHAM, THOS. — Enl., Mar. 28, 1862: Died at sick camp near Richmond, June 11, 1862.

(1)   ELLIOT, W. K. — Dischgd., Aug. 28, 1862, as a non-conscript, underage.

ENGLEKING, S. — W., Antietam (Sept. 17, 1862) and left at Shepardstown, Md.: On extended "wound furlough": Permanently disabled, remained in Tex.

(1)   ESKRIDGE, R. THOS. — W., Gaines' Mill (June 27, 1862): K., Wilderness (May 6, 1864).

EVANS, JACK — Died at sick camp near Richmond, July 6, 1862.

EVANS, RICHARD — Enl., Mar. 28, 1862, at Woodville, Tex.: Captured on patrol, at Stafford C. H., Va., Aug. 8, 1863: Deserted, Aug. 19, 1863.

FELPS, OSCAR — K., Antietam (Sept. 17, 1862).

(1)   FONTAINE, HENRY B. — Transfd. to Co. B, 1st Tex. Inf. Regt., Apr. 26, 1862.

GILDER, U. M. — Enl. at Camp McLeod, Va., Sept. 23, 1861: W., Malvern Hill (July 1, 1862): W., Chickamauga (Sept. 19, 1863): Prom. to Lt. in a Cav. Co. while in Tex. on convalescent furlough.

GOODWYN, WM. — Enl., Apr. 8, 1862 at Woodville, Tex.: Sick in Richmond Hosp., Fall, 1862: Died of pneumonia, Feb. 7, 1863.

GRAHAM, JOHN T. — Prom., 4Cpl., Dec., 1862: Sick in Hosp., Spring, 1863: Reduced to Pvt., June 1, 1863: Died of pneumonia, Mar. 9, 1864, in the CSA Gen'l. Hosp., Danville, Va.

(1)   HAMILTON, EDWARD G. — Dischgd. for disability (chronic diarrhea), Dec. 10, 1861.

HAMILTON, TILFORD A. — See roster, "Hdqtrs., Hood's Tex. Brig."

HANKS, AMOS G. — Enl. at Camp McLeod, Va., Sept. 25, 1861: Prom., 3Sgt., Oct., 1862: W. & POW, Antietam (Sept. 17, 1862): Paroled: Leg amputated, Dec. 10, 1862: Dischgd. for disability, Jan. 8, 1863.

HARVELL, HENRY — W., Gaines' Mill (June 27, 1862): Leg amputated: Furloughed to Tex.: Disabled, unfit for service: Paroled, Houston, July 6, 1865.

(1) HICKS, CHAS. H. — Detailed as orderly to Regmtl. Cmdr.: Prom., 4Cpl.: W. accidentally while scouting: Prom. to Sgt.: K., Chickamauga (Sept. 19, 1863).

HINES, JAS. M. — Enl., Camp McLeod, Va., Sept. 23, 1861: W., Darbytown Rd. (Oct. 7, 1864): Died from wound at Howard's Grove Hosp., Richmond, Oct. 9, 1864.

HOLLIMAN, BURWELL J. — W., Gaines' Mill (June 27, 1862): Died from wound, July 1, 1862.

HOLMES, WM. F. — W., Antietam (Sept. 17, 1862): Missing, Lookout Mtn., Tenn., Oct. 28, 1863: POW, Dade Co., Ga., Nov. 8, 1863: Paroled, Alton, Ill., June 19, 1865.

HOOKER, ROBT. — Enl., Apr. 21, 1862: W., Gaines' Mill (June 27, 1862): Died of pneumonia, Mar. 7, 1863.

HOOKS, GILMORE — Died at sick camp near Richmond, June 21, 1862 (typhoid fever).

JARMON, R. B. — Enl., July 9, 1861 in Richmond: Hospitalized most of 1862: Detailed to Army Intelligence Office, Richmond, Feb., 1863: On duty at Brig. Hdqtrs., Fall, 1863: Detailed to Medical Board, Summer, 1864.

JONES, HENRY C. — Prom., 3Cpl.: W., Chickamauga (Sept. 20, 1863): Died of wound.

(1) JONES, L. SAMUEL — W., Gaines' Mill (June 27, 1862): Detailed as a Brig. teamster, June, 1863: Deserted, Feb. 20, 1864.

KENDALL, JAS. — Enl., Woodville, Tex., Apr. 11, 1862: Dischgd. for disability (ulcer), Oct. 14, 1862.

LANE, A. S. — Enl., Woodville, Tex., Apr. 22, 1862: Died at Goldsboro, No. Car., May 20, 1862.

LLOYD, ROBT. — Enl., Woodville, Tex., Mar. 29, 1862: Detailed as ambulance driver, Summer, 1862: Wardmaster Tex. Hosp., Richmond, Spring, 1863: Transfd. to Navy, Dec., 1863.

(1) LONG, GREEN B. — Present & accounted for until Nov., 1864: Sick in hosp. several times during war.

(1) MARTIN, WM. T. — Enl., May 28, 1861, at New Orleans: Died of typhoid fever in Richmond, Mar. 14, 1863.

(1) McDERMOTT, HUGH — Enl., May 28, 1861, at New Orleans: Dischgd. for disability (consumption), Aug. 12, 1861: Died in Banner Hosp., Richmond, Apr. 19, 1862.

(1) McMILLAN, DUNCAN D. — W., Gaines' Mill (June 27, 1862): Died, July, 1862.

McRAE, C. G. — Enl., Dec., 1861 at Camp Quantico, Va.: W., Gaines' Mill (June 27, 1862): Deserted in E. Tenn., Feb. 17, 1864.

(1) MERCHANT, W. B. — Dischgd., Aug. 28, 1862, as a non-conscript, underage.

MINTER, JOHN — Enl., May 28, 1861 at Woodville, Tex., for 12 mos.: Dischgd. on Surg. Cert. (debility), July 25, 1862: Re-enl. in Tex.: POW, Big Black, Miss., July 13, 1863: Confined at Camp Morton, Indianapolis, Ind.: Died in prison, Jan. 10, 1864, and buried in grave #667 at Greenlawn Cemetery in Indianapolis.

(1) MOORE, HENRY G. — Enl. for 12 mos., May 28 at New Orleans: No other record: Probably dischgd. for disability or expiration of 12 mos. enlmt.

MORELAND, J. T. L. — Died (measles), Mar. 12, 1862.

(1) MORGAN, A. G. — Dischgd., Aug. 28, 1862, as a non-conscript, overage (38).

NEYLAND, A. C. — Enl., May 23, 1861 in the 7th La. Inf. Regt.: Transfd. to Co. F, 1st Tex. Inf., Sept. 1, 1861: Dischgd. for disability (chronic bronchitis), Nov. 21, 1861.

(2) NOBLE, MILTON C. — See list, "Other Officers", above.

(1) OLIVE, O. D. W. — Dischgd. on Surg. Cert. (diarrhea), Aug. 9, 1861.

(1) PATE, ADDISON — W., Malvern Hill (July 1, 1862): Dischgd., Sept. 7, 1862, as a non-conscript, underage (17).

PHILLIPS, JAS. M. — Died in camp near Winchester of cholera, Oct. 10, 1862.

PHILLIPS, JOHN L. — Enl., May 2, 1862: Sick in Petersburg & Danville, Va., hospitals, Spring & Summer, 1863 (ulcers & diarrhea): Sick furlough to Tex., Spring, 1864.

(1) POOL, JOSH W. — Prom., 4Cpl.: W., 2nd Manassas (Aug. 30, 1862): Foot amputated: Returned to Tex., Oct., 1862.

(1) POOL, WM. — Detailed as nurse at Warrenton, Va., after 2nd Manassas: W., Chickamauga (Sept. 19, 1863): Permanently disabled.

(1) PRUITT, ARGALUS P. — Deserted, June 26, 1862 (Enlmt. expired).

(1) RIGSBY, A. J. — See list of "Other Officers" above.

ROUNTREE, W. A. — W., Antietam (Sept. 17, 1862): Prom., 2Cpl., Mar. 1, 1863: Prom., 1Cpl.: W., Gettysburg (July 2, 1863): Retired by Military Examining Board, July 24, 1864.

(1) RUNNELS, PERRY — See list of "Other Officers" above.

SCOTT, WM. F. (or H.) — Enl., Mar. 21, 1862: W. & POW, Antietam (Sept. 17, 1862): Died of wound.

(1) SHIDE, J. H. — Dischgd. as a non-conscript, overage (38).

SIMS, A. C. ("Cubb") — Enl., Apr. 6, 1863: Sick, Jan.-Aug., 1864: W., in Miss., Jan., 1865: Paroled, Macon, Ga., Apr. 30, 1865.

(1) SMITH, ABE — Enl., May 28, 1861 for 12 mos.: Detailed as a hosp. guard at Gaines' Mill (June 27, 1862): Sick in Richmond Hosp., Spring, 1863: Deserted, "about Feb. 17," 1864: Arrested by U.S. Provost Marshal in Bradley County, Ark., May 5, 1864.

(1) SMITH, MILTON A. — Enl., May 28, 1861 at New Orleans: No other record.

SMITH, ZACK — Enl., at Woodville, Tex., Apr. 13, 1862: Died at sick camp near Richmond, June 16, 1862.

(1) SNOW, HENRY — See list of "Other Officers" above.

(2) SNOWDEN, JASPER N. — Enl., Woodville, Tex., Apr. 14, 1862 "for 3 yrs.": Detailed to round-up cattle in No. Va., Apr., 1864: Paroled, Appomattox (Apr. 12, 1865).

(1) STALLINGS, J. J. — Dischgd., Aug. 10, 1861, unfit for duty.

(1) STEDMAN, B. B. ("Bug") — See roster, "Regmtl. Hdqtrs., 1st Tex. Inf."

(1) STEDMAN, ELI T. — W., Eltham's Landing (May 6, 1862): W., Malvern Hill (July 1, 1862): W., Gettysburg (July 2, 1863).

(1) STEDMAN, JOHN T. — Enl., May 25, 1862 for 3 yrs.; W., Gettysburg (July 2, 1863): Died of wound, Mar. 22, 1864.

(1) SWEARINGEN, E. A. — Deserted, June 26, 1862 (enlmt. expired).

TINER, JAMES T. — Enl., Mar. 30, 1862 for 3 yrs.: W., Gettysburg (July 2, 1863): W., Chickamauga (Sept. 19, 1863): Missing, Wilderness (May 6, 1864).

TOLBERT, J. W. — Dischgd. for disability (lung disease), Nov. 21, 1861.

(1) TOMPKINS, D. C. — Dischgd. for disability (chronic diarrhea), Feb. 6, 1862.

(1) TOMPKINS, E. JASPER — See list of "Other Officers" above.

TRAVIS, JOHN — Died of measles, Aug. 18, 1862.

(1) VAN VLECK, JULIUS L. — Detailed to Tex. on recruiting serv., Feb.-Apr., 1863: W., Gettysburg (July 2, 1863): K., Petersburg, Va., June 20, 1864.

WALKER, JAS. W. — Enl., Mar. 22, 1862: Died at sick camp near Richmond, June 4, 1862.

WARD, JOS. — Enl., Apr. 18, 1862: Prom., 3Cpl., Nov., 1862: Detailed to make shoes for government at Petersburg, Va., Nov., 1862: Died, May 29, 1863.

(1) WARE, G. S. — See roster, "Regmtl. Hdqtrs., 1st Tex. Inf."

(1) WELSH, THOS. — K., Wilderness (May 6, 1864).

(1) WEST, A. M. — Detailed to recruiting serv. in Tex., Feb.-Apr., 1862: Prom. to Sgt.: W., 2nd Manassas (Aug. 30, 1862): Died of wound.

WEST, ISAAC — Died of measles, Mar. 22, 1862.

(1) WHITTLESEY, J. R. — AWOL, June 27, 1862: Dischgd., Aug. 28, 1862, as a non-conscript, underage (17).

WIGGINS, WM. D. — Enl., Apr. 23, 1862: Died at Charlottesville, Va., of chronic diarrhea, Oct. 24, 1862.

(1) WOMACK, GREEN — Dischgd., Sept. 6, 1861, Surg. Cert. of disability.

(1) WOOTEN, J. ALBERT — Died of accidental wound, Mar. 7, 1862.

1ST TEX. VOL. INF. REGT.

COMPANY G — *REAGAN GUARDS*

Company was organized in Anderson County, Texas, and mustered into Confederate service "for the war" at Palestine, Texas, June 23, 1861, by Capt. John R. Woodward, CSA.

Key

(1) Original member of Company. (2) Paroled at Appomattox.
K (Killed), W (Wounded), POW (Prisoner of War)
AWOL (Absent Without Leave)

ORIGINAL OFFICERS

(1) WOODWARD, JOHN R. Capt. — See roster of "Regmtl. Hdqtrs., 1st Tex. Inf."

(1)   JEMISON, ELBERT S. 1Lt. — W., Gaines' Mill (June 27, 1862): W., Antietam (Sept. 17, 1862): Elect., Capt., Aug. 9, 1863: Detailed to recruiting serv., Trans-Miss. Dept., Spring, 1864: Resgnd., Aug. 9, 1864.

(1)   DALE, MATT 2Lt. — See roster, "Regmtl. Hdqtrs., 1st Tex. Inf."

(1)   CAMPBELL, BENJ. A. 3Lt. — Detailed to recruiting serv. in Tex., Oct.-Dec., 1862: K., Gettysburg (July 2, 1863).

ORIGINAL NON-COMMISSIONED OFFICERS

(1)   ROSE, T. JEFF 1Sgt. — See list of "Other Officers," following.

(1)   KIMBROUGH, WM. B. 2Sgt. — Reduced to 3Sgt.: Reduced to Pvt.:
(2)   Detailed as "Beef Driver" and "Chief Butcher," Tex. Brig., Fall, 1862: Paroled, Appomattox (April 12, 1865).

(1)   HARRIS, JAS. M. 3Sgt. — Prom., 2Sgt.: Died, Aug. 26, 1862.

(1)   HOLLY, JACK A. 4Sgt. — Died of disease (chronic diarrhea), Richmond, Sept. 1, 1862.

(1)   WRIGHT, CHAS. F. 1Cpl. — Detailed to recruiting serv. in Tex., Feb.-Apr., 1862: W., Wilderness (May 6, 1864): Arm amputated.

(1)   HOPPER, WM. J. 2Cpl. — Enl., June 23, 1861: No other record.

(1)   MONTGOMERY, ROBT. M. 3Cpl. — Dischgd. from service (chronic diarrhea & typhoid fever), Feb. 16, 1862.

(1)   CANTLEY, Z. W. ("Zeb") 4Cpl. — Resgnd. as Cpl., May 31, 1862: W. and POW, Antietam (Sept. 17, 1862): Died of wound.

OTHER OFFICERS

(1)   QUARLES, JOHN JAS. Capt. — Orig. Pvt. in Co.: Prom., 1Sgt., May
(2)   20, 1862: Elect., 2Lt., Apr. 4, 1863: Elect., 1Lt., July 2, 1863: W., Chickamauga (Sept. 19, 1863): Elect., Capt.: Assumed cmd. of Co., Jan. 19, 1864: Paroled, Appomattox (Apr. 12, 1865).

(2)   MYNATT, DONALD M. 1Lt. — Recruited as a Pvt. in Tex., Apr. 2, 1862: Elect., 2Lt., Sept. 25, 1863: Elect., 1Lt., Aug. 7, 1864: Paroled, Appomattox (Apr. 12, 1865).

        MYNATT, W. PARK 2Lt. — See roster, "Regmtl. Hdqtrs., 1st Tex. Inf."

(1)   ROSE, T. JEFF 3Lt. — Orig. 1Sgt. of Co.: Detailed to recruiting serv. in Tex., Feb.-Apr., 1862: Elect., 3Lt., May 20, 1862: W., Antietam (Sept. 17, 1862): Died in Richmond Hosp., Apr. 4, 1863.

PRIVATES

(2)   ADAMS, LEVI A. — Recruited in Tex., Apr. 11, 1862, Age 30: W., Wilderness (May 6, 1864): Paroled, Appomattox (Apr. 12, 1865).

(1)   ALLEN, PHILLIP T. — Sick, Spring, 1863 (acute diarrhea): Sick, Fall, 1863: Deserted, Jan., 1864.

(1)   ASPLEY, MATTHEW JAS. — Prom., 3Sgt.: W. and POW, Antietam (Sept. 17, 1862).

(1)   BARNES, N. R. — Sick (chronic diarrhea), Chimborazo Hosp., Richmond, Apr., 1862: Deserted, June 5, 1862 (enlmt. expired).

(1)   BERGER, JOHN — Died of pneumonia and typhoid fever, March 25, 1862.

(1)   BLACK, SIMEON F. — Prom., 3Cpl., Spring, 1862: W. and disabled,
(2)   2nd Manassas (Aug. 30, 1862): Granted recuperation leave to Tex.: Rejnd. Co., Dec. 14, 1862: Asgnd. as a teamster, Hdqtrs., 1st Tex.: Paroled, Appomattox (Apr. 12, 1865).

(1)   BLACKSHEAR, SILAS L. ("Sebe") — W. and disabled, Antietam (Sept. 17, 1862).

(1)   BOTTOMS, SMITH — K., Antietam (Sept. 17, 1862).

       BOWEN, M. ESTES — Recruited at Palestine, Tex., Apr. 8, 1862, age 31: Died of pneumonia in Richmond, March 17, 1863.

(1)   BOWEN, WILSON P. — Crippled by fall, June, 1863: Detailed to herd
(2)   cattle, Aug., 1863: Prom., 2Sgt., Jan. 1, 1864: Paroled, Appomattox (Apr. 12, 1865).

(1)   BOX, LINA H. — Prom., 5Sgt.: Resgnd. as Sgt., May 20, 1862: Dischgd. for physical disability, Oct., 1862.

(1)   BRADLEY, HENRY F. ("Hy") — Detailed to Pioneer Corps, Nov., 1862: W., Chickamauga (Sept. 20, 1863): Deserted in 1864: Took Fed. oath, Sept. 22, 1864.

(1)   BRIGMAN, WM. H. — Left at Front Royal, Va., July 22, 1863 to attend Gettysburg wounded: K., Chaffin's Farm (Sept. 29, 1864).

       BURROUGHS, SAM RAYMOND — Recruited at Palestine, Tex., Mar. 22, 1862, age 19: POW, Chickamauga (Sept. 19, 1863): Confined at Camp Douglas near Chicago until end of the war.

       BUTLER, RICHARD — Recruited at Palestine, Tex., Mar. 31, 1862, age 17: K., Antietam (Sept. 17, 1862).

       BUTTS, JAS. M. — Recruited at Palestine, Tex., Apr. 8, 1862, age 32: Detailed to Engineer Corps., June 14, 1863: Rejnd. Co.: W. and disabled, Wilderness (May 6, 1864).

       CHAMBERS, A. J. — Recruited at Palestine, Tex., Apr. 11, 1862, age 26, occupation, teacher: Dischgd. for disability (rheumatism & diabetes), Aug. 15, 1862.

(1)   CHAMBERS, D. B. ("Crock") — Present and accounted for until Jan.,
(2)   1864: Furlough, Jan. 15 to Feb. 25, 1864: Paroled, Appomattox (Apr. 12, 1865).

(2)   CHAMBERS, G. WOOD — Recruited at Palestine, Tex., Apr. 8, 1862, age 21: Prom., 1Sgt., Aug. 1, 1864: Paroled, Appomattox (Apr. 12, 1865).

       COLVIN, JIM (or A. W.) — Recruited at Palestine, Tex., Apr. 11, 1862: Deserted.

       CONE, HENRY ("Hy") — Recruited at Palestine, Tex., Mar. 18, 1862, age 37: W. & disabled, Wilderness (May 6, 1864).

(1)   CONE, JOHN ("Jack") — W. & POW, Antietam (Sept. 17, 1862).

(1)   COOK, ABRAM P. — See roster, "Regmtl. Hdqtrs., 1st Tex. Inf."
(2)

(1)   COPELAND, M. B. — Hospitalized in Richmond with "pleuritis," Sept. 13, 1862: K., Wilderness (May 6, 1864).

CORDER, JIM M. — Recruited at Palestine, Tex., Apr. 6, 1862, age 18: W., Antietam (Sept. 17, 1862): Died of wound, Nov. 26, 1862.

(1) CROGAN, JOHN — Enl., June 23, 1861: No other information.

(1) CROMBIE, ANDREW C. — See roster, "Regmtl. Hdqtrs., 1st Tex. Inf."

DAGG, EDWIN — Recruited at Palestine, Tex., Apr. 8, 1862, age 21: Prom., 2Cpl., Nov. 1, 1862: W., Chickamauga (Sept. 20, 1863).

(2) DARNALL, HAYWOOD — Recruited at Palestine, Tex., Apr. 11, 1862, age 19: Sick in hosp. in Richmond, Summer, 1862 with bronchitis: W., Chickamauga (Sept. 19, 1863): Detailed to "pick up stragglers & conscripts, 4th Congr. District, Ga." Spring, 1864: Rejnd. Co.: Paroled, Appomattox (Apr. 12, 1865).

(1) DAVIS, GREEN B. — W., Chickamauga (Sept. 19, 1863): W., Wilderness (May 6, 1864).

(2) DAVIS, JIM W. — Recruited at Palestine, Tex., Apr. 6, 1862, age 29: AWOL, Oct., Nov. & Dec., 1862: Paroled, Appomattox (Apr. 12, 1865).

DEBARD, HERRERA — Recruited at Palestine, Tex., Apr. 8, 1862, age 51: Dischgd., June 4, 1862, overage.

(1) DERDEN, JAS. K. — Hospitalized, Fall & Winter, 1862: Prom., 4Cpl., Sept. 30, 1863: W., Wilderness (May 6, 1864): Dischgd. on Surg. Cert. (chronic diarrhea), Nov. 11, 1864.

(1) DUVALL, JOS. D. — Enl., June 23, 1861: Dischgd. on Surg. Cert. of disability, Aug. 29, 1861.

(1) DUVALL, RICHARD P. W. ("Buck") — Enl., June 23, 1861: Dischgd. on Surg. Cert. of disability, Jan. 23, 1862 (chronic chills).

(1) DUVALL, WM. A. — Prom., Cpl., May 20, 1863: K., Gettysburg (July 2, 1863).

(1) FILES, MANLY M. — Prom., 4Sgt., March 26, 1862: K., Antietam (Sept. 17, 1862).

FONDREN, GILBERT M. — Recruited at Palestine, Tex., Mar. 29, 1862, age 18: Hospitalized, Winter, 1862-63: AWOL in Tex.

GARNER, T. L. — Recruited at Palestine, Tex., Mar. 17, 1862: Sick (dysentery), June, 1862: Dischgd. on Surg. Cert. of disability, July 2, 1862.

GIBSON, L. H. — Recruited at Palestine, Tex., Apr. 8, 1862, age 25: Transfd. to 2nd Ky. Vol. Inf. Regt., Apr. 22, 1864.

GOOD, JAS. O. — Recruited at Palestine, Tex., Apr. 8, 1862, age 24: Prom., 1Cpl., Apr. 7, 1863: W., Gettysburg (July 2, 1863): W., Farmville, Va. (Apr. 7, 1865): Leg amputated.

GOODWIN, CHAS. (or W. S.) — Recruited at Palestine, Tex., Mar. 29, 1862, age 24: Died, July 2, 1863.

(1) GROOMS, LEWIS — Sick (rheumatism), Summer, 1862: W., Chickamauga (Sept. 20, 1863): Died of wound.

(1) HALLUM, BASIL A. ("Bass") — Prom., 2Cpl.: K., Antietam (Sept. 17, 1862).

HAMBY, MARSHALL — Recruited at Palestine, Tex., Mar. 24, 1862, age 32: POW, Chickamauga (Sept. 19, 1863).

HAZELWOOD, W. T. — Recruited at Palestine, Tex., Apr. 3, 1862, age 17: Prom., 4Cpl., July 2, 1863: W., Chickamauga (Sept. 19, 1863): Died of wound, Sept. 28, 1863.

(2)   HENRY, WM. B. — Recruited at Palestine, Tex., Mar. 17, 1862, age 20: W., Gettysburg (July 2, 1863): Paroled, Appomattox (Apr. 12, 1865).

(1)   HEPPERLA, JOHN C. — Enl., June 23, 1862: No other record.

(1)   HICKEY, THOS. C. — From Hill County, age 23: AWOL, Jan. & Feb., 1863: POW, Hagerstown, Md., July 30, 1863: Imprisoned at Ft. Delaware: Died in prison, June 19, 1864 of acute dysentery.

HILL, RICHARD C. — Recruited at Palestine, Tex., Mar. 29, 1862: W., Wilderness (May 6, 1864).

(1)   HOFFMAN, JOHN A. ("Hy") — Asgnd. as litter bearer, Spring, 1863: Deserted, took Federal oath, Sept. 20, 1864.

HOLLOWAY, JIM K. — Recruited at Palestine, Tex., Apr. 8, 1862, age 22: W. & disabled, Gettysburg (July 2, 1863).

HONEYCUTT, H. E. ("Hy") — Recruited at Palestine, Tex., Mar. 24, 1862, age 39: W. & disabled, Wilderness (May 6, 1864).

(1)   HOOVER, WM. P. — Asgnd. to Div. Provost Guard, Spring, 1863: W., Wilderness (May 6, 1864): Died from wound, July 18, 1864.

(1)   HOPKINS, FRANK M. — AWOL, Summer, 1862: Asgnd. to Div.
(2)   Provost Guard, Summer, 1863: Paroled, Appomattox (April 12, 1865).

JOHNSON, JAS. A. — Recruited at Palestine, Tex., Apr. 8, 1862, age 31: Died of lung disease at Richmond, Sept., 1862.

JOHNSON, WM. F. — Enl., June 23, 1861 at Palestine, Tex.: Sick in Fredericksburg Hosp., Apr., 1862: Died of disease, Apr. 12, 1862.

(1)   JORDAN, ROBT. BRUCE — POW (after Gettysburg) at Williamsport, Md., July 13, 1863: Sent to Pt. Lookout, Md.: Paroled, Mar. 3, 1864: Rejnd. Co.

(1)   KEELING, JOHN R. — W., Chickamauga (Sept. 19, 1864): Prom.,
(2)   2Cpl., Sept. 28, 1863: Prom., 1Cpl.: Paroled, Appomattox (Apr. 12, 1865).

(2)   KENNEDY, GEO. W. ("Bud") — Paroled, Appomattox (Apr. 12, 1865): No other information.

(1)   KENNEDY, JAS. H. — See roster, "Regmtl. Hdqtrs., 1st Tex. Inf."

(1)   KNOX, JOS. A. — W., Gettysburg (July 2, 1863): Paroled, Appomattox
(2)   (Apr. 12, 1865).

(1)   KNOX, MARION A. — W., Eltham's Landing (May 7, 1862): W.,
(2)   Antietam (Sept. 17, 1862): Paroled, Appomattox (Apr. 12, 1865).

(1)   KYLE, GEO. — Prom., 2Sgt.: W., Chickamauga (Sept. 19, 1863): Died of wound.

(1)   LATTA, MOSES S. — Died of chronic diarrhea in Richmond, Sept. 8, 1862.

LEATH, DAN P. — Recruited at Palestine, Tex., Apr. 3, 1862, age 19: Sick in hosp., Fall and Winter, 1862: Died of disease, early, 1863.

LEWIS, C. E. ("Cat") — Recruited at Palestine, Tex., Apr. 7, 1862, age 18: Dischgd. for disability, Nov., 1862.

(1)   LINDSEY, JOHN — Sick in hosp. most of 1862: Detailed to CSA Armory as a tinner, Atlanta, Ga., Oct., 1863, disabled for field duty.

(1)   LLEWELLYN, ALF H. M. — No information available.

(1) LLEWELLYN, JOS. E. — On detached serv. as a Brig. carpenter, the
(2)   entire war: Paroled, Appomattox (Apr. 12, 1865).
(1) LYNCH, BARNEY (or BENJ.) — Enl., June 23, 1861: Deserted: POW,
    Warren Co., Miss., July 9, 1863: Sent to Memphis, Tenn. by
    Federals.
(1) MAHLE, HENRY B. — See roster, "Regmtl. Hdqtrs., 1st Tex. Inf."
(1) MAIN, THOS. F. — W., Gettysburg (July 2, 1863): W., Chickamauga
(2)   (Sept. 19, 1863): Paroled, Appomattox (Apr. 12, 1865).
    MALLARD, MARK M. — Enlisted, Dec. 3, 1863: Under arrest, Jan.,
    1864: Deserted near Bull's Gap, Tenn., March, 1864.
(1) MATHEWS, ANDERSON M. — W., Gaines' Mill (June 27, 1862):
    Returned to Tex., disabled.
(2) MATHEWS, FRANK B. — Recruited at Palestine, Tex., Mar. 17, 1862,
    age 19: W., Seven Pines (June 1, 1862): Paroled, Appomattox
    (Apr. 12, 1865).
(1) MATHEWS, JAS. W. — W., Antietam (Sept. 17, 1862): W., Chick-
(2)   amauga (Sept. 19, 1863): Paroled, Appomattox (Apr. 12, 1865).
    McCLANAHAN, REUBEN — Recruited at Palestine, Tex., Apr. 8,
    1862, age 39: Sick last half of 1862: AWOL, Feb., 1863:
    Dropped from rolls, Feb., 1864.
(1) McFARLAND, CALVIN R. — K., Antietam (Sept. 17, 1862).
    McKENZIE, B. THOMPSON — Recruited at Palestine, Tex., Apr. 8,
    1862, age 20: Dischgd. for disability (chronic diarrhea &
    rheumatism), Aug. 5, 1862.
(1) McKENZIE, ROBT. C. — Sick, Winter, 1862-63: Sick furlough to Tex.,
    May, 1863: AWOL: Paroled in Tex., May 6, 1865.
(1) McKNIGHT, ROBT. C. — W., Eltham's Landing (May 6, 1862): W. &
    disabled, Gaines' Mill (June 27, 1862).
(2) MILAM, BART Y. — Enl. at Palestine, Tex., Apr. 8, 1862, age 18: W.,
    Gettysburg (July 2, 1863): Paroled, Appomattox (April 12,
    1865).
    MILAM, JOHN — Enl. at Palestine, Tex., Apr. 5, 1862, age 24: W. &
    POW, Gettysburg (July 2, 1863): Exchanged, Apr. 27, 1864: W.,
    Wilderness (May 6, 1864): Leg amputated.
    MYNATT, DONALD M. — See list of "Other Officers" above.
(1) MYNATT, W. PARK — See list of "Other Officers" above.
(1) NEWSOM, ELIAS — W., Suffolk (Apr., 1863): W., Chickamauga (Sept.
    20, 1863): W. & disabled, Wilderness (May 6, 1864).
    NEWSOM, JOHN — Recruited at Palestine, Tex., Mar. 17, 1862, age
    19: Died, typhoid fever, July 7, 1862.
(1) O'BRIEN, MARTIN — K., Eltham's Landing (May 7, 1862).
    OWENS, H. C. ("Hy") — Enl., Mar. 1, 1862 at Dumfries, Va.: Deserted,
    Oct., 1862.
(1) PARKER, IRA — Prom., 3Cpl., Jan. 24, 1863: W., Gettysburg (July 2,
    1863): W., Chickamauga (Sept. 20, 1863): Died of wound.
(1) PARKER, JOHN — Prom., 4Sgt., Nov. 1, 1862: W., Gettysburg (July 2,
(2)   1863): Paroled, Appomattox (Apr. 12, 1865).
(1) PARKS, BENJ. F. ("Dock") — Enl., June 23, 1861: No other
    information.
(1) PARKS, JOS. — Enl., June 23, 1861: No other information.

(2)   PETTY, JOHN N. — Recruited at Palestine, Tex., Apr. 11, 1862: Paroled, Appomattox (Apr. 12, 1865).

(1)   PETTY, ROBT. B. — Enl., June 23, 1861: Dischgd., Jan. 20, 1862 for disability.

     PITTS, JESSE — Recruited at Palestine, Tex., Apr. 8, 1862, age 20: Absent sick most of 1862: AWOL in Tex. most of 1863: Dropped from rolls, Jan., 1864 for "prolonged absence."

     POSEY, A. J. ("Joe") — Recruited at Palestine, Tex., Mar. 29, 1862, age 22: K., Antietam (Sept. 17, 1862).

(1)   POSEY, JACKSON — Died of typhoid fever in Richmond, May 3, 1862.

     PUGH, ELBERT E. — Recruited at Palestine, Tex., Mar. 29, 1862, age 33: Died of disease in Richmond, Sept., 1862.

     QUARLES, JOHN JAS. — See list of "Other Officers" above.

     RATCLIFF, A. T. — Enl. at Palestine, Tex., Mar. 22, 1862, age 20: W., Gettysburg (July 2, 1863): W., Chickamauga (Sept. 19, 1863).

     REED, N. D. — Enl. at Palestine, Tex., Apr. 2, 1862, age 20: W., Chickamauga (Sept. 19, 1863).

     REED, T. J. — Enl. at Palestine, Tex., Apr. 5, 1862, age 17: W., Chickamauga (Sept. 19, 1863): Transfd. to 2nd Ky. Vol. Inf. Regt., May 23, 1864.

(1)   REEVES, CHAS. L. — Dischgd., Sept. 2, 1861 on Surg. Cert. of disability.

(1)   ROCKWELL, WASH — Enl., June 23, 1861: No other record.

     ROUNDTREE, SAM D. — Enl. at Palestine, Tex., Spring, 1862: K., Gaines' Mill (June 27, 1862).

(1)   RUDD, JOHN S. — No information available.

     SAWYER, W. — Enl., Jan. 1, 1864: Deserted, Feb. 19, 1864.

     SCARBOROUGH, GEO. M. — Enl. at Palestine, Tex., Spring, 1862: Died in hosp. in Richmond, May 22, 1862.

     SCARBOROUGH, J. M. — Enl. at Palestine, Tex., Mar. 22, 1862, age 18: Died of chronic diarrhea, Dec. 26, 1864.

(1)   SCOTT, JOHN G. — See roster, "Regmtl. Hdqtrs., 1st Tex. Inf."

(1)   SEAY, THOS. G. — Detailed as a teamster, July, 1862: Hospitalized,
(2)   Winter, 1862-63 and most of 1863 with chronic diarrhea: Paroled, Appomattox (Apr. 12, 1865).

(1)   SHAMBURGER, THOS. — Died of disease in a Richmond hosp., Spring, 1862.

(1)   SORELL, GEO. C. — AWOL, Summer, 1862: Served as scout for 1st (Longstreet's) Corps, Army of Northern Virginia, Spring, 1864.

(1)   SPRING, LEWIS — Detailed as a nurse, Spring, 1862: Appt. Wardmaster, Tex. Hosp., Richmond, Aug., 1863: Had hernia and was unfit for field service.

(1)   SPURRIER, NATHAN — Died of disease, Apr. 2, 1862.

     STALCUP, JASPER M. — W., Chickamauga (Sept. 20, 1863): W., Chattanooga, Nov. 7, 1863: W. & disabled, Wilderness (May 6, 1864).

(1)   STEVENS, JESSE S. — Enl., June 23, 1861 in Anderson Co.: No other record.

(1)   STINSON, ANDREW J. — Died of double pneumonia & typhoid fever, March 26, 1862.

(1) STINSON, JOHN C. — W., Chickamauga (Sept. 19, 1863): Wound furlough, Winter, 1863-64: Deserted, Dec. 5, 1864.

THOMPSON, ALBERT — Enl. at Palestine, Tex., Mar. 31, 1862, age 28: W., Chickamauga (Sept. 19, 1863): W. & disabled, Wilderness (May 6, 1864).

(1)
(2) WARD, JAS. — W., Antietam (Sept. 17, 1862): Paroled, Appomattox (Apr. 12, 1865).

WARD, R. K. — Enl. at Palestine, Tex., Mar. 17, 1862, age 30: Died of fever, July 2, 1862.

WATTS, A. J. — Enl. at Palestine, Tex., Apr. 5, 1862, age 17: W., Wilderness (May 6, 1864).

WATTS, B. F. — Enl. at Palestine, Tex., Apr. 8, 1862, age 25: Died of rubeola at Lynchburg, Va., hosp., June 12, 1862.

WATTS, F. J. — Enl. at Palestine, Tex., Mar. 29, 1862, age 32: W. & POW, Antietam (Sept. 17, 1862): Exchanged: Absent on wound furlough, May, 1863: W., Chickamauga, Sept. 19, 1863: Furloughed to Tex., Oct. 5, 1864.

(2) WATTS, WILLIS J. — Enl. at Palestine, Tex., Apr. 5, 1862, age 23: W. (3 times), Chickamauga (Sept. 19 & 20, 1863): W., Wilderness (May 6, 1864): Paroled, Appomattox (Apr. 12, 1865).

WILLIAMSON, JAS. E. — Enl. at Palestine, Tex., Mar. 30, 1862, age 37: Sick in Hosp., Summer & Fall, 1862: Died, Spring, 1863.

WOODHOUSE, CHAS. W. — Enl. at Palestine, Tex., Apr. 3, 1862, age 17: W., Gaines' Mill (June 27, 1862): Died of wound.

(1) WOODHOUSE, JOHN F. — Prom., 4Cpl.: Reduced to ranks, May 23, 1863 for straggling: W. & POW, Chickamauga (Sept. 19, 1863): Exchanged: W., Wilderness (May 6, 1864).

(1) WOODHOUSE, WM. D. — Died, Mar. 24, 1862 at Fredericksburg, Va.

(1)
(2) WREN, RICHARD F. ("Little Dick") — Present & accounted for all during war: Paroled, Appomattox (Apr. 12, 1865).

(1) WREN, RICHARD H. ("Big Dick") — Enl., June 23, 1861: No other record.

(1) WREN, WM. C. — Detailed to recruiting serv. in Tex., Feb.-Apr., 1862: Prom., 5Sgt., May 20, 1862: POW, Chickamauga (Sept. 20, 1863).

1ST TEX. VOL. INF. REGT.

COMPANY H — *TEXAS GUARDS*

Company was organized in Anderson County, Texas, and was mustered into Confederate service "for the war" at New Orleans, June 24, 1861 by Lt. John G. Deveroux, CSA.

Key

(1) Original member of Company. (2) Paroled at Appomattox.
K (Killed), W (Wounded), POW (Prisoner of War)
AWOL (Absent Without Leave)

ORIGINAL OFFICERS

(1)   RAINEY, ALEX. T. Capt. — See roster, "Regmtl. Hdqtrs., 1st Tex. Inf."

(1)   MILLER, WM. R. 1Lt. — Resigned, Sept., 1861.

(1)   SPENCER, JOHN L. 2Lt. — Detailed to recruiting serv. in Tex., Feb.-Apr., 1862: K., Eltham's Landing (May 7, 1862), and buried in Hollywood Cemetery, Richmond.

(1)   RHOME, ROMULUS T. 3Lt. — Resigned, Apr., 1862.

ORIGINAL NON-COMMISSIONED OFFICERS

(1)   GASTON, WM. H. 1Sgt. — See list of "Other Officers" following.

(1)   HORTON, ALFRED M. 2Sgt. — See roster, "Regmtl. Hdqtrs., 1st Tex. Inf."

(1)   JONES, JAS. R. 3Sgt. — Reduced to Pvt.: W. & POW, Antietam (Sept. 17, 1862): Paroled: W., Gettysburg (July 2, 1863): POW, Cashtown, Pa., July 5, 1863: Paroled, Mar. 12, 1864.

(1)   PARKS, BEDFORD 4Sgt. — See list of "Other Officers" following.

(1)   HICKMAN, HAYWOOD G. 1Cpl. — Reduced to Pvt.: W., Antietam
(2)   (Sept. 17, 1862): Prom., 5Sgt.: W., Chaffin's Farm (Sept. 29, 1864): Prom., 1Sgt.: Paroled, Appomattox (Apr. 12, 1865).

(1)   BEAUCHAMP, GEO. W. 2Cpl. — Enl., June 24, 1861 at New Orleans: No other record.

(1)   STEVENSON, JOHN 3Cpl. — See list of "Other Officers" following.

(1)   GASTON, ROBT. H. 4Cpl. — See list of "Other Officers" following.

OTHER OFFICERS

GASTON, WM. H. Capt. — Orig. 1Sgt. of Co.: Elect., Capt.: Resgnd., Dec. 4, 1862.

PARKS, BEDFORD Capt. — Orig. 4Sgt. of Co.: Elect., Lt.: Elect., Capt.: W., Chickamauga (Sept. 19, 1863): W., Wilderness (May 6, 1864): Retired for disability on Surg. Cert., Jan. 3, 1865.

GASTON, ROBT. H. 3Lt. — Orig. 4Cpl. of Co.: Elect., 3Lt., May 22, 1862: K., Antietam (Sept. 17, 1862).

SMITH, JOHN T. 3Lt. — Orig. Pvt.: Prom., 1Sgt., Apr. 21, 1862: Elect., 3Lt., Sept. 17, 1862: Detailed to recruiting serv. in Tex., Jan., 1864.

STEVENSON, JOHN 1Lt. — Orig. 3Cpl. of Co.: Elect., 3Lt., Apr. 21, 1862: Elect., 1Lt.

TORBETT, SAM P. 2Lt. — Recruited as a Pvt. in Tex., Spring, 1862: Elect., 3Lt., Dec. 9, 1862: W., Chickamauga (Sept. 20, 1863): W., Va. Defenses, Nov., 1864: Elect., 2Lt.: Paroled, Appomattox (Apr. 12, 1865).

PRIVATES

ADKINSON, A. A. — Recruited at Kickapoo, Tex., Mar. 20, 1862, age 24: Died of pneumonia, July 10, 1862.

ANDERSON, ANTONIO A. — Recruited at Kickapoo, Tex., Mar. 20, 1862, age 24: K., Antietam (Sept. 17, 1862).

ARNWINE, WM. — Enl. at age 21: W., Gettysburg (July 2, 1863): POW, Cashtown, Pa., July 5, 1863: Paroled: Sick in Richmond hosp., Mar., 1864.

BAKER, CHAS. C. — Enl. at Quantico, Va., Oct. 20, 1861: In hosp., Dec., 1862 with chronic diarrhea and in May, 1863 with sciatica: Asgnd. as a Hosp. Wardmaster, May 13, 1863: Returned to Co., Oct. 13, 1864: Prom. to 5Sgt., Spring, 1865: Paroled, Appomattox (Apr. 12, 1865).

BAKER, JOHN G. — Recruited at Kickapoo, Tex., Mar. 7, 1862, age 25: Died at Petersburg, Va., Sept. 15, 1862.

(1) BALDWIN, JAS. W. — Under arrest, Aug. 1, 1862: W., Gettysburg (July 2, 1863): AWOL, Dec., 1863: Dropped from rolls, Feb., 1864.

BARTON, WM. M. — Recruited at Kickapoo, Tex., Mar. 20, 1862, age 25: Dischgd. for disability (TB), Sept. 2, 1862.

BAXLEY, A. C. — Recruited at Kickapoo, Tex., Mar. 20, 1862, age 24: Dischgd. for disability (asthma).

BEARD, W. S. — Recruited at Kickapoo, Tex., Mar. 20, 1862, age 37: Died in hosp., July 27, 1862 (typhoid fever).

(1) BEERS, JOHN R. — Detailed as an ambulance driver, Sept., 1862: Under civil arrest, Oct. 26, 1862: Sick in hosp. most of 1863: Died in hosp., Bristol, Tenn., Apr. 10, 1864.

(1) BELL, J. W. — Left on road near Huntsville, Ala. on way to Richmond, Va., July, 1861 — cause unknown.

(1) BERRY, MILES A. — Prom., 3Cpl.: W., Chickamauga (Sept. 19, 1863).

BIRDWELL, R. R. — Recruited at Kickapoo, Tex., Mar. 20, 1862, age 23: W., Wilderness (May 6, 1864).

(1) BLACKWELL, JOHN M. — Enl., June 24, 1861: In hosp. at Ashland, Va., Apr., 1862: No other record.

(1) BLANTON, PLEASANT A. — W., Wilderness (May 6, 1864): Paroled,
(2) Appomattox (Apr. 12, 1865).

BOLTON, CANADA S. — Recruited at Kickapoo, Tex., Mar. 20, 1862, age 41: W., Antietam (Sept. 17, 1862).

(2) BOLTON, JAS. A. — Transfd. into Co. H from 18th Ga. Inf. Regt.: Paroled, Appomattox (Apr. 12, 1865).

(1) BRIGGS, JAS. — W., Gettysburg (July 2, 1863): W., Williamsburg Rd. (Oct. 27, 1864).

(1) BRILEY, SAMUEL R. — Prom., Cpl.: Prom., 2Sgt., Dec., 1862: POW, Gettysburg (July 3, 1863): Sent to Ft. Delaware, Del.: Paroled, June 9, 1865.

(1) BUSSEY, JOHN B. — Dischgd. for disability (chronic hepatitis), Nov. 18, 1861.

(1) BUTLER, THOS. M. — Dischgd. for disability (chronic diarrhea), Aug. 2, 1862.

CALTON, GEO. — Recruited at Kickapoo, Tex., Mar. 10, 1862, age 19: Present & accounted for until Feb., 1864 when he deserted in Tenn.

(1) CANTRELL, JOHN W. — Enl., June 24, 1861 at New Orleans: No other record.

(1) CANTRELL, STEPHEN J. — Enl., June 24, 1861 at New Orleans: Dischgd. for disability (bronchitis and general physical debility), Oct. 25, 1861.

(1) CAPPS, JOHN Q. A. — Sick in hosp., Summer, 1862 (rheumatism and diarrhea): On detached service at Marshall, Texas as Tanner, Nov., 1862 to end of war.

CECIL, CLEMENT — Orderly for Col. Work, Fall, 1862 & Winter, 1862-63: Deserted, Mar., 1865 at Charleston, West Va., "took amnesty oath and sent North."

(1) CHAPPELL, J. C. — Left on road near Huntsville, Ala. on way to Richmond, Va., July, 1861 — cause unknown.

CLARK, JAS. J. — Recruited at Kickapoo, Tex., Mar. 7, 1862, age 19: Sick in hosp., May, 1862: Died of chronic diarrhea, Aug. 18, 1862.

(1) CORNWELL, SAMUEL B. — K., Eltham's Landing (May 7, 1862).

COTNEY, ISAAC O. — Recruited at Kickapoo, Tex., Jan. 20, 1862, age 35: POW, Williamsburg Rd. (Oct. 27, 1864).

(1) COUNTS, JOHN A. — W., Antietam (Sept. 17, 1862): POW, Gettysburg (July 2, 1863).

COX, A. F. — Recruited at Kickapoo, Tex., Mar. 20, 1862, age 25: Died, buried in Hollywood Cemetery, Richmond.

CRUTCHFIELD, JOHN R. — Recruited at Kickapoo, Tex., Mar. 20, 1862, age 27: Dischgd. for disability (lung disease), July 19, 1862.

CULPEPPER, GEO. WASHINGTON — Recruited at Kickapoo, Tex., Mar. 20, 1862, age 40: W., Antietam (Sept. 17, 1862).

(1) DERROUGH, WM. G. — W., Antietam (Sept. 17, 1862): Missing in action, Darbytown Rd. (Oct. 7, 1864).

DOHERTY, JAS. M. — Recruited at Kickapoo, Tex., Mar. 20, 1862, age 38: K., Gaines' Mill (June 27, 1862).

(1) DONALD, WM. F. — Enl., June 24, 1861: Dischgd. on Surg. Cert. (pneumonia), Mar. 22, 1862.

(2) EDWARDS, T. R. — Recruited at Kickapoo, Tex., Mar. 10, 1862, age 28: Paroled, Appomattox (Apr. 12, 1865).

(1) EMBRY, FELIX M. — W., Gaines' Mill (June 27, 1862): W., Antietam (Sept. 17, 1862): POW, Gettysburg (July 2, 1863): Died in Ft. Delaware Prison, Nov. 2, 1863.

(1) ERWIN, ALONZO F. — W., Gaines' Mill (June 27, 1862): W., Chickamauga (Sept. 19, 1863): W. & POW, Knoxville, Tenn., Nov. 25, 1863.

(1) EVANS, JAS. E. — Prom., 1Cpl., Sept. 17, 1862: W., Chickamauga
(2) (Sept. 19, 1863): Paroled, Appomattox (Apr. 12, 1865).

(1) EVANS, JAS. J. — Enl. at New Orleans, June 24, 1861: Dischgd. for disability, Apr. 27, 1862.

(1) EVANS, LEANDER L. — W., Antietam (Sept. 17, 1862): POW, Gettysburg (July 2, 1863): Sent to Ft. Delaware, July 15, 1863: Paroled, June 9, 1865.

(1) EZELL, ELDRED F. — Prom., 2Cpl.: W., Antietam (Sept. 17, 1862).

(1) FENNELL, ABRAHAM N. — Unfit for field duty (rupture): Detailed as
(2) a Teamster, Feb., 1863: Paroled, Appomattox (Apr. 12, 1865).

(1) FORD, WM. A. — Prom., 3Cpl., Apr. 21, 1862: Prom., 1Sgt., Sept. 17, 1862: K., Wilderness (May 6, 1864).

FOSTER, JOHN J. — Recruited at Kickapoo, Tex., Mar. 7, 1862, age 30: W., Eltham's Landing (May 7, 1862): K., Gaines' Mill (June 27, 1862).

(1) FOSTER, WM. — POW, Gettysburg (July 2, 1863): Sent to Ft. Delaware, July 7, 1863: Died in Prison Camp, Oct. 13, 1863.

(1) FREEMAN, NICHOLAS H. — Enl. at New Orleans, June 24, 1861: No other record.

(1) FRY, ANDREW J. — Prom., Cpl.: W., Gaines' Mill (June 27, 1862):
(2) Reduced to Pvt.: Paroled, Appomattox (Apr. 12, 1865).

(1) GAMBRELL, EZEKIEL M. — Enl. at New Orleans, June 24, 1861: Dischgd. for disability (diarrhea), Sept. 1, 1861.

GIBSON, J. F. — Recruited at Kickapoo, Tex., Mar. 7, 1862: Died, buried in Hollywood Cemetery, Richmond.

GOBLE, B. W. — Recruited at Kickapoo, Tex., Mar. 10, 1862: Deserted, Sept. 16, 1862.

(1) GOLLAHA (or GOLLIHER), JOHN C. — Dischgd. for disability (measles), Sept. 16, 1861.

GRAHAM, J. A. — Recruited at Kickapoo, Tex., Mar. 20, 1862, age 27: W., 2nd Manassas (Aug. 30, 1862): W., Wilderness (May 6, 1864).

(1) GRAY, W. H. — POW, Gettysburg (July 2, 1863).
(1) GREER, JOHN S. — Dischgd. on Surg. Cert. of disability, Sept. 11, 1861: Died, Jan. 18, 1862.

GRESHAM, FULLER — Recruited at Kickapoo, Tex., Mar. 20, 1862, age 46: No other record.

(1) GRESHAM, GEO. W. — Died of typhoid fever, Sept. 12, 1861.

GRIFFIS, J. A. — Recruited at Kickapoo, Tex., Mar. 20, 1862, age 35: Died of measles, June 5, 1862.

(1) GROGGIN, GEO. F. — Enl. at New Orleans, June 24, 1861: No other record.

HAMMER, WM. — Recruited at Kickapoo, Tex., Mar. 10, 1862, age 18: Sick in hosp., Spring & Summer, 1862: Probably dischgd. for disability.

(1) HANKS, JOSHUA B. — K., Gaines' Mill (June 27, 1862).

HARVEY, JOHN O. — Died, buried in Hollywood Cemetery, Richmond, May 19, 1862: No other record.

HAYNES, W. N. — Recruited at Kickapoo, Tex., Mar. 27, 1862, age 23: W., 2nd Manassas (Aug. 30, 1862).

(1) HENRY, JOHN R. — Dischgd. for disability (diarrhea), Sept. 16, 1861.

(1) HERRINGTON, JAS. J. — Hospitalized in Richmond most of 1862 & 1863: Dropped from rolls "on account of protracted absence," Dec., 1863.

(1) HERRINGTON, JOHN M. — W., Antietam (Sept. 17, 1862): W.,
(2) Wilderness (May 6, 1864): Paroled, Appomattox (Apr. 12, 1865).

(1) HICKMAN, JASPER E. — Prom., 4Sgt.: W., Chickamauga (Sept. 19, 1863): Retired for disability, July 20, 1864.

HILL, D. J. — Recruited at Kickapoo, Tex., Mar. 20, 1862, age 35: K., Eltham's Landing (May 7, 1862).

(1) HOLLINGSWORTH, GEO. — W., Gaines' Mill (June 27, 1862): Prom.,
(2) 4Sgt.: W., Cold Harbor (June 1, 1864): Paroled, Appomattox (Apr. 12, 1865).

(1) HOLLINGSWORTH, JOS. C. — Prom., 2Sgt., May 15, 1862: W., 2nd Manassas (Aug. 30, 1862): W., Antietam (Sept. 17, 1862): Died of Antietam wound, Oct. 18, 1862.

(2) HOLLINGSWORTH, NATHAN — Enl., Camp Quantico, Va., Oct. 20, 1861: Appt., 2Sgt., Sept. 17, 1862 to replace wounded brother: W. (through buttocks) at Petersburg, June 22, 1864: Paroled, Appomattox (Apr. 12, 1865).

HOLLINGSWORTH, WM. — Recruited at Kickapoo, Tex., Mar. 20, 1862, age 25: K., Antietam (Sept. 17, 1862).

HONEA, S. S. — Recruited at Kickapoo, Tex., Mar. 20, 1862, age 38: Died, typhoid fever, May 25, 1862.

HONEA, W. A. — Recruited at Kickapoo, Tex., Mar. 20, 1862, age 31: K., Antietam (Sept. 17, 1862).

(2) HONINGSBURGER, I. — Recruited at Kickapoo, Tex., Mar. 7, 1862, age 32: W., Wilderness (May 6, 1864): Paroled, Appomattox (Apr. 12, 1865).

HORNER, WM. — Died and buried in Hollywood Cemetery, Richmond, Jan. 2, 1862: No other record.

HORTON, D. M. — Recruited at Kickapoo, Tex., Mar. 20, 1862, age 32: K., Gettysburg (July 2, 1863).

(1) HORTON, FRED S. — Enl. at New Orleans, June 24, 1861: No other record.

(1) HOWELL, JOS. H. — Sick in hosp. since Oct. 1, 1861: Declared AWOL, Nov., 1862: No other record.

HOWELL, WM. F. — No record.

(1) HUSKEY, JOHN — Dischgd. for disability (chronic diarrhea), Nov. 4, 1861.

JACOBS, M. — Recruited at Kickapoo, Tex., Mar. 20, 1862, age 33: Died and buried in Hollywood Cemetery, Richmond, June 20, 1862: No other record.

(1) JONES, JOHN W. — Enl. at New Orleans, June 24, 1861: No other record.

KING, J. C. — Recruited at Kickapoo, Tex., Mar. 20, 1862, age 20: POW, Gettysburg (July 2, 1863): Died in Ft. Delaware Prison, Apr. 14, 1865.

KNIGHT, ANDREW J. — Recruited at Kickapoo, Tex., Mar. 20, 1862, age 18: Sick in hosp. most of 1862 & 1863: Dropped from rolls, Dec., 1863.

(2) KNIGHT, JOHN A. — Recruited at Kickapoo, Tex., Mar. 20, 1862, age 26: Paroled, Appomattox (Apr. 12, 1865).

(2) KNIGHT, JOS. A. — Recruited at Kickapoo, Tex., Mar. 20, 1862, age 19: Received Texas Gold Medal for bravery, Feb., 1865: Paroled, Appomattox (Apr. 12, 1865).

KNIGHT, WM. H. — Recruited at Kickapoo, Tex., Mar. 20, 1862, age 24: Dischgd., Nov. 26, 1862 for disability (lung disease).

LEE, W. L. — Recruited at Kickapoo, Tex., Mar. 7, 1862, age 30: K., Gaines' Mill (June 27, 1862).

(2) LOFLIN, JAS. — Recruited at Kickapoo, Tex., Mar. 7, 1862, age 34: Paroled, Appomattox (Apr. 12, 1865).

LOVE, S. C. — Enl., Camp Quantico, Va., Oct. 20, 1861: K., Gettysburg (July 2, 1863).

LUMPKIN, G. W. — Enl., Kickapoo, Tex., Mar. 10, 1862, age 20: W., Chickamauga (Sept. 19, 1863): Sick in Richmond hosp., Summer, 1864: Died, Jan. 26, 1865 (pneumonia).

(1) LUMPKIN, JOHN W. — Prom., 3Cpl., Dec. 9, 1862: Prom., 1Sgt., July, 1864: W., Darbytown Rd. (Oct. 7, 1864): Died, Oct. 8, 1864.

(1) MANN, MASSENA V. — Dischgd. for disability (chronic diarrhea), Nov. 10, 1861.

(1) MANSELL, WM. J. — Sick in hosp., Summer, 1862 (rheumatism): Died at Danville, Va., Nov. 23, 1862.

(1) MARSHALL, JAS. H. — Prom., 3Sgt.: K., Antietam (Sept. 17, 1862).

(1) MARTIN, HENRY L. — W., Eltham's Landing (May 7, 1862): Sick in hosp., Fall, 1862: Paroled at Richmond, Apr. 23, 1865.

McBRIDE, CALEB — Recruited at Kickapoo, Tex., Mar. 20, 1862, age 26: K., Antietam (Sept. 17, 1862).

(1) McKINZIE (or McKENZIE), LARKIN G. — Prom., 1Cpl.: Resgnd.,
(2) Sept. 17, 1862: Rejnd. Co. as Pvt.: W., Wilderness (May 6, 1864): Paroled, Appomattox (Apr. 12, 1865).

MENDENHALL, N. A. — Enl. at Camp Quantico, Va., Oct. 20, 1861: Detailed to recruiting serv. in Tex., Feb.-Apr., 1862: K., Chickamauga (Sept. 20, 1863).

(1) MIDDLETON, WM. G. — POW, Gettysburg (July 2, 1863): Confined at Ft. Delaware: Paroled, June 9, 1865.

(1) MILLS, PERRY M. — K., Eltham's Landing (May 7, 1862).

(1) MOON, LEWIS V. — K., Knoxville, Nov. 23, 1863.

(2) MOORE, J. H. — Recruited at Kickapoo, Tex., Mar. 20, 1862, age 16: Prom., 2Cpl.: Paroled, Appomattox (Apr. 12, 1865).

MULLINIX, J. P. — Recruited at Kickapoo, Tex., Mar. 20, 1862, age 24: POW, Gettysburg (July 2, 1863): Sent to Ft. Delaware: Escaped.

NICHOLS, JOHN B. — Recruited at Kickapoo, Tex., Mar. 20, 1862, age 29: Prom., 3Sgt., Sept. 17, 1862: K., Gettysburg (July 2, 1863).

(1) NORRIS, JOS. A. — Transfd. to 3rd Ark. Inf. Regt., Jan. 20, 1863.

OLDHAM, THEO. R. — Recruited at Kickapoo, Tex., Mar. 20, 1862, age 30: K., 2nd Manassas (Aug. 30, 1862).

PATRICK, T. A. — Enl., Camp Quantico, Va., Oct. 20, 1861: Died from disease (measles), June 24, 1862.

(1) PERRY, AMOS C. — Dischgd. for disability (hernia), Nov. 4, 1861.

(1) POLK, ROBT. J. — Dischgd. for disability (chronic diarrhea), Oct. 23, 1861.

(1) POWERS, JOHN H. — Dischgd., Surg. Cert. of disability, Aug. 30, 1861.

(1) REED, JAS. R. — Dischgd. for disability (leg ulcer), July 18, 1862.

(1) REYNOLDS, JAS. W. — Died from typhoid fever, Sept. 2, 1861.

REYNOLDS, MOSES — Recruited at Kickapoo, Tex., Mar. 20, 1862, age 25: Sick, Summer, 1862: Sick furlough, May 10, 1863: Dropped from rolls, Dec., 1863, "protracted absences."

RUDD, J. H. — Enl. in Panola County, Tex., Mar. 18, 1863: W., Wilderness (May 6, 1864): Leg amputated: Died, May 14, 1864.

RUDD, JOS. S. — W., Gaines' Mill (June 27, 1862): POW, Gettysburg (July 2, 1863): Died at Ft. Delaware Prison, Jan. 20, 1864 (inflammation of the stomach).

SCOTT, S. L. — Recruited at Kickapoo, Tex., Mar. 20, 1862, age 21: W., Chickamauga (Sept. 19, 1863): Retired for disability, Oct. 24, 1864.

SIDE (or SIDES), J. E. — Recruited at Kickapoo, Tex., Mar. 20, 1862, age 28: W., 2nd Manassas (Aug. 30, 1862): W., Wilderness (May 6, 1864): Leg amputated.

SIMPSON, REUBEN — Recruited in Kickapoo, Tex., Mar. 20, 1862, age 40: Absent, sick in hosp. most of 1862 with diabetes: Sick furlough, Spring, 1863: Dropped from rolls "on account of protracted absence," Dec., 1863.

SIMPSON, WM. M. — Recruited at Kickapoo, Tex., Mar. 20, 1862, age 18: Died of disease "near the Chickahominy," May 13, 1862.

(1) SMALL, GEO. W. — Prom., 5Sgt., Dec. 9, 1862: W., Chickamauga (Sept. 19, 1863): Died of wound.

(1) SMITH, JARRETT P. — On detached serv. as Teamster, May, 1862: W., Chickamauga (Sept. 19, 1863): Paroled, Augusta, Ga., June 2, 1865.

SMITH, JOE P. — Recruited at Kickapoo, Tex., Mar. 20, 1862, age 27: W., Chickamauga (Sept. 19, 1863).

(1) SMITH, JOHN T. — See list of "Other Officers" above.

(1) STALCUP, JASPER M. — Transfd. to Co. G, 1st Tex. Inf. Regt., Fall, 1861.

STEINCIPHER, J. M. — Recruited at Kickapoo, Tex., Mar. 20, 1862, age 21: K., 2nd Manassas (Aug. 30, 1862).

(1) STEWART, DAVID C. — W., Malvern Hill (July 1, 1862): POW, Bristol, Tenn., Dec. 14, 1864: Took Federal oath.

STROTHER, A. C. — Recruited at Kickapoo, Tex., Mar. 20, 1862, age 25: W., Antietam (Sept. 17, 1862): Wound furlough: Died of wound in Tex., Dec. 1, 1862.

(1)
(2) SURRATT, JOS. P. — W., Gettysburg (July 2, 1863): Hospitalized with chronic diarrhea, July 14, 1863: Paroled, Appomattox (Apr. 12, 1865).

(1) TAYLOR, ASMEL F. — Sick (diarrhea), Mar., 1862: Prom., 4Cpl., Summer, 1863: K., Knoxville, Tenn., Nov. 23, 1863.

(1) TAYLOR, EDWIN M. — Enl. in Anderson County, Tex., June 24, 1861: Sick in hosp. most of 1862: No other record.

(1) THOMAS, ELI. W. — Dischgd. on Surg. Cert. of disability, Nov. 12, 1861.

TILLMAN, JAS. M. — Recruited at Kickapoo, Tex., Mar. 20, 1862, age 23: Died of typhoid fever, May 24, 1862.

TILLMAN, JOS. M. — Recruited at Kickapoo, Tex., Mar. 20, 1862, age 28: Died of typhoid fever, May 26, 1862.

(1) TIPPEN, JAS. G. — K., Antietam (Sept. 17, 1862).

TITUS, FRANK — Transfd. into Co. H, 1st Tex. Inf. from Co. K, Capt. Covington's Co., Ala. Battalion, Feb. 2, 1862: Asgnd. as a Teamster, June, 1862.

(2) TORBETT, SAM P. — See roster, "Other Officers" above.

TRIPP, M. B. — Died, buried in Hollywood Cemetery, Richmond, July 5, 1862: No other record.

(1) TUBB, JAS. — POW, Gettysburg (July 2, 1863): sent to Ft. Delaware: Drowned in an attempt to escape, Nov. 15, 1863.

(1) WATERSON, JOHN L. — Dischgd. for disability (lung disease), Oct. 23, 1861.

(1) WILLIAMS, WM. L. — W., Antietam (Sept. 17, 1862): Died of disease at hosp. in Weldon, N. C., May 3, 1863.

(1) WOFFORD, BENJ. L. — Enl. in Anderson Co., Tex., June 24, 1861: No other record.

WOFFORD, WM. M. — Recruited at Kickapoo, Tex., Mar. 20, 1862, age 25: Sick (hepatitis), Summer, 1862: Sick furlough granted, Sept. 9, 1864.

(1) WOODALL, JAS. T. — Detached service as a wagon driver, Fall, 1862 & Spring, 1863: AWOL, Aug., 1864.

1ST TEX. VOL. INF. REGT.

COMPANY I — *CROCKETT SOUTHRONS*

Company was organized in Houston County, Texas, and mustered into Confederate service "for the war" at New Orleans, June 24, 1861 by Lt. John G. Deveroux, CSA.

Key

(1) Original member of Company. (2) Paroled at Appomattox.
K (Killed), W (Wounded), POW (Prisoner of War)
AWOL (Absent Without Leave)

ORIGINAL OFFICERS

(1) CURRIE, EDW. Capt. — Resgnd., Dec. 20, 1861.

(1) SHERIDAN, JACOB L. 1Lt. — Recruiting duty in Tex., Feb.-Apr., 1862: W., Gaines' Mill (June 27, 1862): Prom., Capt.: Relieved of command by court-martial, Summer, 1863: Cashiered.

(1) WALL, WM. B. 2Lt. — Off. in charge of Regmtl. Store at Ashland, Va., Apr. & May, 1862: W., Gaines' Mill (June 27, 1862): Prom., 1Lt.

(1) COTTON, RICH. W. 3Lt. — Elect., Capt.: W., Antietam (Sept. 17, 1862): Died of wound, Sept. 31, 1862.

ORIGINAL NON-COMMISSIONED OFFICERS

(1) ENGLISH, CROCKETT 1Sgt. — Dischgd. from Service for chronic bronchitis, Oct. 26, 1861.

(1) FOSTER, JON. H. 2Sgt. — W., Gaines' Mill (June 27, 1862): K., Chickamauga (Sept. 19, 1863).

(1) WINGFIELD, JOHN 3Sgt. — Dischgd. for disability (chronic diarrhea), Oct. 15, 1861.
(1) WAGNON, CECIL O. 4Sgt. — W., Gaines' Mill (June 27, 1862): Transfd. from Co. I to Co. M, 1st Tex. Inf. Regt., Feb. 18, 1863.
(1) HARRIS, MORTON V. 1Cpl. — Sick in Richmond hosp., Summer, 1862: Furlough granted, Jan., 1864: Deserted, Feb. 17, 1864.
(1) MONTGOMERY, ALEX. 2Cpl. — W., Gaines' Mill (June 27, 1862): Died of wound, July 14, 1862.
(1) GATES, JOHN C. 3Cpl. — Sick in hosp., Spring & Summer, 1862 and Jan.-Aug., 1863: W., in Va., May 18, 1864: Hospitalized, Columbia, So. Car., May 28, 1864: Paroled, Farmville, Va., Apr. 21, 1865.
(1) HALE, DRURY 4Cpl. — K., Antietam (Sept. 17, 1862).

OTHER OFFICERS

WOOTTERS, JOHN H. Capt. — Orig. Pvt. in Co.: Elect., 3Lt., Spring, 1862: W., Antietam (Sept. 17, 1862): Elect., 1Lt., Summer, 1863: Elect., Capt., Fall, 1863: Recruiting duty in Tex., Aug., 1864.
(2) ALDRICH, ALBERT A. 1Lt. — Orig. Pvt. in Co.: Prom., 5Sgt.: Recruiting duty in Tex., Feb.-Apr., 1862: W., Antietam (Sept. 17, 1862): Elect., 2Lt., July 28, 1863: W., Chickamauaga (Sept. 19, 1863): Elect., 1Lt.: Paroled, Appomattox (Apr. 12, 1865).
(2) BERRYMAN, NEWTON M. 2Lt. — Orig. Pvt. in Co.: Recruiting duty in Tex., Feb.-Apr., 1862: W., Antietam (Sept. 17, 1862): Prom., 4Sgt., Sept. 20, 1863: Elect., 3Lt., March 15, 1864: W., Wilderness (May 6, 1864): Appt., 2Lt.: Paroled, Appomattox (Apr. 12, 1865).
JONES, HENRY N. — Orig. Pvt. in Co.: As a Pvt. cmded. Co. at Malvern Hill (July 1, 1862): W., Antietam (Sept. 17, 1862): Elect., Lt., Oct. 23, 1862: K., Gettysburg (July 2, 1863).

MUSICIANS

(1) BUSH, DAVID B. — Recruited at Milam, Tex., Mar. 7, 1862:
(2) Recruiting duty in Tex., Feb.-Apr., 1862: W., Gaines' Mill (June 27, 1862): Prom., 1Sgt., March 1, 1863: W., Chickamauga (Sept. 19, 1863): Demoted to 5Sgt.: Paroled, Appomattox (Apr. 12, 1865).
(1) HALLMARK, RICHARD M. — Died of typhoid fever in a Richmond hosp., June 21, 1862.

PRIVATES

(1) ALDRICH, ALBERT A. — See list of "Other Officers" above.
(1) ALDRICH, COLLIN Q. — See roster, "Regmtl. Hdqtrs., 1st Tex. Inf."
(2)

(1) ALLEN, WM. J. — Enl. at New Orleans, Aug. 9, 1861: Died of typhoid fever, Sept. 20, 1861.

(1) ANDREWS, ELISHA B. — W., Gaines' Mill (June 27, 1862): Detailed as hosp. nurse, Nov., 1862: Detailed as a nurse in hosp. at Greenville, Tenn., Apr., 1864: POW, Apr. 4, 1865 at Appomattox River: Paroled, June 14, 1865.

BALLENGER, H. — Recruited in Va., Sept. 5, 1861: Hospitalized, Spring, 1863: No other record.

BATY, THOS. — Recruited at Milam, Tex., Mar. 7, 1862: Died of pneumonia, at Danville, Va., July 1, 1862: Left personal effects of $28.30 cash, one pocket book, one pr. pants, one shirt, one pr. drawers, one pr. shoes and one vest.

(1) BECKHAM, FRANKLIN A. — Dischgd. from service for disability (rheumatism), Oct. 26, 1861.

(1) BECKHAM, WM. J. — Dischgd. for disability (chronic bronchitis), Oct. 24, 1861.

BERRYMAN, H. WATTERS — Recruited at Alto, Tex., Mar. 22, 1862: W., (twice), at Wilderness (May 6, 1864): W., (twice), Darbytown Rd., Oct. 7, 1864.

(1) BERRYMAN, NEWTON M. — See list of "Other Officers" above.

BLACKMAN, ROBT. — Recruited at Milam, Tex., Mar. 10, 1862: Died in Richmond hosp., June 20, 1862.

BOONE, TOM A. — Recruited at Alto, Tex., Mar. 22, 1862: W., Antietam (Sept. 17, 1862): POW, Bunker Hill, Va., July 20, 1863: POW, Chickamauga (Sept. 19, 1863): Died in Alto, Tex., from TB. contracted during war.

(1) BOX, FELIX W. — Detailed to Pioneer Corps, May, 1862: K., Antietam (Sept. 17, 1862).

(1) BOX, JOHN P. — Enl. at New Orleans, Aug. 6, 1861: No other record.

BOYKIN, OSBOURN H. — Recruited at New Orleans, La., Apr. 21, 1862: K., Gaines' Mill (June 27, 1862).

(1) BRADSTON, SAMUEL J. — Sick in Richmond hosp., Spring, 1862: Detailed as Regmtl. Wagon Master, Jan., 1864: W., Wilderness (May 6, 1864): Died of wound, May 30, 1864.

(1) BRANDON, WM. M. — Dischgd. for disability (acute diarrhea), Dec. 24, 1861.

(1) BROWN, DANIEL W. — W., Gaines' Mill (June 27, 1862): W., Wilderness (May 6, 1864).

(1) BROWN, JOHN — Dischgd. for disability (chronic diarrhea), Nov. 15, 1861.

BUSH, W. D. — Enl., Apr. 1, 1862 at Milam, Tex.: Sick most of 1862 and 1863: Retired from service, Jan. 24, 1865.

(1) CAIN, DANIEL S. — Sick in hosp., Winter, 1862-63 & Spring, 1863: Deserted, Aug. 12, 1863.

CALLDER, HARTWELL C. — Recruited at Alto, Tex., Mar. 22, 1862: Died near Richmond, June 7, 1862: Buried in Hollywood Cemetery, Richmond, Va.

(1) CARTER, JESSE M. — Died of measles, Sept. 15, 1861.

CHANCE, V. M. — Recruited at Milam, Tex., Apr. 10, 1862: Sick most of 1862 & 1863: Presumed dead, "Missing 12 months."

COLLINS, MONROE P. — Transfd. into Co. I from Co. L, 1st Tex. Inf. Regt., Apr. 19, 1862: Died at Leesburg, Va., Sept. 27, 1862.

(1) CONGLETON, ALLEN A. — K., Antietam (Sept. 17, 1862).
(1) COOK, THOS. J. — K., Antietam (Sept. 17, 1862).
(1) COOK, WM. R. — Enl. at New Orleans, Aug. 9, 1861: No other information.
(1) CORLEY, JAS. M. — W., 2nd Manassas (Aug. 30, 1862): W., Chickamauga (Sept. 19, 1863): Foot amputated.
(1) CUMMINS, JUDGE — Enl. at New Orleans, Aug. 9, 1861: Dischgd. for disability (chronic diarrhea), Nov. 27, 1861.
(1) DeLONG, JOHN — W., Gaines' Mill (June 27, 1862): W., Suffolk, Va. (Apr., 1863): Right leg amputated.
(1) DENMAN, ALBERT H. — Enl., New Orleans, Aug. 9, 1861: Dischgd. for disability (bronchitis), Oct. 26, 1861.
(1) DICKENSON, JOHN W. — Died of disease, Oct. 22, 1861.
     DOUGHERTY, EDW. — Recruited, May 1, 1862 at Crockett, Tex.: Hospitalized in Richmond most of 1864.
     DOUGHERTY, WM. E. — Enl., Richmond, Va., May 1, 1863: K., Wilderness (May 6, 1864).
(2) DRAWHORN, J. M. — Recruited at Milam, Tex., Apr. 10, 1862: Prom., 3Cpl.: W., Chickamauga (Sept. 20, 1863): Prom., 1Cpl.: Paroled, Appomattox (Apr. 12, 1865).
     EASTER, W. C. — Recruited at Alto, Tex., Mar. 22, 1862: Died near Richmond, June 10, 1862.
     ELLISON, M. — Recruited at Milam, Tex., Apr. 10, 1862: Died at Lynchburg, Va., Mar. 7, 1863.
(1) EMMONS, RUFUS F. — Prom., 3Sgt.: W., Chickamauga (Sept. 19,
(2) 1863): Prom., 2Sgt.: Paroled, Appomattox (Apr. 12, 1865).
(1) ENGLISH, WM. R. — Dischgd. for disability (diarrhea, lung disease & measles), Oct. 24, 1861.
(1) FAULDS, ANDREW J. — Sick in hosp., Summer, 1862: Court-Martialed, Apr., 1863: Deserted in Tex., Nov. 10, 1863.
(1) FITTS, LEVI J. — W., Gaines' Mill (June 27, 1862): K., Antietam (Sept. 17, 1862).
(1) FITTS, WM. M. — Died of disease, Winter, 1861-62.
(1) FOSTER, SAMUEL O. — W., Gaines' Mill (June 27, 1862): W., Chickamauga (Sept. 19, 1863): Died of wound, Oct. 14, 1863.
(1) GOMER, LEONIDAS B. — Enl. at New Orleans, Aug. 9, 1861: No other information.
(1) GRIGSBY, DANIEL B. — Dischgd. for disability (lung disease), Oct. 26, 1861.
     HALL, C. W. — Recruited, May 1, 1862 at Crockett, Tex.: Dischgd., Sept. 26, 1862, for chronic diarrhea.
(1) HALL, JOHN J. — Prom., Sgt., Nov. 1, 1863: W., Wilderness (May 6, 1864): Died of wound, May 31, 1864.
(1) HANKS, THOS. A. — W., Gaines' Mill (June 27, 1862): Deserted, Apr. 15, 1864.
     HARRELL, J. R. — Recruited in Milam, Tex., Apr. 1, 1862: Died in Richmond of pneumonia, June 26, 1862.
(1) HARRIS, JOHN — Detailed as a Brig. Teamster, Summer, 1862: POW,
(2) Williamsport, Md., Sept. 15, 1862: Exchanged: W., Chickamauga (Sept. 19, 1863): Paroled, Appomattox (Apr. 12, 1865).
(1) HARRIS, WM. — Regmtl. Mail Carrier, Nov., 1862: Brig. Mail Carrier, Jan., 1863: K., Wilderness (May 6, 1864).

(1) HARRIS, WM. J. L. — W., Gaines' Mill (June 27, 1862): Granted 60 day wound furlough, Jan. 22, 1863.

(1) HART, BENJ. G. — Enl., New Orleans, Aug. 9, 1861: No other information.

HARWELL, JOHN S. — Recruited, May 1, 1862: W., Antietam (Sept. 17, 1862): Two fingers amputated: Died, Oct. 14, 1862.

(1) HOOKER, JESSE — Enl. at New Orleans, Aug. 9, 1861: No other information.

(1) HOUSE, WILEY A. — K., Antietam (Sept. 17, 1862).

HOWARD, Z. M. — Recruited at Milam, Tex., Apr. 10, 1862: Died in Richmond, July 20, 1862 of tuberculosis.

HUGHES, N. G. — Recruited at Alto, Tex., Mar. 22, 1862: Died, buried in Hollywood Cemetery, Richmond, Va., on Nov. 12, 1862.

(1) JARREL, WM. R. — Died of pneumonia, Apr. 12, 1862.

(1) JOHNSON, ROBT. Y. — Transfd. to 18th Va. Heavy Artillery Regt., Aug. 31, 1863.

(1) JONES, GEO. E. — Died of disease in Fredericksburg, Va., Apr. 8, 1862.

(1) JONES, HENRY N. — See list of "Other Officers" above.

JONES, S. J. — Recruited at Milam, Tex., Mar. 22, 1862: Deserted, Feb. 4, 1864.

JORDAN, T. J. — Recruited, May 1, 1862, at Crockett, Tex.: Died in hosp., Aug. 5, 1862, and was buried in Hollywood Cemetery, Richmond, Va., Aug. 20, 1862.

JORDAN, W. W. — Recruited, May 1, 1862: Died of disease in Richmond, June 18, 1862.

(1) KYAL, GEO. W. — Dischgd. from service for hepatitis, Oct. 26, 1861.

LACY, SAMUEL — Recruited at Milam, Tex., Mar. 22, 1862: Detailed as a hosp. nurse, Summer, 1862: AWOL in Tex., Jan., 1863.

LONG, SIMON E. — Recruited at Crockett, Tex., May 1, 1862: Died in Petersburg, Va. of "aneurisma", May 27, 1863.

LOONEY, JIM C. — Recruited at Alto, Tex., Mar. 22, 1862: Died of acute diarrhea, July 25, 1862.

(1) LOVING, BENJ. F. — Died of tuberculosis, Oct. 12, 1861.

LOW, JESSE — Recruited at Milam, Tex., Apr. 10, 1862. Died in Richmond of "disease of chest", June 13, 1862.

(1) LUCKETT, LEVEN W. — POW, Spotsylvania CH. (May 10, 1864). Confined at Camp Elmira, N.Y.: Paroled from Elmira, June 16, 1865.

(1) MANN, GREEN P. — Sick in Richmond hosp. (bronchitis), Spring, 1862: Sick in Richmond hosp. (nephritis), Spring, 1863: W., Chickamauga (Sept. 18, 1863): POW, Petersburg, Apr. 3, 1865: Paroled, June 14, 1865.

(1) MANNING, LEWIS W. — K., Gaines' Mill (June 27, 1862).

(1) MARTIN, JAS. — Dischgd. for chronic rheumatism, Oct. 24, 1861.

MASON, W. B. — Recruited at Milam, Tex., Mar. 22, 1862: K., Chickamauga (Sept. 19, 1863).

McBEE, S. B. — Recruited at Alto, Tex., Mar. 22, 1862: Detailed as nurse at Chimborazo Hosp., Richmond, Fall, 1862: POW, Richmond, Apr. 3, 1865.

(1)　McCALL, THOS. W. H. — Detailed to guard Tex. Depot Baggage, Fall,
(2)　　　1862: Present for duty entire war: Paroled, Appomattox (Apr.
　　　　12, 1865).
　　　McCARTY, JOHN — Recruited at Milam, Tex., Apr. 10, 1862:
　　　　Deserted, June 15, 1862.
(1)　McCASKILL, NEILL E. — Dischgd. for disability (chronic diarrhea),
　　　　Jan. 31, 1862.
(1)　McCLURE, ZACHARIAH T. — Died from chronic diarrhea, Oct. 2,
　　　　1861.
(2)　McLEAN, DANIEL W. — Recruited at Milam, Tex., Apr. 10, 1862: W.,
　　　　Malvern Hill (July 1, 1862): Paroled, Appomattox (Apr. 12,
　　　　1865).
　　　MILLER, A. — Recruited at Milam, Tex., Apr. 10, 1862: Sick at
　　　　Lynchburg, Va. most of 1862: POW, Gettysburg, July 5, 1863:
　　　　Confined at Ft. Delaware: Paroled, June 9, 1865.
(1)　MITCHELL, RUSSELL C. ("Lawyer") — Grandfather of Margaret
　　　　Mitchell, author of *Gone With the Wind:* Prom., 1Sgt.: W.,
　　　　Antietam (Sept. 17, 1862): Reduced to ranks for inefficiency,
　　　　Feb. 28, 1863: Detailed as nurse in hosp. at Atlanta, Ga.,
　　　　Summer, 1863: Never returned to Co.
(1)　MOFFEIT, SOLOMAN D. — Dischgd. for disability (hepatitis), Oct. 22,
　　　　1861.
(1)　MONTGOMERY, ROBT. — W., Gaines' Mill (June 27, 1862).
(1)　MOORE, JAS. A. — Enl. at 16: In Richmond hosp., Fall, 1862:
　　　　Deserted, Sept. 12, 1863.
　　　MOORE, J. T. — Recruited at Crockett, Tex., Mar. 22, 1862: Furlough
　　　　granted, Jan. 8, 1864: Never returned to Co.
(1)　MORRIS, CHRISTOPHER C. — Prom., 5Sgt., July 28, 1863: K.,
　　　　Chickamauga (Sept. 19, 1863).
(2)　MORRIS, F. M. — W., Antietam (Sept. 17, 1862): W., Wilderness (May
　　　　6, 1864): Paroled, Appomattox (Apr. 12, 1865).
　　　MORRIS, J. A. — Recruited at Milam, Tex., Mar. 22, 1862: W.,
　　　　Chickamauga (Sept. 19, 1863).
(1)　MORRIS, WM. G. — K., Gaines' Mill (June 27, 1862).
(1)　MURPHY, MORTIMER — K., Gettysburg (July 2, 1863).
(1)　NORFORD, JAS. W. F. — W., Chickamauga (Sept. 19, 1863): Granted
　　　　"wounded furlough", Feb. 22, 1864.
(1)　NORFORD, JOHN S. — W., Gettysburg (July 2, 1863): W., Wilderness
　　　　(May 6, 1864): Died of wound, May 15, 1864.
(1)　OLIPHANT, S. H. — W. & POW, Gaines' Mill (June 27, 1862): Sent to
　　　　Ft. McHenry, Md.: Exchanged: POW, Gettysburg (July 2, 1863):
　　　　Confined at Ft. Delaware: Paroled, June 19, 1865.
(1)　OLIPHANT, WILFRED — W., Chickamauga (Sept. 20, 1863): W.,
　　　　Wilderness (May 6, 1864).
(1)　OLIVER, ELDRIDGE M. — Detailed as a Regmtl. Teamster, Spring,
　　　　1862: Deserted, Dec. 17, 1862: Captured & court martialed —
　　　　sentenced to work on Richmond defense fortifications: POW,
　　　　Knoxville (Nov. 3, 1863): Confined at Camp Chase, Ohio:
　　　　Paroled, May 23, 1865.
　　　PATRICK, H. C. — Recruited at Milam, Tex., Mar. 22, 1862: W.,
　　　　Antietam (Sept. 17, 1862): Right arm amputated.

PAYNE, W. M. — Transfd. into Co. I, from 2nd Regt. Tex. Mtd. Rifles, Aug., 1862: K., Antietam (Sept. 17, 1862).

PRATT, H. — Recruited at Milam, Tex., Mar. 22, 1862: On sick furlough to Tex., Sept., 1862: Never returned, "Dropped from rolls for protracted absence west of Miss. R.", Dec., 1863.

PRITCHARD, W. P. — Enl., Aug. 9, 1861, at New Orleans: W., Wilderness (May 6, 1864): Retired to Invalid's Corps, Crockett, Tex., Dec. 11, 1864.

(1) PRITCHARD, WM. D. — Prom., 4Cpl.: W., Antietam (Sept. 17, 1862): W., Spotsylvania CH., May 12, 1864. On wounded furlough to No. Car., Fall, 1864: Retired for disability, Feb. 20, 1865.

(1) RABORN, ALEX — Died of typhoid fever at Charlottesville, Va., Oct. 11, 1861.

(1) REEVES, MALACHIAH — W., Antietam (Sept. 17, 1862): Prom., 4Sgt., Apr. 15, 1864: Furlough to Ala., Spring, 1865: Paroled at Centerville, Ala., Apr., 1865.

RENFRO, DAVID K. — Recruited at Milam, Tex., July 28, 1862: Sick in hosp., Spring, 1863: Prom., 3Sgt., Nov., 1863: Present for duty through Aug., 1864.

(1) RENFRO, PETER F. — K., 2nd Manassas (Aug. 30, 1862).

(1) ROACH, BENJ. F. — Dischgd. for disability (diarrhea), Oct. 26, 1861.

RUDICIL, JOS. — Recruited at Milam, Tex., Mar. 7, 1862: W., Antietam (Sept. 17, 1862): K., Chickamauga (Sept. 19, 1863).

RUSSELL, FRANK M. — Recruited at Alto, Tex., Mar. 22, 1862: Sick, Summer, 1862 (rheumatism): Sick, Fall, 1862 (typhoid fever): Dischgd. from service (ulcerated leg), Apr. 14, 1864.

(1) RUSSELL, REUBAN R. — Died (meningitis), Oct. 20, 1861.

(1) RUSSELL, THOS. B. — Dischgd. for disability, Oct. 26, 1861.

(1) SALTER, WM. Y. — Recruiting duty in Tex., Feb.-Apr., 1863: K., Chickamauga (Sept. 19, 1863).

(1) SAMFORD, THOS. P. — Recruiting duty in Tex., Feb.-Apr., 1862.

(1) SCRUGGS, GEO. W. — Enl. at New Orleans, Aug. 9, 1861: No other record.

(2) SCULLY, CHAS. — Recruited at Milam, Tex., Mar. 25, 1862: Sick (pneumonia), May, 1862: Paroled, Appomattox (Apr. 12, 1865).

SELMAN, B. T. — Recruited at Alto, Tex., Mar. 22, 1862: Died in Richmond, June 8, 1862, buried in Hollywood Cemetery, Richmond, Va.

(1) SHAVER, GREEN D. — Enl. at New Orleans, Aug. 9, 1861: No other record.

(1) SHEHANE, WM. R. — Dischgd. for disability (TB), Nov. 7, 1861.

SHERIDAN, JOHN H. — Recruited in Tex., May 1, 1862: W., Antietam (Sept. 17, 1862): POW, Sept. 28, 1862: Confined at Ft. Monroe, Va., Dec. 29, 1862: Paroled: Wound furlough, 90 days, Mar. 15, 1863: Went to Tex., disabled, never rejnd. Co.

SHERIDAN, L. E. — Recruited in Tex., May 1, 1862: Sick in Tex., June, 1862, never jnd. Co. in Va.

(1) SMITH, WM. W. — Enl. at New Orleans, Aug. 9, 1861: No other record.

(1) SPLAWN, WM. — Sick furlough for 60 days granted Feb. 6, 1862: AWOL, since Apr. 25, 1862: No other record.

STEDMAN, JOHN — Recruited at Crockett, Tex., Mar. 22, 1862: Sick in Richmond hosp., Apr., 1862: No other record.

(1) STUART, GEO. — Enl., New Orleans, Aug. 9, 1861: No other record.

(1) THOMPSON, ROBT. W. — Sick in hosp., Charlottesville, Va., June-July, 1862: Sick in hosp., Richmond, July, 1863: Paroled, Montgomery, Ala., June 15, 1865.

(1) TINDALL, ROBT. W. — Prom., 3Sgt., Mar., 1862: Died in Richmond, Va., June 12, 1862.

(1) VAUGHN, THOS. M. — Died at Camp Quantica, Va. of measles, Sept. 18, 1861.

(1) WARE, ABRAM — Dischgd. for disability (hepatitis), Oct. 26, 1861.

WETHERRED, GEO. MARCUS — Recruited at Milam, Tex., Apr. 10, 1862: W., Malvern Hill (July 1, 1862): W. & POW, Chickamauga (Sept. 20, 1863): Died of wound.

WEBSTER, GREEN M. — Recruited at Alto, Tex., Mar. 22, 1862: Died in Winchester, Va., Aug. 3, 1863.

WHITE, H. J. — Recruited at Milam, Tex., Mar. 22, 1862: Sick in hosp., Summer, 1862: Died of pneumonia, Nov. 13, 1862: Buried in Hollywood Cemetery, Richmond, Nov. 18, 1862.

(1) WILLIAMS, FRANCIS M. — W., Malvern Hill (July 1, 1862): Granted sick leave: Listed as deserter, Jan. 3, 1863.

(1) WILLIAMS, WILFRED W. — Dischgd. for disability (TB), Aug. 16, 1862.

(1) WILLIAMSON, ZACHARIAH M. — Dischgd. for disability (rheumatism), Feb., 1862.

WOMACK, L. P. — Recruited at Milam, Tex., Apr. 4, 1862: Sick or on furlough most of 1862 & 1863: Dropped from rolls "on account of protracted absence west of Miss. R.," Dec., 1863.

(1) WOOD, ALFONZO S. — Enl., New Orleans, Aug. 9, 1861: No other record.

(1) WOODS, JAS. G. — Enl., New Orleans, Aug. 9, 1861: No other record.

(1) WOOTTERS, JOHN H. — See list of "Other Officers" above.

WORFORD, J. S. — W., Wilderness (May 6, 1864).

YARBOROUGH, C. F. — Recruited at Milam, Tex., Mar. 10, 1862: No other record.

YATES, J. H. — Recruited at Milam, Tex., Mar. 10, 1862: No other record.

YOUNGBLOOD, M. — Recruited at Milam, Tex., Apr. 10, 1862: W., Antietam (Sept. 17, 1862): Left arm amputated.

COMPANY K — *TEXAS INVINCIBLES*

Company was organized in San Augustine County, Texas, and mustered into Confederate service "for the war" at Griffin's Spring near Richmond, Virginia, Oct. 11, 1861 by Capt. L. R. Page, CSA.

Key

(1) Original member of Company. (2) Paroled at Appomattox.
K (Killed), W (Wounded), POW (Prisoner of War)
AWOL (Absent Without Leave)

ORIGINAL OFFICERS

(1)   BENTON, BENJ. F.   Capt. — K., Gaines' Mill (June 27, 1862).

(1)   PRICE, B. F.   1Lt. — Not re-elected in re-org. of Co., May 16, 1862: Resgnd. and returned to Tex.

(1)   MASSEY, JOHN H.   2Lt. — Elect., 1Lt., May 15, 1862: Elect., Capt., June 27, 1862: W., Antietam (Sept. 17, 1862): K., Wilderness (May 6, 1864).

(1)   BATE, W. W. ("Ben")   3Lt. — Not re-elected when Co. re-org., May 16, 1862: Resgnd. and returned to Tex.

ORIGINAL NON-COMMISSIONED OFFICERS

(1)   PATTON, SAM F.   1Sgt. — See list of "Other Officers" following.

(1)   NOBLE, J. O.   2Sgt. — Enl. at 27: Reduced to Pvt., Aug., 1862: W.,
(2)   Antietam (Sept. 17, 1862): W., Chickamauga (Sept. 19, 1863): Paroled, Appomattox (April 12, 1865).

(1)   FALL, J. CALVIN   3Sgt. — Enl. at 20 at San Augustine, Tex., July 11, 1861: No other record.

(1)   NORVELL, THOS. M.   4Sgt. — Enl. at 27: Died, Jan. 17, 1862.

(1)   PIERCE, JOE E.   5Sgt. — Enl. at 34: Dischgd., Aug. 28, 1862, enlmt. expired.

(1)   BULLOCK, THAD W.   1Cpl. — Reverted to Pvt. at own request, Mar. 11, 1862: W., Darbytown Rd. (Oct. 7, 1864).

(1)   McCLENDON, ALFRED S.   2Cpl. — Enl. at San Augustine, Tex., July 11, 1861 for one year: Died, Nov. 13, 1861.

(1)   STROTHER, W. F.   3Cpl. — Not re-appt. 3Cpl. in re-org. of Co., May, 1862: Reverted to Pvt.: W., Gettysburg (July 2, 1863): Prom.' 1Cpl.: Deserted: Returned: Reduced to Pvt.: W., Wilderness (May 6, 1864), all toes shot off.

(1)   HARRIS, THOS.   4Cpl. — No information available.

OTHER OFFICERS

WILSON, JOHN N. Capt. — Orig. Pvt. in Co.: Elect., 3Lt., May 17, 1862: Elect., 2Lt., June 28, 1862: Elect., 1Lt., Sept. 17, 1862: Elect., Capt.: W., Chickamauga (Sept. 19, 1863): W., Wilderness (May 6, 1864): Paroled, Appomattox (Apr. 12, 1865).

ARDRY, THOS. A. ("Duck") 1Lt. — Orig. Pvt. in Co.: Prom., 2Sgt., May 15, 1862: W., Gaines' Mill (June 27, 1862): Elect., 2Lt., Sept. 17, 1862: On detchd. duty, Fall, 1863: Elect., 1Lt.: Paroled, Appomattox (Apr. 12, 1865).

WATERHOUSE, JAS. 1Lt. — Orig. Pvt. in Co.: Elect., 2Lt., May 15, 1862: Elect., 1Lt., June 27, 1862: W., Gaines' Mill (June 27, 1862): K., Antietam (Sept. 17, 1862).

FORD, HENRY H. 2Lt. — Orig. Pvt. in Co.: Prom., 1Sgt., Dec. 31, 1861: Not re-appt. 1Sgt. in re-org. of Co., May, 1862: Reverted to Pvt.: Elect., 3Lt., Sept. 17, 1862: W., Wilderness (May 6, 1864).

PATTON, SAM F. 3Lt. — Orig. 1Sgt. of Co.: Resgnd. as 1Sgt., Dec. 31, 1861: Prom., 3Lt., June 27, 1862: K., Antietam (Sept. 17, 1862).

MUSICIANS

(1) McCROWSON, JESSE — Fifer: AWOL at Gaines' Mill (June 27, 1862): Reduced to ranks, July 1, 1862: W., Gettysburg (July 2, 1863): Wounded furlough to Athens, Ala.
(1) RIDLEY, JAS. — See roster, "Regmtl. Hdqtrs., 1st Tex. Inf."

PRIVATES

(1) ARDRY, THOS. A. ("Duck") — See list of "Other Officers" above.
(2)
(1) BARNES, JESSE — Died of tuberculosis, Dec. 12, 1861.
(1) BENNETT, HENRY S. — Enl. at 19: Prom., 3Sgt., July 15, 1862: W.,
(2)   Chickamauga (Sept. 19, 1863): W., Wilderness (May 6, 1864): Paroled, Appomattox (Apr. 12, 1865).
(1) BENTON, JESSE, JR. — Died, Apr., 1862.
(1) BRANDON, JOE L. — Enl. at 21: Died, Feb., 1862.
(1) BRANDON, JOHN — W., Chickamauga (Sept. 19, 1863): W., (in face
(2)   with bayonet) Spotsylvania CH. (May 10, 1864): Prom., Cpl., July 10, 1864: Paroled, Appomattox (Apr. 12, 1865).
(1) BROOKS, WM. F. — W., Gettysburg (July 2, 1863): Prom., 4Cpl.:
(2)   Paroled, Appomattox (Apr. 12, 1865).
(1) BROWN, JOHN O. — Present & on duty for entire war, except for
(2)   30-day furlough, Sept., 1863: Paroled, Appomattox (Apr. 12, 1865).
(1) BRYAN, SEBERN — AWOL at Gaines' Mill (June 27, 1862): Dischgd., Sept. 8, 1862.

(1) BRYAN, WM. M. — AWOL at Gaines' Mill (June 27, 1862): POW, South Mountain (Sept. 14, 1862).

(1) BUCKLEY, YOUNG ARCHY — Enl. at 19: Died, Jan., 1862.

(1) BURNAMAN, SAMUEL E. F. — K. near Chattanooga, Tenn., Sept. 25, 1863.

(1) CHAMBERS, W. J. — Prom., 2Cpl., May 15, 1862: K., Gaines' Mill (June 27, 1862).

(1) COE, J. WM. — W., Gaines' Mill (June 27, 1862): Died of wound in Richmond (Chimborazo Hosp.), July 30, 1862.

(1) COLMAN, MASON — Died, Mar., 1862.

(1) COLMAN, WADE H. — Enl. at 19 on July 11, 1861 at San Augustine, Tex.: Died, Dec. 3, 1861: Hearse rental & coffin cost $10.00.

(1) CONNER, ROBT. T. — Prom., 5Sgt., May 15, 1862: W., 2nd Manassas (Aug. 30, 1862): W., Suffolk Campaign (Apr., 1863): Absent on furlough in Tex.: Jnd. Trans-Miss. milt. unit: W., Mansfield (La.) (Apr. 8, 1864).

(1) CURETON, JOHN — Enl. at 19: Died of typhoid fever, Dec. 1, 1861.

(1) CURETON, WM. J. — Prom., 3Cpl., May 17, 1862: W., Gaines' Mill (June 27, 1862): W., Chickamauga (Sept. 19, 1863): W., Wilderness (May 6, 1864): Prom., 2Sgt., July 10, 1864: K., Darbytown Rd. (Oct. 7, 1864).

(1) DAVIDSON, THOS. B. — W., Spotsylvania CH. (May 10, 1864): Prom.,
(2) Cpl., Sept. 1, 1864: Paroled, Appomattox (Apr. 12, 1865).

(1) DAVIDSON, W. R. — W., (in neck with bayonet) Spotsylvania CH. (May 10, 1864): W., Darbytown Rd. (Oct. 7, 1864).

(1) DAVIS, GEO. W., JR. — Enl. at 18: K., Wilderness (May 6, 1864).

DAWSON, J. A. — W., Gettysburg (July 2, 1863): No other record.

(1) DAY, STEPHEN M. — Enl. at 22: W., Antietam (Sept. 17, 1862): Granted wounded furlough, Nov. 14, 1862: Never returned to Co.

(1) DUNHAM, BARZILLIA D. — Detailed as a Wagoneer, May, 1862:
(2) Detailed as a Div. Teamster, Fall, 1864: Paroled, Appomattox (Apr. 12, 1865).

(1) EVANS, JAS. — Enl. at 18: Died of measles & pleurisy, Dec. 7, 1861.

(1) EVANS, ROBT. — Enl. at 20: Died of typhoid pneumonia, Dec. 11, 1861.

(1) FALL, H. VAIL — Dischgd., Sept. 8, 1862, enlmt. expired.

(1) FENLEY, CHAS. WM. — Prom., 1Cpl., May 15, 1862: W., Malvern Hill (July 1, 1862): Sick furlough from Sept., 1862: Reduced to ranks, June 1, 1863.

(1) FORD, HENRY H. — See list of "Other Officers" above.

(1) FORD, JOHN D. — Prom., 1Sgt., May 17, 1862: Captured near Shanghai, Va., July 18, 1863: Died in prison at Camp Chase, Ohio, Oct. 24, 1863.

(1) GRAY, H. N. — Enl. at 33: Dischgd. for disability (bronchitis), Dec. 21, 1861.

(1) GRAY, WM. W. — W., Gaines' Mill (June 27, 1862): W., Antietam (Sept. 17, 1862).

(1) HAIL (or HALE), JESS M. — Enl. at 25: K., Antietam (Sept. 17, 1862).

(1) HAIL (or HALE), JOS. J., JR. — Enl. at 21: "On Police Duty", Spring, 1862: Hospitalized at Farmville, Va., Spring, 1863.
(2) HAIL (or HALE), OSCAR F. — W., Gettysburg (July 2, 1863): Paroled, Appomattox (Apr. 12, 1865).
HAM, GEO. W. — Transfd. to Co. B, 1st Tex. Inf. Regt., Mar. 1, 1863: No other record.
(1) HANKS, O. T. — Prom., 4Cpl., July, 1862: W., Antietam (Sept. 17,
(2) 1862): Prom., 2Sgt., Oct. 7, 1864: Paroled, Appomattox (Apr. 12, 1865).
(1) HAUGHTON, JOHN — W. in accidental firing of gun, June 8, 1862: Left arm amputated: Dischgd., Aug. 10, 1862.
(1) HOOPER, SAMUEL R. — Enl. at 19: Prom., 4Cpl., May 17, 1862: Died, typhoid fever, May 18, 1862.
(1) HOUSMAN, JAS. F. — Enl. at 17: Dischgd., Sept. 8, 1862, enlmt. expired.
(1) HOWARD, WASHINGTON B. — W., Gettysburg (July 2, 1863): Deserted and took Union oath, E. Tenn., Spring, 1864.
(1) HUNT, THOS. C. — Enl. at 17: Dischgd., Sept. 8, 1862, enlmt. expired.
(1) HUSTON, M. T. — Enl. at 32: Dischgd., Sept. 17, 1862 for disability.
(1) IRVING, TORNIL — Enl. at 26: Died, Jan. 17, 1862.
(1) JACOBS, MADISON — Enl. at 26: Prom., 3Sgt., Apr., 1862: Died in Richmond, July 5, 1862.
(1) JOHNSON, WILEY L. — Enl. at 28: Died, Jan. 15, 1862.
(1) JONES, Z. B. — Enl. at 22 at San Augustine, Tex., July 11, 1861: No other record.
(1) LANE, JOS. — Enl. at 18: W., Eltham's Landing (May 7, 1862): K., Malvern Hill (July 1, 1862).
(1) LANIER, C. W. — Enl. at 25: Dischgd., Apr. 11, 1862, tuberculosis.
(1) MASON, LAFAYETTE M. — W., Chickamauga (Sept. 19, 1863): Died of wound, Sept. 22, 1863.
(1) MASSEY, JOEL V. — Enl. at 19: Prom., 4Sgt., Mar., 1862: W., Suffolk Campaign, May 3, 1863: Granted wounded furlough.
(1) MATHEWS, SIMEON — Dischgd. for disability, Sept. 8, 1862.
(1) MATTOX, JOHN CICERO — Enl. at San Augustine, Tex., July 11, 1861: Died, Jan. 17, 1862.
(1) MAYO, LEWIS J. — Prom., 2Cpl., Jan., 1862: Not re-appt. 2Cpl. in re-org. of Co., May, 1862: K., Gaines' Mill (June 27, 1862).
(1) McALISTER, W. A. — Died of "lung congestion", Mar. 1, 1862.
(1) McDONALD, JOHN — Dischgd., Jan. 31, 1862, tuberculosis.
(1) McMAHON, CHAS. F. — W., Malvern Hill (July 1, 1862): Dischgd., Aug. 25, 1862.
(1) McNELLEY, BARNEY — W., Seven Pines (June 1, 1862): Detailed as ambulance driver, Summer, 1863: Deserted while command was in E. Tenn., Winter, 1863-64.
(1) MENEFEE, GEO. W. — W., Gaines' Mill (June 27, 1862): POW, Gettysburg (July 2, 1863): Exchanged, Aug. 17, 1863: Paroled, Appomattox (Apr. 12, 1865).
(1) MENEFEE, JOS. TATUM — Died of typhoid fever, Dec. 5, 1861.
(1) MILLER, EDW. G. ("Ned") — Enl. at 20: W., Antietam (Sept. 17, 1862): W., Wilderness (May 6, 1864): K., Chaffin's Farm (Sept. 29, 1864).

(1) MOSELY, HENRY E. — Enl. at 21: W., Antietam (Sept. 17, 1862): Absent on wound leave: "Transfd. by promotion," Dec. 11, 1863.

(1) MURPHY, B. F. — Enl. at 21: Died, Jan. 17, 1862.

(1) MURPHY, JAS. A. — Enl. at 22: Died in the Globe Hospital, Richmond, Feb. 5, 1862: Personal effects consisted of: 1 pr. shoes, 1 cap, 1 pr. pants, 1 pr. socks, 1 jacket, 1 flannel shirt, 1 overcoat, 1 pr. drawers, 2 shirts, and 3 blankets.

(1) NOBLE, R. L. — Enl. at 18: Dischgd. for disability (asthma), Dec. 15, 1861.

(1) PARKER, JOHN — Enl. at 30: Dischgd., Sept. 8, 1862, enlmt. expired.

(1) PARKER, JULIUS — Enl. at 21: Dischgd. for disability (deafness), Dec. 11, 1861.

(1) PATTON, HENRY P. — Enl. at 19: Dischgd. for "bronchial infection," Dec. 21, 1861.

(1) PATTON, JAS. B. — Enl. at 18: Asgnd. to hosp. duty: No other record.

(1) PATTON, SAM F. — See list of "Other Officers," above.

(1) PETERSON, JOHN M. — Enl. at 26: Died, Jan. 18, 1862.

(1) PETERSON, S. M. — W., Wilderness (May 6, 1864): Paroled,
(2) Appomattox (Apr. 12, 1865).

(1) PITTMAN, J. W. — Enl. at 23: Prom., 4Cpl., Feb., 1862: Not re-appt. 4Cpl. in re-org. of Co., May, 1862: Reverted to Pvt.: Died from disease, June 4, 1862.

(1) POOLE, AMOS N. — Enl. at 44: Dischgd., July 10, 1862, for disability.

(1) POWELL, HENRY C. — Enl. at 19: W., Gaines' Mill (June 27, 1862):
(2) W., Gettysburg (July 2, 1863): W., Wilderness (May 6, 1864): Paroled, Appomattox (Apr. 12, 1865).

(1) PRICE, ELIJAH — Enl. at 18: Dischgd., Sept. 8, 1862, enlmt. expired.

(1) PRISYTHE, J. H. — Enl. at 18: Died, Jan. 15, 1862.

(1) PROSELER, ANDREW J. — Enl. at 22: W., Gaines' Mill (June 27,
(2) 1862): W., Wilderness (May 6, 1864): Paroled, Appomattox (Apr. 12, 1865).

(1) QUINN, WM. O. — W., Antietam (Sept. 17, 1862): POW, near Shanghai, Va., July 18, 1863.

(1) RUDDELL, ISAAC N. ("Ike") — Enl. at 20: Detailed as a sharpshooter, Apr. 29, 1862: Prom., 2Sgt., Sept. 17, 1862: W., Chickamauga (Sept. 19, 1863): Retired for disability, July 10, 1864.

(1) SANDERS, JOHN F. — Enl. at 23: Died at Bristol, Tenn., enroute to Richmond, Sept., 1861.

(1) SHARP, F. MARION — Enl. at 22: K., Gettysburg (July 2, 1863).

(1) SHARPE, W. ANDERSON — Enl. at 21: Prom., 1Cpl., March 11, 1862: Not re-appt. 1Cpl. in re-org. of Co., May, 1862: Reverted to Pvt.: POW, Gettysburg (July 2, 1863): Sent to Ft. Delaware: Deserted, took Union oath.

(1) SHERROD, RANDALL — Enl. at 18: Dischgd., Sept. 8, 1862, enlmt. expired.

(1) SOWELL, JAS. W. J. — Enl. at 41: Dischgd. for disability, Aug. 5, 1862, chronic diarrhea.

(1) STALLINGS, JAS. A. — Enl. at 24: W., Chickamauga (Sept. 19, 1863): W., accidentally, Dec. 10, 1864.

(1) THOMAS, OSCAR E. — Enl. at 18: Dischgd., Sept. 8, 1862, enlmt. expired.

(1) TODD, J. ADDISON — Enl. at 30: Died of typhoid fever, July 3, 1862,

TUCKER, F. H. — Prom., 1Cpl., June 1, 1863: W., Gettysburg (July 2, 1863): W., Chickamauga (Sept. 19, 1863): Prom., 1Sgt., Jan. 1, 1864: W., Wilderness (May 6, 1864): Paroled, Farmersville, Va., Apr. 14, 1865.

TUCKER, R. D. — POW, Gettysburg (July 2, 1863): Sent to Ft. Delaware: Paroled, June 9, 1865.

VICK, IREDELL R. — See roster, "Regmtl. Hdqtrs., 1st Tex. Inf. Regt."

(1) WAFFORD, SAMUEL — Enl. at 26: Died in Richmond hosp., May 24, 1862.

(1) WALKER, J. W. — Enl. at 21: Died of typhoid fever, Dec. 22, 1861.

(1) WATERHOUSE, JAS. — See list of "Other Officers" above.

(2) WATSON, WM. H. — Enl., Apr. 2, 1863: W., Chickamauga (Sept. 20, 1863): Paroled, Appomattox (Apr. 12, 1865).

(1) WEEKS, E. M. — Dischgd., Mar. 6, 1862 for disability.

(1) WHITE, W. T. — Enl. at 23: Appt. Co. Color Guard, Oct., 1862: Prom. to 4Cpl., Nov., 1862: POW near Shanghai, Va., July 19, 1863: Sent to Ft. Delaware, Del.: Paroled, June 10, 1865.

(1) WILSON, A. J. — POW, Antietam (Sept. 17, 1862): Exchanged:
(2) Paroled, Appomattox (Apr. 12, 1865).

(1) WILSON, JOHN N. — See list of "Other Officers" above.
(2)

(1) WILSON, WM. J. — Enl. at 23: Died in Richmond, Sept. 1, 1862 of typhoid fever, buried in Hollywood Cemetery, Richmond.

1ST TEX. VOL. INF. REGT.

COMPANY L — *LONE STAR RIFLES*

Company was organized in Galveston County, Texas, and was mustered into the Confederate service "for the war" on August 30, 1861, near Manassas, Virginia by Capt. Thos. Claiborn, CSA.

Key

(1) Original member of Company. (2) Paroled at Appomattox.
K (Killed), W (Wounded), POW (Prisoner of War)
AWOL (Absent Without Leave)

ORIGINAL OFFICERS

(1) McKEEN, ALFRED C. Capt. — W., Eltham's Landing (May 7, 1862): Resgnd., May 29, 1862, not re-elect. Capt. when Co. re-org.

(1) BEDELL, WM. A. 1Lt. — Detailed to recruiting duty in Tex.,
(2)   Feb.-Apr., 1862: Elect., Capt., May, 1862: W., Malvern Hill (July
        1, 1862): W., Antietam (Sept. 17, 1862): Actg. Maj. of Regt.: W.,
        Wilderness (May 6, 1864): Paroled, Appomattox (Apr. 12, 1865).
(1) THOMPSON, J. C. S. 2Lt. — Elect., 1Lt., May, 1862: K., Antietam
        (Sept. 17, 1862).
(1) BALDWIN, JOHN M. 3Lt. — W., 2nd Manassas (Aug. 30, 1862):
        Elect., 1Lt., Sept., 1862: Elect., Capt., May 26, 1863, and
        transfd. to Engineer Corps, Hood's Division.

ORIGINAL NON-COMMISSIONED OFFICERS

(1) SMITH, ANDREW W. 1Sgt. — Enl. at 20: Reduced to Pvt.: Detailed
        to recruiting duty in Tex., Feb.-Apr., 1862: Elect., Capt. of Co.
        C, 1st Tex. Sharpshooters, Apr., 1862. (This organization is
        unknown to author).
(1) ARMSTRONG, ROBT. R. 2Sgt. — See list of "Other Officers"
        following.
(1) RICHARDSON, W. F. 3Sgt. — See roster, "Hdqtrs. Hood's Tex. Brig."
(1) ROBINSON, W. B. 4Sgt. — Prom., 2Sgt.: W., Chickamauga (Sept. 19,
        1863): Returned to Tex., Fall, 1863: Elect. Treasurer of Ft. Bend
        County, Aug. 1, 1864.
(1) FORSYTHE, A. P. 1Cpl. — See list of "Other Officers" following.
(1) RANDALL, W. P. 2Cpl. — See list of "Other Officers" following.
(1) ROBINSON, R. S. 3Cpl. — Enl. at 22: Prom., 2Cpl.: W., Malvern Hill
        (July 1, 1862): Dischgd. for disability, Aug. 2, 1862, could not
        use left arm.
(1) BRANARD, GEO. A. 4Cpl. — See roster, "Regmtl. Hdqtrs., 1st Tex.
        Inf."

OTHER OFFICERS

VIDOR, CHAS. Capt. — Orig. Pvt. in Co.: Appt. QM clerk, Tex. Brig.:
        Prom., to Capt. in the Confederate QM Dept., Feb. 19, 1864.
ARMSTRONG, ROBT. R. 1Lt. — Orig. 2Sgt. of Co.: Prom., 1Sgt.,
        Apr., 1862: Elect., 3Lt., June 5, 1862: Elect., 2Lt., Sept. 17,
        1862: Elect., 1Lt., May, 1863: W., Chickamauga (Sept. 19,
        1863): W., Wilderness (May 6, 1864): W., Darbytown Rd. (Oct.
        7, 1864): Died from wound, Oct. 20, 1864.
BOLLING, CHAS. L. 2Lt. — Orig. Pvt. in Co.: Enl. at 20: Asgnd. as
        "Ambulance Master," May, 1862: W., Wilderness (May 6, 1864):
        Appt. 3Cpl., Aug., 1864: Prom., 2Lt., Winter, 1864-65: POW,
        Appomattox River, Va., Apr. 3, 1865: Paroled, June 18, 1865.
RANDALL, W. P. 2Lt. — See roster "Hdqtrs., Hood's Tex. Brig."
FORSYTHE, A. P. 3Lt. — See roster, "Regmtl. Hdqtrs., 1st Tex. Inf."

PRIVATES

ALSBROOK, JOS. — Recruited at Galveston, Tex., Mar. 27, 1862, age 24: W., Antietam (Sept. 17, 1862): K., Chaffin's Farm (Sept. 29, 1864).

ATHERON, W. R. — Recruited at Galveston, Tex., Mar. 17, 1862, age 23: Deserted, Apr., 1862.

(1) BAKER, G. B. — Transfd. to Confederate Engineer Corps., June 1, 1863: K., Wilderness (May 6, 1864).

(1) BARBEE, WILSON J. — Asgnd. as "Courier for Gen. Hood": W., Gettysburg (July 2, 1863): K., near Dandridge, Tenn., Jan. 18, 1864. (Awarded CSA Medal of Honor for action at Gettysburg.)

(1) BERNARD, THOS. — Enl. at 28: W., Eltham's Landing (May 7, 1862): Left arm amputated: Discharged for disability, Aug. 28, 1862.

(1) BLESSING, SAMUEL T. — Enl. at 21: W., Antietam (Sept. 17, 1862): W., (both hips) & POW, Darbytown Rd. (Oct. 7, 1864): Sent to Pt. Lookout, Md.: Paroled, June 20, 1865.

(1) BOLLING, CHAS. L. — See list of "Other Officers" above.

(1) BOSS (or BASS), GEO. — K., Antietam (Sept. 17, 1862).

(1) BOURKE, DANIEL — Enl. at 26: Died at Camp Wigfall, Va., Sept. 3, 1861 of chronic dysentery.

BOURKE, JOHN — Sick in hosp., Aug., 1863: No other record.

BOYKAIN (or BOYKIN), W. T. — Transfd. to Co. L from Capt. Bollin's Co., Hubbard's 5th Tex. Inf. Battalion, Apr. 1, 1862.

(1) BRANDT, A. — Enl. at 21: W., Chickamauga (Sept. 20, 1863): Brig. comsy. clerk, Jan., 1864: POW, Spotsylvania CH., May 12, 1864: Paroled, June 16, 1865, at Pt. Lookout, Md.

(1) BROWN, JOHN W. — Enl. at 23: W., Seven Pines (June 1, 1862): W., Gettysburg (July 2, 1863): Thigh amputated: Died, July 10, 1863.

(1) BROWN, JOS. F. — Enl. at 19: K., Eltham's Landing (May 7, 1862).

(1) BUCKLEY, EDWARD C. — See roster, "Hdqtrs., Hood's Texas Brigade".

(1) CADY, D. C. — Enl. at 53: Put in charge of the Tex. Depot, Richmond, by order of Gen. Hood, Mar., 1862.

CARNES, WM. C. — Enl., Apr., 1863 at Galveston, Tex.: Asgnd. to Brig. Provost Guard, Feb., 1864.

(1) CARPENTER, STEPHEN A. — Enl. at 30: Prom., 3Sgt., July, 1862: Appt. Actg. Regmtl. Ordn. Sgt., Sept., 1862: K., Antietam (Sept. 17, 1862).

(1) CARTER, G. W. L. — Enl. at 38: Deserted, May 4, 1862, at Yorktown, Va.

(1) CLARK, SAMUEL — Enl. at 38: W., Wilderness (May 6, 1862):
(2) Paroled, Appomattox (Apr. 12, 1865).

(1) COFFEE, JOHN — W., Eltham's Landing (May 7, 1862): POW, Antietam (Sept. 17, 1862): Exchanged: POW, Chickamauga (Sept. 19, 1864).

(1) COHEN, HENRY — W., Antietam (Sept. 17, 1862), and deserted shortly thereafter.

(1) COLE, FRED T. — Enl. at 18: Asgnd. duty as a Div. Teamster, Mar., 1864: K., Wilderness (May 6, 1864).

(1) COLLINS, MONROE P. — Enl. at 19: Transfd. to Co. I, 1st Tex. Inf. Regt., Apr. 19, 1862.

(1) CRAWFORD, E. C. — Enl. at 18: W., Chickamauga (Sept. 19, 1863): Died of wound, Sept. 24, 1863.

CUMMINGS, JAS. W. — Recruited at Galveston, Tex., Apr. 11, 1862, age 23: W., Gettysburg (July 2, 1863): Retired for disability, Nov., 1864.

(2) CURTIS, R. A. — Recruited at Galveston, Tex., Apr. 11, 1862, age 24: Prom., 1Cpl.: Prom., 5Sgt., May 20, 1863: W., Knoxville, Nov., 1863: W., Petersburg, June, 1864: Reduced to Pvt.: Paroled, Appomattox (Apr. 12, 1865).

(1) DAVIS, JOHN — Enl. at 24: Died at Fredericksburg, Va., Mar. 24, 1862.

(2) DELESDENIER, L. F. — Enl., July 16, 1864 at Galveston, Tex.: Paroled, Appomattox (Apr. 12, 1865).

(1) DILLON, JOHN — Enl. at 24: Present and on duty during entire war:
(2) Paroled, Appomattox (Apr. 12, 1865).

(1) ELMENDORF, DAVID — Enl. at 32: W., Chickamauga (Sept. 19, 1863): Deserted, Mar. 17, 1865.

(1) FARQUAR, ADRIAN M. — Enl. at 21: W. & POW, Gettysburg (July 2, 1863): Exchanged, Mar., 1864.

FRALICH (or FRALISH), JOHN — Recruited at Cypress City, Tex., Apr. 5, 1862, age 20: W., Chickamauga (Sept. 19, 1863): W., Spotsylvania CH. (May 10, 1864).

FRANK, JACOB — Recruited at Houston, Tex., Apr. 1, 1862, age 27: K., Antietam (Sept. 17, 1862).

GADIFFET, GUSTAV — Recruited at Houston, Tex., Apr. 1, 1862, age 22: Deserted, Apr., 1862 at Mobile, Ala.

(1) GARITY (or GARRITY), MICHAEL — POW, Antietam (Sept. 17,
(2) 1862), left with wounded; Exchanged, Nov., 1862: Detailed to Provost Guard, Hood's Division: Paroled, Appomattox (Apr. 12, 1865).

GEARING, F. A. G. — Enl. at Galveston, Tex., Mar., 1864: W., Wilderness (May 6, 1864): Dischgd., Nov. 23, 1864.

(1) GILLIS, JOHN P. — Enl. at 29: W., Antietam (Sept. 17, 1862): W., Chickamauga (Sept. 19, 1863): W., Wilderness (May 6, 1864): W., Chaffin's Farm (Sept. 29, 1864): Left arm amputated.

(1) HAGAN, CHAS. — Enl. at 32: Dischgd., Feb. 1, 1862: Returned to Tex.: Appt. 2Lt. in Co. B, Timmons Regt.

(1) HALLECK, CHAS. B. — Enl. at 23: Detailed to recruiting duty in Tex., Feb.-Apr., 1862: W., Antietam (Sept. 17, 1862): Deserted to enemy — reported as serving with U. S. 6th Corps as Capt. & Subsistence Officer.

(1) HANSON, JOHN — Enl. at 20: Prom., 1Cpl., Apr., 1862: W., Antietam (Sept. 17, 1862): Prom., 3Sgt., July, 1863: Transfd. to Trans-Mississippi Theater.

HARRIS, JOHN — Recruited at Galveston, Tex., Mar. 27, 1862, age 22: Deserted, Apr., 1862 at Galveston, Tex.

HAWKINS, GEO. B. — Recruited at Galveston, Tex., Mar. 20, 1862, age 21: W., Gaines' Mill (June 27, 1862): Disabled and detailed to conscription duty in Tex., Jan., 1863.

(2) HOSKINS, WM. — Recruited at Galveston, Tex., Apr. 11, 1862, age 18: W., Antietam (Sept. 17, 1862): POW, Gettysburg, left with wounded, July 5, 1863: Exchanged: Paroled, Appomattox (Apr. 12, 1865).

(1) HOYLE, CHAS. W. — Enl. at 26: Deserted, Summer, 1862: Rejnd. Co.: POW, Gettysburg (July 2, 1863): Escaped from prison, Jan., 1864: Rejnd. Co.: Deserted, Jan., 1865.

(1) JACKSON, WM. L. — Enl. at 33: Died at Camp Quantico, Va., Dec. 5, 1861.

(1) JACOBLEF, ROBT. — Enl. at 23: Prom., 2Cpl., Sept., 1862: W., Gaines' Mill (June 27, 1862): K., Antietam (Sept. 17, 1862).

JONES, AUSTIN W. — Recruited at Galveston, Tex., Mar. 17, 1862, age 19: W. & POW, Antietam (Sept. 17, 1862): Exchanged, Nov., 1862: POW, Gettysburg, July 5, 1863, left with wounded: Exchanged, May, 1864.

(1) KELSO, AARON — Enl. at 18: W., Chickamauga (Sept. 19, 1863): Prom., 1Cpl.: W. & POW, Darbytown Rd. (Oct. 7, 1864).

KIERAN, L. — Recruited at Galveston, Tex., Apr. 9, 1862, age 27: Deserted, Apr., 1862 at New Orleans, La.

(1) KINGSLEY, CHAS. H. — Enl. at 23: W. & POW, Antietam (Sept. 17, 1862): Exchanged, Nov., 1862: Prom., 5Sgt.: Prom., 1Sgt.: W., Chickamauga (Sept. 19, 1863): POW, Wilderness (May 6, 1864): Died, Pt. Lookout Prison, Md., July, 1864.

(1) LAKE, THOS. W. C. — Enl. at 22: Courier and scout for Gen. Hood: POW, Gettysburg (July 2, 1863): Sent to prison at Pt. Lookout, Md.: Exchanged: Paroled, Winchester, Va., May 8, 1865.

(1) LAZARUS, SALEM S. — Enl. at 32: See roster, "Regmtl. Hdqtrs., 1st Tex. Inf."

(1) LEACH, WM. — Enl. at 18: W., Antietam (Sept. 17, 1862): W., Chickamauga (Sept. 19, 1863): Retired for disability, Dec. 17, 1864: Paroled, Brenham, Tex., Aug., 1865.

(1) LEWIS, JOHN — Enl. at 27: Prom., 3Cpl., July, 1863: K., Chickamauga (Sept. 19, 1863).

LOVELOCK, WM. H. — Recruited at Galveston, Tex., Mar. 27, 1862, age 25: Deserted, Sept. 15, 1862 in Md.

(1) MAHONEY, J. P. — See roster, "Regmtl. Hdqtrs., 1st Tex. Inf."

(1) McCARTY, CHAS. W. — Enl. at 18: Deserted, July 10, 1862.

(2) McCARTY, JOHN M. — Originally a Sgt. in Waul's Tex. Legion: Transfd. into Co. L as Pvt., Oct. 18, 1863: W., Wilderness (May 6, 1864): Paroled, Appomattox (Apr. 12, 1865).

(2) McCARTY, THOS. L. — Recruited at Galveston, Tex., Apr. 12, 1862, age 21: Paroled, Appomattox (Apr. 12, 1865).

(1) McCORQUODALE, EPHRAM A. — Enl. at 25: W., 2nd Manassas (Aug. 30, 1862): POW, Gettysburg, July 5, 1863, left with wounded: Confined at Pt. Lookout, Md.: Exchanged, Oct. 29, 1864.

(1) McGAN, HENRY B. — Enl. at 18: W., Antietam (Sept. 17, 1862): W., Gettysburg (July 2, 1863): Deserted in E. Tenn., Jan., 1864.

(1) MERK (or MERKE), GEO. A. — Enl. at 28: Reported as "wounded and on furlough," Dec., 1862: Paroled, Appomattox (Apr. 12, 1865).

(1) MEYERS, HENRY — Enl. at 26: "Body Servant" (orderly) to Col. Rainey, May 7, 1862: Deserted, May 30, 1862.

(1) MILLARD, WATSON C. — Enl. at 21: Prom., 5Sgt., Sept., 1861: Reduced to ranks, Mar. 31, 1862: W., Malvern Hill (July 1, 1862): Sick in hosp., Nov., 1862 — May, 1863: Deserted, June, 1863: Took Fed. oath, July 17, 1863.

(1) MELLHAUSEN, THEO. H. — Enl. at 18: K., Gettysburg (July 2, 1863).

MURPHY, J. W. — Recruited at Galveston, Tex., Apr. 11, 1862, age 31: W., Chickamauga (Sept. 20, 1863).

(1) NAGLE, JAS. — Enl. at 21: W., Antietam (Sept. 17, 1862): W., Chickamauga (Sept. 20, 1863).

(1) NAGLE, JOS. — Enl. at 19: W., Gaines' Mill (June 27, 1862): Dischgd., Aug., 1862: Re-enl., 1864.

NELSON, JOHN — Recruited at Galveston, Tex., Apr. 11, 1862, age 21: Transfd. to 24th No. Car. Inf. Regt., Apr., 1863.

(1) NICHOLS, FRANKLIN C. — Enl. at 21: W., Eltham's Landing (May 7, 1862): POW near Hagerstown, Md., July 15, 1863: Deserted to enemy.

(1) NICHOLSON, JOHN B. — Enl. at 22: Dischgd. for disability, Jan., 1862.

(1) NOEL, BENJAMIN C. — Enl. at 20: Deserted, Apr. 8, 1862.

(1) PICKETT, JONATHAN — Enl. at 18: Lost leg in railroad accident, Aug. 29, 1862: Died in hosp., Charlottesville, Va., Nov. 16, 1862.

(1) PORTER, WM. H. — Enl. at 46: Prom., 1Sgt., Jan., 1863: K., Gettysburg (July 2, 1863).

POUPART, JOHN — Recruited at Galveston, Tex., Apr. 9, 1862, age 29: K., Gaines' Mill (June 27, 1862).

(1) PRATER, VIRGIL — Enl. at 21: Died at Warrenton, Va., Sept. 22, 1862.

(1)
(2) PRATT (or PRUETT), JAS. C. — Enl. at 22: Prom., 4Cpl., Oct. 1, 1862: W., Chickamauga (Sept. 19, 1863): Prom., 2Cpl.: Prom., 3Sgt.: Paroled, Appomattox (Apr. 12, 1865).

(1) ROBINSON, WALTER M. — Enl. at 27: Detailed as a clerk in the Brig. Comsy. Dept., Jan., 1864: Courier for Col. Bass, July, 1864.

(1) ROGERS, GEO. — Enl. at 22: In hosp. with bronchitis, Nov., 1862: Dischgd. for disability (asthma), June 8, 1863.

ROOKS, NOAH — Recruited at Galveston, Tex., Apr. 11, 1862, age 29: Hospitalized, May, 1862.

(1) ROURKE, JOHN O. — Enl. at 24: W., Antietam (Sept. 17, 1862): Arm amputated: Dischgd., Mar., 1863.

(1) SABLE, JACK — Enl. at 32: Returned to Tex., Fall, 1862: Detailed as ship pilot at Sabine Pass, Tex., Nov., 1862.

(1) SCHADT (or SCHODT), CHAS. — Enl. at 26: K., Eltham's Landing (May 7, 1862).

(1) SCHADT (or SCHODT), WM. — Enl. at 19: W., Chickamauga (Sept. 19, 1863): W. & POW, Wilderness (May 6, 1864).

SCHMIDT, FRANK — Recruited at Cypress City, Tex., Apr. 5, 1862, age 20: W., Chickamauga (Sept. 19, 1863): W., Wilderness (May 6, 1864): Leg amputated: Retired for disability, Nov. 2, 1864.

(2) SCHULTZ, HENRY — Recruited at Cypress City, Tex., Apr. 5, 1862, age 18: W., Antietam (Sept. 17, 1862): W., Wilderness (May 6, 1864): Paroled, Appomattox (Apr. 12, 1865).

(1) SCHULTZ, HENRY P. — Born in Prussia, Enl. at 25: W., Gaines' Mill (June 27, 1862): Prom., 3Cpl., Oct. 1, 1862: POW, Front Royal, Va., July 24, 1863: Deserted, took oath of allegiance to U. S.

(1) SCHWARTING, FRED — Enl. at 27: W., Antietam (Sept. 17, 1862): POW, Gettysburg (July 2, 1863): Took oath of allegiance, enlisted in Federal Army, July, 1863.

(1) SCOTT, ALEXANDER J. — Enl. at 19: Killed in railroad accident, Sept. 10, 1863 (enroute from Wilmington to Atlanta, fell from car and was crushed).

(1) SCOTT, GEO. WASHINGTON — Enl. at 24: Detailed as Hosp. Steward to Dr. Garnett at Dumfries, Va., Dec. 22, 1861.

(2) SHELTON, W. A. — See roster, "Hdqtrs., Hood's Tex. Brig."

(1) SHEPHERD, W. G. — See roster, "Regmtl. Hdqtrs., 1st Tex. Inf."

(1) SIMMS, SMITH D. — Enl. at 17: W., Eltham's Landing (May 7, 1862): POW, Wilderness (May 6, 1864).

SMITH, FRANK — No record found.

SMITH, JOHN — Recruited at Beaumont, Tex., Apr. 14, 1862, age 22: Died of typhoid fever, May 23, 1862.

SMITH, JOHN M. — W., Antietam (Sept. 17, 1862): On furlough to Tex., Feb. 1, 1863: Prom., 1Lt. in Fontain's Light Btry. by Maj.-Gen. Magruder while on furlough to Tex.

(1) SMITH, SIDNEY B. — W., Gaines' Mill (June 27, 1862): Dischgd. in Aug., 1862: Re-enlisted, Oct. 14, 1862: W., & POW, Darbytown Rd. (Oct. 7, 1864): Confined to Pt. Lookout Prison, Md.: Paroled, June 20, 1865.

(1) SOLOMON, NATHANIEL B. — Enl. at 22: Deserted, Aug. 31, 1862.

(1) SOUTHWICK, J. W. — Enl. at 24: Prom., 2Sgt., Apr., 1862: K., Gettysburg (July 2, 1863).

(1) STANSBURY, N. J. — Enl. at 42: Detailed by Secretary of War to arsenal at Augusta, Ga., March 16, 1864.

(1) STARK, W. JASPER — Enl. at 20: Died of measles at Camp Wigfall, Va., Sept. 17, 1861.

(1) STODDARD, BENNETT R. — Enl. at 29: Appt., 2 Cpl., Oct. 1, 1862:
(2) Reduced to Pvt.: Present for duty during entire war: Paroled, Appomattox (Apr. 12, 1865).

(1) TAYLOR, RICHARD H. — Enl. at 21: Sick, Summer, 1862: AWOL, Spring, 1863: Deserted, picked up by Feds. in Shelby Co., Tenn., Mar. 24, 1865.

(1) TAYLOR, WALLACE — Enl. at 19: W. & POW, Gettysburg (July 2, 1863): Exchanged, Mar., 1864: Retired for disability, June, 1864.

THOMPSON, F. LESLIE — Recruited at Houston, Tex., Apr. 7, 1862, age 20: W., Chickamauga (Sept. 19, 1863): W., Wilderness (May 6, 1864).

THOMPSON, LESLIE A. — W., Chaffin's Farm (Sept. 29, 1864): Paroled at Thomasville, Ga., May 9, 1865.

(1) TOWNSEND, J. L. — Enl. at 21: Prom., Cpl., June 5, 1862: W., Gaines' Mill (June 27, 1862): While recovering from wound died of typhoid fever, Aug. 7, 1862.

VARNELL, F. W. — Recruited at Galveston, Tex., Mar. 21, 1862, age 28: Sick, Spring, 1862: AWOL: Deserted, Nov. 1, 1863.

(1) VIDOR, CHAS. — See list of "Other Officers" above.
(1) VON HUTTON, WM. B. — Enl. at 25: Hospitalized, Summer & Fall,
(2)   1864: Paroled, Appomattox (Apr. 12, 1865).
(2) WAGNER, M. L. — Enl. at Galveston, Apr., 1862: Confined in Brig.
        Guard House, Apr. 17, 1864: Paroled, Appomattox (Apr. 12,
        1865).
    WAKELEE, AUGUSTUS — Recruited at Galveston, Tex., Mar. 25,
        1862, age 27: W., Darbytown Rd. (Oct. 7, 1864).
(1) WATERS, JOHN D. — Enl. at 18: K., Gettysburg (July 2, 1863).
(2) WELCH, JAS. — Recruited at Galveston, Tex., Apr. 12, 1862, age 28:
        W., Antietam (Sept. 17, 1862): W., Wilderness (May 6, 1864):
        Paroled, Appomattox (Apr. 12, 1865).
(1) WILLIAMS, CHAS. — Enl. at 28: Dischgd. for disability, Oct. 29, 1861.
    WILSON, ROBT. — Recruited at Houston, Tex., Apr. 12, 1862, age 21:
        Transfd. into Co. L from Capt. Mason's Co. D, Cook's Tex.
        Battery of Artillery: Deserted.
(2) WOOD, ALBERT W. — Recruited at Galveston, Tex., Apr. 12, 1862,
        age 18: W., Gettysburg (July 2, 1863): W., Chickamauga (Sept.
        20, 1863): W., Williamsburg Rd. (Oct. 27, 1864): Paroled,
        Appomattox (Apr. 12, 1865).
(1) WORSHAM, CHAS. S. — Enl. at 19: Transfd. to Co. E, 4th Tex. Inf.
        Regt., Nov. 19, 1861.
(1) WORSHAM, JAS. N. — Enl. at 22: Transfd. to Co. E, 4th Tex. Inf.
        Regt., Oct. 1, 1861.
(1) YOUNG, WM. — Enl. at 18: W., Antietam (Sept. 17, 1862): Transfd. to
        hosp. in Tex., Dec., 1862: Paroled, Galveston, Tex., July 5, 1865.
    ZIMMER, WM. — Recruited at Galveston, Tex., Apr. 12, 1862, age 23:
        Prom., Cpl., June 5, 1862: K., Antietam (Sept. 17, 1862).

1ST TEX. VOL. INF. REGT.

COMPANY M — *SUMTER LIGHT INFANTRY*

Company was organized in Trinity County, Texas, and was
mustered into the Confederate service at Sumter, Texas, May 5,
1862.

Key

(1) Original member of Company. (2) Paroled at Appomattox.
K (Killed), W (Wounded), POW (Prisoner of War)
AWOL (Absent Without Leave)

ORIGINAL OFFICERS

(1) BALLENGER, HOWARD Capt. — W. and POW, Antietam (Sept. 17,
        1862): Exchanged: Disabled and returned home: Resgnd., Apr.,
        1864.

(1) SANFORD, WM. T. 1Lt. — W., Antietam (Sept. 17, 1862): Died of wound.
(1) CECIL, Dr. WM. 2Lt. — Prom., 1Lt., Sept. 17, 1862: W. & POW, Knoxville, Tenn., (Nov., 1863): Died, Nov. 27, 1863.
(1) McMINN, JOS. C. 3Lt. — Prom., 2Lt., Sept. 17, 1862: Resgnd., Jan. 18, 1862, for disability.

ORIGINAL NON-COMMISSIONED OFFICERS

(1) McCLAIN, W. Z. ("Zeb") 1Sgt. — Leave granted, Jan., 1863: AWOL, May, 1863.
(1) ROACH, S. D. ("Shady") 2Sgt. — K., Antietam (Sept. 17, 1862).
(1) MOORE, WM. W. 3Sgt. — AWOL, May, 1863: Reduced to Pvt., Summer, 1863: Asgnd. to office of Adj.-Gen., Trans-Miss., Sept. 12, 1863.
(1) MARTIN, WM. T. 4Sgt. — Dischgd., Sept. 20, 1862, "through a mistake."
(1) BROWNLEE, E. PRESLEY 5Sgt. — Died, Mar. 23, 1863 of smallpox.
(1) PEARY (or PEAVY), THOS. W. 1Cpl. — Hospitalized, Fall, 1862:
(2) Prom., 1Sgt., Winter, 1865: Paroled, Appomattox (Apr. 12, 1865).
(1) WEST, A. JACK 2Cpl. — Sick from July, 1862 to Feb., 1863: Thought to have died.
(1) BENNETT, R. O. 3Cpl. — W., Antietam (Sept. 17, 1862): W., Gettysburg (July 2, 1863).
(1) DAY, JAS. 4Cpl. — Reduced to Pvt.: W., Antietam (Sept. 17, 1862).

OTHER OFFICERS

BLACKSHEAR, WM. N. 3Lt. — Orig. Pvt. in Co.: Prom., 4Sgt., Oct. 1, 1862: Elect., 3Lt., Feb. 9, 1863: W., Wilderness (May 6, 1864).
TOWNES, WM. J. 3Lt. — Orig. Pvt. in Co.: W., Antietam (Sept. 17, 1862): Elect., 3Lt., Oct., 1862: Appt. 2Lt., Feb. 4, 1863: Dischgd. as being "deaf", May 26, 1863.
WAGNON, CECIL O. 3Lt. — Transfd. into Co. M as a Pvt. from Co. I, Feb. 18, 1863: Prom., 4Sgt.: Elect., 3Lt., May 30, 1863: W. & POW, Wilderness (May 6, 1864): Paroled, Ft. Delaware, June 6, 1865.
WAGNON, GEO. H. 3Lt. — Orig. Pvt. in Co.: Elect., 3Lt., May 5, 1862: Died of measles in Miss., June 25, 1862.

MUSICIAN

(1) WATSON, SAM S. — Drummer: Hospitalized several times with
(2) rheumatism & anemia: Paroled, Appomattox (Apr. 12, 1865).

PRIVATES

(1) ADAMS, A. JACK — K., Chickamauga (Sept. 18, 1863).

(1)   BARLEY, JOE ("Kit") — Sick in hosp., May-Dec., 1862: Died of asthma, Dec. 18, 1862.

(1)   BASS, JAS. — W. & POW, Antietam (Sept. 17, 1862): Exchanged: Paroled, Natchitoches, La., June 6, 1865.

(1)   BELLAMY, JOHN F. — Jnd. Regt., Oct. 19, 1862: W., Chickamauga (Sept. 19, 1863): AWOL, Nov., 1863.

(1)   BENNETT, RICHARD O. — Enl., May 5, 1862: W., Antietam (Sept. 17, 1862): POW, Gettysburg (July 3, 1863): Confined at Point Lookout, Md.: Exchanged, Mar. 17, 1865.

(1)   BLACKSHEAR, JOHN H. — Dischgd., Sept. 16, 1862, chronic diarrhea.

(1)   BLACKSHEAR, WM. N. — See list of "Other Officers" above.

(1)   BOON, JOSHUA — K., Antietam (Sept. 17, 1862).

(1)   BOWERS, GEO. B. — Hospitalized with pneumonia, Jan. & Feb., 1863: AWOL, Mar., 1863.

(1)   BOWMAN, T. J. — K., Antietam (Sept. 17, 1862).

(1)   BROWN, ALLEN W. — Dischgd. for disability, Sept. 20, 1862.

(1)   BROWNLEE, A. L. — Dischgd. for disability (ulcers), Feb. 24, 1863.

(1)   BURKE, BENJ. — Sick at Jackson, Miss., Summer & Fall, 1862: AWOL, Jan., 1863.

(1)   BURKE, F. MARION — Sick most of 1862 in Va. & Miss. hospitals: Hospitalized for hepatitis, July, 1863: AWOL, Apr., 1864.

(1)   CAPPS, BOLEWARE J. — POW, Middletown, Md., Sept. 15, 1862:
(2)   Confined at Ft. Delaware: Exchanged: Paroled, Appomattox (Apr. 12, 1865).

(1)   CARLTON, JOHN R. — W., Antietam (Sept. 17, 1862): Prom., 1Cpl.: POW, Knoxville, Tenn. (Dec. 3, 1863): Deserted: Enlisted in U.S. Navy at Rock Island (Ill.) Barracks, Jan. 25, 1864.

(1)   CHAMBERS, W. — Sick, Summer, 1862: AWOL, Mar., 1863: Is reported to have deserted.

(1)   DAVIS, ARCH Y. — Died of disease, Sept. 7, 1862.

(1)   DELANEY, JAS. — Died of asthma, Sept. 13, 1862, Richmond, Va.

(1)   DIAL, EPHRAIM — Sick, Fall & Winter, 1862-63: W., Summer, 1863: Paroled, Greensboro, No. Car., May 5, 1865.

(1)   DOMINY, SEBURN — Present for duty during entire war: Paroled,
(2)   Appomattox (Apr. 12, 1865).

       DUNHAM, M. A. — See roster, "Regmtl. Hdqtrs., 1st Tex. Inf." (served in both Co. B & Co. M).

(1)   DUNLAP, CROCKETT — W., Gettysburg (July 2, 1863): W., Chickamauga (Sept. 19, 1863): Leg amputated: Dischgd. for disability.

(1)   EAVES, E. B. — W., Antietam (Sept. 17, 1862): K., Ft. Gilmer near Richmond, Sept. 21, 1864.

(2)   ENFINGER, W. F. — Paroled, Appomattox (Apr. 12, 1865): No other record.

(1)   EVANS, J. T. — W., Antietam (Sept. 17, 1862): Dischgd. for disability: Returned to Tex. and jnd. Philpot's Co. on the Tex. Frontier.

(1)   EVANS, W. C. ("Button") — Prom., 2Sgt.: Prom., 1Sgt.: W., Antietam (Sept. 17, 1862): K., Petersburg (Bermuda Hundred) by shell fire, June, 1864.

(1)   FORSYTHE, WM. E. — W., Chickamauga (Sept. 19, 1863): W., Wilderness (May 6, 1864).

(1) GOODSON, WM. J. — W., Antietam (Sept. 17, 1862): Hospitalized numerous times during war: Paroled, Lynchburg, Va., Apr. 14, 1865.
(1) GRIMES, W. — Present for duty, May, 1862-Feb., 1864: No other record.
(1) HAMILTON, D. H. — Prom., 5Sgt., Fall, 1864: Paroled, Appomattox
(2) (Apr. 12, 1865).
(1) HARRELL, JOHN B. — Died, May 7, 1863 at Petersburg, Va.
(1) HAMILTON, DAVID H. — Hospitalized, Spring, 1863: Prom., 5Sgt.,
(2) Fall, 1864: Paroled, Appomattox (Apr. 12, 1865).
(1) HAWTHORNE, JAS. — Spent most of 1862 in hosp. with rheumatism: AWOL, Spring, 1863.
(1) HAWTHORNE, TURNER E. — Resgnd., July 10, 1862: Re-enl. in Co.,
(2) Oct. 5, 1862: Paroled, Appomattox (Apr. 12, 1865).
(1) HENDERSON, JOHN T. — Died at Richmond of typhoid fever, Sept. 27, 1862.
(1) HENDERSON, THOS. — Died at Richmond of chronic diarrhea, Sept. 8, 1862.
(1) HILL, ANDREW W. — W., Gettysburg (July 2, 1863): POW, near Knoxville, Tenn., Dec. 3, 1863: Confined at Rock Island, Ill.: Paroled, June 20, 1865.
    HINES, JOS. — Died of disease, Aug. 30, 1861.
(1) HUGHES, W. W. — Dischgd. by Medical Board, Dec. 2, 1862, for tuberculosis.
(1) HUTTO, GEO. F. — Died of pneumonia at Richmond, Dec. 25, 1862.
(1) HUTTO, REASON W. — Deserted in E. Tenn., Dec., 1863: Took Fed. oath, Jan. 2, 1864.
(1) IVY, ELIJAH H. — W., Wilderness (May 6, 1864): POW, Farmville, Va., Apr. 6, 1865: Paroled, Newport News, Va., July 3, 1865.
(1) JERNIGAN, W. A. — Sick most of 1862: AWOL, Aug., 1863.
    JOHNSON, GEO. — Dischgd. for disability, July 20, 1862.
    JOHNSON, THOS. — Enl., June 5, 1862 at Corinth, Tex.: POW, near Spotsylvania CH., May 20, 1864: Imprisoned at Pt. Lookout, Md.: Exchanged, Mar. 14, 1865.
(1) JOHNSON, WM. D. — Dischgd. for disability, Sept., 1862.
(1) JONES, JAS. A. — POW, Sept. 12, 1862 near Frederick, Md.: Exchanged, Nov. 10, 1862: W., Wilderness (May 6, 1864): Right arm amputated: Dischgd. from service, Mar. 13, 1865.
(1) JONES, JOHN W. — W., Wilderness (May 6, 1864): Died of wound.
(1) JONES, WARREN — Died of disease, Jan. 24, 1863.
    KERR, JAS. O. M. — Died, Aug. 23, 1862.
(1) KERR, W. ZED. — Sick, Summer, 1862: AWOL, Oct., 1862.
(1) LANCASTER, JOHN — W., Antietam (Sept. 17, 1862): Died of wound.
(1) LOCKE, J. — Prom., 2Cpl., June, 1863: W., Chaffin's Farm (Sept. 29, 1864).
(1) LONGENO (or LONGINO), B. W. — Died in Richmond of pneumonia, Oct. 11, 1862.
(1) LONGENO (or LONGINO), J. B. — Dischgd. for disability (asthma), Oct. 23, 1862.

(1) LOVETT, ISAIAH D. — W. (in both arms & chest), Darbytown Rd. (Oct. 7, 1864): POW, Richmond, Apr. 3, 1865.

(1) LUNDY, GEO. B. — Prom., 4Cpl.: Prom., 4Sgt., June 1, 1863: W.,
(2) Chickamauga (Sept. 19, 1863): Paroled, Appomattox (Apr. 12, 1865).

LUNDY, H. NEWTON — Died of disease at Camp Lee, Va., July 5, 1862.

(1) LUNDY, J. E. — "Left sick on the march to Maryland" (Sept., 1862): No other information.

MARTIN, JAS. — Prom., Cpl.: Prom., 5Sgt., June 1, 1863: K., Wilderness (May 6, 1864).

(1) McBRIDE, OLIVER — W., Antietam (Sept. 17, 1862): K., Wilderness (May 6, 1864).

(1) McCLAIN, RUFUS R. — Enl., May 5, 1862: Dischgd., Oct. 6, 1862 for chronic hepatitis.

(1) McCLAIN, W. R. — Enl. at 17: Dischgd., Sept., 1862 for disability (bronchitis, chronic diarrhea & measles).

(1) McCLENDON, L. M. — Sick in hosp. from May, 1862 to Sept., 1863: W., Williamsburg Rd. (Oct. 27, 1864).

(1) McENTIRE, F. M. — Dischgd. for disability (ulcerated leg), Dec. 26, 1862.

(1) McMINN, E. — Died, Sept. 1, 1862 of remittent fever.

(1) McMINN, H. — Dischgd. for disability (asthma), Oct. 21, 1862.

(1) MORGAN, GREEN ("Mutt") — W., Chickamauga (Sept. 19, 1863): K., Wilderness (May 6, 1864).

(1) MORROW, DANIEL M. — W., Chickamauga (Sept. 19, 1863).

(1) MOTES, HIRAM — Died of disease in Va., June 12, 1862.

(1) MOTES, J. M. — W., Antietam (Sept. 17, 1862): K., Petersburg, June 22, 1864.

(1) MURRAY, THOS. — Sick, Winter, 1862-63: AWOL, Apr., 1863.

(1) NEWMAN, M. HARVEY — Died of disease, Oct. 14, 1862.

(1) OGLESBY, G. W. — K., Chickamauga (Sept. 19, 1863).

(1) PARKER, JAKE — W., Wilderness (May 6, 1864).

(1) PERRY, ROBT. W. — Died of pneumonia, Jan. 7, 1863: Personal effects — 1 bundle of clothes & 1 pocketbook with $8.00 in notes.

(1) PINSON, HARVEY H. — Left sick on march to Md., Sept., 1862: POW, at Williamsport, Md., Sept. 16, 1862: Exchanged: W., Chickamauga (Sept. 20, 1863).

(1) PONDER, JEFF — AWOL, Nov., 1862: Rejnd. Co.: Lost fingers of one hand in accident: Dischgd. for disability.

(1) POPE, E. — W., Antietam (Sept. 17, 1862): W., Chickamauga (Sept. 19, 1863).

(1) RATCLIFF, JOE — K., Chickamauga (Sept. 19, 1863).

(1) REDDEN, HARMON — Enl., May 5, 1862: Broke arm, Mar. 12, 1863: AWOL, Spring, 1863.

(1) REDDEN, WILLIS T. — K., 2nd Manassas (Aug. 30, 1862).

(1) RIGSBY, A. D. — Died of disease, May 7, 1863.

(1) ROACH, WM. A. — Prom., 2Sgt., May 15, 1863: W., Chickamauga
(2) (Sept. 19, 1863): W., Wilderness (May 6, 1864): Paroled, Appomattox (Apr. 12, 1865).

(1) ROGERS, WM. ROM — Died in Va. of asthma, July 3, 1863.
(1) SANDERS, W. R. — Died "of old age [53]" in Richmond, Apr. 28, 1863.
(1) SHAMBURGER, SAM — Died of disease in Richmond, Apr. 4, 1863.
(1) SKINNER, JESSE — Died of disease at Winchester, Va., Oct. 20, 1862.
(1) SLATER, FRANK M. — Prom., 1Cpl., May, 1863: Prom., 3Sgt., July,
(2)   1863: W., Chickamauga (Sept. 19, 1863): Paroled, Appomattox (Apr. 12, 1865).
(1) STANLEY, J. A. — Died near Culpeper, Va., Nov. 10, 1862.
(1) STEVENS, JOHN D. — K., Chickamauga (Sept. 19, 1863).
(1) STEWART, H. CHAS. — W. "and left on battlefield", Antietam (Sept. 17, 1862): Probably died, not reported on Fed. POW lists.
(1) STEWART, JOHN R. ("Muley") — W., Chickamauga (Sept. 20, 1863).
(1) STORY, JAS. W. — K., Antietam (Sept. 17, 1862).
(1) STROTHER, RICHARD ("Buck") — W., Gettysburg (July 2, 1863): POW, Darbytown Rd. (Oct. 7, 1864).
(1) STROTHER, WM. M. — Sick most of 1863 with rheumatism: Deserted, Spring, 1864.
(1) STUBBLEFIELD, SAM — W., Chickamauga (Sept. 19, 1863): Paroled,
(2)   Appomattox (Apr. 12, 1865).
(1) STUBBLEFIELD, T. J. — Dischgd. for "general disability", Sept. 19, 1862.
(1) SWEAT, J. H. — Died of typhoid fever in Richmond, Mar. 30, 1863.
(1) SYLVESTER, WM. — Prom., 1Cpl., Mar., 1864: POW, Spotsylvania, May 19, 1864: Paroled, Elmira, N. Y., June 14, 1865.
(1) THOMPSON, A. — Sick most of 1862: Dischgd., May 7, 1863 for disability.
(1) TOWNES, WM. J. — See list of "Other Officers" above.
(1) TULLOUS, WILLOUGHBY B. — W., Gettysburg (July 2, 1863):
(2)   Paroled, Appomattox (Apr. 12, 1865).
(1) TURNER, WADE H. — Sick most of 1862: K., Wilderness (May 6, 1864).
    VICK, WM. A. — Died of disease at Camp Lee, Va., Aug. 3, 1862.
(1) WAGNON, GEO. H. — See list of "Other Officers" above.
    WALLACE (or WALLIS), GEO. M. — Died of disease, Aug. 2, 1862.
(1) WALTER, A. — W., Antietam (Sept. 17, 1862): Prom., Cpl., June 1, 1863: W., White Oak Swamp (Aug. 16, 1864).
(1) WHEELINGTON, N. A. — Sick most of 1862: Reported AWOL, Dec., 1862: Dropped from rolls, Aug., 1863.
(1) WHITE, JAS. A. — W., Chickamauga (Sept. 19, 1863): Paroled,
(2)   Appomattox (Apr. 12, 1865).
(1) WHITE, W. THOS. — Prom., 4Sgt.: Resgnd. as 4Sgt., July 18, 1862: W.,
(2)   Chickamauga (Sept. 19, 1863): Paroled, Appomattox (Apr. 12, 1865).
(1) WILSON, JOHN — In & out of hosps. most of 1862 & 1863: Paroled,
(2)   Appomattox (Apr. 12, 1865).
(1) WISBY, V. J. — K., Antietam (Sept. 17, 1862).
(1) WRIGHT, J. E. — AWOL since enlisting, May, 1862: Reported killed in Tex., Aug., 1862.

4TH TEX. VOL. INF. REGT.
HDQTRS. - FIELD, STAFF & BAND

Organized as a Regiment (Cos. A thru K, less J) Sept. 30, 1861, near Richmond, Va.

Key

(1) Original member of Hdqtrs. (2) Paroled at Appomattox.
K (Killed), W (Wounded), POW (Prisoner of War)
AWOL (Absent Without Leave)

OFFICERS, FIELD & LINE

(1)   ALLEN, ROBT. T. P. Colonel
        Orig. Col. of the Regt.: Resgnd. on Sept. 30, 1861, and returned to Tex.

        BANE, JOHN P. Colonel
        Orig. Capt., Co. D: W., Gaines' Mill (June 27, 1862): Appt. Maj., Dec. 29, 1862: Appt. Lt.-Col., July 21, 1863: Appt. Col., April 29, 1864: Absent in Tex. under orders of Sec. of War.

        HOOD, JOHN BELL Colonel
        See roster, "Hdqtrs., Hood's Tex. Brig."

        KEY, JOHN C. G. Colonel
        Orig. Capt. of Co. A: Prom., Maj., March 3, 1862, & asgnd. to Hdqtrs., 4th Tex. Inf. Regt., March 12, 1862: Detailed to recruiting duty in Tex., Feb.-Apr., 1862: W., Gaines' Mill (June 27, 1862): Prom., Lt.-Col., June 27, 1862: Prom., Col., July 10, 1862: Retired, April 29, 1864.

(1)   MARSHALL, JOHN Colonel
        Orig. Lt.-Col. of Regt., appt. Oct. 2, 1861: Prom., Col., March 3, 1862, and took cmd. of Regt., March 12, 1862: K., Gaines' Mill (June 27, 1862).

(1)   WARWICK, BRADFUTE Colonel
        Orig. Maj. of Regt., appt. Oct. 2, 1861: Prom. to Lt.-Col.: W., Gaines' Mill (June 27, 1862): Prom., Col., June 27, 1862: Died from wound, July 6, 1862.

        CARTER, BENJ. F. Lieut.-Colonel
        Orig. Capt. of Co. B: Prom., Maj., June 27, 1862: Prom., Lt.-Col., July 10, 1862: W. & POW, Gettysburg (July 2, 1863): Died from wound, July 21, 1863.

(2)   WINKLER, CLINTON M. Lieut.-Colonel
        Orig. Capt. of Co. I: Detailed to recruiting duty in Tex., Feb.-Apr., 1862 & Feb.-Apr., 1863: Prom., Maj., July 21, 1863: Prom., Lt.-Col., April 29, 1864: Paroled, Appomattox (April 12, 1865).

(2) MARTIN, WM. H. ("Howdy") Major
Orig. Capt. of Co. K: Detailed to recruiting duty in Tex.,
Feb.-Apr., 1862: Prom., Maj., April 29, 1864: W., Darbytown
Rd. (Oct. 7, 1864): Paroled, Appomattox (April 12, 1865).
TOWNSEND, W. P. Major
Orig. Capt. of Co. C: Detailed to recruiting duty in Tex.,
Feb.-Apr., 1862: Prom., Maj., July 10, 1862: W., 2nd Manassas
(Aug. 30, 1862): Foot amputated: Appt. on rotary court-martial
of Gen. Wm. J. Hardee's Corps, Winter, 1862-63: Returned to
Tex., Summer, 1863.
MAKEIG, FRED MILLER Ensign/Lieut.
Orig. Pvt., Co. E: Co. Color-Bearer, 1863-64: Appt. Ens.-Lt., June
25, 1864: W. (both thighs) & POW, Darbytown Rd. (Oct. 7,
1864): Confined at Pt. Lookout, Md.: Paroled, June 14, 1865.

OFFICERS, STAFF

ADJUTANTS

(1) BASSETT, ROBT. H.
Orig. 3Lt., Co. G: Prom., 1Lt., Sept., 1861: Appt. Regmtl. Adj.,
Oct. 2, 1861: Absent on recruiting duty in Tex., Feb.-Apr., 1862:
Prom., Capt., June 29, 1862: W., Chickamauga (Sept. 19, 1863):
Disabled, returned to Tex., June 25, 1864.
BROWN, WM. W.
Orig. 3Sgt., Co. A: Absent on recruiting duty to Tex., Feb.-Apr.,
1862: Prom., 2Lt., Oct. 8, 1862: Appt. Regmtl. Adj., Nov. 14,
1862: K., June 20, 1864 near Petersburg, Va.
PRICE, FRANK L.
Orig. 4Sgt., Co. B: Prom., 1Sgt., Co. B, Oct. 9, 1861: Appt.
Regmtl. Adj., July 24, 1862.
SUTHERLAND, JACK A.
Orig. Pvt., Co. F: Appt. Regmtl. Adj., July 20, 1864: W.,
Darbytown Rd. (Oct. 7, 1864).
(2) BRAHAN, HAYWOOD W.
Orig. 1Sgt., Co. F: Prom., 1Lt., Apr. 8, 1863: Appt. actg. Regmtl.
Adj., Winter, 1863-64: On detchd. serv. to Tex., Spring, 1864:
W., Appomattox CH. (April 9, 1865): Last casualty in Hood's
Tex. Brig.: Paroled, Appomattox (April 12, 1865).

SURGEONS
ESTES, H.
Appt. Regmtl. Surg., Dec., 1861: Appt. Medical Director, Hood's
Div., Nov., 1862.
(1)
(2) JONES, JOHN CURTIS
Orig. Asst. Regmtl. Surg., 4th Tex. Inf. Regt., Appt., Oct. 6,
1861: Appt. Regmtl. Surg., May 22, 1863: Attended Gen. Hood
after his leg was amputated at Chickamauga (Sept. 20, 1863):
Present at all engagements of Hood's Tex. Brig.: Paroled,
Appomattox (April 12, 1865).

SCOTT, A. H.
>Appt. Regmtl. Surg., June, 1862: Transfd. to a Richmond hosp., May 26, 1863.

(1) THOMAS, H. L.
>Orig. Regmtl. Surg., appt. Oct. 2, 1861: Transfd. out of Regt., Nov., 1861.

WIRT, WM.
>Appt. Regmtl. Surg., April, 1862: Transfd. out of Regt., June, 1862.

ASST. SURGEONS

JONES, DAVID C.
>Orig. Pvt., Co. C: Served as Regmtl. Hosp. Steward, Nov. 27, 1861-Jan. 21, 1862: Appt. Asst. Regmtl. Surg., Spring, 1862: Detailed as a Surg. at Richmond, Summer, 1862: See list of "Surgeons," roster of "Regmtl. Hdqtrs., 5th Tex. Inf."

OFFUTT, T. Z.
>Asgnd. as Asst. Regmtl. Surg., June, 1862: Transfd. out of Regt., Feb., 1864.

PARK, JOHN E.
>Enl. at 46 as a Pvt. in Co. D, July 14, 1861: Appt. Asst. Regmtl. Surg., Aug. 11, 1861: On special duty at Conf. Medical Dept., Richmond, Nov. 27, 1861: Dischgd. for disability (rheumatism), July 15, 1862.

TERRELL, ED. THOS.
>Orig. Pvt., Co. G: Appt. Asst. Hosp. Steward, Jan. 21, 1862: W., Gaines' Mill (June 27, 1862): Appt. Asst. Regmtl. Surg., Sept. 1, 1863.

COMMISSARY SUBSISTENCE OFFICERS (ACS)

HAMMAN, WM. H.
>Orig. Pvt., Co. C: Prom., Cpl.: Prom., Regmtl. Color-Sgt., Oct. 16, 1861: Actg. Comsy.-Sgt., July, 1862: Appt. Regmtl. Comsy. Off., Aug. 6, 1862: Office abolished at Regmtl. level by Conf. Govt., Aug., 1863.

(1) OWEN, TOM M.
>Orig. 2Lt., Co. H: Appt. Regmtl. Comsy. Off., Oct. 19, 1861: W., Gaines' Mill (June 27, 1862): Died from wound, Aug. 4, 1862.

QUARTERMASTER OFFICER

(1) WADE, JOS. D.
>Orig. 3Sgt., Co. F: Appt. Regmtl. QM Off., Oct. 2, 1861: Absent, sick, Aug., 1862: Transfd. out of Regt., Oct. 12, 1864.

CHAPLAIN

(1) DAVIS, N. A.
>Orig. Regmtl. Chaplain: Absent on recruiting serv. in Tex., Feb.-Apr., 1862: Absent on duty in Richmond, Summer, 1862-Summer, 1863: Resgnd., Nov., 1863.

NON-COMMISSIONED OFFICERS

SERGEANT-MAJORS

BROWN, CHAS. S.
>Orig. Pvt., Co. F: Prom., 2Sgt., Co. F: Appt. Regmtl. Sgt.-Maj., Oct. 7, 1862: K., Wilderness (May 6, 1864).

(1) CUNNINGHAM, J. T.
>Orig. 2Sgt., Co. F: Prom., Regmtl. Sgt.-Maj., Oct. 1, 1861: Resgnd. position, Feb. 1, 1862: On recruiting serv. to Tex., Feb.-Apr., 1862: W. (shoulder), Gaines' Mill (June 27, 1862): Died of wound, July 10, 1862.

(2) DUNN, M. S.
>Orig. Pvt., Co. D: W., Gaines' Mill (June 27, 1862): POW, 2nd Manassas (Aug. 30, 1862): Exchanged: Appt. Regmtl. Sgt.-Maj., May 6, 1864: POW, Darbytown Rd. (Oct. 7, 1864): Exchanged: Paroled, Appomattox (April 12, 1865).

KNIGHT, GEO. N.
>Orig. Pvt., Co. D: Appt. Regmtl. Sgt.-Maj., Feb. 1, 1862: Elect., 3Lt., Co. D, Sept. 1, 1862: Returned to Co. D: Prom., 2Lt., Oct., 1862: Prom., 1Lt., Dec., 1862: Prom., Capt., May 11, 1863: Asgnd. duty as Provost Marshal, Columbus, Ga., Winter, 1863-64: Retired for disability, Sept. 6, 1864.

COLOR-SERGEANTS

FRANCIS, EDW. M.
>Orig. Pvt., Co. A: Prom., 1Cpl., Oct. 10, 1861: Appt. Regmtl. Color-Sgt., May 12, 1862: W., Gaines' Mill (June 27, 1862): W., 2nd Manassas (Aug. 30, 1862): K., Chickamauga (Sept. 19, 1863).

(1) HAMMAN, WM. H.
>See list of "Commissary (or Subsistence) Officers" above.

QUARTERMASTER-SERGEANTS

ARMSTRONG, D. H.
>Enl. as a Pvt. in Co. D at Seguin, Tex., March 17, 1862: Actg. Regmtl. QM-Sgt., Feb. 20, 1864 to Aug. 30, 1864: No record after this date.

ELLIOTT, JOHN B.
>Orig. Pvt., Co. F: Appt. Regmtl. QM-Sgt., April, 1862 to replace Russell Howard: Returned to Co. F, Nov. 1, 1862: Reduced from QM-Sgt. to Pvt.: Absent on sick furlough to Tex., Nov., 1862.

HOWARD, RUSSELL
>Orig. Pvt., Co. F: Appt. Regmtl. QM-Sgt., Nov. 18, 1861: Appt. Attorney-Gen., Terr. of Arizona (CSA), April, 1862.

POLLEY, JOS. B.
>Orig. Pvt., Co. F: Prom., 3Cpl., Oct. 1, 1861: Prom., 2Cpl.: W., Gaines' Mill (June 27, 1862): Appt. Regmtl. QM-Sgt., Nov. 1, 1862: W., Darbytown Rd. (Oct. 7, 1864): Foot amputated: Retired for disability.

(1) STEWART, WM. H.
>See roster, "Hdqtrs., Hood's Tex. Brig."

WEPPRECHT, CHAS.
  Orig. Pvt., Co. D: Prom., 5Sgt., Summer, 1861: Prom., 3Sgt.,
  Summer, 1862: Appt. Regmtl. QM-Sgt., Fall, 1862.

COMMISSARY SUBSISTENCE SERGEANTS
CADDEL, J. D.
  Orig. 5Sgt., Co. I: W. (foot), Gaines' Mill (June 27, 1862): Asgnd.
  as Regmtl. Comsy-Sgt., Oct., 1863 — Feb., 1864: K., Petersburg,
  July 17, 1864.
JONES, W. A.
  Orig. Pvt., Co. C: Appt. Comsy.-Sgt., Aug. 8, 1862.
(1) WAY, CHAS. BURR
  Orig. Pvt., Co. E: Appt. Comsy.-Sgt., Oct. 1, 1861: Sick in
  Richmond, Oct., 26, 1861: Rejnd. Regt., Dec. 15, 1861: Sick in
  hosp. in Charlotte, No. Car., June 22, 1862: Dischgd. on
  certificate of disability, Aug. 7, 1862.

ORDNANCE-SERGEANTS
BRIETZ, A. C.
  Orig. Pvt., Co. G: Appt. Regmtl. Ordn.-Sgt., July 6, 1862: W.,
  Wilderness (May 6, 1864): Retired for disability, Feb. 5, 1865.
(2) BURGES, WM. H.
  Orig. Pvt., Co. D: Appt. Actg. Regmtl. Ordn.-Sgt., May 6, 1864:
  Paroled, Appomattox (April 12, 1865).

HOSPITAL STEWARDS
JONES, DAVID C.
  See roster of "Surgeons" above.
(2) LEONARD, ROBT. H.
  Orig. Pvt., Co. E: Appt. Actg. Hosp. Steward, Nov. 23, 1862:
  Appt. Hosp. Steward, June 3, 1863: Paroled, Appomattox (April
  12, 1865).
REED, GEO. P. L.
  Orig. Pvt., Co. H: Extra duty at Brig. Hosp., Dec. 15, 1861: Appt.
  Hosp. Steward, June, 1862: Prom., 3Cpl.
TERRELL, ED THOS.
  See roster of "Surgeons" above.

BAND

BANDMASTER
COLLINS, DANIEL
  Orig. musician, Co. G: Appt. Regmtl. Bugler, Oct. 1, 1861: Appt.
  Bandmaster, Winter, 1861-62.

DRUM MAJOR
DOCKSTADER, OSCAR
  Orig. musician, Co. F: Appt. Regmtl. Drum Major, March 1,
  1862.

BRASS BAND MEMBERS
(2) COLLIER, ARTHUR H.
  Recruited for Co. H at Montgomery, Tex., March 14, 1862, age

26: Detailed as litter bearer at Gaines' Mill (June 27, 1862): Asgnd. to Regmtl. Brass Band, Summer, 1862: Paroled, Appomattox (April 12, 1865).
(2) FOSTER, B. H.
Recruited for Co. F at Hallettsville, Tex., March 23, 1862: Detailed to Regmtl. Brass Band, Summer, 1862: Paroled, Appomattox (April 12, 1865).
(2) GOOD, D. J.
Orig. musician, Co. E: Asgnd. to Regmtl. Brass Band, Summer, 1862: Paroled, Appomattox (April 12, 1865).
HERNDON, ED. W.
Orig. musician, Co. C: Asgnd. to Regmtl. Brass Band, June, 1862: Transfd. to Co. G, 5th Tex. Inf., Aug. 1, 1863.
(2) HIRST, T. D.
Orig. musician, Co. E: Asgnd., Regmtl. Brass Band, Summer, 1862: Paroled, Appomattox (April 12, 1865).
(2) JETT, J. R. P.
Orig. musician, Co. H: Detailed as litter bearer, Gaines' Mill (June 27, 1862): Asgnd., Regmtl. Brass Band, Summer, 1862: Paroled, Appomattox (April 12, 1865).
MARSHALL, BENJ. W.
Orig. Pvt. in Co. C: Asgnd. to Regmtl. Brass Band, Spring, 1862.
MELTON, J. E.
Orig. musician, Co. I: Asgnd. to Regmtl. Brass Band, 1863.
MITCHELL, ROBT.
Orig. musician, Co. D: Fifer: Asgnd. to Regmtl. Brass Band, Summer, 1862.
PANGLE, HUGH L.
Orig. Pvt. in Co. A: Hospitalized most of 1862 & 1863, disabled: Detailed to Regmtl. Brass Band, Mar. 20, 1864: Paroled, Washington, D.C., May 20, 1865.
(2) STAMPS, PLEASANT R.
Orig. musician, Co. A: Bugler: Asgnd. to Regmtl. Brass Band, Summer, 1862: Paroled, Appomattox (April 12, 1865).
(2) VEAL, FRANKLIN
Recruited for Co. F at Hallettsville, Tex., March 23, 1862: Asgnd. to Regmtl. Brass Band, June, 1862: Paroled, Appomattox (April 12, 1865).
(2) WARNER, CHAS.
Orig. musician, Co. F: Asgnd. to Regmtl. Brass Band, Summer, 1862: Paroled, Appomattox (April 12, 1865).

SPECIALISTS

ARTIFICER

BECK, JACOB
Orig. Pvt., Co. H: Asgnd. as Regmtl. Artificer, Spring, 1862: Deserted at Bristol, Tenn., Dec. 22, 1864.

FARRIER

KEITH, L. D.
   Orig. Pvt., Co. C: Detailed as Regmtl. Blacksmith, Jan. 8, 1862:
   W., 2nd Manassas (Aug. 30, 1862): W. & POW, Gettysburg (July
   2, 1863): Confined at Ft. Delaware: Exchanged, May 3, 1864.

WAGONMASTER

(2)   SHAFFER, H. E.
   Orig. Pvt., Co. G: On extra duty as a Regmtl. Teamster since Nov.
   19, 1861: Appt. Regmtl. Wagonmaster, Nov. 8, 1862: Paroled,
   Appomattox (April 12, 1865).

FORAGEMASTER

THOMAS, JOHN
   Orig. Pvt., Co. H: Asgnd. as Regmtl. Foragemaster, Feb., 1862:
   Asgnd. as Div. (Hood's) Foragemaster, Apr., 1863: Appt. Asst.
   QM & Foragemaster on Gen. Hood's Staff, Army of Tenn.,
   Summer, 1864.

4TH TEX. VOL. INF. REGT.

COMPANY A — *HARDEMAN RIFLES*

Company was organized in Goliad County, Texas, enrolled there
July 11, 1861, and mustered into the Confederate service "for the
war" at Richmond, Virginia, Sept. 16, 1861, by 2Lt. Waller R.
Bullock, CSA.

Key

(1) Original member of Company. (2) Paroled in Appomattox.
K (Killed), W (Wounded), POW (Prisoner of War)
AWOL (Absent Without Leave)

ORIGINAL OFFICERS

(1)   KEY, JOHN C. G. Capt. — See roster, "Regmtl. Hdqtrs., 4th Tex.
   Inf."
(1)   DARDEN, STEPHEN H. 1Lt. — A State Legislator: On furlough to
   Tex., Oct. 20, 1861 until close of State Legislature (Jan. 14,
   1862): Rejnd. Co., Mar. 25, 1862: Elect., Capt., May 20, 1862:
   Resgnd. & returned to Tex., Oct. 1, 1862, because of ill health:
   Appt. Col., 5th Inf. Regt. of Tex. State Troops, 1863, and served
   along Texas coast: Elect. to Conf. Congress, Nov. 21, 1864.

(1) McKEAN, ANDREW J. 2Lt. — Elect., 1Lt., Mar., 1862: W., Gaines' Mill (June 27, 1862): W., Antietam (Sept. 17, 1862): Elect., Capt., Oct. 8, 1862: Resgnd., May 7, 1863.

(1) BOMAR, RICH. M. 3Lt. — Elect., 2Lt., Mar., 1862: POW in Md., Sept. 10, 1862: Paroled: Elect., 1Lt., Oct. 8, 1862: Prom., Capt., May 9, 1863: K., Wilderness (May 6, 1864).

ORIGINAL NON-COMMISSIONED OFFICERS

(1) MARCHANT, HARRY M. 1Sgt. — See list of "Other Officers" following.

(1) BROWN, ALBERT P. 2Sgt. — W., Gaines' Mill (June 27, 1862): Died of wound, July 16, 1862.

(1) BROWN, WILLIAM W. 3Sgt. — See roster, "Regmtl. Hdqtrs., 4th Tex. Inf."

(1) LYNCH, GEO. W. 4Sgt. — See list of "Other Officers" following.

(1) KEYSER, EZRA 5Sgt. — Designated "Comsy.-Sgt." for Co.: Served as Actg. Asst. Regmtl. QM for short period of time: W., accidentally, shot self in foot.

(1) DEEL, JOHN W. 1Cpl. — Resgnd. as 1Cpl., Oct. 14, 1861: W., Gaines' Mill (June 27, 1862): W., Chickamauga (Sept. 19, 1863).

(1) MARTINDALE, DAVID 2Cpl. — Prom., 3Sgt., May 29, 1862: Prom., 2Sgt.: W. & POW, Antietam (Sept. 17, 1862): Died from wound, Dec. 13, 1862.

(1) THOMAS, ROBT. W. 3Cpl. — Prom., 5Sgt., July 30, 1862: W., 2nd Manassas (Aug. 30, 1862): Prom., 4Sgt.: Prom., 3Sgt., Dec., 1862: Returned to Tex.: Permanently disabled.

(1) CHANDOIN, ALONZO D. 4Cpl. — Appt. 2Sgt., June 10, 1863: Prom., 1Sgt., May 6, 1864.

OTHER OFFICERS

MARCHANT, HARRY M. Capt. — Orig. 1Sgt. of Co.: Elect., 3Lt., May 20, 1862: W., Antietam (Sept. 17, 1862): Prom., 2Lt., Oct. 1, 1862: Prom., 1Lt., May 9, 1863: Prom., Capt., May 6, 1864.

LYNCH, GEO. W. 1Lt. — Orig. 4Sgt. of Co.: Prom., 1Sgt., May 29, 1862: W., 2nd Manassas (Aug. 30, 1862): Elect., 3Lt., June 10, 1863: Prom., 2Lt., July 2, 1863: Prom., 1Lt., May 6, 1864: W., Wilderness (May 6, 1864): Permanently disabled.

GARTH, VIRGIL A. 2Lt. — Orig. Pvt. in Co.: Prom., 4Sgt., May 29, 1862: Prom., 3Sgt.: W. and POW, Antietam (Sept. 17, 1862): Rejnd. Co., Dec. 17, 1862: Prom., 2Sgt.: Elect., 2Lt., May 9, 1863: K., Gettysburg (July 2, 1863).

GRUNDY, JOHN H. 2Lt. — Enl. as a Pvt., Mar. 18, 1862: Elect., 3Lt., Aug., 1863: W., Chickamauga (Sept. 19, 1863): Given wound furlough to Tex.: Prom., 2Lt., May 6, 1864: Paroled, Meridian, Miss., May 16, 1865.

MUSICIANS

(1) STAMPS, PLEASANT R. — See roster, "Regmtl. Hdqtrs., 4th Tex. Inf."

(1) HITE, WALTER H. — Drummer: AWOL, Sept. 1, 1862: Returned to Co.: K., Wilderness (May 6, 1864).

PRIVATES

ADAMS, JOHN — Enl. at Gonzales, Tex., Mar. 18, 1862: W., Gaines' Mill (June 27, 1862): Died from wounds (thigh & wrist), July 20, 1862.

(1) ALFORD, JULIUS W. — Died in Richmond hosp., Nov. 22, 1861 of typhoid fever.

(1) ALLIS, MELVIN H. — Asgnd. to scouting duty near the Occoquon R., Nov., 1861: Asgnd. to duty with Brig. Comsy. Dept., Spring, 1862-Spring, 1863: POW near Knoxville, Tenn., Nov. 20, 1863: Confined at Camp Morton, Ind.: Exchanged, Mar. 2, 1865.

(1) BAKER, SAMUEL H. — Dischgd. for disability, Oct. 19, 1861: Rejnd. Co., Dec. 12, 1862: Detailed to hosp. as nurse, Feb. 13, 1863.

BOSTWICK, JOHN R. — Enl. at 38, Mar. 18, 1862: Dischgd. for disability, Oct. 8, 1862.

(1) BROWN, LYCURGUS M. — Died at Dumfries, Va., Dec. 27, 1861.

BURTON, ANDREW J. — Enl., Mar. 18, 1862: K., Gaines' Mill (June 27, 1862).

CALDWELL, JAS. M. — Enl., Mar. 18, 1862: Appt. 5Sgt.: W. (knee) & POW, Gettysburg (July 2, 1863): Exchanged.

(1) CAMPBELL, JESSE E. — Dischgd. for disability (hernia), Dec. 1, 1861.

CAVITT, WM. C. — Enl., Mar. 18, 1862: POW, Suffolk, Va., Apr., 1863: Exchanged: W., Chickamauga (Sept. 19, 1863): Leg amputated: Returned to Tex.

CHANDOIN, BAILEY P. — Enl., in Gonzales Co., Tex., Mar. 18, 1862: W., Antietam (Sept. 17, 1862): Died of wound, Sept. 27, 1862.

CLARK, JOHN — Enl., Mar. 18, 1862: W., Chickamauga (Sept. 19, 1863): Permanently disabled.

COX, LEROY C. — Enl., Mar. 18, 1862: Died of pneumonia at camp hosp. near Richmond, June 22, 1862.

DAVIS, FRANKLIN — Enl., Mar. 18, 1862: W., Antietam (Sept. 17, 1862): Died from wound.

DEARINGTON, GREEN R. — Enl., Mar. 22, 1862: Died, Nov. 8, 1863. Personal effects 30 cents.

(1)
(2) DEEL, PETER J. — Detailed to Tex. Hosp. in Richmond as nurse: Appt. 3Cpl., June 10, 1863: Appt. 4Sgt., May 6, 1864: Paroled, Appomattox (Apr. 12, 1865).

(1) DEMENT (or DEMITT) JAS. P. — Dischgd. for disability, Dec. 14, 1861.

(1) DIXON, JOHN T. — Prom., 5Sgt., Oct. 8, 1862: Prom., 2Sgt.: Prom., 1Sgt., June 10, 1863: W., Wilderness (May 6, 1864): Died from wound, May 15, 1864.

(1) DOYLE, MICHAEL C. — Deserted in E. Tenn., Dec. 11, 1863.

DOYLE, RICHARD D. — Enl., Mar. 18, 1862: Died of typhoid fever, July 6, 1862.

DRENNAN, JOS. A. — Enl., Mar. 22, 1862: Hospitalized, Winter, 1864-65.

DRENNAN, SHEROD A. — Enl., Mar. 22, 1862: K., Chickamauga (Sept. 19, 1863).

(1) ELDRIDGE, JOHN WESLEY — W., Gaines' Mill (June 27, 1862): Leg amputated on June 28, 1862: Perm. disabled and dischgd.

(1) FIELDS, JOHN MILTON — W. & POW, Gettysburg (July 2, 1863):
(2) Confined at Ft. McHenry, Md.: Exchanged: W., Wilderness (May 6, 1864): Paroled, Appomattox (Apr. 12, 1865).

(1) FINLAY, FRANKLIN — W., Cold Harbor (June 3, 1864): Hospitalized with dysentery, Fall, 1864.

(2) FLETCHER, GEO. W. — Enl., Mar. 18, 1862: Paroled, Appomattox (Apr. 12, 1865).

(1) FRANCIS, EDW. M. — See roster, "Regmtl. Hdqtrs., 4th Tex. Inf."

(1) FRANCIS, WESLEY C. — Detailed to duty at CSA Tanyard in Tenn., Dec. 20, 1863.

(1) FREESTONE, BENJ. F. — Died of tuberculosis, Aug. 4, 1862.

FUTCH, ALBERT G. — POW, Antietam (Sept. 17, 1862): Exchgd. & rejnd. Co., Dec. 18, 1862: W. & POW, Chickamauga (Sept. 19, 1863).

(1) FUTCH, JOHN — Extra duty as nurse, Winter, 1862-63: W., Gettysburg (July 2, 1863): W., Chickamauga (Sept. 19, 1863): Paroled, Meridian, Miss., May 17, 1865.

(1) GARTH, VIRGIL A. — See list of "Other Officers" above.

(1) GOLDSTICKER, JOHN A. — Temp. duty as Hosp. Steward, Sept. 21-Oct. 21, 1862: K., Gettysburg (July 2, 1863).

GROSS, PHILLIP A. — W. & POW, Antietam (Sept. 17, 1862): Died from wound.

GRUNDY, JOHN H. — See list of "Other Officers" above.

(1) GUNN, JOHN HENRY — W., Darbytown Rd. (Oct. 7, 1864): Paroled,
(2) Appomattox (Apr. 12, 1865).

(1) HAGGERTY, JAS. M. — On scouting duty, Occoquon R., Nov., 1861: Asgnd. to Brig. QM Dept., Winter, 1861-62: Dischgd. on Spec. Order of Secy. of War, Aug. 13, 1862.

(1) HAGGERTY, JOHN J. — Sick in Tex., Aug., 1861-May, 1862: Courier for Gen. Hood, Aug., 1862: POW, Gettysburg (July 2, 1863): Confined at Ft. Delaware as a "Rebel spy."

(1) HALL, WM. A. — W., Antietam (Sept. 17, 1862): Paroled, Appomattox
(2) (Apr. 12, 1865).

(1) HAMMONS, RILEY N. — W., Antietam (Sept. 17, 1862): AWOL, Feb., 1864: In arrest, Mar. 20, 1864.

(1) HAPPELL, JAS. A. — Dischgd. for disability, Oct. 19, 1861.

(1) HARDEMAN, THOS. M. — Died in hosp. at Knoxville, Tenn., Aug. 31, 1861.

(1) HARRISON, BENJ. J. — Died of pneumonia near Dumfries, Va., Jan. 7, 1862.

HARRISON, (Dr.) ROBT. B. — A physician by profession: Enl. at Gonzales, Tex., Mar. 18, 1862: Absent on sick furlough to Tex. since Aug. 1, 1862: Remained in Tex. to doctor families of soldiers in & around Gonzales.

HILLIARD, ALEX. H. — Enl. at Yorktown, Va., May 1, 1862: W. (thigh), Gaines' Mill (June 27, 1862): Unfit for field duty.

HINES, JOS. J. — Enl., Mar. 18, 1862: Dischgd. for disability (chronic rheumatism), July 29, 1862.

HOLCOMB, WILSON L. — Enl., Mar. 18, 1862: POW, Gettysburg (July 2, 1863): Confined at Ft. Delaware: Escaped.

HOPKINS, JAS. M. — Enl., Mar. 18, 1862: W., 2nd Manassas (Aug. 30, 1862): Unfit for field duty.

(1) JOHNSON, WM. S. — Sick, Winter, 1862-63: Sick furlough to Miss., Fall, 1863: "Permanently disabled since Oct. 1, 1863."

(1) JONES, JOSHUA S. — W., Petersburg (July, 1864): Paroled, Appo-
(2) mattox (Apr. 12, 1865).

(1) JONES, RICHARD H. — Transfd. from Co. A to Co. D, 4th Tex., Aug. 13, 1862.

(1) JONES, SAMUEL K. — Died in Richmond hosp. of typhoid fever, Nov. 17, 1861.

(1) JONES, WM. A. — Died of pneumonia near Dumfries, Va., Feb. 18, 1862.

(1) KELLY, PETER — Dischgd. for disability, Nov. 14, 1861.

(1) KERR, GEO. W. — Dischgd. for disability, Sept. 12, 1861.

KEY, JOHN H. — Enl. at Fredericksburg, Va., Mar. 15, 1862: W., Gaines' Mill (June 27, 1862): In arrest, Mar. 20, 1864: W., Darbytown Rd. (Oct. 7, 1864): Disabled: Paroled, Lynchburg, Va., Apr. 13, 1865.

(1) KING, HENRY B. — Enl. at 43: Dischgd. for disability ("an inflamed old wound from the Mexican War"), July 25, 1862.

(1) LANGFORD, CHAS. F. — W. and POW, Antietam (Sept. 17, 1862): Confined at Ft. McHenry: Exchanged: W., near Petersburg: Died, June 20, 1864.

(1) LANSDOWN, JOHN J. — Died, typhoid fever, Mar. 26, 1862.

(1) LOCKRIDGE, ROBT. W. — W., Gaines' Mill (Sept. 17, 1862): Retired for disability, May 4, 1864.

(1) LOCKRIDGE, WM. T. — Dischgd. for disability (bronchitis & diarrhea), Dec. 13, 1861.

LYLE, FOUNTAIN E. — Enl., Gonzales Co., Tex., Mar. 18, 1862: W., Gaines' Mill (June 27, 1862): Died of wounds, July 5, 1862.

(1) McALLISTER, PETER — Sick in hosp. in Richmond, Oct., 1861-Apr., 1862: Returned to Tex., sick, Summer, 1862: Dischgd. for disability (typhoid fever & impaired eyesight).

(1) McCARTY, JOS. J. — W., Gaines' Mill (June 27, 1862): Detailed as shoemaker, Nov. 12, 1862: Deserted, Sept. 8, 1863: Under sentence of death for murder in Richmond.

(1) McCATHERIN, JOHN B. — Dischgd. for disability (ulcerated leg), Jan. 7, 1862.

(1) McDONALD, DAN — W. (hand & chest), Gaines' Mill (June 27, 1862): K., Chickamauga (Sept. 19, 1863).

(1) McEACHAN, EVANDER — Dischgd. for disability (asthma), Dec. 1, 1861.

(1) McLARAN, JOHN H. — Dischgd. for disability, Sept. 12, 1861.

(1) McLEAN, DANIEL — Dischgd. for disability, Jan. 23, 1862.

(2) MARTIN, ALEX. J. — Enl., Mar. 18, 1862: Present for duty entire war except for 40 day furlough, Spring, 1864: Paroled, Appomattox (Apr. 12, 1865).

(1) MAYSON, FELIX G. — Enl., Mar. 18, 1862: Dischgd. for disability (chronic rheumatism), July 20, 1862.

MELHORN, ABRAHAM B. — Enl., Mar. 18, 1862: W., Gaines' Mill (June 27, 1862): Died of wound, July 5, 1862.

MILEY, DANIEL — Enl., Mar. 18, 1862: Died of typhoid fever, July, 1862.

(1) MINTER, FRANKLIN M. — Died in a Richmond hosp., Nov. 25, 1861.

(1) MITCHELL, ISAIAH — Detchd. duty with Brig. QM as Foragemaster, Dec. 2, 1861: Died, pneumonia, Mar. 28, 1862.

MONTZ (or MUNCE), CHAS. — Enl., Mar. 18, 1862: W., Gaines' Mill (June 27, 1862): Returned to Tex., disabled.

(1) MOONEY, JAS. M. — Died of typhoid fever, Dec. 9, 1861.

(1) MOONEY, WM. D. — Prom., 5Sgt., Dec. 25, 1862: Prom., 3Sgt., May 6,
(2) 1864: Paroled, Appomattox (Apr. 12, 1865).

(1) MUNFORD, THOS. H. — Sick and on furlough to Tex., Aug. 14, 1861: Rejnd. Co., May 1, 1862: Transfd. to Kelly's Co., Waul's Tex. Legion.

(1) MURPHY, JEREMIAH — W., Gaines' Mill (June 27, 1862): W., Malvern Hill (July 1, 1862).

MUSSY, HART — Jnd. Co. as a Sgt.: Paroled at San Antonio, Sept. 26, 1865.

NATIONS, FRANCIS — Enl., Mar. 18, 1862: W. and POW, Antietam (Sept. 17, 1862): Died of wound.

NATIONS, ROBT. H. — Enl., Mar. 18, 1862: Deserted, Rogersville, Tenn., Dec. 13, 1863.

(1) O'BRIEN, HENRY — Born in London, Eng.: Enl. at age 56: Dischgd. for disability (chronic rheumatism), June 10, 1862.

(1) OWENS, GEO. H. — POW, Gettysburg (July 2, 1863): Imprisoned at Ft. Delaware.

(1) PANGLE, HUGH L. — See roster "Regmtl. Hdqtrs., 4th Tex. Inf."

(2) PITMAN, WM. H. — Enl., Mar. 18, 1862: Present for duty at all times since enlmt.: Paroled, Appomattox (Apr. 12, 1865).

(1) POTEET, ARTHUR N. — Prom., 1Cpl., May 25, 1862: W. & POW, Antietam (Sept. 17, 1862): Exchanged.

(1) RODGERS, JOHN T. — Dischgd. for disability (asthma), Nov. 14, 1861.

(1) SANDIFER, JOHN M. — W. (severely in hand), Wilderness (May 6, 1864): Dischgd. for disability, Sept. 29, 1864.

SCANLON, EDW. R. — Enl., Mar. 18, 1862: W., Antietam (Sept. 17, 1862): K., Wilderness (May 6, 1864).

SCHEIDLE, CHRISTIAN — Enl., Mar. 18, 1862: Died, July, 1862.

(2) SIMMONS, THOS. S. — Enl., Mar. 18, 1862: Paroled, Appomattox (Apr. 12, 1865).

SIMPSON, JOE D. — Enl., Mar. 18, 1862: Present for duty to Aug., 1864: No other record.

STANFIELD, ALPHUS M. — Enl., Mar. 18, 1862: W. & POW, Antietam (Sept. 17, 1862).

(1) STANFIELD, EPHRAIM C. — Died, Dec. 17, 1861 of typhoid fever.

(1) STANFIELD, THOS. B. — W., 2nd Manassas (Aug. 30, 1862): Detailed to duty with the Provost Guard, May 10, 1863: W. (severely in hand), Wilderness (May 6, 1864).

STANFIELD, WM. H. — Enl., Mar. 18, 1862: W., Gaines' Mill (June 27, 1862): Appt. 4Cpl., June 10, 1863: POW, Gettysburg (July 2, 1863): Imprisoned at Ft. Delaware: Paroled, June 9, 1865.

(1) STEGALL, HENRY F. — Dischgd. for disability, Oct. 19, 1861.

STEPHANS, GEO. H. — Enl., Mar. 18, 1862: Died of typhoid fever, May 9, 1862.

(1) STEWART, WM. H. — See roster, "Regmtl. Hdqtrs., 4th Tex. Inf."

(1) STIFFLER, HENRY — Drowned in La. on march to Va., Aug. 24, 1861.

(1) STRINGFIELD, JOHN M. — W., Gettysburg (July 2, 1863): Perm. disabled, returned to Tex.

(1) STRONG, NAPOLEAN A. — Prom., 4Cpl., July 30, 1862: W., 2nd Manassas (Aug. 30, 1862): Prom., 2Cpl.: POW, Chickamauga (Sept. 19, 1863): Escaped and rejnd. Co.: W., Cold Harbor (June 3, 1864).

(1) SURRETT, JAS. A. — Prom., 2Cpl., June 20, 1862: W., Gaines' Mill (June 27, 1862): W., Wilderness (May 6, 1864): Died from wound, May 8, 1864.

TEBBS, ALGERNON S. — Enl., Mar. 18, 1862: Detailed as nurse in Richmond hosp., June 21, 1863: AWOL, Sept. 20, 1863: Presumed deserted.

TERRELL, BENJ. S. — Enl., Mar. 18, 1862: W., Antietam (Sept. 17, 1862): Wound furlough to Tex.: Did not return to Co.: Enl. in Col. Jas. Duff's 33rd Tex. Cav. Regt., May, 1864.

(1) THOMAS, THEOPOLIS J. — W., 2nd Manassas (Aug. 30, 1862): Died from wound, Oct. 5, 1862.

(1) THOMPSON, JAS. E. — Prom., 5Sgt., Oct. 10, 1861: Granted 40-day sick furlough to Tex., Jan. 23, 1862. Rejnd. Co., June 10, 1862: Asgnd. to duty in Adjutant's office, Regmtl. Hdqtrs., 4th Tex. Inf., Feb., 1863: Died while on furlough in Ga., Oct. 1, 1863.

(2) THOMPSON, PERRY — Enl., Mar. 18, 1862: Present for duty since enlisting: Paroled, Appomattox (Apr. 12, 1865).

VANN, QUINTON H. — Enl., Mar. 18, 1862: W., 2nd Manassas (Aug. 30, 1862): On wound furlough to May 7, 1863: POW, Gates Co., No. Car., Mar. 5, 1865: Confined at Pt. Lookout, Md.: Paroled, June 21, 1865.

VANN, THOS. S. — Enl., Mar. 18, 1862: W., 2nd Manassas (Aug. 30, 1862): POW, Chattanooga (Oct. 27, 1863): Confined at Camp Morton, Ind.: Transfd. to Ft. Delaware, Mar. 19, 1864: Paroled, June 9, 1865.

WALKER, E. R. — Enl., Mar. 18, 1862: W., 2nd Manassas (Aug. 30, 1862): Wound furlough to Tex.: Did not return to Co.

(1)
(2) WALKER, PAT. H. — W., Antietam (Sept. 17, 1862): Prom., 3Sgt., Mar. 1, 1864: Prom., 2Sgt.: Paroled, Appomattox (Apr. 12, 1865).

(1)
(2) WALKER, WM. B. — Sick in hosp. several times during war: Paroled, Appomattox (Apr. 12, 1865).

(1) WALLACE, THOS. S. — POW, Antietam (Sept. 17, 1862): Paroled: Appt. 5Sgt.: Detailed to Regmtl. QM office, Aug., 1863.
(1) WARD, MARTIN V. — Dischgd. for disability, Dec. 4, 1861.
(1) WATKINS, JAS. — AWOL, since Feb. 22, 1863: $30 reward offered for his return: Returned of own volition and collected reward: Detailed as scout at Division (Hood's) Hdqtrs., Feb., 1864.
(1) WHARTON, JOHN — Deserted in Knoxville, Tenn., Sept. 4, 1861.
WOOD, JOHN A. — W. (finger shot off), Gaines' Mill (June 27, 1862): Disabled & dischgd., Oct. 8, 1862.

4TH TEX. VOL. INF. REGT.
COMPANY B — *TOM GREEN RIFLES*

Company was organized in Travis County, Texas, enrolled at Camp Clark, Tex., July 11, 1861, and mustered into the Confederate service "for the war" at Richmond, Va., on Sept. 16, 1861, by 2Lt. Waller R. Bullock, CSA.

Key

(1) Original member of Company. (2) Paroled at Appomattox.
K (Killed), W (Wounded), POW (Prisoner of War)
AWOL (Absent Without Leave)

ORIGINAL OFFICERS

(1) CARTER, BENJ. F. Capt. — See roster, "Regmtl. Hdqtrs., 4th Tex. Inf."
(1) WALSH, WM. C. 1Lt. — Prom., Capt., June 27, 1862: W., Gaines' Mill (June 27, 1862): Permtly. disabled, returned to Tex., Summer, 1862: Asgnd. Mar. 21, 1863, by Gen. Magruder as Asst. Commandant of Conscripts in Texas.
(1) McLAURIN, JAS. T. 2Lt. — Prom., 1Lt., June 27, 1862: Prom.,
(2) Capt., Aug. 17, 1863: Hospitalized, chronic dysentery, Fall, 1864: Paroled, Appomattox (Apr. 12, 1865).
(1) LAMBERT, ROBT. J. 3Lt. — Detailed to recruiting duty in Tex., Feb.-Apr., 1862: W., Gaines' Mill (June 27, 1862): Prom., 2Lt., June 27, 1862: Died of wound, July 5, 1862.

ORIGINAL NON-COMMISSIONED OFFICERS

(1) GIRAND, F. W., 1Sgt. — Dischgd. for disability, Oct. 8, 1861.
(1) FLUSSER, OLIVER 2Sgt. — K., Antietam (Sept. 17, 1862).

(1) PLAGGE, C. 3Sgt. — Reduced to ranks, June 16, 1862: Dischgd. for disability (lumbago), Sept. 5, 1862.
(1) PRICE, FRANK L. 4Sgt. — See roster "Regmtl. Hdqtrs., 4th Tex. Inf."
(1) MASTERSON, T. W. 5Sgt. — See list of "Other Officers" following.
(1) McANNELLY, C. W. 1Cpl. — Prom., 4Sgt., Oct. 9, 1861: Prom., 3Sgt., June 16, 1862: W., 2nd Manassas (Aug. 30, 1862): Died from wound at Warrenton, Va., Sept. 22, 1862.
(1) PRICE, JOHN T. 2Cpl. — See list of "Other Officers" following.
(1) BURNHAM (or BURNAM), STEPHEN H. 3Cpl. — W., 2nd Manassas (Aug. 30, 1862): Died from wound at Warrenton, Va., Sept. 22, 1862.
(1) CLEMENTS, ROBT. H. 4Cpl. — W., Antietam (Sept. 17, 1862): Dischgd. for disability, Nov. 10, 1862.

OTHER OFFICERS

PRICE, JOHN T. 1Lt. — Orig. 2Cpl. of Co.: Detailed to recruiting duty in Tex., Feb.-Apr., 1862: Prom., 5Sgt., June 16, 1862: W., Gaines' Mill (June 27, 1862): Prom., 2Lt., July 14, 1862: Prom., 1Lt., May 6, 1863.
MASTERSON, T. W. 2Lt. — Orig. 5Sgt. of Co.: Prom., 4Sgt., June 16, 1862: Prom., 3Lt., July 14, 1862: Detailed to recruiting duty in Tex., Feb.-Apr., 1862: Prom., 2Lt., May 6, 1863: W., Chickamauga (Sept. 20, 1863): Returned to Tex. on wound leave, May 1, 1864: Never returned to Co.: Dropped from rolls, Jan. 7, 1865.
(2) FORD, WM. F. 3Lt. — Orig. Pvt. in Co.: Prom., 2Sgt., 1863: Prom., 3Lt., Apr. 1, 1864: W., Wilderness (May 6, 1864): Prom., 2Lt., June 16, 1864: Paroled, Appomattox (Apr. 12, 1865).

MUSICIANS

(1) BUCHNER, (or BUCKNER), C. A. — Appt. musician, Sept. 1, 1861: Litter bearer at Gaines' Mill (June 27, 1862): POW, Antietam (Sept. 17, 1862): Exchanged and rejnd. Co.: Detchd. duty at Tex. Hosp., Richmond.
(1) HORNE, PAUL — Appt. musician, Sept. 1, 1861: Litter bearer at Gaines' Mill (June 27, 1862): Deserted, Winter, 1862-63.

PRIVATES

(1) ADAMS, A. M. — Dischgd. for disability, June 16, 1862.
(1) ADAMS, R. LEE — Died in Richmond hosp., Nov. 18, 1861.
(1) AMMONS, JACOB C. — Died in Richmond hosp., Nov. 7, 1861: Personal effects, $35.00.
BIGLEY, S. B. — Enl. at Natchez, Miss., Apr. 20, 1863: AWOL, Nov. 1, 1863: No other record.

BLACK, LEMUEL — Died in Huguenot Springs (Va.) hosp., Oct. 12, 1862.

(1) BLAKEY, HART G. — K., Antietam (June 27, 1862).

BONNER, J. C. ("Cal") — Enl. at Austin, Mar. 15, 1862: Detailed as nurse at Warrenton, Va., Aug. 31, 1862, following battle of 2nd Manassas: On leave in Tex., Nov., 1862: Declared AWOL, May 3, 1863: Jnd. Col. Jas. Duff's 33rd Tex. Cav. Regt. in Tex., Oct., 1863.

BONNER, J. W. ("Wash") — Enl. at Austin, Mar. 15, 1862: Sick in hosp., Summer, 1862: Furlough to Tex. granted, Nov., 1862: Declared AWOL in Tex., May 3, 1863: Jnd. Col. Jas. Duff's 33rd Tex. Cav. Regt. in Tex., Oct., 1863.

(1) BONNER, M. C. ("Bud") — Died in Richmond hosp., Nov. 4, 1861.

(1) BROWN, WM. HENRY — Dischgd. for disability, Oct. 31, 1861.

(1) BURDITT, MINUS C. — Died of typhoid fever, Aug. 7, 1863.

(1) BURDITT, TOM P. — Hospitalized, Sept., 1862: No other record.

BURDITT, WM. B. — Enl. at Austin, Mar. 13, 1862: W., Antietam (Sept. 17, 1862): Wound furlough granted, Oct., 1862: Declared AWOL since May 4, 1863: Jnd. Tex. Arty. Btry.: Paroled, Austin, July 27, 1865.

BURKE, JAS. — Enl. at Austin, Apr. 4, 1862: Prom., 3Cpl., Mar. 1, 1864: W., Wilderness (May 6, 1864): Received Texas Gold Star for bravery, Feb., 1865.

BURNHAM (or BURNAM), FRANK M. — Enl. at Austin, Mar. 15, 1862: Sick in Richmond hosp., Winter, 1862-63: On detached serv. near Rapidan Station, Va., Spring, 1863: W., Wilderness (May 6, 1864).

(1) CALHOUN, WM. C. — W., 2nd Manassas (Aug. 30, 1862): W., Antietam (Sept. 17, 1862): POW, Morristown, Tenn., Mar. 20, 1864.

CALLAHAN, JOHN C. — Enl. at Austin, Mar. 14, 1862: W., Gaines' Mill (June 27, 1862): K., Antietam (Sept. 17, 1862).

CAMPBELL, A. G. — Enl. at Austin, Apr. 4, 1862: W., 2nd Manassas (Aug. 30, 1862): Dischgd. for disability (lung disease), Nov. 25, 1862.

CARPENTER, WM. G. — Enl. at Austin, Mar. 15, 1862: Hospitalized most of 1862: W. (thigh), Wilderness (May 6, 1864).

(1) CATER, THOS. E. — Furlough to Tex. granted, Feb. 1, 1863: AWOL, May 14, 1863: Enl. in Tex. State Troops.

(1) CATON, H. W. — Detailed to recruiting duty in Tex., Feb.-Apr., 1862: W. (chest), Gaines' Mill (June 27, 1862): Detailed to duty as "Division (Hood's) Detective," Apr. 4, 1863.

CHANDLER, WM. M. — Enl. at Austin, Apr. 15, 1862: W., 2nd Manassas (Aug. 30, 1862): W. (knee), Wilderness (May 6, 1864).

(1) CHUMNEY, J. K. L. — Died in Richmond hosp., Oct. 21, 1861.

(1) COLVIN, GARLAND ("Snooks") — W., Gaines' Mill (June 27, 1862): Prom., 4Sgt., Sept. 22, 1862: Prom., 1Sgt., May 1, 1863: W., Chickamauga (Sept. 19, 1863): POW, East Tenn., Dec. 3, 1863.

COOK, JONATHON — Enl. at Austin, Mar. 17, 1862: Died of typhoid fever in Richmond hosp., May 29, 1862.

COOKE, J. S. W. — Enl., Culpeper CH., Va., June 6, 1862: W. (thigh) & POW, Gettysburg (July 2, 1863): Exchanged, July 11, 1863: AWOL, Austin, Tex., Dec. 1, 1863: Paroled, July 11, 1865.

COOPER, SAMUEL — Enl. at Austin, Mar. 27, 1862: POW, Gettysburg (July 2, 1863): Confined at Ft. Delaware: Took Fed. oath, Feb. 13, 1865.

(2) COX, LOUIE B. — Enl. at Austin, Mar. 17, 1862: W., Wilderness (May 6, 1864): Paroled, Appomattox (Apr. 12, 1865).

(1) CRONIN, J. C. — Dischgd. by order of Secretary of War, Oct. 28, 1861.

(1) CROZIER, GRANVILLE H. — W. (abdomen), Gaines' Mill (June 27, 1862): W., 2nd Manassas (Aug. 30, 1862): Wound leave to Tex.: AWOL, May 6, 1863: Paroled at Austin, Tex., July 27, 1865.

(1) DAVIDGE, ROBT. A. — POW, Antietam (Sept. 17, 1862): Exchanged: Detailed as clerk in office of Adj., Tex. Brig., Dec. 15, 1862: POW, Chickamauga (Sept. 19, 1863).

(1) DEARING, JAS. H. — Detailed to duty with Regmtl. QM as a teamster, Dec. 12, 1861: Rejnd. Co., Dec. 1, 1862: Prom., 1Cpl.: Detailed as courier to Gen. Micah Jenkins: POW, East Tenn., Mar. 20, 1864: Escaped: K., Darbytown Rd. (Oct. 7, 1864).

(1) DELLEY, JOHN — Dischgd. by order of Secretary of War, Oct. 28, 1861.

(1) DENSON, JAS. H. — Dischgd. for disability, Nov. 6, 1861.

(1) DOHME, C. A. — Sick in hosp., May, 1862-Apr., 1863: Furlough granted to Tex., June, 1863: AWOL, Oct., 1863.

DUNKIN, G. W. — Enl., Bastrop, Tex., Apr. 1, 1862: W., 2nd Manassas (Aug. 30, 1862): Died from wound at Warrenton, Va., Sept. 19, 1862.

(1) DONAHUE, R. G. — Dischgd. for disability, Nov. 14, 1861.

(2) DUNSON, J. K. P. — Enl., Austin, Apr. 1, 1862: Hospitalized, June-Oct., 1862: Paroled, Appomattox (Apr. 12, 1865).

(1)
(2) DURFEE, A. A. — Detailed to duty with QM Section, Tex. Brig., Dec. 15, 1861: Rejnd. Co., May 10, 1862: Detached serv. in hosp., Winter, 1862-63: W. (abdomen), Wilderness (May 6, 1864): Paroled, Appomattox (Apr. 12, 1865).

FALLS, JOHN — Enl. at Austin, Mar. 17, 1862: W. (leg), Gaines' Mill (June 27, 1862): AWOL, Va., Sept., 1862.

(1) FAWCETT, NILES — Prom., 1Cpl., Oct. 9, 1861: W., Gaines' Mill (June 27, 1862): Prom., 4Sgt.: K., 2nd Manassas (Aug. 30, 1862).

(1)
(2) FLANIKEN, WM. J. — Prom., 3Cpl., Sept. 22, 1862: Prom., 2Cpl., 1863: Prom., 5Sgt., Mar. 1, 1864: W., Wilderness (May 6, 1864): Paroled, Appomattox (Apr. 12, 1865).

(1) FORD, WM. F. — See list of "Other Officers" above.

FOSTER, WM. K. — Enl. at Austin, Mar. 13, 1862: POW, Knoxville, Tenn., Dec. 10, 1863: Confined at Camp Chase, Ohio.

(1) FREEMAN, CLEMENT L. — W., Gaines' Mill (June 27, 1862): W., Wilderness (May 6, 1864): POW, Chaffin's Farm (Sept. 29, 1864): Confined at Pt. Lookout, Md.: Paroled, May 13, 1865.

(1) FREEMAN, S. M. ("Pony") — Died of pneumonia in Richmond hosp., Apr. 9, 1862.

GEORGE, ALFRED — Enl. at Houston, Mar. 15, 1863: Prom., 5Sgt., 1863: Prom., 3Sgt., 1864: W., Wilderness (May 6, 1864): Arm amputated.

(1) GILES, VAL C. — W., Gaines' Mill (June 27, 1862): Prom., 4Cpl., Nov. 10, 1862: Prom., 4Sgt., May 1, 1863: POW, Raccoon Mtn. (Oct. 28, 1863): Imprisoned at Camp Morton, Ind.: Escaped and returned to Tex., Nov., 1864.

(1) GLASSCOCK, THOS. A. — W., Antietam (Sept. 17, 1862): W., Chickamauga (Sept. 19, 1863).

GOULD, URIAH — Enl. at Bastrop, Tex., Mar. 23, 1862: W., Antietam (Sept. 17, 1862): Deserted near Dandridge, Tenn., Jan. 18, 1864.

(1) GREGG, ALEXANDER — Died at Dumfries, Va., Dec. 11, 1861.

(1) GRIFFITH, JOHN — W., Gaines' Mill (June 27, 1862): W., Antietam (Sept. 17, 1862): AWOL in Tex., Nov. 1, 1863.

(1) GRUMBLES, PERRY B. — Prom., 5Sgt., Aug. 31, 1862: K., Gettysburg (July 2, 1863).

(1) HAMBY, WM. ROBT. — W., 2nd Manassas (Aug. 30, 1862): Detailed as nurse to wounded at Winchester, Va., Sept. 30, 1862: Dischgd. for disability, Nov. 4, 1862.

HAMILTON, H. — Enl. at Austin, Mar. 27, 1862: Died of typhoid fever, July 4, 1862.

HAMILTON, S. W. — Enl. at Austin, Apr. 2, 1862: Hospitalized, Spring, 1863: Furlough to Tex., June, 1863: Did not return.

(1) HARALSON, CHAS. S. — Dischgd. from Co. B and commissioned as a Lt. in the Conf. States Navy, Mar. 26, 1863. (Haralson attended the U.S. Naval Academy at Annapolis in 1853 & 54).

(1) HARRIS, JOSIAH — Dischgd. for disability, Nov. 6, 1861.

HATHORN, A. J. — Enl. at Austin, Apr. 5, 1862: W., Antietam (Sept. 17, 1862): W. & POW, Gettysburg (July 2, 1863).

(1) HAYNES, J. J. — Transfd. to the 2nd La. Inf. Regt., Oct., 1862.

(1) HENDERSON, J. B. — W., Chickamauga (Sept. 19, 1863): Paroled,
(2)   Appomattox (Apr. 12, 1865).

(1) HERBERT, WM. C. — Dischgd. for disability, Jan. 2, 1862.

(1) HILL, L. D. — Detailed as hosp. orderly, Nov. 27, 1861: Detailed as nurse at sick camp (Va.), June 18, 1862: Detailed to hosp. at Warrenton, Va., Sept., 1862: Detailed to duty in CSA Post Office Dept., Dec. 4, 1863.

(1) HOFFLER, G. W. — W., Antietam (Sept. 17, 1862): Died from wound.

(1) HOLCOMB, CARTER — Dischgd. for disability, Nov. 6, 1861: Died in Richmond, Jan., 1862.

(1) HOLDEN, D. W. — W., Gaines' Mill (June 27, 1862): Left sick near Freeman's Ford, Aug. 20, 1862: Rejnd. Co., Oct. 30, 1862: W., Chaffin's Farm (Sept. 29, 1864).

(1) HOPSON, BRIGGS W. — W., 2nd Manassas (Aug. 30, 1862): W., Antietam (Sept. 17, 1862): Wound furlough to Tex.: AWOL, Tex., Feb. 25, 1863.

(1) HORTON, WARREN H. — W. (head), Gaines' Mill (June 27, 1862): POW, Gettysburg (July 2, 1863): Confined at Ft. Delaware: Paroled, Apr., 1865.

(1) HOWARD, A. JEFF — W., Gaines' Mill (June 27, 1862): W., Chaffin's Farm (Sept. 29, 1864).

(1) HOWARD, ROBT. J. — Dischgd. for disability, Dec. 17, 1861: Enl. in Echol's Btry., Atlanta, Ga., Dec. 2, 1862: Transfd. back to Co. B, 4th Tex., Apr., 1863: W. (abdomen), Gettysburg (July 2, 1863): K., Spotsylvania CH. (May 10, 1864).

HUGHES, JOHN J. — Enl., Austin, Mar. 17, 1862: W. (leg), Gaines' Mill (June 27, 1862): Returned to Tex. on leave & jnd. another unit in Tex.

JONES, A. C. — Enl. at 47 at Austin, Mar. 15, 1862: Dischgd. for chronic rheumatism, Aug. 2, 1862.

(1) JONES, ETANIEL — W. (severely, left leg), Gaines' Mill (June 27, 1862): Dischgd. for disability, Aug. 20, 1863.

(1) JONES, J. K. P. — Sick, Dec., 1861: Present for duty, Jan., 1862 to June, 1863: No other record.

(1) JONES, JOE E. — Appt. 2Cpl., Mar. 1, 1864: Appt. 1Cpl.: Paroled,
(2) Appomattox (Apr. 12, 1865).

KELLER, J. H. — W., Gaines' Mill (June 27, 1862): Wound furlough to Tex.: Arm amputated, Sept., 1862.

(1) KELLER, WM. A. — W. (severely in arm), Gaines' Mill (June 27, 1862): Dischgd. for disability, Sept. 4, 1862.

LESSING, WM. H. — Enl. at Austin, Mar. 13, 1862: W. & POW, Antietam (Sept. 17, 1862): Exchanged: Perm. disabled, returned to Tex.

(1) LIGHTFOOT, W. H. — Detailed to Confederate Comsy. Dept., from Aug., 1862 to end of war.

(1) LUCKETT, ALF. T. — W. (jaw), Wilderness (May 6, 1864): Paroled,
(2) Appomattox (Apr. 12, 1865).

(1) MAIER, HUGO — K., Antietam (Sept. 17, 1862).

(1) MARCKMAN, C. RAMON — W. (throat & shoulders), Gaines' Mill (June 27, 1862): Wound furlough to Tex., Nov. 12, 1862: Disabled, never returned to Co.

(2) MASTERSON, ARCHIBALD R. — Enl. at Houston, Mar. 18, 1863: W. (arm), Darbytown Rd. (Oct. 7, 1862): Prom., 4Cpl.: Paroled, Appomattox (Apr. 12, 1865).

(1) MAYFIELD, E. N. — Dischgd. for disability, Dec. 17, 1861.

(2) MAYFIELD, NEWTON W. ("Old Burnsides") — Enl., Austin, Mar. 15, 1862: W., 2nd Manassas (Aug. 30, 1862): Unfit for field duty: Detailed to Div. Train as a teamster, Dec. 12, 1862: Paroled, Appomattox (Apr. 12, 1865).

McCARTHY, W. C. — Transfd. into Co. B, 4th Tex. Inf. at Winchester, Va., Oct. 15, 1862 from Maj. Inges' Battery of "Miss. Conscripts:" W. (thigh), Gettysburg (July 2, 1863).

(1) McGEHEE, JOHN F. — W., Antietam (Sept. 17, 1862): Wound furlough to Tex. granted Apr. 12, 1863: AWOL, San Marcos, Tex., May 30, 1863: Paroled at San Antonio, Aug. 12, 1865.

(1) McMATH, M. W. — Detchd. serv. to hosp. in Danville, Va., from July, 1862 to Aug., 1864: No other record.

(1) McMULLEN, BERNARD — Detailed to duty in Richmond hosp., May, 1862 to June, 1863: No other record.

McPHALL, CAMPBELL M. — Deserted near Dandridge, Tenn., Jan. 18, 1864.

(1) MILLICAN, EDW. B. — Granted leave to Tex., Nov., 1862: Never returned to Co.: Jnd. Co. A, Cater's Tex. Cav. Btln.: Prom., 1Lt.: Paroled, Austin, Tex., July 27, 1865.

MINOR, ARTHUR L. — Died of typhoid fever & pneumonia, Apr. 16, 1864.

(1) MORRIS, CHAS. L. — W., Gaines' Mill (June 27, 1862): K., Knoxville, Tenn. (Nov., 1864).

(1) MOSELEY, SIDNEY E. — W., Gaines' Mill (June 27, 1862): Prom., 2Cpl., July 24, 1862: Prom., 3Sgt., 1863: Prom., 2Sgt.: W., Wilderness (May 6, 1864): W. & POW, Darbytown Rd. (Oct. 7, 1864): Leg amputated.

(1) MOSS, WM. V. — Sick in Lynchburg, Va., June, 1862-Apr., 1863: AWOL in Va., Jan. 10, 1864: In arrest since March 27, 1864: Rejnd. Co., May, 1864: Paroled, Winchester, Va., June 8, 1865.

NICHOLS, A. W. — Enl. at Austin, Mar. 15, 1862: W., Seven Pines (June 1, 1862): POW, Antietam (Sept. 17, 1862): Exchanged: Granted leave in Tex.: Did not return to Co.: Paroled, Austin, June 27, 1865.

(1) NICHOLS, GEO. W. — W., Gaines' Mill (June 27, 1862): Detailed as orderly to Comdr. of 4th Tex., Sept. 7, 1862: Prom., 4Cpl., May 1, 1863: K., Chickamauga (Sept. 19, 1863).

(1) NORRIS, MOSES T. — Prom., 5Sgt., July 24, 1862: Prom., 2Sgt., May 1, 1863: K., Gettysburg (July 2, 1863).

(1) NUENDORFF, MAX — Dischgd. for disability, July, 1862: Paroled, San Antonio, Tex., Aug. 4, 1865.

(1) PHILIPS, W. J. — Died in Fredericksburg, Va. hosp., Nov. 1, 1861.

PIPER, WM. L. — Enl. at Austin, Mar. 15, 1862: W. (knee), Gaines' Mill (June 27, 1862): W., Antietam (Sept. 17, 1862): Wound furlough granted: AWOL in Tex., May 1, 1863.

(1) POSEY, A. W. — Dischgd. for disability, Dec. 4, 1861.

PUCKETT, LEMUEL — Enl. at Austin, Mar. 17, 1862: Deserted at Suffolk, Va., May 3, 1863.

PURYEAR, WM. E. — Enl. at Austin, Mar. 17, 1862: POW, Gettysburg (July 2, 1863): Confined at Ft. Delaware: Paroled, June 9, 1865.

RAILEY, JOHN D. — Enl. at Bastrop, Tex., Apr. 6, 1862: W., Gaines' Mill (June 27, 1862): Wound furlough granted: AWOL in Tex., May 2, 1863.

(2) RICE, A. R. ("Old Pontoon") — Enl. at Austin, Mar. 22, 1862: Detailed to duty in Richmond hosp., Oct. 27, 1862: Rejnd. Co., Mar. 19, 1863: Extra duty as Provost Guard, Spring, 1863: Paroled, Appomattox (Apr. 12, 1865).

(1) RIPETOE, JAS. M. — Died in Richmond hosp., Nov. 16, 1861.

(1) ROBERTS, ALBERT S. — Enl. at 16: W. & POW, 2nd Manassas (Aug. 30, 1862): Paroled on Nov. 7, 1862: Detailed to duty as courier for Gen. Hood, Nov. 7, 1862: Detailed as courier to Gen. Field, Feb., 1864.

(1) ROBERTSON, GEO. L. — Prom., 1Cpl., July 24, 1862: W. (neck & shoulder) & POW, Antietam (Sept. 17, 1862): Exchanged: Wound furlough granted, Dec., 1862: AWOL in Tex. since May 3, 1863: Paroled, Austin, July 27, 1865.

ROBERTSON, ROBT. R. ("Radway's Ready Relief") — Enl. at Austin, Mar. 13, 1862: Prom., 2Sgt., Sept. 17, 1862: On detchd. serv. at Marshall, Tex., May 12, 1863 to end of the war: Paroled, Austin, July 27, 1865.

(1) ROGERS, J. B. — Dischgd. for disability, Nov. 6, 1861.

(1) ROSE, GEO. W. — Dischgd. for disability (chronic rheumatism), Oct. 3, 1862.

(1) RUSHTON, CHAS. H. — W. (leg), Gaines' Mill (June 27, 1862): POW, Chickamauga (Sept. 19, 1863): Confined at Camp Douglas, Ill.: Paroled, May 17, 1865.

RUST, ROBT. S. — Enl. at Austin, Mar. 18, 1862: Prom., 1Sgt., July 24, 1862: W. & POW, Antietam (Sept. 17, 1862): Exchanged: Reduced to 3Sgt., May 1, 1863.

SCHULER, JOHN — Enl., Austin, Apr. 11, 1862: W. (leg), Gaines' Mill (June 27, 1862): Detailed to duty with CSA Nitre and Mining Bureau, Richmond, Dec., 1862.

(1) SHEPPERD, ELI — Died in a Dumfries, Va. hosp., Dec. 20, 1861.

SIMMONS, EDW. — Enl. at Austin, Apr. 4, 1862: Dischgd. for disability (lunatic), July, 1862. (Simmons was reported to have been a patient at the lunatic asylum in Austin when he enlisted.)

STANLEY, A. E. — Enl. at Austin, Mar. 27, 1862: Sick in hosp., June, 1862-June, 1863: Detailed to duty in QM Dept. as a shoemaker, Feb., 1864: Sick in hosp. in Richmond, Summer, 1864: Retired to Invalid Corps, Dec. 23, 1864 (heart trouble).

(1) STEIN, ISAAC — W., 2nd Manassas (Aug. 30, 1862): Arm amputated: Dischgd. for disability, Feb. 8, 1863.

(1) STEVES, FRANK K. — Sick, Summer, 1862: Asgnd. to duty with Regmtl. QM, Mar. 18, 1863: Deserted near Dandridge, Tenn., Jan. 18, 1864.

STONE, SAMUEL T. C. ("Dock") — Enl., Austin, Mar. 31, 1862: W., 2nd Manassas (Aug. 30, 1862): Unfit for Inf. service due to wounds: Transfd. to Terry's Tex. Rangers (8th Tex. Cav. Regt.), Fall, 1862: Paroled, Talladega, Ala., May 13, 1865.

(1) STROHMER, FRANK — POW, Chickamauga (Sept. 19, 1863): Confined at Camp Douglas, Ill.: Paroled, June 14, 1865.

(1) SUMMERS, JOHN S. — K., Gaines' Mill (June 27, 1862).

(1) TANNEHILL, WM. J. — Hospitalized 8 wks., typhoid fever, Winter,
(2) 1861-62: Prom., 3Cpl., 1863: Prom., 2Cpl., Mar. 1, 1864: Paroled, Appomattox (Apr. 12, 1865).

TATUM, JOHN M. — Enl., Austin, Mar. 15, 1862: Died in Richmond hosp., Jan. 5, 1863.

TAYLOR, SAM C. — Enl., Austin, Mar. 15, 1862: Dischgd. for disability (asthma), July 27, 1862.

(1) TEAGUE, S. P. — Under arrest for charges preferred Nov. 14, 1862: W.
(2) (leg), White Oak Swamp (Aug. 16, 1864): Paroled, Appomattox (Apr. 12, 1865).

(1) THOMAS, JAS. H. — K., 2nd Manassas (Aug. 30, 1862).

(1) THOMAS, MARCUS — W., Gaines' Mill (June 27, 1862): Detailed as a teamster in the Regmtl. QM section, Apr. 1, 1863.

(1) TODD, D. A. — Detailed as nurse for wounded at Winchester, Va., Aug.
(2) 31, 1862: W. (hand), Wilderness (May 6, 1864): Paroled, Appomattox (Apr. 12, 1865).

(1) THORNTON, L. C. — Dischgd. for disability, Oct. 31, 1861.

(1) WAGONER, A. G. — Dischgd. for disability, Nov. 6, 1861.

WALKER, G. W. — Enl., Bastrop, Tex., Apr. 5, 1862: W., Chickamauga (Sept. 19, 1863): W. & POW, Knoxville, Dec. 1, 1863: Died at Fed. hosp. (Middle Brook) near Knoxville, Dec. 5, 1863.

WAX, L. B. — W., Frayser's Farm (June 30, 1862): No other record.
WHEELER, JOHN GILL — Enl., Austin, Apr. 7, 1862: An editor by profession: W., Wilderness (May 6, 1864): Left arm amputated: Retired to Invalid Corps, July 28, 1864.
(1) WHITE, J. A. — Sick most of 1862: Dischgd. for disability (VD), Oct., 1862.
(1) WHITESIDES, HUGH A. — POW, Antietam (Sept. 17, 1862): Exchanged: Detailed to Regmtl. QM as a teamster, Dec. 16, 1862: POW, Cherry Run, Va., July 19, 1863: Took Fed. oath, July 25, 1863.
(1) WILSON, SAM C. — Sent to Charlotte, N. C. to get clothing for Regt., Summer, 1861: W. (side), Wilderness (May 6, 1864): W. (arm), Darbytown Rd. (Oct. 7, 1864).
(1) WOODWARD, F. LOGAN — Died in Richmond hosp., Nov. 10, 1861.
WRIGHT, JAS. A. — Dischgd. for disability (heart trouble), Oct. 20, 1862.
WRIGHT, PEYTON A. — Died in sick camp near Richmond, June 20, 1862.

NEGRO SERVANTS

PRICE, JOHN ("Uncle John") — Body servant and cook to Lt. John T. Price: Had many opportunities to desert to Federals but remained with Lt. Price to the end and returned to Tex. where he voted Democratic "to the end."
JOHNSON, HENRY — Company barber and body servant to Capt. B. F. Carter: Buried his master after Gettysburg: Went to Baltimore to live.

4TH TEX. VOL. INF. REGT.

COMPANY C — *ROBERTSON FIVE SHOOTERS*

Company was organized in Robertson County, Texas, enrolled there July 15, 1861, and mustered into the Confederate service "for the war" at Richmond, Virginia, on Sept. 18, 1861, by 2Lt. Waller R. Bullock, CSA.

Key

(1) Original member of Company. (2) Paroled at Appomattox.
K (Killed), W (Wounded), POW (Prisoner of War)
AWOL (Absent Without Leave)

ORIGINAL OFFICERS

(1) TOWNSEND, WM. P. Capt. — See roster, "Regmtl. Hdqtrs., 4th Tex. Inf."

(1) BARZIZA, DECIMUS ET ULTIMUS 1Lt. — Prom., Capt., June 27, 1862: W., 2nd Manassas (Aug. 30, 1862): W. & POW, Gettysburg (July 2, 1863): Escaped: Retired on Surgeon's Cert., June 21, 1864.

(1) TURNER, BENJ. F. 2Lt. — Prom., 1Lt., June 27, 1862: Resgnd., Aug. 16, 1862.

(1) WOOD, PETER S. 3Lt. — W., Gaines' Mill (June 27, 1862): Prom., 2Lt., July 1, 1862: Leg amputated: Died of wound, July 8, 1862.

ORIGINAL NON-COMMISSIONED OFFICERS

(1) GRIZZLE, JNO. P. 1Sgt. — See list of "Other Officers" following.

(1) DAVIS, H. W. 2Sgt. — Asgnd. to recruiting serv. in Tex., Feb.-Apr., 1862: W., Gaines' Mill (June 27, 1862): W. & POW, Gettysburg (July 2, 1863): Exchanged: Prom., 1Sgt., July 12, 1864.

(1) ROBERTS, JOHN C. 3Sgt. — W., Gaines' Mill (June 27, 1862): Right arm amputated: Dischgd. for disability.

(1) GALLOWAY, JAS. L. 4Sgt. — W., Gaines' Mill (June 27, 1862): W., 2nd Manassas (Aug. 30, 1862): Leg amputated: Dischgd. for disability.

(1) SIMMONS, J. A. 5Sgt. — W., Gaines' Mill (June 27, 1862): K., Chickamauga (Sept. 19, 1863).

(1) STREETMAN, A. P. 1Cpl. — K., Gaines' Mill (June 27, 1862).

(1) HILL, JOHN W. M. P. 2Cpl. — W., Gaines' Mill (June 27, 1862): Arm amputated: Dischgd. for disability.

(1) LIVINGSTON, M. 3Cpl. — See list of "Other Officers" following.

(1) WOOD, EGBERT O. 4Cpl. — Prom., 1Sgt., July 26, 1862: W., 2nd Manassas (Aug. 30, 1862): K., Chickamauga (Sept. 19, 1863).

OTHER OFFICERS

LIVINGSTON, M. Capt. — Orig. 3Cpl. of Co.: Prom., 5Sgt.: Prom., 2Lt., July 15, 1862: Prom., 1Lt., Aug. 12, 1862: W., Gettysburg (July 2, 1863): W., Chickamauga (Sept. 20, 1863): Prom., Capt., June 21, 1864: W., Chaffin's Farm (Sept. 29, 1864).

(2) BOYD, J. C. B. 1Lt. — Orig. Pvt. in Co.: Prom., 3Cpl.: W., Gaines' Mill (June 27, 1862): Prom., 3Lt., Nov. 5, 1862: W., Wilderness (May 6, 1864): Prom., 2Lt., June 12, 1864: W., Chaffin's Farm (Sept. 29, 1864): Prom., 1Lt., Fall, 1864: Paroled, Appomattox (Apr. 12, 1865).

GRIZZLE, JNO. P. 1Lt. — Orig. 1Sgt. of Co.: Prom., 3Lt., July 25, 1862: Prom., 2Lt., Aug. 12, 1862: W., Wilderness (May 6, 1864): Prom., 1Lt., June 21, 1864: W., Darbytown Rd. (Oct. 7, 1864): Died of wound.

MUSICIANS

(1) BAILEY, W. L. — Orig. musician in Co.: W. (chest), Gaines' Mill (June 27, 1862): Wound furlough to Tex., Sept., 1862: Never returned to Co.

(1) HERNDON, ED. W. — See roster, "Regmtl. Hdqtrs., 4th Tex. Inf."
(1) MARSHALL, BENJ. W. — See roster, "Regmtl. Hdqtrs., 4th Tex. Inf."

PRIVATES

(1) ACRUSE, PILER — Dischgd. for disability (chronic rheumatism), Aug. 5, 1862.
(1) ADAMS, J. M. — On duty as a scout, Fall, 1861: Detailed as a Brig.
(2) Provost Guard, Apr., 1863: Prom., 2Sgt.: W., Wilderness (May 6, 1864): Paroled, Appomattox (Apr. 12, 1865).
(1) ADAMS, J. O. — Prom., Cpl., Dec., 1861: K., Gaines' Mill (June 27, 1862).
ALEXANDER, W. J. — Enl., Port Sullivan, Tex., Mar. 4, 1862, age 22: W. (elbow), Antietam (Sept. 17, 1862): Granted wound furlough, Oct. 15, 1862: Dischgd., July 21, 1863.
(1) ALLDAY, PETER R. — Died, Dumfries, Va., Nov. 25, 1861.
(1) ANDERSON, JOHN D. — Dischgd. at Richmond, Dec. 6, 1861.
(1) ANDREWS, A. N. — Asgnd. extra duty as ambulance driver, Fall, 1862: Sick much of 1863: Leave granted to Tex.: AWOL, Feb., 1864.
(1) BARTON, FRANK — W. (arm), Gaines' Mill (June 27, 1862): W. (knee), Chickamauga (Sept. 19, 1863): Wound furlough to Tex.: Never returned to Co.
(1) BARTON, JOHN M. — W., Antietam (Sept. 17, 1862): Right arm amputated: Dischgd. for disability.
(1) BARTON, LEMUEL — W., Antietam (Sept. 17, 1862): Right arm amputated: Dischgd. for disability, April, 1864.
(1) BARZIZA, P. I. — Appt. agent for 4th Tex. Inf. Regt. at the Tex. Depot in Richmond, June, 1862: Prom., 5Sgt.: W., Chickamauga (Sept. 19, 1863): Transfd. to Gen. Magruder's Hdqtrs. in Tex., Winter, 1863-64.
BEAVERS, M. D. — Enl. at Port Sullivan, Tex., Mar. 8, 1862, age 19: Prom., 2Cpl: W. (hand), Gettysburg (July 2, 1863): Wound furlough to Tex.: Prom., 1Cpl., Spring, 1864.
(1) BEAVERS, T. B. — W. (leg), Gaines' Mill (June 27, 1862): Prom., 5Sgt., Feb., 1864: K., Wilderness (May 6, 1864).
(1) BLACKBURN, GREEN P. — Detailed to duty as a teamster with Regmtl. QM, Nov. 19, 1861: W., Wilderness (May 6, 1864): Died from wound, May 10, 1864.
(1) BOYD, J. C. B. — See list of "Other Officers" above.
(1) BROWN, P. A. — K., Gaines' Mill (June 27, 1862).
(1) BURNS, JOE. — Present for duty to June, 1863: No record after that.
(1) BUTLER, T. A. — Died of disease, Jan. 21, 1862.
(1) CHAMBERS, G. J. — K., Antietam (Sept. 17, 1862).
COE, E. N. — Enl. at Port Hudson, Tex., Mar. 16, 1862, age 31: Died of chronic diarrhea at Tex. Hosp., Richmond, June 14, 1862.
COE, L. N. — Enl. at Port Sullivan, Tex., Mar. 29, 1862, age 32: Died at Faison's Depot, Apr. 21, 1862.
(1) CORLEY, WILSON — K., Gaines' Mill (June 27, 1862).
(1) COSGROVE, JAS. H. — W., Wilderness (May 6, 1864): Granted a "furlough of indulgence," Jan. 20, 1865: Hospitalized with pneumonia at Meridian, Miss., Feb. 6, 1865.

(1)   DAVIDSON, RILEY — W., Antietam (Sept. 17, 1862): Died, Frederick City, Md., Feb. 15, 1863.
       DAVIS, LEWIS — Enl. at Port Sullivan, Tex., Mar. 22, 1862, age 18: Dischgd. for disability, Jan., 1863.
       DENNIS, T. E. — Enl. at Port Sullivan, Tex., Mar. 16, 1862, age 28: Died of disease (meningitis), June 25, 1862.
(1)   DRAKE, J. H. — POW, Antietam (Sept. 17, 1862): Exchanged: W., White Oak Swamp (Aug. 16, 1864).
(1)   DRENNAN, J. H. — W. (leg), Gaines' Mill (June 27, 1862): Wound furlough granted, Nov. 5, 1862: W., Cold Harbor (June 3, 1864).
(1)   EASTER, M. L. — W., Gaines' Mill (June 27, 1862): K., Wilderness (May 6, 1864).
(1)   EDDINGTON, H. F. — W., Gaines' Mill (June 27, 1862): K., Darbytown Rd. (Oct. 7, 1864).
(1)   ELDER, GEO. W. — Detailed to duty as a teamster with Regmtl. QM, Nov. 19, 1861: W. & POW, 2nd Manassas (Aug. 30, 1862): Exchanged: W. & POW, Gettysburg (July 2, 1863): Confined at Pt. Lookout, Md.: Exchanged, Mar. 17, 1864: Paroled, Clarksburg, W. Va., Apr. 22, 1865.
(1)   FIELDS, F. L. — W., Antietam (Sept. 17, 1862): K., Gettysburg (July 2, 1863).
(1)   FOSTER, ROBT. V. — Enl. in Robertson Co. Tex., at 17: W., Gaines' Mill (June 27, 1862): Wound furlough granted: POW, Knoxville, Dec. 3, 1863: Confined at Rock Island, Ill.: Paroled, June 20, 1865.
(1)   FOSTER, W. HENRY — W., Gaines' Mill (June 27, 1862): Arm amputated: Dischgd. for disability, Aug., 1862.
(1)   FROST, W. H. — Detailed to duty as a teamster with Regmtl. QM: W., Wilderness (May 6, 1864): Leg amputated.
(1)   GARRETT, JOHN M. — Dischgd., July 19, 1862.
(1)   GARY (or GEARY), WM. — Detailed to duty with Regmtl. Comsy.,
(2)   Apr., 1864: Paroled, Appomattox (Apr. 12, 1865).
(1)   GEER, W. E. — Detailed to duty with CSA Ordn. Dept., Richmond, Feb., 1864: Paroled, Washington, Ga., June 10, 1865.
(1)   GOODMAN, J. H. — W., Gaines' Mill (June 27, 1862): Prom., 2Cpl.: W., Wilderness (May 6, 1864).
(1)   GRIFFIN, J. H. — Left sick at Knoxville, Tenn., Aug., 1861: POW, 2nd Manassas (Aug. 30, 1862): Exchanged: K., Chickamauga (Sept. 19, 1863).
(1)   HAMMAN, WM. H. — See roster, "Regmtl. Hdqtrs., 4th Tex. Inf."
(1)   HARRIS, C. BAZLEY — Died from disease, May 22, 1862.
(1)   HAYNES, RICH. J. — Transfd. to Co. I, 5th Tex. Inf. Regt., Oct. 26, 1861.
(1)   HEARNE, WM. — Appt. courier for Gen. Hood, Summer, 1862: Appt.
(2)   courier for Gen. Chas. Field, Feb., 1864: Paroled, Appomattox (Apr. 12, 1865).
(1)   HENDERSON, J. S. — W., Gaines' Mill (June 27, 1862): Died of wound.
       HERNDON, A. — Enl. in Robertson Co., Tex., Mar. 4, 1862, age 38: K., 2nd Manassas (Aug. 30, 1862).

HERNDON, JACOB W. — Enl. in Robertson Co., Tex., Mar. 22, 1862, age 18: W., Gaines' Mill (June 27, 1862): Appt. courier for Gen. Hood, Spring, 1863: K., Gettysburg (July 2, 1863).

HILL, WM. B. — W., Chickamauga (Sept. 19, 1863): Right arm amputated: Retired for disability.

(1) HIXSON, G. M. — W., Gaines' Mill (June 27, 1862): Detailed to CSA Engineer Corps.: K., Petersburg, June 23, 1864.

(1) HUNTER, W. R. — Detailed to duty as a teamster with Regmtl. QM, Nov. 27, 1861: K., Gaines' Mill (June 27, 1862).

(1) JANUARY, JOHN — Deserted, July 30, 1861.

(1) JONES, (Dr.) DAVID C. — See roster, "Regmtl. Hdqtrs., 4th Tex. Inf."

(1) JONES, J. J. — POW, Antietam (Sept. 17, 1862): Exchanged: K., Chickamauga (Sept. 19, 1863).

(1) JONES, W. A. — See roster, "Regmtl. Hdqtrs., 4th Tex. Inf."

(1) JORDAN, E. — Sick in Richmond hosp., Fall, 1861: Died of typhoid fever, Jan. 15, 1862: Personal effects, $4.00.

(1) KEITH, L. D. — See roster, "Regmtl. Hdqtrs., 4th Tex. Inf."

(1) KINSEY, DANIEL — Detailed to duty as nurse, Nov. 16, 1861: K., Chickamauga (Sept. 19, 1863).

(1) KIRK, WINCHELL S. — W., 2nd Manassas (Aug. 30, 1862): Died of wound, Oct. 5, 1862.

(1) LEE, W. F. — Sick, Spring, 1862: Dischgd. on Surgeon's Cert., July 15, 1862.

(1) LIVINGSTON, W. J. — W., 2nd Manassas (Aug. 30, 1862): W., Gettysburg (July 2, 1863): Two fingers on left hand amputated: Disabled as infantryman, transfd. to Bradford's Regt. of Tex. Cav.

(1) LOFTON, JAS. THOS. — Died of typhoid fever, June 5, 1862.

(1) LOVE, OGLE — Dischgd. by order of Sec. of War, Oct. 10, 1861.

(1) McCLINTON, JAS. C. — Detailed to duty as Regmtl. Butcher, Feb. 3, 1862: Died of typhoid fever at Fredericksburg, Va., Mar. 24, 1862.

McVOYMAN, B. F. — W., Gaines' Mill (June 27, 1862): W., Malvern Hill (July 1, 1862).

(1) MARSH, JOE E. — Dischgd. for chronic dysentery & hemorrhoids, Aug., 1862.

(1) MARSHALL, BENJ. W. — See roster, "Regmtl. Hdqtrs., 4th Tex. Inf."

(1) MARSHALL, W. H. — AWOL, 2nd Manassas (Aug. 30, 1862): POW, Raccoon Mtn. (Oct. 28, 1863).

(1) MARSHALL, W. W. — W., Gaines' Mill (June 27, 1862): Arm amputated: Dischgd. for disability, Oct. 1, 1862.

(1) MERRIMAN, B. F. — W., Gaines' Mill (June 27, 1862): W., Wilderness
(2) (May 6, 1864): Paroled, Appomattox (Apr. 12, 1865).

(1) MITCHELL, S. J. — W., Antietam (Sept. 17, 1862): W., Chickamauga (Sept. 19, 1863): Died of wound near Montgomery, Ala., Oct., 1863.

(2) MONTGOMERY, S. W. ("Whit") — Transfd. into Co. C from Co. I, 5th Tex. Inf. Regt., Feb. 1, 1863: W., Spotsylvania CH. (May 10, 1864): Paroled, Appomattox (Apr. 12, 1865).

(1) MOORE, M. C. — Prom., 2Sgt.: Prom., 1Sgt.: W., Wilderness (May 6, 1864): K., Petersburg, July 12, 1864.

(1) MOORE, R. E. — W. (leg), Petersburg, July 24, 1864: Wound furlough, Sept. 17, 1864: Did not return to Co.

NIXON, G. M. — W., Gaines' Mill (June 27, 1862): No other record.

(1) NOBLE, JAS. R. — Dischgd. on Surgeon's Cert., Apr. 14, 1862.

(1) NORTON, W. — Enl. at 21: Left at Knoxville, Tenn. to attend the sick (Sept., 1861): Prom., 1Cpl., July, 1862: Sick in hosp., Winter, 1862-63: K., Chickamauga (Sept. 19, 1863).

(1) NORWOOD, ALEX — W., Wilderness (May 6, 1864): Died of wound, May 23, 1864.

(1) OLIVER, JESSE NIXON — W. (arm), Gaines' Mill (June 27, 1862): W. (thigh) & POW, Antietam (Sept. 17, 1862): Died of wound.

(1) RAY, Y. B. — Transfd. to Co. G, 5th Tex. Inf., Nov. 13, 1861.

(1) REECE, W. R. — Barefooted and left behind on march to Maryland, Sept., 1862: AWOL, Feb., 1864: Sick in Richmond hosp., Summer, 1864.

(1) REID, ASHLEY — Died of pneumonia at Dumfries, Va., Mar. 7, 1862.

(1) RIMES, B. W. — POW, Antietam (Sept. 17, 1862): Exchanged: Detailed as clerk for Division (Hood's) Surgeon.

(1) ROBERTSON, D. H. — Transfd. to Co. I, 5th Tex. Vol. Inf. Regt., Oct. 26, 1861.

(1) ROBERTSON, FRANK — Transfd. to Co. I, 5th Tex. Vol. Inf. Regt., Oct. 26, 1861.

(1) ROBERTSON, JAS. R. — Detailed to scouting duty, Nov. 23-Dec. 31, 1861: K., Gaines' Mill (June 27, 1862).

(1) RUTHERFORD, ROBT. C. — Sick in hosp., Summer, 1862: No other record.

SMILIE, JACOB — Enl. in Milam County, Tex., Mar. 15, 1862, age 22: W., Wilderness (May 6, 1864): Wound furlough to Tex., May 23, 1864: Did not return.

(1) SMILIE, JAS. R. — Detailed to duty as teamster with Regmtl. QM, Nov. 21, 1861: K., Gaines' Mill (June 27, 1862).

(1) SMILIE, WM. J. — K., Gaines' Mill (June 27, 1862).

(1) SMITH, JOHN A. — Sick, May, 1862-Feb., 1863: W., Chickamauga (Sept. 19, 1863): Died of wound, June 17, 1864.

(1) SNEED, JAS. W. — W., Gaines' Mill (June 27, 1862): Died of wound, Oct., 1862.

(1) STEEL, W. C. — Detailed to scouting duty, Nov. 23, 1861: Prom., 3Sgt.: W., Chickamauga (Sept. 19, 1863): Leg amputated: Retired, disabled.

(1) TALBOT, AUGUSTUS S. — Died at Richmond, Va., Nov. 8, 1861.

(1) TALBOT, Y. O. — K., 2nd Manassas (Aug. 30, 1862).

(1) TINDALL, O. H. — W., Wilderness (May 6, 1864): Leg amputated: Retired, disabled.

(1) VAN DUSEN, H. — W. (head), 2nd Manassas (Aug. 30, 1862): W. (leg) & POW, Antietam (Sept. 17, 1862): Exchanged: W. (hand) & POW, Gettysburg (July 2, 1863): Exchanged.

(1) VAUGHN, P. H. — POW, Boonsboro Gap, Md. (Sept. 14, 1862): Exchanged: Deserted near Franklin Depot, Va., Oct., 1862.

(1) WEBSTER, EDW. — W. (hand), Chaffin's Farm (Sept. 29, 1864).

(1) WELLS, LEWIS — Transfd. to Co. I, 5th Tex. Inf., Oct. 26, 1861.

(1) WHIDDON, W. G. — K., 2nd Manassas (Aug. 30, 1862).

WILKINS, C. D. S. — Enl., Robertson Co., Tex., Mar. 31, 1862, age 26: W. (side), Gaines' Mill (June 27, 1862): POW, Gettysburg (July 2, 1863): Confined at Ft. Delaware: Paroled, June 9, 1865.

(1) WILSON, FRANK — W. & POW, Gettysburg (July 2, 1863): Imprisoned at Ft. Delaware: Died in prison of lung disease, Apr. 7, 1864.
(1) WOOD, BENNETT — W. (face), Gaines' Mill (June 27, 1862): W., Gettysburg (July 2, 1863): Prom., 3Sgt., Mar., 1864: W. (foot), Wilderness (May 6, 1864).
(1) WOOD, JOEL — Dischgd. for lung disease, Oct. 8, 1862.

NEGRO SERVANT

EMBRO (or EMBER) — Served during war with Capt. W. P. Townsend and accompanied Townsend back to Robertson County when the Captain's foot was amputated after 2nd Manassas (Aug. 30, 1862).

4TH TEX. VOL. INF. REGT.

COMPANY D — *GUADALUPE RANGERS OR KNIGHTS OF GUADALUPE COUNTY*

Company was organized in Guadalupe County, Texas, enrolled at Camp Clark, Tex., July 4, 1861, and mustered into the Confederate service "for the war" at Camp Van Dorn, Texas, on July 27, 1861, by 1Lt. A. M. Haskell, CSA.

Key

(1) Original member of Company. (2) Paroled at Appomattox.
K (Killed), W (Wounded), POW (Prisoner of War)
AWOL (Absent Without Leave)

ORIGINAL OFFICERS

(1) BANE, JOHN P. Capt. — See roster, "Regmtl. Hdqtrs., 4th Tex. Inf."
(1) MARTIN, CHAS. L. 1Lt. — Resgnd., Oct. 5, 1861.
(1) HOLLAMON, THOS. H. 2Lt. — K., Gaines' Mill (June 27, 1862).
(1) DUGGAN, ED 3Lt. — Prom., 2Lt., June 27, 1862: Prom., 1Lt., July, 1862: Resgnd. for disability, Oct. 1, 1862.

ORIGINAL NON-COMMISSIONED OFFICERS

(1) DAVIS, R. W. 1Sgt. — Sick in Richmond, Summer, 1862: Dischgd. on Surg. Cert. of disability, Aug. 7, 1862.

(1) JEFFRIES, A. DUDLEY 2Sgt. — See list of "Other Officers" following.

(1) JEFFERSON, JOHN R. 3Sgt. — Dischgd. for being underage (17 years), Nov. 2, 1861.

(1) DIBRELL, CHAS. L., JR. 4Sgt. — Prom., 3Sgt., Nov., 1861: Prom., 1Sgt., Summer, 1862: Confined in Richmond jail, Aug. 20, 1862: Dishonorably dischgd. for theft, Jan. 1, 1863.

(1) DIBRELL, JOHN L. 5Sgt. — Died in camp, Dec. 13, 1861.

(1) HUGGINS, A. V. 1Cpl. — Dischgd. on Surg. Cert. of disability, Nov. 16, 1861.

(1) WILSON, ALEX. E. 2Cpl. — Prom., 4Sgt., Sept. 1, 1862: Prom.,
(2) 2Sgt., Summer, 1862: W., Wilderness (May 7, 1864): Paroled, Appomattox (Apr. 12, 1865).

(1) LeGETTE, JESSE 3Cpl. — Dischgd. for being underage (17 years), Aug. 21, 1862.

(1) SMITH, W. P. 4Cpl. — Enl. at 21: Prom., 3Sgt., Summer, 1863: POW, Gettysburg (July 2, 1863): Confined at Ft. Delaware: Paroled, May 20, 1865.

OTHER OFFICERS

JEFFRIES, A. DUDLEY Capt. — Orig. 2Sgt. of Co.: Prom., 3Lt., July, 1862: Prom., 2Lt., Aug. 30, 1862: W., 2nd Manassas (Aug. 30, 1862): Prom., 1Lt., Oct., 1862: Prom., Capt., Dec., 1862: Resgnd., May 11, 1863.

(2) FRANKS, R. H. Capt. — Orig. Pvt. in Co.: Prom., 3Lt., Aug. 1, 1863: W., Gettysburg (July 2, 1863): W. (thigh), Wilderness (May 6, 1864): Prom., 1Lt., Jan. 9, 1865: Prom., Capt., Jan. 21, 1865: Paroled, Appomattox (Apr. 12, 1865).

KNIGHT, GEO. N. Capt. — See roster, "Regmtl. Hdqtrs., 4th Tex. Inf."

McCLAUGHERTY, WM. H. Capt. — Orig. Pvt. in Co.: Prom., 4Sgt., Dec. 12, 1861: Prom., 1Sgt., Sept. 1, 1862: Prom., 3Lt., Nov. 11, 1862: Prom., 2Lt., Dec., 1862: Prom., 1Lt., May 11, 1863: W., Wilderness (May 6, 1864): Prom., Capt., Sept. 6, 1864: Retired for disability.

MILLER, M. ERSKINE 1Lt. — Recruited as a Pvt., Apr. 11, 1862, at Seguin, Tex.: W. (thigh & arm), Gaines' Mill (June 27, 1862): Prom., 1Lt. and asgnd. as an Enrolling Officer by order of the Sec. of War, Mar. 1, 1864.

REICH, CORNELIUS 1Lt. — Orig. Pvt. in Co.: Prom., 1Lt., Oct. 24, 1861: Detailed to recruiting duty in Tex., Feb.-Apr., 1862: W., Gaines' Mill (June 27, 1862): Died, July 5, 1862.

JOHNSON, T. J. 2Lt. — Orig. Pvt. in Co.: Detailed to recruiting duty in Tex., Feb.-Apr., 1862: Prom., 3Lt., July, 1862: Prom., 2Lt., Aug. 1, 1862: K., 2nd Manassas (Aug. 30, 1862).

WOOD, A. H. 2Lt. — Orig. Pvt. in Co.: Prom., 3Lt., Jan., 1863: Prom., 2Lt., May 11, 1863: W., Gettysburg (July 2, 1863): Retired on Surgeon's Cert., Oct., 1864.

MUSICIANS

(1) MITCHELL, ROBT. — See roster, "Regmtl. Hdqtrs., 4th Tex. Inf."
(1) SMITH, MILES V. — Enl. as a 23 year old Pvt., July 4, 1861: Appt. Co. Drummer, Aug., 1861: Appt. 1Cpl., Sept., 1862: W., Antietam (Sept. 17, 1862): POW, Darbytown Rd. (Oct. 7, 1864): Confined at Pt. Lookout, Md.: Paroled, June 6, 1865.

PRIVATES

(1) AIKEN, WM. R. — Sick much of Winter, 1862-63 with hemorrhoids & chronic diarrhea: Sick furlough, Spring, 1863: Returned to duty, June 1, 1863.
(1) ALLEN, ADOLPHUS J. — Enl. at 17: Died at camp near Dumfries, Va., Dec. 26, 1861.
(1) ANDERSON, C. W. — Enl. at 30: Sick most of the war from chronic dysentery: Last heard from at a hosp. in Hillsboro, N. C., Mar. 6, 1865.
      ARMSTRONG, D. H. — See roster, "Regmtl. Hdqtrs., 4th Tex. Inf."
(1) BAKER, JOHN W. — Asgnd. duty as teamster, CSA QM Dept., Dec., 1861 — Feb., 1863: W. (leg), Wilderness (May 6, 1864).
      BAKER, JOS. — Enl. at Seguin, Tex., Mar. 26, 1862: Dischgd., July, 1862 for chronic diarrhea.
(2) BURGES, GIDEON — Enl. at Seguin, Tex., May 6, 1862: Dischgd., Mar. 4, 1863 for chronic diarrhea.
      BURGES, RICHARD J. — Enl. at New Orleans, Aug. 22, 1861: W. & POW, 2nd Manassas (Aug. 30, 1862): Paroled: Prom., 2Cpl.: Sick in Warrenton, Va., Oct., 1862: Sent to Tex. to recuperate from wound, Spring, 1863: Never returned to Co.
(2) BURGES, ROBT. A. — Enl. at New Orleans, Feb. 27, 1862: Prom., 3Cpl., Nov. 1, 1862: W. (leg), Wilderness (May 6, 1864): Prom., 5Sgt., Summer, 1864: Prom., 3Sgt.: Paroled, Appomattox (Apr. 12, 1865).
(2) BURGES, WM. H. — See roster, "Regmtl. Hdqtrs., 4th Tex. Inf."
(1) BUTLER, GEO. — K., Gaines' Mill (June 27, 1862).
(1) CABANISS, WM. M. — Transfd. to Capt. Flourney's Co., Va. Vols., Oct. 5, 1861.
(1) CALVERT, WM. L. — W., Gaines' Mill (June 27, 1862): Died from wound at Waynesboro, Va., Aug. 26, 1862.
      CAMPBELL, JAS. — Enl. at Seguin, Tex., Apr. 7, 1862: K., Chickamauga (Sept. 19, 1863).
      CODY, E. J. — Enl. at Seguin, Tex., Apr. 26, 1862: Hospitalized, Summer, 1863: K., Chickamauga (Sept. 19, 1863).
(1) COURTNEY, SEYMOUR G. — W. (mouth), Gaines' Mill (June 27, 1862): POW in Va., Aug. 25, 1863: Confined at Ft. McHenry: Took Fed. oath, Sept. 14, 1863.
(1) COX, THOS. H. — W., 2nd Manassas (Aug. 30, 1862): Granted wound furlough to Tex.: POW on *Queen of the West*, on the Red River, La., Feb., 1863: Exchanged, Mar. 1, 1863: Dropped from Co. rolls, Aug. 1, 1863: Paroled, San Antonio, Sept. 17, 1865.

(1)   DANIEL, JOHN S. — Sick on several occasions in late 1861 & early
(2)   1862: Paroled, Appomattox (Apr. 12, 1865).

DAVIDSON, J. J. — Enl. at Seguin, Tex., Mar. 26, 1862: K., Gaines'
Mill (June 27, 1862).

DAVIS, WM. J. — Enl., Richmond, Oct. 15, 1861: K., Antietam (Sept.
17, 1862).

(1)   DIMMETT, ALAMO A. — W. (leg), Gaines' Mill (June 27, 1862):
(2)   Paroled, Appomattox (Apr. 12, 1865).

DIMMETT, JAS. — Enl. at Seguin, Tex., Apr. 26, 1862: W. (foot),
Gaines' Mill (June 27, 1862): Wound furlough to Tex., July,
1862: Dischgd. for disability in Tex., June 30, 1863.

DIMMETT, NAPOLEAN BONAPART — Enl. at Seguin, Tex., Apr. 26,
1862: W., Gaines' Mill (June 27, 1862): Died in hosp. from
wound, Dec. 15, 1862.

DOUGHERTY, GEO. W. — Enl. at Seguin, Tex., Apr. 25, 1862: Died
of chronic diarrhea in Richmond, July 14, 1862.

DUER, A. N. — Enl. at Seguin, Tex., Apr. 25, 1862: K., Gaines' Mill
(June 27, 1862).

(1)   DUNN, M. S. — See roster, "Regmtl. Hdqtrs., 4th Tex. Inf."

EHRINGHAUS, WM. F. M. — Enl. at Seguin, Tex., Apr. 29, 1862:
Dischgd. for disability (St. Vitus Dance), May 26, 1863.

ERSKINE, A. N. — Enl. at Seguin, Tex., Apr. 26, 1862: W. (side),
Gaines' Mill (June 27, 1862): K., Antietam (Sept. 17, 1862).

ERSKINE, ALEC M. — Enl. at Seguin, Tex., Mar. 28, 1862: W., Gaines'
Mill (June 27, 1862): W. (arm), Antietam (Sept. 17, 1862):
Transfd. to Gen. Magruder's Cmd., Trans-Miss. Dept., Feb. 22,
1864, by order of Sec. of War.

(1)   EWING, FINIS Y. — Forty day furlough to Tex. granted, Feb., 1862:
Dischgd. in Tex. for disability, Mar. 18, 1863.

(1)   EWING, THOS. J. — W. (foot), Gaines' Mill (June 27, 1862):
Hospitalized for a year in Richmond recovering from wound.

(1)   FENNELL, ISHAM H. — W., Gaines' Mill (June 27, 1862): Died in
hosp. in Richmond, Oct. 20, 1862.

(1)   FLORES, H. D. — Enl. at 24: Sick much of the war: POW, Antietam
(Sept. 17, 1862): Confined at Ft. Delaware: Exchanged: Paroled,
Richmond, Apr. 12, 1865.

(1)   FRANKS, R. H. — See list of "Other Officers" above.

(1)   GEORGE, MOSES B. — See roster, "Hdqtrs., Hood's Tex. Brig."

(1)   GLAZER, FREDERICK ("Fritz") — Enl. at 22: W., Antietam (Sept.
17, 1862): K., Gettysburg (July 2, 1863).

(1)   GLAZER, JULIUS H. — Enl. at 19: W. (arm), Gaines' Mill (June 27,
1862): W., Chickamauga (Sept. 19, 1863): W. (side), Wilderness
(May 6, 1864).

GORDON, ALONZO A. — Enl. at Seguin, Tex., Apr. 26, 1862: W.
(leg), Gaines' Mill (June 27, 1862): Died of wound in Richmond,
Aug. 15, 1862.

(1)   GREEN, A. G. — W., Gaines' Mill (June 27, 1862): Prom., 2Cpl.,
Spring, 1864: W. (shoulder), Wilderness (May 6, 1864): POW,
Chaffin's Farm (Sept. 29, 1864): Confined at Pt. Lookout, Md.:
Exchanged, Mar. 17, 1865.

(1) GREEN, W. S. — W., Gaines' Mill (June 27, 1862): K., Gettysburg (July 2, 1863).
(1) GREGORY, JOHN B. — Enl. at 37: Present for duty entire war:
(2) Paroled, Appomattox (Apr. 12, 1865).
(1) HARMAN, WM. H. — On duty as carpenter, CSA QM Dept., Dec., 1861 — Mar., 1862: Appt. Asst. Regmt. Comsy. Off., Aug. 5, 1862: W. (side), Wilderness (May 6, 1864): Transfd. to 8th Tex. Cav. Regt., Sept. 28, 1864.
(2) HARMON, ZACK J. — Transfd. from Co. G, 5th Tex. Inf., Nov. 1, 1861: Asgnd. as a carpenter, QM Dept., Dec., 1861: W., Gaines' Mill (June 27, 1862): Prom., 5Sgt.: Paroled, Appomattox (Apr. 12, 1865).
(1) HARRIS, WILLIAM A. — On duty as teamster CSA QM Dept., Nov. 6, 1861 to Apr. 30, 1863: W. (neck), Cold Harbor (June 6, 1864).
HARRISON, W. H. — W., Wilderness (May 6, 1864): No other record.
HARRISON, Z. J. — W., Gaines' Mill (June 27, 1862): No other record.
HENRY, ARCHIBALD W. — Enl. at Seguin, Tex., Apr. 25, 1862: W., Antietam (Sept. 17, 1862): Deserted, Feb. 20, 1864.
HERRON, A. C. — Enl. at Seguin, Tex., Apr. 25, 1862: K., Gettysburg (July 2, 1863).
(1) HERRON, JAS. R. — Died near camp, Dec. 18, 1861.
(2) HODGES, GEO. A. — Enl. at Seguin, Tex., Apr. 25, 1862: W., Wilderness (May 6, 1864): Paroled, Appomattox (Apr. 12, 1865).
(1) HOLMES, JOHN F. — Enl. at 19: Extra duty as Surgeon's Orderly,
(2) Feb., 1863: POW, Suffolk, Va., May, 1863: Exchanged: POW, Gettysburg July 2, 1863): Escaped: Paroled, Appomattox (Apr. 12, 1865).
(1) HUGGINS, GEO. B. — POW, Raccoon Mtn. (Oct. 28, 1863): Confined at Camp Morton, Ind.: Exchanged, Feb. 26, 1865.
JEFFERSON, R. T. — Enl. at Seguin, Tex., Mar. 17, 1862: Present for duty through June, 1863: No other record.
(1) JEFFERSON, THOS. J. — Sick, ordered to the rear, Feb. 26, 1862: Dischgd. for lung disease, Nov., 1862.
(1) JOHNSON, T. J. — See list of "Other Officers" above.
JONES, RICHARD H. — Transfd. to Co. D from Co. A, 4th Tex. Inf., Aug. 13, 1862: W., 2nd Manassas (Aug. 30, 1862): Dischgd. for disability, Dec. 31, 1862.
(1) JONES, S. AUSTIN — W. (hand), Gaines' Mill (June 27, 1862): Asgnd.
(2) to nurse wounded at Warrenton, Va., after 2nd Manassas (Aug. 30, 1862): W., Chickamauga (Sept. 19, 1863): Prom., 4Sgt., Winter, 1864-65: Paroled, Appomattox (Apr. 12, 1865).
(1) JORDON, P. E. — Dischgd., Apr., 1863 for disability.
KING, JAS. W. — Enl. at Seguin, Tex., Apr. 21, 1862: Died of typhoid fever at Petersburg, Va., Aug. 11, 1862.
KING, JOHN M. — Enl. at Seguin, Tex., Apr. 21, 1862: Dischgd. for disability (chronic diarrhea), Aug. 19, 1862.
(1) KNIGHT, GEO. N. — See list of "Other Officers" above.
(1) LACKEY, J. R. — W., Gaines' Mill (June 27, 1862): Died from wound at Richmond, July 28, 1862.
LEONARD, ASA A. — Enl. at Seguin, Tex., Apr. 25, 1862: W., Gaines' Mill (June 27, 1862): Unfit for field duty from wound, detailed as Asst. Brig. Sutler, Apr. 30, 1864.

(1) LEWIS, CHAS. — Died near camp, Dec. 15, 1861.
(2) LITTLE, BENJ. F. — Enl. at Seguin, Tex., Apr. 21, 1862: W., Gaines' Mill (June 27, 1862): W., Darbytown Rd. (Oct. 7, 1864): Paroled, Appomattox (Apr. 12, 1865).
    LONGSTREET, GEO. — Enl. at Seguin, Tex., Apr. 21, 1862: W., Gettysburg (July 2, 1863): Hand amputated: Died, July 27, 1863.
(1) LYNCH, THOS. — On extra duty in Brig. QM Dept. as Blacksmith, since Dec. 8, 1861: AWOL, Apr., 1862: Deserted, Summer, 1863.
(1) McCLAUGHERTY, WM. H. — See list of "Other Officers" above.
    McNEELY, J. D. — Enl. at Seguin, Tex., May 17, 1862: On detached serv. with Brig. QM Dept., 1862 & 1863: Appt. Hosp. Steward in No. Car. hosp., Dec. 31, 1864.
(1) MADDOX, LEVI — Dischgd. on Surg. Cert. by order of Gen. Louis Wigfall, Dec. 14, 1861.
(1) MANNING, S. M. — K., Wilderness (May 6, 1864).
(1) MAYS, J. NELSON — K., Gettysburg (July 2, 1863).
(1) MEANS, REUBEN — Died of typhoid fever at Fredericksburg, Va., Mar. 23, 1862.
    MERRIWEATHER, W. THOS. — Enl. at Seguin, Tex., Mar. 17, 1862: W., Cold Harbor (June 3, 1864): Prom., 1Cpl., Summer, 1864: W., Chaffin's Farm (Sept. 29, 1864).
(1) MILLER, M. ERSKINE — See list of "Other Officers" above.
(1) MILLETT, LEONIDAS — K., Gaines' Mill (June 27, 1862).
(1) MORRISON, ROBT. H. — Dischgd., underage (17 years), Dec. 14, 1861.
(1) PARK, (Dr.) JOHN E. — See roster, "Regmtl. Hdqtrs., 4th Tex. Inf."
(1) PARK, THOS. — W., Gaines' Mill (June 27, 1862): Died from wound at Richmond, July 2, 1862.
    PARRENT, E. J. — Enl. at Seguin, Tex., Apr. 25, 1862: Prom., 4Cpl., Spring, 1863: AWOL, June 1, 1863: Returned to duty: Prom., 3Cpl., Spring, 1864.
(1) PATTERSON, JAS. — Appt. 1Cpl., Nov. 20, 1861: Prom., 2Sgt., Sept. 1, 1862: POW, Antietam (Sept. 17, 1862): Exchanged, Nov. 10, 1862: Prom., 1Sgt., Summer, 1864: Received Texas Gold Star for bravery, Feb., 1865: Paroled, Appomattox (Apr. 12, 1865).
(1) PIERCE, A. L. — K., Gaines' Mill (June 27, 1862).
(1) REAGAN (or RAGER), FRANK — In jail in Richmond, Nov. 8, 1861 — charged with desertion: No other record.
(1) REDUS, WM. — Enl. at 25: Sick, Summer, 1862: Dischgd. for disability (asthma), July 4, 1862.
(1) REICH, CORNELIUS — See list of "Other Officers" above.
    REEVES, J. T. — Enl. at Seguin, Tex., Apr. 21, 1862: W., Wilderness (May 6, 1864): Co. Cmdr. noted on his record, "Good soldier."
    RHOADES, R. A. — Enl. at Seguin, Tex., Apr. 26, 1862: W., 2nd Manassas (Aug. 30, 1862): Dischgd. during Apr., 1863 for disability.
(1) ROGERS, JOHN — Sick much of 1862: Paroled, Appomattox (Apr.
(2) 12, 1865).

(1) ROGERS, MICHAEL — Detailed to duty in CSA QM Dept., Spring, 1862: Died of pneumonia at Richmond, Dec. 14, 1862.
(1) RUSSELL, WM. — Dischgd., Oct. 10, 1861.
(1) RUTLEDGE, A. H. — Carried as "Deserted," Summer, 1862: No other record.
(1) SAUNDERS, FRANK — W. (abdomen), Gaines' Mill (June 27, 1862): Prom., 1Sgt., Winter, 1862-63: Sick at Richmond in Tex. Hosp., Feb. 28, 1863: W. (head & face) & POW, Gettysburg (July 2, 1863): Exchanged: Returned to Tex., disabled: Paroled at Gonzales, Tex., Nov. 25, 1865.
(1) SAUNDERS, GEO. — Died of asthma at Fredericksburg, Va., Mar. 28, 1862.
(1) SAUNDERS, STEWART M. — Dischgd. for asthma, Apr. 4, 1862.
(1) SCHMIDT, BALZER R. — Present for duty during entire war: Paroled,
(2) Appomattox (Apr. 12, 1865).
SHUMATE, WM. M. — Enl. at Seguin, Tex., Apr. 21, 1862: K., Wilderness (May 6, 1864).
(1) SIMMONS, J. WRIGHT — Enl. at 50: Dischgd. "for inability to adjust to army life," Sept. 13, 1861.
SINGLETERRY, J. M. — Enl. at Seguin, Tex., Apr. 29, 1862: Present for duty until Feb., 1863: No other record.
SMITH, E. H. — Enl. at Seguin, Tex., Mar. 20, 1862: Prom., 4Cpl., Nov. 1, 1862: In hosp., Feb. & June, 1863: Died of ulcers, Oct. 10, 1863.
(1) SMITH, JOHN D. — Enl. at 20: Detailed to Litter Corps, Spring, 1862: W. (neck), Williamsburg Rd. (Oct. 29, 1864): Paroled, Charleston, W. Va., June 22, 1865.
(1) SMITH, JOHN W. — Died of disease near camp, Dec. 18, 1861.
(1) SMITH, MILES V. — See list of "Musicians" above.
(1) SMITH, PARIS — W. (arm), Gaines' Mill (June 27, 1862): W., Wilderness (May 6, 1864).
SMITH, THOS. D. — Enl. at Seguin, Tex., Mar. 20, 1862: Died of pneumonia in Richmond, Sept. 18, 1862.
(1) SMITH, WM. R. — Prom., 5Sgt., Summer, 1862: W., Antietam (Sept. 17, 1862): K., Chickamauga (Sept. 19, 1863).
(1) WATSON, THOS. W. — Died of typhoid-pneumonia in hosp. at Newnan, Ga., Feb. 20, 1864.
(1) WEPPRECHT, CHAS. — See roster, "Regmtl. Hdqtrs., 4th Tex. Inf."
(2) WHITE, F. C. — Enl. at Seguin, Tex., Apr. 21, 1862: Present for duty during entire war: Paroled, Appomattox (Apr. 12, 1865).
(1) WHITE, JAS. — Dischgd. for disease (chronic lumbago), Sept. 5, 1862.
(1) WHITE, JAS. M. — W. (arm), Gaines' Mill (June 27, 1862): W. & POW,
(2) Gettysburg (July 2, 1863): Exchanged: Paroled, Appomattox (Apr. 12, 1865).
(1) WHITEHEAD, JAS. W. — K., 2nd Manassas (Aug. 30, 1862).
(1) WILSON, WM. W. — W., Gaines' Mill (June 27, 1862).
(1) WOOD, A. H. — See list of "Other Officers" above.
(1) YOUNG, JOHN T. — W., Gaines' Mill (June 27, 1862): Died of wound in Richmond, Aug. 6, 1862.

COMPANY E — *LONE STAR GUARDS*

Company was organized in McLennan County, Texas, enrolled at Waco, Tex., July 13, 1861, and mustered into the Confederate service "for the war" at Richmond, Va., on Sept. 16, 1861, by Lt. Waller R. Bullock, CSA.

Key

(1) Original member of Company. (2) Paroled at Appomattox.
K (Killed), W (Wounded), POW (Prisoner of War)
AWOL (Absent Without Leave)

ORIGINAL OFFICERS

(1)   RYAN, EDW. D.   Capt. — W., Gaines' Mill (June 27, 1862): Died, July 4, 1862 at St. Francis de Sales Hosp., Richmond, Va.

(1)   BRANDON, J. M.   1Lt. — Detailed to Tex. on recruiting duty, Feb.-Apr., 1862: W., Gaines' Mill (June 27, 1862): Elect., Capt., July 4, 1862: Dischgd. on Surg. Cert. of disability, Oct. 22, 1862 (foot cut by axe in 1849 prevented him from prolonged marching).

(1)   SUBLETT, DAVE L.   2Lt. — See roster, "Hdqtrs., Hood's Texas Brigade."

(1)   BILLINGSLEY, JOS. C.   3Lt. — Elect., 2Lt., May 11, 1862: Elect., 1Lt., July 4, 1862: W., Antietam (Sept. 17, 1862): Elect., Capt., Oct. 22, 1862: K., Chickamauga (Sept. 19, 1863 .)

ORIGINAL NON-COMMISSIONED OFFICERS

(1)   KILLINGSWORTH, ALLEN G.   1Sgt. — See list of "Other Officers" following.

(1)   DOWNS, OSCAR J.   2Sgt. — Sick in Richmond hosp., Winter, 1861-1862: Actg. 1Sgt., Feb. 7, 1862: Procured substitute (N. N. Ripley), Mar. 20, 1862 & returned to Waco, Tex.

(1)   EARLE, SAM S.   3Sgt. — Sick and left in hosp. at Knoxville, Tenn., Sept. 8, 1861: Died, typhoid fever, near Dumfries, Va., Feb. 1, 1862.

(1)   SMITH, JOE C.   4Sgt. — See list of "Other Officers" following.

(1)
(2)   RIPLEY, PAUL M.   5Sgt. — Prom., 3Sgt., Feb., 1862: Appt., 1Sgt., July 15, 1862: W., 2nd Manassas (Aug. 30, 1862): W., Antietam (Sept. 17, 1862): Recommended for prom. to Lt. by Lt. Col. Bane, Mar. 28, 1864: Recommendation not approved: Commanded Co. & paroled, Appomattox (Apr. 12, 1865).

(1)   DUNKLIN, W. W. ("Billie")   1Cpl. — W., Gaines' Mill (June 27, 1862):

(2)   Prom., 2Sgt.: Paroled, Appomattox (Apr. 12, 1865).
(1)   MAJORS, J. B. 2Cpl. — Appt., 1Cpl., Mar. 20, 1862: W., Gaines' Mill
        (June 27, 1862): Deserted in E. Tenn., Feb. 15, 1864.
(1)   YOUNG, SHERWOOD 3Cpl. — Sick, left in hosp. at Knoxville, Tenn.,
        Sept. 8, 1861: Appt. 2Cpl., Mar. 20, 1862: W., Gaines' Mill (June
        27, 1862): Died of wound, July 10, 1862.
(1)   DEAN, R. S. 4Cpl. — Appt. 5Sgt., Mar. 20, 1862: K., 2nd Manassas
        (Aug. 30, 1862).

OTHER OFFICERS

KILLINGSWORTH, ALLEN G. Capt. — Orig. 1Sgt. of Co.: Detailed
    to Tex. on recruiting duty, Feb.-Apr., 1862: Elect., 2Lt., July 10,
    1862: Elect., 1Lt., Oct. 22, 1862: Elect., Capt., Sept. 18, 1863:
    K., Chickamauga (Sept. 19, 1863).
SELMAN, THOS. J. Capt. — Orig. Pvt. in Co.: Elect., 3Lt., Nov. 11,
    1862: On recruiting serv. to Tex., Feb.-Apr., 1863: Prom., 2Lt.,
    July 2, 1863: Prom., 1Lt., Sept. 20, 1863: Elect., Capt., Sept. 21,
    1863: Sick in Richmond hosp., Summer, 1864: On sick leave to
    Ga., Oct., 1864: Paroled, Columbus, Miss., May 19, 1865.
SMITH, JOE C. 1Lt. — Orig. 4Sgt. of Co.: Prom., 2Sgt., Feb., 1862:
    Elect., 3Lt., July 15, 1862: Elect., 2Lt., Oct. 28, 1862: Elect.,
    1Lt., Spring, 1863: K., Gettysburg (July 2, 1863).
(1)   MAKEIG, FREDERICK MILLER 2Lt. — See roster, "Regmtl.
        Hdqtrs., 4th Tex. Inf."
TILLY, EDMUND 2Lt. — Orig. Pvt. in Co.: W., Antietam (Sept. 17,
    1862): Appt. 4Sgt., Dec., 1862: Elect., 2Lt., Sept. 20, 1863:
    Elect., 1Lt., Oct., 1863: K. (hit in stomach), Wilderness (May 6,
    1864).

MUSICIANS

(1)   BLOCKER, JESS C. — AWOL, Feb. 23, 1862: Returned to duty:
        Detached to guard POW's, Spring, 1862: Sick in Richmond hosp.,
        Summer, 1862 & Spring, 1863: AWOL, Oct. 31, 1863, presumed
        deserted.
(1)   GOOD, D. J. — See roster, "Regmtl. Hdqtrs., 4th Tex. Inf."
(1)   HIRST, T. D. — See roster, "Regmtl. Hdqtrs., 4th Tex. Inf."

PRIVATES

(1)   ASHMEAD (or ASHMORE), GEO. L. ("Judge") — Sick at Lynchburg,
        Va., Summer & Fall, 1862: Dischgd. for chronic bronchitis, Dec.
        10, 1862.
(1)   AYCOCK, BURNELL M. — W. (arm & thigh), Gaines' Mill (June 27,
        1862): POW, Darbytown Rd. (Oct. 7, 1864).
(1)   BIBLE, NOAH — W. (leg), Gaines' Mill (June 27, 1862): Disabled,
        returned to Tex., May 8, 1863.

(1) BIBLE, PHIL C. — K., 2nd Manassas (Aug. 30, 1862).
(1) BILLINGSLEY, SAM J. — Detailed to Tex. on recruiting duty,
(2)   Feb.-Apr., 1863: Present for duty with Co. during entire war
        except for recruiting duty in Tex.: Paroled, Appomattox (Apr.
        12, 1865).
(1) BRADFIELD, J. A. — Dischgd. for chronic diarrhea, July 2, 1862.
(1) BURNETT, DANIEL — Transfd. to Co. I, 11th Miss. Inf. Regt., Apr. 1,
        1862.
(1) BURTON, W. H. P. ("Billy") — W., Chickamauga (Sept. 19, 1863):
(2)   Paroled, Appomattox (Apr. 12, 1865).
(1) CHAMBERS, SAM H. — On scouting duty, Nov. 22, 1861: W.,
        Chickamauga (Sept. 19, 1863): Leg amputated.
(1) CHAPMAN, J. BOZE — W., Chickamauga (Sept. 19, 1863): Deserted in
        E. Tenn., Feb. 15, 1864.
(1) CHENAULT, G. N. — Sick much of 1862: Paroled, Appomattox (Apr.
(2)   12, 1865).
(1) CLARK, J. B. — K., 2nd Manassas (Aug. 30, 1862).
    CLARK, J. ED. — Enl. at Waco, Apr. 11, 1862: Detach. serv. at Brig.
        Hdqtrs., Nov., 1862 — Apr., 1863: Died of chronic hepatitis,
        Sept. 20, 1863.
(1) COMBE, J. W. — Died of pneumonia in Richmond hosp., Nov. 26,
        1861.
(1) COWDEN, W. B. — Died of disease (chronic diarrhea), May 21, 1862.
(1) CREED, GEO. — Left at Boonsboro, Md., Sept. 14, 1862: AWOL:
        Deserted.
(1) DECKERD, ALEX. P. — Sick, Summer & Fall, 1861: Dischgd., Aug.
        19, 1862, "for insanity."
(1) DECKERD, DAVID M. — Sick much of 1862: Detailed to Tex. on
        recruiting duty, Feb.-Apr., 1863: K., Spotsylvania CH. (May 12,
        1864).
(1) DELK, W. G. — W., Antietam (Sept. 17, 1862): Furlough to Tex., Mar.
        21, 1864: Did not return to Co.
(1) DONNELLY, H. M. — Actg. hosp. attendant at Brig. hosp., Dumfries,
        Va., Feb., 1862: W., Antietam (Sept. 17, 1862): Died of wound.
(1) DUNCAN, W. E. ("Bill") — Detchd. serv. at Brig. Hdqtrs., Apr., 1862:
        Courier for Gen. Hood, Spring, 1863: Courier for Gen. Chas.
        Field, Spring, 1864: Paroled, Appomattox (Apr. 12, 1865).
(1) DUNKLIN, TIM L. — K., 2nd Manassas (Aug. 30, 1862).
(1) EDWARDS, BINE G. — W., 2nd Manassas (Aug. 30, 1862): Died of
        wound, Sept. 17, 1862.
(1) EVERETT, W. H. — Dischgd. on Surg. Cert. of disability, Dec. 26,
        1861.
(1) FITZHUGH, DUGALD C. ("Champ") — Detailed as Hosp. Orderly,
        Summer, 1862: POW, July 20, 1863 while on furlough in Va.:
        Confined at Pt. Lookout, Md.: Exchanged, Mar. 3, 1864.
(2) FOSSETT, SAM — Enl. in McLennan Co., Tex., Apr. 1, 1862: W.
        (foot), Gaines' Mill (June 27, 1862): W., Gettysburg (July 2,
        1863): W. (hand), Wilderness (May 6, 1864): Paroled, Appo-
        mattox (Apr. 12, 1865).
(1) FREEMAN, R. L. — W., Gaines' Mill (June 27, 1862): Died of wound,
        Aug. 2, 1862.

GREEN, GEO. — Recruited in Va.: K., Gettysburg (July 2, 1863).
HANNAH, W. — Recruited in Va.: Died, June, 1862.
(1) HARRISON, JOHN H. — W. (shoulder), Gaines' Mill (June 27, 1862): Transfd. to Speight's Regt. (15th Tex. Inf.), Jan. 22, 1863.
HICKS, H. K. — Enl. in McLennan County, Tex., Mar. 21, 1862: Died, July 12, 1862.
(1) HICKS, W. M. — Sick, Fall of 1861 & Winter, 1861-62: K., Chickamauga (Sept. 19, 1863).
(1) HILL, ELDON — Prom., Cpl.: W., 2nd Manassas (Aug. 30, 1862): Dischgd., Sept. 16, 1862.
HOLDER, JOHN W. — Enl. in McLennan County, Tex., Mar. 14, 1862: Dischgd. for disability (acute diarrhea), Oct. 1, 1862.
(1) HOLLOWAY, L. DURHAM — W. (shoulder), Gaines' Mill (June 27, 1862): W., Chickamauga (Sept. 19, 1863): Retired for disability, July 8, 1864.
(1) HORNE, LUCK L. — Procured substitute (N. P. Moore), Jan. 1, 1862, and returned to Waco.
(1) HUGHES, JOSIAH — Sick, Summer, 1862: Furlough granted Nov. 20, 1862: No other record.
(1) HUNT, JAS. F. — See roster, "Hdqtrs., Hood's Texas Brigade."
(1) JACKSON, WM. T. — Dischgd. for disability (acute diarrhea), Summer, 1862.
JOHNSON, JOHN — Detached serv. as blacksmith, Fall, 1862: Dischgd., Feb. 11, 1863 for disability.
(1) JOHNSTON, JOHN W. — Appt. 3Cpl., Mar. 1, 1863: Prom., Sgt., Oct., 1863: K., Wilderness (May 6, 1864).
(1) JONES, R. M. ("Dick") — W., 2nd Manassas (Aug. 30, 1862): Arm amputated.
(2) KING, W. M. — Transfd. to Co. E, 4th Tex. Inf., from Co. C, 1st Tex. Inf., Dec. 31, 1863: W., Wilderness (May 6, 1864): Paroled, Appomattox (Apr. 12, 1865).
(1) KIRVEN, WM. H. — Prom., 1Cpl., May 8, 1862: W., Antietam (Sept. 17, 1862): Reduced to ranks, Feb. 27, 1863: POW, Raccoon Mountain (Oct. 28, 1863): Confined at Camp Morton, Ind.: Died in prison, Dec. 23, 1863.
(1) LEHMANN, JOS. — W., Antietam (Sept. 17, 1862): Arm amputated.
(1) LEONARD, ROBT. H. — See roster, "Regmtl. Hdqtrs., 4th Tex. Inf."
(2)
(1) LONG, B. D. — Sick, Summer & Fall, 1861: Dischgd. for disability, Dec. 28, 1861.
(1) LONG, J. H. C. — Appt. 4Cpl., Mar. 20, 1862: Prom., 5Sgt., July, 1862: K., Antietam (Sept. 17, 1862).
(1) LOYD (or LLOYD), WM. J. — Sick, Fall, 1861 & Spring & Summer, 1862: Sick leave to Tex.: Did not return to Co.
McGEE, GREEN — Enl. in McLennan County, Tex., Mar. 10, 1862: Died at Liberty, Va., Jan. 12, 1863.
(1) MADDEN, C. P. — W. (arm), Gaines' Mill (June 27, 1862): Dischgd. on Surg. Cert., Nov. 27, 1862.
(1) MAKEIG, FRED M. — See list of "Other Officers" above.
(1) MANAHAN, JIM H. — Detailed to Tex. on recruiting duty, Feb.-Apr., 1862: Prom., 3Sgt., Dec., 1862: Sick in Richmond, Spring, 1864: 40 day furlough granted, Sept. 3, 1864: Did not return to Co.

(1) MILLER, JOHN D. — Present for duty at all times, was never hospitalized: K., Chickamauga (Sept. 19, 1863).

MOORE, N. P. — (Substitute for Pvt. L. L. Horne): Enl., Jan. 1, 1862 at Dumfries, Va.: W., Gaines' Mill (June 27, 1862): Prom., 5Sgt., Dec. 15, 1862: Prom., 4Sgt., Oct., 1863: K., Knoxville, Tenn., Nov. 24, 1863.

(1) MORGAN, A. B. — Detailed as hosp. Wardmaster, Oct., 1861, "dismissed for drunkenness," Nov., 1861: Sick in Richmond hosp., Spring, 1862 & Winter, 1863: Dischgd. on Surg. Cert., June 3, 1863.

(2) MULLENS, F. COELLA — Enl. at Waco, Tex., Apr. 9, 1863: Paroled, Appomattox (Apr. 12, 1865).

(1) MULLENS, THOS. MACON — Sick, Aug., 1862: Prom., 4Cpl., Dec., 1862: Prom., 1Cpl., Oct., 1863: Sick, June, 1864: Prom., 4Sgt., June 26, 1864: Paroled, Lynchburg, Va., Apr. 14, 1865.

(1) MULLENS, W. T. — Sick in Nashville, Sept.-Nov., 1861: W. (shoulder) & POW, Gettysburg (July 2, 1863): Exchanged: 40 day leave granted Oct. 14, 1863: Sick in hosp., Spring, 1864.

(1) NASH, H. C. — Sick in hosp., Summer & early Fall, 1861: Dischgd. for disability, Nov. 19, 1861.

(1) NORWOOD, TOM L. — K., Chickamauga (Sept. 19, 1863).

(1) ORR, W. L. — Died at Knoxville, Tenn., Oct. 8, 1861.

(1) PAMPLIN, W. A. — W., 2nd Manassas (Aug. 30, 1862): W., Chick-
(2) amauga (Sept. 20, 1863): W. (shoulder), Bermuda Hundred, Va., (June 16, 1864): Paroled, Appomattox (Apr. 12, 1865).

(1) PETERS, LANDON CONRAD — W. (thigh), 2nd Manassas (Aug. 30, 1862): AWOL, Oct. 10, 1863: W. (leg), Spotsylvania CH. (May 12, 1864): Paroled, Clarksburg, W. Va., Apr. 30, 1865.

(1) RAGSDALE, J. B. — Sick, Winter, 1861-62: Took Fed. oath, Washington, D. C., Apr. 10, 1865.

(1) RAMSEY, F. M. — Appt. litter bearer, May 1, 1862: AWOL, Mar. 10, 1864: POW, Morristown, Tenn., Mar. 15, 1864.

(1) REED, J. C. — W., Antietam (Sept. 17, 1862): Died from wound.

(2) RIPLEY, N. N. — (Substitute for 2Sgt. Oscar J. Downs): Enl. at Fredericksburg, Va., Mar. 20, 1862: Detailed to guard baggage in rear, Apr., 1863: W., Wilderness (May 6, 1864): Paroled, Appomattox (Apr. 12, 1865).

(1) ROBERTS, ABNER — K., Gaines' Mill (June 27, 1862).

(1) ROBINSON, J. H. — Dischgd. for disability, Feb. 11, 1862.

(1) ROBINSON, JAS. — See roster, "Hdqtrs., Hood's Tex. Brig."

ROBINSON, JOHN A. — Enl. at Waco, Tex., Apr. 8, 1862: Sick most of 1862: AWOL, July 27, 1863, presumed deserted.

(1) ROBINSON, S. A. — K., Antietam (Sept. 17, 1862).

(1) ROBINSON, W. S. ("Billy") — W., 2nd Manassas (Aug. 30, 1862): W., Antietam (Sept. 17, 1862): Deserted in E. Tenn., Feb. 15, 1864.

(1) ROGERS, H. B. — Sick, Winter, 1861-62: Paroled, Appomattox (Apr.
(2) 12, 1865).

(1) ROGERS, J. L. — Prom., Cpl., July, 1862: W. (leg & hand), 2nd Manassas (Aug. 30, 1862): Leg amputated: Died from wounds at Warrenton, Va., Sept. 20, 1862.

(1) ROGERS, W. D. — W. (side), Gaines' Mill (June 27, 1862): Died of pneumonia, Charlottesville, Va., Dec. 5, 1862.
(1) ROSS, ANDY E. — Died at Dumfries, Va., Nov. 19, 1861.
(1) ROSS, WM. M. — W. (shoulder), Antietam (Sept. 17, 1862): Granted 50 day wound furlough: AWOL, Feb. 2, 1863: Did not return to Co.
(1) ROTAN, W. T. — Detailed as a Brig. Teamster, Nov. 29, 1861: W., Wilderness (May 6, 1864): W. (jaw), Petersburg (June 22, 1864): Retired, disabled, Sept. 26, 1864.
(1) SANDIFER, LAYTON GREEN — Detailed to duty at Gen. G. W. Smith's Hdqtrs., June, 1862: Asgnd. as clerk in Capt. Dudley's Office, Subsistence Dept., Richmond, June, 1863: Asgnd. to QM Depot, Houston, Tex., Winter, 1864-65.
(1) SELMAN, THOS. J. — See list of "Other Officers" above.
(1) SHARP, ELDRED C. — W. (foot), Gaines' Mill (June 27, 1862): Prom.,
(2) 4Cpl., Mar. 1, 1863: Prom., 1Cpl.: Paroled, Appomattox (Apr. 12, 1865).
(1) SMITH, JAS. S. — W. (shoulder), Gaines' Mill (June 27, 1862): Died from wound, July 8, 1862.
(1) SMITH, JOHN S. — See roster, "Hdqtrs., Hood's Texas Brigade."
(1) SMITH, L. (or S.) — Died at Dumfries, Va., Jan. 28, 1862.
(1) TAYLOR, EMZY — Dischgd. for disability (lung disease), Dec. 4, 1861.
(1) TAYLOR, G. M. — W. (arm), Gaines' Mill (June 27, 1862): Sick,
(2) Spring, 1863: Paroled, Appomattox (Apr. 12, 1865).
(1) TERRY, J. C. — W. & POW, Gettysburg (July 2, 1863): Confined at Ft. McHenry, Md.: Paroled, June 5, 1865.
(1) TILLY, EDMUND — See list of "Other Officers" above.
(1) UMBERSON, RUFUS W. — In hosp. several times, Fall, 1861 & Spring,
(2) 1862: Paroled, Appomattox (Apr. 12, 1865).
(1) WAY, CHAS. BURR — See roster, "Regmtl. Hdqtrs., 4th Tex. Inf."
WEST, JOHN C. — Enl. at Waco, Tex., Apr. 9, 1863: W. (mouth), Gettysburg (July 2, 1863): W. (side), Chickamauga (Sept. 19, 1863): Dischgd., Feb. 28, 1864.
(1) WHITEHEAD, CHAS. M. — Detailed as a Brig. Teamster, Nov. 16, 1861: W., 2nd Manassas (Aug. 30, 1862): W., Gettysburg (July 2, 1863): K., Chickamauga (Sept. 20, 1863).
(1) WIDEMAN, C. A. — POW, 2nd Manassas (Aug. 30, 1862): Exchanged: K., Wilderness (May 6, 1864).
(1) WILLIAMS, T. D. — Appt. courier to Gen. Hood, Nov. 12, 1862:
(2) Courier to Gen. Chas. Field, Apr., 1864: On recruiting serv. to Tex., Summer, 1864: Paroled, Appomattox (Apr. 12, 1865).
(1) WILLIS, J. B. — Sick in hosp. on several occasions during war: Returned to Tex. late in war: Paroled at Victoria, Tex., Aug. 8, 1865.
(1) WILSON, G. H. — Died at the Tex. Hosp., Richmond, Va., Apr. 25, 1863 at 9 A.M.
(1) WOLLARD, ANDY J. — Prom., 4Cpl., Feb. 1, 1862: Prom., 3Cpl., Mar. 20, 1862: Prom., Sgt.: W., Chaffin's Farm (Sept. 29, 1864).
WOOD, H. — Enl. in McLennan Co., Tex., Apr. 1, 1862: Sick in hosp., May 27, 1862: "Escaped from hosp. in fit of insanity," June, 1862.

WORSHAM, CHAS. S. — Enl., Aug. 14, 1861 in Co. L, 1st Tex. Inf., transfd. to Co. E, 4th Tex. Inf., Nov. 19, 1861: Prom., 3Cpl., May 15, 1862: W. (shell shocked), Gaines' Mill (June 27, 1862): Prom., 2Cpl., Dec., 1862: AWOL, June 24, 1863, presumed deserted.

(1) WORSHAM, EDW. L. — W. (thigh), Gaines' Mill (June 27, 1862): Prom., 3Sgt.: K., Fredericksburg (Dec. 15, 1862).

WORSHAM, JAS. N. — Enl., Aug. 14, 1861 in Co. L, 1st Tex. Inf., transfd. to Co. E, 4th Tex. Inf., Oct. 1, 1861: Transfd. out of Company, date unknown.

(1) YOUNG, T. H. — Died of typhoid fever in Richmond, June 14, 1862.

4TH TEX. VOL. INF. REGT.

COMPANY F — *MUSTANG GRAYS*

Company was organized in Bexar County, Texas, enrolled at Camp Clark, Tex., July 11, 1861, and mustered into the Confederate service "for the war" at Richmond, Va., Sept. 30, 1861.

Key

(1) Original member of Company. (2) Paroled at Appomattox.
K (Killed), W (Wounded), POW (Prisoner of War)
AWOL (Absent Without Leave)

ORIGINAL OFFICERS

(1) CUNNINGHAM, ED. H. Capt. — W., Antietam (Sept. 17, 1862): Arm amputated: Dischgd. for disability, Nov. 4, 1862.

(1) BROOKS, JOHN F. 1Lt. — W. (thigh), Gaines' Mill (June 27, 1862): Prom., Capt., Nov. 5, 1862: Resgnd., Nov. 7, 1862.

(1) HUGHES, LEMUEL P. 2Lt. — Recruiting serv. in Tex., Feb.-Apr., 1862: W. & POW, Antietam (Sept. 17, 1862): Arm amputated: Paroled, Winchester, Va., Sept. 30, 1862: Prom., 1Lt., Nov. 5, 1862: Prom., Capt., Nov. 7, 1862: Resgnd., Apr. 8, 1863.

(1) LYONS. L. P. 3Lt. — W., Gaines' Mill (June 27, 1862): Died of wound, June 28, 1862.

ORIGINAL NON-COMMISSIONED OFFICERS

(1) BRAHAN, HAYWOOD W. 1Sgt. — See list of "Other Officers"
(2) following.
(1) CUNNINGHAM, J. T. 2Sgt. — See roster, "Regmtl. Hdqtrs., 4th Tex. Inf."
(1) WADE, JOS. D. 3Sgt. — See list of "Other Officers" following.

(1) SAMPSON, EDWIN J. 4Sgt. — K., Gaines' Mill (May 27, 1862).
(1) PENGRA, MARSHALL M. 5Sgt. — W. (groin), Gaines' Mill (June 27, 1862): Sick, Summer & Fall, 1862: POW, Cold Harbor (June 9, 1864): Exchanged, Oct. 29, 1864.
(1) PARK, ELI 1Cpl. — See list of "Other Officers" following.
(1) BENNETT, WALTER A. 2Cpl. — Prom., 1Cpl., Nov., 1861: Prom., 5Sgt., May 1, 1862: Sick in hosp. in Richmond, Va., Fall, 1862: Sick furlough to Tex., Mar. 7, 1863: Never returned to Co.: Paroled, Shreveport, La., June 15, 1865.
(1) MURRAY, JOHN DAVID 3Cpl. — Prom., 3Sgt., Oct. 1, 1862: Prom.,
(2) 2Sgt., Aug., 1862: W., Antietam (Sept. 17, 1862): Prom., 1Sgt., Spring, 1865: Paroled, Appomattox (Apr. 12, 1865).
(1) GOODLOE, CALVIN 4Cpl. — Sick in hosp., Nov., 1861-June, 1862: Reduced to Pvt.: Dischgd. from service, June 27, 1862 for chronic rheumatism, tuberculosis & lumbago.

OTHER OFFICERS

KINDRED, E. T. Capt. — Orig. Pvt. in Co.: Prom., 2Lt., Sept. 11, 1862: Prom., Capt., Apr. 8, 1863: W., Wilderness (May 6, 1864): W., Darbytown Road (Oct. 7, 1864).
(1) WADE, JOS. D. Capt. — See roster, "Regmtl. Hdqtrs., 4th Tex. Inf."
BRAHAN, HAYWOOD W. 1Lt. — See roster, "Regmtl. Hdqtrs., 4th Tex. Inf."
PARK, ELI 1Lt. — Orig. 1Cpl. of Co.: Prom., 1Lt., Apr. 8, 1863: On detchd. serv. to Tex., Spring, 1864, by order of Sec. of War: K., New Market Heights, Aug. 18, 1864.
CRIGLER, REUBEN T. 3Lt. — Enl. as a Pvt. at San Antonio, Tex., Mar. 29, 1862: Prom., 1Cpl.: Elect., 3Lt., May 11, 1863: W., Wilderness (May 6, 1864).

MUSICIANS

(1) DOCKSTADER, OSCAR — See roster, "Regmtl. Hdqtrs., 4th Tex. Inf."
(1) WARNER, CHAS. — See roster, "Regmtl. Hdqtrs., 4th Tex. Inf."

PRIVATES

ADAMS, THOS. J. — Enl. at Columbus, Tex., Apr. 9, 1862: W., Antietam (Sept. 17, 1862): Disabled & dischgd.
(1) ALFORD, JAS. — W. (leg), 2nd Manassas (Aug. 30, 1862): W.,
(2) Gettysburg (July 2, 1863): Paroled, Appomattox (Apr. 12, 1865).
(1) ALLEN, GEO. ("Joel") — W., Gettysburg (July 2, 1863): Arm amputated: Returned to Tex., Jan. 1, 1864.
(2) ARDOUR, S. H. — Paroled, Appomattox (Apr. 12, 1865): No other record.

AYLMER, GERALD G. — Enl., Apr. 9, 1862 at San Antonio: W. (ankle), Gaines' Mill (June 27, 1862): Disabled & dischgd., San Antonio, Apr. 28, 1863.

BEDELL, A. M. — Enl. at San Antonio, Mar. 31, 1862: Left sick on march from Yorktown, May 12, 1862 & "not heard from since."

(1) BRANTLEY, JOHN L. — Sick in hosp., Winter, 1862-63: Deserted, Spring, 1864.

(1) BRECKENRIDGE, A. N. — Transfd. to Capt. J. D. Imboden's Va. Arty. Btry. (Staunton Arty.), Apr. 1, 1862.

BRIEGER, JOHN G. — See roster, "Hdqtrs., Hood's Tex. Brig."

(1) BROOKS, ABRAM — Died at camp near Dumfries, Va., Jan. 13, 1862.

BROOKS, CINCINNATI — Enl., Mar. 31, 1862 at San Antonio, Tex.: W. (head), Cold Harbor (June 5, 1864): Paroled, Washington, D. C., Apr. 14, 1865.

(1) BROWN, CHAS. S. — See roster, "Regmtl. Hdqtrs., 4th Tex. Inf."

(1) BROWN, W. Z. — Dischgd. on Surg. Cert. of disability at Richmond, Va., Nov. 8, 1861.

(1) BUCHANAN, LAFAYETTE — Detailed as nurse at Tex. sick camp, near Richmond, July 20, 1862: Detailed as a Brig. ambulance driver, Jan., 1864: Paroled, Washington, D. C., Apr. 14, 1865.

CAMP, THOS. P. — Enl., Mar. 31, 1862 at La Vernia, Tex.: Sick, Summer, 1862: Sick furlough granted: AWOL, Jan., 1864: Never returned to Co.

CAMPBELL, JOHN M. — Enl., Apr. 1, 1862 at San Antonio: Prom., 3Sgt.: Dischgd., May 20, 1863, substitute furnished (Wm. Christie).

CHRISTIE, WM. — A Virginian who enlisted as a substitute for 3Sgt. John Campbell, May 20, 1863, near the Rapidan River: Deserted, May 22, 1863.

CLARK, JOS. — Enl., May 7, 1862 at Columbus, Tex.: Died of typhoid fever in Tex. Hosp. (Richmond), June 3, 1862.

COHEA, ARCHER T. — Enl., Mar. 13, 1862 at Hallettsville, Tex., Transfd. to CSA Engineer Corps, Capt., Baldwin's Co., Spring, 1863: Transfd. back to Co.: K., Spotsylvania CH. (May 12, 1864).

(1) COOK, JOHN — Left to nurse wounded at Warrenton, Va. following 2nd Manassas (Aug. 30, 1862): Present for duty up to June, 1863: No record after, Summer, 1863.

(1) COPELAND, JOHN — Dischgd. near Dumfries, Va., Dec. 14, 1861.

(1) COPELAND, SOLOMON — Paid $75 in bounty money, Nov. 7, 1862: K., Wilderness (May 6, 1864).

(1) CRENSHAW, MICAJAH — Sick, Fall, 1861: Died at a Richmond hosp., Jan. 25, 1862.

CRIGLER, REUBEN T. — See list of "Other Officers" above.

CROCKETT, ED. R. — Recruited, Mar. 22, 1862 at Hallettsville, Tex.: Prom., 4Sgt.: Prom., 3Sgt., May 20, 1863: W., Wilderness (May 6, 1864).

(1) CURRIE, JOS. B. — Prom., 4Cpl., May 20, 1863: Prom., 2Cpl., Summer, 1863: W., Chickamauga (Sept. 19, 1863): Leg amputated: Retired by Medical Board.

(1) DANSBY, HARRISON — W., Antietam (Sept. 17, 1862): W. (foot), Richmond Defenses, Dec. 13, 1864: Paroled, Jackson, Miss., May 19, 1865.

DIAL, AUGUSTUS A. — Enl., Mar. 23, 1862 at San Antonio: W., Gaines' Mill (June 27, 1862): Dischgd. on Surg. Cert. of disability, Oct. 4, 1862.

DOLLERY, DAVID — Enl., Mar. 20, 1862 at Hopkinsville, Tex.: Sick, May, 1862-June, 1863: Sick leave granted, Summer, 1863: AWOL in Tex.: Never returned to Co.

DOWNING, ED. — Enl., Apr. 25, 1862 at Beaumont, Tex.: K., Gaines' Mill (June 27, 1862).

DREYER (or DWYER), HENRY — Enl., Apr. 2, 1862 at San Antonio: W., Antietam (June 27, 1862): Died of wounds.

(1)
(2) DUNN, WM. H. — Sick in hosp., Fall, 1861: W. & POW, Gettysburg (July 2, 1863): Confined at Pt. Lookout, Md.: Exchanged, Mar. 17, 1865: Paroled, Appomattox (Apr. 12, 1865).

(1) ELLIOT, JOHN B. — See roster, "Regmtl. Hdqtrs., 4th Tex. Inf."

(1) EVATT, JAS. L. — Sick in hosp., Oct. 28, 1862: Dischgd. on Surg. Cert. of disability, Dec. 8, 1861.

(1) FISHBURN, JAS. A. — Enl. at 21: Sick on furlough at Lyons, Tex., Aug. 15, 1861 to May, 1862: On detached service as shoemaker with "CS Shoe Dept.," Richmond, July, 1863-Jan., 1865: On Feb. 17, 1865, shown as a "stable manager" in Patrick Co., Va.

(1) FLOYD, WM. F. — Sick in Richmond, Fall & Winter, 1861: W., Antietam (Sept. 17, 1862): Prom., 3Cpl., May 20, 1863: Decapitated by cannon ball at Gettysburg (July 2, 1863).

FOSTER, B. H. — See roster, "Regmtl. Hdqtrs., 4th Tex. Inf."

(1)
(2) GABBERT, HARMON G. — Extra duty as baker, Feb., 1862: W., Antietam (Sept. 17, 1862): In guard house under charges, Summer, 1863: Confined at Castle Thunder, Richmond, Spring, 1864: Awaiting sentence of Court-martial, Aug., 1864: Paroled, Appomattox (Apr. 12, 1865).

(1) GIVENS, WM. M. — POW, Gettysburg (July 2, 1863): Imprisoned at Ft. Delaware, Md.: Escaped, July 1, 1864, and rejnd. Co.

(1) GOODLOE, WM. — Absent on sick furlough, Winter, 1861-62: Sick in Richmond hosp., Spring, 1862: Dischgd., July 10, 1862, for chronic rheumatism & hepatitis.

GOODWIN, BENJ. — Born in Ireland: Enl. at 40, Apr. 10, 1862 at Sutherland Springs, Tex.: Sick, Fall, 1862: Dischgd. on Surg. Cert., Nov. 19, 1862 for lumbago & chronic rheumatism.

GRAHAM, JOHN C. — Enl., Apr. 10, 1862 at Columbus, Tex.: Sick most of 1862 & Winter, 1862-63: W. (shoulder), Gettysburg (July 2, 1863): Arm amputated: Died, July 29, 1863.

(1) GREEN, WM. A. — W. (thigh), Gaines' Mill (June 27, 1862): Disabled: Wound furlough to Texas, Nov. 15, 1862: Did not return to Co.

(1) HAHN, JOHN — W. (foot), Gettysburg (July 2, 1863): Disabled: Returned to Tex. on furlough: Did not return to Co.

HARBOUR, CALLOWAY — Enl., Mar. 13, 1862 at Hallettsville, Tex.: Died, Dec. 16, 1862, while on leave in Monroe Parish, La.

HARDOIN, ARCH — Enl., Mar. 18, 1862 at Hopkinsville, Tex.: Died of typhoid fever, June 8, 1862.

HARDOIN, SERAND H. — See roster, "Hdqtrs., Hood's Texas Brigade."

HARWELL, J. R. — Enl., Mar. 15, 1862 at Hallettsville, Tex.: W. (groin), Gaines' Mill (June 27, 1862): Dischgd. on Surg. Cert. of disability, Dec. 29, 1862: Paroled, Meridian, Miss., May 11, 1865.

HAYNIE, HENRY M. — Enl., Mar. 23, 1863 at Oso, Tex.: W. (right thigh) & POW, Gettysburg (July 2, 1863): Paroled: W. (right thigh), White Oak Swamp (Aug. 16, 1864).

HENDERSON, BENNETT G. — Enl., Mar. 31, 1862 at La Vernia, Tex.: K., Antietam (Sept. 17, 1862).

HENDERSON, C. F. — Enl., Mar. 31, 1862 at La Vernia, Tex.: K., Gaines' Mill (June 27, 1862).

HENRY, W. R. — Enl., Mar. 22, 1862 at Hallettsville, Tex.: Died of acute diarrhea, July 1, 1862.

(1) HOLLANDER, WM. M. — W. (arm), Antietam (Sept. 17, 1862): Dischgd. for disability, May 8, 1863.

(1) HOUSTON, RUSSELL — Absent on sick furlough, Mar. 7, 1863: Dischgd., Apr., 1864 in Trans-Miss. Dept.

(1) HOWARD, RUSSELL — See roster, "Regmtl. Hdqtrs., 4th Tex. Inf."

HOWARD, WM. — Recruited, Apr. 1, 1862 at San Antonio: POW, Antietam (Sept. 17, 1862): Confined at Ft. Delaware: Took Fed. oath.

(1) JOHNSON, FRANK — Deserted in New Orleans, Sept. 9, 1861.

(1) JOHNSON, JOHN N. — Sick, Summer, 1862: Detailed to Brig. Provost Guard, Spring, 1863: POW, Wilderness (May 6, 1864): Paroled, Ashland, Va., Apr. 22, 1865.

(1) JOHNSON, WM. C. — W., Gaines' Mill (June 27, 1862): Disabled from wounds: Detailed as Wardmaster in Tex. Hosp. at Richmond, Spring, 1863-Summer, 1864: Paroled, Meridian, Miss., May 12, 1865.

(1) JONES, ABSALOM R. — Litter bearer, Sept., 1862-Feb., 1864: POW, No. Anna R., May 20, 1864: Took Fed. oath, Oct. 15, 1864.

(1) JONES, WM. — On extra duty as teamster in CS QM Dept., Fall, 1861: Sick in hosp. at Richmond, Winter & Spring, 1862: Dischgd., July 27, 1862 for "inability to adapt to milt. service."

(1) KAHR, NICHOLAS — K., Gaines' Mill (June 27, 1862).

(1) KINDRED, E. T. — See list of "Other Officers" above.

KINDRED, J. H. — Enl., Mar. 18, 1862 at Hopkinsville, Tex.: W., Antietam (Sept. 17, 1862): Died of wounds.

KINDRED, JAS. B. — Enl., Mar. 12, 1862 at Hallettsville, Tex., W. (shoulder & side), Antietam (Sept. 17, 1862): Disabled, given wound furlough to Tex., Oct. 12, 1862: Did not return to Co.

KINDRED, JOHN S. — Enl., Mar. 7, 1862 at Hopkinsville, Tex.: K., Antietam (June 27, 1862).

KINDRED, JOSHUA P. — Enl., Mar. 7, 1862 at Columbus, Tex.: W. (hand), Gaines' Mill (June 27, 1862): Detailed as Regmtl. Foragemaster, Aug. 31, 1862: POW, Antietam (Sept. 17, 1862), left to take care of wounded: Exchanged: Detailed as Forage-master in Div. (Hood's), Dec. 16, 1862: Prom. to Div. (Hood's) QM Sgt., Apr. 1, 1863.

(1) KOOLBECK, GARRETT — Detailed as a teamster, Fall, 1861 & Spring, 1862: W. (leg), Gaines' Mill (June 27, 1862): Died, spinal meningitis, Sept. 6, 1862.

LOVE, JOS. P. — Enl., Mar. 19, 1862 at Hopkinsville, Tex.: K., Antietam (Sept. 17, 1862).

(1) (2) McALISTER, CHAS. A. — Prom., 4Cpl., May 1, 1862: W. (hand), Gaines' Mill (June 27, 1862): Prom., 1Cpl., Aug. 1, 1862: Courier for Gen. Chas. Field, Spring, 1864: Paroled, Appomattox (Apr. 12, 1865).

(1) McALISTER, DANIEL M. — Prom., 3Cpl., Dec. 1, 1861: Prom., 2Cpl., May 1, 1862: W. (severely in both legs), Gaines' Mill (June 27, 1862): Died of wounds, July 15, 1862.

(1) McCANN, THOS. J. — Detailed as Brig. Butcher, Feb.-Apr., 1862 & Feb.-Apr., 1863: W. (severely in hip), Gaines' Mill (June 27, 1862): Disabled: Appt. Wardmaster in a Petersburg hosp., Spring, 1864.

(1) MADDOX, JOHN Y. — Sick in hosp., Fall, 1861: Died, Feb. 6, 1862.

(1) MASIUS, EDWIN — Died of disease, July 20, 1862.

(1) MAUS, PETER — Sick in hosp., Oct. 28, 1861: W. (ear), Gaines' Mill (June 27, 1862): Prom., 4Cpl., Aug. 1, 1862: K., Antietam (Sept. 17, 1862).

MAYFIELD, JAS. S. — Enlisted, Mar. 2, 1863 at Navasota, Tex.: W. (left thigh) in No. Georgia, Sept. 15, 1863: No other record.

(1) MEISSNER, PAUL — Died at camp near Dumfries, Va., Jan. 28, 1862.

MENGER, OSCAR — Enl., Apr. 5, 1862 at San Antonio: W., Antietam (Sept. 17, 1862): Disabled, given wound furlough to Tex., Jan., 1863: Did not return to Co.

MENEFEE, Q. M. — Enl., Mar. 22, 1862 at Hallettsville, Tex.: W. & POW, Antietam (Sept. 17, 1862): Exchanged: Right leg amputated: Dischgd., Nov. 12, 1862.

(1) MORRIS, WM. — W. (leg), Gaines' Mill (June 27, 1862): Extra duty as Regmtl. QM clerk, Jan., 1863: W. (leg), Wilderness (May 6, 1864): Transfd. to Willis' Btln. of Tex. Cav., Feb. 13, 1865.

MURRAY, JAS. C. — Enl., Mar. 23, 1862 at San Antonio: Prom., 3Cpl., Nov. 22, 1862: Prom., 1Cpl., May 20, 1863: Hospitalized at Charlottesville, Va., with acute diarrhea, Summer, 1863.

(1) MURRAY, ROBT. W. — Sick in hosp., Oct., 1861: W., Antietam (Sept. 17, 1862): Prom., 3Cpl.: W., Wilderness (May 6, 1864): Leg amputated, May 28, 1864.

(1) NAURATH, WM. — On extra duty in Brig. Band: Sick at camp near Richmond, Va., Summer & Fall, 1862: Dischgd., Mar. 5, 1863 for disability (chronic rheumatism) and over-age.

(1) NEWTON, N. M. — Sick in hosp., Oct. 19, 1861: Dischgd. on Surg. Cert., Dec. 9, 1861.

PENN, ABRAHAM C. — Enl., at Burleson, Tex., Mar. 20, 1863: W., Chickamauga (Sept. 19, 1863): Disabled & furloughed to Tex.

(1) PENN, PATRICK J. — Detailed as nurse at hosp. at Winchester, Va., Sept. 20, 1862: Prom., 5Sgt., Nov. 22, 1862: Prom., 4Sgt., May 20, 1863: W., Chaffin's Farm (Sept. 29, 1864): Died from wound, Oct. 1, 1864.

PICKETT, MICHAEL — Enl., Apr. 25, 1862 at Beaumont, Tex.: W., ("stomach bruised by a bomb"), Gaines' Mill (June 27, 1862): Died, Oct. 31, 1863.

(1) POLLEY, JOS. B. — See roster, "Regmtl. Hdqtrs., 4th Tex. Inf."

(2) POGUE, LEVI S. — Enl., Mar. 15, 1862 at Hallettsville, Tex.: Detailed to CSA Pioneer (Engineer) Corps: W., Darbytown Road (Oct. 7, 1864): Paroled, Appomattox (Apr. 12, 1865).

QUICK, JACOB — Enl., Mar. 22, 1862 at Hallettsville, Tex.: Prom., 2Cpl.: Prom., 5Sgt., May 20, 1863: W., Chickamauga (Sept. 19, 1863): Disabled & dischgd.

(1) RECTOR, JAS. P. — Sick on furlough at Columbus, Tex., Summer, 1861: Deserted in Tex., did not go to Va.

(1) RIGGS, JOHN — On extra duty as baker for Regt., Jan. 15, 1862: W., Antietam (Sept. 17, 1862): Died of wound.

(1) RILEY, DAVID W. — Sick in hosp. at Richmond, Fall, 1861: Deserted from hosp., Jan., 1862.

(1) ROBERTS, JOHN — Detailed as a Regmtl. teamster, Mar.-May, 1862: Detailed as a Brig. teamster, May-Aug., 1862: Sick in hosp., Winter, 1862-Summer, 1863: Deserted, Spring, 1864.

(1) ROBINSON, HENRY — Deserted in New Orleans, Sept. 19, 1861.

RUMLEY, JOS. J. — Enl., Mar. 17, 1862 at Hallettsville, Tex., Sick in hosp. most of 1862 & Winter, 1862-63: POW, E. Tenn., Jan. 30, 1864: Confined at Camp Chase, Ohio: Took Fed. oath.

SERGEANT, ANDREW H. — Enl., Mar. 14, 1862 at Lyons, Tex.: Prom., 4Cpl.: Prom., 2Cpl., May 20, 1863: Prom., 1Cpl.: W. (shoulder) & POW, Gettysburg (July 2, 1863): Exchanged: Returned to Texas, disabled.

(1) SCHULTZ, WM. — Dischgd. for disability, Dec. 7, 1861: Reenl.: Asgnd. duty as Apothecary at Gen'l. Hosp. No. 8 (Richmond), Oct. 9, 1862.

(1) SCHWCEIR, GEO. — Sick in hosp., Fall, 1861: W. & POW, Antietam (Sept. 17, 1862): Exchanged: Furlough granted to Tex., Nov. 15, 1862: Never returned to Co.

SELF, M. M. — Enl., Mar. 22, 1862 at Hallettsville, Tex.: Died of pneumonia, June 20, 1862.

(1) SKINNER, RICHARD H. — Prom., 2Cpl., Nov. 1, 1861: Prom., 1Sgt., Nov. 22, 1862: Sent to Tex. on recruiting duty, Feb.-Apr., 1863: W. & POW, Gettysburg (July 2, 1863): Confined at Ft. Delaware: Paroled, Winchester, Va., Apr. 24, 1865.

(1) SMITH, HENRY — W., Antietam (Sept. 17, 1862): POW, Gettysburg (July 2, 1863).

(1) SNEED, ALBERT — W., 2nd Manassas (Aug. 30, 1862): Dischgd., Mar. 30, 1863.

STEPHENS, THOS. — Enl., Feb. 1, 1864 at New Market Rd., Va.: Deserted, Feb. 16, 1864: Took Fed. oath, Feb. 26, 1864.

(1) SULLIVAN, ROBT. A. — K., Gaines' Mill (June 27, 1862).

SUMMERVILLE, JAS. — Enl., Mar. 23, 1862 at San Antonio: W., Cold Harbor (June 10, 1864): Arm amputated, June 12, 1864.

(1) SUTHERLAND, JACK — See roster, "Regmtl. Hdqtrs., 4th Tex. Inf."

(1) SWEET, GEO. H. — Dischgd. by order (S. O. #21) of War Dept., Jan. 27, 1862.

(1) TALLIAFERRO, LAWRENCE — Transfd. to a Fredericksburg, Va. Artillery Co., Oct. 5, 1861.

(1) THORNTON, HOWARD G. — Sick, Fall, 1861: Sick furlough, Winter, 1861-62: Dischgd., Sept. 16, 1862 for lung disease.

(2) VEAL, FRANKLIN — See roster, "Regmtl. Hdqtrs., 4th Tex. Inf."

(1) WALLACE, E. F. — Sick in hosp., Fall, 1861: Missing at Boonsboro, Md. (Sept. 14, 1862).

(1) WEBER, SIMON — Sick at hosp. in Fredericksburg, Nov., 1861-Feb., 1862: Present for duty to June, 1863: No other record.

(1) WEIR, HENRY — POW, Point of Rocks, Md., Sept. 12, 1862: Exchanged: Granted sick furlough, Oct. 16, 1862: Did not return from furlough: As of Apr. 14, 1865, Weir was a Capt. stationed at the CS Arsenal at San Antonio.

(1) WISEMAN, JAS. — Sick, Fall, 1861: W. (hand & thigh) & POW, Gettysburg (July 2, 1863): Exchanged, Aug. 31, 1863: W. (thigh), Wilderness (May 6, 1864): Disabled & returned to Tex.: Paroled, San Antonio, Sept. 11, 1865.

(1) WOLF, SIMON — W., 2nd Manassas (Aug. 30, 1862): Died of wound.

WOOD, GREER W. — Enl., Mar. 22, 1862 at Hallettsville, Tex.: Hospitalized for diarrhea, May, 1862: Hospitalized for typhoid fever, June & July, 1862: POW, Gettysburg (July 2, 1863): Exchanged, Aug. 22, 1863: Hospitalized for asthma, May & June, 1864: Paroled at Columbus, Tex., July 28, 1865.

4TH TEX. VOL. INF. REGT.

COMPANY G — *GRIMES COUNTY GREYS*

Company was organized in Grimes County, Texas, enrolled at Harrisburg, Tex., July 19, 1861, and mustered into the Confederate service "for the war" at Richmond, Va., Sept. 30, 1861.

Key

(1) Original member of Company. (2) Paroled at Appomattox.
K (Killed), W (Wounded), POW (Prisoner of War)
AWOL (Absent Without Leave)

ORIGINAL OFFICERS

(1) HUTCHESON, JOHN W. Capt. — W., Gaines' Mill (June 27, 1862): Died of wound, June 29, 1862.

(1) DUNHAM, JOS. H. 1Lt. — Sick furlough to Tex., Dec. 11, 1861: Resgnd., June 12, 1862.

(1) KENNARD, JOHN R. 2Lt. — Resgnd., Aug. 6, 1861.

(1) BASSETT, ROBT. H. 3Lt. — See roster, "Regmtl. Hdqtrs., 4th Tex. Inf."

ORIGINAL NON-COMMISSIONED OFFICERS

(1) GOULD, JAS. L. 1Sgt. — Demoted to 2Sgt., Jan. 2, 1862: W., Gaines' Mill (June 27, 1862): W. & POW, Gettysburg (July 2, 1863): Died in prison camp in New York.

(1) BOOKMAN, J. M. ("Bob") 2Sgt. — See list of "Other Officers" following.

(1) WOOD, RUFUS H. 3Sgt. — Detailed to recruiting serv. in Tex., Feb.-Apr., 1862: Dischgd. for disability (chronic inflammation of knee), Aug. 5, 1862.

(1) BUTTS, DAVID LEWIS 4Sgt. — See list of "Other Officers" following.

(1) BLACKSHEAR, JAS. J. 1Cpl. — Appt., 3Sgt., Nov. 20, 1861: Sick in
(2) Hanover County, Va., June, 1862: W., Antietam (Sept. 17, 1862): Paroled, Appomattox CH. (Apr. 12, 1865).

(1) BAKER, JESSE W. 2Cpl. — See list of "Other Officers" following.

(1) ATKINSON, JOHN J. 3Cpl. — See list of "Other Officers" following.

(1) McCLENNEY, WM. H. 4Cpl. — Appt. 3Cpl., Jan., 1862: Prom., 5Sgt., Aug. 1, 1862: Reduced to Pvt., Sept. 16, 1862: Prom., 4Sgt., Winter, 1863-64: K., Wilderness (May 6, 1864).

OTHER OFFICERS

(2) BUFFINGTON, THOS. C. Capt. — Orig. Pvt. in Co.: Appt. 2Cpl., Sept. 15, 1861: Appt. 1Cpl., Winter, 1861-62: Elect., 3Lt., June 21, 1862: Prom., 2Lt., June 27, 1862: Prom., 1Lt., July 30, 1862: POW, 2nd Manassas (Aug. 30, 1862): Exchanged, Nov. 10, 1862: Prom., Capt., June 23, 1864: "Leave of indulgence" granted by Gen. Lee, Jan. 24, 1865.

BAKER, JESSE W. 2Lt. — Orig. 2Cpl. in Co.: Elect., 2Lt., Sept. 14, 1861: Sent to rear because of sickness, June 28, 1862: Resigned, July 30, 1862.

BOOKMAN, J. M. 2Lt. — Orig. 2Sgt. of Co.: Appt. 1Sgt., Jan. 7, 1862: Elect., 3Lt., July 12, 1862: Prom., 2Lt., July 30, 1862: K., Chickamauga (Sept. 19, 1863).

(2) ATKINSON, JOHN J. 3Lt. — Orig. 3Cpl. of Co.: Appt. 2Cpl., Winter, 1861-62: Prom., 1Sgt., July 12, 1862: Elect., 3Lt., Feb. 4, 1863: W., Chickamauga (Sept. 19, 1863): W. (thigh), White Oak Swamp (Aug. 16, 1864): Paroled, Appomattox (Apr. 12, 1865).

BARRY, WM. E. 3Lt. — Orig. Pvt. in Co.: W. (arm), Gaines' Mill (June 27, 1862): POW, Antietam (Sept. 17, 1862): Confined at Ft. Delaware: Exchanged, Nov. 10, 1862: Elect., 3Lt., Mar. 7, 1864: W. (arm), Wilderness (May 6, 1864): Retired for disability, Nov. 28, 1864.

BUTTS, DAVID LEWIS 3Lt. — Orig. 4Sgt. of Co.: Elect., 3Lt., Oct. 10, 1861: K., Gaines' Mill (June 27, 1862).

ROACH, JOHN 3Lt. — Orig. Pvt. in Co.: Prom., 3Lt., Aug. 2, 1862: K., Antietam (Sept. 17, 1862).

MUSICIANS

(1) COLLINS, DANIEL — See roster, "Regmtl. Hdqtrs., 4th Tex. Inf."
(1) PINCKNEY, RICH. — Appt. musician, Oct. 1, 1861: Transfd. to Co. A, 10th Tex. Inf. Regt., by order of Sec. of War, May 9, 1863: Served with Conf. Naval Cadets for short period: Reasgnd. to Co. G, 4th Tex. Inf. Regt., Winter, 1863-64: Youngest man in Co.
(1) ROCO, ALBERT C. — Appt. musician, Oct. 1, 1861: POW, Gettysburg (July 2, 1863).

PRIVATES

ADAMS, SAM H. — Enl. at Anderson, Tex., Mar. 2, 1862: Sick in hosp., Spring, 1862: Dischgd. for disability (hemorroids & chronic rheumatism), July 28, 1862.
(2) AIKENS, JAS. O. — Enl. at Anderson, Tex., Mar. 19, 1862: Sick in a Richmond hosp., Summer, 1862: Detailed to Provost Guard, Winter, 1864: Paroled, Appomattox (Apr. 12, 1865).
ALLEN, WM. J. — Enl. at Anderson, Tex., Mar. 13, 1862: Sick, Spring & Summer, 1862: Dischgd. for chronic bronchitis, Oct. 25, 1862.
(1) ARNETT, DAVID — Left sick, Manassas, Va., Aug. 30, 1862: Detailed to Provost Guard, Fall, 1862: Prom., 4Cpl., Feb. 4, 1863: POW, Gettysburg (July 2, 1863): Confined at Ft. Delaware: Paroled, June 9, 1865.
(1) BAINES, TOM N. — Appt. 5Sgt., Sept. 15, 1861: Appt. 4Sgt., Oct. 11, 1861: Died in Richmond, Nov. 7, 1861.
(1) BAINES, WM. M. — Detchd. serv. attending sick in Richmond, Va.,
(2) Oct. 15, 1861: W. (side), Gaines' Mill (June 27, 1862): Prom., 2Sgt., May 1, 1864: W. (hand), Wilderness (May 6, 1864): Paroled, Appomattox (Apr. 12, 1865).
(1) BARKER, JAS. C. — Scout on Occoquan River, Va., Winter, 1861-62: Sick, Richmond, Va., Spring & Summer, 1862: Dischgd. for disability (asthma), Oct. 9, 1862.
(1) BARNES, JOHN T. — Died in Richmond, Dec. 29, 1861.
(1) BARRY, JOHN D. — W., Antietam (Sept. 17, 1862): K., Chickamauga (Sept. 19, 1863).
(1) BARRY, LEWIS HOWARD — Appt. 4Sgt., Oct. 11, 1861: Prom.,
(2) 3Sgt.: W., Antietam (Sept. 17, 1862): Prom., 1Sgt.: W. (arm), Wilderness (May 6, 1864): Paroled, Appomattox (Apr. 12, 1865).
BARRY, THOS. W. — Transfd. into Co. G, 4th Tex. from Co. A, 10th Tex. Inf. Regt., June 14, 1863: No other record.
(1) BARRY, WM. E. — See list of "Other Officers" above.
BASSETT, NOAH — Enl., Mar. 15, 1862 at Anderson, Tex.: Left sick in Tex. by recruiting officer: Detailed as Agent of the Tex. Depot in Richmond, Nov. 17, 1862: Transfd. to a unit in the Trans-Miss. Dept., Mar. 16, 1864.
(1) BEECHER, RUDOLPH A. — Appt. 5Sgt., Sept. 11, 1862: Missing at Boonsboro, Md. (Sept. 14, 1862): Rejnd. Co.: Prom., 1Sgt., Feb. 4, 1863: K., Gettysburg (July 2, 1863).

(2) BLACKSHEAR, DUNCAN R. — Enl. at Anderson, Tex., May 15, 1863: Appt. Sgt.: W. (thigh), Wilderness (May 6, 1864): Paroled, Appomattox (Apr. 12, 1865).

BLACKSHEAR, E. T. — Transfd. into Co. G, 4th Tex. Inf. from Co. A, 10th Tex. Inf. Regt., June 14, 1863: Given 90 day furlough: Died in Thomas County, Ga., before he jnd. Co.

BLACKSHEAR, ROBT. D. — Recruited Mar. 19, 1862 at Anderson, Tex.: Asgnd. to CSA QM Dept., Summer, 1862 & Winter, 1863-64: W., Antietam (Sept. 17, 1862): W. (lower jaw), Spotsylvania CH. (May 12, 1864): Retired for disability, July 11, 1864.

(1) BOOZER, H. D. — Appt. 2Cpl., Oct. 1, 1862: Prom., 4Sgt.: POW, Gettysburg (July 2, 1863): Confined at Ft. Delaware: Escaped, Feb. 27, 1865.

BOWEN, ALLEN — Recruited, Mar. 19, 1862 at Anderson, Tex.: Sick in Richmond, Spring, 1862: Dischgd. for disability (dropsy of chest) at Culpeper, Va., Nov. 2, 1862.

(1) BRIETZ, A. C. — See roster, "Regmtl. Hdqtrs., 4th Tex. Inf."
(1) BUFFINGTON, THOS. C. — See list of "Other Officers" above.
(1) CARLEY, MARTIN F. — Sick in Lynchburg, Va., Spring, 1862: Detailed to Provost Guard, Dec., 1863: Furlough to Wilkinson Co., Miss., Granted, Jan. 1, 1865.

CHAMBERS, G. C. — Recruited, Mar. 10, 1862 at Anderson, Tex.: K., Antietam (Sept. 17, 1862).

CHATHAM, WM. L. — Recruited, Mar. 14, 1862 at Anderson, Tex.: Sick in Richmond, Summer, 1862: Prom., 1Cpl., May 1, 1864: W. (knee), Wilderness (May 6, 1864).

CHURCHWELL, THOS. — Recruited, Mar. 11, 1862 at Anderson, Tex.: K., Chickamauga (Sept. 20, 1863).

CLOSS, THOS. O. — Recruited, Mar. 15, 1862 at Anderson, Tex.: K., Gettysburg (July 2, 1863).

(1) COTTON, HENDERSON T. — Died of pneumonia, Fredericksburg, Va., Mar. 28, 1862.

(2) COOKE, J. J. — Transfd. into Co. G, 1863: Paroled, Appomattox (Apr. 12, 1865): No other record.

CRUSE, A. J. — Recruited, Mar. 18, 1862 at Anderson, Tex.: K., Gaines' Mill (June 27, 1862).

DAFFAN, LAWRENCE A. — Recruited, Mar. 15, 1862 at Anderson, Tex.: POW, Lenore Station, Tenn., Fall, 1863: Confined at Rock Island, Ill.: Paroled, June 19, 1865.

(1) DAMM, FRANK A. — POW, Antietam (Sept. 17, 1862): Confined at Ft. Delaware: Exchanged, Nov. 10, 1862: Detailed to hosp., Spring, 1864: Paroled, Nashville, Tenn., May 22, 1865.

(1) DANCE, JOHN T. — W. (both legs), Gaines' Mill (June 27, 1862): Sick leave to Texas: Returned to duty, Summer, 1864.

(2) DAVIS, ED. C. — Recruited, Mar. 14, 1862 at Anderson, Tex.: Present for duty entire war: Paroled, Appomattox (Apr. 12, 1865).

DAVIS, JOHN A. — Recruited, Mar. 15, 1862 at Anderson, Tex.: Transfd. to Co. B, 49th Va. Inf. Regt., Mar. 12, 1864.

(1) DAWKINS, F. A. — Died, Richmond, Va., Dec. 29, 1861.

(1) DUKE, JOS. G. — Captured Federal flag at 2nd Manassas (Aug. 30, 1862): Sick, Winter, 1862-63: W., Chickamauga (Sept. 19, 1863): Died, Oct. 20, 1863.

EKELLS, WM. R. A. — Recruited, Mar. 6, 1862 at Anderson, Tex.: W., Gaines' Mill (June 27, 1862): Arm amputated.

(1) FERRELL, S. DAVE — W., Gaines' Mill (June 27, 1862): K., Gettysburg (July 2, 1863).

(1) FIELDS, DRURY H. — Sick, Fall & Winter, 1861: Dischgd. for disability (tuberculosis), June 21, 1862.

(1) FINLEY, J. K. — Died, Richmond, Jan. 30, 1862.

(1) FLOURNOY, JAS. J. — W., Gaines' Mill (June 27, 1862): Wound furlough to Tex., July & Aug., 1862: Never returned to Co.: Asgnd. to Invalid Corps in Tex.: Retired for disability, Feb. 22, 1865.

FLOYD, CHAS. E. — Detailed to Div. Ambulance Corps, Spring, 1862: Died of gangrene at Howard Grove Hosp., Richmond, Feb. 26, 1863.

(1) FLOYD, WM. W. — Enl. at Anderson, Tex., July 19, 1861: Sick, Leesburg, Va., Sept., 1862: Died, Atlanta, Ga., Jan., 1863.

FREEMAN, M. P. — Hired as a substitute for A. E. Watson on Nov. 2, 1862: Deserted, Nov. 4, 1862.

(1) GAY, GUS A. — W., Gaines' Mill (June 27, 1862): Dischgd. for disability.

(1) GILES, E. D. — Sick in Richmond, Fall, 1861: Died, Ashland, Va., Apr. 23, 1862.

(1) GILES, J. L. — Died, Ashland, Va., Nov. 10, 1861.

(1) GILES, JOHN J. — Died, Richmond, Va., Apr. 16, 1862.

GREENE, JOHN H. — Recruited, Mar. 10, 1862 at Anderson, Tex.: K., Gettysburg (July 2, 1863).

(1) GRIFFIN, DAVID C. — W. (thigh), Gaines' Mill (June 27, 1862): Disabled for field duty: Asgnd. duty as a teamster, July, 1862-Oct., 1864: Also reported to have died of heart disease, June 21, 1863.

(1)
(2) GRISSETT, WM. J. — Sick in Richmond, Fall, 1861 & Spring, 1862: W., Wilderness (May 6, 1864): Prom. to 2Cpl., May 11, 1864: Prom., 5Sgt.: Paroled, Appomattox (Apr. 12, 1865).

HADDON, JAS. J. — Recruited, Mar. 26, 1862 at Anderson, Tex.: Sick, Richmond, Spring, 1862: Detailed as nurse at Richmond, Aug., 1862: Detailed as shoemaker at Petersburg, Va. QM Depot, Nov., 1862: Transfd. to Columbus, Ga., QM Depot as shoemaker, July, 1863.

(1) HADDON, MACK E. — K., 2nd Manassas (Aug. 30, 1862).

(1) HARRISON, M. M. ("Smokey") — Sick in Richmond, Spring & Summer, 1862: Dischgd. for disability (asthma), Winchester, Va., Oct. 21, 1862.

(1) HASSON, ROBT. — Sick, Fall, 1861; Spring, 1862; & Fall & Winter, 1862-63: Prom., 2Cpl., Mar. 7, 1864: Prom., 5Sgt., May 1, 1864: W. (hand), Wilderness (May 6, 1864): W., Darbytown Rd. (Oct. 7, 1864): Leg amputated.

(1) HELMER, ED. G. — Died, Oct. 23, 1861.

(1) HUBBELL, N. L. — Died in camp near Dumfries, Va., Dec. 26, 1861.

HUGHES, WM. T. — Recruited, Mar. 6, 1862 at Anderson, Tex.: Sick in Hanover County, Va., June, 1862: Died, July 8, 1862.

HYETT, J. W. — Recruited, Mar. 14, 1862 at Anderson, Tex.: Hospitalized with pneumonia, Spring, 1863: W., Gettysburg (July 2, 1863): Three fingers amputated: Dischgd. for disability: Paroled, Selma, Ala., May 25, 1865.

(1) HYMAN, GEO. W. — Detailed to Div. Ambulance Corps: W. (shoulder) & POW, Antietam (Sept. 17, 1862): Confined at Ft. McHenry: Exchanged, early Jan., 1863: Furlough to Tex.: Paroled, Galveston, Tex., Aug. 14, 1865.

(1) JACKSON, ISAAC — Dischgd. for disability (rheumatism), Fredericksburg, Va., Jan. 20, 1862.

(1) JACKSON, JOB — W., 2nd Manassas (Aug. 30, 1862): W., Antietam (Sept. 17, 1862): Leg amputated.

(1) JONES, GEO. W. — Sick in Richmond, Fall, 1861 & Summer, 1862:
(2) Paroled, Appomattox (Apr. 12, 1865).

(1) JONES, ISAAC N. — Prom., 4Cpl., Nov. 20, 1861: Sick, Spring & Summer, 1862: Prom., 1Cpl., July, 1862: Reduced to ranks, Sept. 1, 1862: Asgnd. as nurse, Sept., 1862: Dischgd. for disability (asthma & hepatitis), Oct. 23, 1862.

JONES, N. B. — Recruited, Mar. 22, 1862 at Anderson, Tex.: Sick in Richmond most of 1862: Deserted, Spring, 1863.

JONES, W. S. — Recruited, Mar. 15, 1862 at Anderson, Tex.: K., Gaines' Mill (June 27, 1862).

KAY, ELI — Recruited, Mar. 14, 1862 at Anderson, Tex.: Sick in Culpeper, Va. hosp., Winter, 1862-63: Hospitalized with VD, Jan., 1865: Paroled, Meridian, Miss., May 16, 1865.

(1) KELLY, B. FRANK — W. (arm), Gaines' Mill (June 27, 1862): W.,
(2) Antietam (Sept. 17, 1862): POW, Gettysburg (July 2, 1863): Exchanged, Mar. 3, 1864: W. (abdomen), Darbytown Rd. (Oct. 7, 1864): Hospitalized, Fall, 1864: Paroled, Appomattox (Apr. 12, 1865).

(1) KELLY, SOLOMON P. — Sick in Richmond, Spring & Summer, 1862: W., Antietam (Sept. 17, 1862): Detailed to Brig. Provost Guard, Apr., 1864: W., near Richmond, Apr. 2, 1865: Paroled, Montgomery, Ala., May 21, 1865.

(1) KENDALL, J. L. — Died in camp near Dumfries, Va., Dec. 20, 1861.

(1) KENNARD, A. DREW — Died in Richmond, Nov. 27, 1861.

KING, JOHN H. — Recruited, Mar. 26, 1862 at Anderson, Tex.: Dischgd. for disability (asthma), Oct. 23, 1862.

(1) LAWRENCE, GROCE — W., Antietam (Sept. 17, 1862): Appt. 3Cpl., Oct. 1, 1862: K., Wilderness (May 6, 1864).

LIVINGSTON, ABRAHAM — Recruited, Mar. 10, 1862 at Anderson, Tex.: Sick in Richmond, May, 1862: Dischgd. for disability, Aug. 14, 1862.

LOGGINS, JAS. C. — Recruited, Mar. 10, 1862 at Anderson, Tex.: Sick in Richmond, Summer, 1862: POW, Gettysburg (July 2, 1863): Confined at Ft. Delaware, Md.: Escaped, July 1, 1864, and rejnd. Co.

LOPER, WM. H. — Transfd. into Co. G from Co. H, 4th Tex., Apr. 1, 1862: Sick in Culpeper County, Va., Summer & Fall, 1862: Reported to have deserted in Md., July 6, 1863.

McDANIEL, BEN H. — Recruited, Mar. 25, 1862 at Anderson, Tex.: Sick in Bedford County, Va., June, 1862: Dischgd. for disability (asthma), July 19, 1862.

McGOWAN, JOS. — Former Tex. Ranger: Recruited, Mar. 18, 1862 at Anderson, Tex.: Appt. 4Cpl., Oct., 1862: K., Chickamauga (Sept. 20, 1863).

McGREGOR, WM. B. — Recruited, Mar. 22, 1862 at Anderson, Tex.: Sick (VD), Charlottesville, Va., June, 1862: Sick in Richmond, Aug., 1862: Sick (acute diarrhea), Petersburg, Spring, 1863: Hospitalized (VD), Summer, 1864.

(1)
(2) MARTIN, JOHN F. — Sick, June, 1862: Present for duty rest of the war: Prom., 2Cpl., Winter, 1864-65: Paroled, Appomattox (Apr. 12, 1865).

(1)
(2) MARTIN, WM. A. — Present for duty entire war: W. (shoulder), Wilderness (May 6, 1864): Paroled, Appomattox (Apr. 12, 1865).

(1) MAYS, JOHN W. T. — Sick in Richmond, Nov. 8, 1861: W. ("paralyzed by a bombshell"), Gaines' Mill (June 27, 1862): Appt. Co. Color Guard: W. (leg), 2nd Manassas (Aug. 30, 1862): Missing, Knoxville, Tenn., Nov. 29, 1863: AWOL in Tex.: Thought to have jnd. the Cav.

MIDKIFF, E. P. — Recruited, Mar. 19, 1862 at Anderson, Tex.: K., Gaines' Mill (June 27, 1862).

(1) MIDKIFF, ISAAC A. ("Babe") — Sick in Richmond, Oct. 24, 1861: Detailed to duty as Ambulance Driver, Spring & Summer, 1862: W. (leg), Wilderness (May 6, 1864): Paroled, Appomattox (Apr. 12, 1865).

(1) MONTGOMERY, JOS. W. — W. (leg), Gaines' Mill (June 27, 1862): W. (hand), 2nd Manassas (Aug. 30, 1862): Hospitalized for chronic diarrhea, Spring, 1864.

(2) MOORING, CHAS. G. — Recruited, Mar. 10, 1862 at Anderson, Tex.: Sick in Charlottesville, Va., Summer, 1862: W., Wilderness (May 6, 1864): Paroled, Appomattox (Apr. 12, 1865).

(1) MOORING, JAS. S. ("Bob") — Detailed to QM Dept. as a teamster, Winter, 1861-62: Sick at Frederick Hall, Va., June, 1862: Appt. Surgeon's Orderly, Aug., 1862: Detailed as a Brig. teamster, Mar., 1863: W., Wilderness (May 6, 1864): Lost use of arm & dischgd. for disability.

(1) MORSE, GEO. T. — Dischgd. for disability, Richmond, Nov. 20, 1861.

(1) MULDROW, JOHN T. — Sick in Richmond, Oct., 1861 to June, 1862: W. (ankle), Wilderness (May 6, 1864): Paroled, New Orleans, July 12, 1865).

(1)
(2) MUSE, JAS. T. — W. (forehead), Gaines' Mill (June 27, 1862): Sick in hosp. in Jerusalem, Va., Apr., 1863: Paroled, Appomattox (Apr. 12, 1865).

(1) NEAL, FRANK S. — Sick in Richmond, Oct., 1861: Gave out and fell to rear, June 27, 1862 (Gaines' Mill): Sick in Richmond, Aug., 1862: Prom., Cpl.: Reduced to ranks, Sept. 11, 1862: POW, Gettysburg (July 2, 1863): Confined at Ft. Delaware: Paroled, May 20, 1865.

(1) NELMS, EVERAND P. — Appt. 4Cpl., June 21, 1862: W. (hip), Gaines' Mill (June 27, 1862): Reduced to Pvt., Sept. 11, 1862: Dischgd. for disability, Dec. 12, 1862.

(1) NETTLES, JOS. H. — Sick, sent to rear, Sept. 17, 1862 (Antietam): Duty with CSA Engineer Corps, June, 1863: W., Gettysburg (July 2, 1863): W. (leg), Wilderness (May 6, 1864).

(1) NIX, JOHN L. — Sick in Richmond, Summer, 1862: POW, near Suffolk, Va., Apr., 1863: Exchanged: W. (arm), Gettysburg (July 2, 1863): Recuperation leave to Tex., Sept., 1863: Did not return to Co.

(1) PARNELL, JAS. C. — Transfd. to Co. A, 10th Tex. Inf. Regt., June 1, 1863.

PATTERSON, W. R. — Recruited, Mar. 17, 1862 at Anderson, Tex.: Died, Richmond, June 19, 1862.

(1) PEARCE, BEN W. — W., Antietam (Sept. 17, 1862): Dischgd. for disability (exostosis), Oct. 20, 1862: Paroled, Millican, Tex., July 10, 1865.

(1) PEARCE, ED. W. — W., (Gaines' Mill (June 27, 1862): Hand amputated.

(1) PETEET, JAS. MONROE — W., Gaines' Mill (June 27, 1862): Dischgd. for disability, Apr. 7, 1863.

(1) PETEET, WM. B. — W. (leg), Gaines' Mill (June 27, 1862): Transfd. to Co. E, 5th Ala. Inf. Regt., May 15, 1863.

(1) PINCKNEY, JOHN M. — W., Wilderness (May 6, 1864): Paroled,
(2) Appomattox (Apr. 12, 1865).

(2) PLASTERS, H. FRANK — Enl. at Anderson, Tex., Apr. 16, 1862: Paroled, Appomattox (Apr. 12, 1865): No other record.

(1) PLASTERS, JOS. H. — W. (leg), Gaines' Mill (June 27, 1862): W. (leg), Wilderness (May 6, 1864).

(2) QUALLS, GEO. S. — Recruited, Mar. 6, 1862 at Anderson, Tex.: Sick at Richmond, May, 1862: Appt. Color-Cpl. for Co.: Paroled, Appomattox (Apr. 12, 1865).

(2) REYNOLDS, JAS. S. — Recruited, Mar. 10, 1862 at Anderson, Tex.: Detailed to QM Dept., Winter, 1863-64: Paroled, Appomattox (Apr. 12, 1865).

(1) ROACH, JOHN — See list of "Other Officers" above.

(1) ROBINSON, JOHN H. — Detailed to Pioneer Corps, Dec., 1862: Deserted, Mar., 1864.

(1) ROGERSON, JOHN — K., Gaines' Mill (June 27, 1862).

ROWE, H. T. — Recruited, Mar. 15, 1862 at Anderson, Tex.: W., Antietam (Sept. 17, 1862): Present for duty up to Aug., 1864: No record after that.

(1) SCHULTZ, W. J. — Paid $50.00 bounty, July 24, 1862: Oct. 4, 1862 asgnd. to duty as Apothecary at Gen'l. Hosp. No. 8: Relieved from duty at Gen'l. Hosp. No. 8, Dec. 19, 1862 & ordered to report to Asst. Surg. at Hanover Junction, Va.

(1) SCOTT, GARRETT — K., Antietam (Sept. 17, 1862).

SCOTT, J. B. — Recruited, Mar. 22, 1862 at Anderson, Tex.: W., Gaines' Mill (June 27, 1862): Died of wound, July 5, 1862.

(1) SHAFFER, H. E. — See roster, "Regmtl. Hdqtrs., 4th Tex. Inf."

(1) SILVERBAUGH, D. — W. (elbow), Gaines' Mill (June 27, 1862): K., Chickamauga (Sept. 19, 1863).

SMITH, WM. H. — Recruited, Mar. 17, 1862 at Anderson, Tex.: Sick at Richmond most of 1862: Dischgd. for disability, Spring, 1863: Re-enl. in Tex.: Paroled, Millican, Tex., July 11, 1863.

SPENCER, CHAS. W. — Recruited, Mar. 15, 1862 at Anderson, Tex.: W., Eltham's Landing (May 7, 1862): Died of wound, June 3, 1862.

STACEY, JNO. J. — Recruited, Mar. 12, 1862 at Anderson, Tex.: Appt. Color-Cpl. for Co.: W. & POW, Gettysburg (July 2, 1863): Confined at Ft. Delaware: Exchanged: Prom., 3Cpl., May, 1864: Retired from Invalid Corps, Nov. 30, 1864.

(1) STACEY, WILLIS A. — W. (arm), Gaines' Mill (June 27, 1862): W.
(2) (head), Wilderness (May 6, 1864): Prom. to 3Cpl., May, 1864: Prom., 3Sgt.: Paroled, Appomattox (Apr. 12, 1865).

(1) STEWART, ANDREW JACKSON — W. (thigh), Gettysburg (July 2,
(2) 1863): Paroled, Appomattox (Apr. 12, 1865).

(1) TERRELL, ED. THOS. — See roster, "Regmtl. Hdqtrs., 4th Tex. Inf."

(1) TERRELL, WM. H. — Died (pneumonia), Richmond, Apr. 10, 1862.

(1) THOMAS, ISAAC W. ("Gotch") — W., Boonsboro (Sept. 14, 1862): Sick, sent to Tex. Hosp. at Richmond, Mar. 2, 1863: Left Co. in E. Tenn., Winter, 1863-64: AWOL in Tex.

TIDWELL, WM. C. — Recruited, Mar. 26, 1862 at Anderson, Tex.: Detailed to Div. Ambulance Corps, Summer, 1862: Sick in Richmond, Aug., 1862: Dischgd. for disability (chronic rheumatism), Nov., 24, 1862.

(1) TRANT, JOHN — W., Gaines' Mill (June 27, 1862): K., Antietam (Sept. 17, 1862).

(1) TURNER, JASPER — Died in camp near Dumfries, Va., Dec. 23, 1861. 1861.

(1) TURNER, WESLEY — Sick at Richmond, Oct. 29, 1861: Dischgd. for disability, Nov. 25, 1861.

(2) WALLINGFORD, THOS. G. — Recruited, Mar. 15, 1862 at Anderson, Tex.: Oldest man in Co.: W., Darbytown (Oct. 13, 1864): Paroled, Appomattox (Apr. 12, 1865).

(1) WARD, CHAS. F. — Died in hosp., 1862: No other record.

(1) WATSON, A. E. — Sick in Culpeper, Va., Aug. 20, 1862: Dischgd., Nov. 2, 1862, produced a substitute (M. P. Freeman).

WEBB, FRANK X. — Recruited, Mar. 26, 1862 at Anderson, Tex.: Age 44: Sick, Summer & Fall, 1862: Furlough granted, Spring, 1863: Dischgd. for disability (inflammation of kidneys), Spring, 1864.

(1) WHITE, CALEB — K., Gaines' Mill (June 27, 1862).

(1) WHITE, MATTHEW D. — Died, Dumfries, Va., Dec. 31, 1861.

(1) WHITEHURST, J. K. — Sick numerous times in 1862 & 1863: POW, in East Tenn., Nov., 1863.

(1) WHITESIDE, ASA HOXEY — POW, Gettysburg (July 2, 1863): Drowned trying to escape from Ft. Delaware, Md., Winter, 1864.

(1) WHITLOCK, A. THOS. — Sick in Richmond, Sept. & Oct., 1861: Detached duty as a Brig. teamster, Jan., 1862-Mar., 1864: Hospitalized with heart trouble, Apr., 1864: Died, May 18, 1864 of dropsy.

(2)   WILLIAMS, HENRY F. — Recruited, Mar. 15, 1862 at Anderson, Tex.: Sick at Richmond, Aug., 1862 & Apr., 1864: Paroled, Appomattox (Apr. 12, 1865).

(1)   WILLIAMS, JOS. J. — W. (knee), Gaines' Mill (June 27, 1862): Wound furlough to Tex.: Dischgd. for disability at Houston, July 13, 1863.

WILSON, WALTER — Recruited, Mar. 10, 1862 at Anderson, Tex.: Sick at Richmond, May, 1862: W., 2nd Manassas (Aug. 30, 1862): Furlough granted to Tex.: Dischgd., June 1, 1863 for disability.

(1)   WOMACK, MARK S. — Sick, 1862: POW, Gettysburg (July 2, 1863): Sent to Ft. Delaware: Paroled, June 9, 1865.

(1)   WOOD, DAN A. — Prom., 1Cpl., Oct., 1862: POW, Antietam (Sept. 17, 1862): Confined at Ft. Delaware: Exchanged, Nov. 10, 1862: Prom., 5Sgt., Feb. 4, 1863: W. (neck & leg), Wilderness (May 6, 1864): W. (leg), Chaffin's Farm (Sept. 29, 1864).

4TH TEX. VOL. INF. REGT.

COMPANY H — *PORTER GUARDS*

Company was organized in Walker County, Texas, was enrolled at Huntsville, May 7, 1861, and was mustered into the Confederate service "for the war" at Richmond, Va., Sept. 30, 1861. Company included men from Grimes, Montgomery, and Washington Counties as well as Walker County.

Key

(1) Original member of Company. (2) Paroled at Appomattox.
K (Killed), W (Wounded), POW (Prisoner of War)
AWOL (Absent Without Leave)

ORIGINAL OFFICERS

(1)   PORTER, PROCTOR P. Capt. — W., Gaines' Mill (June 27, 1862): Died of typhoid fever while recuperating from his wound, July 20, 1862.

(1)   HUNTER, JAS. T. 1Lt. — Elect., Capt., July, 1862: W., 2nd Manassas
(2)   (Aug. 30, 1862): Paroled, Appomattox (Apr. 12, 1865): Led 4th Tex. Inf. Regt. back to Tex. after Appomattox.

(1)   OWEN, TOM M. 2Lt. — See roster, "Regmtl. Hdqtrs., 4th Tex. Inf."

(1)   RANDOLPH, BENTON 3Lt. — Elect., 2Lt., Oct. 25, 1861: W., Gaines' Mill (June 27, 1862): Transfd. to Gen. W. C. Hardee's Corps and appt. Judge Advocate of Corps, Feb. 12, 1863.

ORIGINAL NON-COMMISSIONED OFFICERS

(1) JONES, CHAS. E. 1Sgt. — See list of "Other Officers" following.

(1) SMITH, SAM Y. 2Sgt. — Dischgd., May 12, 1862, furnished a substitute (John Smith).

(1) FINLEY, HOWARD 3Sgt. — Resgnd. as Sgt., Dec. 12, 1861: Asgnd. to Brig. Comsy., Dec., 1861-Mar., 1863: Transfd. to Maj. Henry's Arty. Btln., Apr., 1863.

(1) MYER, NELS A. 4Sgt. — Appt. 1Sgt., Oct. 25, 1861: Detailed to recruiting serv. in Tex., Feb.-Apr., 1862: K., Gaines' Mill (June 27, 1862).

(1) REYNOLDS, BENJ. 5Sgt. — See list of "Other Officers" following.

(1) WYNNE, GUS A. 1Cpl. — Appt. 3Sgt., Dec. 12, 1861: W., Gaines' Mill (June 27, 1862): K., Antietam (Sept. 17, 1862).

(1) SAPP, HART T. 2Cpl. — Sick leave, Feb., 1862: W., Eltham's Landing (May 7, 1862): Dischgd. for disability, Sept. 4, 1862: Rejnd. Co., July 2, 1863: Prom., 1Sgt., May 6, 1864: POW, Darbytown Rd. (Oct. 7, 1864): Confined at Pt. Lookout, Md.: Exchanged, Jan. 17, 1865.

(1) LANDRUM, ZACK 3Cpl. — W. (thigh), Gettysburg (July 2, 1863): Permanently disabled.

(1) MORRIS, A. C. 4Cpl. — Died, typhoid fever, Dumfries, Va., Feb. 2, 1862.

OTHER OFFICERS

HOLMES, M. C. 1Lt. — W., 2nd Manassas (Aug. 30, 1862): Retired for disability, Aug. 25, 1864.

(2) SPIVEY, J. SYD 1Lt. — Orig. Pvt. in Co.: W., Gaines' Mill (June 27, 1862): Appt. 4Sgt., Dec. 15, 1862: Elect., 3Lt., Mar. 7, 1863: W., Gettysburg (July 2, 1863): Elect., 1Lt.: Paroled, Appomattox (Apr. 12, 1865).

JONES, CHAS. E. 2Lt. — Enl. in Montgomery County, Tex., July 29, 1861: Orig. 1Sgt. of Co.: Elect., 3Lt., Oct. 25, 1861: Detailed to recruiting serv. in Tex., Feb.-Apr., 1862: Elect., 2Lt., July, 1862: K., 2nd Manassas (Aug. 30, 1862).

REYNOLDS, BENJ. 2Lt. — Orig. 5Sgt. of Co.: Appt. 4Sgt., Oct. 25, 1861: Elect., 3Lt., Oct. 7, 1862: Prom., 2Lt., Mar. 7, 1863: K., Gettysburg (July 2, 1863).

TEDFORD, R. J. 3Lt. — Orig. Pvt. in Co.: Elect., 3Lt.: W., Chickamauga (Sept. 19, 1863): Dischgd. for disability.

MUSICIANS

(2) COLLIER, ARTHUR H. — See roster, "Regmtl. Hdqtrs., 4th Tex. Inf."

(1) HAHN, ADAM — Hospitalized, Fall & Winter, 1861: W. (abdomen), Gaines' Mill (June 27, 1862): W. (back) & POW, Gettysburg (July 2, 1863): Paroled, Aug. 24, 1863: Hospitalized at Lynchburg, Va., from Sept., 1863 to Aug., 1864.

(1) JETT, J. R. P. — See roster, "Regmtl. Hdqtrs., 4th Tex. Inf."
(2)

PRIVATES

(1) ALLEN, BEN H. — K., Gaines' Mill (June 27, 1862).
ANDERS, BURRELL — Enl. at Montgomery, Tex., Apr. 7, 1862, age 33: POW, Antietam (Sept. 17, 1862): Paroled, Sept. 30, 1862: Sick, Winter, 1862-63: W. (leg), Chickamauga (Sept. 19, 1863): Disabled, unfit for field duty: Asgnd. as a teamster, Summer, 1864: Retired, Dec. 17, 1864.
(1) BARZON, HENRY — K., Gaines' Mill (June 27, 1862).
(1) BASCOM, GEO. F. — Appt 5Sgt., Nov. 8, 1861: Died near Dumfries, Va., Dec. 9, 1861.
(1) BECK, JACOB — See roster, "Regmtl. Hdqtrs., 4th Tex. Inf."
(1) BELL, O. W. — Dischgd. (chronic dysentery), July 27, 1862.
(1) BRENT, THOS. A. — K., 2nd Manassas (Aug. 30, 1862).
BRYANT, GOLDEN D. L. — Enl. at Claiborne, Ala., Apr. 27, 1862, age 18: K., Gaines' Mill (June 27, 1862).
(1) BULLOCK, B. F. — Appt 1Cpl., July, 1862: W., 2nd Manassas (Aug. 30, 1862): Prom., 2Sgt., May 6, 1864: W. (foot), Wilderness (May 6, 1864): W., Darbytown Rd. (Oct. 7, 1864). Paroled at Jackson, Miss., May 19, 1865.
CARTWRIGHT, E. W. — K., in railroad accident at Holly Springs, Miss., en route to Va., Sept., 1861.
(1) CARTWRIGHT, JAS. G. W. — Appt. 4Sgt.: POW, Antietam (Sept. 17, 1862): Exchanged, Nov. 8, 1862: Appt. 2Sgt.: K., Wilderness (May 6, 1864).
CARTWRIGHT, L. C. — Enl. at Montgomery, Tex., Mar. 24, 1862, age 25: W., Darbytown Rd. (Oct. 7, 1864): Arm amputated.
CATHEY, BENNETT H. — Enl. at Montgomery, Tex., Apr. 5, 1862, age 23: Died, Apr. 30, 1863.
(1) CHILTON, FRANK B. — Dischgd., Sept. 15, 1862, under age (17): Returned to Tex. & re-enlisted in another Tex. Regt.: Prom. to Capt.: Serving as Chief Ordn. Off. with Gen. J. B. Robertson in Tex. when war ended.
CLEPPER, L. D. — Enl. at Montgomery, Tex., Mar. 18, 1862, age 23: Sick in hosp., Summer, 1862: Leave granted, Nov., 1862: Did not return to Co.
COLLIER, ARTHUR H. — See roster, "Regmtl. Hdqtrs., 4th Tex. Inf."
CONKLING, JAS. R. — Enl. in Walker Co., Tex., Feb. 27, 1863: Appt. 1Cpl., Jan., 1864: K., Wilderness (May 6, 1864).
(1) CONNOLLY, JAS. — Appt. 4Cpl., July, 1862: W. (shoulder), 2nd Manassas (Aug. 30, 1862): Dischgd. for disability.
(1) CONROW, CHAS. M. — Appt. 1Cpl., Dec. 12, 1861: K., Gaines' Mill (June 27, 1862).
(1) COPELAND, W. E. — W., Gaines' Mill (June 27, 1862): Foot amputated: Dischgd. for disability.
CROSS, T. M. — Enl., Apr. 27, 1863: Detailed to recruiting duty in Tex., June-Aug., 1863: Did not return to Co.

CUDE, WM. J. — Enl. at Montgomery, Tex., Apr. 5, 1862, age 23: AWOL in Tex., Spring, 1863.

DALE, G. W. — Enl. at Montgomery, Tex., Mar. 18, 1862, age 33: Appt. 3Sgt., May 6, 1864: W. (arm), Wilderness (May 6, 1864): Hospitalized for ulcers, Fall, 1864.

(1) DAMM, ADAM — Died of disease at Richmond, Apr. 25, 1862.

(1) DAWSON, R. C. — K., 2nd Manassas (Aug. 30, 1862).

(2) DILLARD, THOS. C. — Enl. at Huntsville, Tex., Mar. 24, 1862, age 21: Appt. 5Sgt.: Resgnd. as 5Sgt., Oct. 15, 1862: POW, Gettysburg (July 2, 1863): Exchanged: Appt. 2Cpl., May 6, 1864: Paroled, Appomattox (Apr. 12, 1865).

DOWDY, B. CALEB — Enl. at Huntsville, Tex., Mar. 20, 1862, age 26: W., 2nd Manassas (Aug. 30, 1862): W. (groin), Wilderness (May 6, 1864).

(1) EDMONDSON, T. J. — Died at Richmond, June 4, 1862.

ELLIS, JACK W. — Enl. at Huntsville, Tex., Mar. 20, 1862, age 21: W. (leg) & POW, Gettysburg (July 2, 1863): Died at DeCamp Gen. Hosp., David's Is., N.Y., July 31, 1863.

(1) FARROW, D. D. — Died in hosp. in Dumfries, Va., Dec. 12, 1861.

FARROW, SAM W. — Enl. at Montgomery, Tex., Mar. 20, 1862, age 40: Sick in Richmond, Fall, 1862; Winter, 1862-63 & Summer, 1864: Furlough to Tex.: Did not return to Co.

(1) FAULKNER, ALBERT — Dischgd. at Richmond, Dec. 26, 1861: Re-enl. at Montgomery, Tex., Mar. 29, 1862, age 24: K., Antietam (Sept. 17, 1862).

(1) FISHER, WM. S. ("Billy") — W. (arm), Gaines' Mill (June 27, 1862): Asgnd. to Provost Guard at Winchester, Va., Oct., 1862: W., Chickamauga (Sept. 19, 1863): Perm. disabled.

FOX, RICHARD — Enl. at Montgomery, Tex., Mar. 24, 1862, age 24: K., Antietam (Sept. 17, 1862).

GAFFORD, REUBAN D. — Enl. at Montgomery, Tex., Mar. 15, 1862, age 34: Died of disease at Richmond, May 25, 1862.

(1) GILLIAM, JOHN H. — K., Gaines' Mill (June 27, 1862).

(1) GRIGGS, GREEN — Sick, Summer, 1862: Appt. 5Sgt., Mar. 1, 1863: W. (abdomen), Wilderness (May 6, 1864): Furlough to Tex., Aug., 1864.

(1) HALL, JAS. H. — Sick in Richmond, Spring, 1862: Appt. 4Cpl., May 6,
(2) 1864: Paroled, Appomattox (Apr. 12, 1865).

(1) HARRISON, D. — Hospitalized, Summer, 1862: On leave, Fall, 1862: POW, near Chattanooga, Oct. 27, 1863: Took oath of allegiance to Feds., Nov. 5, 1863.

(1) HATCH, L. B. — Died at hosp. in Dumfries, Va., Dec. 23, 1861.

(1) HOLT, A. C. — Sick in hosp. (frost bite), Winter & Spring, 1862: Dischgd. on a Surg. Cert. of disability, July 28, 1862.

(1) HOPKINS, J. C. — Appt. 2Sgt., Sept., 1863: POW, Knoxville, Tenn., Nov. 20, 1863: Confined at Camp Chase, Ohio: Died of pneumonia, Mar. 13, 1864: Buried south of prison barracks.

(1) HOWARD, C. S. — Died near Dumfries, Va., Dec. 3, 1861.

(1) HOWARD, N. F. — Died of disease (typhoid fever) at Petersburg, Va., Apr. 25, 1862.

JEFFERS, MANLIUS S. — Enl. at Montgomery, Tex., Mar. 18, 1862, age 36: POW, Antietam (Sept. 17, 1862) left to attend the wounded: Exchanged, Sept. 30, 1862: Granted leave to Tex., Nov., 1862: Never returned to Co.: Was asgnd. to CSA QM Depot, Hempstead, Tex., Oct., 1864.

KEEBLE, EDWIN A. — Enl. by Capt. Hunter, Feb. 27, 1863: Transfd. to Co. D, 5th Tex. Inf. Regt., 1864.

(1) KERR, W. C. — Sick, Winter, 1861-62: POW, Gettysburg (July 2, 1863): Confined at Ft. Delaware: Paroled, June 9, 1865.

(1) KEYSER, GEO. W. — Dischgd. (sickness) in Richmond, Jan. 2, 1862.

(2) KEYSER, HENRY — Enl. at Huntsville, Tex., Mar. 18, 1862, age 36: Detailed to Brig. Comsy. Dept. as a butcher, Nov., 1862-Aug., 1864: Paroled, Appomattox (Apr. 12, 1865).

(1) KING, F. G. — Sick in Richmond, July, 1863: No record after Feb., 1864: May have been killed at Wilderness or Spotsylvania.

(1) KING, SAM P. — W. (thigh), 2nd Manassas (Aug. 30, 1862): Died from wound, Oct. 4, 1862.

(1) KIPPS, GEO. W. — Sick, Richmond hosp., Oct., 1861: Appt. 1Sgt., Nov. 1, 1862: Detailed to recruiting in Tex., Feb.-Apr., 1863: Cmded. Co. at Wilderness (May 6, 1864): K., Wilderness (May 6, 1864).

KIRBY, JAS. A. — Enl. at Montgomery, Tex., Mar. 24, 1862, age 27: W. (arm), Gaines' Mill (June 27, 1862): K., Chickamauga (Sept. 19, 1863).

(1) LACKLAND, S. M. — Dischgd. for disability (sick), Nov. 25, 1861.

(1) LANDRUM, WILLIS J. — AWOL, June 1, 1862: Rejnd. Co., July, 1862: "Left in rear at Blackwater River, Va., Apr. 12, 1863": Left service on Surg. Cert. of disability, June 19, 1863: Returned to Co.: AWOL during skirmish at White Oak Swamp, Aug. 16, 1864: Paroled, Ashland, Va., Apr. 26, 1865.

LAWRENCE, J. W. — Appt. 5Sgt.: No other record.

(1) LAWRENCE, W. H. — Deserted at Richmond, Sept. 28, 1861.

LEACH, WM. G. — Enl. at Huntsville, Tex., Mar. 20, 1862, age 25: Died of typhoid fever at Danville, Va., June 20, 1862.

(1) LEMON, J. W. — AWOL, July 15, 1864: Said to have transfd. to a Cav. Co. in Va. in July, 1864.

LEVANTURE, LOUIS — Enl. at New Orleans, Apr. 22, 1862, age 29: W., 2nd Manassas (Aug. 30, 1862): Granted furlough: AWOL in La. since 1863.

(1) LEWIS, CLINT A. — W. (shoulder), Gaines' Mill (June 27, 1862): Died from wound, Aug. 8, 1862.

(1) LEWIS, JAS. L. — Missing at Antietam (Sept. 17, 1862): Believed killed.

LEWIS, WM. — Enl. at Montgomery, Tex., Mar. 24, 1862, age 30: Dischgd., Surg. Cert. of disability (heart trouble), June 28, 1862.

(1) LONG, JOHN — W. (knee), Gaines' Mill (June 27, 1862): Detailed to Div. Pioneer Serv., Dec. 20, 1862: POW, Gettysburg (July 2, 1863): Confined at Ft. McHenry, Md.: Took Fed. oath.

(1) LOPER, WM. H. — Sick, Fall, 1861: Transfd. to Co. G, 4th Tex., Apr., 1862.

LOWN, JACOB — Enl. at Anderson, Tex., Mar. 26, 1862, age 22: W. (side), Gaines' Mill (June 27, 1862): POW, Gettysburg (July 2, 1863): Exchanged: POW, Knoxville, Nov. 30, 1863: Confined at Camp Chase, Ohio: Died, Jan. 18, 1864: Buried in Cave Hill Cemetery near Camp Chase.

(1) MARTIN, W. L. — On duty with Brig. QM, Nov., 1861: K., Gaines' Mill (June 27, 1862).

(1) MATHEWS, T. R. — Sick, Fall, 1861: Dischgd. at Richmond, Dec. 3, 1861.

(1) MAY, D. G. — W. (thigh), Gaines' Mill (June 27, 1862): Granted furlough to Tex.: Never returned to Co.: In Apr., 1864 was still in Tex. "awaiting a decision on an application for transfer."

(1) MAY, R. M. — W. (shoulder), Gaines' Mill (June 27, 1862): Paroled,
(2) Appomattox (Apr. 12, 1865).

(1) MAY, THOS. G. — Physician by occupation: Attended sick, Fall, 1861: Detailed as "surgeon" in charge of the wounded after 2nd Manassas (Aug. 30, 1862) at Warrenton, Va.: Hospitalized, Summer, 1863: Furlough granted, Oct. 21, 1863: Present for duty, 1864.

(1) MAY, W. C. — W., Gaines' Mill (June 27, 1862): W. (chest & arm), 2nd
(2) Manassas (Aug. 30, 1862): Appt. 4Sgt., May 6, 1864: Received Texas Gold Star for bravery, Feb., 1865: Paroled, Appomattox (Apr. 12, 1865).

(1) McCOWAN, A. J. — Sent to the rear because of sickness, Sept. 17, 1862
(2) (Antietam): W. (knee) & POW, Gettysburg (July 2, 1863): Confined at Ft. Delaware: Exchanged, Oct. 31, 1863: W., E. Tenn., 1863: Paroled, Appomattox (Apr. 12, 1865).

(1) McDANIEL, Y. L. — Detailed to Ambulance Corps during battle of Gaines' Mill (June 27, 1862): Sick, Summer, 1863: W. (arm & side), Wilderness (May 6, 1864): Paroled, Lynchburg, Va., Apr., 1865.

(1) McGRAW, WM. — Sick in Richmond hosp., Fall, 1861: Dischgd. at Richmond, Dec. 3, 1861.

(1) MILLICAN, WM. — Dischgd. on Surg. Cert. of disability, Feb. 1, 1862.

MITCHELL, THOS. R. — Enl. at Montgomery, Tex., Mar. 20, 1862, age 27: "Made a hasty retreat to the rear on June 27, 1862" (Gaines' Mill): Deserted, Oct., 1862.

(1) MYERS, MARION F. — W., Gaines' Mill (June 27, 1862): Court-martialed, June, 1863 — lost one month's pay: W., Wilderness (May 6, 1864): AWOL in Tex., Summer, 1864.

MYERS, THOS. J. — Enl. at Huntsville, Tex., Mar. 20, 1862, age 24: Died of chronic diarrhea, Aug. 25, 1862.

NAVIS, HENRY — W., Gaines' Mill (June 27, 1862): Not listed on Bi-Monthly Muster Roll.

(1) NEVILLS, D. E. — Sick, Winter & Spring, 1862: Dischgd. on Surg. Cert. of disability (hemorrhoids), June 26, 1862.

(1) PARKER, WM. A. — Sick, Fall, 1861: Co. Color-Bearer: W. & POW, Boonsboro (Sept. 14, 1862): Died from wound in Fed. hosp. at Frederick, Md., Dec. 18, 1862.

(1) PEACOCK, WM. — Detchd. duty as a Regt. teamster, June, 1862: K., Chickamauga (Sept. 20, 1863).

(1)　PEASLEY, GEO. A. — Sick, Winter, 1861-62: Died at Camp Winder, Va., May 10, 1862.

(1)　PETTY, THOS. T. M. — W. (arm), Gaines' Mill (June 27, 1862): No record after June, 1863: Reported to have died in E. Tenn., Fall, 1863.

　　　QUIGLEY, R. — Enl. at Montgomery, Tex., Mar. 18, 1862, age 24: K., Gaines' Mill (June 27, 1862).

(1)　RANDOLPH, D. J. — Sick in Richmond hosp., Fall, 1861: Dischgd. at Richmond, Dec. 6, 1861.

　　　RANKIN, ROBT. — Enl. at Montgomery, Tex., Mar. 29, 1862, age 30: W., Gettysburg (July 2, 1863): Finger shot off: In Richmond hosp. with ulcerated leg, Winter, 1864-65: POW, Richmond, Apr. 3, 1865.

(1)　RANSOM, R. W. — K., 2nd Manassas (Aug. 30, 1862).

(1)　REED, GEO. P. L. — See roster, "Regmtl. Hdqtrs., 4th Tex. Inf."

(1)　ROGERS, JOHN P. — Died from disease at Richmond, Oct. 17, 1861.

　　　RUDD, J. J. — Appt. 3Sgt.: Transfd. to the artillery in 1861: Not listed on Bi-Monthly Muster Roll.

(1)　SANDERLIN, J. M. — Sick, Fall, 1861: Dischgd. at Richmond, Nov. 23, 1861.

　　　SAUNDERS, C. B. — Enl. at Montgomery, Tex., Mar. 24, 1862, age 47: Dischgd. in Va., July 28, 1862, overage (48).

(1)　SAVAGE, EDW. — Sick, Summer, 1862: Missing at Gettysburg (July 2, 1863), believed killed.

　　　SEARGENT, JAS. B. — Enl. at Montgomery, Tex., Mar. 28, 1862, age 19: W. (leg), Gaines' Mill (June 27, 1862): Detailed as Brig. Mail Carrier, Sept., 1863-Mar., 1865: POW, Richmond, Apr. 3, 1865: Paroled at Pt. Lookout, Md., June 19, 1865.

(1)　SEARGENT, THOS. — Missing since Gaines' Mill (June 27, 1862): Returned to Co.: Served as courier to Gen. Hood, Mar., 1863-Aug., 1864.

(1)　SEAY, A. B. — Sent to rear to attend wounded at Gaines' Mill (June 27, 1862): W. (foot) & POW, Gettysburg (July 2, 1863: Exchanged: W. (hip), Wilderness (May 6, 1864).

(1)　SEWARD, J. R. — Died at Dumfries, Va., Feb. 2, 1862.

(1)　SHARP, JAS. H. — W., 2nd Manassas (Aug. 30, 1862): W., Antietam (June 27, 1862): W., Gettysburg (July 2, 1863): K., Petersburg, June 22, 1864.

　　　SMITH, JOHN — Jnd. Co., May, 1862, as a substitute for 2Sgt. Sam Y. Smith: K., Chickamauga (Sept. 19, 1863).

　　　SMITH, JOHN I. — Enl. at Montgomery, Tex., Mar. 15, 1862, age 23: W., Gaines' Mill (June 27, 1862): Appt. 3Cpl., May 6, 1864: W., Williamsburg Rd. (Oct. 27, 1864).

(1)　SPIVEY, J. SYD. — See list of "Other Officers" above.

　　　STEUSSEY, JACOB — Enl. at Montgomery, Tex., Mar. 25, 1862, age 24: W., Gettysburg (July 2, 1863): Leg amputated.

　　　STEUSSEY, MATHEW — Enl. at Montgomery, Tex., Mar. 25, 1862, age 21: W., Gaines' Mill (June 27, 1862): Arm amputated: Perm. disabled, dischgd. in Tex.

(1) STRATTON, ROBT. R. — W. (leg), Gaines' Mill (June 27, 1862): Perm. disabled and returned to Tex.: Asgnd. as Ordn. Off. "Post of Anderson," Grimes Co., Tex., Aug., 1864.

(1) STUART, JOHN E. — W., Antietam (Sept. 17, 1862): W. (right knee) & POW, Gettysburg (July 2, 1863): Leg amputated, July 7, 1863: Paroled, Nov. 7, 1863: Perm. disabled and honorably dischgd., Apr. 23, 1864.

(1)
(2) STUART, R. H. — Hospitalized, Fall, 1861-62: Appt. 1Cpl., May 6, 1864: W. (arm & side), Wilderness (May 6, 1864): Paroled, Appomattox (Apr. 12, 1865).

(1) TALIAFERRO, J. H. — Sick, Summer & Fall, 1862: W., Gettysburg (July 2, 1863): Retired from serv., July 8, 1864: Asgnd. to duty in Richmond hosp., Jan. 11, 1865: POW, Richmond, Apr. 3, 1865.

TALLEY, JAS. C. — Enl. at Montgomery, Tex., Mar. 15, 1862, age 34: Sick in hosp., Fall, 1862: Died at Danville, Va., 1864.

TALLEY, REUBEN — Enl. at Montgomery, Tex., Mar. 15, 1862, age 31: Present for duty to Aug., 1864: Paroled at Houston, Tex., July 27, 1865.

(1) TAYLOR, ALEX — W. (arm), Wilderness (May 6, 1864): W. (jaw), Petersburg (June 19, 1864): Furlough to Tex., Sept., 1864.

TAYLOR, CHAS. L. — Enl. at Montgomery, Tex., Mar. 20, 1862, age 22: Shot in foot accidentally, Nov. 1, 1862: Disabled.

(1) TEDFORD, R. J. — See list of "Other Officers" above.

(1) THIGPEN, G. C. — Dischgd. for disability, Dec. 2, 1861.

(1) THOMAS, JOHN — See roster, "Regmtl. Hdqtrs., 4th Tex. Inf."

(1) TRAVIS, HENRY — W. (arm), Gaines' Mill (June 27, 1862): Appt. 2Cpl.: K., Wilderness (May 6, 1864).

(1) TUCKER, D. J. — Sick, Spring & Summer, 1862: Appt. courier to Gen. J. B. Robertson, Nov., 1862-Jan., 1864: Appt. courier to Lt. Gen. Longstreet.

(1) TYLER, R. L. — Appt. 5Sgt., Dec. 9, 1861: K., Gaines' Mill (June 27, 1862).

(1) WADE, FRANK H. — Appt. 4Cpl., Feb. 3, 1862: Sick, Summer, 1862: AWOL in Richmond, Nov., 1862: Reported to have transfd. to the arty. in 1863.

(1) WALLACE, JOHN H. — Dischgd. on Surg. Cert. of disability, Nov. 6, 1861.

(1) WALTRIP, CHAS. M. — Sick numerous times during war: W. (leg), near Richmond, Oct. 2, 1864.

WATSON, HENRY C. — Enl. at Huntsville, Tex., Mar. 20, 1862, age 21: K., 2nd Manassas (Aug. 30, 1862).

(1)
(2) WATSON, WM. A. — Appt. 5Sgt., Oct. 15, 1862: Present for duty most of war: Paroled, Appomattox (Apr. 12, 1865).

(1) WILCOX, THOS. W. — Died of disease at Fredericksburg, Va., Apr. 12, 1862.

WILKES, B. B. — Enl. at Montgomery, Tex., Mar. 18, 1862, age 18: W. (finger), 2nd Manassas (Aug. 30, 1862): Finger amputated: Appt. Cpl., Jan., 1864: Dischgd., Mar. 2, 1864: Appt. as actg. Midshipman, CSN, Mar. 2, 1864.

(1) WILKES, T. O. — Appt. 2Sgt.: K., Gaines' Mill (June 27, 1862).
(1) WYNNE, A. J. — Dischgd. for disability (lung disease), Dec. 1, 1861.
     WYNNE, SEROCTUS W. — Enl. at Huntsville, Tex., Mar. 19, 1862, age
          21: W. (chest), 2nd Manassas (Aug. 30, 1862): Died from wound,
          Sept. 15, 1862.
(1) WYNNE, THOS. A. — Enl. at Huntsville, Tex., Mar. 19, 1862, age 23:
(2)   W: (leg), 2nd Manassas (Aug. 30, 1862): W., Wilderness (May 6,
          1864): Paroled, Appomattox (Apr. 12, 1865).

4TH TEX. VOL. INF. REGT.

COMPANY I — *NAVARRO RIFLES*

Company was organized in Navarro County, Texas, enrolled there
on July 17, 1861, and was mustered into the Confederate service
"for the war" at Richmond, Va., Sept. 30, 1861. Company
included men from Ellis, Freestone, and Hill Counties as well as
Navarro County.

Key

(1) Original member of Company. (2) Paroled at Appomattox.
K (Killed), W (Wounded), POW (Prisoner of War)
AWOL (Absent Without Leave)

ORIGINAL OFFICERS

(1) WINKLER, CLINTON M. Capt. — See roster, "Regmtl. Hdqtrs., 4th
(2)   Tex. Inf.
(1) LOUGHRIDGE, J. R. 1Lt. — W. (arm), Gaines' Mill (June 27, 1862):
          Disabled, resgnd., Oct. 11, 1863.
(1) OGILVIE, J. R. 2Lt. — Resgnd., Oct. 31, 1861 "on account of
          inability."
(1) HILL, B. J. C. ("Jeff") 3Lt. — Prom., 2Lt.: Resgnd., Dec. 16, 1861.

ORIGINAL NON-COMMISSIONED OFFICERS

(1) BEASLEY, MATT 1Sgt. — See list of "Other Officers" following.
(1) PENNINGTON, C. W. 2Sgt. — Died en route to Va. at Decatur, Ala.,
          Sept. 15, 1861.
(1) CASADY, J. M. 3Sgt. — Dischgd. for "inability and old age," Oct. 18,
          1861.

(1) JACKSON, WM. C. 4Sgt. — Demoted to ranks, Dec. 24, 1861: POW, Seven Pines (June 1, 1862): Confined at Ft. Delaware: Exchanged, Aug. 5, 1862: Prom., 1Sgt., Feb. 4, 1864: W. (arm), Darbytown Rd. (Oct. 7, 1864).

(1) CADDEL, J. D. 5Sgt. — See "Regmtl. Hdqtrs., 4th Tex. Inf."

(1) BEASLEY, JOHN T. 1Cpl. — Died in hosp., Richmond, Nov. 6, 1861.

(1) TURPIN, CHAS. C. 2Cpl. — Died of pneumonia at Fredericksburg, Va., Mar. 12, 1862.

(1) TOWERS, W. H. 3Cpl. — Died in hosp., Richmond, Nov. 16, 1861.

(1) STEWART, J. D. 4Cpl. — Dischgd. for disability, Nov. 23, 1861.

OTHER OFFICERS

BEASLEY, MATT Capt. — Orig. 1Sgt. of Co.: Prom., 2Lt., Dec. 14, 1861: W., Gaines' Mill (June 27, 1862): Prom., Capt., Summer, 1863: On detchd. duty, Aug. 15, 1864.

(2) MILLS, NAT J. 1Lt. — Orig. Pvt. in Co.: Prom., 3Lt., Dec. 26, 1861: W., Antietam (Sept. 17, 1862): Prom., 1Lt.: Paroled, Appomattox (Apr. 12, 1865).

(2) DUREN, JOHN W. 2Lt. — Orig. Pvt. in Co.: Prom., 1Sgt., Dec. 21, 1861: Prom., 2Lt., Feb. 4, 1864: W., Wilderness (May 6, 1864): Paroled, Appomattox (Apr. 12, 1865).

MUSICIANS

(1) UTZMAN, J. L. — Demoted from musician to ranks, Nov. 20, 1861:
(2) Detchd. serv. as butcher, Mar. 1, 1862: Paroled, Appomattox (Apr. 12, 1865).

(1) MELTON, J. E. — See roster, "Regmtl. Hdqtrs., 4th Tex. Inf."

PRIVATES

(2) ALLEN, WM. B. — Enl., Apr. 3, 1862 in Navarro County, Tex.: Left wrist badly injured in R.R. accident, Mar. 8, 1864: Paroled, Appomattox (Apr. 12, 1865).

(1) ALPHIN, THOS. — Died in hosp., Richmond, Dec. 7, 1861.

(1) ANDERSON, JOHN L. — Died in hosp., Richmond, Nov. 2, 1861.

(1) ARMSTRONG, R. C. — Sick, Fall & Winter, 1861: AWOL, Fall, 1862: POW, Spotsylvania CH. (May 10, 1864): Confined at Pt. Lookout, Md.: Died of pneumonia, Jan. 28, 1865: Personal effects, 10 cents.

(1) ASTIN, J. H. — W. (thigh), Gaines' Mill (June 27, 1862): Detchd. duty as ambulance driver, Feb., 1863: W., Chickamauga (Sept. 19, 1863): Wound furlough to Tex.: Did not return to Co.

(1) BALES, W. H. — W. (abdomen), Gettysburg (July 2, 1863): Detchd. duty as a teamster, Apr.-Sept., 1864.

BAKER, WM. — Enl., Apr. 17, 1862 in Navarro County, Tex.: Died of pneumonia, Chimborozo Hosp. in Richmond, May 22, 1862.

(1) BARNETT, J. H. — Prom., 4Cpl., Sept. 20, 1861: Died in hosp., Fredericksburg, Va., Mar. 12, 1862.
(1) BARRY, AMBROSE — POW, Antietam (Sept. 17, 1862): Confined at Ft. Delaware: Exchanged, Nov. 10, 1862: POW, Chickamauga (Sept. 20, 1863): Confined at Camp Douglas, Ill.: Paroled, June 14, 1865.
(1) BARRY, M. — Present for duty most of the war: Paroled, Appomattox
(2) (Apr. 12, 1865).
(1) BEASLEY, JESSE R. — K., 2nd Manassas (Aug. 30, 1862).
     BLACK, HENRY F. — Enl., Apr. 9, 1862 in Navarro County, Tex.: W., 2nd Manassas (Aug. 30, 1862): Sick, Winter & Spring, 1863: AWOL, Summer, 1863: Never returned to Co.
     BLACK, JAS. R. — Enl., Apr. 3, 1862 in Navarro County, Tex.: Dischgd., Oct. 19, 1862 because of "hemorrhoids of long standing . . . old age . . . and completely broken down."
(1) BOYNTON, G. S. — Dischgd. for disability (chronic bronchitis), Sept. 22, 1862.
(1) BREWSTER, A. J. — Missing after crossing Rapidan River, Va., Aug. 23, 1862: Rejnd. Co.: Sick, Winter, 1862-63: Deserted, Mar. 26, 1864: Also reported as POW.
     BYAS, ANDREW J. — Enl., Mar. 27, 1862 in Navarro County, Tex.: Died (pneumonia), Richmond, Mar. 11, 1863.
     CARROLL, WM. E. — Enl., Mar. 24, 1862 in Navarro County, Tex.: W. (shoulder), Gaines' Mill (June 27, 1862): K., Chickamauga (Sept. 20, 1863).
(1) CHILDRESS, B. F. — Sick, Winter, 1861-62: Typhoid fever, Summer, 1862: K., Chickamauga (Sept. 19, 1863).
(1) CRABB, E. S. — W., 2nd Manassas (Aug. 30, 1862): Furlough granted, Oct., 1862: AWOL, Feb., 1863: Dischgd. for disability: Drowned in Tex., Sept. 4, 1863.
(1) CRABTREE, J. W. — W., Malvern Hill (July 1, 1862): Detchd. duty
(2) with Provost Guard, Apr.-June, 1863: Hospitalized, Fall, 1863: Paroled, Appomattox (Apr. 12, 1865).
(1) CRAWFORD, ROBT. W. — Enl. at 18: Prom., 3Cpl.: POW, 2nd Manassas (Aug. 30, 1862): Prom., 2Sgt.: Granted 70 day furlough to Tex., Jan., 1864: Did not return to Co.: Enl. in a Co. in Tex.
(2) CROSSLAND, A. M. — Enl., Apr. 14, 1863: W., Wilderness (May 6, 1864): W. (arm & thigh), Chaffin's Farm (Sept. 29, 1864): Disabled: Paroled, Appomattox (Apr. 12, 1865).
(1) DILLARD, F. P. — W., Antietam (Sept. 17, 1862): Dischgd. (chronic hepatitis & lung disease), Feb. 13, 1863.
     DOZIER, H. H. — Enl., Mar. 24, 1862 in Navarro County, Tex.: Died (lung disease), Danville, Va., June 7, 1862.
(1) DUNCAN, J. P. — Died in hosp., Richmond, Dec. 9, 1861.
(1) DUREN, JOHN W. — See list of "Other Officers" above.
(1) FAGAN, JAS. G. — Dischgd. (chronic rheumatism), Nov. 20, 1862.
(1) FONDRAN, W. A. — K., Gaines' Mill (June 27, 1862).
     FORSTON, J. R. — Dischgd. for disability (pelvic disease of the kidneys), Dec. 18, 1862.

(1) FOSTER, G. W. — W. & POW, 2nd Manassas (Aug. 30, 1862): Paroled, Warrenton, Va., Sept. 29, 1862: W., Wilderness (May 6, 1864): W. (leg & arm), Darbytown Rd. (Oct. 7, 1864): Dischgd. for disability.

(1) FOSTER, J. A. — Prom., 4Cpl., Apr., 1862: Prom., 2Cpl.: W., 2nd Manassas (Aug. 30, 1862): Leave granted to Tex., Nov., 1862: Dischgd. for disability, Apr. 1, 1863.

(1) FOSTER, M. L. — Sick, Spring, 1862: AWOL, Aug., 1862: Did not return to Co.

(1) FRANKLIN, JAS. — W. (leg), Gaines' Mill (June 27, 1862): Wound leave granted: AWOL, did not return to Co.

FULLER, JOS. L. — Enl., Mar. 24, 1862 in Navarro County, Tex.: W. (hip & arm), Wilderness (May 6, 1864): Died from wounds, June 20, 1864.

(1) FULLER, W. W. — Detchd. duty as a teamster, Nov. & Dec., 1861: Sick, Winter, 1862-63: Granted leave to Tex.: AWOL, did not return to Co.

(1) GARNER, E. M. — W. (head), Gaines' Mill (June 27, 1862): K., Antietam (Sept. 17, 1862).

(1) GREEN, JOHN — Died of typhoid fever at Chimborozo Hosp., Richmond, May 13, 1862.

(1) GREEN, JOHN F. — Detached duty as a teamster, Winter, 1861-62: W., Gaines' Mill (June 27, 1862): POW, Boonsboro (Sept. 15, 1862): Exchanged, Nov. 10, 1862: POW, Chickamauga (Sept. 20, 1863): Confined at Camp Douglas, Ill.: Exchanged, Oct. 7, 1863.

GREGORY, JOHN — Enl., Mar. 21, 1862 in Navarro County, Tex.: W. (chest), Gaines' Mill (June 27, 1862): Granted furlough to Tex.: Did not return to Co.

GREGORY, ROBT. — Enl. at 49, Mar. 24, 1862 in Navarro County, Tex.: Dischgd. (chronic rheumatism), Oct. 19, 1862.

(1) HAGAL, JOS. — Sick, Spring, 1862 & Winter & Spring, 1863: Paroled, Chattanooga, Tenn., May 26, 1865.

(1) HALDERMAN, J. W. — Sick, Summer, 1862: W. (head & arm),
(2) Wilderness (May 6, 1864): Paroled, Appomattox (Apr. 12, 1865).

(1) HAMILTON, JAS. D. — Prom., 3Cpl., Dec. 28, 1861: Dischgd. for chronic diarrhea, July 30, 1862.

HAMILTON, JESSIE L. — Enl., Apr. 1, 1862 in Navarro County, Tex.: Sick, Summer, 1862: Dischgd. (asthma), Sept. 24, 1862.

(1) HARPER, B. FRANK — Died in hosp., Richmond, Nov. 20, 1861.

(1) HARRIS, J. Q. — K., Gettysburg (July 2, 1863).

(1) HARRISON, HENRY — Present for duty most of war: Paroled,
(2) Appomattox (Apr. 12, 1865).

(1) HARRISON, J. J. — Sick, Summer & Fall, 1862: Dischgd. on Surg.
(2) Cert. of disability, Nov. 29, 1862, partial blindness: Paroled, Appomattox (Apr. 12, 1865).

(1) HENDERSON, G. W. — W. (thigh), Wilderness (May 6, 1864): Furlough granted, Oct., 1864.

(1) HERBERT, JAS. H. — W. (shoulder), 2nd Manassas (Aug. 30, 1862): Dischgd. for disability, Mar. 13, 1863.

(1) HILL, JACK — W. (hand), Gaines' Mill (June 27, 1862): Detchd. duty as a teamster, June, 1863: K., White Oak Swamp (Aug. 16, 1864).

(1) HILL, J. H. — W. (arm), Gaines' Mill (June 27, 1862): W. (arm) & POW, Antietam (Sept. 17, 1862): Confined at Ft. McHenry, Md.: Exchanged, Oct. 13, 1862: Arm amputated, Oct. 23, 1862: Dischgd. for disability, Nov. 3, 1862.

(1) HOLLOWAY, ROBT. G. — Prom., 2Cpl., Spring, 1862: W., Antietam
(2) (Sept. 17, 1862): Prom., 4Sgt., Jan., 1864: Paroled, Appomattox (Apr. 12, 1865).

(1) JEFFERSON, W. R. — Sick, Fall & Winter, 1861: POW, Antietam (Sept. 17, 1862): Confined at Ft. Delaware: Exchanged, Oct. 6, 1862: POW, Richmond, Apr. 3, 1865: Paroled, July 25, 1865.

(1) JORDAN, J. C. — Sick, Summer, 1862: Detchd. duty with Brig. Provost Guard, Spring, 1864: Missing on retreat from Richmond, Apr. 3, 1865: Paroled, Apr. 14, 1865.

(1) KENNEDY, THOS. — W., 2nd Manassas (Aug. 30, 1862): Reported AWOL, Winter, 1862-63: Dischgd. for disability, May 30, 1863.

(1) KILLIAN, H. L. W. — W. & POW, Antietam (Sept. 17, 1862): Confined at Ft. McHenry, Md.: Exchanged: Hospitalized, Summer, 1864: Retired, Sept. 27, 1864.

(1) KNIGHT, C. G. — Dischgd. by order of Sec. of War, Nov., 1861.

(1) LANHAM, J. B. — Prom., 1Cpl., Dec. 28, 1861: W., Antietam (Sept. 17, 1862): W. (thigh), Darbytown Rd. (Oct. 7, 1864): Dischgd. for disability.

LEA, P. B. — Enl., Apr. 4, 1863: Missing, Wilderness (May 6, 1864).
(1) LEMMON, A. M. — W. (both thighs), Gaines' Mill (June 27, 1862): Detchd. duty as a teamster, June, 1863 to June, 1864: W. (arm), Chaffin's Farm (Sept. 29, 1864): Furlough to Tex., Oct., 1864.

(1) LUMMUS, J. M. — W., 2nd Manassas (Aug. 30, 1862): Furlough, Winter, 1862-63: Dischgd., Apr. 1, 1863.

(1) McMORRIS, J. M. — K., 2nd Manassas (Aug. 30, 1862).
(1) MASSEY, JAS. H. — W. (arm), in skirmish at Chickahominy River, June 8, 1862: W. (knee), Chickamauga (Sept. 19, 1863): Dischgd. for disability, June 14, 1864.

(1) MEADOR, A. L. — Died in hosp., Richmond, Nov. 11, 1861.
(1) MILLER, R. S. — W., 2nd Manassas (Aug. 30, 1862): POW, Gettysburg (July 2, 1863): Confined at Ft. Delaware: Paroled, June 9, 1865.

(1) MILLS, NAT J. — See list of "Other Officers" above.
(1) MITCHELL, WM. H. ("Lawyer") — Dischgd. for "inability" & asthma, Mar. 20, 1862.

(1) MORRIS, T. R. — Prom., 3Sgt., Nov. 7, 1861: Absent on recruiting duty to Tex., Feb.-Apr., 1862: W., Malvern Hill (July 1, 1862): W., 2nd Manassas (Aug. 30, 1862): Died of wound.

(1) NEAL, J. H. ("Jeff") — Died in hosp., Richmond, Nov. 14, 1861.
(2) ORNDORFF, J. H. — Enl., Mar. 31, 1862 in Navarro County, Tex.: Detchd. duty with Regmtl. Comsy. as a teamster, Nov., 1862 to end of the war: Paroled, Appomattox (Apr. 12, 1865).

(1) OSBORNE, PADDY H. — Sick, Fall, 1861: Dischgd., Nov. 14, 1861.
(1) OSBORNE, T. A. ("Sandy") — Died of typhoid fever, Feb. 20, 1862 near Dumfries, Va.

(1) PELHAM, J. L. — Disabled by a broken leg: Dischgd., Nov. 2, 1861.
PHELPS, FRANKLIN — Enl., Apr. 6, 1862 in Navarro County, Tex.: Died, Winder Hosp., Richmond, "about May 25, 1862."

(1)   PICKETT, JOHN — W. (leg), Gaines' Mill (June 27, 1862): Granted furlough: AWOL in Tex.: Asgnd. to Invalid Corps., Sept. 29, 1864.

(1)   PLATT, J. W. G. — W. (foot), Gaines' Mill (June 27, 1862): Transfd. to 19th La. Inf. Regt., Nov. 1, 1862.

(1)   POLK, J. M. — Absent on recruiting duty to Tex., Feb.-Apr., 1862: W. (arm), Gaines' Mill (June 27, 1862): W., Chickamauga (Sept. 19, 1863): POW, St. Louis, Mo., June 29, 1864.

(1)   PURSELEY, T. LEWIS — Died in hosp., Richmond, Nov. 15, 1861.

     RICE, J. L. — Enl., Mar. 29, 1862 in Navarro County, Tex.: Died, Richmond, July, 1862.

(1)
(2)   RICE, L. W. — Sick, Summer, 1862; Winter & Summer, 1863; & Spring & Summer, 1864: Paroled, Appomattox (Apr. 12, 1865).

(1)   RICE, R. N. — K., 2nd Manassas (Aug. 30, 1862).

(1)   RIGGS, STEPHEN MADISON — Prom., 2Sgt., Sept. 20, 1861: Absent on recruiting serv. to Tex., Feb.-Apr., 1863: W., Chickamauga (Sept. 19, 1863): Leg amputated: Died, Sept. 21, 1863.

     ROBERTSON, J. R. — Enl., Mar. 18, 1862 in Navarro County, Tex.: Dischgd. for disability, Oct., 1862: Not listed on Co. Muster Roll.

     RUSKIN, M. D. L. — Enl., Mar. 24, 1862 in Navarro County, Tex.: Died of smallpox, Richmond Hosp., Jan. 3, 1863.

     SELF, P. P. T. — Enl., Mar. 13, 1863: Deserted, Mar. 14, 1863.

(1)   SESSIONS, E. G. — Absent on furlough, Winter, 1861-62: Transfd., Nov. 12, 1863 to hosp. in Shreveport, La., as Wardmaster.

(1)   SESSIONS, T. J. — Died in hosp., Richmond, Nov. 7, 1861.

(2)   SHAW, J. R. — Enl., Apr. 3, 1862 in Navarro County, Tex.: W. (thigh), Gaines' Mill (June 27, 1862): Paroled, Appomattox (Apr. 12, 1865).

(1)   SIMMONS, J. W. — Sick, Summer, 1862: Dischgd., Mar. 31, 1863, due to poor health (rheumatism).

(1)   SMITH, PULASKY — W., Gettysburg (July 2, 1863): Prom., 3Sgt., Jan., 1864: Paroled, Montgomery, Ala., May 13, 1865.

(1)   SMITH, W. G. — Sick leave, Spring, 1862: Dischgd., Nov. 14, 1862, rheumatism & old age (60).

(1)   SMITH, WM. T. — W., 2nd Manassas (Aug. 30, 1862): K., Gettysburg (July 2, 1863).

(1)   SPENCE, W. P. — Actg. Co. Color-Cpl., Apr., 1862: K., 2nd Manassas (Aug. 30, 1862).

     STOKES, CORNELIUS H. — Enl., Mar. 13, 1863: W., Wilderness (May 6, 1864): K., Cold Harbor (June 3, 1864).

(1)   TEMPLETON, A. N. — Dischgd. for disability, Dec. 30, 1861.

     TEMPLETON, MOSES B. — Enl., Apr. 1, 1862 in Navarro County, Tex.: Sick, May, 1862-June, 1863: AWOL, Jan., 1864: Did not return to Co.

(1)
(2)   TEMPLETON, WM. W. — Sick, Fall & Winter, 1861: Sick, Summer, 1862: W. (shoulder), Wilderness (May 6, 1864): Paroled, Appomattox (Apr. 12, 1865).

(1)   TERRELL, S. B. — Enl., July 17, 1861 in Navarro County: Prom., 4Sgt., Dec. 28, 1861: W., Suffolk, Va., Apr. 21, 1863: Died at Petersburg, June 4, 1863.

(1) TREADWELL, JAS. H. — W. (foot), Gaines' Mill (June 27, 1862):
(2)   Detchd. duty as a teamster, June, 1863-Aug., 1864: Paroled,
        Appomattox (Apr. 12, 1865).
(1) WADE, R. H. — W. (leg & foot), Gaines' Mill (June 27, 1862):
        Disabled: Furlough to Tex. granted: Did not return to Co.
(1) WALKER, H. E. — W. (shoulder), Gaines' Mill (June 27, 1862): K.,
        Wilderness (May 6, 1864).
(1) WALKER, J. C. — Prom., 5Sgt., Dec. 28, 1861: Resgnd. as 5Sgt., Feb.
        24, 1862: Sick, Summer, 1862: No record after June, 1863: May
        have been killed at Gettysburg, July 2, 1863.
    WARREN, BENAJAH — Enl., Mar. 24, 1862 in Navarro County, Tex.:
        AWOL, Winter, 1862-63: Died of lung trouble, Aug. 14, 1863.
    WATERS, EZEKIEL — Enl., Mar. 31, 1862 in Navarro County, Tex.,
        age 32: W. (mouth & leg), Gaines' Mill (June 27, 1862): AWOL,
        Mar., 1863.
(1) WEIL, SOLOMAN — Born in Bavaria, enl. at 45: Detchd. duty with
        Regmtl. Comsy., Oct., 1861-Oct., 1862: Detchd. duty with Div.
        Hdqtrs., Dec., 1862-Nov., 1863: Dischgd. on Surg. Cert. of
        disability (insane), Nov. 18, 1863.
(1) WELCH, JOHN C. — Detchd. duty as a teamster, Nov., 1861: W.
(2)   (thigh), Gaines' Mill (June 27, 1862): W. (knee), Wilderness (May
        6, 1864): Paroled, Appomattox (Apr. 12, 1865).
(1) WELCH, MIKE H. — Dischgd. for disability, Jan. 6, 1862.
(1) WESTBROOK, GEO. W. — Died in hosp., Richmond, Oct. 31, 1861.
(1) WESTBROOK, J. H. — Died in hosp., Richmond, Dec. 5; 1861.
(1) WESTBROOK, J. N. — Died of pneumonia in Fredericksburg Hosp.,
        Mar. 20, 1862.

4TH TEX. VOL. INF. REGT.

COMPANY K — *SANDY POINT MOUNTED RIFLES*

Company was organized in Henderson County, enrolled at Athens,
Tex., July 15, 1861, and was mustered into the Confederate
service "for the war" at Richmond, Va., Sept. 30, 1861.

Key

(1) Original member of Company. (2) Paroled at Appomattox.
K (Killed), W (Wounded), POW (Prisoner of War)
AWOL (Absent Without Leave)

ORIGINAL OFFICERS

(1) MARTIN, WM. H. Capt. — See roster, "Regmtl. Hdqtrs., 4th Tex.
(2)   Inf."

(1)   BURRESS, JOHN T. 1Lt. — Detailed to recruiting serv. in Tex., Feb.-Apr., 1862: W. (face), Gaines' Mill (June 27, 1862): "Right eye destroyed & left arm paralyzed": Resgnd., Jan. 20, 1863.

(1)   CLANAHAN, MATHEW O. 2Lt. — W. (thigh), Gaines' Mill (June 27, 1862): Prom., 1Lt., Jan. 27, 1863: W., Chickamauga (Sept. 19, 1863): Died from wound in an Atlanta, Ga. hosp., Oct. 5, 1863.

(1)   RONNSAVALL, WM. D. 3Lt. — W., Gaines' Mill (June 27, 1862): Right arm amputated: Resgnd., Sept. 13, 1862.

ORIGINAL NON-COMMISSIONED OFFICERS

(1)   DERDEN, WM. L. 1Sgt. — See list of "Other Officers" following.

(1)   JONES, W. B. S. 2Sgt. — Died, Fredericksburg, Va., Nov. 30, 1861.

(1)   OWEN, SAMUAL TINE 3Sgt. — Resgnd. as 3Sgt., June 15, 1862: W., Gaines' Mill (June 27, 1862): Died of wound, July 25, 1862.

(1)   MARTIN, HENRY 4Sgt. — Resgnd. as 4Sgt., Jan. 28, 1862: Appt. 1Sgt., Mar. 20, 1862: K., 2nd Manassas (Aug. 30, 1862).

(1)   BOBO, WM. C. 1Cpl. — Prom., 2Sgt., Dec. 25, 1861: Resgnd. as 2Sgt., Jan. 31, 1862: Appt. 1Sgt., Mar. 18, 1862: Died of pneumonia at Fredericksburg, Va., Mar. 20, 1862.

(1)   CARTER, HUGH 2Cpl. — W., 2nd Manassas (Aug. 30, 1862): Detailed as Ambulance Driver, Feb.-Dec., 1863: POW, near Knoxville, Tenn., Dec. 18, 1863: Confined at Rock Is., Ill.: Paroled, May 23, 1865.

(1)   RONNSAVALL, JOHN A. 3Cpl. — Resgnd. as 3Cpl., Nov. 12, 1861: W. (leg), Gaines' Mill (June 27, 1862): Died of wound, July 27, 1862.

(1)
(2)   CHAMPION, L. D. 4Cpl. — W. (hand), Gaines' Mill (June 27, 1862): POW, Boonsboro (Sept. 14, 1862): Asgnd. to the Pioneer Corps, Winter, 1864: W. (leg), Wilderness (May 6, 1864): Paroled, Appomattox (Apr. 12, 1865).

OTHER OFFICERS

DERDEN, WM. L. 2Lt. — Orig. 1Sgt. of Co.: Resgnd. as 1Sgt., Mar. 18, 1862: Appt. 3Sgt., June 15, 1862: W., Gaines' Mill (June 27, 1862): Elect., 3Lt., Oct. 1, 1862: Prom., 2Lt., Jan. 27, 1863: Tendered resignation, Oct. 15, 1863: AWOL: Dropped by Secy. of War, Apr. 26, 1864.

MARTIN, ROBT. B. 3Lt. — Orig. Pvt. in Co.: Prom., 5Sgt., Jan. 1, 1862: On recruiting serv. to Tex., Feb.-Apr., 1862: Appt. 1Sgt., Oct. 1, 1862: Elect., 3Lt., Jan. 27, 1863: K., Knoxville, Nov., 1863.

MUSICIANS

(1)   MATHEWS, WM. R. — Drummer: Died of typhoid fever at Dumfries, Va., Dec. 9, 1861.

(1)   LOOP, GEO. R. — Fifer: Reduced to ranks, Dec. 8, 1861: Appt. 3Cpl.,
      June 1, 1863.

PRIVATES

ALLEN, JAS. M. — Recruited, Mar. 5, 1862 at Athens, Tex.: K.,
Chickamauga (Sept. 19, 1863).
ALLEN, WM. J. — Recruited, Mar. 14, 1862 at Athens, Tex.: Died at
camp near Richmond, May 5, 1862.
ANDING, JOHN D. — Recruited, Mar. 15, 1862 at Athens, Tex.: Died,
Lynchburg, Va. hosp., June 17, 1862.
AUTLE, MILTON — Recruited, Mar. 7, 1862 at Athens, Tex.: Prom. to
2Cpl.: Prom. to 1Cpl., Feb. 1, 1863: W., Chickamauga (Sept. 19,
1863).

(1)   BAKER, JOS. — Sick in hosp., much of 1862 & 1863: Paroled,
(2)   Appomattox (Apr. 12, 1865).
BALL, BENJ. F. — Recruited, Mar. 23, 1862 at Athens, Tex.: Died of
smallpox, Feb. 2, 1863.

(1)   BANKS, THOS. C. — Appt. 2Cpl., June 1, 1863: W., Gettysburg (July
(2)   2, 1863): Appt. 5Sgt., May 7, 1864: Paroled, Appomattox (Apr.
12, 1865).

(1)   BARHAM, CHAS. J. — W., Yorktown (May 1, 1862): Died of wound.
(1)   BOLES, AXOM — Sick in hosp., Fall, 1861: Appt. 4Sgt., Apr. 10,
(2)   1862: Resgnd. as 4Sgt., June 15, 1862: Sick, Winter & Spring,
1863: Paroled, Appomattox (Apr. 12, 1865).

(1)   BOYD, JAS. — Enl. at 19: In arrest, Dec. 27, 1862: Sick, Spring &
Summer, 1863: Deserted, Apr. 4, 1864.

(1)   BRADLEY, J. F. T. — Appt. 4Sgt., Sept. 15, 1862: Prom., 3Sgt.:
Prom., 1Sgt., Feb. 1, 1863: W. & POW, Gettysburg (July 2,
1863): W., Wilderness (May 6, 1864): Leg amputated: Paroled,
Montgomery, Ala., June 1, 1865.

(2)   BROWN, WM. T. — Recruited, Mar. 25, 1862 at Athens, Tex.: Asgnd.
duty as a shoemaker, Winter, 1863-64: Paroled, Appomattox
(Apr. 12, 1865).

(1)   BUSBY, JAS. H. — Died of bronchitis, Richmond, Apr. 7, 1862.
(1)   BUTLER, C. B. — Deserted, Oct. 14, 1861.
(1)   CAMPBELL, ANDERSON — Died, Aug. 9, 1862 while on furlough in
Ala.

(1)   CAMPBELL, JETHRO E. — W., Gaines' Mill (June 27, 1862): K.,
Wilderness (May 6, 1864).

(1)   CAMPBELL, JOS. M. — W. (chest), Gaines' Mill (June 27, 1862):
(2)   AWOL, Jan.-May, 1864: Returned to Co., June, 1864: Paroled,
Appomattox (Apr. 12, 1865).

(1)   CARGUILE, WM. A. — Sick in hosp. most of 1862: Dischgd., Nov. 23,
1862 for chronic rheumatism.

(1)   CARRIFEE, LEWIS A. — Died of pneumonia at Richmond, Nov. 15,
1861.
CARTER, WM. — Recruited at 56, Apr. 17, 1862 at Athens, Tex.:
Dischgd. for disability (rheumatism & old age), May 23, 1862.
CHAPMAN, JAS. — Recruited, Mar. 14, 1862 at Athens, Tex.: Appt.
4Cpl., May 1, 1864: No other record.

(2)   CHAPMAN, MORGAN — Recruited, Mar. 14, 1862 at Athens, Tex.: Detailed as an Ambulance Driver, Fall, 1862: Furlough to Tex., Jan., 1863: Extra duty as a Brig. Teamster, most of 1864: Paroled, Appomattox (Apr. 12, 1865).

CLANAHAN, WM. R. — Recruited, Mar. 29, 1862 at Athens, Tex.: W., Chickamauga (Sept. 19, 1863): Appt. 4Sgt., May 7, 1864.

(1)   CLARK, JOHN C. — Died, Richmond hosp., Nov. 6, 1861.

(1)   COLLINS, DANIEL B. — Sick in hosp., Oct. 19, 1861: Dischgd. for disability, Nov. 9, 1861.

(1)   COX, BERRY M. — K., Gaines' Mill (June 27, 1862).

EDWARDS, WM. L. — Recruited, Mar. 10, 1862 at Athens, Tex.: W., Gaines' Mill (June 27, 1862): Died of wound, July 15, 1862.

ELLEDGE, HUGH D. — Recruited, Apr. 12, 1862 at Athens, Tex.: K., Gaines' Mill (June 27, 1862).

(2)   ELLEDGE, JOHN F. — Recruited, Mar. 12, 1862 at Athens, Tex.: W. (chest), Wilderness (May 6, 1864): W. (foot), Darbytown Rd. (Oct. 7, 1864): Paroled, Appomattox (Apr. 12, 1865).

(1)   FORRESTER, JOEL — K., Gettysburg (July 2, 1863).

FORRESTER, THOS. — Recruited, Apr. 15, 1862 at Athens, Tex.: Died at Lynchburg, Va., of typhoid fever, July 9, 1862.

(1)   GIBBON, JOS. F. — Present for duty throughout war: Paroled,
(2)   Appomattox (Apr. 12, 1865).

GIEGER, JOHN B. — A musician by profession: Transfd., as a Pvt., into Co. K, 4th Tex. from Co. K, 5th Tex., Dec. 7, 1861: Court-Martialed, Spring, 1863: Sick, Spring, 1864.

GOODWIN, WESLEY — Recruited, Mar. 27, 1862 at Athens, Tex.: Died in camp near Richmond, July 15, 1862.

(1)   GREEN, DAVID N. — Appt. 4Cpl., June 1, 1863: W., Chickamauga (Sept. 19, 1863): Died in field hosp. near Chattanooga, Oct. 9, 1863.

(1)   GREEN, JAS. J. — Sick, Summer & Fall, 1862: Died in hosp., Feb. 6, 1864.

(1)   GUTHRIE, LEWIS J. — W. (arm), Wilderness (May 6, 1864): Paroled,
(2)   Appomattox (Apr. 12, 1865).

(1)   HAMBY, JOHN — Deserted, took Fed. oath, Sept. 20, 1864.

(1)   HEARD, JOS. D. — W. (leg), Gaines' Mill (June 27, 1862): Furlough to Tex.: Did not return to Co., AWOL.

(1)   HIGHT, FRANCIS M. — K., Gaines' Mill (June 27, 1862).

(1)   HILLIARD, ELIAS C. — K., Gaines' Mill (June 27, 1862).

(1)   HOBGOOD, FERDINAND — Died of laryngitis at Richmond, Nov. 7, 1861.

(1)   HOBGOOD, THOS. J. — Deserted, Jan. 3, 1864: No other record.

(1)   HODGE, MAGNUS H. — W., 2nd Manassas (Aug. 30, 1862): W. (thigh),
(2)   Wilderness (May 6, 1864): Appt. 3Sgt., May 7, 1864: Paroled, Appomattox (Apr. 12, 1865).

HOLLAND, F. M. — Recruited, Mar. 19, 1862 at Athens, Tex.: Sick, Fall & Winter, 1862; Fall, 1863 & Winter, 1863-64.

(1)   ISAACS, WM. S. — W. (hip), Gaines' Mill (June 27, 1862): Appt. 4Cpl., Feb. 4, 1863: Reduced to ranks by court-martial, June 1, 1863: AWOL, Winter & Spring, 1863-64.

(1)   JORDON, Z. C. — Sick in hosp., Fall, 1861: Dischgd. for disability, Dec. 30, 1862.

(1) KIMBROUGH, JOHN H. — Prom., 5Sgt.: Appt. 1Sgt., May 7, 1864:
(2)   Paroled, Appomattox (Apr. 12, 1865).
(1) LARUE, ANDREW J. — W., Chickamauga (Sept. 19, 1863): Paroled,
(2)   Appomattox (Apr. 12, 1865).
(1) LARUE, J. H. — Died of typhoid fever at Dumfries, Va., Dec. 10, 1861.
    LENOX, AMOS C. — Recruited, Mar. 28, 1862 at Athens, Tex.: Died
        of typhoid fever near Richmond, July 18, 1862: Personal effects,
        77 cents.
(1) McCALL, JAS. C. — K., Wilderness (May 6, 1864).
(1) McNEELEY, THOS. G. — Appt. Cpl. of the Co. Color Guard, Jan. 10,
        1862: W. (thumb shot off), Gaines' Mill (June 27, 1862).
    MARTIN, ALFRED — Recruited, Mar. 10, 1862 at Athens, Tex.: On
        duty as a shoemaker, Winter, 1863-64: POW, Wilderness (May 6,
        1864): Confined at Elmira, N. Y.: Died, chronic diarrhea, Sept.
        30, 1864.
(1) MARTIN, ROBT. — Died, Richmond hosp., Nov. 15, 1861.
(1) MARTIN, ROBT. B. — See list of "Other Officers" above.
    MESTER, JOEL — K., Gettysburg (July 2, 1863): Not listed on Co.
        Bi-Monthly Muster Roll.
    MILTON A. — Appt. 3Cpl., July 1, 1862: Not listed on Co. Bi-Monthly
        Muster Roll.
    MORSE, WM. — Recruited, Mar. 8, 1862 at Athens, Tex., 51 yrs. old:
        Dischgd. for disability (chronic rheumatism & old age), May 30,
        1862.
    NORVELL, ROBT. F. — Recruited, Mar. 10, 1862 at Athens, Tex.: W.
        (shoulder) & POW, Gettysburg (July 2, 1863): Arm amputated:
        Paroled, Baltimore, Md., Aug. 23, 1862.
(1) OWEN, JOHN D. — Appt. 3Sgt., Sept. 1, 1862: Prom., 2Sgt.: K., Cold
        Harbor (June 2, 1864).
    PAIR, WM. R. — Recruited, Mar. 29, 1862 at Athens, Tex.: POW,
        Gettysburg (July 2, 1863): Confined at Ft. Delaware: Paroled,
        June 9, 1865.
(1) PATTILLO, B. A. — Sick, Winter, 1862-63 & Spring & Summer, 1863:
        POW, Raccoon Mtn., Tenn. (Oct. 28, 1863): Confined at Camp
        Morton, Ind.: Exchanged, Feb. 19, 1865.
(1) PAUL, ROBT. B. — Asgnd. to nursing duties in a Richmond hosp.,
        Oct., 1861: W., Antietam (Sept. 17, 1862): Died of wound, Oct.
        1, 1862.
    PHILLIPS, HARRINGTON — Recruited, Apr. 1, 1862 at Athens, Tex.:
        Appt. 3Cpl., May 1, 1864: No other record.
(1) PICKERING, IRA — Dischgd. for disability, Feb. 22, 1862.
(2) PICKERING, JAS. J. — Recruited, Mar. 17, 1862 at Athens, Tex.:
        Paroled, Appomattox (Apr. 12, 1865): No other record.
(1) PIERCE, W. T. — Died in hosp., Richmond, Oct. 22, 1861.
    PRICE, RUSSELL — Recruited, Apr. 3, 1862 at Athens, Tex.: W.,
        Boonsboro (Sept. 14, 1862): Detailed as a nurse, Spring, 1864:
        Retired on Surg. Cert. of disability (epilepsy & loss of fingers on
        left hand), Feb. 15, 1865.
    PRICE, WM. B. — Recruited, Apr. 1, 1862 at Athens, Tex.: Died of
        pleuritis at Lynchburg, Va., Feb. 4, 1865.

REDMAN, RICHARD — Recruited, Mar. 10, 1862: Sick most of 1862: Asgnd. duty as a shoemaker, Winter, 1863-64: W. (both legs), Wilderness (May 6, 1864).

(1) RICE, JOHN — W. and POW, Antietam (Sept. 17, 1862): Exchanged:
(2) Paroled, Appomattox (Apr. 12, 1865).

(1) RICHARDSON, WM. E. — Sick in hosp., Fall, 1861: Appt. ambulance driver, Summer, 1862: Appt. 4Cpl., Nov. 1, 1862: Appt. 3Cpl., Feb. 1, 1863: In charge of Div. Ambulance Train, Spring, 1863: Resgnd., June 1, 1863: Rejnd. Co.: W. (knee), Wilderness (May 6, 1864).

(1) RICHMOND, WM. ISAAC — Sick in hosp. since Oct. 27, 1861: Dischgd. for disability, Jan. 15, 1862.

(1) ROGERS, A. H. — Appt. 4Cpl., Jan. 12, 1862: W. (arm), Gaines' Mill (June 27, 1862): Appt. 4Sgt., June 15, 1862: Appt. 2Sgt.: W. (chest), 2nd Manassas (Aug. 30, 1862): Reduced to ranks, Oct. 1, 1862: Elect., 4Sgt., Nov. 1, 1862: Prom., 3Sgt., Feb. 1, 1863: W., Chickamauga (Sept. 19, 1863): Retired, Dec. 6, 1864.

(1) ROGERS, SAM S. — Appt. 2Sgt., Oct. 1, 1862: Detailed as an ordnance wagon driver, Winter, 1863-64: POW, Wilderness (May 6, 1864): Confined at Pt. Lookout, Md.: Paroled, June 19, 1865.

(1) RONNSAVALL, ISAAC M. — Appt. 3Cpl., Nov. 1, 1862: Prom., 2Cpl., Feb. 1, 1863: Released from duty, Oct. 5, 1864.

ROSS, CHRISTOPHER C. — Recruited, Apr. 29, 1862 at Athens, Tex.: W. (hand), Wilderness (May 6, 1864): POW, Beverly, W. Va., Sept. 29, 1864: Deserted, took Fed. oath, Oct. 5, 1864.

RUSHING, JAS. H. — Recruited, Apr. 29, 1862 at Athens, Tex.: Dischgd., date unknown: Not carried on Co. Bi-Monthly Muster Roll.

(1) SANDERS, JOHN W. — Sick in hosp., Oct. 27, 1861: Dischgd. for disability, Nov. 7, 1861.

(1) SLOAN, JAS. T. — Died in Richmond hosp., Oct. 20, 1861.

(1) SMITH, FELIX J. — W., Seven Pines (June 1, 1862): Granted furlough to Tex.: AWOL, Spring, 1864: Did not return to Co.

(1) SULLIVAN, WM. M. — Died, Dumfries, Va., Dec. 6, 1861.

(1) SWINDLE, JAS. M. — W. (thigh), Gaines' Mill (June 27, 1862): K., Wilderness (May 6, 1864).

(1) TUBBS, ROBT. — Sick in hosp. since Oct. 27, 1861: Appt. 1Cpl.: Resgnd. as 1Cpl., June 1, 1862: POW, Gettysburg (July 2, 1863), detailed as a nurse to care for wounded: Confined at Pt. Lookout, Md.: Exchanged, Mar. 3, 1864.

(1) VOWELL, J. R. — Sick in hosp., Oct. 22, 1861: Dischgd. for disability, Nov. 9, 1861.

WEISENSEE, CHAS. P. — Recruited, Mar. 10, 1862 at Athens, Tex.: W., 2nd Manassas (Aug. 30, 1862): Appt. 5Sgt., Mar. 15, 1863: Asgnd. to Div. Provost Guard, Spring, 1864: Appt. 2Sgt., May 7, 1864: W. & POW, Darbytown Rd. (Oct. 7, 1864): Confined at Pt. Lookout, Md.: Paroled, June 21, 1865.

WHITAKER, WM. F. — Recruited, Mar. 8, 1862 at Athens, Tex.: W., 2nd Manassas (Aug. 30, 1862).

WIGGINGTON, WM. D. — Recruited, Mar. 10, 1862 at Athens, Tex.: Died at hosp. in Charlottsville, Va., July 7, 1862.

(1)   WILLIAMS, E. J. — Appt. 3Cpl., Nov. 12, 1861: Appt. 2Sgt., Apr. 25, 1862: K., Gaines' Mill (June 27, 1862).

(1)   WILTON, WM. T. — Appt. 1Cpl., Dec. 28, 1861: W. (thigh), Gaines' Mill (June 27, 1862): Appt. 1Cpl., June 1, 1862: Elect., 5Sgt., Nov. 1, 1862: Prom., 4Sgt., Feb. 1, 1863: Died of smallpox at Richmond, Mar. 8, 1863.

5TH TEX. VOL. INF. REGT.

HDQTRS. - FIELD, STAFF & BAND

Organized as a Regiment (Cos. A thru K, less J) Sept. 30, 1861, near Richmond, Va.

Key

(1) Original member of Hdqtrs. (2) Paroled at Appomattox.
K (Killed), W (Wounded), POW (Prisoner of War)
AWOL (Absent Without Leave)

OFFICERS, FIELD & LINE

(1) ARCHER, JAS. J. Colonel
Orig. Col., 5th Tex. Inf. Regt.: Appt. Cmdr., 5th Tex. Inf. Regt., Sept. 30, 1861: See roster, "Hdqtrs., Hood's Tex. Brig."
POWELL, ROBT. M. Colonel
Orig. Capt., Co. D: See roster, "Hdqtrs., Hood's Tex. Brig."
(1) ROBERTSON, JEROME B. Colonel
Orig. Capt., Co. I: Orig. Lt.-Col., 5th Tex. Inf. Regt., appt., Oct. 10, 1861: See roster, "Hdqtrs., Hood's Tex. Brig."
BOTTS, W. BROWN Lieut.-Colonel
Orig. Capt., Co. A: Prom., Maj., Nov. 4, 1861: Prom., Lt.-Col., June 2, 1862: Resgnd. and returned to Tex., July 17, 1862.
BRYAN, KING Lieut.-Colonel
Orig. Capt., Co. F: Prom., Maj., Aug. 30, 1862: W., 2nd Manassas (Aug. 30, 1862): Prom., Lt.-Col., Nov. 1, 1862: W., Gettysburg (July 2, 1863): W. (arm), Wilderness (May 6, 1864).
UPTON, JOHN C. Lieut.-Colonel
Orig. Capt., Co. B: Prom., Maj., June 1, 1862: Prom., Lt.-Col., July 17, 1862: K., 2nd Manassas (Aug. 30, 1862).
(1) QUATTLEBAUM, PAUL J. Major
Orig. Maj., 5th Tex. Inf. Regt.: See roster, "Hdqtrs., Hood's Tex. Brig."
ROGERS, JEFFERSON C. Major
Orig. Capt., Co. G: Prom., Maj., Nov. 1, 1862: Cmded. 5th Tex. Inf. Regt. at Chickamauga (Sept. 19-20, 1863): W. (left side), Chickamauga (Sept. 20, 1863): Convalescent furlough to Selma, Ala.: Disabled, asgnd. to the Invalid Corps in Tex., Oct. 25, 1864.
WHALEY, D. M. Major
Orig. Capt., Co. C: Prom., Maj., July 17, 1862: K., Freeman's Ford (Aug. 22, 1862).

(2) HILL, WM. T. Captain
Orig. 1Lt., Co. D: Detailed to recruiting duty in Tex., Feb.-Apr., 1862: Prom., Capt., Aug. 23, 1862: W. (foot), Gettysburg (July 2, 1863): W. (arm), Wilderness (May 6, 1864): Paroled, Appomattox (Apr. 12, 1865) as Cmdr., 5th Tex. Inf. Regt.
McBRIDE, J. J. Captain
Orig. 1Lt., Co. C: Detailed to recruiting duty in Tex., Feb.-Apr., 1862: Prom., Capt., July 17, 1862: W., 2nd Manassas (Aug. 30, 1862): Actg. Maj., 5th Tex., Spring, 1864: W. (both legs), Wilderness (May 6, 1864): Retired for disability, Dec. 7, 1864.
(2) CLARK, WM. H. Ensign
Enl. as a Pvt. in Co. A at Houston, Tex., Mar. 25, 1862: POW, Boonsboro (Sept. 15, 1862): Confined at Ft. Delaware: Exchanged, Nov. 10, 1862: Hospitalized in Richmond, Spring, 1863: W., Chickamauga (Sept. 20, 1863): Appt. as Ensign by Sec. of War, May 6, 1864 "for gallant and meritorious serv." as color bearer at Gettysburg (July 2, 1863) and Chickamauga (Sept. 19-20, 1863) & asgnd. to Regmtl. Hdqtrs.: W., Wilderness (May 6, 1864): Paroled, Appomattox (Apr. 12, 1865).

OFFICERS, STAFF

ADJUTANTS (AAG)
(1) SELLERS, WM. H. Captain
Orig. Asst. Adj.-Gen., 5th Tex. Inf. Regt., appt., Oct. 6, 1861: See roster, "Hdqtrs., Hood's Tex. Brig."
KERR, JOHN W. 1st Lieutenant
See roster, "Hdqtrs., Hood's Tex. Brig."
(2) McGOWAN, W. P. 2nd Lieutenant
Orig. 2Sgt., Co. A: Prom., 1Sgt., Nov. 7, 1861: Prom., 3Lt., July 8, 1862: Detailed as Regmtl. Adj., July 10, 1863: Prom., 2Lt., Fall, 1863: Appt. Regmtl. Adj., Feb. 19, 1864: W. (hip), Wilderness (May 6, 1864): Paroled, Appomattox (Apr. 12, 1865).
(1) WOOD, CAMPBELL 2nd Lieutenant
Orig. 3Lt., Co. D: Prom., 2Lt., Aug. 23, 1862: Appt. Regmtl. Adj., June, 1862: W. (foot), Gettysburg (July 2, 1863): Three toes amputated: Retired for disability, Dec. 9, 1864: Asgnd. to Enrolling Service: Paroled, Clinton, La.

SURGEONS
(1) BRECKINRIDGE, R. J.
Appt. Regmtl. Surg., Nov. 8, 1861: Temporarily asgnd. to Army Medical Board at Richmond, Mar., 1862: Transfd. from Regmtl. Hdqtrs., 5th Tex. Inf., Fall, 1862, to Hdqtrs., Army of No. Va., as Chief Medical Inspector.
CROSS, GEO. WARREN
See roster, "Hdqtrs., Hood's Tex. Brig."
LEVERETT, S. P.
Appt. Regmtl. Surg., Apr. 10, 1864: Sick in Richmond Hosp., Summer, 1864: Died, July 23, 1864.

ROACH, E. J.
　　Appt. Regmtl. Surg., Spring, 1862: Absent on furlough, Summer, 1863: Asgnd. to duty in Tex. Brig. Hosp., Richmond, Nov., 1863.
(2)　ROBERTS, JOHN J.
　　Orig. Pvt. in Co. E: Appt. Asst. Regmtl. Surg., Nov. 15, 1861: W., Wilderness (May 6, 1864): Appt. Regmtl. Surg., Aug. 10, 1864: Paroled, Appomattox (Apr. 12, 1865).
WATERS, HENRY W.
　　Enl. as a Pvt., Co. I at Independence, Tex., Apr. 7, 1862: W., Gaines' Mill (June 27, 1862): Appt. Asst. Regmtl. Surg., Sept. 23, 1862: Appt. Regmtl. Surg., Nov. 13, 1862: Transfd. to 1st Tex. Inf. Regt., Jan., 1863.

ASST. SURGEONS

BRUCE, J. S.
　　Enl. as a Pvt., Co. B, Mar. 24, 1862: W., 2nd Manassas (Aug. 30, 1862): Appt. Asst. Regmtl. Surg., Oct. 20, 1862.
CLOPTON, JOHN
　　Appt. Asst. Regmtl. Surg., Dec. 24, 1861: Jnd. Regmtl. Hdqtrs., Jan. 2, 1862.
HERNDON, Z. B.
　　See roster, "Hdqtrs., Hood's Tex. Brig."
HUGHES, EDW. C.
　　Enl. as a Pvt. in Co. I at Independence, Tex., Apr. 7, 1862: Asgnd. as a "surg." to the Regmtl. sick camp, June 12, 1862: Detailed to Tex. Hosp. in Richmond, Spring, 1863: Asgnd. as the Tex. Hosp. Druggist, Feb. 15, 1864: W., Wilderness (May 6, 1864): Appt. Asst. Regmtl. Surg., Sept. 1, 1864.
JONES, DAVID C.
　　Transfd. into Regt. from 4th Tex. Inf.: Appt. Asst. Regmtl. Surg., Summer, 1863: On furlough commencing, Oct. 18, 1863: Resgnd., Dec. 31, 1863: See roster of "Regmtl. Hdqtrs., 4th Tex. Inf."
PERRIE, R. E.
　　Orig. Pvt. in Co. A: Appt. Actg. Asst. Regmtl. Surg., Nov. 14, 1861: Dischgd. from serv., Feb. 8, 1862.
(2)　POWELL, WM. P.
　　Enl. as a Pvt. in Co. D at Waverly, Tex., Mar. 20, 1862: W., 2nd Manassas (Aug. 30, 1862): Appt. Actg. Asst. Regmtl. Surg., Mar. 12, 1863: POW, Cashtown, Pa., July 5, 1863, while taking care of the Gettysburg wounded: Exchanged: Returned to Co. D as a Pvt.: W., Chickamauga (Sept. 19, 1863): Appt. Actg. Asst. Regmtl. Surg., May 6, 1864: Paroled, Appomattox (Apr. 12, 1865) as a Pvt.

COMMISSARY SUBSISTENCE OFFICERS (ACS)

BURNS, ROBT.　Captain
　　See roster, "Hdqtrs., Hood's Tex. Brig."
DENNY, W. D.　Captain
　　Orig. 1Sgt., Co. B: Appt. Regmtl. Comsy.-Sgt., Nov. 24, 1861: Prom., Capt. & appt. Regmtl. Comsy. Off., Jan., 1862: K., Eltham's Landing (May 7, 1862).

(1) SETTLE, E. B. Captain
Prom., Capt., Oct. 6, 1861 & appt. Regmtl. Comsy. Off., 5th Tex.
Inf.: Resgnd., Dec. 14, 1861.

QUARTERMASTER OFFICERS
(1) LITTLEFIELD, J. H. Captain
Orig. QM, 5th Tex. Inf. Regt., Appt. Oct. 31, 1861: See roster,
"Hdqtrs., Hood's Tex. Brig."
NORWOOD, WALTER N. Captain
See roster, "Hdqtrs., Hood's Tex. Brig."

NON-COMMISSIONED OFFICERS

SERGEANT-MAJORS
(1) ALLEN, HARDY
Orig. Pvt. in Co. E: Prom., Regmtl. Sgt.-Maj., Oct. 6, 1861: K.,
Antietam (Sept. 17, 1862).
ROBINSON, GEO. JULIUS
Orig. Pvt. in Co. A: Detchd. duty as scout, Nov. 22, 1861: W.,
Gaines' Mill (June 27, 1862): Prom., 3Cpl., Aug. 1, 1862: Prom.,
5Sgt.: Prom., 2Sgt.: Actg. Regmtl. Sgt.-Maj., Winter, 1863-64:
W., Wilderness (May 6, 1864): Shot through both cheeks, tongue
mangled & jaw shattered: Retired for disability, Dec. 2, 1864.
(2) SMITHER, JOHN M.
Orig. Pvt., Co. D: Appt. 4Cpl.: Appt. Actg. Regmtl. Sgt.-Maj.,
Sept. 18, 1862: Appt. Regmtl. Sgt.-Maj., Nov. 1, 1862: W.,
Chickamauga (Sept. 19, 1863): W. (head), Petersburg, June 18,
1864.

COLOR-SERGEANTS
CLARK, W. H.
See list of "Officers, Field & Line" above.
FITZGERALD, T. W.
Enl. as a Pvt. in Co. A, Mar. 28, 1862, Houston, Tex.: Appt.
Regmtl. Color-Sgt., July, 1862: W. (knee & foot) & POW,
Gettysburg (July 2, 1863): Paroled, Sept. 25, 1863: W.
(shoulder), Cold Harbor (June 1, 1864): Retired to Invalid Corps,
Tex., Oct. 16, 1864.
OATS, NATHAN
Orig. Pvt., Co. K: Prom., 1Cpl., Feb. 10, 1862: W., 2nd Manassas
(Aug. 30, 1862): Detailed to Tex. on recruiting serv., Feb.-Apr.,
1863: Appt. 5Sgt., June 22, 1863: Transfd. to Regmtl. Hdqtrs. as
Color-Sgt., Summer, 1863: K., Chickamauga (Sept. 19, 1863).
(1) ONDERDONK, GEO.
Orig. Pvt., Co. A: Appt. Regmtl. Color-Sgt., Nov. 25, 1861:
Prom., 5Sgt., Dec., 1861: Prom., 2Sgt.: W. (arm), Gaines' Mill
(June 27, 1862): Furloughed to Tex.: Did not return to Co.:
Dischgd. for disability, Apr. 6, 1863 by Medical Board in
Trans-Miss. Dept.

QUARTERMASTER-SERGEANTS

(1) DARDEN, W. J.

A lawyer by profession: Orig. Pvt., Co. B: Appt. Regmtl. QM-Sgt., Nov. 1, 1861: Returned to Co. B, Feb. 8, 1862: Detailed to recruiting serv. in Tex., Feb.-Apr., 1862: POW, Eltham's Landing (May 7, 1862): Confined at Ft. Delaware: Exchanged, Aug. 5, 1862: W. (leg) & POW, Antietam (Sept. 17, 1862): Confined at Old Capitol Prison, Wash., D.C.: Paroled, Apr., 1863: 60 day furlough granted to Tex., Apr. 28, 1863: Did not return to Co., AWOL at Columbus, Tex.

WRAY, J. F.

Orig. 5Sgt., Co. E: Appt. Regmtl. QM-Sgt., Feb. 11, 1862: W., Gaines' Mill (June 27, 1862): On detchd. serv. foraging with Brig. QM, in No. Va., Fall, 1864.

COMMISSARY SUBSISTENCE-SERGEANTS

(1) DENNY, W. D.

See preceding list of "Commissary Officers."

(2) STANGER, JAS.

Orig. Pvt., Co. A: Appt. Regmtl. Comsy.-Sgt., Sept. 22, 1862: Returned to Co. A, Summer, 1863, when Comsy. Section was eliminated at Regmtl. level: Paroled, Appomattox (Apr. 12, 1865).

ORDNANCE-SERGEANTS

(2) CROSS, J. T.

Orig. Pvt., Co. I: W., Gaines' Mill (June 27, 1862): Appt. Regmtl. Ordn.-Sgt., July 18, 1862: Paroled, Appomattox (Apr. 12, 1865).

McMURTRY, JOHN A. — See list of "Original Non-Commissioned Officers, Co. A."

HOSPITAL STEWARDS

BOTELER, GEO.

Orig. Pvt., Co. A: Detchd. duty as Regmtl. Hosp. Steward, Apr. 2, 1863.

(2) CHADWICK, W. H. H.

Orig. Pvt., Co. A: Prom., 3Cpl.: Appt. Regmtl. Hosp. Steward, June 2, 1863: Granted 40-day furlough to Ala., Jan., 1864: Paroled, Appomattox (Apr. 12, 1865).

NORTON, J. S.

Orig. Pvt. in Co. A: Appt. Regmtl. Hosp. Steward, Winter, 1861-62: Detailed to Ambulance Corps, Apr., 1862: POW, 2nd Manassas (Aug. 30, 1862): Paroled, Nov. 14, 1862: On extra duty as a Regmtl. Musician, Spring, 1863 to Feb., 1864.

TAYLOR, T. O.

Recruited as a Pvt., Co. B, Mar. 18, 1862, at Columbus, Tex., age 26: Detailed as a clerk at Chimborozo Hosp., Richmond, Summer, 1862: Detailed as Regmtl. Hosp. Steward, Mar. 27, 1864.

TERRELL, CHAS. M.

Recruited, age 40, Mar. 29, 1862 at Columbus, Tex.: Detailed as a Hospital Steward, Sept. 18, 1862: Dischgd. by Gen. G. W. Smith, Nov. 20, 1862.

(1) WRIGHT, JEFFERSON
   Orig. Pvt., Co. E: Detailed as Regmtl. Hosp. Steward, Dec. 20, 1861: Prom., 1Cpl.: Prom., 4Sgt.: Placed in charge of 5th Tex. Inf. Regt. Depot, Richmond: Detailed as Steward, Tex. Hosp., Richmond, Dec. 8, 1862: Deserted, Apr. 8, 1863.

BAND

CHIEF BUGLER

HERNDON, ED. W.
   Musician in Co. G: Transfd. to Regmtl. Hdqtrs., as Chief Bugler, Apr. 1, 1864.

BAND MEMBERS

CARTER, ALBERT H.
   See list of "Privates", Co. B.
NORTON, J. S.
   See list of "Hospital Stewards" above.

SPECIALISTS

FORAGEMASTER

BUNGER, W. G.
   Orig. Pvt., Co. E: Asgnd. to QM Dept., Apr. 16, 1862: Detailed as Regmtl. Foragemaster, Apr., 1864.

WAGONMASTER

BURDEN, JOHN G.
   Orig. Pvt., Co. D: Appt. Regmtl. Wagonmaster, May 2, 1862: W. (leg), Wilderness (May 6, 1864): Dischgd. for disability, June 27, 1864.

FARRIERS OR BLACKSMITHS

HURT, JAS. S.
   Orig. Pvt. in Co. E: Detailed as Asst. Regmtl. Blacksmith, Jan., 1862: K., Antietam (Sept. 17, 1862).
IRWIN, SAMUEL W.
   Orig. Pvt., Co. C: Detailed as Regmtl. Blacksmith, Jan., 1862: W., Gaines' Mill (June 27, 1862): Finger shot off: AWOL, Oct., 1862: Did not return to Co.

5TH TEX. VOL. INF. REGT.

COMPANY A — *BAYOU CITY GUARDS*

Company was organized in Harris County, Texas, enrolled at Houston, July 19, 1861, and mustered into the Confederate service "for the war" at Richmond, Virginia, Sept. 30, 1861.

Key

(1) Original member of Company. (2) Paroled at Appomattox.
K (Killed), W (Wounded), POW (Prisoner of War)
AWOL (Absent Without Leave)

ORIGINAL OFFICERS

(1) BOTTS, W. BROWN Capt. — See roster, "Regmtl. Hdqtrs., 5th Tex. Inf."
(1) SELLERS, WM. H. 1Lt. — See roster, "Regmtl. Hdqtrs., 5th Tex. Inf."
(1) HALE, JOHN R. 2Lt. — Prom., 1Lt., Nov. 7, 1861: Detailed to Pioneer Corps, Dec. 20, 1862: Transfd. to Nitre & Mining Bureau, July 2, 1863.
(1) FARMER, D. C. 3Lt. — Prom., Capt., Nov. 1, 1861: W., Gettysburg (July 2, 1863): Actg. Maj. of Regt., Oct. 31, 1863: Actg. Lt.-Col. of Regt., Dec. 31, 1863: W. (hip), Wilderness (May 6, 1864): On detchd. duty, recruiting in Tex., Summer, 1864.

ORIGINAL NON-COMMISSIONED OFFICERS

(1) CLUTE, J. E. 1Sgt. — See list of "Other Officers" following.
(1) McGOWAN, W. P. 2Sgt. — See list of "Other Officers" following.
(1) CLEVELAND, W. D. 3Sgt. — Prom., 2Sgt.: Dischgd. for disability (hernia), Dec. 18, 1861.
(1) NOBLE, E. A. 4Sgt. — Prom., 3Sgt., Nov. 7, 1861: Prom., 1Sgt., Feb., 1862: W., 2nd Manassas (Aug. 30, 1862): Furlough to Tex.: Dischgd. for disability by Med. Bd. in Trans-Miss.
(1) MOORE, E. R. 1Cpl. — Transfd., Fall, 1861 to Terry's Texas Rangers (8th Tex. Cav. Regt.).
(1) LEVERTON, JOHN 2Cpl. — Prom., 1Cpl.: Prom., 4Sgt., Nov. 7, 1861: Prom., 2Sgt.: Reduced to ranks by request, July 1, 1862: W. (hip) & POW, Gettysburg (July 2, 1863): Exchanged: Retired to Invalid Corps in Tex., Nov. 22, 1864.
(1) DAVIDSON, JUSTUS 3Cpl. — Prom., 2Cpl.: Prom., 1Cpl., Nov. 7, 1861: Detchd. as druggist in hosp., Richmond, Jan. 6, 1862: Reduced to the ranks, Fall, 1862.

(1) McMURTRY, JOHN A. 4Cpl. — Prom., 3Cpl.: Prom., 2Cpl., Nov. 7,
1862: Served extra duty as Regmtl. Ordn.-Sgt., Spring, 1862:
Prom., 4Sgt., July, 1862: W., 2nd Manassas (Aug. 30, 1862):
Died of wound, Nov. 6, 1862.

OTHER OFFICERS

FULLER, B. PUGH 1Lt. — Orig. Pvt. in Co.: Prom., 3Lt., Nov. 7,
1861: Prom., 2Lt., June 27, 1862: Prom., 1Lt., Sept. 1, 1863: W.
(hand), Wilderness (May 6, 1864): Sick in Richmond, Fall, 1864.
CLUTE, J. E. 2Lt. — Orig. 1Sgt. of Co.: Prom., 2Lt., Nov. 7, 1861:
Asgnd. to recruiting serv. in Tex., Feb.-Apr., 1862: K., Gaines'
Mill (June 27, 1862).
GARDNER, C. B. 2Lt. — Orig. Pvt. in Co.: Courier for Gen. Hood:
W., Chickamauga (Sept. 19, 1863): Prom., 2Lt., Dec. 20, 1863,
and asgnd. to the Trans-Miss. Dept.
McGOWAN, W. P. 2Lt. — Orig. 2Sgt. of Co.: See roster, "Regmtl.
Hdqtrs., 5th Tex. Inf."

MUSICIANS

(1) WOOLFE, A. F. — Drummer: Reduced to Pvt., Feb., 1862: W. (arm),
Seven Pines (June 1, 1862): W., skirmish near Richmond, June 9.
1862: W. & POW, Antietam (Sept. 17, 1862): Died of wound,
Oct. 1, 1862, in Fed. hosp.

PRIVATES

ANGEL, ALBERT — Recruited, Mar. 14, 1862 in Harris Co., Tex.: W.,
2nd Manassas (Aug. 30, 1862): Died of wound.
(1) AUERBACH, JACOB — Dischgd. for disability, Nov. 28, 1861.
BACHRACH, WOLF — Recruited, Mar. 11, 1862 in Harris Co., Tex.:
AWOL at Antietam, Sept. 16, 1862: Returned to Co.: Sick in
Tex. Hosp., Richmond, Feb., 1863.
(1) BAILEY, SAMUEL — W., Gaines' Mill (June 27, 1862): W. (hip &
hand) & POW, 2nd Manassas (Aug. 30, 1862): Exchanged: W.
(hip), Gettysburg (July 2, 1863): K., Spotsylvania (May 10,
1864).
(1) BARRON, JASPER — On detchd. duty to transport his "crazy
brother" to Tex., Nov. & Dec., 1861: Sick most of 1862 & 1863:
Paroled at Richmond, May 17, 1865.
(1) BARRON, WM. — Dischgd. by War Dept., Dec. 2, 1861, "for insanity."
BEISLEY (or BEASELEY), JOHN A. — Recruited, Mar. 28, 1862 in
Harris Co., Tex.: Deserted to enemy at Boonsboro (Sept. 14,
1862).
(1) BELL, H. C. — Dischgd. for disability, Dec. 8, 1861.
(1) BELL, JOHN H. — Prom., 4Cpl., May 1, 1862: Prom., 1Cpl., July,
1862: W., 2nd Manassas (Aug. 30, 1862): Died of wounds.

(1) BERRY, M. F. — Died of typhoid pneumonia, Nov. 16, 1861.
(1) BIGBEE, T. E. — POW, Boonsboro (Sept. 14, 1862): Confined at Ft. Delaware: Exchanged, Oct. 6, 1862: Sick in hosp. with "irritable bladder": AWOL, Cleveland, Tenn., Nov. 18, 1863: Returned to Co., June 25, 1864: POW, Farmville, Va., Apr. 6, 1865: Paroled, June 16, 1865.
BILLIG, ISAAC — Recruited, Mar. 11, 1862 in Harris Co., Tex.: Deserted to enemy on retreat from Suffolk, Va., May 3, 1863.
(1) BOTELER, GEO. W. — See roster, "Regmtl. Hdqtrs., 5th Tex. Inf."
(1) BOTTS, C. M. — Dischgd. for disability (blind), Sept. 13, 1861.
BRYAN, THOS. P. — Enl. at Enterprise, Miss., Feb. 2, 1864: K., Wilderness (May 6, 1864).
(1) BURKE, A. J., Jr. — Dischgd. for disability (hernia), Dec. 4, 1861.
BURNS, PATRICK — Recruited, Mar. 16, 1862 in Harris Co., Tex.: Deserted to enemy at Boonsboro (Sept. 14, 1862).
(1) BURNS, ROBT. — See roster, "Regmtl. Hdqtrs., 5th Tex. Inf."
(1) BUTLER, G. J. — Dischgd. by War Dept., Dec. 27, 1861.
(1) CAMERON, J. A. — Sick, Fall, 1862: AWOL, since Dec. 25, 1864.
CAMPBELL, ROBT. — Recruited, Mar. 14, 1862 in Harris Co., Tex.: W. (ankle), 2nd Manassas (Aug. 30, 1862): W. (leg & arm), Chickamauga (Sept. 19, 1863): Detailed as courier at Brig. Hdqtrs., Feb. 27, 1864: W. ("severely — head, knee & body") & POW, Darbytown Rd. (Oct. 7, 1864).
(1) CAPPS, ROBT. M. — Sick furlough, Winter, 1861-62: AWOL, Summer, 1862: Did not return to Co.
CARAN, JAS. — Recruited, Mar. 11, 1862 in Harris Co., Tex.: Deserted before joining Co. in Va.
(1) CHADWICK, W. H. H. — See roster, "Regmtl. Hdqtrs., 5th Tex. Inf."
(1) CLARK, THOS. H. — Sick furlough granted, Jan., 1862: Did not return to Co.: Said to have deserted in Richmond.
(1) CLARK, W. A. — Detailed in Army Intell. Office, Richmond, July, 1862 to Sept., 1863: Detached duty in Telegraph Office, Trans-Miss. Dept., Sept., 1863: Returned to Army Intell. Office in Richmond, Jan., 1864: Died in Richmond of pneumonia, Feb. 24, 1864.
(1) CLARK, W. F. — Dischgd. for disability (lung disease), Dec. 4, 1861.
(1) CLARK, WM. H. — See roster, "Regmtl. Hdqtrs., 5th Tex. Inf."
(1) COHEN, S. — K., Gettysburg (July 2, 1863).
(2) COLEMAN, LEWIS — Recruited, Mar. 11, 1862 in Harris Co., Tex.: W. (right arm), Gettysburg (July 2, 1863): Extra duty as Brig. ambulance driver, Fall, 1864: Paroled, Appomattox (Apr. 12, 1865).
COOK, A. W. — Enlisted at Niblets Bluff, La. by Lt. W. H. Sellers, Sept., 1861: Sick, Winter, 1861-1862: Sick most of 1862, 1863 & 1864 with VD: Paroled, Apr. 29, 1865.
CRAMER, JOS. — W. (thigh) & POW, Gettysburg (July 2, 1863): Confined at U.S. Genl. Hosp., Baltimore, Md.: Exchanged: Wound furlough to Tex., Dec., 1864.
CRAMER, LOUIS — Recruited, Mar. 11, 1862 in Harris County, Tex.: AWOL, May 15, 1862 from Richmond Hosp.

(1)   CURRAN, B. R. — Detailed to Camp Winder, Va. as clerk, Fall, 1862: Dischgd. for bronchitis, Oct. 20, 1864.

(1)   CYRUS, W. HENRY — Furlough granted to Tex., Feb., 1862: AWOL, did not return to Co.

DEALEY, E. C. — Recruited, Mar. 26, 1862 in Harris Co., Tex.: Left in sick camp, Aug., 1862: Returned to Tex.

DE BOLD, ADAM — Recruited, Mar. 10, 1862 in Harris Co., Tex.: Detchd. duty as Hosp. Steward at hosp. in Marietta, Ga., Oct. 19, 1863.

(1)   DEGGS, C. W. — K., Gettysburg (July 2, 1863).

(1)   DE LESDENIER, G. H. — K., Gaines' Mill (June 27, 1862).

(1)   DE LESDENIER, JOHN W. — K., 2nd Manassas (Aug. 30, 1862).

DELOACH, J. C. — W. (head), Wilderness (May 6, 1864): K., Chaffin's Farm (Sept. 27, 1864).

DEVOE, WM. R. — Recruited, Mar. 28, 1862 in Harris Co., Tex.: No other record.

DE YOUNG, JOHN — K., 2nd Manassas (Aug. 30, 1862).

(1)   DOUGLASS, GEO. M. — Sick in Richmond Hosp., Feb., 1862 &
(2)   Summer, 1862: Sick in Richmond Hosp., Spring, 1863: Sick furlough to Tex., Spring, 1864: Sick in Richmond, Fall, 1864: Paroled, Appomattox (Apr. 12, 1865).

(1)   DOWNEY, JAS. — Extra duty as Regmtl. Saddler, Jan. 9, 1862:
(2)   Detailed as litter bearer, Fall, 1863: Detailed as shoemaker at Greenville, Tenn., Feb., 1864: W., Chaffin's Farm (Sept. 27, 1864): W. (arm), Darbytown Rd. (Oct. 7, 1864): Paroled, Appomattox (Apr. 12, 1865).

(1)   DYER, BENJ. L. — Prom., 4Cpl., Aug. 1, 1862: W. (leg) & POW, Antietam (Sept. 17, 1862): Confined at Ft. McHenry, Md.: Exchanged, Feb. 15, 1863: Prom., 1Cpl., Feb., 1863: Leg amputated, Dec. 7, 1863: Dischgd. for disability.

(1)   EDEY, ARTHUR H. — Detchd. duty as Agent for the Regt., at Richmond Depot, Feb. 7, 1862: W. (hip) & POW, Gettysburg (July 2, 1863): Confined at U.S. Convalescent hosp., Ft. Wood, Bedloe's Is., N.Y. Harbor.

(1)   ELSASSER, ISAAC — Dischgd. for disability (rheumatism), Dec. 9, 1861.

EMANUEL, T. S. — Recruited, Mar. 22, 1862 at Houston, Tex.: Died of measles in Richmond, May 26, 1863.

EVES, C. R. — Recruited, Mar. 27, 1862 in Harris Co., Tex.: W., Gaines' Mill (June 27, 1862): Detailed in Telegraph Office in Richmond, Sept. 15, 1862 to end of war.

(1)   FERRELL, WM. B. — Detailed to Tex. Hosp., Richmond, Sept. 19, 1862: POW, Spotsylvania (May 10, 1864): Confined at Pt. Lookout, Md.: Exchanged, Jan. 17, 1865.

FITZGERALD, T. W. — See roster, "Regmtl. Hdqtrs., 5th Tex. Inf."

(1)   FLEMING, D. N. — Died of chronic dysentery, Dec. 23, 1861.

FRAZEE, EMMITT — Recruited, Mar.·27, 1862 in Harris Co., Tex.: W., Gettysburg (July 2, 1863): AWOL, Nov., 1863.

FREY, CHAS. — Recruited, Mar. 12, 1862 in Harris Co., Tex.: Sick during entire enlistment: Died, Dec. 20, 1862 at Richmond, Va.

(1)   FULLER, B. PUGH — See list of "Other Officers" above.

GAFFNEY, WM. — Recruited, Mar. 13, 1862 in Harris Co., Tex.: Deserted before joining Co.

(1) GARDNER, C. B. — See list of "Other Officers" above.

(1) GARRISON, JOHN H. — Prom., 4Cpl., Jan. 1, 1863: Prom., 3Cpl.: POW, Gettysburg (July 2, 1863): Confined at Ft. McHenry, Md.: Paroled, June 9, 1865.

(1) GEORGE, WM. A. — Detailed to Pioneer Corps, Dec., 1862: Paroled,
(2) Appomattox (Apr. 12, 1865).

(1) HARN, C. P. — Duty as scout, Nov., 1861: AWOL, May 23, 1862: In arrest in Richmond, Va., Aug. 10, 1862: Dropped from rolls by Special Order of Gen. Lee, Aug., 1863.

HEALEY, JOHN — Recruited, Mar. 8, 1862 in Harris Co., Tex.: AWOL, July 1, 1862: Returned to Co., Oct. 20, 1863: W. & POW, Darbytown Rd. (Oct. 7, 1864): Took Fed. Oath, Oct. 11, 1864.

HEFFERAN, JOHN — Recruited, Mar. 10, 1862 in Harris Co., Tex.: K., 2nd Manassas (Aug. 30, 1862).

HENRY, GEO. — Deserted at Richmond, Va., Sept. 24, 1861.

(1) HEWES, S. D. — Enl. at age 34: Occupation, "speculator": Detailed to recruiting serv. in Tex., Feb.-Apr., 1862: W. (foot & hip), 2nd Manassas (Aug. 30, 1862): Furlough to Miss. & Tex.: Dischgd. for disability, June 15, 1863.

HICKS, J. M. — Recruited, Mar. 14, 1862 in Harris Co., Tex.: Sick, Fall, 1862: AWOL, July, 1863, at Culpeper, Va.: Said to have jnd. the cavalry.

HILTON, EDW. — Recruited, Mar. 11, 1862 in Harris Co., Tex.: Deserted before joining Co.

(1) HOLBROOK, GEO. C. — Sick furlough granted, Jan., 1862: AWOL, July, 1862: Did not return to Co.

(1) HOWARD, Dr. R. G. — Physician by profession: Actg. Asst. Regmtl. Surg., Oct., 1861: Sick furlough, Winter, 1861-1862: Served as a Pvt. to Feb., 1863: No record after that date.

HOWE, WM. D. — Recruited, Mar. 28, 1862 at Houston, Tex.: Sick, Summer & Fall, 1862: Sick most of 1863 & 1864: POW, Richmond, Apr. 3, 1865: Died, of dysentery in Fed. hosp., July 4, 1865.

(1) HURT (or HURTT), JOHN T. — Sick in hosp. in Richmond, Va.,
(2) Summer, 1862: Sick, Summer, 1864: Paroled, Appomattox (Apr. 12, 1865).

(1) KEESEE, THOS. H. — Dischgd. for disability, Feb. 24, 1862.

(1) KEILEY, WM. — W. (hand), 2nd Manassas (Aug. 30, 1862): AWOL since Dec., 1862: Paroled at Montgomery, Ala., May 23, 1865.

(1) KINNAIRD, J. A. — Detailed as Regmtl. Apothecary, Nov. 2, 1862: Detailed as Apothecary in a Richmond hosp., Feb., 1863: Deserted at Morristown, Tenn., Mar. 29, 1864: Took Fed. oath, Apr. 2, 1864.

KOSSEE, FRANK E. — Recruited, Mar. 29, 1862 in Harris Co., Tex.: K., Antietam (Sept. 17, 1862).

(1) LANDES, JAS. E. — Sick, Fall & Winter, 1862-1863: W., Wilderness
(2) (May 6, 1864): Finger amputated: Paroled, Appomattox (Apr. 12, 1865).

(1)   LANDINGHAM, J. W. — On sick furlough to Tex., Feb. & Mar., 1862: Detchd. duty at Brig. Hdqtrs., Mar. 16, 1862: Transfd. to Army of Tenn., Feb., 1864, as clerk for Lt.-Gen. Hood.

(1)   LEBESQUE, F. — Transfd. on Nov. 4, 1861, to Co. B, Garrett's La. Artillery Battalion (Donaldsonville Arty.).

(1)   LEE, J. M. — Dischgd. for disability, Oct. 24, 1861.

LEVY, ROBT. — Recruited, Mar. 10, 1862 at Harris Co., Tex.: Deserted before joining Co.

(1)   LIVINGSTON, HORACE G. — Dischgd. for disability (rheumatism), Dec. 4, 1861.

LOVE, JOS. E. — Recruited at Houston, Tex., Apr. 1, 1863: K., Gettysburg (July 2, 1863).

(1)   LUBBOCK, THEO. U. — Transfd. out of Co., Fall, 1861, to Terry's Tex. Rangers (8th Tex. Cav. Regt.).

(1)   McCULLOUGH, M. J. — Dischgd. for disability (chronic rheumatism), Dec. 15, 1861.

McCULLOUGH, PAUL E. — Recruited, Mar. 25, 1862 in Harris Co., Tex.: Reported missing in retreat from Yorktown, Va., May 5, 1862: W. (head) & POW, Darbytown Rd. (Oct. 7, 1864): Confined at Pt. Lookout, Md.: Paroled, May 14, 1865.

McDONALD, EDW. — Recruited, Mar. 25, 1862 at Houston, Tex.: Sick most of 1863 & 1864 (chronic ulcer of leg).

(1)   McDOWELL, WM. — W. & POW, Gettysburg (July 2, 1863): Died of wound in Fed. hosp. in Baltimore, Md.

McGRANGE, D. G. — Recruited, Mar. 26, 1862 at Houston, Tex.: Sick in Richmond, Va., May, 1862: AWOL, July 14, 1863, in Md.: Did not rejoin Co.

McKENZIE, ALEX. — Recruited, Mar. 12, 1862 in Harris Co., Tex.: Deserted before joining Co.

MASSENBURG, J. N. — Recruited, Mar. 22, 1862 in Harris Co., Tex.: K., 2nd Manassas (Aug. 30, 1862).

(1)   MAY, J. V. — Asgnd. extra duty as ambulance driver, Fall, 1861 to Summer, 1863: AWOL in Richmond since Sept. 9, 1863.

(1)   MERRIMAN, CHAS. H. — Sick in Richmond, Sept., 1861: Dischgd. on Surg. Cert. (lung disease), Feb. 7, 1862.

MILLER, GEO. C. — Recruited, Mar. 28, 1862 in Harris Co., Tex.: Deserted, Sept. 14, 1862 (Boonsboro) & "is now in Federal uniform."

MONELL, A. G. — Recruited, Mar. 29, 1862 in Harris Co., Tex.: AWOL, since Sept. 28, 1862, at Winchester, Va.

MORRIS, JOHN — Recruited, Mar. 9, 1862 in Harris Co., Tex.: W., Gettysburg (July 2, 1863): W., Chickamauga (Sept. 19, 1863): W. (arm), Petersburg trenches, July 13, 1864: Hospitalized in Richmond: POW, Richmond, Apr. 3, 1865.

MORSE, GEO. W. — Recruited, Mar. 27, 1862 in Harris Co., Tex.: On sick furlough in Tex. since Jan. 30, 1863: AWOL, did not return to Co.

MORSE, HENRY A. — Recruited, Mar. 27, 1862 in Harris Co., Tex.: W. (arm), Darbytown Rd. (Oct. 7, 1864): Granted furlough to Mobile, Ala.: Paroled, Houston, June 28, 1865.

MYERS, HENRY — Recruited, Mar. 28, 1862 at Houston, Tex.: Sick most of 1862: Dischgd. by Medical Bd., Oct. 8, 1863.

NETHERLY, JAS. R. — Recruited, Mar. 25, 1862 in Harris Co., Tex.: W. (side), Malvern Hill (July 1, 1863): Died at Warrenton, Va. of chronic diarrhea, Oct. 4, 1862.

(1) NORTON, J. S. — Enl., July 19, 1861 at Houston, Tex.: See roster, "Regmtl. Hdqtrs., 5th Tex. Inf."

(1) O'DONNELL, THOS. — Detailed as ambulance driver, Nov., 1861 to Dec., 1863: Detailed as courier to Gen. Hood (Army of Tenn.), Feb. 25, 1864.

(1) O'MALLEY, OWEN — A civil engr. by profession: Enl. at 28, July 19, 1861 at Houston: W. & POW, 2nd Manassas (Aug. 30, 1862): Paroled, Sept. 30, 1862: W., Chickamauga (Sept. 19, 1863): Granted furlough to Tex., AWOL, did not return to Co.

(1) ONDERDONK, GEO. — Enl. on July 19, 1861 at Houston: See roster, "Regmtl. Hdqtrs., 5th Tex. Inf."

OTT, FRANCIS — Recruited, Mar. 13, 1862 in Harris Co., Tex.: Deserted before joining Co.

PATTON, J. R. — Recruited, Mar. 12, 1862 in Harris Co., Tex.: W., 2nd Manassas (Aug. 30, 1862): Died (smallpox), Apr. 1, 1863.

(1) PERRIE, R. E. — See roster, "Regmtl. Hdqtrs., 5th Tex. Inf."

(1) PHELPS, R. W. — Sick in Richmond, Va.: Fell to rear, sick, on retreat from Yorktown, May 5, 1862: POW: Co. reported him a deserter, May 12, 1862.

PLUMMER, F. W. — Recruited, Mar. 10, 1862 in Harris Co., Tex.: W., Gaines' Mill (June 27, 1862): Detailed to Brig. Provost Guard: W., Chickamauga (Sept. 20, 1863): Detailed as a shoemaker, Dec. 22, 1863 at St. Clair, Tenn.: Detailed as a shoemaker at Greenville, Tenn., Feb. 21, 1864.

(1) POLAND, F. M. — Detailed as Hosp. Steward at Marietta, Ga., Oct. 19, 1863: Transfd. to Trans-Miss. Medical Dept., Sept. 17, 1864.

(1) POMEROY, NICHOLAS — W. (hand & side) & POW, Gettysburg (July 2, 1863): Confined at Ft. McHenry, Md.: Exchanged, July 31, 1863.

PUCKETT, G. R. — Recruited, Mar. 27, 1863 at Houston, Tex.: AWOL, Nov., 1863, supposed to be in Tex.

REDSALL, JAS. E. — Recruited, Mar. 28, 1862 in Harris Co., Tex.: Appeared to take sick before each major battle: AWOL, Mar., 1864: Said to have deserted.

(1) REILY, JOHN — Dischgd. by order of Sec. of War, Sept. 21, 1861.

(1) REVELY, THOS. H. — Extra duty as wagoneer & courier, Winter, 1861-62: W. (hip) & POW, Gettysburg (July 2, 1863): Paroled, Aug. 24, 1863: Transfd. to the 8th Tex. Cav. Regt. (Terry's Tex. Rangers), Mar. 19, 1864.

RILEY, W. J. — Recruited, Mar. 29, 1862 at Houston, Tex.: W., 2nd Manassas (Aug. 30, 1862): Died of pneumonia at Winchester, Va., Oct. 18, 1862.

(1) ROBBINS, GEO. H. — W. (right arm), Chickamauga (Sept. 19, 1863): Detailed to Invalid Corps in Tex., Oct., 1864: Paroled, Houston, Tex., July 3, 1865.

ROBINSON, GEO. JULIAN — See roster, "Regmtl. Hdqtrs., 5th Tex. Inf."

(1) RODGERS, HIRAM R. — Dischgd. by War Dept., Feb. 6, 1862 for "being a minor."

(1) SALOI, PETER — Dischgd. on Surg. Cert. of disability, Aug. 4, 1861.

SCHAUFF, BENJ. — Recruited, Mar. 9, 1862 in Harris Co., Tex.: Deserted before joining Co.

(1) SETTLE, CHAS. F. — Prom., 4Cpl., Oct. 1, 1862: W. & POW,
(2) Gettysburg (July 2, 1863): Confined at Ft. Delaware: Paroled: Prom., 2Sgt., Nov., 1864: Paroled, Appomattox (Apr. 12, 1865).

(1) SETTLE, H. G. ("Ham") — Prom., 4Cpl., Nov. 7, 1861: Prom., 5Sgt., Sept. 1, 1862: W., Gettysburg (July 2, 1863): Prom., 2Sgt., Mar., 1864: W. (neck), Petersburg (June 13, 1864): Died in Richmond of wound, July 15, 1864, at home of G. W. Smith on 4th Str. between Leigh & Clay.

(1) SHELDON, CHAS. — AWOL, May, 1862: In arrest in Richmond, Aug., 1862 to Feb., 1863: Deserted to enemy on retreat from Suffolk, Va., May 3, 1863.

(1) SHEPHERD, JOS. H. — W., Gaines' Mill (June 27, 1862): Sick, Fall,
(2) 1862 to Spring, 1863: Prom., 1Cpl., Mar. 27, 1864: W. (legs), Wilderness (May 6, 1864): Prom., Sgt., Feb., 1865: Paroled, Appomattox (Apr. 12, 1865).

(1) SIMMS, WM. — Sick, Fall, 1861: Dischgd. by War Dept. on Surg. Cert., Dec. 3, 1861.

(1) SIMPSON, B. C. — Prom., 3Cpl., Nov. 7, 1861: W., 2nd Manassas (Aug. 30, 1862): W. (leg) & POW, Gettysburg (July 2, 1863): Confined at Ft. Delaware: Escaped: Prom., 1Sgt., Apr., 1864: Paroled at Houston, Aug. 1, 1865.

STANGER, JAS. — See roster, "Regmtl. Hdqtrs., 5th Tex. Inf."

STEELE, M. L. — Recruited, Mar. 7, 1862 in Harris Co., Tex.: W. & POW, Chickamauga (Sept. 19, 1863): Confined at Camp Douglas, Ill.: Paroled, May 16, 1865.

STEVENS, CHAS. E. — Recruited, Mar. 17, 1862 in Harris Co., Tex.: Deserted to enemy, Sept. 14, 1862 (Boonsboro).

STEWART, ALEX — Recruited, Mar. 27, 1862 in Harris Co., Tex.: W. (foot), Antietam (Sept. 17, 1862): Leave granted to Tex.: Dischgd. by Medical Bd., Trans-Miss. Dept., June, 1863.

(1) SWEENEY, J. J. — Died on march to Va., Sept. 9, 1861.

SYXE, FRANK — Recruited, Mar. 10, 1862 at Houston, Tex. by Lt. J. E. Clute: Was already a member of Co. D, 2nd Tex. Inf. Regt. at the time of taking oath with Lt. Clute & was paid bounty for joining Co. A: Deserted to rejoin Co. D.

(1) TAYLOR, A. C. M.— Died on march to Va., Sept. 24, 1861.

THOMAS, F. B. — Recruited, Mar. 27, 1862 at Houston, Tex.: Deserted at Yorktown, Va., May 4, 1862.

(1) TOOLE, H. P. — Died of typhoid pneumonia, Dec. 30, 1861.

(1) TRESSAM, JOHN — Left sick in Tex.: Jnd. Co. in Va., Oct., 1861: Sick in Richmond, Nov., 1861: Dischgd. on Surg. Cert. of disability (VD), Dec. 4, 1861.

(1) TRYON, W. A. — Dischgd., Fall, 1861, for inability.

(1)   VAN BERGEN, V. — Dischgd. for disability (lung disease), Apr. 17, 1862.

VIVEN, FRANCIS L. — Recruited, Mar. 27, 1862 in Harris Co., Tex.: Dischgd. for disability (chronic rheumatism), Nov. 11, 1862.

(1)   WALKER, D. W. — K., 2nd Manassas (Aug. 30, 1862).

WATKINS, STEPHEN H. — Recruited, Mar. 28, 1862 at Houston, Tex.: W., Gettysburg (July 2, 1863): POW, Richmond, Apr. 3, 1865: Confined at Pt. Lookout, Md.: Paroled, June 22, 1865.

(1)   WEBBER, S. B. — Extra duty as Pioneer, Nov., 1861: AWOL, July, 1862: Did not return to Co.

WELCH, H. P. — Recruited, Mar. 25, 1862 in Harris County, Tex.: "Deserted to enemy," Sept. 14, 1862 (Boonsboro).

WHITAKER, CHRIS — Dischgd. on Surg. Cert., July 15, 1862.

(1)   WILKINSON, JOHN — Transfd. out of Regt. to an Artillery Co., Fall, 1861.

WILLIAMS, H. W. — Recruited, Mar. 24, 1862 in Harris Co., Tex.: Died of typhoid fever at Richmond, Va., Fall, 1862.

WITHERS, W. L. — Recruited, Mar. 29, 1862 in Harris Co., Tex.: Left at Mobile, Ala., Apr. 17, 1862, disabled by a RR. accident: Dischgd., July 15, 1862.

WOLF, BENJ. — Recruited, Mar. 12, 1862 in Harris Co., Tex.: Sick in Richmond, Va., May, 1862: Sick furlough to Tex.: Dischgd. by Medical Bd., Trans-Miss. Dept., Fall, 1864.

(1)   WRIGHT, R. F. — Died, Mar. 27, 1862 in Richmond, Va. from wound received in "a personal difficulty."

(1)   ZIMMERMAN, T. — Died in Tex., Aug. 31, 1861, before leaving for Va.

5TH TEX. VOL. INF. REGT.

COMPANY B — *No local designation*

Company was organized in Colorado County, Texas, enrolled at Columbus, Tex., July 10, 1861, and mustered into the Confederate service "for the war," at Richmond, Virginia, Sept. 30, 1861.

Key

(1) Original member of Company. (2) Paroled at Appomattox.
K (Killed), W (Wounded), POW (Prisoner of War)
AWOL (Absent Without Leave)

ORIGINAL OFFICERS

(1)   UPTON, JOHN C. Capt. — See roster, "Regmtl. Hdqtrs., 5th Tex. Inf."

(1) ROBERDEAU, J. D. 1Lt. — Detailed to recruiting serv. in Tex., Feb.-Apr., 1862: Prom., Capt., June 7, 1862: W. (right arm), 2nd Manassas (Aug. 30, 1862): W. & POW, Gettysburg (July 2, 1863): Confined at Johnson's Is., Ohio: Transfd. to Pt. Lookout, Md., Mar. 14, 1865.

(1) BULLINGTON, J. H. 2Lt. — Prom., 1Lt., June, 1862: Sent to rear on Surg. Cert., Aug. 20, 1862: Furloughed to Tex.: Resgnd., Feb., 1863.

(1) COLLIER, EDW. 3Lt. — Prom., 2Lt., June 1, 1862: POW, Antietam (Sept. 17, 1862): Paroled, Boonsboro, Md., Oct. 18, 1862: Prom., 1Lt., Feb. 19, 1863: W., Chickamauga (Sept. 19, 1863): W. (left elbow), Cold Harbor (June 5, 1864): Retired for disability, Nov. 30, 1864.

ORIGINAL NON-COMMISSIONED OFFICERS

(1) DENNY, W. D. 1Sgt. — See roster, "Regmtl. Hdqtrs., 5th Tex. Inf."

(1) HARE, WALTER S. 2Sgt. — Sick, Winter, 1861-62; Summer, 1862 & Winter, 1862-63: POW, Gettysburg (July 2, 1863): Confined at Ft. Delaware: Paroled, June 9, 1865.

(1) HENDERSON, D. H. 3Sgt. — See list of "Other Officers" following.

(1) BAKER, BEN M. 4Sgt. — See list of "Other Officers" following.

(1) KINDRED, JOS. C. 5Sgt. — Prom., 1Sgt., July 21, 1862: Sick, Spring,
(2) 1863: Detailed to Div. Comsy. Dept., Mar., 1864: Returned to Co. B as a Pvt.: Paroled, Appomattox (Apr. 12, 1865).

(1) BUCHANAN, J. C. 1Cpl. — Dischgd. for disability, Jan. 24, 1862.

(1) WALL, JOHN B. 2Cpl. — Prom., 4Sgt., Nov. 10, 1861: W. (hand), 2nd Manassas (Aug. 30, 1862): AWOL, since Feb. 8, 1863: Said to have jnd. a Tenn. cavalry company.

(1) MILLER, JOHN S. 3Cpl. — Prom., 2Cpl., July 21, 1862: W. (side), 2nd Manassas (Aug. 30, 1862): K., Gettysburg (July 2, 1863).

(1) PINCHBACK, W. W. 4Cpl. — Prom., 3Cpl., July 21, 1862: W. (stomach), 2nd Manassas (Aug. 30, 1862): Died of wound, Sept. 1, 1862.

OTHER OFFICERS

(2) BAKER, BEN M. 1Lt. — Orig. 4Sgt. of Co.: Prom., 1Sgt., Nov. 10, 1861: Prom., 3Lt., July 20, 1862: W. (hip), 2nd Manassas (Aug. 30, 1862): Prom., 2Lt., Feb. 19, 1863: W. (ear), Chickamauga (Sept. 19, 1863): Prom., 1Lt., Nov., 1864: Paroled, Appomattox (Apr. 12, 1865).

HENDERSON, D. H. 3Lt. — Orig. 3Sgt. of Co.: Elect., 3Lt., Mar. 15, 1863: W. & POW, Gettysburg (July 2, 1863): Died of wound in Fed. prison camp.

MUSICIANS

(1) PRIEST, JOHN — Hospitalized in Richmond, Spring, 1864.

(1) MURPHY, P. M. — W. (thigh), Gaines' Mill (June 27, 1862): POW, Gettysburg (July 2, 1863), left to attend wounded: Confined at Ft. McHenry, Md.: Exchanged, Mar. 17, 1864: Deserted, took Fed. oath at Washington, Apr. 10, 1865.

PRIVATES

(1) AUERBACH, EMORY — Sick, Winter, 1861-62: K., Wilderness (May 6, 1864).

BAKER, A. HICKS — Recruited, age 23, on Mar. 21, 1862 at Columbus, Tex.: W. (leg), Antietam (Sept. 17, 1862), carrying flag at Antietam: Died of wound.

BAKER, JAS. D. — Recruited, age 36, on April 3, 1862 at Columbus, Tex.: Dischgd., Surg. Cert. of disability (VD), Oct. 6, 1862.

BEHNE, G. A. — Recruited, age 33, on Mar. 31, 1862 at Columbus, Tex.: Detailed to Intelligence Office by Sec. of War, July, 1862: Dischgd. for lung disease, Oct. 20, 1863.

BENTLEY, AARON — Recruited, age 32, on Mar. 26, 1862 at Columbus, Tex.: Dischgd. on Surg. Cert. of disability, Aug. 8, 1862.

(1) BESCH, EMIL — W. (arm), Gaines' Mill (June 27, 1862): W. (leg), 2nd
(2) Manassas (Aug. 30, 1862): W. (shoulder & head), Wilderness (May 6, 1864): Paroled, Appomattox (Apr. 12, 1865).

BOSTICK, S. R. — Recruited, age 41, on Mar. 21, 1862 at Columbus, Tex.: Dischgd. by Sec. of War, Sept. 22, 1862, overage.

(1) BRIDGE, W. A. — Dischgd., Dec. 5, 1862 at Dumfries, Va.

BRUCE, J. S. — See roster, "Regmtl. Hdqtrs., 5th Tex. Inf."

BURFORD, ROBT. P. — Recruited, age 17, on Mar. 20, 1862 at Columbus, Tex.: Dischgd. by Sec. of War, Sept. 22, 1862, underage.

BURKS, ROWLAND — Recruited, age 33, on Mar. 22, 1862 at Columbus, Tex.: Detailed to CSA Intelligence Office, Jan. 2, 1862: Died of disease, Lynchburg, Va., Oct. 8, 1862.

(1) BURTON, W. L. — Sick, Summer & Fall, 1862 & Spring & Summer, 1863: K., New Market Hill, Va., by sharpshooter, Aug. 18, 1864.

BYARS, GEO. C. — Recruited, age 18, on Apr. 3, 1862 at Columbus, Tex.: Died of measles & bronchitis, Richmond, May 15, 1862.

(1) CABANISS, MAX — Died of disease, Winter, 1861-62.

(1) CARLTON, W. H. — W. (arm), Gaines' Mill (June 27, 1862): Detailed
(2) as courier for Gen. Hood, Fall, 1863: Detailed as courier for Gen. Field, Spring, 1864: Paroled, Appomattox (Apr. 12, 1865).

(1) CARRELL (or CARROLL), J. L. — W. (knee), Gaines' Mill (June 27, 1862): Detailed as guard to Gen. Hosp. #9, Richmond, Dec. 15, 1863.

(1) CARRIGAN, JOHN — W. (side), 2nd Manassas (Aug. 30, 1862): Died of wound, Oct. 23, 1862.

(1) CARTER, ALBERT H. — W. (arm), Gaines' Mill (June 27, 1862):
(2) Detailed as a musician, Mar. 25, 1863: Paroled, Appomattox (Apr. 12, 1865).

(1) CARTER, A. V. L. — Prom., 4Cpl., July 21, 1862: W. (arm), 2nd Manassas (Aug. 30, 1862): Prom., 2Cpl.: Died from 2nd Manassas wound, May 11, 1863.

(1) CARTER, JAS. T. — Actg. scout: Prom., 2Cpl., Nov. 10, 1861: Prom., 5Sgt., July 21, 1862: Sent to Tex. Hosp., Richmond, Mar. 18, 1863: Prom., 3Sgt.: W. (shoulder) & POW, Gettysburg (July 2, 1863): Died, July 31, 1863 in Fed. hosp.

(1) CHERRY, WESLEY — W. (hip), Antietam (Sept. 17, 1862): W. (arm),
(2) Wilderness (May 6, 1864): W. (head), Darbytown Rd. (Oct. 7, 1864): Paroled, Appomattox (Apr. 12, 1865).

(1) COFFEE, CLEVELAND — Sick, Winter, 1862-1863: Died of pneumonia at Howard Grove Hosp., Va., Sept. 15, 1864.

(1) COLLINS, PAT — W. (left arm), 2nd Manassas (Aug. 30, 1862): W. (leg), Wilderness (May 6, 1864): POW, Darbytown Rd. (Oct. 7, 1864): Confined at Pt. Lookout, Md.: Exchanged, Mar. 17, 1865.

COOPER, A. NEWTON — Recruited, age 26, on Mar. 18, 1862 at Columbus, Tex.: Dischgd. by Sec. of War, Sept. 22, 1862.

COOPER, W. J. — Recruited, age 27, on Mar. 18, 1862 at Columbus, Tex.: Dischgd. by Sec. of War, Sept. 22, 1862 for lung disease.

(1) CURRIE, DAVID M. — Detailed to Litter Corps, Summer, 1862:
(2) Paroled, Appomattox (Apr. 12, 1865).

(1) DAGGETT, MICHAEL — W. (groin), 2nd Manassas (Aug. 30, 1862): Sick, Summer, 1864.

(1) DARDEN, W. J. — See roster, "Regmtl. Hdqtrs., 5th Tex. Inf."

(1) DeGRAFFENRIED, THOS. T. — See roster, "Regmtl. Hdqtrs., 5th
(2) Tex. Inf."

(1) DICKERSON, J. C. — Appt. orderly to Lt.-Col. Upton: Appt. musician, June 15, 1863: Reduced to ranks by Col. J. C. Rogers: Supposed to be POW, since Mar., 1864, and also reported to be with Mosby's Cmd.

(1) DICKEY, G. W. — Dischgd. for disability (tuberculosis), Jan. 9, 1862.

DOLAND, THOS. — Recruited, age 29, on Mar. 13, 1862 at Columbus, Tex.: Sick most of 1862: Deserted in East Tenn., Feb. 24, 1864.

(1) EDGERS, JOS. — Deserted, Nov. 10, 1861, Richmond.

ENKE, AUGUST — Recruited, age 25, on Mar. 25, 1862 at Columbus, Tex.: W. (shoulder), Eltham's Landing (May 7, 1862): Detailed as carpenter at 4th Ga. Hosp., Richmond: Sent to Tex. Hosp., Richmond, Mar. 18, 1863: W. (wrist), Chickamauga (Sept. 19, 1863): Furlough to Tex., Spring, 1864: Did not return to Co.

FLANAGAN, M. — Recruited, age 21, on Mar. 20, 1862 at Columbus, Tex.: W. (arm), 2nd Manassas (Aug. 30, 1862): Accidently shot, Jan. 16, 1863: POW, Gettysburg (July 2, 1863): Confined at Ft. Delaware.

(1) GAINES, J. R. — Detailed as Regmtl. butcher, Nov. 24, 1861: K., Gaines' Mill (June 27, 1862).

GEGENWORTH, GEO. — Recruited, age 30, on Mar. 25, 1862 at Columbus, Tex.: Detailed as cook at sick camp, Summer, 1862: Detailed as cook to Capt. Roberdeau, Co. Cmdr., Oct. 1, 1862: AWOL, Spring, 1864, did not return from furlough in Tex.

(1) GRACE, J. M. — Dischgd. by Surg. Cert. for disability (lung disease), Jan. 9, 1862.

(1)   GRAF, RUDOLPH — Detailed as a Regmtl. butcher, Fall, 1862: W.
       (arm), Wilderness (May 6, 1864): Paroled, Farmville, Va., Apr.
       13, 1865.
(1)   HAGAN, JOHN — Dischgd. for sickness, Nov. 28, 1861.
(1)   HAHN, JACOB — Detailed as a Regmtl. butcher, Feb., 1862: W.
       (foot), Gaines' Mill (June 27, 1862): Furlough granted for "indefinite
       period" to Tex. to recover from wound: Did not return to Co.:
       Paroled, Columbus, Tex., July 13, 1865.
       HANKS, JOHN K. — Recruited, age 39, on Mar. 29, 1862, at
       Columbus, Tex.: Furlough to Tex., Spring, 1863: AWOL,
       Summer, 1863, never returned to Co.: Reported to be at Tyler,
       Tex.
       HARBERT, W. J. — Recruited, age 31, on Apr. 8, 1862 at Columbus,
       Tex.: Dischgd. by Surg. Cert. for disability, July 29, 1862.
       HARRIS, F. K. — Recruited, age 32, on Mar. 11, 1862 at Columbus,
       Tex.: POW, Eltham's Landing (May 7, 1862): Exchanged, Aug. 5,
       1862: W. (thigh), Freeman's Ford (Aug. 22, 1862): Dischgd: by
       order of Gen. Elzey, Feb. 13, 1863.
       HARRIS, T. W. — Recruited, age 41, on Mar. 29, 1862 at Columbus,
       Tex.: Dischgd. by order of Sec. of War, Sept. 22, 1862, overage.
       HART, E. Y. — Recruited, age 28, on Mar. 22, 1862 at Columbus,
       Tex.: Sent to Tex. Hosp., Richmond, Mar., 1863: Detailed as a
       nurse, Winter, 1863-64: W., Wilderness.
(1)   HARVEY, J. B. — AWOL, Spring, 1862 at Whiteville, Tenn.: W.,
       Chickamauga (Sept. 20, 1863): Sick leave granted to Tex.: Did
       not return to Co.: Paroled, Columbus, Tex., Aug. 3, 1865.
(1)   HAYNES, B. W. — Died of disease, Dec. 26, 1861, at Dumfries, Va.
(1)   HAYNES, HENRY — Detailed as am ambulance driver, Summer, 1862:
       W. & POW, Gettysburg (July 2, 1863): Died in Federal prison of
       Gettysburg wound.
(1)   HIGGS, J. F. — Died of chronic dysentery, Richmond, Dec., 1861.
       HOFFMAN, JOS. — Recruited, age 38, on Mar. 14, 1862 at Columbus,
       Tex.: W., Antietam (Sept. 17, 1862): Died of wound.
(1)   HOWARD, J. A. — Prom., 4Cpl., Nov. 7, 1862: K., Gettysburg (July 2,
       1863), "while charging enemy with colors."
       HUMPHREY, R. J. — Recruited, age 31, on Mar. 18, 1862 at
       Columbus, Tex.: W. (thigh), 2nd Manassas (Aug. 30, 1862): W.
       (side), May 31, 1864 near Cold Harbor, Va.: Died from wound,
       June 2, 1864.
       HURLEY, DOMINICK — Recruited, age 30, on Mar. 20, 1862 at
       Columbus, Tex.: W. (thigh), Freeman's Ford (Aug. 22, 1862): W.
       (bayonet in face), Spotsylvania (May 10, 1864): W. (chest),
       Chaffin's Farm (Sept. 29, 1864).
(1)   HURLEY, M. — Detailed to Litter Corps, Aug. 15, 1862: K.,
       Gettysburg (July 2, 1863).
(1)   JENKINS, JOHN M. — Detailed as Actg. Comsy. Clerk, Spring, 1862:
       Dischgd. for disability (inflammation of the hip), Sept. 22, 1862.
(1)   JOHNSON, JOHN W. — W. (leg), 2nd Manassas (Aug. 30, 1862):
(2)   Paroled, Appomattox (Apr. 12, 1865).
(1)   KOEPKE, FRED — Detailed to serv. with Brig. Pack Train, Feb. 7,
       1862: K., Malvern Hill (July 1, 1862).

(1) KOLBOW, JOHN — K., Antietam (Sept. 17, 1862).
(1) LAHEY, JOHN — Detailed to Brig. Provost Guard, Spring, 1864: POW, Farmville, Va., Apr. 6, 1865: Paroled, Newport News, Va., June 16, 1865.
(1) LUNDY, PATRICK — W. (thigh), 2nd Manassas (Aug. 30, 1862): Deserted, Feb. 29, 1864 near Morristown, Tenn., took Fed. oath.
(1) LYNCH, CORNELIUS — W. (shoulder), Gaines' Mill (June 27, 1862): Asgnd. to light duty in hosp. by order of Gen. Longstreet, Aug., 1863: Died of paralysis at Howard Grove Hosp., Va., Dec. 23, 1864.
(1) McCORMICK, J. — Died of disease, Dec. 6, 1861, Dumfries, Va.
McCORMICK, STEPHEN — Recruited, age 29, on Mar. 19, 1862 at Columbus, Tex.: Died of typhoid fever at Chimborazo Hosp., Richmond, June 15, 1862.
(1) McLEOD, M. W. — Sick, Fall, 1861: Dischgd., Dec. 29, 1861, Dumfries, Va.
McMILLAN, A. M. — Recruited, age 42, on Mar. 20, 1862 at Columbus, Tex.: Never joined Co., left sick at Shreveport, La.: Deserted, reported living in Mexico, Nov. 30, 1862.
(1) McNEILLIS, D. — W. (leg), Antietam (Sept. 17, 1862): Died of wound.
(1) MANNHEART, C. M. — Deserted, April 4, 1862, "said to have joined a cavalry co."
MATHEE, FRED — Recruited, age 18, on Mar. 13, 1862 at Columbus, Tex.: K., Freeman's Ford (Aug. 22, 1862).
(1) MONROE, GEO. — Wagoneer since mid-Dec., 1861: Left in Md., after Antietam (Sept. 17, 1862): Deserted, reported to have taken Fed. oath.
(1) MORRISSEY, JOHN — Wagoneer since mid-Dec., 1861: W. (both legs) & POW, Antietam (Sept. 17, 1862): Confined at Ft. McHenry, Md.: Exchanged, Oct. 13, 1862: POW, Chickamauga (Sept. 19, 1863): Confined at Camp Douglas, Ill.: Paroled, May 16, 1865.
NELMS, W. F. — Recruited, age 17, on Mar. 14, 1862 at Columbus, Tex.: W. (knee), 2nd Manassas (Aug. 30, 1862): W. & POW, Gettysburg (July 2, 1863): Leg amputated: Died at Fed. hosp., July 9, 1863.
(1) OBENSHAIN, J. S. — Elect., 1Sgt., July 15, 1863: W., Chickamauga
(2) (Sept. 19, 1863): AWOL, Spring, 1864: Reduced to Pvt.: Paroled, Appomattox (Apr. 12, 1865).
(1) O'NEILL, JOHN — W. (hand), Gaines' Mill (June 27, 1862): K., Gettysburg (July 2, 1863).
(1) PENDLETON, H. G. — Injured in wagon accident, Hanover County, Va., Aug. 14, 1862: Transfd. to 1st Va. Cav. Regt., July 1, 1863.
(1) PERKINS, S. L. — Died of disease, Dec. 21, 1861, Dumfries, Va.
(1) PRATT, HENRY — W. & POW, Gettysburg (July 2, 1863): Confined at Ft. Delaware: Died in prison of "inflammation of the lungs," Oct. 23, 1863.
(1) PUTNEY, D. E. — Prom., 2Sgt., Spring, 1863: AWOL, Summer, 1863: Reported to have jnd. Co. F, Brown's Cav. Regt. in Tex.
(1) RATIGAN, JOHN — Born in Ireland: W. (foot), Gaines' Mill (June 27, 1862): Detailed as Hosp. Steward at Warrenton, Va., Sept. 3, 1862: Transfd. to Navy by Sec. of Navy, June, 1863: Returned to Co.: Detailed to QM Dept., Richmond, by Gen. Longstreet, Mar. 3, 1864.

(1) REYNOLDS, JAS. — Dischgd. for disability (chronic rheumatism), Feb. 6, 1862.

(1) RHEA, JAS. M. — Dischgd. for disability (chronic diarrhea), Feb. 8, 1862.

RHODES, W. L. — Recruited, age 27, on Mar. 31, 1862 at Columbus, Tex.: W., Antietam (Sept. 17, 1862): Died of pneumonia, Nov. 20, 1862.

(1) ROBERTS, T. J. — W. (right leg), Freeman's Ford (Aug. 22, 1862): Furlough granted to Tex.: AWOL, Feb., 1863: Did not return to Co.

RYAN, WM. — Recruited, age 23, on Mar. 17, 1862 at Columbus, Tex.: Murdered in Tex. by a man named Pierce, Mar. 30, 1862.

SANDERS, NEWTON — Recruited, age 27, on Mar. 18, 1862 at Columbus, Tex.: Sent to rear, May 28, 1862: AWOL, not heard from again.

SCHERER, RILEY L. — Recruited, age 27, on Apr. 11, 1862 at Columbus, Tex.: K., Eltham's Landing (May 7, 1862).

SENNE, HENRY — Recruited, age 25, on Apr. 2, 1862 at Columbus, Tex.: W. (left arm), Eltham's Landing (May 7, 1862): POW, Farmville, Apr. 6, 1865: Paroled, Newport News, Va., June 18, 1865.

(1) SHEPHERD, WEBB. — W. (neck), 2nd Manassas (Aug. 30, 1862): Prom., 4Cpl., Mar. 15, 1863: Wound furlough to Mobile, Ala.: Detailed to Brig. Comsy. Dept., Apr., 1864: Paroled, Montgomery, Ala., May 9, 1865.

SHIELDS, CHAS. — Recruited, age 38, on Mar. 27, 1862 at Columbus, Tex.: Dischgd. by Sec. of War, Sept. 22, 1862, overage.

(1) SHORT, JAS. — Deserted, Nov. 10, 1861.

SLAYTON, F. W. — Recruited, age 23, on Mar. 18, 1862 at Columbus, Tex.: Died (rheumatism), Richmond, May 27, 1862.

(1) SLOAN, A. G. — Asgnd. as a Regmtl. Wagoneer, Mar. 8, 1862: K., Gettysburg (July 2, 1863).

SLONEKER, W. J. — Recruited, age 31, on Mar. 15, 1862 at Columbus, Tex.: AWOL, Summer, 1863: Dischgd., Jan. 8, 1864 at Staunton, Va., for disability (stomach trouble).

(1) SMITH, JOHN — W. (leg), Gaines' Mill (June 27, 1862): W. (arm), 2nd Manassas (Aug. 30, 1862): W. & POW, Gettysburg (July 2, 1863): Died in Fed. prison of wound.

(1) SNELL, WM. T. — W. (arm), 2nd Manassas (Aug. 30, 1862): POW, Farmville, Va., Apr. 6, 1865: Paroled, Newport News, Va., June 16, 1865.

STAFFORD, R. E. — Recruited, age 28, on Apr. 8, 1862 at Columbus, Tex.: Wounded by a man named Conner, Apr., 1862 & left at Niblets Bluff, La.: Dischgd. on Surg. Cert. of disability, June 2, 1863.

(1) STEVENSON, W. R. — Died of disease, Dec. 25, 1861, Dumfries, Va.

STROUD, B. F. — Enl. at Columbus, Tex., Mar. 20, 1862, age 24: Sick, Summer, 1862: Died, 1864, no other record.

(1) TANN, M. W. — Died, Bird Island Hosp., Richmond, Apr. 3, 1862.

(1) TANNER, C. B. — Dischgd. for disability, Nov. 28, 1861.

(1) TATUM, H. A. — Detailed as scout, Nov. 21, 1861: Dischgd., Sept. 22, 1862, chronic rheumatism.

TAYLOR, H. M. — Recruited, at 31, on Mar. 27, 1862 at Columbus, Tex.: AWOL, June, 1863, seen in Pa.: Believed to have deserted to Federals.

TAYLOR, T. O. — See roster "Regmtl. Hdqtrs., 5th Tex. Inf."

TERRELL, CHAS. M. — See roster, "Regmtl. Hdqtrs., 5th Tex. Inf."

(1)   TERRELL, HUNT — W., Eltham's Landing (May 7, 1864): W. (back & neck) & POW, Gettysburg (July 2, 1863): Confined at Ft. Delaware: Paroled, June 9, 1865.

TRAINOR (or TRAYNOR), JOHN — Recruited, age 28, on Mar. 13, 1862 at Columbus, Tex.: W. (neck), 2nd Manassas (Aug. 30, 1862): POW, Gettysburg (July 2, 1863): Confined at Ft. Delaware: Paroled, June 9, 1865.

(1)   UMBARGER, J. P. — W., 2nd Manassas (Aug. 30, 1862): Died of wound, Sept. 23, 1862.

WALLACE, R. C. — POW, June 30, 1863 in Pa.: Took Fed. oath.

(1)   WELCH, PATRICK — Deserted, May 31, 1862.

(1)   WHITEHEAD, J. H. — Prom., 1Cpl., Jan. 24, 1862: W. (foot), 2nd Manassas (Aug. 30, 1862): Prom., 5Sgt., Mar. 15, 1863: Prom., 4Sgt.: W. (both feet) & POW, Gettysburg (July 2, 1863): Prom., 3Sgt.: Retired by Medical Bd., July 26, 1864.

WILSON, W. B. — W. & POW, Gettysburg (July 2, 1863): Died in Fed. prison from Gettysburg wound.

(1)   WOODHOUSE, PATRICK — W. (leg), 2nd Manassas (Aug. 30, 1862): POW, Gettysburg (July 2, 1863): Confined at Ft. Delaware: Paroled, June 9, 1865.

5TH TEX. VOL. INF. REGT.

COMPANY C — *THE LEON HUNTERS*

Company was organized in Leon County, Texas, enrolled at Centerville, July 11, 1861, and mustered into the Confederate service "for the war," Aug. 2, 1861 at Camp Van Dorn, Tex., by A. M. Haskell, 1Lt., CSA.

Key

(1) Original member of Company. (2) Paroled at Appomattox.
K (Killed), W (Wounded), POW (Prisoner of War)
AWOL (Absent Without Leave)

ORIGINAL OFFICERS

(1)   WHALEY, D. M. Capt. — See roster, "Regmtl. Hdqtrs., 5th Tex. Inf."

(1) McBRIDE, J. J. 1Lt. — See roster, "Regmtl. Hdqtrs., 5th Tex. Inf."
(1) WALLACE, W. G. 2Lt. — Cmded. Co. at Gaines' Mill (June 27, 1862):
    W., Gaines' Mill: Arm amputated: Prom., 1Lt.: Died of wound at
    Chimborazo Hosp., Richmond, July 28, 1862.
(1) ANDERSON, J. E. 3Lt. — Prom., 2Lt., July 17, 1862: Prom., 1Lt.,
(2) July 28, 1862: Prom., Capt., Dec. 17, 1864: Paroled, Appo-
    mattox (Apr. 12, 1865): Present for duty during entire war.

ORIGINAL NON-COMMISSIONED OFFICERS

(1) TUBB, LEE 1Sgt. — Dischgd. by Surg. Cert. of disability (chronic
    dysentery), Dec. 1, 1861.
(1) LOGAN, Z. L. 2Sgt. — See list of "Other Officers" following.
(1) PRIDGEN, T. J. 3Sgt. — Sick most of 1862: Transfd. to Co. C, 36th
    N. C. Inf. Regt., Feb. 16, 1863.
(1) MOSS, N. P. 4Sgt. — Resgnd. as 4Sgt., Dec. 1, 1861: Appt. 2Sgt., Apr.
    20, 1863: POW, Gettysburg (July 2, 1863): Confined at Ft.
    Delaware: Took Fed. oath, Jan. 17, 1865.
(1) BLACK, E. W. 5Sgt. — Resgnd. as 5Sgt., Dec. 1, 1861: Transfd. to
    Capt. Black's Co., 20th Tex. Cav. Regt., Oct. 7, 1862.
(1) PRUITT, W. A. 1Cpl. — Detailed to extra duty as a wagonmaster,
    Dec., 1861: Died, Feb. 10, 1862 at a private home near Dumfries,
    Va.
(1) ADKINSON, J. T. 2Cpl. — Sick, Winter, 1861-62: W., 2nd Manassas
    (Aug. 30, 1862): Furlough granted, Oct., 1862: Did not return to
    Co.
(1) COX, JOHN C. 3Cpl. — Resgnd. as 3Cpl., Jan. 1, 1862: Appt. 5Sgt.,
    Mar. 1, 1862: W., 2nd Manassas (Aug. 30, 1862): Prom., 4Sgt.,
    July 1, 1862: W., Antietam (Sept. 17, 1862): Prom., 1Sgt., Apr.
    26, 1863: W., Chickamauga (Sept. 19, 1863): Dischgd. for
    disability, Dec. 14, 1863.
(1) BORDER, G. F. 4Cpl. — See list of "Other Officers" following.

OTHER OFFICERS

NEW, JOS. S. 1Lt. — Orig. Pvt. in Co.: Prom., 3Lt., July 19, 1862:
    Prom., 2Lt., July 28, 1862: Died, Gen. Hosp. #10, Richmond,
    Va., of pneumonia, Apr. 16, 1863.
BORDER, G. F. 2Lt. — Orig. 4Cpl. of Co.: Prom., 2Sgt., Dec. 1,
    1861: W., 2nd Manassas (Aug. 30, 1862): Elect., 3Lt., Oct. 25,
    1862: Prom., 2Lt., Apr., 1863: W., near Knoxville, Tenn., Nov.
    25, 1863: Retired for disability, Apr. 25, 1864.
LOGAN, Z. L. 2Lt. — Orig. 2Sgt. of Co.: Prom., 1Sgt., Dec. 1, 1861:
    Detailed to recruiting serv. in Tex., Feb.-Apr., 1862: POW,
    Brandy Sta., Va., Aug. 24, 1862: Exchanged: Elect., 3Lt., Apr.
    26, 1863: W., Chickamauga (Sept. 19, 1863): Prom., 2Lt., May 1,
    1864: AWOL, since Aug., 1864: Paroled, Demopolis, Ala., June
    23, 1865.

BOYD, HENRY W. 3Lt. — Orig. Pvt. in Co.: Prom., 4Sgt., Dec. 1, 1861: Reduced to ranks by Col. J. B. Robertson, June 25, 1862: Elect., 3Lt., Aug. 4, 1862: Killed, Antietam (Sept. 17, 1862).

MUSICIANS

(1) ALRICK, H. L. — Died at St. Charles Hosp., Richmond, Oct. 7, 1861: Not listed on Co. Bi-Monthly Roster.
(1) WEBB, R. F. — Sick, Dec., 1861 & May & June, 1862: Furlough granted, Apr., 1864: Did not return to Co.

PRIVATES

ALLEN, ROBT. — Recruited, age 30, on Mar. 17, 1862 at Centerville, Tex.: W., 2nd Manassas (Aug. 30, 1862): Died, Aug. 31, 1862 of wound.
(1) ALLISON, ARTHUR B. — POW, Gettysburg (July 2, 1863): Confined at Ft. McHenry, Md.: Paroled, June 7, 1865.
(1) ALLISON, JOHN T. — W., 2nd Manassas (Aug. 30, 1862): W. & POW, Boonsboro (Sept. 14, 1862): Exchanged: W. (arm), Wilderness (May 6, 1864): Paroled, Appomattox (Apr. 12, 1865).
(1) ANDERSON, JESS M. — W. (side), 2nd Manassas (Aug. 30, 1862): W. & POW, Gettysburg (July 2, 1863): Confined at Ft. McHenry: Exchanged: July 31, 1863: W. (leg), Spotsylvania (May 10, 1864): W. (leg), Chaffin's Farm (Sept. 29, 1864): On wound furlough, Oct., 1864: Paroled, Demopolis, Ala., June 14, 1865.
BARBEE, JAS. B. — Recruited, age 35, on Apr. 3, 1862 at Centerville, Tex.: Died of chronic diarrhea at Danville, Va., Aug. 17, 1862.
(1) BELL, EDW. — Died of pneumonia, Tex. Hosp., Richmond, Mar. 27, 1863.
(1) BELL, ZEBULON P. — Died of pneumonia, Tex. Hosp., Richmond, Mar. 16, 1863.
(1) BOYD, HENRY W. — See list of "Other Officers" above.
BOYKIN, T. J. — W., Gettysburg (July 2, 1863): W., Bermuda Hundred, Va., June 14, 1864: POW, Farmville, Apr. 6, 1865: Died at U.S. hosp. at Farmville on Apr. 29, 1865.
BOYKIN, WM. F. — Recruited, age 20, on Mar. 15, 1862 at Centerville, Tex.: Died in camp, July 14, 1862.
(1) BRADEN, F. M. — Dischgd. for disability (lung disease), Dec. 1, 1861.
BRAIM, WM. — Recruited, age 26, on Mar. 26, 1862 at Centerville, Tex.: Died of acute diarrhea, Gen. Hosp., Danville, Va., Aug. 3, 1862.
(1) BRASHEAR, A. B. — Died (chronic diarrhea), Chimborazo Hosp., Richmond, Apr. 5, 1862.
(1) BREWER, J. H. — Died, field hosp., near Camp Neabsco, Va., Dec. 2, 1861.
BRISTOW, B. W. — Jnd. by transfer from Co. E, 20th Miss. Inf. Regt.: W. (hip), 2nd Manassas (Aug. 30, 1862): Dischgd., June 10, 1863, disabled from Manassas wound.

BRISTOW, E. H. — Jnd. by transfer from Co. E, 20th Miss. Inf. Regt.: W. (arm & back), Gaines' Mill (June 27, 1862).

(1) COPELAND, J. M. — W. (head), Cold Harbor (June 3, 1864): K., skirmish on Charles City Rd. near White Oak Swamp, Aug. 16, 1864.

(2) COPELAND, JOHN P. — Recruited, age 19, on Mar. 26, 1862 at Centerville, Tex.: Paroled, Appomattox (Apr. 12, 1865).

COSTIN, DOYLE O. H. — Recruited, age 18, on Mar. 15, 1862 at Centerville, Tex.: W. & POW, Gettysburg (July 2, 1863): Confined at Ft. Delaware: Exchanged, Oct. 31, 1864.

(1) COSTIN, J. F. — Detailed as nurse at sick camp, July, 1862: Appt. 1Cpl., Aug. 1, 1863: Furlough to Tex., Fall, 1864.

(1) COZBY (or COSBY), JOHN S. — Dischgd., May 25, 1862 for disability: Died, Sept. 27, 1862 at Danville, Va.

DEATTEY (or DEATLEY), JAS. — Recruited, age 18, on Apr. 4, 1862 at Centerville, Tex.: Died in Richmond Hosp., May 26, 1862.

(1) DEZELL, E. M. — W., Antietam (Sept. 17, 1862): Sent home on convalescent leave: Died at home, Leon County, Tex. of smallpox, Dec. 4, 1862.

(1) DEZELL, Z. Y. — W. (side), Gaines' Mill (June 27, 1862): Appt. 5Sgt., Apr. 30, 1863: K., Gettysburg (July 2, 1863).

DICKSON, JOS. C. — Recruited, age 19, on Mar. 29, 1862 at Centerville, Tex.: Dischgd. for disease, Oct. 31, 1862 at Genl. Hosp. #2, Lynchburg, Va.

(1) DRISCOLL, HENRY T. — W., Gettysburg (July 2, 1863): Paroled,
(2) Appomattox (Apr. 12, 1865).

(1) DRISCOLL, J. P. — W., 2nd Manassas (Aug. 30, 1862): W. (back) & POW, Gettysburg (July 2, 1863): Paroled, Nov. 12, 1863.

DUNKIN, M. V. B. — Recruited, age 21, on Apr. 3, 1862 at Centerville, Tex.: Sick most of 1862: Absent on sick furlough most of 1863: Did not return to Co.

DUNLAP, ANDREW J. — Recruited, age 44, on Mar. 22, 1862 at Centerville, Tex.: Dischgd. for disability (heart trouble), Aug. 31, 1862.

(1) DUNN, H. B. — W., 2nd Manassas (Aug. 30, 1862): Died from wound at Warrenton, Va., Sept. 10, 1862.

DURGAN, JAS. B. — Recruited, age 25, on Mar. 13, 1862 at Centerville, Tex.: Deserted from Bird Island Hosp., Richmond, Va., Oct. 21, 1862.

ELKINS, BENJ. P. — Recruited, age 27, on Mar. 22, 1862 at Centerville, Tex.: Died (May 18, 1862), Bird Island Hosp., Richmond, Va.

ELLIS, COMPTON A. — Recruited, age 32, on Mar. 26, 1862 at Centerville, Tex.: Sick much of 1862: Sick furlough, Oct., 1863: Did not return to Co.

(1) ELLIS, JOHN E. — Detailed as a Regmtl. Wagoneer: W. (side), Wilderness (May 6, 1864): Paroled, Lynchburg, Va.

(1) FARRIS, JOHN B. — Under arrest for theft, Sept., 1862: Deserted, Nov. 5, 1862 between Winchester & Culpeper, Va.: POW, Nov. 30, 1862: Confined at Ft. McHenry, Md.: Escaped from prison, Feb. 19, 1863: Re-captured, confined at Ft. McHenry, Feb. 25, 1863.

(1) FOLEY, THOS. — Dischgd., Dec. 1, 1862 for disability ("injuries received before entering the service").

FRYER, JAS. A. J. — Recruited, age 42, on Mar. 25, 1862 at Centerville, Tex.: Dischgd. for disability (chronic rheumatism), Sept. 19, 1862.

GARRISON, JOHN W. — Recruited, age 21, on Mar. 22, 1862 at Centerville, Tex.: Sick most of 1862 & 1863: W. (hand), Wilderness (May 6, 1864): POW, North Anna River, May 21, 1864: Confined at Pt. Lookout, Md.: Took Fed. oath, June 8, 1864.

GOUGH, JOHN J. — Enl., Mar. 5, 1863: W., Chickamauga (Sept. 20, 1863): W. & POW, Campbell Station, Tenn., Dec. 5, 1863: Died at Ft. Delaware, Md., Mar. 13, 1864, of "inflammation of the lungs."

GRAHAM, JAS. R. — Recruited, age 24, on Mar. 29, 1862 at Centerville, Tex.: Died of typhoid fever, June 4, 1862 at Chimborazo Hosp., Richmond.

GRAHAM, STRICKLING — Recruited, age 19, on Mar. 29, 1862 at Centerville, Tex.: Died of typhoid fever, June 8, 1862 at Chimborazo Hosp.

GRAHAM, WILEY — Recruited, age 22, on Mar. 29, 1862 at Centerville, Tex.: Dischgd. for disability (epilepsy), Oct. 8, 1862.

GREEN, JAS. G. — Recruited, age 18, on Mar. 22, 1862 at Centerville, Tex.: Under arrest and detained in Tex. for having enlisted previously in another Tex. organization (13th Tex. Cav. Regt.): Never jnd. Co.

(1)
(2) GREEN, JOHN A. — An artist by profession, enl. at 22: On scouting serv. with "Guerrilla Co." since Nov. 25, 1861: W. (side), 2nd Manassas (Aug. 30, 1862): Appt. 5Sgt., Aug. 1, 1863: Prom., 3Sgt., Sept., 1864: W. (thigh), Chaffin's Farm (Sept. 29, 1864): On "furlough of indulgence," Dec. 27, 1864: Prom., 2Sgt., Feb., 1865: Paroled, Appomattox (Apr. 12, 1865).

(1) GUNN, J. N. M. — Sick, Winter, 1861-62: Home on sick furlough, Mar., 1862 & assisted in procuring recruits while there: Dischgd. for disability (chronic hepatitis), Sept. 23, 1862.

(1) HAILEY, JOHN H. — W. (right knee), Freeman's Ford (Aug. 22, 1862): Sent to Globe Hosp., Richmond: Dischgd. for disability, Jan. 13, 1863.

(1) HAYS, R. H. — Died from apoplexy at Seabrook Hosp., Richmond, Dec. 3, 1862.

HENRY, WM. B. — Recruited, age 32, on Mar. 15, 1862 at Centerville, Tex.: Died at Gen. Hosp., Liberty, Va., Aug. 18, 1862.

(1) HICKS, BERRY — Sick, Fall, 1861 & Spring, 1862: AWOL, May, 1862: Never returned to Co.

HOUGH, WM. B. — Recruited, age 23, on Apr. 2, 1862 at Centerville, Tex.: Died of pneumonia, June 4, 1862.

IRWIN, G. W. — Transfd. to Co. C from the 34th Miss. Inf. Regt., Nov. 1, 1862: POW, East Tenn., Apr. 3, 1864.

(1) IRWIN, SAMUEL W. — See roster, "Regmtl. Hdqtrs., 5th Tex. Inf."

(1)
(2) JAMES, E. W. — Detailed to Pioneer Corps: Sick most of 1863: W. (neck), White Oak Swamp (Aug. 16, 1864): Paroled, Appomattox (Apr. 12, 1865).

(1) JOHNSON, CALLOWAY — Dischgd. for disability, Dec. 3, 1861.
(1) JONES, A. A. — Died of pneumonia at Richmond, Va., June 20, 1862.
(1) LACEY, JAS. E. — W., 2nd Manassas (Aug. 30, 1862): W. (face), Wilderness (May 6, 1864): Deserted to enemy, Sept. 7, 1864.
(1) LAWSON, ASBURY — W. & POW, Gettysburg (July 2, 1863): Exchanged, Sept. 17, 1863: Deserted to enemy, Sept. 7, 1864.
LEE, THOS. M. — Recruited, age 32, on Mar. 13, 1862 at Centerville, Tex.: POW, Chickamauga (Sept. 19, 1863): Confined at Camp Douglas, Ill.: Took Fed. oath.
LOGAN, W. J. — Recruited from Yazoo County, Miss.: Paroled, Demopolis, Ala., June 10, 1865.
LONG, WM. L. — Recruited, age 18, on Mar. 24, 1862 at Centerville, Tex.: Under arrest and detained in Tex. for having enlisted previously in another Tex. organization: AWOL.
(1) LUSK, P. LACEY — Dischgd. for disability from St. Charles Hosp., Va., Dec. 5, 1861.
(1) McGARY, M. M. — Died, St. Charles Hosp., Richmond, Sept. 23, 1861.
(1) McKENZIE, P. K. — Dischgd. for disability (ulcer on leg), May 21, 1862.
(1) McKENZIE, RANSOM — Dischgd. for disability from St. Charles Hosp., Richmond, (date unknown).
MEREDITH, JOHN L. — Recruited, age 27, on Mar. 20, 1862 at Centerville, Tex.: W. in skirmish near Richmond on June 8, 1862: Died from wound, June 12, 1862.
(1) MILLS, G. W. — Dischgd. for disability, June 28, 1862.
MOODY, STERLING D. — Recruited, at 19, on Mar. 19, 1862 at Centerville, Tex.: Dischgd. for disability, July 20, 1862.
(1) MOORE, J. D. — Appt. 5Sgt., Jan. 1, 1862: Resgnd., Mar. 1, 1862: Died in hosp. at Fredericksburg, Va., Mar. 15, 1862.
MOORE, WM. M. — Recruited, age 19, on Mar. 15, 1862 at Centerville, Tex.: Died (chronic diarrhea), in Danville, Va. hosp., June 24, 1862: Personal effects, 10 cents.
(1) MULHOLLAND, B. E. — Appt. 1Cpl., Jan. 11, 1862: Died, Jan. 26, 1862, at Dumfries, Va. in camp hosp.
MURCHISON, WM. — Recruited, age 20, on Mar. 31, 1862 at Centerville, Tex.: Died, Aug. 3, 1862 of pneumonia at Genl. Hosp., Camp Winder, Div. #2, Richmond, Va.
(1) NEIGHBORS, JAS. W. — W. & POW, Antietam (Sept. 17, 1862): Confined at Ft. McHenry: Exchanged, Apr. 27, 1863: W., Chickamauga (Sept. 19, 1863).
(1) NEIGHBORS, JOHN L. — Died of typhoid fever in camp near Dumfries, Va., Feb. 1, 1862.
(1) NEW, JOS. S. — See list of "Other Officers" above.
(1) NUNNERY, BENJ. D. — W., Antietam (Sept. 17, 1862): W. & POW, Gettysburg (July 2, 1863): Confined at Pt. Lookout, Md.: Paroled at Baltimore, Aug. 16, 1863: Did not rejoin Co.: Paroled, Meridian, Miss., May 10, 1865.
(1) PAGE, R. D. — Died, St. Charles Hosp., Richmond, Nov. 14, 1861.
PARKER, ELISHA P. — Recruited, age 19, on Mar. 29, 1862 at Centerville, Tex.: AWOL, Sept., 1862: Did not return to Co.
PERRY, BENJ. R. — Recruited, age 36, on Mar. 13, 1862 at Centerville, Tex.: K., Chickamauga (Sept. 19, 1863).

(1) PERRY, PHILO B. — Appt. 3Cpl., Jan. 1, 1862: Reduced to ranks by Gen. Robertson, June 14, 1862: W. (side & back), 2nd Manassas (Aug. 30, 1862): Wound leave to Tex.: Did not return to Co.

(1) PERRY, W. B. — Died, Union Hosp., Richmond, Nov. 7, 1861.

PHILIPS, POLASKI G. — Recruited, Mar. 29, 1862 at Centerville, Tex.: W., 2nd Manassas (Aug. 30, 1862): Deserted, June 29, 1863 while on march to Gettysburg.

(1) PISTOLE, THOS. R. — W., 2nd Manassas (Aug. 30, 1862): W. & POW,
(2) Gettysburg (July 2, 1863): Confined at Ft. McHenry, Md.: Exchanged, Sept. 18, 1863: Paroled, Appomattox (Apr. 12, 1865).

POOL, JAS. H. — Recruited, age 20, on Mar. 26, 1862 at Centerville, Tex.: W. (chest), Gettysburg (July 2, 1863): Died, July 3, 1863.

(1) PRICE, DAVID — Deserted from Camp Bragg near Richmond, Va., Nov. 10, 1861.

PRIDGEN, JOHN J. — Recruited, age 21, on Apr. 4, 1862 at Centerville, Tex.: K., Spotsylvania (May 10, 1864).

(1) ROBINSON, T. M. — Asgnd. to scouting duty, Nov. 25, 1861: Appt. 1Cpl., Feb. 1, 1862: POW, Brandy Station, Va. (Aug. 24, 1862): Exchanged: Reduced to ranks, July 20, 1863 by Maj. Rogers: W., Chickamauga (Sept. 19, 1863): Transfd., Mar. 15, 1862 to 8th Tex. Cav. Regt. (Terry's Tex. Rangers), no longer fit for inf. duty.

ROSE, JOS. — Recruited, age 20, on Mar. 22, 1862 at Centerville, Tex.: Died of measles, June 9, 1862.

ROSS, JOS. L. — Recruited, age 40, on Mar. 13, 1862 at Centerville, Tex.: W., 2nd Manassas (Aug. 30, 1862): W. (head) by shell, Fredericksburg (Dec. 14, 1862): Dischgd. for disability, May 8, 1863.

(1) SAWYERS, ELBERT H. — Died of typhus, Feb. 25, 1862, in camp near Dumfries, Va.

SCOTT, GEO. M. — Recruited, age 20, on Mar. 28, 1862 at Centerville, Tex.: AWOL, Dec., 1862: Did not return to Co.

(1) SHILLINGS, G. A. — Prom., 4Cpl., Dec. 1, 1861: W., Antietam (Sept. 17, 1862): POW, Gettysburg (July 2, 1863): Confined at Ft. Delaware: Paroled, June 9, 1865.

(1) SIMMONS, W. B. — Prom., 3Cpl., July 1, 1862: Prom., 2Sgt., Oct. 25, 1862: W. (knee), by shell at Fredericksburg, Va., Dec. 14, 1862: K., accidentally shot near Suffolk, Va., Apr. 12, 1863.

SKINNER, JOHN S. — Recruited, age 26, on Mar. 14, 1862 at Centerville, Tex.: W., Chickamauga (Sept. 19, 1863): Died of wound.

(1) STEPHENS, J. D. — AWOL, Dec., 1862: Rejnd. Co., Mar., 1863: W., Chickamauga (Sept. 19, 1863): AWOL, June, 1864, went to Tex. on forged furlough papers: Deserted.

STUART, SAMUEL B. — Recruited, age 28, Apr. 2, 1862 at Centerville, Tex.: Prom., 5Sgt., July 1, 1862: K., Antietam (Sept. 17, 1862).

(1) SWINDLER, JAS. E. — Detailed to Div. Provost Guard, Dec., 1863:
(2) Paroled, Appomattox (Apr. 12, 1865).

(1) THOMAS, SAMUEL P. — Died, St. Charles Hosp., Richmond, Va., Nov. 29, 1861.

(1) TRAWEEK, C. C. — Dischgd. for disability from St. Charles Hosp., Richmond, Dec. 8, 1861.

(1) TRAWEEK, H. P. — On detchd. serv. to nurse wounded, Sept.,
(2) 1862-Feb., 1864: W. (head), Wilderness (May 6, 1864): Paroled, Appomattox (Apr. 12, 1865).

TURNER, RICHARD — Recruited, age 35, on Mar. 29, 1862 at Centerville, Tex.: W., Antietam (Sept. 17, 1862): W., Wilderness (May 6, 1864): Leg amputated.

UNDERWOOD, JAS. H. — Recruited, age 42, on Mar. 20, 1862 at Centerville, Tex.: Died of measles, June 7, 1862 at Chimborazo Hosp., Richmond.

WALKER, VIRGIL J. — Recruited, age 24, on Apr. 3, 1862 at Centerville, Tex.: Died of pneumonia at Chimborazo Hosp., June 11, 1862.

(1) WALLACE, J. M. — W., 2nd Manassas (Aug. 30, 1862): POW, Gettysburg (July 2, 1863): Confined at Ft. Delaware: Exchanged, Sept. 18, 1864.

(1) WATSON, WM. — K., by Yankee sharpshooter, Apr. 24, 1862, while on picket near Yorktown, Va.

(1) WELCH, M. T. — W. (chest), Gaines' Mill (June 27, 1862): Died in Chimborazo Hosp. of wound, July 27, 1862.

(1) WEST, P. H. — Sick, Dec., 1861: Paroled at Appomattox (Apr. 12,
(2) 1865).

(1) WHALEY, C. M. C. — Transfd. to Capt. White's Va. Cav. Co., Loudon County, Va., no date given.

(1) WILLIAMS, F. M. — Appt. 3Cpl., Oct. 25, 1862: Prom., 3Sgt., Apr. 30, 1863: W. (elbow), Gettysburg (July 2, 1863): W. (jaw & neck), Petersburg (June 20, 1864): Dischgd. for disability, Oct. 20, 1864.

(1) WILLIAMS, JAS. — Asgnd. extra duty as a Pioneer: Dischgd., Dec. 31, 1861 for disability (hernia).

WILLIAMS, WM. KING — Enlisted near Dumfries, Va., Jan. 1, 1862: K., Gaines' Mill (June 27, 1862).

(1) WYCHE, HENRY C. — W. & POW, Knoxville, Tenn., Dec. 4, 1863: Confined at Rock Island, Ill.: Paroled, June 21, 1865.

(1) YELDELL, J. R. — Asgnd. extra duty as a Regmtl. wagoneer: Died of chronic diarrhea at Danville, Va., June 18, 1862.

(1) YOW, ELI — W., Chickamauga (Sept. 19, 1863): W. & POW, Darbytown Rd. (Oct. 7, 1864): Confined at Pt. Lookout, Md.: Paroled, June 22, 1865.

COMPANY D — *WAVERLY CONFEDERATES*

Company was organized in Walker County, Texas, and was mustered into the Confederate service "for the war," in that county on Aug. 2, 1861. The Company also included men from Montgomery County.

Key

(1) Original member of Company. (2) Paroled at Appomattox.
K (Killed), W (Wounded), POW (Prisoner of War)
AWOL (Absent Without Leave)

ORIGINAL OFFICERS

(1)   POWELL, ROBT. M. Capt. — See roster, "Regmtl. Hdqtrs., 5th Tex. Inf."

(1)   HILL, WM. T. 1Lt. — See roster, "Regmtl. Hdqtrs., 5th Tex. Inf."

(1)   WOODALL, A. C. 2Lt. — Prom., 1Lt., Aug. 23, 1862: W. (arm), Cold Harbor (June 3, 1864): W. (arm), Darbytown Rd. (Oct. 7, 1864): Retired for disability from wounds, Dec. 7, 1864.

(1)   WOOD, CAMPBELL 3Lt. — See roster, "Regmtl. Hdqtrs., 5th Tex. Inf."

ORIGINAL NON-COMMISSIONED OFFICERS

(1)   LEWIS, W. H. 1Sgt. — Resgnd. as 1Sgt., Nov. 1, 1861: K., Wilderness (May 6, 1864).

(1)   MURRAY, J. A. 2Sgt. — Prom., 1Sgt., Aug. 23, 1862: Transfd. out of Co., May 9, 1863 by promotion to 1Lt. & asgnd. as Aide de Camp to Gen. Magruder.

(1)   CAMPBELL, J. W. 3Sgt. — Dischgd. for disability (tuberculosis), Jan. 26, 1862.

(1)   ABERCROMBIE, M. B. 4Sgt. — Dischgd. for disability, Dec. 1, 1862.

(NOT DESIGNATED) 5Sgt.

(1)   CAMPBELL, W. B. 1Cpl. — Prom., 4Sgt., Dec. 1, 1861: Prom., 3Sgt., Feb. 1, 1862: Prom., 2Sgt., Aug. 23, 1862: POW, near Knoxville, Tenn., Dec. 21, 1863: Confined at Rock Island, Ill.: Paroled, May 23, 1865.

(1)   BRANTLEY, R. A. 2Cpl. — Prom., 1Cpl., Feb. 1, 1862: Color bearer, Summer, 1862: W. (abdomen), 2nd Manassas (Aug. 30, 1862): Prom., 5Sgt., Apr. 30, 1863: POW, Gettysburg (July 2, 1863): Confined at Ft. Delaware: Paroled, June 7, 1865.

(1)   SMITH, W. O. 3Cpl. — W., 2nd Manassas (Aug. 30, 1862): Prom., 3Cpl., Sept. 20, 1863: Prom., 2Cpl., Nov., 1863: Detailed as courier to Gen. Chas. Field, Feb. 10, 1864: Paroled at Montgomery, Ala., May 23, 1865.

(1)   HUME, F. CHAS. 4Cpl. — Asgnd. to scouting duty, Nov. 22, 1861: W. (leg), June 8, 1862 near Richmond: W. (thigh), 2nd Manassas (Aug. 30, 1862): Transfd. out of Co., Dec. 7, 1862, to be Adj. of the 32nd Va. Cav. Regt.

OTHER OFFICERS

(1)   CALDWELL, O. P. 3Lt. — Orig. Pvt. in Co.: Prom., 1Sgt., Nov. 1, 1861: Elect., 3Lt., Aug. 23, 1862: W. (hand), 2nd Manassas (Aug. 30, 1862): Deserted with 1Sgt. A. M. Hinson while at winter quarters near Morristown, Tenn., Feb. 1, 1864: Sec. of War ordered name dropped from rolls, Apr. 15, 1864.

MUSICIANS

(1)   ALLEN, W. H. — Died of smallpox, Richmond, Jan. 16, 1863.
      SHACKLEFORD, E. — Orig. Pvt. in Co.: Detailed as a musician, Apr. 7, 1863.

PRIVATES

ABERNATHY, H. C. — Recruited, Mar. 20, 1862 at Huntsville, Tex.: K., Gettysburg (July 2, 1863).

ADICKS, E. J. — Recruited, Mar. 20, 1862 at Huntsville, Tex.: Furlough to Tex., Spring, 1863: While on leave (Nov., 1863) was detailed as a tax collector in Walker County, Tex. by Gen. Magruder.

(1)   ALSTON, A. D. — K., Gaines' Mill (June 27, 1862).

(1)   ALSTON, R. H. — Died, Regmtl. Hosp., Dec. 16, 1861.

ALSTON, W. W. — Recruited, Mar. 20, 1862 at Huntsville, Tex.: Sick most of 1862: W. (leg), Wilderness (May 6, 1864): Dischgd. for disability, Nov. 1, 1864.

ALVERSON, JOHN T. — Recruited, Mar. 25, 1862 at Huntsville, Tex.: K., Spotsylvania (May 10, 1864).

ARCHER, R. P. — Recruited, Mar. 20, 1862 at Huntsville, Tex.: Sick, Winter, 1863-64: AWOL, Feb. 1, 1864: Dischgd. as unfit for milt. serv. (chronic rheumatism), May 30, 1864.

(1)   ARRINGTON, J. W. — Dischgd. for "inability," June 13, 1862.

(1)   BASS, J. M. — Dischgd., Jan. 26, 1862, as unfit for service (effects of typhoid fever & pneumonia).

(2)   BIRDWELL, THOS. J. — Recruited, Mar. 25, 1862 at Huntsville, Tex.: Sick, Spring, 1864: Paroled, Appomattox (Apr. 12, 1865).

(1)   BOWDEN, J. G. — Dischgd. for disability, Dec. 1, 1861.

BROWN, G. W. — Recruited, Mar. 20, 1862 at Huntsville, Tex.: Died of typhoid fever at Richmond, Sept. 25, 1862.

(1) BROWN, M. C. — POW, Suffolk, Va., Apr. 12, 1863: Exchanged: In arrest & confinement, July, 1863: Court Martialed, Aug., 1863: K., Chickamauga (Sept. 19, 1863).

BROWN, R. C. — Recruited, Apr. 29, 1862 in Va.: W. (hands), Malvern Hill (July 1, 1862): Amputated, 2 fingers and thumb on left hand, and 1st finger on right hand: Detailed in C.S. Treasury Dept., Apr. 1, 1863: Dischgd. for Malvern Hill wounds, Dec. 8, 1864.

(1) BURDEN, JOHN G. — See roster, "Regmtl. Hdqtrs., 5th Tex. Inf."

(1) BURDEN, JOS. C. — W. (side), 2nd Manassas (Aug. 30, 1862): Died of wound, Aug. 31, 1862.

(1) BURK, Z. — Dischgd. for "physical inability," Fall, 1861.

(1) BURKE, E. — Detailed as ambulance driver, Apr. 1, 1863: POW, Gettysburg (July 2, 1863): Confined at Ft. McHenry, Md.: Paroled, June 9, 1865.

(1) CALDWELL, O. P. — See list of "Other Officers" above.

(1) CAMPBELL, DOUGLAS — Dischgd. for "inability," June 28, 1862.

(1) CARRINGTON, BERNARD — W. (arm & side), Wilderness (May 6,
(2) 1864): Paroled, Appomattox (Apr. 12, 1865).

COLEMAN, W. G. — Recruited, Mar. 20, 1862 at Huntsville, Tex.: Detailed as a Pioneer, Dec., 1862: W. (thigh), Gettysburg (July 2, 1863): Detailed as a Brig. shoemaker, Spring, 1864: Furlough to Alabama, July, 1864: Foot amputated, Nov., 1864: Paroled at Talladega, Ala., May 20, 1865.

(1) COTTON, JOHN — W. (head), 2nd Manassas (Aug. 30, 1862).

COTTON, JOHN W. — Recruited, Mar. 20, 1862 at Huntsville, Tex.: W. & POW, Gettysburg (July 2, 1863): Confined at Ft. Delaware: Exchanged: Procured substitute (A. Lee), July 27, 1863.

(1) COTTON, ROBT. — Detailed to recruiting serv. in Tex., Feb.-Apr., 1862: Transfd. to Co. B, 32nd Battalion, Va. Cav., Feb. 10, 1863.

(1) COX, LOUIS — Dischgd. for disability (diarrhea), Dec. 13, 1861.

(1) CUNNINGHAM, F. M. — Died of pneumonia, Jan. 4, 1862.

(1) CUNNINGHAM, NATHANIEL G. — Dischgd., Feb. 14, 1862, "for want of physical development."

DeCAPREE, J. A. — Recruited, Mar. 20, 1862 at Huntsville, Tex.: Detailed as an army baker, Richmond, Va., May, 1862: Furlough granted, Apr., 1863: Dischgd. in Tex. for disability.

(1) DICKIE, J. A. — Detailed to scouting duty, Nov. 22, 1861: Detailed to recruiting duty in Tex., Jan.-Mar., 1863: Detailed as scout for Gen. Hood, May 15, 1863: W., Chickamauga (Sept. 19, 1863): Detailed as a scout for Gen. S. B. Buckner: POW, Mar. 25, 1864 near Morristown, Tenn.: Confined at Camp Chase, Ohio: Exchanged, Feb. 25, 1865.

(1) DOUGLAS, N. — Detchd. duty as a Regmtl. teamster: W. (chest), 2nd Manassas (Aug. 30, 1862): K., Gettysburg (July 2, 1863).

(1) DYKEMAN, WM. — Dischgd. for disability (hernia), Jan. 20, 1862.

(1) EDWARDS, T. J. — K., Antietam (Sept. 17, 1862).

(1) ELMORE, J. F. — Died of paralysis, Jan. 6, 1862.

ESKRIDGE, G. W. — Recruited, Mar. 20, 1862 at Huntsville, Tex.: K., Gettysburg (July 2, 1863).

(1) ESTILL, BEN P. — W. (chest), 2nd Manassas (Aug. 30, 1862): Died of Manassas wound, Sept. 12, 1862.

(1) ESTILL, BLACK — Died of disease, May 24, 1862.

EUTSLER, C. C. — Recruited, Mar. 21, 1862 at Huntsville, Tex.: Detailed as a nurse in Richmond from Aug., 1863 to end of war.

(1) EWING, J. W. — Detailed to Div. Provost Guard, June, 1863: Paroled,
(2) Appomattox (Apr. 12, 1865).

(1) FARTHING, W. G. W. — Prom., 5Sgt., Apr., 1863: W. & POW, Gettysburg (July 2, 1863): Exchanged: Left leg amputated, Nov. 18, 1863: Dischgd. for wounds, Apr. 26, 1864.

(1) FRANKLIN, S. J. — Detailed as a clerk to Regmtl. Adj., May 1, 1862: Transfd. to Co. A, Cobb's Arty., Cobb's Legion, Nov., 1862.

GILBERT, J. E. — Recruited, Mar. 26, 1862 at Huntsville, Tex.: W. (arm), Antietam (Sept. 17, 1862): W., Chickamauga (Sept. 19, 1863): W. (thigh) & POW, Wilderness (May 6, 1864): Confined at Elmira, N. Y.: Exchanged, Oct. 11, 1864.

(2) GILBERT, MARTIN L. — Recruited, Mar. 26, 1862 at Huntsville, Tex.: W., Chickamauga (Sept. 19, 1863): Paroled, Appomattox (Apr. 12, 1865).

(1) GOLDING, ANTHONY F. — W. (side), 2nd Manassas (Aug. 30, 1862):
(2) Paroled, Appomattox (Apr. 12, 1865).

(1) GRANT, GEO. A. — W. (thigh), Gaines' Mill (June 27, 1862): POW, Gettysburg (July 2, 1863): Confined at Ft. Delaware: Exchanged: W. (back), Chaffin's Farm (Sept. 29, 1864): Retired, Mar. 7, 1865.

(1) GREEN, G. H. — Detailed as nurse in Brig. Hosp., at Dumfries, Va., Fall, 1861: Died, May 5, 1862 at Ashland, Va.

(1) GRIFFIN, R. H. — W. (thigh), 2nd Manassas (Aug. 30, 1862): K., Wilderness (May 6, 1864).

(1) GUYNN, WM. — Dischgd. for disability, Dec. 1, 1861.

(1) HARDY, RICHARD — Sick, Fall, 1861: W., Gettysburg (July 2, 1863):
(2) Appt. 2Cpl., May, 1864: W. (ankle), Chaffin's Farm (Sept. 29, 1864): Paroled, Appomattox (Apr. 12, 1865).

(1) HARPER, W. E. — Prom., 5Sgt., Nov. 1, 1861: Died at Regmtl. Hosp., Dec. 27, 1861.

HARRIS, JAS. K. P. — Recruited, Nov. 10, 1861, in Va.: POW, Yorktown, May 4, 1862: Exchanged, Aug. 11, 1862: W. (thigh), 2nd Manassas (Aug. 30, 1862): Died of wound, Sept. 20, 1862.

(1) HARRISON, J. S. — Prom., 3Cpl., Feb. 1, 1862: W. in hand accidentally, June 5, 1862: Prom., 2Cpl., Aug. 23, 1862: Detailed as nurse in Winder Hosp., Winter, 1863-64: Dischgd. for disability, May 25, 1864.

(1) HAWK, A. G. — Dischgd. while on the march (June, 1863) for drunkenness: No other record.

(1) HENRY, Z. P. — Asgnd. extra duty as a Regmtl. teamster, Feb. 8, 1861: K., near Williamsport, Md., July 6, 1863 by enemy cavalry.

HEWITT, ROBT. — POW, near Bunker Hill, Va., July 18, 1863. Confined at Camp Chase, Ohio: Escaped.

(1) HIGHTOWER, J. O. — Dischgd. for disability (asthma), Dec. 24, 1861.

HILL, A. T. — Recruited, Apr. 17, 1862 at Huntsville, Tex.: Procured substitute (John Welch), Apr. 28, 1863.

HILL, C. T. — Recruited, Apr. 20, 1862 at Huntsville, Tex.: Procured
    substitute (John Murphy), Apr. 27, 1863.
(1) HILL, JOHN C. — Prom., 1Sgt., Apr., 1864: W. (face), Cold Harbor
(2)   (June 4, 1864): Paroled, Appomattox (Apr. 12, 1865).
(1) HINSON, ABNER M. — Prom., 1Cpl., Dec. 1, 1861: Prom., 1Sgt., Apr.
(2)   30, 1863: AWOL while in winter quarters near Morristown,
    Tenn., Feb. 1, 1864: Returned to Co.: Reduced to Pvt.: W.
    (shoulder), Cold Harbor (June 3, 1864): W. (hip), Darbytown Rd.
    (Oct. 7, 1864): Paroled, Appomattox (Apr. 12, 1865).
(1) IRVINE, H. R. — Died at Camp Winder, Richmond, July 1, 1862.
(1) KEARSE, CALHOUN — POW, Gettysburg (July 2, 1863): Confined at
    Ft. Delaware: Paroled, May 31, 1865.
    KEEBLE, EDWIN A. — Transfd. into Co. D, 5th Tex. from Co. H, 4th
    Tex., Summer, 1863: W., Wilderness (May 6, 1864): Wound
    furlough granted to Tex.: AWOL, did not return to Co.
(1) KEENAN, W. A. — Detailed as a Provost Guard, Jan. 22, 1863:
    Wounded accidentally, Sept. 5, 1863: W. (ankle), Darbytown Rd.
    (Oct. 7, 1864): Wound furlough granted to Tex.: AWOL, did not
    return to Co.
(1) LACKMAN, E. — W. (arm), 2nd Manassas (Aug. 30, 1862): K.,
    Gettysburg (July 2, 1863).
(1) LAMPKIN, M. A. — Sick, Spring, 1862: W. (shoulder), 2nd Manassas
(2)   (Aug. 30, 1862): Transfd. to cavalry, July 10, 1863: Transfd.
    back to Co. D: Paroled, Appomattox (Apr. 12, 1865).
    LEE, A. — Substitute for J. W. Cotton, July 27, 1863: AWOL, June 1,
    1864: Not on Co. Bi-Monthly Muster Roll.
(2) LEWIS, THOS. J. — Recruited, Mar. 20, 1862 at Huntsville, Tex.: W.,
    Chickamauga (Sept. 19, 1863): Paroled, Appomattox (Apr. 12,
    1865).
(1) LEWIS, WM. E. — Asgnd. as courier to Col. Robt. Powell, Nov. 8,
    1862: Appt. 4Cpl., Oct. 1, 1863: Prom., 2Cpl., Spring, 1864: K.,
    Wilderness (May 6, 1864).
(1) LUCAS, L. R. — Sick furlough to Tex. granted, Dec., 1861: AWOL,
    Apr., 1862: Did not return to Co.
(1) McDADE, J. A. — K., Gettysburg (July 2, 1863).
(1) McGILVARY, WM. T. — W. & POW, Gettysburg (July 2, 1863):
    Confined at Ft. Delaware: Paroled, June 9, 1865.
(1) McKINNY, A. W. — Deserted, Summer, 1861 before leaving Tex.
(1) McKINNY, M. — Deserted, Summer, 1861 before leaving Tex.
(1) MALONE, H. F. — Dischgd. for disability, Nov. 5, 1861.
(1) MASS, LEWIS — K., 2nd Manassas (Aug. 30, 1862).
(1) MINSHEW, JOEL — Sick, Fall, 1861: W. (thigh) & POW, Gettysburg
    (July 2, 1863): Paroled from Fed. Gen. Hosp. at David's Is., N.
    Y., Aug. 24, 1863: Sick, Winter, 1863-64.
    MITCHELL, C. J. — Recruited, Apr. 1, 1862 in Robertson County,
    Tex.: Prom., 4Cpl., Dec. 1, 1861: Dischgd. for disability
    (asthma), June 20, 1862.
(1) MITCHELL, L. A. — Prom., 2Cpl., Feb. 1, 1862: Prom., 1Cpl., Aug.
    23, 1862: W., 2nd Manassas (Aug. 30, 1862): POW, Gettysburg
    (July 2, 1863): Confined at Ft. Delaware: Exchanged, Feb. 27,
    1865: Paroled, Montgomery, Ala., May 10, 1865.

MORRIS, ROBT. — Enlisted, Mar. 14, 1863 in Tex.: Detailed to Brig. Provost Guard, Apr. 6, 1864.

MORRISON, C. T. — Transfd. to cavalry, July 10, 1863: Not on Co. Bi-Monthly Muster Roll.

MURPHY, JOHN — Enl. as a substitute for C. T. Hill, Apr. 27, 1863: W. & POW, Gettysburg (July 2, 1863): Deserted, took Fed. oath, Feb. 24, 1865.

(1) MURRAY, J. H. — Dischgd. for "inability," May 1, 1862.

MYERS, W. H. H. — Recruited, Mar. 20, 1862 at Huntsville, Tex.: Sick, most of 1862: W. (both thighs), Wilderness (May 6, 1864).

NELMS, JESSE C. — Recruited, Apr. 5, 1862 at Waverly, Tex.: POW, Gettysburg (July 2, 1863): Confined at Ft. Delaware: Exchanged, Feb. 18, 1865.

NELMS, W. M. — Recruited, Mar. 28, 1862 at Waverly, Tex.: W. (leg), 2nd Manassas (Aug. 30, 1862): Leg amputated: Died of wound, Sept. 8, 1862.

(1) NETHERLY, T. W. — Died, Richmond, Mar. 31, 1862.

(1) PAGE, K. J. — W. (leg), 2nd Manassas (Aug. 30, 1862): POW, Gettysburg (July 2, 1863): Confined at Ft. McHenry: Exchanged: Furlough granted, Oct., 1864: AWOL.

(1) PARKER, ISAAC ("Ike") — W. (arm), Gettysburg (July 2, 1863): W., Chickamauga (Sept. 19, 1863): POW, near Mossyback, Tenn., Mar. 4, 1864: Confined at Camp Chase, Ohio: Paroled, Apr. 13, 1864.

(1) PEARCE, W. J. C. — POW, Gettysburg (July 2, 1863): Died in Federal prison, Jan. 1, 1864.

(1) PERKINS, E. F. — Sick (VD) most of enlistment: Deserted, Oct. 9, 1863.

(1) PERRIE, R. E. — See roster, "Regmtl. Hdqtrs., 5th Tex. Inf."

PIRTLE, SAM — Recruited, Mar. 28, 1862 at Waverly, Tex.: K., Antietam (Sept. 17, 1862).

POWELL, WM. P. — See roster, "Regmtl. Hdqtrs., 5th Tex. Inf."

(1) RANDALL, S. B. — W. (chest & thigh) & POW, Gettysburg (July 2, 1863): Sent to Fed. Gen. Hosp., David's Is., N. Y.: Paroled, Oct. 22, 1863: Dischgd. for wounds, Sept. 13, 1864.

REYNOLDS, R. M. — Recruited, Mar. 20, 1862 at Huntsville, Tex.: AWOL at Frederick, Md., on march to Antietam, Sept. 10, 1862.

(1) RIDGWAY, F. M. — K., Antietam (Sept. 17, 1862).

(1) ROBERTSON, JOHN R. — Dischgd. for disability, Mar. 14, 1862.

(1) ROBINSON, J. M. — Prom., 4Sgt., Feb. 1, 1862: W. (arm), 2nd Manassas (Aug. 30, 1862): Prom., 3Sgt., Sept., 1862: W., Chickamauga (Sept. 19, 1863): Leg amputated.

ROME, W. B. — Recruited, Mar. 26, 1862 at Huntsville, Tex.: POW, Antietam (Sept. 17, 1862): Paroled, Sept. 20, 1862: Detailed as clerk to Regmtl. Adj., Apr. 6, 1864: W., Wilderness (May 6, 1864): Leg amputated.

ROSE, J. D. — Recruited, Apr. 8, 1862 at Waverly, Tex.: Died of sickness, June 3, 1862.

(1) ROSS, S. T. — W. (abdomen), 2nd Manassas (Aug. 30, 1862): Died of wound, Aug. 31, 1862.

(1) RUSSELL, E. — Dischgd. for disability, Nov. 5, 1861.

(1) SAUNDERS (or SANDERS), ALONZO — Died, Nov. 2, 1861 at Regmtl. Hosp., Richmond.

(1) SAUNDERS (or SANDERS), WM. — Detailed as scout for Gen. Longstreet, May 1, 1863: K., Knoxville, Tenn., Nov. 25, 1863.

(1) SCOTT, J. F. — Dischgd. for disability (chronic diarrhea), July 1, 1862.

(1) SCOTT, T. B. — W., Gaines' Mill (June 27, 1862): W. (leg), Malvern Hill (July 1, 1862): Leg amputated: Dischgd. for disability, Oct. 30, 1862.

SEALES, J. R. — Recruited, Mar. 20, 1862 at Huntsville, Tex.: W. (side), 2nd Manassas (Aug. 30, 1862): Detailed as nurse at Winder Hosp., Richmond, Aug., 1863-Jan., 1864: W. (hip), Jan. 29, 1864: Retired for disability, May 31, 1864.

(1) SHACKELFORD, E. — See "Musicians," above.

SHANOSKI, CHAS. — Recruited, Mar. 20, 1862 at Huntsville, Tex.: AWOL, Jan. 16, 1863: W. & POW, Gettysburg (July 2, 1863): Exchanged: AWOL, Aug. 26, 1864: Dropped from rolls, Dec. 1, 1864.

SHAW, J. T. — Recruited, Mar. 20, 1862 at Huntsville, Tex.: K., Spotsylvania (May 10, 1864).

(1) SHERMAN, W. L. — Dischgd. for "inability," Feb. 1, 1862.

SMITH, RODUM — Recruited, Mar. 20, 1862 at Huntsville, Tex.: Died in hosp., Winter, 1862-63.

SMITH, SIMEON — Recruited, Mar. 26, 1862 at Huntsville, Tex.: K., Mar. 29, 1862 at Huntsville before joining Co.

(1) SMITHER, JOHN M. — See roster, "Regmtl. Hdqtrs., 5th Tex. Inf."

(1) SPIVEY, W. F. — W. ("in rump"), 2nd Manassas (Aug. 30, 1862): Died of wound, Sept. 12, 1862.

(1) STANTON, ROBT. — Detailed as a Regmtl. Artificer (ammunition maker), Dec. 10, 1861: Detailed as a Brig. carpenter, Oct. 10, 1862: Detailed as a Div. Artificer: POW, Wilderness (May 6, 1864): Confined at Point Lookout, Md.: Exchanged, Feb. 12, 1865: Paroled, Appomattox (Apr. 12, 1865).

STRAYHORN, W. N. — Recruited, Mar. 31, 1862 at Waverly, Tex.: Died (acute diarrhea), June 29, 1862, Charlottesville, Va.

TOMLINSON, JAS. — Recruited, Mar. 28, 1862 at Waverly, Tex.: Died of disease, Richmond, Va., May 26, 1862.

TOMLINSON, JOHN — Recruited, Mar. 28, 1862 at Waverly, Tex.: Hospitalized for sickness, Fall, 1862 to Summer, 1863: K., Chickamauga (Sept. 19, 1863).

(1) TRAYLOR, ALEX H. — Enl. at 19: W., Chickamauga (Sept. 19, 1863): W. (arm), Wilderness (May 6, 1864): Dischgd. for wounds, June 20, 1864.

(1) TRAYLOR, J. H. — Sick, Winter, 1861-62: Dischgd. for disability, Oct. 1, 1862.

(2) TRAYLOR, WM. A. — Recruited, Mar. 28, 1862 at Waverly, Tex.: W. (arm), Wilderness (May 6, 1864): W. (thigh), Darbytown Rd. (Oct. 7, 1864): Paroled, Appomattox (Apr. 12, 1865).

(1) TURNER, WM. — W. (hip & groin) & POW, Gettysburg (July 2, 1863): Died, July 6, 1863.

(2) UNDERWOOD, ALFRED W. — Recruited, Apr. 10, 1862 at Patrick's Ferry, Tex.: Paroled, Appomattox (Apr. 12, 1865).

(1) WALKER, W. C. — Appt. 4Cpl., Dec., 1863: Appt. 1Cpl., May, 1864: W. (leg), Wilderness (May 6, 1864).

WALLACE, T. R. — Recruited, Mar. 28, 1862 at Waverly, Tex.: Died, Richmond, June 12, 1862.

(1) WARREN, W. L. — Dischgd. for disability (chronic diarrhea), July 1, 1862.

(1) WATSON, T. L. — Appt. 4Cpl., Nov. 1, 1862: Prom., 3Cpl.: K., Chickamauga (Sept. 19, 1863).

WELCH, JOHN — Enl., Apr. 28, 1863 as substitute for A. T. Hill: Deserted, May 4, 1863, on march from Suffolk, Va.

WILLIAMS, D. M. — Recruited, Mar. 20, 1862 at Huntsville, Tex.: Deserted, Feb. 23, 1864 while on march from Strawberry Plains, Tenn.

WILLIAMS, W. P. — Recruited, Mar. 25, 1862 at Huntsville, Tex.: No other record.

(1) WILLIAMSON, P. G. — W., Antietam (Sept. 17, 1862): W. (knee) & POW, Gettysburg (July 2, 1863): Died of wound, July 9, 1863.

WILSON, C. N. — Paroled, June 8, 1865 at Montgomery, Ala.: No other record.

(1) WILSON, LUTE — Detailed as a Brig. teamster, Dec., 1861: Deserted on retreat from Yorktown, May 4, 1862.

(2) WILSON, WM. P. — Detailed as a litter bearer, Apr., 1863: Detailed as a Regmtl. teamster, Jan., 1864: Paroled, Appomattox (Apr. 12, 1865).

(1) WOOD, R. L. — Dischgd. for disability (rheumatism), Jan. 26, 1862.

(1) WOODSON, C. T. — Appt. 4Cpl., Feb. 1, 1862: Prom., 3Cpl., Aug. 23, 1862: Detailed as nurse at Winder Hosp., Richmond, Oct., 1862: Prom., 2Cpl., Mar., 1863: Transfd. to cavalry, July 10, 1863.

(1) WYNNE, W. D. — K., 2nd Manassas (Aug. 30, 1862).

(1) YOAKUM, GEO. — Died at Richmond of typhoid fever, Apr. 6, 1863.

5TH TEX. VOL. INF. REGT.

COMPANY E — *DIXIE BLUES*

Company was organized in Washington County, Texas, July 19, 1861 and was mustered into the Confederate service in that county "for the war," Aug. 8, 1861.

Key

(1) Original member of Company. (2) Paroled at Appomattox.
K (Killed), W (Wounded), POW (Prisoner of War)
AWOL (Absent Without Leave)

ORIGINAL OFFICERS

(1) ROGERS, JOHN D. Capt. — Resgnd., July 22, 1862.
(1) BABER, THOS. A. 1Lt. — Prom., Capt., July 22, 1862: W., Antietam (Sept. 17, 1862): Detailed to recruiting serv. in Tex., Summer, 1864: W. (arm), Darbytown Rd. (Oct. 7, 1864): Retired for disability, Dec. 15, 1864.
(1) HARPER, R. THOS. 2Lt. — Detailed to Tex. on recruiting serv., Feb.-Apr., 1862: Prom., 1Lt., July 22, 1862: W. (thigh & shoulder) & POW, Gettysburg (July 2, 1863): Confined at Camp Chase, Ohio: Transfd. to Pt. Lookout, Md., Mar. 14, 1865.
(1) NASH, THOS. 3Lt. — W. (arm), Gaines' Mill (June 27, 1862): Prom., 2Lt., July 22, 1862: W., 2nd Manassas (Aug. 30, 1862): Detailed to Tex. on recruiting serv., Feb.-Apr., 1863: K., Wilderness (May 6, 1864).

ORIGINAL NON-COMMISSIONED OFFICERS

(1) LITTLEFIELD, J. H. 1Sgt. — See roster, "Regmtl. Hdqtrs., 5th Tex. Inf."
(1) STEVENS, A. J. 2Sgt. — Detailed to Tex. on recruiting serv., Feb.-Apr., 1862: Detailed as a nurse in the Tex. Hosp., Richmond, June 20, 1863: Transfd. by Sec. of War to secret service work in Trans-Miss. Dept.
(1) NORWOOD, WALTER N. 3Sgt. — See list of "Other Officers" following.
(1) HALL, A. J. 4Sgt. — Dischgd. for disability (chronic bronchitis), Dec. 14, 1861.
(1) WRAY, J. F. 5Sgt. — See roster, "Regmtl. Hdqtrs., 5th Tex. Inf."
(1) GEORGE, W. B. W. 1Cpl. — Prom., 4Sgt., Dec. 4, 1861: Prom., 3Sgt., Aug., 1862: Prom., 2Sgt., Feb., 1863: W. (hand), Wilderness (May 6, 1864): Prom., 1Sgt., Aug., 1864: POW, Darbytown Rd. (Oct. 7, 1864): Confined at Pt. Lookout, Md.: Paroled, June 6, 1865.
(1) FELDER, MIERS M. 2Cpl. — W., 2nd Manassas (Aug. 30, 1862): Dischgd. for disability at Columbia, S. Car., Feb. 14, 1863.
(1) GAY, MILAM 3Cpl. — Died, Dec. 2, 1861.
(1) SEDGLEY, J. T. 4Cpl. — W., Chickamauga (Sept. 19, 1863): Furlough granted to Miss., Oct., 1863: Never returned to Co.: Paroled in Tex., June 27, 1865.

OTHER OFFICERS

COFFIELD, SAM T. 1Lt. — Orig. Pvt. in Co.: W., Gaines' Mill (June 27, 1862): Prom., 1Lt., Jan., 1864 & transfd. to Capt. H. B. Coffield's Co., Tex. Vols., Trans-Miss. Dept.

(2)   ELDRIDGE, BOLLING 3Lt. — Orig. Pvt. in Co.: W., Gaines' Mill
      (June 27, 1862): Prom., 3Lt., May 16, 1863: W. (shoulder),
      Wilderness (May 6, 1864): Prom., 2Lt., May 6, 1864: Paroled,
      Appomattox (Apr. 12, 1865): Last survivor of Hood's Tex. Brig.,
      died, Oct. 28, 1938.
      NORWOOD, WALTER N. 3Lt. — See roster, "Hdqtrs., Hood's Tex.
      Brig."

MUSICIANS

(1)   CARTMELL, JAS. A. — W. (leg), 2nd Manassas (Aug. 30, 1862):
      Wound furlough to Tex., Oct., 1862: AWOL.
(1)   COUSINS, J. W. — Declared unfit for infantry service: Transfd. to Co.
      D, 15 Va. Cav. Regt., Jan. 12, 1863.
(1)   FIELDS, JOHN G. — Detailed to Litter Corps, Summer & Fall, 1862:
(2)   Left to attend W. at Gettysburg, POW (July 4, 1863): Exchanged,
      Apr. 27, 1864: Paroled, Appomattox (Apr. 12, 1865).
(2)   HARDEMAN, JAS. H. — Orig. Pvt. in Co.: Detailed as a musician, Fall,
      1863: Paroled, Appomattox (Apr. 12, 1865).
      ZANTGROFT, AUGUST — Recruited, Mar. 24, 1862 at Washington,
      Tex.: Sick most of 1862 & 1863: Detailed as a musician, Fall,
      1863: Furlough granted, Feb., 1864: AWOL, did not return to
      Co.

PRIVATES

(1)   ADAIR, D. F. — Dischgd. for disability (heart disease), Dec. 27, 1861.
(1)   ALLEN, C. C. — Detailed as a Regmtl. teamster, Nov., 1861-Dec.,
      1864.
(1)   ALLEN, HARDY — See roster, "Regmtl. Hdqtrs., 5th Tex. Inf."
(1)   ALLEN, R. L. — K., 2nd Manassas (Aug. 30, 1862).
(1)   ARMITAGE, T. J. — W. (hand), Gettysburg (July 2, 1863): Finger
      amputated: Disabled, detailed to QM Dept., Montgomery, Ala.:
      Paroled at Montgomery, May 12, 1865.
      BAKER, JAS. — Recruited, Mar. 24, 1862 at Washington, Tex.:
      Dischgd., Oct. 3, 1862, for disability (VD).
      BATTE, DAN E. — Recruited, Mar. 29, 1862 at Washington, Tex.: W.,
      Gaines' Mill (June 27, 1862): W., Malvern Hill (July 1, 1862):
      Detailed to QM Dept., Spring, 1863: W. (arm), Petersburg June
      28, 1864: Paroled, Jackson, Miss., May 19, 1865.
(1)   BOOTHE, JOHN — K., Gettysburg (July 2, 1863).
(1)   BROWN, CHAS. — Dischgd. on Surg. Cert., Apr. 9, 1862.
(1)   BUNGER, W. G. — See roster, "Regmtl. Hdqtrs., 5th Tex. Inf."
(1)   BUSTER, J. C. — Prom., 1Cpl., May, 1862: Prom., 5Sgt., July, 1862:
      W., 2nd Manassas (Aug. 30, 1862): Leg amputated: Dischgd.,
      Oct. 23, 1862.
(1)   CHRISTIE, C. C. — Not listed on Co. Bi-Monthly Muster Rolls.
      CHRISTIE, R. J. — Recruited, at 46, Mar. 22, 1862, at Washington,
      Tex.: Sick, Summer, 1862: Dischgd., Oct. 8, 1862 for "general
      debility from old age."

(1) CLAY, ATREUS M. — Deserted at Friend's Station, East Tenn., Feb. 13, 1864.

(1) COFFIELD, SAM T. — See preceeding list of "Other Officers."

(1) COOPER, GEO. R. — Died, Jan. 7, 1862.

(1) COOPER, MOSES — K., Gaines' Mill (June 27, 1862).

(1) COUNTS, GEO. W. — W., Gaines' Mill (June 27, 1862): Detailed as a Provost Guard, Sept., 1862: Prom., 3Cpl.: W. & POW, Gettysburg (July 2, 1863): Died of wound in Fed. hosp.

DANIELS, JOHN L. — Enl. as a substitute for Geo. Ewing, Nov. 1, 1862, Culpeper Court House, Va.: W., Fredericksburg (Dec. 13, 1862): W., Gettysburg (July 2, 1863): W. (face), Wilderness (May 6, 1864).

(1) DEAN, SAM H. — W. (chest & thigh), 2nd Manassas (Aug. 30, 1862): Died of wounds, Sept. 21, 1862.

DRUMMELLA, A. W. — Recruited, Mar. 22, 1862 at Washington, Tex.: Transfd. to Co. E, 4th Va. Cav. Regt., Feb. 8, 1863: Procured Harris Peters as a substitute, Feb. 14, 1863.

DULANEY, JOHN T. — Recruited, Mar. 29, 1862 at Washington, Tex.: W., Gaines' Mill (June 27, 1862): Disabled and dischgd., July 15, 1862.

(1) ELDRIDGE, BOLLING — See list of "Other Officers" above.

(1) ELDRIDGE, FRANK — W. (arm), Fredericksburg (Dec. 13, 1862): Prom., 4Sgt.: W., Chickamauga (Sept. 20, 1863): Prom., 3Sgt.: W. (thigh), Darbytown Rd. (Oct. 7, 1864): Dischgd. for disability, Dec. 13, 1864.

(1) EVANS, M. A. J. — Detailed to ambulance serv., Apr., 1862: Detailed
(2)   as litter bearer, June, 1862: W., Chickamauga (Sept. 20, 1863): Paroled, Appomattox (Apr. 12, 1865).

EWING, GEO. — Recruited, Mar. 29, 1862 at Washington, Tex.: Sick most of 1862: Procured substitute, John Daniels, Nov. 1, 1862, at Culpeper Court House, Va.

EWING, JOHN F. — Recruited, Mar. 24, 1862 at Washington, Tex.: Sick most of 1862: Hospitalized, July-Dec., 1863: POW, Richmond hosp., Apr. 3, 1865.

(1) FARMER, JAS. P. — W. (leg), Malvern Hill (July 1, 1862): Disabled from wound: Furlough to Tex.: Did not return to Co.

(1) FARQUHAR, C. E. — K., Wilderness (May 6, 1864).

(1) FARQUHAR, FELIX — W. (thigh), Gettysburg (July 2, 1863): Wound furlough to Tex.: AWOL, Feb., 1864: Did not return to Co.

(1) FELDER, RUFUS K. — Sick, Spring & Summer, 1862: Present for all
(2)   battles: Paroled, Appomattox (Apr. 12, 1865).

(1) GARRETT, JOHN T. — Died, Jan. 22, 1862.

(1) GEE, JAS. B. — W., Chickamauga (Sept. 19, 1863): Wound furlough to Tex.: AWOL, Dec., 1863: Did not return to Co.

(1) GEE, JOHN — W., 2nd Manassas (Aug. 30, 1862): Transfd. to Gen. B. H. Robertson's Cav. Brig., Dec. 27, 1862.

(1) GEE, LEONARD G. — Sick at Winchester, Va., Fall & Winter, 1862: Detailed as courier for Gen. J. B. Robertson, Oct., 1863: W. (arm), Wilderness (May 6, 1864): Furlough granted to Miss.

GEORGE, JOEL W. — Recruited, Mar. 24, 1862 at Washington, Tex.: Dischgd., Surg. Cert. of disability, July 11, 1862.

GOGGANS, D. JACK — Recruited, Mar. 22, 1862 at Washington, Tex.: Sick, Spring, 1862: Died, Aug. 15, 1862 at Scottsville, Va. of asthma.

(1) GOODWIN, C. S. — Sick, Winter, 1861-62: Died, Louisa Court House, Va., June 1, 1862.

(1) GOODWIN, ROBT. — Deserted at Friend's Station, East Tenn., Feb. 13, 1864.

(1) GRAY, W. H. H. — Prom., 4Cpl.: W., 2nd Manassas (Aug. 30, 1862): Prom., 2Cpl.: Detailed by Maj. Hamilton (Brig. Comsy. Off.) to drive cattle: Paroled, Appomattox (Apr. 12, 1865).

GRIFFON (or GRIFFIN), A. G. — Substitute for Leonidas Holliday, enl. in Co., Feb., 1863: Died at Tex. Hosp., Richmond, June 20, 1863.

HALL, JOHN W. — Recruited, Apr. 6, 1862 at Washington, Tex.: Furlough to Tex., May, 1863: AWOL, June, 1863.

(1) HARDEMAN, JAS. H. — See preceding list of "Musicians."

(1) HARGROVE, R. W. — Detailed to Cavalry Recruiting Service in Tex., Spring, 1862.

(1) HARPER, R. G. — Detailed to duty on staff of Gen. C. M. Wilcox, Spring, 1862: Dischgd., Aug. 5, 1862.

(1) HENDERSON, JOHN NATHANIEL — Prom., 3Cpl., May, 1862: W., Antietam (Sept. 17, 1862): Left arm amputated: Returned to Tex., prom., Lt. and served on staff of Gen. J. B. Robertson in Tex., 1864-65.

(1) HENDLEY, F. M. — Died, Feb. 2, 1862.

(1) HENRY, J. E. — Dischgd. for disability (perm. injury of foot), Jan. 22, 1862.

(1) HILL, ANDERSON — Furlough granted to Tex., Fall, 1862: Died of smallpox, Nov. 10, 1862, at Cherokee, Tex., Rusk County.

HILL, J. S. — Recruited, Mar. 29, 1862 at Washington, Tex.: Furlough to Tex., June, 1863: Sick in hosp. in Gaston, Ga., Jan.-Aug., 1864: Returned to Co., Sept., 1864.

(1) HOLLIDAY, LEONIDAS B. — W., 2nd Manassas (Aug. 30, 1862): Procured substitute (A. G. Griffon), Feb., 1863.

HONEA, THOS. — Recruited, Mar. 22, 1862 at Washington, Tex.: Died (acute diarrhea), Danville, Va., Jan. 12, 1863: Personal effects — coat, hat, shoes & $20.00.

(1) HURT, JAS. S. — See roster, "Regmtl. Hdqtrs., 5th Tex. Inf."

(1) HUTCHINSON, J. H. — W., 2nd Manassas (Aug. 30, 1862): Died of wound, Sept. 23, 1862.

(1) HUTCHINSON, JAS. S. — W. (knee), 2nd Manassas (Aug. 30, 1862): Died, Sept. 23, 1862.

(1) INNIS, WM. H. — Detailed as clerk in QM Dept. from Feb., 1862 to the end of war: Paroled, Appomattox (Apr. 12, 1865).

(1) KAVANAUGH, B. Y. — W., accidentally, June 1, 1862: W., 2nd Manassas (Aug. 30, 1862): Paroled, Montgomery, Ala., May 23, 1865.

(1) LeGRAND, WM. C. — W. (hand), Antietam (Sept. 17, 1862): Prom., 3Cpl.: W., Chickamauga (Sept. 20, 1863): Prom., 3Sgt.: Paroled, Appomattox (Apr. 12, 1865).

(1) LOCKETT, S. S. — W. (side), Gettysburg (July 2, 1863): Died, July 6, 1863.

(1) LOTT, JESSE B. — W., Gaines' Mill (June 27, 1862): Sick, Fall & Winter, 1862.
(1) LOTT, JOHN W. — W., 2nd Manassas (Aug. 30, 1862): Deserted at Friend's Station, East Tenn., Feb. 13, 1864.
(2) LOTT, WM. R. — Recruited, Mar. 22, 1862 at Washington, Tex.: Left sick at Chattanooga: Sick most of 1862: Sent to Atlanta, Ga., Nov. 1, 1863: Returned to Co.: W. (leg), Wilderness (May 6, 1864): Paroled, Appomattox (Apr. 12, 1865).
(1) McCALISTER, WM. H. — W., Gaines' Mill (June 27, 1862): W. (leg),
(2) Wilderness (May 6, 1864): Paroled, Appomattox (Apr. 12, 1865).
(1) McCOY, THOS. — Detailed as a cook in a Richmond hosp., Winter, 1861-62: Detailed to QM Dept., Spring, 1862: AWOL, June 8, 1862: Did not return to Co.
(1) McPHERSON, D. W. — Detailed as a Regmtl. teamster, Feb., 1862: W. (hand), at Petersburg, Va., July 3, 1864.
(1) MADDOX, T. E. — W., Chickamauga (Sept. 20, 1863): Died of wounds.
MARSHALL, E. M. — Recruited, Mar. 22, 1862 at Washington, Tex.: Sent to hosp., Nov. 14, 1862, died later. Personal effects, $3.00.
MARSHALL, S. J. — Recruited, at 28, Mar. 22, 1862 at Washington, Tex.: Physically disabled for field duty: Detailed as a shoemaker, by order of Gen. Longstreet, Nov., 1862.
(1) MAXEY, ERASTUS E. — Missing at Malvern Hill (July 1, 1862): Detailed as a scout for Gen. Hood, Oct., 1863: POW, New Market, Ala., Nov., 1863: Confined at Ft. Delaware: Exchanged, Nov. 13, 1863: Detailed as scout for Gen. Chas. Field: Detailed, Aug., 1864 by Sec. of War for "special serv." with Gen. Hood.
(1) MAY, JOHN R. — Sick, Winter, 1862-63: Granted furlough to Ark., May, 1863: AWOL, "supposed to be in Ark."
(1) MAYFIELD, JOHN M. — Died of pneumonia, Feb. 2, 1862.
(1) MEADOR, PEYTON R. — W., Gaines' Mill (June 27, 1862): Furlough to Tex., Oct., 1862: Did not return to Co.
(1) MONCRIEF, C. E. — K., 2nd Manassas (Aug. 30, 1862).
MOORE, L. P. — Recruited, Mar. 29, 1862 at Washington, Tex.: Died at Tex. Hosp., Richmond, May 20, 1863.
(1) MUIR, W. A. — Detailed to nurse sick, Fall, 1861: Died, Apr. 25, 1862 at Ashland, Va.
(1) MULLINS, N. W. — K., 2nd Manassas (Aug. 30, 1862).
(1) MULLINS, T. H. — W., Antietam (Sept. 17, 1862): W., Chickamauga (Sept. 19, 1863): W. (chest), Cold Harbor (June 1, 1864): W. (neck), Bermuda Hundreds, June 17, 1864: W. (arm), White Oak Swamp (Aug. 16, 1864).
(1) MUSE, W. T. — Died of disease, Nov., 1861.
(1) NASH, FRANK M. — Dischgd. for sickness ("permanent stricture of the urethra"), Mar. 19, 1862.
(1) NIBLETT, R. S. — Sick (VD & diarrhea), Farmersville, Va., Summer, 1862 & Summer, 1864: Furlough to Miss., Fall, 1864.
(1) PATRICK, DAVID O. — W., Gaines' Mill (June 27, 1862): W. (shoulder
(2) & chest), Darbytown Rd. (Oct. 7, 1864); Paroled, Appomattox (Apr. 12, 1865).
(1) PATRICK, SIDNEY V. — Prom., 3Cpl., Aug., 1862: Prom., 1Cpl., Nov., 1862: Sick, Winter, 1862-63: Prom., 4Sgt., Nov., 1864: Paroled, Appomattox (Apr. 12, 1865).

(1) PEARSON, R. W. — K., Gaines' Mill (June 27, 1862).
PETERS, HARRIS — Enl., Feb. 14, 1863 as a substitute for A. W.
Drummella: Deserted, Apr. 7, 1863.
(1) PETTEY, V. E. — Prom., 3Sgt., Dec., 1861: Prom., 1Sgt., Aug., 1862:
W., 2nd Manassas (Aug. 30, 1862): Died of wound, Sept. 1, 1862.
POLLOCK, HENRY — Recruited, Mar. 29, 1862 at Washington, Tex.:
AWOL, Jan., 1863: Did not return to Co.
(1) RANDLE, JOHN A. — Sick, Fall, 1862: Sick leave granted, Oct., 1862:
AWOL, Nov., 1862: Never returned to Co.
REEDY, W. S. — Recruited, Mar. 29, 1862 at Washington, Tex.: Died,
Richmond, Aug. 15, 1862.
(1) RICE, CHAS. J. — Dischgd. for disability (chronic rheumatism), Dec.
14, 1861.
(1) RINGGOLD, R. M. — K., Gaines' Mill (June 27, 1862).
(1) ROBERTS, JOHN H. — W. (both legs) & POW, Gettysburg (July 2,
1863): Exchanged: Dischgd. for wounds, June 1, 1864.
(1) ROBERTS, JOHN J. — A physician by profession: See roster, "Regmtl.
Hdqtrs., 5th Tex. Inf."
(1) ROBERTS, JOHN L. — Dischgd. for disability (lung disease), Dec. 14,
1861.
(1) ROGERS, P. H. — Transfd. to Terry's Tex. Rangers (8th Tex. Cav.
Regt.), Oct. 25, 1861.
RUARK, W. A. — Recruited, Mar. 22, 1862 at Washington, Tex.: Died
of typhoid fever, July 8, 1862.
(1) SENSEBAUGH, WM. — Asgnd. as a scout, Dec., 1861: W. (thigh), 2nd
Manassas (Aug. 30, 1862): Leg amputated: Died, July 21, 1863.
(1) SHERMAN, JOS. W. — K., Malvern Hill (July 1, 1862).
(1) SMITH, B. F. — Transfd. to the 14th No. Car. Inf. Regt., July 22, 1862
as Regmtl. QM.
(1) SMITH, FRANK M. — Detailed to Regmtl. QM, Summer, 1862:
(2) Detailed as a wagon driver for Hood's (Field's) Div., Mar., 1864:
Paroled, Appomattox (Apr. 12, 1865).
SMITH, J. J. — Prom., 2Cpl.: W. (arm), 2nd Manassas (Aug. 30, 1862):
Prom., 3Sgt.: W., Gettysburg (July 2, 1863): Disabled: Furloughed to Tex.
(1) SMITH, SIMON B. — W. (shoulder), Gaines' Mill (June 27, 1862):
(2) Paroled, Appomattox (Apr. 12, 1865).
(1) SPANN, JAS. W. — Sick, Winter & Spring, 1863: W., Chickamauga
(Sept. 19, 1863): Died of wound.
STEVENS, W. E. — Recruited, Mar. 22, 1862 at Washington, Tex.: W.
(both legs & right hip) & POW, Gettysburg (July 2, 1863): Died
of wounds at Camp Letterman, USA Genl. Hosp., Gettysburg,
Pa., Sept. 4, 1863.
STUTSMAN, DAVID — Recruited, Mar. 22, 1862 at Washington, Tex.:
Died of measles, Richmond, June 28, 1862.
TOLAND, J. F. — W., 2nd Manassas (Aug. 30, 1862): On sick leave to
Atlanta, Ga., Nov., 1863: AWOL: Did not return to Co.
(1) TOLAND, R. S. — K., Antietam (Sept. 17, 1862).
TOWNSEND, D. E. — Recruited, Apr. 22, 1862 in La.: Leave granted,
June, 1862: AWOL: Did not return to Co.
(1) TRANER, A. J. — Died of pneumonia, Lynchburg, Va., June 15, 1862.

(1) WALLACE, JOS. W. — W., Chickamauga (Sept. 19, 1863): Detailed to Brig. Comsy. Dept., May 1, 1864: Paroled, Appomattox (Apr. 12, 1865).

WALTHALL, J. J. — Recruited, Mar. 22, 1862 at Washington, Tex.: Prom., 5Sgt.: W., accidentally, July 5, 1863: Died of wound.

(1) WATSON, SAM H. — W., Gaines' Mill (June 27, 1862): W. (arm) & POW, Gettysburg (July 2, 1863): Arm amputated: Died of wound, Sept. 13, 1863.

WEATHERSBY, THOS. — Recruited, Mar. 29, 1862 at Washington, Tex.: K., Gettysburg (July 2, 1863).

(1) WILCOX, JOHN L. — Died, Richmond, June 2, 1862.

(1) WILKINSON, R. D. — Dischgd. on Surg. Cert. for rheumatism, Jan. 10, 1862.

(1) WILLIAMS, GEO. B. — Detailed as a wagon driver, Nov., 1861: W., 2nd
(2) Manassas (Aug. 30, 1862): W. (both legs), Wilderness (May 6, 1864): Prom., 5Sgt.: Paroled, Appomattox (Apr. 12, 1865).

(1) WILLIAMSON, F. M. — Prom., 5Sgt., June, 1862: Prom., 1Sgt., Oct., 1862: Transfd. to Co. E, 1st Tenn. Cav. Regt.

(1) WRIGHT, JEFFERSON — See roster, "Regmtl. Hdqtrs., 5th Tex. Inf."

ZANTGROFT, AUGUST — See preceding list of "Musicians."

5TH TEX. VOL. INF. REGT.

COMPANY F — *COMPANY INVINCIBLES*

Company was organized in Washington County, Texas, July 11, 1861 and was mustered into the Confederate service there "for the war," Aug. 11, 1861. Company included men from Jefferson and Liberty Counties as well as Washington County.

Key

(1) Original member of Company. (2) Paroled at Appomattox.
K (Killed), W (Wounded), POW (Prisoner of War)
AWOL (Absent Without Leave)

ORIGINAL OFFICERS

(1) BRYAN, KING Capt. — See roster, "Regmtl. Hdqtrs., 5th Tex. Inf."

(1) WILLIAMS, WATSON DUGAT 1Lt. — Detailed to recruiting serv. in
(2) Tex., Feb.-Apr., 1862: In charge of Regmtl. sick camp, June 11, 1862: Prom., Capt., Aug. 30, 1862: Sick, sent to Tex. Hosp., Richmond, Aug., 1863: W. (leg), Darbytown Rd. (Oct. 7, 1864): Paroled, Appomattox (Apr. 12, 1865).

(1) COBB, J. E. 2Lt. — Prom., 1Lt., Aug. 30, 1862: POW, Gettysburg (July 2, 1863): Confined at Johnson Is., Ohio: Paroled, May 17, 1865.

(1) BRYAN, PRYOR L. 3Lt. — Died, May 28, 1862, in a private home in Va.

ORIGINAL NON-COMMISSIONED OFFICERS

(1) EVANS, WM. S. 1Sgt. — Sick, Summer & Fall, 1862: K., Chickamauga (Sept. 19, 1863).

(1) CHURCH, J. F. 2Sgt. — W., 2nd Manassas (Aug. 30, 1862): Died of wound, Oct. 22, 1862.

(1) CROSBY, GILBERT 3Sgt. — Dischgd. for VD, Dec. 21, 1861.

(1) STEPHENSON, W. S. ("Shake") 4Sgt. — Dischgd., Nov. 14, 1861 for "homesickness."

(1) DILLON, J. M. 5Sgt. — Prom., 3Sgt., Dec. 21, 1861: W., 2nd Manassas (Aug. 30, 1862): W., Chickamauga (Sept. 20, 1863): W. (leg), Wilderness (May 6, 1864): W. (head), Chaffin's Farm (Sept. 29, 1864): K., Darbytown Rd. (Oct. 7, 1864).

(1) ANGELL, HENRY V. 1Cpl. — Sick in Warwick Hosp., Richmond,
(2) Oct., 1861: Appt. 5Sgt., Jan. 1, 1862: Prom., 1Sgt.: W. (groin), Chickamauga (Sept. 19, 1863): Paroled, Appomattox (Apr. 12, 1865).

(1) McCARTY, WM. J. 2Cpl. — Died of tuberculosis, Richmond, Jan. 8, 1862.

(1) PRUETT, EDMOND 3Cpl. — Sick, Fall & Winter, 1861: Dischgd. for sickness, Mar. 19, 1862.

(1) KEITH, EDMUND N. 4Cpl. — Died, Dec. 1, 1861.

OTHER OFFICERS

LEONARD, R. H. 2Lt. — Orig. Pvt. in Co.: Detailed as a Brig. teamster, Dec., 1861: Elect., 2Lt., Sept. 14, 1862: AWOL in Tex., Apr., 1863: Dropped from rolls by special order from Richmond, July 20, 1864.

McCALLY, CHAS. 2Lt. — Orig. Pvt. in Co.: Appt. 1Cpl., Jan. 1, 1862: Prom., 5Sgt., Nov. 1, 1862: Detailed as clerk to Regmtl. Adj.: Prom., 2Lt., Apr. 2, 1864, & transfd. to the Engineering Corps, Trans-Miss. Dept.

STRICKLAND, MACK 2Lt. — Orig. Pvt. in Co.: Elect., 2Lt., July 22, 1862: W., Antietam (Sept. 17, 1862): Died of wound, Sept. 19, 1862.

McKINNON, R. J. 3Lt. — Orig. Pvt. in Co.: Elect., 3Lt., Oct. 16, 1862: W., Wilderness (May 6, 1864): W. (face & arm), Chaffin's Farm (Sept. 29, 1864): W., Darbytown Rd. (Oct. 7, 1864): W., Williamsburg Rd. (Oct. 27, 1864): Died from wound, Jan. 31, 1865.

MUSICIANS

(1) SANDERS, J. B. — Detailed to Ambulance Corps, June, 1862: Sick, Apr., 1862-July, 1863: Died on leave in a hosp. in Ala., Aug., 1863.

(1) SMITH, JOHN — POW, 2nd Manassas (Aug. 30, 1862): Exchanged, Sept. 29, 1862: Detailed to duty in Harness Shop at Clarksville, Va., Oct., 1862: Detailed to duty as a shoemaker, Greenville, Tenn., Feb., 1864: W. (arm), Darbytown Rd. (Oct. 7, 1864): Paroled, Jackson, Miss., May 19, 1865.

PRIVATES

(1) ALLNOCH, WM. — Detailed as an ambulance driver, Dec., 1861: Sick, most of 1863: Detailed as a Provost Guard, Dec., 1863: AWOL, Dec., 1864.

(1) ATCHISON, J. M. — Died, Richmond, Aug. 1, 1862.

(1) BAUDWIN, ALBERT — Sick, Summer, 1862: K., Gettysburg (July 2, 1863).

(1) BECKMAN, JULIUS — W., Chickamauga (Sept. 19, 1863): Extra duty
(2) as a beef driver for Maj. Hamilton, Brig. Comsy. Off.: Paroled, Appomattox (Apr. 12, 1865).

(1) BENJAMIN, GEO. — Died of chronic diarrhea, Charlottesville, Va., Nov. 15, 1862.

(1) BERRY, E. M. — Dischgd. for disability (chronic diarrhea), Nov. 10, 1861: Recruited again Mar. 31, 1862 at Liberty, Tex. by Lt. W. D. Williams: Sick, Summer, 1862: Dischgd. a second time for disability (chronic diarrhea), July 28, 1863.

(1) BOOTH, JAS. — W. (thigh), Gettysburg (July 2, 1863): Disabled: Returned to Tex., Jan., 1865.

(1) BOSTWICK, J. A. — Died of disease, Dec. 20, 1861.

(1) BOUCH, E. R. — W. (head) & POW, Gettysburg (July 2, 1863): Paroled: W., Wilderness (May 6, 1864).

(1) BRASHEAR, BASIL CROW — Dischgd. for disability (chronic
(2) rheumatism), Nov. 10, 1861: Recruited again Mar. 10, 1862 at Liberty, Tex.: W., Gaines' Mill (June 27, 1862): W. (side), Darbytown Rd. (Oct. 7, 1864): Paroled, Appomattox (Apr. 12, 1865).

(1) BRASHEAR, CHAS. D., Jr. — Extra duty as Company Commissary: K., Gettysburg (July 2, 1863).

(1) BROWN, J. H. — Asgnd. as a butcher in Longstreet's Cmd., Oct., 1862: W. (hip) & POW, Gettysburg (July 2, 1863): Confined at Letterman Gen'l. Hosp., Gettysburg, Pa.: Paroled, Nov. 12, 1863: Transfd. to 8th Tex. Cav. Regt. (Terry's Tex. Rangers).

BRYAN, ANDREW — Recruited, Mar. 12, 1862 at Liberty, Tex.: Dischgd. for asthma, Aug. 6, 1862.

BRYAN, J. K. ("Dallis") — Recruited, Mar. 6, 1862 at Liberty, Tex.: W., 2nd Manassas (Aug. 29, 1862): Dischgd. for underage, Oct. 17, 1862.

BRYAN, THOS. W. — Recruited, Mar. 12, 1862 at Liberty, Tex.: W., Chaffin's Farm (Sept. 29, 1864): Granted wound furlough, Oct., 1864: Did not return to Co.

BRYAN, W. M. — Died of asthma, Richmond, July 8, 1862.

(1) BUXTON, PINKNEY C. — K., Chickamauga (Sept. 19, 1863).

(1) CARLOCK, JAS. M. — Prom., 3Cpl., Aug., 1862: Prom., 2Sgt., Feb., 1863: W. (hand), Darbytown Rd. (Oct. 7, 1864): Granted wound furlough, Oct., 1864: Did not return to Co.

(1) CHAISON, JEFF — Recruiting serv. in Tex., Feb.-Apr., 1862: W., Gaines' Mill (June 27, 1862): W. & POW, Antietam (Sept. 17, 1862): Confined at Ft. Delaware: Exchanged, Nov. 10, 1862: W. (hand), Wilderness (May 6, 1864): W. (foot & hand) & POW, Darbytown Rd. (Oct. 7, 1864): Exchanged, Mar. 17, 1865: Paroled, Charlestown, W. Va., May 15, 1865.

(1) CHOATE, PRYOR — In arrest at Jonesboro, Tenn., July, 1862: Returned to duty, order of Gen. Hood: Sick in Tex. Hosp., Richmond, Apr.-Oct., 1863: W. (side), Wilderness (May 6, 1864): Furlough granted to Tex.: Did not return to Co.

COOGAN, THOS. — Recruited, Mar. 18, 1862 at Liberty, Tex.: W., Chickamauga (Sept. 19, 1863): Leg amputated.

(1) COOKE, Dr. J. P. — Detailed to Med. Corps, June 15, 1862: Asgnd. to duty with 48th Ala. Inf. Regt., Jan., 1863: Commissioned an Asst. Surg., Feb. 13, 1863: Asst. Surg., Law's Brig., Fall, 1864.

COPAL, OCTAVE — Recruited, Mar. 17, 1863: W., Wilderness (May 6, 1864): Arm amputated.

(1) CRAWFORD, J. C. — Dischgd. on Surg. Cert. of disability, Apr. 14, 1862.

CURVILLO, A. — Recruited, Mar. 17, 1863: W. (arm), Wilderness (May 6, 1864): W. (arm & side), Darbytown Rd. (Oct. 7, 1864).

DORIAN, NEAL — Recruited, Mar. 18, 1862 at Liberty, Tex.: W. (thigh) & POW, Gettysburg (July 2, 1863): Confined at Fed. hosp. at David's Is., N. Y.: Paroled: Absent on wound furlough since Oct. 1, 1863.

(1) DUGAT, ALBERT G. — K., 2nd Manassas (Aug. 30, 1862).

DUGAT, BEASLEY — Recruited, Mar. 12, 1862 at Liberty, Tex.: Died, Richmond, May 27, 1862.

(1) FINK, CHAS. — Died of pneumonia at Richmond, Dec. 28, 1861.

(1) FITZGERALD, MILAM M. — Appt. 2Cpl., Jan. 1, 1862: Detailed to Comsy. Dept. at Warrenton, Va., Oct., 1862: Detailed as forager for Maj. Hamilton, Brig. Comsy. Off., Jan., 1864: Courier for Gen. Chas. Field, July 11, 1864.

(1) FLAKE, F. — Deserted about Sept. 15, 1861, in New Orleans.

(1) FLETCHER, W. A. — W., 2nd Manassas (Aug. 30, 1862): Paroled, Sept. 29, 1862: Prom., 5Sgt., Oct., 1863: W., Chickamauga (Sept. 19, 1863): Transfd., on account of unfitness for inf. duty, to 8th Tex. Cav. Regt. (Terry's Tex. Rangers), Apr., 1864.

FORTESCUE, C. G. — Recruited, Mar. 22, 1862 at Liberty, Tex.: W., 2nd Manassas (Aug. 30, 1862): Died of wound, Sept. 18, 1862.

(1) FRAZIER, ROBT. — Died, Niblett's Bluff, Tex., Sept. 1, 1861.

(1) GILDAY, FRANK — Dischgd. for tuberculosis, Dec. 21, 1861.

(1) GILMAN, JOHN J. — Died of pneumonia, Aug. 15, 1862, at Richmond.

(1) GOODWIN, SAM — Deserted from Tex. Hosp., Richmond, about Feb. 15, 1863.

GRIFFITH, HENRY — Recruited, Mar. 8, 1862 at Liberty, Tex.: W. & POW, 2nd Manassas (Aug. 30, 1862): Paroled, Sept. 29, 1862: AWOL, Nov., 1862.

GUEDRY, S. — Recruited, Mar. 16, 1862 at Liberty, Tex.: No other record.

GUNNING, THOS. — Recruited, Mar. 16, 1862 at Liberty, Tex.: POW, Antietam (Sept. 17, 1862): Confined at Ft. Delaware: Took oath of allegiance to Federal govt.

(1) HALL, W. S. — K., Gaines' Mill (June 27, 1862).

(1) HAMILTON, FRANK — Dischgd. on Surg. Cert. of disability, Nov. 15, 1861.

HARRIOTT, R. R. — Recruited, Mar. 16, 1862 at Liberty, Tex.: No other record.

HART, EDWIN — Recruited, Mar. 8, 1862 at Liberty, Tex.: Died of chronic diarrhea, Lynchburg, Va., Nov. 28, 1862.

(1) HOWELL, JAS. — Died of typhoid fever, Charlottesville, Va., July 5, 1862.

(1) JAMES, GEO. W. — Dischgd., Nov. 14, 1861.

JIRON, JOS. — Recruited, Mar. 16, 1862 at Liberty, Tex.: Sick furlough granted to Tex.: AWOL, Nov., 1862: Did not return to Co.

(1) JIRON, SEVAN — W. (both thighs) & POW, Gettysburg (July 2, 1863): Confined at Fed. Hosp. at David's Is., N. Y.: Paroled, Aug. 24, 1863: W., Darbytown Rd. (Oct. 7, 1864): Paroled, Lynchburg, Va., Apr. 13, 1865.

JOHNSON, JAS. — Recruited, Mar. 28, 1862 at Liberty, Tex.: W. (both thighs), Malvern Hill (July 1, 1862): Died, pneumonia, Richmond, Va., May 20, 1863.

(1) JOHNSTON, H. BLAIR — Appt. 3Cpl., Feb. 6, 1862: K., 2nd Manassas (Aug. 30, 1862).

(1) JOHNSTON, M. H. — Dischgd., Oct. 18, 1862, underage.

KAUFFMAN, MATHEW — Recruited, Mar. 12, 1862 at Liberty, Tex.: POW, Dandridge, Tenn., Jan. 20, 1864: Confined at Rock Is. Barracks, Ill.: Took Fed. oath, Mar. 23, 1865.

(1) KEY, PHILIP — Courier, Dec., 1861: Sick, Spring & Summer, 1862: Dischgd., Sept. 15, 1862 for "gen'l. debility."

(1) KNAPP, G. W. — W., Gaines' Mill (June 27, 1862): Leg amputated.

(1) LEONARD, R. H. — See preceding list of "Other Officers."

LINSCOTT, ISAAC — Recruited, Mar. 6, 1862 at Liberty, Tex.: Transfd. to Conf. Navy, Mar. 20, 1863.

(1) LITTLE, JOHN — W., 2nd Manassas (Aug. 30, 1862): Died of wound, Sept. 1, 1862.

(1) LORISCH, ALBERT — Drowned before starting to Va. at Harrisburg, Tex., Sept. 10, 1861.

(1) LYONS, G. W. — Dischgd., Nov. 19, 1861.

(1) LYONS, MIKE L. — Elect. an officer in Co. I of the 28th La. Inf. Regt.: Transfd. to new regt., Nov. 5, 1862.

(1) McCALLY, CHAS. — See preceding list of "Other Officers."

(1) McCARTY, ED. V. — Sick, Winter & Spring, 1863: In arrest & confinement in prison, Richmond, since June, 1863: Died of pneumonia at Gen. Hosp. #13, Richmond, Jan. 4, 1864.

(1) McCARY, W. L. — Detailed as a company cook, Spring, 1863: Prom., 5Sgt.: W., Chickamauga (Sept. 20, 1863): Absent on convalescent furlough since Mar. 15, 1864: Never returned to Co.: Paroled, Houston, Tex., June 30, 1865.

(1) McCOLL, THOS. — K., Antietam (Sept. 17, 1862).
(1) McDONALD, ALEXANDER — Dischgd. on Surg. Cert. of disability (asthma), Apr. 15, 1862.
(1) McKINNON, R. J. — See preceding list of "Other Officers."
    McVEY, WM. — Recruited, Mar. 18, 1862 at Liberty, Tex.: W., Chickamauga (Sept. 19, 1863): Leg amputated.
(1) MALLORY, PETER — Orderly for Lt.-Col. King Bryan (cmdr., 5th Tex. Inf.), Spring, 1863: Courier for Brig.-Cmdr., Gen. John Gregg, Aug., 1864: K., Darbytown Rd. (Oct. 7, 1864).
(1) MEADOWS (or MEADOURS), J. S. — Sick (rheumatism), Nov., 1862: Sick furlough granted, Dec., 1862: Did not return to Co.
(1) MERRIMAN, A. C. ("Gus") — Sick at Fredericksburg, Va., Winter, 1861-62: Died, Liberty, Va., July 16, 1862.
(1) MILLER, JOHN J. — Died of disease, Nov. 20, 1861.
    MILLINGTON, J. A. — POW, 2nd Manassas (Aug. 30, 1862): No other record.
    MOBRAY, JOS. — Recruited, Mar. 11, 1862 at Liberty, Tex.: Furlough granted to Tex., Oct., 1862: AWOL, never returned to Co.
    MOODIE, JOHN R. — Recruited, Mar. 10, 1862 at Liberty, Tex.: W., Gaines' Mill (June 27, 1862): Asgnd. duty as a Div. Provost Guard, June, 1863: Deserted near Russellville, Tenn., Dec. 8, 1863: Took Fed. oath, Jan. 9, 1864.
(1) MULDOON, JOHN — W., Malvern Hill (July 1, 1862): Vanished in Richmond: Reported as a deserter.
(1) NOBLES, J. C. — Asgnd. duty as a Brig. teamster, Dec., 1861: W. (arm), Malvern Hill (July 1, 1862): W., 2nd Manassas (Aug. 30, 1862): Asgnd. as a litter bearer, May, 1863: Prom., Sgt.: K., White Oak Swamp (Aug. 16, 1864).
(1) NOE, J. W. — Dischgd. on Surg. Cert. at Harrisburg, Tex., July 11, 1861.
(1) NORTON, ALONZO B. — Died of pneumonia, Feb. 5, 1862.
(1) O'BRYAN, GEO. W. — Dischgd. for measles, Dec. 10, 1861.
    OXFORD, ISAAC — Recruited, Mar. 22, 1862 at Liberty, Tex.: Died of diarrhea, June 5, 1862.
    PELON, EDW. — Recruited, Mar. 6, 1862 at Liberty, Tex.: Dischgd. for rheumatism, Sept. 19, 1862.
(1) PEMBERTON, I. W. — W., 2nd Manassas (Aug. 29, 1862): Died in Tex., of wound while on convalescent furlough in 1863.
(1) PERLEY, SAM E. — Asgnd. as a Brig. teamster, Nov., 1861 and
(2) continued on this asgnmt. entire war: Paroled, Appomattox (Apr. 12, 1865).
    PERRYMAN, R. M. — Recruited, Mar. 7, 1862 at Liberty, Tex.: Died of VD in Richmond, Aug. 15, 1862.
(1) PRICE, SAM — Asgnd. as a Brig. teamster, Dec. 23, 1861: Broke leg on march from Fredericksburg to Yorktown, Apr. 8, 1862: Detailed to Richmond Navy Yard as a ship's carpenter, Dec., 1862.
    PRUE, MARSHAL — Recruited, Mar. 7, 1862 at Liberty, Tex.: K., Gettysburg (July 2, 1863).
(1) RACHAL, DARIUS C. — Detailed to Ambulance Corps, Aug., 1862: Appt. Cpl., Feb., 1863: Granted furlough "of indulgence" to Tex., Feb., 1864: AWOL, did not return to Co.: Jnd. another unit in Tex.

(1) READ, A. J. — Died of disease, Dec. 19, 1861.
(1) REESE, JAS. — Died of disease, Nov. 28, 1861.
(1) ROBERTS, A. B. — Detailed as wardmaster at hosp. in Newman, Ga., Oct., 1863: Deserted in East Tenn., Mar. 5, 1864.
    ROSAS, SANTOS — Recruited, Mar. 17, 1863: W. (leg), Wilderness (May 6, 1864): W., Darbytown Rd. (Oct. 7, 1864): POW, Petersburg, Apr. 4, 1865: Paroled, June 14, 1865.
(2) ROSS, JOS. C. — Recruited, Mar. 7, 1862 at Liberty, Tex.: W. (leg), Gaines' Mill (June 27, 1862): W. (leg), Darbytown Rd. (Oct. 7, 1864): Paroled, Appomattox (Apr. 12, 1865).
(1) RYAN, JAS. — Asgnd. as a Brig. carpenter, Nov., 1861: Sick much of 1862: Detailed for 60 days to work on a gunboat (James River), Feb., 1863: Deserted, Feb. 18, 1865.
(1) SCHULTZ, WM. — Died of pneumonia at Warrenton, Va., Sept. 10, 1862.
(2) SHEA, HENRY C. — Recruited, Mar. 20, 1862 at Liberty, Tex.: W., 2nd Manassas (Aug. 30, 1862): POW, Gettysburg (July 2, 1863): Confined at Ft. Delaware: Released, Aug., 1864: Paroled, Appomattox (Apr. 12, 1865).
(1) SIMMONS, THOS. — Died of typhoid fever, June 27, 1861.
(1) SLOAN, JOHN V. — W. (neck), Gaines' Mill (June 27, 1862): W.
(2) (head), Cold Harbor (June 2, 1864): Paroled, Appomattox (Apr. 12, 1865).
    SMITH, T. F. — Recruited, Mar. 7, 1862 at Liberty, Tex.: Detailed as teamster, June, 1862: Sick furlough granted, Apr., 1863: Dischgd. in Tex. with chronic rheumatism.
    SPENCER, JOS. — Recruited, Mar. 6, 1862 at Liberty, Tex.: W. & POW, Antietam (Sept. 17, 1862): No other record.
(1) STARK, L. M. — Sick, Winter, 1861-62: Dischgd., Dec. 4, 1862 on Surg. Cert. of disability (chronic hepatitis).
(1) STARNES, G. W. ("Wash") — Appt. 4Sgt., Dec. 21, 1861: W. & POW, 2nd Manassas (Aug. 30, 1862): Paroled, Sept. 29, 1862: Died from wound, Dec. 21, 1862.
(1) STRAHAN, J. N. — Sick, Fall & Winter, 1861-62 & Summer & Fall, 1862: Detailed as company cook, June, 1863: Sick, Fall, 1864.
(1) STRICKLAND, MACK — See preceding list of "Other Officers."
(1) SWINNEY, RANSOM — Detailed as an ordnance wagoneer: W.,
(2) Chaffin's Farm (Sept. 29, 1864), finger shot off: Paroled, Appomattox (Apr. 12, 1865).
(1) TAYLOR, H. L. — W., Chickamauga (Sept. 19, 1863): Deserted, East Tenn., Mar. 5, 1864.
(1) TAYLOR, THOS. W. — Sick, Winter, 1862-63: W. (shoulder), Wilder-
(2) ness (May 6, 1864): Paroled, Appomattox (Apr. 12, 1865).
    TAYLOR, WM. M. — Recruited, Mar. 10, 1862 at Liberty, Tex.: Sick, Summer, 1862: Furlough granted to Tex.: Dischgd. for disability in Tex., July, 1864.
    TILTON, DAVID — Recruited, Mar. 8, 1862 at Liberty, Tex.: Detailed as nurse in hosp. at Morristown, Tenn., Dec., 1863: Deserted at Morristown, Feb. 25, 1864.
(1) TOUPS, DEMOSTHENES — A native Frenchman: Detailed as a Regmtl. butcher: K., Chickamauga (Sept. 19, 1863): Toups was the French cousin of Capt. W. D. Williams. Co. Cmdr.

(1) TRUAX, A. M. — Detailed as an ambulance driver, Dec., 1861: Dischgd. on Surg. Cert., Aug. 6, 1862.

(1) TUCKER, E. T. — Detailed as an ordnance wagoneer, Jan. 23, 1863: W. (leg & foot), Wilderness (May 6, 1864): Furlough granted to Tex.: Paroled, Jackson, Miss., May 19, 1865.

(1) TUTT, JOHN C. — W. (shoulder), Malvern Hill (July 1, 1862): POW, near Knoxville, Tenn., Nov. 20, 1863: Confined at Rock Island, Ill.: Paroled, June 20, 1865.

VARIN, PAUL — Paroled at Winchester, Va., Apr. 19, 1865: No other record.

(1) VAUGHN, A. N. — Sick, Winter & Spring, 1862: Sick, Fall & Winter, 1863: W. (leg), Wilderness (May 6, 1864): Agent for 5th Tex. Regt. Depot in Richmond, Nov., 1864: Paroled, Montgomery, Ala., May 9, 1865.

(1) VAUGHN, A. R. — Transfd. out of Co., Nov. 12, 1861: No other record.

WALKER, J. — Recruited, Mar. 9, 1862 at Liberty, Tex.: Deserted, Mar. 21, 1862, before leaving for Va.

(1) WALLACE, W. W. — Died of pneumonia at Huguenot Springs, Va., June 12, 1861.

(1) WILBORN (or WELLBORN), CADMUS — Appt. 4Cpl., Nov. 1, 1862:
(2) Prom., 3Sgt.: Prom., 2Sgt.: Received Tex. Medal for Bravery, Feb., 1865: Paroled, Appomattox (Apr. 12, 1865).

WHALAN (or WHALEN), M. — Recruited, Mar. 18, 1862 at Liberty, Tex.: W., Boonsboro (Sept. 14, 1862): Little finger amputated: Deserted, East Tenn., Feb. 25, 1864.

(1) WHITE, JOHN O. — Sick during entire 11 months of service: Dischgd., June 5, 1862 for "feeble constitution, great emaciation and debility."

(1) WHITLOCK, BENARD — Dischgd. for disability, Nov. 19, 1861.

(1) WHITLOCK, HENRY — Spent most of serv. in hosp.: Died of pneumonia, Jan. 17, 1863.

(1) WHITTINGTON, FRANK J. — Shell-shocked at Gaines' Mill (June 27,
(2) 1862): W., 2nd Manassas (Aug. 30, 1862): W., Chickamauga (Sept. 19, 1863): Paroled, Appomattox (Apr. 12, 1865).

(1) WILSON, JOHN — POW, 2nd Manassas (Aug. 30, 1862), left with wounded: Paroled: Detailed to Pioneer Corps, Jan., 1863: POW, Gettysburg (July 1, 1863): Confined at Ft. McHenry: Took Fed. oath.

(1) WOODS, GEO. N. — K., Gaines' Mill (June 27, 1862).

(1) YATES, F. O. — Sick, Winter, 1861-62: Prom., 5Sgt., July, 1863: W. (thigh) & POW, Gettysburg (July 2, 1863): Sent to the Hammond Gen'l. Hosp. at Pt. Lookout, Md.: Paroled, Apr. 27, 1864: Furlough granted to Springville, Ala.

COMPANY G — *MILAM COUNTY GREYS*

Company was organized at Cameron in Milam County, Texas, July 15, 1861 and was mustered into the Confederate service "for the war," by 1Lt. A. M. Haskell, CSA Inf., at Houston, Texas, Aug. 29, 1861.

Key

(1) Original member of Company. (2) Paroled at Appomattox. K (Killed), W (Wounded), POW (Prisoner of War) AWOL (Absent Without Leave)

ORIGINAL OFFICERS

(1)   ROGERS, JEFFERSON C. Capt. — See roster, "Regmtl. Hdqtrs., 5th Tex. Inf."

(1)   SMITH, JOHN 1Lt. — Asgnd. to recruiting serv. in Tex., Feb.-Apr., 1862: Prom., Capt., Nov. 1, 1862: Asgnd. to recruiting serv. in Tex., Feb.-Apr., 1863: On permanent recruiting serv. in Tex. since Aug. 15, 1864.

(1)   STREETMAN, SAM 2Lt. — Left sick on march to Richmond, June 25, 1862: Asgnd. to recruiting duty in Tex., Oct. 12, 1862: K., Chickamauga (Sept. 19, 1863).

(1)   BATTE, LU 3Lt. — Sick, Winter, 1861-62: Resgnd. on acct. of ill health, Mar. 26, 1862.

ORIGINAL NON-COMMISSIONED OFFICERS

(1)   TERRY, W. J. 1Sgt. — See list of "Other Officers" following.

(1)   NABORS, WM. A. 2Sgt. — Prom., 1Sgt., Mar. 28, 1862: Reduced to
(2)   Pvt., Dec. 3, 1862: Detailed as litter bearer, July, 1863: Paroled, Appomattox (Apr. 12, 1865).

(1)   GREEN, BEN. M. 3Sgt. — Enl. at 19: Reduced to ranks, Jan. 1, 1863: W. (right lung) & POW, Gettysburg (July 2, 1863): Sent to Fed. hosp. at David's Is., N. Y.: Confined at Ft. Wood, N. Y. Harbor.

(1)   JACKSON, ISAAC 4Sgt. — Asgnd. as Regmtl. wagoneer, June, 1862: W. (forearm), Gettysburg (July 2, 1863): Disabled, nerves in arm injured.

(1)   NABORS, B. F. 1Cpl. — Died of pneumonia, Jan. 13, 1862.

(1)   STEWART, J. L. 2Cpl. — Sick, Fall, 1862 & Winter, 1862-63: POW, Chickamauga (Sept. 20, 1863): Confined at Camp Douglas, Ill.: Paroled, New Orleans, May 23, 1865.

(1)   SMITH, JAS. P. 3Cpl. — Sick, Winter, 1861-62 & Summer, 1862:
(2)   Asgnd. to Div. Provost Guard, May 12, 1863: Paroled, Appomattox (Apr. 12, 1865).

(1) BROWN, A. H. 4Cpl. — Reduced to the ranks, Oct. 31, 1861: W. (arm & face) & POW, Gettysburg (July 2, 1863): Sent to Fed. hosp. on David's Is., N. Y. Harbor: Paroled, City Point, Va., Sept. 27, 1863: Dischgd. on Surg. Cert. of disability, Aug. 7, 1864.

OTHER OFFICERS

TERRY, W. J. 1Lt. — Orig. 1Sgt. of Co.: Prom., 3Lt., Mar. 28, 1862: Left on march, sick, June 25, 1862: Prom., 2Lt., Nov. 1, 1862: Prom., 1Lt.: K., White Oak Swamp (Aug. 16, 1864).
(2) WILLIAMS, EDW. D. 1Lt. — Recruited, age 37, Mar. 25, 1862 in Milam County, Tex.: Appt. 5Sgt., Dec. 1, 1862: Elect., 3Lt., Oct. 17, 1863: W. (head), Wilderness (May 6, 1864): Prom., 2Lt.: Prom., 1Lt., Sept. 13, 1864: Paroled, Appomattox (Apr. 12, 1865).
BEAN, E. M. 2Lt. — Orig. Pvt. in Co.: Appt. 1Cpl., Feb. 1, 1862: Prom., 2Sgt., Mar. 27, 1862: Elect., 3Lt., Nov. 1, 1862: W. & POW, Gettysburg (July 2, 1863): Confined in U.S. Hosp. at Baltimore: Transfd. to Pt. Lookout, Md., Jan. 23, 1864: Exchanged, May 3, 1864: Prom., 2Lt., Sept. 19, 1863: W., Petersburg, July, 1864: Retired, disabled, Sept. 13, 1864.

MUSICIANS

HERNDON, E. W. — Transfd. into Co. G from Co. C, 4th Tex. Inf. Regt., Aug. 1, 1863: See roster, "Regmtl. Hdqtrs., 5th Tex. Inf."
(1) LAWRENCE, J. J. — Drummer: K., Gaines' Mill (June 27, 1862).
(1) POOL, JAS. — Fifer: Prom., 2Cpl., July, 1862: W., Antietam (Sept.
(2) 17, 1862): Appt. 4Sgt., May 1, 1863: Detailed to work in a sawmill, Dec., 1864: Paroled, Appomattox (Apr. 12, 1865).

PRIVATES

ADAMS, C. G. — Recruited, Mar. 22, 1862 in Milam County, Tex.: K., 2nd Manassas (Aug. 30, 1862).
ALLEN, J. W. — Recruited, Mar. 15, 1862 in Milam County, Tex.: W., 2nd Manassas (Aug. 30, 1862): Arm amputated: Dischgd., Oct. 17, 1862.
(1) ALLISON, S. P. — W. & POW, Gettysburg (July 2, 1863): Confined at Ft. Delaware: Paroled, June 9, 1865.
ANDERSON, W. P. — Recruited, Mar. 24, 1862 in Milam County, Tex.: K., Gettysburg (July 2, 1863).
ANSLEY, J. T. — Recruited, Mar. 12, 1862 in Milam County, Tex.: Sick entire time in the service: Died, Apr. 28, 1863.
(2) AUSTIN, JOHN T. — Recruited, Mar. 15, 1862 in Milam County, Tex.: W., Chickamauga (Sept. 19, 1863): Paroled, Appomattox (Apr. 12, 1865).
(1) BAGWELL, C. L. — Sick, Summer, 1862: K., Chickamauga (Sept. 19, 1863).

(2)   BARNARD, GEO. A. — Recruited, Mar. 22, 1862 in Milam County, Tex.: W. (knee), Gettysburg (July 2, 1863): W. (leg), Wilderness (May 6, 1864): Paroled, Appomattox (Apr. 12, 1865).

      BASS, J. E. — Recruited, Mar. 24, 1862 in Milam County, Tex.: No other record.

(1)   BEAL, D. R. — W., 2nd Manassas (Aug. 30, 1862): W. (back) & POW, Gettysburg (July 2, 1863): Confined in U.S. hosp., David's Is., N. Y.: Paroled, Aug. 24, 1863: Appt. 1Cpl., Dec. 1, 1864.

(1)   BEAN, E. M. — See list of "Other Officers" above.

(1)   BELLER, SAM H. — W. (arm), Wilderness (May 6, 1864): Retired for disability, Nov. 1, 1864.

      BENGE, J. J. — Recruited, Mar. 22, 1862 in Milam County, Tex.: K., Gaines' Mill (June 27, 1862).

(1)   BIGBY, T. M. — Enl. at 24: Prom., 4Cpl., May, 1862: POW, Gettysburg (July 2, 1863): Confined at Ft. Delaware: Paroled, City Pt., Va., Sept. 17, 1863: W. (leg), Wilderness (May 6, 1864): W. (shoulder) & POW, Darbytown Rd. (Oct. 7, 1864): Exchanged, Feb. 13, 1865.

(1)   BLACKBURN, W. T. — Transfd. out of Co. G and into Co. I, 5th Tex. Inf. Regt., Nov. 1, 1861.

(1)   BLACKMAN, M. W. — Sick, Spring & Summer, 1862 & Winter & Spring, 1863: K., Gettysburg (July 2, 1863).

(1)   BLACKMAN, W. J. — Died of typhoid fever at Dumfries, Va., Dec. 14, 1861.

(1)   BOLINGER, F. M. — K., 2nd Manassas (Aug. 30, 1862).

(1)   BOUNDS, J. H. — Died of brain fever, Jan. 4, 1862 at Neabsco Creek Camp, Va.

(1)   BRACKEN, J. B. — Sick in various hospitals throughout the war, saw little active duty.

(1)   BRACKEN, T. E. — W., Gaines' Mill (June 27, 1862): Arm amputated: Wound furlough granted to Tex.

      BRYAN, J. E. — Enl., age 33, in Milam County, Tex., Mar. 24, 1862: W., 2nd Manassas (Aug. 30, 1862): Detailed as a shoemaker in East Tenn., Winter, 1863-64: Deserted at Strawberry Plains, Tenn., Mar. 20, 1864.

(2)   CALDWELL, L. W. — Recruited, Mar. 22, 1862 in Milam County, Tex.: W., 2nd Manassas (Aug. 30, 1862): Appt. 1Sgt., Dec. 3, 1862: W. (head), Wilderness (May 6, 1864): Paroled, Appomattox (Apr. 12, 1865).

(1)   CARSON, D. H. — Sick, Spring, 1862: Detailed to Regmtl. Adj.'s Office, Dec., 1862: POW, Gettysburg (July 2, 1863): Confined at Ft. Delaware.

      CHANCE, D. M. C. — Recruited, Mar. 22, 1862 in Milam County, Tex.: Detailed as a shoemaker in East Tenn., Winter, 1863-64: Deserted near Knoxville, Mar. 20, 1864.

(1)   CLARK, J. F. — K., Gettysburg (July 2, 1863).

(1)   CONVERSE, G. W. — Died of typhoid fever at Fredericksburg, Va., Dec. 1, 1861.

      COOK, J. B. — Recruited, Mar. 22, 1862 in Milam County, Tex.: Sick, Spring, 1863: Sick furlough to Tex., June, 1863: AWOL, did not return to Co.

(1) COOPER, W. V. L. — W., Gaines' Mill (June 27, 1862): Disabled from wound and dischgd. for disability, Oct. 20, 1862.

(1) COWLEY, BENJ. — Asgnd. as a Regmtl. wagoneer, Mar. 14, 1862: Detailed to QM Dept., Aug., 1862: Asgnd. as a Brig. wagonmaker, Feb. 2, 1864: Missing, Darbytown Rd. (Oct. 7, 1864).

(1) CROSS, ANTONIO — Died of typhoid fever at Camp Neabsco, Va., Dec. 28, 1861.

(1) CUNNINGHAM, A. P. — W. (leg) & POW, Gettysburg (July 2, 1863): Sent to Fed. Gen. hosp. at David's Is., N. Y. Harbor: Paroled, City Pt., Va., Sept. 27, 1863: Disabled & retired, Aug. 28, 1864.

(1) DITTO, ALEX. — Died of measles at Camp Neabsco, Oct. 20, 1861.

DUKE, J. W. — Recruited, Mar. 26, 1862 in Milam County, Tex.: Dischgd. for tuberculosis, May 1, 1862.

(2) DYER, WM. T. — Recruited, Mar. 22, 1862 in Milam County, Tex.: Asgnd. as an ambulance driver, Dec., 1862 to end of war: Paroled, Appomattox (Apr. 12, 1865).

EDWARDS, JAS. — Recruited, Mar. 10, 1862 in Milam County, Tex.: Dischgd. for tuberculosis, Mar. 13, 1862.

EVANS, D. M. — Recruited, Mar. 15, 1862 in Milam County, Tex.: Died of disease, Richmond, Va., June 17, 1862.

(1) EVANS, JAS. W. — Sick, Winter, 1862-63: W. (thigh), Wilderness (May 6, 1864): Furlough granted to Jefferson, Miss.

(1) FLEMING, N. H. — Hospitalized almost all of 1862 with "congestive fever, pneumonia, & debilitas": Died, Chimborazo Hosp., Richmond, Mar., 1863.

(1) FORD, G. M. — Died of measles at St. Charles Hosp., Richmond, Oct. 26, 1861.

(1) FORD, J. G. — Dischgd. on Surg. Cert. of disability, Dec. 26, 1861.

(1) FORD, J. L. — Died of typhoid fever at Chimborazo Hosp., Richmond, Oct. 24, 1861.

FRAZIER, JAS. — Recruited, Mar. 22, 1862 in Milam County, Tex.: Disabled for field duty: Asgnd. as a Div. wagoneer, June, 1863 and remained so for rest of the war: Paroled, Farmville, Va., Apr. 13, 1865.

(1) GAFFORD, J. C. — Sick, Aug., 1862-Feb., 1863: W (hand), Wilderness (May 6, 1864): Appt. 5Sgt., Dec. 1, 1864: Paroled, Millican, Tex., July 7, 1865.

(1) GARRETT, G. W. — Died of measles at St. Charles Hosp., Richmond, Nov. 9, 1861.

GARRETT, M. D. — Recruited, Mar. 24, 1862 in Milam County, Tex.: W., 2nd Manassas (Aug. 30, 1862): W., Chickamauga (Sept. 19, 1863): W., Wilderness (May 6, 1864): Leg amputated: Furlough granted to Covington, Ga., July, 1864.

GOULD, E. PETER — Enl. in Milam Co., Tex., Aug. 6, 1862: Died of pneumonia at the Tex. Hosp., Richmond, Jan. 15, 1863.

(1) GRIFFIN, ROBT. — Sick, Spring, 1863: W., Gaines' Mill (June 27, 1862): W., Malvern Hill (July 1, 1862): K., Chickamauga (Sept. 19, 1863).

(1) HAIRSTON, A. B. — K., while on leave in Alabama, when he fell from R.R. car, Feb. 6, 1864.

(1) HALE, CHAS. — Dischgd. on Surg. Cert. of disability, Dec., 1861.

(1) HARDCASTLE, JAS. — Asgnd. to recruiting serv. in Tex., Feb.-Apr., 1862: Furlough granted to Tex., May, 1863: Did not return to Co.

(1) HARMAN, ZACK J. — Transfd. to Co. D, 4th Tex. Inf. Regt., Nov. 1, 1861.

(1) HAWKINS, J. H. — Detailed as a Regmtl. wagoneer, Nov., 1861: W. (side), Gaines' Mill (June 27, 1862): Dischgd. because of wound, May, 1863.

HENDERSON, R. B. — Recruited, Mar. 12, 1862 in Milam County, Tex.: POW, Gettysburg (July 2, 1863): Confined at Ft. Delaware: Died in prison, Feb. 4, 1864 of "inflammation of the lungs" and "buried on the Jersey Shore opposite the Post."

HERNDON, E. W. — Transfd. to Co. G, 5th Tex., from Regmtl. Hdqtrs., 4th Tex. Inf., Aug. 1, 1863: See roster, "Regmtl. Hdqtrs., 5th Tex. Inf."

(1) HILL, JOHN C. — Transfd. to Co. I, 5th Tex. Inf. Regt., Nov. 1, 1861.

(1) HILL, WM. B. — Transfd. to Co. I, 5th Tex. Inf. Regt., Nov. 1, 1861.

(1) HILL, W. W. — Appt. 1Cpl., Mar. 29, 1862: POW, Gettysburg (July 2, 1863): Confined at Ft. Delaware: Exchanged, July 31, 1863: Reduced to ranks, Jan. 11, 1864: W. (shoulder), Wilderness (May 6, 1864): Detailed as a blacksmith, Feb., 1864: Furlough granted to Ga., Dec., 1864: Did not return to Co.

(1) HOBBS, O. P. — Sick furlough granted, Winter, 1861-62: Asgnd. as a Provost Guard, May, 1863: Deserted, E. Tenn., Dec., 1863.

(1) HUFFMAN, ALEX. — W. (shoulder), Gaines' Mill (June 27, 1862): Asgnd. as orderly for Maj. Rogers, May, 1863: W. (both legs), Wilderness (May 6, 1864).

JACKSON, ANDREW — Recruited, Mar. 17, 1862 in Milam County, Tex.: W., Antietam (Sept. 17, 1862): W. (head) & POW, Gettysburg (July 2, 1863): Died of wound in Fed. hosp. at Gettysburg, July 23, 1863.

(1) JACKSON, C. J. — W., Gaines' Mill (June 27, 1862): POW, Raccoon Mtn., Tenn. (Oct. 28, 1863): Sent to Camp Morton, Ind., Nov., 1863: Transfd. to Ft. Delaware, Mar. 22, 1864: Paroled, June 9, 1865.

(1)
(2) JACKSON, H. C. — Paroled, Appomattox (Apr. 12, 1865). Claimed after the war he was never absent during a battle, records substantiate his claim. Miraculously, he was never wounded or endured a prolonged spell of sickness during his four years of service.

(1) JOLLY, JOHN A. — Appt. 4Cpl., Nov. 1, 1861: W., Antietam (Sept. 17, 1862): K., Gettysburg (July 2, 1863).

JONES, A. G. — Recruited, Mar. 9, 1862 in Milam County, Tex.: Sick, Spring & Summer, 1862: W., Chickamauga (Sept. 20, 1863): Wound furlough to Greensborough, Ga., Aug., 1864: Paroled, Meridian, Miss., May 12, 1865.

(1) JONES, G. A. — K., Gettysburg (July 2, 1863).

(1) JONES, H. E. — Died of flux at Chimborazo Hosp., Richmond, Winter, 1862-63.

(1) JONES, M. P. — Dischgd. on Surg. Cert. of disability (rheumatism), Dec. 30, 1861.

JONES, W. C. — Recruited, Mar. 24, 1862 in Milam County, Tex.: K., Gettysburg (July 2, 1863).

(1) JONES, WASHINGTON — W. & POW, Gettysburg (July 2, 1863): Leg amputated: Confined in U.S. Gen'l. hosp. at Baltimore: Exchanged: Paroled, Meridian, Miss., May 12, 1865.

(1) KING, B. D. — Died, in Richmond, Sept. 28, 1861.

LANGFORD (or LANKFORD), D. J. — Recruited, Mar. 22, 1862 in Milam County, Tex.: Sick in hosp. most of 1862 & Winter & Spring, 1863: Deserted, near Knoxville, Tenn., Mar. 20, 1864.

LANGFORD (or LANKFORD), T. A. — Recruited, Mar. 22, 1862 in Milam County, Tex.: Died of pneumonia, Nov. 15, 1862.

LESTER, TRAVIS — Recruited, Mar. 20, 1862 in Milam County, Tex.: Died of tuberculosis, Danville, Va.

(1) LEWIS, JONATHAN — Dischgd. on Surg. Cert. of disability, Dec. 18, 1861.

LOCKLIN, J. D. — Recruited, Mar. 24, 1862 in Milam County, Tex.: Missing, Gettysburg (July 2, 1863): Probably killed, not reported on Fed. POW list.

LONG, G. T. — Recruited, Mar. 15, 1862 in Milam County, Tex.: W. & POW, 2nd Manassas (Aug. 30, 1862): Arm amputated: Dischgd. for disability, Oct. 23, 1862.

(1) MAYES, DAVID H. — W., Gaines' Mill (June 27, 1862): W. (leg) &
(2) POW, Gettysburg (July 2, 1863): Sent to Fed. hosp. at David's Is., N. Y. Harbor: Paroled at City Pt., Va., Sept. 27, 1863: Rejnd. Co.: Paroled, Appomattox (Apr. 12, 1865).

(1) MAYES, R. B. — W., 2nd Manassas (Aug. 30, 1862): POW, Chickamauga (Sept. 20, 1863): Confined at Camp Douglas, Ill.: Paroled, May 23, 1865.

(1) McALISTER, J. H. — Asgnd. as a Regmtl. wagoneer from Dec., 1861 to Spring, 1863: Died of bronchitis, Dec. 25, 1863.

(2) McANNICH, ELIAS B. — Enl., age 33, Mar. 22, 1862 in Milam Co., Tex.: Paroled, Appomattox (Apr. 12, 1865).

(1) McDONALD, DANIEL — Sick, Winter, 1861-62: W. (foot) & POW, Gettysburg (July 2, 1863): Exchanged, Ft. Monroe, Va., May 18, 1863: W., Petersburg trenches (July, 1864): W. (leg), White Oak Swamp (Aug. 16, 1864): Paroled, Appomattox (Apr. 12, 1865).

(1) McDONALD, ELISHA, Jr. — W. (knee), 2nd Manassas (Aug. 30, 1862): Died of wound at Warrenton, Va., Nov. 21, 1862.

(1) McDONALD, ELISHA, Sr. — K., Gaines' Mill (June 27, 1862).

(1) McKINNEY, JAS. — Dischgd. on Surg. Cert. of disability, Nov. 9, 1861.

(1) McKNIGHT, EDW. — Transfd. from Co. G into Co. I, 5th Tex. Inf. Regt., Nov. 1, 1861.

McPRUETT, WILSON — Recruited, Mar. 22, 1862 in Milam County, Tex.: Sick, Winter, 1861-62: Detailed as a nurse, June, 1864: Retired for physical disability, Dec. 20, 1864.

(1) MIDDLETON, N. D. — Dischgd. on Surg. Cert. of disability, Nov. 18, 1861.

MILLER, L. W. — Recruited, Mar. 24, 1862 in Milam County, Tex.: W., Antietam (Sept. 17, 1862): Detailed as a shoemaker in East Tenn., Jan. 8, 1864: W. (arm), Wilderness (May 6, 1864).

MOORE, G. W. — Recruited, Mar. 22, 1862 in Milam County, Tex.: Died of smallpox at Tex. Hosp. in Richmond, Winter, 1862-63.

MOORE, JOHN — Recruited, Mar. 24, 1862 in Milam County, Tex.: W., 2nd Manassas (Aug. 30, 1862): POW, Gettysburg (July 2, 1863): Confined at Ft. Delaware: Exchanged: AWOL, May, 1864.

(1) MOREY, HARVEY — W., Gettysburg (July 2, 1863): Dischgd. for disability, Nov. 3, 1864.

MUNROW (or MONROE), JOHN — Recruited, Mar. 12, 1862 in Milam County, Tex.: Died of pleurisy, Dec. 22, 1862.

(1) NANCE, CONSTANTINE P. — Asgnd. as a Regmtl. wagoneer, Dec. 21,
(2) 1861: W. (leg, bone splintered), Gaines' Mill (June 27, 1862): AWOL, East Tenn., Winter, 1863-64: W. (arm), Darbytown Rd. (Oct. 7, 1864): Paroled, Appomattox (Apr. 12, 1865).

NORMAN, P. W. — Died of erysipelis at Warrenton, Va., Sept. 5, 1862.

NORWOOD, JOHN — Enl., Feb. 2, 1864 near Knoxville, Tenn., deserted 2 days later.

ODUM, J. H. — Recruited, Mar. 26, 1862 in Milam County, Tex.: Did not join Co. until May, 1863: Missing, Chickamauga (Sept. 20, 1863).

(1) OGDEN, MILTON — Died of typhoid fever at St. Charles Hosp., Richmond, Nov. 8, 1861.

(1) PEEKS, W. W. — Sick, Fall & Winter, 1861: K., Wilderness (May 6, 1864).

(1) PEMBERTON, W. J. — Dischgd. on Surg. Cert. of disability (tuberculosis), at Neabsco Creek, Va., Jan. 27, 1862.

(1) PENDARVIS, WM. — Dischgd. at Dumfries, Va., on Feb. 24, 1862: Elect., 2Lt., 29th Ga. Inf. Regt.

POOL, ELBERT — Recruited, Mar. 26, 1862 in Milam County, Tex.: W. (knee), 2nd Manassas (Aug. 30, 1862): W. (hand), Wilderness (May 6, 1864).

(1) POOL, I. M. — Dischgd. on Surg. Cert. of disability (tuberculosis), Feb. 7, 1862.

PRICE, FREDERICK — Recruited, Mar. 26, 1862 in Milam County, Tex.: W. (hand), 2nd Manassas (Aug. 30, 1862): Granted wound furlough to Tex., Nov., 1862: AWOL, did not return to Co.

PRICE, ROBT. D. — Recruited, Mar. 26, 1862 in Milam County, Tex.: Died, Richmond, June 17, 1862.

RAY, R. A. — Recruited, Mar. 26, 1862 in Milam County, Tex.: K., 2nd Manassas (Aug. 30, 1862).

RAY, Y. B. — Transfd. into Co. G from Co. C, 4th Tex. Inf. Regt., Nov. 13, 1861: K., 2nd Manassas (Aug. 30, 1862).

RICHARDSON, S. W. — Recruited, Mar. 22, 1862 in Milam County, Tex.: W., 2nd Manassas (Aug. 30, 1862): Granted wound furlough to Tex., Oct., 1862: AWOL, did not return to Co.

(1) RICHEY, R. W. — Dischgd. on Surg. Cert. of disability (acute diarrhea), Dec. 18, 1861: Re-enl., Aug. 9, 1862 at Columbia, So. Car.: W., Gettysburg (July 2, 1863): Dischgd., Dec. 25, 1864 as unfit for military service.

ROSS, D. C. — Recruited, at age 24, on Mar. 22, 1862 in Milam County, Tex.: Appt. 2Cpl., May 1, 1863: W., Gettysburg (July 2, 1863): Finger amputated: Granted wound furlough to Meridian, Miss., Sept., 1863: AWOL, did not return to Co.

(1)   ROWE, H. H. — Appt. to Div. Engineering Staff, June 12, 1863: K., Chickamauga (Sept. 19, 1863).

SHARP, H. H. — Recruited, Mar. 12, 1862 in Milam County, Tex.: Sick furlough to Tex., June, 1863: AWOL, did not return to Co.

(1)   SHARP, J. A. — Shoemaker by trade: Detailed as a nurse, Spring, 1863: W. (hand), Wilderness (May 6, 1864): AWOL in Tex. since July, 1863: Did not return to Co.: Paroled, Sullivan's Ford, Brazos River, July 21, 1865.

(1)   SHARP, ROBT. — Died of pneumonia at Camp Wigfall, Va., Apr. 2, 1862.

(1)   SHARP, S. W. — K., Malvern Hill (July 1, 1862).

(1)   SHELTON, J. D. — W., 2nd Manassas (Aug. 30, 1862): Wound furlough to Tenn. granted, Spring, 1863: AWOL, did not return to Co.

SHEPPARD, T. H. — Recruited, Mar. 12, 1862 in Milam County, Tex.: Dischgd. for tuberculosis, June, 1863.

(1)   SHERRILL, ALFRED — W. (arm & hand), 2nd Manassas (Aug. 30, 1862): Disabled and dischgd., May 26, 1863.

(1)   SHERRILL, D. M. — Detailed as a litter bearer, Summer, 1862: K., near Howlett's House, Chesterfield, Va. (Bermuda Hundred), June 17, 1864.

(1)   SHERRILL, J. G. — Appt. 2Sgt., Nov. 9, 1862: W. (thigh), Wilderness (May 6, 1864): W. (thigh), Chaffin's Farm (Sept. 29, 1864).

(1)   SHERRILL, JAS. — Died of measles at Bird Island, Va., Oct. 28, 1861.

SHIRLEY, R. L. — Recruited, Mar. 23, 1862 in Milam County, Tex.: Died, Richmond, May 20, 1862.

SHIRLEY, T. M. — Recruited, Mar. 24, 1862 in Milam County, Tex.: Died of pneumonia at Richmond, May 26, 1862.

SIMPSON, THOS. — Enl., Feb. 20, 1864 near Knoxville, Tenn.: Deserted 2 days later.

(1)   SMALL, JOHN B. — W. (thigh), Antietam (Sept. 17, 1862): Appt. to
(2)   Division Engineering Staff, June 12, 1863: Returned to Co. G: W. (head), Spotsylvania (May 10, 1864): Paroled, Appomattox (Apr. 12, 1865).

(1)   SMITH, WM. W. — Appt. 3Sgt., Jan. 16, 1863: POW, Suffolk, Va., Apr., 1863: Exchanged, May 18, 1863: W. (chest) & POW, Gettysburg (July 2, 1863): Exchanged: Detailed to Div. QM Guard, July, 1864: Appt. Div. Foragemaster, Dec., 1864: Paroled, Appomattox (Apr. 12, 1865).

(1)   STEDHAM, J. M. — W., 2nd Manassas (Aug. 30, 1862): Dischgd. for disability (tuberculosis), July 23, 1863.

(1)   STEDHAM, LEWIS — Died of "congestion of the brain," Fredericksburg, Dec. 1, 1861.

STILES, JOHN — Recruited, Mar. 22, 1862 in Milam County, Tex.: Died, June 10, 1862, Richmond, Va.

(1)   TARVER, W. H. — Prom., 4Sgt.: W., 2nd Manassas (Aug. 30, 1862): Granted wound furlough to Tex., Oct., 1862: AWOL, did not return to Co.

THOMPSON, JOHN W. — Recruited, Mar. 22, 1862 in Milam County, Tex.: Transfd. to Co. I, 5th Tex. Inf. Regt., July 1, 1863: POW, Gettysburg (July 2, 1863), left to care for wounded: Confined at Pt. Lookout, Md.: Exchanged, Mar. 3, 1864.

(1) THORNTON, J. E. — Recruited, Mar. 22, 1862 in Milam County, Tex.: Died of measles, Jan. 4, 1862 at Robertson Hosp., Richmond, Va.

(2) TOMLINSON, ANDREW JACKSON — Transfd. into Co. G from Co. I, 5th Tex. Inf. Regt., Nov. 1, 1861: W., Eltham's Landing (May 7, 1862): Paroled, Appomattox (Apr. 12, 1865), & also paroled at Montgomery, Ala., May 13, 1865.

(1) TOMLINSON, J. B. — W. (arm), Wilderness (May 6, 1864): K., Cold Harbor (June 4, 1864).

(1) TURNHAM, R. C. — Appt. 5Sgt., Jan. 1, 1862: Reduced to ranks because of constant sickness, Dec. 1, 1862: Detailed as a Brig. Provost Guard, Feb. 27, 1864: W. (chest), Chaffin's Farm (Sept. 29, 1864).

(1) TUTTLE, W. P. — Prom., 5Sgt., Fall, 1861: Dischgd. on Surg. Cert. of disability (tuberculosis) at Camp Neabsco, Va., Dec. 31, 1861.

(1) VALLIANT, W. A. — Dischgd. on Surg. Cert. of disability (erysipelas), Dec. 24, 1861.

(1) WALKER, S. H. — Scouting duty, Dec., 1861: W., 2nd Manassas (Aug. 30, 1862): W. & POW, Gettysburg (July 2, 1863): Confined at Fort Delaware.

(1) WALKER, W. T. — K., Antietam (Sept. 17, 1862).

WARD, CHAS. — Recruited, Mar. 15, 1862 in Milam County, Tex.: K., Gaines' Mill (June 27, 1862).

WATSON, D. M. — Recruited, Mar. 12, 1862 in Milam County, Tex.: Dischgd. for diabetes & chronic rheumatism, Aug. 6, 1862.

WATSON, J. H. — Recruited, Mar. 26, 1862 in Milam County, Tex.: W., Antietam (Sept. 17, 1862): Furlough to Tex., Dec., 1863: AWOL, did not return to Co.

(1) WATSON, R. E. — Died of typhoid fever, Jan. 10, 1862.

(1) WEBB, J. W. — W. (leg), Gaines' Mill (June 27, 1862): W. (neck), Gettysburg (July 2, 1863): Died of wound at Richmond, Va., Aug. 7, 1863.

(1) YOUNG, WM. — Died of disease at Richmond, July 13, 1862.

5TH TEX. VOL. INF. REGT.

COMPANY H — *TEXAS POLK RIFLES*

Company was organized at Cold Spring, Polk County, Texas, July, 1861, and was mustered into the Confederate service "for the war," Aug. 29, 1861. Company included men from Liberty, Trinity, and Walker Counties, as well as Polk County.

Key

(1) Original member of Company. (2) Paroled at Appomattox.
K (Killed), W (Wounded), POW (Prisoner of War)
AWOL (Absent Without Leave)

ORIGINAL OFFICERS

(1) CLEVELAND, JOHN C. Capt. — Detailed to recruiting serv. in Tex., Feb.-Apr., 1862: W., 2nd Manassas (Aug. 30, 1862): W., Chickamauga (Sept. 20, 1863): Briefly cmded. 5th Tex. Inf. Regt. at Chickamauga, Sept. 19 & 20, 1863, before being wounded: Granted convalescent leave to Tex., Feb., 1864: Retired for disability, Mar. 16, 1865.

(1) MAXCY (or MAXEY), W. S. 1Lt. — Died of pneumonia in a private residence near Dumfries, Va., Jan. 17, 1862.

(1) ROBINSON, WM. 2Lt. — Prom., 1Lt., Feb. 11, 1862: W., 2nd Manassas (Aug. 30, 1862): W., Wilderness (May 6, 1864): Died from Wilderness wound on May 7, 1864.

(1) BYRD, A. B. 3Lt. — Died in Richmond, Nov. 26, 1861.

ORIGINAL NON-COMMISSIONED OFFICERS

(1) STANLEY, S. S. 1Sgt. — See list of "Other Officers" following.

(1) McALEXANDER, JOHN 2Sgt. — Died, Nov. 11, 1861 at Richmond.

(1) JENNINGS, J. A. 3Sgt. — Sick, May, 1863: K., Chickamauga (Sept. 20, 1863).

(1) HOUGH, F. T. 4Sgt. — Sick, Winter, 1861-62: Died of pneumonia at Chimborazo Hosp., Richmond, Apr. 18, 1862.

(1) McCORMICK, MAXEY 5Sgt. — K., Antietam (Sept. 17, 1862).

(1) ROSS, J. B. 1Cpl. — Died of disease in Richmond, Dec. 2, 1861.

(1) GRACE, JOHN W. 2Cpl. — Dischgd., Feb. 2, 1862: Provided a substitute (M. B. Grace).

(1) STEVENSON (or STEPHENSON), W. L. 3Cpl. — Dischgd. on Surg. Cert. of disability, Dec. 19, 1861.

(1) STONE, J. S. 4Cpl. — W., 2nd Manassas (Aug. 30, 1862): POW, Mar. 11, 1863: Exchanged: Detailed as a Div. teamster, Jan., 1864: W., Wilderness (May 6, 1864): Absent, sick, since Sept., 1864.

OTHER OFFICERS

(2) DARBY, WILLIS B. 2Lt. — Orig. Pvt. in Co.: Prom., 2Sgt., Nov., 1862: Prom., 3Lt., Jan. 1, 1863: AWOL in Tex., Feb., 1864: Prom., 2Lt., July, 1864: Dropped from rolls by order of War Dept., Aug. 27, 1864: Re-enl. as a Pvt.: Paroled, Appomattox (Apr. 12, 1865).

SPROTT, T. B. 2Lt. — Orig. Pvt. in Co.: Prom., 3Lt., Jan. 9, 1862: W., 2nd Manassas (Aug. 30, 1862): Prom., 2Lt., Feb., 1863: W., Chickamauga (Sept. 20, 1863): Retired for disability.

STANLEY, S. S. 2Lt. — Orig. 1Sgt. of Co.: Prom., 2Lt., Jan. 1, 1862: W., Antietam (Sept. 17, 1862): Resgnd. as 2Lt. for reason of "feeble health," Jan. 22, 1863.

(2) McDONALD (or McDONNELL), D. W. 3Lt. — Orig. Pvt. in Co.: W., Antietam (Sept. 17, 1862): Prom., 2Lt., July 11, 1864: Paroled, Appomattox (Apr. 12, 1865).

MUSICIANS

(2) COOPER, WM. — Recruited, Feb. 24, 1862 in Trinity County, Tex.: Detailed as a musician, Winter, 1863: Paroled, Appomattox (Apr. 12, 1865).
(1) CORLEY, P. — Sick, Fall, 1861: Dischgd. for disability, Dec. 27, 1861.
(1) McLAIN, JOHN — Detailed as nurse at Dumfries, Va., Dec., 1861: Died of typhoid fever at Charlottesville, Va., July 5, 1862.

PRIVATES

BAINES, R. R. — Recruited, Mar. 27, 1862 in Trinity County, Tex.: K., 2nd Manassas (Aug. 30, 1862).
(1) BALL, WM. — Sick, Summer & Fall, 1862: K., Darbytown Rd. (Oct. 7, 1864)"in a charge near New Market Road."
(1) BARBER, JONATHAN — Overseer by occupation: W., 2nd Manassas (Aug. 30, 1862): W., Chickamauga (Sept. 20, 1863): Wound furlough granted, Sept. 23, 1863: Hospitalized, Spring, 1864: Paroled, Salisbury, N. C., May 3, 1865.
(1) BASS, JAS. F. — W., Chickamauga (Sept. 19, 1863): W. (hand), Cold Harbor (June 3, 1864): Wound furlough granted, July, 1864: Did not return to Co.
BASS, NATHAN S. — Recruited, Apr. 2, 1862 in Walker County, Tex.: Sick in Richmond during entire enlistment: Died of intermittent fever, Aug. 11, 1862.
(1) BELL, E. R. — W., 2nd Manassas (Aug. 30, 1862): Absent sick since June, 1864: Reported to have deserted to the enemy, Sept. 7, 1864.
(2) BRINKLEY, A. D. — Recruited, Mar. 31, 1862 at Sumter, Trinity County, Tex.: Sick, Summer & Fall, 1862; Winter, 1863-64 & Spring, 1864: Paroled, Appomattox (Apr. 12, 1865).
BRINKLEY, CHRISTIAN — Recruited, Mar. 19, 1862 in Trinity County, Tex.: Died of typhoid fever, July 7, 1862.
(2) BUTLER, ALMARINE H. — Recruited, Apr. 17, 1863 in Polk County: Paroled, Appomattox (Apr. 12, 1865).
(1) CARR, JAS. — Died of disease, Dec. 23, 1861 at Camp Neabsco, Va.
(1) CARTER, G. M. T. — Died of disease at Dumfries, Va., Mar. 11, 1862.
(2) CHESSER, JAS. A. — Recruited, Mar. 18, 1862 in Trinity County, Tex.: Deserted, Nov. 7, 1863: Prisoner under Div. guard, Winter, 1863-64: W. (arm), Wilderness (May 6, 1864): Paroled, Appomattox (Apr. 12, 1865).
(1) CONNOVER, CHAS. — Died, Dec. 15, 1861 at Camp Neabsco, Va.
(1) CUNNINGHAM, PETER — Detailed as a Regmtl. wagoneer, Mar., 1862: W., East Tenn., Jan. 27, 1864: Leg amputated: Died, Feb. 18, 1864.
(2) CURRY, JAS. C. — Recruited, Mar. 27, 1862 at Sumter, Trinity County, Tex.: Detailed to Litter Corps, Aug., 1862: W., 2nd Manassas (Aug. 30, 1862): Paroled, Appomattox (Apr. 12, 1865).
(1) DANSBY, URIAH — Died, St. Charles Hosp., Richmond, Oct. 27, 1861.

DARBY, WILLIS D. — See list of "Other Officers" above.
(1) DAUGHERTY, JAS. — Sick, Fall, 1861: Died, Dumfries, Va., Mar. 12, 1862.
(1) DAVIS, W. D. — Dischgd. for VD, Nov. 6, 1861.
DOOLEY, THOS. B. — Recruited, Mar. 17, 1862 at Newport, Walker County, Tex.: Absent, sick, Winter, 1862-63: Deserted in East Tenn., Nov., 1863, took Fed. oath at Knoxville, Dec. 29, 1863.
DOUGHTEN, C. B. — Recruited, Mar. 29, 1862 in Trinity County, Tex., age 26: Detailed as a "Division guard," Apr., 1863: Paroled, Talladega, Ala., June 5, 1865.
(1) DROFFER, GEO. — Dischgd. (double hernia), Richmond, Va., Mar. 28, 1862.
FERREL, W. B. — Recruited, Mar. 29, 1862 at Sumter, Trinity County, Tex.: Died of pneumonia, May 22, 1863 in Orange County, Va.
(1) FITZGERALD, FRANK M. — K., Gettysburg (July 2, 1863).
(1) FITZGERALD, LUCIOUS — Dischgd. for disability at Richmond, Nov. 16, 1861.
(1) FITZGERALD, TILMON — K., Gaines' Mill (June 27, 1862).
(1) FLOYD, W. R. — Died in Warwick Hosp., Richmond, Oct. 27, 1861.
(2) FOSTER, MILTON — Recruited, Mar. 27, 1862 in Trinity County, Tex.: POW, Hagerstown, Md., Sept. 15, 1862: Confined at Ft. Delaware: Exchanged, Nov. 10, 1862: Paroled, Appomattox (Apr. 12, 1865).
FREEMAN, BENJ. — Recruited, Apr. 3, 1862 at Cold Springs, Polk County, Tex.: K., 2nd Manassas (Aug. 30, 1862).
(1) FRIDGE, J. R. — W., Gettysburg (July 2, 1863): Hospitalized for wound at Augusta, Ga.: Retired, Oct. 12, 1864, by Medical Examiner's Board: POW, Savannah, Ga., Dec. 27, 1864: Confined at Ft. Delaware: Paroled, June 9, 1865.
GAINES, W. H. — Recruited, Apr. 3, 1862 in Trinity County, Tex.: Dischgd. for sickness, July 19, 1862.
(1) GIBSON, B. B. — Absent sick from Dec., 1861 to Feb., 1863: Absent sick, Nov., 1863 to May, 1864: Dischgd. for disability, Feb. 20, 1865.
GILLIAM, LEMUEL — Recruited, Mar. 30, 1862 at Dayton, Polk County, Tex.: Asgnd. to Litter Corps, Jan., 1863: POW, Aug. 18, 1863 at Fairmont, Va.: Confined at Ft. Delaware: Paroled, June 9, 1865.
(1) GOREE, EDW. KING — Detailed as Surg's. Orderly, July, 1862: Furlough to Tex., Jan. 21, 1863 for 60 days: W., Wilderness (May 6, 1864): Leg amputated: Paroled, Lynchburg, Va., Apr. 15, 1865.
(1) GOREE, LANGSTON JAS. — Prom., 4Cpl., May, 1862: W., 2nd Manassas (Aug. 29, 1862): Dischgd. on Surg. Cert. of disability, Dec. 20, 1862.
(2) GOREE, PLEASANT KITTRELL ("Scrap") — Recruited at 16, Aug. 11, 1863 in Polk County, Tex.: Detailed as Div. courier, Dec. 1, 1863: W. (arm), White Oak Swamp (Aug. 16, 1864): Paroled, Appomattox (Apr. 12, 1865).

GRACE, M. B. — Substitute for 2Cpl. John W. Grace, Feb. 2, 1862: W. (leg), 2nd Manassas (Aug. 30, 1862): Absent most of 1863, sick & disabled: Transfd. to 8th Tex. Cav. Regt. (Terry's Tex. Rangers), Mar. 14, 1864.

GRAVES, JOHN C. — Recruited, Mar. 10, 1862 at Cold Springs, Polk County, Tex.: W. (thigh), Gettysburg (July 2, 1863): Absent sick since, May, 1864: Paroled, Montgomery, Ala., May 9, 1865.

(1) GRAYLESS, J. A. — Died of disease, Dec. 2, 1861 at Camp Neabsco, Va.

(1) GRAYLESS, WM. M. — Prom., 4Cpl.: Deserted, Nov. 7, 1863: Prisoner
(2) under Div. guard, Winter, 1863-64: Released: Appt. 3Sgt., Dec. 1, 1864: Paroled, Appomattox (Apr. 12, 1865).

HALL, C. L. — Recruited, Apr. 10, 1862 at Cold Springs, Polk County, Tex.: K., 2nd Manassas (Aug. 30, 1862).

HAMPTON, T. L. — Recruited, age 23, Mar. 17, 1862 at Newport, Walker County, Tex.: W., 2nd Manassas (Aug. 30, 1862): W. (leg), Wilderness (May 6, 1864): Died, Nov. 6, 1864 at Orangeburg, S. C.

(1) HARRIS, B. E. — Asgnd. to scouting duty, Dec., 1861: Sick, Summer & Fall, 1862: Transfd. to Co. K, 12th Ala. Inf. Regt., Feb. 6, 1863.

(1) HAYNIE, THOS. S. — POW, Boonsboro (Sept. 15, 1862): Confined at
(2) Ft. Delaware: Exchanged at Aikens Landing, Va., Nov. 10, 1862: Granted furlough of indulgence, Apr., 1864: Paroled, Appomattox (Apr. 12, 1865).

(1) HEMPHILL, JACOB — W., 2nd Manassas (Aug. 30, 1862): W.,
(2) Antietam (Sept. 17, 1862): Prom., 3Cpl.: W. (arm), Wilderness (May 6, 1864): Prom., 1Sgt.: W., White Oak Swamp (Aug. 16, 1864): Granted wound furlough, Sept., 1864: Received Tex. Medal for bravery, Feb., 1865: Paroled, Appomattox (Apr. 12, 1865).

(1) HENRY, S. E. — Dischgd., Jan. 14, 1862 on Surg. Cert. of disability (gen'l. debility).

(1) HINDMAN, S. M. — Dischgd. for disability (bronchitis), Dec. 27, 1861.

(1) HOUSE, WM. M. — On recruiting serv. to Tex., Feb.-Apr., 1862: Prom., 1Cpl., May, 1862: K., Antietam (Sept. 17, 1862).

(1) HUBERT, M. D. — Died of disease, Nov. 20, 1861 at Richmond, Va.

(1) HUFFMAN, J. E. — Died of disease, Nov. 26, 1861 at Fredericksburg, Va.

(1) JACKSON, BENJ. F. — Died of pneumonia at Dumfries, Va., Feb. 2, 1862.

(1) JENNINGS, B. W. — Dischgd. on Surg. Cert. of disability (debilitas & old age), Dec. 5, 1862.

(1) JETT, VALENTINE — Died of disease at Camp Neabsco, Va., Jan. 24, 1862.

(1) JETT, WM. L. — Dischgd., Feb. 4, 1862 on Surg. Cert. of disability (debilitas).

(1) JOHNSON, GEO. H. — Asgnd. as a Brig. teamster, Nov., 1861: Served
(2) in this capacity throughout the war: Paroled, Appomattox (Apr. 12, 1865).

JOHNSON, JONATHAN — Recruited, Mar. 24, 1862 at Cold Springs, Polk County, Tex.: Died, May, 1862 at Camp Winder, Richmond.

JONES, W. J. — Recruited, Feb. 26, 1863 in Liberty County, Tex.: K., Spotsylvania (May 11, 1864).

(1)
(2) KELLY, THOMPSON — Furlough granted, Dec., 1861: Present for duty, except for furlough, entire war: Paroled, Appomattox (Apr. 12, 1865).

(1) KEYS, JOHN — Enl. in Polk County, Tex., Aug. 20, 1861: Prom., 2Cpl., June, 1862: Sick, Aug., 1862: Furlough granted, Jan., 1863: AWOL, May, 1863: Reported to be sick in hosp. in Tex.

KIRBY, JOS. — Recruited, Mar. 18, 1862 in Trinity County, Tex.: Deserted, Dec. 2, 1863 near Knoxville, Tenn.: Took Fed. oath at Nashville, Jan. 3, 1864.

KIRGAN (or KERGAN), E. M. L. — Recruited, Apr. 4, 1862 at Sumter, Trinity County, Tex.: Deserted in E. Tenn., Nov. 18, 1863: Took Fed. oath at Nashville, Dec. 29, 1863.

(1) LEE, R. E. — Sick, Winter, 1861-62: W., 2nd Manassas (Aug. 30, 1862): W., Chickamauga (Sept. 19, 1863): Permanently disabled, retired.

LEWIS, G. A. — Recruited, Mar. 11, 1862 in Trinity County, Tex.: Died of disease at sick camp near Richmond, July 12, 1862.

(1) LEWIS, JAS. — Sick, Winter, 1861-62: Absent sick, Fall & Winter, 1863: Reported to have died.

LOUIS, JAS. — Enl., Mar. 20, 1862 in Trinity County, Tex.: Sick most of enlmt.: Died at Richmond, Aug. 25, 1862.

McCANN, WASHINGTON — Recruited, Mar. 18, 1862 in Trinity County, Tex.: Died of disease, June 27, 1862.

(1) McCRACKEN, DAVID — W. (both legs), Wilderness (May 6, 1864): POW, Farmville, Va. (Apr. 6, 1865): Paroled, Newport News, Va., June 16, 1865.

(1) McDONALD (or McDONNELL), D. W. — See list of "Other Officers" above.

McDONALD (or McDONELL), J. F. — Recruited, Mar. 10, 1862 at Cold Springs, Polk County, Tex.: Prom., 5Sgt.: W. & POW, Gettysburg (July 2, 1863): Died from wound.

(1) McGEE, JESSE — Dischgd. for disability (rheumatism), Dec. 21, 1861.

(1) McGEE, WM. — Died, Nov. 18, 1861, Richmond, Va.

(1) McNEELEY, JOHN — Dischgd. for disability (hernia), Nov. 8, 1861.

(1) McNULTY, FRANK — Asgnd. as a Regmtl. wagoneer, Dec., 1861: Deserted, took Fed. oath, Mar. 20, 1865.

(1) MARTIN, A. S. — Sick, Spring & Summer, 1862: Granted furlough to Tex., Mar., 1863: AWOL in Tex., since July, 1863: Dropped from rolls for prolonged absence.

(1) MARTIN, D. G. — K., Antietam (Sept. 17, 1862).

(1) MAXCY (or MAXEY), G. F. — Dischgd. for tuberculosis, Dec. 26, 1861.

(1) MILLS, JAS. H. — Died of sickness, Nov. 2, 1861, Richmond, Va.

(1) MORRIS, C. J. — Dischgd. for disability, Nov. 22, 1861.

(1) MORRISON, DAN — Sick, Winter, 1861-62: Dischgd., July 19, 1862, intermittent fever.

NEW, JOHN — Recruited at 28, Mar. 15, 1862 at Cold Springs, Polk County, Tex.: W., 2nd Manassas (Aug. 30, 1862): AWOL in Tex., since July, 1863: Dropped from rolls for prolonged absence: Asgnd. to Conscription Bureau in Tex.

OBARR, G. D. — Recruited, Mar. 31, 1862 at Sumter, Trinity County, Tex.: Died at Camp Winder, Richmond, Va., May, 1862.

(1) OSBURN, ELIAS M. — Prom., 4Sgt., May, 1862: W., 2nd Manassas (Aug. 30, 1862): Deserted, Dec. 2, 1863, near Knoxville, Tenn.: Took Fed. oath at Nashville, Jan. 3, 1864.

(1) OSTEEN, J. P. — Dischgd., Jan. 20, 1862 on Surg. Cert. of disability (chronic hepatitis).

(1) PANNEL, DAVID — K., 2nd Manassas (Aug. 30, 1862).

PINSON, J. N. — Recruited, Feb. 25, 1863 in Trinity County, Tex.: W., Wilderness (May 6, 1864): W. (chest) & POW, Darbytown Rd. (Oct. 7, 1864): Died, Oct. 29, 1864.

PINSON, J. WESLEY — Recruited, Mar. 29, 1862 at Sumter, Trinity County, Tex., age 30: Absent sick during entire enlistment: Died, on or about June 1, 1863.

RAINES, ENOCH — Recruited, Mar. 27, 1862 in Trinity County, Tex.: Dischgd., Jan. 13, 1863 on Surg. Cert. of disability.

(1) READER, JOHN — Sick, Summer, 1862: Asgnd. as Gen. Robertson's
(2) groom, Oct., 1862: Paroled, Appomattox (Apr. 12, 1865).

ROBINETT, JAS. — Recruited, Mar. 10, 1862 at Cold Springs, Polk County, Tex.: W. & POW, Gettysburg (July 2, 1863): Confined at Ft. Delaware: Paroled, July 30, 1863: W. (leg), Wilderness (May 6, 1864): Paroled, Montgomery, Ala., May 24, 1865.

(1) ROSE, HARVEY — W. (leg), Gaines' Mill (June 27, 1862): W.,
(2) Chickamauga (Sept. 19, 1863): Paroled, Appomattox (Apr. 12, 1865).

(1) ROSS, MADISON — Prom., 3Sgt.: Prom., 2Sgt.: POW, Bunker Hill, Va., July 17, 1863: Exchanged: AWOL in Tex., since Feb. 29, 1864: Dropped from rolls "for prolonged absence from his command."

RUFF, ALLEN — Recruited, Mar. 19, 1862 in Trinity County, Tex.: Died of pneumonia, Apr. 7, 1863 at Richmond, Va.

(1) SCOREFIELD (or SCOFIELD), W. C. — Sick, Summer, 1861: Dischgd. for disability, Nov. 25, 1861.

SEROIS, JAS. — Died, Spring, 1863, (date and cause unknown): Not listed on Co. Bi-Monthly Muster Roll.

(1) SHAW, J. ALEXANDER — W. (arm), Wilderness (May 6, 1864):
(2) Paroled, Appomattox (Apr. 12, 1865).

(2) SHIELDS, ISAIAH — Recruited, Mar. 17, 1862 at Newport, Walker County, Tex.: W., Antietam (Sept. 17, 1862): Paroled, Appomattox (Apr. 12, 1865).

SIMMONS, T. J. — Recruited, Mar. 29, 1862 at Sumter, Trinity County, Tex.: K., Chickamauga (Sept. 19, 1863).

SIMMONS, WILEY W. — Recruited, Apr. 4, 1862 at Sumter, Trinity County, Tex.: Died of disease (measles) at Richmond, July 13, 1862.

(1) SIMPSON, HIRAM — See roster, "Hdqtrs., Hood's Tex. Brig."

(1) SIMS, G. M. — Sick, Winter & Spring, 1862: Prom., 2Cpl., July, 1863:
(2) Prom., 3Sgt., Mar., 1864: W. (jaw & shoulder), Cold Harbor (June 3, 1864): Prom., 2Sgt.: Paroled, Appomattox (Apr. 12, 1865).
(2) SMALL, JAS. M. — Recruited, Feb. 24, 1863 in Trinity County, Tex.: Detailed to Regmtl. Adj.'s office, Apr. 20, 1863: Appt. 4Sgt., Dec. 1, 1864: Paroled, Appomattox (Apr. 12, 1865).
(2) SMALL, SAM W. — Recruited, Apr. 3, 1862 in Trinity County, Tex.: Detailed as cook at CSA shoe factory, Apr. 8, 1864: Prom., 4Sgt., Dec. 1, 1864: Paroled, Appomattox (Apr. 12, 1865).
SPIARS (or SPIRES), S. A. — Recruited, Mar. 27, 1862 in Trinity County, Tex.: Deserted, Dec. 2, 1863, near Knoxville, Tenn.: Took Fed. oath, Jan. 3, 1864.
(1) SPROTT, T. B. — See list of "Other Officers" above.
(1) STEEL, A. J. — Died of disease, Nov. 16, 1861 at Camp Neabsco, Va.
(1) STEEL, GEO. — Died of disease, Dec. 7, 1861 at Richmond, Va.
STEPHENSON, J. A. — Recruited, Apr. 3, 1862 in Trinity County, Tex.: Died, Camp Bragg, Richmond, Va., May, 1862.
STEVENSON, S. V. — Recruited, Mar. 27, 1862 at Cold Springs, Polk County, Tex.: K., Gettysburg (July 2, 1863).
(1) TARKINGTON, JOHN — POW, Antietam (Sept. 17, 1862): Confined at Ft. McHenry, Md.: Exchanged: W., Gettysburg (July 2, 1863): W., Wilderness (May 6, 1864): Detailed as a wagon guard, Nov., 1864.
(1) TEMPLEMAN, MADISON MONROE — Asgnd. to scouting duty, Nov., 1861: W., Antietam (Sept. 17, 1862): K., in skirmish at Thoroughfare Gap, Va., May 1, 1863.
(1) WALTERS, S. E. — W., 2nd Manassas (Aug. 30, 1862): Asgnd. as a
(2) Brig. teamster, Jan., 1864: Paroled, Appomattox (Apr. 12, 1865).
(1) WEATHERS, J. R. — Prom., 1Cpl., Sept., 1862: K., Gettysburg (July 2, 1863).
WHITMIRE, JESSIE — Recruited at 18, Mar. 20, 1862 in Trinity County, Tex.: Sick most of 1862: AWOL on sick furlough, Jan., 1863: Dropped from rolls for prolonged absence, Sept., 1864.
WICKS, L.,B. — Recruited, Mar. 10, 1862 at Cold Springs, Polk County, Tex.: K., Hazel Run, Va., Aug. 21, 1862.
WILLIAMS, D. R. — Recruited, Mar. 15, 1862 at Cold Springs, Polk County, Tex.: Died, of tuberculosis, Sept. 5, 1862.
(2) WILSON, ROBT. T. — Enrolled, Aug. 20, 1861, Liberty, Tex.: Sick in Tex. Hosp., Richmond, Spring, 1863: Paroled, Appomattox (Apr. 12, 1865).
(1) WOODALL, L. H. — Prom., 1Sgt.: W., 2nd Manassas (Aug. 30, 1862): K., Cold Harbor (June 6, 1864).
(1) WOODS, WM. — Prom., 3Cpl., Jan., 1862: W., Antietam (Sept. 17, 1862): W. (arm), Gettysburg (July 2, 1863): Detailed most of 1864 to QM Dept. as a shoemaker and a saddler: Paroled, Appomattox (Apr. 12, 1865).

COMPANY I — *TEXAS AIDES*

Company was organized at Independence, Washington County, Texas, and was mustered into the Confederate service "for the war," Sept. 7, 1861.

Key

(1) Original member of Company. (2) Paroled at Appomattox.
K (Killed), W (Wounded), POW (Prisoner of War)
AWOL (Absent Without Leave)

ORIGINAL OFFICERS

(1) ROBERTSON, JEROME BONAPARTE Capt. — See roster, "Regmtl. Hdqtrs., 5th Tex. Inf."

(1) CLAY, TACITUS T. 1Lt. — Prom., Capt., Oct. 23, 1861: Granted 60-day sick leave, Jan. 15, 1862: W., Gaines' Mill (June 27, 1862): Detailed to Tex. on recruiting serv., Spring, 1863: Actg. Lt.-Col. and Col. of 5th Tex. Inf. Regt. at various times during 1863 and 1864: W. (hand), Wilderness (May 6, 1864): W., Darbytown Rd. (Oct. 7, 1864): Leg amputated: Resigned, Jan. 9, 1865.

(1) KERR, JOHN W. 2Lt. — See roster, "Regmtl. Hdqtrs., 5th Tex. Inf."

(1) FRANKLIN, BEN. I. 3Lt. — Prom., 2Lt., Oct. 23, 1861: Detailed to recruiting serv. in Tex., Feb.-Apr., 1862: Prom., 1Lt., Aug. 1, 1862: W., 2nd Manassas (Aug. 30, 1862): Furlough to Tex., Jan., 1863: In hosp., Spring, 1863: Detailed to Tex., Spring, 1864, "to collect absentees": Rejnd. Co., Summer, 1864: W. (arm), Darbytown Rd. (Oct. 7, 1864): Paroled, Appomattox (Apr. 12, 1865).

ORIGINAL NON-COMMISSIONED OFFICERS

(1) DRAKE, J. P. 1Sgt. — See list of "Other Officers" following.

(1) TARVER, H. S. 2Sgt. — Appt. 1Sgt., Sept. 1, 1862: W. (thigh) & POW, Gettysburg (July 2, 1863): Sent to U.S. Gen'l. Hosp., Chester, Pa.: Transfd. to Pt. Lookout, Md.: Exchanged, Mar. 3, 1864: Furlough to Tex., Mar., 1864.

(1) HAIRSTON, J. T. 3Sgt. — Detailed to recruiting serv. in Tex., Feb.-Apr., 1862: Prom., 2Sgt.: Transfd to Co. B, Brown's Tex. Cav. Battalion (later, 35th Tex. Cav. Regt.), May 1, 1863.

(1) BARTON, OLIVER P. 4Sgt. — See roster, "Hdqtrs., Hood's Tex. Brigade."

(1) PARK, ROBT. A. 5Sgt. — Prom., 4Sgt., Sept., 1862: W. (shoulder) & POW, Antietam (Sept. 17, 1862): Paroled, Sept. 30, 1862: Dischgd., July 23, 1863, disabled by Antietam wound.
(1) GRAHAM, C. A. 1Cpl. — See list of "Other Officers" following.
(1) MONTGOMERY, S. W. ("Whit.") 2Cpl. — Prom., 1Cpl., Nov., 1862: Transfd. to Co. C, 4th Tex. Inf. Regt., Feb. 1, 1863.
(1) MORGAN, WM. O. 3Cpl. — W. (arm), 2nd Manassas (Aug. 30, 1862):
(2) Prom., 1Cpl., Jan. 27, 1863: W., Gettysburg (July 2, 1863): Prom., 5Sgt., Aug. 1, 1863: Prom., 3Sgt., Oct. 31, 1864: Prom., 2Sgt., Winter, 1864-65: Paroled, Appomattox (Apr. 12, 1865).
(1) HOLMES, WM. H. 4Cpl. — Died, Fredericksburg, Va., Apr. 9, 1862.

OTHER OFFICERS

(2) PONCE, D. R. 1Lt. — Orig. Pvt. in Co.: Prom., 3Cpl., Jan. 22, 1863: Prom., 3Lt., May 8, 1863: Prom., 2Lt., July 16, 1863: Prom., 1Lt., Winter, 1864-65: Paroled, Appomattox (Apr. 12, 1865).
(1) GRAHAM, C. A. 2Lt. — Orig. 1Cpl. of Co.: Prom., 3Lt., Oct. 23, 1861: W. (chest), 2nd Manassas (Aug. 30, 1862): Prom., 2Lt., Aug. 1, 1862: W., Gettysburg (July 2, 1863): Died of wound, July 15, 1863.
(1) DRAKE, J. P. 3Lt. — Orig. 1Sgt. of Co.: Prom., 3Lt., Sept. 1, 1862: W. & POW, Antietam (Sept. 17, 1862): Died of wound, Oct. 5, 1862.
(1) FLANIKEN (or FLANAGAN), JOHN W. 3Lt. — Orig. Pvt. in Co.: Prom., 1Cpl., Oct. 23, 1861: Prom., 5Sgt., Nov., 1862: Prom., 3Lt., Jan. 16, 1863: Died of chronic diarrhea at Lynchburg, Va., Jan. 27, 1863.

MUSICIANS

ANDERSON, R. J. — Transfd. into Co. I, on Oct. 17, 1863 from Co. D, 24th Tex. Cav. Regt.: Deserted in E. Tenn., Christmas Day, 1863.
(1) HUDSON, D. W. — Reduced to ranks & detailed as a nurse in Chimborazo Hosp., Richmond, Nov., 1861: Ordered back to Co. I, Nov., 1862, but did not report: Remained a nurse the entire war. Paroled, Richmond, Va., May 18, 1865.
(1) LEE, ABRAHAM B. — A dentist by profession: Enl. at age 40: Detailed as a nurse to hosp. at Warrenton, Va., Aug., 1862: Granted furlough to Tex., Oct., 1862: AWOL, did not return to Co.

PRIVATES

(1) ALLEN, D. B. — Detailed as teamster, Dec., 1861: W., 2nd Manassas (Aug. 30, 1862): Granted furlough, May, 1863: Reported as POW.

(1) ANDREWS, W. H. — Detailed as a Brig. teamster, Feb., 1862: Detailed for ambulance duty, Summer, 1862: Detailed as a Div. carpenter, Dec., 1862: Detailed as a teamster most of 1864.

(1) ATKINSON, J. S. — Dischgd. on Surg. Cert. of disability: Enl. in Waul's Tex. Legion.

(1) BAKER, BAT — W. & POW, Antietam (Sept. 17, 1862): Died of wound.

(1) BALDWIN, BEN. J. — W., 2nd Manassas (Aug. 30, 1862): W.,
(2) Chickamauga (Sept. 19, 1863): W. (arm), Wilderness (May 6, 1864): Paroled, Appomattox (Apr. 12, 1865).

BALDWIN, WM. GEO. — Recruited, Mar. 24, 1862 at Independence, Tex.: W., 2nd Manassas (Aug. 29, 1862): K., Wilderness (May 6, 1864).

BANNER, MARTIN A. — Recruited, Mar. 17, 1862 at Independence, Tex.: Died of pneumonia, Chimborazo Hosp., Richmond, May 28, 1862.

(1) BANNER, THOS. T. — Died of disease in Brig. Hosp. at Camp Neabsco, Va., Dec. 21, 1861.

(1) BARLOW, W. R. — W. (abdomen), Wilderness (May 6, 1864): Retired for disability, Winter, 1864-65.

(1) BATES, THOS. — W., 2nd Manassas (Aug. 30, 1862): K., Gettysburg (July 2, 1863).

(1) BEAUMONT, ALEX G. — Dischgd. (tuberculosis), Sept. 25, 1862.

(2) BETTIS, FRITZ W. — Enl., Feb. 5, 1862 in Washington Co., Tex.: Detailed to nurse wounded, Fall, 1863 to Spring, 1864: Paroled, Appomattox (Apr. 12, 1865).

BISHOP, RICH. B. — Recruited, Mar. 22, 1862 at Independence, Tex., age 25: Granted sick furlough to Tex., Oct., 1863: Disabled, did not return to Co.

BLACKBURN, WM. T. — Transfd. into Co. I from Co. G, 5th Tex. Inf. Regt., Nov. 1, 1861: Hospitalized several times during 1863 & 1864: W. (thigh) & POW, Chaffin's Farm (Sept. 29, 1864): Confined at Pt. Lookout, Md.: Exchanged, Jan. 17, 1865.

BLUE, CORNELIUS D. — Recruited, Mar. 17, 1862 at Independence, Tex.: Dischgd. (tuberculosis), July 26, 1862.

BLUE, J. HARVE — Recruited, Mar. 26, 1863 in Washington County, Tex.: Asgnd. as a courier, during battle of Gettysburg: W., Gettysburg (July 2, 1863): Dischgd. on Surg. Cert., Mar. 5, 1864, disabled by wound.

(1) BLUE, JEROME R. — Enl. at 24: Hospitalized numerous times during war for various ills including chronic diarrhea, scurvy & diphtheria.

(1) BLUE, WILLIS G. — Asgnd. as orderly to Col. Robertson: Asgnd. as
(2) courier for Gen. Robertson, Oct., 1862: Returned to Co., Dec., 1863: W. (arm), Wilderness (May 6, 1864): Paroled, Appomattox (Apr. 12, 1865).

BOYLES, DUFF — Recruited, Mar. 15, 1862 at Independence, Tex.: Died of measles at the Chimborazo Hosp., Richmond, May 17, 1862.

(1) BRADY, JAS. — Detailed as a hosp. nurse, June, 1862: Missing after Chickamauga (Sept. 20, 1863): Granted furlough to Tex., June, 1864: POW, near Rodney, Miss., July, 1864: Exchanged, Aug. 5, 1864: Disabled, detailed as a nurse in Richmond hosp., Dec., 1864.

(2) CARTER, DAN H. — Recruited, Mar. 29, 1862 at Independence, Tex.: Clerk for Brig. Asst. Adj. Gen., Fall, 1862 to end of war: Paroled, Appomattox (Apr. 12, 1865).

CHASE, OSCAR — Dischgd. for disability: Not listed on Co. Bi-Monthly Muster Rolls.

(1)
(2) CLAMPETT, GEO. W. — POW, 2nd Manassas (Aug. 30, 1862): Paroled, Warrenton, Va., Sept. 30, 1862: Appt. 5Sgt., Jan. 1, 1863: W., Gettysburg (July 2, 1863): W. (leg), Wilderness (May 6, 1864): Paroled, Appomattox (Apr. 12, 1865).

(1)
(2) CLIETT, JAS. R. — W., Seven Pines (May 31, 1862): W. (hand), Darbytown Rd. (Oct. 7, 1864): Paroled, Appomattox (Apr. 12, 1865).

(1) CONNOR, JOHN — Sick, Winter, 1861-62: Detailed to Pioneer Corps, Feb., 1863: W. (leg), Wilderness (May 6, 1864): POW, Farmville, Va., Apr. 6, 1865: Paroled at Newport News, Va., June 16, 1865.

CONWAY, RICH. N. — Recruited, Mar. 15, 1862 at Independence, Tex.: Dischgd. ("chronic inflammation of bladder"), Sept. 15, 1862.

(1) COOKE, T. J. — Sick, Winter, 1861-62: Dischgd. on Surg. Cert. of disability (hepatitis), June 27, 1862.

CRABTREE, WM. — Recruited at 33, Mar. 22, 1862 at Independence, Tex.: W. (knee), 2nd Manassas (Aug. 30, 1862): W., Chickamauga (Sept. 19, 1863): Died of Chickamauga wound, Sept. 23, 1863.

(1) CROSS, J. T. — See roster, "Regmtl. Hdqtrs., 5th Tex. Inf."

(1) DALLAS, J. W. — Enl. at 19: W. & POW, 2nd Manassas (Aug. 30, 1862): Paroled at Warrenton, Va.: Granted wound furlough to Tex.: Disabled, did not return to Co.

DAVIS, JOHN — Recruited, age 31, Mar. 17, 1862 at Independence, Tex.: W., Chickamauga (Sept. 19, 1863): K., Wilderness (May 6, 1864).

(1)
(2) DEAN (or DEANE), JOHN WATT — W. (face), Wilderness (May 6, 1864): Paroled, Appomattox (Apr. 12, 1865).

(1) DEGGS, JAS. R. — Dischgd. on Surg. Cert. of disability (rheumatism), Mar. 1, 1862.

DICK, JOHN — Recruited, Mar. 22, 1862 at Independence, Tex.: W. (arm), 2nd Manassas (Aug. 30, 1862): Disabled, granted wound furlough to Tex.: Dischgd., Aug. 12, 1863.

(1) DRISCOLL, STEPHEN S. — W., 2nd Manassas (Aug. 30, 1862): POW, Chickamauga (Sept. 19, 1863): Confined at Camp Douglas, Ill; Died in prison of tuberculosis, June 21, 1864.

DUDLEY, T. P. — Enl., Mar. 20, 1863 in Washington Co., Tex.: W., Knoxville, Tenn., Nov. 25, 1863: W. (thigh), Cold Harbor (June 3, 1864): K., Darbytown Rd. (Oct. 7, 1864).

(1) DUNN, EDW. R. — W. & POW, Antietam (Sept. 17, 1862): Died of wound in Fed. prison camp.

(2) EATMAN, JAS. A. — Recruited, Mar. 22, 1862 at Independence, Tex.: Hospitalized, Winter, 1862-63: Paroled, Appomattox (Apr. 12, 1865).

EDNEY, FERNANDO C. — Recruited, Mar. 22, 1862 at Independence, Tex.: W. (chest), Seven Pines (May 31, 1862): Dischgd., Aug. 23, 1862.

(2) FITZGERALD, BENJ. S. — Recruited, Mar. 22, 1862 at Independence, Tex.: Furlough granted to Tex., Aug., 1862: AWOL: Returned, Spring, 1864: Paroled, Appomattox (Apr. 12, 1865).

(1) FITZGERALD, ROBT. E. — Detailed to care for wounded, Winter,
(2) 1863-64: Paroled, Appomattox (Apr. 12, 1865).

(1) FLANIKEN (or FLANAGAN), D. W. — Detailed as hosp. nurse, July, 1862: Furlough to Tex. granted, Feb., 1864: Did not return to Co.

(1) FLANIKEN (or FLANAGAN), JOHN W. — See list of "Other Officers" above.

(2) FLEMING, ROBT. — Recruited, age 30, Mar. 24, 1862 at Independence, Tex.: POW, 2nd Manassas (Aug. 30, 1862): Paroled, Warrenton, Va., Sept. 29, 1862: W. (hand), Wilderness (May 6, 1864): Paroled, Appomattox (Apr. 12, 1865).

(1) GOODLETT, F. PAT — Dischgd. on Surg. Cert. of disability (tuberculosis), Jan. 4, 1862.

GOODWIN, J. B. — Recruited, Mar. 22, 1862 at Independence, Tex.: Asgnd. to mfg. shoes in Richmond, Nov., 1862: Dischgd., Dec. 24, 1862 — furnished a substitute (name not known).

GRANT, J. S. — Recruited, Apr. 1, 1863 in Burleson County, Tex.: W. (arm & thigh), Wilderness (May 6, 1864): Transfd. to 8th Tex. Cav. Regt. (Terry's Tex. Rangers), Mar. 26, 1865.

GRANT, JOSH F. — Recruited, Apr. 1, 1863 in Burleson County, Tex.: Dischgd., May 16, 1863 — furnished a substitute (name not known).

GRAVES, CHAS. H. — Recruited, Apr. 1, 1862 at Independence, Tex.: W. (hand), May 12, 1862: Prom. to 3Lt. & transfd. to Col. Chas. Bradford's Tex. Cav. Regt., June 1, 1864.

GRAVES, JUNIUS W. — Recruited, Mar. 22, 1862 at Independence, Tex.: Prom., 3Cpl., June 23, 1863: Prom., 2Cpl.: K., Chickamauga (Sept. 20, 1863).

(1) GUEST, JAS. N. — Dischgd. on Surg. Cert. of disability, Jan. 13, 1862.

(2) HAFNER, JOHN S. — Recruited, Mar. 17, 1862 at Independence, Tex.: POW, Antietam (Sept. 17, 1862), detailed to attend wounded: Prom., 4Cpl., June 23, 1863: W., Gettysburg (July 2, 1863): Prom., 5Sgt., Oct. 31, 1864: Prom., 4Sgt.: Paroled, Appomattox (Apr. 12, 1865).

HALEY, WM. — Recruited, Mar. 22, 1862 at Independence, Tex.: W., 2nd Manassas (Aug. 30, 1862): K., Gettysburg (July 2, 1863).

(1) HALLUM, JOE A. — W., Gaines' Mill (June 27, 1862): W. (thigh), Darbytown Rd. (Oct. 7, 1864).

(1) HARDY, HAMMETT — Dischgd., Feb. 27, 1862 on Surg. Cert. of disability (gen'l. debility).

(1) HARDY, JOHN H. — Died of typhoid fever at Camp Neabsco, Va., Nov. 27, 1861.

(1) HARRIS, W. T. — W., Gaines' Mill (June 27, 1862): W. (leg) & POW, 2nd Manassas (Aug. 30, 1862): Paroled, Warrenton, Va., Sept. 29, 1862: Granted wound furlough to Tex.: Did not return to Co.: Asgnd. to duty with the 20th Tex. Cav. Regt., Summer, 1864, by Gen. E. K. Smith.

(1) HARTMAN, H. L. — Dischgd. on Surg. Cert. of disability (effects of typhoid fever), Jan., 1862.

HAYNES, RICH. J. — Transfd. into Co. I from Co. C, 4th Tex. Inf. Regt., Nov. 1, 1861: W., Gaines' Mill (June 27, 1862): Died of wound, July 1, 1862.

(1) HIGGASON, R. A. — Prom. to 1Lt. & transfd. to Nitre and Mining Bureau, Richmond, June 10, 1863.

(1) HILL, GREEN W. — Died of typhoid pneumonia, Nov. 4, 1861 at Chimborazo Hosp., Richmond.

HILL, JOHN C. — Transfd. into Co. I from Co. G, 5th Tex. Inf. Regt., Nov. 1, 1861: Died, Medical College Hosp., Richmond, Apr. 17, 1862.

HILL, WM. B. — Transfd. into Co. I from Co. G, 5th Tex. Inf. Regt., Nov. 1, 1861: Dischgd. on Surg. Cert. of disability (hernia), Jan. 26, 1862.

(1) HOLMES, CURRAN — Detailed as orderly for Col. Robertson, July,
(2) 1862: Detailed as courier for Gen. Robertson, Oct. 22, 1862: Returned to Co., Jan., 1864: Paroled, Appomattox (Apr. 12, 1865).

HOLMES, JAS. D. — W., Gettysburg (July 2, 1863): W., Chickamauga (Sept. 19, 1863): W. (hand), Cold Harbor (June 3, 1864): W., Chaffin's Farm (Sept. 29, 1864).

HOLMES, JAS. L. — Transfd. into Co. I from Co. C, 20th Tex. Inf., May 1, 1863: W., Gettysburg (July 2, 1863): Died of wound, July 5, 1863.

(1) HOLMES, WM. A. — W., Chickamauga (Sept. 19, 1863): W. (leg), Wilderness (May 6, 1864): Present for duty on last Muster Roll entry, Dec., 1864.

HOLMES, WM. S. — Recruited, Mar. 15, 1862 at Independence, Tex.: Dischgd. on Surg. Cert. of disability, June 12, 1862.

(2) HOLT, A. W. — Recruited, Mar. 18, 1863 in Burleson County, Tex.: W., Chickamauga (Sept. 20, 1863): Paroled, Appomattox (Apr. 12, 1865).

(1) HOOD, A. B. — W. (hand), Wilderness (May 6, 1864): Wound furlough to Tex., Jan., 1865: Present for duty entire war until Wilderness wound.

(1) HOWELL, JOHN D. — W., Antietam (Sept. 17, 1862): W. (head),
(2) Wilderness (May 6, 1864): Paroled, Appomattox (Apr. 12, 1865).

(1) HOWELL, ROBT. N. — Detailed as a nurse in Brig. hosp. at Dumfries, Va., Winter, 1861-62: W., Antietam (Sept. 17, 1862): Furlough granted to So. Car.: Detailed to Conscript Dept., in So. Car.: Detailed to QM Dept., Aug., 1864 by Sec. of War.

HUGHES, EDW. C. — See roster, "Regmtl. Hdqtrs., 5th Tex. Inf."

(1) JACKSON, HUGH — Dischgd. on Surg. Cert. of disability (chronic rheumatism), Jan. 15, 1862.

JONES, JAS. — Enl., Dec. 24, 1862 at Fredericksburg, Va.: Procured substitute (name not known), Dec. 24, 1862.

(1) KERR, R. WALTER — Dischgd., June 17, 1862 on Surg. Cert. of disability.

KILBY, JOHN W. — Recruited, Apr. 7, 1862 at Independence, Tex.: K., Chickamauga (Sept. 19, 1863).

LIPSCOMB, Dr. M. Q. — Enl., Mar. 20, 1863 in Burleson Co., Tex.: Transfd. to Co. D, 24th Tex. Cav. Regt., Fall, 1863.

(2) LOVE, JOHNATHAN A. — Recruited, Apr. 7, 1862 at Independence, Tex.: Detailed to work in tanyard in Tenn., Jan., 1864: Paroled, Appomattox (Apr. 12, 1865).

(1) MACK, J. A. — Deserted at Richmond, Va., May 20, 1862.

MARTIN, HARMON C. — Transfd. into Co. I from Brown's Tex. Cav. Battalion (later 35th Tex. Cav. Regt.), May 1, 1863: POW, Gettysburg (July 2, 1863): Confined at Ft. Delaware: Paroled, June 9, 1865.

(1) McFARLAND, JOHN A. — Dischgd. on Surg. Cert. of disability (chronic rheumatism), Feb. 5, 1862.

(1) McKEE, H. — Died, Jan. 4, 1862 in Regmtl. Hosp.

McKNIGHT, ED. H. — Transfd. into Co. I from Co. G, 5th Tex. Inf. Regt., Nov. 1, 1861: W. & POW, 2nd Manassas (Aug. 30, 1862): Paroled at Warrenton, Va., Sept. 29, 1862: Prom., 2Cpl., Jan. 22, 1863: Detailed as a teamster, May, 1863 to Feb., 1864: Transfd. to Co. I, 8th Tex. Cav. Regt. (Terry's Tex. Rangers), Mar. 12, 1864.

(1) McNEESE, PARRIOT GEO. WASHINGTON — Sick furlough granted, Jan., 1862: Dischgd. on Surg. Cert., July 12, 1862.

(1) McREE, WM. ROBT. — W., Freeman's Ford (Aug. 22, 1862): W. &
(2) POW, 2nd Manassas (Aug. 30, 1862): Paroled at Warrenton, Va., Sept. 29, 1862: W. (head), Cold Harbor (June 3, 1864): Paroled, Appomattox (Apr. 12, 1865).

MITCHELL, JOHN — Recruited, Mar. 25, 1862 at Independence, Tex.: Left, disabled (lacerations) at Staunton, Va., June 21, 1862 & died there on June 29.

MITCHELL, ROBT. — Died at Dumfries, Va., Winter, 1861-62: Does not appear on Co. Bi-Monthly Muster Rolls.

MITCHELL, THOS. H. — Recruited, Mar. 22, 1862 at Independence, Tex.: Detailed as a Div. Ordn. teamster, Oct., 1862 to Dec., 1864: Paroled, Meridian, Miss., May 11, 1865.

(1) MONTGOMERY, T. JEFF — Died of disease, July 23, 1862 in camp near Richmond, Va.

(1) MORGAN, DREW F. — W. & POW, Antietam (Sept. 17, 1862): Exchanged: Prom., 4Cpl., Jan. 22, 1863: Prom., 5Sgt., June 6, 1863: Prom., 3Sgt., July, 1864: W. (groin), Darbytown Rd. (Oct. 7, 1864): Died from wound (bladder punctured & thigh lacerated), Oct. 26, 1864.

(1) MORRISS (or MORRIS), S. A. — Dischgd. on Surg. Cert. of disability (dysentery), Nov. 26, 1861.

(1) NEWMAN, THOS. J. — W. & POW, Antietam (Sept. 17, 1862): Paroled: Left arm amputated: Disabled, granted wound furlough to Tex.: Never returned to Co.: AWOL.

(1) PARKER, HUGH M. — Sick practically all of 1862, 63 & 64: Present for duty, Sept., 1864: Paroled, Quincy, Fla., May 24, 1865.

(1) PERKINS, DELL P. — Dischgd. on Surg. Cert. of disability, Dec. 26, 1861.

(1) PETERSON, PETER — Dischgd. for "exhausted constitution," July 25, 1862.

(1) PONCE, D. R. — See list of "Other Officers" above.

POWELL, J. W. — Recruited, Mar. 22, 1862 at Independence, Tex.: W., Wilderness (May 6, 1864): Died from wound.

(1) QUALLS, BEN W. — Dischgd. on Surg. Cert. of disability (measles), Jan. 9, 1862.

(1) RAINEY, R. R. — Dischgd., July 16, 1862 on Surg. Cert. of disability.

ROBERTSON, D. H. — Transfd. into Co. I from Co. C, 4th Tex. Inf. Regt., Oct. 26, 1861: Detailed as scout, Nov. 23 to Dec. 30, 1861: W. & POW, 2nd Manassas (Aug. 30, 1862): Paroled at Warrenton, Va., Sept. 29, 1862: Disabled, granted furlough to Tex.: Did not return to Co.: AWOL.

ROBERTSON, FRANK — Transfd. into Co. I from Co. C, 4th Tex. Inf. Regt., Oct. 26, 1861: Detailed as nurse at Warrenton, Va. Hosp., Aug. 30, 1862 to care for 2nd Manassas wounded: Transfd. to Co. C, 20th Tex. Inf. Regt., May 1, 1863.

(1) ROBERTSON, H. O. — Detailed as scout, Nov. 23 to Dec. 31, 1861: Detailed as clerk for Medical Examiners Board, Mar., 1863: W. & POW, Gettysburg (July 2, 1863): Sent to Fed. hosp. at Pt. Lookout, Md.: Paroled at City Point, Va., Apr. 27, 1864: Prom., 2Sgt., May, 1864: Retired, July 1, 1864.

(1) ROYSTON, W. B. — W., 2nd Manassas (Aug. 30, 1862): Died of wound, Sept. 15.

(1) SEWARD, COLUMBUS DIGHTON — Asgnd. as nurse for Capt. T. T. Clay, June 28, 1862: Asgnd. to special duty with Gen. Robertson, Oct. 22, 1862: Asgnd. to special duty with Gen. Gregg, Mar., 1864: K., Cold Harbor (June 3, 1864).

SHORT, JOHN — Recruited at age 19 on Mar. 25, 1862 at Independence, Tex.: W., 2nd Manassas (Aug. 30, 1862): K., Chickamauga (Sept. 20, 1863).

(1) SHORT, WM. H. — W. (arm & chest) & POW, Gettysburg (July 2, 1863): Sent to U.S. Gen'l. Hosp. at Baltimore: Paroled at City Pt., Va., Apr. 27, 1864: Retired for disability, Sept. 6, 1864: Paroled, Meridian, Miss., May 12, 1865.

(1) SPENCE, ROBT. H. — W., 2nd Manassas (Aug. 30, 1862): K., near Knoxville, Tenn., Nov. 25, 1863.

(1) STEPHENS, JERRY H. — Dischgd. on Surg. Cert. of disability (tuberculosis), Nov. 25, 1862.

(1) STEPHENS, WILL S. — Sent to hosp., Feb., 1863: Granted sick furlough to Tex., May, 1863: Joined a milt. unit in Tex., did not return to Co.

(1) SUTHERLAND, TOM N. — Died, Fredericksburg, Va., Apr. 1, 1862, "dropped dead with heart attack on march."

THOMAS, JAS. R., Jr. — Enl., May 1, 1863 in Milam Co., Tex., as a substitute for his father (Jas. R. Thomas, Sr.): POW, Gettysburg (July 2, 1863): Confined at Ft. Delaware: Paroled, June 9, 1865.

THOMAS, JAS. R., Sr. — Dischgd., Sept. 5, 1863: Furnished his son as substitute (Jas. R. Thomas, Jr.).

(1) THOMAS, JAS. W. — Hospitalized, Summer & Fall, 1862 & Winter, 1862-63: POW, Gettysburg: Paroled: Furlough to Tex., Mar., 1864: Did not return to Co.: AWOL.

(1) THOMAS, WM. FRANCIS — Asgnd. to work on R.R. bridges in Tenn., for the year, 1864: Deserted, took Fed. oath, Dec. 14, 1864.

THOMPSON, JOHN W. — Transfd. into Co. I from Co. G, 5th Tex. Inf. Regt., July 1, 1863: POW, Gettysburg (July 2, 1863), left to nurse wounded: Confined at Pt. Lookout, Md.: Exchanged, Mar. 3, 1864: Granted "parole furlough" to Tex.: Did not return to Co.: AWOL.

(1) TOMLINSON, ANDREW JACK — Transfd. from Co. I to Co. G, 5th Tex. Inf. Regt., Nov. 1, 1861.

TOOLEY, J. W. — Enl., age 39, Mar. 26, 1863, in Burleson Co., Tex.: W., Chickamauga (Sept. 19, 1863): Granted 60 day furlough to Augusta, Ga., Feb., 1865.

(1) WARD, F. M. ("Coot") — Dischgd. on Surg. Cert. of disability (chronic laryngitis), Jan. 3, 1862.

WATERS, HENRY W. — See roster, "Regmtl. Hdqtrs., 5th Tex. Inf."

WEATHERLY, SAM S. — Recruited, Mar. 28, 1862 at Independence, Tex.: Sick much of 1862: Died of typhoid fever, Lynchburg, Va., Jan. 27, 1863.

WELLS, LEWIS — Transfd. into Co. I from Co. C, 4th Tex. Inf. Regt., Oct. 26, 1861: W. (foot), Gaines' Mill (June 27, 1862): Disabled, granted wound furlough to Tex.: Did not return to Co.: AWOL.

(1) WELSH, J. — Deserted at Houston, Tex., Sept. 8, 1861.

(1) WIEBUSCH, C. — Dischgd., tuberculosis, Sept. 8, 1862.

(1) WILLIAMS, SAM D. — Asgnd. to duty as ambulance driver, Dec.,
(2) 1862: Detailed as baggage guard, Spring, 1863: Prom., 2Cpl., June 23, 1863: Prom., 4Sgt., Oct. 31, 1864: Prom., 3Sgt., Winter, 1864-65: Paroled, Appomattox (Apr. 12, 1865).

(1) WILSON, JOHN J. — Deserted at Camp Bragg, Richmond, Va., Oct. 20, 1861.

5TH TEX. VOL. INF. REGT.

COMPANY K —
POLK COUNTY FLYING ARTILLERY

Company was organized at Livingston, Polk County, Texas, in July, 1861, and was mustered into the Confederate service "for the war," Sept. 9, 1861 at Camp Van Dorn, Tex. Company included men from Liberty, Livingston, and Trinity Counties, as well as Polk County.

Key

(1) Original member of Company. (2) Paroled at Appomattox.
K (Killed), W (Wounded), POW (Prisoner of War)
AWOL (Absent Without Leave)

ORIGINAL OFFICERS

(1) TURNER, IKE N. M. Capt. — At 22, the youngest Co. Cmdr. in the Tex. Brig.: Actg. Maj., Winter, 1862-63: Selected to cmd. special battalion of Tex. sharpshooters in the Tex. Brig., Mar. 23, 1863: K., Suffolk, Va., Apr. 14, 1863.

(1) HUBERT, R. W. 1Lt. — Asgnd. to recruiting duty in Tex., Feb.-Apr., 1862: Prom. to Capt., Apr. 15, 1863: POW, Gettysburg (July 2, 1863): Confined at Johnson's Is., Ohio: Transfd. to Pt. Lookout, Md., Mar. 14, 1865: Paroled.

(1) THORNTON, SAM B. 2Lt. — Died of apoplexy, Oct. 12, 1861 at Richmond.

(1) JONES, J. F. 3Lt. — Prom., 2Lt., Oct. 12, 1861: Died at Richmond, June 6, 1862.

ORIGINAL NON-COMMISSIONED OFFICERS

(1) HENRY, B. W. 1Sgt. — See list of "Other Officers" following.

(1) TURNER, JOS. 2Sgt. — See list of "Other Officers" following.

(1) BEARD, JOHN C. 3Sgt. — W., Freeman's Ford (Aug. 22, 1862): Appt. 2Sgt., Dec. 11, 1862: W. (head), Fredericksburg (Dec. 13, 1862): Appt. 1Sgt., June 22, 1863: K., Chickamauga (Sept. 19, 1863).

(1) McKINNON, NEILL B. 4Sgt. — W., 2nd Manassas (Aug. 30, 1862): Appt. 3Sgt., Dec. 11, 1862: Appt. 2Sgt., June 22, 1863: POW, Gettysburg (July 2, 1863): Confined at Ft. Delaware: Paroled, June 9, 1865.

(1) BOYLES, W. N. 5Sgt. — Prom., 1Sgt., Feb. 10, 1862: Reduced to ranks, Dec. 11, 1862, & asgnd. to the 5th Tex. Depot in Richmond: K., Darbytown Rd. (Oct. 7, 1864).

(1) BLOUNT, TRACY 1Cpl. — Dischgd., Jan. 1, 1862: Not listed on Co. Bi-Monthly Muster Rolls.

(1)
(2) MEECE, T. F. 2Cpl. — Prom., 5Sgt., Feb. 10, 1862: W., 2nd Manassas (Aug. 30, 1862): Appt. 4Sgt., Dec. 11, 1862: Appt. 3Sgt., June 22, 1863: W. (arm) & POW, Gettysburg (July 2, 1863), left with wounded: W. (neck & left lung), White Oak Swamp (Aug. 16, 1864): Prom., 1Sgt., Winter, 1864-65: Paroled, Appomattox (Apr. 12, 1865).

(1) CRAIG, Z. Q. 3Cpl. — Died, Camp Neabsco, Va., Jan. 15, 1862.

(1) COCHRAN, J. W. 4Cpl. — Dischgd. for disability, Jan. 9, 1862: Died, June 2, 1862.

OTHER OFFICERS

(1) HURT, BEAUFORD H. N. 1Lt. — Orig. Pvt. in Co.: Elect., 3Lt., July 14, 1862: Prom., 2Lt., Aug. 30, 1862: Prom., 1Lt., Apr. 15, 1863: POW, Gettysburg (July 2, 1863): Confined at Johnson's Is., Ohio, July 18, 1863: Transfd. to Pt. Lookout, Md., Mar. 14, 1865: Paroled.

(2) ALEXANDER, J. M. 2Lt. — Orig. Pvt. in Co.: Elect., 3Lt., Sept. 13, 1862: W. (mouth & thighs) & POW, Antietam (Sept. 17, 1862): Exchanged: Actg. Regmtl. Adj., Jan.-Apr., 1863: Prom., 2Lt., Apr. 15, 1863: POW, Gettysburg (July 2, 1863): Confined at Ft. Delaware — transfd. to Johnson's Is.: Exchanged, Feb. 9, 1864: W. & POW, Darbytown Rd. (Oct. 7, 1864): Sent to Ft. Delaware, escaped enroute: Paroled, Appomattox (Apr. 12, 1865).

(1) HENRY, B.,W. 2Lt. — Orig. 1Sgt. of Co.: Prom., 2Lt., Feb. 10, 1862: K., 2nd Manassas (Aug. 30, 1862).

(1) TURNER, JOS. 3Lt. — Orig. 2Sgt. of Co.: W., 2nd Manassas (Aug. 30, 1862): W., Antietam (Sept. 17, 1862): Appt. 1Sgt., Dec. 11, 1862: Prom., 3Lt., June 8, 1863: W., Chickamauga (Sept. 19, 1863): Granted wound furlough, Dec., 1863 for 6 months: Did not return to Co.

MUSICIANS

(1) HERVEY (or HERVY), VIRGIL T. — Orig. Pvt. in Co.: Asgnd. duty as a musician, Mar., 1862: POW, Boonsboro (Sept. 14, 1862): Deserted, took Fed. oath.

(2) SANDALL (or SANDELL), W. S. — Orig. Pvt. in Co.: W., Antietam (Sept. 17, 1862): Asgnd. as a musician, Dec. 12, 1863: Paroled, Appomattox (Apr. 12, 1865).

(2) SMITH, J. WESLEY — Orig. Pvt. in Co.: Prom., 3Cpl., Feb. 10, 1862: W., 2nd Manassas (Aug. 30, 1862): Appt. musician, Spring, 1863: Paroled, Appomattox (Apr. 12, 1865).

PRIVATES

(1) ADAMS, J. J. — Died of disease, Nov. 29, 1861, at Camp Neabsco, Va.

(1) ALEXANDER, J. M. — See list of "Other Officers" above.

(1) ALLBRITTON, L. — Died of disease, Nov. 3, 1861, Richmond, Va.

(1) ARMOUR, JOHN H. C. — Asgnd. to recruiting duty in Tex., Feb.-Apr., 1862: Asgnd. as a teamster, Jan., 1863 to Spring, 1865: Unfit for field duty.

(1) ASHLEY, R. A. — W. (hip) & POW, Gettysburg (July 2, 1863): Sent to
(2) U.S. Gen'l. Hosp., David's Is., N. Y.: Paroled: W. (thigh), White Oak Swamp (Aug. 16, 1864): Paroled, Appomattox (Apr. 12, 1865).

BEST, M. W. — Recruited, Mar. 14, 1862 in Livingston County, Tex.: Sick, Summer, 1862: Sick furlough to Tex., Aug., 1862: Did not return to Co., AWOL.

(1) BOWEN, J. M. — Sick, Fall, 1861: W., 2nd Manassas (Aug. 30, 1862):
(2) Asgnd. to Brig. Provost Guard, Apr. 1, 1864: Paroled, Appomattox (Apr. 12, 1865).

BRASWELL, WM. N. — Recruited, Mar. 14, 1862 in Polk County, Tex.: W., 2nd Manassas (Aug. 30, 1862): Retired by Medical Examiners' Board, Nov. 11, 1864, because of "chronic enlargement of ankle joint from injury in early childhood." Recommended he join the cavalry.

(1) BURCH, JOS. — Died of disease, Nov. 20, 1861, Richmond, Va.
(1) BURROUGHS, T. J. — Sick, Winter, 1861-62: Prom., 4Cpl., Feb. 10, 1862: Accidentally wounded in hand, May 12, 1862: Dischgd. for disability, July 9, 1862.
BUTLER, AARON — Recruited, Mar. 19, 1862 in Trinity County, Tex.: Died, May 17, 1862, Richmond, Va.
BUTLER, FREDERICK — Recruited, Mar. 19, 1862 in Trinity County, Tex.: W., 2nd Manassas (Aug. 30, 1862): W., Chickamauga (Sept. 20, 1863): Retired, July 6, 1864 by Med. Exam. Bd.
BUTLER, JAS. — Recruited, Mar. 19, 1862 in Trinity County, Tex.: Hospitalized, Summer & Fall, 1862: POW, Gettysburg (July 2, 1863): Confined at Ft. Delaware: Exchanged, Feb. 18, 1865.
BUTLER, JOHN T. — Recruited, Apr. 6, 1862 in Polk County, Tex.: W., Gaines' Mill (June 27, 1862): Died of wound, July 4, 1862.
(2) CALVERT, J. D. — Recruited, Apr. 5, 1862 in Polk County, Tex.: W., Gettysburg (July 2, 1863): Under arrest by order of Lt. Walker, AAG, Gary's Cav. Brig., Dec., 1864: Paroled, Appomattox (Apr. 12, 1865).
CALVERT, THOS. — Recruited, Mar. 14, 1862 in Polk County, Tex.: Died at Chimborazo Hosp., Richmond on June 25, 1862.
(1) CANON, J. J. — Dischgd. for disability, Nov. 6, 1861.
(1) CARR, A. B. — Died of disease, Jan. 4, 1862 at Camp Neabsco, Va.
CLARK, B. C. — Recruited, Mar. 8, 1862 in Liberty County, Tex.: Dischgd. for physical disability (asthma), Oct. 16, 1862.
(1) COLLINS, R. B. — K., Antietam, (Sept. 17, 1862).
(1) CROUCH, HENRY — Died of pneumonia, Mar. 1, 1862.
(1) CROUCH, JULIUS A. — Sick, Winter, 1861-62: Died, Mar. 1, 1862, Richmond.
(1) DAVIS, A. C. — Dischgd. for disability (tuberculosis), Feb. 4, 1862 at Dumfries, Va.
(1) DAVIS, B. F. — Dischgd. for disability (chronic hepatitis), Jan. 1, 1862 at Richmond, Va.
(1) DAVIS, F. H. — Dischgd. for disability, Apr. 1, 1862 at Richmond, Va.
(1) DeWALT, N. B. — Died, Dec. 10, 1861, Richmond, Va.
(1) DeWALT, WATERS — Died, Nov. 10, 1861, Richmond, Va.
(1) DORSEY, C. C. — Dischgd., Dec. 14, 1861.
(1) DORTCH, L. B. — W., 2nd Manassas (Aug. 30, 1862): Prom., 3Cpl., June 22, 1863: Prom., 2Cpl.: W. (both eyes shot out) & POW, Chickamauga (Sept. 19, 1863).
(1) DUNN, ALFRED W. — W., 2nd Manassas (Aug. 30, 1862): W. (arm),
(2) Wilderness (May 6, 1864): Paroled, Appomattox (Apr. 12, 1865).
(1) DUNN, JOHN W. — Died of pneumonia, Richmond, Va., May 26, 1862.
DUNN, SIM — Enl., Apr. 6, 1862 in Polk Co., Tex.: K., Gettysburg (July 2, 1863).
(1) EASTERLING, H. A. — W., 2nd Manassas (Aug. 30, 1862): Died of wound, Sept. 12, 1862).
(1) FAIRCHILDS, A. J. — Sick, Sept., 1862 to Aug., 1862: W. (shoulder),
(2) Chickamauga (Sept. 19, 1863): Paroled, Appomattox (Apr. 12, 1865).

FIELDS, RANDOLPH R. — Recruited, Mar. 8, 1862 in Liberty County, Tex.: Deserted, Howard's Gap, Tenn., Mar. 27, 1864.

(1) FIELDS, V. B. — Dischgd. on Surg. Cert., Dec. 26, 1861, Richmond.

FIELDS, W. H. H. — Recruited, Mar. 8, 1862 in Liberty County, Tex.: W. (chest & shoulder) & POW, Gettysburg (July 2, 1863): Died of wound in Fed. hospital.

(1) FORD, J. F. — W. (left hip & right thigh) & POW, Gettysburg (July 2,
(2) 1863): Exchanged, Sept. 25, 1863: Prom., 4Cpl.: W. (head), Chaffin's Farm (Sept. 29, 1864): Paroled, Appomattox (Apr. 12, 1865).

(1) FRASIER (or FRAZIER), WM. — AWOL, Sept., 1861: Reported to have deserted.

(1) GIEGER, JOHN B. — Transfd. from Co. K, 5th Tex. Inf. to Co. K, 4th Tex. Inf., Dec. 7, 1861.

(1) GREEN, A. B. — Salesman by occupation: Prom., 2Cpl., Feb. 10,
(2) 1862: W., 2nd Manassas (Aug. 30, 1862): Prom., 1Cpl., June 22, 1863: Prom., 5Sgt., Apr. 1, 1864: W. (arm & side), Wilderness (May 6, 1864): Paroled, Appomattox (Apr. 12, 1865).

(1) GREEN, H. R. — Dischgd. for disability (tuberculosis), Dec. 10, 1861.

(1) HAM, GEO. W. — Sick, Winter & Spring, 1862: POW, Boonsboro (Sept. 14, 1862): Confined at Ft. Delaware: Exchanged at Aikens Landing, Va., Nov. 10, 1862: Transfd. from Co. K, 5th Tex. Inf. to Co. B, 1st Tex. Inf., Mar. 1, 1863.

HENDLEY, J. A. — Recruited, Mar. 8, 1862 in Liberty County, Tex.: Died, near Richmond, July 24, 1862.

(1) HENDLEY, W. D. C. — Enl. at 22: Sick, Fall, 1861: W., Antietam
(2) (Sept. 17, 1862): Granted wound furlough: Paroled, Appomattox (Apr. 12, 1865).

(1) HENRY, THOS. W. — Sick with typhoid fever, Fall, 1861: K., Wilderness (May 6, 1864).

(1) HERVEY (or HERVY), VIRGIL T. — See list of "Musicians" above.

HESTER, JASPER N. — Recruited, Mar. 19, 1862 in Trinity County, Tex.: Sick, Spring & Summer, 1863: Dischgd. for disability (ulcer of the cornea), Nov. 2, 1863.

(1) HICKS, A. — Died of disease, Nov. 15, 1861, Richmond, Va.

(1) HIRAMS, HENRY C. — Enl. at 24: Sick, Winter, 1861-62: W.,
(2) Antietam (Sept. 17, 1862): Granted wound furlough: W. (hand), Wilderness (May 6, 1864): Granted wound furlough: Detailed to Div. Supply Train, Nov. 1, 1864: Paroled, Appomattox (Apr. 12, 1865).

(1) HIRAMS, S. C. — Sick, Fall, 1861: Dischgd. for sickness, Jan. 4, 1862.

HOBBS, JAS. D. — Recruited, Mar. 8, 1862 in Liberty County, Tex.: Died of disease, Richmond, Va., June 6, 1862.

(1) HOLTON, D. — Died of disease, Dumfries, Va., Jan. 11, 1862.

(1) HUBERT, BENJ. C. — Detailed as a shoemaker, June, 1863 to May, 1864: W. (leg), Wilderness (May 6, 1864): "Deserted to enemy near Chaffin's Farm," Va., Aug. 9, 1864.

(2) HUBERT, MARK A. — Recruited, Mar. 21, 1863 in Livingston County, Tex.: W. (thigh) & POW, Gettysburg (July 2, 1863): Exchanged: W., Aug. 8, 1864, near Richmond: Paroled, Appomattox (Apr. 12, 1865).

(1) HUDSON, E. T. — Died, Jan. 11, 1862 at Camp Neabsco, Va.
(1) HURT, BEAUFORD H. N. — See list of "Other Officers" above.
(1) HUTTON, G. A. — Dischgd. for heart trouble, Nov. 21, 1861.
(1) JEWELL, WM. E. — Sick constantly throughout war: Sick furlough granted, Aug., 1862: Took Fed. oath at Chattanooga, Tenn., Nov. 18, 1863.
(1) JOHNSON, J. H. — Dischgd. for disability, Dec. 14, 1861.
    JONES, J. M. — Recruited, Mar. 13, 1862 in Polk County, Tex.: Sent to rear sick, Oct. 29, 1862: POW, Chester Gap, Va., July 21, 1863: Confined at Pt. Lookout, Md.: Exchanged, Nov. 1, 1864.
(1) JULIEN (or JULIAN), E. H. — Sick, Fall, 1861: Deserted, Zollicoffer, Tenn., Apr. 14, 1864.
(1) JULIEN (or JULIAN), JOHN — POW, Gettysburg (July 2, 1863): Confined at Ft. Delaware, Md.: Paroled, June 9, 1865.
(1) KALE, JOHN P. — Asgnd. as a nurse, Fall, 1861: W., 2nd Manassas (Aug. 30, 1862): Procured a substitute (name unknown), Oct. 29, 1862.
    KEITH, JOHN C. — Recruited, Apr. 4, 1862 in Polk County, Tex.: POW, Gettysburg (July 2, 1863): Confined at Ft. Delaware: Paroled: Deserted, Howard's Gap, Tenn., Mar. 27, 1864.
(1) KILLINGSWORTH, J. M. — Died of disease, Nov. 5, 1861, Richmond, Va.
(2) KIRKLAND, E. — Recruited, Mar. 21, 1863 in Livingston County, Tex.: Sick, Winter, 1863-64: Paroled, Appomattox (Apr. 12, 1865).
(1) KNOX, A. Z. — Detailed as hosp. nurse, Fall, 1861: Died of acute diarrhea, Richmond, Va., Apr. 18, 1862.
    LEWIS, GEO. W. — Recruited, Mar. 28, 1862 in Polk County, Tex.: Dischgd. for chronic bronchitis, Richmond, Va., Aug. 26, 1862.
(1) LEWIS, J. M. — Died, Nov. 17, 1861, Richmond, Va.
    LOCKHEART (or LOCKHART), C. H. — Recruited, Mar. 8, 1862 in Polk County, Tex.: W., Eltham's Landing (May 7, 1862): Fingers cut off in accident, Aug. 7, 1862: AWOL in Tex., since Dec., 1862: Never returned to Co.
    LOCKHEART (or LOCKHART), J. W. — Recruited, Mar. 8, 1862 in Polk County, Tex.: Died of disease, Richmond, Summer, 1862.
    LOCKHEART (or LOCKHART), WESLEY — Recruited, Mar. 28, 1862 in Polk County, Tex.: Died of disease, Richmond, Va., June 6, 1862.
(1) LOTT, J. T. — Dischgd. for tuberculosis, Richmond, Va., Aug. 26, 1862.
(1) MATTHEWS, JOHN W. — POW, Gettysburg (July 2, 1863): Confined at Ft. Delaware: Paroled, June 9, 1865.
(1) MATTHEWS, T. C. — W., 2nd Manassas (Aug. 30, 1862): Under arrest, Winter, 1862: K., Gettysburg (July 2, 1863).
(1) MATTHEWS, W. H. — POW, Gettysburg (July 2, 1863): Confined at Ft. Delaware: Paroled, June 9, 1865.
    McCLENNY, ELIJAH C. — Recruited, Mar. 8, 1862 in Polk County, Tex.: Died of disease, Richmond, Va., Summer, 1862.
(1) McCORMICK, W. J. — Sick, Fall, 1861: AWOL, Fall, 1862: Dischgd. on Surg. Cert., Dec. 2, 1861, Richmond, Va.

(1) McCOY, J. W. — W., 2nd Manassas (Aug. 30, 1862): POW, Chickamauga (Sept. 19, 1863): Confined at Camp Douglas, Ill.: Paroled, May 23, 1865.

(1) McCOY, W. J. — Dischgd. (chronic ulcer), Nov. 20, 1861.

(1) McCRORY, T. W. — Sick, Winter, 1861-62: K., Wilderness (May 6, 1864).

(1) McDONALD, WM. M. — Detailed to Div. Comsy. Dept., June, 1864:
(2) Paroled, Appomattox (Apr. 12, 1865).

(1) McKEE, JOHN FRANCIS — W., 2nd Manassas (Aug. 30, 1862): Hospitalized, Spring & Summer, 1863: K., Wilderness (May 6, 1864).

MEECE, CALVIN W. — Transfd. into Co. K, 5th Tex. Inf., From Co. B, 1st Tex. Inf., Mar. 1, 1863: POW, Gettysburg (July 2, 1863): Died as POW at Ft. Delaware, Md., June 15, 1864.

MEECE, J. P. — Recruited, Mar. 21, 1863 in Livingston County, Tex.: W. & POW, Gettysburg (July 2, 1863): Died of wound in prison camp.

(1) MEEKINS, BEN. F. — Sick, Winter, 1861-62: W., 2nd Manassas (Aug.
(2) 30, 1862): POW, Gettysburg (July 2, 1863): Confined at Ft. McHenry: Exchanged, Sept. 18, 1864: On "parole furlough," Sept. 20, 1864: Paroled, Appomattox (Apr. 12, 1865).

MYERS, B. G. — Recruited, Apr. 5, 1862 in Polk County, Tex.: Died of disease, Richmond, Va., June 3, 1862.

NAULTY, THOS. — Enl., Oct. 16, 1861 at Richmond: Detailed as nurse at Dumfries, Va., Feb., 1862: Sick, Spring, 1862: Dischgd. for heart trouble, June 21, 1862.

(1) NETTLES, J. H. — Died, Nov. 29, 1861 at Camp Neabsco, Va.

(1) NETTLES, W. D. S. — Furlough, Winter, 1862-63: W., Chickamauga (Sept. 19, 1863): AWOL, East Tenn., near Howard's Gap, Mar. 27, 1864: Did not return to Co.

(1) OATS, NATHAN — See roster, "Regmtl. Hdqtrs., 5th Tex. Inf."

OATS, W. J. — Recruited, Mar. 21, 1863 in Livingston County, Tex.: Died of pneumonia at Gen'l. Receiving Hosp., Gordonsville, Va., June 18, 1863.

OLIVER, JOS. G. — Recruited at 36, Apr. 10, 1862 in LaGrand County, Tex.: Detached service as a harness maker, May, 1862 to July, 1864: Deserted to enemy at New Market Heights, Va., Sept. 11, 1864: Took Fed. oath at Wash., D.C., Sept. 15, 1864.

(1) PEEBLES, JAS. W. — Sick, Winter, 1861-62: W., Gaines' Mill (June 27, 1862): Granted wound furlough: Jaw fractured, Apr., 1864: Returned to Co. for "light duty", Sept., 1864: Retired by Med. Exam. Bd., Dec. 6, 1864 & asgnd. to Invalid Corps in Tex.

(1) PIERROT, GUSTAVUS — Left to nurse wounded at 2nd Manassas (Aug. 30, 1862): K., Cold Harbor (June 3, 1864).

(1) REESE, J. F. — Died, Fredericksburg, Va., Jan. 11, 1862.

(1) RITCHIE (or RICHY), A. H. — Dischgd. on Surg. Cert., Dec. 26, 1861, Richmond, Va.

(1) RITTER, LEWIS — Died of tuberculosis, Nov. 19, 1861, Richmond, Va.

(1) ROANE (or RHONE), JERRY — Dischgd., Nov. 7, 1861: Re-enl., Mar. 31, 1862 in Polk County, Tex.: W., 2nd Manassas (Aug. 30, 1862): Dischgd. on Surg. Cert. of disability, Mar. 21, 1864.

(1) ROWE, DENNIS A. — W., 2nd Manassas (Aug. 30, 1862): Appt. 5Sgt.,
(2) Dec. 11, 1862: W., Apr. 10, 1863, near Suffolk, Va.: Appt. 4Sgt., June 22, 1863: W., Gettysburg (July 2, 1863): Prom., 3Sgt.: W. (leg), Wilderness (May 6, 1864): W. (hand & thigh), Darbytown Rd. (Oct. 7, 1864): Paroled, Appomattox (Apr. 12, 1865).

(1) SALLES, B. A. — Transfd., Nov. 9, 1861 to Donaldson's Flying Arty., La. Vols.: No other information.

(1) SANDALL (or SANDELL), W. S. — See list of "Musicians" above.

(1) SAWYER, JOS. H. — Nurse in Chimborazo Hosp., Richmond, Fall, 1861: AWOL, in Tex. since July, 1863: Deserted at Resaca, Ga., Dec., 1863: Took Fed. oath, Jan. 4, 1864.

(1) SCHOOLER, SAM — Dischgd. for disability, Dec. 2, 1861.

(1) SIMPSON, L. — Died of measles, Nov. 20, 1861, Richmond, Va.

SLATTER, LEWIS W. — Recruited, Mar. 17, 1862 in Polk County, Tex.: Died, Aug., 1862 at St. Francis De Sales Hosp. in Richmond.

(1) SMITH, J. P. — W., Gaines' Mill (June 27, 1862): Detailed as a teamster, Feb., 1863.

(1) SMITH, J. WESLEY — See list of "Musicians" above.

SOUTH, N. J. — Recruited, Apr. 5, 1862 in Polk County, Tex.: Died, Danville, Va. hosp., May 17, 1863 of bronchitis: Personal effects included "8 plugs of tobacco."

(1) SPEIGHTS, C. A. — Died, Dec. 15, 1861, Richmond, Va.

(1) STARLING, JOHN — Died, Dec. 2, 1861, Richmond, Va.

(2) STEPHENSON, URIAH P. — Recruited, Mar. 22, 1862 in Liberty County, Tex.: W. (head), Cold Harbor (June 3, 1864): W. (leg), Chaffin's Farm (Sept. 29, 1864): Paroled, Appomattox (Apr. 12, 1865).

STERLING, MALCOM — Recruited, Mar. 15, 1862 in Polk County, Tex.: Nursed wounded after 2nd Manassas (Aug. 30, 1864): Dischgd. for heart trouble, July 31, 1863.

(1) STEVENS, ISAAC ("Ike") — Nurse in Johnson's Hosp., Dumfries, Va., Nov., 1861: Dischgd., June 17, 1862 for "bronchitis, spinal disease and kidney trouble."

STEVENS, JOHN W. — Recruited, Mar. 9, 1862 in Liberty County, Tex.: Appt. 4Cpl., Oct. 1, 1862: Appt. 2Cpl., June 22, 1863: POW, Gettysburg (July 2, 1863): Confined at Ft. Delaware: Exchanged: Prom., 1Cpl., May, 1864.

(1) STEWART, WILEY — W., 2nd Manassas (Aug. 29-30, 1862): Died in Howard Grove Hosp., Va., Feb. 6, 1863 of smallpox.

(1) SUTTLES, ISAAC — Died, Dec. 14, 1861, Richmond, Va.: Personal effects, $5.00.

(1) TOWNS, JOHN R. — Sick, Winter, 1861-62: Appt. 4Cpl., June 22, 1863: POW, Gettysburg (July 2, 1863): Confined at Ft. Delaware: Paroled, June 9, 1865.

TREADWAY, RICHARD — Recruited, Mar. 8, 1862 in Polk County, Tex.: Died of pneumonia, Dec. 26, 1862.

TURNER, C. H. — Recruited, Mar. 21, 1863 in Livingston County, Tex.: Hospitalized most of 1863: Sick furlough, Apr., 1864: Retired for chronic diarrhea, Mar. 22, 1865.

(1) TURNER, W. H. — Dischgd., Aug. 7, 1862, Richmond, Va.: Not listed on Co. Bi-Monthly Muster Roll.

(1) WALDROP, S. D. — W. (mouth), Gaines' Mill (June 27, 1862):
(2) "Straggled out of fight of Manassas" (Aug. 30, 1862): W. (leg), Wilderness (May 6, 1864): Paroled, Appomattox (Apr. 12, 1865).

(1) WALKER, J. A. — Died (pneumonia), Oct. 31, 1861 in Warwick Hosp., Richmond, Va.

(1) WALKER, WM. A. — W., Antietam (Sept. 17, 1862): Died of wound, Oct. 3, 1862.

(1) WARD, W. J. — W., 2nd Manassas (Aug. 30, 1862): Died of wound, Sept. 12, 1862.

WILEY, NELSON — Recruited, Mar. 19, 1862 in Trinity County, Tex.: W., Boonsboro (Sept. 14, 1862): W. (abdomen), Wilderness (May 6, 1864): Died from wound.

WILSON, J. B. — Recruited, Feb. 26, 1862 in Monroe, La.: W., Freeman's Ford (Aug. 22, 1862): Died of wound, Lynchburg, Va., Oct. 25, 1862.

WILSON, W. W. — Recruited, Mar. 8, 1862 in Liberty County, Tex.: Died, Richmond, Va., Spring, 1862.

(2) YOUNG, WES B. — Recruited, Mar. 29, 1862 in Polk County, Tex.: W. (thigh), Wilderness (May 6, 1864): W. (leg), Chaffin's Farm (Sept. 29, 1864): Paroled, Appomattox (Apr. 12, 1865).

3RD ARK. VOL. INF. REGT.

SHORT HISTORY

The 3rd Arkansas Volunteer Infantry Regiment developed from Captains Van H. Manning's and William H. Tebbs' Companies that were organized in Ashley County, Arkansas in the Spring of 1861. These two companies were initially mustered on May 20, 1861 at Portland (Ashley County), Arkansas. Manning's and Tebbs' Companies became part of the infantry regiment organized and raised by Albert Rust, a well known Arkansas political leader from Union County. The ten companies that comprised Rust's 3rd Arkansas Infantry Regiment were raised primarily in 5 counties located in Southeast Arkansas, namely, Ashley, Dallas, Drew, Hot Springs and Union Counties. The Regiment was expanded to an overstrength organization when a Company (L) of Arkansans, commanded by Captain Joseph D. Christian of Ashley County, joined Rust's command in Virginia on August 14, 1861. All of the companies, except Company H, were composed wholly of Arkansans. Company H was comprised of men from both Kentucky and Arkansas.

The first official muster of the Regiment was held on June 9, 1861. Following this date the companies departed Arkansas for Virginia at varying times. All had left by the last of June and had reached their rendezvous point in the East, Lynchburg, Virginia, by early July. On July 3 and 4, company and regimental officers were "officially" appointed and elected, and on July 5 the Regiment was mustered into Confederate service "for the war." Albert Rust was elected Colonel and the Regimental Commander and Seth M. Barton, a West Point Graduate (Class of 1849), was appointed Lieutenant Colonel of the Regiment. Barton, a Virginian, had been assigned by the Confederate War Department to the Arkansas Regiment. Van H. Manning, Captain of Company K, was appointed the Major of the Regiment. Company commanders (captains) elected were: Co. A, William H. Tebbs; Co. B, James H. Capers; Co. C, Thomas M. Whittington; Co. D, Capt. Robert S. Taylor; Co. E, Thomas F. Nolan; Co. F, Daniel A. Newman; Co. G, John W. Reedy; Co. H, Samuel V. Reid; and Co. I, George D. Alexander.

Two organizational changes took place during 1862 that effected the makeup of the 3rd Arkansas Infantry. During January of 1862, five new companies of Arkansas troops arrived in

Virginia. These troops, known as the 2nd Battalion, Arkansas Infantry, were commanded by Major Wm. N. Bronaugh. This Battalion saw much action during the Peninsular Campaign of 1862 and suffered very heavy casualties at the battles of Seven Pines (May 31-June 1), Beaver Dam Creek or Mechanicsville (June 26) and at Gaines' Mill on June 27. On July 18, 1862, the 133 survivors of the 2nd Battalion, Arkansas Infantry, were assigned to and amalgamated with the 3rd Arkansas Infantry Regiment. The second organizational change took place in late September. At the Battle of Antietam (Sept. 17, 1862) Companies A and L of the 3rd Arkansas were decimated. On September 25, the few survivors of Company L were transferred into Company A and Company L ceased to exist. Thus, the Regiment was reduced to ten companies, the normal complement for an infantry regiment.

The 3rd Arkansas Infantry, prior to being assigned to Hood's Texas Brigade in late November, 1862 had seen only limited action in the Eastern Theater. Rust's command was assigned to various brigades and divisions during the first year and a half after it arrived in Virginia. The Regiment participated in the ill-fated Western Virginia Campaign during the Fall of 1861 and Winter of 1861-62. In the early Spring of 1862 the Arkansas troops traveled to the North Carolina coastal area to counter a Federal invasion attempt. In late May, Rust's Regiment moved back to Virginia and occupied a position near Drewry's Bluff on the James River south of Richmond. The 3rd Arkansas mostly marched and counter-marched during the Seven Days Battle (June 26-July 1), missed Second Manassas (Aug. 30), but did see much action at bloody Antietam (September 17) where it, along with Lee's entire army, suffered heavy casualties.

The Army of Northern Virginia was reorganized during November of 1862. Among other organizational changes, the reorganization involved both the promotion and reassignment of senior officers and the realignment of regiments within brigades. The goal of the War Department was to have regiments from the same states brigaded together. This was not possible in all cases, for instance the 3rd Arkansas Infantry was the only "Razorback" Regiment in Virginia. Fortunately, however, there were only three Texas Regiments under Lee's command so a perfect combination was worked out involving the two contiguous frontier states. During the organization shuffle, Hood's Texas Brigade lost the infantry companies of Hampton's South Carolina Legion to General Micah Jenkins' South Carolina Brigade, and the 18th Georgia Infantry Regiment was reassigned to General T. R. R.

Cobb's Georgia Brigade. The 3rd Arkansas was transferred into Hood's Texas Brigade, thus bringing that famous Brigade up to its full strength of four regiments. The Texans and Arkansans remained brigaded together until the final curtain at Appomattox. The Texans in Hood's Brigade generally referred to their Arkansas "cousins" as "the 3rd Texas."

3RD ARK. VOL. INF. REGT.

HDQTRS. - FIELD, STAFF & BAND

Regiment was formed in Ashley County, Ark., in June, 1861, and was mustered into the Confederate Service at Lynchburg, Va., July 5, 1861 by Maj. H. L. Clay, CSA.

Key

(1) Original member of Hdqtrs. (2) Paroled at Appomattox.
K (Killed), W (Wounded), POW (Prisoner of War)
AWOL (Absent Without Leave)

OFFICERS, FIELD & LINE

(1) MANNING, VAN H. Colonel
    Orig. Cmdr., Co. K: Prom., Maj., July 9, 1861: Orig. Maj. of Regt.: Prom., Col., Mar. 11, 1862: W. (thigh) & POW, Wilderness (May 6, 1864): Confined at Ft. Delaware: Paroled, July 24, 1865.
(1) RUST, ALBERT Colonel
    Orig. Col. of Regt.: Not with Regt. when it was asgnd. to Hood's Tex. Brig., Nov., 1862.
(1) BARTON, SETH M. Lieut.-Colonel
    Orig. Lt.-Col. of Regt.: Not with Regt. when it was asgnd. to Hood's Tex. Brig., Nov., 1862.
(2) TAYLOR, ROBERT S. Lieut.-Colonel
    Orig. Cmdr., Co. D, age 35: Prom., Maj., Apr. 23, 1862: Prom., Lt.-Col., Jan. 11, 1863: Asgnd. to recruiting serv. in Ark., Feb.-Apr., 1863: POW, Madison Parish, La., Apr. 8, 1863: Confined at Ft. Delaware: Exchanged: Hospitalized for chronic rheumatism, Mar., 1865: Paroled, Appomattox (Apr. 12, 1865).
     TEBBS, WILLIAM H. Lieut.-Colonel
    Orig. Cmdr., Co. A, age 40: Prom., Lt.-Col., Mar. 11, 1862: Resgnd., Jan. 11, 1863, and returned to Ark.

REEDY, JOHN W. Major
    Orig. Capt., Co. G, age 31: Prom., Maj., Jan. 19, 1863: K.,
    Chickamauga (Sept. 19, 1863).
WILKINS, WM. K. Major
    Orig. Capt., Co. K: Prom., Maj., Sept. 19, 1863: K., Wilderness
    (May 6, 1864).
(2) JONES, ALEXANDER C. Captain
    Orig. 1Lt., Co. G: Prom., Capt., Jan. 19, 1863: W. (right arm),
    Wilderness (May 6, 1864): Temporarily cmded. Regt. last few
    months of the war: Paroled, Appomattox (Apr. 12, 1865).

OFFICERS, STAFF

ADJUTANTS (AAG)
BUTLER, HENRY A. Captain
    Orig. 2Lt., Co. I, age 24: Appt. Capt., and Regmtl., AAG, Nov. 4,
    1863: Retired to Invalid Corps, Oct. 6, 1864.
BUTLER, LEWIS P.
    Orig. Pvt., Co. I: Appt Regmtl. Adj., Sept., 1862: Relieved from
    duty, Dec. 30, 1863.
(2) MILES, JOSEPHUS 1st Lieutenant
    Orig. Pvt., Co. H: Prom., 3Lt., Feb. 13, 1863: Prom., 2Lt., July
    2, 1863: W. (forearm), Wilderness (May 6, 1864): Appt. AAG
    and 1Lt., Winter, 1864-65: Paroled, Appomattox (Apr. 12,
    1865).
(1) SEMMES, T. M. 1st Lieutenant
    Orig. Adj. of Regt.: Not with Regt. when it was asgnd. to Hood's
    Tex. Brig., Nov., 1862.

SURGEON
(1) BROWN, JOHN R.
(2)   Orig. 2Lt., Co. G: Orig. Asst. Surg. of Regt., Appt. Nov. 15,
    1861: Prom., Surg., July 25, 1864: Paroled, Appomattox (Apr.
    12, 1865).
ASST. SURGEONS
HALE, J. J.
    Appt. Asst. Regmtl. Surg., Dec. 21, 1862: Resgnd., May 7, 1863.
(2) KLEINSCHMIDT, CARL H. A.
    Appt. Asst. Regmtl. Surg., Mar. 3, 1863: Paroled, Appomattox
    (Apr. 12, 1865).
(1) RAMSEY, J. W.
    Appt. Asst. Surg., Oct. 29, 1861: Arrested, May 29, 1863, at
    Monroeton, Pa. as a Conf. spy: Confined at Ft. McHenry, Md.

COMMISSARY SUBSISTENCE OFFICERS (ACS)
STONE, THOS. H. C. Captain
    Orig. Pvt., Co. D, age 18: Asgnd. extra duty, Regmtl. ACS Dept.,
    July, 1861: Prom., Capt. & asgnd. as Regmtl. ACS, Dec. 5, 1862:
    Office abolished by Conf. Govt., July 31, 1863: Transfd. to
    Hood's Corps, Army of Tenn.: Not reappt. ACS Off., July 17,
    1864: Returned to Ark. & jnd. a home guard unit.

(1)   STONE, WM. M. Captain

> Orig. Regmtl. Comsy./Subs. Off.: Not with Regt. when it was asgnd. to Hood's Tex. Brig., Nov., 1862.

QUARTERMASTER OFFICERS

(1)   HOLLOWAY, JOHN D.

> Orig. 1Sgt., Co. E, age 43: Appt. Regmtl. QM, July 13, 1861: Resgnd., Nov. 20, 1861: Not member of the Regmt. when it joined Hood's Tex. Brig.

       RUST, JAS. A.

> Enl. as a Pvt., Co. C, age 34: Prom. to Capt., & appt. Regmtl. Asst. QM, Nov. 23, 1861: Detached serv. to Div., Mar., 1864: Resgnd., Sept. 15, 1864.

CHAPLAINS

(2)   BUTLER, GEORGE E.

> Clergyman by profession: Orig. Pvt., Co. I, age 24: Appt. Regmtl. Chaplain, Jan. 15, 1863: POW, left with wounded at Gettysburg (July 2, 1863): Confined at Ft. McHenry, Md.: Released from Ft. McHenry: Paroled, Appomattox (Apr. 12, 1865).

(1)   MADISON, B. F.

> Orig. Regmtl. Chaplain, appt. July 9, 1861: Resgnd., Jan. 15, 1863.

NON-COMMISSIONED OFFICERS

SERGEANT-MAJOR

(1)   LAWRENCE, F.

> Orig. Regmtl. Sgt.-Maj., appt. Aug. 24, 1861: Not a member of the Regt. when it joined Hood's Tex. Brig.

COLOR-SERGEANTS

None identified as such on Company or Regimental Bi-Monthly Muster Rolls.

QUARTERMASTER-SERGEANTS

(1)   GIBSON, S.

> Orig. Regmtl. QM-Sgt., appt. Aug. 23, 1861: Not a member of the Regt. when it joined Hood's Tex. Brig.

       SPEARS, JOHN B.

> Orig. Pvt., Co. G, age 26: Appt. QM-Sgt., Nov., 1862 & held position to Aug., 1864: No other records after this date.

COMMISSARY SUBSISTENCE-SERGEANT

(2)   RUST, ROBT. S.

> Enl. as a Pvt. in Co. C, at Austin, Tex., Mar. 18, 1862: Prom., Regmtl. Comsy. Sgt., Aug. 1, 1863: Paroled, Appomattox (Apr. 12, 1865). Note: See Co. B, 4th Tex. Inf. (page 110).

ORDNANCE-SERGEANTS

SKIPPER, EVERETT
>Recruited at age 31, Apr. 12, 1862 at Cut Off, Ark.: Appt. Ordn.-Sgt., Jan. 25, 1862: Transfd. to Miss. by order of Secy. of War, Jan. 24, 1864.

WORTHINGTON, WARREN W.
>Served as Regmtl. Ordn.-Sgt., Oct., 1862-Jan., 1863: See list of "Officers," Co. G.

HOSPITAL STEWARDS

(2)   WHITE, HAMP C.
>Orig. 3Sgt., Co. K, age 24: Transfd. to Regmtl. Band, Feb. 28, 1862: Appt. Hosp. Steward, Sept. 17, 1863: Paroled, Appomattox (Apr. 12, 1865).

(1)   CRAIG, PETER G.
>Orig. Pvt., Co. G: Appt. a Regmtl. Hosp. Steward, July 19, 1861: POW in Ark., May 29, 1864: Confined at Rock Island, Ill.

BAND

BANDMASTER

BAILEY, JAMES AUGUSTUS
>Actor by profession: Transfd. to Regmtl. Hdqtrs., 3rd Ark. as Bandmaster from 44th Ala. Inf. Regt., May 20, 1862: Granted leave to Wilmington, No. Car., Jan. 28, 1865. Wrote famous marching song of Hood's Tex. Brig., "The Old Gray Mare."

BAND MEMBERS

(2)   BAILEY, GEO. A.
>Transfd. to Regmtl. Hdqtrs., 3rd Ark. Inf. as a musician from 44th Ala. Inf. Regt., May 20, 1862: Paroled, Appomattox (Apr. 12, 1865).

(2)   BAILEY, RICH. J.
>Enl. as a Pvt. in Co. H, Apr. 8, 1862 at Richmond: Transfd. to Regmtl. Hdqtrs. as a musician, Nov., 1862: Paroled, Appomattox (Apr. 12, 1865).

CLYDE, ROBT. B.
>Enl. as a Pvt. in Co. K: Transfd. to Regmtl. Band, Feb. 28, 1862: POW, Antietam (Sept. 17, 1862); Exch., Oct. 27, 1862: Sick most of 1863.

DELANNAY (or DELANEY), GEO. W.
>Orig. Pvt. in Co. K: Transfd. to Regmtl. Band, Feb. 28, 1862: POW, Antietam (Sept. 17, 1862): Exchanged, Oct. 27, 1862: Deserted, Feb., 1864, in E. Tenn.: Took Fed. oath, Feb. 29, 1864.

FILES, JAS. S.
>Enl. as a musc. in Co. K, Mar. 1, 1862: POW, Antietam (Sept. 17, 1862): Exchanged, Oct. 20, 1862: Transfd. to Regmtl. Band, Jan., 1863: Sick, Summer, 1863.

(2) JACKSON, J. B.
  Orig. Pvt., Co. K: Transfd. to Regmtl. Band, July 28, 1862: POW, Antietam (Sept. 17, 1862): Exchanged: Paroled, Appomattox (Apr. 12, 1865).
JOHNSON, JOS.
  Orig. Pvt., Co. A: Dropped from rolls, Aug., 1864, AWOL.
(2) LOWRY, ROBT. J.
  Enl. as a Pvt. in Co. G, Mar. 1, 1862 at Three Creeks, Ark.: Transfd. to Regmtl. Band, Sept., 1863: Paroled, Appomattox (Apr. 12, 1865).
McKINNEY, L. B.
  Enl. as a musician in Co. K, Mar. 1, 1862: Transfd. to Regmtl. Band, Summer, 1862: POW, Antietam (Sept. 17, 1862): Exchanged: Sick, Spring, 1863.
(2) MELTON, GEO. F.
  Enl. as a member of the Regmtl. Band, Mar. 1, 1862 at Madison CH., Va., Mar. 1, 1862: Paroled, Appomattox (Apr. 12, 1865).
(2) RANDLE, JOHN D.
  Orig. 4Cpl., Co. A: Reduced to Pvt., June 1, 1861: POW, Antietam (Sept. 17, 1862): Exchanged, Oct. 18, 1862: Transfd. to Regmtl. Band, Summer, 1863: Paroled, Appomattox (Apr. 12, 1865).
(2) WARD, BENJAMIN F.
  Orig. Pvt., Co. F: Transfd. to Regmtl. Band, May 1, 1863: Paroled, Appomattox (Apr. 12, 1865).
(2) WARD, FRANCIS M.
  Orig. Musician, Co. E, age 18: Appt. to Regmtl. Band, June, 1864: Paroled, Appomattox (Apr. 12, 1865).
WARD, WM. J.
  Orig. musician (drummer), Co. F, age 18: Transfd. to Regmtl. Hdqtrs., June, 1863 and appt. "Chief Musician": No record after Aug., 1864.
WHITE, D. R.
  Orig. Pvt., Co. K: Transfd. to Regmtl. Band, Feb. 28, 1862: POW, Antietam (Sept. 17, 1862): Exchanged, Oct. 27, 1862: Paroled, Memphis, Tenn., May 16, 1865.
WHITE, HAMP C.
  See list of "Hospital Stewards" above.
WOOD, AUGUSTUS BALDWIN
  Enl. as a Musician in Co. K, Mar. 1, 1862: POW, Antietam (Sept. 17, 1862): Exchanged, Oct. 20, 1862: Transfd. to Regmtl. Band as "Chief Musician," Feb., 1863. No record after Aug., 1863.
WOOD, S. B.
  Orig. 3Cpl., Co. K: Transfd. to Regmtl. Band, Feb. 28, 1862: W., Gettysburg (July 2, 1863): POW, Conway Co., Ark., Jan. 27, 1865: Died of pneumonia at Fed. Prison, Little Rock, Ark., Feb. 23, 1865.
WOOD, W. H.
  Enl. as a Regmtl. Musician, Feb. 15, 1863 at Hamburg, Ark.: Shown on Bi-Monthly Muster Roll, Aug., 1863: No other record.

* * * * *

MEMBERS OF HEADQUARTERS, 3RD ARK. INF. REGT., WHO WERE NOT PRESENT FOR DUTY DURING THE PERIOD THAT THE REGIMENT WAS ASSIGNED TO HOOD'S TEXAS BRIGADE (NOV., 1862-APR., 1865)

OFFICERS

(1) Rust, Albert, Col. (Orig. Col. of the Regt.: Prom., Mar., 1862)
(1) Barton, Seth M., Lt.-Col. (Orig. Lt.-Col. of the Regt.: Resgnd., Nov., 1861)
Capers, James H., Maj. (Orig. Capt., Co. B: Resgnd., Apr., 1862)
(1) Semmes, T. M., 1Lt. (Orig. Adj. of Regt.: Returned to VMI, Jan., 1862)

Wright, William G., Surgeon (No record)
Brevarde, T., Asst. Surgeon (No record)
Pusley, _____, Asst. Surgeon (Resgnd., 1861)
Stone, Wm. M., ACS (No record)
Madison, B. F., Chaplain (Transfd., July, 1861)

NON-COMMISSIONED OFFICERS

Lawrence, F., Sgt.-Maj. (AWOL, Oct., 1862)

Gibson, S., QM-Sgt. (Dischgd., Oct., 1861)

3RD ARK. VOL. INF. REGT.

COMPANY A

Company was organized in Ashley County, Arkansas, enrolled there on May 20, 1861, and was mustered into the Confederate service, "for the war," at Lynchburg, Va., July 5, 1861, by Maj. H. L. Clay, CSA.

Key

(1) Original member of Company. (2) Paroled at Appomattox.
K (Killed), W (Wounded), POW (Prisoner of War)
AWOL (Absent Without Leave)

OFFICERS

(1) JOHNSON, BART, Jr. Capt. — Orig. 2Lt. of Co.: Prom., 1Lt., Mar. 11, 1862: Prom., Capt., Sept. 18, 1862: Furlough granted to

Ark., Jan., 1864: POW, Pt. Coupee, La.: Escaped, July 4, 1864: Never returned to Co.: Reported to have org. cavalry company in Trans-Miss.

(1) TEBBS, WM. H. Capt. — See roster, "Regmtl. Hdqtrs., 3rd Ark. Inf."

ARCHER, J. A. Lt. — POW, Port Hudson, La., July 9, 1863: Confined at Johnson's Is., Ohio: No other record.

(1) CAMERON, JOHN A. 2Lt. — Orig. 2Sgt. of Co., age 27: Prom., 2Lt., Winter, 1862-63: W., Chickamauga (Sept. 19, 1863): Granted leave furlough: Did not return to Co.

(1) SCOGGIN, WM. D. 2Lt. — Orig. 3Lt. of Co.: Prom., 2Lt., Mar. 11, 1862: POW, Richmond, Apr. 4, 1865: Took Fed. oath, Apr. 11, 1865.

NON-COMMISSIONED OFFICERS

(1) BUTLER, JAMES P. 3Sgt. — Orig. Pvt. in Co.: Appt. 3Sgt., Nov., 1862: W., Chickamauga (Sept. 19, 1863).

(1) CAMERON, JOHN A. 2Sgt. — See list of "Officers" above.

FISHER, IRA W. 3Cpl. — Orig. Pvt. in Co., age 18: W. (shoulder) & POW, Antietam (Sept. 17, 1862): Confined at Ft. McHenry, Md.: Exchanged, Mar. 13, 1863.

(1) HARRIS, CHAS. A. 4Sgt. — Enl., age 22: Orig. 4Sgt. of Co.: Absent sick, Jan.-June, 1863: Reduced to Pvt.: Dropped from rolls, Aug., 1864 for being AWOL.

MARTIN, STEPHEN A. Cpl. — Died of wound, July 26, 1863 in U.S. Milt. hosp., Memphis, Tenn.: No other record.

PUGH, JOHN D. 1Sgt. — Orig. Pvt. in Co., age 25: Prom., 1Sgt., Jan., 1863: W. (thigh), Wilderness (May 6, 1864).

(2) RALPH, HARRISON A. 5Sgt. — Orig. Pvt. in Co., age 20: Prom., 5Sgt., June 30, 1863: Paroled, Appomattox (Apr. 12, 1865).

(1) RANDLE, JOHN D. 4Cpl. — See roster, "Regmtl. Hdqtrs., 3rd Ark. Inf."

(1) SWEENEY, JAS. A. 1Cpl. — Orig. 1Cpl. of Co., age 28: Reduced to Pvt., Aug., 1861: Absent sick most of 1862: Asgnd. as cook at a Petersburg hosp., Aug., 1862.

(1) TURNBOE, JOS. E. 2Sgt. — Orig. 3Cpl. of Co., age 22: Prom., 2Sgt., Nov., 1862: W., Chickamauga (Sept. 19, 1863): Retired to Invalid Corps, Oct. 24, 1864.

PRIVATES

BAILEY, JOHN A. — Paroled, Lynchburg, Va., Apr. 14, 1865.

(1) BAGLEY, JAS. A. — On detached serv., Fredericksburg, Va., Jan., 1863.

(1) BANKS, JOHN S. — Enl. at 18: W., Antietam (Sept. 17, 1862): W.,
(2) Wilderness (May 6, 1864): Absent sick, Richmond, Summer, 1864.

BARLOW, GEO. W. — Enl. at Portland, Ark., Feb. 15, 1862: Absent sick, Richmond, Summer, 1864: POW, Amelia CH., Apr. 6, 1865: Paroled, Nashville, Tenn., May 24, 1865.

BEAVERS, HENRY J. — Enl., age 23: W., Chickamauga (Sept. 20, 1863): Retired for disability, Dec. 24, 1864.

BILLINGSLY, ROBT. — Enl., age 25: POW, Gettysburg (July 2, 1863): Confined at Ft. Delaware.

BOWMAN, R. N. — Deserted, E. Tenn.: Took Fed. oath, Jan. 6, 1864 at Knoxville, Tenn.

BOYER, F. W. — POW, Gettysburg (July 2, 1863): Confined Pt. Lookout, Md.

BULL, WM. — Enl., Mar. 10, 1863 at Hamburg, Ark.: W. (neck) & POW, Gettysburg (July 2, 1863): Died, July 12, 1863.

BUTLER, JAS. P. — See list of "Non-Commissioned Officers" above.

CALDELEUGH, R. A. H. — Enl., Feb. 25, 1863 at Hamburg, Ark.: POW, Darbytown Rd. (Oct. 7, 1864): Confined at Pt. Lookout, Md.: Exch., Feb. 10, 1865.

(1) CALHOUN, MILTON — W., Greenbrier River (Oct. 3, 1861): POW, Suffolk, May 4, 1863.

(1) CARROLL, DAVID V. — Enl., age 22: Absent sick, Richmond, Winter, 1862-63 & Winter, 1863-64: AWOL, Summer, 1864: Dropped from rolls, Aug., 1864.

(1) CARROLL, THOS. S. — Enl., age 23: Dropped from rolls for prolonged absence, Aug., 1864.

CARTER, JAS. E. — Enl., Apr. 2, 1862, age 23, at Hamburg, Ark.: W., Chickamauga (Sept. 19, 1863): Dischgd. for disability, May 2, 1864.

CLARY, NATHAN C. — Enl., Apr. 2, 1862 at Hamburg, Ark.: K., Wilderness (May 6, 1864).

DALY, HENRY — Transfd. to Co. A from 2nd Ark. Btln., July 18, 1862: Transfd. to Co. F, 3rd Ark. Inf., May 1, 1863.

DANIEL, JESSE T. — Enl., age 16, Mar. 22, 1862, Hamburg, Ark.: W., Chickamauga (Sept. 19, 1863): K., Williamsburg Rd. (Oct. 27, 1864).

(2) DAY, JAS. — Enl., age 30, Apr. 4, 1862 at Hamburg, Ark.: Paroled, Appomattox (Apr. 12, 1865).

DONIPHON, JAS. A. — Enl. at Hamburg, Ark., Mar. 9, 1863: No other record.

ELAM, RICHARD — Enl., age 47, Mar. 20, 1862 at Hamburg, Ark.: POW, Chickamauga (Sept. 20, 1863): Confined at Camp Douglas, Ill.: Took Fed. oath and enl. in 6th U.S. Vol. Inf. Regt., May 5, 1865.

(1) FISHER, IRA W. — See list of "Non-Commissioned Officers" above.

(2) GEDDIE, JOS. — Enl., age 30, Apr. 8, 1862 at Hamburg, Ark.: Present for duty during entire war: Paroled, Appomattox (Apr. 12, 1865).

GERRIN, JOHN — Transfd. to Co. A, from 2nd Ark. Btln., July 18, 1862: Sick much of 1863 & 1864: Detailed as nurse at Howard's Grove Hosp., Richmond, Mar. 25, 1865: POW, Richmond, Apr. 3, 1865: Paroled, Apr. 12, 1865.

(2) GREGORY, W. E. — Enl., age 19: Absent sick, Winter, 1863-64: Paroled, Appomattox (Apr. 12, 1865).

(2) HANNAH, W. C. — Transfd. to Co. A from Co. L, Sept. 25, 1862: Paroled, Appomattox (Apr. 12, 1865).

(1) HARROLD, CHESTER A. — Enl., age 18: Detached duty as courier for
(2) Gen. Robertson, Spring, 1863: POW, E. Tenn., Mar., 1864:
Exchanged: Paroled, Appomattox (Apr. 12, 1865).
HAYS, ROBT. F. — Enl., Feb. 14, 1862 at Hamburg, Ark.: W. (arm),
Wilderness (May 6, 1864): POW, Amelia CH., Apr. 6, 1865:
Paroled, Nashville, Tenn., May 24, 1865.
(1) HAZARD, FRANK — Enl., age 22: Dropped from rolls, Aug., 1864.
JOHNSTON, F. J. — POW, Suffolk, Va., Apr., 1863: Exchanged, May
13, 1863: Sick, Spring, 1864.
JONES, HENRY — Deserted in E. Tenn.: Took Fed. oath, Dec., 1863.
(2) KELLY, JOHN A. — Transfd. to Co. A from Co. L, Sept. 25, 1862:
Paroled, Appomattox (Apr. 12, 1865).
(1) KELLY, JOS. D. — Enl., age 34: W., Antietam (Sept. 17, 1862):
(2) Paroled, Appomattox (Apr. 12, 1865).
KIMBALL, THOS. G. — Enl., age 22, at Hamburg, Ark., Apr. 8, 1862:
No record after June, 1863.
KISER, CHAS. — POW, Little Rock, Ark., Sept. 11, 1863.
LEWIS, ABRAHAM — Paroled at Springfield, Mo., Jan. 14, 1863.
McCRAY, J. C. — POW, Knoxville, Tenn., Mar. 26, 1864: Died of
diarrhea in prison camp, Oct. 25, 1864.
McPHAIL, RUFUS — Enl., Mar. 10, 1863 at Hamburg, Ark.: Deserted,
May 4, 1863, took Fed. oath.
McRAE, JOHN C. — Enl., June 1, 1862 in Ashley County, Ark.:
Present for duty to Feb., 1864: No records after that date.
MILLAIN, THOS. F. — POW, Helena, Ark., July 4, 1863: Confined at
Ft. Delaware: Exchanged, Mar. 7, 1865.
(1) MINSCHEW, JOHN R. — Enl., age 21: Died of pneumonia at Farmville,
Va., May 4, 1863.
(1) MOCK, GEO. Y. — W., Antietam (Sept. 17, 1862): Paroled, Appo-
(2) mattox (Apr. 12, 1865).
(2) MORRIS, HENRY N. — Enl., age 23, at Hamburg, Ark., Apr. 8, 1862:
Paroled, Appomattox (Apr. 12, 1865).
MOORE, JOEL — Deserted, E. Tenn.: Took Fed. oath, Feb. 24, 1864.
(1) MOORE, S. DUNK — Enl., age 22: Detached duty as a Brig. teamster,
Spring, 1863: No other record.
(1) MOORE, W. ALLEN — Enl., age 20: W., Chickamauga (Sept. 19,
(2) 1863): Div. Foragemaster, Summer & Fall, 1864: Paroled,
Appomattox (Apr. 12, 1865).
(1) MUNDY, MIKE — Enl., age 24: Deserted at Suffolk, Va., May 4, 1863:
Took Fed. oath.
MULVEY, MICHAEL — Enl., age 42, July 15, 1861: Dischgd. for
chronic rheumatism, Jan. 13, 1863.
NEVILLS, THOS. G. — Enl., age 36, at Hamburg, Ark., Apr. 6, 1862:
Paroled, Chattanooga, Tenn., May 21, 1865.
(1) PARKER, MADISON D. — Enl., age 21: Asgnd. to build cabins, Winter,
1861-62: Paroled, Monroe, La., June 9, 1865.
(2) PARKS, WASHINGTON — Enl., age 20: Detailed as a Regmtl. & Brig.
teamster most of war: Paroled at Appomattox (Apr. 12, 1865).
PRESTON, WM. — Deserted in E. Tenn.: Took Fed. oath, Feb. 29,
1864.
(1) PUGH, JOHN D. — See list of "Non-Commissioned Officers" above.

(1) PUGH, ROBT. A. — Enl., age 22: Sick in hosp., Winter, 1862-63: Detailed as wagon guard, Nov., 1863: Paroled, Monroe, La., June 7, 1865.

(1) RALPH, HARRISON A. — See list of "Non-Commissioned Officers" above.

(1) RAMSOUR, WM. P. — Enl., age 24: W., Chickamauga (Sept. 19, 1863): Paroled, Charlotte, No. Car., May 12, 1865.

(1) REINHARDT, ALEX S. — Enl., age 22: Present for duty to June, 1863: No records after that date, may have been killed at Gettysburg.

SANES, J. F. — Deserted in E. Tenn.: Took Fed. oath, Feb. 29, 1864: No other record.

SCORBIN, WM. J. — POW, Gettysburg (July 2, 1863): Confined at Ft. Delaware: Died in prison, Mar. 7, 1865.

(1) SMITH, G. W. — Enl., age 20: Sick, Winter, 1861-62: Paroled,
(2) Appomattox (Apr. 12, 1865).

(1) STEPHENS (or STEVENS), S. FRANK — Enl., age 19: W., Greenbrier
(2) River, W. Va. (Oct. 3, 1861): W., Chickamauga (Sept. 19, 1863): Paroled, Appomattox (Apr. 12, 1865).

(1) TAYLOR, J. H. M. — Enl., age 22: W., Wilderness (May 6, 1864).

(1) TAYLOR, J. W. J. — Enl., age 22: W. (foot), Chickamauga (Sept. 19, 1863): Foot amputated: Dischgd. for disability, Nov. 30, 1864.

THOMPSON, MITCHELL — Deserted, E. Tenn., Winter, 1863-64: Took Fed. oath, Jan. 6, 1864.

(1) TRULY, BENNET R. — Enl., age 23: Detach. serv. as a provost guard, Spring, 1862 & as a teamster, Fall, 1862: AWOL, Feb., 1864: Dropped from rolls, Aug., 1864: Paroled, Natchitoches, La., June 20, 1865.

(1) VENTERS, JOHN — Enl., age 22: Present for duty until June, 1863: No record after that date, may have been killed at Gettysburg.

WALLACE, RICHARD — Enl. at Portland, Ark., Feb. 14, 1862: W., Chickamauga (Sept. 19, 1863): Wound furlough granted: AWOL, dropped from rolls, Aug., 1864.

(1) WARD, JAS. W. — Enl., age 18: Asgnd. to build cabins, Dec., 1861: W. (side) & POW, Wilderness (May 6, 1864): Died in prison.

WILSON, MICHAEL — POW, Missionary Ridge, Tenn., Nov. 25, 1863: Confined in Fed. prison at Louisville, Ky.: Took Fed. oath, Dec. 29, 1863, Knoxville, Tenn.

WOLFIN, W. F. — POW, Knoxville, Tenn., Mar. 26, 1864: Confined at Camp Chase, Ohio: Paroled, May 7, 1865.

WORTHINGTON, ROBT. — Enl., at Hamburg, Ark., Feb. 14, 1862: Sick most of year 1863 & much of year 1864: Paroled at Albany, Ga., May 18, 1865.

(2) WRIGHT, G. LEWIS — Transfd. into Co. A from Co. L, Sept. 25, 1862: Arrested for forgery, Dec. 12, 1862: Charges dropped: On detached serv. in Richmond as a shoemaker, Nov., 1862 to July, 1864: Paroled, Appomattox (Apr. 12, 1865).

*　*　*　*　*

MEMBERS OF COMPANY A, 3RD ARK. INF. REGT., WHO WERE NOT PRESENT FOR DUTY DURING THE PERIOD THAT THE REGIMENT WAS ASSIGNED TO HOOD'S TEXAS BRIGADE (NOV., 1862-APR., 1865)

OFFICERS

(1) Harris, Sampson L., 1Lt./Capt. (K., Antietam)

NON-COMMISSIONED OFFICERS

(1) Austin, Jas. F., 3Sgt. (D., Feb., 1862)
(1) Cammack, Jas. C., Cpl. (AWOL, Sept., 1862)
(1) Cook, Jos. M., 2Cpl. (Dischgd., July, 1861)
(1) Price, Thos. S., 1Sgt. (D., July, 1861)

Tompkins, Herbert B., 1Sgt. (No record)
Worsham, Wm. L., 1Sgt. (Transfd.)
(1) Worthington, Fred J., Cpl. (K., Antietam)

MUSICIANS

(1) Fisher, Jas. M. (Dischgd., July, 1861)

(1) Sherer, Jas. C. (Dischgd., Dec., 1861)

PRIVATES

Baker, Jos. (Deserted)
Beasley, Wm. C. (No record)
Black, Simeon B. (POW)
(1) Blackburn, Jas. M. (Dischgd., Aug., 1862)
Brazeale, David R. (D., Nov., 1862)
(1) Britton, John D. (D., Mar., 1862)
(1) Caldeleugh, Jas. S. (Dischgd., Sept., 1862)
Caldeleugh, R. A. H. (No record)
Cammack, Michael (Disabled, Antietam)
(1) Cammack, W. Edward (D., July, 1862)
Campbell, Chas. P. (Deserted)
Carter, Reubin A. (K., Antietam)

(1) Chavers, Matthew (D., Feb., 1862)
Clary, John C. (No record)
(1) Cleveland, Jos. (Dischgd., Aug., 1861)
Daniel, Wm. Walter (K., Antietam)
(1) Drake, Holden J. (Dischgd., Sept., 1862)
Edgman, Abner (No record)
Edgman, John (No record)
Gibson, Wm. A. (No record)
Gray, Madison (No record)
(1) Harris, Ptolemy T. (D., Aug., 1861)
(1) Hartsfield, Jas. M. (D., Feb., 1862)
(1) Herren, Patrick C. (No record)
Herren, R. Pink (D., Mar., 1862)

(1) Hogue, J. W. P. (K., Antietam)
(1) Hogue, M. G. (Dischgd., Dec., 1861)
(1) Holloway, Jas. M. (D., July, 1861)
(1) Holloway, P. M. L. (No record)
Ivins, Henry H. (No record)
Jackson, Jesse B. (No record)
Jacobs, Henry (No record)
(1) Keen, L. B. (Dischgd., Dec., 1861)
Lewis, Elisha (Dischgd., date unk.)
(1) McCain, Andrew J. (K., Antietam)
(1) Mears, Wm. A. (D., June, 1861)
(1) Mulise, F. M. (Dischgd., Sept., 1861)
O'Connell, Michael (No record)
(1) O'Neill, Sidney W. (Dischgd., Aug., 1861)

Owen, E. M. (D., Oct., 1862)
(1) Porter, King D. (D., Feb., 1862)
(1) Ramsour, Francis E. (Missing, Antietam)
Reynolds, G. M. (No record)
Shaver, Noah (Deserted)
Smoot, Wm. H. (Dischgd., Oct., 1862)
Stephens, Charleston W. (Dischgd., Apr., 1862)
(1) Taylor, Geo. A. (D., June, 1861)
(1) Tebbs, Obediah B. (AWOL, Feb., 1862)
(1) Venters, Augustus (D., Greenbrier R., Oct., 1861).
Villines, Robt. (No record)
Wilson, John E. (D., Aug., 1862)
(1) Wiltshire (or Wilshire), Geo. W. (D., Dec., 1861)

3RD ARK. VOL. INF. REGT.

COMPANY B

Company was organized in Ashley County, Arkansas, was enrolled there June 9, 1861 and was mustered into the Confederate service "for the war" at Lynchburg, Va., July 5, 1861, by Maj. H. L. Clay, CSA.

Key

(1) Original member of Company. (2) Paroled at Appomattox.
K (Killed), W (Wounded), POW (Prisoner of War)
AWOL (Absent Without Leave)

OFFICERS

FOOTE, WM. A. Capt. — Orig. 1Sgt., Co. B, age 33: Prom., Capt., Mar. 11, 1862: Resgnd., June 16, 1863.
JONES, J. WHITE Capt. — Orig. 2Cpl., Co. B, age 25: Prom., 2Lt., Apr. 4, 1862: Prom., 1Lt., Dec. 10, 1862: Prom., Capt., June 16, 1863.

HENSON, JOHN T. 1Lt. — Orig. 4Sgt., Co. B, age 22: Prom., 2Lt., Dec. 20, 1862: Prom., 1Lt., June 16, 1863: Died, Oct. 1, 1863.
(1) KEESEE, WM. H. 1Lt. — Orig. 3Lt., Co. B, age 21: Prom., 1Lt., Mar. 11, 1862: Died at Richmond of smallpox, Dec. 10, 1862.
SEALE, CHAS. J. 1Lt. — Orig. Pvt., Co. B, age 27: Prom., 2Lt., June 16, 1863: Prom., 1Lt., Oct. 1, 1863: K., Wilderness (May 6, 1864).
JOHNSON, WM. PIZZARRO 2Lt. — Orig. Pvt., Co. B, age 18: Asgnd. to build cabins, Nov., 1861: Prom., 2Lt., Winter, 1864-65: Paroled in Miss., May 6, 1865.

NON-COMMISSIONED OFFICERS

(1) ASHWORTH, JOS. J. 4Cpl. — Orig. 4Cpl., Co. B: Reduced to ranks, Nov., 1862: K., Spotsylvania (May 13, 1864).
BROWN, THOS. C. 1Sgt. — Orig. Pvt., Co. B, age 22: Prom., 1Sgt., Jan., 1863: Present for duty as of May 31, 1863: No record after that.
BUGG, WM. T. Sgt. — Record not available.
(1) BULLARD, CHAS. M. C. 3Sgt. — Orig. 3Sgt., Co. B: No other record.
CHANDLER, JOSH S. 2Sgt. — Enl., at Berlin, Ark., Mar. 3, 1862: Prom., 2Sgt., Nov., 1862: Died of diphtheria, Fredericksburg, Va., Feb. 16, 1863.
(1) FOOTE, WM. A. 1Sgt. — See list of "Officers" above.
GOODWIN, THEOPHILUS 4Sgt. — Orig. Pvt., Co. B, age 21: Prom., 4Sgt., Feb. 16, 1863: W., Chickamauga (Sept. 19, 1863): Wound furlough, Macon, Miss.: AWOL in Ark., Dec., 1863.
(1) HENSON, JOHN T. 4Sgt. — See list of "Officers" above.
(1) JONES, J. WHITE 2Cpl. — See list of "Officers" above.
(2) LINDSEY, HARRISON 5Sgt. — Orig. Pvt., Co. B: Enl., age 19: Asgnd. as a Regmtl. teamster, Nov., 1862 to Aug., 1863: Sick, Summer, 1864: Prom., 5Sgt., Winter, 1864-65: Paroled, Appomattox (Apr. 12, 1865).
(2) McMURRAY, ROBT. E. 1Sgt. — Orig. Pvt., Co. B, age 20: Prom., 5Sgt., Mar. 1, 1864: Prom., 1Sgt., Winter, 1864-65: Paroled, Appomattox (Apr. 12, 1865).
MILENDER, JASPER N. 4Cpl. — Orig. Pvt., Co. B, age 24: Prom., 4Cpl., Nov., 1862: Present for duty to June, 1863: No records after that, may have been killed at Gettysburg.
MORRIS, ANDREW J. 2Sgt. — Orig. Pvt., Co. B, age 21: Prom., 3Sgt., July, 1863: Prom., 2Sgt., July, 1864: POW, Richmond hosp., Apr. 3, 1865: Paroled, Richmond, May 30, 1865.
MURRAY, JASPER N. 2Sgt. — Orig. Pvt., Co. B, age 22: Prom., 3Sgt., Jan., 1863: Prom., 2Sgt., July, 1863: Died, Oct., 1863.
(1) SAWYER, JAS. H. 3Cpl. — Orig. 3Cpl., Co. B, age 19: Reduced to ranks, July, 1863: Granted sick furlough, Apr., 1863: AWOL, Aug., 1863.
SEALE, JAS. 4Sgt. — Orig. Pvt., Co. B, age 24: Sick, Winter, 1862-63: Prom., 1Cpl., June, 1863: W., Gettysburg (July 2, 1863): Wound furlough to Greenville, Ala.: Prom., 4Sgt., Jan., 1864: Retired for disability, Greenville, Ala., Nov. 28, 1864.

(1) WYATT, WM. B. 1Cpl. — Orig. 1Cpl., Co. B, age 33: Absent sick in Richmond hosp., Oct., 1862 to Aug., 1863: Reduced to ranks, June, 1863: No record after Aug., 1863, may have been killed at Chickamauga.

PRIVATES

(1) ARMSTRONG, THOS. D. — Furloughs granted, Feb., 1862 & Jan., 1863: Absent sick at Berlin, Ark., Mar., 1863: Did not return to Co.

(1) BAKER, DENNIS — K., Darbytown Rd. (Oct. 7, 1864).

(1) BROWN, THOS. C. — See list of "Non-Commissioned Officers" above.

BURNEY, J. C. — Enl., at Berlin, Ark., Mar. 3, 1862: Sick in hospitals at Petersburg, Farmville and Danville, Va., Nov., 1862 to July, 1863: Sick furlough to Ark., July, 1863: Did not return to Co.

(1) COBB, SAMUEL D. — Enl., age 28: Present for duty entire war:
(2) Paroled, Appomattox (Apr. 12, 1865).

(1) COOPER, NORPHLET H. — Enl., age 18: POW, E. Tenn., Nov. 19, 1863: Took Fed. oath, Dec. 29, 1863.

(1) DENTON, GREEN B. — W. (right hand), Wilderness (May 6, 1864): POW, Chaffin's Farm (Sept. 29, 1864): Confined at Pt. Lookout, Md.: Exchanged, Feb. 10, 1865.

(1) FULLER, NELSON J. — Enl., age 21: Present for duty most of the
(2) war: Paroled, Appomattox (Apr. 12, 1865).

(1) GILLESPIE, WM. H. H. — Enl., age 20: W., Chickamauga (Sept. 19, 1863): Died of wound at Marietta, Ga., Oct. 11, 1863.

(1) GOLDSMITH, DANIEL R. — Enl., age 20: POW, Antietam (Sept. 17, 1862): Confined at Ft. McHenry, Md.: Exchanged, Oct. 27, 1862: AWOL from Chimborazo Hosp., Richmond, July 22, 1863.

(1) GOODWIN, THEOPHILUS — See list of "Non-Commissioned Officers" above.

(1) GRIFFIN, GEO. G. — Enl., age 20: Died of pneumonia at Richmond, Apr. 8, 1863.

(1) HAYNES, ALBERT — Enl., age 21: W. & POW, Gettysburg (July 2, 1863): Confined, Fed. hosp. in Baltimore: Exchanged, Oct. 15, 1863: Retired to Invalid Corps, Nov. 3, 1864.

(1) HAYNES, JESSE F. — Enl., age 18: W. & POW, Gettysburg (July 2, 1863): Confined, Fed. hosp. in Baltimore: Exchanged, Nov. 12, 1863.

(1) HUGHES, JAS. P. — Enl., age 20: Present for duty entire war: Paroled,
(2) Appomattox (Apr. 12, 1865).

JOHNSON, JOHN J. — Enl., age 26, in Carroll Co., Ark., Feb. 16, 1863: POW, Carroll Co., Mar. 31, 1863: Refused to take Fed. oath: Paroled, June 7, 1863.

(1) JOHNSON, WM. PIZZARRO — See list of "Officers" above.

JONES, H. H. — Enl., Mar. 3, 1862 in Ashley Co., Ark.: POW, Wilderness (May 6, 1864): Confined at Pt. Lookout, Md.: Exchanged, Oct. 29, 1864.

KINNARD, JAS. P. — Enl., Berlin, Ark., Dec. 16, 1861: W. (arm), Gettysburg (July 2, 1863): Wound furlough to Macon, Miss., Oct., 1863: Did not return to Co.

(1) KITCHENS, JAS. F. — Enl., age 26: Present for duty entire war:
(2) Paroled, Appomattox (Apr. 12, 1865).
(1) LINDSEY, HARRISON — See list of "Non-Commissioned Officers"
above.
LYLER, ANDREW L. — POW, Helena, Ark., July 4, 1863: Confined at
Fed. prison, Alton, Ill.: No other record.
(1) MARTIN, JOHN H. — Enl., age 21: POW, Antietam (Sept. 17, 1862):
Exchanged: K., Suffolk, Va., Apr. 22, 1863.
(1) MILENDER, JASPER N. — See list of "Non-Commissioned Officers"
above.
McARTHUR, CHAS. — POW, Gettysburg (July 2, 1863): No other
record.
(1) McMURRAY, ROBT. E. — See list of "Non-Comm. Officers" above.
MONCRIEF, STERLING P. — Enl., in Ashley Co., Ark., Mar. 3, 1862:
Sick, Spring & Summer, 1863: No record after Aug., 1863, may
have been killed at Chickamauga.
(1) MOORE, HARRISON — Enl., age 30: Transfd. to Co. K, 3rd Ark. Inf.
from Co. B, June 6, 1863.
(1) MORRIS, ANDREW J. — See list of "Non-Commissioned Officers"
above.
MOUND, JOHN — Paroled, Shreveport, La., June 7, 1865: No other
record.
MURPHY, P. — POW, Gettysburg (July 2, 1863): No other record.
(1) MURRAY, JASPER N. — See list of "Non-Commissioned Officers"
above.
NICHOLAS, BENJ. F. — POW, Green Co., Mo., Feb. 2, 1864: Confined
at Fed. prison, Alton, Ill.: Paroled, Mar. 2, 1865.
(1) NORRIS, JOHN T. — Enl., age 23: Asgnd. as a Regmtl. teamster, Mar.,
1862 to Feb., 1863: No record after June, 1863, may have been
killed at Gettysburg.
(1) OGLETREE, JAS. A. — Enl., age 28: Asgnd. as a Regmtl. teamster
most of 1862: W. (arm), Wilderness (May 6, 1864).
(1) OWEN, JESSE — Enl., age 19: Missing at Gettysburg (July 2, 1863):
No other record, probably killed at Gettysburg.
(1) POGUE, THOS. A. — Enl., age 31: POW, E. Tenn., Jan., 1864: Took
Fed. oath, Jan. 11, 1864.
(1) PURSLEY, SAMUEL C. — Enl., age 18: Appt. Steward of hosp. at
Chattanooga, Tenn., Feb. 18, 1863: No other record.
(1) REED, JASPER — Enl., age 24: Sick much of 1864 with chronic
diarrhea: No record after Sept., 1864.
REEVES, SAMUEL R. — POW, Madison Co., Ark., Oct. 20, 1863:
Confined at Pt. Lookout, Md.: Exchanged, Feb. 17, 1865.
(2) REID, JAS. W. — Enl. at Berlin, Ark., Mar. 3, 1862: Detached duty as a
shoemaker, Winter, 1862-63: Paroled, Appomattox (Apr. 12,
1865).
REID, JOHN L. — Enl. in Ashley Co., Ark., Mar. 3, 1862: Sick much of
1862 & 1863: No record after Feb., 1864.
(1) SANDERS, JOHN W. — Enl., age 21: Asgnd. to build cabins, Oct.,
1861: W. (thigh) & POW, Wilderness (May 6, 1864).

SAWYER, WEYMAN P. — Enl., in Ashley Co., Ark., Mar. 3, 1862: Dischgd., Jan. 22, 1863, underage.
(1) SEALE, CHAS. J. — See list of "Officers" above.
(1) SEALE, JAS. — See list of "Non-Commissioned Officers" above.
SHEARER, JOHN A. — Enl., at Berlin, Ark., Dec. 16, 1861: W., Antietam (Sept. 17, 1862): Granted furlough, June, 1863: Did not return to Co.
SLOVER, JOHN — POW, Barry Co., Mo., Mar. 25, 1863: Sentenced to hard labor and confined at the U.S. Milt. Prison, Alton, Ill.: Died in prison of anemia.
(1) SMITH, ALFRED — K., Bermuda Hundred, Va., June 16, 1864.
STACK, JAMES Q. — Died, Spring, 1863.
(1) WALDEN, J. F. — Sick in Richmond, Winter, 1862-63: AWOL, May, 1863: Did not return to Co.
WALDEN, JOHN — Enl., Mar. 21, 1862, at Berlin, Ark.: Hospitalized, Summer, 1864: No record after Aug., 1864.
(1) WALDEN, THOS. J. — Enl., age 18: Absent sick in Ark., Mar., 1863: No record after Aug., 1863.
WALDEN, WM. — Enl., Mar. 21, 1862, at Berlin, Ark.: W., Gettysburg (July 2, 1863): No other record.
(1) WALDRUP, FRANCIS M. — K., Bermuda Hundred, Va. (June 16, 1864).
(1) WALKER, JOHN H. — Enl. at 18: W. (thigh), Antietam (Sept. 17, 1862): Confined at Ft. McHenry, Md.: Exchanged, Mar. 13, 1863: Wound furlough to Ark., Apr., 1863: Did not return to Co.
(1) WALLACE, STEPHEN — Enl. at 26: W., Antietam (Sept. 17, 1862): W. (elbow & thigh), Gettysburg (July 2, 1863): Left arm amputated: Died from wounds, Aug. 22, 1863.
WALLING, J. — Enl. in Ashley Co., Ark., Mar. 21, 1862: Hospitalized, Dec., 1862 & Aug. & Sept., 1864: No other record.
WILHITE, L. P. — Enl., Mar. 22, 1862 in Ashley Co., Ark.: Dischgd. by order of Col. Manning, Dec. 30, 1862.
WILLIAMS, A. J. — Enl., Dec. 16, 1861 at Berlin, Ark.: Died of pneumonia at a hosp. in Richmond, Apr. 6, 1863.
(1) WILLIAMS, ROBT. — W., Antietam (Sept. 17, 1862): POW, Mechanics-ville, Va., Apr. 3, 1865: Confined at Pt. Lookout, Md.: Paroled, June 22, 1865.
(1) YOUNG, THOS. J. — Enl., age 21: POW, Kingston, Ga., Nov. 19, 1863: Confined in Fed. prison at Louisville, Ky.: Took Fed. oath, Dec. 29, 1863.
YOUNG, WM. — Enl., Mar. 3, 1862: W., Chickamauga (Sept. 19, 1863): Granted wound furlough to Ark., Dec., 1863: Did not return to Co.

★   ★   ★   ★   ★

MEMBERS OF COMPANY B., 3RD ARK. INF. REGT., WHO WERE NOT PRESENT FOR DUTY DURING THE PERIOD THAT THE REGIMENT WAS ASSIGNED TO HOOD'S TEXAS BRIGADE (NOV., 1862-APR., 1865)

OFFICERS

(1) Key, Drury H., Capt. (Orig. 1Lt. of Co.: Resgnd., Oct., 1862)

(1) Byrd, Young, 2Lt. (Orig. 2Lt. of Co.: Resgnd., Oct., 1861)

NON-COMMISSIONED OFFICERS

(1) Bailey, W. Julian, 2Sgt. (AWOL, Nov., 1862)
Biven, Robt., Sgt. (POW, Tenn., Dec., 1862)

(1) Keesee, Benton, 1Sgt. (K., Antietam)
(1) Sawyer, W. E., 3Sgt. (POW, Antietam)

MUSICIANS

(1) Chandler, Leonard M. (No record)

Johnson, Alfred (No record)

PRIVATES

(1) Attaway, John A. (No record)
Chandler, W. L. (No record)
Cranford, W. P. (POW, Antietam)
(1) Donaldson, Peter L. (D., Feb., 1862)
Englishby, Thos. A. (D., July, 1862)
(1) Ferguson, Wm. H. (No record)
(1) Fleming, James L. (No record)
(1) Fogle, Wm. A. (No record)
(1) Gaston, John N. (No record)
(1) Gillespie, Seaburn (D., July, 1861)
(1) Hamilton, David T. (No record)
(1) Hill, George W. (No record)
Holcomb, T. C. (D., Apr., 1862)
Holt, F. M. (D., Jan., 1862)
(1) Holt, Jonathan (D., July, 1861)
Hughes, Wm. P. (No record)
(1) Kenner, Benjamin (No record)
Marsh, W. E. (No record)
McKee, James (POW, Miss., Oct., 1862)
(1) McKain, James F. (No record)
Milender, Wm. D. (D., Feb., 1862)
(1) Nance, James W. (No record)
(1) Neel, James M. (No record)

(1) Radcliff, John C. (POW, Antietam)
(1) Ramsey, Thomas (No record)
Rayburn, Benjamin (No record)
Rayburn, Wm. J. (Disabled, Nov., 1862)
(1) Reaves, Jesse W. (D., Jan., 1862)
Reid, Jas. M. (D., Apr., 1862)
Reid, Wm. E. (Dischgd., Oct., 1862)
(1) Rogers, Wm. A. (No record)
(1) Sandford, Jesse L. (Provided substitute)
(1) Shippy, Wm. H. (No record)
(1) Slack, Jas. Q. (No record)
(1) Spears, Edw. (D., Jan., 1862)
(1) Stover, Elijah (No record)
(1) Tarply, David J. (D., July, 1861)
(1) Waits, Alford B. (Disabled, May, 1862)
Walling, W. (No record)
Watson, Geo. (POW, Tenn., 1862)
Watson, Jas. (No record)
(1) White, Stuart (No record)
(1) White, W. J. (Dischgd., Nov., 1862)

(1) Wilson, Chas. E. (Disabled, Jan., 1862)

3RD ARK. VOL. INF. REGMT.
COMPANY C

Company was organized in Drew County, Arkansas in early June, 1861, and was mustered into the Confederate Service, "for the war," at Lynchburg, Va., June 20, 1861, by Maj. H. L. Clay, CSA.

Key

(1) Original Member of Company. (2) Paroled at Appomattox
K (Killed), W (Wounded), POW (Prisoner of War)
AWOL (Absent Without Leave)

OFFICERS

FERRING, W. A. Capt. — Paroled, Augusta, Ga., May 18, 1865: No other record.

(1)
(2) HIGHTOWER, JOSHUA Capt. — Orig. 3Lt., Co. C: Prom., 2Lt., June 20, 1861: Prom., 1Lt., Nov., 1862: Prom., Capt., Dec. 1, 1862: W., Chickamauga (Sept. 19, 1863): Paroled, Appomattox (Apr. 12, 1865).

(1) WHITTINGTON, THOS. M. Capt. — Orig. Capt. of Co., age 27: Sick, Winter, 1861-1862: Resgnd., Dec. 1, 1862.

(1) WILLIAMS, MARK A. Capt. — Orig. 1Lt. of Co., age 25: Prom., Capt., Dec. 1, 1861: Died, Nov. 20, 1862.

HUDSPETH, HENRY S. 1Lt. — Orig. 1Sgt. of Co., age 22: Prom., 2Lt., June 20, 1861: Prom., 1Lt.: W., Antietam (Sept. 17, 1862): Prom., 1Lt., Dec. 1, 1862: Detailed to recruiting serv. in Ark., Summer, 1864.

BARKER, DAVID E. 2Lt. — Orig. Pvt. in Co.: Prom., 1Sgt., Dec. 17, 1861: Elect., 2Lt., Jan., 1863: W. (thigh), Gettysburg (July 2, 1863): Wound furlough, Aug., 1864: Retired, Dec. 5, 1864.

HAYNES, FRANK D. 2Lt. — Orig. Pvt. in Co., age 23: Prom., 2Lt., Summer, 1862: Resgnd. for disability (tuberculosis), June 1, 1863.

(1) PALMER, ABRAHAM W. 3Lt. — Enl. as a Pvt., age 30, at Monticello, Ark.: Appt. Sgt., Dec. 19, 1862: Appt. 3Lt., June 12, 1863: No record after June, 1863, may have been killed at Gettysburg.

NON-COMMISSIONED OFFICERS

(2) CONLEY, WM. E. 1Sgt. — Orig. Pvt. in Co.: Prom., 1Cpl., Nov., 1862: Prom., 3Sgt., Feb., 1864: Prom., 1Sgt., Winter, 1864-65: Paroled, Appomattox (Apr. 12, 1865).

(1) HUDSPETH, HENRY S. 1Sgt. — See list of "Officers" above.

(1) JETER, CHAS. W. 1Cpl. — Orig. 2Cpl. in Co., age 22: Present for duty
(2) during entire war: Paroled, Appomattox (Apr. 12, 1865).
MILLARD, NATHANIEL 2Sgt. — Orig. Pvt. in Co., age 24: Prom.,
3Cpl., Feb. 2, 1862: Prom., 3Sgt., Dec. 19, 1862: No record after
Aug., 1864.
PAYNE, THOMAS M. 3Sgt. — Enl., Aug. 31, 1861 at Camp Bartow,
Va., as a substitute for 3Sgt. John Gaston: No record after June
30, 1863, may have been killed at Gettysburg.
WATERS, WM. T. 1Sgt. — Orig. Musician in Co., age 19: Prom., 1Sgt.,
Dec. 9, 1862: W. (foot) & POW, Gettysburg (July 2, 1863): Last
two toes of left foot amputated: Confined at Fed. hosp., Davids
Is., N.Y. Harbor: Exchanged: Asgnd. duty with QM Depot,
Macon, Ga.
WELCH, ROBT. L. 3Cpl. — Orig. Pvt. in Co., age 18: Prom., 3Cpl.,
Dec. 19, 1862: AWOL, Dec., 1863: Dropped from rolls, Aug.,
1864.
WILSON, ELIAS N. 4Cpl. — Orig. Pvt. in Co., age 23: Prom., 4Cpl.,
Apr. 30, 1862: W. (groin) & POW, Wilderness (May 6, 1864):
Paroled, Griffin, Ga., May 19, 1865.

MUSICIANS

(1) SUMNER, SIMON P. — Enl., age 26: "Deserted the battle field at
Chickamauga," Sept. 19, 1863: Dropped from rolls.
(1) WATERS, WM. T. — See list of "Non-Comm. Officers" above.

PRIVATES

BALDY, THOS. H. — Enl. at Monticello, Ark., Mar. 31, 1862: POW,
Falling Waters, Md., July 21, 1863: Took Fed. oath at
Washington, Mar. 22, 1864.
(2) BARDEN, JAS. T. — W. (shoulder), Darbytown Rd. (Oct. 7, 1864):
Paroled, Appomattox (Apr. 12, 1865).
(1) BARKER, DAVID E. — See list of "Officers" above.
BARNES, NATHANIEL H. — Enl. at 50, Mar. 22, 1862 at Monticello,
Ark.: Died in Va., Apr. 17, 1863.
(1) BENNETT, JAS. M. — Enl., age 22: Sick, Fall, 1862: AWOL, Nov.,
1862: Deserted, Memphis, Tenn., Feb. 16, 1864.
(1) BOATNER, JOHN L. — Enl., age 22: Sick, Winter, 1862-63: AWOL,
Winter, 1863-64: Dropped from rolls, Feb., 1864.
BOYLES, ROBT. — Died of disease, June, 1863 in Fed. Prison.
BRADLEY, WM. M. — Enl., age 22, at Monticello, Ark., Dec. 9, 1862:
POW, Memphis, Feb. 9, 1865.
BRIDGES, HIRAM — Enl. at Monticello, Ark., Feb. 9, 1863: W.
(hand), Gettysburg (July 2, 1863): AWOL, Sept. 20, 1863,
dropped from rolls.
BRIDGES, WILEY — Enl., age 41, at Monticello, Ark., Mar. 5, 1862:
Hospitalized, Summer, 1863 (chronic diarrhea).
CARPENTER, HENRY L. — Enl., age 34 at Monticello, Ark., Mar. 17,
1862: K., Suffolk, Va. (May 3, 1863).

(1) CASH, THOS. B. — Enl., age 18: Died (dysentery), May 30, 1863 in a Petersburg hosp.

(1) COLLINS, ANDREW J. — Enl., age 21: POW: Exchanged at Chattanooga, Jan. 11, 1863.

(1) CONLEY, WM. E. — See list of "Non-Commissioned Officers" above.

CRAIN, HOWELL P. — Enl., age 33 at Gaines Lodge, Ark., Apr. 2, 1862: Transfd. to Co. D, 3rd Ark. Inf., Nov., 1862.

(1) CRYER, THOS. E. — Dischgd., for disability (heart trouble) at Petersburg, Va., Oct. 1, 1862: Re-enl. in Co. D, 3rd Ark. Inf., Feb. 27, 1863.

CULLEN, C. — Paroled, Charlotte, No. Car., May, 1865: No other record.

(1) CUNNINGHAM, JAS. M. — Enl., age 23: Deserted in E. Tenn., Nov. 25, 1863: Took Fed. oath, Pine Bluff, Ark., Apr. 6, 1864.

(1) CUNNINGHAM, JOSHUA W. — Enl., age 19: Deserted, E. Tenn., Nov., 1863: Took Fed. oath at Knoxville, Dec. 29, 1863.

(1) DIKES, HECTOR M. — Enl., age 21: Died, Aug. 5, 1863.

DOUGLAS, WM. R. — Enl., age 22 at Monticello, Ark., Mar. 20, 1862: Deserted, E. Tenn., Nov. 18, 1863: Took Fed. oath in Drew Co., Ark.

DRAPER, W. B. — Paroled, June 13, 1865 at Shreveport, La.: No other record.

DURHAM, HENRY F. — Enl., age 23: Absent sick, Richmond, Mar., 1863: AWOL, Nov., 1863.

(2) FERGUSON, JOHN A. — Enl., age 23 at Monticello, Ark., Mar. 22, 1862: AWOL, Winter, 1862-63: Sick, Winter, 1863-64: Paroled, Appomattox (Apr. 12, 1865).

(1) FRY, JOS. — Enl., age 34: W. & POW, Antietam (Sept. 17, 1862): Exchanged: Dischgd. for disability, June 21, 1863.

(1) GLOSSUP, BEN. F. — Enl., age 22: Detailed as a teamster, Summer & (2) Fall, 1863: W. (right shoulder), Bermuda Hundred, Va., June 19, 1864: Paroled, Appomattox (Apr. 12, 1865).

HALE, J. T. — Enl., age 21, at Carroll, Mo., June 29, 1862: POW, Carroll Co., Ark., Apr. 3, 1863: Exchanged, City Pt., Va., June 2, 1863: Paroled, Meridian, Miss., May 14, 1865.

(1) HAYNES, FRANK D. — See list of "Officers" above.

(1) HAYNES, THOS. W. — Enl., age 18: Deserted, E. Tenn., Nov. 18, 1863: Took Fed. oath at Knoxville, Dec. 29, 1863.

(1) HEREFORD, THOS. — Enl., age 24: POW, Gettysburg (July 2, 1863): Confined at Ft. Delaware: Took Fed. oath, Apr. 19, 1864.

HYATT, ROBT. F. — Enl., age 17 at Monticello, Ark., Mar. 15, 1862: W. & POW, Antietam (Sept. 17, 1862): Confined at Ft. McHenry, Md.: Exchanged, Jan. 31, 1863.

(1) JACKSON, PHINEAS T. — Enl., age 23: W., Chickamauga (Sept. 19, 1863).

JAMES, JASPER J. — Enl., age 19 at Cut Off, Ark., Apr. 1, 1862: POW, Gettysburg (July 2, 1863): Confined at Ft. Delaware, Md.

(1) JOHNSON, JOHN M. — Enl., age 19: Nursed sick in Richmond, Summer, 1861: Present for duty to June, 1863: No other record.

(1) JORDAN, CLAYBORN — Died of measles, Mar. 10, 1863.

(1) LAW, PEYTON — Enl., age 50: Dischgd. for disability, Mar. 24, 1863.

(2) LAW, WYATT S. (or L.) — Enl. at Monticello, Ark., Feb. 7, 1863:
Paroled, Appomattox (Apr. 12, 1865).

LITTLETON, SAMUEL H. — Enl., age 36 at Monticello, Ark., Dec. 9,
1862: AWOL since Mar., 1864 in Ark.: Deserted, took Fed. oath
at Pine Bluff, Ark., Apr., 1864.

McCALL, JAS. R. — Enl., age 20, at Monticello, Ark., Mar. 26, 1862:
Died of apoplexy at Petersburg, May 21, 1863.

McCALL, JOHN F. — Enl., age 18, at Monticello, Ark., Mar. 22, 1862:
AWOL, Winter, 1863-64: Dropped from rolls, Feb., 1864.

McCAMMUR, J. W. — POW, Shelbyville, Tenn., June 27, 1863:
Confined at Ft. Delaware: No other record.

(1) MILLARD, NATHANIEL — See list of "Non-Comm. Officers" above.

MITCHELL, JOS. N. — Enl., Mar. 5, 1863: POW, Tuscaloosa, Ala., May
18, 1865: Paroled.

(1) NEAL, REASON L. — Enl., age 27: Sick, most of enlistment: Sick
furlough granted, Oct., 1863: AWOL, dropped from rolls, Feb.,
1864.

NICHOLS, FRANCIS M. — Enl., age 18, at Monticello, Ark., Mar. 8,
1863: Dischgd. for tuberculosis, Oct. 26, 1863.

(1) OTTS, SAMUEL P. — Enl., age 24: Extra duty as a teamster, Dec.,
(2) 1861: Sick, Spring, 1863 & Summer, 1864: Paroled, Appomattox
(Apr. 12, 1865).

(1) PARKER, JOHN B. — Enl., age 25: Detailed to Div. Pioneer Corps,
Winter, 1862-63: POW, Richmond, Apr. 3, 1865.

(1) PATTON, JOHN W. — Enl., age 18: K., Suffolk, Va., May 3, 1863.

PHILLIPS, JOAB L. — Enl., age 23, at Monticello, Ark., June 10, 1862:
Detailed at various times as a Regmtl. foragemaster, carpenter &
wheelwright, May, 1862 to July, 1864.

(1) PRICE, JOHN R. — Enl., age 19: W., Chickamauga (Sept. 19, 1863):
Disabled by wound & dischgd.

(1) PRITCHARD, BARTON R. — Enl., age 24: Detailed as orderly for Col.
Van Manning: No record after June, 1863, may have been killed
at Gettysburg.

(1) REYNOLDS, WM. M. — Enl., age 28: Detailed as a Provost Guard,
Spring, 1862: Hospitalized, Spring, 1863: Sick furlough to Ark.,
June, 1863: AWOL: Dropped from rolls, Feb., 1864.

(1) ROBERTSON, AARON T. — Enl., age 23: W., Antietam (Sept. 17,
1862): Little finger amputated: No record after, June, 1863, may
have been killed at Gettysburg.

REDMOND, S. M. — POW, Vicksburg (July 4, 1863): No other record.

(1) ROBERTSON, AMOS T. — Enl., age 22: Deserted in E. Tenn., Jan. 15,
1864.

(1) ROBERTSON, JAS. B. — Enl., age 20: W. (leg), Wilderness (May 6,
(2) 1864): Paroled, Appomattox (Apr. 12, 1865).

(1) ROWLAND, SUMTER — K., Suffolk, Va., May 3, 1863.

(1) RUST, JAS. A. — See roster, "Regmtl. Hdqtrs., 3rd Ark. Inf."

RUST, ROBT. S. — See roster, "Regmtl. Hdqtrs., 3rd Ark. Inf."

(1) SAWYERS, HARRISON H. — Enl., age 18: W. (back) & POW,
Gettysburg (July 2, 1863): Confined at Fed. hosp. at Davids Is.,
N.Y. Harbor: Paroled, Aug. 24, 1863: No other record.

(1) SINCLAIR, JOHN A. — Enl., age 23: K., Cold Harbor (June 2, 1864).

THOMPSON, SAMUEL D. — Enl., age 32, at Gaines Lodge, Ark., Apr. 2, 1862: Present for duty until Feb., 1864: No record after that date.

(1) THOMPSON, THOS. L. — Enl., age 26: POW, Gettysburg (July 2, 1863): Confined at Ft. Delaware: Took Fed. oath, Nov. 15, 1863: Jnd. U.S. Navy, Mar. 16, 1864.

(1) TUGGLE, ROBT. L. — W., Chickamauga (Sept. 19, 1863): Wound furlough granted: Did not return to Co.

(2) TUGGLE, WM. T. — Enl., age 20, at Monticello, Ark., Mar. 28, 1862: Sick, Spring & Summer, 1863: Paroled, Appomattox (Apr. 12, 1865).

VICK, IREDELL R. — A minister by profession: Enl. as a Pvt. at Monticello, Ark., Mar. 22, 1863: Transfd. to Co. K, 1st Tex. Inf. Regt., June 13, 1863.

(1) VICK, THADDEUS W. — Enl., age 22: W., Antietam (Sept. 17, 1862): W. (foot), Wilderness (May 6, 1864): Foot amputated: Dischgd. for disability, Dec. 15, 1864.

(1) VINING, OREGON J. — Enl., age 17: K., Petersburg trenches, June 22, 1864.

(1) WALKER, JOHN A. — Enl., age 26: W. (thigh) & POW, Gettysburg (July 2, 1863): Left leg amputated: Retired to Invalid Corps, Nov. 11, 1864.

(1) WALKER, WM. P. — Enl., age 28: POW, Gettysburg (July 2, 1863), left as nurse for wounded: Paroled: Furlough to Ark.: AWOL, dropped from rolls.

WARD, S. J. — POW, Mercer Co., Ky., June 9, 1862: Paroled, Aug. 4, 1863 at Ft. Monroe, Va.: No other record.

(1) WELCH, ROBT. L. — See list of "Non-Comm. Officers" above.

(1) WELLS, THOS. L. S. — Enl., age 22: W. (back) & POW, Gettysburg (July 2, 1863): Paroled, Davids Is., N.Y. Harbor, Aug. 24, 1863: Wound furlough to Ark.: AWOL: Dropped from rolls, Feb., 1864.

(1) WILSON, ELIAS N. — See list of "Non-Comm. Officers" above.

(1) WILSON, HENRY S. — Enl., age 19: Detailed as a teamster, Apr., 1862 to Feb., 1863: Deserted at Suffolk, Va., May 3, 1863.

(1) WILSON, THOS. J. — Enl., age 24: W. (hand), Bermuda Hundred, June
(2) 17, 1864: Paroled, Appomattox (Apr. 12, 1865).

(1) YOUNG, SPENCER — Enl., age 18: W. (thigh), Wilderness (May 6, 1864): W. (groin), Chaffin's Farm (Sept. 29, 1864): Retired for disability, Mar. 15, 1865.

★ ★ ★ ★ ★

MEMBERS OF COMPANY C, 3RD ARK. INF. REGT. WHO WERE NOT PRESENT FOR DUTY DURING THE PERIOD THAT THE REGIMENT WAS ASSIGNED TO HOOD'S TEXAS BRIGADE (NOV., 1862-APR., 1865).

OFFICERS

(1) Burks, Wm. P., 2 Lt. (Orig. 2Lt.
of Co.: Resgnd., Sept.,
1862.)

NON-COMMISSIONED OFFICERS

(1) Allen, Riley P., Cpl. (Dischgd.
for sickness, Sept., 1862)
(1) Baker, John A., Cpl. (Dischgd.
for disability)
Crain, Geo. W., Cpl. (No
record)
Dumbow, J. E., 3Cpl. (No
record)
(1) Easley, Dunbar T., Sgt. (No
record)

(1) Gaster, John, Sgt. (No record)
(1) Gibson, Samuel, Sgt. (Dischgd.,
Oct. 12, 1861)
(1) Hyatt, Ben F. J., Sgt.-Maj. (Dischgd., Feb. 10, 1862)
Parker, John A., 4Cpl. (No
record)
(1) Wells, Frank S., 2Sgt. (D., Sept.
25, 1861)

PRIVATES

(1) Baldy, Stephen S. (K., July,
1861)
Barker, Cornelius W. (POW)
Barker, Jas. C. (Dischgd., disability, July, 1862)
(1) Barnes, Jas. A. (D., Sept., 1861)
(1) Barnett, Jas. D. (D., Mar.,
1862)
(1) Biggs, Benj. (No record)
(1) Boring, John M. (No record)
(1) Bowden, Edw. (Dischgd., disability, Aug., 1862)
(1) Boyd, David J. (D., Nov., 1861)
(1) Brooks, James W. (W. & POW,
Greenbrier R., Oct., 1861)
(1) Bullock, Cyprian (Dischgd.,
unfit)
(1) Burtons, Jas. J. (No record)
Carpenter, Samuel H. (Dischgd.,
underage, 15)
Carter, Lafayette (No record)
Chambers, Ransom L. (Dis-
chgd., Antietam wound)
Champlain, Hugh (No record)
Clink, Benhart (No record)
(1) Coatney, John S. (No record)
(1) Collier, Needham B. (Transfd.
out)

Collins, Pleasant B. (No record)
(1) Cox, Archibald G. (D., Aug.,
1861)
(1) Davis, Daniel W. (Dischgd.,
Sept., 1861)
(1) Denton, Matthew (No record)
Dial, J. (No record)
(1) Ellis, Wm. G. (D., Oct., 1861)
(1) Erwin, Jas. A. (D., Jan., 1862)
(1) Fartheree, Jas. M. (D., Aug.,
1861)
Ferguson, Elijah H. (No record)
(1) Ferguson, Jas. O. (D., Dec.,
1861)
(1) Flemister, Jas. H. (Dischgd.,
May, 1862)
Fulks, Geo. S. (No record)
(1) Furguson, Edw. R. (No record)
(1) Furguson, Marmaduke E. (W.,
Antietam, AWOL)
(1) Furguson, Wm. F. (No record)
(1) Gibson, Wm. (K., Antietam)
Harmon, Milford L. (W. &
POW, Antietam)
Hemingway, Sullivan S. (Took
Fed. oath)
Holkersmith, T. D. (No record)
(1) House, Robt. (D., Apr., 1862)

(1) Hyatt, Elijah L. (K., Antietam)
(1) Ivy, Henry C. (W., Antietam, AWOL)
Johnson, S. T. (POW, Oct., 1862)
(1) Jones, Jas. B. R. (AWOL)
(1) Jordan, Jas. T. (Took Fed. oath)
Kanady, Wm. H. (No record)
(1) Kidd, Robt. A. (Rejected, unfit)
(1) Kimbro, Wm. C. (Dischgd., disability)
(1) Lewis, Hampton W. (Dischgd., disability)
McAlister, Francis M. (Dischgd., disability)
McCall, Wm. K. (No record after Mar., 1862)
(1) McClure, Christopher C. (D., Feb., 1862)
(1) McFarland, Dennis (D., Aug., 1861)
(1) Middleton, John W. (D., Jan., 1862)

(1) Nelson, Arnold J. (D., Aug., 1861)
O'Hara, E. C. (No record)
(1) Palmer, Daniel L. (POW, Antietam)
(1) Powell, John B. (D., July, 1861)
Rasberry, John L. (AWOL)
(1) Sacket, John (Dischgd., disability)
Scott, W. M. (D., Dec., 1862 in Miss.)
Shores, J. D. (No record)
(1) Summers, Jas. M. (D., Aug., 1861)
(1) Veasey, Leonidas S. (Disabled, Antietam)
(1) Wade, Wm. W. (K., Antietam)
(1) Walker, John C. (Rejected for service in Va.)
Watts, Francis B. (No record)
(1) White, Chas. L. (No record)
Wootan, Bailey L. (K., Antietam)

3RD ARK. VOL. INF. REGT.

COMPANY D

Company was organized in Drew County, Arkansas in early June, 1861 and was mustered into the Confederate service, "for the war," at Lynchburg, Va., July 2, 1861, by Maj. H. L. Clay, CSA.

Key

(1) Original member of Company. (2) Paroled at Appomattox.
K (Killed), W (Wounded), POW (Prisoner of War)
AWOL (Absent Without Leave)

OFFICERS

FITZGERALD, WILEY Capt. — Orig. 1Sgt. of Co., age 24: Prom., 1Lt., Sept. 7, 1861: On recruiting serv. to Ark., Spring, 1862: Prom., Capt., Apr. 23, 1863: Resgnd., May 19, 1863.

(1) HARRELL, SAMUEL C. Capt. − Orig. 3Lt. of Co., age 27: Prom.,
2Lt., Apr. 23, 1862: Prom., 1Lt., June 12, 1862: Prom., Capt.,
May 19, 1863: K., Petersburg trenches, July 1, 1864.

MARTIN, AMOS G. Capt. − Enl. as a Pvt., at Memphis, Tenn., Feb.
21, 1862: Elect., 3Lt., Nov. 6, 1862: Prom., 1Lt. & Capt., July 1,
1864: POW, Darbytown Rd. (Oct. 7, 1864): Confined at Ft.
Delaware: Paroled, June 17, 1865.

(1) TOUCHSTONE, PEMBROKE S. 1Lt. − Orig. Pvt. in Co., age 31:
Elect., 2Lt., Nov. 6, 1862: Elect., 1Lt., May 19, 1863: Deserted
in E. Tenn., Feb. 5, 1864: Dropped from rolls, June 27, 1864.

RODGERS, ALBERT W. 2Lt. − POW (place unk.): Exchanged,
Springfield, Mo., June 16, 1863: No other record.

NON-COMMISSIONED OFFICERS

BREEDLOVE, JOHN M. 1Sgt. − Orig. Pvt. in Co., age 21: Prom.,
1Sgt., Apr., 1864: K., Wilderness (May 6, 1864).

BREEDLOVE, WM. E. 1Cpl. − Orig. Pvt. in Co., age 23: W.,
Gettysburg (July 2, 1863): Prom., 1Cpl., Summer, 1864.

CARTER, WM. J. 1Cpl. − Orig. Pvt. in Co., age 23: Prom., 1Cpl.,
May, 1863: K., Chickamauga (Sept. 19, 1863).

DONALDSON, JAS. P. 2Sgt. − Orig. Pvt. in Co., age 23: Prom., 1Cpl.,
Jan., 1863: Sick (acute diarrhea), Summer, 1863: Prom., 2Sgt.,
May, 1864: POW, Darbytown Rd. (Oct. 7, 1864): Confined at Pt.
Lookout, Md.: Died in Prison, Apr. 21, 1865.

(1) FITZGERALD, WILEY − See list of "Officers" above.

(1) HARRELL, JAS. A. 1Sgt. − Orig. 3Cpl. of Co., age 23: W. (head),
(2) Wilderness (May 6, 1864): Paroled, Appomattox (Apr. 12, 1865).

McLEAR, JOHN Sgt. − POW, Shelbyville, Tenn., June 27, 1863:
Confined at Ft. Delaware: Exchanged, July 20, 1863: No other
record.

(1) PRUITT (or PREWIT), CASS 1Sgt. − Orig. 3Sgt. of Co., age 24: POW,
Antietam (Sept. 17, 1862): Paroled, Sept. 19, 1862: Prom.,
1Sgt., May, 1863: W. & POW, Gettysburg (July 2, 1863):
Confined, U.S. Gen'l. Hosp., Chester, Pa.: Exchanged, Sept. 17,
1863.

(1) ROWELL, GEO. W. 1Sgt. − Orig. Pvt. in Co., age 25: Prom., 1Sgt.,
Jan., 1863: Reduced to ranks, June 16, 1863: Deserted, E. Tenn.,
Feb. 22, 1864.

WILLIAMS, L. Cpl. − POW, Helena, Ark., July 4, 1863: Confined, Ft.
Delaware: Exchanged, Mar. 7, 1865.

MUSICIAN

(1) WHITE, JOHN H. − Orig. Musc. in Co., age 27: Reduced to Pvt., Mar.,
(2) 1862: Paroled, Appomattox (Apr. 12, 1865).

PRIVATES

(1) (2) ANDERSON, WM. T. — Enl., age 21: Sick most of 1862: Paroled, Appomattox (Apr. 12, 1865).

ATKERSON (or ATKINSON), THOS. — Enl., Mar. 14, 1862 at Warren, Ark.: W., Gettysburg (July 2, 1862): Paroled, Salisbury, No. Car., May 19, 1865.

BARRETT, J. L. — Enl., Mar. 13, 1863 at Cut Off, Ark.: POW, Gettysburg (July 2, 1863): Confined at Ft. Delaware: Died in prison of measles, Aug. 23, 1863.

BARRETT, THOS. — Deserted, E. Tenn., Mar. 14, 1864.

(1) BOYD, FRANK M. — Enl., age 21: POW, Gettysburg (July 2, 1863), left with wounded: Confined at Pt. Lookout, Md.: Paroled, Feb. 23, 1865.

(1) BREEDLOVE, JOHN M. — See list of "Non-Comm. Officers" above.

(1) BREEDLOVE, WM. E. — See list of "Non-Comm. Officers" above.

(1) (2) BUSH, JAS. — Enl., age 22: W., Wilderness (May 6, 1864): Unfit for field duty: Paroled, Appomattox (Apr. 12, 1865).

(1) CARTER, DELTON H. — Enl., age 20: W., Chickamauga (Sept. 19, 1863): Paroled, Augusta, Ga., May 25, 1865.

CARTER, J. P. — Enl., Mar. 21, 1863 at Cut Off, Ark.: Died of "congestion of the brain," June 5, 1863 at Rapidan River, Va.

(1) CARTER, WM. J. — See list of "Non-Commissioned Officers" above.

(1) CHILDERS, JOHN H. — Enl., age 21: W., Gettysburg (July 2, 1863): Granted leave to Petersburg, Fall, 1863: Did not return to Co.: Paroled at Petersburg, Va.

CRAIN, HOWELL P. — Transfd. to Co. D from Co. C, Nov., 1862: Detailed as cook, unfit for field service: Paroled, Chattanooga, May 21, 1865.

(1) (2) CROW, THOS. T. — Enl. at 17: Present for duty most of the war: Paroled, Appomattox (Apr. 12, 1865).

CRYER, THOS. E. — Orig. Pvt. in Co. C: Discharged: Re-enl. in Co. D, Feb. 27, 1863: W., Gettysburg (July 2, 1863): Asgnd. to hosp. duty, Spring, 1864.

DILBY, J. W. — POW, Gettysburg (July 2, 1863): No other record.

(1) DONALDSON, JAS. P. — See list of "Non-Comm. Officers" above.

(1) FORRESTER, JOHN — Enl., age 21: POW, Knoxville, Mar. 26, 1864: Confined at Camp Chase, Ohio: Paroled, May 10, 1865.

(1) FRAZER, ANDREW J. — Enl., age 28: W., Gettysburg (July 2, 1863): W. (head), Williamsburg Rd. (Oct. 27, 1864): Died from wound, Nov. 11, 1864.

(1) HARLE, ARMSTEAD B. — Enl., age 36: W. (arm), Chickamauga (Sept. 19, 1863): W. (leg), Wilderness (May 6, 1864): Paroled, Nashville, May 22, 1865.

(1) JONES, MARION C. — Enl., age 18: W., Jan. 4, 1862: W. (thigh), Chickamauga (Sept. 20, 1863): K., Petersburg trenches (July 13, 1864).

(1) KERR, JOHN D. — POW, E. Tenn., Feb. 13, 1864: Confined at Alton, Ill. Prison.

(1) LEVEL, LYCURGUS T. — Enl., age 20: Asgnd. duty as a Div. teamster, Winter, 1863-64: Deserted, E. Tenn., Apr. 2, 1864.

(1) LUSBY, JOHN B. — Enl., age 27: POW, Cheat Mtn., Va. (Aug. 22, 1861): Exchanged: Died of a brain hemmorhage, Lynchburg, Va., Mar. 2, 1863.

LUSBY, WM. G. — Enl., age 21: Present for duty until Fall, 1864: K., Darbytown Rd. (Oct. 7, 1864).

LYTLE, J. T. — Enl., age 23, at Gaines Lodge, Ark., Apr. 2, 1862: Deserted, E. Tenn., Feb. 22, 1864.

(1) LYTLE, TREVALON L. — Enl., age 17: W. (neck), Gettysburg (July 2, 1863): Deserted, E. Tenn., Feb. 22, 1864.

MARTIN, AMOS G. — See list of "Non-Comm. Officers" above.

(1) McDUFFEY, PATRICK — Enl., age 31: W. (hand), Suffolk (Apr. 12, 1863): AWOL: Dropped from rolls for "protracted absence," Aug., 1864.

McGUIRE, HENRY — POW, Jonesboro, Ga., Sept. 1, 1864: Confined at Camp Douglas, Ill.: Paroled, May 17, 1865.

McKINNEY, EDMON J. — Enl., age 32 at Gaines' Lodge, Ark., Apr. 2, 1862: Detailed as a blacksmith, Spring, 1862: Sick, Winter, 1862-63: W., Chickamauga (Sept. 19, 1863): Retired for disability.

(1) MITCHELL, WM. — Enl., age 22: Deserted, Morristown, E. Tenn., Mar. 15, 1864: No other records.

NEELY, JOHN ISIAH — POW, Harrison Landing, Va., Aug. 16, 1863: Confined at Ft. Delaware.

(1) PASCHALL, MICHAEL E. — Enl., age 20: POW, Gettysburg (July 2, 1863): Confined, Ft. Delaware: Took Fed. oath, Jan., 1865.

(1) PITMAN, GILES C. — Enl., age 25: Detailed as a nurse in hosp. at Emory, Va., Mar., 1864: Transfd. to Capt. Chisholm's Co. of Florida Scouts, Jan. 11, 1865.

(1) ROWELL, GEO. W. — See list of "Non-Comm. Officers" above.

(1) TINER, JACOB H. — Enl., age 25: Present for duty entire war: Paroled,
(2) Appomattox (Apr. 12, 1865).

(1) TINER, LUKE M. — Enl., age 17: W., Chickamauga (Sept. 19, 1863): Retired from service, "totally disqualified."

(1) TINSLEY, WM. N. — Enl., age 23: Sick, Spring, 1863: No record after Aug., 1863, may have been killed at Chickamauga.

(1) TOUCHSTONE, PEMBROKE S. — See list of "Officers" above.

(1) TRIBBLE, BENJ. F. — Enl., age 38: Sick much of 1863: Died at Greensboro, Ga., Feb. 11, 1864.

WEATHERALL, J. M. — Enl. at Cut Off, Ark., Mar. 7, 1863: Detailed to special duty at Culpeper, Va., June 13, 1863: No other record.

(1) WILLIAMS, JOHN G. — Enl., age 19: Dropped from rolls for prolonged absence, Aug., 1864.

(1) WILSON, THOS. E. — Enl., age 19: Present for duty until Feb., 1864, no record after that date.

WISE, EPHRAIM A. — POW, Chattanooga, Oct. 2, 1863: Confined at Camp Morton, Ind.: Exchanged, Feb. 19, 1865.

(1) YATES, WM. H. — Enl., age 16: W., Gettysburg (July 2, 1863): Hospitalized in Richmond, Summer, 1864.

* * * * *

MEMBERS OF COMPANY D, 3RD ARK. INF. REGT. WHO WERE NOT PRESENT FOR DUTY DURING THE PERIOD THAT THE REGIMENT WAS ASSIGNED TO HOOD'S TEXAS BRIGADE (NOV., 1862-APR., 1865).

OFFICERS

(1) Stone, John L., 1Lt. (Orig. 1Lt. of Co.: Dischgd. for disability, June, 1862).

(1) Tillar, J. Thos. W., 2Lt. (Orig. 2Lt. of Co.: Resgnd., June, 1862).

(1) Walker, John A., 2Lt. (Orig. Pvt. in Co: K., Antietam).

NON-COMMISSIONED OFFICERS

(1) Lytle, Harmon O., Cpl. (No record)

(1) Mason, Jesse, Sgt. (No record)

(1) Phillips, David P., Sgt. (D., Feb., 1862).

(1) Wiley, Edw., Sgt. (Dischgd., disability, Oct., 1861).

MUSICIANS

(1) Harper, Darins M. (Dischgd., disability, Jan., 1862).

PRIVATES

(1) Arrington, West A. (W. & POW, Antietam)

(1) Bartlett, Jos. R. (No record)

(1) Beckerdite, Oliver C. (Dischgd., disability, June, 1862)

(1) Beshires, Wm. (AWOL, Winter, 1862-63)

(1) Bond, John F. (Transfd. to Co. E, Dec., 1861)

(1) Boyd, Jas. M. (No record)

(1) Breedlove, Ransom S. (Dischgd., disability, July, 1862)

(1) Breedlove, Richard L. (No record)

(1) Bush, Jesse D. (Dischgd., disability, Dec., 1861)

(1) Carrick, Thos. J. (W., W. Va., Jan. 4, 1862)

(1) Carter, Martin V. (Dischgd., disability, Apr., 1862)

(1) Claypole, Jerry (No record)

(1) Donaldson, Alex. (D., Dec., 1861)

(1) Harris, Isham H. (POW, Cheat Mtn., Va., Fall, 1861)

(1) Henderson, John (Dischgd., disability, Jan., 1862)

(1) Holcomb, Dennis (No record)

Kerby, Wm. E. P. (POW)

Marshbanks, C. C. (No record)

Murphy, Vinson W. (POW)

(1) Nations, Thos. J. (No record)

(1) Paschall, John W. (No record)

(1) Peacock, Lovett M. (K., Antietam)

(1) Peacock, Walter G. (Dischgd., Feb., 1862)

Ragisdis, L. L. (No record)

Rankin, R. N. (No record)

Shears, W. B. (No record)

Stiles, Jas. R. (D., Mar., 1862)

(1) Touchstone, Geo. W. (AWOL)

COMPANY E

Company was organized in Union County, Arkansas, in early June, 1861 and mustered into the Confederate Service "for the war," at Lynchburg, Va., July 2, 1861, by Maj. H. L. Clay, CSA.

Key

(1) Original member of Company. (2) Paroled at Appomattox.
K (Killed), W (Wounded), POW (Prisoner of War)
AWOL (Absent Without Leave)

OFFICERS

(2) HARRISON, WM. H. Capt. — Orig. Pvt. in Co., age 24: Elect., 3Lt., Mar. 3, 1863: Prom., 2Lt., July 30, 1863: Prom., Capt., May 26, 1864: Paroled, Appomattox (Apr. 12, 1865).

(1) TUCKER, BARNARD H. Capt. — Orig. 2Lt. of Co., age 28: Prom., 1Lt., Apr. 1, 1862: Prom., Capt., Nov., 1862: Released from service, Jan. 20, 1863.

STEVENS, JAS. M. Capt. — Orig. Pvt. in Co., age 28: Prom., 2Lt., Apr. 10, 1862: Prom., 1Lt., May, 1862: Prom., Capt., Nov., 1862: In arrest, Aug., 1863.

(2) PICKENS, JAS. D. 1Lt. — Transfd. into Co. E. as a Pvt. from 2nd Btln. Ark. Inf., July 18, 1862: Prom., 2Lt., Mar. 4, 1864: Prom., 1Lt., May 26, 1864: W. (hand), Darbytown Rd. (Oct. 7, 1864): Paroled, Appomattox (Apr. 12, 1865).

SMITH, THOS. J. 1Lt. — Orig. 4Sgt. of Co., age 23: Elect., 2Lt., May, 1862: Elect., 1Lt., Oct. 28, 1862: Arrested, Feb. 14, 1863: Court-Martialed: Cashiered from service, July 30, 1863: Conscripted, Aug. 1, 1863: Transfd. to Co. K, Cobb's Legion of Cav., Sept. 3, 1863.

NON-COMMISSIONED OFFICERS

AMASON, JESSE T. 1Cpl. — Orig. Pvt. in Co., age 23: Prom., 2Cpl., Nov., 1862: POW, Gettysburg (July 2, 1863): Exchanged: Prom., 1Cpl., Apr., 1864: POW, Wilderness (May 6, 1864): Confined at Ft. Delaware: Exchanged, Feb. 23, 1865.

(2) AMASON, JONES 3Cpl. — Orig. Pvt. in Co., age 26: Appt. 3Cpl., Dec. 1, 1862: Reduced to ranks, Aug. 1, 1863: Paroled, Appomattox (Apr. 12, 1865).

(2) DUKE, LITTLETON C. 4Cpl. — Orig. Pvt. in Co., age 19: W., Wilderness (May 6, 1864): Prom., 4Cpl., Winter, 1864-65: Paroled, Appomattox (Apr. 12, 1865).

(2) DUMAS, WM. H. 5Sgt. — Transfd. as a Pvt. into Co. E from 2nd Ark. Btln., July 18, 1862: Appt. 4Cpl., Aug. 16, 1864: Prom., 5Sgt., Winter, 1864-65: Paroled, Appomattox (Apr. 12, 1865).

(1) GROOMS, JAS. S. 1Sgt. — Orig. 2Cpl. of Co., age 22: Prom., 3Sgt.,
(2) Nov., 1862: W., Darbytown Rd. (Oct. 7, 1864): Prom., 1Sgt., Winter, 1864-65: Paroled, Appomattox (Apr. 12, 1865).

HAILE (or HALE), BENJ. B. 3Cpl. — Orig. Pvt. in Co., age 42: Detailed to duty as "Enrolling Officer" for Amherst Co., Va., Feb., 1863: Prom., 3Cpl., Aug., 1864: Paroled, Amherst Co., Va., May 29, 1865.

(2) HILL, JESSE W. 3Sgt. — Orig. Pvt. in Co., age 21: Prom., 5Sgt., Jan., 1862: W., Gettysburg (July 2, 1863): W., Wilderness (May 6, 1864): W. (ankle), White Oak Swamp (Aug. 16, 1864): W., Darbytown Rd. (Oct. 7, 1864): Prom., 3Sgt., Winter, 1864-65: Paroled, Appomattox (Apr. 12, 1865).

HINDLY, JAS. M. Cpl. — POW: Exchanged, Springfield, Mo., June 16, 1863: No other record.

(1) HOLLOWAY, JOHN D. 1Sgt. — See roster, "Regmtl. Hdqtrs., 3rd Ark. Inf."

(1) KADLE, JEREMIAH D. 1Cpl. — Orig. 1Cpl. of Co., age 27: Reduced to ranks, June 30, 1863: W., Chickamauga (Sept. 19, 1863): POW, Mt. Sterling, Ky. (June 10, 1864): Confined at Rock Is., Ill.: Died in prison of dysentery, Sept. 1, 1864.

KELLY, JAS. T. 5Cpl. — Orig. Pvt. in Co., age 22: Appt. 5Cpl., Aug. 1, 1863: No other record.

(2) KING, JOHN T. 4Sgt. — Orig. Pvt. in Co., age 18: Appt. 5Sgt., Dec. 1, 1862: W., Wilderness (May 6, 1864): Appt. 4Sgt., Winter, 1864-65: Paroled, Appomattox (Apr. 12, 1865).

McLENDON, ISAAC C. P. 1Sgt. — Orig. Pvt. in Co.: Appt. 1Sgt., Dec. 1, 1862: Reduced to ranks, Jan., 1863 & detailed as a clerk in CSA Comsy. Dept.: Paroled, Nashville, May 4, 1865.

MURPHY, HENRY C. 1Cpl. — Transfd. to Co. E from 2nd Ark. Btln., July 18, 1862: Appt. 1Cpl., June 30, 1863: POW, Spotsylvania (May 12, 1864): Confined at Elmira, N.Y.: Exchanged, Feb. 13, 1865.

NABORS, JOHN B. 2Sgt. — Orig. Pvt. in Co., age 21: Prom., 2Sgt., Apr. 30, 1862: W., Gettysburg (July 2, 1863): Hospitalized in Richmond.

PERRY, BENJ. J. 3Cpl. — Orig. Pvt. in Co., age 19: Prom., 3Cpl., Feb., 1864: W., Wilderness (May 6, 1864): Paroled, Montgomery, Ala., June 7, 1865.

(1) PERDUE, GEO. 4Cpl. — Orig. 4Cpl. of Co., age 22: Reduced to ranks, Apr. 10, 1862: W., Wilderness (May 6, 1864): Paroled, Montgomery, Ala., June 7, 1865.

(1) SMITH, THOS J. 4Sgt. — See list of "Officers" above.

SNYDER, THOS. J. 1Sgt. — Orig. Pvt. in Co., age 27: Prom., 1Sgt., Jan. 10, 1863: W., Chickamauga (Sept. 19, 1863): Disabled: Asgnd. as a baggage guard at Lynchburg, Va., Apr., 1864: Paroled, Apr. 10, 1865.

MUSICIANS

(1)   HILL, JAS. W. — Orig. musician of Co.: Present for duty record good:
(2)   Paroled, Appomattox (Apr. 12, 1865).

PRIVATES

(1)   AMASON, JAS. H. — Enl., age 22: K., Gettysburg (July 2, 1863).
(1)   AMASON, JESSE T. — See list of "Non-Commissioned Officers" above.
(1)   AMASON, JONES — See list of "Non-Commissioned Officers" above.
(1)   ANDERSON, ALBERT A. — Detach. serv. as shoemaker in Richmond, Nov., 1862 to Mar., 1863: Transfd. to Little Rock, Ark. as shoemaker, Mar. 13, 1863.
(1)   AVERA, JAS. — W. (back) & POW, Gettysburg (July 2, 1863): Confined at Federal hosp., Davids Is., N.Y. Harbor: Exchanged: Dischgd. for disability, July 12, 1864.
       BELL, THOS. B. — POW, Carroll Co., Ark., Mar. 29, 1863: Escaped from prison, June 20, 1863.
(1)   BRINTON, CALEB — Enl., age 20: W., Chickamauga (Sept. 19, 1863): Retired by Medical Board, May 4, 1864.
       BROWN, WM. A. — Transfd. to Co. E from 2nd Ark. Btln., July 18, 1862: Paroled, Burkeville Junction, Va., Apr. 27, 1865.
(1)   BURNSIDE, SAMUEL N. — Enl., age 21: POW, E. Tenn., Dec. 3, 1863: Confined at Ft. Delaware: Exchanged, Mar. 7, 1865.
       CALAWAY (or CALLOWAY), HENRY C. — Transfd. to Co. E from 2nd Ark. Btln., July 18, 1862: W., Summer, 1864: Retired to Invalid Corps, Sept. 18, 1864.
       CLOWER, DANIEL M. — POW, Jefferson County, Ark., Sept. 11, 1864: Confined at Rock Is., Ill.: Exchanged, Feb. 25, 1865.
       CRAVY, THOS. H. — Transfd. to Co. E from 2nd Ark. Btln., July 18, 1862: W., Seven Pines (June 1, 1862): W., Wilderness (May 6, 1864): Died from wound, May 15, 1864.
       CRAWFORD, N. S. — Transfd. to Co. E from 2nd Ark. Btln., July 18, 1862: Hospitalized much of 1863 and 1864.
       CRAWFORD, THOS. B. — Enl., May 13, 1862 at Monroe, Ala.: W., Wilderness (May 6, 1864): W., Bermuda Hundred (June 17, 1864).
       DAMAR, GEO. — Paroled, Charlotte, No. Car., May, 1865: No other record.
       DAVIS, JOHN H. — Transfd. to Co. E from 2nd Ark. Btln., July 18, 1862: W. & POW, Wilderness (May 6, 1864).
(1)   DUKE, LITTLETON C. — See list of "Non-Comm. Officers" above.
       DUMAS, WM. H. — See list of "Non-Commissioned Officers" above.
       DUNN, J. B. — POW, Larkinville, Ala., Aug. 29, 1863: Took Fed. oath at Louisville, Ky., Sept. 16, 1863.
       EMERSON, THOS. — POW, Spotsylvania (May 12, 1864): Confined at Elmira, N.Y.: Exchanged, Feb. 13, 1865.
       ESTES, JOHN — POW, Lawrence Co., Mo., Feb. 17, 1864: Took Fed. oath.
       FIELD, J. — POW, Gettysburg (July 2, 1863): No other record.

(1) FREEMAN, JAS. E. — Enl., age 18: K., Petersburg trenches, June 30, 1864.

FULTIS, JACOB — POW, Carroll Co., Ark., Mar. 29, 1863: Paroled, June 2, 1863.

GILBERT, ALBERT — Transfd. to Co. E from 2nd Ark. Btln., July 18, 1862: K., Wilderness (May 6, 1864).

GOODARD, J. P. — POW, Helena, Ark., July 4, 1863: Died in prison, Sept. 11, 1863.

GOODWIN, M. J. — POW, Van Buren Co., Ark., Dec. 14, 1864: Died of measles in prison.

(1) GREGORY, JOHN T. — Enl., age 27: W., Gettysburg (July 2, 1863): W., Wilderness (May 6, 1864): Leg amputated, May 10, 1864: Retired for disability, Sept. 21, 1864.

GUNLIN, DANIEL — POW, Carroll Co., Ark., Apr. 7, 1863: No other record.

(1) HAILE (or HALE), BENJ. B. — See list of "Non-Commissioned Officers" above.

(1) HARRISON, WM. H. — See list of "Officers" above.

(1) HEATHERMAN, THOS. — Enl., age 32: W., Antietam (Sept. 17, 1862): Asgnd. to guard duty in Richmond, Summer, 1863: Retired by Medical Bd., July 12, 1864.

(1) HILL, JESSE W. — See list of "Non-Commissioned Officers" above.

(1) JESTER, JAS. R. — Enl., age 18: Dischgd. for disability (chronic
(2) rheumatism), May 5, 1862: Re-enlisted: Paroled, Appomattox (Apr. 12, 1865).

JESTER, JOHN H. — Enl., age 20 at Campagnolle, Ark., Mar. 4, 1862: AWOL, Spring, 1864: Deserted, took Fed. oath at Chattanooga, July 11, 1864: Requested to be released north of the Ohio R.

(1) JESTER, OLIVER W. — Enl., age 23: Sick, Winter, 1862-63: Paroled,
(2) Appomattox (Apr. 12, 1865).

(1) JESTER, THOS. F. — Enl., age 18: Deserted, E. Tenn., about Jan. 15, 1864.

(1) JESTER, THOS. P. — Enl., age 32: POW, Gettysburg (July 2, 1863): Confined, Ft. Delaware: Paroled, May 15, 1865.

(2) JESTER, WM. V. — Enl., age 18: Sick, Spring, 1863: Paroled, Appomattox (Apr. 12, 1865).

JONES, THOS. J. — Transfd. to Co. E from 2nd Ark. Btln., July 18, 1862: No record after June, 1863, may have been killed at Gettysburg.

(1) KELLY, JAS. T. — See list of "Non-Commissioned Officers" above.

(1) KING, BERRY H. — Enl., age 18: Present for duty record good: Paroled, Montgomery, Ala., May 25, 1865.

(1) KING, HENRY F. — Enl., age 22: Detailed as guard for supply train,
(2) Winter, 1863-64: Paroled, Appomattox (Apr. 12, 1865).

(1) KING, JOHN T. — See list of "Non-Commissioned Officers" above.

(1) KUNDERT, JOHN U. — Enl., age 29: POW, Chaffin's Farm (Sept. 29, 1864): Confined at Pt. Lookout, Md.

(1) LOGAN, WM. — Transfd. to Co. E from 2nd Ark. Btln., July 18, 1862: Transfd. to Co. H, 3rd Ark. Inf., Feb. 1, 1863.

(1) McCAIN, JOHN H. — Enl., age 20: Died of pneumonia, Dec. 15, 1862.

McELROY, THOS. — Transfd. to Co. E from 2nd Ark. Btln., July 18, 1862: Detailed as a guard for Richmond hosp., Feb.-Dec., 1863: Sick, transfd. to Ark., Dec., 1863.

(1) McELVEEN, JOHN M. — Enl., age 25: W., Bermuda Hundred (June 17, (2) 1864): Paroled, Appomattox (Apr. 12, 1865).

(1) McGOWAN, JOHN — Enl., age 22: Detached duty guarding R.R. bridges in No. Car., Spring, 1862: Asgnd. hosp. duty, Spring & Summer, 1864.

McHENRY, W. L. — Transfd. to Co. E from 2nd Ark. Btln., July 18, 1862: No record after June, 1863, may have been killed at Gettysburg.

(1) McLENDON, ISAAC C. P. — See list of "Non-Comm. Officers" above.

MIERS, LORENZO A. — Transfd. to Co. E from 2nd Ark. Btln., July 18, 1862: W., White Oak Swamp (Aug. 16, 1864).

(1) MONTGOMERY, JAS. — Enl., age 32: W. (thigh) & POW, Gettysburg (July 2, 1863): Confined at Pt. Lookout, Md.: Took Fed. oath, Feb. 19, 1864.

MOODY, URBIN E. — Transfd. to Co. E from 2nd Ark. Btln., July 18, 1862: AWOL in Ark., Aug., 1863.

MOORE, W. G. — Paroled, Goldsboro, No. Car., May 15, 1865: No other record.

(1) MORGAN, JACKSON S. — Enl., age 23: W. & POW, Wilderness (May 6, 1864): Retired to Invalid Corps, Mar. 15, 1865: Paroled, Talladega, Ala., May 23, 1865.

(1) NABORS, JOHN B. — See list of "Non-Commissioned Officers" above.

NORRIS, GEO. W. — Enl., age 35: Transfd. to Co. E from 2nd Ark. Btln., July 18, 1862: Dischgd. for disability, Dec. 12, 1862.

NORRIS, JOHN — Transfd. to Co. E from 2nd Ark. Btln., July 17, 1862: K., near Knoxville, Dec. 5, 1863.

NORRIS, JOS. — Transfd. to Co. E from Co. H, 1st Tex. Inf. Regt., Jan. 20, 1863: Sick, Spring, 1863: No other record.

NORRIS, PASCHAL — Transfd. to Co. E from 2nd Ark. Btln., July 18, 1862: W., Chickamauga (Sept. 19, 1863): Retired for disability, Oct. 6, 1864, "totally disqualified."

OLIVER, ALFRED — POW, Carroll Co., Ark., Mar. 29, 1862: Exchanged, City Pt., Va.

(1) PERRY, BENJ. J. — See list of "Non-Commissioned Officers" above.

PICKENS, JAS. D. — See list of "Officers" above.

PICKETT, JEPTHA S. — Enl., age 19, at Champagnolle, Ark., Mar. 4, 1862: K., Gettysburg (July 2, 1863).

(1) QUINNEY, JAS. A. — Enl., age 23: W., Gettysburg (July 2, 1863): W., Wilderness (May 6, 1864): Disabled for field duty.

RAY, HARRIS — Transfd. to Co. E from 2nd Ark. Btln., July 18, 1862: W., Bermuda Hundred (June 17, 1864).

(2) REYNOLDS, PHILLIP H. — Transfd. to Co. E from 2nd Ark. Btln., July 18, 1862: Paroled, Appomattox (Apr. 12, 1865).

SALYERS, ERASTUS — Transfd. to Co. E from 2nd Ark. Btln., July 18, 1862: Asgnd. as teamster, Winter, 1862-63: Died in Richmond of typhoid fever, Apr. 30, 1863.

(1) SCHMIDT, KASPER — Enl., age 24: Unfit for field duty: Asgnd. duty as a blacksmith, Mar., 1863 to Dec., 1864.

SCOTT, B. S. — Paroled, Goldsboro, No. Car., May 15, 1865: No other record.

(1) SLAUGHTER, RICH. J. — Enl., age 29: Sick most of 1862 & 1863: Died at Rome, Ga., Jan. 12, 1864 of pneumonia "as a result of a gunshot wound."

(1) SLONE (or SLOAN), WM. — Enl., age 18: POW, Gettysburg (July 2, 1863): Confined at Ft. Delaware: Took Fed. oath and enl. in the 1st Conn. Cav. Regt.

SMITH, A. C. — POW, Gettysburg (July 2, 1863): Confined at Ft. Delaware: No other record.

SMITH, JAS. MONROE — Transfd. to Co. E from 2nd Ark. Btln., July 18, 1862: POW, Gettysburg (July 2, 1863): Confined at Ft. Delaware: Exchanged, Feb., 1864.

(2) SMITH, K. — Paroled, Appomattox (Apr. 12, 1865): No other record.

(1) SNYDER, THOS. J. — See list of "Non-Commissioned Officers" above.

(1) STAPLES, JOHN D. — Enl., age 20: W., Wilderness (May 6, 1864):
(2) Paroled, Appomattox (Apr. 12, 1865).

(1) STAPLES, WM. J. — Enl., age 18: Dischgd. for disability, July 17, 1861: Re-enl., Mar. 4, 1862 at Champagnolle, Ark.: Died, Petersburg, Va., Spring, 1863.

(1) STATHAM, JOHN — Enl., age 30: POW, Antietam (Sept. 17, 1862): Paroled, Sept. 26, 1862: Present for duty through Aug., 1864.

STEPHEN, W. — Paroled, Memphis, Tenn., May 31, 1865: No other record.

(1) STEVENS, BENJ. F. — Enl., age 31: Detached duty as teamster, Jan.,
(2) 1862 to end of war: Paroled, Appomattox (Apr. 12, 1865).

(1) STEVENS, JAS. M. — See list of "Officers" above.

STEVENS, THOS. J. — Enl. at Champagnolle, Ark., Jan. 19, 1863: K., Gettysburg (July 2, 1863).

STEVENSON, JESSE A. — Transfd. to Co. E from 2nd Ark. Btln., July 18, 1862: W. (arm), Antietam (Sept. 17, 1862): K., Suffolk, Va. (May 3, 1863).

TATUM, CHAS. J. — Enl. at Camden, Ark., Feb. 2, 1863: POW, Spotsylvania (May 8, 1864): Confined at Elmira, N.Y.: Paroled, May 5, 1865.

TATUM, TIMOTHY P. — Transfd. to Co. E from 2nd Ark. Btln., July 18, 1862: Sick much of 1863 & 1864: No records after Aug., 1864.

TIERNEY, THOS. — Enl., age 27: POW, Chickamauga (Sept. 19, 1863): Confined at Rock Is., Ill.: Took Fed. oath, Mar. 18, 1864 to join U.S. Navy: Rejected by Fed. Navy.

(1) WARD, FRANCIS M. — See roster, "Regmtl. Hdqtrs., 3rd Ark. Inf."

WATKINS, THOS. N. — Transfd. to Co. E from 2nd Ark. Btln., July 18, 1862: Asgnd. duty as a teamster, Feb., 1863.

WELCH, TURNER G. — Tranfs. to Co. E from 2nd Ark. Btln., July 18, 1862: W., Chickamauga (Sept. 20, 1863): Disabled from wound, dischgd. from service, Feb. 21, 1864.

(1) WHITE, MARTIN V. — Enl., age 23: POW, Gettysburg (July 2, 1863): Died of pneumonia while a prisoner, July 10, 1863.

(1) WRIGHT, WM. J. — Enl., age 24: K., Spotsylvania (May 12, 1864).

MEMBERS OF COMPANY E, 3RD ARK. INF. REGT., WHO WERE NOT PRESENT FOR DUTY DURING THE PERIOD THAT THE REGIMENT WAS ASSIGNED TO HOOD'S TEXAS BRIGADE (NOV., 1862-APR., 1865).

OFFICERS

(1) Key, Drury H., Capt. (Orig. 1Lt., Co. B: Prom., Capt., Co. E, Mar. 3, 1862: Resgnd., Oct. 28, 1862).
(1) Nolan, Thos. F., Capt. (Orig. Capt., Co. E: Resgnd., Feb. 25, 1862).

Davis, H. H., 1Lt. (No record)
(1) Lamkin, Romulus, 1Lt. (Orig. 1Lt. of Co.: Resgnd., Mar. 9, 1862).
(1) Kelly, Vincent L., 2Lt. (Orig. 3Lt. of Co.: Resgnd., Apr. 28, 1862).

NON-COMMISSIONED OFFICERS

Greenhaw, Jos. D., 1Sgt. (D., Sept., 1861)
Owen, Wm. C., 3Cpl. (Dischgd. for disability, June, 1862)

Pumphry, Lewis, Sgt. (K., Antietam)
Holloway, John D., 1Sgt. (Appt. Regmtl. QM, July, 1861).

PRIVATES

(1) Amason, Wm. J. (Dischgd., disability, Aug., 1862)
Andrews, Wm. A. (POW)
Bell, John (POW)
(1) Bennett, Patrick (No record)
(1) Binford, Henry (Dischgd., disability, Dec., 1861)
(1) Bloxton, Jas. H. (No record)
(1) Bloxton, Jos. P. (No record)
(1) Bond, John F. (No record)
(1) Brackin, Barnard B. (D., Jan., 1862)
(1) Burnett, Lafayette (No record)
Burns, Wm. A. (No record)
Caldwell, J. W. (No record)
(1) Carmack, Michael O. (No record)
Cobb, Hosea (Dischgd., disability, July, 1862)
(1) Cole, Wm. H. (D., Fall, 1861)

Crawford, Alex G. (Transfd. from 2nd Ark. Btln., July, 1862: No other record)
Davis, John (Dischgd., disability, July, 1862)
(1) Davis, Randolph H. (D., Mar., 1862)
Dixon, Thos. (POW, Aug., 1862)
Doss, Washington C. (D., Mar., 1862)
(1) Dresher, Jos. (No record)
Easter, Wm. (POW)
Estes, W. J. (Paroled, Md., Jan., 1863)
(1) Fitzpatrick, Mahone (No record)
Fowler, Henry D. (No record)
Geathers, R. H. M. (POW)
(1) Gorman, Robt. E. (D., Sept., 1861)

(1) Hammond, Thos. F. (D., Oct., 1861)
(1) Hancock, Geo. W. (D., Jan., 1862)
(1) Hill, Alex. B. (No record)
(1) Hoslie, Belthasa (D., Nov., 1862)
Hotchkiss, G. B. (No record)
Hughey, Jas. P. (POW)
Hulsey, Armstead (POW)
Ingraham, R. P. (Transfd. from 2nd Ark. Btln.: K., Antietam)
(1) Jester, Benj. F. (D., Sept., 1861)
(1) Jester, Wm. R. (No record)
Jones, J. C. (No record)
(1) Lambert, Jonathan (D., Feb., 1862)
Lee, T. J. (POW, Oct., 1862)
Lipps, G. W. (POW)
(1) Lodge, J. R. (Mar., 1862)
Lynch, John H. (No record)
Mathews, Alcany B. (POW)

(1) Moore, T. L. (D., Sept., 1861)
(1) Morgan, Jos. F. (D., Dec., 1861)
Murphy, John (POW)
(1) Newton, Lewis D. (Dischgd., Feb., 1862)
Nickols, A. C. (No record)
Peel, Thos. H. (POW)
Pig, M. M. (POW)
(1) Pumphrey, Dennis D. (Dischgd., disability, July, 1862)
Raines, Jas. L. (POW)
Rainey, John H. (Last record, Mar., 1862)
Rains, John C. (POW)
Ross, A. C. (POW)
Ross, W. F. (No record)
(1) Sharp, Henry (D., Mar., 1862)
(1) Sledge, Thos. A. H. (No record)
Stamphill, S. P. (POW)
Witherington, Wm. J. (Dischgd., Jan., 1862)
Yarborough, Wm. (No record)
(1) Young, John (D., Jan., 1862)

3RD ARK. VOL. INF. REGT.

COMPANY F — *HOT SPRINGS HORNETS*

Company was organized in Hot Springs Co., Ark., in early June, 1861, and was mustered into the Confederate Service, "for the war," at Lynchburg, Va., July 5, 1861 by Maj. H. L. Clay, CSA.

Key

(1) Original member of Company. (2) Paroled at Appomattox.
K (Killed), W (Wounded), POW (Prisoner of War)
AWOL (Absent Without Leave)

OFFICERS

(2) ANDERSON, FRANKLIN A. Capt. — Orig. Pvt. in Co., age 31: Prom., 3Lt., Nov., 1862: Prom., 1Lt., June 16, 1863: Prom., Capt., July 27, 1864: Paroled, Appomattox (Apr. 12, 1865).

THRASHER, THOS. J. Capt. — Orig. 1Sgt. of Co., age 24: W., Antietam (Sept. 17, 1862): Prom., Capt., Sept., 1862: Granted ninety days leave to Ark. to recruit & to arrest deserters, Feb.-Apr., 1864: AWOL, May, 1864: Dropped from rolls, July 27, 1864.

(1) FARRIS, THOS. D. 1Lt. — Orig. 1Lt. of Co., age 40: Resigned & returned to Ark., Apr. 8, 1863.

(2) STRIBLING, RICH. M. 1Lt. — Orig. Pvt. in Co., age 21: W. (leg), Wilderness (May 6, 1864): Prom., 1Lt., July 27, 1864: Paroled, Appomattox (Apr. 12, 1865).

BURGANER, ISAAC 2Lt. — Orig. Pvt. in Co., age 23: Prom., 5Sgt., Jan., 1862: Prom., 2Lt., May, 1863: No record after June, 1863, may have been killed at Gettysburg.

(1) MILLER, JOHN A. 2Lt. — Orig. 2Lt. of Co., age 23: Resigned, Surg. Cert. of disability (chronic rheumatism), June 16, 1863.

NON-COMMISSIONED OFFICERS

(2) ADAIR, WM. S. 1Sgt. — Orig. Pvt. in Co., age 19: Prom., 4Cpl., May, 1863: W., Spotsylvania (May 10, 1864): Prom., 4Sgt., Aug., 1864: Prom., 1Sgt., Spring, 1865: Paroled, Appomattox (Apr. 12, 1865).

BRYAN, CHAS. K. 2Cpl. — Orig. Pvt. in Co., age 21: Prom., 4Cpl., Aug., 1863: W. (foot), Chickamauga (Sept. 19, 1863): Prom., 2Cpl., Aug., 1864.

CHAMBERLAIN, EWEL 3Sgt. — Orig. Pvt. in Co., age 25: W., Antietam (Sept. 17, 1862): Prom., 3Sgt., Feb., 1864: W., Wilderness (May 6, 1864): Died of wound, June 16, 1864.

(1) FRANCE, JAS. B. 5Sgt. — Orig. 1Cpl. of Co., age 25: Prom., 5Sgt., June, 1863: K., Gettysburg (July 2, 1863).

(1) JOHNSON, SIMEON B. 3Cpl. — Orig. 4Cpl. of Co., age 22: Prom., 3Cpl., Apr., 1862: W. (forearm), Chickamauga (Sept. 20, 1863): Dischgd. for disability, Feb., 1865: Paroled, Selma, Ala., June, 1865.

(1) PHELPS, AUSTIN 2Sgt. — Orig. Pvt. in Co., age 18: Present for duty
(2) entire war: Prom., 5Sgt., Summer, 1864: Prom., 2Sgt., Spring, 1865: Paroled, Appomattox (Apr. 12, 1865).

(1) THRASHER, THOS. J. 1Sgt. — See list of "Officers" above.

MUSICIANS

(1) SPARKS, JAS. E. — Orig. musician in Co.: POW, Amelia CH. (Apr. 7, 1865): Confined at Pt. Lookout, Md.: Paroled, June 19, 1865.

(1) WARD, WM. J. — See roster, "Regmtl. Hdqtrs., 3rd Ark. Inf."

PRIVATES

(1) ADAIR, WM. S. — See list of "Non-Commissioned Officers" above.

(1) ANDERSON, FRANKLIN A. – See list of "Officers" above.
(1) ASHBROOK, JACOB – Enl., age 26: Died, Winter, 1862-63.
(1) BARNES, WM. C. – W., Chickamauga (Sept. 19, 1863): No other record.
(1) BASEY, GRANVILLE – POW, Antietam (Sept. 17, 1862): Confined at Ft. McHenry, Md.: Exchanged: Detailed as teamster, Sept., 1863: AWOL: Dropped from rolls, July, 1864.
(1) BEAUCHAMP, SAMUEL M. – POW, Gettysburg (July 2, 1863): Confined at Ft. Delaware: Exchanged, Mar. 7, 1865.
    BROADWAY, WM. – K., Gettysburg.
(1) BROWN, LARKIN C. – Enl., age 21: Deserted, dropped from rolls, Aug., 1864.
(1) BRYAN, CHAS. K. – See list of "Non-Commissioned Officers" above.
(1) BURGANER, ISAAC – See list of "Officers" above.
(2) BUSTER, C. R. – Enl., Sept. 17, 1861 at Hot Springs, Ark.: Detach. Serv. at Div. Hdqtrs., June, 1863: Paroled, Appomattox (Apr. 12, 1865).
(1) CHAMBERLAIN, EWEL – See list of "Non-Comm. Officers" above.
(1) CLEM, MASON C. – Enl., age 24: W. (leg) & POW, Gettysburg (July 2, 1863): Confined at Fed. hosp., Davids Is., N.Y. Harbor: Exchanged, Aug., 31, 1863.
(1) COFFMAN, HARRISON C. – W. & POW, Gettysburg (July 2, 1863): Confined at Fed. hosp., Davids Is., N.Y. Harbor: Lost left eye: Exchanged, City Pt., Va., Aug. 28, 1863: Retired from service as "totally disqualified."
    CUMMINGS, W. A. – Enl., Oct. 18, 1863 at Cross Plains, Ala.: W., Bermuda Hundred (June 17, 1864): W. (knee), White Oak Swamp (Aug. 16, 1864).
    DALY, HENRY – Transfd. to Co. F from Co. A, May 1, 1863: Deserted in Pa., June 30, 1863: Took Fed. oath.
(1) DAVIS, MARTIN J. – Enl., age 19: W. & POW, Gettysburg (July 2, 1863): Confined at Fed. hosp. at Davids Is., N.Y. Harbor: Exchanged, Sept. 7, 1863.
(1) DEWBERRY, WM. H. – W., Antietam (Sept. 17, 1862): Wound furlough granted: Disabled, remained in Ark.
(1) DOWNEY, WM. H. C. – Enl., age 19: K., Gettysburg (July 2, 1863).
(1) ELLIOTT, JAS. H. – Enl., age 18: AWOL, dropped from rolls, Summer, 1864: Paroled, New Orleans, June, 1865.
(1) ELMORE, OVERTON – Enl., age 19: Absent sick, Jan., 1864: Deserted at Washington, D.C., Apr. 12, 1865.
(1) EMERSON, SAM H. – Enl., age 18: W., Wilderness (May 6, 1864):
(2) Paroled, Appomattox (Apr. 12, 1865).
    GLENN, C. T. – Transfd. to Co. F from 2nd Ark. Btln., July 18, 1862: Detach. Serv. at Div. Hdqtrs., Dec., 1863: Deserted, Mar. 5, 1865: Took Fed. oath in Celine Co., Ark.
    GILES, GEO. – Transfd. to Co. F from 2nd Ark. Btln., July 18, 1862: K., Suffolk, Va., June 2, 1863.
(1) GRIGSBY, ANDREW J. – Enl., age 21: Present for duty entire war:
(2) Paroled, Appomattox (Apr. 12, 1865).
    GUERIN, JAS. – Transfd. to Co. F from 2nd Ark. Btln., July 18, 1862: POW, Antietam (Sept. 17, 1862): Exchanged: K., Suffolk, Va., June 2, 1863.

(1) HALL, ELIJAH B. — Enl., age 20: Sick, Summer, 1861: Dischgd. for disability, Mar. 21, 1863.

HAMILTON, W. D. — Enl., age 42: Transfd. to Co. F from 2nd Ark. Btln., July 18, 1862: Discharged for disability (infected leg), Jan. 30, 1863.

HARP, WM. C. — W. (leg) & POW, Gettysburg (July 2, 1863): POW, Wilderness (May 6, 1864): Confined at Fed. hosp. at Davids Is., N.Y. Harbor.

HARRY, DEMPSEY C. — Enl., Mar. 15, 1862 at Rockport, Ark.: Sick, Winter & Spring, 1863: Died, Apr. 17, 1863.

HEFLY, JOHN — Transfd. to Co. F from 2nd Ark. Btln., July 18, 1862: W., Chickamauga (Sept. 20, 1863): Deserted, Richmond, Apr. 3, 1865.

(1) HEILBRON, HENRY — POW, Hagerstown, Md., July 12, 1863: Took Fed. oath, Jan. 12, 1864.

HENSON, J. W. — Transfd. to Co. F from 2nd Ark. Btln., July 18, 1862: W. & POW, Gettysburg (July 2, 1863): Took Fed. oath, July 17, 1863.

(1) HULTSMAN (or HOLTZMAN), BENJ. N. — Enl., age 19: POW, Spotsylvania (May 15, 1864): Confined at Elmira, N.Y.: Exchanged, Feb. 16, 1865.

(1) KING, ALFRED B. — Enl., age 24: POW, E. Tenn., Nov. 20, 1863: No other record.

(1) MAGBY, CHAS. — POW, Cheat Mtn., Va., Sept. 12, 1861: Exchanged, Aug. 25, 1862: Deserted, Richmond, Apr. 3, 1865.

MARSH, _____ — Paroled: Wounded, admitted to Fed. hosp., June 21, 1865: No other record.

(1) McCLENNEN, ELI — Enl., age 20: POW, Chickamauga (Sept. 20, 1863): Confined at Fed. Prison, Louisville, Ky.: Paroled, New Orleans, May 4, 1865.

MEACHAM, S. M. — POW, Gettysburg (July 2, 1863): Confined at Ft. Delaware.

(1) MILLER, HENRY C. — Enl., age 27: Died of pneumonia, Chimborazo Hosp., Richmond, Jan. 1, 1863.

(1) NEWMAN, CHRISTOPHER G. — Enl., age 19: POW, near Chattanooga, Dec. 26, 1863: Confined at Rock Island, Ill.

(1) O'CONNOR, RODERICK W. — Detach. duty as a nurse at a hosp. in Liberty, Va., Sept., 1862 to Nov., 1864.

(1) PHELPS, ALFRED — Enl., age 25: AWOL, Feb., 1863: Dropped from rolls, Summer, 1864.

(1) PHELPS, AUSTIN — See list of "Non-Commissioned Officers" above.

(1) ROLAND, GEO. W. — Enl., age 32: POW, Antietam (Sept. 17, 1862): Confined at Ft. McHenry, Md.: Exchanged, Oct. 14, 1862: POW, Amelia CH. (Apr. 5, 1865): Confined at Pt. Lookout, Md.: Paroled, June 17, 1865.

(1) SMITH, HIRAM G. — Enl., age 18: W. (neck), Bermuda Hundred (June 17, 1864): Wound furlough, June, 1864.

SPEAR, F. M. — Transfd. to Co. F from 2nd Ark. Btln., July 18, 1862: W. (arm), Wilderness (May 6, 1864): POW, Jeterville, Va., (Apr. 4, 1865): Confined at Pt. Lookout, Md.: Paroled, June 19, 1865.

STANER, WILLIS — Transfd. to Co. F from 2nd Ark. Btln., July 18, 1862: K., Wilderness (May 6, 1864).

(2) STANLEY, WM. — Enl. at Rockport, Ark., Feb. 1, 1862: W. (thigh), Wilderness (May 6, 1864): Paroled, Appomattox (Apr. 12, 1865).

(1) STRIBLING, RICH. M. — See list of "Officers" above.

TAYLOR, W. A. — Transfd. to Co. F from 2nd Ark. Btln., July 18, 1862: No record after June, 1863, may have been killed at Gettysburg.

(1) THOMPSON, ENNIS — Enl., age 28: W., Chickamauga (Sept. 19, 1863): Took Fed. oath, Mar. 5, 1865 at Hot Springs, Ark.

(1) THOMPSON, WM. — Enl., age 25: W. (hand), Wilderness (May 6, 1864): Retired to Invalid Corps, Mar. 2, 1865.

TILLERY, HUGH — Transfd. to Co. F from 2nd Ark. Btln., July 18, 1862: No record after June, 1863, may have been killed at Gettysburg.

(1) TYLER, JOHN W. — Enl., age 18: W., Chickamauga (Sept. 20, 1863): Wound furlough granted: AWOL, Mar., 1864.

(1) WARD, BENJ. F. — See roster, "Regmtl. Hdqtrs., 3rd Ark. Inf."

(1) WHITE, ANDREW P. — Enl., age 23: POW, Falling Water, Md., July 14, 1863: Took Fed. oath and "sent north," Dec. 17, 1863.

(2) WHITE, T. J. — Transfd. to Co. F from 2nd Ark. Btln., July 18, 1863: Paroled, Appomattox (Apr. 12, 1865).

(1) WILLIAMS, RUSSELL — Enl., age 20: W., Antietam (Sept. 17, 1862): Wound furlough granted: AWOL, dropped from rolls.

(1) WOODS, JOHN G. — Enl., age 28: No record after June, 1863, may have been killed at Gettysburg.

WORTHINGTON, WM. S. — Enl., at Three Creeks, Ark., Dec. 20, 1862: AWOL, Nov., 1863: Dropped from rolls, July, 1864.

* * * * *

MEMBERS OF COMPANY F, 3RD ARK. INF. REGT., WHO WERE NOT PRESENT FOR DUTY DURING THE PERIOD THAT THE REGIMENT WAS ASSIGNED TO HOOD'S TEXAS BRIGADE (NOV., 1862-APR., 1865)

OFFICERS

Gurley, John W., Capt. (POW)
(1) Newman, Daniel A., Capt. (Orig. Capt.: Resgnd., July, 1862)

(1) Whitaker, Jas. C., 2Lt. (Orig. 3Lt.: Resgnd. for disability, May, 1862).
Wiggins, Calvin, 2Lt. (POW)

NON-COMMISSIONED OFFICERS

(1) Gaines, Wm. C., Cpl. (Orig. 3Cpl., No other record)
(1) Lee, Wm. C. Sgt. (No record)

Newton, Richard M., Sgt. (AWOL)
Waits, Browder B., Cpl. (D., Aug., 1861)

PRIVATES

(1) Baldwin, Wm. (Rejected in Va.)
(1) Beason, Jesse (POW, Antietam)
(1) Beason, Jonathan (No record)
Beauchamp, Samuel M. (No record)
Brown, Mathew (No record)
(1) Burks, Wm. (D., Feb., 1862)
Burns, John H. (POW, Ark.)
(1) Cain, J. C. (No record)
(1) Chastain, Larkin D. V. (No record)
Collier, John B. (D., Nov., 1862)
(1) Collier, Wm. A. (D., Feb., 1861)
Cooper, J. (Dischgd., disability, Aug., 1861)
Crawford, John W. (Dischgd., disability, July, 1862)
Denham, Alfred (D., Dec., 1861)
(1) Elliott, Jackson (D., Dec., 1861)
Elmore, Overton (No record)
(1) Engram (or Ingraham), Lawson (No record)
(1) Ewing, Newton C. (D., Aug., 1861)
Gallahare (or Gallagher), J. H. (No record)
(1) Gibbs, Geo. W. (Dischgd., Apr., 1862)
Glenn, A. S. (Dischgd., July, 1862)
Godwin, John (Dischgd., disability, July, 1862)
(1) Gooden, Monroe (Deserted)
Grant, T. F. (No record)
Green, D. H. (Dischgd., Aug., 1862)
Green, Thos. (Deserted)
Guerin, J. P. (Dischgd., disability, Aug., 1862)

Guest, J. V. (Dischgd., disability, July, 1862)
Hefly, Andrew (No record)
Hulin, J. C. (Dischgd., disability, July, 1862)
Hurst, C. R. (Dischgd., disability)
Jenkins, A. (POW)
Johnson, Jas. (D., Aug., 1861)
Keller, A. M. (POW)
(1) King, David R. (D., Mar., 1862)
(1) Levering, Henry E. (D., July, 1861)
Lockett, E. S. (Dischgd., July, 1862)
(1) McClure, John H. (D., Aug., 1861)
McCollum, John (Dischgd., Aug., 1862)
Page, Hosey (No record)
(1) Power, Reuben J. H. (D., Apr., 1862)
Pruitt, W. A. (Dischgd., wound, Aug., 1862)
Ray, Isaac (No record)
(1) Reynolds, Elijah (D., July, 1862)
(1) Roberson, Wm. H. (Dischgd., disability, July, 1862)
Scarborough, Wm. (No record)
(1) Thompson, Willis (D., Dec., 1861)
(1) Turner, John A. (Deserted, July, 1861)
White, John R. (Dischgd., disability, July, 1862)
Williams, Wm. D. (D., Fall, 1862)

3RD ARK. VOL. INF. REGT.
COMPANY G

Company was organized in Union County, Ark. in early June, 1861, and was mustered into the Confederate Service, "for the war," at Lynchburg, Va., July 5, 1861 by Maj. H. L. Clay, CSA.

Key

(1) Original member of Company. (2) Paroled at Appomattox.
K (Killed), W (Wounded), POW (Prisoner of War)
AWOL (Absent Without Leave)

OFFICERS

(1) JONES, ALEXANDER C. Capt. — Orig. 1Lt. of Co.: See roster, "Regmtl. Hdqtrs., 3rd Ark. Inf."
JONES, JAS. A. 1Lt. — Orig. 1Cpl. of Co., age 23: Prom., 3Lt., Mar. 6, 1862: Prom., 2Lt., Jan. 19, 1863: Prom., 1Lt., July 2, 1863: W., Chickamauga (Sept. 19, 1863): Disabled.
THOMPSON, PLEASANT H. 1Lt. — Orig. 2Sgt. of Co., age 23: Prom., 1Lt., Jan. 19, 1863: K., Gettysburg (July 2, 1863).
(2) MEEK, JAS. S. 2Lt. — Orig. 1Sgt. of Co., age 24: Elect., 3Lt., July 10, 1863: Prom., 2Lt., Sept. 19, 1863: W. (face & neck), Wilderness (May 6, 1864): Paroled, Appomattox (Apr. 12, 1865).
WORTHINGTON, WARREN W. 2Lt. — Orig. Pvt. in Co., age 20: Prom. to Regmtl. Ordn. Sgt., Oct., 1862: Elect., 3Lt., Jan. 23, 1863: Returned to Co.: Prom., 2Lt., July 2, 1863: K., Chickamauga (Sept. 19, 1863).

NON-COMMISSIONED OFFICERS

(1) BARKER, WM. M. 3Sgt. — Orig. 3Sgt. of Co.: Sick, Spring & Summer, 1863: W., Chickamauga (Sept. 19, 1863): Granted sick leave: AWOL, Reduced to ranks and dropped from rolls, Aug., 1864: Paroled, Montgomery, Ala., June 14, 1865.
BLACK, JOHN A. 2Sgt. — Orig. Pvt. in Co., age 22: Prom., 2Sgt., Apr. 4, 1862: K., Wilderness (May 6, 1864).
CANTERBERY, JAS. H. Cpl. — Enl. as a Pvt., Sept. 28, 1861 at El Dorado, Ark.: Appt. Cpl., July 4, 1863: W., Chickamauga (Sept. 19, 1863).
(1) COURTNEY, EUGENE 1Sgt. — Orig. 4Cpl. of Co., age 21: Prom., 1Sgt., Apr. 4, 1862: W., Chickamauga (Sept. 20, 1863): Disabled in hosp. in Atlanta: Reduced to ranks, Aug., 1864: Paroled, New Orleans, June, 1865.
ELLIOTT, JOSH Sgt. — Paroled, June, 1865: No other record.

(1) JONES, JAS. A. 1Cpl. — See list of "Officers" above.

LEWIS, FREEMAN 1Cpl. — Orig. Pvt. in Co., age 24: Prom., 1Cpl., Nov., 1862: K., Wilderness (May 6, 1864).

LOWRY, JOHN F. 3Sgt. — Orig. Pvt. in Co., age 22: Prom., 3Sgt., Apr. 14, 1862: W. (hand), Gettysburg (July 2, 1863): On wound leave & disabled, Jackson, Miss.

(2) MASSEY, HENRY A. 5Sgt. — Enl. as a Pvt. on Mar. 1, 1862 at Three Creeks, Ark.: Prom., 5Sgt., Winter, 1864-65: Paroled, Appomattox (Apr. 12, 1865).

(1) McDONALD, RICHARD M. 4Cpl. — Orig. Pvt. in Co., age 18: Prom.,
(2) 4Cpl., Apr. 14, 1862: W. (hip) & POW, Gettysburg (July 2, 1863): Confined at Fed. hosp., Davids Is., N.Y. Harbor: Exchanged, Aug. 31, 1863: Paroled, Appomattox (Apr. 12, 1865).

(1) MEEK, JAS. S. 1Sgt. — See list of "Officers" above.

MOORE, GEO. W. 2Sgt. — Orig. Pvt. in Co., age 19: Prom., 2Sgt., Aug., 1864: Sick in Richmond hosp., Jan., 1865.

STEDMAN, STEPHEN S. 5Sgt. — Orig. Pvt. in Co., age 18: Prom., 5Sgt., Apr. 14, 1862: POW, Spotsylvania (May 10, 1864): Confined at Elmira, N.Y.: Exchanged, Feb. 13, 1865.

(1) THOMPSON, PLEASANT H. 2Sgt. — See list of "Officers" above.

(1) WARWICK, LUCIAN C. 4Sgt. — Orig. Pvt. in Co., age 25: Prom.,
(2) 4Sgt., Winter, 1864-65: Paroled, Appomattox (Apr. 12, 1865).

(1) WHITE, ROBT. A. 1Sgt. — Orig. 3Cpl. in Co., age 29: W. (side), Wilderness (May 6, 1864): W. (shoulder) & POW, Darbytown Rd. (Oct. 7, 1864): Died in prison from wound, Nov. 7, 1864.

PRIVATES

(2) ALDERSON, W. J. — Enl., Mar. 1, 1862 at Three Creeks, Ark.: Appt. courier for Gen. John Gregg, Feb., 1864: W. (chest), Darbytown Rd. (Oct. 7, 1864): Paroled, Appomattox (Apr. 12, 1865).

BEEMAN, CHRISTOPHER C. — Enl., Mar. 9, 1863 at El Dorado, Ark.: W., Gettysburg (July 2, 1863): Died of wound, July 10, 1863.

(1) BEEMAN, PHILLIP A. — POW, Gettysburg (July 2, 1863): Exchanged:
(2) W. (foot), Darbytown Rd. (Oct. 7, 1864): Paroled, Appomattox (Apr. 12, 1865).

BEESON, JONATHAN E. — Enl., Mar. 1, 1862 at Three Creeks, Ark.: W. (arm), Darbytown Rd. (Oct. 7, 1864): Disabled.

(1) BLACK, JOHN A. — See list of "Non-Commissioned Officers" above.

(1) BOOTH, DERENSELLEAR R. — Enl., age 16: W., Chickamauga (Sept. 20, 1863): Disabled, asgnd. to Invalid Corps: Paroled, Montgomery, Ala., May 23, 1865.

(1) BROOKS, JOHN F. — Enl., age 23: W. (leg), Wilderness (May 6, 1864):
(2) Paroled, Appomattox (Apr. 12, 1865).

CANTERBERY, JAS. H. — See list of "Non-Comm. Officers" above.

CARTER, SAMUEL — Enl., Mar. 1, 1862 at Three Creeks, Ark.: Detchd. serv. as clerk in Brig. QM, June, 1862: AWOL, Oct., 1863: Dropped from rolls, Aug., 1864.

(1) COURSON, JOHN H. — Enl., age 21: Sick, Spring, 1863 and Fall, 1864: No record after Sept., 1864.

(2) COURTNEY, FRANKLIN — Enl., Mar. 1, 1862 at Three Creeks, Ark.: Paroled, Appomattox (Apr. 12, 1865): Present for duty most of war.

(1) COURTNEY, JUNIUS — Enl., age 19: W., Antietam (Sept. 17, 1862): Granted wound furlough, Jan., 1863: AWOL, dropped from rolls, Aug., 1864: Paroled, New Orleans, June, 1865.

(1) CRAIG, PETER G. — Enl., age 30: Detailed as a Regmtl. Hosp. Steward from Oct., 1861 to Aug., 1863: See roster, "Regmtl. Hdqtrs., 3rd Ark. Inf."

(1) CRAVY, RICHARD N. — Enl., age 22: Sick, Feb. & Mar., 1864 at Bristol, Va.: K., Chaffin's Farm (Sept. 29, 1864).

(1) CRUMPLER, MARCUS L. — Enl., age 21: Sick, Winter, 1862-63 &
(2) Spring & Summer, 1863: Dropped from rolls for prolonged absence, AWOL, Aug., 1864: Paroled, Appomattox (Apr. 12, 1865).

(2) CUMMINGS, ALEXANDER P. — Transfd. to Co. G from 2nd Ark. Btln., July 18, 1862: Paroled, Appomattox (Apr. 12, 1865).

(1) FERGUSON, HENRY J. P. — Enl., age 18: W. (knee), Antietam (Sept.
(2) 17, 1862): Detach. duty as a teamster, Nov., 1862: W. (arm), Darbytown Rd. (Oct. 7, 1864): Paroled, Appomattox (Apr. 12, 1865).

(1) FOYLE, ALFRED — Enl., age 19: Asgnd. to build cabins, Oct. & Nov., 1861: Sick, Winter, 1862-63: Deserted in E. Tenn., Jan. 25, 1864.

(2) FULLER, GEO. W. — Transfd. to Co. G from 2nd Ark. Btln., July 18, 1862: W. (both legs), Wilderness (May 6, 1864): Paroled, Appomattox (Apr. 12, 1865).

(1) GRAHAM, NORMAN A. — Enl., age 20: Sick, Petersburg hosp., Spring & Summer, 1863: Detailed as clerk to Medical Bd. at Selma, Ala., Oct., 1863: POW, paroled at Farmville, Va., mid-Apr., 1865.

(1) GRAY, JOHN F. — Enl., age 20: W. (neck) & POW, Gettysburg (July 2, 1863): Confined at Fed. hosp., Davids Is., N.Y. Harbor: W. (arm), Wilderness (May 6, 1864): Retired for disability, Sept. 27, 1864: Paroled, Montgomery, Ala., May 22, 1865.

(1) HORN, JESS M. — Enl., age 23: POW, Antietam (Sept. 17, 1862): Paroled, Sept. 19, 1862: W. (foot) & POW, Gettysburg (July 2, 1863): Confined at Fed. hosp. in Baltimore: Exchanged, Nov. 12, 1863: Wound furlough granted, Dec., 1864.

(1) JEANS, JOHN J. — Enl., age 23: W. (face) & POW, Gettysburg (July 2, 1863): Confined at Fed. hosp., Davids Is., N.Y. Harbor.

(1) JEANS, ROBT. M. — Enl., age 19: W. (thigh), Petersburg (July 7, 1864): Left leg amputated: Retired for disability, Aug. 29, 1864.

JEFFRIES, CHAS. A. — Enl. at Three Creeks, Ark., Dec. 19, 1862: W. (leg) & POW, Gettysburg (July 2, 1863): Confined at Fed. hosp., Davids Is., N.Y. Harbor.

JOLLY, JAS. S. — Enl. at Three Creeks, Ark., Dec. 19, 1862: W., Wilderness (May 6, 1864): Granted wound leave.

(1) JONES, HILL — Enl., age 19: W. (leg), Bermuda Hundred (June 16,
(2) 1864): Paroled, Appomattox (Apr. 12, 1865).

JONES, WM. K. — Enl., Mar. 1, 1862 at El Dorado, Ark.: Transfd. to Co. G from the 19th Ark. Inf. Regt., Feb. 3, 1863 as a replacement for John F. Meek: K., Chaffin's Farm (Sept. 29, 1864).

(2) KEELING, WM. J. — Transfd. to Co. G from 2nd Ark. Btln., July 18, 1862: W. (hand), Wilderness (May 6, 1864): Paroled, Appomattox (Apr. 12, 1865).

(1) KING, JOHN H. — Enl., age 24: W., Chickamauga (Sept. 19, 1863): Granted wound furlough: Did not return to Co.

(1) LAUDERDALE, JOHN F. — Enl., age 22: W. (shoulder & arm),
(2) Wilderness (May 6, 1864): Paroled, Appomattox (Apr. 12, 1865).

(2) LEWIS, DIXON H. — Enl., at Little Rock, Ark., Mar. 30, 1863: Paroled, Appomattox (Apr. 12, 1865): No other record.

(1) LEWIS, FREEMAN — See list of "Non-Commissioned Officers" above.

(1) LEWIS, PERRY — Enl., age 23: W. (leg) & POW, Gettysburg (July 2, 1863): Leg amputated: Confined at Fed. hosp. at Baltimore: Exchanged: Dischgd. for disability, Nov., 1863.

(1) LOWRY, JOHN F. — See list of "Non-Commissioned Officers" above.

LOWRY, ROBT. JAS. — Enl., Mar. 1, 1862 at Three Creeks, Ark.: See roster, "Regmtl. Hdqtrs., 3rd Ark. Inf."

MASSEY, HENRY A. — See list of "Non-Comm. Officers" above.

(1) MASSEY, JABEZ C. — Enl., age 19: W. (thigh), Darbytown Rd. (Oct. 7, 1864): POW, Richmond, Apr. 3, 1865: Paroled, July 31, 1865.

McCOY, HILLIARD — Enl., Mar. 20, 1863 at Three Creeks, Ark.: Died of typhoid fever, Aug. 10, 1863.

McDONALD, MORRIS — Enl., Mar. 1, 1862 at Three Creeks, Ark.: Detailed as a teamster, Apr., 1862: Detailed as a nurse, Feb., 1863: Dischgd., Mar. 10, 1863.

(1) McDONALD, RICHARD M. — See list of "Non-Commissioned Officers" above.

McGEE, M. P. — Paroled at New Orleans, June, 1865: No other record.

McGOOGAN, MALCOLM D. — Transfd. to Co. G from 2nd Ark. Btln., July 18, 1862: W., Chickamauga (Sept. 19, 1863): Dischgd. for disability, Feb. 20, 1864.

(1) MITCHELL, ELIAS, Jr. — Enl., age 22: Present for duty most of the
(2) war: Paroled, Appomattox (Apr. 12, 1865).

MITCHELL, WM. — Enl. at Three Creeks, Ark., Mar. 1, 1862: W. & POW, Wilderness (May 6, 1864): Confined at Elmira, N.Y.: Exchanged, Feb. 25, 1865.

MOODY, ANDERSON — Transfd. to Co. G from 2nd Ark. Btln., July 18, 1862: Died of pneumonia, Jan. 15, 1863.

(1) MOORE, GEO. W. — See list of "Non-Commissioned Officers" above.

(1) MOORE, JAS. A. — Enl., age 21: Sick, Spring, 1863 & Fall, 1864:
(2) Paroled, Appomattox (Apr. 12, 1865).

(1) NORMAN, JOHN P. — Enl., age 22: Sick, Winter, 1863-64: Paroled at Montgomery, Ala., May 13, 1865.

OWENS, JOHN P. — W. & POW, Gettysburg (July 2, 1863): No other record.

(1) PEAVY, JOHN A. — Enl., age 22: Detailed as a teamster, Spring, 1862: W. (chest), Darbytown Rd. (Oct. 7, 1864): Paroled, May 9, 1865 at Montgomery, Ala.

PHARR, JESSE — Enl., Sept. 23, 1861 at El Dorado, Ark.: No records after Feb., 1863.

PHARR, SAMUEL J. — Enl., Sept. 23, 1861 at El Dorado, Ark.: Present for duty until Aug., 1863: No records after that date.

PICKERING, JOHN W. — Transfd. to Co. G from 2nd Ark. Btln., July 18, 1862: W. (chest), Wilderness (May 6, 1864): Wound furlough to Miss., July, 1864.

(1) POWERS, JOHN — Enl., age 28: W. (foot) & POW, Gettysburg (July 2, 1863): Confined at Fed. hosp. at Davids Is., N.Y. Harbor: Exchanged: Paroled, June 2, 1865 at Mobile, Ala.

(1) PUGH, WHITTINGTON T. — Sick furlough to Atlanta granted, Sept., 1863: AWOL, dropped from rolls, Aug., 1864.

(1) REED, JAS. C. — Enl., age 18: W. (left side) & POW, Gettysburg (July 2, 1863): Confined at Fed. hosp., Davids Is., N.Y. Harbor: Paroled, Aug. 24, 1863.

(1) SHANNON, SAMUEL S. — Enl., age 25: Detchd. duty as cook for the Co. Cmdr., Apr., 1862: Died, Oct. 31, 1863.

SHORT, DREWRY B. — Enl., age 30: Sick much of 1863: Sick in Ala., Apr., 1864: No other record.

SINGLETON, WM. O. — Enl., age 22: Detached service as a nurse, Summer & Fall, 1863: No record after Sept., 1863.

(1) SMITH, ROBT. — Enl., age 19: K., Gettysburg (July 2, 1863).

STEADMAN, F. L. — Issued clothing, Apr. 23, 1864: No other record.

(1) STEDMAN, STEPHEN S. — See list of "Non-Comm. Officers" above.

THOMAS, JOHN H. — Transfd. to Co. G from 2nd Ark. Btln., July 18, 1862: POW, Falling Waters, Md., July 14, 1863: Confined at Pt. Lookout, Md.

TURLEY, THOS. W. — Enl., Mar. 1, 1862: Died of pneumonia at Chimborazo Hosp., Apr. 5, 1863.

(1) WARWICK, LUCIAN C. — See list of "Non-Comm. Officers" above.

WARWICK, NATHANIEL A. — Enl., Mar. 20, 1863 at Three Creeks, Ark.: W., Petersburg trenches (July 17, 1864): Several fingers and toes shot off: Paroled, Farmville, Va., Apr. 14, 1865.

(1) WARWICK, VIRGIL T. — Enl., age 21: Sick, Winter, 1863-64 at
(2) Bristol, Va.: Paroled, Appomattox (Apr. 12, 1865).

(1) WILHELM, JOHN F. — Enl., age 25: W., Boonsboro (Sept. 14, 1862): Wound leave to Ark.: Detailed to Div. Engr. Corps, June, 1863.

(1) WORTHINGTON, WARREN W. — See list of "Officers" above.

* * * * *

MEMBERS OF COMPANY G, 3RD ARK. INF. REGT., WHO WERE NOT PRESENT FOR DUTY DURING THE PERIOD THAT THE REGIMENT WAS ASSIGNED TO HOOD'S TEXAS BRIGADE (NOV., 1862-APR., 1865).

OFFICERS

(1) Sturgis, Jas. M. D., 2Lt. (Orig. 3Lt.: Resgnd., Jan., 1862)

(1) Brown, John R., 2Lt. (Orig. 2Lt.: See roster, "Regmtl. Hdqtrs., 3rd Ark. Inf.")

NON-COMMISSIONED OFFICERS

(1) Crumpler, Jas. A., Cpl. (POW, Antietam)

(1) Medlock, Thos. L., 4Sgt. (Orig. 4Sgt.: D., Apr., 1862)

Plethandhal, S., Cpl. (POW)

(1) Sheppard, Lewis, Cpl. (Orig. 2Cpl.: Did not go to Va.)

PRIVATES

(1) Avery, Benj. (Dischgd., Jan., 1862)

Binder, John Lewis (No record)

Booth, Derensellear R. (No record)

Boulden, Thos. T. (No record)

Brown, Aesop (POW)

Cameron, John T. (Dischgd., July, 1862)

Cates, Jefferson (D., July, 1862)

(1) Chandler, Henry L. (No record)

Cornish, A. J. (No record after July, 1862)

(1) Crawford, John L. (No record)

Crumpler, Henry B. (D., July, 1862)

Farr, S. J. (No record after July, 1862)

(1) Fogle, Alfred J. (No record)

(1) Foster, Geo. W. (Dischgd., Apr., 1862)

(1) Galbreath, Daniel M. (Dischgd., May, 1862)

(1) Gammel, Marcellus A. (D., Dec., 1862)

(1) Gibson, Chas. W. (Dischgd., Oct., 1861)

Glenn, John (POW)

(1) Glenn, Wm. A. (No record)

(1) Hammontree, Wm. M. (Dischgd., June, 1862)

(1) Hardy, Benj. A. (D., Aug., 1861)

Gray, J. W. (No record after July, 1862)

Hare, Stephen (No record after July, 1862)

Higgins, Wm. (No record)

(1) Home, Osker S. (No record)

Huley, Chas. W. (POW)

Johnston, Jas. M. (D., Apr., 1862)

Jones, Martin M. (Dischgd., July, 1862)

Lewis, Albert P. (No record after Nov., 1862)

Lowry, Leander S. (POW)

Lowry, Samuel M. (D., Apr., 1862)

(1) McCorvy, Bouie A. (D., July, 1861)

(1) McDonald, Nathaniel B. (POW)

(1) Meek, Boswell M. (Dischgd., Apr., 1862)

Meek, Isaac C. (No record after Oct., 1862)

(1) Meek, John T. (Dischgd., Feb., 1862)

(1) Meek, Wm. S. (No record)

(1) Michael, Elias, Sr. (D., Apr., 1862)

(1) New, Robt. E. (D., Oct., 1861)

(1) Norman, Yewan A. (D., Mar., 1862)

Padgette, A. L. (POW)

(1) Parker, Wm. M. (Dischgd., Jan., 1862)

Perkins, Wm. Henry H. (No record after Oct., 1862)

(1) Phillips, Wm. L. (No record after Apr., 1862)

(1) Ray, David L. (D., Aug., 1861)

Rush, Shederick C. (Dischgd., July, 1862)

(1) Russell, Jesse D. (Dischgd., June, 1862)

(1) Spears, Willie M. (Dischgd., Mar., 1862)

(1) Tisdale, Francis M. (Dischgd., Aug., 1861)

Tisdale, Wm. S. (No record after Mar., 1862)
Vick, Lawson (No record after July, 1862)
Walker, Jas. G. (D., Apr., 1862)
Welch, Jas. (Dischgd., July, 1862)

(1) Wesson, Thos. J. (Dischgd., July, 1862)
(1) Wilson, Flavius J. (No record)
(1) Wilson, Jas. M. (D., Apr., 1862)
(1) Yancey, Thos. H. (D., Fall, 1861)
(1) Young, Perry D. (D., Apr., 1861)

3RD ARK. VOL. INF. REGT.

COMPANY H

Company was organized in Drew County, Ark., in early June, 1861, and was mustered into the Confederate Service, "for the war," at Lynchburg, Va., July 5, 1861 by Maj. H. L. Clay, CSA.

Key

(1) Original member of Company. (2) Paroled at Appomattox.
K (Killed), W (Wounded), POW (Prisoner of War)
AWOL (Absent Without Leave)

OFFICERS

ALLEN, LAFAYETTE J. Capt. — Orig. 3Lt. of Co., age 29: Asgnd. to recruiting service in Ark., Feb.-Apr., 1862: Prom., 2Lt. & 1Lt., Summer, 1862: Prom., Capt., Feb. 12, 1863: K., Gettysburg (July 2, 1863).

(1) REID, SAMUEL V. Capt. — Orig. Capt. of Co., age 26: Resgnd., Feb. 12, 1863: Detailed to CSA Comsy. Dept.

(2) THACH, FRANK Capt. — Orig. 2Sgt. of Co., age 25: Detailed to recruiting serv. in Ark., Feb.-Apr., 1862: Prom., 2Lt., Summer, 1862: Prom., 1Lt., Feb. 12, 1863: Prom., Capt., July 2, 1863: Sick much of war: Paroled, Appomattox (Apr. 12, 1865).

(1) TALIAFERRO, JOHN R. 1Lt. — Orig. 2Cpl. of Co., age 29: Prom., 3Lt., Summer, 1862: Prom., 2Lt., Feb. 12, 1863: Prom., 1Lt., July 2, 1863: W. (leg), Gettysburg (July 2, 1863): Detailed to recruiting serv. in Ark., Winter, 1864-65.

MILES, JOSEPHUS 2Lt. — See roster, "Regmtl. Hdqtrs., 3rd Ark. Inf."

NON-COMMISSIONED OFFICERS

(1) ANDERSON, WM. H. 3Sgt. — Orig. 3Sgt. of Co.: Reduced to Pvt., Summer, 1862: Transfd. to Co. E, 6th Ky. Inf. Regt., Jan. 16, 1863.

BRASHEAR, RICHARD H. 4Sgt. — Orig. Pvt. in Co., age 18: Prom., 4Cpl., Dec. 1, 1862: Prom., 4Sgt., Spring, 1863: W. & POW, Gettysburg (July 2, 1863): Confined at Fed. hosp. in Baltimore: Leg amputated: Exchanged, Nov., 1863: Paroled, Liberty, Va., May 25, 1865.

BUTLER, JOEL 1Cpl. — Enl. as a Pvt., Mar. 8, 1862: Prom., 1Cpl., Fall, 1863: Deserted, E. Tenn., Feb. 22, 1864.

CASTLEMAN, JAS. W. 4Sgt. — Orig. Pvt. in Co., age 18: Prom., 4Sgt., Summer, 1862: W. (thigh) & POW, Gettysburg (July 2, 1863).

(2) HAYGOOD, THOS. W. 4Sgt. — Orig. Pvt. in Co., age 21: Prom., 1Cpl., Spring, 1864: Prom., 4Sgt., Spring, 1865: Paroled, Appomattox (Apr. 12, 1865): Also paroled at Memphis, Tenn., June 9, 1865.

KING, HENRY R. 3Sgt. — Orig. 4Cpl. of Co., age 23: Prom., 3Sgt., Summer, 1862: No record after June, 1863, may have been killed at Gettysburg.

(1) OLIVE, JOHN 4Sgt. — Orig. Pvt. in Co., age 22: Prom., 1Cpl., Fall, 1863: Prom., 4Sgt., Spring, 1864: W., Wilderness (May 6, 1864): Leg amputated.

(1) TALIAFERRO, JOHN R. 2Cpl. — See list of "Officers" above.

(1) THACH, FRANK 2Sgt. — See list of "Officers" above.

(1) TSHEAR, NAPOLEON 1Sgt. — Orig. Pvt. in Co., age 32: Prom., 1Sgt., Summer, 1862: W. & POW, Gettysburg (July 2, 1863): Shoulder amputated, Nov., 1863: Paroled, Liberty, Va., May 25, 1865.

WELLS, WILLIS D. 4Cpl. — Transfd. as a Pvt. to Co. H from 2nd Ark. Btln., July 18, 1862: Prom., 4Cpl., Mar., 1863: No record after June, 1863, may have been killed at Gettysburg.

(1) WHITE, DAVID A. 2Sgt. — Orig. Pvt. in Co., age 25: Prom., 5Sgt., Summer, 1862: Prom., 2Sgt., Fall, 1863: W., Chickamauga (Sept. 19, 1863): Right leg amputated: Retired to Invalid Corps, July 23, 1864.

MUSICIANS

(1) MULVEY, MICHAEL — Orig. Musician in Co., age 27: Absent sick (VD) in Richmond, Summer, 1863: No record after Sept. 9, 1863.

PRIVATES

AUSTIN, ISAIAH — Enl., Mar. 10, 1862 at Tyro, Ark.: AWOL, absent sick, Mar., 1863: Dropped from rolls, Aug., 1863.

BAILEY, JOHN — Enl., Mar. 17, 1862 at Lynchburg, Va.: Detailed as a Regmtl. teamster, Sept., 1862: Paroled, Lynchburg, Apr. 15, 1865.

BAILEY, RICH. J. — See roster, "Regmtl. Hdqtrs., 3rd Ark. Inf."

BRASHEAR, RICH. H. — See list of "Non-Comm. Officers" above.

BURNS, ISHAM L. — Enl., Mar. 7, 1862 at Tyro, Ark.: Sick, Spring, 1863: Deserted, E. Tenn., Mar. 26, 1864.

(1) BURNS, JAS. M. — Enl., age 21: W. (wrist & side), Chickamauga (Sept. 19, 1863): Dropped from rolls, Aug., 1864 "for protracted absence without leave."

(1) BURNS, JAS. W. — Enl., Mar., 1863 at Tyro, Ark.: Deserted, E. Tenn., Dec., 1863: Took Fed. oath at Louisville, Feb. 29, 1864.

BUTLER, JOEL — See list of "Non-Commissioned Officers" above.

(1) CASTLEMAN, JAS. W. — See list of "Non-Comm. Officers" above.

CAY, BUFORD — Enl., Mar. 31, 1862 at Lynchburg, Va.: K., Spotsylvania (May 10, 1864).

CAY, SAMUEL — Enl., Mar. 19, 1862 at Lynchburg, Va.: POW, Chickamauga (Sept. 19, 1863): Confined at Camp Morton, Ind.: Exchanged, Mar. 15, 1865.

(2) COOK, JOS. W. — Enl., Mar. 15, 1861 at Tyro, Ark.: Present for duty during entire enlistment: Paroled, Appomattox (Apr. 12, 1865).

(1) DODD, GEO. B. — Enl., age 18: W., Antietam (Sept. 17, 1862): Transfd. to Co. E, 6th Ky. Inf. Regt., Jan. 16, 1863.

EAGAR (or EDGAR), WM. D. — Enl., Mar. 8, 1862 at Tyro, Ark.: Deserted in E. Tenn., Feb. 22, 1864.

FORD, McDONALD — Enl., Mar. 15, 1862 at Tyro, Ark.: Deserted in E. Tenn., Mar. 24, 1864: Took Fed. oath at Knoxville, Mar. 28, 1864.

FORRESTER, T. J. — Deserted in E. Tenn., Mar. 26, 1864: Took Fed. oath at Knoxville, Mar. 28, 1864: No other record.

(1) GOODRICH, JOHN H. — Deserted at Suffolk, Va., May 3, 1863: No other record.

GRAHAM, ZACCHEUS — Enl., Mar. 17, 1862 at Lynchburg, Va.: W. (arm), Wilderness (May 6, 1864): W. (arm), Darbytown Rd. (Oct. 7, 1864).

(1) HAYGOOD, THOS. W. — See list of "Non-Comm. Officers" above.

JACKSON, RALSEY M. — Enl., Mar. 31, 1862 at Hamburg, Ark.: POW, Ashley Co., Ark., Nov. 20, 1863: Took Fed. oath, Nov. 28, 1863.

(1) KING, GEO. F. — Enl., age 23: W., Antietam (Sept. 17, 1862): No records after June, 1863, may have been killed at Gettysburg.

(1) LEMASTER, JOHN T. — Enl., age 22: W., Chickamauga (Sept. 19, 1863): Arm amputated.

(1) LOGAN, WM. — Enl., age 29: Transfd. to Co. H, Feb. 1, 1863: Deserted at Suffolk Va., May 3, 1863.

(1) MATHENY, SAMUEL N. — Enl., age 24: W. (hip) & POW, Gettysburg (July 2, 1863): Confined at Fed. hosp., Davids Is., N.Y. Harbor: Paroled, Sept. 27, 1863.

MAY, GEO. W. — Enl., Mar. 15, 1862 at Tyro, Ark.: Detached. serv. as a nurse in a Richmond hosp., Feb., 1863 to Aug., 1864: POW, Richmond, Apr. 3, 1865.

(2) MAY, JOS. N. — Enl., Mar. 15, 1862 at Tyro, Ark.: Present for duty during entire enlistment: Paroled, Appomattox (Apr. 12, 1865).

McDANIEL, SAMUEL — Enl. at Lynchburg, Va., on Mar. 17, 1862: POW, Antietam (Sept. 17, 1862): Exchanged: Detailed as a shoemaker at Salem, Va., Mar., 1863-Sept., 1864.

(1) McDONALD, GREENBERRY P. — W. (thigh) & POW, Gettysburg
(2)   (July 2, 1863): Exchanged: Accidentally wounded (hand),
        Petersburg trenches, July 2, 1864.
        McDONALD, J. M. — POW, Gettysburg (July 2, 1863): Confined at Ft.
        Delaware: No other record.
(1) McMILLEN, WM. P. — Enl., age 37: W. & POW, Gettysburg: Paroled at
        City Pt., Va., Sept. 27, 1863: AWOL, dropped from rolls, Aug.,
        1864: Took Fed. oath at Memphis, Mar. 27, 1865.
(1) MILES, JOSEPHUS — See list of "Officers" above.
        OGLETREE, WM. T. — Enl., Mar. 7, 1862 at Tyro, Ark.: Died near
        Fredericksburg, Va., Dec. 28, 1862.
(1) OLIVE, JOHN — See list of "Non-Commissioned Officers" above.
(1) ORM, JEREMIAH — Present for duty until June, 1863: No record after
        that date, may have been killed at Gettysburg.
        PENCE, GEO. W. — Enl., June 15, 1862 at Lynchburg, Va.: W. (thigh)
        & POW, Antietam (Sept. 17, 1862): Paroled from Ft. McHenry,
        Nov. 12, 1862: Returned to duty, Apr., 1863.
        PEARCE, JOHN A. — Enl., Apr. 24, 1862 at Goldsboro, No. Car.:
        POW, Gettysburg (July 2, 1863): Confined at Ft. Delaware.
        QUESSENBERRY, GEO. W. — Enl., Mar. 17, 1862 at Lynchburg, Va.:
        Sick, Summer, 1863: Transfd. to Co. E, 29th Va. Inf. Regt., Feb.
        1, 1865.
        REYNOLDS, EDMOND W. — Enl., Mar. 7, 1862 at Tyro, Ark.: W. (leg)
        & POW, Gettysburg (July 2, 1863): Paroled: W. (knee), E. Tenn.,
        Mar., 1864.
(1) SHEAN, ALEX. CRITTENDEN — Enl., age 19: POW, Gettysburg (July
        2, 1863): Confined at Ft. Delaware: Took Fed. oath, Apr. 15,
        1864.
(1) SMITH, GILBERT G. — Enl., age 27: Sick, Winter, 1862-63: Deserted
        in E. Tenn., Nov., 1863: Took Fed. oath at Louisville, Nov. 29,
        1863.
        SMITH, JOS. K. — Transfd. to Co. H from 2nd Ark. Btln., July 18,
        1862: Retired to Invalid Corps, July 6, 1864: Paroled at
        Salisbury, N.C., May 22, 1865.
(1) SOUTHWORTH, LEWIS E. — Enl., age 18: AWOL, E. Tenn., Feb.,
        1864: Deserted, Apr. 3, 1864.
        STARNES,._____ — Paroled, Talladega, Ala., May 19, 1865: No
        other record.
(1) STATOM, JOHN W. — Enl., age 26: POW, Falling Waters, Md., July 14,
        1863: Confined at Pt. Lookout, Md.
(1) TSHEAR, NAPOLEAN — See list of "Non-Comm. Officers" above.
        THOMAS, DAVID W. — Enl. at Lynchburg, Va., Mar. 17, 1862: K.,
        Gettysburg (July 2, 1863).
(2) THORNBERRY, JEFFERSON — Enl., Nov. 13, 1861 at Tyro, Ark.:
        W., Antietam (Sept. 17, 1862): Paroled, Appomattox (Apr. 12,
        1865).
(1) TOWNSEND, JOHN M. — Enl., age 20: Hospitalized with VD, Fall,
        1862: W., Gettysburg (July 2, 1863): Deserted, Apr. 13, 1864.
        TYLER, THOS. — Paroled, Jackson Port, Ark., June 5, 1865, age 25:
        No other record.
(1) VARNARSDALE, CORNELIUS C. — Furlough, Spring, 1862: No
        record after Apr., 1863.

VICORY (or VICKERY), JAS. B. — Enl., Sept. 3, 1861 at Memphis, Tenn.: POW, Gettysburg (July 2, 1863): Confined at Ft. Delaware.

WALLACE, OAKLEY M. — Enl., Mar. 10, 1862 at Tyro, Ark.: Died of pneumonia at Chimborazo Hosp., Apr. 13, 1863.

WELLS, WILLIS D. — See list of "Non-Commissioned Officers" above.

(1) WHITE, DAVID A. — See list of "Non-Commissioned Officers" above.

WHITTINGTON, JOHN M. — Enl., Mar. 8, 1862 at Tyro, Ark.: Died in Gen. Hosp. No. 8, Goldsboro, No. Car., Sept. 5, 1863.

WILKERSON, JOHN A. — Transfd. to Co. H from 2nd Ark. Btln., July 18, 1862: W. (leg & face) & POW, Gettysburg (July 2, 1863): Confined at Fed. hosp. in Baltimore: Exchanged: Retired to Ark., permanently disabled.

(1) WILKES, JAS. D. — Enl., age 32: W., Antietam (Sept. 17, 1862): Paroled, Oct. 14, 1862: Sick in hosp., Summer, 1864.

WILKS, JOHN M. — Enl., at Tyro, Ark. on Mar. 13, 1862: Deserted, E. Tenn., Mar. 26, 1864.

WITHERS, JOHN — Enl. at Tyro, Ark. on Mar. 31, 1862: Detached duty as teamster, Feb., 1863: Deserted in E. Tenn., Mar. 26, 1864.

(1) WOLF, ABRAHAM — Enl., age 39: Detailed as nurse at the Gen'l. Hosp. in Richmond, Summer, 1862: Permanently disabled with myopia & lumbago: No record after Oct., 1863.

* * * * *

MEMBERS OF COMPANY H, 3RD ARK. INF. REGT., WHO WERE NOT PRESENT FOR DUTY DURING THE PERIOD THAT THE REGIMENT WAS ASSIGNED TO HOOD'S TEXAS BRIGADE (NOV., 1862-APR., 1865).

OFFICERS

(1) Gibson, John G., 1Lt. (Orig. 1Lt. of Co.: Resgnd., Aug., 1862)

(1) Hughes, Jas. E., 2Lt. (Orig. 2Lt. of Co.: Resgnd., June, 1862)

NON-COMMISSIONED OFFICERS

(1) Applegate, David Thos., Jr., 1Sgt. (Orig. 1Sgt. of Co.: No record after Apr., 1862)

(1) Cogar, Andrew J., Sgt. (Orig. 1Cpl. of Co.: No other record)

(1) Head, Jesse S., Sgt. (Orig. 3Cpl. of Co.: K., Antietam)

(1) Humphries, Franklin W., Sgt. (W., Antietam)

(1) Love, John A., Cpl. (No record after Apr., 1862)

(1) Miles, Wyatt S., Sgt. (Orig. 4Sgt. of Co.: D., Oct., 1862)

(1) Olive, Jas. H., Cpl. (K., Antietam)

PRIVATES

(1) Applegate, Jos. M. (W., Antietam)

(1) Arnold, Wm. C. (No record after Sept., 1861)

(1) Ball, John K. (Transfd. to 3rd Tenn. Inf.)

Barnes, T. W. (No record)

(1) Blocker, John E. (No record)

(1) Blocker, Thos. G. (No record)

(1) Blocker, Wm. O. (K., Greenbrier R., Oct., 1861)

Bowlin, Eli (D., Aug., 1862)

(1) Boy, Geo. (Dischgd., Feb., 1862)

Brintle, Wm. H. (D., May, 1862)

Brown, G. W. (POW)

Burgess, Kennedy (No record)

Burns, Bennett W. (Dischgd., Aug., 1862)

(1) Burns, Wm. B. (Dischgd., Feb., 1862)

(1) Byrd, Lemuel P. (W., Antietam)

Byrd, Richard (No record)

Carroll, John (Deserted)

Carter, John G. (W. & POW)

(1) Carter, John (No record)

Cockman, J. W. (Dischgd., Aug., 1862)

Cockman, W. S. (AWOL)

(1) Daniel, Jas. R. (No record)

Dodd, John E. (No record)

Evans, Green S. (AWOL)

(1) Hart, Frank (No record)

(1) Haygood, Jesse H. (D., Nov., 1862)

(1) Horne, Robt. E. (No record)

Howell, Wm. B. (W., Antietam)

(1) Huff, Thomas A. (No record)

(1) Humphries, Felix V. (Dischgd., May, 1862)

Mann, Augustus M. (No record after Apr., 1862)

(1) Marshall, Lafayette (Transfd. to 8th Ky. Inf.)

McGowan, Jos. J. (Dischgd., July, 1862)

Melton, T. R. (Dischgd., Aug., 1862)

Mullany, Thos. (No record)

Myers, Newel (D., Aug., 1862)

(1) Olive, Peter H. (Dischgd., Feb., 1862)

Pickery, J. B. (No record)

Roberts, J. L. (Dischgd., July, 1862)

(1) Sexsmith, Wm. T. (No record after Apr., 1862)

Smith, Benj. F. (Dischgd., Mar., 1862)

(1) Smith, Claiborne W. (D., Apr., 1862)

Smith, Reuben (D., Apr., 1862)

Stughleman, Andrew J. (K., Antietam)

Wilkes, John A. (D., Spring, 1862)

Wilks, J. T. (D., Apr., 1862)

(1) Williams, Benj. Franklin (Missing, Antietam)

Winchester, D. G. (Dischgd., Aug., 1862)

(1) Wingfield, Jos. S. (Transfd. to 8th Ky. Inf.)

COMPANY I – *TULIP RIFLES*

Company was organized in Dallas County, Ark., in early June, 1861 and was mustered into the Confederate Service, "for the war," at Lynchburg, Va., July 5, 1861 by Maj. H. L. Clay, USA.

Key

(1) Original member of Company. (2) Paroled at Appomattox.
K (Killed), W (Wounded), POW (Prisoner of War)
AWOL (Absent Without Leave)

OFFICERS

SMITH, SAMUEL W. Capt. – Orig. 4Sgt. of Co., age 21: Prom., 1Lt., Feb. 6, 1862: Prom., Capt., June 24, 1862: W. (thigh), Gettysburg (July 2, 1863): Prom., Maj., May 6, 1864: Retired to Invalid Corps, Dec. 3, 1864.

ALLEN, BENJ. T. 1Lt. – Orig. 1Sgt. of Co.: Prom., 1Lt., Dec. 6, 1862: W. (arm), Wilderness (May 6, 1864).

(1) EATON, JOHN R. 1Lt. – Orig. 3Lt. of Co., age 27: Resgnd., Dec. 6, 1862.

BROWN, TYREE H. 2Lt. – Orig. Pvt. in Co., age 18: Prom., 2Lt., Dec., 1862: W., Chickamauga (Sept. 19, 1863): Disabled: Resgnd., Aug. 18, 1864.

(1) BUTLER, HENRY A. 2Lt. – See roster, "Regmtl. Hdqtrs., 3rd Ark. Inf."

PRIOR (or PRYOR), SAM W. 2Lt. – Orig. Pvt. in Co., age 25: Prom., 1Cpl., Feb., 1862: W., Antietam (Sept. 17, 1862): Prom., 3Lt., Dec. 25, 1862: W., Gettysburg (July 2, 1863): Prom., 2Lt., Dec., 1863: Paroled, Lynchburg, Apr. 15, 1865.

NON-COMMISSIONED OFFICERS

(1) ALLEN, BENJ. T. 1Sgt. – See list of "Officers" above.

JOYNER, JAS. L. 1Sgt. – Orig. Pvt. in Co., age 33: Appt. Cpl., Feb., 1862: Appt. 5Sgt., Dec., 1862: Appt. 1Sgt., Feb., 1864: K., Wilderness (May 6, 1864).

LATHAM, WM. P. 2Cpl. – Orig. Pvt. in Co., age 23: Prom., 2Cpl., Feb., 1862: W., Gettysburg (July 2, 1863): W. (leg), Chaffin's Farm (Sept. 29, 1864).

(1) LITTLE, LOFTON M. 4Sgt. – Enl. as a 4Sgt., age 25: Not fit for field duty, asgnd. as messenger in War Dept., Nov., 1864.

(2) LOCKHART, WM. G. 4Sgt. – Transfd. as a Pvt. to Co. I from 2nd Ark. Btln., July 18, 1862: Appt. Cpl., July, 1863: Appt. 4Sgt., Aug., 1864: Paroled, Appomattox (Apr. 12, 1865).

MARSHALL, WILLIS S. 1Cpl. — Orig. Pvt. in Co., age 23: Appt. 1Cpl., Jan. 1, 1863: W., Chickamauga (Sept. 20, 1863): No record after Aug. 1864.

McNEILL, ALEX. H. Cpl. — Orig. Pvt. in Co.: Appt. Cpl., Feb. 7, 1862: Reduced to Pvt., Nov., 1862: AWOL, May, 1864.

(2) NEWBERN, BRADFORD B. 3Cpl. — Transfd. as a Pvt. to Co. I from 2nd Ark. Btln., July 18, 1862: Appt. 3Cpl., Mar. 10, 1863: W. (leg), Wilderness (May 6, 1864): Paroled, Appomattox (Apr. 12, 1865).

PAISLEY, WM. 3Cpl. — Orig. Pvt. in Co., age 19: W. (arm), Antietam (Sept. 17, 1862): Disabled: Dischgd., May 25, 1863.

(1) SMITH, SAMUEL W. 4Sgt. — See list of "Officers" above.

STEWARD, ORTON Cpl. — W. (head) & POW, Helena, Ark., July 4, 1863: Confined at Fed. hosp. at Memphis: Died in hosp., July 25, 1863.

TOMME, WM. W. 5Sgt. — Transfd. as a Pvt. to Co. I from 2nd Ark. Btln., July 18, 1862: K., Wilderness (May 6, 1864).

WATSON, JAS. H. 5Sgt. — Orig. Pvt. in Co., age 22: Prom., 3Cpl., Aug., 1861: Prom., 5Sgt., Feb., 1862: W. (mouth) & POW, Gettysburg (July 2, 1863): Confined at Fed. hosp., Davids Is., N.Y. Harbor: Exchanged: Retired for disability, Oct. 24, 1864: Paroled, May 19, 1865.

(2) WILLIAMS, JOS. SIM 1Sgt. — Orig. Pvt. in Co., age 17: Prom., 1Sgt., July 1, 1863: W. (leg), Petersburg trenches (June 22, 1864): Paroled, Appomattox (Apr. 12, 1865).

MUSICIAN

McDERMOTT, EDW. — Enl., age 24: Orig. Pvt. in Co.: Appt. musician, July 12, 1861: Dischgd. for disability, Jan. 25, 1863.

PRIVATES

BARKER, C. — POW, Gettysburg (July 2, 1863): Confined at Ft. McHenry, Md.: No other record.

BARKER, WM. — Transfd. to Co. I from 2nd Ark. Btln., July 18, 1862: W. (thigh) & POW, Gettysburg (July 2, 1863): Confined at Davids Is., N.Y. Harbor: Paroled.

BEARD, ROBT. — Enl., Jan. 12, 1863 at Camden, Ark.: Sick most of 1863: Deserted in E. Tenn.: Took Fed. oath at Louisville, Dec. 23, 1863.

(1) BENTON, WM. — W. (chest) & POW, Gettysburg (July 2, 1863): Confined at Davids Is., N.Y. Harbor: Paroled, Aug. 28, 1863.

(1) BERRY, JAS. M. — POW, Falling Waters, Md. (July 14, 1863): Confined at Pt. Lookout, Md. & Elmira, N.Y. prisons: Paroled from latter, May 15, 1865.

BLACK, GEO. W. — Enl., Mar. 26, 1863 at Camden, Ark.: Absent, sick, much of 1863: Detailed to duty as a nurse, Dec., 1863.

(2) BREWER, WM. T. — Enl., Mar. 10, 1863 at Camden, Ark.: Sick, Winter, 1864-65: Paroled, Appomattox (Apr. 12, 1865).

(1)   BROWN, TYREE H. — See list of "Officers" above.

BURTON, JAS. W. — Enl., Mar. 12, 1863 at Camden, Ark.: Deserted in E. Tenn.: Took Fed. oath, Feb. 29, 1864.

BUTLER, CHAS. A. — Enl., Apr. 14, 1862 in Dallas County, Ark.: POW, Gettysburg (July 2, 1863): Confined at Ft. Delaware.

BUTLER, GEO. E. — See roster, "Regmtl. Hdqtrs., 3rd Ark. Inf."

(1)   BUTLER, LEWIS P. — See roster, "Regmtl. Hdqtrs., 3rd Ark. Inf."

CAMARA, JAS. L. — POW, Little Rock, Ark., Sept. 11, 1863, "deserted the Rebels." No other record.

(1)   CHAPPELL, COLEMAN H. — Enl., age 18: K., Cold Harbor (June 5, 1864).

CLEMENTS, J. W. — Enl., Mar. 17, 1863 at Camden, Ark.: Sick most of 1863: Dischgd. by Med. Bd., Jan. 25, 1864.

CLEMENTS, JAS. B. — Enl., Mar. 26, 1863 at Camden, Ark.: W. (face & thigh) & POW, Gettysburg (July 2, 1863): Confined at Fed. hosp. on Davids Is., N.Y. Harbor: Paroled, Fall, 1863.

(1)   CLEVELAND, WILEY B. — Enl., age 21: POW, Antietam (Sept. 17, 1862): Exchanged: W., Suffolk (Apr. 28, 1863).

COCHRAN, P. R. — Enl., Mar. 26, 1863 at Camden, Ark.: POW, Gettysburg (July 2, 1863): Confined at Ft. McHenry, Md.

DANIEL, H. H. — Enl., Mar. 16, 1863 at Camden, Ark.: W., on picket near Chattanooga, Oct. 18, 1863: Hospitalized at Augusta, Ga.

DAVIS, DAVID A. — Transfd. to Co. I from 2nd Ark. Btln., July 18, 1862: POW, Gettysburg (July 2, 1863): Confined at Pt. Lookout, Md.: Exchanged, Oct. 11, 1864: Died of chronic dysentery, Oct. 24, 1864.

DAUGHERTY, JOS. — Enl., age 14 at Zollicoffer, Tenn. on Apr. 18, 1864: Dischgd. by Med. Bd., Sept. 9, 1864, as being "small of stature and unfit for any duty."

DOUGAL, BENJ. M. — Enl., Mar. 14, 1863 at Camden, Ark.: Died at hospital in Weldon, N. Car. of "congestive fever," Apr. 26, 1863.

ELLISON, WM. G. — Enl., Mar. 26, 1863 at Camden, Ark.: AWOL, Aug., 1863, "supposed to have gone to Gen. Bragg's Army."

FIPPS, S. C. — POW, Helena, Ark., July 4, 1863: Confined at Alton, Ill. Prison Camp: Died, Jan. 10, 1864 in prison hosp. of gangrene.

(1)   FITZHUGH, EZEKIEL — Enl., age 20: Missing since Oct. 28, 1863, "while skirmishing with enemy at Lookout Mtn.:" No other record.

FULENWIDER, JOHN A. — Enl., Mar. 20, 1863 at Camden, Ark.: POW, Wilderness (May 6, 1864): Confined at Fed. prison, Elmira, N.Y.: Died at prison of pneumonia, Feb. 17, 1865.

GAMMILL, WM. — Enl., Mar. 26, 1863: W. (eye), Bermuda Hundred (June 17, 1864): W., Chester, Va., July 18, 1864: W. (shoulder), Chaffin's Farm (Sept. 29, 1864).

(2)   GARNER, MOSES — Transfd. to Co. I from 2nd Ark. Btln., July 18, 1862: Paroled, Appomattox (Apr. 12, 1865).

(1)   GOZA, ELIJAH D. — Enl., age 30: Present for duty entire war:
(2)   Paroled, Appomattox (Apr. 12, 1865).

HARPER, JOHN S. — Enl., Mar. 11, 1863 at Camden, Ark.: W. & POW, Chickamauga (Sept. 20, 1863): Died in Fed. prison, Dec. 23, 1863 of tuberculosis.

HERNSBERGER, ADAM — POW, Gettysburg: No other record.

(1) HOOD, WM. C. — Enl., age 22: W. (leg) & POW, Gettysburg (July 2, 1863): Confined at the Fed. hosp. on Davids Is., N.Y. Harbor: Exchanged: Retired to Invalid Corps, Dec. 15, 1864.

(1) HOUSE, GREEN D. — Enl., age 18: W. (face), Bermuda Hundred (June 17, 1864).

HOUSE, M. C. — Enl., Mar. 11, 1863 at Camden, Ark.: Sick in Richmond, Spring, 1865: POW, Richmond hosp., Apr. 3, 1865: Died in military prison hosp. at Newport News, Va., June 9, 1865: Buried on P. West's farm.

JOHNSON, ANDREW JACKSON — Enl., age 46 at Camden, Ark., Mar. 8, 1863: Sick, Weldon, N. Car., Apr. 15, 1863: AWOL: POW, Randolph County, Va., Aug. 13, 1863: Confined at Atheneum Prison, Wheeling, W. Va.

JOHNSON, PLEASANT M. — Enl., Mar. 26, 1863 at Camden, Ark.: POW, Gettysburg (July 2, 1863): Died at Ft. Delaware Prison of chronic bronchitis on Aug. 14, 1863.

(1) JONES, JAS. W. — Enl., age 24: POW, Chickamauga (Sept. 20, 1863): Confined at Camp Morton, Ind.: Paroled, May 10, 1865.

(2) JONES, JOHN C. — Transfd. to Co. I from 2nd Ark. Btln., July 18, 1862: Paroled, Appomattox (Apr. 12, 1865).

(1) JOYNER, JAS. L. — See list of "Non-Comm. Officers" above.

(1) KELLEY, JAS. — Enl., age 24: W. (hip), Suffolk (May 1, 1863): Granted wound furlough to Ark.: No record after Aug., 1864.

(1) LANTORN, ZACHARIAH J. — Enl., age 22: W. (arm), Wilderness (May 6, 1864): Hospitalized, Summer, 1864.

(1) LATHAM, WM. P. — See list of "Non-Comm. Officers" above.

LITEZ, CALEB — Transfd. to Co. I from 2nd Ark. Btln., July 18, 1862: Dischgd., Dec. 23, 1862.

(1) LITTLE, JOHN C. R. — Enl., age 22: W. (arm), Wilderness (May 6, 1864): Paroled, Burkeville Junction, Va., Apr. 21, 1865.

LOCKHART, WM. G. — See list of "Non-Comm. Officers" above.

LYBRAND, GODFREY N. — Transfd. to Co. I from 2nd Ark. Btln., July 18, 1862: W. (leg), Wilderness (May 6, 1864): Leg amputated: Paroled, Augusta, Ga., May 14, 1865.

(1) MARSHALL, WILLIS S. — See list of "Non-Comm. Officers" above.

(1) McDERMOTT, EDW. — See "Musician" above.

(1) McNEILL, ALEX. H. — See list of "Non-Comm. Officers" above.

MILLS, M. J. — Enl., Mar. 23, 1863: POW, Wilderness (May 6, 1864): Confined at Elmira, N.Y.: Died in prison hosp. of pneumonia, Sept. 20, 1864.

(1) MONTGOMERY, JAS. W. — Enl., age 19: W., Antietam (Sept. 17, 1862): Hospitalized, Spring, 1865: POW, Ashland Station, Va., Apr. 3, 1865: Paroled, May 18, 1865.

(2) MORGAN, WM. G. H. — Enl., Mar. 14, 1863 at Camden, Ark.: Paroled, Appomattox (Apr. 12, 1865): No other record.

(1) MORRIS, LEROY M. — Enl., age 21: W. & POW, Gettysburg (July 2, 1863): Confined at Fed. hosp., Davids Is., N.Y. Harbor.

MORRIS, WM. B. — Transfd. to Co. I from 2nd Ark. Btln., July 18, 1862: W., Chickamauga (Sept. 19, 1863): Retired for disability, Dec. 14, 1864.

NAWLS, BRYANT — Enl., Mar. 12, 1863 at Camden, Ark.: AWOL from Hosp., Ringgold, Ga., Sept., 1863.

NEWBERN, BRADFORD B. — See list of "Non-Comm. Officers" above.

NORRIS, FRANCIS M. — Transfd. to Co. I from 2nd Ark. Btln., July 18, 1862: Died of pneumonia in Richmond, Dec. 15, 1862.

(1)   PAISLEY, WM. — See list of "Non-Comm. Officers" above.

PALLMAN, ANTHONY — Enl., Mar. 26, 1863 at Camden, Ark.: W. & POW, Gettysburg (July 2, 1863): Confined at Ft. Delaware: Died in prison hosp. of typhoid fever, Sept. 1, 1863.

PARKER, CALIHAN — Enl., Mar. 14, 1863 at Camden, Ark.: W. & POW, Gettysburg (July 2, 1863): Confined at Ft. Delaware: Died in prison hosp., July 30, 1863.

PERKINS, CULLEN W. — Enl., Mar. 26, 1863 at Camden, Ark.: POW, Gettysburg (July 2, 1863): Confined at Ft. Delaware: Exchanged, July 31, 1863: AWOL from Williamsburg, Va. hosp., Aug., 1863.

(1)   POWERS, JOHN — Enl., age 28: On detached service as a shoemaker from Nov., 1862 to Aug., 1864.

(1)   PRIOR (or PRYOR), SAM W. — See list of "Officers" above.

RAINES, M. W. — Enl., Feb. 23, 1863 at Camden, Ark.: POW, Falling Waters, Md., July 14, 1863: Took Fed. oath at Washington, D.C., Dec. 13, 1863 and sent north.

(2)   RATTERREE, ROBT. — Transfd. to Co. I from 2nd Ark. Btln., July 18, 1862: Detailed to Provost Guard, June, 1863: Paroled, Appomattox (Apr. 12, 1865).

(1)   RHODES, JAS. W. — Not listed on Co. Bi-Monthly Muster Rolls.
(2)
(1)   ROBERTSON, JAS. M. — Enl., age 29: Paroled, Appomattox (Apr. 12,
(2)   1865): No other record.
(2)   SHIRLEY, ISAAC S. — Enl., Mar. 23, 1863 at Camden, Ark.: Paroled, Appomattox (Apr. 12, 1865).

(1)   SMITH, RICHARD J. — Enl., age 20: POW, Gettysburg (July 2, 1863): Confined at Ft. Delaware: Died in Fed. prison, Mar. 7, 1865.

TATUM, HARDY L. — Transfd. to Co. I from 2nd Ark. Btln., July 18, 1862: AWOL, dropped from rolls, July, 1864.

THURMON, RILEY W. — Transfd. to Co. I from 2nd Ark. Btln., July 18, 1862: Deserted in E. Tenn., Feb. 23, 1864: Took Fed. oath, Feb. 29, 1864.

TINER, JOHN P. — Transfd. to Co. I from 2nd Ark. Btln., July 18, 1862: Died of chronic diarrhea, Feb. 18, 1863.

TOMME, WM. W. — See list of "Non-Comm. Officers" above.

(1)   VANDERSLICE, JOHN — Enl., age 19: AWOL, May, 1864: Dropped from rolls, Aug., 1864: Reported to have joined cavalry unit in Ark.

(1)   WATSON, JAS. H. — See list of "Non-Comm. Officers" above.

WEST, T. J. — Enl., Mar. 26, 1863 at Camden, Ark.: POW, Gettysburg (July 2, 1863): Confined at Ft. Delaware.

(1)   WHITEMORE, JAS. — Enl., age 30: Missing since May 3, 1863 on march from Suffolk.

WILLIAMS, H. L. — Enl., Mar. 11, 1863 at Camden, Ark.: Died of fever at Weldon, N. Car., Apr. 20, 1863.

(1) WILLIAMS, JOS. SIM — See list of "Non-Comm. Officers" above.
     WILSON, J. C. — Deserted in E. Tenn., Mar. 20, 1864.
(1) WILSON, TEMPECOLA — Sick, Spring & Summer, 1863: AWOL, from
     hosp. at Atlanta, Sept. 17, 1863.

* * * * *

MEMBERS OF COMPANY I, 3RD ARK. INF. REGT., WHO WERE NOT PRESENT FOR DUTY DURING THE PERIOD THAT THE REGIMENT WAS ASSIGNED TO HOOD'S TEXAS BRIGADE (NOV., 1862-APR., 1865).

OFFICERS

(1) Alexander, George D., Capt. (Orig. Capt. of Co.: W., Capon Bridge, Jan., 1862)

(1) Taylor, Howell L., 1Lt. (Orig. 1Lt. of Co.: Resgnd., Jan., 1862)

NON-COMMISSIONED OFFICERS

(1) Davidson, Robt. A., 3Cpl. (Orig. 3Cpl.: Dischgd., disability, Sept., 1861)
    Harges, Henry C., Cpl. (POW, Oct., 1862)
(1) Littlejohn, Thos. B., 2Sgt. (Orig. 2Sgt.: Dischgd., July, 1861)
    Moore, Jas. W., Cpl. (Orig. 4Cpl.: D., Feb., 1862)
(1) Reid, Wm. H., 3Sgt. (Orig. 3Sgt.: Dischgd., Feb., 1862)

(1) Smith, John M., Sgt. (Orig. 1Cpl.: Dischgd., Mar., 1862)
(1) Smith, Wm. N., Sgt. (Transfd. out, Sept., 1862)
(1) Somerville, Willis L., Sgt. (K., Antietam, Sept., 1862)
(1) Sullenberger, Jos. P., Cpl. (K., Capon Bridge, Jan., 1862)
(1) Williams, Erastus B., 2Cpl. (Orig. 4Cpl.: Dischgd., Nov., 1861)

MUSICIANS

(1) Schadd, Henry M. (Orig. Pvt., Appt. Drummer, Apr., 1862: No other record.

PRIVATES

Barker, Stephen (Dischgd., Nov., 1862)
(1) Baugh, Wm. B. (Dischgd., Oct., 1861)
(1) Boyd, Jas. F. (No record)
(1) Brown, Wm. (AWOL, Mar., 1862)

(1) Bryan, Larkin W. (K., Antietam)
    Bryant, Michael W. (Transfd. out, Mar., 1862)
(1) Bullock, Thos. S. (Dischgd., Nov., 1861)
(1) Bush, Jas. (No record)
    Crassett, Robt. (No record after July, 1862)

(1) Durham, Duncan R. (D., Sept., 1861)

Ezell, Wm. F. (No record)

(1) Floyd, John M. (D., July, 1862)

Foreman, F. M. (Did not join Co. in Va.)

Goad, C. P. (No record after Nov., 1862)

Goad, W. H. (No record after Nov., 1862)

(1) Green, Dudley P. (Dischgd., disability, Aug., 1861)

(1) Hall, Jas. (K., Antietam)

Harris, Solomon (No record after July, 1862)

Huett, John (No record after July, 1862)

Huett, Wm. (No record after July, 1862)

(1) Hutchinson, Wm. B. (Dischgd., Sept., 1862)

(1) Jones, Nicholas A. (D., July, 1861)

Kenady (or Kennedy), Wm. H. (D., Nov., 1862)

Kuykendall, Jas. W. (D., Nov., 1861)

(1) Leiper, Wm. D. (Dischgd., July, 1861)

(1) Overton, Jas. G. (No record)

Overton, Wm. (D., Oct., 1861)

(1) Pattillo, Robt. G. (Dischgd., Aug., 1861)

(1) Phillips, John H. (Dischgd., Oct., 1861)

(1) Phillips, Thos. P. (Dischgd., Oct., 1861)

Pitman, John (Did not report in Va.)

(1) Porterfield, Jos. R. (AWOL, Mar., 1862)

Purnell, John J. (D., Oct., 1862)

(1) Pryor, Wm. (D., Aug., 1861)

(1) Robertson, Jos. (D., Sept., 1861)

(1) Ross, David C. (POW, Antietam, Sept., 1862)

(1) Scott Anderson (Dischgd., wound, May, 1862)

(1) Sims, Jas. F. (K., Antietam, Sept., 1862)

(1) Smith, Lemuel P. (Transfd., Apr., 1862)

(1) Somerville, John M. (AWOL, Oct., 1862)

Strother, Eli (Did not report in Va.)

(1) Stroud, Holston S. (Dischgd., disability, Feb., 1862)

Taylor, Fred P. (AWOL, Dec., 1862)

Taylor, Giles (No record after July, 1862)

(1) Turner, John F. (Dischgd., July, 1861)

(1) Underwood, Elijah V. (D., Oct., 1861)

Wilson, Andrew (Dischgd., disability, July, 1862)

(1) Winston, Franklin (No record)

Woodie, Jas. W. (K., Antietam)

(1) Wright, G. L. (D., Aug., 1861)

Yates, George (Dischgd., Aug., 1862)

3RD ARK. VOL. INF. REGT.

COMPANY K – *ARKANSAS TRAVELERS*

Company was organized in Ashley County, Ark. in early June, 1861, and was mustered into the Confederate Service "for the war," at Lynchburg, Va., July 5, 1861 by Maj. H. L. Clay, CSA.

Key

(1) Original member of Company. (2) Paroled at Appomattox.
K (Killed), W (Wounded), POW (Prisoner of War)
AWOL (Absent Without Leave)

OFFICERS

HADLEY, THOS. J. Capt. — Orig. 2Sgt. of Co.: Prom., 2Lt., Sept. 17, 1862: Prom., 1Lt., Sept. 26, 1862: W. (head), Petersburg trenches, July 16, 1864: Prom., Capt., Winter, 1864-65: POW, Richmond, Apr. 3, 1865.

(1)
(2) NORRIS, JESSE W. Capt. — Orig. 1Lt. of Co.: Prom., Capt., Sept. 19, 1863: W. (thigh), Wilderness (May 6, 1864): Paroled, Appomattox (Apr. 12, 1865).

(1) LOWE, BENJ. F. 1Lt. — Orig. 2Lt. of Co.: Prom., 1Lt., Sept. 19, 1863: AWOL, Winter, 1864-65: Paroled, Montgomery, Ala., June, 1865.

(2) BREWER, THOS. P. 2Lt. — Orig. Pvt. in Co.: Prom., 2Sgt., Nov., 1862: AWOL, Winter, 1862-63: Prom., 2Lt., Winter, 1864-65: Paroled, Appomattox (Apr. 12, 1865).

COCKRAN, WM. W. 2Lt. — Orig. 1Sgt. of Co.: Prom., 3Lt., Dec., 1862: Prom., 2Lt., Jan., 1864: Reduced to ranks, Aug., 1864: W. (shoulder), Darbytown Rd. (Oct. 7, 1864).

NON-COMMISSIONED OFFICERS

(1) BATMAN, PETER F. 4Cpl. — Orig. 4Cpl. of Co.: Reduced to Pvt.: Transfd. out of 3rd Ark. Inf., Jan. 11, 1863: K., Gettysburg (July 2, 1863).

(1) COCHRAN, WM. W. 1Sgt. — See list of "Officers" above.

(2) DENSON, N. C. 1Sgt. — Orig. Pvt. in Co.: Appt. 2Sgt., Feb., 1864: W. (head), Spotsylvania (May 10, 1864): Appt. 1Sgt., Winter, 1864-65: Paroled, Appomattox (Apr. 12, 1865).

(1)
(2) GOLDSBY, JOS. H. 4Sgt. — Orig. 4Sgt. of Co.: Abs. sick, Aug., 1864: AWOL, dropped from rolls: Rejnd. Co. as a Pvt., Jan. 24, 1865: Paroled, Appomattox (Apr. 12, 1865).

(1) HADLEY, THOS. J. 2Sgt. — See list of "Officers" above.

(2) HILL, J. L. F. Sgt. — Orig. Pvt. in Co.: Prom., Sgt.: Paroled, Appomattox (Apr. 12, 1865).

MAYS, S. H. 4Sgt. — Orig. Pvt. in Co.: Prom., 4Sgt., Summer, 1864: W. (hip), Darbytown Rd. (Oct. 7, 1864).

(2) McCURDY, M. L. 5Sgt. — Orig. Pvt. in Co.: Prom., 5Sgt., Apr., 1864: W. (thigh), Wilderness (May 6, 1864): Paroled, Appomattox (Apr. 12, 1865).

McGUIRE, MICHAEL 2Sgt. — Orig. Pvt. in Co.: Prom., 2Sgt., Spring, 1862: Fell off of horse, hospitalized, Aug. & Sept., 1862: Reduced to ranks, Oct. 31, 1862: POW, Gettysburg (July 2, 1863): Confined at Ft. Delaware: Exchanged, Mar. 7, 1865.

MORGAN, JAS. H. 4Cpl. — Orig. Pvt. in Co.: W., Antietam (Sept. 17, 1862): Prom., 4Cpl., July, 1863: Died of disease at Petersburg, June 23, 1864.

NOBLE, JAS. S. 5Sgt. — Orig. Pvt. in Co.: Prom., 5Sgt., Jan., 1862: W. (thigh) & POW, Gettysburg (July 2, 1863): Died in Fed. hosp., July 7, 1863.

(1) SAWYER, R. L. 4Cpl. — Orig. Pvt. in Co.: Prom., 4Cpl., Summer, 1862: K., Gettysburg (July 2, 1863).

(1) WHITE, HAMP C. 3Sgt. — See roster, "Regmtl. Hdqtrs., 3rd Ark. Inf."

WILLIAMS, JAS. V. 1Sgt. — Orig. Pvt. in Co.: Prom., 1Sgt., Summer, 1862: W., E. Tenn., Winter, 1863-64: Wound furlough, Mar., 1864: Did not return to Co.

WILSON, AUGUSTUS H. 4Sgt. — Orig. Pvt. in Co.: Prom., 4Sgt., Feb., 1862: W., Chickamauga (Sept. 19, 1863): AWOL, dropped from rolls, Aug., 1864.

(1) WOOD, S. B. 3Cpl. — See roster, "Regmtl. Hdqtrs., 3rd Ark. Inf."

MUSICIANS

(1) BIGHAM, E. L. — Orig. Musician of Co.: Paroled, Appomattox (Apr.
(2)   12, 1865).
(1) FILES, JAS. S. — See roster, "Regmtl. Hdqtrs., 3rd Ark. Inf."
(1) McKINNEY, L. B. — See roster, "Regmtl. Hdqtrs., 3rd Ark. Inf."
(1) WOOD, AUGUSTUS BALDWIN — See roster, "Regmtl. Hdqtrs., 3rd Ark. Inf."

PRIVATES

(2) ALBRIGHT, JOHN H. — Transfd. to Co. K from 2nd Ark. Btln., July 18, 1862: AWOL since Oct. 1, 1863: Under arrest, Summer, 1864: Paroled, Appomattox (Apr. 12, 1865).

(1) BENNETT, A. P. — Good present for duty record: Paroled,
(2) Appomattox (Apr. 12, 1865).

(1) BLACKBURN, JAS. S. — W., Chickamauga (Sept. 19, 1863): Dischgd. for disability, Aug. 4, 1864.

BLAIR, JAS. L. — Enl., Mar. 1, 1862, age 35: Dischgd. for disability, 1864: Paroled, Talladega, Ala., May 22, 1865.

(1) BREWER, THOS. P. — See list of "Officers" above.

(1) CAMERON, A. W. H. — AWOL, dropped from rolls, Oct., 1864: No other record.

(1) CAMERON, WM. — Died, Jerusalem, Va., May 14, 1863.

(2) CAMPBELL, J. H. — Enl. at Bull's Gap, Tenn., Mar. 12, 1864: Paroled, Appomattox (Apr. 12, 1865).

CLARK, JOHN — POW, Washington Co., Ark., Apr 1, 1864: Confined at Alton, Ill. prison: Exchanged, Feb. 17, 1865.

(1) CLYDE, ROBT. B. — See roster, "Regmtl. Hdqtrs., 3rd Ark. Inf."

CLYDE, W. T. — Enl., Feb. 15, 1863 at Hamburg, Ark.: No other record.

(1) COLE, JAS. — Detach. duty as teamster, Summer, 1863: Paroled, Lynchburg, Va., Apr. 13, 1865.
(1) CRAIG, J. W. — Abs. sick, Summer, 1863: AWOL, Oct., 1863: Died of dyspesia at Cross Plains, Ala., Dec. 27, 1863.
      CRUMPTON, THOS. — Enl., Sept. 17, 1861 at Hot Springs, Ark.: W. (thigh & face) & POW, Gettysburg: No other record.
(1) DeLANNAY (or DeLANEY), GEO. W. — See roster, "Regmtl. Hdqtrs., 3rd Ark. Inf."
(1) DENSEN, N. C. — See list of "Non-Comm. Officers" above.
(1) DONOHO, DENNIS — Deserted at Suffolk, Va., May 3, 1863.
(1) DURHAM, A. A. — Died of wounds received at Wilderness (May 6, 1864).
(2) EVERETT, W. D. — Enl., Feb. 15, 1863 at Hamburg, Ark.: Paroled, Appomattox (Apr. 12, 1865).
      FERGUSON, ROBT. S. — Paroled at Charlotte, No. Car., May 19, 1865: No other record.
(1) FOUNTAIN, J. H. J. — W., Darbytown Rd. (Oct. 7, 1864): Paroled,
(2) Appomattox (Apr. 9, 1865).
      FOWLER, WM. — Enl. at Hot Springs, Ark., Sept. 17, 1861: W. & POW, Wilderness (May 6, 1864): Confined at Elmira, N.Y.: Paroled, June 16, 1865.
(1) GILCREASE, JOHN A. — W., Gettysburg (July 2, 1863): Retired for disability, May 24, 1864.
(1) GILLIAM, JAS. C. — W., Williamsburg Rd. (Oct. 27, 1864): Paroled,
(2) Appomattox (Apr. 12, 1865).
(1) HILL, J. L. F. — See list of "Non-Comm. Officers" above.
(1) HOLCOMB, A. W. — W., Chickamauga (Sept. 19, 1863): Paroled,
(2) Appomattox (Apr. 12, 1865).
      HOLLAND, JOHN G. — Transfd. to Co. K from 2nd Ark. Btln., July 18, 1862: Deserted, took Fed. oath at Hot Springs, Ark., Mar. 5, 1865.
      HOYT, THOS. — POW, Spotsylvania (May 12, 1864): Confined at Elmira, N.Y.
      HUGHES, JAS. W. — Enl., July 15, 1861 in Ashley Co., Ark., age 19: POW, E. Tenn., Nov. 25, 1863: Confined at Rock Island, Ill.: Paroled, Dec. 9, 1863.
(2) JACKSON, GEO. — Enl. at Bull's Gap, Tenn., Mar. 28, 1864: Paroled, Appomattox (Apr. 12, 1865).
(1) JACKSON, J. B. — See roster, "Regmtl. Hdqtrs., 3rd Ark. Inf."
(1) JOHNSON, JOHN W. — Detached duty as a shoemaker at Columbus, Ga., Nov., 1861 to end of war.
      LANDERS, JOHN — POW, Hellena, Ark., July 4, 1863: Exchanged, Mar. 7, 1865.
(1) LANG, CONRAD — Deserted at Suffolk, Va., May 3, 1863.
      LANGLEY, WM. — POW, Little Rock, Ark., Sept. 11, 1863: No other record.
(1) MANNING, JAMISON A. — Absent, furlough, Aug., 1861: John C. Bull, Co. L served as substitute.
(1) MAYS, S. H. — See list of "Non-Comm. Officers" above.
(1) McALLISTER, J. D. — Served as temp. Regmtl. QM Sgt., July 16 to Aug. 16, 1861: POW, Gettysburg (July 2, 1863): Escaped: Recaptured, Aug. 1, 1863: Paroled, Aug. 13, 1863.

(1) McCRORY, E. A. — Sick, Winter of 1862-63 & most of 1864: No record after Aug., 1864.

(1) McCURDY, M. L. — See list of "Non-Comm. Officers" above.

McGREGOR, MICHAEL — POW, Gettysburg (July 2, 1863): Confined at Ft. Delaware.

(1) McGUIRE, MICHAEL — See list of "Non-Comm. Officers" above.

(1) McKINNEY, H. H. — Asgnd. temporarily to 3rd Ark. Regmtl. Band, Jan. 1 to Feb. 28, 1863: Under arrest, Jan., 1864, sentenced to 3 mos. hard labor on fortifications: W. (head), Wilderness (May 6, 1864): POW, Amelia Springs (Apr. 7, 1865): Confined at Pt. Lookout, Md.: Paroled, June 29, 1865.

McKINNEY, L. B. — See roster, "Regmtl. Hdqtrs., 3rd Ark. Inf."

(1) MOORE, G. W. — Died, Danville, Va., of chronic diarrhea & bronchitis, Feb. 18, 1863.

(1) MOORE, HARRISON — Enl., age 30: Transfd. to Co. K from Co. B, June 6, 1863: POW, Chickamauga (Sept. 20, 1863): Confined at Camp Douglas, Ill.: Exchanged, Oct. 2, 1863.

(1) MORGAN, JAS. H. — See list of "Non-Comm. Officers" above.

(1) MORRIS, THOS. — Present for duty entire war: Paroled, Appomattox
(2) (Apr. 12, 1865).

(1) MYRICK, F. B. — POW, Falling Waters, Md., July 14, 1863: Confined at Pt. Lookout, Md.: Took Fed. oath, Feb. 25, 1864.

NOBLE, DALLAS — Enl., Mar. 1, 1862 at Hamburg, Ark.: W., Gettysburg (July 2, 1863): W. (leg), Darbytown Rd. (Oct. 7, 1864).

NOBLE, J. B. — Enl., Mar. 1, 1862 at Hamburg, Ark.: AWOL, dropped from rolls, Aug., 1864.

(1) NOBLE, JAS. S. — See list of "Non-Comm. Officers" above.

NOBLE, L. R. — Enl., Mar. 1, 1862 at Hamburg, Ark.: POW, Gettysburg (July 2, 1863), left with wounded: Exchanged: Dropped from rolls, for protracted absence, Aug., 1864.

(1) NOBLE, R. P. — Detached duty at Div. Comsy., Jan., 1864: Paroled at
(2) Appomattox (Apr. 12, 1865).

NOBLE, S. P. — Enl., Feb. 15, 1863 at Hamburg, Ark.: Dropped from rolls for AWOL, Dec., 1863: Rejnd. Co., Jan. 9, 1864 at Morristown, Tenn.: W. (leg), Wilderness (May 6, 1864).

PALMER, JACKSON — Paroled, Shreveport, La., June 13, 1865: No other record.

(1) PHILLIPS, JOHN C. — Enl., Mar. 1, 1862 at Hamburg, Ark.: Detach. Serv. with Div. Pioneer Corps, June, 1863: Paroled, Appomattox (Apr. 12, 1865).

(1) REEVES, M. — W. (hip) & POW, Gettysburg (July 2, 1863): Died in Fed. prison, July 18, 1863.

ROBERTS, C. R. — Enl., Mar. 1, 1862 at Hamburg, Ark.: Sick furlough, Aug., 1863: AWOL.

ROBERTS, JOS. R. — Enl., Mar. 1, 1862 at Hamburg, Ark.: POW: Took Fed. oath, Apr. 8, 1865 at Clarksburg, W. Va.

(1) ROBERTS, R. M. — W., Suffolk (May 3, 1863): Paroled, Appomattox
(2) (Apr. 12, 1865).

SAWYER, J. D. — Enl., Mar. 1, 1862 at Hamburg, Ark.: W., Chickamauga (Sept. 19, 1863): No other record.

(1) SAWYER, R. L. — See list of "Non-Comm. Officers" above.
(1) SIMPSON, B. F. — Present for duty until Aug., 1864: Sick (dysentery), Aug., 1864: Sick leave to Tannersville, Ala., Sept. 8, 1864.
(1) STELL, WM. B. — W. (wrist), Malvern Hill (July 1, 1862): W. (arm), Wilderness (May 6, 1864): Arm amputated: Dischgd. for disability, Nov. 2, 1864.
(1) STROOPE, S. F. — Sick, Mar. to Aug., 1863 & Summer, 1864: Paroled as hosp. patient, May 11, 1865, Greensboro, N.C.
     WATSON, A. W. — Transfd. to Co. K, from 2nd Ark. Btln., July 18, 1862: W., Chickamauga (Sept. 19, 1863): AWOL: Paroled, Montgomery, Ala., May 9, 1865.
(1) WHITE, D. R. — See roster, "Regmtl. Hdqtrs., 3rd Ark. Inf."
(1) WHITE, D. T. — Paroled, Appomattox (Apr. 12, 1865): No other
(2) record.
(1) WHITE, T. T. — POW, Wilderness (May 6, 1864): Confined at Elmira, N.Y.: Exchanged, Feb. 13, 1865.
(1) WILLIAMS, D. G. — W., Spotsylvania (May 10, 1864): Died from wound (May 27, 1864).
(1) WILLIAMS, JAS. V. — See list of "Non-Comm. Officers" above.
     WILLIAMS, W. B. — POW, Franklin, Tenn., June 12, 1863: Confined at Ft. Delaware, July 14, 1863.
(1) WILSON, AUGUSTUS H. — See list of "Non-Comm. Officers" above.
     WOOD, A. J. — W., Chickamauga (Sept. 19, 1863): Wound furlough: AWOL: Dropped from rolls, Aug., 1864.
     WOOD, ASHLEY — Enl. at Hamburg, Ark., Feb. 15, 1863: W., Gettysburg (July 2, 1863): Died of wound, July 15.
(1) WOODS, M. G. — POW, Gettysburg (July 2, 1863): Confined at Ft. Delaware: Exchanged, Mar. 7, 1865.
(1) WOODS, W. H. H. — W., Chickamauga (Sept. 19, 1863): W., Spotsylvania (May 10, 1864): Disabled.

* * * * *

MEMBERS OF COMPANY K, 3RD ARK. INF. REGT., WHO WERE NOT PRESENT FOR DUTY DURING THE PERIOD THAT THE REGIMENT WAS ASSIGNED TO HOOD'S TEXAS BRIGADE (NOV., 1862-APR., 1865).

OFFICERS

NONE

NON-COMMISSIONED OFFICERS

Bell, W. W., 3Cpl. (Orig. 2Cpl. of Co.: AWOL, Apr., 1862)

Erwin, W. B., Cpl. (Orig. 1Cpl. of Co.: W., Antietam)

PRIVATES

(1) Bailey, S. W. (No record)
(1) Barham, W. O. (Dischgd., Jan., 1862)
(1) Barefield, Chas. S. (Dischgd., Apr., 1862)
Beasley, A. P. (No record)
(1) Beasley, E. A. (Dischgd., Apr., 1862)
(1) Bell, Jos. (Transfd. to Co. L, Feb., 1862)
(1) Carlock, F. C. (AWOL)
(1) Cole, S. S. (Dischgd., Apr., 1862)
(1) Davis, P. H. (No record)
(1) Denson, J. N. (POW, Antietam)
(1) Denson, N. E. (No record)
(1) Farther, C. C. (No record)
(1) Fleming, C. L. (No record)
(1) Fleming, M. M. (Dischgd., Oct., 1862)
Gearin, Arch (Dischgd., July, 1862)
(1) Gearin, F. M. (Dischgd., Spring, 1862)
(1) Gibbs, B. D. (Dischgd., Nov., 1861)
(1) Gillam, Jo. G. (Dischgd., Apr., 1862)
(1) Griffin, W. P. (Dischgd., July, 1861)
(1) Guice, E. S. (Dischgd., Jan., 1862)
Hairwood, T. J. (No record)
(1) Hamilton, L. T. (K., Antietam)
Hanks, J. M. (Dischgd., July, 1862)

Harmon, H. H. (No record)
(1) Harmon, J. D. (D., Nov., 1862)
Hogan, M. C. (No record)
(1) Maddox, G. W. (No record after Oct., 1862)
(1) Manning, J. B. (No record)
McCurdy, J. H. (No record after Oct., 1862)
McCurdy, W. R. (No record after Apr., 1862)
(1) McLarren, M. (No record)
(1) McLeod, J. (No record)
Neal, John N. (No record)
(1) Nichols, W. O. (No record after Apr., 1862)
Park, Amzi (No record in Va.)
(1) Patterson, J. B. (D., Nov., 1862)
Philan, Jackson T. (Dischgd., May, 1862)
(1) Pippen, T. J. (No record)
Pitts, W. A. (D., Aug., 1861)
(1) Reeves, J. W. (No record)
(1) Reynolds, L. (No record after Apr., 1862)
(1) Rogers, C. B. (Dischgd., July, 1861)
Shelton, Jas. (D., Aug., 1861)
Stillwell, R. S. (Dischgd., Spring, 1862)
(1) Stinson, Wm. M. (W., Antietam)
(1) Vernon, T. I. (Dischgd., Nov., 1861)
(1) Wilson, Elias (K., Jan., 1862)
Wilson, Marion (D., June, 1861)

3RD ARK. VOL. INF. REGT.

COMPANY L – *RUST GUARDS*

Company was organized in Ashley County, Arkansas in late June, 1861 and was mustered into the Confederate Service, "for the war" at Lynchburg, Va., July 30, 1861 by Maj. H. L. Clay, CSA. Company L was consolidated with Co. A, Sept. 25, 1862, and ceased to exist as a Company after that date.

Key

(1) Original member of Company. (2) Paroled at Appomattox. K (Killed), W (Wounded), POW (Prisoner of War) AWOL (Absent Without Leave)

OFFICERS

There were no officers present for duty in Company L when the 3rd Ark. Inf. Regt. was assigned to Hood's Texas Brigade in mid-Nov., 1862. Two months previously Company L had been transferred into Company A.

NON-COMMISSIONED OFFICERS

HANNAH, JOHN A. Cpl. — Enl. as a Cpl., Dec. 12, 1861 as a substitute for Columbus C. Wolf: K., Petersburg trenches, June 20, 1864.

SCARBOROUGH, WM. J. 4Cpl. — Orig. Pvt. in Co., age 19: Appt. 4Cpl., Mar. 1, 1862: No record after Apr., 1863.

SMITH, WM. Cpl. — Orig. Pvt. in Co., age 22: Transfd. to Co. A, Sept., 1862: Prom., Cpl., Feb. 1, 1864: W., Cold Harbor (June 3, 1864).

SWAYZE, JAS. S. 2Cpl. — Orig. Pvt. in Co., age 21: Transfd. to Co. A, Sept., 1862: Prom., 4Cpl., May 30, 1863: Prom., 2Cpl., Spring, 1864.

WATKINS, SAMUEL Cpl. — Enl. as a Pvt., Sept. 25, 1861 in Ashley County, Ark.: Transfd. to Co. A, Sept., 1862: POW, Chaffin's Farm (Sept. 29, 1864): Confined at Pt. Lookout, Md.: Exchanged, Feb. 13, 1865: Paroled, May 18, 1865.

MUSICIAN

(2) KELLY, JOHN A. — Orig. Pvt. in Co., age 24: Appt. Musician, Winter, 1861-62: Reduced to ranks, Apr., 1862: Paroled, Appomattox (Apr. 12, 1865).

PRIVATES

(1) BERRYMAN, WM. L. — Transfd. to Co. A, Sept., 1862: W., Gettysburg (July 2, 1863): Sick , Summer, 1864.

(1) BROWN, JAS. — Enl., age 36: Transfd. to Co. A, Sept., 1862: W., Winter, 1864-65: POW, Lynchburg, Va., Apr. 13, 1865.

(2) BULL, JOHN C. — Transfd. to Co. A, Sept., 1862: W. (arm), Gettysburg (July 2, 1863): Detached duty to Div. Hdqtrs., Aug., 1864: Paroled, Appomattox (Apr. 12, 1865): Substitute for Jamison A. Manning (Orig. Pvt. in Co. K).

BULL, ROBT. C. — Transfd. to Co. A, Sept., 1862: W., Chickamauga (Sept. 19, 1863).

(1) CASH, HENRY C. — Enl., age 18: Hospitalized, Summer, 1863: No record after June, 1863.

(1) CONNER, THOS. J. — Enl., age 22: Transfd. to Co. A, Sept., 1862: Deserted at Suffolk (May 4, 1863): Took Fed. oath.

(1) DANIEL, WM. H. — Enl., age 25: Sick, Winter & Spring, 1863: Sick furlough to Ark., Nov., 1863: AWOL, dropped from rolls, Aug., 1864.

(1) GREGORY, JOSHUA P. — Enl., age 21: Transfd. to Co. A, Sept., 1862: W., Chickamauga (Sept. 19, 1863): Retired, Sept. 6, 1864 at Selma, Ala.

(1) GREGORY, WM. E. — Enl., age 19: Transfd. to Co. A, Sept., 1862:
(2) Sick, Spring & Summer, 1864: Paroled, Appomattox (Apr. 12, 1865).

(2) HANNAH, WM. C. — Enl., Sept. 25, 1861: Transfd. to Co. A, Sept., 1862: Sick, Winter, 1862-63: Paroled, Appomattox (Apr. 12, 1865).

(1) JOHNSON, SOLOMON S. — Enl., age 27: W., E. Tenn., Nov. 17, 1863:
(2) Paroled, Appomattox (Apr. 12, 1865).

(1) KELLY, JOHN A. — See "Musician" above.

MANNING, ELIND S. — Transfd. to Co. L from Co. K, Sept. 20, 1861: Transfd. to Co. A, Sept., 1862: AWOL, Oct., 1863: Dropped from rolls, Aug., 1864.

(1) McGILL, ELIJAH J. W. — Enl., age 21: Transfd. to Co. A, Sept., 1862: No record after June, 1863, may have been killed at Gettysburg.

(1) McGINTY, THOS. J. — Enl., age 25: Transfd. to Co. A, Sept., 1862: No record after June, 1863, may have been killed at Gettysburg.

(1) McPHAIL, JAS. A. — Enl., age 26: Transfd. to Co. A, Sept., 1862: Deserted at Suffolk, May 4, 1863: Took Fed. oath.

(2) MOCK, GEO. Y. — Transfd. to Co. L from Co. K, Sept. 20, 1861: W., Antietam (Sept. 17, 1862): Transfd. to Co. A, Sept., 1862: Paroled, Appomattox (Apr. 12, 1865).

(1) PARKS, WASHINGTON — Enl., age 20: Asgnd. duty as teamster,
(2) Winter, 1861-62: Transfd. to Co. A, Sept., 1862: Paroled, Appomattox (Apr. 12, 1865).

PILES, WM. — Transfd. to Co. A, Sept., 1862: POW, North Anna R. (May 24, 1864): Confined at Pt. Lookout, Md.

(1) ROBERTS, JAS. B. — Enl., age 51: Asgnd. as cook for Brig. teamsters, Feb., 1862: Retired on Surg. Cert., Mar. 15, 1865.

(1) SANDERS, JOHN P. — Enl., age 19: Transfd. to Co. A, Sept., 1862: POW, E. Tenn., Oct. 12, 1863: Took Fed. oath at Nashville, Oct. 23, 1863.

(1) SAUCER, WM. J. — Enl., age 22: Transfd. to Co. A, Sept., 1862: Died of pneumonia, June 14, 1864 at Richmond.

(1) SCARBOROUGH, WM. J. — See list of "Non-Comm. Officers" above.

(1) SMITH, GEO. W. — Enl., age 20: Transfd. to Co. A, Sept., 1862:
(2) Present for duty during entire war: Paroled, Appomattox (Apr. 12, 1865).

SMITH, JAS. (or JOHN) — Deserted in Roane Co., Tenn., Dec. 29, 1863: No other record.

(1) SMITH, WM. P. — See list of "Non-Comm. Officers" above.

(1)   SULLIVAN, JACKSON — Enl., age 24: Transfd. to Co. A, Sept., 1862:
          Dischgd. for disability (tuberculosis), Aug. 17, 1863.
(1)   SWAYZE, JAS. S. — See list of "Non-Comm. Officers" above.
          WATKINS, LEMARCUS — Transfd. to Co. A, Sept., 1862: POW,
          Chaffin's Farm (Sept. 29, 1864): Confined at Pt. Lookout, Md.:
          Exchanged, Mar. 17, 1865.
(1)   WHITEHEAD, WM. B. — Sick, Fall & Winter, 1861: Transfd. to Co. A,
          Sept., 1862: Last record dated, Feb., 1864.
(1)   WILSON, PETER W. — Enl., age 44: Transfd. to Co. A, Sept., 1862:
          Sick much of war.
(1)   WRIGHT, GEO. S. — Enl., age 23: Transfd. to Co. A, Sept., 1862: On
(2)   detached service making shoes at Richmond, Nov., 1862 to Feb.,
          1864: Paroled, Appomattox (Apr. 12, 1865).

★   ★   ★   ★   ★

MEMBERS OF COMPANY L, 3RD ARK. INF. REGT., WHO WERE NOT PRESENT FOR DUTY DURING THE PERIOD THAT THE REGIMENT WAS ASSIGNED TO HOOD'S TEXAS BRIGADE (NOV., 1862-APR., 1865).

OFFICERS

Bell, Jos. H., Capt. (Orig. Pvt. Co. K: Resgnd., Oct., 1862)

(1) Christian, Jos. D., Capt. (Orig. Capt. of Co.: Resgnd., Fall, 1861)

(1) Hundley, Epenetus S., Capt. (Orig. 1Lt. of Co.: D., Jan., 1862)

(1) Barnes, Jas., Lt. (Orig. 2Sgt. of Co.: K., Antietam.

(1) Moore, Jackson, 1Lt. (Orig. 4Sgt. of Co.: Resgnd., June, 1862)

(1) Stillwell, Thos. S., 2Lt. (Orig. 2Lt. of Co.: Resgnd., Apr., 1862)

(1) Wallace, John G., 2Lt. (Orig. 3Lt. of Co.: Resgnd., Aug., 1861)

NON-COMMISSIONED OFFICERS

Bell, Wm. N., 2Cpl. (AWOL, Apr., 1862)

Aiken, Samuel T., 3Sgt. (POW, Antietam)

Anderson, Wm., 1Cpl. (No record)

Barnes, Wm. A., Cpl. (D., 1862)

Hundley, Thaddeus M., 1Sgt. (D., Jan., 1862)

Manning, John W., Sgt. (Transfd. out of Co., Sept., 1862)

Utley, Robt. G., Cpl. (No record after Apr., 1862)

Wiley, Robt G., 2Cpl. (No record)

Wolf, Columbus C., 4Cpl. (Procured substitute, Dec., 1861)

PRIVATES

Clements, Jos. (No record)

Coker, Levi G. (D., Aug., 1861)

Danes, H. Daniel (POW, Antietam)

Daniel, Jas. A. (No record)

Dowling, Wm. J. (Dischgd., disability, Apr., 1862)

Finlayson, Angus (No record)

Garon, John (POW, Greenbrier R., Oct., 1861)

Glenn, Abraham (No record)

Johnson, Jos. (No record after Apr., 1862)

Johnson, Silas G. (K., Antietam)

McCarthy, Wesley L. (AWOL)

McCloud, John (Dischgd., disability, Aug., 1862)

Owens, Erasmus M. (D., Oct., 1861)

Randolph, Zachariah (D., Aug., 1861)

Scarborough, Jas. S. (K., Antietam)

Wainwright, Geo. W. (D., Aug., 1861)

White, Wm. (No record)

Whitehead, Madison L. (D., Aug., 1861)

Wolf, Wm. P. (Dischgd. for wound, July, 1862)

Young, Jas. T. (Did not arrive in Va.)

18TH GA. VOL. INF. REGT.

SHORT HISTORY

The 18th Georgia Volunteer Infantry Regiment was comprised of men from seven counties located in the Central and Western parts of the State. Bartow County in the northwestern section of Georgia furnished four companies to the Regiment. Cobb, Dooly, Dougherty, Gordon, Jackson and Newton Counties each raised one company.

The companies rendezvoused at Camp McDonald in Cobb County in early June, 1861. Here they were augmented by recruits and trained during June and July. On August 3 the ten companies entrained for Richmond, arriving at the Confederate Capitol on August 8. The Georgians went into camp near the Reservoir on the outskirts of the city. The Regimental Headquarters was officially organized here on or about August 9. Colonel William T. Wofford, a lawyer-legislator from Cassville, Georgia, was appointed the Regimental Commander. S. Z. Ruff and Jefferson Johnson were appointed lieutenant-colonel and major, respectively. Wofford, Ruff and Johnson all had the same date of rank — April 25, 1861. The ten companies of the 18th Georgia were mustered into the Confederate service "for three years" at Richmond on or about August 9.

The Regiment was briefly employed near Goldsboro, North Carolina in late October and early November, 1861 to counter a Federal invasion attempt along the Carolina coast. Wofford's command returned to Richmond on November 9 & 10 and was immediately sent to northern Virginia to help defend the "Potomac River Line." On November 20 while encamped near Dumfries, Virginia, the 18th Georgia Infantry was assigned as the fourth regiment to the Texas Brigade, thus bringing this Brigade up to full strength. The Texas Brigade, at the time, was commanded by Brig.-General Louis T. Wigfall.

The Georgian's remained assigned to the Texas Brigade for a year. They fought alongside the Texans in three of the bloodiest battles of the war — Gaines' Mill (June 27, 1862), Second Manassas (August 30, 1862), and Antietam (September 17, 1862). Like the three Texas regiments in the Brigade, the Georgia Regiment suffered heavy casualties in these sanguinery engagements. Colonel Wofford, as the senior colonel led the Texas

Brigade at both Boonsboro (Sept. 14, 1862) and Antietam. When the Army of Northern Virginia was reorganized in November, 1862, the 18th Georgia Infantry Regiment was reassigned to the Georgia Brigade commanded by Brig-General T. R. R. Cobb.

The Georgia Regiment fought in the Army of Northern Virginia for the rest of the war. Following Wofford's promotion to brigadier general on January 17, 1863, the 18th Georgia was commanded in turn by Colonels S. Z. Ruff and Joseph Armstrong. The command of the Brigade to which the Regiment was assigned passed to Wofford after Cobb was killed at Fredericksburg. Wofford commanded the Brigade until he was reassigned to a command in Georgia in January, 1865. At Appomattox the Georgia Brigade was commanded by Brig.-General D. M. DuBose.

By April, 1865, the 18th Georgia Infantry Regiment was decimated. It was commanded by a lieutenant, G. I. Lasseter, and only 48 men were present for duty when Robert E. Lee surrendered his Army at Appomattox. Like the three Texas regiments with which it had been brigaded earlier in the war, the 18th Georgia fought in all of the major engagements in which the Army of Northern Virginia had participated, except Chancellorsville.

18TH GA. VOL. INF. REGT.
HDQTRS. - FIELD, STAFF & BAND

The Headquarters of the 18th Georgia Volunteer Infantry Regiment was organized at Richmond on or about August 9, 1861. At this time the officers and non-commissioned officers assigned to Headquarters were mustered into the Confederate service "for three years."

Key

(1) Original member of Hdqtrs. (2) Paroled at Appomattox
K (Killed), W (Wounded), POW (Prisoner of War)
AWOL (Absent Without Leave)

OFFICERS, FIELD & LINE

ARMSTRONG, JOS. Colonel
  Orig. Capt., Co. I: W. (hip), Gaines' Mill (June 27, 1862): W., Fredericksburg (Dec. 13, 1862): Prom., Col., Jan. 6, 1864: Paroled, Petersburg, Va., Apr. 15, 1865.

(1) RUFF, S. Z. Colonel
       Orig. Lt.-Col. of Regt.: Elect., Col., Jan. 17, 1863: K., near
       Knoxville, Nov. 29, 1863.
(1) WOFFORD, WM. T. Colonel
       Orig. Col. of Regt.: As Senior Colonel, commanded Texas Brig. at
       Boonsboro & Antietam: Prom., Brig.-Gen., Jan. 17, 1863:
       Paroled, Resaca, Ga., May 2, 1865.
     FORD, FRANK Lieut.-Colonel
       Orig. Capt., Co. H: Prom., Lt.-Col., Mar. 25, 1864: Paroled,
       Kingston, Ga., May 12, 1865.
     CALLAHAN, W. G. Major
       Orig. 2Lt., Co. C: Elect., 2Lt., June 27, 1862: Elect., 1Lt., Sept.
       6, 1862: Elect., Capt., Mar. 27, 1863: Prom., Maj. & transfd. to
       Regmtl. Hdqtrs., Mar. 19, 1864: K., Saylor's Creek (Apr. 6,
       1865).
(1) JOHNSON, JEFFERSON Major
       Orig. Maj. of Regmt.: Resgnd., Surg. Cert. of disability, Mar. 29,
       1862.
     STEWART, JOS. A. Major
       Orig. Capt., Co. B: W., Chancellorsville (May 3, 1863): Elect.,
       Maj. & transfd. to Regmtl. Hdqtrs., May 27, 1863: Resgnd.,
       appt. Surg. by Gov. of Ga., Jan. 4, 1864.
     ROGERS, WM. G. 1st Lieutenant
       Orig. Pvt. in Co. I: Appt. Regmtl. Color-Bearer, Dec., 1863:
       Prom., Ensign & asgnd. to Regmtl. Hdqtrs., May 24, 1864: Elect.,
       2Lt., Nov. 24, 1864: Elect., 1Lt., Spring, 1865: POW, Burkeville,
       Va., Apr. 6, 1865: Confined at Johnson's Is., Ohio: Paroled, June
       19, 1865.

OFFICERS, STAFF

ADJUTANTS (AAG)

     EVERETT, EDW. N.
       Orig. Pvt., Co. I: W., Antietam (Sept. 17, 1862): W., Fredericks-
       burg (Dec. 13, 1862): Appt. 3Sgt., Jan. 22, 1864: W., Cold
       Harbor (June 1, 1864): Appt. Regmtl. Adj., June 15, 1864: POW,
       Saylor's Creek (Apr. 6, 1865): Confined at Johnson's Is., Ohio:
       Paroled, June 18, 1865.
(1) GRIFFIS, JOHN C. Major
(2)   Orig. AAG of Regt.: Elect., Maj., Feb. 17, 1863: Appt. ACS, Apr.
       7, 1863: Paroled, Appomattox (Apr. 12, 1865).
     PATTON, A. H. 2nd Lieutenant
       Orig. 2Lt., Co. E: Appt. Regmtl. Adj., Apr. 7, 1862: Prom., Capt.
       & appt. AAG, Wofford's Brig., Feb. 17, 1863: K., Chancellorsville
       (May 3, 1863).
     WOOLLEY, ANDREW F., Jr.
       Orig. 2Lt., Co. F: Elect., 1Lt., Oct. 1, 1861: W., Antietam (Sept.
       17, 1862): Appt. Aide-de-Camp for Gen. Wofford: Prom., Capt.
       & appt. Regmtl. AAG, May 23, 1863.

SURGEONS

BROWN, JAS. BROYLES
    Orig. Asst. Surg. of Regt.: Prom., Surgeon, Mar. 23, 1863: No
    record after Aug., 1863.

(1)   ROACH, ELISHA JAS.
    Orig. Surg. of Regt.: Transfd. to 5th Tex. Inf. Regt., Spring,
    1862: See roster, "Regmtl. Hdqtrs., 5th Tex. Inf."

ASSISTANT SURGEONS

(1)   BROWN, JAS. BROYLES
    See list of "Surgeons" above.

BROYLES, J. J.
    Jnd. Regt. as an Asst. Surg. at Fredericksburg, Va., Nov., 1862:
    Transfd. to hosp. at Dalton, Ga., June 7, 1863.

COMMISSARY SUBSISTENCE OFFICERS (ACS)

GRIFFIS, JOHN C.
    See list of "Adjutants (AAG)" above.

(1)   WIKLE, JESSE R.   Captain
    Orig. ACS of Regmt.: Resgnd., Aug. 6, 1862 because of poor
    health.

WOFFORD, T. J.
    Jnd. Regmtl. Hdqtrs., as ACS, Aug. 5, 1862: Staff agency
    abolished by Act of Conf. Cong., 1863.

QUARTERMASTER OFFICERS (AQM)

BELL, H. W.   Captain
    Orig. 2Sgt., Co. C: Appt. 1Sgt., Oct. 17, 1861: W. (arm), Gaines'
    Mill (June 27, 1862): Prom., 2Lt., Mar. 27, 1863: Prom., 1Lt.,
    Mar. 19, 1864: Prom., Capt. & asgnd. as Regmtl. AQM, Summer,
    1864.

LUMPKIN, F.   Captain
    Not listed on Bi-Monthly Muster Rolls.

POWERS, JAS. M.   Captain
    Orig. 3Lt., Co. G: Elect., 2Lt., May 13, 1862: Elect., 1Lt., Sept.
    5, 1862: Elect., Capt. & Regmtl. AQM, Oct. 14, 1862: Resgnd.
    for disability, Oct. 27, 1864.

(1)   VAUGHN, JAS. A.   Captain
    Appt. Regmtl. AQM, June 14, 1861: Prom., Capt., July 19,
    1862: Resgnd. for disability, Aug. 12, 1862.

CHAPLAIN

(1)   DOLL, PENFIELD
    Appt. Regmtl. Chaplain, Sept. 23, 1861: Resgnd. for disability,
    Dec. 24, 1863.

NON-COMMISSIONED OFFICERS

SERGEANT-MAJORS

(1)   LOUDERMILK, JOHN
    Orig. Pvt., Co. K: Appt. Sgt.-Maj., Oct., 1861: No record after
    Mar., 1862.

WEEMS, SAMUEL C.
Orig. 5Sgt., Co. E: Appt. 3gt., Dec. 9, 1861: Appt. Regmtl.
Sgt.-Maj., June 11, 1864: Elect., 2Lt., Co. K, Dec., 1864: Elect.,
1Lt., Co. K, Jan. 30, 1865: Elect., Capt., Co. K, Feb. 21, 1865:
POW, Saylor's Cr. (Apr. 6, 1865): Confined at Johnson's Is.,
Ohio: Paroled, June 20, 1865.

COLOR SERGEANT
ROGERS, WM. G.
See list of "Officers, Field & Line" above.

QUARTERMASTER-SERGEANTS
(2) FORD, J. V.
Orig. 3Sgt., Co. H: W., Fredericksburg (Dec. 13, 1862): Appt.
1Sgt., 1863: Appt. Regmtl. QM Sgt., Mar. 1, 1864: Paroled,
Appomattox (Apr. 12, 1865).
WOFFORD, JOHN T.
Orig. 4Sgt., Co. H: Appt. Regmtl. QM Sgt., Apr. 1, 1862: No
further record.

COMMISSARY SUBSISTENCE-SERGEANT
(2) BARRON, AUGUSTUS L.
Orig. Pvt., Co. H: Appt. 4Sgt., Oct., 1861: W., Malvern Hill (July
1, 1862): Reduced to ranks, Aug. 4, 1862: Appt. Regmtl. Comsy.
Sgt., June 11, 1864: Paroled, Appomattox (Apr. 12, 1865).

ORDNANCE-SERGEANTS
(2) GAY, JOHN FLOYD
Orig. 4Sgt. of Co. B: Appt. Regmtl. Ordn. Sgt., June 11, 1862:
Paroled, Appomattox (Apr. 12, 1865).
HARRIS, Z. N.
Orig. Pvt., Co. G: Appt. 5Sgt., Sept. 14, 1861: Appt. Ordn.-Sgt.,
May 25, 1862: Elect., 2Lt., Co. G., July 4, 1862: Prom., 1Lt.,
Mar. 26, 1863: Resgnd., Mar. 26, 1863.
LYONS, PETER
Orig. Pvt., Co. G: W., Gaines' Mill (June 27, 1862): Appt.
Ordn.-Sgt., July 22, 1862: Prom., 2Lt., Co. G., Oct., 1862:
Prom., 1Lt., Nov., 1863: W., Cold Harbor (June 1, 1864): Died
of Chronic diarrhea at Ft. Delaware, Mar. 13, 1865.

HOSPITAL STEWARD
WATSON, W. A.
Orig. Pvt., Co. C: Detailed as Hosp. Steward, Aug. 1, 1861:
Dischgd. for disability, Jan. 3, 1862.

BAND

BANDMASTER
LAWLESS, GEO. W.
Orig. Musician, Co. H: Appt. Regmtl. Bandmaster, June, 1864:
Granted "furlough of indulgence" to Ark., Mar. 11, 1865.

MAIL CARRIER

WILHITE, J. M.
> Orig. Pvt., Co. C: Appt. Regmtl. Mail Carrier, Jan., 1862: Present for duty as late as Nov., 1864.

★ ★ ★ ★ ★

MEMBERS OF HEADQUARTERS, 18TH GA. INF. REGT., WHO WERE NOT PRESENT FOR DUTY DURING THE PERIOD THAT THE REGIMENT WAS ASSIGNED TO HOOD'S TEXAS BRIGADE (NOV., 1861-NOV., 1862).

NON-COMMISSIONED OFFICERS

HOSPITAL STEWARD

(1) Scott, H. M. (Orig. Pvt., Co. A:
Appt. Hosp. Stew., June,
1861: Dischgd., disability,
Sept. 30, 1861.)

18TH GA. VOL. INF. REGT.

COMPANY A – *ACWORTH RIFLES*

Company was organized in Cobb County, Georgia, during the Spring of 1861. It rendezvoused, recruited and trained at Camp McDonald, Cobb County, in late June and in July. The Company was mustered into the Confederate service at Richmond, "for three years," on or about August 9, 1861.

Key

(1) Original member of Company. (2) Paroled at Appomattox.
K (Killed), W (Wounded), POW (Prisoner of War)
AWOL (Absent Without Leave)

OFFICERS

(1) LEMON, JAMES LILE Capt. – Orig. 2Lt. of Co.: Elect., 1Lt., June 5, 1862: Elect., Capt., Mar. 5, 1863: POW, Knoxville, Nov. 29, 1863: Confined at Camp Chase, Ohio: Paroled, June 12, 1865.

(1)   O'NEILL, J. B. Capt. — Orig. Capt. of Co.: W., 2nd Manassas (Aug. 30, 1862): Resgnd., disabled, Mar. 5, 1863.

(1)   JACKSON J. 1Lt. — Orig. 1Lt. of Co.: Resgnd., June 5, 1862.

TANNER, LEE H. 1Lt. — Orig. Pvt. in Co.: Elect., 2Lt., June 5, 1862: Prom., 1Lt., Mar. 5, 1863: POW, Cedar Creek (Oct. 19, 1864): Paroled, June 17, 1865.

FANNIN, J. T. 2Lt. — Orig. Pvt. in Co.: Elect., 2Lt., Mar. 5, 1863: POW, Saylor's Creek (Apr. 6, 1865): Confined at Johnson's Is., Ohio: Paroled, June 18, 1865.

PHILLIPS, MATHEW M. 2Lt. — Orig. 1Sgt. of Co.: Elect., 3Lt., Jan. 15, 1863: Prom., 2Lt., Mar. 5, 1863: POW, Saylor's Cr. (Apr. 6, 1865): Confined at Johnson's Is., Ohio: Paroled, June 19, 1865.

(1)   AVERY, N. 3Lt. — Orig. 3Lt. of Co.: Resgnd., disability (rheumatism), May 30, 1862.

GRAGG, HAMILTON D. 3Lt. — Orig. Pvt. in Co.: Elect., 3Lt., June 5, 1862: W. (foot), Gaines' Mill (June 27, 1862): Wound furlough granted: AWOL: Tendered resignation, Nov. 25, 1862: Dropped from rolls, Jan. 12, 1863.

NON-COMMISSIONED OFFICERS

ABNEY, J. M. 4Cpl. — Orig. Pvt. in Co.: W. (shoulder), Gaines' Mill (June 27, 1862): Prom., 4Cpl., Sept. 1, 1864: POW, Cedar Cr. (Oct. 19, 1864): Confined at Pt. Lookout, Md.: Paroled, Mar. 28, 1865.

BORING, A. N. 5Sgt. — Orig. Pvt. in Co.: Prom., 5Sgt., Sept. 1, 1864: POW, Cedar Cr. (Oct. 19, 1864): Confined at Pt. Lookout, Md.: Paroled, June 24, 1865.

CHEATHAM, J. R. T. Cpl. — Orig. Pvt. in Co.: No record after Aug., 1864.

(1)   CROSSLEY, J. E. 3Sgt. — Orig. 3Sgt. of Co.: POW, Burkeville (Apr. 6, 1865): Paroled, June 14, 1865.

EMBRY, WM. P. 2Cpl. — Orig. Pvt. in Co.: Deserted, E. Tenn., Jan. 29, 1864: Took Fed. oath, Feb. 25, 1864.

GARRISON, M. W. 3Cpl. — Orig. Pvt. in Co.: W., Chancellorsville (May 3, 1863): Prom., 3Cpl., June 5, 1863: K., Wilderness (May 6, 1865).

(1)   HARDAGE, T. J. 1Sgt. — Orig. 2Sgt. of Co.: Granted furlough, Jan., 1865: Jnd. Ga. Militia Cav. Regt. (J. Johnson's), Feb., 1865: Paroled, Kingston, Ga., May 12, 1865.

(1)   HARPER, D. B. 3Sgt. — Orig. 2Cpl. of Co.: Appt. 3Sgt., 1864: Deserted, Feb., 1865: Took Fed. oath, Feb. 15, 1865.

(1)   HOLCOMBE, WM. W. 1Cpl. — Orig. 1Cpl. of Co.: W., Antietam (Sept. 17, 1862): POW, Gettysburg (July 2, 1863): Confined at Pt. Lookout, Md., Exchanged, Feb. 18, 1865.

McLAIN, JOHN M. 3Sgt. — Enl., Sept. 1, 1861 at Richmond: Appt. 3Sgt.: W. (leg) & POW, Gettysburg (July 2, 1863): Exch., Sept. 27, 1863: Transfd. as a Pvt. to the 1st Ga. Cav. Regt., Aug., 1864.

(2) NICHOLS, A. 2Cpl. — Orig. Pvt. in Co.: W. (thigh), Gaines' Mill (June 27, 1862): W., Front Royal, Va. (Aug. 16, 1864): Paroled, Appomattox (Apr. 12, 1865).
(1) O'NEILL (or O'NEAL), J. J. 4Sgt. — Orig. 4Sgt. of Co.: Dischgd., furnished substitute, Dec. 1, 1862.
     OWENS, THOS. M. 5Sgt. — Orig. Pvt. in Co.: Prom., 5Sgt., Sept. 12, 1861: W. (head), Gaines' Mill (June 27, 1862): Reduced to ranks, Apr. 1, 1864: Paroled at Chattanooga, May 24, 1865.
(1) PHILLIPS, MATHEW M. 1Sgt. — See list of "Officers" above.
(1) SHELTON, J. E. 3Cpl. — Orig. 3Cpl. of Co.: Elect., 2Lt., Co. E, 3rd Btln., Ga. Sharpshooters & transfd. out of Co., Mar. 1, 1863.
     STEELE, M. W. 3Cpl. — Enl., Feb. 21, 1862 at Acworth, Ga.: Appt. 3Cpl., May 6, 1864: W., Cold Harbor (June 1, 1864).
(1) TINSLEY, I. N. 4Cpl. — Orig. 4Cpl. of Co.: Died, Sept. 4, 1862.

MUSICIANS

(1) JENKINS, J. T. — Orig. Musician in Co.: Reduced to ranks, Winter,
(2) 1864-65: Paroled, Appomattox (Apr. 12, 1865).
(1) SUMMERS, F. M. — Orig. Musician in Co.: W. (foot), Gaines' Mill (June
(2) 27, 1862): Reduced to ranks, Winter, 1864-65: Paroled, Appomattox (Apr. 12, 1865).

PRIVATES

(1) ABNEY, J. M. — See list of "Non-Comm. Officers" above.
(1) BABB, J. N. — No record after Aug., 1864.
(1) BAKER, HIRAM S. — Died, typhoid fever, Oct. 3, 1862.
     BALAN, WM. C. — POW, Boonsboro (Sept. 15, 1862): Confined at Ft. Delaware, Md.: Exchanged, Nov. 10, 1862.
     BARNES, WESLEY — No record after Apr., 1862.
     BARRETT, MILTON — Enl., June 13, 1862: Transfd. to 3rd Btln., Ga. Sharpshooters, June 8, 1863.
(1) BENNETT, T. J. — K., Malvern Hill (July 1, 1862).
(1) BORING, A. N. — See list of "Non-Comm. Officers" above.
(1) BORING, FRANCIS A. — W. (shoulder), Antietam (Sept. 17, 1862): POW, Roswell, Ga., July 9, 1864.
(1) BORING, L. H. — Died, May, 1862.
(1) BROWN, J. G. — POW, Burkesville (Apr. 6, 1865): Paroled, June 25, 1865.
     BROWN, JOHN — Enl., Feb. 16, 1862 at Acworth, Ga.: W., Gettysburg (July 2, 1863): W., Cedar Cr. (Oct. 19, 1864): Lost eye.
(1) BROWN, T. P. — W., 2nd Manassas (Aug. 30, 1862): K., E. Tenn., Nov. 27, 1863.
     BROWN, W. F. — Enl., Aug. 21, 1861 at Richmond, Va.: No record after Aug., 1864.
(1) BURNETT, A. F. — Deserted, E. Tenn., Jan. 29, 1864.
     CHANNELL, H. C. — Enl., Feb. 21, 1862 at Acworth, Ga.: Died, Oct. 31, 1862.

(1) CHEATHAM, J. R. T. — See list of "Non-Comm. Officers" above.
(1) COPELAND, R. D. — Died of typhoid fever at Richmond, Nov. 28, 1861.
(1) DABBS, C. T. — Dischgd., furnished substitute (Jas. R. Thacker), Feb. 6, 1862.
(1) DABBS, W. M. — Died of typhoid fever at Richmond, Dec. 9, 1861.
   DAVENPORT, M. L. — Enl., Feb. 19, 1862 at Acworth, Ga.: K., Antietam (Sept. 17, 1862).
   DAVENPORT, WM. — Enl., Feb. 19, 1862 at Acworth, Ga.: K., Antietam (Sept. 17, 1862).
(1) DEMPSEY, A. G. — W. (hand), Gaines' Mill (June 27, 1862): No record after Dec., 1863.
(1) DURHAM, ALFRED — W., 2nd Manassas (Aug. 30, 1862): K., Gettysburg (July 2, 1863).
   DURHAM, JAS. P. — Enl., May 16, 1862 at Atlanta: W., 2nd Manassas (Aug. 30, 1862): W., Gettysburg (July 2, 1863): Retired.
   DURHAM, L. H. — Enl., Sept. 2, 1862: Died of smallpox in Richmond, Dec. 4, 1862.
   DURHAM, L. W. — Enl., Aug. 6, 1862 at Calhoun, Ga.: POW, E. Tenn., Dec. 5, 1863: Died in Fed. hosp. near Knoxville, Dec. 25, 1863.
   DURHAM, WM. P. — Enl., Feb. 17, 1862 at Acworth, Ga.: POW, Cedar Cr. (Oct. 19, 1864): Died, Pt. Lookout, Md., May 12, 1865.
(1) EMBRY, WM. P. — See list of "Non-Comm. Officers" above.
(1) FANNIN, J. T. — See list of "Officers" above.
   GARRISON, A. J. — Enl., Feb. 18, 1862 at Acworth, Ga.: POW, Burkeville (Apr. 6, 1865): Paroled, June 25, 1865.
   GARRISON, JOHN — Enl., Sept. 20, 1862 at Acworth, Ga.: W. (hand), Chancellorsville (May 3, 1863): POW, Cedar Cr. (Oct. 19, 1864); Exch., Mar. 28, 1865.
(1) GARRISON, M. W. — See list of "Non-Comm. Officers" above.
(1) GLADDEN, J. D. — Died of chronic dysentery at Lynchburg, July 13, 1862.
   GOODWIN, J. S. — Enl., Feb. 24, 1862 at Acworth, Ga.: Transfd. out of Co., June 8, 1863.
(1) GRAGG, HAMILTON D. — See list of "Officers" above.
(1) GRAVES, G. L. — AWOL, Aug., 1864: No later record.
   GRISHAM (or GRESHAM), G. W. — Enl., May 16, 1862 at Atlanta: W., Gaines' Mill (June 27, 1862): W., Fredericksburg (Dec. 13, 1862): POW, Gettysburg (July 2, 1863): Died of tuberculosis at Ft. Delaware Fed. prison.
   HAFL, SAMUEL — POW, 2nd Manassas (Aug. 30, 1862): No other record.
(1) HARRIS, J. B. — POW, Boonsboro (Sept. 14, 1862); Exch., Nov. 10, 1862: Died of erysipelas, July 31, 1863 at Liberty, Va.
(1) HICKS, T. A. — W. (shoulder) & POW, 2nd Manassas (Aug. 30, 1862): Died of wound, Sept. 23, 1862.
(1) HOUSE, GROGAN — POW, Burkeville (Apr. 6, 1865): Paroled, June 25, 1865.
   HOUSE, H. — Enl., Sept. 15, 1861 at Acworth, Ga.: POW, Burkeville (Apr. 6, 1865): Paroled, June 25, 1865.

HOUSE, R. — Enl., Feb. 19, 1862 at Acworth, Ga.: Died, May 14, 1864.

(1) HULL, GEO. S. — Transfd. to 3rd Btln., Ga. Sharpshooters, June 8, 1863.

JACKSON, JOHN E. — Enl., Sept. 1, 1861 at Richmond: K., Gaines' Mill (June 27, 1862).

(1) JACKSON, M. H. — Dischgd., disability, Dec. 1, 1862: Re-enl.: W., 2nd Manassas (Aug. 30, 1862): No later record.

JACKSON, WESLEY H. — Enl., Feb. 18, 1862 at Acworth, Ga.: W., 2nd Manassas (Aug. 30, 1862): Leg amputated.

(1) JOHNSON, RICH. — Transfd. to Phillips' Legion Ga. Inf., Aug., 1862 in exchange for Benj. R. Whitfield.

(1) KENDRICK, T. E. — W. (arm), Wilderness (May 6, 1864): POW, Tallahassee, Fla., May 10, 1865.

LANMON (or LANDMON), ARCHER — Enl., Jan. 1, 1862 at Dumfries, Va.: Died, Feb. 21, 1862 of typhoid fever at Dumfries.

LANMON (or LANDMON), J. N. — Enl., Jan. 1, 1862 at Dumfries, Va.: Dischgd. for disability, July 21, 1862.

LANMON (or LANDMON), O. L. — Enl., July 1, 1862 at Calhoun, Ga.: Sick most of war: POW, Cedar Cr. (Oct. 19, 1864): Exch., Mar. 28, 1865.

(1) LANMON (or LANDMON), R. A. — POW, Gettysburg (July 2, 1863).

(1) MASON, J. S. — POW, Burkeville (Apr. 6, 1865): Paroled, June 14, 1865.

MASON, M. S. — Enl., Aug. 21, 1861 at Richmond: W., 2nd Manassas (Aug. 30, 1862): POW, Cobb Co., Ga.: Took Fed. oath, Feb. 25, 1864.

(1) McEVER, JOS. — AWOL, Oct., 1863 to Aug., 1864: No other record.

McLAIN, JAS. — Enl., Sept. 15, 1861 at Acworth, Ga.: W., Knoxville, Nov. 28, 1863: POW, Louden, Tn., Jan., 1864: Paroled from Ft. Delaware, Sept. 14, 1864: AWOL, Jan., 1865.

McLAIN, JOHN M. — See list of "Non-Comm. Officers" above.

(1) MILLER, JOS. — W. (arm), Wilderness (May 6, 1864): POW, Carroll Co., Ga.

(1) MIMS, J. P. — K., Spotsylvania (May 10, 1864).

MORRIS, WM. W. — Enl., Feb. 21, 1862 at Acworth, Ga.: Died of yellow jaundice at Farmville, Va., July 11, 1862.

MULL, G. S. — POW, 2nd Manassas (Aug. 30, 1862): No other record.

(1) MULLINS, J. D. — K., 2nd Manassas (Aug. 30, 1862).

(1) MULLINS, R. D. — Dischgd. for disability, 1864.

(1) NICHOLS, A. — See list of "Non-Comm. Officers" above.

NICHOLS, J. C. — Enl., Aug. 21, 1861 at Richmond: K., Knoxville, Oct. 29, 1863.

NORTHCUTT, T. H. — Enl., Aug. 21, 1861 at Richmond: W., Antietam (Sept. 17, 1862): Dischgd., Feb. 23, 1863.

(1) OWENS, GEO. S. — Transfd. to 3rd Btln., Ga. Sharpshooters, June 8, 1863.

(1) OWENS, THOS. M. — See list of "Non-Comm. Officers" above.

(1) PATTERSON, G. M. — W., Fredericksburg (Dec. 13, 1862): Retired to Invalid Corps, July 30, 1864.

PEACOCK, L. C. — Enl., Feb. 16, 1862 at Acworth, Ga.: POW, Burkeville (Apr. 6, 1865): Paroled, June 25, 1865.

(1) PETERS, T. M. — W. (hand), Gaines' Mill (June 27, 1862): Present for duty until Nov., 1864.

(1) PHILLIPS, C. C. — POW while on furlough in Ga., Summer, 1864.

PHILLIPS, F. T. — Enl., May 4, 1862 at Richmond: Present for duty until Oct., 1864.

PRICE, T. D. — Enl., Aug. 21, 1861 at Richmond: K., Gaines' Mill (June 27, 1862).

(1) PRIEST, M. V. — POW, hosp. in Richmond, Apr. 3, 1865: Paroled, June 25, 1865.

(1) PRIEST, PINKNEY C. — W. & POW, 2nd Manassas (Aug. 30, 1862): Paroled, Sept. 29, 1862: Foot amputated.

(1) PYRON, CHAS. W. — Paroled, Appomattox (Apr. 12, 1865): No other
(2) record.

(1) PYRON, THOS. JEFF. — W., Antietam (Sept. 17, 1862): Detailed to ambulance Corps.

(1) RHODES, N. J. — POW, Burkeville (Apr. 6, 1865): Paroled, June 25, 1865.

RHODES, W. J. — Enl., Aug. 21, 1861 at Richmond: POW, High Bridge (Apr. 6, 1865).

ROBERSON (or ROBERTSON), ELIJAH N. — Enl., Mar. 8, 1862 at Acworth, Ga., Dischgd. for disability, May 27, 1862.

(1) ROBERTSON, F. J. — W., Antietam (Sept. 17, 1862): K., Spotsylvania (May 12, 1864).

(1) SCOTT, JOHN D. — W. & POW, Antietam (Sept. 17, 1862): Paroled, Sept. 30, 1862: K. near end of war.

SHELLEY, J. A. — Enl., Oct. 1, 1862 at Acworth, Ga.: POW, Farmville (Apr. 6, 1865): Paroled, June 25, 1865.

(1) SHERBURNE, GEO., Jr. — Dischgd., disability (rheumatism), July 31, 1862.

SHERMAN, GEO. — Dischgd., Mar. 3, 1862 for old age.

SHINN, JOHN H. — Enl., Feb. 15, 1862 at Acworth, Ga.: AWOL, Aug., 1864.

SMITH, G. H. — On duty June 30, 1862: No other record.

SMITH, GEO. A. — Enl., Mar. 1, 1862 at Acworth, Ga.: Transfd. to 3rd Btln., Ga. Sharpshooters, June 8, 1863: Paroled, Greensboro, No. Car., May 12, 1865.

SMITH, J. W. — Transfd. to Co. A from Co. H, Oct. 23, 1861: W. (throat), Gaines' Mill (June 27, 1862): No record after Aug., 1863.

SMITH, ROBT. — Returned to duty, Apr. 19, 1862 after being hospitalized: No other record.

STANLEY, WM. P. — Enl., Feb. 18, 1862 at Acworth, Ga.: W. (arm), Gaines' Mill (June 27, 1862): Present & accounted for as late as Jan., 1865.

(1) STANSELL, J. B. — On detail at Richmond, Jan. 30, 1865: No other record.

(1) STANSELL, WM. S., Sr. — K., Gaines' Mill (June 27, 1862).

STEELE, M. W. — See list of "Non-Comm. Officers" above.

STEELE, W. A. — Enl., Feb. 18, 1862 at Acworth, Ga.: W. (thigh) & POW, 2nd Manassas (Aug. 30, 1862): POW, Burkeville (Apr. 6, 1865): Paroled, June 25, 1865.

(1) STOKES, SYLVANUS — POW, Gettysburg (July 2, 1863): Confined at Ft. McHenry.

(1) TANNER, J. M. — W., Malvern Hill (July 1, 1862): POW, Farmville (Apr. 6, 1865): Paroled, June 25, 1865.

(1) TANNER, JOHN Q. — POW, Burkeville (Apr. 6, 1865): Paroled, June 25, 1865.

(1) TANNER, LEE H. — See list of "Officers" above.

TANNER, W. J. — W. (leg), Gaines' Mill (June 27, 1862): No record after Aug., 1863.

THACKER, JAS. R. — Enl., Feb. 1, 1862 at Dumfries: Substitute for C. T. Dabbs: W. (foot), Gaines' Mill (June 27, 1862): Transfd. to 3rd Btln., Ga. Sharpshooters, June 8, 1863.

(1)
(2) THOMPSON, BEN. F. — Paroled, Appomattox (Apr. 12, 1865)

THOMPSON, R. S. — Enl., Feb. 20, 1862 at Acworth, Ga.: POW, Cold Harbor (June 3, 1864): Exchanged, Mar. 14, 1865.

TURNER, R. E. — Enl., Feb. 4, 1862 at Acworth, Ga.: W. (thigh), Gaines' Mill (June 27, 1862): W. ("bruised by a shell"), Malvern Hill (July 1, 1862): AWOL, Spring, 1864.

WALRAVEN, ELIJAH — Enl., Feb. 21, 1862: Transfd. to 2nd Btln., Ga. Sharpshooters, June 8, 1863.

WALRAVEN, ELISHA C. — Enl., Feb. 21, 1862 at Acworth, Ga.: Died (measles), May 21, 1862 at Richmond.

(1) WHEELER, J. W. — W. (thigh), Antietam (Sept. 17, 1862): Retired to Invalid Corps, July 26, 1864.

(1) WHITE, W. W. — W. (head), Malvern Hill (July 1, 1862): POW, Burkeville (Apr. 6, 1865): Paroled, June 25, 1865.

(1) WHITENER, J. R. — W., 2nd Manassas (Aug. 30, 1862): Died of wound, Sept. 6, 1862 at Warrenton, Va.

WHITFIELD, BEN R. — Transfd. to Co. A from Phillips Ga. Inf. Legion, Aug., 1862 in exchange with Pvt. Rich. Johnson: W., 2nd Manassas (Aug. 30, 1862): Dischgd. for disability, Oct. 27, 1863.

(1)
(2) WHITFIELD, D. B. — W., 2nd Manassas (Aug. 30, 1862): Paroled, Appomattox (Apr. 12, 1865).

(1) WHITFIELD, WM. F. — Died of disease at Richmond, May 22, 1862.

WIMMS, JOHN — W. (arm), Gaines' Mill (June 27, 1862).

(1) WINN, W. T. — Dischgd., July 4, 1864 "on account of over-age."

$$\star \quad \star \quad \star \quad \star \quad \star$$

MEMBERS OF COMPANY A, 18TH GA. INF. REGT., WHO WERE NOT PRESENT FOR DUTY DURING THE PERIOD THAT THE REGIMENT WAS ASSIGNED TO HOOD'S TEXAS BRIGADE (NOV., 1861-NOV., 1862).

OFFICERS

Whites, M. B., 1Lt. (POW, Strasburg, Va., Oct. 19, 1864).

NON-COMMISSIONED OFFICERS

Cook, John H., Cpl. (D., Apr.
1865)
Hacker, H. C., Cpl. (No record
prior to Gettysburg)

Lewis, Jas., Cpl. (No record prior
to Nov., 1863)
McCormack, J., Sgt. (No record
prior to Aug., 1864)

MUSICIANS

(1) Moseley, E. L. (No record after
Oct., 1861)

PRIVATES

Blackwell, John A. (Dischgd.,
disability, Sept., 1861)
Bowie, J. M. (Fever, Summer,
1863: No other record)
Brooks, Ryal (or Royal)'
(Dischgd. for disability,
Nov., 1861)
Brown, J. A. (Hospitalized,
July, 1864: No other
record)
Fitzgerald, J. P. (Enl., Jan. 1,
1863)
Gooding, I. M. (No record prior
to May, 1865)
Graham, P. E. (No record after
Oct., 1861)
Helton, T. J. (Enl., Apr., 1863)
Henderson, S. S. (D., Sept.,
1861)
Hirsch, Henry (Dischgd., dis-
ability, Nov., 1861)
Jarvis, J. B. (No record prior to
Feb., 1865)
Keheley, J. S. (D., Oct., 1861)
Leazer, W. J. (No record prior to
Feb., 1863)

Peacock, G. W. (Enl., Apr.,
1863)
Peters, M. S. (Transfd. into Co.
A, Jan., 1863)
Phillips, T. D. (No record prior
to Aug., 1863)
Priest, P. W. (No record after
Oct., 1861)
Rousseau, A. (Dischgd., dis-
ability, Nov., 1861)
Scott, H. M. (Dischgd., dis-
ability, Sept., 1861)
(2) Stansell, E. C. (Enl., Jan., 1863)
Stephens, D. J. (No record prior
to May, 1865)
(1) Toler, W. L. (D., Sept., 1861)
Tully, J. A. (No record prior to
June, 1864)
Williams, J. N. (Enl., Dec.,
1862)
Willoughby, Thos. (Not listed
on Bi-Monthly Muster Roll)
(1) Wooten, W. J. (Deserted, Oct.,
1861)

COMPANY B – *NEWTON RIFLES*

Company was organized in Newton County, Georgia, during the Spring of 1861. It rendezvoused, recruited & trained at Camp McDonald, Cobb County, Georgia in late June and in July. The Company was mustered into the Confederate Service, "for three years," at Richmond, Va., on or about Aug. 9, 1861.

Key

(1) Original member of Company. (2) Paroled at Appomattox.
K (Killed), W (Wounded), POW (Prisoner of War)
AWOL (Absent Without Leave)

OFFICERS

(1)　STUART (or STEWART), JOS. A.　Capt. – Orig. Capt. of Co.: W., Chancellorsville (May 3, 1863): Resgnd., Jan. 6, 1864.

　　　TREADWELL, F. S.　Capt. – Orig. 3Sgt. of Co.: Elect., 3Lt., Aug. 7, 1862: Elect., 2Lt., Oct. 1, 1862: Prom., 1Lt., Apr. 1, 1863: Prom., Capt., May 27, 1863: POW, Saylor's Cr. (Apr. 6, 1865): Paroled, June 20, 1865.

(1)　CRUMLEY, M. F.　1Lt. – Orig. 3Lt. of Co.: Elect., 2Lt., Aug. 2, 1862: Prom., 1Lt., Oct. 1, 1862: Transfd. to 3rd Btln., Ga. Sharpshooters, Apr. 1, 1863.

　　　DOSS, S. P.　1Lt. – Orig. 1Sgt. of Co.: W. (foot), Gaines' Mill (June 27, 1862): W., Antietam (Sept. 17, 1862): Prom., 3Lt., Oct. 1, 1862: Prom., 2Lt., Apr. 1, 1863: Prom., 1Lt., May 3, 1863: AWOL: Dropped from rolls, Jan. 31, 1865.

(1)　EDWARDS, S. A.　1Lt. – Orig. 2Lt. of Co.: Elect., 1Lt., Aug. 2, 1862: Resgnd., disability, Oct. 3, 1862.

(1)　GLENN, JOHN JAS. W.　1Lt. – Orig. 1Lt. of Co.: Resgnd. for disability (chronic dysentery), Aug. 2, 1862.

　　　RICHARDSON, JAS.　Lt. – W., Gaines' Mill (June 27, 1862): Dischgd. on Surg. Cert. of disability, Oct. 23, 1862.

　　　CHANDLER, E. W.　2Lt. – Orig. Pvt. in Co.: W., Gaines' Mill (June 27, 1862): Elect., 2Lt., Apr. 1, 1863: W. (head) & POW, Knoxville (Dec., 1863): Died, Dec. 6, 1863.

　　　SWAN, WM. W.　2Lt. – Enl., Feb. 22, 1862, age 26: Prom., 2Lt., Jan. 21, 1864: POW, Strasburg, Va. (Oct. 19, 1864): Paroled, June 17, 1865.

　　　SWAN, M. F.　3Lt. – Orig. Pvt. in Co.: Elect., 3Lt., Jan. 21, 1864: W., Cold Harbor (June 3, 1864).

NON-COMMISSIONED OFFICERS

BARTLETT, BLAKE 4Cpl. — Enl. as a Pvt., Feb. 15, 1862: Appt. 4Cpl., 1863: POW, Burkeville, Va. (Apr. 6, 1865): Paroled, June 25, 1865.

(1) DOSS, S. P. 1Sgt. — See list of "Officers" above.

(1) DOWDY, F. H. 1Cpl. — Orig. 1Cpl. of Co.: Reduced to ranks: Paroled,
(2) Appomattox (Apr. 6, 1865).

(1) GUINN, T. D. 1Sgt. — Orig. 2Sgt. of Co.: W., Gaines' Mill (June 27, 1862): Prom., 1Sgt., Oct., 1862: Transfd. to 3rd Btln., Ga. Sharpshooters, Apr. 1, 1863.

(1) McDONALD, ROBT. F. 2Cpl. — Orig. 2Cpl. of Co.: W., Malvern Hill (July 1, 1862): Transfd. to 3rd Btln., Ga. Sharpshooters, Apr. 1, 1863.

(1) OVERTON, JAS. M. 5Sgt. — Orig. 3Cpl. of Co.: W., Fredericksburg (Dec. 13, 1862): Appt. 5Sgt., 1863: POW, Burkeville, Va. (Apr. 6, 1865): Paroled, June 14, 1865.

POLSTON (or POLSON), F. M. 2Sgt. — Orig. Pvt. in Co.: Appt. 4Sgt., June 1, 1862: Appt. 2Sgt., Apr. 1, 1863: Transfd. to 17th Ga. Inf. Regt.

REAGIN, W. B. 3Sgt. — Orig. Pvt. in Co.: Appt. 3Sgt., 1863: No record after Nov., 1864.

(1) STANSELL, JOEL J. 1Cpl. — Orig. 4Cpl. of Co.: Appt. 1Cpl.:
(2) Paroled, Appomattox (Apr. 12, 1865).

(1) TREADWELL, FRANKLIN S. 3Sgt. — See list of "Officers" above.

TRIMBLE, W. H. 4Sgt. — Orig. Pvt. in Co., age 26: Dischgd., Nov. 18, 1861: Re-enl., Feb. 22, 1862: W. (leg), Gaines' Mill (June 27, 1862): Appt. 4Sgt., 1864: POW, Farmville (Apr. 6, 1865).

(2) WILLINGHAM, J. T. 2Cpl. — Orig. Pvt. in Co.: Appt. 2Cpl., Apr. 1, 1863: Paroled, Appomattox (Apr. 12, 1865).

YARBRAY, L. H. 3Cpl. — Orig. Pvt. in Co.: Appt. 3Cpl., 1863: No record after Nov., 1864.

PRIVATES

(1) ALMAN, J. WALKER — W., Gaines' Mill (June 27, 1862): W., Knoxville (Nov. 29, 1863): W., Spotsylvania (May 10, 1864).

(1) ALMAND, ELIHU (or ELISHA) — W. (hip), Gaines' Mill (June 27, 1862): Died of wound, Sept., 1862.

(1) ALMAND, JOHN W. — W. (knee, hand & shoulder), Gaines' Mill (June 27, 1862): POW, Burkeville (Apr. 6, 1865).

(1) ANCHORS, SNOWDEN EDW. T. — Shown on duty, Winter, 1864-65: No other record.

ARNOLD, STEPHEN — Enl., Feb. 15, 1862: No other record.

BARTLETT, BLAKE — See list of "Non-Comm. Officers" above.

(1) BLAKE, C. A. — W., Spotsylvania (May 12, 1864): No record after Jan., 1865.

(1) BLAKE, JOHN A. — POW, Strasburg (Oct. 19, 1864): Exchanged, Mar. 17, 1865.

BRADLEY, ISAAC — Enl., May 14, 1862 at Richmond: Died (typhoid fever), Nov. 26, 1862.

(1) BROOKS, JOHN J. — POW, Gettysburg (July 2, 1863): Exchanged, Feb. 18, 1865.

BUTLER, JAS. M. — Enl., May 14, 1862 at Conyers, Ga.: No record after Aug., 1864.

CAMP, J. A. — Enl., Sept. 2, 1861 at Richmond: Dischgd. on Surg. Cert., Aug. 5, 1862.

CHANDLER, CLARK S. — Enl., Feb. 25, 1862, age 23: No other record.

(1) CHANDLER, E. W. — See list of "Officers" above.

(1) CHRISTIAN, H. J. B. — Paroled, Appomattox (Apr. 12, 1865): No
(2) other record.

CHRISTIAN, JOHN W. — Enl., Feb. 15, 1862, age 18: POW, Burkeville (Apr. 6, 1865): Paroled, June 25, 1865.

CHRISTIAN, W. W. — Pvt., 1862: No other record.

(1) CRAWFORD, WM. C. — Transfd. to Co. B, 35th Ga. Inf. Regt., Sept. 1, 1862.

CRISWELL, SAMUEL (or DANIEL) — Enl., Feb. 15, 1862: No other record.

CRISWELL, W. H. H. — Enl., Feb. 15, 1862 at Conyers, Ga.: W. (hand), Wilderness (May 6, 1864).

(1) CRUMLY, WM. V. — Appt. courier to Gen. L. McLaws: No record after Aug., 1864.

(1) DANIEL, ISAAC N. — Court-martialed, Nov. 12, 1862: K., Knoxville (Dec. 1, 1863).

(1) DANIEL, JOHN F. — Died (typhoid fever), May 18, 1862.

DEMPSEY, H. L. — Enl., May 14, 1862 at Conyers, Ga.: Court-martialed, Nov. 12, 1862: POW, Burkeville (Apr. 6, 1865).

DENARD, FRANCIS M. — Enl., Feb. 24, 1862, age 26: W., Seven Pines (June 1, 1862): Died of wound, June 13, 1862.

DENARD, WILEY F. — Enl., Feb. 24, 1862, age 21: Died, Apr. 14, 1862.

DOBY, MALON J. — Enl., Feb. 22, 1862, age 22: Dischgd. on Surg. Cert., Aug. 5, 1862.

(1) ELLIS, J. F. — W., Fredericksburg (Dec. 11, 1862): Transfd. to 3rd Btln., Ga. Sharpshooters, June 8, 1863.

FLOYD, LORENZO D. — Enl., Feb. 22, 1862 at Conyers, Ga.: Died, Fredericksburg, Va., Apr. 18, 1862.

(1) FORMBY, M. G. — POW, Strasburg (Oct. 19, 1864): Exchanged, Mar. 28, 1865.

(1) GAINES, R. A. — Asgnd. to Clothing Bureau at Richmond: Transfd. to Clothing Bureau at Atlanta, Oct. 12, 1863: Dischgd. on Surg. Cert. (epilepsy), July 2, 1864.

(1) GALLOWAY, M. — POW: Died at Camp Chase, Ohio, Mar. 10, 1865.

GOREE, JOHN WM. — Enl., Sept. 30, 1861 at Richmond: Transfd. to 3rd Btln., Ga. Sharpshooters, June 8, 1863.

(1) GUINN, JOHN — W. (leg), Gaines' Mill (June 27, 1862): Transfd. to 3rd Btln., Ga. Sharpshooters, June 8, 1863.

(1) GUINN, R. A. — Dischgd., Surg. Cert. of disability, Aug. 7, 1862.

HALLING, G. W. — On sick leave, Nov., 1862: No other record.

(1) HANEY, JOHN C. — Dischgd. on Surg. Cert., July 17, 1862.
(2) HARDEN (or HARDIN), J. D. — Enl., Feb. 22, 1862 at Conyers, Ga.:
Paroled, Appomattox (Apr. 12, 1865).
HARDEN (or HARDIN), WM. F. — Enl., Feb. 22, 1862 at Conyers,
Ga.: POW, Cedar Cr. (Oct. 19, 1864): Exch., Mar. 28, 1865.
HARRIS, J. R. — Hospitalized, Oct., 1862: No other record.
(1) HENDRY, ANDREW J. — W. (shoulder), Gaines' Mill (June 27, 1862):
Died of wound, July 15, 1862.
(1) HICKS, JOS. H. — Died of disease, Winter, 1861-62.
HILL, JOHN D. — Enl., Feb. 24, 1862: W., Gaines' Mill (June 27,
1862): Died of wound, July 5, 1862.
(1) HILL, RICHARD — K., Gaines' Mill (June 27, 1862).
(1) HILL, S. A. — W. (face), Gaines' Mill (June 27, 1862): W., Antietam
(2) (Sept. 17, 1862): Paroled, Appomattox (Apr. 12, 1865).
(1) HILL, T. M. — POW, Burkeville (Apr. 6, 1865): Paroled, June 25, 1865.
HILL, WM. J. — Enl., Feb. 22, 1862, age 19: Transfd. to the 3rd Btln.,
Ga. Sharpshooters, June 8, 1863.
HOLLINGSWORTH, GEO. W. — Enl., May 14, 1862: Present for duty,
Jan. 30, 1865.
HOLLINGSWORTH, ROBT. — Enl., Feb. 22, 1862 at Conyers, Ga.:
W., Antietam (Sept. 17, 1862): Granted wound furlough.
HOLLINGSWORTH, ROBT. H. — Enl., Feb. 22, 1862 at Conyers, Ga.:
Dischgd. for tuberculosis, Apr. 22, 1863.
(1) HOLLINGSWORTH, WM. — W., Wilderness (May 6, 1864): Died of
wound, June 7, 1864.
(1) HUMPHRIES, C. H. — W., Fredericksburg (Dec. 11, 1862): Transfd. to
3rd Btln., Ga. Sharpshooters, June 8, 1863.
HUMPHRIES, EDWIN — Enl., Aug. 24, 1861 at Richmond: W., Second
Manassas (Aug. 30, 1862).
(1) HUTCHINSON, JOHN L. — W., near Malvern Hill, July 5, 1862:
Detailed to light duty on account of wound.
(1) JOHNSON, N. G. — W., Cold Harbor (June 1, 1864): Arm amputated.
JOHNSON, THOS. L. — Enl., Aug. 5, 1862 at Calhoun, Ga.: W.,
Wilderness (May 6, 1864): POW, Burkeville (Apr. 6, 1865).
(1) JOHNSON, W. T. — POW, paroled Newton, N. Car., Apr. 19, 1865: No
other record.
KING, JOEL W. — Enl., Feb. 22, 1862 at Conyers, Ga.: POW, Saylor's
Cr. (Apr. 6, 1865).
KNIGHT, W. J. — Enl., May 14, 1862 at Conyers, Ga.: All fingers on
left hand amputated, Summer, 1864: Retired, disabled, Dec. 22,
1864.
LESTER, W. J. — Enl., Feb. 24, 1862 at Conyers, Ga.: W., Gaines' Mill
(June 27, 1862): Died of wounds, July 13, 1862.
(1) LEWIS, DREWRY — POW, E. Tenn., Mar., 1864: No other record.
(1) LEWIS, JOHN H. — Dischgd. for disability, Dec. 9, 1861.
(2) MANN, JAS. MOSES — Enl., Apr. 1, 1862 at Fredericksburg, Va.:
Paroled, Appomattox (Apr. 12, 1865).
MANN, GILBERT S. — Enl., Oct. 8, 1862 at Atlanta, Ga.: K.,
Knoxville, Nov. 29, 1863.
(1) MANN, LEWIS — Died at Richmond, Apr. 1, 1862.

MANN, SAMUEL F. — Enl., Feb. 22, 1862, age 19: Died (smallpox), Feb. 27, 1863.

McDONALD, B. E. — Enl., Feb. 22, 1862: W., Gaines' Mill (June 27, 1862): Present for duty, Nov., 1864.

McDONALD, THOS. J. — Enl., Feb. 22, 1862: Died, Apr. 8, 1862.

(1) McKEE, WM. M. — W., Malvern Hill (July 1, 1862): POW, Antietam (Sept. 17, 1862): Paroled: Deserted, E. Tenn.: Took Fed. oath, Jan. 5, 1864.

(1) MILLER, H. — W., Gaines' Mill (June 27, 1862): Transfd. to 3rd Btln., Ga. Sharpshooters, June 8, 1863.

MILLER, JULIUS A. — Enl., Feb. 15, 1862: W., Gaines' Mill (June 27, 1862): POW, 2nd Manassas (Aug. 30, 1862): Paroled: W., Chancellorsville (May 3, 1863): Arm amputated, died, June 2, 1863.

MITCHELL, W. J. — Enl., May 14, 1862: In hosp., Aug., 1864: No other record.

MORGAN, R. D. — Hospitalized, Fall, 1862: No other record.

MORGAN, RICH. L. — Enl., Aug. 17, 1862: K., Spotsylvania (May 12, 1864).

MORGAN, THOS. J. — Enl., Feb. 15, 1862, age 26: W., Gaines' Mill (June 27, 1862): Transfd. to 3rd Btln., Ga. Sharpshooters, June 8, 1863.

(1) MORGAN, W. J. — W. (leg), Gaines' Mill (June 27, 1862): Transfd. to 17th Ga. Inf. Regt., Nov. 1, 1862.

MURRAY, JAS. — Died of fever, Nov. 20, 1862 at Richmond.

(1) NELMS, H. E. — Enl., age 17: Dischgd. on Surg. Cert., Dec. 9, 1861.

NUTT, WARREN — Enl., Aug. 1, 1862: Died, disease, Oct. 15, 1862.

OSBURN (or OSBORNE), D. E. — Enl., July 26, 1862: Dischgd., disability, Dec. 15, 1862.

OSBURN (or OSBORNE), E. ALEX. — Enl., July 7, 1862: W. (thigh), Saylor's Cr. (Apr. 6, 1865): Paroled, Burkeville, Va., mid-Apr., 1865.

(1) OSBURN (or OSBORNE), JAS. ROBT. — Transfd. to Cobb's Legion (Cav.), Co. I, Mar. 7, 1863.

OVERTON, JAS. H. — Enl., May 14, 1862: Dischgd., disability, July 15, 1862: Employed at the Atlanta Arsenal.

(2) OVERTON, WM. M. — Enl., Feb. 15, 1862: Paroled, Appomattox (Apr. 12, 1865).

PARKER, GEO. W. — Enl., Feb. 15, 1862, age 36: Transfd. to 3rd Btln., Ga. Sharpshooters, June 8, 1863.

PARKER, W. S. — Enl., Aug. 19, 1862: Dischgd. for tuberculosis, Nov. 12, 1862.

PATTERSON, ELISHA H. — Enl., Feb. 22, 1862: Deserted, E. Tenn., Jan., 1864.

(2) PENN, H. C. — Enl., Sept. 20, 1861 at Richmond: Paroled, Appomattox (Apr. 12, 1865).

PHELPS, WM. N. — Enl., Feb. 22, 1862: W., Gaines' Mill (June 27, 1862): W. & POW, Antietam (Sept. 17, 1862): Paroled: Transfd. to 3rd Btln., Ga. Sharpshooters, June 8, 1863.

(1) PHILLIP, J. — W., Farmville (Apr. 7, 1865): Died of wound.

PLUNKETT, C. T. — Enl., Feb. 24, 1862: Died, Apr. 13, 1862.
(1) PLUNKETT, L. — W., Fredericksburg (Dec. 13, 1862).
PLUNKETT, W. F. — Enl., Feb. 22, 1862, age 21: W., Fredericksburg (Dec. 13, 1862): Died of wound.
POLSTON (or POLSON), F. M. — See list of "Non-Comm. Officers" above.
(1) POLSTON (or POLSON), G. MACK. — K., 2nd Manassas (Aug. 30, 1862).
POLSTON (or POLSON), JONATHAN — Enl., Feb. 15, 1862: W. & POW, Knoxville (Dec. 5, 1863): Exch., Feb. 24, 1865.
(1) POLSTON (or POLSON), TRUSTIN P. — Died of typhoid fever, Dec. 31, 1861.
PRATHER, WM. V. — Enl., Feb. 20, 1862, age 20: Died of measles, Apr. 7, 1862.
(1) REAGIN, W. B. — See list of "Non-Comm. Officers" above.
RHODES, EDW. A. — Enl., Feb. 22, 1862, age 27: K., Wilderness (May 6, 1864).
RICE, A. G. — Enl., Sept. 2, 1861: Detailed as a wagonmaster, Dec., 1861: Paroled, Greensboro, No. Car., May 1, 1865.
RICE, DAVID D. — Enl., Feb. 22, 1862, age 18: W. (foot), Cedar Cr. (Oct. 19, 1864): Perm. disabled.
(1) RICHARDSON, A. K. — W. (leg), Gaines' Mill (June 27, 1862): POW, Burkeville (Apr. 6, 1865): Died in Fed. prison hosp., June 30, 1865.
RICHARDSON, JAS. M. — Enl., Feb. 20, 1862, age 27: Dischgd. for tuberculosis, Oct. 23, 1862.
RICHARDSON, OLIVER P. — Enl., May 14, 1862: Dischgd. for tuberculosis, Jan. 4, 1863.
(1) RICHARDSON, S. J. — W. (chest), Gaines' Mill (June 27, 1862): W. (hand), Chancellorsville (May 3, 1863): Transfd. to 3rd Btln., Ga. Sharpshooters, June 8, 1863.
RICHARDSON, THOS. L. — Enl., Feb. 15, 1862: POW, Cedar Cr. (Oct. 19, 1864): Paroled, May 14, 1865.
(1) RICHARDSON, WM. T. — Died at home on furlough, Dec. 23, 1862.
SCOTT, J. F. — Admitted to Chimborazo Hosp. for "debilitas," Dec. 12, 1862: No other record.
SCOTT, S. F. — Enl., May 14, 1862: W., 1862: POW, Farmville (Apr. 6, 1865).
SEAMANS, JOHN W. — Enl., Feb. 22, 1862: Died (pneumonia), Aug. 1, 1862.
SEWELL, JAS. R. G. — Enl., Sept. 20, 1861: K., 2nd Manassas (Aug. 30, 1862).
SHAW, JOHN — Enl., July 7, 1862: POW, Burkeville (Apr. 6, 1865).
(1) SHAW, WM. H. — W. (shoulder), Malvern Hill (July 1, 1862): Paroled,
(2) Appomattox (Apr. 12, 1865).
SIMONS, J. M. (or S. H.) — Returned to duty from hosp., Sept. 23, 1862: No other record.
SIMS, RICH. SIMPSON — Enl., Feb. 24, 1862: Transfd. to 3rd Btln., Ga. Sharpshooters, June 8, 1863.

(1) SMITH, DOCK M. — Court-martialed, Nov. 12, 1862: Paroled,
(2)   Appomattox (Apr. 12, 1865).
(1) SMITH, GEO. T. — Transfd. to 3rd Btln., Ga. Sharpshooters, June 8,
          1863.
   SMITH, J. B. — Enl., Feb. 15, 1862, age 18: Signed for clothing, Nov.,
          1864: No other record.
   SMITH, J. J. — POW, 2nd Manassas (Aug. 30, 1862): No other record.
(1) SMITH, JAS. T. — W., 2nd Manassas (Aug. 30, 1862): Present for "light
          duty," Summer, 1864.
   SMITH, P. T. — Enl., Feb. 22, 1862, age 23: Transfd. to 3rd Btln., Ga.
          Sharpshooters, June 8, 1863.
   SMITH, WM. B. — Enl., Aug. 2, 1862 at Decatur, Ga.: W., Knoxville:
          Paroled, Appomattox (Apr. 12, 1865).
   SPINKS, R. THOS. — Enl., May 14, 1862: W. (side), 2nd Manassas
          (Aug. 30, 1862): Died of wound, Sept. 19, 1862.
   STANSELL, RICHARD A. — Enl., Feb. 25, 1862, age 22: Transfd. to
          3rd Btln., Ga. Sharpshooters, June 8, 1863.
   STANSELL, WM. S. — Enl., Feb. 25, 1862, age 18: Transfd. to 3rd
          Btln., Ga. Sharpshooters, June 8, 1863.
   STEARNS, WM. B. — W. (chest), Gaines' Mill (June 27, 1862): No
          other record.
   STEPHENSON, ROBT. O. — Enl., Feb. 25, 1862, age 26: Died of
          measles, Apr. 1, 1862.
   ST. JOHN, FRANK M. — Enl., May 14, 1862: Died (pneumonia), Jan.
          11, 1863.
   ST. JOHN, GEO. W. — Enl., Feb. 14, 1862: Hospitalized, Spring, 1863:
          No other record.
(1) ST. JOHN, J. M. — POW, Gettysburg (July 2, 1863); Exchanged, Jan.
          17, 1865.
   ST. JOHN, JAS. M. — Transfd. to Co. B, May 14, 1862, from 35th Ga.
          Inf. Regt.: POW, Fisher's Hill (Sept. 19, 1864).
   ST. JOHN, WM. T. — Enl., May 14, 1862: POW, Knoxville, Dec. 3,
          1863: Died of smallpox in Fed. prison at Rock Is., Ill., Feb. 27,
          1864.
(1) STOWERS, HENRY H. — Transfd. to 3rd Btln., Ga. Sharpshooters,
          Apr. 1, 1863.
   STOWERS, WM. B. — Enl., Feb. 22, 1862, age 20: K., Gaines' Mill
          (June 27, 1862).
(1) STUART, J. A. B. — Detailed to "light duty," Summer, 1864: No other
          record.
(1) SUMMERS, J. J. — Died in Richmond, 1862.
(1) SWAN, M. F. — See list of "Officers" above.
   SWAN, WM. W. — See list of "Officers" above.
   TANNER, HUGH M. — Enl., Feb. 15, 1862, age 23: K., Spotsylvania
          (May 12, 1864).
   TAYLOR, JOHN H. — Enl., Feb. 15, 1862, age 24: Transfd. to 3rd
          Btln., Ga. Sharpshooters, June 8, 1863.
   TESTER, W. J. — W. (foot & thigh), Gaines' Mill (June 27, 1862): No
          other record.

(1)   THORN, H. G. B. — Transfd. to 3rd Btln., Ga. Sharpshooters, June 8, 1863.

(1)   THRASHER, DAVID R. — Enl., age 27: POW, 2nd Manassas (Aug. 30, 1862): Paroled, Sept. 29, 1862: POW, Strasburg (Oct. 19, 1864).

(1)   THRASHER, T. T. — W., 2nd Manassas (Aug. 30, 1862): Leg amputated.

       TOWELL, J. R. G. — Enl., Sept. 30, 1861 at Richmond: K., 2nd Manassas (Aug. 30, 1862).

(1)   TREADWELL, WM. E. — Sick furlough, Winter, 1861-62: No other record.

(1)   TRIMBLE, J. H. — Dischgd., Nov. 18, 1861: Re-enl., Aug. 20, 1862: Died, 1864.

(1)   TRIMBLE, W. H. — See list of "Non-Comm. Officers" above.

(1)   VEAL, GEO. — POW, Frederick, Md., Sept. 12, 1862: Exchanged: POW, Knoxville, Dec. 3, 1863: Died (smallpox), Fed. prison, Jan. 14, 1864.

(1)   VEAL, JAS. T. — W., Gaines' Mill (June 27, 1862): Arm amputated.

       WALDROP, WM. H. — Enl., Feb. 22, 1862, age 21: Died at Richmond, June 19, 1862.

       WARREN, JAS. F. — Enl., Feb. 22, 1862, age 23: Died of typhoid fever at Richmond, Apr. 22, 1863.

       WARREN, WM. L. — Enl., Feb. 22, 1862: Died, Apr. 23, 1862.

       WATKINS, EDW. — Enl., Feb. 15, 1862, age 19: K., 2nd Manassas (Aug. 30, 1862).

(1)   WATKINS, J. B. — K., Gaines' Mill (June 27, 1862).

(1)   WATKINS, THOS. B. — Absent on furlough, Summer, 1864: No other record.

       WHITE, HUGH L. — Enl., Feb. 15, 1862, age 23: POW, Williamsburg (May 6, 1862): Exchanged: Transfd. to 3rd Btln., Ga. Sharpshooters, June 8, 1863.

       WILKINS, T. J. — Died, Jan. 31, 1863 of pneumonia: No other record.

(1)   WILLIAMS, A. A. — Died, July 1, 1862: No other record.

       WILLIAMS, BENJ. J. — Enl., Feb. 15, 1862: POW, Cold Harbor (June 1, 1864).

       WILLIAMSON, A. W. — POW, Gettysburg (July 3, 1863): Exchanged, Mar. 7, 1865.

(1)   WILLINGHAM, J. T. — See list of "Non-Comm. Officers" above.

(1)   WINBURN, H. D. — W. & POW, Antietam (Sept. 17, 1862).

(1)   WINBURN, J. A. — W. (thigh), Gaines' Mill (June 27, 1862): Transfd. to 3rd Btln., Ga. Sharpshooters, June 8, 1863.

(1)   WINFIELD, JAS. LUCIUS — W., Spotsylvania (May 12, 1864): Died of wound, May 25, 1864.

(1)   WOOLLEY, H. D. — Enl., Oct. 2, 1861: Died, Apr. 29, 1862 at Richmond.

(1)   WRIGHT, JAS. — Dischgd., Mar. 22, 1862, cause unknown.

(1)   YARBRAY, L. H. — See list of "Non-Comm. Officers" above.

       YARBRAY, W. LUM. — Enl., May 14, 1862: POW, Farmville (Apr. 6, 1865).

*   *   *   *   *

MEMBERS OF COMPANY B, 18TH GA. INF. REGT., WHO WERE NOT PRESENT FOR DUTY DURING THE PERIOD THAT THE REGIMENT WAS ASSIGNED TO HOOD'S TEXAS BRIGADE (NOV., 1861-NOV., 1862)

OFFICERS

NONE

NON-COMMISSIONED OFFICERS

Marran, Peter, Sgt. (No record prior to Oct., 1864)

Mines, P., Sgt. (No record prior to Dec., 1864)

PRIVATES

Anchors, A. M. (Enl., Dec., 1862)
Bailey, J. M. (No record prior to Sept., 1864)
Bramlet, L. W. (Enl., Jan., 1863)
(1) Braswell, Lace (Dischgd., Sept., 1861)
(1) Braswell, N. J. (Dischgd., Oct., 1861)
Elliott, Daniel (No record)
(1) Ficquett, R. E. (D., Sept., 1861)
Gray, H. F. (No record prior to Apr., 1865)
Hammon, L. M. (No record prior to Nov., 1864)
Harvey, Jas. (No record prior to Oct., 1864)
(1) Henry, J. C. (No record)
(1) Henry, W. P. (No record after Oct., 1861)
(1) Hudson, D. (D., Sept., 1861)
(1) Hudson, H. C. (Dischgd., July, 1861)
Knowles, C. C. (No record prior to July, 1863)
Mann, F. (No record prior to Nov., 1862)
(1) Mitchell, John T. (Dischgd., disability, Aug., 1861)

Morgan, B. G. (No record prior to Nov., 1862)
(1) Morgan, L. J. (Dischgd., Oct., 1861)
Mote, W. M. (Enl., Dec., 1862)
(1) Nixon, R. L. (D., Oct., 1861)
Norris, John (No record prior to Oct., 1864)
(1) Penn, W. B. (AWOL, Dec., 1861)
Rice, E. D. (No record prior to Nov., 1864)
Spinks, H. D. (Enl., Dec., 1862)
Spinks, Jas. W. (Enl., May, 1864)
(1) Thompson, A. R. (D., Sept., 1861)
Thorn, J. F. (No record prior to Aug., 1864)
Treadwell, John A. (Enl., Dec., 1862)
Trent, G. (No record prior to Oct., 1864)
(2) Wade, J. M. (Only record, paroled, Appomattox, Apr. 12, 1865).
Watson, John (No record prior to Oct., 1864)
(1) Wilson, Wm. T. (Dischgd., disability, Aug., 1861)

COMPANY C – *JACKSON COUNTY VOLS.*

Company was organized in Jackson County, Georgia, during the Spring of 1861. It rendezvoused, recruited & trained at Camp McDonald, Cobb County, Georgia, in late June & in July. The Company was mustered into the Confederate service, "for three years," at Richmond, Va., on or about Aug. 9, 1861.

Key

(1) Original member of Company. (2) Paroled at Appomattox.
K (Killed), W (Wounded), POW (Prisoner of War)
AWOL (Absent Without Leave)

OFFICERS

(2)   ESPY, J. F. Capt. — Orig. 3Cpl. of Co.: Prom., 3Lt., July 12, 1862: Prom., 2Lt., Sept. 6, 1862: Prom., 1Lt., Mar. 27, 1863: Prom., Capt., Mar. 19, 1864: Paroled, Appomattox (Apr. 12, 1865): Commanded DuBose's Brig. at Appomattox.

(1)   JARRETT, D. L. Capt. — Orig. Capt. of Co.: W. (thigh), 2nd Manassas (Aug. 30, 1862): Died of wound, Sept. 6, 1862.

(1)   SILMAN, J. B. Capt. — Orig. 2Lt. of Co.: W. (arm), Gaines' Mill (June 27, 1862): Prom., 1Lt., June 27, 1862: Prom., Capt., Sept. 6, 1862: Resgnd., Mar. 27, 1863.

(1)   McCULLOCH, L. A. 1Lt. — Orig. 1Lt. of Co.: K., Gaines' Mill (June 27, 1862).

      MORGAN, J. P. 2Lt. — Enl. as a Pvt., Sept. 2, 1861 at Richmond: Prom., 2Lt., Mar. 19, 1864: AWOL, dropped from rolls, Dec. 30, 1864.

NON-COMMISSIONED OFFICERS

      BARNETT, H. C. 4Sgt. — Enl. as a Pvt., Mar. 3, 1862 at Jefferson, Ga.: Appt. 4Sgt., 1864: POW, Burkeville (Apr. 6, 1865): Paroled, June 25, 1864.

      DAVIS, JOHN L. 5Sgt. — Enl. as a Pvt., Feb. 25, 1862 at Jefferson, Ga., age 32: Appt. 1Cpl., July 20, 1862: Appt. 5Sgt., 1864: POW, Burkeville (Apr. 6, 1865): Died of chronic diarrhea in milt. prison at Newport News, Va., June 12, 1865.

      de la PERRIERE, A. A. 4Cpl. — Orig. Pvt. in Co.: Appt. 4Cpl., 1863: W. (shoulder), Spotsylvania (May 10, 1864).

(1)   DOSTER, J. W. 4Cpl. — Orig. 4Cpl. in Co.: AWOL, Spring, 1864: Reduced to Pvt.: Detached duty, Aug., 1864.

(1) ESPY, J. F. 3Cpl. — See list of "Officers" above.
(1) EUSTACE, E. M. 3Sgt. — Orig. 3Sgt. of Co.: W. (side), Gaines' Mill (June 27, 1862): POW, Knoxville, Dec. 3, 1863: Took Fed. oath & enl. in U.S. Navy, Rock Is., Ill.
(1) HARRISON, T. L. 4Sgt. — Orig. 4Sgt. of Co.: AWOL, Aug., 1864, "term of service expired."
(1) HUTCHINS, L. J. 5Sgt. — Orig. 5Sgt. of Co.: Dischgd. by Medical Bd. (tuberculosis), Oct. 4, 1862.
McELHANON, J. C. 5Sgt. — Orig. Pvt. in Co.: Prom., 5Sgt., Summer, 1862: K., 2nd Manassas (Aug. 30, 1862).
MORGAN, DANIEL M. 2Sgt. — Orig. Pvt. in Co.: Appt. 2Sgt., 1862: POW, Cold Harbor (June 1, 1864): Died of smallpox in Fed. milt. prison at Elmira, N.Y., Jan. 29, 1865.
POTTER, R. P. 3Cpl. — Orig. Pvt. in Co.: Appt. 3Cpl., 1864: Present for duty until Nov., 1864.
SHOCKLEY, W. S. 2Cpl. — Orig. Pvt. in Co.: Appt. 2Cpl., July 20, 1861: W., Antietam (Sept. 17, 1862): POW, Cold Harbor (June 1, 1864): Died of pneumonia in the Fed. milt. prison at Elmira, N.Y., Feb. 5, 1865.
STRICKLAND, JESSE WHITE 1Sgt. — Enl. as a Pvt. in Co., Feb. 25, 1862, age 22: Appt. 1Sgt., 1864: Absent on furlough (AWOL), Jan., 1865.
(2) WIER, JOHN G. 2Cpl. — Orig. Pvt. in Co.: W. & POW, Gaines' Mill (June 27, 1862): Paroled: Appt. 2Cpl.: W., Spotsylvania (May 12, 1864): Paroled, Appomattox (Apr. 12, 1865).
(2) WILHITE, O. M. 1Cpl. — Orig. Pvt. in Co.: Appt. 1Cpl., 1864: Paroled, Appomattox (Apr. 12, 1865).
WILHITE, W. T. 3Sgt. — Orig. Pvt. in Co.: W., Chancellorsville (May 3, 1863): Appt. 3Sgt., Jan. 25, 1864: Wound furlough, Winter, 1864-65.
WILLIAMSON, J. H. 1Cpl. — Orig. Pvt. in Co.: Appt. 1Cpl.: Died, Oct. 13, 1862.
WORSHAM, JOHN L. 2Sgt. — Orig. Pvt. in Co.: Prom., 2Sgt., Oct. 17, 1861: Reduced to Pvt., Nov. 25, 1861 & asgnd. as a teamster.

PRIVATES

ADAMS, GEO. F. — Enl., Feb. 19, 1862 in Jackson Co., Ga., age 35: Died at Dumfries, Apr. 22, 1862.
(1) ADAMS, JAS. T. — Died of asthma, Feb. 27, 1862.
ADDINGTON, JESSE R. — Enl., Feb. 25, 1862 in Jackson Co., Ga.: K., Antietam (Sept. 17, 1862).
(1) ADDINGTON, JOHN M. — AWOL, Summer, 1863, "supposed to be dead."
(1) ANGLIN, WILLIS — K., Gaines' Mill (June 27, 1862).
(1) ANGLIN, W. W. — Deserted, Gettysburg (July 3, 1863): POW, near Chambersburg, Pa., July 26, 1863: Confined at Ft. Mifflin, Pa.: Escaped, July 12, 1864.
(1) APPLEBY, JAS. T. — K., Gaines' Mill (June 27, 1862).

BACON, ALEXANDER E. – Enl., Mar. 3, 1862 in Jackson Co., Ga.: Died, May 1, 1862.

BACON, H. E. – Enl., Mar. 3, 1862 in Jackson Co., Ga.: Died, Apr. 1, 1862.

BARNETT, H. C. – See list of "Non-Comm. Officers" above.

(1)
(2) BARRON, WM. L. – AWOL, Winter, 1861-62: Paroled, Appomattox (Apr. 12, 1865).

BATES, FRANCIS M. – Enl., Feb. 25, 1862 at Jefferson, Ga., age 18: W., Gaines' Mill (June 27, 1862): POW, Cold Harbor (June 1, 1864): Exchanged, Oct. 28, 1864.

BELL, ANDREW JACKSON – Enl., May 15, 1862 at Augusta, Ga.: AWOL, most of 1864.

BENNETT, E. F. – Enl., Mar. 3, 1862: Died of measles at Ashland, Va., Apr. 1, 1862.

BENNETT, THOS. – Enl., Mar. 1, 1862 at Jefferson, Ga.: POW, 2nd Manassas (Aug. 30, 1862): Paroled.

BENTON, THOS. J. – Enl., Feb. 25, 1862 at Jefferson, Ga.: POW, Harper's Ferry, June 4, 1863: Took Fed. oath & enl. in the 3rd Maryland Cav. Regt., USA.

(1) BOWLES, THOS. C. – W. (thigh), Gaines' Mill (June 27, 1862): POW, Burkeville (Apr. 6, 1865).

(1) CALLAHAN, JOHN H. – W., Fredericksburg (Dec. 13, 1862): Died of measles, Richmond, Feb. 19, 1863.

CLANTON, WM. – Transfd. to Co. C from the 16th Ga. Inf. Regt., Sept. 1, 1861: K., 2nd Manassas (Aug. 30, 1862).

(1) COHEN, M. A. – Died of fever near Dumfries, Dec. 9, 1861.

DAILEY (or DALEY), JONES D. – Enl., Feb. 25, 1862 at Jefferson, Ga., age 44: AWOL, Summer, 1864.

(1) DAVIS, EPHRAIM – Dischgd. for disability, July 29, 1862.

DAVIS, JOHN L. – See list of "Non-Comm. Officers" above.

(2) DAVIS, H. PIERCE – Enl., Sept. 1, 1861: Paroled, Appomattox (Apr. 12, 1865).

(1) DAVIS, WM. C. – POW, Knoxville, Dec. 3, 1863: Took Fed. oath & enl. in U.S. Navy at Rock Is., Ill.

(1) de la PERRIERE, A. A. – See list of "Non-Comm. Officers" above.

ERWIN (or IRVIN), ELIJAH A. – Enl., Feb. 25, 1862, age 30: POW, Cold Harbor (June 1, 1864): Paroled, Elmira, N.Y., June 21, 1865.

(1) ESPEY, JAS. A. – W., 2nd Manassas (Aug. 30, 1862): Foot amputated: Died from operation, Sept. 11, 1862.

(1) EVANS, J. H. – Died, Nov. 1, 1862.

(1) EVANS, J. T. – Died, Apr. 1, 1862.

EVANS, W. L. – Enl., Feb. 25, 1862 at Jefferson, Ga.: Died of tuberculosis, Aug. 17, 1862.

FOSTER, JAS. W. – Hospitalized, Summer, 1862: No other record.

(1) FRANKLIN, D. B. – AWOL, Winter, 1861-62: POW, Cold Harbor (June 1, 1864): Paroled, July 11, 1865.

(1) GILBERT, H. C. – POW, Knoxville, Dec. 3, 1863: Took Fed. oath & enl. in the U.S. Navy at Rock Is., Ill.

GREEN, HENRY – POW, near Fredericksburg, Va., Mar. 10, 1863: Took Fed. oath, May 30, 1863.

HARDIN, WM. — Enl., Aug. 5, 1861 at Richmond: Died, Apr. 7, 1862.

HARRIS, GEO. J. — Enl., Mar. 13, 1862 at Jefferson, Ga.: W., Antietam (Sept. 17, 1862): Died from wound, Oct. 24, 1862.

HARRIS, GEO. W. — Enl., Feb. 25, 1862 in Jackson Co., Ga.: Died of pneumonia at Charlottesville, Va., July 15, 1862.

HARRIS, I. G. — Died, Aug. 1, 1862: No other record.

HARRIS, JESSE M. — Enl., Feb. 25, 1862 in Jackson Co., Ga.: Died, Apr. 18, 1862.

HARRIS, W. G. — Enl., Feb. 25, 1862 at Jefferson, Ga.: Died, July 15, 1862.

HARRIS, W. H. — Hospitalized, Fall, 1862: No other record.

HARRISON, WM. C. — Enl., Feb. 25, 1862 in Jackson Co., Ga.: Died, Apr. 12, 1862.

(1) HARWELL, ANDREW C. — W., Antietam (June 27, 1862): Leg amputated: Died from operation.

HARWELL, WM. — Enl., Feb. 25, 1862 at Jefferson, Ga.: Died, Sept. 1, 1862.

(1) HELTON, ELIJAH — K., Spotsylvania (May 12, 1864).

(1) HELTON, R. H. — AWOL, Winter, 1863-64.

(1) HELTON, WM. — POW, Cold Harbor (June 1, 1864): Exchanged: AWOL, Summer, 1864.

HOOD, WM. W. — Enl., Feb. 25, 1862 in Jackson Co., Ga.: POW, Burkeville (Apr. 6, 1865).

(1) HOWARD, JOHN R. — K., 2nd Manassas (Aug. 30, 1862).

IRVIN, E. A. — Enl., Feb. 25, 1862 at Jefferson, Ga.: W. (thigh), Gettysburg (July 3, 1863): POW, Cold Harbor (June 1, 1864).

(1) KINNEY (or KENNEY), JOHN A. — W., Fredericksburg (Dec. 13, 1862): POW, Knoxville, Dec. 3, 1863: Took Fed. oath, enl. in U.S. Navy at Rock Is., Ill.

LEATH, J. S. — Enl., May 10, 1862 at Savannah, Ga.: No other record.

LONG, T. H. — Enl., Feb. 14, 1862 in Jackson Co., Ga.: No other record.

LORD, J. S. — Enl., Mar. 5, 1862 at Jefferson, Ga.: W., Fredericksburg (Dec. 13, 1862): Died of wound, Jan. 4, 1863.

LORD, JAS. W. — Enl., Mar. 1, 1862: POW, Knoxville, Dec. 3, 1863.

(2) LORD, PHILLIP — Enl., Feb. 25, 1862: Paroled, Appomattox (Apr. 12, 1865).

LORD, W. T. — Enl., Feb. 25, 1862: Died at Richmond, Oct. 1, 1862.

(1) McELHANON, J. C. — See list of "Non-Comm. Officers" above.

(1) McELHANON, H. W. — K., Gaines' Mill (June 27, 1862).

MICHAEL, BENJ. — Transfd. to Co. C from 16th Ga. Inf. Regt., Sept. 18, 1861: POW, Mine Run, Va. (Aug. 29, 1864).

MILLER, JOHN H. — Enl., Feb. 25, 1862 at Jefferson, Ga.: K., 2nd Manassas (Aug. 30, 1862).

(1) MILLER, W. P. — Died of chronic diarrhea at Petersburg, Aug. 14, 1862.

(1) MITCHELL, J. R. — W. & POW, 2nd Manassas (Aug. 30, 1862): Thigh amputated, Sept., 1862: Paroled, Sept. 29, 1862.

(1) MOORE, J. J. — K., Gaines' Mill (June 27, 1862).

MOORE, J. T. — Enl., May 3, 1862: POW, Falling Waters, Md., July 14, 1863: Exchanged: POW, Cedar Cr. (Oct. 19, 1864): Exchanged.

MOORE, S. F. — Hospitalized, Spring, 1862: No other record.

(1) MORGAN, B. B. — Enl., Aug. 2, 1861: Paroled, Appomattox (Apr. 12,
(2) 1865).

MORGAN, DAN. M. — See list of "Non-Comm. Officers" above.

MORGAN, GEO. D. — Enl., Mar. 30, 1862, age 16: K., Fredericksburg
(Dec. 13, 1862).

MORGAN, J. P. — See list of "Officers" above.

(1) NOBLACK, THOS. H. — W. & POW, 2nd Manassas (Aug. 30, 1862):
(2) Paroled, Appomattox (Apr. 12, 1865).

OLIVER, ANDREW G. — Enl., Feb. 25, 1862, age 18: K., Gettysburg
(July 2, 1863).

(1) OLIVER, JAS. H. — K., 2nd Manassas (Aug. 30, 1862).

OLIVER, JOHN M. — Enl., Feb. 25, 1862 at Jefferson, Ga., age 33:
POW, Harper's Ferry (June 15, 1863): Took Fed. oath & jnd. 1st
Conn. Cav. Regt.

(1) ORR, JOS. M. — W. (leg), Gaines' Mill (June 27, 1862): Paroled,
(2) Appomattox (Apr. 12, 1865).

(1) PALMER, JOS. A. — Transfd. to 16th Ga. Inf. Regt., Jan. 1, 1863.

(1) PATMAN, THOS. H. — POW, Cold Harbor (June 1, 1864): Paroled,
Oct. 11, 1864.

PERRY, WM. O. — Died, Apr. 9, 1862.

PERRY, WM. R. — Enl., Feb. 25, 1862 in Jackson Co., Ga.: No other
record.

PETTYJOHN, M. G. — Enl., Feb. 25, 1862: Died, June 1, 1862.

PHARR, SAM M. — Enl., Feb. 30, 1862, age 30: Died of typhoid fever,
Nov. 13, 1862 at Richmond.

(1) POTTER, R. P. — See list of "Non-Comm. Officers" above.

POTTER, WM. M. — Enl., July 26, 1861: W. (foot), Gaines' Mill (June
27, 1862): POW, in Richmond hosp., Apr. 3, 1865: Paroled, Apr.
20, 1865.

POTTS, A. WAYNE — Enl., Sept. 2, 1861 at Richmond: POW,
Gettysburg (July 2, 1863): Confined at Ft. Delaware.

POTTS, JOHN M. — Enl., Feb. 25, 1862 at Jefferson, Ga.: K.,
Fredericksburg (Dec. 13, 1862).

RAILEY (or REILLY), SAMUEL A. — Enl., Feb. 25, 1862 at
Jefferson, Ga., age 20: Dischgd. for disability (chronic
bronchitis), July 26, 1862: Died.

ROBERTS, J. A. — Enl., Feb. 25, 1862, age 18: W., Antietam (Sept.
17, 1862).

RODGERS, J. A. — Enl., July 20, 1862 at Augusta, Ga.: Paroled, Apr.
15, 1865.

RODGERS, JAS. A. — Enl., Feb. 25, 1862 in Jackson Co., Ga., age 18:
Died, Apr. 26, 1862.

ROGERS, ROBT. T. — Enl., Feb. 25, 1862 in Jackson Co., Ga., age 18:
W. (hip & abdomen), Gaines' Mill (June 27, 1862).

(1) ROUSE, ELIAS — Died, May 16, 1862.
(1) ROUSE, H. F. — Dischgd., Dec. 9, 1861.

SHELLEY, RICHARD — Enl., Aug. 5, 1861 at Richmond: Present for
duty until Oct., 1862: No other record.

SHOCKLEY, J. H. — Hospitalized with bronchitis, Nov., 1862 to Feb.,
1863: No other record.

(1)   SHOCKLEY, W. S. — See list of "Non-Comm. Officers" above.

        STANLEY, WM. S. — Enl., Feb. 25, 1862 in Jackson Co., Ga., age 26: "Died in line of duty," Apr. 11, 1862.

(1)   STAPLER, A. D. — Dischgd. (rheumatism), Aug. 4, 1862.

        STRICKLAND, JESSE WHITE — See list of "Non-Comm. Officers" above.

        THURMOND, A. M. — Enl., Feb. 25, 1862: POW, Cold Harbor (June 1, 1864): Paroled, July 7, 1865.

(1)   THURMOND, JAS. H. — K., Gaines' Mill (Jun 27, 1862).

        THURMOND, WM. T. — Transfd. to Co. C from the 16th Ga. Inf. Regt., Aug. 2, 1861: W., 2nd Manassas (Aug. 30, 1862).

(1)   TOLBERT, A. J. — POW, Knoxville, Nov. 29, 1863: Confined at Rock Is., Ill.: Took Fed. oath: Enl. in U.S. Navy, Jan., 1864.

(1)   VANDIVER, C. C. — Absent, sick, Summer, 1862: Died, 1862.

        WALTON, W. L. — Present for duty, June, 1862: No other record.

        WARSHAM (or WORSHAM), W. W. — POW, 2nd Manassas (Aug. 30, 1862): Paroled, Warrenton, Va., Sept. 29, 1862.

        WATSON, W. A. — See roster, "Regmtl. Hdqtrs., 18th Ga. Inf."

        WELLS, M. L. — Died of measles in Richmond, June 22, 1862.

(1)   WHITE, J. M. — Dischgd. on Surg. Cert., Nov. 7, 1861: Re-enl., Feb. 25, 1862: W., Gaines' Mill (June 27, 1862): AWOL, Summer, 1864.

(1)   WIER, JOHN G. — See list of "Non-Comm. Officers" above.

        WILHITE, JOHN M. — See roster, "Regmtl. Hdqtrs., 18th Ga. Inf."

(1)   WILHITE, O. M. — See list of "Non-Comm. Officers" above.

(1)   WILHITE, W. T. — See list of "Non-Comm. Officers" above.

        WHITEHEAD, MADISON — Enl., Feb. 25, 1862 at Jefferson, Ga., age 24: W., Wilderness (May 6, 1864): Died of wound, June 18, 1864.

        WILBANKS, TILLISON — Enl., Mar. 3, 1862: Died, Apr. 19, 1862.

        WILLIAMSON, B. C. — In Chimborazo Hosp., Sept., 1862: No other record.

(1)   WILLIAMSON, C. C. — Deserted: Took Fed. oath, Feb. 18, 1864.

(1)   WILLIAMSON, J. H. — See list of "Non-Comm. Officers" above.

        WILLIAMSON, JOHN N. — Enl., Mar. 3, 1862 in Jackson Co., Ga., age 27: W., 2nd Manassas (Aug. 30, 1862).

(1)   WILLIAMSON, R. N. — K., 2nd Manassas (Aug. 30, 1862).

        WILLS, MARTIN L. — Enl., May 5, 1862 at Jefferson, Ga.: Died of measles in Richmond, June 22, 1862.

        WILSON, EZRA A. — Enl., Mar. 3, 1862: Died, Apr. 1, 1862.

        WILSON, FENUEL S. — Enl., Sept. 2, 1861: Sick, Fall, 1862: Dischgd., Feb. 1, 1863.

        WILSON, MICHAEL M. — Enl., Mar. 3, 1862, age 29: Died of typhoid pneumonia.

        WILSON, HENRY W. — Enl., Feb. 25, 1862: POW, Winchester, Va., Oct. 19, 1864.

(1)   WILSON, WM. O. — W., 2nd Manassas (Aug. 30, 1862): Died from wound, Oct. 10, 1862.

(1)   WINGFIELD, J. E. — Died of pneumonia at Richmond, Apr. 28, 1862.

(1)   WINGFIELD, JOHN N. — Enl., July 15, 1861: POW, Cedar Cr. (Oct. 19, 1864): Paroled, June 22, 1865.

WOFFORD, B. B. — Sick at Richmond, Nov., 1862: No other record.
WOFFORD, JAS. H. — Enl., Feb. 25, 1862 at Jefferson, Ga., age 33: Died of typhoid fever at Richmond, July 19, 1862.
WOFFORD, T. H. — Enl., Feb. 25, 1862 at Jefferson, Ga., age 19: K., Rapidan Sta., Va., Aug. 17, 1862.
(1) WORSHAM, JOHN L. — See list of "Non-Comm. Officers" above.
(1) WORSHAM, WM. N. — Transfd. to 3rd Btln., Ga. Sharpshooters, June 8, 1863: POW, Saylor's Cr. (Apr. 6, 1865).

* * * * *

MEMBERS OF COMPANY C, 18TH GA. INF. REGT., WHO WERE NOT PRESENT FOR DUTY DURING THE PERIOD THAT THE REGIMENT WAS ASSIGNED TO HOOD'S TEXAS BRIGADE (NOV., 1861-NOV., 1862).

OFFICERS

Scwen, T. F., Capt. (Not on Bi-Monthly Muster Roll)

NON-COMMISSIONED OFFICERS

Foster,_____, Cpl. (No record)
(1) Hardy, Andrew J., 1Cpl. (Orig. 1Cpl. of Co.: D., Sept., 1861)

(1) Park, W. A., 2Cpl. (Orig. 2Cpl. of Co.: Transfd. out, July, 1861)
(1) Story, J. M., 1Sgt. (Orig. 1Sgt. of Co.: Dischgd. (rheumatism), Oct. 17, 1861)

PRIVATES

Adair, J. O. (Deserted, Nov., 1861)
Adair, W. A. (D., Sept., 1861)
Addington, J. C. (No record prior to Nov., 1862)
Allen, J. B. (Dischgd., July, 1861)
Anglin, W. T. (D., Oct., 1861)
Bates, J. C. (Enl., May, 1864)
Cheek, L. M. (Dischgd., July, 1861)
Connell, Jas. S. (No record prior to Mar., 1864)
Estes, Obediah N. (D., Sept., 1861)

Evans, Geo. E. (No record before Apr., 1865)
Evans, J. R. (No record)
Evans, T. H. (No record before July, 1863)
(1) Franklin, M. D. (D., Aug., 1861)
(1) Freeman, S. A. (D., Sept., 1861)
Gooden, A. M. (Enl., Apr., 1864)
Harris, J. G. (No record)
Holmes, J. H. (Enl., Dec., 1862)
Irwin, T. H. (No record prior to Mar., 1865)
Jarrett, N. M. (D., Nov., 1861)

Ledford, Adam (Enl., Feb., 1864)

Ledford, Jesse (Enl., Mar., 1864)

Lindsey, Jas. (D., Sept., 1861)

Lord, James W. (Enl., Mar., 1863)

Loyd, John (D., Dec., 1861)

Matthews, C. W. (Dischgd., Nov., 1861)

McLester, W. W. (Enl., Jan., 1864)

Milligan, R. J. (Transfd. out, July, 1861)

North, John R. (Transfd. out, July, 1861)

Nowke, R. C. (No record prior to May, 1865)

Pettyjohn, Thos. J. (D., Sept., 1861)

Phillips, B. M. (No record prior to Mar., 1865)

Quattlebaum, A. M. (No record prior to June, 1864)

Ross, D. A. (No record prior to Apr., 1865)

Rouse, B. O. W. (No record after Oct., 1861)

Saunders (or Sanders), Jas. E. (Transfd. out, Sept., 1861)

Spencer, Absalom (Transfd. out, July, 1861)

Strickland, Ansel (Enl., Feb., 1863)

White, H. S. (Enl., Oct., 1863)

Whitehead, J. T. (Enl., Apr., 1864)

Williams, J. N. (D., Nov., 1861)

Willingham, Albert (Not on Bi-Monthly Muster Roll)

Wilson, T. F. (No record after Oct., 1861)

Winfield, J. R. (No record)

Winters, J. W. (Enl., Oct., 1863)

18TH GA. INF. REGT.

COMPANY D – *DAVIS INVINCIBLES*

Company was organized in Dougherty County, Georgia, during the Spring of 1861. It rendezvoused, recruited & trained at Camp McDonald, Cobb County, Georgia, in late June & in July. The men were mustered into the Confederate service, "for three years," at Richmond, Va., on or about Aug. 9, 1861.

Key

(1) Original member of Company. (2) Paroled at Appomattox.
K (Killed), W (Wounded), POW (Prisoner of War)
AWOL (Absent Without Leave)

OFFICERS

GILBERT, WM. G. Capt. – Orig. 1Sgt. of Co.: Elect., 3Lt., Jan., 1862: Elect., 2Lt., July 16, 1862: W., Antietam (Sept. 17, 1862): Prom., 1Lt., Apr., 1863: Prom., Capt., Feb. 7, 1865: POW, Sayler's Cr. (Apr. 6, 1865): Confined at Johnson's Is., Ohio: Paroled, June 18, 1865.

(1)   IRVIN, SAMUEL D. Capt. — Orig. Capt. of Co.: Resgnd., ill health, July 16, 1862.

(1)   LAWS, ELVIS R. Capt. — Orig. 1Lt. of Co.: Elect., Capt., July 16, 1862: W., 2nd Manassas (Aug. 30, 1862): Resgnd., Apr., 1863.

(1)   MACON, GIDEON H. Capt. — Orig. 2Lt. of Co.: Elect., 1Lt., July 16, 1862: W., Antietam (Sept. 17, 1862): Elect., Capt., Apr., 1863: AWOL, Apr., 1864: Dropped from rolls, Feb., 1865.

       ADAMS, MAT H. 2Lt. — Orig. Pvt. in Co.: W., Antietam (Sept. 17, 1862): Elect., 3Lt., May, 1863: Prom., 2Lt.: Transfd. to CSA Navy, Sept. 3, 1863.

(1)   TWITTY, PETER W. 2Lt. — Resgnd., ill health, Dec. 6, 1861.

       RHODES, OWEN R. 3Lt. — Orig. Pvt. in Co.: Appt. 2Cpl., Jan., 1861: Elect., 3Lt., July 16, 1862: W., 2nd Manassas (Aug. 30, 1862): POW, Fredericksburg (Dec. 13, 1862): Died, Apr., 1863.

NON-COMMISSIONED OFFICERS

       BRINSON, ISAAC 4Cpl. — Orig. Pvt. in Co.: Appt. 4Cpl., Jan., 1862: Paroled, May 15, 1865.

(1)   BROOM, ASGILL 1Cpl. — Orig. 3Cpl. of Co.: Appt. 1Cpl., Jan., 1862: W. & POW, 2nd Manassas (Aug. 30, 1862): Paroled, Sept. 29, 1862: Died (chronic diarrhea), Nov. 8, 1862.

(1)   CAIN, HIRAM 5Sgt. — Orig. 2Cpl. of Co.: Appt. 5Sgt., Jan., 1862: W., Fredericksburg (Dec. 13, 1862): W. & POW, Gettysburg (July 2, 1863): Paroled: POW, Burkeville, Va. (Apr. 6, 1865).

       GILBERT, R. T. Sgt. — Orig. Pvt. in Co.: Prom. to Sgt.: W. & POW, Gettysburg (July 2, 1863): Leg amputated: Retired to Invalid Corps, Nov. 4, 1864.

(1)   GILBERT, WM. G. 1Sgt. — See list of "Officers" above.

(1)   HURLY, GREEN C. 3Sgt. — Orig. 4Sgt. of Co.: Appt. 3Sgt., Jan. 1, 1862: No record after Feb., 1862.

       HIGGINBOTHAM, J. E. 2Cpl. — Orig. Pvt. in Co.: Appt. 2Cpl., July 16, 1862: W., 2nd Manassas (Aug. 30, 1862): No record after Nov., 1862.

(1)   HOBBS, WM. W. 4Sgt. — Orig. 5Sgt. of Co.: Prom., 4Sgt., Jan., 1862: W. (chest), Gaines' Mill (June 27, 1862): W., Cedar Cr. (Oct. 19, 1864): POW, Burkeville, Va. (Apr. 6, 1865).

       MARCHMAN, J. A. 5Sgt. — Orig. Pvt. in Co.: W., Fredericksburg (Dec. 13, 1862): Appt. 5Sgt., 1864: POW, Burkeville, Va. (Apr. 6, 1865).

(1)   MATHEWS, WM. M. 1 Cpl. — Orig. 1Cpl. of Co.: Reduced to ranks, Feb. 15, 1862: Died in Richmond, Nov. 11, 1862.

(1)   MURRAY, WM. A. 2Sgt. — Orig. 3Sgt. of Co.: Appt. 2Sgt., Jan. 1, 1862: K., Gaines' Mill (June 27, 1862).

       PENICK, CLIFTON 2Sgt. — Orig. Pvt. in Co.: Appt. 2Cpl., Jan., 1862: W. & POW, 2nd Manassas (Aug. 30, 1862): Paroled: Appt. 2Sgt.

       PIERCE, W. J. 2Cpl. — Orig. Pvt. in Co.: W., Antietam (Sept. 17, 1862): POW, Gettysburg (July 2, 1863): Confined at Elmira, N.Y.: Prom., 2Cpl., Spring, 1864: Died of fever at Elmira prison, Aug. 1, 1864.

TAYLOR, A. J. 2Cpl. — Orig. Pvt. in Co.: W., Antietam (Sept. 17, 1862): W., Chancellorsville (May 3, 1863): Prom., 3Cpl., Winter, 1863-64: Prom., 2Cpl., Spring, 1864: POW, Burkeville, Va. (Apr. 6, 1865).

WEST, WM. 4Cpl. — Orig. Pvt. in Co.: W., Gaines' Mill (June 27, 1862): POW, Burkeville, Va. (Apr. 6, 1865).

WOODALL, JESSE A. 3Sgt. — Orig. Pvt. in Co.: W. (arm), Chancellorsville (May 3, 1863): W. (leg), Spotsylvania (May 12, 1864): Appt. 3Sgt., 1864: POW, Cold Harbor (June 1, 1864).

(1) WOODALL, SAMUEL H. 1Sgt. — Orig. 2Sgt. of Co.: Appt. 1Sgt., Jan. 1, 1862: W. & POW, Antietam (Sept. 17, 1862): Paroled: POW, Cold Harbor (June 3, 1864): Exchanged.

PRIVATES

(1) ADAMS, A. G. — In arrest, Feb., 1862: Dischgd., overage (46), July, 1864.

(1) ADAMS, MARTIN — Sick in hosp., Summer, 1862: No other record.

(1) ADAMS, MAT H. — See list of "Officers" above.

(1) BAILEY, ANGUISH — W. (hip), Gaines' Mill (June 27, 1862): No record after Jan., 1863.

(1) BAILEY, SILAS B. — Dischgd. on Surg. Cert., Jan. 6, 1862: Re-enl.: POW, Gettysburg (July 2, 1863): Exchanged, Mar. 3, 1864: Dischgd., Sept. 23, 1864.

(1) BENNETT, THOS. J. — Dischgd., disability, Jan. 6, 1862.

(1) BLIZZARD, JAS. — Paroled, Lynchburg (Apr. 15, 1865).

(1) BRACK, AUGUSTUS L. — W., Chancellorsville (May 3, 1863): POW, Loudon, Tenn., Dec. 23, 1863: Took Fed. oath at Rock Is., Ill., Oct. 13, 1864 & "enlisted in U.S. Army for frontier duty."

BRINSON, ISAAC — See list of "Non-Comm. Officers" above.

BROOME, M. — POW, Knoxville, Dec. 18, 1863: No other record.

(1) CLEMENTS, THOS. — Died of pneumonia, Apr. 9, 1862.

(1) CLIFTON, REDDICK C. — W., Antietam (Sept. 17, 1862): Arm amputated.

(1) COOK, ALONZO G. — POW, Gettysburg (July 4, 1863): Paroled: POW, E. Tenn.: Took Fed. oath, Dec., 1863.

(1) CORD, G. — Died, Richmond, Dec. 25, 1864.

(1) CRAWFORD, PETER — Dischgd. for disability, Jan. 6, 1862.

(1) DANCER, JOHN M. — W., Gaines' Mill (June 27, 1862): W., Fredericksburg (Dec. 13, 1862): POW, E. Tenn., Jan. 31, 1864: Took Fed. oath.

(1) DANCER, WM. R. — W. (arm), Gaines' Mill (June 27, 1862): Arm amputated.

(1) DERISO, GEO. H. — W. & POW, Cold Harbor (June 1, 1864).

(1) DOYLE, THOS. — No record after Feb., 1862.

EARLY, W. P. — W., Antietam (Sept. 17, 1862): No other record.

(1) FAIRCLOTH, CALVIN — W. (hip), Gaines' Mill (June 27, 1862): Paroled, Albany, Ga., May 17, 1865.

FAIRCLOTH, W. R. — Enl., Mar. 4, 1862: W. (leg), Gaines' Mill (June 27, 1862): Paroled, Albany, Ga., May 17, 1865.

(1) FRAZIER, BENJ. — Died, Apr., 1862.
(1) GILBERT, R. T. — See list of "Non-Comm. Officers" above.
(1) GRAY, REDDING — POW, 2nd Manassas (Aug. 30, 1862): Paroled,
    Sept. 29, 1862: W. (foot), Gettysburg (July 2, 1863): Retired for
    disability, Jan. 25, 1865.
(1) GREEN, JOHN C. — W., Fredericksburg (Dec. 13, 1862): AWOL,
    Summer, 1864.
(1) GREEN, W. H. — No record after Aug., 1862.
    GRIFFIN, W. W. — W. (hip) & POW, Gettysburg (July 2, 1863): No
    other record.
(1) HAMMOND, N. M. — W., Chancellorsville (May 3, 1863): POW,
    Farmville (Apr. 6, 1865).
    HAYNIE, J. Z. — Dischgd. by Surg. for chronic diarrhea, July 19, 1862.
(1) HAYS, JAS. — W., 2nd Manassas (Aug. 30, 1862): W., Antietam (Sept.
    17, 1862): POW, Gettysburg (July 2, 1863): Took Fed. oath, jnd.
    U.S. 3rd Md. Cav. Regt.
(1) HEARST (or HURST), J. W. J. — W., 2nd Manassas (Aug. 30, 1862).
(1) HENNEGAN, JOHN — Deserted, Mar., 1865.
(1) HIGGINBOTHAM, J. E. — See list of "Non-Comm. Officers" above.
(1) HUDNALL, J. A. — Died, June 3, 1862, of "remittent fever."
(1) JOHNSON, D. J. — Died at Richmond, July 30, 1864.
(1) JOHNSON, J. J. — POW, Gettysburg (July 2, 1863): Took Fed. oath,
    jnd. U.S. 3rd Md. Cav. Regt.
(1) JOHNSON, JEREMIAH — W. (thigh) & POW, Knoxville, Dec. 5, 1863:
    Leg amputated: Died from operation while a POW at Middle
    Brook Hosp., near Knoxville, Feb. 15, 1864.
(1) JONES, ALLEN — W. & POW, Antietam (Sept. 17, 1862): Died of
    wound at Fed. hosp., Oct. 17, 1862.
    KNIGHT, JAS. M. — Enl., Mar. 10, 1862: Died, Richmond, June 10,
    1862.
(1) KNIGHT, JOS. A. — W., 2nd Manassas (Aug. 30, 1862): POW, Cold
    Harbor (June 2, 1864).
(1) MARCHMAN, J. A. — See list of "Non-Comm. Officers" above.
(1) MATHEWS, WM. M. — See list of "Non-Comm. Officers" above.
(1) MAUND, JOHN — Deserted, Mar. 1, 1863: No other record.
(1) McCRAY, JOHN — W., Fredericksburg (Dec. 13, 1862): Arm
    amputated.
    McCUE, W. M. — W., Antietam (Sept. 17, 1862).
(1) McDOWELL, P. H. — Transfd. to the 17th Ga. Inf. Regt., Dec. 10,
    1862.
(1) MERCHANT, WM. — Absent on furlough, Aug., 1864: No further
    record.
(1) MERRITT, M. E. — AWOL, Aug., 1864: No further record.
(1) MERRITT, W. ELMORE — W., Chancellorsville (May 3, 1863).
(1) MILLS, J. H. — Dischgd., Dec. 10, 1861: No other record.
    MILROY, JOHN — Sick at Winchester, Va., Nov., 1862: No other
    record.
    MITCHELL, GEO. W. — Paroled, Ft. Delaware, Apr. 27, 1865: No
    other record.

(1) MITCHELL, JOHN — POW, Gettysburg (July 2, 1863): Died as POW at Ft. Delaware, Dec. 19, 1864.

(1) MUSGROVE, MILES — K., Chancellorsville (May 3, 1863).

(1) MUSGROVE, SAMPSON G. — W., Chancellorsville (May 3, 1863): POW, Cold Harbor (June 1, 1864): Exchanged, Nov. 15, 1864.

(1) NEWSOM, JOEL — Dischgd. (rheumatism), Aug. 4, 1862.

(1) PENICK, CLIFTON — See list of "Non-Comm. Officers" above.

(1) PIERCE, W. J. — See list of "Non-Comm. Officers" above.

(1) REID, W. J. — W., 2nd Manassas (Aug. 30, 1862): Dischgd., Sept. 15, 1863, unfit for field duty.

(1) RHODES, GEO. W. — W., Gaines' Mill (June 27, 1862): Two fingers amputated.

RHODES, JAS. R. — Enl., Mar. 4, 1862 at Fredericksburg: W., Gaines' Mill (June 27, 1862): POW, Spotsylvania (May 22, 1864): Exchanged: Died of tuberculosis at Richmond, Oct. 9, 1864.

(1) RHODES, OWEN R. — See list of "Officers" above.

(1) SALTER, W. L. — Dischgd. (liver ailment), Aug. 7, 1862.

SANDERS, E. S. — Enl., Sept. 5, 1861: K., near Fredericksburg (Dec. 18, 1862).

(1) SAPP, HENRY — W., 2nd Manassas (Aug. 30, 1862): Leg amputated.

SHAW, HENRY — Enl., July 22, 1861: Died from typhoid fever, Jan. 8, 1862.

SIMMS, J. N. — Hospitalized, Fall, 1862: No other record.

(1) SMITH, A. W. — W., Wilderness (May 6, 1864).

(1) SOUTHEIMER, ISAAC — POW, Falling Waters (July 14, 1863): Took Fed. oath, Dec. 17, 1863.

(1) STUCKEY, JAS. — Died of pneumonia, at Dumfries, Dec. 13, 1861.

(1) TAYLOR, A. J. — See list of "Non-Comm. Officers" above.

(1) TEMPLE, WM. T. — Died of pneumonia, at Richmond, Jan. 3, 1863.

(1) WADE, JESSE — Died of chronic diarrhea, at Richmond, Sept. 12, 1862.

(1) WARD, D. P. — POW, Gettysburg (July 5, 1863), left with wounded: Exchanged, Feb. 18, 1865.

(1) WEST, WM. — See list of "Non-Comm. Officers" above.

WILLIAMS, A. — Died, Summer, 1864: No other record.

(1) WINDHAM, J. H. (or J. A.) — Present for duty, Aug., 1862: No other record.

(1) WOODALL, JESSE A. — See list of "Non-Comm. Officers" above.

★ ★ ★ ★ ★

MEMBERS OF COMPANY D, 18TH GA. INF. REGT., WHO WERE NOT PRESENT FOR DUTY DURING THE PERIOD THAT THE REGIMENT WAS ASSIGNED TO HOOD'S TEXAS BRIGADE (NOV., 1861-NOV., 1862)

OFFICERS

NONE

NON-COMMISSIONED OFFICERS

Collins, G. W., Cpl. (No record prior to Apr., 1865)
(1) Duncan, Miles M., 4Cpl. (Dischgd., disabled, Sept., 1861)
Force, Peter, 1Sgt. (No record before July, 1863)

Lane, Jas., Cpl. (No record before Apr., 1865)
(1) Wicket, John S., Color Cpl. (D., Oct., 1861)

PRIVATES

(1) Edwards, Benj. F. (Dischgd. for disability, Oct., 1861)
English, J. G. (No record before Oct., 1864)
Lane, T. W. (No record before Apr., 1865)
Mathews, Daniel J. (or H.) (Dischgd., disability, Nov., 1861)

(1) McKinney, Isaiah (D., July, 1861)
Merritt, J. M. (Enl., Aug., 1864)
Murray, Jos. (Dischgd., disability, Oct., 1861)
Penick, Spencer R. (D., Sept., 1861)
Royal, Jas. R. (D., Sept., 1861)
Savage, Reuben (Enl., Mar., 1863)

18TH GA. VOL. INF. REGT.

COMPANY E – *STEPHENS INFANTRY*

Company was organized in Gordon County, Georgia, during the Spring of 1861. It rendezvoused, recruited & trained at Camp McDonald, Cobb County, Georgia, in late June & in July. The Company was mustered into the Confederate service at Richmond, "for three years," on or about Aug. 9, 1861.

Key

(1) Original member of Company. (2) Paroled at Appomattox.
K (Killed), W (Wounded), POW (Prisoner of War)
AWOL (Absent Without Leave)

OFFICERS

(1) STARR, E. L. Capt. – Orig. Capt. of Co.: W., Antietam (Sept. 17, 1862): Appt. Enrolling Officer in Ga., Nov., 1862.
(1) CRAWFORD, M. J. 1Lt. – Orig. 1Lt. of Co.: W., Chancellorsville (May 3, 1863): AWOL, Fall, 1864.
(1) BROWN, E. L. 2Lt. – Orig. 3Lt. of Co.: Prom., 2Lt., Apr. 7, 1862: K., 2nd Manassas (Aug. 30, 1862).

PUTNAM, O. W. 2Lt. — Orig. 2Sgt. of Co.: W. (chest), Gaines' Mill (June 27, 1862): Elect., 3Lt., July 12, 1862: Elect., 2Lt., Aug. 30, 1862: W. (arm) & POW, Gettysburg (July 2, 1863): Arm amputated.

RAMSAUR, D. H. 2Lt. — Orig. 1Sgt. of Co.: Elect., 2Lt., May 12, 1863: Present for duty, Aug., 1864.

LANGLEY, JOHN J. 3Lt. — Enl. as a Pvt., Aug. 3, 1861: Appt. 5Sgt., Dec. 9, 1861: Elect., 3Lt., Sept. 5, 1862: Dropped from rolls, May 1, 1863.

NON-COMMISSIONED OFFICERS

ARNOLD, MARTIN 2Cpl. — Orig. Pvt. in Co.: W. (head), Antietam (Sept. 17, 1862): Prom., 2Cpl.: POW, Burkeville (Apr. 6, 1865).

BOUGHAN (or BAUGHAN), B. F. 2Sgt. — Orig. Pvt. in Co.: Appt. 2Sgt., July 1, 1862: W., Wilderness (May 6, 1864).

BRYSON, JOHN S. 4Cpl. — Orig. Pvt. in Co.: Appt. 4Cpl., Aug. 31, 1861: Died of tetanus, Apr. 3, 1862.

COLLINS, M. S. 3Cpl. — Orig. Pvt. in Co.: Appt. 3Cpl., Jan., 1862: K., 2nd Manassas (Aug. 30, 1862).

CRAWFORD, W. H. 2Cpl. — Orig. Pvt. in Co.: Appt. 2Cpl., Jan., 1862: Reduced to ranks: Dischgd., July 4, 1864.

DOVER, THOS. C. 3Cpl. — Orig. Pvt. in Co.: Appt. 3Cpl., Winter, 1862-63: Court-martialed for AWOL, Apr., 1863: POW, Cold Harbor (June 1, 1864): Exchanged, March 2, 1865: Took Fed. oath, Apr. 3, 1865.

(1) FULLER, J. T. 1Sgt. — Orig. 1Cpl. of Co.: Appt. 1Sgt.: W., Wilderness (May 6, 1864): Died in Fed. prison, Pt. Lookout, Md., Feb. 13, 1865.

HOLCOMBE, ABSOLOM 3Sgt. — Orig. Pvt. in Co.: W., Antietam (Sept. 17, 1862): Appt. 3Sgt., 1863: W., Cedar Cr. (Oct. 19, 1864).

JOHNSON, N. T. 4Cpl. — Orig. Pvt. in Co.: Prom., 4Cpl.: Reduced to ranks: No record after Sept., 1864.

NAVE, J. A. 1Cpl. — Orig. Pvt. in Co.: W., Gaines' Mill (June 27, 1862): POW, E. Tenn., Nov. 29, 1863: Confined at Rock Is., Ill.: Enl. in U.S. Army "for frontier service," Oct. 4, 1864.

(1) NORWOOD, F. W. 1Cpl. — Orig. 2Cpl. of Co.: Prom., 1Cpl., 1862: Died, July, 1862.

(1) PUTNAM, O. W. 2Sgt. — See list of "Officers" above.

(1) RAMSAUR, D. H. 1Sgt. — See list of "Officers" above.

SANDERS, B. F. Cpl. — Orig. Pvt. in Co.: W., 2nd Manassas (Aug. 30, 1862): Prom., Cpl., Fall, 1863: AWOL, Aug., 1864: Took Fed. oath at Clarksburg, W.V., Nov. 20, 1864.

(1) WEEMS, FRANCIS A. 1Sgt. — Orig. 4Sgt. of Co.: W., 2nd Manassas (Aug. 30, 1862): Prom., 1Sgt., May, 1863: POW, Carterville, Ga., Sept. 3, 1864.

(1) WEEMS, SAM C. Sgt.-Maj. — See roster, "Regmtl. Hdqtrs., 18th Ga. Inf."

PRIVATES

(1)   ALEXANDER, J. L. — POW, Spotsylvania (May 22, 1864): Exchanged, Nov. 15, 1864.

(1)   ALLEN, JOHN E. — AWOL, since Feb., 1862.

(1)   ARNOLD, MARTIN — See list of "Non-Comm. Officers" above.

(1)   BALLARD, JOS. — POW, Gettysburg (July 3, 1863): Exchanged, Jan. 17, 1865.

(1)   BALLEW, W. C. — K., Spotsylvania (May 10, 1864).

(1)   BAXTER, R. N. — Died, Nov. 18, 1863, at Rome, Ga.

(1)   BEAUCHAMP, JOS. — Transfd. to Co. H, 18th Ga. Inf., Aug., 1862.

(1)   BOUGHAN (or BAUGHAN), ALONZO — W., 2nd Manassas (Aug. 30, 1862): Paroled, Lynchburg, Va., Apr. 13, 1865.

(1)   BOUGHAN (or BAUGHAN), B. F. — See list of "Non-Comm. Officers" above.

(1)   BROOKS, JOHN B. — W. & POW, Antietam (Sept. 17, 1862): Paroled, Sept. 27, 1862: Died of wound, Oct. 12, 1862.

(1)   BRYSON, JOHN S. — See list of "Non-Comm. Officers" above.

(1)   CALDWELL, JOHN W. — W., Boonsboro (Sept. 14, 1862), "while on picket:" Retired, June 10, 1864.

(2)   COLLINS, D. M. — Paroled, Appomattox (Apr. 12, 1865): No other record.

(1)   COLLINS, J. A. — Transfd. to 23rd Ga. Inf., 1864: No other record.

(1)   COLLINS, M. S. — See list of "Non-Comm. Officers" above.

(1)   COLLINS, T. W. — POW, Boonsboro (Sept. 15, 1862): Exchanged: No record after Sept., 1864.

     CONDESS, W. L. — Sick in hosp., Oct., 1862: No other record.

     COOK, BENJ. F. — Enl., Aug. 11, 1861 at Richmond: POW, E. Tenn., Nov. 28, 1863: Died of chronic diarrhea at Fed. prison, Rock Is., Ill.

     COOK, E. F. — Hospitalized, Spring, 1862: No other record.

     COOK, H. C. — Enl., Aug. 11, 1861 at Richmond: W. (neck), Spotsylvania (May 12, 1864).

(1)   CRAWFORD, W. H. — See list of "Non-Comm. Officers" above.

     DOBBIN, J. H. — Hospitalized, Dec., 1861: No other record.

(1)   DOVER, THOS. C. — See list of "Non-Comm. Officers" above.

(1)   EDDLEMAN, SAMUEL — W., 2nd Manassas (Aug. 30, 1862): W., Chancellorsville (May 3, 1863): Paroled, Apr. 19, 1865 at Newton, No. Car.

     ELLIS, M. M. — Hospitalized, Fall, 1862: No other record.

(1)   ELLIS, R. F. — W., Wilderness (May 6, 1864): POW, Cedar Cr. (Oct. 19, 1864): Exchanged, Mar. 28, 1865.

(1)   ELLIS, W. H. — Died, Apr. 15, 1862: No other record.

(1)   ELROD, W. H. — Enl., Camp McDonald, Ga., date unknown: Present for duty, Summer, 1864: No other record.

(1)   FREEMAN, JAS. — No record after Aug., 1862.

(1)   GIBSON, J. L. — Transfd. out of Co. E to Co. D, 23rd Ga. Inf. Regt., Jan. 1, 1862.

     GREEN, F. M. — Enl., June 25, 1862 at Calhoun, Ga.: W., Front Royal, Va., Sept. 19, 1864.

GUYTON, J. S. — Enl., Aug. 11, 1861: W., 2nd Manassas (Aug. 30, 1862): POW, Cold Harbor (June 1, 1864): Exchanged, Mar., 1865.

(1) HALL, THOS. A. — Missing, believed killed, Antietam (Sept. 17, 1862).

HARRIS, W. O. — Enl., Aug. 11, 1861 at Richmond: W. (mouth), Gaines' Mill (June 27, 1862): Paroled, Newton, No. Car., Apr. 19, 1865.

(1) HICKMAN, J. O. A. — Dischgd. (epilepsy), Feb. 18, 1862.

(1) HOLCOMBE, ABSOLOM — See list of "Non-Comm. Officers" above.

(1) HOUK, WM. — W. (leg), Gaines' Mill (June 27, 1862): AWOL, Summer, 1864: Took Fed. oath, Nov. 20, 1864.

(1) JARRETT, JOHN J. — K., 2nd Manassas (Aug. 30, 1862).

JOHNSON, J. T. — Hospitalized, Fall, 1862: No other record.

(1) JOHNSON, N. T. — See list of "Non-Comm. Officers" above.

(1) JOHNSON, NATHAN — Present for duty, Aug., 1862: No other record.

(1) KELLEY, DANIEL — AWOL, Aug., 1864: No other record.

KELLEY, F. M. — Enl., June 25, 1862: AWOL, Aug., 1864: Paroled, Talladega, Ala., May 29, 1865.

KELLEY, MARION — Enl., July 29, 1862: No other record.

(1) KELLEY, W. J. — K., 2nd Manassas (Aug. 30, 1862).

(1) KENNEDY, CHAS. S. — Dischgd. (tuberculosis), Oct. 31, 1862.

(1) KING, F. R. — W., Fredericksburg (Dec. 13, 1862): AWOL, Jan., 1864.

(1) LANGLEY, JOHN J. — See list of "Officers" above.

LEDFORD, MILAS — Enl., July 30, 1861: W., Fredericksburg (Dec. 18, 1862): POW, Gettysburg (July 5, 1863): Paroled, July 31, 1865.

(1) LOWERY, A. J. — W. (neck), Antietam (Sept. 17, 1862): W., accidentally by his own file leader, July 28, 1864: Several fingers amputated.

LUSK, JOHN — Enl., Aug. 11, 1861 at Richmond: Dischgd., Sept. 20, 1864.

(1) MARTIN, MALACHI — W., 2nd Manassas (Aug. 30, 1862): No record after Nov., 1862.

(1) MURDOCK, E. F. M. — Paroled, Nashville, May 6, 1865: No other record.

(1) NAVE, J. A. — See list of "Non-Comm. Officers" above.

(1) NORWOOD, JOS. W. — Died, Apr. 25, 1862.

(1) PANNEL, WM. L. — W., 2nd Manassas (Aug. 30, 1862): Paroled, Newton, No. Car., Apr. 19, 1865.

(1) PERKINS, WM. — W., Gettysburg (July 2, 1863): POW, Cold Harbor (June 1, 1864): Exchanged, Feb. 20, 1865.

RICHEY, JAS. A. — Enl., Nov. 14, 1861 at Calhoun, Ga.: POW, Cold Harbor (June 1, 1864): Paroled, July 7, 1865.

RUSSAU (or ROUSSEAU), R. H. V. B. — Enl., July 2, 1861: W., 2nd Manassas (Aug. 30, 1862): AWOL, Aug., 1864.

SAMPSON, F. M. — Enl., Aug. 11, 1861: W., Gaines' Mill (June 27, 1862): Arm amputated.

(1) SANDERS, B. F. — See list of "Non-Comm. Officers" above.

(1) SHIPMAN, SAMUEL — W. (knee & arm), Chancellorsville (May 3, 1863): AWOL, Sept., 1863.

(1)   SILK, (or SILKS), WM. — On detached duty, Summer, 1862: No other record.

SMITH, E. M. — Transfd. to Co. E, 18th Ga. Inf., from 23rd Ga. Inf. Regt., Aug. 31, 1861: K., 2nd Manassas (Aug. 30, 1862).

(1)   SMITH, JAS. M. — W. (hip & stomach), Gaines' Mill (June 27, 1862): Died, July 9, 1862, from wounds.

SMITH, T. J. — Transfd. to Co. E, 18th Ga. Inf., from 23rd Ga. Inf. Regt., Jan. 1, 1862: K., 2nd Manassas (Aug. 30, 1862).

UNDERWOOD, E. J. — Enl., Sept. 28, 1862 at Calhoun, Ga.: AWOL, May, 1864.

VERNON, J. C. — Enl., Sept. 28, 1862 at Calhoun, Ga.: AWOL, Jan., 1864.

(1)   WILLIS, D. — Died at Richmond, May 19, 1862.

★   ★   ★   ★   ★

MEMBERS OF COMPANY E, 18TH GA. INF. REGT., WHO WERE NOT PRESENT FOR DUTY DURING THE PERIOD THAT THE REGIMENT WAS ASSIGNED TO HOOD'S TEXAS BRIGADE (NOV., 1861-NOV., 1862)

OFFICERS

NONE

NON-COMMISSIONED OFFICERS

Blackstone, R. M., Sgt. (No record prior to Sept., 1863)

(1) Pritchett, Jas. R., 4Cpl. (Transfd. out, Sept., 1861)

(1) Smith, Wm. T., 3Cpl. (No record after Nov., 1861)

(1) Swann, M. S., 3Sgt. (Transfd. out, Dec., 1861)

Vaughn, B. F., Sgt. (No record prior to July, 1864)

PRIVATES

(1) Alexander, Thos. P. (Dischgd., Oct., 1861)

(1) Ballentine, Josiah J. (D., Sept., 1861)

(1) Ballentine, W. H. (D., Oct., 1861)

Childers, H. Curtis (Enl., Sept., 1863)

Collins, E. M. (No record prior to Apr., 1865)

Davis, T. C. (No record prior to Apr., 1865)

(1) Dooly, Thos. B. (Dischgd., Nov., 1861)

Doyal, John (Dischgd., disability, Sept., 1861)

(1) Ellis, B. F. (No entry after June, 1861)

Goodman, C. S. (D., Aug., 1861)

Grant, R. R. (No record after Oct., 1861)

Guyton, M. J. (Enl., Mar., 1863)
Hassett, John M. (Enl., June, 1863)
Kelly, John W. (Enl., May, 1864)
(1) Nally, Benson (Dischgd., Nov., 1861)
(1) Nave, D. W. (Dischgd., Dec., 1861)
(1) Nave, W. R. (Deserted, July, 1861)
Nesbit, J. S. (Enl., May, 1864)
(1) Pannel, J. L. (Dischgd., disability, Aug., 1861)
Ramblit, F. P. (No record prior to Feb., 1863)
(1) Satterfield, J. L. (Dischgd., July, 1861)

(1) Smith, J. S. (Dischgd., disability, July, 1861)
(1) Smith, W. S. (Deserted, July, 1861)
(1) Smith, W. T. (Deserted, July, 1861)
Rooks, Arch. (No record prior to May, 1864)
Thompson, C. C. (Deserted, July, 1861)
(1) Walker, M. L. (Dischgd., July, 1861)
Warwick, T. J. (Dischgd., disability (rheumatism), Nov., 1861)

18TH GA. VOL. INF. REGT.

COMPANY F − *DAVIS GUARDS*

Company was organized in Bartow County, Georgia, during the Spring of 1861. It rendezvoused, recruited & trained at Camp McDonald, Cobb County, Georgia, in late June & in July. The men were mustered into the Confederate service, "for three years," at Richmond, Va., on or about Aug. 9, 1861.

Key

(1) Original member of Company. (2) Paroled at Appomattox.
K (Killed), W (Wounded), POW (Prisoner of War)
AWOL (Absent Without Leave)

OFFICERS

(1)   HARDIN, JOHN F. Capt. − Orig. 3Lt. of Co.: Elect., 2Lt., Oct. 31, 1861: W., 2nd Manassas (Aug. 30, 1862): Prom., 1Lt., Feb. 17, 1863: Prom., Capt., Nov. 26, 1863: No record after Feb., 1865.
(1)   ROPER, JOEL COLE, Sr. Capt. − Orig. Capt. of Co.: W., 2nd Manassas (Aug. 30, 1862): Resgnd. commission, Nov. 26, 1863: Elect., Repr. in Ga. Legislature from Bartow County.
REYNOLDS, JOHN C. 1Lt. − Orig. 4Sgt. of Co.: W., Gaines' Mill (June 27, 1862): W., Antietam (Sept. 17, 1862): Elect., 2Lt., Feb. 17, 1863: Elect., 1Lt., Nov. 26, 1863: No record after Jan., 1865.

(1)   WOOLLEY, ANDREW F., Jr. 1Lt. — See roster, "Regmtl. Hdqtrs., 18th Ga. Inf."

BRANDON, JEFFERSON R. 2Lt. — Orig. Pvt. in Co.: Elect., 3Lt., Mar., 1863: Prom., 2Lt., Nov. 26, 1863: POW, Sayler's Cr. (Apr. 6, 1865): Confined at Johnson's Is., Ohio: Paroled, June 18, 1865.

REYNOLDS, BENJ. F. 3Lt. — Orig. Pvt. in Co.: Elect., 3Lt., Oct. 1, 1861: Died, Mar. 6, 1862.

ROLAND, JOHN 3Lt. — Orig. 1Sgt. of Co.: Elect., 3Lt., Mar. 6, 1862: Cashiered, Nov. 13, 1862.

WHITAKER, FOUNTAIN 3Lt. — Enl. as a Pvt., Feb. 26, 1862: Elect., 3Lt., Jan. 22, 1864: POW, Cedar Cr. (Oct. 19, 1864): Confined at Ft. Delaware: Paroled, June 17, 1865.

NON-COMMISSIONED OFFICERS

ARNOLD, LARKIN B. 2Cpl. — Orig. Pvt. in Co.: Prom., 2Cpl., Dec. 15, 1861: K., Antietam (Sept. 17, 1862).

BOYCE, JAS. R. 4Cpl. — Orig. Pvt. in Co.: Prom., 4Cpl., Aug., 1862: W., 2nd Manassas (Aug. 30, 1862): Died of wound.

BRADFORD, WM. J. 4Sgt. — Orig. Pvt. in Co.: Appt. 4Cpl.: W., Chancellorsville (May 3, 1863): Appt. 4Sgt.: POW, Burkeville, Va. (Apr. 6, 1865): Paroled, June 25, 1865.

(1)   BRANDON, WM. JOS. 2Sgt. — Orig. 1Cpl. of Co.: Appt. 2Sgt., Jan., 1862: POW, E. Tenn., Dec. 5, 1863: Confined at Rock Is., Ill.: Paroled, June 17, 1865.

(1)   CANTRELL, JAS. A. 5Sgt. — Orig. 5Sgt. of Co.: Reduced to Pvt.: POW, Gettysburg (July 2, 1863): Escaped: POW, Burkeville (Apr. 6, 1865): Paroled, June 14, 1865.

DURHAM, FRANCIS M. 2Cpl. — Orig. Pvt. in Co.: W., Gaines' Mill (June 27, 1862): Appt. 2Cpl., 1862: W., Fredericksburg (Dec. 13, 1862): Arm amputated.

(1)   EARP, A. J. 3Sgt. — Orig. 3Sgt. of Co.: W., Gaines' Mill (June 27, 1862): K., Fredericksburg (Dec. 13, 1862).

(1)   FORREST, J. W. 2Sgt. — Orig. 2Sgt. of Co.: Resgnd. as Sgt., Dec. 5, 1861: Detailed to Blacksmith Shop: POW, E. Tenn., Dec. 4, 1863.

FOSTER, JOHN D. 2Cpl. — Orig. Pvt. in Co.: W., Gaines' Mill (June 27, 1862): W. (chest) & POW, Antietam (Sept. 17, 1862): Paroled, Sept. 30, 1862: Dischgd. on Surg. Cert.

(1)   GALPHIN, THOS. 5Sgt. — Orig. 3Cpl. of Co.: Prom., 2Sgt., Dec. 1, 1861: W., 2nd Manassas (Aug. 30, 1862): Prom., 5Sgt.: No record after Nov., 1864.

HOWARD, FRANCIS M. 5Sgt. — Orig. Pvt. in Co.: POW, Winchester, Va. (Dec. 22, 1862): Paroled, Jan., 1863: Appt. 5Sgt., Jan. 1, 1864: K., Wilderness (May 6, 1864).

KENNEDY, JOS. J. 4Cpl. — Enl. as a Pvt., July 19, 1861 at Richmond: Appt. 4Cpl., Mar. 1, 1864: No record after Nov., 1864.

McBRYDE (or McBRIDE), ISAAC W.   1Sgt. — Transfd. to Co. F as a Pvt. from the 12th Miss. Inf. Regt., Oct. 11, 1861: Appt. 5Sgt., Jan., 1862: Appt. 1Sgt., Jan. 1, 1864: Paroled, Augusta, Ga., May 19, 1865.

(1) MURCHISON, JOHN D.   4Cpl. — Orig. 4Cpl. of Co.: Dischgd. for inefficiency, Dec. 11, 1861.

MOSTELLER, A. H.   Sgt. — Enl. as a Pvt., Apr. 1, 1862: Appt. Sgt.: W. & POW, Sayler's Cr. (Apr. 6, 1865).

PINSON, AUGUSTINE F.   3Cpl. — Enl. as a Pvt., July 30, 1861: Appt. 3Cpl., 1863: AWOL, Summer, 1864.

RAMSEY, RANDALL   1Cpl. — Orig. Pvt. in Co.: Appt. 1Cpl., Dec. 17, 1861: No other record.

(1) REYNOLDS, JOHN C.   4Sgt. — See list of "Officers" above.

REYNOLDS, LARKIN B.   2Cpl. — Orig. Pvt. in Co.: Appt. 2Cpl., Nov. 10, 1861: Dischgd., Aug., 1862: Ruffin Earp his substitute.

(1) ROLAND, JOHN   1Sgt. — See list of "Officers" above.

PRIVATES

(1) ALLEN, ZACHARIAH T. — Dischgd. for disability, Dec. 7, 1861.

(1) ARNOLD, LARKIN B. — See list of "Non-Comm. Officers" above.

(1) BOYCE, JAS. R. — See list of "Non-Comm. Officers" above.

(1) BRADFORD, WM. J. — See list of "Non-Comm. Officers" above.

BRANDON, DAVID P. — Enl., Apr. 1, 1862 at Kingston, Ga.: W., 2nd Manassas (Aug. 30, 1862): W., Antietam (Sept. 17, 1862): POW, Sayler's Cr. (Apr. 6, 1865).

(1) BRANDON, JEFFERSON R. — See list of "Officers" above.

BREWER, J. HARRISON — Enl., May 12, 1862 at Kingston, Ga.: Died at Richmond of typhoid fever, June 22, 1864.

(1) BROCK, JAS. N. — W., 2nd Manassas (Aug. 30, 1862): W., Antietam (Sept. 17, 1862): POW, E. Tenn., Dec. 5, 1863: Died in Fed. prison of smallpox, Feb. 8, 1864.

(1) BROOKS, SAMPSON — W., Antietam (Sept. 17, 1862): Died of wound, Sept. 20, 1862.

BYERS, WM. — Enl., Oct. 23, 1861 at Calhoun, Ga.: W., Gaines' Mill (June 27, 1862): Deserted, took Fed. oath, Feb., 1865.

CALDWELL, J. W. — Enl., Feb. 18, 1862 in Bartow County, Ga.: W., Antietam (Sept. 17, 1862): Died of wound, Oct. 15, 1862.

(1) CALVERT, JAS. — K., 2nd Manassas (Aug. 30, 1862).

(1)
(2) CANTRELL, MOSES M. — Paroled, Appomattox (Apr. 12, 1865): No other record.

CANTRELL, SAMUEL C. — Enl., Oct. 23, 1861 at Calhoun, Ga.: W. (hand), Antietam (Sept. 17, 1862): Finger amputated: AWOL, Spring, 1864.

(1) CONN, GEO. W. — W., 2nd Manassas (Aug. 30, 1862): Died from wound, Jan. 14, 1863.

(1) CONN, JAS. M. — W., 2nd Manassas (Aug. 30, 1862): Transfd. to 3rd Btln., Ga. Sharpshooters, June 8, 1863.

(1) CONN, THOS. N. — Sick, Feb., 1862: Dischgd., Apr., 1862.

CRYER, WM. — Hospitalized, Oct., 1862: No other record.

(1) DAWSON, THOS. — W., 2nd Manassas (Aug. 30, 1862): W., Antietam
(2) (Sept. 17, 1862): Paroled, Appomattox (Apr. 12, 1865).

(2) DICKERSON, JOS. G. — Enl., Mar. 13, 1862 in Bartow Co., Ga.: W., Antietam (Sept. 17, 1862): Paroled, Appomattox (Apr. 12, 1865).

DRUMMOND, S. H. — Enl., Feb. 26, 1862 at Kingston, Ga.: POW, Cedar Cr. (Oct. 19, 1864): Exchanged, Jan. 17, 1865.

DRUMMOND, W. H. — Enl., Sept. 1, 1862 at Calhoun, Ga.: POW, Cold Harbor (June 1, 1864): Died in Fed. prison, Sept. 19, 1864.

(1) DURHAM, FRANCIS M. — See list of "Non-Comm. Officers" above.

EARP, RUFFIN — Enl., Aug. 15, 1862 at Richmond: Substitute for 2Cpl. Larkin B. Reynolds: AWOL, Spring, 1864.

(1) EAVES, L. P. — K., Antietam (Sept. 17, 1862).
(1) ELLIOTT, DAVID W. — Died in Bartow County, Ga., Feb. 17, 1862.
(1) ELLIS, J. V. — AWOL, June, 1864: No other record.
(1) ELLIS, JOHN C. — Present for duty, Feb., 1862: No other record.
(1) ELLIS, WM. M. — Present for duty, Aug., 1864: No other record.

FORSEE, JOHN — Enl., Oct. 23, 1861: AWOL, Oct., 1862.

(1) FOSTER, JOHN D. — See list of "Non-Comm. Officers" above.

FREEMAN, Z. — Enl., Feb. 26, 1862 at Kingston, Ga.: W., Gaines' Mill (June 27, 1862): Disabled.

(1) GAINES, J. BENJ. — Paroled, Appomattox (Apr. 12, 1865): No other
(2) record.

(1) GREEN, ROBT. G. — Died, Ashland, Va., Apr. 27, 1862.

(1) GUEST, WM. G. — W., 2nd Manassas (Aug. 30, 1862): AWOL, Aug., 1864.

HACKETT, G. T. — Hospitalized, Fall, 1862: No other record.

(1) HACKETT, THOS. J. — W., Gaines' Mill (June 27, 1862): K., Fredericksburg (Dec. 13, 1862).

HANIE, JOHN — Enl., Mar. 17, 1862 in Bartow Co., Ga.: Dischgd. for disability, Aug. 4, 1862.

HAY, WM. — Enl., Feb. 19, 1862 in Bartow Co., Ga.: W., 2nd Manassas (Aug. 30, 1862).

HAYS, JASPER — Enl., Feb. 26, 1862 in Bartow Co., Ga.: POW, Cedar Cr. (Oct. 19, 1864): Exchanged, Mar. 28, 1865.

HENDERSON, ANDREW P. — Enl., Aug. 6, 1861 at Richmond: W. (arm), Chancellorsville (May 3, 1863).

HENDERSON, J. P. — Hospitalized, Summer, 1862: No other record.

(1) HOWARD, FRANCIS M. — See list of "Non-Comm. Officers" above.

HUBBERTS, C. J. — W., Gaines' Mill (June 27, 1862): No other record.

JACKSON, JERRY — Enl., Mar. 15, 1862 at Fredericksburg: Died of typhoid fever, Aug. 20, 1862 at Lynchburg, Va.

JACKSON, JOS. N. — Enl., Mar. 15, 1862 at Fredericksburg: Died, acute diarrhea, May 27, 1862.

JACKSON, PRUITT — Enl., Aug. 20, 1861 at Richmond: Died, Winter, 1862-63.

JACKSON, WM. A. — Enl., July 19, 1861: W., Gaines' Mill (June 27, 1862): Died from wound.

KAY, WM. — Enl., Feb. 26, 1862 at Kingston, Ga.: W., Fredericksburg (Dec. 13, 1862): POW, Cedar Cr. (Oct. 19, 1864).

KENNEDY, GEO. H. — Enl., Mar. 12, 1862: Died at Ashland, Va., July 31, 1862.

KENNEDY, JAS. L. — Enl., Mar. 15, 1862 in Bartow Co., Ga.: W., 1862: Died at Richmond, July 31, 1862.

KENNEDY, JOS. J. — See list of "Non-Comm. Officers" above.

KING, ALONZO A. — Enl., July 19, 1861: W., 2nd Manassas (Aug. 30, 1862): Present for duty, Nov., 1864.

(1)   KING, JAS. M. — POW, Cold Harbor (June 1, 1864): Paroled, July 7, 1865.

(1)   LAWSON, JASPER B. — Transfd. to 3rd Btln., Ga. Sharpshooters, June 8, 1863.

(1)   LINDSEY, JACOB — Sick, Summer, 1862: Present for duty, Jan., 1865.

LONG, BYRAM — POW, Winchester, Dec. 22, 1862: No other record.

LOVELESS, R. B. — Hospitalized, Spring, 1862: No other record.

(1)   LOWREY, JOHN — POW, E. Tenn., Dec. 3, 1863: Paroled, June 19, 1865.

(1)   LUMPKIN, A. J. — Dischgd. for dropsy, Aug. 4, 1862.

LUMPKIN, G. M. — Present for duty, Nov., 1862: No other record.

LUMPKIN, HORACE W. — Present for duty, Nov., 1862: No other record.

(1)   LUMPKIN, JESSE M. — W., 2nd Manassas (Aug. 30, 1862): W., Antietam (Sept. 17, 1862): No record after Jan., 1863.

LUMPKIN, WILSON — Enl., Feb. 28, 1862 at Kingston, Ga.: Died of typhoid fever, Sept. 13, 1863.

(1)   MATHEWS, ANDREW J. — Died, Apr. 18, 1862.

McBRYDE (or McBRIDE), ISAAC W. — See list of "Non-Comm. Officers" above.

McDANIEL, ALLEN — Enl., Sept. 19, 1862 at Calhoun, Ga.: POW, Burkeville, Va. (Apr. 6, 1865).

McFADDEN, C. D. — Enl., Apr. 1, 1862 in Bartow Co., Ga.: W., Chancellorsville (May 3, 1863): Died of wounds, May 23, 1863.

(1)   MEDLOCK, JAS. — Deserted, 1863.

MEEKS, WM. S. — Enl., Mar. 4, 1862 at Kingston, Ga.: POW, Boonsboro (Sept. 15, 1862): Exchanged, Oct. 2, 1862: POW, Knoxville, Jan. 21, 1864: Took Fed. oath, Feb. 14, 1865.

MILWOOD, J. — Hospitalized, Fall, 1862: No other record.

(1)   MOONEY, JAS. PETER — Dischgd., Mar., 1862: Provided substitute, L. C. Smith.

(1)   MOONEY, W. A. — Dischgd. (chronic erysipelas), June 26, 1862.

(1)   MOORE, JOHN H. — W. (knee), Spotsylvania (May 17, 1864).

MOSTELLER, A. H. — See list of "Non-Comm. Officers" above.

MOSTELLER, EZEKIEL — Enl., Apr. 25, 1862: K., 2nd Manassas (Aug. 30, 1862).

MOSTELLER, GEO. M. — Enl., Oct. 23, 1861: W., 2nd Manassas (Aug. 30, 1862): Present for duty, Nov., 1864.

(1)   MOTES, WM. A. — K., Chancellorsville (May 3, 1863).

(1)   NICHOLS, LINDSEY J. — W. (hand), Gaines' Mill (June 27, 1862): Court-martialed, Aug. 21, 1863: Present for duty, Nov., 1864.

(1)   NOWLIN, DAVID W. — K., Fredericksburg (Dec. 13, 1862).

NOWLIN, SAMUEL — Transfd. to Co. F from the 8th Ga. Inf. Regt., Oct. 8, 1862: Substitute for Wm. F. Parish: POW, Cold Harbor (June 1, 1864).

OWENS, ALFRED — Enl., Mar. 1, 1862 in Bartow Co., Ga.: POW, Gettysburg (July 2, 1863): Paroled, Aug. 24, 1863: Deserted, Mar., 1865.

(1) PARISH, WM. F. — W., Gaines' Mill (June 27, 1862): Transfd. to the 8th Ga. Inf. Regt. in exchange for Samuel Nowlin, Oct. 8, 1862.

PINSON, AUGUSTINE F. — See list of "Non-Comm. Officers" above.

(1) PINSON, JASPER — W., Fredericksburg (Dec. 13, 1862): Court-martialed, Aug. 21, 1863: Present for duty, Aug., 1864.

POWELL, J. — Hospitalized, Spring, 1862: No other record.

(1) RAMSEY, RANDALL — See list of "Non-Comm. Officers" above.

(1) REED, A. J. — W. (hip), Gaines' Mill (June 27, 1862): Died of wound, Dec. 15, 1864.

(1) REYNOLDS, BENJ. F. — See list of "Officers" above.

(1) REYNOLDS, JAS. C. — Present for duty, Summer, 1862: No other record.

REYNOLDS, JAS. F. — Enl., Mar. 3, 1862 at Kingston, Ga.: Dischgd., Feb. 29, 1864.

(1) REYNOLDS, JOHN A. — Dischgd. (bronchitis), Sept. 7, 1861: Re-enl., May, 1862: Present for duty, Winter, 1864-65.

(1) REYNOLDS, JOHN CASWELL — Died at Richmond, June 6, 1862.

(1) REYNOLDS, LARKIN B. — See list of "Non-Comm. Officers" above.

SARTER, A. G. — W., 2nd Manassas (Aug. 30, 1862).

(1) SARTER, ANDREW J. — W., Gaines' Mill (June 27, 1862): AWOL, Fall, 1864.

SMITH, L. C. — Enl., Jan., 1862 at Fredericksburg: Substitute for Jas. P. Mooney: W., Gaines' Mill (June 27, 1862): Died from wound.

(1) SPENCE, MALACHI — AWOL, Nov., 1862: No other record.

STONE, J. P. — Enl., Feb. 27, 1862 in Bartow Co., Ga.: Present for duty, Jan., 1865.

STONE, W. G. — Enl., Feb. 27, 1862 in Bartow, Ga.: POW, Burkeville, Va. (Apr. 6, 1865).

TEMPLETON, WM. A. — Enl., Sept. 2, 1861 at Richmond: Died of pneumonia, May 16, 1862 at Farmville, Va.: Buried in Holly-wood Cemetery, Richmond.

(1) THOMPSON, JOHN W. — POW, Spotsylvania (May 22, 1864): Paroled, Elmira prison, N.Y., June 14, 1865.

(1) UNDERWOOD, ABNER J. — Dischgd. for "inefficiency," Jan. 25, 1862.

WHITAKER, FOUNTAIN — See list of "Officers" above.

WINGO, WM. — Enl., Feb. 26, 1862 in Bartow Co., Ga.: POW, Antietam (Sept. 17, 1862): Exchanged, Nov. 10, 1862: W., Chancellorsville (May 3, 1863): Leg amputated: Died, June 1, 1863.

WOOD, WILEY — Enl., Aug. 19, 1862 at Calhoun, Ga.: W. & POW, E. Tenn., Nov. 29, 1863: Paroled from Ft. Delaware, Feb., 1865.

(1) WRIGHT, RICHMOND B. — POW, near Knoxville, Dec. 3, 1863: Paroled from Rock Is., Ill., June 20, 1865.

* * * * *

MEMBERS OF COMPANY F, 18TH GA. INF. REGT., WHO WERE NOT PRESENT FOR DUTY DURING THE PERIOD THAT THE REGIMENT WAS ASSIGNED TO HOOD'S TEXAS BRIGADE (NOV., 1861-NOV., 1862)

OFFICERS

(1) Center, W. B., 1Lt. (Orig. 1Lt. of Co.: Resgnd., Sept. 11, 1861)

NON-COMMISSIONED OFFICERS

(1) Dodd, Thos. W., 2Cpl. (Orig. 2Cpl. of Co.: Transfd. out, Nov., 1861)

PRIVATES

(1) Barker, Marcus (Dischgd., July, 1861)
(1) Brooks, J. J. (D., Sept., 1861)
(1) Butler, Jas. B. (Dischgd., Nov., 1861)
Connell, J. (No record prior to Nov., 1863)
(1) Crocker, A. (Dischgd., Oct., 1861)
Davis, L. P. (No record after June, 1861)
(1) Earp, Wm. (Dischgd., Nov., 1861)
(1) Fuller, John (AWOL, Oct., 1861)
Kay, Geo. (Enl., Feb., 1863)
Kennedy, W. G. (Enl., July, 1864)
King, Jasper A. (Enl., Dec., 1863)
Lawson, T. (No record prior to Nov., 1862)
Lindsey, John (Enl., Apr., 1863)
Lindsey, L. (No record after July, 1861)
Lowrey, Wm. W. (Dischgd., Oct., 1861)
Lumpkin, H. H. (No record after June, 1861)
Lumpkin, H. V. (No record after June, 1861)
Mackerson, F. (No record prior to Apr., 1865)
Melton, Hiram (Enl., Aug., 1863)
Mosteller, Andrew J. (Enl., Mar., 1864)
Parker, S. T. (Enl., Jan., 1863)
Phillips, T. J. (D., Sept., 1861)
Pitts, W. S. (D., Sept., 1861)
Saye, J. F. (No record)
Walker, Wm. (Enl., Nov., 1863)
Wheeler, B. Y. (No record prior to May, 1865)
Whitley, Jas. L. (No record after Nov., 1861)
Wilton, H. (No record prior to June, 1864)

18TH GA. VOL. INF. REGT.

COMPANY G — *LEWIS VOLUNTEERS*

Company was organized in Bartow County, Georgia, during the Spring of 1861. It rendezvoused, recruited and trained at Camp McDonald, Cobb County, Georgia in late June and in July. The men were mustered into the Confederate service, "for three years," at Richmond, Va., on or about August 9, 1861.

Key

(1) Original member of Company. (2) Paroled at Appomattox.
K (Killed), W (Wounded), POW (Prisoner of War)
AWOL (Absent Without Leave)

OFFICERS

MADDOX, JAS. F. Capt. — Orig. 3Sgt. of Co.: Elect., 3Lt., Sept. 5, 1862: Elect., 1Lt., Nov. 4, 1862: Prom., Capt., Dec. 8, 1863: Deserted, June, 1864: Dropped from the rolls, Feb., 1865.

(1) MADDOX, JOHN COOK Capt. — Orig. Capt. of Co.: W. (side), Gaines' Mill (June 27, 1862): Resgnd., disabled, Aug. 28, 1862.

(1) MADDOX, GEO. W. Capt. — Orig. 2Lt. of Co.: Elect., 1Lt., May 13, 1862: Prom., Capt., Sept. 5, 1862: W., Antietam (Sept. 17, 1862): Resgnd. due to ill health, Dec. 8, 1863.

LYON, T. H. 1Lt. — POW, Cold Harbor (June 1, 1864): No other record.

LYONS, PETER C. 1Lt. — Orig. Pvt. in Co.: W., Gaines' Mill (June 27, 1862): Appt. Regmtl. Orderly Sgt., July 22, 1862: Prom., 2Lt., Nov. 4, 1862: Prom., 1Lt., Dec. 8, 1863: POW, Cold Harbor (June 1, 1864): Died of chronic diarrhea, Mar. 13, 1865 at Fed. prison, Ft. Delaware.

(1) TATE, FARISH CARTER 1Lt. — Orig. 1Lt. of Co.: Died at Richmond, May 13, 1862.

WELLS, JOHN S. 2Lt. — Orig. Pvt. in Co.: Appt. 5Sgt., Oct. 27, 1861: Elect., 3Lt., May, 1863: Prom., 2Lt., Dec. 8, 1863: POW, Cold Harbor (June 1, 1864): Paroled, June 17, 1865.

HARRIS, Z. N. 3 Lt. — Orig. Pvt. in Co.: Appt. Regmtl. Ordn. Sgt., May 25, 1862: Elect., 2Lt., July 4, 1862: Appt., 1Lt., Mar. 26, 1863: Refused appt. claiming "incompetency & disability": Resgnd: See Roster, "Regmtl. Hq., 18th Ga. Inf."

JONES, WM. 3Lt. — Orig. 1Sgt. of Co.: Elect., 3Lt., May 13, 1862: W. (hip), Gaines' Mill (June 27, 1862): Died from wound, July 1.

NON-COMMISSIONED OFFICERS

BAKER, W. B. 2Cpl. — Orig. Pvt. in Co.: Prom., 2Cpl., Winter, 1862-63: Deserted, E. Tenn., Nov. 4, 1863: No other record.

(1) BRAWNER, H. M. 1Cpl. — Orig. 1Cpl. of Co.: Reduced to ranks: POW, Cold Harbor (June 1, 1864): Paroled, June 21, 1865.

(1) BUISE, JAS. B. 1Sgt. — Orig. 2Sgt. of Co.: Reduced to ranks, Oct. 27, 1861: Appt. 1Sgt., May 13, 1862: No record after Aug., 1864.

CARNEY, JOHN Cpl. — Orig. Pvt. in Co.: W. (shoulder), Gaines' Mill (June 27, 1862): Prom., Cpl., Winter, 1862-63.

(1) DYKES, JOHN 2Cpl. — Orig. 2Cpl. of Co.: Dischgd., disability, Dec. 14, 1861: Re-enl., Mar., 1862 in Cav. Btln. of Phillips' Legion.

GRAY, JAS. 1Cpl. — Orig. Pvt. in Co.: POW, Boonsboro (Sept. 14, 1862): Exchanged, Nov. 10, 1862: Deserted, Nov. 14, 1863 in E. Tenn.

HARDIN, J. M. 4Sgt. — Orig. Pvt. in Co.: Appt. 4Sgt.: AWOL, Sept., 1863.

HARRIS, J. H. 2Sgt. — Orig. Pvt. in Co.: Appt. 2Sgt., Sept. 5, 1862: POW, Burkeville, Va. (Apr. 6, 1865).

(1) JONES, WM. 1Sgt. — See list of "Officers" above.

(1) MADDOX, JAS. F. 3Sgt. — See list of "Officers" above.

MAJOR, J. E. 5 Sgt. — Orig. Pvt. in Co.: Appt. 5Sgt., Oct. 27, 1861: K., Antietam (Sept. 17, 1862).

MORRIS, J. M. 3Cpl. — Orig. Pvt. in Co.: Appt. 3Cpl., Dec. 1, 1861: K., Gaines' Mill (June 27, 1862).

MYERS, A. L. 3Cpl. — Orig. Pvt. in Co.: Appt. 3Cpl.: W., Antietam (Sept. 17, 1862): POW, Farmville, Va. (Apr. 6, 1865).

PRATHER, E. J. 2Cpl. — Orig. Pvt. in Co.: Appt. 2Cpl., Dec. 9, 1861: W. & disabled at Jericho Ford, Va., May 23, 1864.

(1) RIPLEY, THOS. E. 2Sgt. — Orig. 4Sgt. of Co.: Appt. 3Sgt., Oct. 27, 1861: POW, near Knoxville, Dec. 3, 1863: Took Fed. oath at Rock Is., Ill. & enl. in the U.S. Army "for Frontier Service."

STRADLEY, D. M. 4Sgt. — Orig. Musician (drummer) of Co.: Appt. 4Sgt., Oct. 27, 1861: Reduced to Pvt.: Paroled, Newton, N.C., Apr. 19, 1865.

TITTLE, L. P. 3Cpl. — Orig. Pvt. in Co.: Appt. 3Cpl.: No record after Aug., 1862.

(1) TURNER, JAS. G. 1Cpl. — Orig. 4Cpl. of Co.: Appt. 1Cpl.: Died in Va., May 18, 1862.

MUSICIANS

BARNES, JAS. H. — Orig. Pvt. in Co.: Appt. Co. Fifer, Nov. 2, 1861: Died, Oct. 16, 1862 from injuries received in a R.R. accident.

(1) STRADLEY, D. M. — See list of "Non-Comm. Officers" above.

PRIVATES

(1) ALLEN, ANDREW J. — Deserted, took Fed. oath, Mar. 26, 1864.

ATERS, JOE J. — Hospitalized, Nov., 1862: W., near Fredericksburg (Dec. 18, 1862).

(1) BAGGETT, F. E. — POW, Spotsylvania (May 22, 1864): Took Fed. oath, jnd. U.S. Army, May 31, 1864.

(1) BAKER, W. B. — See list of "Non-Comm. Officers" above.

(1) BALLEW, THOS. P. — POW, Chattanooga, Dec. 4, 1863: Took Fed. oath, Nov. 6, 1864: Enl. in U.S. Navy.

(1) BARNES, ANDREW J. — W., 2nd Manassas (Aug. 30, 1862): POW, Knoxville, Tenn., Dec. 3, 1863: Paroled, June 17, 1865.

(1) BARNES, JAS. H. — See list of "Musicians" above.

(1) BARNES, WM. — No record after Aug., 1862.

(1) BARNES, WM. H. — POW, near Knoxville, Dec. 3, 1863: Paroled, June 17, 1865.

BISHOP, W. J. — No record after Oct., 1862.

(1) BISHOP, W. P. — Deserted, Aug. 1, 1864: Took Fed. oath, Sept. 13, 1864.

(1) BRADFORD, F. M. — Died (nephritis) at Petersburg, Feb. 27, 1863.

(1) BROWN, G. E. — AWOL, Summer, 1864: No other record.

(1) BROOM, J. E. — POW, Burkeville, Va. (Apr. 6, 1865).

(1) BURON, WM. H. — No record after Oct., 1862.

(1) CANTRELL, BANISTER — W. (thigh), Gaines' Mill (June 27, 1862): Transfd. to 23rd Ga. Inf. Regt., Aug. 1, 1862.

CANTRELL, P. — POW, Knoxville, Tenn., Dec. 3, 1863: Took Fed. oath, Oct. 17, 1864 & jnd. U.S. Army "for Frontier Service."

(1) CARNEY, JOHN — See list of "Non-Comm. Officers" above.

CARSON, M. T. — No record after Dec., 1862.

CARNER, LORENZO O. — Transfd. to Co. G, Dec. 1, 1861 from 23rd Ga. Inf. Regt.: POW, Knoxville, Tenn., Dec. 3, 1863.

(1) COLBERT, W. C. — Appt. courier for Gen. Wofford: Dischgd., July, 1864.

COLLINS, J. C. — POW, Antietam: Paroled, Nov. 12, 1862: No other record.

(1) DALTON, CLAIBORNE — Dischgd. (old age), Mar. 31, 1862.

(1) DAVIS, D. A. — POW, Knoxville, Tenn., Dec. 25, 1863: Died in Fed. prison of chronic diarrhea, Feb. 20, 1864.

(1) DAVIS, J. J. M. — POW, Strousburg, Va. (Oct. 19, 1864).

(1) DAVIS, JAS. E. — POW, Cold Harbor (June 1, 1864).

(1) DAVIS, NATH. O. — Deserted, Sept. 30, 1863.

DAVIS, W. V. — K., Fredericksburg (Dec. 13, 1862).

(1) DIXON, S. W. — W. (face), Gaines' Mill (June 27, 1862): Dischgd. for disability, Aug. 6, 1862.

DOBBS, ASA A. — Enl., Aug. 9, 1861 at Richmond: AWOL, Aug., 1864.

(1) DUCKETT, G. W. — Deserted at New Creek, W. Va., Mar., 1865: Took Fed. oath and sent north.

(1) DOUGLAS, HIRAM — No record after Aug., 1862.

(1) DUNAWAY, W. H. — Died at Manassas Junction, Va., Feb. 11, 1863.

(1) ERWIN, ABEL — Deserted, Jan. 28, 1865: POW, Feb. 10, 1865: Took Fed. oath.

(1) ETTERS, J. J. — Deserted, July 1, 1861: Arrested & returned to Co., July 12, 1861: AWOL, 1863.

FOWLER, J. W. — Enl., Oct. 2, 1861 in Va.: Died of typhoid fever in Richmond, Nov. 7, 1862.

(1) GLAYSON (or GLEASON), JOHN — POW, near Knoxville, Dec. 3, 1863: Took Fed. oath, Rock Is., Ill., and released: Volunteered for frontier service in the U.S. Army but was rejected.

(1) GRAY, JAS. — See list of "Non-Comm. Officers" above.

(1) HARDIN, J. M. — See list of "Non-Comm. Officers" above.

HARRIS, J. H. — See list of "Non-Comm. Officers" above.

(1) HARRIS, Z. N. See list of "Officers" above.

(1) HARWELL, VINES, Jr. — W. (ankle), Gaines' Mill (June 27, 1862): Died of wound, July 8, 1862.

HENDY, A. J. — W. (shoulder & back), Gaines' Mill (June 27, 1862).

(1) HILL, WM. — W. (leg), Gaines' Mill (June 27, 1862): W., Cedar Cr. (Oct. 19, 1864): Paroled, Apr. 30, 1865.

(1) HILLBORN, N. G. — No record after Oct., 1862.

(1) HILLS, WM. J. — W., Gaines' Mill (June 27, 1862).

(1) HUBBORD (or HUBBARD), W. P. — W. (pelvis) & POW, Gettysburg (July 2, 1862): No further record.

(1) JONES, BARNABAS — W. (eye), Malvern Hill (July 1, 1862): No record after Sept., 1862: May have been killed at Antietam.

(1) JONES, JAS. R. — Sick most of his enlistment: Transfd. out of the 18th Ga. Inf., Apr. 14, 1863.

KENDALL, J. B. — W. (thigh), Gaines' Mill (June 27, 1862): No other record.

(1) KEYS, E. A. — W., 2nd Manassas (Aug. 30, 1862): Deserted, E. Tenn., Mar. 15, 1864.

(1) LEE, O. G. — W., Jan. 31, 1862: No further record.

(1) LOVELADY, M. JACKSON — Transfd. to Co. G, Nov. 18, 1861 from the 23rd Ga. Inf. Regt.: AWOL, July, 1862.

(1) LYONS, PETER C. — See list of "Officers" above.

(1) MAJOR, J. E. — See list of "Non-Comm. Officers" above.

(1) MARSH, JOS. J. — Paroled, Talladega, Ala., May 24, 1865.

(1) MAXWELL, JAS. M. — Deserted, Nov. 4, 1863 in E. Tenn.: Took Fed. oath, Dec. 28, 1863 at Louisville, Ky.

McCARTY, JOS. M. — Enl., Sept. 27, 1861: POW, Knoxville, Dec. 3, 1863: Confined at Rock Is., Ill.: Exchanged, Mar. 2, 1865.

(1) MELTON, J. W. — Died, Richmond, Aug. 30, 1862.

MITCHELL, JOHN F. — Transfd. to Co. G, Dec. 1, 1861 from the 23rd Ga. Inf. Regt.: Died (typhoid fever), July 19, 1862 at Charlottesville, Va.

(1) MORRIS, J. M. — See list of "Non-Comm. Officers" above.

(1) MORRIS, MARTIN — W. (hand), Gaines' Mill (June 27, 1862): POW, Spotsylvania (May 22, 1864): Deserted, jnd. U.S. Army, May 31, 1864.

(1) MYERS, A. L. — See list of "Non-Comm. Officers" above.

(1) ODUM, J. C. — W. & POW, Gettysburg (July 2, 1863): Died in Fed. prison there, July 12, 1863.

(1) PATTERSON, ROBT. A. — No record after Oct., 1862.

(1) POTTS, JEFFERSON — POW, Cold Harbor (June 1, 1864): Paroled, June 21, 1865.

(1) PRATHER, E. J. — See list of "Non-Comm. Officers" above.

(1) PRINCE, J. M. — W. (head), Gaines' Mill (June 27, 1862).

(1) ROBERTS, J. S. — Paroled, Appomattox (Apr. 12, 1865).
(2)
(1) SMITH, ALBERT — Dischgd., Jan. 14, 1862 on Surg. Cert.: Re-enl.: W., 2nd Manassas (Aug. 30, 1862): Leg amputated: Paroled, Kingston, Ga., May 12, 1865.
(1) SMITH, EURICHUS — Deserted, 1863: No other record.
(1) SMITH, JOHN H. — Deserted, took Fed. oath, Feb. 29, 1864 at Chattanooga.
(1) STARNES, L. L. — Absent, sick, Jan., 1865: No other record.
     TAPP, E. S. — Transfd. to Co. G, Dec. 1, 1861 from the 23rd Ga. Inf. Regt.: Died at Dumfries, Va. from pneumonia, Dec. 15, 1861.
     TAYLOR, L. M. — Enl., Oct. 27, 1861 in Ga.: Deserted, "Gone Yankee," late 1863: Took Fed. oath, Mar. 14, 1864 at Chattanooga.
     THOMPSON, A. — POW, Ft. Delaware: Exchanged, Nov. 10, 1862: No other record.
(1) THOMPSON, NATHAN — W. (hip), Gaines' Mill (June 27, 1862): POW, Fredericksburg (June 11, 1864): Paroled, June 21, 1865.
(1) TITTLE, L. P. — See list of "Non-Comm. Officers" above.
     WARD, RICHARD M. — Enl., Feb. 18, 1862 at Ringgold, Ga.: Dischgd. for disability, Aug. 5, 1862.
(1) WELLS, JOHN S. — See list of "Officers" above.
(1) WHITMORE, E. T. — W. (knee), Spotsylvania (May 15, 1864): No other record.
(1) WHITTEN, G. W. — W., Antietam (Sept. 17, 1862): AWOL, Fall, 1863.
(1) WHITWORTH, S. W. — Dischgd., Jan. 14, 1862 for physical disability.
(1) WIGGINS, J. M. — Dischgd., Jan. 11, 1865: Paroled, May 20, 1865 at Bainbridge, Ga.

* * * * *

MEMBERS OF COMPANY G, 18TH GA. INF. REGT. WHO WERE NOT PRESENT FOR DUTY DURING THE PERIOD THAT THE REGIMENT WAS ASSIGNED TO HOOD'S TEXAS BRIGADE (NOV., 1861 TO NOV., 1862).

OFFICERS

(1) Powers, Jesse, Lt. (See roster, "Regmtl. Hdqtrs., 18th Ga. Inf.")

NON-COMMISSIONED OFFICERS

(1) Kelley, A. M. D., 3Cpl. (Orig. 3Cpl. of Co.: Transfd. to the 23rd Ga. Inf. Regt., Nov. 1, 1861)

MUSICIANS

(1) Harwell, Buck (Dischgd., Nov., 1861)

PRIVATES

Baker, A. M. (Deserted, Aug., 1861)

Bishop, J. H. (No record prior to July, 1864)

Burt, Jas. A. (D., Sept. 6, 1861)

Campbell, Isaac (Dischgd., Aug., 1861)

(1) Cantrell, Silas (Dischgd., disability, Nov., 1861)

(1) Cox, Geo. W. (Transfd. out, Fall, 1861)

(1) Cox, Jas. M. (Dischgd., Nov., 1861)

Crawford, W. L. (No record prior to June, 1864)

(1) Dowdy, A. S. (Transfd. out, Nov., 1861)

(1) Ferguson, Wm. (Transfd. out, Nov., 1861)

(1) Grady, G. W. (Deserted, Aug., 1861)

(1) Harney, John (No record after Oct., 1861)

Hawkins, E. (Only record is clothing receipt, Feb., 1864)

(1) Kerney, John (No record after Nov., 1861)

Major, J. M. (No record after Oct., 1861)

Martin, W. A. (Dischgd., disability, Aug., 1861)

McClinton, John F. (No record prior to 1864)

Mitts, C. (No record prior to Gettysburg)

Roach, Jas. (Transfd. out, Nov., 1861)

Roberts, Jas. (No record prior to June, 1864)

Roberts, Stephen T. (Transfd. out, Nov., 1861)

Rogers, J. (Dischgd., May, 1861)

Vineyard, T. A. (No record prior to Nov., 1862)

Wade, Wm. (No record after Aug., 1862)

18TH GA. VOL. INF. REGT.

COMPANY H — *ROWLAND HIGHLANDERS*

Company was organized in Bartow County, Georgia, during the Spring of 1861. It rendezvoused, recruited & trained at Camp McDonald, Cobb County, Georgia, in late June & in July. The men were mustered into the Confederate Service, "for three years," at Richmond, Va., on or about Aug. 9, 1861.

Key

(1) Original member of Company. (2) Paroled at Appomattox.
K (Killed), W (Wounded), POW (Prisoner of War)
AWOL (Absent Without Leave)

OFFICERS

(1) FORD, FRANK M. Capt. — Orig. Capt. of Co.: Elect., Lt. Col. & transfd. out, Mar. 25, 1864.

(1) GRANT, JOHN Capt. — Orig. 2Lt. of Co.: W. (face), Gaines' Mill (June 27, 1862): W., Antietam (Sept. 17, 1862): Elect., 1Lt., Jan. 17, 1863: Prom., Capt., Mar. 25, 1864: AWOL, Jan., 1865.

SMITH, GEO. R. 1Lt. — Orig. Pvt. in Co.: W. (leg), Gaines' Mill (June 27, 1862): Elect., 3Lt., Jan. 17, 1863: Prom., 2Lt., May, 1863: Prom., 1Lt., Mar. 25, 1864: Furlough to Georgia, Feb., 1865.

(1) WOFFORD, WM. L. 1Lt. — Orig. 1Lt. of Co.: W., 2nd Manassas (Aug. 30, 1862): Appt. Aide-de-Camp for Gen. Wofford & 1Lt., May 25, 1863.

KING, F. A. 2Lt. — Orig. Pvt. in Co.: W. (chest), Gaines' Mill (June 27, 1862): Elect., 3Lt., May 17, 1863: Elect., 2Lt., Jan. 21, 1864: No record after Feb., 1865.

MILLER, N. J. 2Lt. — Orig. Pvt. in Co.: Elect., 2Lt.: Deserted, 1863: POW, Western Virginia, July 23, 1863: Dropped from rolls.

(1) SMITH, W. D. 2Lt. — Orig. 3Lt. of Co.: Elect., 2Lt., Jan. 17, 1863: Resgnd., May, 1863.

WATERS, W. H. H. 3Lt. — Orig. Pvt. in Co.: Appt. 1Sgt., Mar. 1, 1864: Prom., 3Lt., Oct. 12, 1864: Reported to have been aide-de-camp for Gen. Wofford in Ga.

NON-COMMISSIONED OFFICERS

ANTHONY, A. H. 2Sgt. — Orig. Pvt. in Co.: W., Fredericksburg (Dec. 11, 1862): Appt. 2Sgt., 1864: POW, Cedar Cr. (Oct. 19, 1864): Confined at Pt. Lookout, Md.: Died in prison, May 8, 1865.

BELL, HENRY W. 2Cpl. — Orig. Pvt. in Co.: Appt. 2Cpl., Aug. 14, 1862: POW, Cartersville, Ga., Aug. 9, 1864: Reduced to Pvt.: Died of pneumonia, Dec. 9, 1864, in Fed. prison at Camp Douglas, Ill.

COCHRAN, A. 1Cpl. -- Orig. Pvt. in Co.: POW, 7 Pines (May 31, 1862): Exchanged, Aug. 5, 1862: Appt. 1Cpl.: W., Chancellorsville (May 3, 1863): POW, Burkeville, Va. (Apr. 6, 1865).

COLLUM, WM. T. 2Cpl. — Orig. Pvt. in Co.: W., Fredericksburg (Dec. 13, 1862): Appt. 2Cpl.: No record after Jan., 1865.

(1)
(2) COTTON, WM. W. 1Sgt. — Orig. 1Sgt. of Co.: Reduced to ranks: Paroled, Appomattox (Apr. 12, 1865).

DYSART, L. N. 4Sgt. — Orig. Pvt. in Co.: Appt. 4Sgt.: Died at Richmond, Jan. 30, 1863.

(1) FORD, J. V. 3Sgt. — See roster, "Regmtl. Hdqtrs., 18th Ga. Inf."

(1) HAMPTON, S. R. 5Sgt. — Orig. 5Sgt. of Co.: Dischgd. for disability, Aug. 7, 1862.

(1) HOLDEN, F. M. 4Cpl. — Orig. 4Cpl. of Co.: W. (leg), Gaines' Mill (June 27, 1862): K., Antietam (Sept. 17, 1862).

KING, W. J. 4Cpl. — Orig. Pvt. in Co.: Prom., 4Cpl.: W. (arm), Wilderness (May 6, 1864): Wound furlough, Aug., 1864.

LEECHMAN, JAS. L. 4Sgt. — Orig. Pvt. in Co.: W., 2nd Manassas (Aug. 30, 1862): POW, Cold Harbor (June 1, 1864): Exchanged: Appt. 4Sgt., Dec. 4, 1864.

MERRILL, J. R. 3Cpl. — Orig. Pvt. in Co.: Appt. 3Cpl., Oct. 1, 1861: W., Antietam (Sept. 17, 1862): POW, Cedar Cr. (Oct. 19, 1864): Exchanged, Mar. 30, 1865.

(1) MILLER, H. K. 1Cpl. — Orig. 1Cpl. of Co.: POW, Big Hill, Ky., July 30, 1863: Took Fed. oath, Oct. 4, 1864 & furnished transp. to Cleveland, Ohio.

NALLEY, A. J. 3Cpl. — Orig. Pvt. in Co.: W., 7 Pines (June 1, 1862): Appt. 3Cpl.: POW, Farmville (Apr. 6, 1865).

SAYE, D. M. 3Sgt. — Orig. Pvt. in Co.: W., Fredericksburg (Dec. 18, 1862): Appt. 3Sgt., 1864: POW, Burkeville, Va. (Apr. 6, 1865).

(1) VAUGHN, JASPER 2Sgt. — Orig. 2Sgt. of Co.: W. (shoulder), Gaines' Mill (June 27, 1862): Died of wound, July 6, 1862.

WINDSOR, JAS. M. 4Sgt. — Orig. Pvt. in Co.: Appt. 4Sgt., Aug., 1862: W., 2nd Manassas (Aug. 30, 1862): W., Antietam (Sept. 17, 1862): POW, near Cartersville, Ga. (Sept. 28, 1864): Died of smallpox at Camp Chase, Ohio, Dec. 14, 1864.

(1) WINDSOR, W. H. 3Sgt. — Orig. 2Cpl. of Co.: Appt. 3Sgt., June 27, 1862: W., 2nd Manassas (Aug. 30, 1862): POW, Frederick, Md. (Sept. 12, 1862): Exchanged, Nov. 10, 1862: K., Chancellorsville (May 3, 1863).

WILLIAMS, DAVID 5Sgt. — Orig. Pvt. in Co.: Appt. 5Sgt., Aug. 1, 1862: K., Chancellorsville (May 3, 1863).

(1) WOFFORD, JOHN T. 4Sgt. — See roster, "Regmtl. Hdqtrs., 18th Ga. Inf."

(1) WHITE, AMOS T. 3Cpl. — Orig. 3Cpl. of Co.: Dischgd., disability (chronic rheumatism), Aug. 1, 1862.

MUSICIANS

(1) RICH, JAS. R. — Orig. Musician in Co.: Reduced to ranks: Paroled,
(2) Appomattox (Apr. 12, 1865).
(1) LAWLESS, GEO. W. — See roster, "Regmtl. Hdqtrs., 18th Ga. Inf."

PRIVATES

(1) ABERNATHY, ELIJAH — Died, May, 1862.

ABERNATHY, HENRY — Enl., Mar. 26, 1862: W., Fredericksburg (Dec. 13, 1862): AWOL, Nov., 1863: Deserted, "Gone to the Yankees," July, 1864.

(1) ABERNATHY, J. J. — W., Malvern Hill (July 1, 1862): W., 2nd Manassas (Aug. 30, 1862): Died of typhoid fever, Nov. 12, 1862.

ADDINGTON, WM. D. — Enl., Aug. 23, 1862: K., near Fredericksburg (Dec. 18, 1862).

ALLEN, J. W. — Enl., May 1, 1862: W., Gettysburg (July 2, 1863): Arm amputated: POW, Burkeville, Va. (Apr. 6, 1865).

ANTHONY, A. H. — See list of "Non-Comm. Officers" above.

(1) ANTHONY, C. P. — W., Fredericksburg (Dec. 13, 1862): AWOL, Aug., 1864.

ANTHONY, JOSEPHUS P. — Hospitalized, Spring, 1862: No other record.

(1) ATKINSON, A. NICHOLAS — W. & POW, Gettysburg (July 2, 1863): Paroled: AWOL, Nov., 1863: Deserted, 1864.

(1) ATKINSON, J. F. — Enl., Mar. 17, 1862: W., Antietam (Sept. 17,
(2) 1862): Paroled, Appomattox (Apr. 12, 1865).

BARNES, WM. H. — Enl., June 14, 1862 in Cass Co., Ga.: No record after Aug., 1862.

(1) BARRON, W. H. H. — POW, Cedar Cr. (Oct. 19, 1864): Paroled, June 9, 1865.

BEAUCHAMP, JOS. — Transf. into Co. H. from Co. E, Aug. 1862.

(1) BELK, H. C. — Transfd. to 3rd Btln., Ga. Sharpshooters, June 8, 1863: POW, Deep Bottom, Va. (Aug. 16, 1864).

BELK, S. J. — Enl., July 18, 1862: W., 2nd Manassas (Aug. 30, 1862); Transfd. to 3rd Btln., Ga. Sharpshooters, June 8, 1863: POW, Gettysburg (July 2, 1863).

(1) BELL, HENRY W. — See list of "Non-Comm. Officers" above.
(1) BIAS, W. L. — Present for duty, Jan., 1865: No other record.
(1) BRADSHAW, W. T. — Deserted to the enemy, Sept. 19, 1863.
(1) BURNS, B. L. — W., Antietam (Sept. 17, 1862): Finger amputated: W., Fredericksburg (Dec. 13, 1862): No record later than Nov., 1864.
(1) BUTLER, J. B. — POW, Richmond, Va., Apr. 3, 1865: No other record.
(1) CARVER, RILEY — Died of general debility at Farmville, Va., Aug. 16, 1862.
(1) CHUMBLEY, M. V. — W., 2nd Manassas (Aug. 30, 1862): Present for duty, Jan., 1865.
(1) CLARK, W. W. — W., 2nd Manassas (Aug. 30, 1862): Died of disease at Cassville, Ga., Dec. 19, 1862.
(1) COCHRAN, A. — See list of "Non-Comm. Officers" above.

COCHRAN, B. — Enl., Mar. 3, 1862: No record after Aug., 1862.

(1) COLLUM, WM. T. — See list of "Non-Comm. Officers" above.
(1) CORBIN, EDLEY D. — POW, 2nd Manassas (Aug. 30, 1862): Paroled, Sept. 29, 1862: AWOL, July, 1863.

COTTON, ARTHUR L. — Enl., May 10, 1862: Died of typhoid fever at Lynchburg, Va., June 28, 1862.

COTTON, J. L. — Received bounty on May 1, 1862: No other record.

(1) COTTON, MATHEW B. — W., Fredericksburg (Dec. 13, 1862): Died, Dec. 19, 1862.
(1) COUCH, ARTHUR — Dischgd. for disability, Aug. 1, 1862.
(1) COX, MONROE — POW, Burkeville, Va. (Apr. 6, 1865).
(1) COX, W. T. — W., 1864: On wound furlough: No record after June, 1864.

CROSS, ALFRED — Enl., Aug. 20, 1862 in Cass Co., Ga.: K., Antietam (Sept. 17, 1862).

DOYAL, J. S. — Enl., Aug. 20, 1862 in Cass Co., Ga.: Served as a substitute for Dock Glasgow who was reported as missing at Antietam (Sept. 17, 1862): No other record.

DOYAL, THOS. T. — Enl., Feb. 23, 1862: Dischgd., May, 1863.

(1) DYKES, JAS. L. — POW, Burkeville, Va. (Apr. 6, 1865).
(1) DYSART, AMERICUS — Died, May, 1862.

(1) DYSART, JAS. M. — Transfd. to 3rd Btln., Ga. Sharpshooters, June 8, 1863.

(1) DYSART, L. N. — See list of "Non-Comm. Officers" above.

EDDLEMAN, L. H. — Hospitalized, July, 1862: No other record.

(1) EDLEMAN, WM. H. — W. (ankle), Gaines' Mill (June 27, 1862): W., Fredericksburg (Dec. 13, 1862): K., Chancellorsville (May 3, 1863).

FERGUSON, A. — Enl., Mar. 3, 1862 at Cartersville, Ga.: W., Chancellorsville (May 3, 1863): Deserted, May 24, 1863.

FORD, M. — Enl., Mar. 4, 1862 at Pine Log, Ga.: W., Fredericksburg (Dec. 13, 1862): Present for duty, Jan., 1865.

FOSTER, E. G. — Enl., June 14, 1862 in Cass Co., Ga.: K., Antietam (Sept. 17, 1862).

(1) FOSTER, J. V. — W., Gaines' Mill (June 27, 1862): Died from wound, July 2, 1862.

(1) FOX, A. J. — Deserted, Mar. 15, 1865: No other record.

FOX, ANDREW — Enl., Mar. 26, 1862 at Etowah, Ga.: W., Gaines' Mill (June 27, 1862): W., Fredericksburg (Dec. 13, 1862).

(1) GARDNER, D. B. — W. (shoulder), Gaines' Mill (June 27, 1862): Paroled, Nashville, July 15, 1865.

GILBERT, JOHN — W. (leg), Gaines' Mill (June 27, 1862): No other record.

(1) GILLSTRAP, Y. B. — K., Spotsylvania (May 10, 1864).

(1) GORDON, CHAS. P. — Transfd. to 3rd Btln., Ga. Sharpshooters, June 8, 1863.

(1) HAMMETT, GEO. W. — W., Gaines' Mill (June 27, 1862): K., Chancellorsville (May 3, 1863).

(1) HENSON (or HINSON), J. THADDEUS — Detached duty at Selma, Ala., Aug., 1864: No other record.

(1) HIGHT (or HITE), JAS. — Died of measles at Ashland, Va., Apr. 26, 1862.

HIGHT (or HITE), WM. — Enl., Feb. 28, 1862: W. (chest), Gaines' Mill (June 27, 1862): Dischgd., disability, Apr. 27, 1863.

(1) HIGHT (or HITE), WYATT — Died, May 23, 1862.

HINSON, C. J. — Returned to duty from hosp., Nov., 1862: No other record.

HOLMES, J. B. — Enl., Mar. 4, 1862 at Pine Log, Ga.: Present for duty, Nov., 1864.

(1) JENKINS, ELI — W., Fredericksburg (Dec. 13, 1862): W. (hand), Chancellorsville (May 3, 1863): Transfd. to 3rd Btln., Ga. Sharpshooters, June 8, 1863.

(1) JENKINS, JOS. N. — POW, Antietam (Sept. 17, 1862): Paroled, Oct. 2, 1862: Took Fed. oath at Chattanooga, Feb. 14, 1864.

JOHNSON, JOHN — Enl., Aug. 20, 1862 in Cass Co., Ga.: Substitute for J. M. Wofford: Deserted, Spring, 1864.

JORDAN, WM. — Died, Fall, 1862: No other record.

(1) KING, D. G. — POW, Frederick, Md. (Sept. 15, 1862): Exchanged, Nov. 10, 1862: POW, Gettysburg (July 2, 1863).

(1) KING, F. A. — See list of "Officers" above.

KING, J. D. — Enl., Aug. 20, 1862: POW, Antietam (Sept. 17, 1862).

(1) KING, W. J. — See list of "Non-Comm. Officers" above.
(1) KIRK, D. — Deserted: No other record.
(1) KIRK, RICHARD B. — W., 2nd Manassas (Aug. 30, 1862): Took Fed. oath, June 26, 1864.
KNIGHT, JAS. P. — Enl., Mar. 6, 1862 at Etowah, Ga.: POW, Cold Harbor (June 1, 1864).
(1) KUYKENDALL, J. W. — "Absent, supposed to be in hands of enemy": No other record.
LEACHMAN, JAS. L. — Enl., Oct. 18, 1861 at Richmond: W., Fredericksburg (Dec. 13, 1862): POW, Cold Harbor (June 1, 1864).
(1) LEAK, W. B. — W. & POW, Antietam (Sept. 17, 1862): Died of wounds, Sept., 1862.
LEECHMAN, C. J. — Enl., Oct. 18, 1861 at Richmond: W., 2nd Manassas (Aug. 30, 1862): Took Fed. oath, Feb. 18, 1865.
LEECHMAN, H. F. — Enl., Feb. 26, 1862 in Carr County, Ga.: K., 2nd Manassas (Aug. 30, 1862).
(1) LEECHMAN, JAS. L. — See list of "Non-Comm. Officers" above.
(1) MANN, L. M. — W., Chancellorsville (May 3, 1863): Transfd. to 3rd Btln., Ga. Sharpshooters, June 8, 1863.
(1) MANN, R. J. — POW, Burkeville, Va. (Apr. 6, 1865).
(1) MANN, W. H. — W. (hand), 2nd Manassas (Aug. 30, 1862): W., Chancellorsville (May 3, 1863): Leg amputated: Died from amputation, May 22, 1863.
(1) MANN, W. L. — W., Antietam (Sept. 17, 1862): Deserted, Aug. 3, 1864.
(1) MERRILL, J. R. — See list of "Non-Comm. Officers" above.
(1) MILERS, JAS. E. — W., 2nd Manassas (Aug. 30, 1862): Leg amputated: Died, Sept. 18 from amputation.
(1) MILLER, N. J. — See list of "Officers" above.
(1) MORRIS, E. L. — On detached duty, Jan. 31, 1865: No other record.
(1) NALLEY, A. J. — See list of "Non-Comm. Officers" above.
(1) OVERLOCK, E. — POW, Richmond hosp., Apr. 3, 1865.
(1) OWENS, HENRY S. — W., 2nd Manassas (Aug. 30, 1862): W., Fredericksburg (Dec. 13, 1862): On wound furlough, Jan., 1865.
(1) PARTIN, HUBBART — Deserted, 1863.
(1) PAUL, R. K. — W., Chancellorsville (May 3, 1863): Present for duty, Jan., 1865.
(1) PAYNE, JAS. — Died of pneumonia at Fredericksburg, Dec. 11, 1861.
(1) PIERCE, GEO. H. — Dischgd. on Surg. Cert., Nov. 6, 1861: Re-enl., Mar. 4, 1862 at Cartersville, Ga.: Hospitalized, Winter, 1864-65.
(1) PONDER, P. H. — Died at Fredericksburg, Mar. 20, 1862.
(1) RICE, JAS. M. — W. (arm), Gaines' Mill (June 27, 1862): Took Fed. oath, Feb. 21, 1865.
(1) RICH, ARCH — No record after Feb., 1863.
(1) RICH, WM. W. — W. (side), Gaines' Mill (June 27, 1862): W.,
(2) Fredericksburg (Dec. 13, 1862): Paroled, Appomattox (Apr. 12, 1865).
SARNEY, D. M. — W., Gaines' Mill (June 27, 1862): No other record.
SAYE, ALEXANDER C. — Enl., May 10, 1862 at Augusta, Ga.: Died, Dec. 28, 1862 of tuberculosis.

(1) SAYE, D. M. — See list of "Non-Comm. Officers" above.
(1) SAYE, GEORGE — Dischgd., Jan. 24, 1862 for "inability to perform the duties of a soldier."
SAYE, JOHN — Enl., May 10, 1862 at Augusta, Ga.: No record after Aug., 1862, may have been killed at 2nd Manassas.
(1) SAYE, ROBT. — K., near Fredericksburg, Dec. 18, 1862.
SIMS, J. C. — Present for duty, Spring, 1862: No other record.
(1) SMITH, A. J. — No record after Feb., 1862.
(1) SMITH, GEO. — No record after Feb., 1862.
(1) SMITH, GEO. R. — See list of "Officers" above.
SMITH, JELU — POW, 2nd Manassas (Aug. 30, 1862): Paroled, Sept. 29, 1862.
(1) SMITH, P. C. — W., Malvern Hill (July 1, 1862): POW, 2nd Manassas (Aug. 30, 1862): Paroled, Sept. 29, 1862: Transfd. to 3rd Btln., Ga. Sharpshooters, June 8, 1863.
(1) SMITH, W. H. — Died, Richmond, July 22, 1862.
(1) STACY, AARON O. — W. (ankle & arm) & POW, Antietam (Sept. 17, 1862): Paroled, Oct. 19, 1862: AWOL, Dec., 1862.
STANFORD, JAS. C. — Enl., Mar. 4, 1862 at Pine Log, Ga.: W., Chancellorsville (May 3, 1863): POW, Farmville, Va. (Apr. 6, 1865).
(1) STEWART, LEANDER — W. (face & arm), Gaines' Mill (June 27, 1862): No record after Nov., 1862.
(1) STRAIN, JAS. — K., Gaines' Mill (June 27, 1862).
(1) STROUP, DRURY — W., Gaines' Mill (June 27, 1862): W., 2nd Manassas (Aug. 30, 1862): Arm amputated.
STROUP, JOHN — Enl., Mar. 8, 1862 at Cartersville, Ga.: W. (shoulder), 2nd Manassas (Aug. 30, 1862): Present for duty, Jan., 1865.
SUGGS, E. L. — Enl., Mar. 17, 1862 at Etowah, Ga.: Deserted, Summer, 1864.
(1) TIERCE, D. S. — Hospitalized, Winter, 1861-62: No other record.
TOLBERT, G. W. — Enl., Feb. 28, 1862 at Etowah, Ga.: POW, 7 Pines (June 1, 1862): Exchanged: K., Antietam (Sept. 17, 1863).
(1) UNDERWOOD, D. L. — Sick furlough, Feb., 1865: No other record.
(1) UNDERWOOD, F. W. — W., Malvern Hill (July 1, 1862): Died from wound.
(1) UPSHAW, J. M. — Transfd. to 3rd Btln., Ga. Sharpshooters, June 8, 1863.
(1) VAUGHN, S. L. — W., Chancellorsville (May 3, 1863): AWOL, Aug., 1863.
(1) VINING, WM. E. — K., Chancellorsville (May 3, 1863).
WARD, JOHN — Enl., Nov. 22, 1862 in Bartow County, Ga.: W., 7 Pines (June 1, 1862): Transfd. to 3rd Btln., Ga. Sharpshooters, June 8, 1863.
WARD, WM. — Enl., Nov. 4, 1861 at Richmond: Dischgd. for "inability to perform the duties of a soldier," Jan. 26, 1862.
(2) WATERS, J. M. — Paroled, Appomattox (Apr. 12, 1865): No other record.
(1) WATERS, J. N. — W. (arm), Chancellorsville (May 3, 1863): Present for duty, Summer, 1864.

(1) WATERS, W. H. H. — See list of "Officers" above.
(1) WELCH, W. A. — POW, Cold Harbor (June 1, 1864): Paroled, Elmira, N.Y., July 7, 1865.
(1) WHITMORE, L. C. — Present for duty, Summer, 1864: No other record.
     WILLIAMS, E. R. — Enl., Mar. 4, 1862 at Etowah, Ga.: Died, May, 1863.
     WILLIAMS, DAVID — See list of "Non-Comm. Officers" above.
     WILLIAMS, ELIJAH — Enl., Mar. 26, 1862: No other record.
(1) WILLIAMS, JAS. F. — W. (shoulder), Gaines' Mill (June 27, 1862): "Fingers shot off."
(1) WINDSOR, JAS. M. — See list of "Non-Comm. Officers" above.
     WOFFORD, J. M. — Procured John Johnson as a substitute, Aug. 20, 1862: No other record.
(1) WOFFORD, JAS. C. — Dischgd., disability, Jan. 11, 1862: Re-enl. in 40th Ga. Inf. Regt., Mar. 4, 1862.
(1) WOFFORD, WM. B. — Transfd. to 3rd Btln., Ga. Sharpshooters, June 8, 1863.
(1) WOODALL, THOS. J. — W., 2nd Manassas (Aug. 30, 1862): Arm amputated.
(1) YOUNG, DARIUS — W. (arm), Gaines' Mill (June 27, 1862): Arm amputated.
     YOUNG, HENRY — Transfd. to Co. H, Nov. 19, 1861 from 23rd Ga. Inf. Regt.: Detailed to recruiting service, Feb. 28, 1862.

* * * * *

MEMBERS OF COMPANY H, 18th GA. INF. REGT. WHO WERE NOT PRESENT FOR DUTY DURING THE PERIOD THAT THE REGIMENT WAS ASSIGNED TO HOOD'S TEXAS BRIGADE (NOV., 1861-NOV., 1862).

OFFICERS
NONE

NON-COMMISSIONED OFFICERS

Miles, A. L., Cpl. (No record prior to Apr., 1865)

Smith, J. W., Color Guard (Transfd. out, Oct., 1861)

PRIVATES

Adams, H. (No record prior to Feb., 1864)

Bishop, C. (No record prior to Apr., 1863)

Bowman, Benj. T. (No record prior to July, 1864)

Bryant, Benj. (Enl., Jan., 1864)

Calton, W. W. (No record prior to Apr., 1865)

Chastain, John (Enl., 1865)

Donohoe, Wm. (D., Oct., 1861)

Harban, Baalam (No record prior to Dec., 1864)

Jenkins, J. P. (No record prior to May, 1863)

Powers, S. (No record prior to June, 1864)

Strain, J. W. (No record prior to May, 1863)

(1) Tate, W. N. (D., Nov., 1861)

Walben, J. (No record prior to Aug., 1863)

(1) Young, B. L. (Transfd. out, Nov., 1861)

(1) Younge, Wm. (D., Sept., 1861)

18TH GA. VOL. INF. REGT.

COMPANY I – *DOOLY LIGHT INFANTRY*

Company was organized in Dooly County, Georgia, during the Spring of 1861. It rendezvoused, recruited & trained at Camp McDonald, Cobb County, Georgia, in late June & in July. The men were mustered into the Confederate service "for three years" at Richmond, Va., on or about Aug. 9, 1861.

Key

(1) Original member of Company. (2) Paroled at Appomattox. K (Killed), W (Wounded), POW (Prisoner of War) AWOL (Absent Without Leave)

OFFICERS

(1) GILBERT, PATRICK E. Capt. — Orig. 3Lt. of Co.: Prom., 2Lt., May 5, 1862: Prom., 1st Lt., Aug. 22, 1863: Prom., Capt., Jan. 6, 1864: W., Spotsylvania (May 12, 1864): Absent, wounded, Aug., 1864.

BARTON, JAS. S. 1Lt. — Orig. Pvt. in Co.: Prom., 4Sgt., July 1, 1862: Elect., 3Lt., Dec. 9, 1862: Elect., 2Lt., Aug. 22, 1863: Elect., 1Lt., Jan. 6, 1864: K., Petersburg, June 9, 1864.

(1) COLEY, REDDING T. 1Lt. — Orig. 1Lt. of Co.: W., 2nd Manassas (Aug. 30, 1862): Resgnd., Aug. 22, 1863.

(2) LASSITER, GIDEON I. 1Lt. — Orig. 3Sgt. of Co.: W., 2nd Manassas (Aug. 30, 1862): Elect., 3Lt., Jan. 21, 1864: Elect., 1Lt., June 9, 1864: Paroled, Appomattox (Apr. 12, 1865): Commanded Regt. at Appomattox.

(1) CARTER, JAS. W. 2Lt. — Orig. 2Lt. of Co.: Resgnd., May 5, 1862.

CONE, THOS. J. 3Lt. — Orig. 5Sgt. of Co.: Elect., 3Lt., May 5, 1862: W., Gaines' Mill (June 27, 1862): Leg amputated: died from amputation, July 7, 1862.

WILLIAMS, DAVID B. 3Lt. — Orig. Pvt. in Co.: Elect., 3Lt., June 27, 1862: Died of disease, Winchester, Va., Nov. 4, 1862.

ROGERS, WILLIAM G. Ensign — See roster, "Regmtl. Hdqtrs., 18th Ga. Inf."

NON-COMMISSIONED OFFICERS

BENNETT, WM. F. 3Sgt. — Orig. Pvt. in Co.: Prom., 3Cpl., Feb. 6, 1862: W., Antietam (Sept. 17, 1862): POW, Burkeville, Va. (Apr. 6, 1865).

BULLINGTON, JOHN L. 3Cpl. — Orig. Pvt. in Co.: Appt. 3Cpl., Feb. 6, 1862: Died, Dec., 1862.

(1) CONE, ANDREW J. 4Sgt. — Orig. 4Sgt. of Co.: Appt. 1Sgt., Jan. 22, 1864: POW, Cedar Cr. (Oct. 19, 1864): Reduced to ranks: Exchanged, Mar. 17, 1865.

(1) CONE, THOS. J. 5Sgt. — See list of "Officers" above.

FLOYD, GEO. W. 2Cpl. — Orig. Pvt. in Co.: W. (foot), 2nd Manassas (Aug. 30, 1862): Appt. 2Cpl.: POW, Cedar Cr. (Oct. 19, 1864).

(1) GRAHAM, JOHN T. 1Cpl. — Orig. 4Cpl. of Co.: Prom. to 1Cpl.: POW, Burkeville, Va. (Apr. 6, 1865).

HARVARD, B. A. Sgt. — Jnd. Co. as a Sgt.: W., 2nd Manassas (Aug. 30, 1862): No further record.

HARVARD, VIRGIL A. 5Sgt. — Orig. Pvt. in Co.: Appt. 2Cpl., Nov. 5, 1861: W., 2nd Manassas (Aug. 30, 1862): Prom., 5Sgt.: Died of tuberculosis at Farmville, Va., June 18, 1863.

(1) LASSITER, GIDEON I. 3Sgt. — See list of "Officers" above.

(1) ROBERTS, MILTON 1Cpl. — Orig. 1Cpl. of Co.: K., Chancellorsville (May 3, 1863).

(1) WINN (or WYNN), ELBERT W. , 2Sgt. — Orig. 2Sgt. of Co.: W. (head), Gaines' Mill (June 27, 1862): Died of wound.

PRIVATES

(2) ARMSTRONG, G. W. — Enl., Apr. 4, 1862: Paroled, Appomattox (Apr. 12, 1865).

(1) AMMONS, THOS. A. — Dischgd., Nov. 24, 1861.

(1) ARNETT, ALBERT W. — POW, 2nd Manassas (Aug. 30, 1862): Paroled, Sept. 29, 1862.

BAIRD, JAS. C. — POW, Williamsport, Md. (Sept. 16, 1862): Exchanged, Nov. 10, 1862.

(1) BARTON, JAS. S. — See list of "Officers" above.

(1) BELL, JOHN THOS. — D., Apr., 1862: No other record.

BENNETT, L. H. — Enl., Sept. 25, 1864 in Twiggs Co., Ga.: POW, Burkeville, Va. (Apr. 6, 1865).

(1) BENNETT, WM. F. — See list of "Non-Comm. Officers" above.

(1) BLANCHARD, NATHAN — AWOL, Fall, 1861: Died, Winter, 1861-62.

(1) BULLINGTON, JOHN L. — See list of "Non-Comm. Officers" above.

(1) BULLINGTON, THOS. R. — W., Chancellorsville (May 3, 1863): POW, Cedar Cr. (Oct. 19, 1864): Exchanged, Mar. 19, 1865.

(1) BUTLER, FORT W. — W., 2nd Manassas (Aug. 30, 1862): POW, Knoxville, Nov. 29, 1863.

(1)
(2) CARROLL, WM. J. — W., Chancellorsville (May 3, 1863): Paroled, Appomattox (Apr. 12, 1865).

(1) CHRISTMAS, DANIEL J. — W., Cold Harbor (June 3, 1864): POW, Burkeville, Va. (Apr. 6, 1865).

(1)   CLARKE, JOHN D. — Dischgd., disability, Jan. 2, 1862.

(1)   CLEMMONS, DAVID G. — W. (hand), Gaines' Mill (June 27, 1862): Deserted, E. Tenn., Dec. 18, 1863.

(1)   COLLINS, JESSE M. — Dischgd., July, 1862.

(1)   CONE, JAS. A. — Missing, E. Tenn., Nov. 29, 1863: POW.

(1)   CONE, KADWELL BATTO — K., Jericho Ford, Va., May 25, 1864.

CONE, WM. G. — Enl., Sept. 1, 1862: Died (tuberculosis) at Staunton, Va., Jan. 14, 1863.

(1)   COPPEDGE, JOHN H. — K., Antietam (Sept. 17, 1862).

(1)   CRINN, J. J. — Died, Richmond, Aug. 26, 1864: Buried in Hollywood Cemetery.

(1)   CROSIER, WM. J. — W. (foot), Gaines' Mill (June 27, 1862): Paroled,
(2)   Appomattox (Apr. 12, 1865).

(1)   CRUMPLER, JAS. M. — W., 2nd Manassas (Aug. 30, 1862): Paroled, Sept. 29, 1862: AWOL, Spring, 1864.

(1)   CRUMPLER, JOHN — Dischgd., Dec. 9, 1861 from effects of typhoid fever.

(1)   DAVIS, NATHANIEL S. — W., Chancellorsville (May 3, 1863): POW, Cold Harbor (June 1, 1864): Died, chronic diarrhea, in Fed. prison at Elmira, N.Y., Oct. 13, 1864.

DAVIS, R. A. — Enl., May 20, 1862 in Dooly County, Ga.: Died, typhoid fever, at Richmond, June 11, 1863.

ELERS (or EILERS), I. — POW, 2nd Manassas (Aug. 30, 1862): Paroled, Sept. 29, 1862.

EVES, LAWSON P. — Present for duty as of Dec. 31, 1861: No other record.

(1)   FAIL, THOS. — W., Knoxville, Nov. 29, 1863: Paroled, Appomattox
(2)   (Apr. 12, 1865).

(1)   FLOYD, GEO. W. — See list of "Non-Comm. Officers" above.

(1)   GARVIN, JOHN D. — W., 2nd Manassas (Aug. 30, 1862): W., Petersburg (June 9, 1864): POW, Burkeville, Va. (Apr. 6, 1865).

GILBERT, JOHN G. — Enl., Mar. 4, 1862 at Vienna, Ga.: W., Gaines' Mill (June 27, 1862): W., 2nd Mannassas (Aug. 30, 1862): Paroled, Lynchburg, Va., Apr. 13, 1865.

(1)   GRAHAM, JOS. W. — POW, Burkeville, Va. (Apr. 6, 1865).

(1)   HALL, WM. L. — Died, Apr., 1862.

(1)   HALL, ZACHARIAH B. — Died, Apr., 1862.

(1)   HAM, Judge MARTIN VAN BUREN — W. (arm), 7 Pines (June 1, 1862): POW, Cold Harbor (June 1, 1864).

(1)   HAMMOND, VIRGIL A. — Hospitalized, Apr., 1863: No other record.

(1)   HARVARD, JOHN R. — No record after Aug., 1862.

(1)   HARVARD, JOS. P. — W., Fredericksburg (Dec. 13, 1862): POW, Cedar Cr. (Oct. 19, 1864).

(1)   HARVARD, VIRGIL A. — See list of "Non-Comm. Officers" above.

(1)   HATCHER, GREEN B. — Died of pneumonia at Chimborazo Hosp., Jan. 9, 1862.

(1)   HENDERSON, GEO. W. — W., 2nd Manassas (Aug. 30, 1862): Died of debility at Richmond, Apr. 28, 1863.

(1)   HERRING, FRANCIS M. — POW, Burkeville, Va. (Apr. 6, 1865).

(1)   HERRING, GEO. F. — W. (arm & side), Gaines' Mill (June 27, 1862): K., Knoxville, Nov. 29, 1863.

(1)   HOOKS, WM. L. — POW, Cold Harbor (June 1, 1864): Paroled, July 7, 1865.

(1)   HOWARD, J. P. — POW, Spring, 1864: No other record.

       IVEY, AUGUSTUS I. — Enl., Aug. 7, 1861 at Bristol, Tenn.: POW, 2nd Manassas (Aug. 30, 1862): Paroled, Sept. 29, 1862: Present for duty, Jan., 1865.

       IVY, JAS. M. — Enl., Aug. 7, 1861 at Bristol, Tenn.: W., Chancellorsville (May 3, 1863): Absent, sick, Summer, 1864.

(1)   IVY, SAMUEL A. — Dischgd., disability (chronic bronchitis), Dec. 16, 1861.

       KING, M. S. — Enl., Mar. 4, 1862 in Dooly Co., Ga.: K., Chancellorsville (May 3, 1863).

(1)   LEWIS, JAS. S. — Dischgd. on Surg. Cert., Aug. 11, 1862.

(1)   LOCKE, JOS. F. — Missing, Antietam (Sept. 17, 1862): No other record.

(1)   LOCKERMAN, JOHN — Died, Apr., 1862.

(1)   LOCKERMAN, JOHN A. — W., Antietam (Sept. 17, 1862): POW, Cedar Cr. (Oct. 19, 1864): Exchanged, Mar. 28, 1865.

(1)   LUPO, NATHANIEL G. — K., Knoxville (Nov. 29, 1863).

(1)   MATTOX, WM. J. — Dischgd. for disability (lung disease), Dec. 23, 1861.

(1)   McCULLOCH, NEIL C. — Died, typhoid fever, Nov. 30, 1861.

       McRAY, F. — POW, Frederick, Md., Sept., 1862: Exchanged, Nov. 10, 1862.

(1)   MERCER, JESSE W. — W., Antietam (Sept. 17, 1862): POW, Cold Harbor (June 1, 1864): Exchanged, Mar. 21, 1865.

(1)   NORRIS, ISAIAH E. — Dischgd., Mar. 19, 1862.

(1)   PEAVY, ELI B. — POW, Knoxville (Nov. 29, 1863): Died in Fed. prison in Ky. of smallpox, Jan. 6, 1864.

       PEAVY, H. W. — Hospitalized, Spring, 1862: No other record.

       PEAVY, JAS. M. — Enl., Mar. 4, 1862 in Dooly Co., Ga.: K., 2nd Manassas (Aug. 30, 1862).

(1)   POLLOCK, JAS. THOS. — K., Gaines' Mill (June 27, 1862).

       PRICE, JOHN — Hospitalized, Fall, 1862: No other record.

(1)   REYNOLDS, DANIEL M. — Dischgd. (lung disease), Dec. 23, 1861.

(1)   RIDLEY, JOS. W. — W., 2nd Manassas (Aug. 30, 1862): Leg amputated.

(1)   ROGERS, THOS. P. — Present for duty, Winter, 1861-62: No other record.

(1)   ROGERS, WM. G. — See list of "Officers" above.

(1)   ROWLAND, DANIEL — W., Chancellorsville (May 3, 1863): No record after June, 1864.

       ROWLAND, EASON — Enl., Feb. 20, 1862 at Vienna, Ga.: Dischgd. for disability caused by a head wound at either Gaines' Mill (June 27, 1862) or 2nd Manassas (Aug. 30, 1862).

(1)   SPRADLEY, WM. H. — Accidentally wounded, Dec., 1862: No other record.

(1)   STEVENS (or STEPHENS), ISAAC T. — AWOL, Winter, 1864-65: No other record.

(1)   TATUM, FRANCIS A. — Missing, Antietam (Sept. 17, 1862): No other record.

(1) TATUM, JAS. J. — W., Yellow Tavern (May 11, 1864): POW, Burkeville, Va. (Apr. 6, 1865).

(1) WARREN, JOHN M. — W., Fredericksburg (Dec. 13, 1862): Died from wound, Jan. 8, 1863.

(1) WATERS, AARON J. — W. (hip) & POW, Knoxville (Dec. 5, 1863): Exchanged, Sept. 18, 1864.

(1) WHITE, GEO. B. — Died of measles, 1862.

(1) WILLIAMS, DAVID B. — See list of "Officers" above.

(1) WINDWARD, GILES M. — Transfd. to the 51st Ga. Inf. Regt., Jan. 5, 1863.

(1) WOODWARD, JAS. M. — W., Chancellorsville (May 3, 1863): Paroled,
(2) Appomattox (Apr. 12, 1865).

★ ★ ★ ★ ★

MEMBERS OF COMPANY I, 18TH GA. INF. REGT., WHO WERE NOT PRESENT FOR DUTY DURING THE PERIOD THAT THE REGIMENT WAS ASSIGNED TO HOOD'S TEXAS BRIGADE (NOV., 1861-NOV., 1862).

OFFICERS

NONE

NON-COMMISSIONED OFFICERS

(1) Ballard, Thos. A. (Orig. 3Cpl. of Co.: Dischgd., Nov., 1861)

(1) Collin, Thos. F. (Orig. 1Sgt. of Co.: No record after Oct., 1861)

(1) Collins, Divin L. (Orig. 2Cpl. of Co.: D., Sept., 1861)

Woodward, G. T., Cpl. (No record prior to May, 1863)

PRIVATES

Adkinson, H. F. (No record prior to Apr., 1865)

Arnett, N. C. (Enl., Nov., 1863)

Bealle, V. (No record prior to Feb., 1865)

(1) Bell, Harris P. (D., Sept., 1861)

Bullington, Francis M. (Deserted, Nov., 1861)

Bullington, J. M. (Enl., June, 1864)

Christian, C. (No record prior to June, 1864)

Christmas, J. T. (No record before Nov., 1864)

Cobb, Jas. (No record prior to June, 1865)

(1) Cone, WM. T. (D., Sept., 1861)

Dickson, J. M. (Enl., Apr., 1864)

Dupree, J. J. (Enl., Apr., 1864)

(1) Dupree, Thos. R. (Dischgd., Nov., 1861)

(1) Harrison, Benj. F. (D., Aug., 1861)

Herring, A. T. (No record prior to Aug., 1863)
Holcombe, J. (Enl., Feb., 1863)
Jones, J. B. (Enl., June, 1863)
Lassiter, Isaac S. (Enl., Apr., 1864)
Mason, W. T. (Enl., Apr., 1864)
Maven, Robert H. (Enl., Oct., 1864)
Moate, J. W. (No record prior to Apr., 1865)
(1) Monroe, John P. (Deserted, Nov., 1861)
Parks, Wm. (Enl., Sept., 1864)

(1) Peacock, John H. (Died, Aug., 1861)
Phelps, John (Enl., July, 1864)
Phelps, Wm. (No record prior to June, 1865)
Smith, J. G. (No record prior to June, 1865)
Tippet, William J. (Dischgd., Nov., 1861)
Trippe, E. M. (No record prior to Apr., 1865)
Turner, Samuel (No record prior to Feb., 1865)

18TH GA. VOL. INF. REGT.

COMPANY K – ROWLAND INFANTRY

Company was organized in Bartow County, Georgia, during the Spring of 1861. It rendezvoused, recruited & trained at Camp McDonald, Cobb County, Georgia, in late June & in July. The men were mustered into the Confederate Service, "for three years," at Richmond, Va., on or about Aug. 9, 1861.

Key

(1) Original member of Company. (2) Paroled at Appomattox.
K (Killed), W (Wounded), POW (Prisoner of War)
AWOL (Absent Without Leave)

OFFICERS

BROWN, WM. Capt. – Orig. 5Sgt. of Co.: W., 2nd Manassas (Aug. 30, 1862): Elect., 2Lt., Sept. 30, 1862: Elect., 1Lt., Dec. 13, 1862: W., Fredericksburg (Dec. 13, 1862): Elect., Capt., Apr. 27, 1864: AWOL, Jan., 1865.
(1) CRAWFORD, JOHN A. Capt. – Orig. Capt. of Co.: W., Antietam (Sept. 17, 1862): Retired to Invalid Corps, Apr. 25, 1864 & asgnd. as Commandant of Conscripts, State of Georgia.
McMURRAY, A. J. 1Lt. – Orig. 2Sgt. of Co.: W., Malvern Hill (July 1, 1862): Elect., 3Lt., Sept. 30, 1862: Elect., 2Lt., Dec. 13, 1862: Elect., 1Lt., Apr. 27, 1864: K., Deep Bottom, Va. (Aug. 16, 1864).
SMITH, SAMUEL V. 1Lt. – Orig. Pvt. in Co.: Elect., 1Lt., Sept. 3, 1861: W., Malvern Hill (July 1, 1862): K., 2nd Manassas (Aug. 29, 1862).

(1) WOFFORD, NAT T. 1Lt. — Orig. 3Lt. of Co.: Prom., 2Lt., June 27, 1862: Prom., 1Lt., Aug. 29, 1862: K., Fredericksburg (Dec. 13, 1862).

(1) DOWTIN, THOS. 2Lt. — Orig. 2Lt. of Co.: K., Gaines' Mill (June 27, 1862).

UNDERWOOD, T. C. 2Lt. — Orig. 1Sgt. of Co.: Elect., 3Lt., Aug. 1, 1862: Elect., 2Lt., Aug. 29, 1862: K., Antietam (Sept. 17, 1862).

BAKER, JAS. M. 3Lt. — Enl. as a Pvt., Sept. 3, 1861 at Richmond: Elect., 3Lt., Apr. 4, 1863: W., Chancellorsville (May 3, 1863): Leg amputated.

BAKER, THOS. H. 3Lt. — A physician by profession: Enl. as a Pvt., Aug. 3, 1861 at Cartersville, Ga.: Elect., 3Lt., Jan. 13, 1863: Resgnd., Aug. 31, 1863 to follow his profession.

CLEVELAND, JAS. M. D. 3Lt. — Orig. Pvt. in Co.: Appt. 3Sgt., Nov. 30, 1861: Elect., 3Lt., Sept. 10, 1862: K., Antietam (Sept. 17, 1862).

NON-COMMISSIONED OFFICERS

BOX, JOHN W. 4Cpl. — Orig. musician in Co.: Prom., 4Cpl.: K., Wilderness (May 6, 1864).

(1) BROWN, WM. 5Sgt. — See list of "Officers" above.

DAVIS, JOHN F. 1Sgt. — Orig. Pvt. in Co.: Appt. 4Sgt., Oct. 15, 1861: Appt. 1Sgt., Aug. 1, 1862: W., 2nd Manassas (Aug. 30, 1862): K., Chancellorsville (May 3, 1863).

DEATON, ELIJAH 1Sgt. — Enl. as a Pvt.: Aug. 3, 1861: Dischgd., disability, Mar. 31, 1862: Re-enl., Aug. 1, 1862: Appt. 1Sgt., June 8, 1863: POW, Cold Harbor (June 1, 1864).

DEMPSEY, G. A. Sgt. — Enl. as a Pvt., Feb. 19, 1862: Appt. Sgt.: Reduced to ranks: No record after Nov., 1864.

DRAKE, B. T. 2Sgt. — Orig. Pvt. in Co.: W. (thigh), Antietam (Sept. 17, 1862): Appt. 2Sgt., Sept. 30, 1862.

HARDY, W. F. 1Cpl. — Enl. as a Pvt., Feb. 21, 1862: Appt. 1Cpl., Feb. 24, 1862: W., Fredericksburg (Dec. 17, 1862): Took Fed. oath, Mar., 1865.

JONES, THOS. 1Sgt. — Only record shows that he was paid for period of service as a 1Sgt. from May to Dec., 1862.

(1) LANGLEY, BAYLUS M. 1Cpl. — Orig. 1Cpl. of Co.: Dischgd., furnished Geo. C. Windsor as a substitute, Feb. 24, 1862.

LOUDERMILK, HENRY Cpl. — Orig. Pvt. in Co.: Prom., Cpl.: W., Gaines' Mill (June 27, 1862): Leg amputated.

(1) McMURRAY, A. J. 2Sgt. — See list of "Officers" above.

SLATON, W. F. 2Sgt. — Orig. Pvt. in Co.: Appt. 2Sgt., 1864: POW, Burkeville, Va. (Apr. 6, 1865).

(1) SCOTT, JOHN B. 3Cpl. — Orig. 3Cpl. of Co.: POW, 2nd Manassas (Aug. 30, 1862): Paroled: W., Chancellorsville (May 3, 1863): Disabled.

(1) SMITH, J. V. 2Cpl. — Orig. 2Cpl. of Co.: Resgnd. as Cpl. to drive forage wagon, Nov. 27, 1861: W., Chancellorsville (May 3, 1863): AWOL, June, 1863.

(1)   SLAUGHTER, T. B. 1Sgt. — Orig. Pvt. in Co.: W., Antietam (Sept. 17, 1862): Appt. 1Sgt., May 3, 1863: Transfd. to 3rd Btln., Ga. Sharpshooters, June 8, 1863.

SQUIRES, J. W. Sgt. — Enl. as a Pvt., Sept. 13, 1862 at Merlenburg, Ga.: Prom. to Sgt.: Hospitalized, Spring, 1863: No other record.

UNDERWOOD, G. L. 3Sgt. — Enl. as a Pvt., Mar. 23, 1862 in Bartow Co., Ga.: Appt. 3Sgt., Fall, 1863: POW, near Knoxville (Nov. 29, 1863): Died as a POW, Mar. 4, 1864, at Rock Is., Ill.

UNDERWOOD, JOHN H. 2Cpl. — Orig. Pvt. in Co.: Appt. 2Cpl.: W., Chancellorsville (May 3, 1863): Leg amputated.

(1)   UNDERWOOD, T. C. 1Sgt. — See list of "Officers" above.

WILLIAMS, J. V. 4Sgt. — Enl. as a Pvt., Feb. 21, 1862: Appt. 4Sgt., Oct. 14, 1861: POW, Burkeville, Va. (Apr. 6, 1865).

MUSICIANS

(1)   ANDERSON, JOHN M. — Orig. Musician in Co.: Reduced to ranks: POW, Burkeville, Va. (Apr. 6, 1865).

(1)   BOX, JOHN W. — See list of "Non-Comm. Officers" above.

PRIVATES

ABERNETHY, GEHU — Died, May 10, 1862: No other record.

(1)   ALLEN, J. R. — Transfd. to 3rd Btln., Ga. Sharpshooters, June 8, 1863.

ALLEN, R. D. — No record after Nov., 1862.

(1)   ARMSTRONG, GARVIN A. — POW, Cedar Cr. (Oct. 19, 1864).

ARMSTRONG, T. A. — No record after June, 1862.

ARTHER, B. J. — No record after Oct., 1862.

ATWOOD, A. — No record after July, 1862.

ATWOOD, WM. H. — Enl., Aug. 30, 1861 at Richmond: Deserted, took Fed. oath, Nov. 5, 1864.

(1)   AUSTIN, JOHN H. — K., Antietam (Sept. 17, 1862).

BAKER, JAS. M. — See list of "Officers" above.

BAKER, THOS. H. — See list of "Officers" above.

BARNES, J. M. (or W.) — No record after Nov., 1862.

BARNES, WM. WESLEY — Enl., Feb. 23, 1862 in Bartow Co., Ga.: W., Wilderness (May 6, 1864): AWOL, July, 1864.

(1)   BARTON, J. F. — D., Aug., 1862.

(1)   BARTON, JOHN W. — Sick most of 1862: No record after Feb., 1863.

BEARDEN, F. M. — Enl., Aug. 3, 1862 at Dalton, Ga.: W. (hand), Gaines' Mill (June 27, 1862): AWOL, Nov., 1862.

(1)   BLACK, A. J. — K., 2nd Manassas (Aug. 30, 1862).

BRACT (or BROCK), W. M. — No record after Nov., 1862.

(1)   BRADLEY, WM. C. — W. (side & leg), Gaines' Mill (June 27, 1862): Died from wounds, June 29, 1862.

BRAMLETT, G. W. — No record after Nov., 1862.

(1)   BRAMLETT, J. W. — Died of typhoid fever, Richmond, June, 1862.

BRANSON, JOHN C. — Transfd. to Co. K from cavalry co. in Phillips Ga. Legion, Aug. 2, 1862: Dischgd. for disability, May 27, 1862.

(1) BRANTLEY, JOHN B. — Died, Nov. 12, 1862, cause unknown.

BROCK, ELEAZER — Enl., June 19, 1862 at Stilsboro, Ga.: Dischgd., disability, Oct. 23, 1862.

BROCK, J. H. — Enl., Feb. 23, 1862 in Bartow Co., Ga.: W., Antietam (Sept. 17, 1862): POW, Burkeville, Va. (Apr. 6, 1865).

BROCK, WM. R. — Enl., Feb. 23, 1862 in Bartow Co., Ga.: Present for duty, Jan., 1865.

(2) BROWN, HENRY M. — Enl., Apr. 16, 1862 in Bartow Co., Ga.: Paroled, Appomattox (Apr. 12, 1865).

BROWN, W. H. — Listed on Bi-Monthly Muster Roll as being present at Antietam (Sept. 17, 1862).

BURNETT, WM. P. — Enl., Aug. 3, 1861 at Adairsville, Ga.: W. (head), Antietam (Sept. 17, 1862): Transfd. to 3rd Btln., Ga. Sharpshooters, June 8, 1863.

(1) BURT, JOHN H. — Hospitalized, Summer, 1864.

(1) CAMPBELL, JAS. H. — Died, Mar. 24, 1862.

(1) CARROLL, J. H. — W., 7 Pines (June 1, 1862): W. (shoulder), Gaines' Mill (June 27, 1862): W., Chancellorsville (May 3, 1863).

CARROLL, WM. M. — Enl., Sept. 3, 1861 at Richmond: W. (thigh), Gaines' Mill (June 27, 1862): Deserted, took Fed. oath, Mar. 25, 1865.

CLEVELAND, A. B. — Enl., Feb. 23, 1862 in Bartow Co., Ga.: W. (side), Gaines' Mill (June 27, 1862): W. (arm), Wilderness (May 6, 1864): AWOL, July, 1864.

(1) CLEVELAND, JAS. M. D. — See list of "Officers" above.

COLLENDER, W. J. — W., Antietam (Sept. 17, 1862): No other record.

(1) COLLINS, J. H. — W. (foot), Gaines' Mill (June 27, 1862): POW, Gettysburg (July 2, 1863): Died, Ft. Delaware, Oct. 8, 1863.

(1) COOK, C. — Died at Richmond, June 4, 1862.

COOK, DAWSEY (or DORSEY) — Enl., Apr. 5, 1862 in Bartow Co., Ga.: On detached service, Jan., 1865: No other record.

COOK, J. S. — Enl., June 20, 1862: Transfd. to 3rd Btln., Ga. Sharpshooters, June 8, 1863: POW, Farmville, Va. (Apr. 6, 1865).

(1) COOK, WM. R. — W., 2nd Manassas (Aug. 30, 1862): Disabled: POW, Bartow Co., Ga. (Oct. 28, 1864).

(1) DAVIS, JOHN F. — See list of "Non-Comm. Officers" above.

DEATON, ELIJAH — See list of "Non-Comm. Officers" above.

DEMPSEY, G. A. — See list of "Non-Comm. Officers" above.

(1) DRAKE, B. T. — See list of "Non-Comm. Officers" above.

(1) FORD, DARBY D. — W. (chest & leg), Gaines' Mill (June 27, 1862): POW, Cold Harbor (June 1, 1864).

FORD, JOHN G. — Enl., June 2, 1862: W., Gaines' Mill (June 27, 1862): POW, Knoxville (Dec. 5, 1863).

(1) FOWLER, P. K. — Transfd. to 3rd Btln., Ga. Sharpshooters, May 8,
(2) 1863: Paroled, Appomattox (Apr. 12, 1865).

FRANKS, J. S. — Enl., Feb. 22, 1862: Transfd. to 3rd Btln., Ga. Sharpshooters, June 8, 1863.

FREEMAN, J. E. — Enl., Feb. 19, 1862: Present for duty, Jan., 1865.

GADDIS, WM. H. — Enl., Feb. 19, 1862: K., Gaines' Mill (June 27, 1862).

(2) GARRISON, J. N. — Enl., June 22, 1862: W., Wilderness (May 6, 1864): AWOL, Summer, 1864: Paroled, Appomattox (Apr. 12, 1865).

(1) GARRISON, JAS. M. — W., 2nd Manassas (Aug. 30, 1862): W., Chancellorsville (May 3, 1863): POW, Missionary Ridge, Tenn. (Nov. 25, 1863): D. of pneumonia in prison, May 16, 1864.

(1) GODDARD, R. T. — Died, Fall, 1862.

HARDY, W. F. — Enl., Feb. 21, 1862: See list of "Non-Commissioned Officers" above.

HARLING, EDMUND — Enl., Feb. 17, 1862: W. (thigh), Gaines' Mill (June 27, 1862): Leg amputated.

HARRIS, JOHN Y. — K., Antietam (Sept. 17, 1862).

HARRIS, S. — W., Antietam (Sept. 17, 1862).

HARRIS, THOS. — Enl., Feb. 2, 1862: POW, Knoxville (Dec. 3, 1863): Died of smallpox at Rock Is., Ill., Jan. 22, 1864.

HARRISON, SAMPSON — Enl., Feb. 6, 1862: W., 2nd Manassas (Aug. 30, 1862): AWOL, Aug., 1863.

(1) HAWKINS, A. M. — No record after July, 1863.

HAYES, N. T. — Enl., May 6, 1862: POW, Cold Harbor (June 1, 1864).

(1) HEADDEN, JOS. W. — W. (hand), Fredericksburg (Dec. 13, 1862): No record after Jan., 1865.

(1) HEADDEN, JOHN T. — Deserted, Dec. 18, 1863.

(1) HEATON, W. R. D. — AWOL: Jnd. Co. B, 37th Btln., Va. Cav., Mar. 30, 1863: Deserted, Nov. 10, 1864.

(1) HENDERSON, A. M. — No record after Feb., 1862.

(1) HENDERSON, LEVI D. — Transfd. to 3rd Btln., Ga. Sharpshooters, June 8, 1863.

HENDERSON, W. M. — Enl., Aug. 16, 1862: AWOL, Aug., 1864.

HICKBY, B. T. — W., Gaines' Mill (June 27, 1862): No record after Nov., 1862.

HIGHFILL, T. P. — Enl., July 2, 1862: Sick much of the war.

HOLBROOKS, JOHN R. — Enl., Mar. 12, 1862: W., Chancellorsville (May 3, 1863): Died of wound, May 13.

HORN, T. S. — Enl., Aug. 3, 1861: W., Antietam (Sept. 17, 1862): W., Spotsylvania (May 12, 1864): AWOL, Aug., 1864.

HUFFMAN, JOHN W. — Hospitalized, July, 1862: No other record.

HUSH, JOHN — W., Antietam (Sept. 17, 1862).

(1) JOHNSON, HOSEA — W., Gaines' Mill (June 27, 1862): "Leg amputated in pvt. home behind enemy lines."

(1) (2) JOHNSON, JAS. A. — Paroled, Appomattox (Apr. 12, 1865): No other record.

(1) JOHNSON, JOHN P. — Dischgd., overage (50 yrs. old), July 14, 1864.

(1) JOHNSON, WM. M. — POW, Fredericksburg (Dec. 13, 1862): Paroled.

(1) JONES, JAS. H. — W. (knee) & POW, 2nd Manassas (Aug. 30, 1862): Paroled, Sept. 29, 1862: Died of wound, Oct. 1, 1862.

(1) JONES, MANON — W., Cold Harbor (June 1, 1864): AWOL, Aug., 1864.

(1) JONES, R. F. — W., 2nd Manassas (Aug. 30, 1862): POW, Farmville, Va. (Apr. 6, 1865).

(1) JONES, WM. — Hospitalized, Summer, 1862: No other record.

LANDERS, F. M. — Enl., Mar. 12, 1862: W. (thigh), Gaines' Mill (June 27, 1862): Died from wound, July 9.

(1) LANDERS, WM. J. — W. (head), Cold Harbor (June 1, 1864): Died from wound, June 24.

(1) LANGLEY, JOSIAH — W. (leg), Gaines' Mill (June 27, 1862): AWOL, Oct., 1863.

(1) LANGLEY, LOCH, Jr. — W. (shoulder & arm), Chancellorsville (May 3, 1863): Transfd. out of Co.: Deserted, took Fed. oath, July 1, 1864.

(1) LANGLEY, THOS. — Died in Richmond, Feb. 4, 1863.

(1) LAWLESS, G. W. — Died, Mar., 1862.

(1) LEDBETTER, CHAS. — W., Antietam (Sept. 17, 1862): Transfd. to 3rd Btln., Ga. Sharpshooters, June 8, 1863.

(1) LEDBETTER, DANIEL — W. (shoulder & chest) & POW, 2nd Manassas (Aug. 30, 1862): Paroled: Transfd. to 3rd Btln., Ga. Sharpshooters, June 8, 1863.

(1) LEDBETTER, RICHARD — POW, 2nd Manassas (Aug. 30, 1862): Paroled: Transfd. to 3rd Btln., Ga. Sharpshooters, June 8, 1863.

LEDBETTER, WM. — Enl., Sept. 3, 1861 at Ringgold, Ga.: Transfd. to 3rd Btln., Ga. Sharpshooters, June 8, 1863.

(1) LOUDERMILK, HENRY — See list of "Non-Comm. Officers" above.

(1) LOUDERMILK, JOHN — See roster, "Regmtl. Hdqtrs., 18th Ga. Inf."

McMURRY, A. G. — Transfd. to Co. K from Co. B (cav.), Phillip's Ga. Legion, Sept. 4, 1861: W., Antietam (Sept. 17, 1862).

(1) MORGAN, ANDREW — Died, Mar. 4, 1862 at Calhoun, Ga.

MORGAN, JOHN — Dischgd. on Surg. Cert., Dec. 18, 1861.

MORRIS, JOHN W. — Enl., Aug. 26, 1862 at Calhoun, Ga.: POW, Burkeville, Va. (Apr. 6, 1865).

(1) MORROW, JOHN — W., 2nd Manassas (Aug. 30, 1862): Leg amputated: Died from amputation, Sept. 17, 1862.

(1) NEWMAN, D. J. — Died, Oct., 1862.

NOLES, JOHN — Enl., Feb. 11, 1862: W., Malvern Hill (July 1, 1862): W. (leg), Fredericksburg (Dec. 13, 1862).

OWEN, H. C. — Enl., Sept. 3, 1861 at Richmond: POW, Spotsylvania (May 22, 1864): Exchanged.

PATTERSON, WM. E. — Enl., Feb. 24, 1862 at Dumfries, Va.: W. (thigh) & POW, Antietam (Sept. 17, 1862).

PELHAM, W. L. — Enl., Apr. 20, 1862: W., 2nd Manassas (Aug. 30, 1862).

PENNY, J. H. — Enl., Feb. 28, 1862: W. (finger), Chancellorsville (May 2, 1863): W. (wrist), Wilderness (May 6, 1864).

(1) PETTIT, J. P. — W., 2nd Manassas (Aug. 30, 1862): Deserted, Aug., 1864.

(1) PIERCE, CHESTER — W. (hip), Gaines' Mill (June 27, 1862): W., 2nd Manassas (Aug. 30, 1862): POW, Antietam (Sept. 17, 1862): Exchanged, Oct. 17, 1862: POW, Gettysburg (July 2, 1863): Confined at Ft. Delaware: Escaped: Recaptured & confined at Ft. McHenry, Md.: Exchanged, Jan. 17, 1865.

POOR, JOHN L. — Enl., Feb. 23, 1862: Died of sickness at Ashland, Va., Apr. 21, 1862.

POPHAM, W. L. — Enl., Apr. 30, 1862: Died of pneumonia, Jan. 23, 1863.

(1) RAGAN, JAS. W. — W. (hand), Fredericksburg (Dec. 13, 1862): Transfd. to 3rd Btln., Ga. Sharpshooters, June 8, 1863: POW, Gettysburg (July 2, 1863).

(1) RICE, G. W. — Transfd. to 3rd Btln., Ga. Sharpshooters, June 8, 1863.

(1) RICHIE (or RICHEY), B. T. — W. (hand), Gaines' Mill (June 27, 1862): Disabled, dischgd., Apr. 17, 1863.

ROBERTSON, DAN — Enl., Apr. 26, 1862: Died, Dec. 1, 1862.

(1) SCOTT, GEO. W. — W., Gaines' Mill (June 27, 1862): Died from wound.

(1) SCOTT, JOHN B. — Enl. at Camp McDonald, Ga., June 21, 1861: See list of "Non-Commissioned Officers" above.

SCOTT, N. L. — W., Gaines' Mill (June 27, 1862): No other record.

(2) SCOTT, SAM M. — Enl., Feb. 2, 1862: W., Gaines' Mill (June 27, 1862): Paroled, Appomattox (Apr. 12, 1865).

SCOTT, W. L. — Enl., June 21, 1862: POW, Cedar Cr. (Oct. 19, 1864).

SEWARD, JOHN — W., Gaines' Mill (June 27, 1862): No other record.

(1) SHAW, E. C. — W., Gaines' Mill (June 27, 1862): Deserted, Dec. 18, 1863.

SHAW, E. D. — Enl., Apr. 10, 1862: AWOL, Dec., 1862.

SLANDERS, W. — W., 2nd Manassas (Aug. 30, 1862): Wound furlough to Ga.: Did not return to Co.

(1) SLATON, W. F. — See list of "Non-Comm. Officers" above.

SLAUGHTER, DAVID W. — Enl., Feb. 20, 1862: W., Gaines' Mill (June 27, 1862): Exchanged: POW, Antietam (Sept. 17, 1862): Paroled: Dischgd. on a Surg. Cert.

SLAUGHTER, M. (or W.) B. — Enl., Apr. 26, 1862: W., Gaines' Mill (June 27, 1862): K., Antietam (Sept. 17, 1862).

(1) SLAUGHTER, T. B. — See list of "Non-Comm. Officers" above.

SMITH, J. M. — Enl., Sept. 3, 1861 at Richmond: Died, June, 1864.

(1) SMITH, JAS. S. — W., Gaines' Mill (June 27, 1862): W., 2nd Manassas (Aug. 30, 1862): POW, Antietam (Sept. 17, 1862): Exchanged, Nov. 10, 1862: W. (hand), Wilderness (May 6, 1864): POW, Cass Co., Ga., July 15, 1864: Took Fed. oath, July 18, 1864.

(1) SMITH, JOS. N. — W., 2nd Manassas (Aug. 30, 1862): Transfd. to 3rd Btln., Ga. Sharpshooters, June 8, 1863.

SMITH, R. W. — Enl., Feb. 2, 1862: Deserted: Took Fed. oath at Washington, D.C., Mar. 30, 1865.

(1) SMITH, SAMUEL V. — See list of "Officers" above.

SMITH, WM. H. C. — Enl., Apr. 10, 1862: W. (hip), Gaines' Mill (June 27, 1862): W., Fredericksburg (Dec. 13, 1862): Transfd. to 3rd Btln., Ga. Sharpshooters, June 8, 1863.

(1) SMITH, WM. K. — Dischgd. for rheumatism, Jan. 6, 1862.

(1) SORRELLS, JOHN C. (or E.) — W., Malvern Hill (June 1, 1862): Deserted, Mar., 1865.

SPIKES, H. M. — Enl., Mar. 21, 1862: W., Fredericksburg (Dec. 13, 1862).

SQUIRES, J. W. — See list of "Non-Comm. Officers" above.

STEDMAN, A. G. — Enl., Apr. 26, 1862: Transfd. to 3rd Btln., Ga. Sharpshooters, June 8, 1863.

(1) STEADMAN, JOSIAH — Dischgd., disability, Aug. 1, 1862.

(1) SUGGS, J. H. — Died (heart attack), July 1, 1862, Lynchburg, Va.

(1) SUMMERELL, CHANCY — K., Gaines' Mill (June 27, 1862).

(1) SUMMERELL, M. O. — Died of pneumonia, Richmond, Feb., 1863.

SUTTON, N. F. — Enl., Apr. 10, 1862: POW, Gettysburg (July 2, 1863): Exchanged, May 3, 1864: Paroled, Lynchburg, Va., Apr. 15, 1865.

(1) TATE, F. M. — K., Gaines' Mill (June 27, 1862).

(1) TONEY, W. J. — K., 2nd Manassas (Aug. 30, 1862).

TRAMP, JOHN — W., 2nd Manassas (Aug. 30, 1862): No other record.

(1) TUCKER, J. W. — POW, Fredericksburg (Dec. 13, 1862): Exchanged: K., Chancellorsville (May 3, 1863).

TURNER, BARNEY S. — Enl., Apr. 28, 1862: AWOL, Apr., 1864.

TURNER, M. — Enl., Apr. 10, 1862: Paroled, May 28, 1865.

(1) UNDERWOOD, A. JACK — W., Malvern Hill (July 1, 1862): POW, Lincoln Co., Tenn., Dec. 6, 1863: Took Fed. oath, Oct. 11, 1864.

(1) UNDERWOOD, D. H. — W., 2nd Manassas (Aug. 30, 1862): W., Antietam (Sept. 17, 1862): Disabled.

UNDERWOOD, G. L. — See list of "Non-Comm. Officers" above.

(1) UNDERWOOD, JOHN H. — See list of "Non-Comm. Officers" above.

(1) UNDERWOOD, STEPHEN — W. (eye), Gaines' Mill (June 27, 1862): Lost sight of one eye: Deserted: Took Fed. oath, Mar. 2, 1865.

(1) UNDERWOOD, WM. J. — K., Cold Harbor (June 7, 1864).

(1) WADE, GEO. W. — W. (hip), Gaines' Mill (June 27, 1862): No record after Aug., 1863.

(1) WHEELER, WM. — W., 2nd Manassas (Aug. 30, 1862): Died of disease while on furlough to Ga., May, 1864.

(1) WILEY, WM. — Died of fever at Shepardstown, Va., Sept. 16, 1862.

WILLIAMS, J. V. — See list of "Non-Comm. Officers" above.

WILLIAMS, J. W. — W., Fredericksburg (Dec. 13, 1862): No other record.

WILLIS, J. V. — Enl., Apr. 6, 1862: POW, Cold Harbor (June 1, 1864).

WINDSOR, GEO. C. — Enl., Feb. 24, 1862 at Dumfries, Va., as a substitute for Cpl. Baylus Langley: POW, Boonsboro (Sept. 15, 1862): Exchanged: Deserted, E. Tenn., Nov., 1863: Took Fed. oath, Dec. 4, 1863.

WYLEY (or WILEY), SAMUEL — Enl., Apr. 6, 1862: W., Gaines' Mill (June 27, 1862): Arm amputated.

★   ★   ★   ★   ★

MEMBERS OF COMPANY K, 18TH GA. INF. REGT., WHO WERE NOT PRESENT FOR DUTY DURING THE PERIOD THAT THE REGIMENT WAS ASSIGNED TO HOOD'S TEXAS BRIGADE (NOV., 1861-NOV., 1862).

OFFICERS

(1) Smith, W. G., 1Lt. (Orig. 1Lt. of
Co.: D., Aug., 1861)

NON-COMMISSIONED OFFICERS

(1) Price, E. P., 3Sgt. (Orig. 3Sgt. of
Co.: Transfd. out of Co.,
Nov., 1861)
(1) Smith, J. P., 4Cpl. (Orig. 4Cpl.

of Co.: No record after Oct.,
1861)
(1) Smith, M. A., 4Sgt. (Orig. 4Sgt.
of Co.: D., Oct., 1861)

MUSICIANS

(1) Floyd, D. R. (Orig. Musician in
Co.: D., Sept., 1861)

PRIVATES

(1) Brewster, Jas. N. (D., Aug.,
1861)
Brown, W. (No record prior to
July, 1863)
(1) Brummett, E. (Dischgd., disability, Oct., 1861)
(1) Burnett, B. E. B. (No record
after June, 1861)
(1) Chadwick, J. T. (D., Nov., 1861)
Cleveland, F. M. (Enl., Aug.,
1863)
(1) Cook, A. M. (D., Oct., 1861)
Cowen, H. C. (No record)
Davidson, Jas. (No record)
(1) Davis, W. M. (Deserted, Oct.,
1861)
(1) Fowler, B. R. (No record after
Oct., 1861)
Frank, J. (No record prior to
Dec., 1862)
Freeman, J. A. (No record prior
to Mar., 1865)
Garrison, J. A. (Enl., June,
1863)
(1) Harmon, A. H. (Dischgd., disability, Oct., 1861)
(1) Henderson, H. M. (No record
after Oct., 1861)

Johnson, J. M. K. (No record
prior to May, 1863)
Jones, John L. (Enl., Feb., 1863)
(1) Langley, Loch, Sr. (Dischgd.,
disability, Oct., 1861)
Ledbetter, B. (No record prior to
Nov., 1862)
McMikle, John C. (Enl., Feb.,
1864)
Price, E. M. (No record prior to
May, 1864)
Purser, H. F. (Enl., Apr., 1864)
Quinn, D. S. (Deserted, Oct.,
1861)
Scott, M. (No record prior to
July, 1863)
Simerell, C. (No record after
Nov., 1861)
Smith, J. D. (No record prior to
May, 1863)
Taylor, Jas. (Dischgd., disability,
Nov., 1861)
(1) Terrell, John (No record after
Oct., 1861)
Topham, W. L. (No record prior
to Jan., 1863)
Wethers, B. M. (No record prior
to Jan., 1865)

Whitten, John (No record prior to Sept., 1863)

Yarbrough, W. E. (No record prior to Nov., 1862)

Yarman, J. B. (No record prior to Nov., 1862)

Yonson (or Johnson), J. M. (No record prior to Nov., 1862)

HAMPTON'S SO. CAR. LEGION (INF. BTLN.)

SHORT HISTORY

The Hampton Legion South Carolina Volunteers was organized June 12, 1861 with an Infantry Battalion of eight companies, A through H; a Cavalry Battalion of four companies, A through D, and an Artillery Battalion of two companies, A and B.

On August 22, 1862, the Cavalry Battalion was assigned to the 2nd Regiment of South Carolina Cavalry. The Artillery Battalion became separate and independent companies sometime prior to August 25, 1862; Company A became Hart's Company, Horse Artillery, South Carolina, and Company B became Bachman's Company, South Carolina Artillery.

The eight infantry companies of the Hampton Legion were assigned to Hood's Texas Brigade immediately following the Battle of Seven Pines (May 31-June 1, 1862). These South Carolina companies fought with the Texas Brigade in the battles of Second Manassas (Aug. 30, 1862); Boonsboro (Sept. 14, 1862); and Antietam (Sept. 17, 1862). In mid-November, 1862, when the Army of Northern Virginia was reorganized, the South Carolina infantry of Hampton's Legion was transferred to Brig.-Gen. Micah Jenkins' Brigade. Also, at this time, the eight companies were augmented by Companies I and K (13th Battalion, South Carolina Infantry) to form a regiment.

Prior to joining Hood's Texas Brigade, the Hampton Legion had participated in two major battles, First Manassas (July 21, 1861) and Seven Pines (May 31-June 1, 1862). After its assignment to Jenkins' Brigade in mid-November, 1862, the Legion fought in the battles engaged in by the Army of Northern Virginia (except Chancellorsville) and in the Chickamauga and E. Tennessee Campaigns under Longstreet in the Fall of 1863 and Winter of 1863-64.

In the Spring of 1864, this South Carolina Infantry Regiment was mounted and transferred to the cavalry service. It was paroled at Appomattox, April 12, 1865, as "Hampton's Legion Mounted Infantry, South Carolina Volunteers."

HAMPTON'S SO. CAR. LEGION (INF. BTLN.)

HDQTRS. - FIELD, STAFF & BAND

Organized as an overstrength Infantry Battalion of eight companies (A thru H) near Columbia, South Carolina in early June, 1861. When the Battalion left Hood's Texas Brigade in mid-November, 1862, two more companies were added (I & K) increasing the Battalion to a regiment.

Key

(1) Original member of Hdqtrs. (2) Paroled at Appomattox.
K (Killed), W (Wounded), POW (Prisoner of War)
AWOL (Absent Without Leave)

OFFICERS, FIELD & LINE

GARY, MARTIN W.   Colonel
> Orig. Capt., Co. B, age 30: Prom., Lt.-Col., June 16, 1862: Prom., Col., Aug. 25, 1862: Appt. Brig.-Gen., May 19, 1864.

LOGAN, T. M.   Colonel
> Orig. 2Lt., Co. A, age 20: Prom., Capt., Sept. 3, 1861: W. (foot), Gaines' Mill (June 27, 1862): Prom., Maj., Sept. 17, 1862: Prom., Lt.-Col., Dec. 13, 1862: Prom., Col., May 19, 1864: Appt. Brig.-Gen., Feb. 15, 1865.

NICHOLSON, BENJ. E.   Colonel
> Orig. 1Sgt., Co. B, age 20: Elect., 2Lt., Aug. 15, 1861: Prom., 1Lt., June 16, 1862: Prom., Capt., Sept. 17, 1862: Prom., Maj., Sept. 3, 1864: W., Darbytown Rd. (Oct. 7, 1864): Prom., Col., Winter, 1864-65: Paroled, May 23, 1865 at Augusta, Ga.

(2)   ARNOLD, ROBT. B.   Lieut.-Colonel
> Orig. 1Lt., Co. E, age 27: Prom., Capt., Sept. 14, 1861: Prom., Lt.-Col., Dec. 13, 1862: Paroled, Appomattox (Apr. 12, 1865).

(1)   GRIFFIN, JAS. B.   Lieut.-Colonel
> Orig. Maj. of Btln.: Prom., Lt.-Col., July 21, 1861: Declined prom. to Col.: No record after May, 1864.

OFFICERS – STAFF

ADJUTANTS (AAG)

(1)   BARKER, THEO. G.   Captain
> Orig. AAG of Btln.: Transfd. to 2nd So. Car. Cav. Regt., Nov. 15, 1862.

(2)   BALL, BEAUFORT W. 1st Lieutenant
        Enl. as a Pvt. in Co. B, at Richmond, July 10, 1861: Appt. Btln.
        Adj., Nov. 15, 1862: Paroled, Appomattox (Apr. 12, 1865).

SURGEON
(1)   DARBY, JOHN T. Major
        Orig. Surg. of Btln.: Transfd. to Hood's Div. as Div. Surg., Nov.
        24, 1862.

ASST. SURGEONS
(2)   BOZEMAN, JOHN J. Captain
        Orig. Pvt., Co. E, age 25: Appt. Asst. Surg., Winter, 1862-63:
        Paroled, Appomattox (Apr. 12, 1865).
(1)   TAYLOR, BENJ. WALTER Captain
        Orig. Asst. Surg. of Btln.: Hospitalized, Spring, 1862: Appears on
        a Nov., 1864 roster: No other record.

COMMISSARY SUBSISTENCE OFFICER (ACS)
(1)   BEGGS, THOS. C. Captain
        Orig. Btln. ACS Officer: No record after Aug., 1862.

QUARTERMASTER OFFICERS (AQM)
(1)   GOODWIN, CLAUDIUS L. Captain
        Orig. Btln. AQM: No record after June 30, 1862.
        MAULDIN, WM. H.
        Orig. 2Lt., Co. D, age 22: Elect., 1Lt., Spring, 1862: Appt. Btln.
        AQM, Nov., 1864.

CHAPLAIN
(1)   JOHNSON, RICHARD Captain
        Orig. Btln., Chaplain: Transfd. to cavalry, Dec., 1862.

NON-COMMISSIONED OFFICERS

SERGEANT-MAJORS
ANCRUM, JAS. H., Jr.
        Orig. Pvt., Co. A, age 18: Prom., Btln., Sgt.-Maj., Nov. 7, 1862:
        Prom., 2Lt. of arty., July 29, 1864.
(1)   GAILLARD, SAM J.
        Orig. 1Sgt., Co. C, age 29: Prom., Btln., Sgt.-Maj., Sept. 21, 1861:
        Dischgd., Nov. 7, 1862.

QUARTERMASTER SERGEANT (AQM)
HAMILTON, A. HUGHES
        Enl., Mar. 18, 1862 at Williamston, So. Car.: No record after
        Aug., 1863.

ORDNANCE SERGEANTS

GARRISON, DAVID

    Orig. 4Sgt., Co. F, age 21: Prom., 3Sgt., Fall, 1861: Prom., 1Sgt., Spring, 1862: W. (finger), 7 Pines (June 1, 1862): Prom., Btln. Ordn.-Sgt., Winter, 1863-64: No record after Oct., 1864.

GREENE, JOHN SAMUEL

    Orig. Pvt., Co. A, age 24: Prom., 5Cpl., Oct. 9, 1861: Prom., 3Sgt., Summer, 1862: Prom. Btln. Ordn.-Sgt., July 1, 1862: No record after Aug., 1863.

HOSPITAL STEWARD

McLAURIN, HENRY J.

    Orig. Pvt., Co. C, age 23: Appt. Hosp. Steward, Spring, 1863: No record after Sept., 1863.

BAND

BANDMASTER

(2)   GRIFFIN, BENJ. F.

    Orig. Pvt., Co. D, age 25: Prom., 3Cpl., Fall, 1861: Reduced to ranks, Spring, 1862: Appt. "Chief Musician," July, 1862: Paroled, Appomattox (Apr. 12, 1865).

BAND MEMBERS

(2)   ACKER, RICHMOND

    Orig. Pvt., Co. D, age 21: Appt. Btln. Musician, Aug., 1862: Paroled, Appomattox (Apr. 12, 1865).

(2)   BARNETT, JOHN M.

    Orig. Pvt., Co. D, age 23: Appt. Btln. Musician, Spring, 1862: Paroled, Appomattox (Apr. 12, 1865).

(2)   CRYMES, JOHN W.

    Orig. Pvt., Co. D, age 27: Appt. Btln. Musician, Spring, 1862: Paroled, Appomattox (Apr. 12, 1865).

(2)   CRYMES, THOS. W.

    Orig. Pvt., Co. D, age 23: Appt. Btln. Musician, Spring, 1862: Paroled, Appomattox (Apr. 12, 1865).

(2)   GREEN, JORDAN G.

    Orig. Pvt., Co. D, age 23: Appt. Btln. Musician, Summer, 1862: Paroled, Appomattox (Apr. 12, 1865).

HARBOT, J. VALENTINE

    Orig. Pvt., Co. D, age 22: Appt. Btln. Musician, Summer, 1862: No record after Oct., 1864.

(2)   HOKE, CHAS. F.

    Orig. Pvt., Co. D, age 22: Appt. Btln. Musician, Dec., 1852: Prom., 1Cpl., Fall, 1864: Paroled, Appomattox (Apr. 12, 1865).

HOWARD, JAS. F.

    Enl. as a Musician in Co. D, Feb. 25, 1862: Transfd. to Btln. Hdqtrs., Summer, 1863.

MASTERSON, EDW. T.

    Orig. Pvt., Co. A, age 25: Appt. Btln. Musician, Summer, 1863.

(2)   PARKINS (or PERKINS), THOS.
            Orig. Pvt., Co. D, age 20: Appt. Btln. Musician, Fall, 1862:
            Paroled, Appomattox (Apr. 12, 1865).
(2)   SMITH, BENNETT F.
            Orig. Pvt., Co. D, age 26: W., 1st Manassas (July 21, 1861): Appt.
            Btln. Musician, Summer, 1862: Paroled, Appomattox (Apr. 12,
            1865).
(2)   WALKER, WM. E.
            Orig. Pvt., Co. D, age 21: Appt. Btln. Musician, Feb., 1862:
            Paroled, Appomattox (Apr. 12, 1865).

★   ★   ★   ★   ★

MEMBERS OF HEADQUARTERS, HAMPTON'S SO. CAR. LEGION (INF. BTLN.) WHO WERE NOT PRESENT FOR DUTY DURING THE PERIOD THAT THE BATTALION WAS ASSIGNED TO HOOD'S TEXAS BRIGADE (JUNE 2-NOV. 15, 1862).

OFFICERS

(1) Hampton, Wade, Col. (Orig. Col. Hampton's Legion: Prom. Brig.-Gen., May, 1862 & transfd. out)

Conner, Jas., Col. (Orig. Capt., Co. A, age 31: Prom., Maj., July 21, 1861: Prom., Col., June 1, 1862 & asgnd. cmd. of the 22nd No. Car. Inf. Regt.)

(1) Johnson, Benj. J., Lt.-Col. (Orig. Lt.-Col. of Btln.: K., 1st Manassas (July 21, 1861)

(2) Green, W. P., Asst. Surg. (No record prior to Apr., 1865)

Moore, Henry W., Asst. Surg. (Orig. Pvt. in a Cav. Co.: No record after Apr., 1862)

(1) Goodwin, W. C., AQM (No record after June, 1861)

(1) Johnson, W. B., Chap. (No record after June, 1861)

Thomas, _____ , Chap. (No record prior to Sept., 1864)

NON-COMMISSIONED OFFICERS

(1) Hughes, F. P., Sgt.-Maj. (Dischgd., disability, Apr., 1862)

McLeon, J. O., Hosp. Stew. (No record prior to Sept., 1864)

BAND

Buchanan, Geo. (No record prior to Aug., 1864)

Griffin, Holbert A. (Enl., Mar., 1863)

(2) Humbert, I. V. (No record prior to Apr., 1865)

(2) McGee, Geo. W. (Enl., Mar., 1863)

HAMPTON'S SO. CAR. LEGION (INF. BTLN.)
COMPANY A – *WASHINGTON LIGHT INF. VOL*

Company was mustered into the Confederate Service on June 12, 1861 at Charleston, So. Carlonia, "for one year," by Lt. Jas. Conner.

Key

(1) Original member of Company. (2) Paroled at Appomattox.
K (Killed), W (Wounded), POW (Prisoner of War)
AWOL (Absent Without Leave)

OFFICERS

THOMAS, EUGENE A. Capt. — Orig. 4Cpl. of Co., age 21: Prom., 1Lt., June 8, 1862: W., 2nd Manassas (Aug. 30, 1862): Prom., Capt., Sept. 17, 1862.

McELROY, JAS. 1Lt. — Orig. Pvt. in Co.: Prom., 3Lt., Summer, 1862: W., 2nd Manassas (Aug. 30, 1862): Prom., 2Lt., Sept. 12, 1862: Prom., 1Lt., Jan. 8, 1863.

O'CONNOR, W. EDMUND 1Lt. — Orig. Pvt. in Co., age 26: Prom., 2Lt., June 8, 1862: W. (arm), Antietam (Sept. 17, 1862): Prom., 1Lt., Sept. 17, 1862: Resgnd., Jan. 8, 1863.

ALBERGOTTIE, THOS. C. 2Lt. — Orig. Pvt. in Co., age 25: Prom., 2Lt.: W. (head), Summer, 1864: No other record.

GIBBS, JAS. P. 2Lt. — Enl. as a Pvt., Aug. 24, 1861: Prom., 3Lt., Summer, 1863: W., Wills Valley, Tenn. (Oct. 28, 1863): Prom., 2Lt., Nov. 18, 1863: Retired, Dec. 15, 1864.

HENNING, W. ALSTON 2Lt. — Orig. Pvt. in Co., age 23: W., near Richmond, 1861: Elect., 3Lt., Feb. 8, 1863: Prom., 2Lt., Feb. 15, 1863: K., Campbell's Sta., Tenn., Nov. 18, 1863.

ROY, ROBT. 2Lt. — Orig. Pvt. in Co., age 26: W., Antietam (Sept. 17, 1862): Prom., 2Lt., Jan. 20, 1863: Resgnd., Feb. 8, 1863.

COPES, JOEL 3Lt. — Orig. 3Sgt. of Co., age 21: Elect., 3Lt., June 30, 1864: W., Darbytown Rd. (Oct. 13, 1864).

NON-COMMISSIONED OFFICERS

(2) COACHMAN, FRANCIS G. 5Sgt. — Enl. as a Pvt., Aug. 24, 1861: W., 7 Pines (June 1, 1862): Prom., 5Sgt., Fall, 1864: Paroled, Appomattox (Apr. 12, 1865).

(1) COPES, JOEL 3Sgt. — See list of "Officers" above.

DANIELS, GEO. W. 3Sgt. — Enl. as a Pvt., at Richmond, June 26, 1861: Prom., 1Cpl., Aug. 6, 1862: Prom., 3Sgt., Spring, 1864: POW, Burkeville, Va. (Apr. 6, 1865).

(1) GARDNER, JOHN H. 1Sgt. — Orig. 2Sgt. of Co., age 23: Appt. 1Sgt., Aug. 30, 1861: Reduced to ranks, Summer, 1862: Dischgd., Oct. 1, 1862, appt. to Commissary Subsistence Dept., CSA.

JONES, C. E. 3Sgt. — Orig. Pvt. in Co.: W., 7 Pines (June 1, 1862): Prom., 1Cpl., Aug. 1, 1862: W., 2nd Manassas (Aug. 30, 1862): Prom., 3Sgt., Winter, 1862-63: Dischgd., disability, Aug., 1863.

JONES, WM. 3Cpl. — Orig. Pvt. in Co., age 23: W. & POW, Manassas (Aug. 30, 1862): Paroled: Prom., 3Cpl., Fall, 1864.

MUSTARD, ROBT. W. 1Cpl. — Orig. Pvt. in Co., age 26: POW, 7 Pines (June 1, 1862): Exchanged: W., 2nd Manassas (Aug. 30, 1862): Prom., 1Cpl., Fall, 1864: W., New Market Heights (Sept. 29, 1864).

POPPENHEIM, CHRISTOPHER P. 2Cpl. — Orig. Pvt. in Co., age 24: Prom., 2Cpl., Aug. 1, 1862: W., Antietam (Sept. 17, 1862).

(2) STOCKER, SAMUEL H. 1Sgt. — Enl. as a Pvt., July 29, 1861: W., Antietam (Sept. 17, 1862): Prom., 2Sgt., Fall, 1862: W., E. Tenn. (Jan. 17, 1864): Prom., 1Sgt., Fall, 1864: Paroled, Appomattox (Apr. 12, 1865).

STROHECKER, OSWELL 1Cpl. — Orig. Pvt. in Co., age 24: Prom., 1Cpl., Winter, 1863-64: K., 9 Mile Rd., Va. (Oct. 27, 1864).

(1) THOMAS, EUGENE 4Cpl. — See list of "Officers" above.

VERNER, SOLOMON S. 2Cpl. — Orig. Pvt. in Co. A, age 24: Prom., 2Cpl., Fall, 1864: Present for duty, Dec., 1864.

WEAR, GEO. 3Sgt. — Orig. Pvt. in Co., age 32: Prom., 3Cpl., Nov. 1, 1862: Prom., 3Sgt., Fall, 1864.

WHILDEN, GEO. T. 4Sgt. — Enl. as a Pvt., Sept. 1, 1861: W., 7 Pines (June 1, 1862): Prom., 4Sgt., Fall, 1864.

YATES, EDW. 2Sgt. — Enl. as a Pvt., Sept. 1, 1861: W., 2nd Manassas (Aug. 30, 1862): Prom., 3Cpl., Aug. 1, 1862: Prom., 2Sgt., 1864.

PRIVATES

(1) ALBERGOTTIE, THOS. C. — See list of "Officers" above.

ALLEN, BARNETT B. — Enl. at Richmond, June 26, 1861: W. & POW, Manassas (Aug. 30, 1862): Paroled.

(1) ASHER, HENRY — Enl., age 20: Dischgd., Aug. 12, 1862.

(1) ATKINSON, JONAH A. — Dischgd., disability, June 12, 1862.

(1) AVEILHE, L. SIDNEY — W., 7 Pines (June 1, 1862): W. (leg), 2nd Manassas (Aug. 30, 1862): Dischgd., Surg. Cert., Nov. 26, 1862: Jnd. crew of CSA Privateer, "Rattlesnake."

(1) BECKMAN, JACOB S. — Enl., age 26: W., 2nd Manassas (Aug. 30,
(2) 1862): Paroled, Appomattox (Apr. 12, 1865).

(1) BIRD, W. COOPER — Enl., age 26: Dischgd. (rheumatism), June 16, 1862.

(1) BLUM, JOHN A. — Died of disease at Charleston, Fall, 1862.

BRANTLY, BEVERLY B. — Enl., July 29, 1861: K., 2nd Manassas (Aug. 30, 1862).

(2) BRINSON, HENRY L. — Enl., Nov. 30, 1861: Paroled, Appomattox (Apr. 12, 1865).

(1) BROWN, BURNETT — Deserted, Jan. 23, 1865: No other record.

(1) BROWN, JAS. H. — Enl., age 22: Returned from sick furlough, Fall, 1863: No other record.

(1) BRUEN, HALSEY F. — Enl., age 26: Dischgd., June 6, 1862.

(1) BRUEN, WM. R. H. — Enl., age 24: Dischgd., sick, Nov. 12, 1863.

BUNCH, JAS. S. — Enl., June 26, 1861 at Richmond: Present for duty, Dec., 1864, no further record.

(1) CAY, THADDEUS LANDRY — Enl., age 24: Died of disease, Sept. 9, 1862.

(1) CLARK, JOS. A. — Transfd. out of Co., Summer, 1862.

(1) COACHMAN, EDGAR F. — W. (arm & back), Mechanicsville (June 26, 1862): Arm amputated: Died, Aug. 6, 1862.

COACHMAN, FRANCIS G. — See list of "Non-Comm. Officers" above.

(1) CONTERIER, J. E. — Enl., age 20: Transfd. to 2nd So. Car. Inf. Regt., Dec. 5, 1864.

(1) COX, CHAS. E. — Dischgd., June 21, 1862: Re-enl., Apr. 6, 1863: K., Petersburg, July 28, 1864.

(1) CUTTINO, WM. H. — Enl., age 22: W., Antietam (Sept. 17, 1862).

DANIELS, GEO. W. — See list of "Non-Comm. Officers" above.

DANIELS, HENRY — Enl., Feb. 1, 1862: POW, Burkeville, Va. (Apr. 6, 1865).

DIBBLE, W. JASPER — Enl., Sept. 1, 1861: W., 2nd Manassas (Aug. 30, 1862).

(1) EASTERLING, EDW. C. — Present for duty most of war: Paroled,
(2) Appomattox (Apr. 12, 1865).

(1) EDIE, JAS. A. — W. (foot), Gaines' Mill (June 27, 1862).

EDWARDS, J. G. — Enl., Sept. 24, 1861 at Columbia, S.C.: Present for duty, Nov. & Dec., 1864: No further record.

EMANUEL, E. M. — Enl., Apr. 30, 1862: Present for duty, Nov. & Dec., 1864: No further record.

(1) ERICKSON, CHAS. — Deserted, jnd. U.S. Army, Oct. 14, 1864.

(1) FERRELL, HENRY C. — POW, 1st Manassas (July 21, 1861): Exchanged, Nov., 1861: W. & POW, Wills Valley, Tenn. (Oct. 28, 1863): Died of wound in Fed. prison.

(1) FORD, STEPHANUS — Present for duty most of war: Paroled,
(2) Appomattox (Apr. 12, 1865).

FORD, THOS. S. — Enl., Aug. 24, 1861: W., 7 Pines (June 1, 1862): Dischgd., Jan. 31, 1863.

FORD, WM. H. — Enl., June 26, 1861 at Richmond: W., 7 Pines (June 1, 1862): Dischgd. because of wound, Nov. 22, 1862.

GIBBS, JAS. P. — See list of "Officers" above.

(1) GREEN, JOHN H. — Transfd. to 6th So. Car. Cav. Regt., May 21, 1863.

HASELL, P. GADSDEN — Enl., Sept. 1, 1861: Present for duty, Nov. & Dec., 1864: No further record.

(1) HENNING, W. ALSTON — See list of "Officers" above.

(1) HERIOT, WM. CLARKSON — Enl., age 33: Dischgd., Sept. 12, 1862 (overage).

(1) HOWE, JONAS — Enl., age 24: Dischgd., June 21, 1862.

(1) HUCKABEE, JOHN P. — No record after Nov. & Dec., 1864.

HUGHES, F. P. — See Roster, "Hdqtrs., Hampton's Legion": Re-enl., Nov., 1862: W., Darbytown Rd. (Oct. 7, 1864): Died of wound, Oct. 14.

(1) HUGHES, WM. L. — Enl., age 20: W., 2nd Manassas (Aug. 30, 1862): Provided a substitute, dischgd., Feb. 28, 1863.

HUMAN, B. T. — Enl., Apr. 1, 1862 at Columbia, S.C.: Transfd. to 2nd So. Car. Inf. Regt., Dec. 15, 1864.

HUMAN, E. S. — Enl., Apr. 1, 1862 at Columbia, S.C.: Present for duty, Nov. & Dec., 1864.

JENKINS, JAS. H. — Enl., June 26, 1861 at Richmond: Present for duty, Nov. 7 Dec., 1864.

(1) JONES, C. E. — See list of "Non-Comm. Officers" above.

(1) JONES, WM. — See list of "Non-Comm. Officers" above.

(2) KENNEDY, J. E. — Enl., Apr. 12, 1862: Paroled, Appomattox (Apr. 12, 1865).

(1) KENYON, WM. A. — W. & POW, near Chattanooga, Oct. 29, 1863.

(1) LaCOSTE, CHAS. P. — Transfd. to 25th So. Car. Inf. Regt., Oct. 24, 1864.

LAMBERT, CHAS. — Enl., Aug. 31, 1862 at Richmond: POW, Amelia CH. (Apr. 6, 1865).

McCARLY, THOS. H. — Enl., Apr. 30, 1862: Present for duty, Nov. & Dec., 1864.

McCUTCHEON, R. G. — Enl., Mar. 27, 1862: POW, Richmond, Apr. 3, 1865.

(1) McELROY, JAS. — See list of "Officers" above.

(1) McGEE, JAS. W. — Enl., age 25: W., 2nd Manassas (Aug. 30, 1862): Died from wound, Sept. 10, 1862.

(1) McINTOSH, J. — Present for duty, Sept. & Oct., 1863: No other record.

(1) McQUADE, JAS. — Enl., age 30: W., Antietam (Sept. 17, 1862): Dischgd., Sept. 29, 1862, "never acquired a domicile."

MORRISON, RICH. T. — Enl., Nov. 1, 1861: Present for duty, Nov. & Dec., 1864.

(1) MORRISON, ROBT. V. — Enl., age 20: W. (ankle), Louisa CH., Va., Summer, 1861: No record after Dec., 1864.

(1) MULKAI, THOS. D. — Enl., age 26: Present for duty, Dec., 1864.

(1) MUSTARD, ROBT. W. — See list of "Non-Comm. Officers" above.

(1) MYERS, JACOB S. — Enl., age 24: W. & POW, Wills Valley, Tn. (Oct. 28, 1863).

(1) O'CONNOR, W. EDMUND — See list of "Officers" above.

OWENS, JAS. B. — Enl., Sept. 1, 1861: Dischgd. for chronic diarrhea, Mar. 17, 1863.

(2) PARKER, JAS. — Enl., Aug. 1, 1862: Paroled, Appomattox (Apr. 12, 1865).

PARKER, SAMUEL — Enl., Feb. 1, 1862: Paroled, Charlotte, N. Car., May 11, 1865.

PEARSON, MOSES — Enl., Apr. 3, 1862: Present for duty, Dec., 1864.

(1) POPPENHEIM, CHRISTOPHER P. — See list of "Non-Comm. Officers" above.

POPPENHEIM, JOHN L. — Enl., Aug. 17, 1861: Present for duty, Dec., 1864.

PORCHER, CHAS. P. — Enl., Aug. 24, 1861: Elect. a Cadet (Ensign?) in Co. K, Nov., 1863.

POSTELL, J. G. — Enl., Sept. 1, 1861: W., 2nd Manassas (Aug. 30, 1862).

(1) POYAS, JOHN E. — Dischgd., Sept. 5, 1862, overage.

REED, J. O. — Enl., Aug. 15, 1861: Dischgd., Sept. 5, 1862, underage.

(1) ROUX, HENRY — Enl., age 22: K., 2nd Manassas (Aug. 30, 1862).

(1) ROY, ROBT. — See list of "Officers" above.

SAWYER, L. — Enl., Apr. 4, 1862, age 46: Dischgd., chronic diarrhea, Oct. 17, 1862.

(1) SCRIVEN, R. H. — Present for duty, Dec., 1864: No other record.

SEAFORD, M. H. — Enl., Oct. 15, 1861: K., E. Tenn., Jan. 17, 1864.

(1) SNOW, JOS. R. — Enl., age 23: Dischgd. on Surg. Cert., June 19, 1862.

SPEER, G. W. — Enl., July 20, 1861: Present for duty, Dec., 1864.

STOCKER, SAMUEL H. — See list of "Non-Comm. Officers" above.

(1) STROHECKER, OSWELL — See list of "Non-Comm. Officers" above.

TAYLOR, GEO. B. — Enl., June 26, 1861: Dischgd., Sept. 5, 1862, underage.

(1) THOMPSON, JULIUS A. — Enl., age 20: W. (thigh), Antietam (Sept. 17, 1862).

(1) TODD, WM. H. — Enl., age 22: W., 2nd Manassas (Aug. 30, 1862): Died of wound, Aug. 31.

(1) TUPPER, JAS. — Enl., age 18: W., 7 Pines (June 1, 1862): Dischgd., Sept. 12, 1862, underage.

(2) TYSON, B. H. — Enl., Mar. 5, 1862: Paroled, Appomattox (Apr. 12, 1865).

(1) VERDIER, HENRY E. — Enl., age 30: W., 2nd Manassas (Aug. 30, 1862).

(1) VERNER, SOLOMON S. — See list of "Non-Comm. Officers" above.

(1) WALKER, F. DOUGLAS — Dischgd., Aug. 7, 1862, "never acquired a domicile," and "being a subject of Gr. Brit."

(1) WALKER, THOS. K. — Enl., age 30: Present for duty, Dec., 1864.

(1) WEAR, GEO. — See list of "Non-Comm. Officers" above.

WHILDEN, GEO. T. — See list of "Non-Comm. Officers" above.

WHITE, GEO. — Enl., Nov., 1861: Transfd. to 15th So. Car. Inf. Regt., Dec. 3, 1864.

(1) WHITNEY, ALONZO G. — W., 1st Manassas (July 21, 1861): No record after Dec., 1864.

WITHERSPOON, R. S. — Enl., age 41, Jan. 1, 1862: No record after Dec., 1864.

(1) YATES, CHAS. L. — Present for duty most of war: Paroled,
(2) Appomattox (Apr. 12, 1865).

YATES, EDW. — See list of "Non-Comm. Officers" above.

* * * * *

MEMBERS OF COMPANY A, HAMPTON'S SO. CAR. LEGION (INF. BTLN.) WHO WERE NOT PRESENT FOR DUTY DURING THE PERIOD THAT THE REGIMENT WAS ASSIGNED TO HOOD'S TEXAS BRIGADE (JUNE 2-NOV. 15, 1862).

OFFICERS

(1) Klinck, Theodore, 1Lt. (Orig. 3Lt. of Co.: W. & POW, 7 Pines, June 1, 1862: Died as POW)
(1) Lowndes, Jas., 1Lt. (Orig. 1Lt. of Co.: Dropped from rolls, Apr., 1862)

(1) Dotterer, Wm. A., 2Lt. (Orig. 1Sgt. of Co.: Dropped from rolls, Apr., 1862)
(1) Simkins, Wm. S., Lt. (Orig. Pvt. in Co.: No record after Aug. 6, 1861)

NON-COMMISSIONED OFFICERS

(1) Adams, Wm. T., Sgt. (No record after June, 1861)
(1) Anderson, Andrew J., Sgt. (No record after Feb., 1862)
(1) Baker, Henry G., 2Cpl. (Orig. 2Cpl. of Co.: Dischgd., sick, Jan., 1862)
(1) Bomar, Robt. A., Sgt. (Orig. 1Cpl. of Co.: Dischgd., wound, Oct., 1861)

(1) Condy, Jas. Ancrum, 3Sgt. (Orig. 4Sgt. of Co.: No record after Apr., 1862)
Lloyd, Angus M., 3Cpl. (Orig. 3Cpl. of Co.: Dischgd. (TB), Sept., 1861)
Taylor, Frank E., 4Cpl. (Enl., Pvt., Aug., 1863)

PRIVATES

(1) Adams, Jas. T. (No record after Aug., 1861)
(1) Adams, Sam D. (No record after Feb., 1862)
(1) Adams, Wm. J. (No record after Feb., 1862)
Addison, Jas. W. (Dischgd., rheumatism, Aug., 1861)
Anderson, H. M. (No record prior to Oct., 1863)
(1) Arnau, Robt. M. (No record after Feb., 1862)
Arnholter, Fred (No record after May, 1862)
(1) Asher, Harris (No record after Feb., 1862)
(1) Atkinson, Chas. (W., 1st Manassas, dischgd., July, 1861)
(1) Baker, Thos. D. (W., 1st Manassas: Dischgd., Nov., 1861)
(2) Barnham, Rich. P. (Enl., Aug., 1863)
(1) Beck, Arthur (No record after Oct., 1861)
(1) Bessellieu, Chas. M. (Transfd. out, Oct., 1861)

(1) Bidault, Jos. A. (D., Aug., 1861)
Blankensee, David (K., 1st Manassas)
Butt, Richard F. (Dischgd., sick, May, 1862)
(1) Calvitt, Edw. S. (Dischgd., Nov., 1861)
Carlisle, A. R. (Enl., May, 1864)
(1) Chapin, J. Russell (W., 1st Manassas: Died, Sept., 1861)
Clairdy, M. F. (Enl., May, 1863)
Clarkson, Edw. McC. (Transfd. out, Nov., 1861)
Clarkson, John M. (Dischgd., Dec., 1861)
Clarkson, Walt. B. (Dischgd., Sick, Dec., 1861)
Coachman, Stephen F. (Enl., Jan., 1864)
Coffin, Ebin (W., 7 Pines: Dischgd.)
Conley, John D. (Enl., May, 1863)
(2) Cook, T. O. N. (No record prior to Apr., 1865)

(2) Crawford, D. H. (No record prior to Apr., 1865)

Daniels, Thos. (No record prior to Jan., 1865)

Eggleston, Wm. (No record prior to Nov., 1864)

Emanuel, P. A. (Enl., Nov., 1864)

Floyd, J. E. (Enl., May, 1863)

(1) Glover, Washington P. (Dischgd., Sick, Dec., 1861)

Gore, A. (Enl., May, 1863)

Graham, W. H. (Enl., May, 1863)

(1) Green, Jas. W., Jr. (W., 1st Manassas: Dischgd., Aug., 1861)

Hall, E. O. (Enl., Jan., 1864)

Hall, Jesse (No record before Sept., 1864)

Hardwick, S. P. (Enl., May, 1863)

Heyward, A. R. (Enl., Aug., 1863)

Holmes, Andrew (Enl., May, 1863)

Holmes, D. H. (Enl., Apr., 1863)

Hunt, A. L. (Enl., May, 1864)

Hunt, A. W. (Enl., May, 1864)

Hunter, Geo. V. (Enl., Apr., 1863)

(1) Hutson, Chas. W. (POW, 7 Pines)

Inglesby, Thos. S. (Enl., July, 1863)

Ivey, Jas. M. (W., 7 Pines: Dischgd.)

Jenkins, T. H. (Enl., May, 1863)

(1) Jervey, Gabriel C. (W., 1st Manassas: D., July, 1861)

Jones, Cadwallader (Transfd. out, Nov., 1861)

(1) Jones, Chas. A. (No record after Dec., 1861)

Jones, Iredell (No record after Oct., 1861)

(1) Jones, J. Quincy (D., June, 1862)

Jones, W. H. (Enl., May, 1863)

(1) Kennedy, Henry E. (Dischgd., Aug., 1861)

Kennedy, John (Dischgd., May, 1862)

Kirby, Jas. (Enl., Apr., 1863)

Lieber, Oscar M. (No record after Apr., 1862)

Lewis, Peter C. (No record prior to Jan., 1865)

(1) Lloyd, Julius S. (Dischgd. (TB), Sept., 1861)

Logan, D. W. (Enl., Apr., 1863)

(1) Lowndes, Edw. (Dischgd., Oct., 1861)

Lundy, Wm. (Enl., June, 1863)

Marsh, Malcomb (Enl., Oct., 1864)

McDonald, Alex G. (K., 7 Pines)

(1) Middleton, Henry A., Jr. (K., 1st Manassas)

Missroon, Jas. (Enl., Aug., 1863)

Page, Wm. B. (Enl., June, 1863)

(1) Phelps, Geo. L. (K., 1st Manassas)

Pitts, Chas. (Enl., Apr., 1863)

Rhodes, A. (No record prior to Sept., 1864)

Roper, Geo. W. (Enl., Apr., 1863)

(1) Russell, John B. (W., 1st Manassas: Dischgd., Oct., 1861)

Shackelford, J. B. (Enl., May, 1863)

Skipper, E. M. (Enl., May, 1863)

Skrine, Thos. B. (Enl., Aug., 1863)

Smith, Richard Y. (No record after Dec., 1861)

(1) Smith, Thos. H. (W., 1st Manassas: No record after Apr., 1862)

Smith, W. J. (Enl., Apr., 1863)

Somers, Richard H. (Dischgd. (TB), July, 1861)

(1) Sprague, Wm. B. (Dischgd., heart trouble, Nov., 1861)

(1) Stoney, Edgar G. (Dischgd., asthma, May, 1862)

Suggs, Arthur (Enl., May, 1863)

(1) Sweat, Robt. S. (W., 1st Manassas: D., Aug., 1861)

(1) Taylor, Henry C. (D., May, 1862)

Thomlinson, Robt. J. (Enl., Apr., 1864)

(1) Thompson, John M. (W., 1st Manassas: Dischgd., Dec., 1861)

Tupper, Wm. (No record before July, 1864)

Turner, Theo. H. (Enl., June, 1863)

(2) Watson, R. P. (Transfd. into Co., Sept., 1864)

West, J. E. (Enl., June, 1863)

(1) Wharton, John (Dischgd., May, 1862)

White, Julius (No record prior to Jan., 1865)

(1) Whitney, Eli G. (Dischgd., July, 1861: Appt. Midshipman in CS Navy)

(1) Whittemore, Wm. (D., typhoid fever, Dec., 1861)

Whitten, L. P. (Enl., Apr., 1863)

Williams, J. W. (Enl., May, 1864)

Wilson, R. G. (Enl., May, 1863)

(1) Wilson, Wm. G. (Dischgd., Mar., 1862: Appt. Midshipman in CS Navy)

(1) Wolf (or Wolfe), Sam M. (Dischgd., Nov., 1861)

Yearden, R., Jr. (K., 7 Pines)

HAMPTON'S SO. CAR. LEGION (INF. BTLN.)

COMPANY B — *WATSON GUARDS*

Company was mustered into the Confederate Service on June 12, 1861 at Charleston, South Carolina, "for one year," by Capt. Martin W. Gary.

Key

(1) Original member of Company. (2) Paroled at Appomattox. K (Killed), W (Wounded), POW (Prisoner of War) AWOL (Absent Without Leave)

OFFICERS

(1) GARY, MARTIN W. — See Roster, "Regmtl. Hdqtrs., Hampton's So. Car. Legion."

(2) TOMPKINS, R. AUGUSTUS Capt. — Orig. 2Sgt. of Co.: Appt. 1Sgt., Aug. 15, 1861: Elect., 2Lt., Apr. 25, 1862: Prom., 1Lt., Sept. 17, 1862: Prom., Capt., Sept. 3, 1864: Paroled, Appomattox (Apr. 12, 1865).

(1) TOMPKINS, ROBT. W. Capt. — Orig. 1Lt. in Co.: Prom., Capt., June 16, 1862: K., Antietam (Sept. 17, 1862).

TULLY, LOVET A. 1Lt. — Orig. Pvt. in Co.: Prom., 3Lt., Summer, 1862: Prom., 2Lt., Sept. 17, 1862: Prom., 1Lt., Sept. 3, 1864.

(2) BOUKNIGHT, BENJ. J. 2Lt. — Orig. Pvt. in Co.: W. (head), Antietam (Sept. 17, 1862): Appt. 3Lt., Fall, 1862: Appt. 2Lt., Sept. 3, 1864: Paroled, Appomattox (Apr. 12, 1865).

HARMON, THOS. PICKENS 2Lt. — Orig. Pvt. in Co.: Appt. 5Sgt., Sept. 23, 1862: Prom., 2Lt., Sept. 3, 1864: No record after Dec., 1864.

NON-COMMISSIONED OFFICERS

BRIGGS, R. PICKENS Cpl. — Orig. Pvt. in Co.: Prom., Cpl., Spring, 1862: W., Antietam (Sept. 17, 1862): Died of W., Sept. 27.

(1) BURKHALTER, JOHN E. 2Cpl. — Orig. 2Cpl. of Co.: Reduced to Pvt.: K., Gaines' Mill (June 27, 1862).

(1) CORLEY, S. WILSON 4Cpl. — Orig. 4Cpl. of Co., age 41: Reduced to ranks: W., 7 Pines (June 1, 1862): Dischgd. (overage), Sept. 20, 1862.

DEAN, L. YANCEY 4Sgt. — Orig. Pvt. in Co.: Prom., 5Cpl., Fall, 1861: Prom., 4Sgt., Summer, 1862: W. (thigh), Gaines' Mill (June 27, 1862): Leg amputated: Dischgd., July 10, 1862.

DORN, JAS. MARION 3Sgt. — Orig. Pvt. in Co.: Prom., 2Cpl., Fall, 1862: Prom., 3Sgt., Nov., 1864: No further record.

DORN, WM. R. 1Sgt. — Orig. Pvt. in Co.: Prom., 4Sgt., Summer, 1862: W., 2nd Manassas (Aug. 30, 1862): Prom., 2Sgt., Fall, 1862: Prom., 1Sgt., Fall, 1864.

(1) HERLONG, VASTINE A. 1Cpl. — Orig. 1Cpl. of Co.: Reduced to ranks, Aug. 5, 1861: No record after Dec., 1864.

JENNINGS, JOHN WESLEY 1Sgt. — Orig. Pvt. in Co.: Appt. 1Sgt., Apr. 25, 1862: W., E. Tenn., Oct., 1863: Leg amputated.

(2) LILES, THOS. D. 5Cpl. — Orig. Pvt. in Co.: Prom., 5Cpl., Fall, 1864: Paroled, Appomattox (Apr. 12, 1865).

MEDLOCK, A. PICKENS 5Sgt. — Orig. Pvt. in Co.: Prom., 5Sgt., 1861: W. & POW, 7 Pines (June 1, 1862): Exchanged: Dischgd., Sept. 17, 1862, overage.

(1)
(2) NICHOLSON, ALBERT R. Sgt. — Orig. Sgt. in Co.: Reduced to Pvt.: Fall, 1862: Prom., 3Cpl., Winter, 1863-1864: Paroled, Appomattox (Apr. 12, 1865).

(1) PADGET, MANFRED A. 3Cpl. — Orig. 3Cpl. of Co.: Reduced to ranks, Summer, 1862: AWOL, Summer, 1863.

(2) PRICE, THOS. DAN 4Sgt. — Orig. Pvt. in Co.: W., Chickamauga (Sept. 20, 1863): Prom., 4Sgt., Fall, 1864: Paroled, Appomattox (Apr. 12, 1865).

STEVENS, BENJ. J. 5Sgt. — Orig. Pvt. in Co.: Prom., 3Cpl., Sept. 23, 1862: Prom., 5Sgt., Winter, 1863-64.

STONE, HENRY 4Cpl. — Orig. Pvt. in Co.: W. (shoulder), Antietam (Sept. 17, 1862): Prom., 4Cpl., Winter, 1863-64.

STURKEY, DANIEL PRESLEY 3Sgt. — Orig. Pvt. in Co.: W., 7 Pines (June 1, 1862): Prom., 3Sgt., Fall, 1862: K., E. Tenn., Oct., 1863.

(1) TOMPKINS, JOHN W. 4Cpl. — Orig. 4Cpl. in Co.: POW, 7 Pines (June 1, 1862): Exchanged: Dischgd. for disability, Aug. 7, 1862.

(1) TOMPKINS, R. AUGUSTUS 2Sgt. — See list of "Officers" above.

TUCKER, G. PICKETT 3Sgt. — Orig. Pvt. in Co.: Prom., 3Sgt.,
Summer, 1862: W., 2nd Manassas (Aug. 30, 1862): Died, Sept. 7.
TURNER, ROBT. A. 2Sgt. — Orig. Pvt. in Co.: Prom., 1Cpl., Summer,
1862: Prom., 2Sgt., Winter, 1863-64.
WARREN, FRANKLIN M. 2Cpl. — Orig. Pvt. in Co.: Prom., 5Cpl.,
Sept. 27, 1862: Prom., 2Cpl., Winter, 1863-64: Reduced to
ranks.
WELLS, F. PICKENS 1Cpl. — Orig. Pvt. in Co.: W. (shoulder),
Antietam (Sept. 17, 1862): Prom., 4Cpl., Sept. 23, 1862: Prom.,
1Cpl., Winter, 1863-64.

PRIVATES

ALBRECHT, EMIL — Enl., Aug. 26, 1861: Nursed wounded, Summer,
1862.
(1) BAUGUS, ROBT. — Carried on rolls until Dec., 1864.
(1) BOUKNIGHT, BENJ. J. — See list of "Officers" above.
(1) BRADLEY, HENRY M. — Dischgd., Sept. 8, 1862, reason unknown.
(1) BRIGGS, R. PICKENS — See list of "Non-Comm. Officers" above.
BRIGGS, THOS. J. — Died (dysentery), Sept. 25, 1862.
(1) BROWN, MALCOLM — POW, 2nd Manassas (Aug. 30, 1862): Paroled,
Sept. 29, 1862.
(1) BROWN, NICHOLAS E. — W., 2nd Manassas (Aug. 30, 1862): Arm
amputated.
(1) BROWNING, THOS. N. — Present for duty most of war: On sick
furlough, Fall, 1864.
(1) BURTON, NATHAN N. — Dischgd., underage (18), Sept. 9, 1862.
(1) CARROLL, ROBT. T. — K., Gettysburg (July 4, 1863).
(1) CARTER, WM. T. — W. (arm), Gaines' Mill (June 27, 1862): Dischgd.,
underage, Sept. 6, 1862.
(1) CARTLEDGE, MALCOLM — Dischgd., disability, June 12, 1862.
(1) COLEMAN, JOHN L. — Dischgd., overage, Sept. 6, 1862.
(1) CORLEY, CLEMENT — Present for duty as of Dec., 1864: No further
record.
(1) CORLEY, HEZEKIAH F. — POW, Deep Bottom, Va. (Sept. 29, 1864):
Exchanged, Mar. 17, 1865.
(1) CORLEY, JOEL — Present for duty, Nov. & Dec., 1864: No further
record.
(1) DAY, JAS. S. — Paroled, Augusta, Ga., May 18, 1865.
(1) DEAN, L. YANCEY — See list of "Non-Comm. Officers" above.
(1) DORN, DAVIS W. — Died, Nov. 14, 1863.
(1) DORN, GEO. E. — Present for duty most of war: Paroled, Appomattox
(2) (Apr. 12, 1865).
(1) DORN, JAS. MARION — See list of "Non-Comm. Officers" above.
(1) DORN, JOHN RUFUS — Enl., age 15: Present for duty as of Nov. &
Dec., 1864: No further record.
(1) DORN, WM. R. — See list of "Non-Comm. Officers" above.
(1) FRANKLIN, A. PRESTON — Present for duty to Aug., 1862: No
further record.

(1)	FREEMAN, THADDEUS W. — POW, Deep Bottom, Va. (Sept. 29, 1864): Exchanged, Mar. 17, 1865.
(1) (2)	GILBERT, JAS. S. — Paroled, Appomattox (Apr. 12, 1865): No other record.
	GILLESPIE, MICHAEL — K., 2nd Manassas (Aug. 30, 1862).
(1)	GILLFILLAN (or McGILFILLAN), JOHN — POW, Chaffin's Farm (Sept. 30, 1864).
(1)	GRAY, JAS. W. — Dischgd., underage (16), Sept. 27, 1862.
(1)	HAMILTON, GEO. W. — Paroled, Augusta, Ga., May 30, 1865.
(1)	HARMON, THOS. PICKENS — See list of "Officers" above.
(1) (2)	HARMON, WM. D. — Paroled, Appomattox (Apr. 12, 1865).
(1)	HAVIRD, GEO. W. — Present for duty most of the war: No record after Dec., 1864.
	HEMMINGWAY, THOS. — Enl., July 6, 1861: W., Antietam (Sept. 17, 1862): W., Chickamauga (Sept. 19, 1863).
(1)	HERLONG, DANIEL H. — Absent on furlough, Dec. 1, 1864: No further record.
(1) (2)	HITT, MALCOLM C. — W., Aug. 15, 1864: Paroled, Appomattox (Apr. 12, 1865).
(1)	JAIRO, JAS. — W. (side), Antietam (Sept. 17, 1862).
	JENNINGS, JOHN — Enl., July 11, 1861: Present for duty as of Dec., 1864.
(1)	JENNINGS, JOHN WESLEY — See list of "Non-Comm. Officers" above.
	JENNINGS, WM. — W. (arm), Antietam (Sept. 17, 1862): Dischgd. for disability, Oct. 2, 1862.
(1)	JOHNSON, WILEY S. — Present for duty as of Dec., 1864.
(1)	KING, SAMSON — Present for duty as of Aug., 1862: No further record.
	LAMOTTE, THOS. J. — Enl., July 11, 1861: Transfd. to 17th So. Car. Inf. Regt., July 28, 1864.
(1)	LANDRUM, FRANCIS W. — POW, Chambersburg, Pa., Aug. 8, 1863: Took Fed. oath, Nov. 24, 1863.
(1)	LILES, THOS. D. — See list of "Non-Comm. Officers" above.
(1)	LIVINGSTON, JOHN — No record after Dec., 1864.
	LUMPKIN, WM. T. — Enl., July 12, 1861: No record after Dec., 1864.
(1)	LYLES, MILLEDGE B. — K., Antietam (Sept. 17, 1862).
(1) (2)	LYON, JOHN — W., Spring, 1863: Paroled, Appomattox (Apr. 12, 1865).
(1)	MALLET, PRESTON S. — Dischgd., underage, Sept. 6, 1862.
(1)	MEDLOCK, A. PICKENS — See list of "Non-Comm. Officers" above.
(1)	OUZTS (or OUTZ), CALEB PINKNEY — Present for duty most of war: Paroled, Augusta, Ga., May 30, 1865.
	PALMER, GEO. P. — Enl., Aug. 26, 1861: W. (knee), 7 Pines (May 31, 1862): POW, Deep Bottom, Va. (Sept. 29, 1864): Died as a POW, Nov., 1864.
(1)	PRICE, BARTHOLOMEW F. — W., Antietam (Sept. 17, 1862): Died, acute dysentery, Aug. 11, 1863.
(1)	PRICE, THOS. DAN — See list of "Non-Comm. Officers" above.

(1)   ROBERTSON, FRANK M. — Enl., June 22, 1862: On sick leave, Dec., 1864.

(1)   ROBERTSON, GEO. W. — Present for duty as late as Dec., 1864.

(1)   ROTTEN, WM. S. — W., Antietam (Sept. 17, 1862): Present for duty as of Dec., 1864.

(1)   SELF, JOHN M. — Shown as "abs. on furlough," Dec., 1864.

(1)   SMITH, JOHN T. — Present for duty most of the war.

(1)   STEVENS, BENJ. J. — See list of "Non-Comm. Officers" above.

(1)   STONE, HENRY — See list of "Non-Comm. Officers" above.

(1)   STONE, WM. R. — Present for duty as late as Dec., 1864.

(1)   STURKEY, DANIEL P. — See list of "Non-Comm. Officers" above.

      STURKEY, MARION B. — Enl., Aug. 26, 1861: W. (hip), Cold Harbor (June, 1864).

      STURKEY, WM. O. — Enl., Aug. 26, 1861: POW, June 14, 1864, St. Mary's Church, Va.

(1)   TALBERT, WM. L. — Paroled, Appomattox (Apr. 12, 1865): No other
(2)   record.

      TOMPKINS, JAS. S. — Enl., Oct. 24, 1862: Shown as "abs., sick," Dec., 1864.

(2)   TOMPKINS, S. JAS. — Enl., Oct. 24, 1862: Paroled, Appomattox (Apr. 12, 1865).

(1)   TUCKER, G. PICKETT — See list of "Non-Comm. Officers" above.

(1)   TULLY, LOVET A. — See list of "Officers" above.

(1)   TULLY, WM. J. — W. (hip), July 17, 1863: Paroled, Augusta, Ga., June 2, 1865.

(1)   TURNER, ROBT. A. — See list of "Non-Comm. Officers" above.

(1)   WALTON, MARION — Present for duty most of war: Paroled, Augusta, Ga., May 20, 1865.

(1)   WALTON, WM. T. — Paroled, Farmville, Va., mid-Apr., 1865.

(1)   WARREN, FRANKLIN M. — See list of "Non-Comm. Officers" above.

(1)   WATKINS, EPHRAIM — Present for duty most of war: Paroled, Newton, No. Car., Apr. 19, 1865.

(1)   WATSON, STANMORE — Present for duty most of the war: Paroled, Newton, No. Car., Apr. 19, 1865.

(1)   WATSON, WM. — Present for duty most of the war: Paroled, Augusta, Ga., May 24, 1865.

(1)   WELLS, F. PICKENS — See list of "Non-Comm. Officers" above.

★ ★ ★ ★ ★

MEMBERS OF COMPANY B, HAMPTON'S SO. CAR. LEGION (INF. BTLN.), WHO WERE NOT PRESENT FOR DUTY DURING THE PERIOD THAT THE REGIMENT WAS ASSIGNED TO HOOD'S TEXAS BRIGADE (JUNE 2-NOV. 15, 1862).

OFFICERS

(1) Bates, Andrew D., 2Lt. (Orig. 2Lt. of Co.: Resgnd., Apr., 1862)

(1) Jennings, Wm. D., 3Lt. (Orig. 3Lt. of Co.: Resgnd., Aug. 6, 1861).

NON-COMMISSIONED OFFICERS

(1) Eidson, Milledge B., 2Sgt. (K., 7 Pines)
Holstein, Moses N., Sgt. (Dischgd., disability, July 18, 1861)

Nicholson, John T., 2Sgt. (Dischgd., disability, Nov. 20, 1861)

PRIVATES

(1) Abney, Ezras (Dischgd., sick, Nov., 1861)

(1) Abney, Jacob (D., Sept., 1861)

(2) Adams, I. T. (No record prior to Apr., 1865)

(1) Adams, Robt. (No record after May, 1862)

(1) Adams, Thos. S. (Transfd. out, July, 1861)

(1) Armstrong, Jas. (Dischgd., old age, Aug., 1861)

(1) Arnold, Jefferson (Dischgd., sick, Nov., 1861)

(1) Ashmore, Wm. H. (No record after July, 1861)

(1) Austin, John P. (D., May, 1862)
Barden, Genus (D., Apr., 1862)
Boatwright, Sumpter (Enl., Apr., 1864)

(1) Bodie, Davis S. (Dischgd., Aug., 1861)
Bouknight, Daniel P. (Enl., July, 1863)

(1) Bryan, Jas. J. (No record after Apr., 1862)

(2) Chamberlain, Thos. (Enl., Aug., 1864)

(1) Coleman, Wm. B. (No record after Apr., 1862)
Collier, Abner G. (Enl., Sept., 1863)

(1) Corley, Wm. C. (Dischgd., Aug., 1861)

(2) Crooks, T. H. (Enl., Nov., 1864)
Dorn, L. Yancy (Dischgd., sick, Nov., 1861)
Dowden, John W. (Enl., Aug., 1863)
Durisoe, Peter L. (Enl., Apr., 1864)
Eichelberger, Walter (Enl., Apr., 1864)
Fortson, Jas. (Enl., Oct., 1864)

(1) Freeman, Wm. W. (D., Feb., 1862)
Gill, Wm. T. (Enl., Aug., 1863)
Golightly, Melville V. (Enl., Apr., 1863)

(1) Gossett, Jas. (Dischgd. for disability, Sept., 1861)

(1) Grant, Gilson W. D. (No record after, Apr., 1862)
Gribble, Jas. H. (Enl., May, 1863)
Griffin, Lemuel L. (Enl., Apr., 1863)

(1) Griffith, Matthew A. (No record after May, 1862)

(1) Harrington, G. W. (Dischgd., disability, Jan., 1862)
Hatton, Frank D. (D., Aug., 1861)
Hatton, Jas. J. (Dischgd., disability, Sept., 1861)

(1) Irwin, W. J. (Enl., June, 1864)
Jairo, Augustus (Enl., Apr., 1864)

Jennings, R. T. (No record prior to Apr., 1864)

Jennings, Thos. (Enl., Apr., 1864)

(1) Jeter, Edmund (Dischgd., sick, Sept., 1861)

Jones, Chas. (Enl., Jan., 1864)

Jones, Curren E. (Enl., Aug., 1863)

Kinnaird, Wm. T. (Enl., Apr., 1864)

Lewis, Archy (No record prior to Apr., 1865)

(1) Lumpkin, Andrew J. (K., 7 Pines)

(1) Martin, Ambrose (K., 7 Pines)

(1) Martin, Louis (No record after June, 1861)

May, Thos. A. (K., 1st Manassas)

(1) Miller, J. Abney (Dischgd., sick, Nov., 1861)

(1) Myers, David (Dischgd., sick, June, 1862)

(2) Parden, C. E. (No record prior to Apr., 1865)

Parker, Horace (Enl., Apr., 1864)

Payne, D. J. (Enl., Apr., 1864)

Perryman, E. R. (Enl., Nov., 1864)

Price, John (Enl., Apr., 1864)

(1) Price, Thos. (Dischgd., sick, July, 1861)

Reems, Benj. L. (Enl., Aug., 1863)

(1) Rhodes, Jas. W. (Dischgd., sick, Sept., 1861)

Richardson, Walter (Enl., Apr., 1864)

Roach, T. Jefferson (Enl., Apr., 1864)

(1) Rochelle, John W. (Dischgd., June, 1862)

Rogers, Wm. A. (Enl., Apr., 1863)

Rutledge, Barney C. (Enl., Mar., 1864)

Seigler, Elias (Enl., July, 1864)

Sellers, John S. (Enl., May, 1863)

Still, Wm. A. (Enl., Aug., 1863)

Stone, Francis M. (Enl., Apr., 1864)

(1) Stone, Jesse (Dischgd., W., Sept., 1861)

(1) Stone, Wm. (No record after Apr., 1862)

(1) Strom, Wm. B. (No record after June, 1861)

Sturkey, Thos. J. (Enl., Mar., 1863)

Talbert, Wm. J. (Enl., Sept., 1864)

Teague, B. Hammet (Enl., Apr., 1864)

Tompkins, Dan (Enl., Apr., 1864)

(1) Turner, John W. (Dischgd., sick, Nov., 1861)

(1) Watkins, Benj. C. (Dischgd., sick, Aug., 1861)

Watkins, John S. (Enl., Aug., 1863)

Watson, Milton A. (Enl., Sept., 1864)

Watts, Augustus W. (Enl., Mar., 1864)

Whittle, Oratio (Enl., Apr., 1863)

(2) Wright, I. P. (No record prior to Apr., 1865)

COMPANY C – *MANNING GUARDS*

Company was mustered into the Confederate Service on June 19, 1861 at Columbia, So. Car., "for one year," by Capt. Brown Manning.

Key

(1) Original member of Company. (2) Paroled at Appomattox.
K (Killed), W (Wounded), POW (Prisoner of War)
AWOL (Absent Without Leave)

OFFICERS

(1)   HUGGINS, GEORGE A.   Capt. – Orig. 1Lt. of Co.: Elect., Capt., Apr. 25, 1862: Resgnd., Aug. 14, 1862.

JAMES, JOHN H. M.   Capt. – Orig. Pvt. in Co.: Elect., 2Lt., June 20, 1862: Prom., 1Lt., Sept. 14, 1862: Prom., Capt., Nov. 1, 1864.

LESESNE, WM. THEO.   Capt. – Orig. 4Sgt. of Co.: Elect., 2Lt., Apr. 25, 1862: Prom., 1Lt., June 20, 1862: Prom., Capt., Aug. 14, 1862: W., Aug., 1864: Resgnd., Nov. 1, 1864.

CAMPBELL, RICHARD S.   1Lt. – Orig. Pvt. in Co., age 22: Appt. 2Lt., Oct. 4, 1862: Appt. 1Lt., Nov. 1, 1864: No further record.

(1)   DINGLE, J. HERVEY   1Lt. – Orig. 2Lt. of Co.: Elect., 1Lt., Apr. 25, 1862: K., Antietam (Sept. 17, 1862).

KELLY, JAS. D.   2Lt. – Orig. 4Cpl. of Co.: Prom., 2Lt., June 20, 1862: Died, Sept. 11, 1862, cause of death unknown.

WITHERSPOON, WM. V.   2Lt. – Orig. Pvt. in Co.: Prom., Bvt. 3Lt., Fall, 1862: Prom., 3Lt., Winter, 1862-63: Prom., 2Lt., Nov. 1, 1864.

NON-COMMISSIONED OFFICERS

BILLUPS, ROBT. L.   1Sgt. – Orig. Pvt. in Co.: Prom., 2Sgt., May, 1862: Prom., 1Sgt., Spring, 1864: On duty, Dec., 1864.

CLARK, JOHN W.   1Cpl. – Orig. Pvt. in Co.: Prom., 4Cpl., Spring, 1863: Prom., 1Cpl., Spring, 1864: On duty, Dec., 1864.

(2)   CONNORS, CHAS. C.   5Sgt. – Orig. Pvt. in Co.: Prom., 5Sgt., Spring, 1864: Paroled, Appomattox (Apr. 12, 1865).

COOGLER, FRANCIS J.   2Sgt. – Orig. Pvt. in Co.: Prom., 3Sgt., Fall, 1862: Prom., 2Sgt., Spring, 1864: W. (neck), Darbytown Rd. (Oct. 7, 1864): Paroled, Appomattox (Apr. 12, 1865).

DARBY, A. ELLIOTT   1Sgt. – Orig. Pvt. in Co.: Prom., 3Sgt., Sept. 20, 1861: Prom., 2Sgt., Spring, 1862: Prom., 1Sgt., Summer, 1862: Dischgd. on Surg. Cert., Dec. 18, 1862.

DAVIS, THOS. N. 3Sgt. — Enl. as a Pvt., July 5, 1861: W., Gaines'
Mill (June 27, 1862): Prom., 5Sgt., Winter, 1862-63: Prom.,
3Sgt., Winter, 1863-64.

DEAN, HUGH W. 3Cpl. — Orig. Pvt. in Co.: Prom., 5Cpl., Summer,
1863: Prom., 3Cpl., Winter, 1863-64: On duty, Dec., 1864.

DORRITY, ANDREW J. 1Sgt. — Orig. Pvt. in Co.: Appt. 1Sgt., Apr.
27, 1862: POW, E. Tenn., Dec. 5, 1863: Died, pneumonia, Jan. 8,
1864.

(2) HARVIN, WM. J. T. 4Sgt. — Orig. Pvt. in Co.: Prom., 4Sgt., Fall,
1862: Reduced to ranks: Paroled, Appomattox (Apr. 12, 1865).

KELLY, BENJ. P. 2Cpl. — Enl. as a Pvt., Mar. 25, 1862: Prom., 2Cpl.,
Winter, 1863-64.

KELLY, HENRY M. 4Cpl. — Orig. Pvt. in Co.: Prom., 5Cpl., Winter,
1863-64: Prom., 4Cpl., Fall, 1864.

(1) KELLY, JAS. D. 4Cpl. — See list of "Officers" above.

(1) LESESNE, WM. THEO. 4Sgt. — See list of "Officers" above.

(2) MAHONEY, HENRY D. 4Sgt. — Orig. Pvt. in Co.: Prom., 4Sgt., Fall,
1864: Paroled, Appomattox (Apr. 12, 1865).

McCALL, C. S. 5Cpl. — Orig. Pvt. in Co.: Prom., 5Cpl., Winter,
1864-65.

PATTERSON, SAMUEL 2Cpl. — Orig. Pvt. in Co.: Prom., 2Cpl., Apr.
26, 1862: Missing, 2nd Manassas (Aug. 30, 1862): No further
record.

SULLIVAN, SAMUEL W. 2Sgt. — Orig. Pvt. in Co.: Appt. 4Sgt., Sept.
20, 1861: Prom., 2Sgt., Summer, 1862: Dischgd., Sept. 8, 1862,
overage (38).

PRIVATES

(1) ANDERSON, W. J. — Paroled, Greensboro, No. Car., May 1, 1865.

(1) BAGNAL, JOHN C. — POW, 7 Pines (June 1, 1862): Exchanged, Aug.
(2) 5, 1862: Paroled, Appomattox (Apr. 12, 1865).

(1) BILLUPS, ROBT. L. — See list of "Non-Comm. Officers" above.

(1) BOCHETT, THOS. J. — Absent on wound furlough, Spring, 1863.
(Prob. W. at Antietam or Fredericksburg).

BOWERS, J. V. — Enl., Sept. 10, 1861: POW, Knoxville, Tn., Dec. 5,
1863: Died at Camp Chase, Ohio, of pneumonia, Feb. 15, 1865.

(1) BRADY, PATRICK — Paroled, Appomattox (Apr. 12, 1865): No other
(2) record.

(1) CAMPBELL, RICHARD S. — See list of "Officers" above.

(1) CHANDLER, S. THOMAS — K., Mill Cr., Va. (June 26, 1862).

(1) CLARK, JOHN W. — See list of "Non-Comm. Officers" above.

CLARY, MICHAEL — Enl., Oct. 23, 1861: Dischgd. (underage), Nov.,
1862.

(1) COBIA, WM. F. — Dischgd., overage, Sept. 8, 1862.

(1) COCHRAN, JAS. B. — Dischgd., Surg. Cert., June 18, 1862.

(1) COLE, SIDNEY F. — Deserted, took Fed. oath, Mar. 30, 1865.

(1) CONNORS, CHAS. C. — See list of "Non-Comm. Officers" above.

(1) COOGLER, FRANCIS J. — See list of "Non-Comm. Officers" above.

(1) COOK, J. T. — Present for duty Mar. to Sept., 1863: No other record.
(1) DARBY, A. ELLIOTT — See list of "Non-Comm. Officers" above.
DAVIS, S. JAS. — Enl., Oct. 23, 1861: K., 2nd Manassas (Aug. 29, 1862).
DAVIS, THOS. N. — See list of "Non-Comm. Officers" above.
(1) DEAN, HUGH W. — See list of "Non-Comm. Officers" above.
(1) DERAKIN, SAMUEL — POW on Steamer *Katskill,* Aug. 5, 1862: Dischgd., Nov., 1862.
(1) DORRITY, ANDREW J. — See list of "Non-Comm. Officers" above.
(1) EIKERENKOETTER, JOHN F. — W. (hand), Gaines' Mill (June 27, 1862): POW, Frederick, Md., Sept. 12, 1862: Exchanged, Nov. 10, 1862: On duty, Dec., 1864.
FORD, J. — Enl., May 3, 1862: On duty, Oct., 1864.
FORD, S. — Enl., May 3, 1862: On duty, Dec., 1864.
(1) FRITH, THOS. — Sick in hosp., Fall, 1862: No other record.
GAMBLE, J. M. — Enl., May 9, 1862: Transfd. to 25th So. Car. Inf. Regt., Nov. 5, 1864.
(1) GRAHAM, JOS. E. — W. (chest), Petersburg: Died of wound, July 31, 1864.
(1) HARVIN, SEPTOMIE A. — Present for duty most of the war: POW, Darbytown Rd. (Oct. 8, 1864): Exchanged, Feb. 18, 1865.
(1) HARVIN, WM. J. T. — See list of "Non-Comm. Officers" above.
(1) HODGE, JOHN W. — W., 1st Manassas (July 21, 1861): Retired, Dec., 1864.
(1) HORTON, JOS. W., Jr. — Enl., age 17: Discharged, underage, Sept. 5, 1862.
(1) HUMPHREY, SAMUEL R. — K., 2nd Manassas (Aug. 30, 1862).
(1) JACOBS, ABRAM L. — No record after Oct., 1863.
(1) JAMES, JOHN H. M. — See list of "Officers" above.
(1) JOHNSON, ROBT. R. — W. at either Antietam or Fredericksburg: Died from wound, Apr. 6, 1863.
KELLY, BENJ. P. — See list of "Non-Comm. Officers" above.
(1) KELLY, HENRY M. — See list of "Non-Comm. Officers" above.
(1) KING, FELIX L. — Furnished a substitute, Jan. 12, 1864.
(1) KING, R. R. — Died, Winchester, Va., Fall, 1862.
(1) LESESNE, C. FRED — Enl., age 47: Dischgd., June 9, 1862, overage.
(2) LESESNE, JAS. I. — Enl., Aug. 18, 1861: Paroled, Appomattox (Apr. 12, 1865).
(1) MAHONEY, HENRY D. — See list of "Non-Comm. Officers" above.
(1) McCALL, C. S. — See list of "Non-Comm. Officers" above.
(1) McKNIGHT, ROBT. M. — Enl., age 17: POW, 7 Pines (May 31, 1862): Exchanged, Aug. 5: Dischgd., Sept. 9, 1862, underage.
(1) McLAURIN, J. F. — POW, Bennettsville, So. Car., Mar. 6, 1865.
(1) McLEOD, A. S. — W., Fall, 1864: On duty, Dec., 1864.
(1) McLEOD, JAS. G. — Dischgd. (chronic diarrhea), June 18, 1862.
(1) McLEOD, JOHN C. — Present for duty most of war: Paroled,
(2) Appomattox (Apr. 12, 1865).
(1) MESSER, J. M. — W. (arm), Petersburg, 1864: Absent, sick, Dec., 1864.
MOSES, A. DeLEON — Enl., Jan. 1, 1862: W., Antietam (Sept. 17, 1862): Transfd. to CS Navy, Aug. 25, 1863.

(1) NELSON, R. MANNING — Hospitalized, Feb., 1864: No further record.
(1) NELSON, THEO. M. — K., 2nd Manassas (Aug. 30, 1862).
(1) O'HARA, JOHN — Enl., age 45: Dischgd. (overage), Dec. 20, 1862.
(1) PACK, BENJ. JOS. — W., 2nd Manassas (Aug. 30, 1862): Died from wound, Sept. 18, 1862.
(1) PATTERSON, SAMUEL — See list of "Non-Comm. Officers" above.
(1) PLOWDEN, G. WHITFIELD — W., E. Tenn., Fall, 1863: Paroled,
(2) Appomattox (Apr. 12, 1865).
(1) PLOWDEN, J. BELTON — W., 2nd Manassas (Aug. 30, 1862): Died from wound, Sept. 19.
(1) RAGIN, JOHN F. — Dischgd. (hernia), June 18, 1862.
(1) RAGIN, RUFUS A. — Sick, Dec., 1864: No further record.
(1) RICHBOURG, ELI N. — W., Gaines' Mill (June 27, 1862): Died from wound, Dec. 31, 1862.
(1) RICHBOURG, RUFUS N. — Dischgd., sick, Aug. 20, 1862.
RIDGEWAY, LAURENCE M. — Enl., Oct. 23, 1861: Dischgd., Sept. 9, 1862, overage.
(1) RIDGILL, WM. J. W. — W., Gettysburg (July, 1863): On detached duty, Dec., 1864.
ROLLINS, WM. L. D. — Enl., Mar. 19, 1862: On duty, Mar., 1864.
SANDERS, M. P. — Enl., July 12, 1862: On leave, Dec., 1864.
STEPHENS, C. — Enl., Mar. 19, 1862: On duty, Mar., 1864.
(1) STUART, SAMUEL — K., Gaines' Mill (June 27, 1862).
(1) STUKES, JOHN M. — Present for duty most of war: Paroled,
(2) Appomattox (Apr. 12, 1865).
(1) SULLIVAN, SAMUEL W. — See list of "Non-Comm. Officers" above.
THAMES, THOS. L. — Enl., Apr. 15, 1862: Died, Mar. 10, 1863.
(1) THOMAS, J. N. — On duty as of Dec., 1864.
THOMAS, WM. — Enl., Aug. 14, 1861: No record after Oct., 1863.
(1) THOMPSON, JOHN D. — Dischgd. (chronic rheumatism), June 18, 1862.
THOMPSON, WM. B. — Enl., Aug. 8, 1861: AWOL, Fall, 1864.
TOUCHBERRY, JOS. E. — Enl., July 2, 1861: POW, hosp. in Richmond, Apr. 3, 1865.
(1) WARD, HEZEKIAH — Dischgd. (chronic bronchitis), June 20, 1862.
WHITE, I. H. — POW, Williamsburg (May 6, 1862): Exchanged, Aug. 15, 1862: No further record.
WHITWORTH, JOHN S. — Enl., June 30, 1862: K., 2nd Manassas (Aug. 30, 1862).
WILLOUGHBY, P. — Enl., Oct. 17, 1861: POW, Burkeville, Va. (Apr. 6, 1865): Died as POW, May 7, 1865.
(1) WILSON, JOS. C. — W., E. Tenn., Jan., 1864: POW, Richmond hosp., Apr. 3, 1865.
(1) WINECOFF, MARCUS W. — Transfd. to 7th No. Car. Inf. Regt., Feb. 13, 1863.
(1) WITHERSPOON, CHAS. L. — Enl., age 17: POW on Steamer *Katskill*, Aug. 5, 1862: Exchanged: Dischgd., Sept. 8, 1862, underage.
(1) WITHERSPOON, WM. V. — See list of "Officers" above.
(1) WOODS, JOHN H. — No record after Feb., 1863.

WOOTEN, M. I. — POW, 2nd Manassas (Aug. 30, 1862): Paroled, Sept. 29, 1862.

★ ★ ★ ★ ★

MEMBERS OF COMPANY C, HAMPTON'S SO. CAR. LEGION (INF. BTLN.), WHO WERE NOT PRESENT FOR DUTY DURING THE PERIOD THAT THE REGIMENT WAS ASSIGNED TO HOOD'S TEXAS BRIGADE (JUNE 2-NOV. 15, 1862).

OFFICERS

(1) Manning, Brown, Capt. (Orig. Capt. of Co.: Dropped from rolls, Apr., 1862).
(1) Benbow, Henry L., 2Lt. (Transfd. out, Nov., 1861)
(1) Haynsworth, John R., 2Lt. (W., 1st Manassas: Died of W., Aug., 1861)
(1) Nelson, Wm. Calvin, 2Lt. (Dropped from rolls, Apr., 1862)

NON-COMMISSIONED OFFICERS

(1) Hammet, Wm. J. W., 1Sgt. (No record after Apr., 1862)
(1) Hayneworth, George E., 2Sgt. (Dischgd., Sept., 1861)
(1) Martin, Charles W., 3Cpl. (Dischgd., disability, Oct., 1861)
(1) McKnight, W. Hilliard, 1Cpl. (K., 7 Pines)
(1) Singleton, Thos. D., 1Cpl. (Died, pneumonia, Feb., 1862)

PRIVATES

Alexander, W. (Enl., Nov., 1864)
Alford, J. M. L. (No record prior to Dec., 1864)
Alford, R. (No record prior to Dec., 1864)
Allen, F. A. (Enl., July, 1864)
(1) Baggett, Benj. H. (Dischgd., disability, Jan., 1862)
(1) Barwick, Benj. J. (Dischgd., Surg. Cert., Sept., 1861)
(1) Barwick, L. Newton (Dischgd., hernia, Sept., 1861)
Berry, N. T. (Enl., June, 1863)
Bethea, R. C. (Enl., Apr., 1863)
(2) Biggart, W. A. (Enl., Apr., 1863)
Bowers, N. J. (Enl., Aug., 1863)
(1) Brailsford, Theo. W. (Dischgd., Oct., 1861)
Brigman, T. J. (Enl., June, 1863)
Bullard, C. W. (Enl., Feb., 1863)
Bullard, G. W. (Enl., Feb., 1863)
(1) Burgess, R. Warren (No record after Apr., 1862)
(1) Burgess, Samuel E. (D., Sept., 1861)
(1) Burgess, William R., Jr. (Dischgd, TB, Aug., 1861)
Calder, A. (Enl., Feb., 1863)
Calder, Robt. (Enl., Feb., 1863)
Calder, S. (Enl., Oct., 1863)
Calder, W. (Enl., Jan., 1863)
Calhoun, D. C. (Enl., Oct., 1863)
Cantrell, J. T. (Enl., June, 1863)
Clopton, G. W. (Transfd. out, Spring, 1862)

Creighton, J. D. (Enl., Apr., 1863)

Crow, Jas. (Enl., May, 1863)

Cutter, J. F. (No record prior to Apr., 1865)

Dave, W. (Enl., Apr., 1863)

Davis, W. H. (Enl., Feb., 1863)

Davis, Wm. A. (D., May, 1862)

Dean, Robt. (Enl., July, 1863)

Dinkins, Wm. E. (Dischgd., Aug., 1861)

DuBose, David St. P., Jr. (Dischgd., Feb., 1862)

Dukes, Geo. H. (Dischgd., Oct., 1861)

Duncan, J. B. (Enl., Apr., 1863)

Dunkins, S. (POW, 7 Pines)

Felder, Wm. E. (No record after June, 1861)

Fletcher, J. D. (Enl., Aug., 1863)

Fletcher, J. K. (Enl., Aug., 1863)

Floyd, O. (Enl., Apr., 1864)

Ford, Jacob (No record prior to Sept., 1864)

Francis, Jas. (No record prior to Dec., 1863)

Gayle, D. C. (Enl., May, 1864)

(1) Geddings, Abraham W. (Dischgd., Nov., 1861)

(1) Gee, Samuel (Transfd. out, Apr., 1862)

Gorns, J. R. (Enl., Apr., 1863)

Griffin, Lawrence M. (Dischgd., Aug., 1861)

Griffin, Robt. H. (Dischgd., Aug., 1861)

Gruver, J. R. (No record prior to Sept., 1864)

(1) Habersham, Rich. W. (No record after Apr., 1862)

Hammet, J. H. (Enl., Apr., 1864)

Harrington, J. J. (Enl., May, 1863)

Harrison, J. T. (Enl., Apr., 1863)

(1) Harvin, J. Jos. (D., Jan., 1862)

Hodge, S. D. (Enl., Nov., 1863)

Horton, C. C. (Enl., June, 1863)

Horton, J. J. (Enl., Apr., 1863)

Horton, W. S. (Enl., Apr., 1863)

(1) James, Robt. B. (No record)

Jennings, H. (No record prior to Nov., 1863)

(1) Jenkins, Wm. W. (No record)

Johnson, John W. (D., Apr., 1862)

(1) King, Wm. C. (No record)

Lamb, W. D. (No record prior to Nov., 1864)

Lemaster, J. M. (Enl., Nov., 1864)

(1) Lesesne, Neighbor D. (D., Aug., 1861)

(2) Lipscomb, W. B. (No record prior to Apr., 1865)

(1) Livingston, John B. (Dischgd., Sept., 1861)

(1) Lynch, Thos. (No record)

(1) Manning, Rich. I., Jr. (No record)

Martin A. (Enl., May, 1864)

Martin, W. T. (Enl., Feb., 1864)

(2) McAbee, A. (No record prior to Apr., 1865)

McCall, W. H. (No record prior to Sept., 1864)

(1) McFaddin, J. M. (Dischgd., Aug., 1861)

McIntosh, Ed (Enl., May, 1863)

McNeil, A. (Enl., June, 1863)

Miller, J. M. (Enl., June, 1863)

Miller, S. (Enl., June, 1863)

Monihan, Thos. (Enl., Apr., 1863)

Moses, Isaac Calhoun (No record after Dec., 1861)

Plowden, W. B. (No record prior to Nov., 1864)

Pool, S. (No record prior to Nov., 1864)

Readon, J. J. (Enl., May, 1863)

(1) Rhame, Jas. O. (D., Nov., 1861)

(1) Rhame, John B. (D., Aug., 1861)

Rice, J. P. (No record prior to Feb., 1863)

(1) Richardson, Rich. C., Jr. (Dischgd., Oct., 1861)

(1) Richbourg, Augustus B. (No record after Apr., 1862)

(1) Richbourg, Edwin N. (K., 7 Pines)
Robertson, R. T. (Enl., Apr., 1863)
Rogers, P. (Enl., Apr., 1863)
Rosier, J. R. (Enl., May, 1863)
(1) Scarborough, Jas. H. (No record)
Sinclair, D. (Enl., Feb., 1864)
(1) Sings, John W. (D., Apr., 1862)
(1) Skinner, Benj. W. (No record after Dec., 1861)
Small, Samuel (Enl., Apr., 1863)
Smith, J. C. (No record prior to Sept., 1864)
(2) Sonis, I. R. (No record prior to Apr., 1865)
(1) Strange, John P. (Dischgd., Oct., 1861)
(1) Strange, Jos. D. (D., Sept., 1861)
(1) Stukes, Samuel J. (No record after Apr., 1862)
(1) Thames, Rufus M., Jr. (D., Sept., 1861)
(2) Thrift, T. E. (No record prior to Apr., 1865)

(1) Tindall, Benj. M. (Dischgd., Feb., 1862)
(1) Tindall, Henry L. (No record after Apr., 1862)
Tindall, J. J. (No record prior to Sept., 1864)
Tindall, R. W. (Enl., Apr., 1864)
Touchberry, Jas. J. (K., 1st Manassas)
Wade, W. D. (No record prior to Nov., 1864)
Ward, Jas. (Enl., May, 1863)
Watts, J. J. (Enl., Apr., 1863)
Webb, Lewis (Enl., May, 1863)
(1) Wells, Francis A. (D., Dec., 1861)
Williams, Geo. W. (No record after Mar., 1862)
(1) Wise, A. Jackson (No record)
(1) Wise, Thos. J. (D., Jan., 1862)
(1) Witherspoon, Jas. W. (Dischgd., arm amputated, Aug., 1861)
Wright, R. (Enl., Apr., 1864)
Wright, S. (Enl., Apr., 1863)

HAMPTON'S SO. CAR. LEGION (INF. BTLN.)

COMPANY D – *GIST RIFLES*

Company was mustered into the Confederate Service on June 15, 1861 at Columbia, So. Car., "for one year" by Capt. Henry J. Smith.

Key

(1) Original member of Company. (2) Paroled at Appomattox.
K (Killed), W (Wounded), POW (Prisoner of War)
AWOL (Absent Without Leave)

OFFICERS

AUSTIN, WM. H. Capt. — Orig. Pvt. in Co.: Prom., 2Lt., Sept. 21, 1862: Prom., 1Lt., Jan., 1863: Prom., Capt., June 17, 1864.
BOWEN, ELIJAH B. Capt. — Pvt. in Co.: Elect., 2Lt., Apr. 25, 1862: Elect., 1Lt., Fall, 1862: Elect., Capt., Winter, 1862-63: Resgnd., disabled, Jan. 3, 1863.

McNEELY, JOSIAH K. Capt. — Orig. Pvt. in Co.: Prom., 2Lt., July 5, 1862: Prom., 1Lt., Sept. 21, 1862: Prom., Capt., Jan. 23, 1863: W. (shoulder), Petersburg (June 13, 1864): Died from wound, June 17, 1864.

(1) SMITH, HENRY J. Capt. — Orig. Capt. of Co.: K., Antietam (Sept. 17, 1862).

(2) STRINGER, ANDREW J. 1Lt. — Orig. Pvt. in Co.: Prom., 2Lt., Jan. 19, 1863: Prom., 1Lt., June 17, 1864: Paroled, Appomattox (Apr. 12, 1865).

(1) ACKER, ELIHU H. 2Lt. — Orig. 3Lt. of Co.: Elect., 2Lt., June 12, 1861: Dischgd., Sept. 29, 1862.

DONALDSON, JOHN T. 2Lt. — Orig. Pvt. in Co.: Prom., 1Sgt., Spring, 1862: Prom., 3Lt., Winter, 1862-63: Prom., 2Lt., June 17, 1864.

FARMER, NATHAN O. 2Lt. — Orig. Pvt. in Co.: Prom., 3Lt., Winter, 1863-64: Prom., 2Lt., June 23, 1864: Paroled, Farmville, Va., mid-Apr., 1865.

NON-COMMISSIONED OFFICERS

(2) BENNETT, THOS. B. 1Cpl. — Orig. Pvt. in Co.: W. & POW, Gaines' Mill (June 27, 1862): Paroled: Appt. 1Cpl., Oct., 1864: Paroled, Appomattox (Apr. 12, 1865).

BENNETT, W. DRAYTON 1Cpl. — Orig. Pvt. in Co.: W., 7 Pines (May 31, 1862): Prom., 1Cpl., Jan., 1863: K., Wills Valley, Tenn., Oct. 28, 1863.

(2) BRADLEY, AMBROSE J. 2Sgt. — Orig. Pvt. in Co.: Prom., 2Sgt., Spring, 1864: Paroled, Appomattox (Apr. 12, 1865).

BRUCE, JOHN C. 1Sgt. — Orig. Pvt. in Co.: Appt. 1Sgt., Spring, 1864.

(1) BURDINE, JAS. H. 2Cpl. — Orig. 2Cpl. of Co.: W. (foot), Antietam (Sept. 17, 1862): W. (leg) & POW, Lookout Valley, Tn., Nov. 25, 1863: Exchanged, Jan. 1, 1864: Reduced to Pvt.

COPELAND, JAMES B. 3Sgt. — Orig. Pvt. in Co.: Prom., 3Sgt., Spring, 1864: On duty as of Dec., 1864.

CRYMES, BENJ. L. 4Cpl. — Orig. Pvt. in Co.: Present for duty most of the war: Prom., 4Cpl., Spring, 1864.

DICKSON, THOS. J. 1Sgt. — Orig. Pvt. in Co.: W. & POW, Antietam (Sept. 17, 1862): Paroled, Oct. 14, 1862: Prom., 1Sgt., Jan. 23, 1863: POW, E. Tenn., Oct. 29, 1863: Died in prison camp of pneumonia, Dec. 18, 1863.

(1) GIBBS, WM. W. 2Sgt. — Orig. 2Sgt. of Co.: Reduced to ranks, Spring, 1862: Dischgd., Sept. 8, 1862.

(2) GLENN, JAS. P. 2Cpl. — Orig. Pvt. in Co.: W. & POW, Antietam (Sept. 17, 1862): Exchanged: Prom., 2Cpl., Winter, 1863-64: Paroled, Appomattox (Apr. 12, 1865).

IRBY, CHAS. G., Jr. 4Cpl. — Orig. Pvt. in Co.: Appt. 4Cpl., Jan. 1, 1863: Died, Jan. 3, 1864.

(1) KENNEDY, RUFUS C. 2Sgt. — Orig. 3Sgt. of Co.: Prom., 2Sgt., Spring, 1862: K., Antietam (Sept. 17, 1862).

(1) KOHLER, HEINRICH 2Sgt. — Orig. 4Cpl. of Co.: Prom., 2Cpl., Fall, 1861: POW, 7 Pines (June 1, 1862): Exchanged, Aug., 1862: Prom., 2Sgt., Fall, 1862: W., E. Tenn., Fall, 1863.

(1) LAWSON, JOHN W. 3Cpl. — Orig. 3Cpl. of Co.: Reduced to ranks, Spring, 1862: AWOL, Fall, 1864.

MARONEY, WARREN D. 1Cpl. — Orig. Pvt. in Co.: Prom., 1Cpl., Fall, 1862: Reduced to ranks, July 1, 1863: Prom., 1Cpl., Fall, 1864.

(2) MAULDIN, LABIN 5Cpl. — Orig. Pvt. in Co.: Prom., 5Cpl., Fall, 1864: Paroled, Appomattox (Apr. 12, 1865).

(2) PICKENS, ISRAEL W. 5Sgt. — Orig. Pvt. in Co.: Prom., 5Sgt., Winter, 1863-64: W. (arm), Petersburg, July 28, 1864: Paroled, Appomattox (Apr. 12, 1865).

ROPER, D. H. 5Cpl. — Enl. as a Pvt., Mar. 19, 1862: Prom., 5Cpl., Summer, 1862: Deserted, Jan., 1863.

STEWART, SAMUEL D. 4Sgt. — Enl. as a Pvt., Aug. 29, 1861: W. (hand), Antietam (Sept. 17, 1862): Prom., 4Sgt., Fall, 1864.

WILLIAMS, J. BERRY 4Sgt. — Orig. Pvt. in Co.: W. & POW, 2nd Manassas (Aug. 30, 1862): Paroled, Sept. 29, 1862: Prom., 4Sgt., Winter, 1862-63: K., Campbell Sta., E. Tenn. (Nov. 16, 1863).

PRIVATES

(1) ARIAL, WM. H. — On detached duty, Dec., 1864: No other record.

AUGUSTINE, JAS. A. — Enl., July 5, 1861: Died, Feb. 18, 1865, gunshot wound in head.

(1) AUSTIN, WM. H. — See list of "Officers" above.

(1) BARNETT, H. O'NEILL — Died, blood poisoning, Sept. 10, 1863.

(1) BARNETT, W. BENJ. J. — W. (arm), 7 Pines (May 31, 1862): Dischgd. for wound, Feb. 12, 1863.

(1) BENNETT, THOS. B. — See list of "Non-Comm. Officers" above.

(1) BENNETT, W. DRAYTON — See list of "Non-Comm. Officers" above.

BOGGS, BENJ. F. — Enl., June 25, 1861: W. (foot), Gaines' Mill (June 27, 1862).

(1) BOGGS, THOS. K. — Present for duty most of the war.

BOWEN, ELIJAH B. — See list of "Officers" above.

(1) BRADLEY, AMBROSE J. — See list of "Non-Comm. Officers" above.

(1) BRADLEY, R. NEWTON — Died, Richmond, Summer, 1863.

(1) BROWN, GEO. W. M. — Died, Richmond, Summer, 1863.

(1) BRUCE, JOHN C. — See list of "Non-Comm. Officers" above.

(1) BRUCE, WM. T. — Present for duty most of the war: Paroled,
(2) Appomattox (Apr. 12, 1865).

(1) CARSON, NATHAN C. — W. (thigh), Chaffin's Farm (Sept. 29, 1864): Died from wound.

CLAYTON, F. V. — Enl., Mar. 15, 1862: Present for duty, Dec., 1864.

(1) COPELAND, JAS. B. — See list of "Non-Comm. Officers" above.

(1) CRYMES, BENJ. L. — See list of "Non-Comm. Officers" above.

(1) DAVENPORT, SAM. R. — Dischgd., Sept. 6, 1862, underage (17): Re-enl., May 6, 1863.

DEALE, MILTON H. — Enl., Aug. 27, 1861: Dischgd., Sept. 8, 1862, overage.

(1) DICKSON, THOS. J. — See list of "Non-Comm. Officers" above.

(1) DONALDSON, JOHN T. — See list of "Officers" above.

(1) ERWIN, THOS. — Dischgd., Sept. 22, 1862, overage (38).

(2) FARMER, GADDIS — Enl., May 23, 1862: W. (back) & POW, Lookout Mtn., Tenn. (Oct. 29, 1863): Exchanged: Paroled, Appomattox (Apr. 12, 1865).

(1) FARMER, NATHAN O. — See list of "Officers" above.

(1) GARY, SAMUEL J. — No record after June 30, 1862.

(2) GILLHAM, G. P. — Enl., Mar. 29, 1862: Paroled, Appomattox (Apr. 12, 1865).

GILLHAM, JOHN F. — Enl., Aug. 27, 1861: Present for duty, Dec., 1864.

(1) GLAZE, WM. HENRY — Present for duty most of the war: Paroled,
(2) Appomattox (Apr. 12, 1865).

(1) GLENN, JAS. P. — See list of "Non-Comm. Officers" above.

GOWER, I. C. — POW, 2nd Manassas (Aug. 30, 1862): Paroled, Sept. 29, 1862.

(2) GREEN, B. F. — Enl., Mar. 29, 1862: W. (thigh), Gaines' Mill (June 27, 1862): Paroled, Appomattox (Apr. 12, 1865).

(1) GREEN, GEO. A. — Present for duty most of the war.

(1) HAMILTON, HENRY H. — Dischgd., Fall, 1862, underage (17).

HARRIS, T. Y. — Enl., Jan. 6, 1862: On furlough, Fall, 1864.

(1) HENDRICKS, JAS. F. — On duty most of the war: Paroled,
(2) Appomattox (Apr. 12, 1865).

HOLDER, WM. W. — Enl., June 12, 1862: Dischgd., Sept. 8, 1862, overage (35).

HOWARD, IRBY — Enl., Mar. 19, 1862: Transfd. to 18th So. Car. Inf. Regt., June 17, 1864.

HOWARD, JAS. F. — See roster, "Btln. Hdqtrs."

(1) HOWARD, JOHN M. — Transfd. to the 18th So. Car. Inf. Regt., June 17, 1864.

(1) HOWARD, M. LAFAYETTE — Died, Aug. 22, 1863.

(1) IRBY, CHAS. G., Jr. — See list of "Non-Comm. Officers" above.

KELLY, M. PINKNEY — Enl., Jan. 12, 1862: On detached serv., Fall, 1864.

KELLY, MANSEL — Enl., Aug. 27, 1861: Transfd. to Capt. Clark's Cav. Co., June 13, 1862.

(1) KENNEDY, A. ROSS — W., 2nd Manassas (Aug. 30, 1862): W., E.
(2) Tenn., Fall, 1863: Paroled, Appomattox (Apr. 12, 1865).

(1) KING, ROBT. R. — Present for duty as of Dec., 1862.

(1) KING, VAN B. — Present for duty as of Dec., 1864.

KNIGHT, JOHN G. — Enl., Aug. 27, 1861: Dischgd., Sept. 8, 1862, overage.

LEE, WM. F. — Enl., Mar. 13, 1862: Paroled, Farmville, Va., Apr., 1865.

LIGON, JAS. H. — Enl., Dec. 3, 1861: On furlough, Fall, 1864.

(1) LIPFORD, WM. C. — POW, Richmond hosp., Apr. 3, 1865.

(1) MADDOX, WM. M. — W., Gaines' Mill (June 27, 1862): Died of wound, July 13.

(1) MARONEY, WARREN D. — See list of "Non-Comm. Officers" above.

(1) MAULDIN, ANDREW M. — Dischgd., Sept. 8, 1862, overage.
(1) MAULDIN, JOHN E. — K., Wills Valley, Tenn. (Oct. 28, 1863).
(1) MAULDIN, LABIN — See list of "Non-Comm. Officers" above.
(1) MAULDIN, VARDRY — Present for duty most of the war.
(1) MAXWELL, D. S. — Present for duty, Dec., 1864: No other record.
(1) McCLELLION, JOHN P. — Present for duty most of the war.
   McNEELY, JOHN O. — Enl., Dec. 3, 1861: POW, Deep Bottom, Va.,
      Aug. 17, 1864: Exchanged, Oct. 11, 1864.
(1) McNEELY, JOSIAH K. — See list of "Officers" above.
(1) MOORE, DAVID — Dischgd., Sept. 8, 1862, overage: Re-enl., May 3,
      1864.
(2) MOORE, JEFF — Enl., Mar. 30, 1862: Paroled, Appomattox (Apr. 12,
      1865).
   MURPHY, W. S. — Enl., Dec. 11, 1861: Absent on furlough, Fall,
      1864.
(1) MURRELL, CHAS. P. — Dischgd., Sept. 8, 1862, overage (35).
(1) NEIGHBORS, HENRY T. — K., Antietam (Sept. 17, 1862).
(2) O'NEAL, JOEL T. — Enl., Mar. 8, 1862: Paroled, Appomattox (Apr.
      12, 1865).
   PACE, JOHN F. — Enl., Mar. 7, 1862: Absent, sick, Nov., 1863.
(1) PARKINS, DANIEL — Missing after Antietam (Sept. 17, 1862).
   PATTERSON, ANDREW J. — Enl., Aug. 27, 1861: Dischgd., Sept. 10,
      1862, overage (45).
(1) PICKENS, ISRAEL W. — See list of "Non-Comm. Officers" above.
(1) PITTMAN, DAVID T. — Absent on furlough, Nov., 1863: No other
      record.
   POOR, A. JACKSON — Enl., Mar. 19, 1862: Present for duty, Dec.,
      1864.
(1) POSEY, W. N. — Transfd. to Co. E., Hampton's Legion, Summer, 1863.
   POWERS, WM. T. — Enl., Aug. 27, 1861: No record after June 30,
      1862.
(1) RILEY, JOHN J. — W. 7 Pines (May 31, 1862): POW, Petersburg, July
      28, 1864.
(1) ROGERS, DAVID, Jr. — K., near Dandridge, Tenn., Jan. 17, 1864.
(1) ROGERS, LEWIS — W. (arm), Antietam (Sept. 17, 1862): Retired,
      Sept. 15, 1864.
   ROPER, D. H. — See list of "Non-Comm. Officers" above.
   ROPER, L. H. — Enl., Mar. 19, 1862: W. (face), Antietam (Sept. 17,
      1862): On detached serv., Dec., 1864.
(1) SCOTT, WM. M. — Present for duty most of the war: Paroled,
(2) Appomattox (Apr. 12, 1865).
(1) SESSIONS, JOHN G. — No record after Apr., 1863.
(1) SPENCE, SAMUEL A. — W., E. Tenn., Fall, 1863: Absent, wound,
      Dec., 1864.
   STEWART, SAMUEL D. — See list of "Non-Comm. Officers" above.
(1) STRINGER, ANDREW J. — See list of "Officers" above.
   TAYLOR, JOHN R. — Enl., Aug. 27, 1861: On furlough, Dec., 1864.
(1) TIMBS, GARRISON — W., 7 Pines (May 31, 1862): W., 2nd Manassas
      (Aug. 30, 1862): Paroled: Absent, sick, Nov., 1863.
(1) TIMBS, JOHN — Dischgd., Aug. 1, 1862, overage (55).
(1) TUMBLIN, JOHN — No record after Aug., 1863.

(1) TURNER, HIRAM — Deserted, took Fed. oath, Jan., 1865.
(1) WARREN, JOHN H. — K., Campbell Sta., Tenn. (Nov. 16, 1863).
WHITE, BENJ. F. — Enl., Mar. 31, 1862: Present for duty, Dec., 1864.
WHITT, JOHN V. — Enl., Aug. 27, 1861: Paroled, Farmville, Va. (mid-Apr., 1865).
(1) WILLIAMS, J. BERRY — See list of "Non-Comm. Officers" above.

* * * * *

MEMBERS OF COMPANY D, HAMPTON'S SO. CAR. LEGION (INF. BTLN.), WHO WERE NOT PRESENT FOR DUTY DURING THE PERIOD THAT THE REGIMENT WAS ASSIGNED TO HOOD'S TEXAS BRIGADE (JUNE 2-NOV. 15, 1862)

OFFICERS

(1) Hudgins, Reuben, R., 1Lt. (Dropped from rolls, Apr., 1862)

Smith, W. S., 2Lt. (No record prior to Jan., 1863)

NON-COMMISSIONED OFFICERS

(1) Burdine, Wm. C., Cpl. (Dischgd., Sept., 1861)

(1) Wilson, John H., 2Cpl. (K., 7 Pines)

MUSICIAN

Scotie, Geo. B. (Transfd. to Co. D, Feb., 1863)

PRIVATES

Abernathy, A. L. (Enl., Apr., 1864)
Acken, E. H. (Enl., Apr., 1863)
(1) Acker, Wm. B. (W., 7 Pines, arm amputated)
(1) Allen, Pinckney M. (Dischgd., Oct., 1861)
(2) Anderson, J. M. (No record prior to Apr., 1865)
Anderson, Wm. (Enl., Apr., 1864)
Attison, Wm. (Enl., Aug., 1863)

Blake, Kennedy H. (Dischgd., Feb., 1862)
Boggs, H. D. (Enl., Aug., 1863)
Boggs, J. A. (Enl., Feb., 1863)
(1) Brock, Jos. (W., 1st Manassas)
(2) Broom, A. J. (Enl., Aug., 1863)
(2) Broom, W. J. (Enl., Aug., 1863)
Bruce, Horatio (Enl., Apr., 1864)
Burdine, J. W. (Enl., Apr., 1864)
(2) Campbell, A. P. (Enl., Oct., 1863)

(2) Campbell, J. F. (Enl., Apr., 1864)
Carr, John J. (K., 7 Pines)
Cobb, Jas. A. (Dischgd., May, 1862)
Cooley, Wm. (Enl., Apr., 1864)
Cox, Thos. (Enl., Sept., 1863)
Crenshaw, W. H. (Enl., May, 1864)
Crymes, Wm. A. (D., Oct., 1861)
Duckworth, B. F. (Enl., Apr., 1864)
Duckworth, J. M. (Enl., Apr., 1864)
Duckworth, W. R. (Enl., Aug., 1863)
Eaton, H. L. (Enl., May, 1864)
Eaton, J. J. (Enl., Nov., 1864)
Evans, W. R. (Enl., Aug., 1863)
Fielding, J. B. (Enl., Nov., 1864)
Gary, Wm. (Enl., Apr., 1864)
Glaspy, A. (Enl., Apr., 1864)
Glaze, A. (Enl., Apr., 1864)
Glenn, John M. (Enl., Oct., 1863)
Green, Lewis (K., 7 Pines)
Green, Thos. (K., 7 Pines)
Green, Wm. L. (W., 1st Manassas: Dischgd., Sept., 1861)
Hackett, W. W. (Enl., Sept., 1864)
(1) Hallums, Clark, Jr. (K., 1st Manassas)
Hamilton, Andy M. (W., 7 Pines: No further record)
(1) Hamilton, David A. (D., Aug., 1861)
Hamilton, E. H. (Enl., Sept., 1864)
Hamilton, J. H. (Enl., Feb., 1864)
(1) Hammond, Alfred J. (D., Dec., 1861)
Harris, L. D. (Enl., Nov., 1864)
Hart, J. Millidge (Dischgd., Aug., 1861, 1st Manassas W.)
James, Howard (Enl., Aug., 1863)
Janes, W. F. (Enl., Apr., 1864)
Jolly, L. F. (Enl., Nov., 1864)
Kelly, D. C. (Enl., Mar., 1863)

Kelly, Wm. Harvey (Missing, 7 Pines)
Kennemor, Jacob (Enl., Apr., 1863)
(1) Kitsinger, Andrew J. (D. Nov., 1861)
Knight, S. Thos. (Enl., Oct., 1863)
Lee, John W. (Enl., Mar., 1863)
Lee, Robt. A. (D., Dec., 1861)
Loving, Thos. F. (Enl., Aug., 1863)
Major, J. A. (Enl., Aug., 1863)
Manley, Jas. L. (Enl., Oct., 1863)
Martin, T. W. (Enl., Mar., 1863)
Mattison, N. Cobb (Enl., Oct., 1863)
(1) Mattison, Wyatt (D., Aug., 1861)
(1) Mauldin, L. Epps (Dischgd., June, 1861)
Mayfield, Wm. N. (Enl., July, 1863)
McCall, Howard (Enl., Aug., 1863)
McNeely, J. M. (Enl., Apr., 1864)
McWhorter, J. M. (Enl., Apr., 1864)
McWhorter, Wm. F. (K., 7 Pines)
Morehead, Wm. (Enl., Nov., 1864)
Myres, Z. E. (Enl., July, 1863)
Newton, J. S. (Enl., Apr., 1864)
Orr, J. B. (Enl., Sept., 1863)
Orr, Wm. (Enl., Nov., 1864)
(1) Pickens, A. Monroe (D., May, 1862)
Poor, Samuel E. (Enl., Apr., 1863)
Pope, D. (Enl., Nov., 1864)
Rabb, Jas. K. (Dischgd., sick, Aug., 1861)
(1) Rankin, Robinson W. (Dischgd., sick, Apr., 1862)
(1) Richardson, Chas. P. (No record after Dec., 1861)
(2) Richardson, I. F. (No record prior to Apr., 1865)
(1) Robinson, Albert B. (K., 1st Manassas)

(1) Roebuck, Wm. P. (Dischgd., W., 1st Manassas, Sept., 1861)
Rogers, J. P. (Enl., Apr., 1864)
Rogers, Milton P. (Dischgd., W., 1st Manassas, Sept., 1861)
Roper, A. W. (Enl., Aug., 1863)
Simpson, G. C. (No record prior to Nov., 1864)
(1) Simpson, Jas. A. (D., Aug., 1861)
Slaton, J. R. (Enl., Sept., 1864)
(1) Smith, Archer M. (AWOL, June, 1862)
Smith, J. F. (Enl., July, 1864)
Snead, Wm. (Enl., Feb., 1864)
Spence, David C. (Enl., July, 1863)

Spivy, Wm. (Enl., Aug., 1863)
Stephens, A. C. (Enl., Apr., 1864)
Stewart, Wm. C. (Enl., Aug., 1863)
(2) Taylor, S. F. (No record prior to Apr., 1865)
Taylor, T. F. (Enl., Apr., 1864)
Todd, H. C. (Enl., Nov., 1864)
Turner, J. B. (Enl., Nov., 1864)
Wilkins, Robt. (Enl., July, 1863)
Wilson, J. R. (Enl., Oct., 1863)
Wilson, John (No record after Dec., 1861)
Wilson, Reuben (K., 7 Pines)
Young, R. S. (Enl., Nov., 1864)

HAMPTON'S SO. CAR. LEGION (INF. BTLN.)

COMPANY E – *BOZEMAN GUARDS*

Company was mustered into the Confederate Service on June 19, 1861 at Columbia, So. Car., "for one year," by Capt. T. L. Bozeman.

Key

(1) Original member of Company. (2) Paroled at Appomattox.
K (Killed), W (Wounded), POW (Prisoner of War)
AWOL (Absent Without Leave)

OFFICERS

(1) (2) DAVENPORT, WM. A. B. Capt. – Orig. 2Lt. of Co.: Prom., 1Lt., Sept. 19, 1861: W. (hip), Antietam (Sept. 17, 1862): Prom., Capt., Dec. 13, 1862: W. (thigh), Petersburg (June 13, 1864): Paroled, Appomattox (Apr. 12, 1865).

(2) NESBIT, CYRUS D. 1Lt. – Orig. 4Sgt. of Co.: W., 1st Manassas (July 21, 1861): Appt. 1Sgt., Oct. 28, 1861: Prom., 3Lt., Apr. 25, 1862: Prom., 2Lt., Aug. 21, 1862: Prom., 1Lt., Dec. 13, 1862: Paroled, Appomattox (Apr. 12, 1865).

HOWARD, OLIVER P. 2Lt. – Orig. 2Sgt. of Co.: Prom., 2Lt., Oct. 27, 1861: Dischgd., disability, Sept. 3, 1862.

HUFF, JAS. R. 2Lt. — Orig. Pvt. in Co.: Prom., 3Lt., Sept. 13, 1862: Prom., 2Lt., Dec. 12, 1862: K., Petersburg (June, 1864).

THOMPSON, MOSES W. 2Lt. — Orig. Pvt. in Co.: Prom., 1Sgt., Summer, 1862: Prom., 3Lt., Summer, 1863: Prom., 2Lt., June 20, 1864.

NON-COMMISSIONED OFFICERS

(1) (2) ALLISON, ROBT. B. 4Cpl. — Orig. 4Cpl. of Co.: W. (foot), Gaines' Mill (June 27, 1862): Paroled, Appomattox (Apr. 12, 1865).

AUSTIN, FRANCIS M. Sgt. — Orig. Pvt. in Co.: Appt. Sgt., Sept. 1, 1862: No record after Dec., 1864.

BABB, THOS. D. 2Cpl. — Orig. Pvt. in Co.: Prom., 2Cpl., Summer, 1863: W. (hip), Darbytown, Va. (Oct. 13, 1864).

(2) ESKEW, SAMUEL A. 2Cpl. — Orig. Pvt. in Co.: Appt. 2Cpl., Sept. 23, 1861: Reduced to ranks, Summer, 1862: POW, 2nd Manassas (Aug. 30, 1862): Exchanged: Paroled, Appomattox (Apr. 12, 1865).

GODFREY, JAS. R. 3Cpl. — Orig. Pvt. in Co.: Appt. 3Cpl., Sept. 23, 1861: Dischgd., Sept. 5, 1862.

(1) HARRISON, JOHN L. 2Cpl. — Orig. 2Cpl. of Co.: Reduced to ranks, Summer, 1862: Died, Sept. 4, 1863.

HIETT, JOHN S. 1Cpl. — Orig. Pvt. in Co.: Appt. 1Cpl., Sept. 12, 1861: Reduced to ranks, Summer, 1862: W., Antietam (Sept. 17, 1862): Present for duty, Fall, 1864.

(1) HOWARD, OLIVER P. 2Sgt. — See list of "Officers" above.

MARSHALL, WM. L. 5Sgt. — Orig. Pvt. in Co.: Prom., 5Sgt., Dec. 30, 1861: Died, Aug. 15, 1862.

MEEKS, JAS. S. 5Cpl. — Enl. as a Pvt., Sept. 7, 1861: Appt. 5Cpl., Summer, 1862: Reduced to Pvt., Summer, 1863.

(1) NESBIT, CYRUS D. 4Sgt. — See list of "Officers" above.

PARLER, LEWIS E. 1Sgt. — Enl. as a Pvt., July 5, 1861: Prom., 1Sgt., May 1, 1863: On duty, Dec., 1864.

PINSON, JOS. D. 3Sgt. — Orig. Pvt. in Co.: Prom., 3Sgt., Spring, 1863: Shown absent, Dec., 1864.

TERRY, C. WILLSON 5Cpl. — Enl. as a Pvt., Apr. 5, 1862: Prom., 5Cpl., Fall, 1863: Present for duty, Feb., 1864.

TERRY, T. F. 3Sgt. — Enl. as a Pvt., Sept. 7, 1861: Prom., 3Sgt., Summer, 1862: Died on furlough to So. Car., Feb. 18, 1863.

THOMPSON, JOHN P. 2Sgt. — Orig. Pvt. in Co.: Prom., 2Sgt., Summer, 1862: W., 2nd Manassas (Aug. 30, 1862): On duty, Dec., 1864.

VAUGHN, JOS. J. 3Cpl. — Orig. Pvt. in Co.: W. (hip), Antietam (Sept. 17, 1862): Prom., 3Cpl., Summer, 1863: On duty, Dec., 1864.

VOGT, THOS. P. 4Cpl. — Enl. as a Pvt., July 5, 1861: Appt. 4Cpl., Sept. 23, 1861: Reduced to ranks, Summer, 1862: No record after Oct., 1863.

PRIVATES

(2) ACKER, NEWTON — Enl., Aug. 16, 1862: Paroled, Appomattox (Apr. 12, 1865).

AUSTIN, CHISOLM — Enl., May 20, 1862: Present for duty, Dec., 1864.

(1) AUSTIN, FRANCIS M. — See list of "Non-Comm. Officers" above.

(1) AUTRY, WM. — Dischgd., Sept. 5, 1862, overage (38).

(1) BABB, THOS. D. — See list of "Non-Comm. Officers" above.

BRIEL, J. A. — POW, 7 Pines (May 31, 1862): Exchanged, Aug. 5, 1862.

BRUNSON, R. S. — Enl., June 30, 1862: On furlough, Dec., 1864: No other record.

(1) CHAPMAN, IRA C. — POW, E. Tenn., Oct. 29, 1863: Exchanged:
(2) Paroled, Appomattox (Apr. 12, 1865).

(1) CHAPMAN, JOHN T. — Present for duty most of war: Paroled,
(2) Appomattox (Apr. 12, 1865).

(1) COKER, HUGH S. — Present for duty most of war.

(1) COKER, MARSHALL — Present for duty most of war.

(1) COKER, ROBT. — Died, typhoid fever, Nov. 9, 1864.

COKER, WILSON — Enl., Sept. 7, 1861: On sick furlough, Fall, 1864.

(1) DAVENPORT, CHAS. — W., 7 Pines (May 31, 1862): POW, near Westover Church, Aug. 7, 1864: Exchanged, Mar. 17, 1865.

(1) DAVENPORT, JOHN — W., 7 Pines (May 31, 1862): Paroled, mid-Apr., 1865.

(1) DAVENPORT, JOS. — Present for duty most of the war.

DAVENPORT, MARTIN — Enl., Sept. 7, 1861: Present for duty, Dec., 1864.

(1) DAVENPORT, W. PINCKNEY — Dischgd., Sept. 5, 1862, underage.

DAVENPORT, WILLIS — Enl., Sept. 7, 1861: Dischgd., Sept. 5, 1862, underage.

(1) DAVIS, GEO. W. — Dischgd., Aug. 18, 1862, underage (17).

(1) DAVIS, WM. — Present for duty most of the war: Paroled, Appomattox
(2) (Apr. 12, 1865).

(1) DAWSON, STEPHEN — Transfd. to the 7th So. Car. Inf. Regt., Sept. 9, 1862.

(1) EMENS, AUSTIN — POW, 7 Pines (May 31, 1862): Exchanged, Aug. 5, 1862: W., Chickamauga (Sept. 20, 1863).

(1) ESKEW, SAMUEL A. — See list of "Non-Comm. Officers" above.

(1) ESKEW, YOUNG D. — Dischgd., Aug. 18, 1862, underage: Re-enl.,
(2) Mar. 5, 1863: Paroled, Appomattox (Apr. 12, 1865).

(1) ESTES, JAS. — W. (leg), Antietam (Sept. 17, 1862): Died, typhoid fever, Nov. 15, 1862.

FELDER, JAS. D. — Enl., July 5, 1861: K., 2nd Manassas.

FOWLER, J. J. — Enl., May 20, 1862: W. & POW, 2nd Manassas (Aug. 30, 1862): Died from wound, Oct. 1, 1862.

(1) GODFREY, JAS. R. — See list of "Non-Comm. Officers" above.

(1) HIETT, JOHN S. — See list of "Non-Comm. Officers" above.

(2) HINDMOND, A. D. — Enl., Apr. 1, 1862: Paroled, Appomattox.

(1) HOWARD, JOS. D. — Died, typhoid fever, Dec. 11, 1862.

(1) HUFF, JAS. R. — See list of "Officers" above.

JACKSON, E. BELLINGER — Enl., July 5, 1861: W., Culpeper CH.: Dischgd., wound, Jan. 31, 1862.

KIRBY, JESSE P. — Enl., Sept. 7, 1861: W. (back), Gaines' Mill (June 27, 1862): Present for duty, Dec., 1864.

(1) (2) LEE, D. M. — Present for duty most of the war: Paroled, Appomattox (Apr. 12, 1865).

(2) LIVINGSTON, WM. O. — Enl., July 5, 1861: Present for duty most of the war: Paroled, Appomattox (Apr. 12, 1865).

(1) MARSHALL, WM. L. — See list of "Non-Comm. Officers" above.

MATTISON, L. W. — Enl., Sept. 7, 1861: Died, Fall, 1862.

MATTISON, T. S. — Enl., Sept. 7, 1861: POW, E. Tenn., Jan. 17, 1864.

(1) (2) McCOY, IRA C. — Present for duty most of war: Paroled, Appomattox (Apr. 12, 1865).

MEARS, S. M. — Enl., Apr. 5, 1862: Present for duty, Dec., 1864.

(1) MEARS, WYATT — POW, near Chattanooga, Oct. 29, 1863: Exchanged, Mar., 1865.

MEEKS, JAS. S. — See list of "Non-Comm. Officers" above.

MOSELY, W. C. — Enl., Nov. 4, 1861: Present for duty, Dec., 1864.

(1) NELSON, ROBT. M. — Present for duty most of the war.

(1) NELSON, T. F. — W. (hand), Darbytown Rd. (Oct. 7, 1864).

PARLER, LEWIS E. — See list of "Non-Comm. Officers" above.

PATTERSON, JOHN B. — Enl., July 5, 1861: W. (arm & shoulder), Darbytown Rd. (Oct. 7, 1864).

(1) PEDEN, HUGH L. — W., Antietam (Sept. 17, 1862): Big toe amputated (ingrown toenail), Oct., 1864.

(1) PEDEN, ROBT. C. — W., 2nd Manassas (Aug. 30, 1862): W., Petersburg, July, 1864: Paroled, Farmville, Va. (mid-Apr., 1865).

PERKINS, THOS. C. — Enl., July 5, 1861: No record after Oct., 1863.

PHILIPS, G. A. — Transfd. to Co. E. from 7th So. Car. Inf. Regt., Sept., 1862.

(1) PINSON, JOS. D. — See list of "Non-Comm. Officers" above.

PLYMALE, A. — Enl., Apr. 11, 1862: No record after Dec., 1862.

POSEY, W. N. — Transfd. into Co. E from Co. D, Summer, 1863: W. & POW, Wills Valley, Tenn. (Oct. 28, 1863): Died as POW from W., Nov. 11, 1863.

(1) RAMSEY, JAS. W. — W. (foot), Antietam (Sept. 17, 1862): Died of wound, Nov. 22, 1862.

RAMSEY, JOHN — Enl., May 20, 1862: Present for duty, Aug., 1863.

(1) RICE, JOHN P. — W., 7 Pines (May 31, 1862): W., Petersburg (July, 1864).

(1) RODGERS, ROBT. — W. (thigh), Antietam (Sept. 17, 1862): Present for duty as of Dec., 1864.

(1) SATTERFIELD, JOHN B. O. — W. (knee), Antietam (Sept. 17, 1862): POW, 9-Mile Road, Va., Oct. 27, 1864.

(1) SMITH, EZEKIEL — Dischgd., Sept. 5, 1862, overage (36).

(1) SMITH, W. J. — W. (hip), 2nd Manassas (Aug. 30, 1862): Died, Fall, 1862.

STONE, E. G. — Enl., Aug. 1, 1862: No record after Oct., 1863.

STONE, ROBT. M. — Enl., July 5, 1861: Died (chronic diarrhea), Sept. 12, 1862.

STROKE, SAMUEL B. — Enl., July 5, 1861: Died, Feb. 14, 1863, in So. Car. while on furlough.
(1) TARRANT, JAS. — W. (leg), Gaines' Mill (June 27, 1862): Dischgd., Sept. 5, 1862, overage.
TERRY, C. WILLSON — See list of "Non-Comm. Officers" above.
(1) TERRY, GEO. F. — Present for duty most of the war: Paroled,
(2) Appomattox (Apr. 12, 1865).
(2) TERRY, JOHN M. — Enl., Apr. 5, 1862: Paroled, Appomattox (Apr. 12, 1865).
TERRY, T. F. — See list of "Non-Comm. Officers" above.
TERRY, TANDY — Enl., May 20, 1862: Died (chronic diarrhea), Sept. 17, 1862.
THOMASON, G. W. — Enl., May 20, 1862: Died, Dec. 31, 1862.
(1) THOMPSON, HARRIS — Present for duty most of the war.
(1) THOMPSON, JOHN P. — See list of "Non-Comm. Officers" above.
(1) THOMPSON, MOSES W. — See list of "Officers" above.
(1) THOMPSON, W. DRAYTON — W. (leg), Gaines' Mill (June 27, 1862): Absent on sick furlough, Dec., 1864.
(1) THOMPSON, WM. — Present for duty most of the war.
TOLLISON, ABRAHAM — Enl., May 20, 1862: Dischgd. (TB), June 25, 1863.
(1) TOLLISON, FRANCIS M. — K., Antietam (Sept. 17, 1862).
(1) TUMBLIN, JOHN G. — W. (back), Gaines' Mill (June 27, 1862): No record after Apr., 1863.
TURBYFILL, T. P. — Enl., Sept. 7, 1861: On furlough, Dec., 1864.
(1) VAUGHN, JOS. J. — See list of "Non-Comm. Officers" above.
VOGT, THOS. P. — See list of "Non-Comm. Officers" above.
(1) WALDRUP, ANDERSON — Dischgd., Sept. 5, 1862, overage (35).
(1) WASSON, JOSIAH B. — W. (lung), Petersburg (July, 1864): Paroled,
(2) Appomattox (Apr. 12, 1865).
(1) WHITLOCK, ROBT. — POW, Richmond hosp., Apr. 5, 1865.
(1) WILLIS, GIDEON P. (or T.) — POW, Chattanooga, Oct. 29, 1863: Escaped, Nov. 14, 1864.
(1) WOODSON, AZARIAH — W. & POW, 2nd Manassas (Aug. 30, 1862): Dischgd., Apr. 2, 1863.

* * * * *

MEMBERS OF COMPANY E, HAMPTON'S SO. CAR. LEGION-(INF. BTLN.), WHO WERE NOT PRESENT FOR DUTY DURING THE PERIOD THAT THE REGIMENT WAS ASSIGNED TO HOOD'S TEXAS BRIGADE (JUNE 2 - Nov. 15, 1862).

OFFICERS

Adams, Thomas, Capt. (No record after July, 1861)

(1) Bozeman, Toliver L., Capt. (Dischgd., Sick, July, 1861)

(1) Baker, Thos. P., 2Lt. (No record after May, 1862)

(1) Stenhouse, John T., 3Lt. (D., W., Aug., 1861)

NON-COMMISSIONED OFFICERS

(2) Farnandis, Harry, 5Cpl. (Enl., Apr., 1864)

(1) Fowler, Jas. W., 4Sgt. (D., Dec., 1861)

(1) Fowler, Robt. A., 4Sgt. (K., 7 Pines)

(1) Hammond, John S., 1Sgt. (Dischgd., Oct., 1861)

(1) Kirby, W. Vincent, 1Cpl. (D., Sept., 1861)

(1) Ownes, Archibald P., 1Cpl. (No record after June, 1862)

(1) Peden, Alex. M., 2Sgt. (Dischgd., May, 1862)

(1) Peden, David T., 2Sgt. (Dischgd., Sept., 1861)

PRIVATES

Acker, E. H. (Enl., Aug., 1863)

Allison, Jas. (Enl., Jan., 1864)

(1) Anderson, Sam L. (Dischgd., Sept., 1861)

(1) Austin, Thos. (Dischgd., June, 1861)

(1) Austin, Wm. T. (Dischgd., Summer, 1861)

(1) Autry, Robt. C. (K., 1st Manassas)

(1) Babb, Martin (Dischgd., Sept., 1861)

(1) Baker, J. Harvey (Dischgd., Feb., 1862)

(1) Berry, Andrew J. (Dischgd., Aug., 1861)

Berry, C. P. (Enl., Nov., 1864)

Blye, J. W. (Enl., May, 1864)

Bookhart, Joel T. (Died, W., 1861)

Boyd, J. S. (Enl., Mar., 1864)

Carson, Jos. (Enl., May, 1863)

(1) Ceicly, Hamilton W. (Dischgd., Aug., 1861)

Chandler, J. M. (Enl., Apr., 1863)

(1) Chandler, Pinckney L. (Dischgd., Oct., 1861)

(1) Chapman, Elias (D., Jan., 1862)

Chapman, Hewitt (Enl., Jan., 1864)

(1) Chapman, Jas. W. (Dischgd., Sept., 1861)

(1) Chapman, Solomon (Dischgd., June, 1861)

Chapman, W. A. (Enl., Jan., 1864)

Coker, Barnett (Enl., Nov., 1864)

Coker, Thurman (Enl., May, 1863)

Cox, John (Enl., Aug., 1864)

Davenport, F. M. (Enl., Feb., 1863)

Davenport, H. B. (Enl., Mar., 1864)

Davenport, Irvin (Enl., Mar., 1864)

Davis, J. T. (No record prior to Apr., 1865)

Davenport, Dunklin (Enl., Jan., 1864)

(1) Eskew, Jas. R. (Dischgd., June, 1861)

Eskew, Simeon (Enl., Nov., 1864)

(1) Farmer, Robt. H. (D., Aug., 1861)

Fowler, M. T. (Enl., Mar., 1864)

(1) Fuller, Wm. S. (Dischgd., June, 1861)

(1) Gambrill, Norman W. (D., Dec., 1861)

(1) Goldsmith, Jas. W. (No record after Oct., 1861)

(1) Gunnels, Robt. (Dischgd., June, 1861)

Guthry, Wm. (Enl., Oct., 1864)
(1) Gwin, John (Deserted, June, 1861)
Holiday, Jas. J. (Dischgd., Sept., 1861)
(1) Jenkins, Jas. H. (D., Oct., 1861)
Johnson, J. H. (Enl., Jan., 1864)
Johnson, W. H. (Enl., Feb., 1863)
Jones, Jas. L. (D., Apr., 1862)
Kasler, Andrew (Enl., Aug., 1863)
Kasler, John (Enl., Aug., 1863)
King, Wm. (Transfd. out, July, 1861)
(1) Kirby, Jesse (D., Sept., 1861)
Livingston, Abednego P. (D., Aug., 1861)
Livingston, Thos. (Dischgd., Oct., 1861)
Martin, Wm. (Enl., May, 1864)
McCullough, Jas. (Enl., Feb., 1863)
McDougle, Robt. (Transfd. out, Aug., 1861)
Mise, Jeremiah (Enl., Feb., 1863)
(1) Nash, Edw. W. (Dischgd., Aug., 1861)
(1) Neill, Edw. F. (D., Dec., 1861)
(1) Nesbit, John P. (Dischgd., Sept., 1861)
Owens, M. D. (Enl., Mar., 1864)
Patterson, John (Dischgd., July, 1861)
Patterson, Nathaniel (Dischgd., July, 1861)
Patterson, Preston B. (Dischgd., W., Aug., 1861)
(1) Peden, David M. (Dischgd., Nov., 1861)

(1) Ramsey, Wm. (D., Dec., 1861)
(1) Reid, Christopher R. (Dischgd., July, 1861)
Rice, Thos. (Enl., Oct., 1864)
Roberts, Peter C. (K., 1st Manassas)
Rush, David H. (Dischgd., W., Oct., 1861)
Scott, Jas. (Enl., Oct., 1863)
(2) Smith, H. L. (No record prior to Apr., 1865)
(1) Smith, Jasper W. (D., Apr., 1862)
Sullivan, W. D. (Enl., Oct., 1864)
Switzer, _____ (Enl., Nov., 1864)
Templeton, D. McDuffee (D., Oct., 1861)
(1) Terry, Jas. A. (POW, 7 Pines)
Terry, W. C. (Enl., Mar., 1864)
Thompson, C. E. (Enl., July, 1863)
(1) Thompson, Mathew (Dischgd., June, 1861)
(1) Thompson, Wilson T. (No record after June, 1861)
Tollison, E. T. (Enl., Aug., 1863)
Traynham, T. W. (Enl., Aug., 1863)
Vaughn, F. H. (No record prior to May, 1863)
(1) Vaughn, Wm. H. (K., 1st Manassas)
(1) West, L. Marion (Died, W., July, 1861)
Whitlock, Drury (Enl., Sept., 1863)
(1) Woods, Brewer (D., Jan., 1862)
Ze, I. M. (No record prior to May, 1865)

COMPANY F – *DAVIS GUARDS*

Company was mustered into the Confederate Service, "for one year," at Columbia, So. Car., June 13, 1861 by Capt. Wm. L. M. Austin.

Key

(1) Original member of Company. (2) Paroled at Appomattox.
K (Killed), W (Wounded), POW (Prisoner of War)
AWOL (Absent Without Leave)

OFFICERS

(1) AUSTIN, JAS. S. Capt. – Orig. Capt. of Co.: Resgnd., Mar. 24, 1863, passed over for promotion.
 CHARLES, WM. B. Capt. – Orig. 3Sgt. of Co.: Prom., 2Lt., Apr. 25, 1862: Prom., 1Lt., Mar. 23, 1863: Prom., Capt., Mar. 24, 1863: W. (leg), Petersburg, June 13, 1864.
(1) AUSTIN, JOHN W. 1Lt. – Orig. 2Lt. of Co.: Prom., 1Lt., Apr. 25, 1862: No record after Aug., 1862.
 CLEVELAND, JEREMIAH 1Lt. – Orig. Pvt. in Co.: Prom., 2Lt., Apr. 25, 1862: Prom., 1Lt., Mar. 24, 1863: Present for duty up to Dec., 1864.
(2) MORGAN, BENJ. P. 2Lt. – Orig. Pvt. in Co.: Prom., 3Lt., Summer, 1863: Prom., 2Lt., July 22, 1864: Paroled, Appomattox (Apr. 12, 1865).
 THOMASON, ROBT. 2Lt. – Orig. Pvt. in Co.: Prom., 3Lt., Fall, 1862: Prom., 2Lt., Mar. 24, 1863: Died, July 22, 1864.
 GRESHAM, WM. P. 3Lt. – Orig. Pvt. in Co.: Elect., 3Lt., July 22, 1864: Absent on furlough, Fall, 1864.

NON-COMMISSIONED OFFICERS

 ALEXANDER, WM. J. Cpl. – Orig. Pvt. in Co.: Appt. Cpl., Apr. 25, 1862: Dischgd., enlmt. expired, Nov. 6, 1862.
 ASHMORE, PASCHAL A. 1Sgt. – Orig. Pvt. in Co.: Prom. to 1Sgt., Sept., 1864: Present for duty most of the war.
(1) AUSTIN, WM. M. 2Sgt. – Orig. 2Sgt. of Co.: Prom., 1Sgt., Fall, 1861: Reduced to ranks, Apr., 1862: Dischgd., Sept. 7, 1862.
 BRAMLETT, JOHN T. 1Cpl. – Orig. Pvt. in Co.: W. (side & arm), Antietam (Sept. 17, 1862): Prom., 1Cpl., Nov., 1862: Dischgd., Mar. 24, 1864.
 CABEEN, RICH. 2Cpl. – Enl. as a Pvt., July 16, 1861: Prom., 2Cpl.: K. near Campbell's Sta., Tenn., Nov. 16, 1863.
(1) CHARLES, WM. B. 3Sgt. – See list of "Officers" above.

CURETON, THOS. J. 4Cpl. — Orig. Pvt. in Co.: Prom., 4Cpl., Spring, 1864: W. (leg), Petersburg, mid-Aug., 1864.
(1) DACUS, DAVID N. M. 2Cpl. — Orig. 2Cpl. of Co.: Reduced to ranks: W. (both hips), Petersburg, June, 1864: Died of wounds, June 15, 1864.
(2) DILLARD, LEMUEL G. 2Cpl. — Orig. Pvt. in Co.: Prom., 2Cpl., Fall, 1861: Reduced to ranks, Apr. 25, 1862: W. (arm & leg) & POW, Antietam (Sept. 17, 1862): Paroled, Appomattox (Apr. 12, 1865).
FOWLER, JAS. F. 2Cpl. — Orig. Pvt. in Co., age 18: Prom., 5Cpl., Mar. 24, 1863: Prom., 2Cpl., Winter, 1863-64.
(2) GREEN, JAS. D. 3Cpl. — Enl. as a Pvt., Aug. 29, 1861: Prom., 3Cpl., Winter, 1863-64: Paroled, Appomattox (Apr. 12, 1865).
(1) HUNTER, HENRY L. 5Sgt. — Orig. 5Sgt. of Co.: Reduced to ranks, Apr. 25, 1862: No record after Aug., 1862.
JOHNSON, FRANCIS A. 1Cpl. — Orig. Pvt. in Co.: Appt. 1Cpl., Apr. 25, 1862: Transfd. to 2nd So. Car. Cav. Regt., Oct. 10, 1862.
MARTIN, ALBERT R. 4Sgt. — Orig. Pvt. in Co.: Appt. 2Cpl., Spring, 1862: POW, Boonsboro (Sept. 14, 1862): Paroled: Appt. 1Cpl., Spring, 1863: Prom., 4Sgt., Fall, 1864.
SATTERFIELD, JAS. H. 3Sgt. — Orig. Pvt. in Co.: Appt. 3Cpl., Apr. 25, 1862: W., 2nd Manassas (Aug. 30, 1862): Prom., 3Sgt., Winter, 1863-64.
SOWELL, H. F. 2Sgt. — Enl. as a Pvt., Aug. 29, 1861: Prom., 5Sgt., Spring, 1862: W. (foot & knee), Antietam (Sept. 17, 1862): Prom., 2Sgt., Winter, 1863-64.
STORY, JOHN F. 5Sgt. — Orig. Pvt. in Co.: Appt. 4Cpl., Apr. 25, 1862: Prom., 5Sgt., Winter, 1863-64.
TARRANT, WM. W. 5Cpl. — Orig. Pvt. in Co.: Prom., 5Cpl., July 27, 1864: POW (date & place unknown).
THACKSTON, WM. P. 3Cpl. — Orig. Pvt. in Co.: Prom., 3Cpl., Fall, 1861: Reduced to ranks, Spring, 1862: POW, 7 Pines (May 31, 1862): Exchanged, Aug. 5, 1862: W. (head & legs), Antietam (Sept. 17, 1862).
WALLACE, WM. D. 1Cpl. — Orig. Pvt. in Co.: Prom., 5Cpl., Fall, 1862: Prom., 4Cpl., Summer, 1863: Prom., 1Cpl., Spring, 1864.
YEARGIN, BENJ. F. 4Sgt. — Orig. Pvt. in Co.: Appt. 4Sgt., Apr. 25, 1862: Died (chronic diarrhea), Oct. 17, 1862.

PRIVATES

(1) ACKER, JAS. A. — Enl., age 17: W. (finger shot off), Gaines' Mill (June 27, 1862): Dischgd., Sept., 1862.
(1) ALEXANDER, WM. J. — See list of "Non-Comm. Officers" above.
ASHMORE, D. J. — Enl., July 15, 1862: Absent since Nov., 1862.
(1) ASHMORE, PASCHAL A. — See list of "Non-Comm. Officers" above.
(1) ATKINSON, JOHN W. — No records after Aug., 1863.
(1) ATKINSON, WM. A. — Enl., age 17: Died, Richmond, Mar. 17, 1863.
(1) AUSTIN, ANDERSON M. — Died (typhoid fever), Sept. 30, 1862.

AUSTIN, J. M. — Enl., July 1, 1862: No record after Dec., 1864.
(2)   AUSTIN, LAUTHAN B. — Enl., Aug. 29, 1861: Paroled, Appomattox (Apr. 12, 1865).
AUSTIN, THOS. — Enl., Apr. 5, 1862: Died, typhoid fever, June 30, 1862.
(1)   AUSTIN, WILEY NELSON — W., Antietam (Sept. 17, 1862): On detached serv., Dec., 1864.
BENNETT, DECATUR C. — Enl., Sept. 4, 1861: Present for duty most of the war.
(1)   BENSON, PERRIN — Dischgd., Sept. 7, 1862.
(1)   BRAMLETT, JOHN T. — See list of "Non-Comm. Officers" above.
BRAMLETT, R. — Enl., Apr. 5, 1862: Died, tuberculosis, Dec. 4, 1862.
(1)   BRAMLETT, WM. A. — Present for duty most of the war.
BRICE, THOS. — Enl., July 6, 1861: No record after Aug., 1862.
CABEEN, RICH. — See list of "Non-Comm. Officers" above.
(1)   CHAPMAN, JOHN — Present for duty, Dec., 1864: No other record.
(1)   CHAPMAN, JOHN C. — Present for duty most of the war.
(1)   CHAPMAN, WM. M. — W., Antietam (Sept. 17, 1862).
(1)   CHILDERS, PATTERSON Z. — Hospitalized, Spring, 1863: No other record.
CHRISTIAN, ROBT. — Enl., July 6, 1861: Dischgd., sick, Nov. 26, 1862.
(1)   CLEVELAND, JEREMIAH — See list of "Officers" above.
CLEVELAND, VANNOY — Enl., July 6, 1861: POW, 2nd Manassas (Aug. 30, 1862): Paroled: W., Winter, 1862-63.
CLINE, W. B. — Enl., Mar. 28, 1862: Present for duty, Dec., 1864.
(1)   COX, LEWIS — Enl., age 18: Dischgd., Sept. 7, 1862.
CRAINE (or CRANE), THRUSTON — Enl., July 1, 1862: Missing, Antietam (Sept. 17, 1862).
(1)   CRUMPTON, PINCKNEY — POW, 2nd Manassas (Aug. 30, 1862): Paroled: W., Fredericksburg (Dec. 13, 1862): Detached service, Fall, 1864.
(1)   CURETON, THOS. J. — See list of "Non-Comm. Officers" above.
DALTON, AMOS H. — Enl., Sept. 4, 1861: POW, Chattanooga, Oct. 28, 1863: Died (acute diarrhea) in Fed. prison, Mar. 23, 1864.
(1)   DARBY, WM. J. — Enl., age 17: Dischgd. (underage), Sept. 7, 1862.
(1)   DILLARD, LEMUEL G. — See list of "Non-Comm. Officers" above.
DOBSON, RUFUS — Enl., Mar. 28, 1862: Present for duty, Dec., 1864.
EASTERS, A. — Enl., May 1, 1862: Present for duty, Dec., 1864.
(1)   FOWLER, JAS. F. — See list of "Non-Comm. Officers" above.
GREEN, JAS. D. — See list of "Non-Comm. Officers" above.
(1)   GRIDLEY, EDW. — Transfd. to the 16th So. Car. Inf. Regt., Nov. 24, 1862.
(1)   GRESHAM, WM. P. — See list of "Officers" above.
(1)   HICKS, CHAS. — Died, Fall, 1862.
HILL, J. T. — Enl., Mar. 16, 1862: Present for duty, Dec., 1864.
(1)   HOLLAND, ROBT. H. — Died, Fall, 1862.
(1)   HUDSON, W. A. — Absent, sick, Dec., 1863.
(1)   HUGHES, ROBT. L. — Died (chronic dysentery), Sept. 12, 1862.
HUTCHINGS, DAVID A. — Enl., Aug. 29, 1861: Dischgd. for age, Sept. 7, 1862.

(1) HUTCHINGS, WM. P. — Present for duty to Aug., 1863.
(1) JOHNSON, FRANCIS A. — See list of "Non-Comm. Officers" above.
JONES, WM. — Enl., Aug. 29, 1861: W., 7 Pines (June 1, 1862): Dischgd., Sept., 1862.
LEAGUE, WM. — Enl., Aug. 29, 1861: Present for duty, Dec., 1864.
(1) LENDERMAN, JACOB H. — Dischgd. (epilepsy), Oct. 3, 1862.
(1) MARTIN, ALBERT R. — See list of "Non-Comm. Officers" above.
MARTIN, JOHN — Enl., Jan. 8, 1862: On sick furlough, Dec., 1864.
McDOUGLE, ROBT. — Transfd. into Co. F, Aug., 1861: No record after Aug., 1862.
(1) McHUGH, HARRISON — W., Antietam (Sept. 17, 1862): Died (pneumonia), Dec. 30, 1862.
(1) MOORE, WM. — Present for duty most of the war: Paroled,
(2) Appomattox (Apr. 12, 1865).
(1) MORGAN, BENJ. P. — See list of "Officers" above.
(2) NEVINS, JAS. — Enl., Mar. 28, 1862: Paroled, Appomattox (Apr. 12, 1865).
(1) NIX, W. HENRY — Present for duty most of the war: Paroled,
(2) Appomattox (Apr. 12, 1865).
(1) PAYNE, JAS. P. — Present for duty most of the war: On detached serv., Dec., 1864.
(1) PAYNE, JOHN W. — Enl., age 18: Present for duty, Dec., 1864.
POOL, J. H. — Enl., Oct. 10, 1861: On duty as of Dec., 1864.
(1) ROARK, JOHN — Present for duty as of Dec., 1864.
ROBERTS, WM. G. — Dischgd., underage (17), Aug. 18, 1862.
(1) RODGERS, GEO. W. — K., Lookout Valley, Tenn. (Nov. 28, 1863).
ROPER, DAVID — Transfd. to Co. F from the 2nd So. Car. Rifle Regt., Oct. 10, 1862: Transfd. out of Co. F, Feb., 1863.
ROSEMAN, W. N. — Enl., Dec. 12, 1861: Paroled, Newton, No. Car., Apr. 19, 1865.
(1) RUNION (or RUNYON), ANDREW M. — Enl. at 18: W. (hand), Antietam (Sept. 17, 1862): Present for duty as of Aug., 1863.
(1) SATTERFIELD, JAS. H. — See list of "Non-Comm. Officers" above.
SMITH, B. F. — Enl., Apr. 5, 1862: No other record.
SMITH, S. CHRISTOPHER — Enl., Aug. 29, 1861: Present for duty most of the war.
(1) SMITH, STEPHEN — Enl., age 45: No record after Apr., 1863.
SMITH, WM. J. — Enl., Aug. 29, 1861: Dischgd., underage (17), Nov. 6, 1862.
SOWELL, H. F. — See list of "Non-Comm. Officers" above.
(1) STORY, JOHN F. — See list of "Non-Comm. Officers" above.
(1) TARRANT, WM. W. — See list of "Non-Comm. Officers" above.
THACKSTON, C. G. — Enl., Dec. 30, 1861: Present for duty, Dec., 1864
THACKSTON, J. H. — Enl. Dec. 30, 1861: POW, Burkeville, Va. Apr. 6, 1865.
(1) THACKSTON, WM. P. — See list of "Non-Comm. Officers" above.
(1) THOMASON, B. WESLEY — W., Chickamauga (Sept. 20, 1863): POW, E. Tenn. (Nov., 1863).
(1) THOMASON, CHURCHWELL — POW, 2nd Manassas (Aug. 30, 1862): Paroled: Died, Nov. 12, 1862.

(1)   THOMASON, ROBT. — See list of "Officers" above.

TIMBS, J. E. — Enl., Jan. 12, 1862: Deserted, Sept. 7, 1864.

(1)   TOWNES, ALEX S. — Present for duty as of Dec., 1864.

VAUGHN, J. M. — Enl., Aug. 29, 1861: Absent on sick furlough, Dec., 1864.

VAUGHN, MARSHALL — Enl., Sept. 4, 1861: POW, 2nd Manassas (Aug. 30, 1862): Paroled.

(1)   VAUGHN, SAMUEL — POW, Deep Bottom, Va. (Sept. 29, 1864): Exchanged.

(1)   VERDIN, LEDFORD N. — Dischgd., Sept. 7, 1862.

(1)   WALDRIP, ISRAEL — W., Antietam (Sept. 17, 1862): Transfd. out of Co., Sept., 1863.

(1)   WALKER, HENRY A. — W. & POW, 2nd Manassas (Aug. 30, 1862): Paroled: Died of Manassas Wound, Feb. 2, 1863.

(1)   WALLACE, WM. D. — See list of "Non-Comm. Officers" above.

(2)   WATSON, JAS. F. — Enl., Aug. 29, 1861: W., 7 Pines (June 1, 1862): Paroled, Appomattox (Apr. 12, 1865).

WEST, T. J. — Enl., May 20, 1862: No record after Dec., 1864.

WILSON, W. — Enl., July 6, 1861: Deserted, Aug., 1862.

(1)   WOOD, JOS. T. — Absent sick, Oct., 1863: No other record.

(1)   WOOD, THOS. C. — Absent furlough, Dec., 1864: No other record.

WOODS, HASTIN — Enl., Jan. 8, 1862: W. (foot), Richmond (Aug. 17, 1864).

(1)   WOODS, THOS. — Present for duty, Aug., 1862: No other record.

(1)   YEARGIN, BENJ. F. — See list of "Non-Comm. Officers" above.

YEARGIN, T. — Enl., age 16, Apr. 5, 1862: Dischgd., Sept. 7, 1862.

YEARGIN, W. M. — Enl., Nov. 27, 1861: Absent on sick furlough, Dec., 1864.

★   ★   ★   ★   ★

MEMBERS OF COMPANY F, HAMPTON'S SO. CAR. LEGION (INF. BTLN.) WHO WERE NOT PRESENT FOR DUTY DURING THE PERIOD THAT THE REGIMENT WAS ASSIGNED TO HOOD'S TEXAS BRIGADE (JUNE 2-NOV. 15, 1862)

OFFICERS

(1) Austin, Wm. L. M., Capt. (Orig. Capt. of Co.: K., July 6, 1861)

(1) Lester, Geo. W., 1Lt. (Orig. 1Lt. of Co.: Dropped, Apr., 1862)

Austin, William, 2Lt. (Orig. 1Sgt. of Co.: Dropped, Apr., 1862)

(1) Yeargin, D. Wm., 2Lt. (Orig. 2Lt. of Co.: K., 1st Manassas)

NON-COMMISSIONED OFFICERS

(1) Garrison, Obadiah W., 3Cpl. (Orig. 3Cpl. of Co.: Dischgd., Feb., 1862)

(1) Barrison, Wm. D., Cpl. (Orig. Cpl. in Co.: Dischgd., Sept., 1861)

(1) McDaniel, Jas. A., 4Cpl. (Orig. 4Cpl. of Co.: D., Aug., 1861) Smyer, Miles A., 1Cpl. (Orig. Pvt. in Co.: No record after Apr., 1862)

PRIVATES

Alexander, N. B. (Enl., May, 1863)

(1) Baldwin, Willis A. J. (No record after June, 1861)

Beam, Franklin (D., Nov., 1861)

Brice, Jas. P. (D., Nov., 1861)

(1) Bright, Jacob (No record)

(1) Burdett, Jesse J. (W., 7 Pines)

Burdett, Reuben (No record after Apr., 1862)

(1) Burgess, Jas. (D., Spring, 1862)

(1) Charles, David S. (Dischgd., Oct., 1861)

Charles, J. T. (Enl., Mar., 1864)

(1) Charles, Jas. F. (D., Aug., 1861)

(1) Clark, Jas. (Dischgd., Aug., 1861)

(1) Cobb, David (Dischgd., May, 1862)

(1) Cox, John (Dischgd., Apr., 1862)

Crosby, Chas. (No record before Nov., 1864)

Crumpton, J. M. (Enl., May, 1864)

Dalton, L. R. (Enl., Apr., 1864)

Davis, L. P. (Enl., Nov., 1863)

Dent, Benj. W. (Dischgd., Sept., 1861)

(1) Dunigan, Thos. A. (No record after Apr., 1862)

(1) Farmer, Jas. A. (D., Sept., 1861)

(1) Forrester, John E. (Dischgd., Aug., 1861)

(1) Garrett, Patella G. (D., Sept., 1861)

Garrison, B. D. (Enl., Feb., 1864)

(1) Garrison, Henry D. (No record after June, 1861)

Garrison, J. B. (Enl., Apr., 1864)

(1) Garrison, Wm. (Dischgd., Nov., 1861)

(1) Gary, Wm. D. (D., Aug., 1861)

Graham, A. A. (Enl., May, 1863)

Graham, G. W. (Enl., May, 1863)

Green, J. T. (Enl., Apr., 1864)

Griffith, Devoreaux (D., Apr., 1862)

(1) Griffith, John (No record)

Grissam, Jas. L. (Dischgd., Apr., 1862)

(1) Henderson, Oliver P. (Dischgd., July, 1861)

Henderson, W. H. (Enl., Oct., 1863)

(1) Hill, Chas. J. (Dischgd., Aug., 1861)

Hunnicut, W. A. (Enl., May, 1864)

Jones, J. A. (Enl., Feb., 1863)

Jones, Madison J. (D., Dec., 1861)

King, Nath. L. (D., Mar., 1862)

(1) Kinman, Jas. B. (D., Aug., 1861)

(1) League, Joshua (D., Apr., 1862)

League, L. M. (Enl., July, 1863)

Lemons, Harvey (Enl., May, 1863)

(1) Manaffee, J. Manning (No record after Apr., 1862)

McDaniel, A. James (No record after Apr., 1862)

McNeal, J. (No record prior to Sept., 1864)

Morgan, G. (Enl., July, 1864)

Morgan, Wm. E. (K., 1st Manassas)

Morris, Jos. (Enl., May, 1863)

(1) Nelson, Terry (Transfd. out, Aug., 1861)

Nix, J. L. (Enl., Mar., 1863)

(1) Nunnely, Francis F. (Dischgd., Sept., 1861)

Orr, Andrew (Enl., May, 1863)

Patterson, Sam P. (No record after Dec., 1861)

Roark, Alex (Enl., Oct., 1863)

Roberts, J. A. (Enl., Aug., 1863)

Rochester, A. M. (Enl., May, 1864)

(1) Rodgers, Wm. R. (No record)

Roon, J. H. (No record prior to May, 1865)

Runion (or Runyon), Jas. M. (Dischgd., May, 1862)

Sarvis, J. M. (Enl., May, 1863)

Schutz, John (Enl., May, 1863)

Sloan, J. R. (Enl., Aug., 1863)

Smith, M. E. A. (Enl., Apr., 1864)

Smith, M. F. (No record prior to May, 1865)

(2) Smith, W. B. (Paroled, Appomattox)

Smith, W. Z. (Enl., June, 1864)

(1) Spillers, Geo. E. (D., Apr., 1862)

(1) Story, Wm. L. (K., 1st Manassas)

Stroud, W. M. (Enl., July, 1863)

Tarrant, C. B. (Enl., Aug., 1863)

Tarrant, J. A. (Enl., Apr., 1863)

(1) Thackston, Thos. M. (Dischgd., wound, Aug., 1861)

(1) Thackston, Wm. S. (No record)

Thomason, Austin (No record)

Thomason, David (D., Nov., 1861)

Thomason, J. B. (Enl., Apr., 1864)

Thomason, J. F. (No record)

Times, J. T. (No record)

Vaughn, Archibald (Dischgd., Sept., 1861)

Vaughn, D. (Enl., Apr., 1864)

Walker, Geo. (Enl., Feb., 1864)

Walker, Jas. (Enl., Oct., 1864)

(1) Walker, Jesse A. (D., Oct., 1861)

Walker, Warren D. (Dischgd., Sept., 1861)

Walton, Thos. J. (Dischgd., Mar., 1862)

Watson, Wm. H. (Enl., Oct., 1864)

West, W. W. (Enl., July, 1864)

White, Jos. (Enl., May, 1863)

Whitney, J. C. (Enl., May, 1864)

Woodard, Chas. (Enl., May, 1863)

(1) Yeargin, Benj. F., Jr. (Dischgd., wound, July, 1861)

HAMPTON'S SO. CAR. LEGION (INF. BTLN.)

COMPANY G – *CLAREMONT RIFLES*

Company was mustered into the Confederate Service, "for one year," at Columbia, So. Car., Aug. 19, 1861 by Capt. Jas. G. Spann.

Key

(1) Original member of Company. (2) Paroled at Appomattox.
K (Killed), W (Wounded), POW (Prisoner of War)
AWOL (Absent Without Leave)

OFFICERS

CARSON, E. SCOTT Capt. — Orig. 1Cpl. of Co.: Appt. 2Sgt., Winter, 1861-62: Appt. 3Lt., Fall, 1862: Elect., 2Lt., Jan. 29, 1863: Prom., Capt., Apr. 1, 1864: Paroled, Farmville, mid-Apr., 1865.

COUNCILL, WM. B. Capt. — Orig. 3Sgt. of Co.: Prom., 2Lt., Apr. 25, 1862: Prom., 1Lt., Sept. 17, 1862: Prom., Capt., Jan. 29, 1863: No record after Oct., 1863.

(1) MOORE, ISHAM Capt. — Orig. 2Lt. of Co.: Prom., Capt., Apr. 25, 1862: Resgnd., Jan. 24, 1863 (lumbago).

BRACEY, J. W. 1Lt. — Orig. 4Sgt. of Co.: Prom., 3Lt., Winter, 1861-62: Prom., 2Lt., Sept. 17, 1862: Prom., 1Lt., Jan. 29, 1863: Paroled, Farmville, mid-Apr., 1865.

EXUM, JAS. J. 1Lt. — Orig. 1Sgt. of Co.: Elect., 1Lt., Apr. 25, 1862: K., Antietam (Sept. 17, 1862).

(2) McEACHERN, JAS. A. 2Lt. — Orig. 2Cpl. of Co.: Prom., 3Sgt., Spring, 1862: Elect., 3Lt., Jan. 26, 1863: Elect., 2Lt., Apr., 1864: Paroled, Appomattox (Apr. 12, 1865).

NON-COMMISSIONED OFFICERS

ALLEN, E. E. Cpl. — Orig. Pvt. in Co.: W., Gaines' Mill (June 27, 1862): Prom., Cpl.: Died in So. Car., Oct. 24, 1864.

ALLISON, R. M. Cpl. — Enl. as a Pvt., Aug. 20, 1861: Prom., Cpl.: Present for duty most of the war.

ATKINSON, WM. M. Sgt. — Orig. Pvt. in Co.: Prom., Cpl., Apr. 25, 1862: Prom., Sgt., 1863: No record after Oct., 1863.

(1)
(2) BALLARD, J. R. 1Sgt. — Orig. 2Sgt. in Co.: Prom., 1Sgt., Spring, 1862: Reduced to Pvt., Spring, 1863: Paroled, Appomattox (Apr. 12, 1865).

(1) BRACEY, J. W. 4Sgt. — See list of "Officers" above.

BROWN, JOHN F. 3Sgt. — Orig. Pvt. in Co.: Appt. Cpl., Feb. 28, 1863: Appt. 3Sgt., Spring, 1864.

(1) CARSON, E. SCOTT 1Cpl. — See list of "Officers" above.
(1) COUNCILL, WM. B. 3Sgt. — See list of "Officers" above.

EVELEIGH, W. R. 3Cpl. — Orig. Pvt. in Co.: Prom., 3Cpl., Feb., 1863: No record after Oct., 1863.

EXUM, J. W. 4Cpl. — Orig. Pvt. in Co.: Prom., 4Cpl., Apr. 25, 1862: Died, Sept. 18, 1864.

(1) EXUM, JAS. J. 1Sgt. — See list of "Officers" above.
(2) GOLDING, J. F. 3Cpl. — Orig. Pvt. in Co.: Prom., 4Cpl., Summer, 1861: Prom., 3Cpl., Fall, 1864: Paroled, Appomattox (Apr. 12, 1865).

(2) LANGSTON, R. W. 1Cpl. — Orig. Pvt. in Co.: Prom., 1Cpl., Winter, 1863-64: W., Petersburg (June 14, 1864): Paroled, Appomattox (Apr. 12, 1865).

(1) McEACHERN, JAS. A. 2Cpl. — See list of "Officers" above.

MORSE, W. W. 1Cpl. — Enl. as a Pvt., Aug. 26, 1861: Prom., 1Cpl., Winter. 1862-63: No record after Oct., 1863.

(2) OWENS, J. J. 4Sgt. — Orig. Pvt. in Co.: Prom., 4Sgt., Winter, 1863-64: W. (arm), White Oak Swamp (Aug. 16, 1864): Paroled, Appomattox (Apr. 12, 1865).

ROBERTS, J. DeB. 4Sgt. — Orig. Pvt. in Co.: W., 2nd Manassas (Aug. 30, 1862): Prom., 1Cpl., Fall, 1862: Prom., 4Sgt., Feb. 28, 1863.

RUSS, W. H. 5Sgt. — Orig. Pvt. in Co.: W. (side), Antietam (Sept. 17, 1862): Prom., 5Sgt., Feb. 28, 1863: No record after Oct., 1863.

(1) SANDERS, M. C. 1Sgt. — Orig. 4Cpl. of Co.: Prom., 3Cpl., Summer, 1861: Prom., 5Sgt., Apr. 25, 1862: Prom., 1Sgt., Feb. 12, 1863.

SPANN, H. M. 2Sgt. — Orig. Pvt. in Co.: Prom., 4Cpl., Fall, 1862: Prom., 2Sgt., Winter, 1863-64.

(1) SPANN, T. D. 3Sgt. — Orig. 3Cpl. of Co.: Prom., 4Sgt., Apr. 25, 1862: W. (knee), 7 Pines (May 31, 1862): Prom., 3Sgt., Fall, 1862: No record after Oct., 1863.

STEPHENS, J. A. 3Cpl. — Orig. Pvt. in Co.: Prom., 3Cpl., Spring, 1862: Dischgd., overage (34), Sept. 8, 1862.

PRIVATES

(1) ALLEN, E. E. — See list of "Non-Comm. Officers" above.

ALLISON, R. M. — See list of "Non-Comm. Officers" above.

(2) ANDERSON, J. G. — Enl., Mar. 22, 1862: AWOL at Gettysburg (July 3, 1863): Paroled, Appomattox (Apr. 12, 1865).

(2) ANDERSON, J. J. — Enl., June 8, 1862: AWOL at Gettysburg (July 3, 1863): Paroled, Appomattox (Apr. 12, 1865).

(1) ATKINSON, JOHN S. — POW, Farmville, Va. (Apr. 6, 1865): No other record.

(1) ATKINSON, SAMUEL — Died, Spring, 1863.

(1) ATKINSON, WM. M. — See list of "Non-Comm. Officers" above.

(1) BALLARD, J. R. — See list of "Non-Comm. Officers" above.

(1) BARTLETT, RICH. — POW, Petersburg, July 26, 1864: Exchanged: Mar., 1865.

BAUGHMAN, H. H. — Enl., July 14, 1862: POW, Lexington CH., Feb. 14, 1865.

BAUGHMAN, R. H. — Enl., Apr. 1, 1862: Deserted, Apr. 5, 1865.

BELK, H. A. — Enl., Sept. 22, 1861: Dischgd. for age, Sept. 8, 1862.

(1) BELK, SUMTER — Dischgd., underage (17), Sept. 8, 1862.

(1) BOSSARD, JOHN — Dischgd., overage (35), Sept. 5, 1862.

BRACEY, J. H. — Enl., Jan. 14, 1862: Absent "on detail," Dec., 1864.

(1) BROWN, JOHN F. — See list of "Non-Comm. Officers" above.

(1) BROWN, R. S. — Dischgd., Sept. 5, 1862.

COATS, SAMUEL — Enl., Aug. 19, 1862: K., Antietam (Sept. 17, 1862).

DAVIDSON, NOAH — Enl., Feb. 12, 1862: Absent "on detail," Dec., 1864.

(1) DEASE, J. L. — Died, Sept. 1, 1862.

DENNIS, J. S. — Enl., Aug. 19, 1861: Dischgd., overage (36), Sept. 8, 1862.

(2) DOROTHY, J. W. — Enl., Aug. 19, 1861: Present for duty most of the war: Paroled, Appomattox (Apr. 12, 1865).

(1) DUTTON, B. Z. — Exchanged for H. T. Kelley, 2nd So. Car. Inf. Regt., Aug. 1, 1862.

ELLIS, E. P. — Enl., Apr. 24, 1862: Died (TB), Mar. 19, 1865.

(1) EVELEIGH, J. E. — W., 7 Pines (May 31, 1862): W. & POW, 2nd Manassas (Aug. 30, 1862): Arm amputated.

(1) EVELEIGH, W. R. — See list of "Non-Comm. Officers" above.

(1) EXUM, J. W. — See list of "Non-Comm. Officers" above.

(1) FITZGERALD, D. — Dischgd., overage (60), July 25, 1862.

(1) FITZGERALD, R. — No record after Oct., 1863.

GARY, J. A. — Enl., Jan. 20, 1862: POW, Richmond, Apr. 3, 1865: Died as POW, May 28, 1865.

(1) GOLDING, J. F. — See list of "Non-Comm. Officers" above.

(1) GREEN, R. R. — Present for duty most of the war: Paroled, Farmville, Va. (mid-Apr., 1865).

HOWELL, W. L. — Enl., Aug. 26, 1861: Dischgd., Sept. 25, 1862.

HUCKS, J. — Enl., Jan. 1, 1862: Present for duty, Dec., 1864.

KELLEY, H. T. — Transfd. out of Co., Aug. 1, 1862.

(1) LANGSTON, R. W. — See list of "Non-Comm. Officers" above.

(1) MARSHALL, ELIJAH — Dischgd. for disability, Jan. 1, 1864.

McELWEE, J. W. — Enl., Aug. 20, 1861: Present for duty, Dec., 1864.

(1) McGEE, J. B. — Dischgd., Sept. 5, 1862, overage.

(1) McGEE, J. E. — Died (bronchitis), June 3, 1862.

McGEE, P. A. W. — Dischgd., Sept. 8, 1862, underage (17).

(1) MINTZ, C. H. — Present for duty, Dec., 1864: No other record.

(1) MITCHUM, T. B. — Present for duty, Oct., 1864: No other record.

(1) MOODY, E. A. — Died (typhoid-pneumonia), Dec. 24, 1862.

(1) MOODY, M. E. — Died in So. Car., Jan. 24, 1863.

MORSE, W. W. — See list of "Non-Comm. Officers" above.

(1) NETTLES, C. B. — W., Chaffin's Farm (Sept. 29, 1864): Paroled, Farmville, Va. (mid-Apr., 1865).

(2) NIPPER, D. W. — Enl., June 1, 1862: Paroled, Appomattox (Apr. 12, 1865).

(1) NORTON, E. — Dischgd., Sept. 25, 1862.

(1) OWENS, J. J. — See list of "Non-Comm. Officers" above.

(1) PATTERSON, D. R. — W., 7 Pines (May 31, 1862): Dischgd., Sept. 29, 1862, overage (51).

(1) POOLE, FELIX — Present for duty as of Oct., 1863.

PORTER, D. A. — Enl., Dec. 28, 1861: Present for duty as of Dec., 1864.

PORTER, J. A. — Enl., Dec. 30, 1861: Present for duty as of Dec., 1864.

PORTER, W. — Enl., June 20, 1862: Present for duty as of Dec., 1864.

(1) ROBERTS, J. DeB. — See list of "Non-Comm. Officers" above.

ROSE, WM. P. — Enl., Jan. 1, 1862: Present for duty as of Dec., 1864.

(1) RUSS, W. H. — See list of "Non-Comm. Officers" above.

(1) SANDERS, T. P. — Dischgd., underage (17), Sept. 5, 1862.

(1) SHAYLOR, J. D. — K., Antietam (Sept. 17, 1862).

(2) SPIERS, G. — Enl., Dec. 21, 1861: Paroled, Appomattox (Apr. 12, 1865).

SPIERS, M. — Enl., Dec. 21, 1861: Present for duty as of Dec., 1864.

SMITH, J. — Enl., Nov. 16, 1861: On detail as of Dec., 1864.

(1) SMITH, J. J. — Died in So. Car., Feb. 12, 1863.
(1) SPANN, H. M. — See list of "Non-Comm. Officers" above.
(1) STEPHANS, J. A. — See list of "Non-Comm. Officers" above.
(1) SULLIVAN, W. J. — Dischgd., Sept. 7, 1862.
(1) TAYLOR, ELIAS — Dischgd., disability, Aug. 13, 1863.
(1) TAYLOR, J. D. — K., Antietam (Sept. 17, 1862).
(1) TURNER, H. R. — Present for duty, 1864.
(1) WILSON, HEROD — W., Antietam (Sept. 17, 1862): Died, E. Tenn.,
      Spring, 1864.

★ ★ ★ ★ ★

MEMBERS OF COMPANY G, HAMPTON'S SO. CAR. LEGION (INF. BTLN.) WHO WERE NOT PRESENT FOR DUTY DURING THE PERIOD THAT THE REGIMENT WAS ASSIGNED TO HOOD'S TEXAS BRIGADE (JUNE 2-NOV. 15, 1862).

OFFICERS

(1) Spann, Jas. G., Capt. (Orig. Capt. of Co.: Resgnd., Apr., 1862)
(1) Spann, Ransom D., 1Lt. (Orig. 1Lt. of Co.: Resgnd., Apr., 1862)

(1) Murray, John, 2Lt. (Orig. 3Lt. of Co.: Resgnd., Jan., 1862)
(2) Zimmerman, D., 2Lt. (No record prior to Apr., 1864)

NON-COMMISSIONED OFFICERS

Bailey, J. W., 5Sgt. (Enl., May, 1863)
Dunn, J. H., 3Cpl. (Enl., Sept., 1863)

Simmons, J. H., 3Cpl. (Enl., May, 1863)

PRIVATES

(1) Allen, J. J. L. (Dischgd., overage, May, 1862)
Anderson, J. H. (Enl., May, 1863)
Anderson, Jas. E. (No record prior to Aug., 1864)
Anderson, W. H. (Enl., May, 1863)
(1) Atkinson, A. (D., Dec., 1861)
Axon, M. (Enl., Mar., 1863)
Baker, M. M. (Enl., July, 1863)

Bishop, Isaac (Enl., Jan., 1863)
Blackwell, M. J. (Enl., May, 1863)
(1) Bostick, L. T. (K., 7 Pines)
(1) Bowen, W. B. (D., Nov., 1861)
Bracey, J. M. (Enl., Nov., 1864)
Brown, G. W. (Enl., Apr., 1864)
(1) Brown, H. M. (D., Apr., 1862)
Buckhalter, J. W. (Enl., May, 1863)
Bunch, J. V. (Enl., Sept., 1863)

Calder, P. (Enl., June, 1863)
Cannaday, S. R. (Enl., Sept., 1863)
(2) Cape, W. D. (Enl., May, 1863)
Carter, J. J. (Enl., May, 1863)
Cauthen, P. (Enl., May, 1863)
Clark, W. R. (Enl., Feb., 1864)
Davis, E. L. (Enl., May, 1863)
Davis, Joel (D., Jan., 1862)
Davis, Jos. (D., Jan., 1862)
(2) Dennis, J. H. (Enl., Apr., 1863)
Denson, J. J. (Enl., May, 1863)
Easley, A. (Enl., Apr., 1863)
Elliott, T. (Enl., May, 1864)
Evans, J. H. (Enl., Feb., 1864)
(1) Eveleigh, H. (D., May, 1862)
Finklea, S. R. (Jnd. Co., May, 1864)
(1) Galloway, J. W. (D., Apr., 1862)
Gerald, W. H. (Enl., May, 1863)
(1) Gowdy, B. L. (Dischgd., Apr., 1862)
Graham, P. J. (Enl., May, 1863)
Graham, S. F. (Enl., May, 1863)
Graham, T. (Enl., May, 1863)
Grant, J. B. (Enl., May, 1863)
Grimsley, J. A. (Enl., Dec., 1863)
Hardy, J. B. (Enl., May, 1863)
Hodge, J. D. (Enl., May, 1863)
(1) Hodges, T. (Enl., Nov., 1863)
Holmes, A. (Enl., May, 1863)
Lambeth, J. C. (Enl., May, 1863)
(1) Lawhorn, Jos. (D., Nov., 1861)
(1) Lawhorn, Thos. L. (Dischgd., Oct., 1861)
Lee, J. S. (Enl., May, 1863)
(1) Lenoir, R. M. (Dischgd., Feb., 1862)
Leopold, John (Enl., Sept., 1863)
Long, G. W. H. (Enl., May, 1863)
(1) Jones, E. (Dischgd., Feb., 1862)
(1) Jones, G. (D., Jan., 1862)
Jones, J. A. (Enl., Sept., 1863)
Jones, W. J. (Enl., May, 1863)
Kitchens, C. E. (Enl., June, 1863)
Knight, S. (Enl., Sept., 1863)
Martin, C. B. (Enl., May, 1865)

Maull, C. M. (Enl., Sept., 1863)
McDaniel, M. (Enl., June, 1863)
McDonald, D. (Enl., Sept., 1864)
McRay, L. P. (Enl., May, 1863)
Metts, H. (Enl., Apr., 1864)
Mitchum, J. (Enl., July, 1863)
Mitchum, S. (Enl., Dec., 1863)
(1) Moody, E. R. (No record after Dec., 1861)
Murrell, O. (No record prior to Sept., 1864)
(2) Nipper, A. (No record prior to Apr., 1865)
(1) Norris, Alex (Dischgd., Nov., 1861)
Nunnery, R. M. (Enl., Oct., 1863)
Page, D. (Jnd. Co., July, 1864)
Patrick, D. E. (Enl., May, 1863)
Pitts, C. (Enl., May, 1863)
Pool, J. (No record)
Powell, W. L. (No record prior to Apr., 1865)
Reynolds, E. W. (Enl., May, 1863)
(2) Reynolds, T. (No record prior to Apr., 1865)
Rhodes, J. D. (Enl., May, 1863)
Rivers, R. S. (Enl., Mar., 1863)
Sandifer, A. J. (Enl., May, 1863)
(1) Sansbery, Wm. (Dischgd., Nov., 1861)
Sellers, L. J. (Enl., May, 1863)
Sellers, T. B. (Enl., May, 1863)
Shaylor, John (Enl., Nov., 1864)
Shealey, G. W. (Enl., May, 1863)
Simmons, E. A. H. (Enl., Sept., 1863)
Sistrunk, N. E. W. (Enl., Oct., 1863)
Snelling, W. H. (Enl., May, 1863)
(1) Spann, W. A. (Dischgd., Feb., 1862)
(1) Sparrow, A. (Dischgd., Mar., 1862)
Spiers, A. (Enl., Nov., 1863)
Streeter, E. H. (No record prior to Sept., 1864)
(1) Thompson, Wm. (No record after Apr., 1862)

Ursery, John C. (Enl., May, 1863)
Wallace, Henry (Dischgd., Oct., 1861)
Walter, A. B. (Enl., Mar., 1864)
(1) Welch, David (D., Jan., 1862)
Whindham, J. H. (Enl., May, 1863)

Whitfield, G. V. (Enl., May, 1863)
Williams, J. F. (Enl., June, 1863)
Williamson, D. A. (Enl., Feb., 1863)
(1) Wright, T. J. (K., 7 Pines)

HAMPTON'S SO. CAR. LEGION (INF. BTLN.)

COMPANY H – *SO. CAR. ZOUAVE VOLS.*

Company was mustered into the Confederate Service, "for the war," at Charlestown, So. Car., Sept. 7, 1861 by Capt. L. C. McCord.

Key

(1) Original member of Company. (2) Paroled at Appomattox.
K (Killed), W (Wounded), POW (Prisoner of War)
AWOL (Absent Without Leave)

OFFICERS

GARDNER, WM. G. Capt. – Orig. Pvt. in Co.: Elect., 2Lt., Oct. 2, 1862: Prom., 1Lt., Jan. 23, 1863: Prom., Capt., Jan. 17, 1864.
(1) McCORD, L. CHEVES Capt. – Orig. Capt. of Co.: Died, Jan. 23, 1863.
(1) PALMER, JOHN D. Capt. – Orig. 1Lt. of Co.: W., 2nd Manassas (Aug. 30, 1862): Prom., Capt., Jan. 23, 1863.
(1) CLARKE, T. A. G. 1Lt. – Orig. 2Lt. of Co.: Prom., 1Lt., Apr. 12, 1862: W., 2nd Manassas (Aug. 30, 1862): K., E. Tenn., Jan. 17, 1864.
(2) WELCH, S. ELLIOTT 1Lt. – Orig. 1Sgt. of Co.: W. (head), Antietam (Sept. 17, 1862): Reduced to ranks, Summer, 1862: Appt. 2Sgt., Jan. 2, 1863: Elect., 2Lt., Jan. 31, 1863: Prom., 1Lt., Jan. 17, 1864: Paroled, Appomattox (Apr. 12, 1865).
SNIDER, A. M. 2Lt. – Orig. Pvt. in Co.: Appt. Cpl., Feb. 1, 1863: Prom., 5Sgt., Oct. 6, 1864: Prom., 2Lt., Dec., 1864.

NON-COMMISSIONED OFFICERS

ARANT, H. C. 1Sgt. – Orig. Pvt. in Co.: Appt. Cpl., Jan. 25, 1862: Prom., 1Sgt., Dec. 15, 1864.

(1) AULD, D. J. 2Sgt. — Orig. 2Sgt. of Co.: Reduced to ranks: Paroled,
(2)   Appomattox (Apr. 12, 1865).
    CARSON, B. A. 3Sgt. — Orig. Pvt. in Co.: Appt. 5Sgt., Jan. 25, 1862:
         Appt. 3Sgt., Fall, 1864.
(1) CURTIS, J. M. 1Cpl. — Orig. 1Cpl. of Co.: POW, Chickamauga (Sept.
         20, 1863): Took Fed. oath, Jan. 15, 1864.
    DANNELLY, M. P. 4Sgt. — Orig. Pvt. in Co.: Appt. 4Sgt., June 9,
         1863: K., near Richmond, Fall, 1863.
    DeCAMPS, P. E. 2Sgt. — Orig. Pvt. in Co.: Appt. 2Sgt., Feb. 1, 1863:
         Dischgd. (heart trouble), June 30, 1863.
    DUMARESA, E. J. 1Sgt. — Orig. Pvt. in Co.: Appt. 3Sgt., Summer,
         1862: Appt. 1Sgt., Feb. 1, 1863: Reduced to ranks, Fall, 1864.
(2) FELDER, J. D. 2Cpl. — Orig. Pvt. in Co.: W., 2nd Manassas (Aug. 30,
         1862): Appt. 2Cpl., Nov. 24, 1864: Paroled, Appomattox (Apr.
         12, 1865).
    GARDNER, THOS. 4Cpl. — Orig. Pvt. in Co.: Appt. 4Cpl., Feb. 27,
         1862: Reduced to ranks by courtmartial, July 26, 1863: POW,
         Apr., 1865.
(1) GELLING, G. B. 3Sgt. — Orig. 3Sgt. of Co.: Reduced to ranks,
         Summer, 1862: W. & POW, Antietam (Sept. 17, 1862): Ex-
         changed: W., Lookout Valley, Tenn., Fall, 1863: Present for
         duty, Mar., 1864.
    HALL, W. D. 4Sgt. — Orig. Pvt. in Co.: Prom., 4Sgt., Fall, 1861:
         Reduced to Pvt. "at own request," June 9, 1863: POW,
         Chattanooga, Oct. 29, 1863: Died of pneumonia, Nov. 26, 1863.
(2) KENNERLY, A. J. 4Sgt. — Orig. Pvt. in Co., age 17: Prom., 1Cpl.,
         Winter, 1863-64: Prom., 4Sgt., Nov. 24, 1864: Paroled, Appo-
         mattox (Apr. 12, 1865).
(2) KENNERLY, T. F. Cpl. — Orig. Pvt. in Co.: Prom., Cpl.: Paroled,
         Appomattox (Apr. 12, 1865).
    NETTLES, H. B. 2Sgt. — Orig. Pvt. in Co.: Appt. 2Sgt., Nov. 24,
         1864.
(1) SANDERS, H. J. 1Cpl. — Orig. 2Cpl. of Co.: Prom., 1Cpl., Summer,
         1862: W., 2nd Manassas (Aug. 30, 1862): Died, Jan. 5, 1863.
    SIMMONS, WM. H. 2Sgt. — Orig. Pvt. in Co., age 17: Appt. 2Sgt.,
         June 9, 1863: K., Chaffin's Farm (Sept. 29, 1864).
(1) STALEY, J. H. 4Cpl. — Appt. 4Cpl., Nov. 24, 1864: POW, Mar.,
         1865: Took Fed. oath.
(2) SUTCLIFFE, L. W. 4Cpl. — Orig. Pvt. in Co.: Appt. 4Cpl., Aug. 24,
         1863: Reduced to Pvt., Winter, 1863-64: Paroled, Appomattox
         (Apr. 12, 1865).
    THOMAS, W. E. 2Cpl. — Orig. Pvt. in Co.: Appt. 3Cpl., Feb. 27,
         1862: Prom., 2Cpl., Summer, 1863: Reduced to ranks, Winter,
         1863-64.
    TUCKER, J. T. 4Cpl. — Orig. Pvt. in Co.: Prom., 4Cpl., Fall, 1861:
         Reduced to ranks, Dec. 21, 1861: POW, Aug. 14, 1864.
(1) WELCH, S. ELLIOTT 1Sgt. — See list of "Officers" above.
    WOLFE, T. D. 3Cpl. — Orig. Pvt. in Co.: Appt. 3Cpl., Oct. 6, 1864.

PRIVATES

(1)	ARANT, H. C. — See list of "Non-Comm. Officers" above.
(1)	ARANT, J. G. — Died, White Plains, Va., Sept. 13, 1862.
(1)	ASHTON, L. — Present for duty most of the war.
(1)	AULD, D. J. — See list of "Non-Comm. Officers" above.
(1)	AYERS, D. W. — Enl., age 17: Present for duty most of war: Paroled,
(2)	Appomattox (Apr. 12, 1865).
(1)	AYERS, S. L. — W., 2nd Manassas (Aug. 30, 1862): Retired to Invalid Corps, Jan. 17, 1865.
(2)	BARADHA, J. — Present for duty most of war: Paroled, Appomattox (Apr. 12, 1865).
(1)	BARS, B. J. — K., Wills' Valley, Tenn. (Oct. 28, 1863)
	BARS, D. — Enl., Jan. 22, 1862: Died, Aug. 23, 1864.
	BARS, D. W. — Enl., Jan. 22, 1862: W., Wills' Valley, Tenn. (Oct. 28, 1863): Asgnd. as a Pioneer, Dec., 1864.
(1)	BINNICKER, N. B. — Died in Va., Spring, 1863.
(1)	BOLEN, H. D. — W., Lookout Valley, Tenn. (Oct. 28, 1863): Paroled,
(2)	Appomattox (Apr. 12, 1865).
(1)	BONNETT, C. F. — Present for duty most of the war: Paroled,
(2)	Appomattox (Apr. 12, 1865).
(1)	BRANDES, HENRY — W. (abdomen), Antietam (Sept. 17, 1862): POW, Oct. 1, 1864.
(1)	BRIDGER, CHAS. — In arrest, Charleston, Spring, 1863: On duty, Oct., 1863.
(1)	BROWN, J. D. — Present for duty most of the war: Paroled, Farmville, Va. (mid-Apr., 1865).
(1)	BROWN, W. C. — K., 2nd Manassas (Aug. 30, 1862).
(1)	CARN, L. C. — W. (leg), Antietam (Sept. 17, 1862): Paroled, Apr. 26, 1865.
(1)	CARSON, B. A. — See list of "Non-Comm. Officers" above.
(1)	CARSON, JACOB — Present for duty most of the war.
(1)	CARSON, WM. — Died (pneumonia), Mar. 28, 1863.
(2)	COONER, R. — Enl., Apr. 11, 1862: Paroled, Appomattox (Apr. 12, 1865).
	CULCLEASURE, A. D. — Enl., Apr. 11, 1862: POW, Frederick, Md., Sept. 12, 1862: Exchanged, Nov. 10, 1862.
(1)	CULCLEASURE, D. J. — Present for duty as of Dec., 1864.
(1)	CULCLEASURE, J. F. — POW, Frederick, Md., Sept. 12, 1862: Exchanged, Nov. 10, 1862: Present for duty as of Oct., 1863.
	DANNELLY, D. S. — Enl., Nov. 19, 1861: Asgnd. as a Scout, Fall, 1864.
	DANNELLY, J. J. — Enl., Nov. 19, 1861: Died, Sept. 1, 1862.
(1)	DANNELLY, M. P. — See list of "Non-Comm. Officers" above.
(1)	DAVIS, A. M. — Present for duty most of the war.
(1)	DAVIS, G. J. — W., Chaffin's Farm (Sept. 29, 1864): Arm amputated.
(1)	DAVIS, T. E. — Dischgd., disability, June 20, 1862.
(1)	DeCAMPS, P. E. — See list of "Non-Comm. Officers" above.
(1)	DOVER, J. J. — AWOL, Aug., 1862.
(1)	DRAWDY, DAN L. — POW, Richmond, Apr. 3, 1865.
(1)	DUMARESA, E. J. — See list of "Non-Comm. Officers" above.

(1) DUVA, W. H. — Present for duty most of the war.
(1) FELDER, J. D. — See list of "Non-Comm. Officers" above.
(1) FLEISHMAN, H. F. — Court-Martialed, Apr. 29, 1862: Asgnd. as orderly to Gen. Gary.
(1) FOGLE, W. C. — W., 2nd Manassas (Aug. 30, 1862): POW, Edisto R., So. Car., Feb. 10, 1865.
(1) FOGLE, W. D. — Enl., age 17: Court-Martialed, Apr. 29, 1862: W., 2nd Manassas (Aug. 30, 1862): W., Chaffin's Farm (Sept. 29, 1864): Retired to Invalid Corps, Oct. 28, 1864.
(1) GARDNER, THOS. — See list of "Non-Comm. Officers" above.
(1) GARDNER, WM. G. — See list of "Officers" above.
(1) GARRICK, J. A. — W. (thigh), Antietam (Sept. 17, 1862): Paroled, mid-Apr., 1865.
(1) GARRICK, J. M. — Enl., age 17: W. & POW, Lookout Valley, Tenn. (Oct. 28, 1863): Died (smallpox) as a POW, Mar. 23, 1864.
GLEATON, J. P. — Enl., Dec. 17, 1861: Present for duty, Oct., 1863.
(1) GREGORY, C. A. — W. (wrist), Antietam (Sept. 17, 1862): W., Lookout Valley, Tenn. (Oct. 28, 1863).
(1) GREGORY, O. F. — Enl., age 17: W., 2nd Manassas (Aug. 30, 1862): POW, Knoxville (Dec. 5, 1863).
GRUVER, G. W. — Enl., Mar. 21, 1862: W., Chaffin's Farm (Sept. 29, 1864).
(1) HALL, W. D. — See list of "Non-Comm. Officers" above.
HAMER, P. M. — Enl., July 1, 1862: Absent, sick, Dec., 1864.
HERNDON, B. O. — Enl., June 30, 1862: Present for duty, Dec., 1864.
HEUSTESS, A. — Enl., Oct. 17, 1862: Present for duty, Dec., 1864.
(1) HORTON, E. R. — W., 2nd Manassas (Aug. 30, 1862): Present for duty, Oct., 1864.
(1) HUGHES, E. — W., Lookout Valley, Tenn. (Oct. 28, 1863): AWOL, Fall, 1864.
(1) HUGHES, J. W. — Died, Nov. 10, 1862.
HUNGERPELER, J. S. — W., 2nd Manassas (Aug. 30, 1862): Died from wound, Sept. 19, 1862.
(1) HUTTO, D. H. — Present for duty most of the war.
(1) HUTTO, J. J. — Enl., age 17: W., 2nd Manassas (Aug. 30, 1862):
(2) Paroled, Appomattox (Apr. 12, 1865).
(1) HUTTO, W. C. — POW, Lookout Valley, Tenn. (Oct. 28, 1863): Exchanged, Mar. 4, 1865.
(1) JOHN, D. C. — Present for duty as of Dec., 1864: No other record.
JOHN, P. T. — Enl., May 1, 1862: W., Petersburg (July 8, 1864).
(1) KELLER, W. H. — Enl., age 17: POW, Frederick, Md., Sept. 12, 1862: Exchanged: K., Lookout Valley, Tenn. (Oct. 28, 1863).
(1) KENNERLY, A. J. — See list of "Non-Comm. Officers" above.
(1) KENNERLY, A. V. — W. & POW, Antietam (Sept. 17, 1862): Died of wound in prison camp, Dec. 13, 1862.
KENNERLY, L. D. S. — Enl., May 8, 1862: POW, Richmond hosp., Apr. 3, 1865.
(1) KENNERLY, T. F. — See list of "Non-Comm. Officers" above.
(1) LOCKWOOD, H. A. — Enl., age 16: W. & POW, 2nd Manassas (Aug. 30, 1862): Paroled: Died of wound, Oct. 7, 1862.
(1) LOWE, D. — Present for duty, Oct., 1864.

MICHE, W. H. — POW, Boonsboro (Sept. 14, 1862): Exchanged, Nov. 10, 1862.

MURROW, O. H. — Enl., Feb. 7, 1862: Dischgd., disability, Sept. 28, 1862.

(1) NETTLES, H. B. — See list of "Non-Comm. Officers" above.

(1) PARRY, J. G. — W., 2nd Manassas (Aug. 30, 1862): Present for duty, Dec., 1864.

(1) PEARSON, J. A. — Absent, sick, Dec., 1864.

(1) RAY, J. D. — Dischgd., Surg. Cert., Dec. 9, 1862.

(1) RICKENBACKER, H. K. — K., Antietam (Sept. 17, 1862).

(1) RICKENBACKER, P. H. — Present for duty most of the war.

RICKENBACKER, W. J. — Enl., Apr. 30, 1862: K., Antietam (Sept. 17, 1862).

(1) ROBINSON, JAS. — POW, Frederick, Md., Sept. 12, 1862: Exchanged,
(2)   Nov. 10, 1862: Paroled, Appomattox (Apr. 12, 1865).

(1) ROBINSON, WM. — POW, Chattanooga (Oct. 29, 1863): Died (pneumonia) in prison camp, Jan. 16, 1864.

(1) SANFORD, W. L. — K., 2nd Manassas (Aug. 30, 1862).

(1) SIMMONS, WM. H. — See list of "Non-Comm. Officers" above.

(1) SLEVIN, WM. — Died, May 19, 1863 of bronchitis.

(1) SNIDER, A. M. — See list of "Officers" above.

(1) SPENCER, G. H. — On detached service with Hood's Corps, Fall, 1863.

(1) STALEY, D. N. — POW, Harper's Farm, Apr. 6, 1865.

(1) STALEY, J. H. — See list of "Non-Comm. Officers" above.

(1) STURKIE, D. G. — W. (thigh), Antietam (Sept. 17, 1862): Paroled,
(2)   Appomattox (Apr. 12, 1865).

(1) STURKIE, L. J. — W., Lookout Mtn., Oct., 1863: Paroled, Appo-
(2)   mattox (Apr. 12, 1865).

(1) SUTCLIFFE, L. W. — See list of "Non-Comm. Officers" above.

THOMAS, JOE — Enl., Feb. 5, 1862: Present for duty, Dec., 1864.

(1) THOMAS, W. E. — See list of "Non-Comm. Officers" above.

(1) TUCKER, J. T. — See list of "Non-Comm. Officers" above.

(1) TURNER, H. E. — W., Lookout Valley, Tenn. (Oct. 28, 1863): Paroled,
(2)   Appomattox (Apr. 12, 1865).

(1) WALKER, W. A. — Enl., age 17: Present for duty, Dec., 1864.

WALLING, JAS. — Enl., Nov. 10, 1861: W. (side), Antietam (Sept. 17, 1862): Transfd. to 25th So. Car. Inf. Regt., Aug. 15, 1864.

(1) WATKINS, J. C. — Present for duty, Apr., 1863.

(1) WALTERS, S. S. — POW, Burkeville, Va., Apr. 6, 1865.

(1) WELCH, JOHN F. — POW, Cumberland Gap, Tenn., Jan. 12, 1864: Exchanged, Feb. 15, 1865.

(1) WILLIAMS, W. W. — Dischgd. (heart trouble), Sept. 27, 1862.

(1) WOLFE, T. D. — See list of "Non-Comm. Officers" above.

(1) YOUNG, H. J. N. — K., near Richmond, 1864.

★   ★   ★   ★   ★

MEMBERS OF COMPANY H, HAMPTON'S SO. CAR. LEGION (INF. BTLN.) WHO WERE NOT PRESENT FOR DUTY DURING THE PERIOD THAT THE REGIMENT WAS ASSIGNED TO HOOD'S TEXAS BRIGADE (JUNE 2-NOV. 15, 1862).

OFFICERS

Hammond, S. L., Lt. (Resgnd., Apr. 17, 1862).

NON-COMMISSIONED OFFICERS

Crossland, T. L., 1Cpl. (Enl., Jan., 1864)

PRIVATES

Brown, J. J. (Enl., Aug., 1863)
Carroll, Z. (No record prior to Nov., 1864)
Cate, J. J. (Enl., Aug., 1863)
Clifford, Sam R. (No record prior to Nov., 1864)
(1) Cook, H. P. (No record after Feb., 1862)
(1) Cook, J. B. (No record after Apr., 1862)
Coxe, Edwin (Enl., Apr., 1864)
Crossland, C. (Enl., Jan., 1864)
Cudworth, J. W. (No record)
Dannelly, G. W. (Enl., Apr., 1864)
Davis, W. C. (Enl., Feb., 1863)
(1) Dervane, P. (No record after Apr., 1862)
(1) Doling, John (Dischgd., sick, Feb., 1862)
Dumas, Edward (No record)
(1) Fairey, G. W. B. (Dischgd., Feb., 1862)
(1) Hall, C. H. (No record)
(1) Hall, S. (No record after Apr., 1862)

(1) Hammond, A. L. (Dischgd., overage, Mar., 1862)
(1) Hankers, Francis (No record after Dec., 1861)
(1) Hennon, W. H. (Dischgd., sick, Jan., 1862)
Hogan, P. (No record)
Hughes, W. L. (Enl., May, 1863)
John, J. T. (Enl., Aug., 1863)
(1) Kittrell, J. B. (No record)
Neal, B. (Enl., Sept., 1863)
Pate, J. (Enl., Jan., 1864)
Price, _____ (No record prior to Sept., 1864)
Quick, J. (Enl., Feb., 1863)
(1) Reynolds, S. (Dischgd., Dec., 1861)
(1) Robinson, C. S. D. (No record after Apr., 1862)
(2) Sears, D. (No record prior to Apr., 1865)
Spears, J. E. (Enl., Mar., 1864)
West, G. H. (No record prior to Apr., 1865)

SERVANTS

(1) Andrew, (Cook) (No record after Dec., 1861)
(1) Andy, (Servant) (No record after Dec., 1861)

(1) Simon, (Cook) (No record after Dec., 1861)

1ST NO. CAR. ARTY. REGT.

COMPANY D — *ROWAN ARTILLERY*

SHORT HISTORY

This light artillery battery was originally organized in Rowan County, North Carolina, May 18, 1861, as the "Rowan Artillery." The Company was called to active service at Salisbury, North Carolina, May 3, 1861 and moved to Weldon, North Carolina where on June 15, it was mustered into the Confederate service "for three years or the war." Captain James Reilly assumed command of the Battery on June 28, 1861, and moved it to Manassas Junction, Va., July 27, 1861.

The Battery was assigned to Brigadier-General W. H. C. Whiting's Brigade (later Brigadier-General Evander Law's Brigade) until the re-organization of the Army of Northern Virginia in the fall of 1862. At this time "Reilly's Battery" was assigned to Major-General John B. Hood,'s Division as part of Major B. W. Frobel's Artillery Battalion. Reilly's Battery was regarded by the members of Hood's Texas Brigade as part of its organization for its six guns gave the Texas Brigade close support during several major engagements. The North Carolina artillerists and Texas infantrymen first became acquainted when both were in winter quarters near Dumfries, Virginia, during the winter of 1861-62. Captain Reilly and his men supported Hood's Texas Brigade at 2nd Manassas (August 29-30, 1862), Antietam (September 17, 1862), Fredericksburg (December 13-15, 1862), the latter stages of the Suffolk Campaign (April 11-May 4, 1863), and the battle of Gettysburg (July 2-3, 1863). At Gettysburg, Reilly's Battery was assigned to Maj. M. W. Henry's Artillery Battalion.

Reilly's Battery did not accompany the Texas Brigade (Longstreet's Corps) when it moved west to fight at Chickamauga (September 18-20, 1863) and in East Tennessee (Winter, 1863-64). The two organizations were never closely associated after the Gettysburg Campaign. However, the Texans never forgot the North Carolinians and when the survivors of Hood's Texas Brigade formed their veterans association in the early 1870s, the survivors of Reilly's Battery were invited to join the organization and participate in the annual reunions.

James Reilly was promoted to major in early September, 1863, and command of the Battery passed to Capt. John A.

Ramsay, original 1st Lieutenant of the unit. The Battery was present during most of the engagements of the Army of Northern Virginia in 1864 and was paroled at Appomattox on April 12, 1865. When supporting the Texas Brigade, the Battery was armed with two, 24-pounder Dahlgrens; two, 10-pounder Parrotts; and two, 3-inch Rifles. At Gettysburg, on July 2 & 3, 1863, Reilly maintained such a hot fire (800 rounds) that one of his 3-inch Rifles burst. Late in the war the Rowan Artillery had been assigned three, 10-pounder Parrotts; one, 12-pounder Whitworth; and two, 8-pounder Armstrongs.

Key

(1) Original member of Co. or Btry. (2) Paroled at Appomattox.
K (Killed), W (Wounded), POW (Prisoner of War)
AWOL (Absent Without Leave)

OFFICERS

(1) REILLY, JAS. Capt. — Orig. memb., Co. A, 1st N. C. Arty. Regt.: Prom., Capt., May 16, 1861: Assumed cmd. of Co. D, June 28, 1861: Prom., Maj., Sept. 7, 1863 & transfd. to Regmtl. Hdqtrs., 1st. No. Car. Arty.

(1) RAMSAY, JOHN A. Capt. — Orig. Capt. of Btry.: Reduced to 1Lt. by Gov. Ellis: W., 2nd Manassas (Aug. 30, 1862): Prom., Capt., Sept. 7, 1863: Paroled, Salisbury, N. C., June 19, 1865.

(1) MYERS, WM. W. 1Lt. — Orig. 2Lt. of Btry.: Appt. 1Lt., May 16, 1861: Paroled, Salisbury, N. C., June 14, 1865.

(1) WOODWARD, JESSE F. 1Lt. — Orig. 2Lt. of Btry.: Prom., 1Lt., Sept.
(2) 7, 1863: Paroled, Appomattox (Apr. 12, 1865).

MITCHELL, LUICO 2Lt. — Appt. 2Lt., Jan. 17, 1863: Appt. Actg. Adj. of Btln., July-Aug., 1863: Prom., 1Lt. & Transfd. to 46th N. C. Inf. Regt.

SCHAFFER, FRANCIS C. 2Lt. — Appt. 5Sgt., July 1, 1861: Appt. QM-Sgt., Summer, 1862: Prom., 2Lt., Sept. 7, 1863: Paroled, Salisbury, N. C., May 31, 1865.

NON-COMMISSIONED OFFICERS

SERGEANTS

(1) BAILEY, JOHN T. Sgt. — Orig. Pvt. in Co.: Appt. Cpl., May 30, 1862: Prom., Sgt., Dec. 1, 1863.

(2) COOPER, HENRY QM-Sgt. — Transfd. into Co. D from Co. G, 3rd N. C. Arty. Regt., Oct. 8, 1862 as a Pvt.: Appt., Cpl., Nov. 1, 1862: Prom., QM-Sgt., Dec. 1, 1863: Paroled, Appomattox (Apr. 12, 1865).

(1) CROWELL, JAS. M. Sgt. — Orig. Pvt. in Co.: Appt. Cpl., July 15, 1861: Prom., Sgt., June 15, 1862: Reduced to ranks, Oct., 1862: POW, Amelia CH. (Apr. 5, 1865): Paroled, Pt. Lookout, Md., June, 1865.

(1) DICKS, WM. RUFUS 1Sgt. — Orig. 1Sgt. of Co.: Reduced to Sgt., Dec. 15, 1861: Prom., 1Sgt., July 19, 1862: Actg. 2Lt., Sept. 7, 1863-Feb. 28, 1864: Resumed Sgt. status, Mar. 1, 1864: POW, Amelia CH., Apr. 5, 1865: Paroled, Pt. Lookout, Md., June 12, 1865.

(1) BOTTRAL, WM. H. Sgt. — Orig. Pvt. in Co.: Appt. Cpl., Dec. 15, 1861: Prom., Sgt., May 30, 1862: Reduced to ranks, Feb. 24, 1863.

(1) GARMAN, JAS. A. Sgt. — Orig. Pvt. in Co.: Appt. Cpl., May 30,
(2) 1862: Prom., Sgt., July 19, 1862: Paroled, Appomattox (Apr. 12, 1865).

(1) LOWDER, ISAAC D. J. Sgt. — Orig. 3Sgt. of Co.: POW, Amelia CH., Apr. 5, 1865: Paroled, Pt. Lookout, Md., June 28, 1865.

(1) MOYLE, MATTHEW Sgt. — Orig. 1Cpl. of Co.: Prom., Sgt., May 30, 1862: POW, Amelia CH., Apr. 5, 1865: Parole, June 29, 1865 at Pt. Lookout, Md.

(1) OLDHAM, JOSIAH Sgt. — Orig. Pvt. in Co.: Appt. Cpl., Nov. 1, 1862: Prom., Sgt., Feb. 1, 1863: Reduced to ranks by court-martial, Feb. 27, 1864.

RIGGS, JOHN Sgt. — Appt. Sgt., Summer, 1863: POW, Amelia CH., Apr. 5, 1865: Paroled, Pt. Lookout, Md., June 17, 1865.

(1) SCHOESSER, IGNATZ Sgt. — Orig. Pvt. in Co.: Appt. Cpl., June 15, 1862: W., Malvern Hill (July 1, 1862): Prom., Sgt., Nov. 1, 1862: Reduced to ranks, Feb. 1, 1863 & confined by court-martial.

(1) SHEPPERD, SILAS Sgt. — Orig. Pvt. in Co.: Appt. 4Sgt., July 15,
(2) 1861: Reduced to ranks, Dec. 10, 1861: Paroled, Appomattox (Apr. 12, 1865).

(2) WILCOX, EDW. W. 1Sgt. — Transfd. as Pvt. into Co. D from Co. G, 3rd N. C. Arty. Regt., Oct. 8, 1862: Appt. Sgt., Oct. 15, 1862: Prom., 1Sgt., Dec. 1, 1863: Paroled, Appomattox (Apr. 12, 1865).

CORPORALS

(1) BELL, JOS. F. Cpl. — Orig. Pvt. in Co.: Appt. Cpl., June 15, 1862: Reduced to Pvt., Nov., 1862 due to sickness: Died, Lynchburg, Va., Jan. 8, 1863.

(2) CRANFORD, WM. H. Cpl. — Enl. as a Pvt., Feb. 28, 1862, age 21: Appt. Cpl., Nov. 1, 1862: POW, Amelia CH., Apr. 5, 1865: Escaped: Paroled, Appomattox (Apr. 12, 1865).

CROWELL, HENRY H. Cpl. — Enl. as Pvt., age 28, Feb. 27, 1862: Appt. Cpl., July 19, 1862: POW, Amelia CH., Apr. 5, 1865: Paroled, Pt. Lookout, Md., June 24, 1865.

GRIFFIN, JAS. H. Cpl. — Transfd. as a Cpl. into Co. D from Co. G, 3rd N. C. Arty. Regt., Oct. 8, 1862: No other record.

HARDISTER, JONATHAN Cpl. — Enl. in Randolph Co., N. C., Mar. 10, 1862 as a Pvt., age 20: W., Malvern Hill (July 1, 1862): Appt. Cpl., Nov. 1, 1862: W., Gettysburg (July 3, 1863): Granted convalescent leave: Paroled, Salisbury, N. C., June 28, 1865.

HARWELL, JAS. S. Cpl. — Transfd. as a Pvt. into Co. D from Co. G, 3rd N. C. Arty Regt., Oct. 8, 1862: Appt. Cpl., Summer, 1863: POW, Amelia CH., Apr. 5, 1865: Paroled, Pt. Lookout, Md., June 15, 1865.

(1) IRBY, WM. H. Cpl. — See "Specialists" following.

(1) McCOMBS, WM. M. Cpl. — Orig. Pvt. in Co.: Appt. Cpl., May 30, 1862: POW, Amelia CH., Apr. 5, 1865: Paroled, June 29, 1865 at Pt. Lookout, Md.

PEELER, ALFRED Cpl. — Enl. in Rowan County as a Pvt., Feb. 17, 1862, age 26: Appt. Cpl., Feb. 1, 1863: POW, Amelia CH., Apr. 5, 1865: Paroled, June, 1865 at Pt. Lookout, Md.

PITTMAN, JOS. W. Cpl. — Transfd. as a Pvt. into Co. D from Co. G, 3rd N. C. Arty. Regt., Oct. 8, 1862: Appt. Cpl., Nov. 1, 1862: No other record.

(1) SKILLICORN, WM. H. Cpl. — Orig. Pvt. in Co.: Appt. Cpl., May 30, 1862: W., Spotsylvania (May 13, 1864): POW, Amelia CH. (Apr. 5, 1865): Paroled, Pt. Lookout, Md., June, 1865.

STAMPER, JOS. J. Cpl. — Transfd. as Pvt. into Co. D from Co. G, 3rd N. C. Arty Regt., Oct. 8, 1862: Appt. Cpl., Nov. 1, 1862: POW, Amelia CH. (Apr. 5, 1865): Paroled, Pt. Lookout, Md., June, 1865.

SPECIALISTS

AGNER, HENRY C. Saddler & Bugler — Enl. as a Pvt. in Co., June 1, 1862: Appt. Bugler: Appt. Saddler, Nov. & Dec., 1863: Appt. Guidon, Jan. & Feb., 1864: Reduced to ranks, Sept. 1, 1864: POW, Amelia CH. (Apr. 5, 1865): Paroled, Pt. Lookout, Md., June, 1865.

HODGE, ABRAHAM A. Farrier — Enl. as a Pvt., Mar. 19, 1862, age 29: Appt. Farrier, June 15, 1862: W., Antietam (Sept. 17, 1862): POW, Amelia CH. (Apr. 5, 1865): Paroled, Pt. Lookout, Md., June, 1865.

HUFF, WM. H. Farrier — Transfd. as a Pvt. to Co. D from Co. K, 4th Regt. N. C. Troops, July 19, 1861: Appt. Farrier, Sept. 1, 1861: Reduced to ranks, June, 1862: W., Malvern Hill (July 1, 1862): POW, Amelia CH. (Apr. 5, 1865): Paroled, Pt. Lookout, Md., June, 1865.

(1) IRBY, WM. H. Artificer — Orig. Pvt. in Co., Appt. Artificer, Aug. 12, 1861: Prom., Cpl., Dec. 1, 1863: Retired to Invalid Corps, Jan. 25, 1865.

MILLER, URIAH Bugler — Enl. as a Pvt., Feb. 25, 1862, age 18: Appt. Bugler, Feb. 1, 1865: POW, Amelia CH. (Apr. 5, 1865): Paroled, Pt. Lookout, Md., June, 1865.

(1) MORGAN, CAMY W. Saddler — Enl. as a Pvt., June 15, 1862: Appt. Saddler, Jan. 1, 1862: Present or accounted for until Feb., 1865.

(1)
(2) PIERCE, JEREMIAH M. Artificer — Enl. as an Artificer, June 15, 1861: Paroled, Appomattox (Apr. 12, 1865): No other record.

PRIVATES

ALFORD, JESSE — Transfd. into Co. D from Co. G, 3rd N. C. Arty. Regt., Oct. 8, 1862: No other record.

(1)
(2) ALMAN, ROBT. — W., Antietam (Sept. 17, 1862): Paroled, Appomattox (Apr. 12, 1865).

AUTRY, JOHN — Conscripted, July 22, 1862: POW, Amelia CH. (Apr. 5, 1865): Paroled, Pt. Lookout, Md., June, 1865.

AUTRY, LOVE — Conscripted, July 22, 1862: POW, Amelia CH. (Apr. 5, 1865): Paroled, Pt. Lookout, Md., June, 1865.

BAGGETT, WASHINGTON — Conscripted, July 22, 1862: POW, Amelia CH. (Apr. 5, 1865): Paroled, Pt. Lookout, Md., June, 1865.

(1) BAME, DAVID — POW, Amelia CH. (Apr. 5, 1865): Died of acute diarrhea in prison camp at Pt. Lookout, Md.

(1) BASINGER, JEREMY W. — Dischgd., Jan. 6. 1863, for disability, deformed foot.

BASS, JAS. OLIN — Conscripted, July 22, 1862: Transfd., Nov. 5, 1864, to 2nd N. C. Arty. Regt.

BEAVER, CHAS. W. — Enl., Mar. 19, 1862: POW, Amelia CH. (Apr. 5, 1865): Paroled, Pt. Lookout, Md., June, 1865.

BELL, McGILBREY — Transfd. into Co. D from Co. G, 3rd Regt. N. C. Arty., Oct. 8, 1862: Died at Richmond, Jan. 4, 1863.

BELL, WM. H. — Transfd. into Co. D from Co. G, 3rd Regt. N. C. Arty., Oct. 8, 1862: No other record.

BEST, JOHN H. L. — Transfd. into Co. D from Co. G, 3rd Regt. N. C. Arty., Oct. 8, 1862: POW, Amelia CH. (Apr. 5, 1865): Paroled, Pt. Lookout, Md., June, 1865.

BILLUPS, DAVID T. — Transfd. into Co. D from Co. G, 3rd Regt. N. C. Arty., Oct. 8, 1862: W., Hanover Junction, Va., May 25, 1864: POW, Amelia CH. (Apr. 5, 1865): Paroled, Pt. Lookout, Md., June, 1865.

BILLUPS, JOS. H. — Transfd. into Co. D from Co. G, 3rd Regt. N. C. Arty., Oct. 8, 1862: POW, Amelia CH. (Apr. 5, 1865): Paroled, Pt. Lookout, Md., June, 1865.

(1) BLACK, WM. H. — Died, typhoid fever, Oct. 10, 1862, near Fairfax CH., Va.

BOGGS, PETER — Enl. as a Pvt., Mar. 19, 1862, age 18: Paroled, Salisbury, N. C., May 2, 1865.

BOST, JESSE M. — Enl. as a Pvt., Mar. 3, 1862, age 18: Died, Liberty, Va., Sept. 18, 1862.

(1) BRADY, BENJAMIN — Paroled, Salisbury, N. C., May 2, 1865.

BRADY, CALVIN — Enl. as a Pvt., Mar. 11, 1862, age 22: Died, Dec. 8, 1862.

BRADY, DAVID — Enl. as a Pvt., Mar. 19, 1862, age 30: Paroled, Salisbury, N. C., May 2, 1865.

BRADY, JOHN A. — Enl. as a Pvt., Mar. 11, 1862, age 22: POW, Amelia CH. (Apr. 5, 1865): Paroled, Pt. Lookout, Md., June, 1865.

BRADY, JOS. A. — Enl. as a Pvt., Mar. 11, 1862, age 21: POW, Amelia CH. (Apr. 5, 1865): Paroled, Pt. Lookout, Md., June, 1865.

(1) BRADY, MOSES C. — POW, Amelia CH. (Apr. 5, 1865): Paroled, Pt. Lookout, Md., June, 1865.

(1) BRINGLE, JOHN H. — W., Antietam (Sept. 17, 1862): POW, Amelia CH. (Apr. 5, 1862): Paroled, Pt. Lookout, Md., June, 1865.

BRITT, JOHN J. — Transfd. into Co. D from Co. G, 3rd Regt. N. C. Arty., Oct. 8, 1862: POW, Amelia CH. (Apr. 5, 1865): Paroled, Pt. Lookout, Md., June, 1865.

BRITT, WM. — Transfd. into Co. D from Co. G, 3rd Regt. N. C. Arty., Oct. 8, 1862: Died, pneumonia, Va., June 8, 1863.

BROWN, CALVIN L. — Enl., Feb. 26, 1862, age 21: Paroled, Salisbury, N. C., May 2, 1865.

BROWN, RICHARD L. — Enl., Feb. 14, 1862, age 19: POW, Amelia CH. (Apr. 5, 1865): Paroled, Pt. Lookout, Md., June, 1865.

(1) BULLABOA, LORENZO — Died, Winchester, Va., Oct. 10, 1862 "from injuries rec'd. when ammunition chest exploded."

(2) BUNN, WM. F. — Enl., Feb. 22, 1862, age 19: Paroled, Appomattox (Apr. 12, 1865).

BURAGE, JAS. — Enl., Rowan Co., July 15, 1861: Died, Richmond, Dec. 23, 1862 of disease.

BYRUM, JOHN — Transfd. into Co. D from Co. G, 3rd Regt. N. C. Arty., Oct. 8, 1862: No other record.

CAMPBELL, WM. — Enl., Rowan Co., Mar. 11, 1862, age 22: W., Gettysburg (July 3, 1863): Retired, Invalid Corps, Oct. 18, 1864: Paroled, Salisbury, N. C., May 16, 1865.

CANUP, CALEB — Enl., Rowan Co., Mar. 10, 1862, age 17: W. (both arms & shoulder), Amelia CH. (Apr. 5, 1865).

CARR, E. — Paroled, Goldsboro, N. C., May 27, 1865: No other record.

(1) CAUBLE, HENRY M. — Orig. Pvt. in Co.: POW, Amelia CH. (Apr. 5, 1865): Paroled, Mt. Lookout, Md., June, 1865.

CLAMPIT, JOHN A. — Enl., Aug. 24, 1861: POW, Amelia CH. (Apr. 5, 1865): Paroled, Pt. Lookout, Md., June, 1865.

(1) CORL, ALEXANDER — Orig. Pvt. in Co.: Deserted, Downsville, Md., July 14, 1863.

CREIGSLER, JESSE L. — POW, Southside R.R. (Apr. 5, 1865): Paroled, Pt. Lookout, Md., June, 1865.

(1) CROWELL, RICH. E. — W., 2nd Manassas (Aug. 30, 1862): Dischgd. on Surg. Cert., Nov. 10, 1862 because of "gunshot wound of the lungs which upon exertion produces hemorrhage."

CROWELL, THOS. JEFFERSON — Enl., Mar. 19, 1862, age 22: POW, Amelia CH. (Apr. 5, 1862): Paroled, Pt. Lookout, Md., June, 1865.

(1) CROWELL, WM. — Paroled, Salisbury, N. C., May 2, 1865: No other record.

CRUSE, ADAM — Enl., Mar. 12, 1862, age 42: W., Malvern Hill (July 1, 1862): POW, Amelia CH. (Apr. 5, 1865): Paroled, Pt. Lookout, Md., June, 1865.

DANIELS, AMOS M. — Enl., Aug. 26, 1861: Paroled, Salisbury, N. C., May 18, 1865.

(2) DAUGHTRY, ALLEN — Enl., July 22, 1862: Paroled, Appomattox (Apr. 12, 1865).

DAVIS, WM. H. — POW, Amelia CH. (Apr. 5, 1865): Paroled, Pt. Lookout, Md., June, 1865.

DOWNING, JAS. H. — Transfd. into Co. D from Co. G, 3rd Regt. N. C. Arty., Oct. 8, 1862: POW, Amelia CH. (Apr. 5, 1865): Paroled, Pt. Lookout, Md., June, 1865.

(2) DOWNING, THADDEUS — Transfd. into Co. D from Co. G, 3rd Regt. N. C. Arty., Oct. 8, 1862: Paroled, Appomattox (Apr. 12, 1865).

(1) EARNHART, JAS. P. — POW, Amelia CH. (Apr. 5, 1865): Paroled, Pt. Lookout, Md., June, 1865.

(2) EARNHART, ROBT. — Enl., Apr. 15, 1862, age 23: Paroled, Appomattox (Apr. 12, 1865).

EARNHART, WILEY — Enl., Apr. 11, 1862, age 25: Present & accounted for until Feb., 1865.

(1) ELKINS, OREN L. — Present & accounted for until Feb., 1865.

(1) ELLER, FARLEY — W., Hanover Junction, Va., May 25, 1864: Retired to Invalid Corps, Dec. 15, 1864: Paroled, Salisbury, N. C., May 11, 1865.

(1) ELLER, JACOB — POW, Amelia CH. (Apr. 5, 1865): Paroled, Pt. Lookout, Md., June, 1865.

(1) ELLER, JAS. I. — Paroled, Farmville, Va., Apr., 1865.

ELLER, MILAS — Enl., Mar. 19, 1862, age 28: POW, Amelia CH. (Apr. 5, 1865): Paroled, Pt. Lookout, Md., June, 1865.

ELLER, WM. A. — Enl., Mar. 8, 1862, age 21: POW, Amelia CH. (Apr. 5, 1865): Paroled, Pt. Lookout, Md., June, 1865.

(2) EVERETT, JOHN — Transfd. into Co. D from Co. G, 3rd Regt. N. C. Arty., Oct. 8, 1862: Paroled, Appomattox (Apr. 12, 1865).

FLOOD, ROBT. — Transfd. into Co. D from Co. G, 3rd Regt. N. C. Arty., Oct. 8, 1862: Present & accounted for until Feb., 1865.

FRICK, LEVI — Enl., July 19, 1861: POW, Amelia CH. (Apr. 5, 1865): Paroled, Pt. Lookout, Md., June, 1865.

FRICK, MOSES — Enl., Mar. 19, 1862, age 22: Paroled, Salisbury, N. C., May 2, 1865.

GRICE, WM. D. — Conscripted, July 22, 1862: Transfd. to Co. B, 2n Btln. N. C. Defense Troops, Nov. 5, 1864.

(2) HALL, CONSTANT — Conscripted, July 22, 1862: Detchd. Serv., July 21, 1863-Feb., 1865: Paroled, Appomattox (Apr. 12, 1865).

HALL, LIVINGSTON — Conscripted, July 22, 1862: Transfd. to Co. B, 2nd Btln. N. C. Defense Troops, Nov. 6, 1864.

HARPER, ALLEN — Transfd. into Co. D from Co. G, 3rd Regt. N. C. Arty., Oct. 8, 1862: POW, Amelia CH. (Apr. 5, 1865): Paroled, Pt. Lookout, Md., June, 1865.

(2) HARTMAN, DANIEL — Enl., Mar. 19, 1862, age 22: Paroled, Appomattox (Apr. 12, 1865).

HARTMAN, JOHN H. — Enl., Mar. 19, 1862, age 19: POW, Amelia CH. (Apr. 5, 1865): Paroled, Pt. Lookout, Md., June, 1865.

HATHAWAY, BENJ. J. — Transfd. into Co. D from Co. G, 3rd Regt. N. C. Arty., Oct. 8, 1862: POW, Amelia CH., Apr. 5, 1865: Paroled, Pt. Lookout, Md., June, 1865.

HAYNES, EATON — Transfd. into Co. D from Co. G, 3rd Regt. N. C. Arty., Oct. 8, 1862: W., Spotsylvania (May 9, 1864): POW, Hatcher's Run (Apr. 5, 1865): Paroled, Pt. Lookout, June, 1865.

HESS, BENJAMIN — Enl., Mar. 20, 1862, age 18: Paroled, Salisbury, N. C., May 2, 1865.
HESS, CHAS. — Enl., Mar. 3, 1862, age 30: Paroled, Salisbury, N. C., May 2, 1865.
HESS, JOHN H. — Enl., Mar. 19, 1862, age 25: POW, Amelia CH. (Apr. 5, 1865): Paroled, Pt. Lookout, Md., June, 1865.
HESS, RICHARD — Enl., Mar. 19, 1862, age 24: Paroled, Salisbury, N. C., May 2, 1865.
HOFFNER, NATHAN J. — Enl., Mar. 19, 1862, age 22: POW, Amelia CH. (Apr. 5, 1865): Paroled, Pt. Lookout, Md., June, 1865.
HOFFNER, WM. H. — Enl., Mar. 19, 1862, age 24: K., Gettysburg (July 2, 1863).
HOLLAND, KENNETH — Transfd. into Co. D from Co. G, 3rd Regt. N. C. Arty., Oct. 8, 1862: POW, Amelia CH. (Apr. 5, 1865): Paroled, Pt. Lookout, Md., June, 1865.
(2) HOLLAND, WM. T. — Transfd. into Co. D from Co. G, 3rd Regt. N. C. Arty., Oct. 8, 1862: Paroled, Appomattox (Apr. 12, 1865).
(1) HOLSHOUSER, ALEXANDER — Enl., June 15, 1861: POW, Amelia CH. (Apr. 5, 1865): Paroled, Pt. Lookout, Md., June, 1865.
(1) HOLSHOUSER, CRISENBERY — POW, Amelia CH. (Apr. 5, 1865).
(1) HOLSHOUSER, MICHAEL — POW, Amelia CH. (Apr. 5, 1865): Paroled, Pt. Lookout, Md., June 14, 1865.
(1) HOLSHOUSER, RUFUS — W., Antietam (Sept. 17, 1862): Paroled, Salisbury, N. C., May 2, 1865.
(1) HONBARGER, JOHN — Paroled, Salisbury, N. C., June 10, 1865.
(1) HOWARD, ANDREW M. — W., Gettysburg (July 2, 1863): POW, Amelia CH. (Apr. 5, 1865): Paroled, Pt. Lookout, June, 1865.
(2) HOWELL, JAS. — Transfd. into Co. D from Co. G, 3rd Regt. N. C. Arty., Oct. 8, 1862: Paroled, Appomattox (Apr. 12, 1865).
HOWELL, JOHN H. — Transfd. into Co. D from Co. G, 3rd Regt. N. C. Arty., Oct. 8, 1862: POW, Amelia CH. (Apr. 5, 1865): Paroled, Pt. Lookout, Md., June, 1865.
(2) HYDE, JAS. THOS. — Transfd. into Co. D from Co. G, 3rd Regt. N. C. Arty., Oct. 8, 1862: Paroled, Appomattox (Apr. 12, 1865).
INGRAM, JOHN S. — Enl., July 22, 1862: Present & accounted for through Feb., 1865.
(1) JACKSON, ANDREW — On detchd. service, May, 1863-Feb., 1865: No other record.
JACKSON, OLIN — Enl., July 22, 1862: Transfd. to Co. A, 2nd Regt. N. C. Arty., Nov. 5, 1864.
JOHNSON, CHAS. K. — Conscripted, July 22, 1862: Transfd. to Co. B, 2nd Btln. N. C. Local Defense Troops, Nov. 5, 1864.
JOHNSON, DANIEL J. — Conscripted, July 22, 1862: Transfd. to Co. B, 2nd Btln. N. C. Local Defense Troops, Nov. 5, 1864.
(2) JONES, ANDREW J. — Transfd. into Co. D from Co. G, 3rd Regt. N. C. Arty., Oct. 8, 1862: Paroled, Appomattox (Apr. 12, 1865).
(1) JULIAN, JAS. — POW, Amelia CH. (Apr. 5, 1865): Paroled, Pt. Lookout, Md., June, 1865.
KEPLEY, GEO. C. — Enl., Feb. 28, 1862, age 19: W., Antietam (Sept. 17, 1862): Died of wound, Dec. 8, 1862.

KESLER, DANIEL — Enl., Mar. 19, 1862, age 25: POW, Amelia CH. (Apr. 5, 1865): Paroled, Pt. Lookout, Md., June, 1865.

(1) KESLER, HENRY R. — POW, Southside R.R. (Apr. 5, 1865): Paroled, Pt. Lookout, Md., June, 1865.

(1) KINNEY, CALVIN S. — Deserted, Downsville, Md., July 14, 1863: Took Fed. oath, Dec. 13, 1863.

KLUTTS, HENRY W. — Enl., Mar. 5, 1862, age 23: POW, So. Mountain, Md., July 7, 1863.

KLUTTS, JACOB — Enl., Mar. 19, 1862, age 25: POW, Amelia CH. (Apr. 5, 1865): Paroled, Pt. Lookout, Md., June, 1865.

KLUTTS, MOSES A. — Enl., Mar. 19, 1862, age 18, as a substitute for Jas. Holshouser: POW, Amelia CH. (Apr. 5, 1865): Paroled, Pt. Lookout, Md., June 28, 1865.

(1) KLUTTS, RUFUS, JR. — Died, Winchester, Va., Sept. 27, 1862.

(1) KLUTTS, RUFUS, SR. — Died, Petersburg, May 29, 1863.

LEE, JOSIAH — Conscripted, July 22, 1862: POW, Amelia CH. (Apr. 5, 1865): Paroled, Pt. Lookout, Md., June, 1865.

(1) LINN, JAS. F. — POW, Amelia CH. (Apr. 5, 1865): Paroled, Pt. Lookout, Md., June, 1865.

LOCKERMAN, WM. — Conscripted, July 22, 1862: Present & accounted for until Feb., 1865.

(1) LYERLY, JOS. M. — POW, Antietam (Sept. 17, 1862): Exchanged, Oct. 4, 1862: POW, Amelia CH. (Apr. 5, 1865): Paroled, Pt. Lookout, Md., June, 1865.

MATHEWS, BLACKMAN — Conscripted, July 22, 1862: POW, Amelia CH. (Apr. 5, 1865): Paroled, Pt. Lookout, Md., June, 1865.

(1) MAY, CALVIN — POW, Amelia CH. (Apr. 5, 1865): Paroled, Pt. Lookout, Md., June, 1865.

(1) MAY, ROBT. — W., Malvern Hill (July 1, 1862): W., 2nd Manassas (Aug. 30, 1862): POW, Amelia CH. (Apr. 5, 1865): Paroled, Pt. Lookout, Md., June, 1865.

MEEKS, JOSHUA — Transfd. into Co. D from Co. G, 3rd Regt. N. C. Arty., Oct. 8, 1862: Broke leg, retired to Invalid Corps, Dec. 3, 1864.

(2) MILLER, CALEB A. — Enl., Mar. 19, 1862, age 23: Paroled, Appomattox (Apr. 12, 1865).

MILLER, DAVID L. — Enl., Feb. 25, 1862, age 23: POW, Amelia CH., Apr. 5, 1865: Paroled, Pt. Lookout, Md., June, 1865.

MILLER, HARRISON — Enl., Mar. 12, 1862, age 20: W., Aug. 12, 1863: Present or accounted for until Feb., 1865.

(1) MILLER, HENRY M. — K., Antietam (Sept. 17, 1862).

(1) MILLER, ROLAND — POW, Amelia CH. (Apr. 5, 1865): Paroled, Pt. Lookout, Md., June, 1865.

MISENHEIMER, DAN. J. — Enl., July 15, 1861: K., Antietam (Sept. 17, 1862).

MORGAN, DANIEL P. — Enl., Mar. 19, 1862, age 21, as a substitute for Leonard Hofferer: POW, Amelia CH. (Apr. 5, 1865): Paroled, Pt. Lookout, Md., June, 1865.

(1)
(2) MORGAN, JOS. — Paroled, Appomattox (Apr. 12, 1865).

OWENS, HENRY W. — Enl., Mar. 7, 1862, age 19: K., Gettysburg (July 2, 1863).

(2) PARKER, MARK — Transfd. into Co. D from Co. G, 3rd Regt. N. C. Arty., Oct. 8, 1862: Paroled, Appomattox (Apr. 12, 1865).

PARKS, JOHN F. — Enl., Mar. 19, 1862, age 18: POW, Amelia CH. (Apr. 5, 1865): Paroled, Pt. Lookout, Md., June, 1865.

(1) PARKS, JOS. D. — POW, Amelia CH. (Apr. 5, 1865): Paroled, Pt. Lookout, Md., June, 1865.

PARKS, WM. A. — Enl., Mar. 13, 1862, age 31: W., Antietam (Sept. 17, 1862): POW, Amelia CH. (Apr. 5, 1865): Paroled, Pt. Lookout, Md., June, 1865.

(1) PEELER, DANIEL — Paroled, Appomattox (Apr. 12, 1865): No other
(2) record.

PIERCE, ADAM A. — Enl., Feb. 27, 1862, age 23: Died, Winchester, Va., Oct. 15, 1862.

(2) PITT, BENJ. F. — Transfd. into Co. D from Co. G, 3rd Regt. N. C. Arty., Oct. 8, 1862: Paroled, Appomattox (Apr. 12, 1865).

PONDS, ROBT. — Transfd. into Co. D from Co. G, 3rd Regt. N. C. Arty., Oct. 8, 1862: POW, Amelia CH. (Apr. 5, 1865): Paroled, Pt. Lookout, Md., June, 1865.

(1) POOL, HENRY C. — W., Antietam (Sept. 17, 1862): Paroled, Salisbury, N. C., May 2, 1865.

(2) PORTER, OTHO N. — Enl., Mar. 14, 1862, age 20: Paroled, Appomattox (Apr. 12, 1865).

(1) RICHARDS, JOHN — Deserted, Downsville, Md., July 14, 1863.

RICKERTS, WM. — Enl., Feb. 12, 1862, age 21: Paroled, Salisbury, N. C., May 2, 1865.

(1) RIGGS, ZADOC — W., Cold Harbor (June 3, 1864): Died of wound, Richmond, June 17, 1864.

(1) ROWE, BENJ. C. — POW, Amelia CH. (Apr. 5, 1865): Paroled, Pt. Lookout, Md., June, 1865.

(1) ROSE, STEPHEN A. — POW, Southside R.R. (Apr. 5, 1865): Paroled, Pt. Lookout, Md., June, 1865.

(2) RUTH, ANDREW J. — Enl., Mar. 16, 1862, age 23: W., Malvern Hill (July 1, 1862): Paroled, Appomattox (Apr. 12, 1865).

SAVAGE, JOHN HENRY — Transfd. into Co. D from Co. G, 3rd Regt. N. C. Arty., Oct. 8, 1862: Transfd. to Co. H, 1st Regt. N. C. Arty., Dec., 1864.

SAVAGE, JOS. B. — Transfd. into Co. D from Co. G, 3rd Regt. N. C. Arty., Oct. 8, 1862: Present & accounted for through Feb., 1865.

SESSOMS, NATHAN H. — Transfd. into Co. D from Co. G, 3rd Regt. N. C. Arty., Oct. 8, 1862: POW, Amelia CH. (Apr. 5, 1865): Paroled, Pt. Lookout, Md., June, 1865.

STALLINGS, EASON — Transfd. into Co. D from Co. G, 3rd Regt. N. C. Arty., Oct. 8, 1862: POW, Amelia CH. (Apr. 5, 1865): Paroled, Pt. Lookout, Md., June, 1865.

(1) TERRELL, THOS. — Transfd. to C.S. Navy, Apr. 6, 1864.

THOMAS, THOS. — Enl., Mar. 19, 1862, age 28: Paroled, Salisbury, N. C., May 2, 1865.

THOMPSON, SYLVESTER — Enl., Feb. 12, 1862, age 19: POW, Falling Waters, Va., July 14, 1863: Deserted to Federals, Feb. 5, 1864.

THOMPSON, THOS. C. — Enl., Aug. 26, 1861: POW, Amelia CH. (Apr. 5, 1865): Paroled, Pt. Lookout, Md., June, 1865.

THORNTON, ETHARD — Enl., July 22, 1862: Present or accounted for through Feb., 1863.

TREXLER, ALFRED M. — Enl., Mar. 19, 1862, age 23: POW, Amelia CH. (Apr. 5, 1865): Paroled, Pt. Lookout, Md., June, 1865.

(1) TREXLER, ALLEN — W., 7 Pines (June 1, 1862): Retired to Invalid Corps, Dec. 15, 1864.

TREXLER, DAVID — Enl., Mar. 17, 1862, age 35: POW, Amelia CH. (Apr. 5, 1865): Paroled, Pt. Lookout, Md., June, 1865.

TREXLER, JAS. — Enl., Mar. 8, 1862, age 19: POW, Amelia CH. (Apr. 5, 1865): Paroled, Pt. Lookout, Md., June, 1865.

(1) TREXLER, JESSE L. — POW, Amelia CH. (Apr. 5, 1865): Paroled, Pt. Lookout, Md., June, 1865.

TREXLER, PETER M. — Enl., Feb. 14, 1862, age 18: POW, Amelia CH. (Apr. 5, 1865): Paroled, Pt. Lookout, Md., June, 1865.

TROUTMAN, DANIEL O. — Enl., Feb. 27, 1862, age 29: POW, Burkeville, Va., Apr. 5, 1865.

(1) TROUTMAN, RUFUS — POW, Amelia CH. (Apr. 5, 1865): Paroled, Pt. Lookout, Md., June, 21, 1865.

TROUTMAN, RUFUS P. — Enl., Feb. 13, 1862, age 27: Present & accounted for through Feb., 1865.

(2) TURNER, ALEXANDER — Transfd. into Co. D from Co. G, 3rd Regt. N. C. Arty., Oct. 8, 1862: Paroled, Appomattox (Apr. 12, 1865).

VESTUS, NATHAN H. — Transfd. into Co. D from Co. G, 3rd Regt. N. C. Arty., Oct. 8, 1862: POW, Amelia CH. (Apr. 5, 1865): Paroled, Pt. Lookout, Md., June, 1865.

(1) WALLER, CRUSOE — POW, Amelia CH. (Apr. 5, 1865): Paroled, Pt. Lookout, Md., June, 1865.

WALLER, DR. FRANKLIN — Enl., Mar. 10, 1862, age 20: Paroled, Salisbury, N. C., May 2, 1865.

WALLER, HENRY C. — Enl., Mar. 19, 1862, age 24: POW, Amelia CH. (Apr. 5, 1865): Paroled, Pt. Lookout, Md., June, 1865.

(1) WALLER, LEWIS A. — Present & accounted for through Feb., 1865.

(1) WARK, ISAAC — Born in Ireland, enl. at age 53: Dischgd. for disability (rheumatism), Jan. 31, 1864.

(2) WATKINS, GEO. — Transfd. into Co. D from Co. G, 3rd Regt. N. C. Arty., Oct. 8, 1862: Paroled, Appomattox (Apr. 12, 1865).

(1) WEAVER, TOBIAS — W., Gettysburg (July 3, 1863): Paroled, Salisbury, N. C., June 24, 1865.

(1) WILKERSON, WM. A. — Paroled, Salisbury, N. C., May 2, 1865.

(1) WILKINS, ORRIN LEWIS — Paroled, Apr., 1865.

WILLIAMS, WM. — Enl., July 22, 1862: POW, Amelia CH. (Apr. 5, 1865): Paroled, Pt. Lookout, Md., June, 1865.

WILLIFORD, WARREN — Enl., July 22, 1862: POW, Amelia CH. (Apr. 5, 1865): Paroled, Pt. Lookout, Md., June, 1865.

(1) WOOTSMAN, SOLOMON — POW, Southside R.R. (Apr. 5, 1865): Paroled, Pt. Lookout, Md., June, 1865.

WYATT, ELI — Enl., Feb. 22, 1862, age 21: W., 2nd Manassas (Aug. 30, 1862): POW, Amelia CH. (Apr. 5, 1865): Paroled, Pt. Lookout, Md., June, 1865.

NEGRO SERVANT

WARD, LAWRENCE Cook — Negro Slave: POW, Plymouth, Va., Oct. 31, 1864.

★ ★ ★ ★ ★

MEMBERS OF CO. D, 1ST REGT. NO. CAR. ARTY, WHO WERE NOT PRESENT FOR DUTY DURING THE PERIOD THAT THE COMPANY SUPPORTED HOOD'S TEXAS BRIGADE (SEPT. 1862-JULY, 1863).

OFFICERS

Saunders, Wm. L. 2Lt.

NON-COMMISSIONED OFFICERS

Buckett, Wm. H. Cpl.

PRIVATES

Bowden, J. N.
Brown, David
Brown, Henry M.
Canup, Daniel
Carter, John E.
Casper, Alexander
Chandley, Wm.
Cowan, Richard R.
Denton, Thos. H.
Draughorn, John W.
Earnhart, Abraham
Fraley, Wm. W.
Gibson, Robt. E.

Glover, Richard M.
Goodman, Tobias
Hall, S. H.
Hall, Stockton
Hardister, Thos. H.
Hofferer, Leonard
Holshouser, Jas.
Ireland, Jos. M.
Klutts, Peter
Lemly, Jacob
Lewis, Wm.
Linebarger, Henry R.
Lockerman, Sion
Mitchell, Wm. J.

Monday, P. C.
Myers, Wm. H.
Neal, Chas. E.
Neal, David
Parks, Daniel
Parks, Milas, J. S.
Puller, Jas.
Rands, R. H.
Rodgers, Wm.
Rufty, Milas A.
Ruth, Lorenzo D.
Seaford, Daniel A.
Sinclair, Roland
Williams, Jas.

Part Two

Illustrations

BRIG. GEN. LOUIS T. WIGFALL

Brig. Gen. Louis T. Wigfall commanded the First Texas Infantry Battalion (later regiment) before his appointment as the first commander of the Texas Brigade in Oct., 1861. He resigned his commission in February, 1862, to assume a seat in the Confederate Senate from Texas

BRIGADE COMMANDERS

BRIG.-GEN. JAMES ARCHER

Col. James Archer, original commander of Fifth Texas Regiment, 1861-1862, commanded the Texas Brigade Feb. 20 to March 12, 1862. Archer, who was succeeded in command by John B. Hood, was promoted to Brig.-Gen. and assigned to Hatton's Tenn. Brig. in June, 1862.

BRIGADE COMMANDERS

GEN. JOHN BELL HOOD

Gen. John Bell Hood commanded the Texas Brigade in the spring of 1862 and at its first great victory at Gaines' Mill (June 27, 1862). He was promoted to division commander before Second Manassas (Aug. 30, 1862). Prior to his promotion to Brigade Commander he served as the Colonel of the Fourth Texas Infantry Regiment. During the war Hood rose in rank from first lieutenant to full general, the most rapid rise in rank of any officer in the Confederate Army.

BRIGADE COMMANDERS

BRIG.-GEN. WILLIAM T. WOFFORD

Brig.-Gen. William T. Wofford, commanded the Eighteenth Georgia Infantry Regiment. Due to his seniority he commanded the Texas Brigade at the battles of Boonsboro and Antietam in the summer of 1862. He was the only commander of the Brigade not from Texas.

BRIGADE COMMANDERS

BRIG. GEN. JEROME BONAPARTE ROBERTSON

Brig-Gen. Jerome Bonapart Robertson commanded the Fifth Tex. Inf. Regt. prior to his promotion to Brigade Commander in November, 1862. He led the Brigade at Gettysburg, Chickamauga, and through the East Tennessee campaign of 1863-4, longer than any other commander. Gen. Robertson was relieved of his command in early 1864 and returned to Texas where he commanded the State Reserve Forces.

BRIGADE COMMANDERS

BRIG.-GEN. JOHN GREGG

Brig-Gen. John Gregg was transferred from the Army of Tennessee to command the Texas Brigade in early 1864. He led the Texans through the savage fighting of the Wilderness, Spotsylvania, and Grant's advance to Petersburg in the summer of 1864. Brig-Gen. Gregg was killed as he led his troops in the battle of Darbytown Road, Oct. 7, 1864. He was the only Texas Brigade Commander to die in battle.

LT. COL. C. M. WINKLER
At the battle of Darbytown Road on Oct. 7, 1864, Lt. Col. C. M. Winkler, commander of the Fourth Tex. Inf. Regt., assumed temporary command of the Brigade following the death of Gen. John Gregg and the wounding of Col. Frederick S. Bass (picture not available). Col. Winkler originally commanded Company 1, Fourth Texas Infantry.

BRIGADE COMMANDERS

COL. ROBERT M. POWELL

Col. Robert M. Powell rose from Captain of Co. D, Fifth Tex. Inf. Regt., in 1861 to Colonel, commanding the Fifth Texas in 1862. Wounded and captured at Gettysburg, he was paroled in Mar., 1865, and assumed command of the Texas Brigade. Powell commandetd the Brigade at Appomattox.

BRIGADE STAFF

COL.
WILLIAM H. SELLERS

Assistant Brigade Adjutant General (AAG), 1861-1862. He was the original ILT of Co. A, Fifth Tex. Inf. Regt.

CAPT.
WALTER N. NORWOOD

Assistant Brigade Quartermater (AQM), 1864. He was the original 3Sgt. of Company E, Fifth Tex. Inf. Regt.

FIRST TEXAS INFANTRY REGIMENT

COL. ALEXIS T. RAINEY

Commander of the First Texas, Jan. to June, 1862. Original commander of Co. H, First Texas Infantry.

LT. COL. HUGH McLEOD

Original Lt.-Col. of the First Texas. Died of pneumonia, Jan. 2, 1862.

FIRST TEXAS INFANTRY REGIMENT

LT. COL. PHILIP A. WORK

Original Commander of Co. F, First Texas. Promoted to Lt-Col. and assgd. to Regmtl. Hdqtrs., May 19, 1862.

CAPT. GEORGE T. TODD

Rose from private in Co. A, First Texas, to Commander of the Company in 1862.

FIRST TEXAS INFANTRY REGIMENT

**1ST LT.
WILLIAM W. HENDERSON**

Company D, First Texas.

3RD LT. C. R. CARTRIGHT

Company D, First Texas.

FIRST TEXAS INFANTRY REGIMENT

CAPT. ELBERT S. JEMISON

Company G, First Texas.

**CAPT.
WILLIAM H. GASTON**

Company H, First Texas.

FIRST TEXAS INFANTRY REGIMENT

CAPT. EDWARD CURRIE

Company I, First Texas.

1ST LT. B. F. PRICE

Company K, First Texas.

FIRST TEXAS INFANTRY REGIMENT

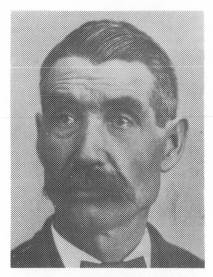

CPL. JAMES W. WILLIAMS
Company C, First Texas

SGT. THOMAS P. OCHILTREE
Company E, First Texas
Later Major in Trans-Mississippi and
U.S. Congressman 1883-85.

PVT. JOHN BURKE
Company E, First Texas
Lee's Scout & served on Gov. Murrah's staff in 1864 & 65.

(l) **PVT. WILLIAM L. LANGLEY**
Killed at Gettysburg
(r) **PVT. THOMAS H. LANGLEY**
Company E, First Texas

FIRST TEXAS INFANTRY REGIMENT

PVT. FRANKLIN MAYS
Company E, First Texas

CPL. HOWARD E. PERRY
Company E, First Texas
Killed at Antietam

PVT. EUGENE O. PERRY
Company E, First Texas
Shown here in the uniform of
Kentucky Military Institute

CPL. RHODES B. STEPHENS
Company E, First Texas
Discharged for underage, but fought
and was killed at Second Manassas.

FIRST TEXAS INFANTRY REGIMENT

PVT. ANDREW J. KNIGHT

PVT. JOHN A. KNIGHT

PVT. JOE A. KNIGHT
Winner of Texas Gold Star for
Bravery — 1865

PVT. WILLIAM H. KNIGHT

THE KNIGHT BROTHERS
of Company H, First Texas

FIRST TEXAS INFANTRY REGIMENT

PVT. SAM R. BURROUGHS
Company G, First Texas

PVT. JOSEPH P. SURRATT
Company H, First Texas

MALACHIAH REEVES
Co. I, First Texas

SGT. GEORGE BRANARD
Company L, First Texas
Regimental Color — Sgt.

FIRST TEXAS INFANTRY REGIMENT

SGT. EDWARD BUCKLEY
Company L, First Texas

SGT. D. H. HAMILTON
Company M, First Texas

PVT. WILLIAM R. McCLAIN
Company M, First Texas

CPL. J. GEORGE LOCKE
Company M, First Texas

WINTER QUARTERS

Company L, First Texas near Dumfries, Va., 1861-1862
(l to r) Pvt. Charles McCarty; Pvt. Joseph Nagle, wounded at Gaines' Mill; Sgt. James W. Southwick, killed at Gettysburg; and James Nagle, wounded at Antietam and Chickamauga.

FOURTH TEXAS INFANTRY REGIMENT

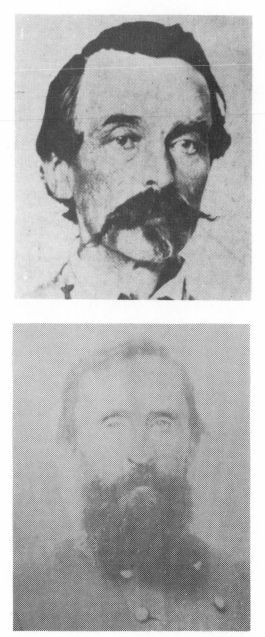

COL. ROBERT T. P. ALLEN

Original commander of the Fourth Texas, 1861.

COL. JOHN MARSHALL

Commander of Fourth Texas, March 3 to June 27, 1862. Killed at Gaines' Mill, June 27, 1862.

FOURTH TEXAS INFANTRY REGIMENT

COL.
BRADFUTE WARWICK

Served with Garibaldi in Italy in the 1850's. Original Major of Fourth Texas. Died of wounds at Gaines' Mill.

MAJ. WILLIAM
H. ("Howdy") MARTIN

Original Captain of Co. K, Fourth Texas. Prom. to Maj. and asgnd. to Regmtl. Hdqtrs., Apr. 29, 1864. Led Brigade to Texas after Appomattox. Served in U.S. Congress, 1887-1891.

FOURTH TEXAS INFANTRY REGIMENT

MAJ. WILLIAM P. TOWNSEND

Original Captain of Co. C, Fourth Texas. Prom. to Maj. and asgnd. to Regmtl. Hdqtrs., July 10, 1862: Lost foot at Second Manassas.

1ST LT. STEPHEN H. DARDEN

Company A, Fourth Texas. Served in Texas Legislature, 1861-62 and Confederate Congress, 1864-65.

FOURTH TEXAS INFANTRY REGIMENT

SURGEON JOHN C. JONES

Fourth Texas. Attended Gen. Hood after the loss of his leg at Chickamauga.

**CAPT.
HENRY M. MARCHANT**

Company A, Fourth Texas.

FOURTH TEXAS INFANTRY REGIMENT

**CAPT. DECIMUS
ET. ULTIMUS BARZIZA**

Company C, Fourth Texas.

LT. EDMUND DUGGAN

Company D, Fourth Texas.

FOURTH TEXAS INFANTRY REGIMENT

**2ND LT.
THOMAS J. JOHNSON**

Company D, Fourth Texas.
Killed at Second Manassas.

CAPT. THOMAS SELMAN

Company E, Fourth Texas.

FOURTH TEXAS INFANTRY REGIMENT

LT. FREDERICK M. MAKEIG

Company E, Fourth Texas.

CAPT. E. T. KINDRED

Company F, Fourth Texas.

FOURTH TEXAS INFANTRY REGIMENT

CAPT. LEMUEL P. HUGHES

Company F, Fourth Texas.
Lost arm at Antietam.

CAPT. THOMAS C. BUFFINGTON

Company G, Fourth Texas.

FOURTH TEXAS INFANTRY REGIMENT

LT. WILLIAM E. BARRY

Company G, Fourth Texas.

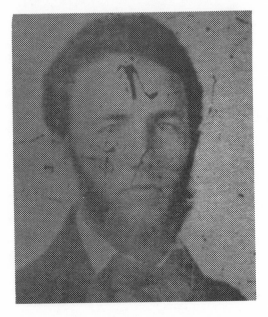

**CAPT. PROCTOR P.
PORTER**

Company H, Fourth Texas.
Died of typhoid after being
wounded at Gaines' Mill.

FOURTH TEXAS INFANTRY REGIMENT

CAPT. JAMES T. HUNTER

Company H, Fourth Texas. Led Brigade to Texas after Appomattox.

LT. J. R. LOUGHRIDGE

Company I, Fourth Texas.

FOURTH TEXAS INFANTRY REGIMENT

(l) SGT. ALBERT P. BROWN
(r) LYCURGUS M. BROWN
Company A, Fourth Texas

PVT. THOMAS B. STANFIELD
Company A, Fourth Texas

PVT. VAL GILES
Company B, Fourth Texas

CPL. JOSEPH E. JONES
Company B, Fourth Texas

FOURTH TEXAS INFANTRY REGIMENT

PVT. WILLIAM R. HAMBY
Company B, Fourth Texas

PVT. L. D. HILL, M.D.
Company B, Fourth Texas

PVT. ASA J. HOWARD
Company B, Fourth Texas

PVT. WILLIAM H. LESSING
Company B, Fourth Texas

FOURTH TEXAS INFANTRY REGIMENT

PVT. JOHN F. McGEHEE
Company B, Fourth Texas

SGT. J. M. ADAMS
Company C, Fourth Texas

PVT. JOHN H. DRENNAN
Company C, Fourth Texas

SGT. JAMES L. GALLOWAY
Company C, Fourth Texas

FOURTH TEXAS INFANTRY REGIMENT

PVT. RODERICK E. MOORE
Company C, Fourth Texas

SGT. WILLIAM H. BURGES
Company D, Fourth Texas

PVT. JOHN W. SMITH
Company D, Fourth Texas
Died of disease, Dec., 1861.

PVT. WILLIAM R. SMITH
Company D, Fourth Texas
Brother of John W. Smith. Killed at
Chickamauga.

FOURTH TEXAS INFANTRY REGIMENT

PVT. GEORGE A. HODGES
Company D, Fourth Texas

PVT. J. A. BRADFIELD
Company E, Fourth Texas

PVT. JOHN C. WEST
Company E, Fourth Texas

PVT. THOMAS M. MULLENS
Company E, Fourth Texas

1ST SGT. JOHN D. MURRAY
Company F, Fourth Texas

CPL. JAMES C. MURRAY
Company F, Fourth Texas

CPL. ROBERT W. MURRAY
Company F, Fourth Texas
Lost leg at Wilderness

SGT. JOSEPH B. POLLEY
Company F, Fourth Texas
Lost foot at Darbytown Road.

FOURTH TEXAS INFANTRY REGIMENT

SGT. JACOB C. QUICK
Company F, Fourth Texas

PVT. LAWRENCE A. DAFFAN
Company G, Fourth Texas

PVT. ALBERT SNEED
Company F, Fourth Texas

PVT. JAMES C. LOGGINS
Company G, Fourth Texas

FOURTH TEXAS INFANTRY REGIMENT

RICHARD PINCKNEY — Musician
Company G, Fourth Texas

PVT. JOHN M. PINCKNEY
Company G, Fourth Texas

PVT. GEORGE S. QUALLS
Company G, Fourth Texas

PVT. MARK S. WOMACK
Company G, Fourth Texas

FOURTH TEXAS INFANTRY REGIMENT

PVT. JOHN LONG
Company H, Fourth Texas

PVT. JACOB F. LOWN
Company H, Fourth Texas
Died as a POW

PVT. WILLIAM A. WATSON
Company H, Fourth Texas

FOURTH TEXAS INFANTRY REGIMENT

FRANK B. CHILTON — Company H, Fourth Texas

At age 52 — 1907 Navasota Convention of Hood's Texas Brigade Association

At age 17 — Discharged for being underage, 1862.

Frank B. Chilton was an active member of Hood's Texas Brigade Association, was most responsible for the Brigade monument in Austin, and served as President of the Association 1910-11.

FOURTH TEXAS INFANTRY REGIMENT

A WARTIME ROMANCE
MR. and MRS. JOHN C. ROBERTS

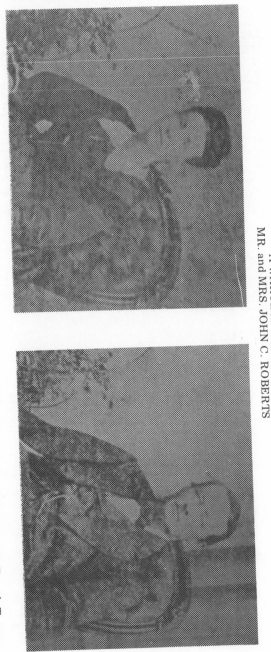

Mrs. John C. Roberts (Mary Louisa Walker)

Sgt. John C. Roberts — Company C, Fourth Texas

During the Texas Brigade's breakthrough of the Federal line at Gaines' Mill, Sgt. John C. Roberts was struck by a minie ball in his right arm. Taken to a Richmond hospital, his mangled limb was amputated above the elbow. Two days after the battle, the wounded Texan met Mary Louisa Walker, a nurse in the hospital, who waited on him until he was able to leave for home. Miss Walker smuggled needed medicines to the hospital from Baltimore beneath her clothing. After the war the couple were married at her home in Lancaster, Pennsylvania. The Roberts settled at Bremond, Texas.

FOURTH TEXAS INFANTRY REGIMENT

MEMBERS OF COMPANY B (Tom Green Rifles), FOURTH TEXAS
Taken at Austin, February, 1866 — less than a year after their return to Texas.
Front row l to r — Capt. William C. Walsh, disabled at Gaines' Mill; Sgt. Sidney E. Mosley, leg amputated at Darbytown Road; Cpl. George L. Robertson, wounded and POW, Antietam; Unidentified officer.
Back row l to r — Capt. James T. McLaurin; Pvt. J. H. Keller, lost arm at Gaines' Mill; Lt. John T. Price; Unidentified man; Pvt. Clemet L. Freeman, Federal POW, 1864-1865.

FOURTH TEXAS INFANTRY REGIMENT

MEMBERS OF COMPANY B (Tom Green Rifles), FOURTH TEXAS
Photo taken at Austin, Texas, February, 1866
Front row l to r — Sgt. Garland "Snooks" Colvin, Pvt. Frank Strohmer, Pvt. Thomas E. Cater and Sgt. Robert R. (Radway's Ready Relief) Robertson.
Back row l to r — Pvt. Charles L. Haralson, Pvt. William K. Foster, and Pvt. Granville H. Crozier.

MEMBERS OF COMPANY B (Tom Green Rifles), FOURTH TEXAS
Nashville, Tenn., Nov., 1897

Front row l to r — Pvt. Isaac Stein, arm lost at 2nd Manassas; C. A. Dohme; and C. A. Buchner, musician.
Middle row l to r — Pvt. Frank Strohmer; Pvt. Albert W. Nichols; Pvt. William R. Hamby; Pvt. Val Giles; Pvt. George L. Robertson, and Pvt. Lum Bonner (not listed on Muster Roll).
Back row l to r — Lt. John T. Price, Pvt. D. A. Todd, Pvt. Samuel T. Stone; Pvt. John G. Wheeler, arm amputated, Wilderness; Pvt. Garland Colvin; and Pvt. Thomas E. Cater.

FOURTH TEXAS AND OTHER TEXAS CONFEDERATE AMPUTEES

l to r Pvt. J. B. Polley, Company F, Fourth Texas Inf. — lost a foot at Darbytown Road, 1864.
B. G. Rosser, 32nd Texas Cavalry — lost left arm
John McDaniel, 32nd Texas Cavalry — lost left arm
Capt. Lemuel P. Hughes, Company F, Fourth Texas Inf. — lost his left arm at Antietam, 1862.

FOURTH TEXAS INFANTRY REGIMENT

THE FIGHTING HERBERT FAMILY

1870

Front row l to r — Pvt. James H. Herbert, Co. I, Fourth Texas, wounded at
Second Manassas; Mary Herbert, later married G. W. Carmichael, 4th Tenn.
Cavalry; and John Herbert, 20th Texas Infantry.

Back row l to r — J. L. Herbert, no service, too young; George S. Herbert, 8th
Texas Cavalry (Terry's Texas Rangers) and Coleman's Scouts; David C.
Herbert, 11th Tenn. Cavalry; and Robert N. Herbert, McClung's Artillery.

1903

Front row l to r — James H. Herbert, Mary Herbert Carmichael, and Robert N.
Herbert.

Back row l to r — George S. Herbert, David C. Herbert, and J. L. Herbert.

FIFTH TEXAS INFANTRY REGIMENT

ACTING COL.
TACITUS T. CLAY

Acting Commander, Fifth Texas, 1863-64. Captain of Company I, Fifth Texas.

LT. COL. JOHN C. UPTON

Original Captain of Company B, Fifth Texas. Asgnd. to Regmtl. Hdqtrs., June 1, 1862. Killed at Second Manassas.

FIFTH TEXAS INFANTRY REGIMENT

ASST. SURGEON
WILLIAM P. POWELL

Enlisted as Private in Company D, Fifth Texas. Asgnd. to Regmtl. Hdqtrs. as an Asst. Surg., Mar. 12, 1863.

ACTG. ASST. SURGEON
PVT. JOHN J. CANON

Enlisted as a private in Company K, Fifth Texas. Actg. Asst. Surgeon, 1861, discharged for disability. Later led 22nd Inf. Regt. (Waul's Legion) at Mansfield, La., as Lt. Colonel.

FIFTH TEXAS INFANTRY REGIMENT

CAPT. D. C. FARMER

Orig. 3Lt., Company A, Fifth Texas. Acting Lt.-Col., Fifth Texas, 1863.

1LT. B. PUGH FULLER

Orig. Pvt., Company A, Fifth Texas. Prom., 1Lt. Sept., 1863.

FIFTH TEXAS INFANTRY REGIMENT

CAPT. J. D. ROBERDEAU

Orig. 1Lt., Company B, Fifth Texas. Prom., Capt., June, 1862.

1LT. BEN M. BAKER

Orig. 4Sgt., Company B, Fifth Texas. Prom., 1Lt., Nov., 1864.

FIFTH TEXAS INFANTRY REGIMENT

CAPT. WILLIAM T. HILL

Orig. 1Lt., Company D, Fifth Texas. Prom., Capt., Aug., 1862. Company D, Fifth Texas. Last commander of Fifth Texas Regiment, 1865.

1ST LT. SAM T. COFFIELD

Orig. Pvt., Company E, Fifth Texas. Prom., 1Lt., Jan., 1864.

FIFTH TEXAS INFANTRY REGIMENT

CAPT. IKE TURNER

Orig. Capt., Company K, Fifth Texas. Killed at Suffolk, Va., 1863. Youngest (22) of the original company commanders, Hood's Tex. Brig.

CAPT. R. W. HUBERT

Orig. 1Lt., Company K, Fifth Texas. Prom., Capt., Apr., 1863. Captured at Gettysburg.

FIFTH TEXAS INFANTRY REGIMENT

PVT. JACOB HAHN
Company B, Fifth Texas

SGT. R. A. BRANTLEY
Company D, Fifth Texas

PVT. WILLIAM H. MYERS
Company D, Fifth Texas

PVT. BILLY PEARCE
Company D, Fifth Texas
POW at Gettysburg — died in prison.

FIFTH TEXAS INFANTRY REGIMENT

1ST SGT. W. B. W. GEORGE
Company E, Fifth Texas

PVT. LEONARD G. GEE
Company E, Fifth Texas

PVT. JESSE B. LOTT
Company E, Fifth Texas

PVT. WILLIAM R. LOTT
Company E, Fifth Texas

FIFTH TEXAS INFANTRY REGIMENT

PVT. JOHN H. ROBERTS
Company E, Fifth Texas
(Last President of Hood's Texas
Brigade Assn., 1925-1933)

PVT. JACOB HEMPHILL
Company H, Fifth Texas
Texas Gold Star Medal Winner

PVT. EDWIN K. GOREE
Company H, Fifth Texas

PVT. LANGSTON J. GOREE
Company H, Fifth Texas

FIFTH TEXAS INFANTRY REGIMENT

PVT. CHARLES H. GRAVES
Company I, Fifth Texas
(Later Lt. in Buford's Texas Cavalry)

PVT. JAMES R. THOMAS, JR.
Company I, Fifth Texas
POW, Gettysburg

PVT. A. B. GREEN
Company K, Fifth Texas

SGT. T. F. MEECE
Company K, Fifth Texas

FIFTH TEXAS INFANTRY REGIMENT

SGT. DENNIS A. ROWE
Company K, Fifth Texas

CPL. JOHN W. STEVENS
Company K, Fifth Texas

(l) PVT. RUFUS K. FELDER
(r) CPL. MIERS M. FELDER
Company E, Fifth Texas

JOHN N. HENDERSON
Company E, Fifth Texas

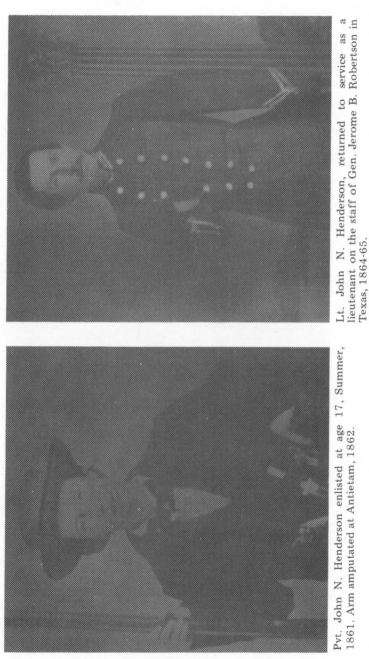

Lt. John N. Henderson, returned to service as a lieutenant on the staff of Gen. Jerome B. Robertson in Texas, 1864-65.

Pvt. John N. Henderson enlisted at age 17, Summer, 1861. Arm amputated at Antietam, 1862.

THE FIGHTING GOREE BROTHERS — 1910

l to r — Pvt. Pleasant K. "Scrap" Goree, a graduate of Washington College (later Washington and Lee, Lexington, Va.) after the war, enlisted at age 15, Co. H, Fifth Texas; Pvt. Edward K. "Pegleg" Goree, Company H, Fifth Texas; and Pvt. Robert D. Goree, Gould's Battalion, Randal's Brigade, Walker's Division (Trans-Mississippi). (Photograph was taken Oct., 1910 at Austin, Texas.)

FIFTH TEXAS INFANTRY REGIMENT

LT. BOLLING ELDRIDGE

Company E, Fifth Texas
Last survivor of Hood's Texas
Brigade.

Lt. Eldridge's Tombstone — Prairie Lea Cemetery, Brenham, Texas

LAST TEXAN RECRUITED FOR
HOOD'S TEXAS BRIGADE
Company I, Fourth Texas

GEORGE T. JESTER

The last recruit for Hood's Texas Brigade was George T. Jester, who was on his way to Virginia when Gen. Lee surrendered at Appomattox. After the war he served in the Texas legislature and as Lieutenant-Governor from 1894-1898. He was the father of Beauford H. Jester, Governor of Texas, 1946-1949.

THIRD ARKANSAS INFANTRY REGIMENT

CPL. BENJAMIN J. PERRY

Company E, Third Arkansas.

**MUSICIAN
ROBERT J. LOWRY**

Company G, Third Arkansas.

HAMPTON'S SO. CAR. LEGION (INF. BTLN.)

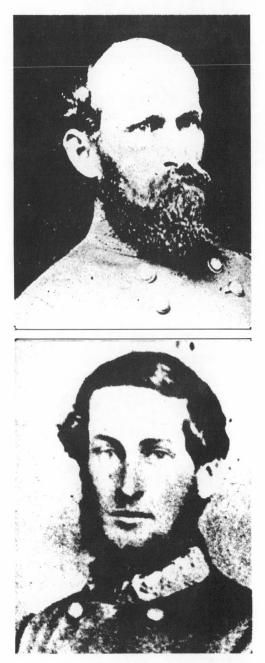

COL. MARTIN W. GARY

Orig. Capt. of Co. B. Prom. to Lt.-Col. & asgnd. to Btln. Hdqtrs., June 16, 1862. Prom. to Brig-Gen., May, 1864.

COL. THOS. M. LOGAN

Orig., 1Lt. of Co. E. Prom. to Major & asgnd. to Btln. Hdqtrs. Sept. 17, 1862. Prom. to Brig.-Gen., Feb., 1865.

Part Three

Statistical Charts & Summaries

COMPANY STATISTICS

Compared to modern wars, the companies of Hood's Texas Brigade suffered frightfully high casualty rates, though they were common for that period. A random sampling of the companies killed, wounded, captured, and missing reveal that Co. B, 1st Texas, had an appalling 28.9% killed or died of wounds — the highest of the Brigade. The decline in manpower from 1861 to 1865 by Company B illustrates the attrition suffered by all of Lee's Army and the cause of the final collapse of the Confederacy. From 79 officers and men who left Polk County, Texas, in the spring of 1861, and the 23 more who were recruited during 1862, the roster dwindled until not a single man answered the roll call at Appomattox in April, 1865.

At the Wilderness, Co. G, 4th Texas reported of the 37 men present for duty, 21 were killed or wounded.

At Antietam, companies of the First Texas were almost depleted of men. After the battle, Company F had no one to answer roll call, Company A had one man, Company C had two, and Company M had the most, eleven men. At this battle the 1st Texas Infantry Regiment suffered the highest casualty rate for any regiment, North or South during the war, 82.3%.

Of the 32 Texas Companies of Hood's Brigade, 19 of them suffered more than 60% total casualties each, and 23 had more than 10% killed.

* * * * * *

ESTIMATED NUMBER OF MILES TRAVELED BY COMPANY "E," FOURTH TEXAS INFANTRY, ON ORDERED MOVES

YEAR	ON FOOT	BY SHIP	BY CART	BY RAIL	TOTAL
1861	260	100	20	1,512	1,892[1]
1862	736			251	987
1863	1,119			933	2,052
1864	355			272	627
1865	605	800		443	1,848[2]
Total	3,075	900	20	3,411	7,406

[1] Includes the estimated 230 miles traveled by foot, 100 by ship, 20 by cart, and 1,450 by rail on the trip from Waco, Texas, to Richmond, Virginia.

[2] Includes the estimated 505 miles traveled by foot, 800 by ship and 415 by rail on the trip from Appomattox Court House, Virginia, to Waco, Texas.

CHART 1

REGIMENTAL BATTLE CASUALTIES FOR THE 1ST, 4TH & 5TH TEXAS INFANTRY REGIMENTS, 1861-65

Regiment	Total Assigned	Killed		Mortally Wounded		Total Killed in Battle		Wounded		Total Wounds[1]		POWS		Missing		Total Battle Casualties	
		No.	%	No.	%	No.	%	No.	%	No.	%	No.	%	No.	%	No.	%
First Texas	1564	187	12.	61	3.9	248	15.9	453	29.	586	—	129	8.2	7	.45	837	53.5
Fourth Texas	1343	178	13.2	78	5.8	256	19.0	486	35.9	606	—	162	12.0	5	.4	909	67.7
Fifth Texas	1439	154	10.7	78	5.4	232	15.4	492	34.2	736	—	214	14.9	3	.2	941	65.4
Total	4346	519	11.9	217	4.9	736	16.9	1431	32.6	1928	—	505	11.5	15	.36	2687	61.7

1. Numerous soldiers were wounded more than once during a battle

CHART II

REGIMENTAL LOSSES, OTHER THAN BATTLE, FOR THE 1ST, 4TH & 5TH TEXAS INFANTRY REGIMENTS, 1861-65

Regiment	Total Assigned	Died of Disease [1]		Died of Other causes		Discharged [2]		Desertions [3]		Total	
		No.	%	No.	%	No.	%	No.	%	No.	%
First Texas	1564	189	12.	5	.31	337	21.	147	9.3	678	43.4
Fourth Texas	1343	161	11.9	3	.22	251	18.	51	3.	466	34.7
Fifth Texas	1439	293	20.3	7	.43	260	18.	84	5.7	644	44.8
Total	4346	643	14.8	15	.36	848	19.	282	6.4	1788	41.0

1 See Chart IV for details.

2 See Chart VI for details.

3 Most of the desertions occured on the march to Virginia in 1861, during the East Tennesse Campaign (October, 1863–April, 1864), and during the final days of the war in the Richmond trenches and the march to Appomattox.

CHART III
CASUALTIES FOR SIX MAJOR BATTLES

Regiments	Gaines' Mill June 27, 1862				Second Manassas Aug. 30, 1862				Antietam Sept. 17, 1862			
	Killed	Wounded	POW	Total	Killed	Wounded	POW	Total	Killed	Wounded	POW	Total
First Texas	21	63	1	85	11	20	0	31	57	130	23	210
Fourth Texas	79	190	0	269	35	68	9	112	32	83	39	154
Fifth Texas	22	55	0	77	54	143	17	214	21	46	19	86
Eighteenth Georgia	27	131	1	159	29	101	21	151	16	57	12	85
Hampton's South Carolina Legion (Inf. Btln.)	3	17	1	21	14	45	11	70	11	45	6	62
Third Arkansas	*	*	*	*	*	*	*	*	*	*	*	*
Totals	152	456	3	611	143	377	58	578	137	361	99	597

Regiments	Gettysburg July 2, 1863				Chickamauga Sept. 19-20, 1863				Wilderness May 6, 1864				Total			
	Killed	Wounded	POW	Total	Killed	Wounded	POW	Total	Killed	Wounded	POW	Total	Killed	Wounded	POW	Total
First Texas	30	50	45	125	39	122	9	170	26	89	6	121	184	374	84	642
Fourth Texas	25	57	58	140	34	40	3	77	26	95	3	124	228	533	145	906
Fifth Texas	37	102	115	254	22	66	8	96	18	92	2	112	172	514	161	847
Eighteenth Georgia	*	*	*	*	*	*	*	*	*	*	*	*	72	289	34	395
Hampton's South Carolina Legion (Inf. Btln.)	*	*	*	*	*	*	*	*	*	*	*	*	28	107	18	153
Third Arkansas	33	71	83	187	5	52	10	67	15	55	13	83	53	178	106	337
Totals	125	280	301	706	100	280	30	410	85	331	24	440	737	1995	548	3280

*Regiment not in the Texas Brigade at time of battle.

CHART IV
REGIMENTAL MORTALITY BY DISEASE — — 1ST, 4TH & 5TH TEXAS INFANTRY REGIMENTS
1861-1865

Regiment	Typhoid Fever	Respiratory Disease 1	Measles	Digestive & Intestinal Disease 2	Small Pox	Neurological Disease 3	Other Diseases 4	Unknown	Died of Disease No.	%
First Texas	25	42	10	12	1	2	5	92	189	12
Fourth Texas	29	31	—	8	3	2	1	87	161	11.9
Fifth Texas	20	55	13	17	6	6	6	170	293	20.3
Total	74	128	23	37	10	10	12	349	643	14.8

1 Respiratory diseases - - pneumonia, asthma, bronchitis, dropsy, laryngitis, pleuritis, inflamation of lungs, tuberculosis.

2 Digestive & intestinal diseases - - dysentery, diarrhea, cholic, hepatitis, flux, "Texas trots."

3 Neurological diseases - - brain disease, meningitis, brain fever, condition of brain, cerebritas, paralysis, apoplexy.

4 Other known causes for death by disease include: VD (1), typhus (1), malaria (2), heart attack (4), cholera (1), rheumatism (2), & old age (1).

Regiment	Abdomen	Arm	Back	Chest	Face	Fingers	Foot	Groin	Hand	Head	Hip	Knee	Leg	Neck	Shoulder	Side	Thigh	Toes	Throat	Wrist	Total Wounds	Amputations
First Texas		11		8	6	1	3		15	3	1	2	18		7	10	5	11[1]	1	1	103	14
Fourth Texas	2	18	1	4	2	1	6	2	6	3	2	7	20	1	5	5	9				94	5
Fifth Texas	2	21		1	6	1	1		15	4	1		38		5	5	7				106	3
Third Arkansas	FIGURES BY WOUND NOT AVAILABLE																					
Total Number	4	50	1	13	14	2	10	2	36	10	4	9	76	1	17	20	21	11	1	1	303	22
Percentage	1.3	16.	.3	4.3	4.6	.6	3.3	.6	11.	3.3	1.3	2.9	25.	.3	5.6	6.6	6.9	3.4	.3	.3		

1 Ten toes were lost by one man.

CHART VI
CAUSES FOR DISCHARGES FOR THE 1ST, 4TH & 5TH TEXAS REGIMENTS
1861-1865

Regiment	Total	Wounds		Sickness		Reorganization [1]		Enlistment Terminated [1]		Underage		Overage		Unknown		Other [2]		Total	
		No.	%	No.	%	No.	%	No.	%	No.	%	No.	%	No.	%	No.	%	No.	%
First Texas	1564	56	3.6	130	8.9	12	.76	46	2.9	15	.98	24	1.5	44	2.8	10	.63	337	21.0
Fourth Texas	1343	75	5.6	139	10	—	—	—	—	4	.29	2	.15	18	1.3	13	.81	251	18.0
Fifth Texas	1439	44	3.	117	8	—	—	—	—	4	.27	4	.27	74	5.1	17	1.1	260	18.0
Total	4346	175	4.0	386	8.8	12	.27	46	1.	23	.52	30	.68	136	3.1	40	.89	848	19.0

1 First Texas enlistments were for one year originally — to 1862; the Fourth and Fifth Texas enlistments, however, were for the duration of the war.

2 Other causes include: "incapable," "deaf," "mistake," "cashiered," "insanity," "previous injury," "physical development," "drunkenness," "homesickness," "exhausted," and "feeble condition."

Part Four
Brigade Trivia

FIRST KILLED

Sgt. John Wimberly, Co. A, 1st Texas, was killed near the Potomac River in late 1861. He was the first member of the Brigade to die due to enemy action.

* * * * * *

RECRUITED TWICE

Both Privates E. M. Berry and Basil C. Brashear, Co. F, 5th Texas, were recruited twice. Both were discharged November 10, 1861, for illness and both re-enlisted in March, 1862. Berry was again discharged for chronic diarrhea; but Brashear, though wounded twice, served to Lee's surrender at Appomattox.

* * * * * *

ONE OF A KIND

Pvt. J. S. W. Cooke, Co. B, 4th Texas, was the only member of the Brigade to be conscripted — all others were volunteers. Cooke was conscripted at Culpeper Court House, Va. on June 6, 1862.

* * * * * *

GONE WITH THE WIND

The grandfather of Margaret Mitchell, author of *Gone With the Wind,* Russell C. Mitchell, served as 1Sgt. of Co. I, 1st Texas, during 1861-62. He was wounded at Antietam (Sept. 17, 1862), but later was reduced to the ranks for "inefficiency." Mitchell left the Brigade in the summer of 1863 to serve as a nurse in Atlanta.

* * * * * *

GONE!

Lt. J. M. Alexander, Co. K, 5th Texas, was captured three times (twice while wounded) at Antietam (Sept. 17, 1862), Gettysburg (July 2, 1863), and Darbytown Road (Oct. 8, 1864). He escaped each time to rejoin his company and served until his parole at Appomattox.

* * * * * *

FICKLE MEMBER

Pvt. Charles W. Hoyle, Co. L, 1st Texas, deserted in the summer of 1862, but later rejoined his company. He was captured at Gettysburg, but escaped from prison to rejoin company, only to desert a final time in Jan., 1865.

* * * * * *

KILLED BY BAYONET

Pvt. Rube Blalock, Co. D, 1st Texas, was killed at Spotsylvania Court House, May 10, 1864, by a bayonet thrust. Blalock was the only member of the Brigade to die from cold steel.

* * * * * *

NO SURVIVOR

Co. B, 1st Texas, had no one present of its total of 102 members to surrender at Appomattox on April 12, 1865.

All nine of the original non-commissioned officers of Co. I, 4th Texas, within a year, had suffered death, wounds, capture, or discharge for disability. One died en route to Virginia, three died of pneumonia in Virginia, and three were either wounded or captured during the defense of Richmond in the spring of 1862.

* * * * * *

PLENTY OF TOOTERS BUT FEW SHOOTERS

Of the eighteen members of the 3rd Arkansas Regimental Band, eight were captured at Antietam (Sept. 17, 1862).

* * * * * *

HOOD'S BEQUEATH

During his fatal illness, General John B. Hood left his already motherless eleven children to the care of "the old Texas Brigade."

* * * * * *

BRIGADE INSPIRES SONG

Colonel William L. Prather, President of the University of Texas 1899-1905, exhorted the student body with, "On one occasion during the Civil War it fell the lot of a Texas Troop (Hood's Brigade) to be reviewed by General Robert E. Lee. The officer in charge gave this command. 'Forward, men of Texas, the eyes of General Lee are upon you.' I would like to paraphrase that utterance," continued Prather, "and say to you 'Forward, young men and women of the University, the eyes of Texas are upon you!'"

In 1903 John Long Sinclair, inspired by the President's words, wrote the verses of the famous Texas University alma mater.

* * * * * *

VERSATILE SOLDIERS

During the first half of 1863, the foot soldiers of Hood's Brigade fought against gunboats, engaged in the first trench warfare in American history, and one regiment, the Third Arkansas, was briefly mounted as a cavalry unit.

* * * * * *

ENOUGH IS ENOUGH

Pvt. James S. Smith, Co. K, 18th Georgia, who was wounded in three battles and captured twice, took the Federal loyalty oath in 1864.

* * * * * *

DEFIANT TO THE END

At Appomattox, the 602 survivors of Hood's Texas Brigade surrendered only 348 rifles to the Federals — many had smashed their guns against trees rather than give them up.

* * * * * *

BETTER LATE THAN NEVER

1st Lieutenant Mark A. Williams, original 1st Lieutenant, Co. C, 3rd Arkansas Infantry, died November 20, 1862 and was promoted to Captain, December 1, 1862, eleven days after he died!

* * * * * *

GENERAL HOOD'S LEG

General John B. Hood entrusted Arthur H. Collier, Co. H, 4th Texas, with the dubious honor of shipping his severed right leg to friends in Texas following the general's wound at Chickamauga (Sept. 20, 1863).

Men of the 1st, 4th, & 5th Texas, Hampton's Legion & the 3rd Arkansas, donated $4,910.50 to buy Hood an artificial leg after the loss of his right limb at Chickamauga. Hood never adjusted to wearing the cork leg and had it strapped to the saddle of his spare mount. The aggressive commander preferred to use a crutch to get around on.

* * * * * *

ENLISTED MEN AS COMMANDERS

1Sgt. George W. Kipps commanded his company, Co. H, 4th Texas, at the Wilderness (May 6, 1864), as there were no officers present for duty.

Pvt. H. N. Jones, Co. I, and Pvt. Sam Patton, Co. K, 1st Texas, commanded their respective companies at Malvern Hill (July 1, 1862), due to heavy casualties a few days prior at Gaines' Mill (June 27, 1862). Both were later promoted to lieutenant, but were both killed in battle, Patton at Antietam (Sept. 17, 1862) and Jones at Gettysburg (July 2, 1863).

* * * * * *

MARKS ON THE LAND

Places in Texas named for members of the Texas Brigade include Hood County, and Fort Hood, (Bell & Coryell Counties) for General John B. Hood; Winkler, Texas (Navarro County) and Winkler County for Lt. Col. Clinton M. Winkler of the 4th Texas; Upton County for Lt. Col. John C. Upton of the 5th Texas; and Gregg County was named for Gen. John Gregg, who commanded the Brigade in 1864.

* * * * * *

100% ATTENDANCE

H. C. Jackson, Co. G, 5th Texas, claimed after the war that he was never absent during a battle: records substantiate his claim. Miraculously, he was never wounded or endured a prolonged spell of sickness during his four years of service.

* * * * * *

WIDE RANGE

Co. H, 4th Texas, had enlistments from nine Texas counties when the company was organized in 1861.

* * * * * *

FAITHFUL FRIEND

Thad W. Bullock, original 1Cpl., Co. K, 1st Texas, reverted back to private at his own request to accompany the remains of a comrade, Pvt. Jesse Benton, Jr., to San Augustine, Texas. Bullock later rejoined his company and suffered a wound at Darbytown Road, Oct. 7, 1864. He never regained his corporal stripes.

* * * * * *

WHAT'S IN A NAME

Proud parents of the 19th Century frequently chose distinguished names for their offspring, drawing upon the classics and American history, the Bible, and popular figures of the day for inspiration. Among the men of Hood's Texas Brigade were George Washingtons, Thomas Jeffersons, Andrew Jacksons, John Adams, Benjamin Franklins, James Madisons, James Monroes, one John Quincy Adams, Martin Van Buren, William H. Harrison and a Madison Monroe Templeton. Other American heroes who inspired namesakes were Alexander Hamilton, Albert Gallatin (Jefferson's Secretary of the Treasury), Columbus, de Leon, Pulaski, Lafayette, Stephen Decatur and the Seminole chief, Osceola. There were also numerous Clays, Calhouns, and Websters, as well as a John Marshall, a Ben Franklin, and an Alamo Dimmett.

From the rolls of Hampton's South Carolina Legion appear the namesakes of the Palmetto State's Revolutionary War heroes, "The Swamp Fox," Francis Marion; the "Gamecock," Thomas Sumter; the "Wizzard Owl," Andrew Pickens; the hero of Fort Sullivan, Sgt. William Jasper; and many Pinckneys, for the statesmen and diplomats of that name.

The Brigade had on its roster such military giants as Napoleon, Jerome and Lucian Bonaparte, Alexander, Darius, Augustus, Pizzarro, Hector and Constantine. Other classical heroes who found namesakes among the soldiers were Horatio (of the bridge), Cincinnatus, Leonidas of Thermopylae, Leander, Lucian, Massena, Claudius, Theophilus, and Romulus T. Rhome was named for the legendary founder of the Eternal City. The classical orators Demosthenes, Lycurgus, and Cicero found their way into the rolls of the Brigade, as did the poets, Virgil, John Milton and Robert Burns. The clergy was well represented by the English divine John Wesley the Scottish religious reformer, Alexander Campbell, and several John Calvins. The French scientist, Paschal also had a namesake.

From the holy scriptures, parents found appropriate names for Adam Damm and Noah Bible. The names of the patriarchs Abraham, Isaac, and Jacob abounded among the troops; and the sons of Israel provided Simeon, Levi, Ruben, Benjamin, Joseph, Ephriam and Manassa, to the roster. Moses and Aaron of the exodus, Joshua and Caleb of the conquest of Caanan, Phineas, Gideon, Joab, Solomon, Sampson, Jeptha, Ezra, and Job had namesakes, as did the Old Testament prophets Elijah or Elias, Isaiah, Ezekiel, Jeremiah, Daniel, Jonah, Zachariah, Hosea, Amos, Joel and Malachi. More obscure Hebrew prophets, priests, and kings who inspired names for Brigade members were, Enock, Uriah, Eli, Micajah, Ebenezer, Nathan, Elihu, Jabez, Hezekiah,

Josiab and Josephus. Of course, there were many Davids and Samuels.

From the Christian era comes the names Cross, Christian and Christmas, as well as Matthew, Mark, Luke and John. Common names like Peter, Andrew, James, Thomas, Nathaniel and Paul abound in profusion, but few were named for the gentile convert Cornelius, the beggar Lazarus, Erastus, the publican Zaccheus, Bartholomew and Barnebus.

Many were the parents who provided names unique to the annals of namedom — they tickle the fancy, trip the tongue, and play a light fantastic upon the ear. Imagine, if you please, Argalus Pruitt, Barzillia Dunham, Bradfute Warwick, Seroctus Wynne, Evander McEachan, Eli Yow, Willoughby Tullous, Boleware Capps, Atreus Clay, Cadmus Wilborn, Seaborne Davenport, and J. Pink O'Rear.

One ponders the disposition of Pleasant Blanton, the voice of Octave Copal, the physique of Handsom Hendricks, the amorous propensity of Valentine Jett, the age of Young Archy Buckley, and the agrarian powers of Rich Cotton.

The First Texas Infantry appeared to have more of the unusual given, last, and nicknames than the other regiments of the Brigade. Company A boasted an "Argyle Campbell"; a "Winkfield Shropshire"; and Co. D a "John Drumgoole." Company F had the three Chance Brothers, "Dock," "Zeke," and "Dan" while the Reagan Guards (Co. G) featured a "Smith Bottoms," "Jasper Stalcup," and an Elbert E. Pugh." Company H listed on its muster roll "George Washington Culpepper," "Johan Steincipher," and "Ignatz Honingsburger." Company M carried on its rolls "Reason Hutto," and three privates that would have made Damon Runyon smile, "Button" Evans, "Mutt" Morgan, and "Shady" Roach.

The Brigade record for names belonged to John W. M. P. Hill and R. H. V. B. Rousseau but no doubt the most unique name in the entire Texas Brigade was that of Captain Decimus Et Ultimus Barziza, Co. C, 4th Texas Regiment. His given names translated from the Latin, mean "Tenth and Last," for he was the tenth child of his parents, and as it did turn out, the last.

The Texas Brigade could proudly boast of a Cardinal, a Victory, a Buffalo, a Canada, a Coffee, and a John Bull, but also had a Grumbles, a Trimble, and a Boozer.

Nicknames abounded among the young soldiers who applied monikers with wild abandon to describe physical, moral, or professional characteristics. One gets a visual image of "Sandy" Osborne, "Ruddy" Connally, and "Gotch" Thomas from their nicknames, while one wonders about "Shake" Stephenson, "Snooks" Colvin, "Coot" Ward, and "Scrap" Goree. The First Texas Regiment had a "Big" Griffin, and a "Little" Wren, while the entire Brigade provided, "Bass" Hallum, "Buck" Duvall, "Bug" Stedman, "Babe" Midkiff, and "Bose" Chance. Nicknames gave "Duck" Ardry, "Pet" Cook, "Muley" Stewart, "Pony" Freeman, "Bull" Crawford, and "Cat" Lewis qualities associated with those animals.

Colorful names like "Old Burnside" Mayfield defy understanding today, but R. R. "Redway's Reddy Relief" Robertson was named for a popular patent medicine with the same initials, and "Howdy" Martin for his wave-like salute.

Pvt. J. E. Swindler, Co. C, 5th Texas, was detailed to the Provost Guard for a good part of the war.

Pvt. John C. Goforth, Co. A, 1st Texas, was a Regimental Teamster — on many forage details.

Cpl. T. W. Bullock, Co. K, 1st Texas, was assigned as Regimental Butcher.

Charley Sharp and Paul Horne were musicians in the 1st and 5th Texas Regimental Bands.

Members of the 3rd Arkansas could boast a few unusual names. Company D had a Lycurgus Level, Trevalon Lytle, and Pembroke Touchstone. Company G had a Derensellear Booth, Malcolm McGoogan, and Whittington Pugh. Company H had on its rolls a Napolean Tshear and a Cornelius C. Varnarsdale, while Company I listed a Tempecola Wilson.

The 18th Georgia was not without its unusual names with Penfield Doll, Sylvanus Stokes, Fenuel Wilson and Pinckney Priest all in Company A. There was Snowden E. T. Anchors in Company B, A. A. de la Perriere in Co. C, and Asgill Broom in Co. D. Company D had an Anguish Bailey and Co. G furnished Farish Carter Tate to the roll. In Companies G through I were Eurichus Smith, Americus Dysart, Gehu Abernethy and Kadwell Batto Cone.

The Palmetto State provided its share of unusual names from the troops of Hampton's Legion. Though the great majority of the South Carolinians were of English, Irish and Scottish stock, there were numerous Germans who lent the roster a Teutonic sound with names of Christopher Poppenheim, Oswell Strohecker, Caleb Pinkney Ouzts, Heinrich Kohler, J. S. Hungerpeler, and John F. Eikerenkoetter. There were Italians like Thomas C. Albergotte and distinctive sounding names of the like of Thaddeus Landry Cay, Jasper Dibble, Vastine Herlong, Daniel Presley Sturkey, Septomie A. Harvin, Azariah Woodson, and Valentine Harbot.

* * * * * *

POINTS OF ORIGIN (NATIONALITIES)

The ethnic makeup of Hood's Texas Brigade proved the truth of the parody on "Dixie" that went,

> *"This is the land of the Anglo-Saxon,*
> *The land of Davis, Lee, and Jackson . . ."*

for by far the overwhelming majority of men came from English, Welsh, and Scottish stock to produce such names as **Ephram McCorquondale** and **Argyle Campbell**. However, the Irish and German immigrants of the 1840's and '50's found their way to the Lone Star State and into the Texas Brigade. The Germans made up the largest minority group in the Texas Regiments of the Brigade with an estimated 215 or almost 5%, with Teutonic names like Prussian born **Henry Schultz, Gustav Gadiffet, Theo Melhausen,** and **Oscar Dockstader**. Running the Germans a close second were the Irish with an estimated 193 or 4.4%, and with such likely Celtic names as **Patrick Murphy, Michael O'Rourke,** and **John Muldoon**. The Third Arkansas had few minorities — 11 Irish, 7 Germans, 2 Jews, and one each of French and Mexican origin.

Perhaps due to the close proximity of French Louisiana, there was a large number of French in the Texas regiments, some 69 or 1.6%, with names like **Rosseau, Currie, Proseler,** and **Delesdinier**. Minor ethnic groups represented were Jewish with 37, Mexican with 9, 5 had Dutch and 5 Italian names, and there was one each Czech, Pole, and American Indian. These groups provided the roster with the names **Van Vleck, Solomon, Flores, Van Dusen, Masius, Shanoski, Rosas,** and **Battise**. Ike Battise, the sole Indian, was a member of the Alabama-Coushatta tribe of East Texas and served in Company B, First Texas Regiment.

Company E, 4th Texas, from McLennan County, a typical company of Hood's Texas Brigade, consisted of men from every Confederate state except Florida, as well as from Connecticut, Ohio, and Indiana. More than 30 percent were born in Tennessee, 15 percent each from Mississippi and Alabama, less than 10 percent were native born Texans, and 6 percent were German born.

* * * * * *

BLACKS WHO SERVED

Contrary to popular beliefs, many Blacks served the South during the War Between the States. A number of Negroes were with Hood's Texas Brigade, from Texas to Virginia — and from Gaines' Mill to Appomattox.

Embro or **Ember**, Co. C, 4th Texas, served with Capt. W. P. Townsend and accompanied Townsend back to Robertson Co. when the Captain's foot was amputated after 2nd Manassas (Aug. 30, 1862).

John Price (Uncle John), Co. B, 4th Texas, was a body servant and cook to Lt. John T. Price. Uncle John had many opportunities to escape to the Federals, but remained with Lt. Price to the end of the war and returned to Texas where he voted "Democratic to the end."

Henry Johnson, Co. B, 4th Texas, Company barber and body servant to Capt. B. F. Carter, buried his master after Gettysburg. Afterward he went to Baltimore where he died in 1864.

In Company H, Hampton's South Carolina Legion, three blacks, **Andrew, Andy** and **Simon**, served as cooks and servants for the first year of the war.

Henderson Howard, a cook of Co. H, 4th Texas, was recognized as a member of the Brigade, he served all through the war and was in most of the battles. Known as "the expert blanket toter," he was presented a certificate of membership in Hood's Texas Brigade Association after the war.

Noah Barnes and **Bob Johnson**, Co. D, Fifth Texas, and **Dan Winston**, Co. E, Fifth Texas all served as cooks during the war. After the war they were all recognized as members of the Brigade, and attended the Brigade reunions. According to the minutes of the meeting, Winston was awarded a badge at the Bryan reunion of Hood's Texas Brigade Association in 1902.

* * * * * *

PEACH FUZZ AND GRAY BEARDS
(Under and Over Age)

Fifteen men of Co. K, 1st Texas, were discharged in the Summer and Fall of 1862 for being over or under age (17-35) and 63 men were released in the entire 1st Texas Regiment for this same reason.

Pvt. William Carter, Co. K, 4th Texas, recruited at 56, April 17, 1862, was discharged for disability (rheumatism and old age), May 23, 1862.

Pvt. William Morse, Co. K, 4th Texas, recruited at 51, March 8, 1862, was discharged for disability (chronic rheumatism and old age), May 30, 1862.

In Co. D, 4th Texas, of the original 84 who enlisted in 1861, 25 (30%) were teenagers, 3 Sgts., 3 Cpls., and 3 Pvts. were 17: 2 Cpls. and 7 Pvts. were 18; and 1 Sgt. and 12 Pvts. were 19 — but one member was aged 50 and another 46.

In Co. K, 1st Texas, 30 out of 98 privates were less than 20 years of age, and in Co. L, 1st Texas, 21 out of 84 original privates were teenagers.

In August, 1862, twelve members of the Brigade were notified of their discharges as non-conscript (being either over or under age). Ten of these left for home on August 28, the day before 2nd Manassas; however, two members of Co. E, 1st Texas, elected to stay behind. Pvts. D. M. Walker, and Rhodes B. Stephens, who were both under 18, chose to go into battle "one last time with their comrades." Both were killed in the battle.

The youngest original company commander in the Texas Brigade was I. N. M. "Ike" Turner, Co. K, 5th Texas, age 22.

Pvt. W. R. Sanders, Co. M, First Texas, died of "old age" at 53.

Joseph Daugherty, Co. I, 3rd Arkansas, enlisted at the age of 14 at Zollicoffer, Tennessee. He was later discharged for "being underage, small of stature, and unfit for any duty."

* * * * * *

ANCHORS AWEIGH

Several members of Hood's Texas Brigade later served in the Confederate or Federal navies.

Pvt. Charles Haralson, Co. B, 4th Texas, left his Texas comrades in March, 1863 to become a Lt. Commander in the CSA Navy.

Pvt. J. S. Vandergraff, Co. E, 1st Texas, transferred to the navy in April, 1863, and later rose to the rank of Lieutenant.

Pvt. Thomas Thompson, Co. C, Third Arkansas, was captured at Gettysburg, took the Federal oath and joined the Federal Navy in 1864.

Pvt. Thomas Tierney, Third Arkansas, captured at Chickamauga, took the Federal oath, tried to enlist in the Federal Navy but was rejected.

Musician Dick Pinckney, Co. G, 4th Texas, served with the Confederate Naval Cadets, 1863-64, before he was reassigned to the Brigade.

Pvt. J. C. K. Mullay, Co. E, 1st Texas, was on detached duty to the Navy Dept. during the winter of 1863-64.

Sgt. E. M. Eustace and privates William C. Davis, H. C. Gilbert, and John A. Kinney, members of Company C, 18th Georgia, were captured and joined the Federal Navy.

Two members of Hampton's South Carolina Legion later joined the Confederate Navy, Pvts. De Leon Moses and Sidney Aveilhe. The latter joined the crew of the Privateer **Rattlesnake**.

* * * * * *

THE OVER THE HILL GANG
(AWOLS and Desertions)

3Lt. O. P. Caldwell and 1Sgt. A. M. Hinson of Co. D, 5th

Texas went AWOL together at Morristown, Tennessee, Feb. 1, 1864.

In Co. C, 1st Texas, privates Higgins, Hindle, Hodge, and Howard deserted in New Orleans, May 21, 1861. Eight more men of the company deserted the following day — but fortunately the company picked up 27 new recruits before leaving the Crescent City.

Pvt. Charles B. Halleck, Co. L, 1st Texas, deserted to the enemy after being wounded at Antietam, and was later reported as serving with the Federal 6th Corps as a captain and Subsistence Officer.

Both musicians of Co. K, 1st Texas, Jesse McCrowson (flutist) and James Ridley (drummer) went over-the-hill during the Battle of Gaines' Mill, June 27, 1862.

Pvt. M. P. Freeman, Co. G, 4th Texas, hired as a substitute for A. E. Watson on November 2, 1862, deserted two days later, November 4, 1862.

Capt. Thomas J. Thrasher, commander of Co. F, 3rd Arkansas Infantry was ordered to Arkansas in February, 1864, to arrest deserters and bring back AWOL's. The Captain, however, went AWOL himself and did not return to his company.

Pvt. Joseph McCarty, Co. A, 4th Texas, deserted, 1863, while under a sentence of death for murder in Richmond.

A number of the Third Arkansas soldiers who were captured took the Federal oath and enlisted in the 1st Connecticut Cavalry Regiment.

* * * * * *

UNUSUAL DISCHARGES

Wm. Martin, Company M, 1st Texas, was discharged "through an error."

Henry B. King, Co. A, 4th Texas (age 43), was discharged "for an inflamed old wound from the Mexican War."

Pvt. James R. Black, Co. I, 4th Texas, was discharged because of "hemorrhoides of long standing — old age — and completely broken down."

Pvt. J. Wright Simmons, Co. D, 4th Texas, was discharged "for inability to adjust to army life."

Edward Simmons, Co. B, 4th Texas, was discharged for being a "lunatic," July, 1862. He was a patient in a lunatic asylum in Austin when he was recruited.

J. A. Logan, Co. C, 1st Texas, was discharged, in New Orleans, as "incompetent to do duty."

Pvt. Michael O'Rourke, Co. C, 1st Texas, was discharged in Dec., 1862, as "never having acquired domicile."

Luke M. Tiner, 3rd Arkansas, age 17, "Retired from service for being "totally disqualified."

* * * * * *

IT TOOK ALL TYPES

Wide and varied were the pre-war civilian occupations of the Texans. Company E, 4th Texas enlisted merchants, farmers, lawmen, students, clerks, farm laborers, ranchers, a cabinet maker, printer, gunsmith, cowboy, teacher, bootmaker, and an overseer. Numerous lawyers, doctors, a few dentists, preachers, professors, and the editor of the *Texas State Gazette* all fought with Hood's Brigade.

* * * * * *

PHYSICIANS

Eleven physicians served as privates in the Texas Regiments in Hood's Brigade. Brigade commander, Brig-Gen. Jerome B. Robertson, was a physician as was Capt. Albert G. Clopton, Commander of Co. D, 1st Texas.

* * * * * *

DENTISTS

Abraham B. Lee, a musician in Co. I, 5th Texas, was a dentist by profession and Pvt. Thomas De Graffenreid was detailed as the Brigade Dentist during the winter of 1864 and 1865.

* * * * * *

ON TO BETTER THINGS

Pvt. Russell Howard, Co. F, 4th Texas, became Attorney-General of the Arizona Territory (CSA).

3Lt. Benton Randolph, Co. H, 4th Texas, became Judge-Advocate General of General W. C. Hardee's Corps, Army of Tennessee, 1863.

Lt. Stephen H. Darden, Co. A, 4th Texas, was elected to the Texas State Senate, 1861. He became Colonel of the 5th Regiment of Texas State Troops in 1863. He later served as a Confederate Congressman from Texas in 1864.

Pvt. John Burke, Co. E, 1st Texas, became one of the war's most famous scouts. He scouted for Stuart, was a "confidential scout" for Lee and Jackson and later served on the staff of Governor Pendleton Murrah of Texas, Spring, 1864.

George Taylor Jester of the 4th Texas was the last recruit of Hood's Brigade — recruited in early spring of 1865, he was on his way to Virginia when Lee surrendered. He later served in the Texas Legislature and as Lt. Governor, 1894-1898. He was the father of Governor Buford H. Jester, 1947-1949.

Decimus Et Ultimus (10th and Last) Barziza, 1Lt. of Co. C, 4th Texas, served in the 14th and 15th Texas Legislatures after the war.

Col. Clinton M. Winkler, 4th Texas, served in the Texas Legislature in 1848 and in 1872, and became a judge of the Court of Appeals in 1876.

Maj. William "Howdy" Martin, 5th Texas, served in the U.S. Congress, 1887-1891; as did Lt. John Pinckney, 1901-1905, until he was assassinated by an anti-prohibitionist at Hempstead, Texas, 1905.

Frank B. Chilton, Co. B, Fourth Texas, headed the Texas State Immigration Bureau after the war.

Capt. John A. Crawford of the 18th Georgia, left his regiment to become Commandant of Conscripts for the State of Georgia.

* * * * * *

FAMILIES

The large family sizes prevalent in 19th century America are evident in the rolls of Hood's Texas Brigade. Brothers, cousins, fathers, and sons enlisted, fought and sometimes suffered and died with each other. Some of the largest family groups represented in the Brigade are as follows:

The four Knight brothers of Co. H, 1st Texas, left a record of service and sacrifice — two were discharged for sickness, while the two remaining served until their paroles at Appomattox. One (Joseph) received the Texas Gold Star for bravery after being wounded four times.

There were eight Jester brothers in Co. E, 3rd Arkansas.

There were five Robinson brothers in Co. E, 4th Texas.

The three Dimmett brothers of Co. D, 4th Texas, Alamo A., James, and Napolean Bonapart (sic) were all wounded at Gaines' Mill — Napolean died of his wound, James was later discharged for his disabled foot, but Alamo recovered from his leg wound and he was paroled at Appomattox in 1865.

Of the seven Olivers of Co. D, 1st Texas — two died of pneumonia, one was killed at Chickamauga, one was taken prisoner at Gettysburg, three were wounded in the war, and two served until paroled at Appomattox.

In Reilly's North Carolina Battery, there were: five Crowells, five Earnharts, five Ellers, six Holshousers, six Klutts (father and five sons), six Millers, six Trexlers, and five Parks.

* * * * * *

THE GALLANT THREE HUNDRED

Approximately 4,350 Texans served in Hood's Brigade from 1861 to 1865, but only 300 served through the entire war to its conclusion at Appomattox. Of the 300, 235 were privates when they enlisted in 1861 and 176 were still privates four years later. However, one private rose to major, three to captain, ten to lieutenant, thirty to sergeant, and fifteen to corporal.

* * * * * *

FAMILY TRAGEDIES

Privates John and Lemuel Barton, brothers, of Co. C, 4th Texas had both of their right arms amputated after being wounded at Antietam (Sept. 17, 1862).

The three Crier brothers of Co. F, 1st Texas, were killed in the last half of 1863 — M. T. at Gettysburg in July, Emanuel at Chickamauga in September, and William at Knoxville in November, 1863.

Three brothers of Co. I, 4th Texas, the Westbrooks, died of disease within a five month period, from October, 1861 to March, 1862, as did the three Giles boys of Co. G, 4th Texas from November, 1861 to April, 1862.

Only one of the six Kindred brothers of Co. F, 4th Texas escaped from bloody Antietam unharmed. Two were killed, two were wounded, and one was captured. The untouched survivor, Capt. E. T. Kindred, was wounded twice later in the war.

Two brothers, Joseph and James Tillman, enlisted in Co. H, 1st Texas, on the same day, March 20, 1862, and died of typhoid fever two days apart, two months later.

Father and son of Co. G, 5th Texas — Pvt. Elisha McDonald, Sr. was killed at Gaines' Mill and his son, Pvt. Elisha McDonald, Jr. was mortally wounded at 2nd Manassas two months later.

At Gaines' Mill, June 27, 1862, Pvt. Jake Smilie borrowed Gen. Hood's horse to perform the grisly task of moving the bodies of his two brothers, James and William, to a spot where they could be buried together.

Brothers Edward and Zebulon Bell, Co. C, 5th Texas, died in the Texas Hospital in Richmond, Va., of pneumonia within one week of each other.

In the 18th Georgia Regiment, there were five St. John brothers in Company B. Of the five, one died of pneumonia, one died in a Federal prison and three were captured.

* * * * * *

BRAVEST OF THE BRAVE

Nine color bearers of the 1st Texas Infantry Regiment were shot down in Miller's Cornfield at Antietam on September 17, 1862. The flag finally fell on the field where it was secured by the Federal troops who eventually overran the field.

Lt. Whit Randall, 1st Texas, was hit by five bullets before he died at the Wilderness.

Samuel Bailey, Co. A, 5th Texas, lost his right thumb at Gettysburg in July, 1863, and was exempted from further service. However, he rejoined the Brigade after a long convalescence a few days before the battle of the Wilderness in May, 1864. At Spotsylvania Court House on May 12, a cannon ball decapitated Bailey, spattering his brains over his comrades and driving his rifle barrel through the body of the man next to him.

In Miller's Corn Field at bloody Antietam, Pvt. Nicholas Pomeroy, Co. A, 5th Texas, heard the cry of a comrade in agony. The private spotted Lt. T. B. Boyd, shot through both legs, and lying helpless in the open field which was being swept by intense enemy artillery and rifle fire. Pomeroy ran back to the field of carnage, lifted the stricken man to his shoulder and brought the lieutenant to safety through a hail of shot and shell.

Capt. J. J. McBride, commander of Co. C, 5th Texas, was badly wounded in both legs at the Wilderness. Faced with a double amputation "and only fifteen days to survive," he requested to be placed back on his cot with the admonishment, ". . . the Yankee has never been born to kill Capt. J. J. McBride."

The plucky Captain remained in a hospital for over a year before he could return to Texas. Though his legs were three inches shorter, due to his severe wounds, he eventually learned to walk without crutches or cane.

Pvt. E. K. Goree, Co. H, 5th Texas, had his leg shattered by a bullet at the Wilderness. Left for dead, he was discovered by a burial party the following day. On the way to a field hospital, the stricken soldier fainted, fell from a horse, and was again left for dead. After several hours, Goree was picked up a second time and carried to the surgeons who amputated his leg. After his parole in April, 1865, he carved a crutch from a forked peach tree limb and walked back to Texas, a journey that took him 13 months to May, 1866.

Pvt. L. B. Dortch, Co. K, 5th Texas, had both eyes shot out at Chickamauga, September 19, 1863.

Pvt. Robert Campbell, Co. A, 5th Texas, suffered the most wounds of the brigade — six — one at 2nd Manassas, two (leg & arm) at Chickamauga, and three (head, knee, and body) at Darbytown Road (Oct. 7, 1864). However, Pvt. W. F. Strother, Co. K, 1st Texas, could have claimed that distinction when he lost all ten toes at the Wilderness (May 6, 1864).

* * * * * *

UNUSUAL DEATHS

Pvt. Asa H. Whiteside, Co. G, 4th Texas, and Pvt. James Tubb, drowned while trying to escape from Ft. Delaware, a Federal Prison, in 1864. The prison was located on an island in the Delaware River.

Asst. Surgeon, Andrew C. Crombie, 1st Texas Infantry, was killed in a train wreck on the way to Georgia for the battle of Chickamauga, and Pvt. Jas. Cartwright, Co. H, 4th Texas, was killed on the way from Texas to Virginia when his saber snagged on the door throwing him beneath the car, the wheels passing over both his legs.

Pvt. Tom N. Sutherland, Co. I, 5th Texas, dropped dead with a heart attack while on the march.

At Thoroughfare Gap, Aug. 29, 1862, two men of the Fourth

Texas were killed when hit by an unexploded tin case of grapeshot.

* * * * * *

SICK CALL

Greer W. Wood, Co. F, 4th Texas, enlisted March, 1862. He was committed to the hospital for diarrhea, May, 1862; he was in the hospital with typhoid fever, June-July, 1862; was a POW, July-August, 1863; and was in the hospital with asthma, May-June, 1864. He was out of action 7 out of 40 months in service.

On Nov. 20, 1861, 47 men from Co. K, 5th Texas were sick in a Richmond hospital and by Dec. 31, 1861, out of an assigned strength of 73, only 5 were present for duty.

Thirty members of Co. K, 5th Texas died of typhoid fever during the first six months of service.

In February and April, 1864 (East Tennessee Campaign), only one private of Co. B, 1st Texas was present for duty. The rest were absent due to sickness, on leave for wounds, and on detached duty.

Pvt. W. N. Bracknell, Co. A, 1st Texas, was sick with lung disease and rheumatism in hospitals all over the South during 1863 — Chimborazo in Richmond, General Hospitals in Lynchburg, and Farmville, Va., Episcopal Hospital at Williamsburg, and C.S.A. Hospital in Atlanta, Ga. He was reported AWOL, Nov. 1, 1863, was captured at Rodney, Miss., Nov. 7, 1863, and confined at Camp Morton, Ind. "for rest of war."

Of the thirty-seven recruits who joined Co. G, 4th Texas, in May, 1862, only eight participated in the Battle of Gaines' Mill on June 27, 1862. Twenty-nine of them were left sick in hospitals from Texas to Virginia.

* * * * * *

CLOSE CALLS

At Gaines' Mill (June 27, 1862) several men of Co. F of the 5th Texas had narrow escapes from serious wounds or death. Pvt.

J. K. "Dallas" Bryan, had both his canteen and haversack pierced by Federal bullets; while two leaden missiles passed through the blanket Pvt. Pete Mallory carried across his shoulder. At the same battle a bullet ricocheted off the cap top of Pvt. William Schultz but left him unharmed, as was Pvt. A. N. Vaughn, who had half of his mustache cut off by a rifle ball ("a close shave"). Lt. R. J. McKinnon was struck between the eyes by a spent ball but it only broke the flesh.

Capt. Samuel T. Blessing, Co. L, 1st Texas, carried a New Testament throughout the war. The testament, a gift of three young ladies of Galveston, had a corner shot off while Blessing fought at the battle of Darbytown Road, October 7, 1864.

Michael Pickett, Co. F, 4th Texas, suffered a bruised stomach by a "bomb" at Gaines' Mill (June 27, 1862).

Dick Childers, Co. E, First Texas, though unharmed, had a knapsack full of foraged biscuits torn from his back and scattered up and down the company line by a Federal cannonball at Gettysburg (July 2, 1863).

Pvt. R. E. Turner, Co. A, 18th Georgia was "bruised by a shell" during combat with Hood's Brigade.

* * * * * *

MULTIPLE WOUNDS

There were many soldiers who earned their "Red Badge of Courage" on numerous fields — the following are examples of the types of multiple wounds found in both armies during the war:

2Lt. J. M. Alexander, Co. K, 5th Texas, was wounded in the mouth and both thighs and captured at Antietam. Later exchanged, he was captured again at Gettysburg and exchanged again. He then was wounded and captured a third time at Darbytown Road, but escaped to serve until his parole at Appomattox.

Pvt. Emil Besch, Co. B, 5th Texas, had four wounds in three battles — arm at Gaines' Mill, leg at 2nd Manassas, and shoulder and head at the Wilderness.

Pvt. Wesley Cherry, Co. B, 5th Texas was wounded in the hip at Antietam, arm at Wilderness, and head at Darbytown Road.

3Lt. R. J. McKinnon, Co. F, 5th Texas, was wounded four times in a five-month period of 1864 — Wilderness, May 6; Chaffin's Farm, September 29; Darbytown Road, October 7; and Williamsburg Road, October 29.

Sgt. E. C. Powell was wounded five times (three at Chickamauga).

Sgt. Dennis A. Rowe, Co. K, 5th Texas, was wounded five times.

Pvt. Jeff Chaison, Co. F, 5th Texas, was wounded four times — Gaines' Mill, Antietam, Wilderness (hand), Darbytown Road (foot and hand), and captured twice, in 1862 and again in 1864.

T. H. Mullins, Co. F, 5th Texas, was wounded five times — Antietam, Chickamauga, Cold Harbor (chest), Bermuda Hundred (neck), and White Oak Swamp (arm).

George J. Robinson, Co. A, 5th Texas, was hit in the face at the battle of the Wilderness (May 6, 1864). The ball passed through both cheeks, and nearly severed his tongue, and broke both jaws. He had to be fed with a straw for the rest of his life.

Willis Watts was wounded six times in nine months — three at Chickamauga and three at the Wilderness. He was a member of Co. D, 5th Texas.

* * * * * *

KILLING ON TWO FRONTS

Cpl. M. T. Norris, Co. B, 4th Texas, received a furlough to Austin in the winter of 1861-62, and while there killed a man who had insulted his aunt. He later returned to the East, was promoted, and was killed at Gettysburg.

* * * * * *

IF LIFE WAS CHEAP, THEN DEATH WAS CHEAPER

When Pvt. Wade H. Coleman, Co. E, 1st Texas, died, his hearse rental and coffin cost only ten dollars.

Pvt. N. J. South, Co. K, 5th Texas, left behind eight plugs of tobacco when he died; while Pvt. William Moore of Co. C of the same regiment bequeathed only 10¢ to his heirs.

* * * * * *

TEXAS GOLD STAR MEDALS

In January, 1865, nine members of the Texas Brigade were chosen by their fellow soldiers to receive an award as the bravest men of the Brigade. The awards were gold stars sent to the Brigade by an unidentified Texas lady and presented to the nine men by brigade commander, Col. Frederick S. Bass, acting upon the orders of Gen. Robert E. Lee. Each regiment received two stars, except the Fourth Texas which received three.

The Texas Gold Star was presented to the following brave men:

First Texas Regiment
Pvt. William Durham, Co. D
Pvt. Joseph Knight, Co. H

Fourth Texas Regiment
Cpl. James Burke, Co. B
Sgt. James Patterson, Co. D
Cpl. W. C. May, Co. H

Fifth Texas Regiment
Sgt. Cadmus Wellborn, Co. F
Sgt. Jacob Hemphill, Co. H

Third Arkansas Regiment
Pvt. J. D. Staples, Co. E
Pvt. J. W. Cook, Co. H

* * * * * *

U.S. CONGRESSIONAL MEDALS OF HONOR
For Action Against Hood's Texas Brigade

Pvt. Samuel Johnson, Co. G, 9th Penn. Reserves was awarded the MOH for the capture of two battle flags of the First Texas Infantry Regiment, at Antietam, Md., September 17, 1862.

Sgt. Thomas Murphy, Co. G, 158th New York Infantry was

awarded America's highest award for valor for the capture of a flag from Gregg's (Hood's) Texas Brigade, probably the Third Arkansas battle flag, at Chaffin's Farm, Va., September 29, 1864.

Lt. Morton A. Read, Co. D, 8th New York Cavalry won the coveted medal for the capture of the Confederate battle flag of the First Texas Infantry Regiment, at Appomattox Station, Va., April 8, 1865.

* * * * * *

CONFEDERATE MEDAL OF HONOR

The Confederate Congress, in 1862, authorized a Confederate Medal of Honor to be awarded along similar lines as the U.S. Congressional Medal of Honor, however, none were awarded before the end of the war. In 1976, the Sons of Confederate Veterans meeting in national convention at Memphis, Tenn., revived the Confederate Medal of Honor to be awarded to the memory of Southern heroes of the Army and Navy.

At the 1977 SCV national convention at Dallas, Texas, the Confederate Medal of Honor was awarded to Pvt. Wilson J. Barbee, Company L, First Texas, Hood's Texas Brigade, for bravery beyond the call of duty and risk of his own life during action at Gettysburg, July 2, 1863.

Barbee was the fourth Confederate soldier to be awarded the medal. His MOH, however, was the first to be awarded publicly. The medal and citation was presented to Colonel Harold B. Simpson for permanent display at the Confederate Research Center, Hill Junior College, Hillsboro, Texas.

* * * * * *

LAST CASUALTY

Regimental Adjutant of the 4th Texas, Haywood W. Brahan, was wounded at Appomattox Court House, April 9, 1865 — the day of Lee's surrender.

* * * * * *

LAST SURVIVOR

Lt. Bolling Eldridge, Co. E, 5th Texas, fought throughout the war, was wounded twice, and was the last survivor of Hood's Texas Brigade. Eldridge passed away October 28, 1938, at Brenham, Texas.

Bibliography

PRIMARY SOURCES

GOVERNMENT DOCUMENTS AND PAPERS

Muster Rolls (bi-monthly). All companies of the First, Fourth, and Fifth Texas Volunteer Infantry Regiments; Third Arkansas Volunteer Infantry Regiment; Eighteenth Georgia Volunteer Infantry Regiment; Infantry Companies, Hampton's South Carolina Legion; Reilly's Battery, Rowan Artillery, First North Carolina Artillery Regiment, June 30, 1861-Dec. 31, 1864. Old Records Section, National Archives, Washington, D.C.

United States War Department.
The War of the Rebellion; Official Records of the Union and Confederate Armies. 128 Vols. and Atlas. Washington: Government Printing Office 1880-1901. Series I., Volumes I-LI, Part II Supplement; Series II, Vol. I; and Series IV, Volumes I-II.

_____. Collection of Confederate Records Muster and Pay Rolls-Texas. Record Group 109.

_____. Compiled Service Records of Confederate Soldiers who served in organizations from Arkansas. Micro Copy No. 317: Rolls 62-70. National Archives.

_____. Compiled Service Records of Confederate Soldiers who served in organizations from Georgia. Micro-copy No. 266; Rolls 308-314. National Archives.

_____. Compiled Service Records of Confederate Soldiers who served in organizations from North Carolina. Micro-copy No. M-270: Rolls 49-60. National Archives.

_____. Compiled Service Records of Confederate Soldiers who served in organizations from South Carolina. Micro-copy No. 267; Rolls 362-37. National Archives.

_____. Compiled Service Records of Confederate Soldiers who served in organizations from Texas. Micro-copy No. 323; Rolls 246-257, 283-293, 295-370. National Archives.

_____. Compiled Service Records of Confederate Generals and Staff Officers and Nonregimental Enlisted Men. Micro-copy No. 331; Rolls 18, 111, 131, 201, 214, 267, 271, and 272. National Archives.

BOOKS AND MANUSCRIPTS

Chilton, Frank B. (comp.) *Unveiling and Dedication of Monument to Hood's Texas Brigade and Minutes Thirty-Ninth Annual Reunion of Hood's Texas Brigade Association.* Houston: F. B. Chilton, 1911.

Davis, Nicholas A. *Chaplain Davis and Hood's Texas Brigade.* Edited by Donald E. Everett. San Antonio: Principia Press of Trinity University, 1962.

Fletcher, William A. *Rebel Private Front and Rear.* Austin: University of Texas Press, 1954.

Giles, Val C. and Mary Lasswell (ed.). *Rags and Hope.* New York: Coward-McCann, 1961.

Hamilton, D. H. *History of Company M, First Texas Volunteer Infantry, Hood's Brigade.* Waco: W. M. Morrison, 1962.

Johnson, Sid S. *Texans Who Wore the Gray.* Tyler, Texas: privately printed, 1907.

Lubbock, Francis J. *Six Decades in Texas.* Edited by C. W. Raines. Austin: Ben C. Jones Co., 1900.

Polley, J. B. *Hood's Texas Brigade.* New York: Neale, 1910.

West, John C. *A Texan In Search of a Fight.* Waco: Texian Press, 1969.

Winkler, Mrs. A. V. *The Confederate Capital and Hood's Texas Brigade.* Austin: Von Boeckmann, 1894.

ARTICLES

Hamby, Wm. R., "Hood's Texas Brigade at Sharpsburg." *Confederate Veteran,* XVI (Jan., 1908), 19-22.

——————, "Story of Hood's Texas Brigade." *Confederate Veteran,* XVIII (Dec., 1910), 563-66.

Todd, George A. "A Sketch of History. The First Texas Regiment, Hood's Brigade, Army of Northern Virginia.: *Jefferson Jimplicute,* April 2-June 11, 1909. Serialized weekly.

NEWSPAPERS

Galveston Daily News, May 8, 1874.

Galveston News, June 28, 1900.

Houston Post, Dec. 9, 1893.

Richmond Dispatch, Feb. 15 & 27, 1865.

Texas Republican, April 20, 1861.

UNPUBLISHED MATERIAL
(All material below is located in the Confederate
Research Center, Hill Junior College, Hillsboro, Tex.,
except where otherwise noted)

Bentley, R. A., "The Seven Days' Battle Around Richmond." Manuscript, N. D.

Blanton, B. H. Letters.

Bookman, I. M. Letters.

Burke, A. J. Letter, October 29, 1861.

Chilton, Frank B. Letters and Papers. (Mrs. Irene Traylor, Houston, Tex.).

Clay, Tacitus T. Letters.

Dale, Matt, Letter, June 7, 1862.

Downs, Oscar J., Diary, 1861-1862.

Edwards, William L. Letters.

Green, A. B., Diary, 1865.

Guinn, R. A. "History of the Important Movements and Incidents of the Newton Rifles." Manuscript,no date.

Hanks, O. T. "History of Captain B. F. Benton's Company, 1861-1865." Manuscript, 1921.

Hendrick, James Henry. Letters.

Joskins, Joe, "A Sketch of Hood's Texas Brigade," Manuscript written at Huntsville, Texas, 1865. Manuscript in possession of R. H. Porter Estate, Austin, Texas.

Landrum, Zach. Letters.
Murray, Jim C. Letters.
O'Neill, Miss L. D. "A Brief History of the Military Career of Her Father, J. J. O'Neill." Unpublished manuscript in the Georgia State Archives, n.d.
Owen, Samuel Tine. Letters.
Pomeroy, Nicholas, "War Memoirs." Manuscript, no date.
Quigley, R. Letters.
Rainey, A. T. Collection of letters and documents.
Sims, A. C., "Recollection of the Civil War." Manuscript. Part of the Manuscript appeared in the Jasper (Texas) *News Boy* of May 17, 1911.
Smith, Miles V. "Reminiscences of the Civil War." Manuscript, circa 1915. Manuscript in possession of R. H. Porter Estate, Austin, Texas.
Smither, J. Mark. Letters.
Tannehill, William J. Letters.
Townsend, William P. Letters.
Travis, Henry. Letters.
Williams, Watson Dugat. Letters.

OTHER SOURCES

Annual Meeting Folders, Hood's Texas Brigade Association, 1874-1933. Archives of the Confederate Research Center, Hill Junior College, Hillsboro, Texas.

Company Folders, Hood's Texas Brigade. Miscellaneous data on the various companies of Hood's Texas Brigade. Includes newspaper clippings, National Archives Material, fragments of letter and roster data. Archives of the Confederate Research Center, Hill Junior College, Hillsboro, Texas.

SECONDARY SOURCES

BOOKS

Boatner, Mark Mayo, III. *The Civil War Dictionary.* New York: David McKay Co. Inc., 1959.

Collier, Calvin L. *They'll Do To Tie To.* Jacksonville, Arkansas: Maj. James D. Warren, 1959.

Ferguson, Joseph O. (comp.). *To Those Who Wore the Gray.* Wilmington: Delaware Civil War Roundtable, 1960.

Heitman, Francis Bernard. *Historical Register and Dictionary of the United States Army.* Washington: U. S. Government Printing Office, 1903.

Johnson, Frank W. *A History of Texas and Texans.,* V Vols. N. Y.: The American Historical Society, 1914.

Kelley, Dayton. *General Lee and Hood's Texas Brigade at the Battle of the Wilderness.* Hillsboro, Texas: Hill Junior College Press, 1969.

Simpson, Harold B. *Hood's Texas Brigade: Lee's Grenadier Guard.* Waco, Texas: Texian Press, 1970.

——————. *Touched with Valor.* Hillsboro, Texas: Hill Junior College Press, 1964.

——————. *Gaines Mill to Appomattox.* Waco: Texian Press, 1963.

——————. *Hood's Texas Brigade in Poetry and Song.* Hillsboro, Texas: Hill Junior College Press, 1968.

_____ . *Hood's Texas Brigade in Reunion and Memory.* Hillsboro, Texas: Hill Junior College Press, 1974.

_____ . *The Marshall Guards.* Marshall, Texas: The Port Caddo Press, 1967.

Warner, Ezra. *Generals in Gray.* Baton Rouge: Louisiana State University Press, 1959.

Wright, Marcus J. and Harold B. Simpson (ed). *Texas in the War 1861-1865.* Hillsboro, Texas: Hill Junior College Press, 1965.

Webb, Walter P. (ed.). *The Handbook of Texas.* 2 vols. Austin: Texas State Historical Association, 1952.

UNPUBLISHED MATERIAL

Reese, Morgan M. "John Bell Hood and the Texas Brigade." Unpublished Master's Thesis, Department of History, Southwest Texas State Teachers College, 1941.

Index

Brown, J.G., 330
Brown, J.H., 212
Brown, J.J., 453
Brown, Jas., 319
Brown, Jas. Broyles, 326
Brown, Jas. H., 404
Brown, John, 66
Brown, John, 330
Brown, John F., 443, 444
Brown, John O., 73
Brown, John R., 2Lt., 254
298
Brown, John W., 79
Brown, Jos. F., 79
Brown, Larkin C., 290
Brown, Lycurgus M., 98,
Photo., 498
Brown, M.C., 198
Brown, Malcolm, 411
Brown, Mathew, 293
Brown, Nicholas E., 411
Brown, P.A., 113
Brown, R.C., 198
Brown, R.S., 444
Brown, Richard L., 460
Brown, T.P., 330
Brown, Thos. C., 265-266
Brown, Tyree H., 2Lt., 306
308
Brown, W., 395
Brown, W.C., 450
Brown, W.F., 330
Brown, W.H., 390
Brown, W.Z., 132
Brown, Wm., 311
Brown, Wm., Capt., 387
388
Brown, Wm. A., 283
Brown, Wm. Henry, 105
Brown, Wm. T., 162
Brown, Wm. W., 91, 97
Browning, R. Henry, 17
Browning, Thos. N., 411
Brownlee, A.L., 86
Brownlee, E. Presley, 85
Broyles, J.J., 326
Bruce, Horatio, 427
Bruce, J.S., 169, 183
Bruce, John C., 423-424
Bruce, Wm. T., 424
Bruen, Halsey F., 404
Bruen, Wm. R.H., 404
Brummett, E., 395
Brunson, R.S., 431
Bryan, Andrew, 212
Bryan, Chas. K., 289-290
Bryan, Felix B., 34
Bryan, J. E., 220
Bryan, J. K., 212, 559
Bryan, Jas. J., 414
Bryan, King, Lt.-Col., 167,
210
Bryan, Larkin W., 311
Bryan, Pryor L., 3Lt., 211
Bryan, Sebern, 73
Bryan, Thos. J., 34
Bryan, Thos. P., 175
Bryan, Thos. W., 212
Bryan, W.M., 212
Bryan, Wm. M., 74
Bryant, Benj., 381
Bryant, Golden D.L., 148

Bryant, Michael W., 311
Bryson, John S., 358, 359
Buchanan, Geo., 401
Buchanan, J.C., 182
Buchanan, Lafayette, 132
Buchner, C.A., 104, Photo
511
Buckett, Wm. H., 466
Buckhalter, J.W., 446
Buckley, Edw. C., 7, 8, 79
Photo., 486
Buckley, Young Archy, 74,
545
Buckner, A.W., 1Lt., 25, 26
Buckner, C.A. (See Buchner,
C.A.).
Buckner, J. B., 26
Buffalo, David, 17
Buffington, Thos. C., Capt.,
138, 140, Photo., 495
Bugg, Wm. T., 265
Buise, Jas. B., 370
Buley, Nathan, 45
Bull, John C., 319, 545
Bull, Robt. C., 319
Bull, Wm., 260
Bullaboa, Lorenzo, 460
Bullard, C.W., 420
Bullard, Chas. M.C., 265
Bullard, G.W., 420
Bullington, Francis M., 386
Bullington, J.H., 2Lt., 182
Bullington, J.M., 386
Bullington, John L., 383
Bullington, Thos. R., 383
Bullock, B.F., 148
Bullock, Cyprian, 275
Bullock, Jas. H., 40
Bullock, Jas. M., 45
Bullock, Thad W., 72, 543,
546
Bullock, Thos. S., 311
Bullock, Waller R., 2Lt., 96,
103, 111, 124
Bunch, J.V., 446
Bunch, Jas. S., 404
Bunger, W.G., 172, 205
Bunn, Wm. F., 460
Burage, Jas., 460
Burch, Jos., 245
Burden, John G., 172, 198
Burden, Jos. C., 198
Burdett, Jesse J., 441
Burdett, Reuben, 441
Burdine, J.W., 427
Burdine, Jas. H., 423
Burdine, Wm. C., 427
Burditt, Minus C., 105
Burditt, Tom P., 105
Burditt, Wm. B., 105
Burford, Robt. P., 183
Burganer, Isaac, 2Lt., 289-
290
Burges, Gideon, 119
Burges, Richard J., 119
Burges, Robt. A., 119
Burges, Wm. H., 94, 119,
Photo., 501
Burgess, Jas., 441
Burgess, Kennedy, 305
Burgess, R. Warren, 420
Burgess, Samuel E., 420

Burgess, Wm. R., Jr., 420
Burk, Z., 198
Burkhalter, John E., 410
Burke, A.J., Jr., 175
Burke, Benj., 86
Burke, E., 198
Burke, F. Marion, 86
Burke, Jas., 105, 561
Burke, John, 40, 553, Pho
482
Burke, Thos., 21
Burks, Rowland, 183
Burks, Wm., 293
Burks, Wm. P., 2 Lt., 275
Burnam, Frank M. (see Bu
ham, Frank M.
Burnaman, Sanuel E.F., 7
Burnam, Stephen H. (See
ham, Frank M.)
Burnaman, Samuel, E. F.,
Burnett, B.E.B., 395
Burnett, Dan., 126
Burnett, Lafayette, 287
Burnett, Wm. P., 390
Burney, J.C., 266
Burnham, Frank M., 105
Burnham, S.H., 40
Burnham, Stephen H., 10
Burns, A.D., Sr., 3Lt., 38
Burns, B.L., 377
Burns, Bennett W., 305
Burns, Isham L., 302
Burns, Jas. M., 302
Burns, Jas. W., 302
Burns, Joe., 113
Burns, John, 40
Burns, John H., 293
Burns, Patrick, 175
Burns, R.S., 40
Burns, Robt., Maj., 6, 169
175, 544
Burns, Wm. A., 287
Burns, Wm. B., 305
Burnside, Samuel N., 283
Buron, Wm. H., 371
Burress, John T., 1Lt., 16
Burroughs, J.J., Lt., 45
Burroughs, Sam Raymond
Photo., 485
Burroughs, T.J., 245
Burt, Jas. A., 374
Burt, John H., 390
Burton, Andrew J., 98
Burton, Jas. W., 308
Burton, Nathan N., 411
Burton, W.H.P. ("Billy"),
Burton, W.L., 183
Burtons, Jas. J., 275
Busby, Jas. H., 162
Bush, David B., 65
Bush, G. H., 15
Bush, Jas., 45
Bush, Jas., 278
Bush, Jas., 311
Bush, Jesse D., 280
Bush, W.D., 66
Bussey, John B., 58
Buster, C.R., 290
Buster, J.C., 205
Butler, Aaron, 245
Butler, Almarine H., 228
Butler, C.B., 162

Durham, Thos., 46
Durham, Wm. L., 34, 561
Durham, Wm. P., 331
Durisoe, Peter L., 414
Dutton, B. Z., 445
Duva, W. H., 451
Duvall, Jos. D., 52
Duvall, Richard P. W.,
  ("Buck"), 52, 546
Duvall, Wm. A., 52
Dwyer, Henry (see Dreyer,
  Henry)
Dwyer, Jos. E., 7
Dyer, Benj. L., 176
Dyer, Wm. T., 221
Dykeman, Wm., 198
Dykes, Jas. L., 377
Dykes, John, 370
Dysart, Americus, 377, 546
Dysart, Jas. M., 378
Dysart, L. N., 375, 378

E

Eagar, Wm. D., 302
Earle, Sam J., 124
Early, W. P., 354
Earnhart, Abraham, 466
Earnhart, Jas. P., 461
Earnhart, Robt., 461
Earnhart, Wiley, 461
Earp, A. J., 363
Earp, Ruffin, 365
Earp, Wm., 368
Easley, A., 447
Easley, Dunbar T., 275
Easley, Jas. S., 34
Easter, M. L., 114
Easter, W. C., 67
Easter, Wm., 287
Easterling, Edw. C., 404
Easterling, H. A., 245
Easters, A., 438
Eatman, Jas. A., 238
Eaton, H. L., 428
Eaton, J. J., 428
Eaton, John R., 1Lt., 306
Eaves, E. B., 86
Eaves, L. P., 365
Eddington, H. F., 114
Eddleman, L. H., 378
Eddleman, Samuel, 359
Edey, Arthur H., 176
Edgers, Jos., 184
Edgman, Abner, 263
Edgman, John, 263
Edie, Jas. A., 404
Edleman, Wm. H., 378
Edmondson, T. J., 149
Edney, Fernando C., 238
Edwards, Benj. F., 357
Edwards, Bine G., 126
Edwards, J. G., 404
Edwards, Jas., 221
Edwards, S. A., 1Lt., 336
Edwards, T. J., 198
Edwards, T. R., 59
Edwards, Wm. L., 163
Eggleston, Wm., 408
Ehringhaus, Wm. F. M., 120
Eichelberger, Walter, 414
Eidson, John, W. M., 17

Eidson, Milledge B., 414
Eikerenkoetter, John F.,
  418, 547
Eilers, I. (see Elers, I.)
Ekells, Wm. R. A., 141
Elam, Richard, 260
Elder, Geo. W., 114
Eldridge, Bolling, 3Lt., 205,
  206, 562, Photo., 527
Eldridge, Frank, 206
Eldridge, John Wesley, 99
Elers, I., 384
Elkins, Benj. P., 191
Elledge, Hugh D., 163
Elledge, John F., 163
Elkins, Oren L., 461
Eller, Farley, 461
Eller, Jacob, 461
Eller, Jas. I., 461
Eller, Milas, 461
Eller, Wm. A., 461
Elliot, John B., 133
Elliot, W. K., 46
Elliott, Daniel, 344
Elliott, David W., 365
Elliott, Jackson, 293
Elliott, Jas. H., 290
Elliott, John B., 93
Elliott, Josh, 294
Elliott, T., 447
Elliott, W. A., 17
Ellington, W. M., 34
Ellis, B. F., 361
Ellis, Compton A., 191
Ellis, E. P., 445
Ellis, J. F., 338
Ellis, J. V., 365
Ellis, Jack W., 149
Ellis, John C., 365
Ellis, John E., 191
Ellis, M. M., 359
Ellis, R. F., 359
Ellis, Richard H., 22
Ellis, W. H., 359
Ellis, Wm. G., 275
Ellis, Wm. M., 365
Ellison, Wm., 67
Ellison, Wm. G., 308
Elmendorf, David, 80
Elmore, J. F., 198
Elmore, Overton, 290, 293
Elrod, W. H., 359
Elsasser, Isaac, 176
Emanuel, E. M., 404
Emanuel, P. A., 408
Emanuel, T. S., 176
Ember (see Embro)
Embro, 117, 548
Embry, Felix M., 59
Embry, Wm. P., 329, 331
Emens, Austin, 431
Emerson, Sam H., 290
Emerson, Thos., 283
Emmons, Rufus F., 67
Enfinger, W. F., 86
Engleking, S., 46
English, Crockett, 64
English, J. G., 357
English, Wm. R., 67
Englishby, Thos. A., 269
Engram, Lawson, 293
Enke, August, 184

Enlaw, J. D., 27
Enright, Thos., 27
Epperson, H. J., Pvt., 17
Erickson, Chas., 404
Ernest, E. A., 39
Erskine, A. N., 120
Erskine, Alec M., 120
Erskine, J. H., 5
Erwin, Abel, 371
Erwin, Alonzo F., 59
Erwin, Elijah A., 347
Erwin, Jas. A., 275
Erwin, Thos., 425
Erwin, W. B., 317
Escan, John, 27
Eskew, Jas. R., 434
Eskew, Samuel A., 430
Eskew, Simeon, 434
Eskew, Young D., 431
Eskridge, G. W., 198
Eskridge, R. Thos., 46
Espey, Jas. A., 347
Espy, J. F., Capt., 345,
  346
Estes, H., 91
Estes, Jas., 431
Estes, John, 283
Estes, Obediah N., 351
Estes, W. J., 287
Estill, Ben P., 199
Estill, Black, 199
Etley, John, 17
Etters, J. J., 371
Eutsler, C. C., 199
Eustace, E. M., 346, 550
Evans, D. M., 221
Evans, Geo. E., 351
Evans, Green S., 305
Evans, J. H., 347
Evans, J. H., 447
Evans, J. R., 351
Evans, J. T., 86
Evans, J. T., 347
Evans, Jack, 46
Evans, Jas., 74
Evans, Jas. E., 59
Evans, Jas. J., 59
Evans, Jas. M., 22
Evans, Jas. W., 221
Evans, Leander L., 59
Evans, M. A. J., 206
Evans, Richard, 46
Evans, Robt., 74
Evans, T. H., 351
Evans, W. C. ("Button"),
  86, 545
Evans, W. L., 347
Evans, W. R., 428
Evans, Wm. S., 211
Evatt, Jas. L., 133
Eveleigh, H., 447
Eveleigh, J. E., 445
Eveleigh, W. R., 443, 445
Everett, Edw. N., 325
Everett, John, 461
Everett, W. D., 315
Everett, W. H., 126
Eves, C. R., 176
Eves, Lawson P., 384
Ewell, Benj. S., Col., 4
Ewing, A., Surg., 11, 17
Ewing, E. H., Maj., 6

Gray, W. H. H., 207
Gray, Wm. W., 74
Grayless, J. A., 230
Grayless, Wm. M., 230
Green, A. B., 246, Photo., 523
Green, A. G., 120
Green, B. F., 425
Green, Ben. M., 218
Green, D. H., 293
Green, David N., 163
Green, Dudley P., 312
Green, F. M., 359
Green, G. H., 199
Green, Geo., 127
Green, Geo. A., 425
Green, Henry, 347
Green, H. R., 246
Green, J. T., 441
Green, Jas. D., 437
Green, Jas. G., 192
Green, Jas. J., 163
Green, Jas. W., Jr., 408
Green, John, 157
Green, John A., 192
Green, John C., 355
Green, John F., 157
Green, John H., 404
Green, Jordan G., 400
Green, Lewis, 428
Green, R. R., 445
Green, Robt. G., 365
Green, Thos., 293
Green, Thos., 428
Green, W. H., 355
Green, W. P., 401
Green, W. S., 121
Green, Wm. A., 133
Green, Wm. L., 428
Greene, John H., 141
Greene, John Samuel, 400
Greenhaw, Jos. D., 287
Greer, John S., 60
Gregg, Alexander, 107
Gregg, John, B-Gen., 2, 3, 543, Photo., 473
Gregory, C. A., 451
Gregory, John, 157
Gregory, John B., 121
Gregory, John T., 284
Gregory, Joshua P., 320
Gregory, O. F., 451
Gregory, W. E., 260
Gregory, Wm. E., 320
Gregory, Robt., 157
Gresham, Fuller, 60
Gresham, G. W. (see Grisham, G. W.)
Gresham, Geo. W., 60
Gresham, Wm. P., 3Lt., 436
Gribble, Jas. H., 414
Grice, Wm. D., 461
Gridley, Edw., 438
Griffin, A. G. (see Griffon, A. G.)
Griffin, Benj. F., 400
Griffin, David C., 141
Griffin, Geo. G., 266
Griffin, Holbert A., 401
Griffin, J. H., 114
Griffin, J. L., 27
Griffin, Jas. B., Lt. Col., 398

Griffin, Jas. H., 457
Griffin, Lawrence M., 421
Griffin, Lemuel L., 414
Griffin, R. H., 199
Griffin, Robt., 221
Griffin, Robt. H., 421
Griffin, W. P., 318
Griffin, W. W., 355
Griffis, J. A., 60
Griffis, John C., Maj., 325, 326
Griffith, Devoreaux, 441
Griffith, Henry, 213
Griffith, John, 107
Griffith, John, 441
Griffith, Matthew A., 414
Griffon, A. G., 207
Griggs, Green, 149
Grigsby, Andrew J., 290
Grimes, W., 87
Grimsley, J. A., 447
Grisby, Daniel B., 67
Grisham, G. W., 331
Grissam, Jas. L., 441
Grissett, Wm. J., 141
Grizzle, Jno. P., 1Lt., 112
Grogard, Thos. F., 35
Groggin, Geo. F., 60
Grooms, Jas. S., 282
Grooms, Lewis, 52
Gross, Phillip A., 99
Grumbles, Perry B., 107
Grundy, John H., 2Lt., 97, 99
Gruver, G. W., 451
Gruver, J. R., 421
Guedry, S., 214
Guerin, J. P., 293
Guerin, Jas., 290
Guest, J. V., 293
Guest, Jas. N., 238
Guest, Wm. G., 365
Guice, E. S., 318
Guinn, John, 338
Guinn, R. A., 338
Guinn, T. D., 337
Gunlin, Daniel, 284
Gunn, J. N. M., 192
Gunn, John Henry, 99
Gunnels, Robt., 434
Gunning, Thos., 214
Gurley, John W., Capt., 292
Guthrie, Lewis J., 163
Guthry, Wm., 435
Guy, Wm., 27
Guynn, Wm., 199
Guyton, J. S., 360
Guyton, M. J., 362
Gwin, John, 435

H

Habersham, Rich. W., 421
Hacker, H. C., 335
Hackett, G. T., 365
Hackett, Thos. J., 365
Hackett, W. W., 428
Haddon, Jas. J., 141
Haddon, Mack E., 141
Haden, J. E., 22
Hadley, Thos. J., Capt., 313
Hafl, Samuel, 331

Hafner, John S., 238
Hagal, Jos., 157
Hagan, Chas., 80
Hagan, John, 185
Haggerty, Jas. M., 99
Haggerty, John J., 99
Hahn, Adam, 147
Hahn, Jacob, 185, Photo., 520
Hahn, John, 133
Hail, Jess M., 74
Hail, Jos. J., Jr., 75
Hail, Oscar F., 75
Haile, Benj. B., 282, 284
Hailey, John H., 192
Hairston, A. B., 221
Hairston, J. T., 234
Hairwood, T. J., 318
Halderman, J. W., 157
Hale, Benj. B. (see Haile, Benj. B.)
Hale, Chas., 221
Hale, Drury, 65
Hale, J. J., 254
Hale, J. T., 272
Hale, Jess M. (see Hail, Jess M.)
Hale, John R., 2Lt., 173
Hale, Jos. J., Jr. (see Hail, Jos. J., Jr.)
Hale, Oscar F. (see Hail, Oscar F.)
Haley, Wm., 238
Hall, A. J., 204
Hall, C. H., 453
Hall, C. L., 230
Hall, C. W., 67
Hall, Constant, 461
Hall, E. O., 408
Hall, Elijah B., 291
Hall, Jas., 312
Hall, Jas. H., 149
Hall, Jesse, 408
Hall, John J., 67
Hall, John W., 207
Hall, Livingston, 461
Hall, S., 453
Hall, S. H., 466
Hall, Stockton, 466
Hall, Thos. A., 360
Hall, W. D., 449, 451
Hall, W. S., 214
Hall, Wm. A., 99
Hall, Wm. L., 384
Hall, Zachariah B., 384
Halleck, Chas. B., 80, 551
Halling, G. W., 338
Hallmark, Richard M., 65
Hallum, Basil A. ("Bas"), 52, 546
Hallum, Joe A., 238
Hallums, Clark, Jr., 428
Ham, Geo. W., 22, 75, 246
Ham, Judge Martin Van Buren, 384
Hamby, John, 163
Hamby, Marshall, 52
Hamby, Wm. Robt., 107, 511, Photo., 499
Hamer, P. M., 451
Hamilton, A. Hughes, 399
Hamilton, Andy M., 428
Hamilton, D. H., 87, Photo., 486

Hill, A. T., 199
Hill, Alex. B., 288
Hill, Anderson, 207
Hill, Andrew W., 87
Hill, B. J. C., 3Lt., 154
Hill, C. T., 200
Hill, Chas. J.; 441
Hill, D. J., 60
Hill, Eldon, 127
Hill, Geo. W., 269
Hill, Green W., 239
Hill, J. H., 158
Hill, J. L. F., 313, 315
Hill, J. S., 207
Hill, J. T., 438
Hill, Jack, 157
Hill, Jas. C., 18
Hill, Jas. W., 283
Hill, Jesse W., 282, 284
Hill, John C., 200, 222, 239
Hill, John D., 339
Hill, John W. M. P., 112,
545
Hill, L. D., 107, Photo.,
499
Hill, Richard, 339
Hill, Richard C., 53
Hill, S. A., 339
Hill, T. M., 339
Hill, W. W., 222
Hill, Wm., 372
Hill, Wm. B., 115, 222, 239
Hill, Wm. J., 339
Hill, Wm. T., Capt., 168,
196, Photo., 518
Hillborn, N. G., 372
Hilliard, Alex H., 100
Hilliard, Elias C., 163
Hills, Wm. J., 372
Hilton, Edw., 177
Hindle, H., 27
Hindly, Jas. M., 282
Hindman, S. M., 230
Hindmond, A. D., 431
Hines, Ben C., 35
Hines, Jas. M., 47
Hines, Jos., 87
Hines, Jos. J., 100
Hines, S. M., Pvt., 18
Hines, Sy, 22
Hinnant, Boynton C., Pvt.,
18
Hinnant, Henry H., Pvt.,
18
Hinson, Abner M., 200, 550
Hinson, C. J., 378
Hinson, J. Thaddeus (see
Henson, J. Thaddeus)
Hirams, Henry C., 246
Hirams, S. C., 246
Hirsch, Henry, 335
Hirst, T. D., 95, 125
Hite, Jas. (see Hight, Jas.)
Hite, Walter H., 98
Hite, Wm. (see High, Wm.)
Hite, Wyatt (see Hight,
Wyatt)
Hitt, Malcolm C., 412
Hixson, G. M., 115
Hobbs, Jas. D., 246
Hobbs, O. P., 222
Hobbs, Wm. W., 353
Hobgood, Ferdinand, 163

Hobgood, Thos. J., 163
Hodge, Abraham A., 458
Hodge, J. D., 447
Hodge, John W., 418
Hodge, Magnus H., 163
Hodge, R., 27
Hodge, S. D., 421
Hodges, Geo. A., 121,
Photo., 502
Hodges, T., 447
Hofferer, Leonard, 466
Hoffman, F. L., 1Lt., 25,
27
Hoffman, John A., 53
Hoffman, Jos., 185
Hoffler, G. W., 107
Hoffner, Nathan J., 462
Hoffner, Wm. H., 462
Hogan, M. C., 318
Hogan, P., 453
Hogue, J. W. P., 264
Hogue, M. G., 264
Hoke, Chas. F., 400
Halbrook, Geo. C., 177
Holbrooks, John R., 391
Holcomb, A. W., 315
Holcomb, Carter, 107
Holcomb, Dennis, 280
Holcomb, T. C., 269
Holcomb, Wilson L., 100
Holcombe, Absolom, 358,
360
Holcombe, J., 387
Holcombe, Wm. W., 329
Holden, D. W., 107
Holden, F. M., 375
Holder, John W., 127
Holder, Wm. W., 425
Holiday, Jas. J., 435
Holkersmith, T. D., 275
Hollamon, Thos. H., 2Lt.,
117
Holland, B. F., 18
Holland, F. M., 163
Holland, John G., 315
Holland, Kenneth, 462
Holland, Robt. H., 438
Holland, Wm. T., 462
Hollander, Wm. M., 134
Holliday, Leonidas B., 207
Holliman, Burwell J., 47
Hollingsworth, Geo., 60
Hollingsworth, Geo. W., 339
Hollingsworth, Jos. C., 61
Hollingsworth, Nathan, 61
Hollingsworth, Robt., 339
Hollingsworth, Robt. H.,
339
Hollingsworth, Wm., 61
Hollingsworth, Wm., 339
Holloway, Jim K., 53
Holloway, L. Durham, 127
Holloway, Jas. M., 264
Holloway, John D., 255,
282, 287
Holloway, P. M. L., 264
Holloway, Robt. G., 158
Holly, Bernard, 27
Holly, Jack A., 50
Holly, N. T., 27
Holmes, A., 447
Holmes, Andrew, 408
Holmes, Curran, 239

Holmes, D. H., 408
Holmes, J. B., 378
Holmes, Jas. D., 239
Holmes, Jas. L., 239
Holmes, John F., 121
Holmes, J. H., 351
Holmes, M. C., 1Lt., 147
Holmes, Wm. A., 239
Holmes, Wm. F., 47
Holmes, Wm. H., 235
Holmes, Wm. S., 239
Holshouser, Alexander, 462
Holshouser, Crisenbery,
462
Holshouser, Jas., 466
Holshouser, Michael, 462
Holshouser, Rufus, 462
Holstein, Moses N., 414
Holt, A. C., 149
Holt, A. W., 239
Holt, D., 27
Holt, F. M., 269
Holt, Jonathan, 269
Holton, D., 246
Holtzman, Benj. N. (see
Hultsman, Benj. N.)
Home, Osker S., 299
Honbarger, John, 462
Honea, S. S., 61
Honea, Thos., 207
Honea, W. A., 61
Honeycutt, H. E., 53
Honingsburger, J., 61, 545
Hood, A. B., 239
Hood, John Bell, Gen., 2,
3, 90, 541, 542, 543,
Photo., 470
Hood, Wm. C., 309
Hood, Wm. W., 348
Hooker, Jesse, 68
Hooker, Robt., 47
Hooks, Gilmore, 47
Hooks, Wm. L., 385
Hooper, Samuel R., 75
Hoover, Wm. P., 53
Hope, Adam, 3Lt., 39, 41
Hopkins, F. Columbus, 35
Hopkins, Frank M., 53
Hopkins, J. C., 149
Hopkins, Jas. M., 99
Hopper, Wm. J., 50
Hopson, Briggs W., 107
Horn, Jess M., 296
Horn, T. S., 391
Horne, Luck L., 127
Horne, Paul, 104, 546
Horne, Robt. E., 305
Horner, Wm., 61
Horton, Alfred M., 12, 57
Horton, C. C., 421
Horton, D. M., 61
Horton, E. R., 451
Horton, Fred S., 61
Horton, Jos. W., Jr., 418
Horton, J. J., 421
Horton, Jos. W., Jr., 418
Horton, W. S., 421
Horton, Warren H., 107
Hoslie, Belthasa, 288
Hotchkiss, G. B., 288
Hough, F. T., 227
Hough, Wm. B., 192
Houk, Wm., 360

Millard, Nathaniel, 271, 273
Millard, Watson C., 82
Miller, A., 69
Miller, Caleb A., 463
Miller, David L., 463
Miller, Edw. G., 75
Miller, Geo. C., 178
Miller, H., 340
Miller, H. K., 376
Miller, Harrison, 463
Miller, Henry Benj., 2Lt., 25 29
Miller, Henry C., 291
Miller, Henry M., 463
Miller, Horatio, 24
Miller, J. Abney, 415
Miller, J. M., 421
Miller, John, 41
Miller, John A., 2Lt., 289
Miller, John D., 128
Miller, John H., 348
Miller, John J., 215
Miller, John S., 182
Miller, Julius A., 340
Miller, L. W., 223
Miller, M. Erskine, 1Lt., 118, 122
Miller, N. J., 2Lt., 375, 379
Miller, R. S., 158
Miller, Poland, 463
Miller, S., 421
Miller, Uriah, 458
Miller, W. P., 348
Miller, Wm. R., 1Lt., 57
Millett, Leonidas, 122
Miller, Jos., 332
Millican, Edw. B., 108
Millican, Larkin, 35
Millican, Wm., 151
Milligan, R. J., 352
Millington, J. A., 215
Mills, C. Styles, 12, 41
Mills, G. W., 193
Mills, Jas. H., 231
Mills, J. H., 355
Mills, M. J., 309
Mills, Nat J., 1Lt., 155, 158
Mills, Perry, M., 62
Milton A., 164
Milwood, J., 366
Mims, J. P., 332
Mines, P., 344
Minor, Arthur L., 108
Minshew, Joel, 200
Minschew, John R., 261
Minter, Franklin M., 101
Minter, John, 47
Mintz, C. H., 445
Mise, Jeremiah, 435
Misenheimer, Dan. J., 463
Missroon, Jas., 408
Mitchell, B. Frank, 35
Mitchell, C. J., 200
Mitchell, Elias, Jr., 297
Mitchell, Geo. W., 355
Mitchell, Isaiah, 101
Mitchell, John, 356
Mitchell, John, 240
Mitchell, John F., 372
Mitchell, John T., 344
Mitchell, Jos. N., 273

Mitchell, J. R., 348
Mitchell, L. A., 200
Mitchell, Luico, 2Lt., 456
Mitchell, Robt., 95, 119
Mitchell, Robt., 240
Mitchell, Russell C., 69, 540
Mitchell, S.J., 115
Mitchell, Thos. H., 240
Mitchell, Thos. R., 151
Mitchell, W. J., 340
Mitchell, Wm., 279
Mitchell, Wm., 297
Mitchell, Wm. H., 158
Mitchell, Wm. J., 466
Mitchum, J., 447
Mitchum, S., 447
Mitchum, T. B., 445
Mitts, C., 374
Mixon, C. M., 36
Moate, J. W., 387
Mobray, Jos., 215
Mock, Geo. Y., 261, 320
Moffeit, Soloman D., 69
Moncrief, C. E., 208
Moncrief, Sterling P., 267
Monday, P. C., 466
Monell, A. G., 178
Monihan, Thos., 421
Monroe, Geo., 186
Monroe, John (see Munrow, John)
Monroe, John P., 387
Montgomery, Alex., 65
Montgomery, Jas., 285
Montgomery, Jas. W., 309
Montgomery, Jos. W., 143
Montgomery, Robt., 69
Montgomery, Robt. M., 50
Montgomery, S. W., 115, 235
Montgomery, T. Jeff, 240
Montz, Chas., 101
Moodie, John R., 215
Moody, Anderson, 297
Moody, E. A., 445
Moody, E. R., 447
Moody, M. E., 445
Moody, Sam. O., 36
Moody, Sterling D., 193
Moody, Urbin E., 285
Moon, Lewis V., 62
Mooney, Jas. M., 101
Mooney, Jas. Peter, 366
Mooney, W. A., 366
Mooney, Wm. D., 101
Moore, David, 426
Moore, D. D., Capt., 20
Moore, E. R., 173
Moore, G. W., 224
Moore, G. W., 316
Moore, Geo. W., 295, 297
Moore, Harrison, 267, 316
Moore, Henry G., 48
Moore, Henry W., 401
Moore, Isham, Capt., 443
Moore, J. D., 193
Moore, J. H., 62
Moore, J. J., 348
Moore, J. T., 69
Moore, J. T., 348
Moore, Jackson, 1Lt., 321
Moore, Jas. A., 69

Moore, Jas. A., 297
Moore, Jas. W., 311
Moore, Jeff, 426
Moore, Joel, 261
Moore, John, 224
Moore, John B., 36
Moore, John H., 366
Moore, L. P., 208
Moore, M. C., 115
Moore, N. P., 128
Moore, R. E., 115, Photo., 501
Moore, S. Dunk, 261
Moore, S. F., 349
Moore, Thos. L., 288
Moore, W. Allen, 261
Moore, W. G., 285
Moore, W. O., 36
Moore, Wm., 439, 561
Moore, Wm. M., 193
Moore, Wm. W., 85
Mooring, Chas. G., 143
Mooring, Jas. S., 143
Morehead, Wm., 428
Moreland, J. T. L., 48
Morey, Harvey, 224
Morgan, A. B., 128
Morgan, A. G., 48
Morgan, Andrew, 392
Morgan, B. B., 349
Morgan, B. G., 344
Morgan, Benj. P., 436, 439
Morgan, Camy W., 458
Morgan, Dan. M., 349
Morgan, Daniel M., 346
Morgan, Daniel P., 463
Morgan, Drew F., 240
Morgan, G., 441
Morgan, Geo. D., 349
Morgan, Green, 88, 545
Morgan, J. P., 2Lt., 345, 349
Morgan, Jackson S., 285
Morgan, Jas. H., 314, 316
Morgan, John, 392
Morgan, Jos., 463
Morgan, Jos. F., 288
Morgan, L. J., 344
Morgan, R. D., 340
Morgan, Rich. L., 340
Morgan, Thos. J., 340
Morgan, W. J., 340
Morgan, Wm. E., 442
Morgan, Wm. G. H., 309'
Morgan, Wm. O., 235
Morris, A. C., 147
Morris, Andrew J., 265, 267
Morris, Benj. F., 23
Morris, C. J., 231
Morris, Chas. L., 109
Morris, Christopher C., 69
Morris, E. L., 379
Morris, F. M., 69
Morris, Henry N., 261
Morris, J. A., 69
Morris, J. M., 370, 372
Morris, John, 178
Morris, John W., 392
Morris, Jos., 442
Morris, Leroy M., 309
Morris, Martin, 372
Morris, Robt., 201

Morris, S. A. (see Morriss, S. A.)
Morris, T. R., 158
Morris, Thos., 316
Morris, W. L., 23
Morris, Wm., 135
Morris, Wm. B., 309
Morris, Wm. G., 69
Morris, Wm. W., 332
Morrison, C. H., 41
Morrison, C. T., 201
Morrison, Dan, 231
Morrison, Rich. T., 405
Morrison, Robt. H., 122
Morrison, Robt. V., 405
Morriss, S. A., 240
Morriss, Simon, 32
Morrissey, Jas., 29
Morrissey, John, 186
Morrow, Daniel M., 88
Morrow, John, 392
Morse, Geo. T., 143
Morse, Geo. W., 178
Morse, Henry A., 178
Morse, W. W., 443, 445
Morse, Wm., 164, 549
Moseley, E. L., 335
Moseley, Sidney E., 109, Photo., 509
Mosely, Henry E., 76
Mosely, W. C., 432
Moses, A. DeLeon, 418, 550
Moses, Isaac Calhoun, 421
Moss, A. M., 36
Moss, G. F., 36
Moss, Henry E., Capt., 33, 36
Moss, N. P., 189
Moss, Wm. O., 36
Moss, Wm. V., 109
Mosteller, A. H., 364, 366
Mosteller, Andrew J., 368
Mosteller, Ezekiel, 366
Mosteller, Geo. M., 366
Mote, W. M., 344
Motes, Hiram, 88
Motes, J. M., 88
Motes, Wm. A., 366
Mound, John, 267
Moyle, Matthew, 457
Muir, W. A., 208
Muldoon, John, 215, 547
Muldrow, John T., 143
Mulholland, B. E., 193
Mulise, F. M., 264
Mulkai, Thos. D., 405
Mull, G. S., 332
Mullany, Thos., 305
Mullay, J. C. K., 42, 550
Mullens, F. Coella, 128
Mullens, Thos. Macon, 128, Photo., 502
Mullens, W. T., 128
Mullinix, J. P., 62
Mullins, J. D., 332
Mullins, N. W., 208
Mullins, R. D., 332
Mullins, T. H., 208, 560
Mulvey, Jos. P., 29
Mulvey, Michael, 301
Munce, Chas. (see Montz, Chas.)

Mundy, Mike, 261
Munford, Thos. H., 101
Munroe, August, 29
Munrow, John, 224
Murchison, John D., 364
Murchison, R. J., 29
Murchison, Wm., 193
Murdock, E. F. M., 360
Murphy, B. F., 76
Murphy, Henry C., 282
Murphy, J. W., 82
Murphy, Jas. A., 76
Murphy, Jeremiah, 101
Murphy, John, 201
Murphy, John, 288
Murphy, Mortimer, 69
Murphy, P., 267
Murphy, P. M., 183
Murphy, Pat, 29
Murphy, Patrick, 18, 547
Murphy, Thos., 561
Murphy, Vinson W., 280
Murphy, W. S., 426
Murray, J. A., 196
Murray, J. H., 201
Murray, Jas., 340
Murray, Jas. C., 135, Photo., 503
Murray, Jasper N., 265, 267
Murray, John, 2Lt., 446
Murray, John David, 131, Photo., 503
Murray, Jos., 357
Murray, Robt. W., 135, Photo., 503
Murray, Thos., 88
Murray, W. W., 36
Murray, Wm. A., 353
Murrell, Chas. P., 426
Murrell, O., 447
Murrow, O. H., 452
Muse, Jas. T., 143
Muse, W. T., 208
Musgrove, Miles, 356
Musgrove, Sampson G., 356
Mussy, Hart, 101
Mustard, Robt. W., 403, 405
Myer, Nels A., 147
Myers, A. L., 370, 372
Myers, B. G., 248
Myers, David, 415
Myers, Henry, 179
Myers, Jacob S., 405
Myers, Marion F., 151
Myers, Newel, 305
Myers, Thos. J., 151
Myers, W. H. H., 201
Myers, Wm. H., 466, Photo., 520
Myers, Wm. W., 1Lt., 456
Mynatt, Donald M., 1Lt., 50, 54
Mynatt, W. Park, 2Lt., 13, 50, 54
Myres, Z. E., 428
Myrick, F. B., 316

Mc

McAbee, A., 421

McAlexander, John, 227
McAlister, Chas. A., 135
McAlister, Daniel M., 135
McAlister, Francis M., 276
McAlister, J. H., 223
McAlister, W. A., 75
McAllister, J. D., 315
McAllister, Peter, 100
McAlpine, Jas. M., 2Lt., 33, 35
McAlpine, Thos. J., 35
McAnally, Thos., 23
McAnnelly, C. W., 104
McAnnich, Elias B., 223
McArthur, Chas., 267
McBee, S. B., 68
McBride, Caleb, 62
McBride, Isaac W. (see McBryde, Isaac W.)
McBride, J. J., Capt., 168, 189, 556
McBride, Oliver, 88
McBryde, Isaac W., 364, 366
McCain, Andrew J., 264
McCall, Howard, 428
McCall, Jas. R., 273
McCall, John F., 273
McCain, John H., 284
McCalister, Wm. H., 208
McCall, C. S., 417, 418
McCall, Jas. C., 164
McCall, Thos. W. H., 69
McCall, W. H., 421
McCall, Wm. K., 276
McCally, Chas., 2Lt., 211, 214
McCammur, J. W., 273
McCann, Thos. J., 135
McCann, Washington, 231
McCarly, Thos. H., 405
McCarter, J. D. P., 28
McCarthy, Ed, 28
McCarthy, W. C., 108
McCarthy, Wesley L., 322
McCarty, Chas. W., 81, Photo., 487
McCarty, Ed. V., 214
McCarty, John, 69
McCarty, John M., 81
McCarty, Jos. J., 100, 551
McCarty, Jos. M., 372
McCarty, Thos. L., 81
McCarty, Wm. J., 211
McCary, W. L., 214
McCaskill, Neill E., 69
McCatherin, John B., 100
McCelon, Wm. K., 35
McClain, Rufus R., 88
McClain, W. R., 88, Photo., 486
McClain, W. Z., 85
McClanahan, Reuben, 54
McClannahan, Jas. E., 23
McClaugherty, Wm. H., Capt., 118, 122
McClellion, John P., 426
McClelland, Wm. K. (see McCelon, Wm. K.)
McClendon, Alfred S., 72
McClendon, L. M., 88
McClennen, Eli, 291

McMillan, A. M., 186
McMillan, Duncan D., 47
McMillen, Wm. P., 303
McMinn, E., 88
McMinn, H., 88
McMinn, Jos. C., 3Lt., 85
McMorris, J. M., 158
McMullen, Bernard, 108
McMurray, A. J., 1Lt.,
387, 388
McMurray, Robt. E., 265,
267
McMurry, A. G., 392
McNeely, J. M., 428
McMurtry, John A., 171,
174
McNeal, J., 441
McNeeley, John, 231
McNeely, John O., 426
McNeely, Josiah K., Capt.,
423, 426
McNeeley, Thos. G., 164
McNeely, J. D., 122
McNeese, Parriot Geo.
Washington, 240
McNelley, Barney, 75
McNeil, A., 421
McNeill, Alex. H., 307, 309
McNeillis, D., 186
McNew, G. W., 29
McNulty, Frank, 231
McNulty, Haines, 23
McPhail, Jas. A., 320
McPhail, Rufus, 261
McPhall, Campbell M., 108
McPherson, D. W., 208
McPruett, Wilson, 223
McQuade, Jas., 405
McQueen, Geo., 41
McRae, C. G., 29
McRae, C. G., 47
McRae, John C., 261
McRay, F., 385
McRay, L. P., 447
McRee, Wm. Robt., 240
McRunnels, W. A., 18
McVey, Wm., 215
McWhorter, J. M., 428
McWhorter, Wm. F., 428
McVoyman, B. F., 115

N

Nabors, B. F., 218
Nabors, John B., 282, 285
Nabors, Wm. A., 218
Nadle, W. B., 1Lt., 25, 29
Nagle, Jas., 82, Photo., 487
Nagle, Jos., 82, Photo., 487
Nalley, A. J., 376, 379
Nally, Benson, 362
Nance, Constantine P., 224
Nance, Jas. W., 269
Nash, Edw. W., 435
Nash, Frank M., 208
Nash, H. C., 128
Nash, Thos., 3Lt., 204
Nations, Francis, 101
Nations, Robt. H., 101
Nations, Thos. J., 280
Naulty, Thos., 248
Naurath, Wm., 135

Nave, D. W., 362
Nave, J. A., 358, 360
Nave, W. R., 362
Navis, Henry, 151
Nawls, Bryant, 310
Neal, B., 453
Neal, Chas. E., 466
Neal, David, 466
Neal, Frank S., 143
Neal, J. H., 158
Neal, John N., 318
Neal, Reason L., 273
Neel, Jas. M., 269
Neely, John Isiah, 279
Neighbors, Henry T., 426
Neighbors, Jas. W., 193
Neighbors, John L., 193
Neil, J. P., 29
Neill, Edw. F., 435
Nelms, Everand, P., 144
Nelms, H. E., 340
Nelms, Jesse C., 201
Nelms, W. F., 186
Nelms, W. M., 201
Nelson, Arnold J., 276
Nelson, J. W., 29
Nelson, John, 82
Nelson, R. Manning, 419
Nelson, Robt. M., 432
Nelson, T. F., 432
Nelson, Terry, 442
Nelson, Theo. M., 419
Nelson, Wm. Calvin, 2Lt.,
420
Nesbit, Cyrus D., 1Lt.,
429-430
Nesbit, J. S., 362
Nesbit, John P., 435
Netherly, Jas. R., 179
Netherly, T. W., 201
Nettles, C. B., 445
Nettles, H. B., 449, 452
Nettles, J. H., 248
Nettles, Jos. H., 144
Nettles, W. D. S., 248
Nettles, W. Thos., 20
Nevills, D. E., 151
Nevills, Thos. G., 261
Nevins, Jas., 439
New, John, 232
New, Jos. S., 1Lt., 189, 193
New, Robt. E., 299
Newbern, Bradford B.,
307, 310
Newman, Christopher G.,
291
Newman, D. J., 392
Newman, Daniel A., Capt.,
251, 292
Newman, J. F., 36
Newman, M. Harvey, 88
Newman, Thos. J., 240
Newman, Wm., 29
Newsom, Elias, 54
Newsom, Joel, 356
Newsom, John, 54
Newton, J. S., 428
Newton, Lewis D., 288
Newton, N. M., 135
Newton, Richard M., 292
Neyland, A. C., 48
Niblett, R. S., 208

Nicholas, Benj. F., 267
Nichols, A., 330, 332
Nichols, A. W., 109, Photo.,
511
Nichols, Francis M., 273
Nichols, Franklin C., 82
Nichols, Geo. W., 109
Nichols, J. C., 332
Nichols, John B., 62
Nichols, Lindsey J., 366
Nichols, W. O., 318
Nicholson, Albert R., 410
Nicholson, Benj. E., Col.,
398
Nicholson, Jackson, 29
Nicholson, John B., 82
Nicholson, John T., 414
Nickols, A. C., 288
Nipper, A., 447
Nipper, D. W., 445
Nix, J. L., 442
Nix, John L., 144
Nix, W. Henry, 439
Nix, W. P., 44
Nixon, G. M., 116
Nixon, R. L., 344
Noblack, Thos. H., 349
Noble, Dallas, 316
Noble, E. A., 173
Noble, J. B., 316
Noble, J. O., 72
Noble, Jas. R., 116
Noble, Jas. S., 314, 316
Noble, L. R., 316
Noble, Milton C., 2Lt.,
6, 45, 48
Noble, R. L., 76
Noble, R. P., 316
Noble, S. P., 316
Nobles, J. C., 215
Noe, J. W., 215
Noel, Benjamin C., 82
Nolan, Thos. F., Capt., 251,
287
Noles, John, 392
Norford, Jas. W. F., 69
Norford, John S., 69
Norman, John P., 297
Norman, P. W., 224
Norman, Yewan A., 299
Norris, Alex, 447
Norris, Francis M., 310
Norris, Geo. W., 285
Norris, Isaiah E., 385
Norris, Jesse W., Capt.,
313
Norris, John, 285
Norris, John, 344
Norris, John T., 267
Norris, Jos., 285
Norris, Jos. A., 62
Norris, Moses T., 109, 560
Norris, Paschal, 285
North, John R., 352
Northcutt, T. H., 332
Norton, Alonzo B., 215
Norton, E., 445
Norton, J. S., 171, 172,
179
Norton, W., 116
Norvell, Robt. F., 164
Norvell, Thos. M., 72

Piper, Wm. L., 109
Pippen, T. J., 318
Pirtle, Sam, 201
Pistole, Thos. R., 194
Pitman, Giles C., 279
Pitman, John, 312
Pitman, Wm. H., 101
Pitt, Benj. F., 464
Pittman, David T., 426
Pittman, J. W., 76
Pittman, Jos. W., 458
Pitts, C., 447
Pitts, Chas., 408
Pitts, Jesse, 55
Pitts, W. A., 318
Pitts, W. S., 368
Plagge, C., 104
Plasters, H. Frank, 144
Plasters, Jos. H., 144
Platt, J. W. G., 159
Plethandhal, S., 299
Plowden, G. Whitfield, 419
Plowden, J. Belton, 419
Plowden, W. B., 421
Plummer, F. W., 179
Plunkett, C. T., 341
Plunkett, L., 341
Plunkett, W. F., 341
Plymale, A., 432
Poague, Jas. R., 42
Pogue, Levi S., 136
Pogue, Thos. A., 267
Poland, F. M., 179
Polk, J.M., 159
Polk, Robt. J., 62
Polley, Jos. B., 93, 136, 512, Photo., 503
Pollock, Henry, 209
Pollock, Jas. Thos. 385
Polson, F. M. (see Polston, F. M.)
Polson, G. Mack (see Polston, G. Mack)
Polson, Jonathan (see Polston, Jonathan)
Polson, Trustin P. (see Polston, Trustin P.)
Polston, F. M., 337, 341
Polston, G. Mack, 341
Polston, Jonathan, 341
Polston, Trustin P., 341
Pomeroy, Nicholas, 179, 556
Ponce, D. R., 1Lt., 235, 241
Ponder, Jeff, 88
Ponder, P. H., 379
Ponds, Robt., 464
Pool, Elbert, 224
Pool, Henry C., 464
Pool, I. M., 224
Pool, J., 447
Pool, J. H., 439
Pool, Jas. H., 194
Pool, Jas. M., 219
Pool, Josh W., 48
Pool, S., 421
Pool, Wm., 48
Poole, Amos N., 76
Poole, Felix, 445
Poor, A. Jackson, 426
Poor, John L., 393
Poor, Sam. E., 428
Pope, A. W., Lt., 32, 38, 44

Pope, Ben S., 42
Pope, D., 428
Pope, E., 88
Pope, Jas. W., Capt., 6, 12, 42
Popham, W. L., 393
Poppenheim, Christopher P., 403, 405, 547
Poppenheim, John L., 405
Porcher, Chas. P., 406
Porter, D. A., 445
Porter, J. A., 445
Porter, J. W., 36
Porter, King D., 264
Porter, Otho N., 464
Porter, Proctor P., Capt., 146, Photo., 496
Porter, W., 445
Porter, Wm. H., 82
Porterfield, Jos. R., 312
Posey, A. J., 55
Posey, A. W., 109
Posey, Jackson, 55
Posey, W. N., 426, 432
Postell, J. G., 406
Postlewaite, Chas. S., 3Lt., 15, 16
Poteet, Arthur N., 101
Potter, R. P., 346, 349
Potter, Wm. M., 349
Potts, A. Wayne, 349
Potts, Jefferson, 372
Potts, John M., 349
Poupart, John, 82
Powell, E. C., 36, 560
Powell, Henry C., 76
Powell, J., 367
Powell, J. W., 241
Powell, John B., 276
Powell, Robt. M., Col., 2, 4, 167, 196, Photo., 475
Powell, T. D., 1 Lt., 16
Powell, W. L., 447
Powell, Wm. P., 169, 201, Photo., 515
Powers, Jas. M., Capt., 326
Powers, Jesse, Lt., 373
Powers, John, 298
Powers, John, 310
Powers, John H., 62
Powers, Reuben J. J., 293
Powers, S. ————, 382
Powers, Wm. T., 426
Poyas, John E., 406
Prater, Virgil, 82
Prather, E. J., 370, 372
Prather, Wm. L., Col., 541
Prather, Wm. V., 341
Pratt, H., 70
Pratt, Henry, 186
Pratt, Jas. C., 82
Prescott, W. D., 39
Preston, W. B., 39
Preston, Wm., 261
Prewit, Cass (see Pruitt, Cass)
Price, ————, 453
Price, B. F., 1Lt., 72, Photo., 481
Price, Bartholomew F., 412
Price, David, 194
Price, E. M., 395
Price, E. P., 395

Price, Elijah, 76
Price, Francis L., Capt., 4
Price, Frank L., 91, 104
Price, Frederick, 224
Price, John, 385
Price, John, 111, 548
Price, John, 415
Price, John R., 273
Price, John T., 1Lt., 104, 548, Photo., 509, 511
Price, Robt. D., 224
Price, Russell, 164
Price, Sam, 215
Price, T. D., 333
Price, Thos., 415
Price, Thos. Dan, 410, 412
Price, Thos. S., 263
Price, Wm. B., 164
Pridgen, John J., 194
Pridgen, T. J., 189
Priest, M. V., 333
Priest, P. W., 335
Priest, Pinkney C., 333, 546
Prince, J. M., 372
Prior, Sam W., 2Lt., 306, 310
Pritchard, Barton R., 273
Priest, John, 182
Prisythe, J. H., 76
Pritchard, W. P., 70
Pritchard, Wm. D., 70
Pritchett, Jas. R., 361
Probert, John, 23
Proseler, Andrew J., 76
Prue, Marshal, 215
Pruett, Edmond, 211
Pruett, Jas. C. (see Pratt, Jas. C.)
Pruitt, Argalus P., 48, 545
Pruitt, Cass, 277
Pruitt, W. A., 293
Pryor, Sam W. (see Prior, Sam W.)
Pryor, Wm., 312
Puckett, G. R., 179
Puckett, Lemuel, 109
Pugh, Elbert E., 55, 545
Pugh, John D., 259, 261
Pugh, Robt. A., 262
Pugh, Whittington T., 298, 546
Puller, Jas., 466
Pumphrey, Dennis D., 288
Pumphrey, Lewis, 287
Puritt, W. A., 189
Purnell, John J., 312
Purnell, W. T., 42
Purseley, T. Lewis, 159
Purser, H. F., 395
Pursley, Samuel C., 267
Pursley, ————, 258
Puryear, Wm. E., 109
Putnam, O. W., 2Lt., 358
Putney, D. E., 186
Pyron, Chas. W., 333
Pyron, Thos. Jeff., 333

Q

Qualls, Ben W., 241
Qualls, Geo. S., 144, Photo., 505

Schuler, John, 110
Schultz, Henry, 82, 547
Schultz, Henry P., 83
Schutz, John, 442
Schultz, W. J., 144
Schultz, Wm., 136
Schultz, Wm., 216, 559
Schwarting, Fred, 83
Schwceir, Geo., 136
Scoggin, Wm. D., 2Lt., 259
Scofield, W. C. (see Scorefield, W. C.)
Scorbin, Wm. J., 262
Scorefield, W. C., 232
Scotie, Geo. B., 427
Scott, A. H., 92
Scott, Alexander J., 83
Scott, Anderson, 312
Scott, B. S., 286
Scott, Garrett, 144
Scott, Geo. M., 194
Scott, Geo. W., 393
Scott, Geo. Washington, 83
Scott, H. M., 328
Scott, H. M., 335
Scott, J. B., 144
Scott, J. F., 202
Scott, J. F., 341
Scott, Jas., 435
Scott, Jas., 30
Scott, John B., 388
Scott, John B., 393
Scott, John D., 333
Scott, John G., 7, 13, 55
Scott, M., 395
Scott, N. L., 393
Scott, S. F., 341
Scott, S. L., 63
Scott, Sam M., 393
Scott, T. B., 202
Scott, Thos. J., 23
Scott, W. C., 42
Scott, W. L., 393
Scott, W. M., 276
Scott, Wm. F. (or H.), 48
Scott, Wm. G., 23
Scott, Wm. M., 426
Scriven, R. H., 406
Scruggs, Geo. W., 70
Scully, Chas., 70
Scwen, T. F., Capt., 351
Seaford, Daniel A., 466
Seaford, M. H., 406
Seale, Chas. J., 1Lt., 265, 268
Seale, Jas., 265, 268
Seales, J. R., 202
Seamans, John W., 341
Seargent, Jas. B., 152
Seargent, Thos., 152
Searle, Edwin B., 25
Sears, D., 453
Seay, A. B., 152
Seay, Thos. G., 55
Sedberry, J. D., 19
Sedgley, J. T., 204
Seigler, Elias, 415
Self, John M., 413
Self, M. M., 136
Self, P. P. T., 159
Seller, John S., 415

Sellers, L. J., 447
Sellers, T. B., 447
Sellers, Wm. H., Col., 5, 168, 173, Photo., 476
Selman, B. T., 70
Selman, Thos. J., Capt., 125, 129, Photo., 493
Semmes, T. M., 1Lt., 254, 258
Senne, Henry, 187
Sensebaugh, Wm., 209
Sergeant, Andrew H., 136
Serois, Jas., 232
Sessions, E. G., 159
Sessions, John G., 426
Sessions, T. J., 159
Sessoms, Nathan H., 464
Setser, P., 19
Settle, Chas. F., 180
Settle, E. B., Capt., 170
Settle, H. G., 180
Sewall, Jas. R. G., 341
Seward, Columbus Dighton, 241
Seward, J. R., 152
Seward, John, 393
Sexsmith, Wm. T., 305
Shackelford, J. B., 408
Shackleford, E., 197, 202
Shaffer, H. E., 96, 144
Shamburger, Sam, 89
Shamburger, Thos., 55
Shannon, Samuel S., 298
Shanoski, Chas., 202
Sharp, Charley F., 14, 45, 546
Sharp, Eldred C., 129
Sharp, F. Marion, 76
Sharp, H. H., 225
Sharp, Henry, 288
Sharp, J. A., 225
Sharp, Jas. H., 152
Sharp, Robt., 225
Sharp, S. W., 225
Sharpe, W. Anderson, 76
Shaver, Green D., 70
Shaver, Noah, 264
Shaw, E. C., 393
Shaw, E. D., 393
Shaw, Henry, 356
Shaw, J. Alexander, 232
Shaw, J. R., 159
Shaw, J. T., 202
Shaw, John, 341
Shaw, John A., 37
Shaw, Wm. H., 341
Shaylor, J. D., 445
Shaylor, John, 447
Shea, Henry C., 216
Shealey, G. W., 447
Shean, Alex. Crittenden, 303
Shearer, John A., 268
Shears, W. B., 280
Shehane, Wm. R., 70
Sheldon, Chas., 180
Shelley, J. A., 333
Shelley, Richard, 349
Shelton, J. D., 225
Shelton, J. E., 330
Shelton, Jas., 318
Shelton, Wm. A., 8, 83
Shepard, W. G., 14

Shepherd, Jos. H., 180
Shepperd, Silas, 457
Shepherd, W. G., 83
Shepherd, Webb, 187
Sheppard, Lewis, 299
Sheppard, T. H., 225
Shepperd, Eli, 110
Sherburne, Geo., Jr., 333
Sherer, Jas. C., 263
Sheridan, Jacob L., 1Lt., 64
Sheridan, John H., 70
Sheridan, L. E., 70
Sherman, Geo., 333
Sherman, Jos. W., 209
Sherman, W. L., 202
Sherrill, Alfred, 225
Sherrill, D. M., 225
Sherrill, J. G., 225
Sherrill, Jas., 225
Sherrod, Randall, 76
Shide, J. H., 48
Shields, Chas., 187
Shields, Isaiah, 232
Shillings, G. A., 194
Shinn, John H., 333
Shipman, Samuel, 360
Shippy, Wm. H., 269
Shirley, Isaac S., 310
Shirley, R. L., 225
Shirley, T. M., 225
Shockley, J. H., 349
Shockley, W. S., 346, 350
Shores, J. D., 276
Short, Drewry B., 298
Short, Jas., 187
Short, John, 241
Short, Wm. H., 241
Shotwell, John I., Capt., 5, 20
Shotwell, Thos. B., 20
Shotwell, Wm. B., 20
Shropshire, J. Winkfield, 11, 32, 545
Shumate, Wm. M., 123
Sicorby, Jas., 30
Side, J. E., 63
Sides, J. E. (see Side, J. E.)
Silk, Wm., 361
Silks, Wm. (see Silk, Wm.)
Silman, J. B., Capt., 345
Silverbaugh, D., 145
Simerell, C., 395
Simkins, Wm. S., Lt., 407
Simmons, E. A. H., 447
Simmons, Edw., 110, 552
Simmons, J. A., 112
Simmons, J. H., 446
Simmons, J. W., 159
Simmons, J. Wright, 123, 552
Simmons, T. J., 232
Simmons, Thos., 216
Simmons, Thos. S., 101
Simmons, W. B., 194
Simmons, Wiley W., 232
Simmons, Wm. H., 449, 452
Simms, Dave F., 37
Simms, J. N., 356
Simms, Smith D., 83
Simms, Wm., 180
Simon, 454, 548

Simons, J. M. (or S. H.), 341
Simpson, B. C., 180
Simpson, B. F., 317
Simpson, Hiram, 9, 232
Simpson, G. C., 429
Simpson, Harold B., 562
Simpson, Jas. A., 429
Simpson, Joe D., 101
Simpson, L., 249
Simpson, Reuben, 63
Simpson, Thos., 225
Simpson, Wm. M., 63
Sims, A. C., 48
Sims, J. C., 380
Sims, G. M., 233
Sims, Jas. F., 312
Sims, Rich. Simpson, 341
Sinclair, D., 422
Sinclair, John A., 273
Sinclair, John Long, 541
Sinclair, Roland, 466
Singleterry, J. M., 123
Singleton, Thos. D., 420
Singleton, Wm. O., 298
Sings, John W., 422
Sistrunk, N. E. W., 447
Skidmore, Jos., 30
Skillicorn, Wm. H., 458
Skinner, Benj. W., 422
Skinner, Jesse, 89
Skinner, John S., 194
Skinner, Richard H., 136
Skipper, E. M., 408
Skipper, Everett, 256
Skrine, Thos. B., 408
Slack, Jas. Q., 269
Slade, Thos. C., 37
Slanders, W., 393
Slater, Frank M., 89
Slaton, J. R., 429
Slaton, W. F., 388, 393
Slatter, Lewis W., 249
Slaughter, Dan. S., 19
Slaughter, David W., 393
Slaughter, E., 19
Slaughter, M. (or W.) B., 393
Slaughter, Rich. J., 286
Slaughter, T. B., 389, 393
Slayton, F. W., 187
Sledge, Thos. A. H., 288
Slevin, Wm., 452
Sloan, A. G., 187
Sloan, J. R., 442
Sloan, Jas. T., 165
Sloan, John V., 216
Sloan, T. M., 42
Sloan, Wm. (see Slone, Wm.)
Slone, Wm., 286
Sloneker, W. J., 187
Slover, John, 268
Small, Geo. W., 63
Small, Jas. M., 233
Small, John B., 225
Small, Sam W., 233
Small, Samuel, 422
Smilie, Jacob, 116, 555
Smilie, Jas. R., 116
Smilie, Wm. J., 116
Smith, A. C., 286
Smith, A. J., 380

Smith, A. W., 356
Smith, Abe, 48
Smith, Albert, 373
Smith, Alfred, 268
Smith, Andrew W., 78
Smith, Archer M., 429
Smith, B. F., 209
Smith, B. F., 439
Smith, Benj. F., 305
Smith, Bennett F., 401
Smith, Chas. W., 30
Smith, Claiborne W., 305
Smith, D. W., 19
Smith, Dock M., 342
Smith, E. H., 123
Smith, E. M., 361
Smith, Ed. D., 19
Smith, Eurichus, 373, 546
Smith, Ezekiel, 432
Smith, Felix J., 165
Smith, Frank, 83
Smith, Frank M., 209
Smith, G. H., 333
Smith, G. W., 262
Smith, Geo., 380
Smith, Geo. A., 333
Smith, Geo. R., 1Lt., 375, 380
Smith, Geo. T., 342
Smith, Geo. W., 320
Smith, Gilbert G., 303
Smith, H. L., 435
Smith, Henry, 136
Smith, Henry J., Capt., 422-423
Smith, Henry W., 30
Smith, Hiram G., 291
Smith, J., 445
Smith, J. B., 342
Smith, J. C., 422
Smith, J. D., 395
Smith, J. F., 429
Smith, J. G., 387
Smith, J. H., 19
Smith, J. J., 209
Smith, J. J., 342
Smith, J. J., 446
Smith, J. M., 393
Smith, J. P., 395
Smith, J. P., 249
Smith, J. S., 362
Smith, J. V., 388
Smith, J. W., 37
Smith, J. W., 333
Smith, J. W., 381
Smith, J. Wesley, 244, 249
Smith, Jas. (or John), 320
Smith, Jas. M., 361
Smith, Jas. Monroe, 286
Smith, Jas. P., 218
Smith, Jas. S., 129
Smith, Jas. S., 393, 542
Smith, Jas. T., 342
Smith, Jarrett P., 63
Smith, Jasper W., 435
Smith, Jelu, 380
Smith, Joe C., 1Lt., 124, 125
Smith, Joe P., 63
Smith, John, 42
Smith, John, 83
Smith, John, 152
Smith, John, 187

Smith, John, 212
Smith, John, 1Lt., 218
Smith, John A., 116
Smith, John D., 123
Smith, John H., 373
Smith, John I., 152
Smith, John M., 311
Smith, John M., 83
Smith, John S., 7, 129
Smith, John T., 3Lt., 57, 63
Smith, John T., 413
Smith, John W., 42
Smith, John W., 123, Photo., 501
Smith, Jos. K., 303
Smith, Jos. N., 393
Smith, Judson, 37
Smith, K., 286
Smith, L. (or S.), 129
Smith, L. C., 367
Smith, Lemuel P., 312
Smith, M. A., 395
Smith, M. E. A., 442
Smith, M. F., 442
Smith, Miles V., 119, 123
Smith, Milton A., 48
Smith, P. C., 380
Smith, P. T., 342
Smith, Paris, 123
Smith, Pulasky, 159
Smith, R. W., 393
Smith, Reuben, 305
Smith, Richard J., 310
Smith, Richard Y., 408
Smith, Robt., 298
Smith, Robt., 333
Smith, Rodum, 202
Smith, S. Christopher, 439
Smith, Sam Y., 147
Smith, Samuel V., 1Lt., 387, 393
Smith, Samuel W., Capt., 306, 307
Smith, Sidney B., 83
Smith, Simeon, 202
Smith, Simon B., 209
Smith, Stephen, 439
Smith, T. F., 216
Smith, T. J., 361
Smith, Thos. D., 123
Smith, Thos. H., 408
Smith, Thos. J., 1Lt., 281-282
Smith, Uriah, 23
Smith, W. B., 442
Smith, W. D., 2Lt., 375
Smith, W. G., 159
Smith, W. G., 1Lt., 395
Smith, W. H., 380
Smith, W. Henegar, 30
Smith, W. J., 408
Smith, W. J., 432
Smith, W. O., 197
Smith, W. P., 118
Smith, W. S., 362
Smith, W. S., 2Lt., 427
Smith, W. T., 362
Smith, W. V., 44
Smith, W. Z., 442
Smith, Wm., 319, 320
Smith, Wm. B., 342
Smith, Wm. H., 145

Smith, Wm. H. C., 393
Smith, Wm. J., 439
Smith, Wm. K., 393
Smith, Wm. N., 311
Smith, Wm. R., 123,
    Photo., 501
Smith, Wm. T., 159
Smith, Wm. T., 361
Smith, Wm. W., 70
Smith, Wm. W., 225
Smith, Zack, 48
Smither, John M., 170, 202
Smoot, Wm. H., 264
Smyer, Miles A., 441
Snead, Wm., 429
Sneed, Albert, 136, Photo.,
    504
Sneed, Jas. W., 116
Snelgrove, J. P., 37
Snell, Wm. T., 187
Snellgrove, J. P. (see
    Snelgrove, J. P.)
Snelling, W. H., 447
Snider, A. M., 2Lt., 448,
    452
Snow, Geo. L., 37
Snow, Henry, 12, 45, 48
Snow, Jos. R., 406
Snow, Robt. M., 37
Snow, Wm. M., 37
Snowden, Jasper N., 48
Snyder, Thos. J., 282, 286
Solomon, Nathaniel B., 83
Somers, Richard H., 408
Somerville, John M., 312
Somerville, Willis L., 311
Sonis, I. R., 422
Sorell, Geo. C., 55
Sorrells, John C. (or E.),
    393
South, N. J., 249, 561
Southeimer, Isaac, 356
Southwick, J. W., 83,
    Photo., 487
Southworth, Lewis E., 303
Sowell, H. F., 437, 439
Sowell, Jas. W. J., 76
Spann, H. M., 444, 446
Spann, Jas. G., Capt., 442,
    446
Spann, Jas. W., 209
Spann, Ransom D., 1Lt.,
    446
Spann, T. D., 444
Spann, W. A., 447
Sparks, Jas. E., 289
Sparrow, A., 447
Spear, F. M., 291
Spears, Edw., 269
Spears, J. E., 453
Spears, John B., 255
Spears, Willie M., 299
Speer, G. W., 406
Speights, C. A., 249
Soence, David C., 429
Spence, Malachi, 367
Spence, Robt. H., 241
Spence, Samuel A., 426
Spence, W. P., 159
Spencer, Absalom, 352
Spencer, Chas. W., 145
Spencer, G. H., 452

Spencer, John L., 2Lt., 57
Spencer, Jos., 216
Spiars, S. A., 233
Spiers, A., 447
Spiers, G., 445
Spiers, M., 445
Spikes, H. M., 393
Spinks, H. D., 344
Spinks, Jas. W., 344
Spinks, R. Thos., 342
Spillers, Geo. E., 442
Spires, S. A. (see Spiars,
    S. A.)
Spivey, J. Syd, 1Lt., 147,
    152
Spivy, Wm., 429
Spivey, W. F., 202
Splawn, Wm., 70
Spradley, Wm. H., 385
Sprague, Wm. B., 408
Spratting, J. B., 43
Spring, Lewis, 55
Sprott, T. B., 2Lt., 227,
    233
Spurrier, Nathan, 55
Squires, J. W., 389, 394
Stacey, Jno. J., 145
Stacey, Willis A., 145
Stack, Jas. Q., 268
Stacy, Aaron O., 380
Stafford, R. E., 187
Stalcup, Jasper M., 55, 63,
    545
Staley, D. N., 452
Staley, J. H., 449, 452
Stallings, Eason, 464
Stallings, J. J., 48
Stallings, Jas. A., 76
Stamper, Jos. J., 458
Stamper, Wm. T., 30
Stamphill, S. P., 288
Stamps, Pleasant R., 95, 98
Staner, Willis, 292
Stanfield, Alphus M., 101
Stanfield, Ephraim C., 101
Stanfield, Thos. B., 102,
    Photo., 498
Stanfield, Wm. H., 102
Stanford, Jas. C., 380
Stanger, Jas., 171, 180
Stanley, A. E., 110
Stanley, J. A., 89
Stanley, S. S., 2Lt., 227
Stanley, Wm., 292
Stanley, Wm. P., 333
Stanley, Wm. S., 350
Stansbury, N. J., 83
Stansell, E. C., 335
Stansell, J. B., 333
Stansell, Joel J., 337
Stansell, Richard A., 342
Stansell, Wm. S., 342
Stansell, Wm. S., Sr., 333
Stanton, Robt., 202
Stapler, A. D., 350
Staples, John D., 286, 561
Staples, Wm. J., 286
Stark, L. M., 216
Stark, W. Jasper, 83
Starling, John, 249
Starnes, _____, 303
Starnes, G. W., 216

Starnes, L. L., 373
Starr, E. L., Capt., 357
Statham, John, 286
Statom, John W., 303
Stauts, G. W., 39 (3Lt.)
Steadman, F. L., 298
Steadman, Josiah, 394
Stearns, Wm. B., 342
Stedham, J. M., 225
Stedham, Lewis, 225
Stedman, A. G., 394
Stedman, B. B., 14, 48, 546
Stedman, Eli T., 48
Stedman, John, 70
Stedman, John T., 48
Stedman, Stephen S., 295,
    298
Steel, A. J., 233
Steel, Geo., 233
Steel, Thos. J., 43
Steel, W. C., 116
Steele, M. L., 180
Steele, M. W., 330, 333
Steele, W. A., 334
Stegall, Henry F., 102
Stein, Isaac, 110, Photo.,
    511
Steincipher, J. M., 63, 545
Stell, Wm. B., 317
Stenhouse, John T., 3Lt.,
    434
Stephans, Geo. H., 102
Stephens, A. C., 429
Stephen, W., 286
Stephens, C., 419
Stephens, Charleston W.,
    264
Stephens, D. J., 335
Stephens, Isaac T. (see
    Stevens, Isaac T.)
Stephens, J. A., 444, 446
Stephens, J. D., 194
Stephens, Jerry H., 241
Stephens, Rhodes B., 43,
    549, Photo., 483
Stephens, S. Frank, 262
Stephens, Thos., 136
Stephens, Will S., 241
Stephenson, J. A., 233
Stephenson, Robt. O., 342
Stephenson, Uriah P., 249
Stephenson, W. L. (see
    Stevenson, W. L.)
Stephenson, W. S., 211, 541
Stept, Goldson, 19
Sterling, Malcom, 249
Steussey, Jacob, 152
Steussey, Mathew, 152
Stevens, A. J., 204
Stevens, Benj. F., 286
Stevens, Benj. J., 410, 413
Stevens, Chas. E., 180
Stevens, Isaac, 249
Stevens, Isaac T., 385
Stevens, Jas. M., Capt., 281
Stevens, Jas. P., 23
Stevens, Jesse S., 55
Stevens, John D., 89
Stevens, John W., 249,
    Photo., 524
Stevens, S. Frank (see
    Stephens, S. Frank)

Tanner, W. J., 334
Tapp, E. S., 373
Tarkington, John, 233
Tarply, David J., 269
Tarrant, C. B., 442
Tarrant, J. A., 442
Tarrant, Jas., 433
Tarrant, Wm. W., 437, 439
Tarver, H. S., 234
Tarver, W. H., 225
Tate, F. M., 394
Tate, Farish Carter, 1Lt., 369, 546
Tate, W. N., 382
Tatum, Chas. J., 286
Tatum, Francis A., 385
Tatum, H. A., 187
Tatum, Fardy L., 310
Tatum, Jas. J., 386
Tatum, John M., 110
Tatum, Timothy P., 286
Taylor, A. C. M., 180
Taylor, A. J., 354, 356
Taylor, Alex, 153
Taylor, Arch, 11
Taylor, Asmel F., 63
Taylor, Benj. Walter, Capt., 399
Taylor, Chas. L., 153
Taylor, Edwin M., 63
Taylor, Elias, 446
Taylor, Emzy, 129
Taylor, Frank E., 407
Taylor, Fred P., 312
Taylor, G. M., 129
Taylor, Geo. A., 264
Taylor, Geo. B., 406
Taylor, Giles, 312
Taylor, H. L., 216
Taylor, H. M., 188
Taylor, Henry C., 408
Taylor, Howell L., 1Lt., 311
Taylor, J. D., 446
Taylor, J. H. M., 262
Taylor, J. K., 2Lt., 38
Taylor, J. M., 43
Taylor, John R., 426
Taylor, J. W. J., 262
Taylor, Jas., 395
Taylor, John H., 342
Taylor, Jos., 31
Taylor, L. M., 373
Taylor, Richard H., 83
Taylor, Robert S., Lt.-Col., 251, 253
Taylor, S. F., 429
Taylor, Sam C., 110
Taylor, T. F., 424
Taylor, T. O., 171, 188
Taylor, Thos. W., 216
Taylor, W. A., 292
Taylor, Wallace, 83
Taylor, Wm. H., 37
Taylor, Wm. M., 216
Teague, B. Hammet, 415
Teague, S. P., 110
Tebbs, Algernon S., 102
Tebbs, Obediah B., 264
Tebbs, William H., Capt., 251, 253, 259
Tedford, R.J., 3Lt., 147, 153

Temple, Wm. T., 356
Templeman, Madison Monroe, 233
Templeton, A. N., 159
Templeton, D., 435
Templeton, Moses B., 159
Templeton, Wm. A., 367
Templeton, Wm. W., 159
Terrell, Benj. S., 102
Terrell, Chas. M., 171, 188
Terrell, Ed. Thos., 92, 94, 145
Terrell, Hunt, 188
Terrell, John, 395
Terrell, S. B., 159
Terrell, Thos., 464
Terrell, Wm. H., 145
Terry, C. Willson, 430
Terry, Geo. F., 433
Terry, J. C., 129
Terry, Jas. A., 435
Terry, John M., 433
Terry, T. F., 430
Terry, Tandy, 433
Terry, W. C., 435
Terry, W. J., 1Lt., 218, 219
Tester, W. J., 342
Thach, Frank, Capt., 300-301
Thacker, Jas. R., 334
Thackston, C. G., 439
Thackston, J. H., 439
Thackston, Thos. M., 442
Thackston, Wm. P., 437, 439
Thackston, Wm. S., 442
Thames, Rufus M., Jr., 422
Thames, Thos. L., 419
Therrell, Abe S., 37
Thigpen, G. C., 153
Thomas, ———, 401
Thomas, David W., 303
Thomas, Eli. W., 63
Thomas, Eugene A., Capt., 402, 403
Thomas, F. B., 180
Thomas, H. L., 92
Thomas, Isaac W., 145, 545
Thomas, J. N., 419
Thomas, Jack M., 32, 33
Thomas, Jas. H., 110
Thomas, Jas. R., Jr., 241, Photo., 523
Thomas, Jas. R., Sr., 241
Thomas, Jas. W., 242
Thomas, Joe, 452
Thomas, John, 96, 153
Thomas, John H., 298
Thomas, Lucian W., 37
Thomas, Oscar E., 77
Thomas, Marcus, 110
Thomas, Robt. W., 97
Thomas, Samuel P., 194
Thomas, Theopolis J., 102
Thomas, Thos., 464
Thomas, W. E., 449, 452
Thomas, Wm., 419
Thomas, Wm. Francis, 242
Thomason, Austin, 442
Thomason, B. Wesley, 439
Thomason, C. G., 31
Thomason, Churchwell, 439
Thomason, David, 442

Thomason, G. W., 433
Thomason, H. J., 23
Thomason, J. B., 442
Thomason, J. F., 442
Thomason, Robt., 2Lt., 436, 440
Thomlinson, Robt. J., 409
Thompson, A., 89
Thompson, A., 373
Thompson, A. R., 344
Thompson, Albert, 56
Thompson, Ben. F., 334
Thompson, C. C., 362
Thompson, C. E., 435
Thompson, Ennis, 292
Thompson, F. Leslie, 83
Thompson, G. B., 2Lt., 16, 19
Thompson, Harris, 433
Thompson, J. C. S., 2Lt., 78
Thompson, Jas. E., 102
Thompson, John D., 419
Thompson, John M., 409
Thompson, John P., 430
Thompson, John W., 225, 242
Thompson, John W., 367
Thompson, Julius A., 406
Thompson, Mathew, 435
Thompson, Mitchell, 262
Thompson, Moses W., 2Lt., 430
Thompson, Nathan, 373
Thompson, Perry, 102
Thompson, Pleasant H., 1Lt., 294-295
Thompson, R. S., 334
Thompson, Robt. W., 71
Thompson, Samuel D., 274
Thompson, Sylvester, 465
Thompson, Thos. C., 465
Thompson, Thos. L., 274, 550
Thompson, W. Drayton, 433
Thompson, Wm., 433
Thompson, Wm., 292
Thompson, Wm., 447
Thompson, Wm. B., 419
Thompson, Willis, 293
Thompson, Wilson T., 435
Thorn, H. G. B., 343
Thorn, J. F., 344
Thornton, Ethard, 465
Thornberry, Jefferson, 303
Thornton, Howard G., 137
Thornton, J. E., 226
Thornton, L. C., 110
Thornton, Sam B., 2Lt., 243
Thrasher, David R., 343
Thrasher, T. T., 343
Thrasher, Thos. J., Capt., 289, 551
Thrift, T. E., 422
Thurmon, Riley W., 310
Thurmond, A. M., 350
Thurmond, Jas. H., 350
Thurmond, Wm. T., 350
Tidwell, Wm. C., 145
Tierce, D. S., 380
Tierney, Thos., 286, 550

Best Regards,

Col. Harold B. Simpson